DATE DUE

DEMCO 38-296

Statistical Record
OF Women
Worldwide

ISSN 1082-7811

Statistical Record OF Women Worldwide

Second Edition

Linda Schmittroth, Editor

An International Thomson Publishing Company

Changing the Way the World Learns

NEW YORK • LONDON • BONN • BOSTON • DETROIT • MADRID
MELBOURNE • MEXICO CITY • PARIS • SINGAPORE • TOKYO
TORONTO • WASHINGTON • ALBANY NY • BELMONT CA • CINCINNATI OH

Linda Schmittroth, *Editor*

Editorial Code and Data, Inc. Staff

Gary Alampi, *Programmer Analyst*

Gale Research Inc. Staff

Anna Sheets, *Developmental Editor*
Neil Schlager, *Managing Editor, Multicultural Team*

Mary Beth Trimper, *Production Director*
Shanna Heilveil, *Production Assistant*

C.J. Jonik, *Desktop Publisher*

∞™ This book is printed on acid-free paper that meets the minimum requirements of American National Standard for Information Sciences-Permanence Paper for Printed Library Materials, ANSI Z39.48-1984.

✿ This book is printed on recycled paper that meets Environmental Protection Agency Standards.

Library of Congress Cataloging-in-Publication Data

Statistical record of women worldwide / compiled and edited by Linda
Schmittroth. -- 2nd ed.
    p.   cm.
    Includes bibliographical references and index.
    ISBN 0-8103-8872-3 (alk. paper)
    1. Women--Statistics   2. Women--United States--Statistics.
I. Schmittroth, Linda.
HQ1150.S73 1995
305.4'021--dc20
                                                    95-37853
                                                    CIP

I(T)P™   Gale Research Inc., an International Thomson Publishing Company.
         ITP logo is a trademark under license.

10 9 8 7 6 5 4 3 2 1

TABLE OF CONTENTS

Preface xxix
Introduction xxxii

CHAPTER 1 - ATTITUDES AND OPINIONS 1
Abortion 1
    Table 1   Is Abortion Murder? 1
    Table 2   Southerners' Views on Abortion 2
    Table 3   Views on Abortion-I 2
    Table 4   Views on Abortion-II 3
    Table 5   Views on Abortion-III 5
    Table 6   Views on Abortion-IV 6
    Table 7   Views on Abortion-V 7
    Table 8   Views on Abortion-VI 7
    Table 9   Views on Abortion-VII 8
    Table 10 Views on Abortion-VIII 9
Economy 11
    Table 11 Which Tax Is the Worst? 11
Home, Family, Community 12
    Table 12 Do You Feel Your Contributions Are Valued? 12
    Table 13 Gift Preferences 12
    Table 14 Is It Necessary to Delay Marriage for Financial Security? . . . 13
    Table 15 Modern Families 14
    Table 16 Single or Married Life the Best? 14
    Table 17 Use of Husband's Last Name 15
    Table 18 What Makes You Feel Successful at Home? 16
International Opinion Polls 17
    Table 19 British Women on Health 17
    Table 20 British Women on Sexual Harassment at Work-I 18
    Table 21 British Women on Sexual Harassment at Work-II 19
    Table 22 British Women on the Battle of the Sexes 20
    Table 23 Canadian Women on Women's Status 20
    Table 24 Canadian Women on Working Mothers 21
    Table 25 German Women on Equal Rights 22
    Table 26 German Women on Politics 22
    Table 27 German Women on Work 23
    Table 28 German Women on Working Women-I 24
    Table 29 German Women on Working Women-II 24
    Table 30 Japanese Women on Children 25
    Table 31 Japanese Women on Reasons to Work 27
    Table 32 Japanese Women on Work 28

CHAPTER 1 - ATTITUDES AND OPINIONS continued:

Major Concerns 29
    Table 33   Biggest Worries 29
    Table 34   What Are Major Economic Worries? 30
    Table 35   What Are Women's Top Concerns? 31
Politics and Government 32
    Table 36   Approval Ratings of President Reagan 32
    Table 37   Approval Ratings of Presidents 33
    Table 38   Dissatisfaction with Major Political Parties 34
    Table 39   Opinions on Political Issues: 1981-1983 34
    Table 40   Opinions on Political Issues: 1986-1988 36
    Table 41   Opinions on Political Issues: 1990-1992 39
    Table 42   Opinions on Political Parties: 1987-1988 42
    Table 43   What Is a Top Priority for Government? 43
    Table 44   Which Level of Government Is the Least Effective? 44
    Table 45   Would the Country Be Better Off with Women Leaders? 44
Religion 45
    Table 46   Sisters on the Sisterhood and Morality 45
    Table 47   Women Pastors? 48
Sex Roles 48
    Table 48   Teenagers and Sex Roles 48
    Table 49   Traditional Sex Roles in Modern Society 50
Sexual Harassment 51
    Table 50   What Should Be Done About It? 51
Work 53
    Table 51   Commitment to a Job by Minority Status 53
    Table 52   Employee Ratings of Female Managers: 1995 54
    Table 53   How Is A Career Advanced? 55
    Table 54   Is It Important to Work Close to Home? 56
    Table 55   Perceptions About Work 56
    Table 56   Perceptions About Work by Minority Status 57
    Table 57   Responsible for Improving Own Job Performance? 58
    Table 58   What Are the Biggest Problems at Work? 59
    Table 59   What Do People Want from Work? 59
    Table 60   What Do Working Women Want More Time For? 60
    Table 61   What Do You Like Best About Your Job? 60
    Table 62   What Is Important About Your Job? 61
    Table 63   What Makes You Feel Successful at Work? 61
    Table 64   What Problems Do You Have at Work? 62
    Table 65   What Would You Like to See Changed in Your Workplace? . . . 63
    Table 66   Why Was a Promotion Denied? 64
    Table 67   Will Present Job Skills be Useful in Five Years? 64
    Table 68   Women Executives on Work-I 65
    Table 69   Women Executives on Work-II 65
    Table 70   Women Executives on Work-III 66
    Table 71   Women Executives on Work-IV 67
    Table 72   Women Executives on Work-V 68
    Table 73   Would You Work If You Didn't Have To? 70
Young Women 71
    Table 74   Political Views of Women Entering College: 1994-I 71

CHAPTER 1 - ATTITUDES AND OPINIONS continued:

Table 75   Political Views of Women Entering College: 1994-II 71
Table 76   Self Esteem: Black Girls and White Girls 72
Table 77   Self-Assessments of Women Entering College: 1994 73
Table 78   Student Satisfaction with the Local High School: 1994 74
Table 79   Which Values Are Important? 75

CHAPTER 2 - BUSINESS AND ECONOMICS 77
Corporate Officers/Executives 77

Table 80   Asian/Pacific Islander Industry Leaders-I 77
Table 81   Asian/Pacific Islander Industry Leaders-II 78
Table 82   Asian/Pacific Islander Industry Leaders by Industry 78
Table 83   Asian/Pacific Islander Industry Leaders' Income-I 79
Table 84   Asian/Pacific Islander Industry Leaders' Income-II 80
Table 85   Executive Suites at Major Corporations 82
Table 86   Heads of Billion-Dollar Businesses 82
Table 87   Hispanic Origin Industry Leaders by Industry 84
Table 88   Hispanic Origin Industry Leaders' Income 85
Table 89   Income of Business Executives and Managers 86
Table 90   Industry Leaders by Educational Attainment 87
Table 91   Industry Leaders by Major Industry Category 87
Table 92   Industry Leaders by Race/Ethnicity 88
Table 93   Industry Leaders by Race/Ethnicity and Educational Attainment 90
Table 94   Industry Leaders' Income by Educational Attainment and Race 91
Table 95   Industry Leaders' Income by Industry and Race 92
Table 96   Industry Leaders' Income Disparities by Race/Ethnicity 92
Table 97   Industry Leaders' Occupational Achievement Compared to Education 93

Legal Matters 94

Table 98   Breast Implant Settlement Approved 94

Sales of Contraceptives 95

Table 99   The Market for Norplant 95

Shopping 96

Table 100   Getting a Second Opinion 96

The Media 97

Table 101   Media Reviews of Mystery Writers 97
Table 102   Smoking Linked to Advertising 98
Table 103   Top Online Services 99

Women Business Owners 100

Table 104   Women-Owned Businesses: 1990 and 1994 100

CHAPTER 3 - CRIME, LAW ENFORCEMENT, AND LEGAL JUSTICE 101
Crime and Criminals 101

Table 105   Arrestees' Age and Race: 1988 101
Table 106   Arrestees' Offenses: 1988-I 102
Table 107   Arrestees' Offenses: 1988-II 102
Table 108   Arrestees' School Dropout History: 1988 103
Table 109   Convicted Felons: 1992 104
Table 110   Correctional Institution Population: 1992 105
Table 111   Jail Inmates' Criminal History: 1983 and 1989 106
Table 112   Jail Inmates' Employment and Income Source: 1989 106

CHAPTER 3 - CRIME, LAW ENFORCEMENT, AND LEGAL JUSTICE continued:

Table 113	Jail Inmates' Offenses: 1989	108
Table 114	Jail Inmates' Prior Sentences: 1989	109
Table 115	Jail Inmates' Use of Jail Time: 1989	110
Table 116	Jail Inmates: 1983 and 1989	111
Table 117	Mothers in Prison: 1991	112
Table 118	Offenders, Characteristics: 1987-1991	113
Table 119	Prisoners of State or Federal Authorities: 1993	114
Table 120	Prisoners Sentenced to Death, State and Race: 1993	115
Table 121	Prisoners Sentenced to Death: 1993	116
Table 122	Sentenced Prisoners: 1980-1992	116
Table 123	Sentences of Jail Inmates: 1989	117
Table 124	State Prison Inmates' Abuse History and Types of Crimes: 1991	118
Table 125	State Prison Inmates' Abuse History: 1991	119
Table 126	State Prison Inmates' Abuse Types: 1991	120
Table 127	State Prison Inmates' Criminal History: 1991	121
Table 128	State Prison Inmates' Family Characteristics: 1991	122
Table 129	State Prison Inmates' Offenses by Drug Use History: 1991	123
Table 130	State Prison Inmates' Offenses: 1986 and 1991	124
Table 131	State Prison Inmates' Prior Sentences: 1991	126
Table 132	State Prison Inmates' Sentences: 1991	126
Table 133	State Prison Inmates: 1986 and 1991	127
Drugs		129
Table 134	Arrestees' Alcohol and Marijuana Use: 1988	129
Table 135	Arrestees' Cocaine and Crack Use: 1988	130
Table 136	Arrestees' Cocaine Use: 1991	130
Table 137	Arrestees' Drug Use By Type of Drug: 1988	131
Table 138	Arrestees' Drug Use: 1988	132
Table 139	Arrestees' Use of Injected Drugs: 1988	134
Table 140	Jail Inmates' Drug Use: 1989	135
Table 141	Prison Inmates' Drug Use: 1986 and 1991	137
Juveniles		138
Table 142	Child Rape Victims, Relationship to Offender: 1992	138
Table 143	Child Rape Victims: 1992	139
Table 144	Dating Violence Among High School Students	140
Table 145	Incest and Paternal Caregiving	140
Table 146	Juvenile Delinquency Trends: 1986-1991	141
Table 147	Juvenile Prostitution	142
Table 148	Juveniles in Custody: 1991	143
Table 149	Juveniles' Use of Drugs: 1992-I	144
Table 150	Juveniles' Use of Drugs: 1992-II	144
Table 151	Juveniles' Use of Drugs: 1992-III	145
Table 152	Juveniles' Use of Drugs: 1992-IV	145
Table 153	Victimizations at School	146
Table 154	Victims of Childhood Sexual Abuse, Recall	147
Table 155	Sexually Molested as a Child	148
Law Enforcement		149
Table 156	Resolution of EEOC Complaints: 1993	149
Victims		150
Table 157	Battered Women	150

CHAPTER 3 - CRIME, LAW ENFORCEMENT, AND LEGAL JUSTICE continued: 151
   Table 158 Jail Inmates' Victims: 1989 151
   Table 159 Murder Victims and Defendants: 1988 152
   Table 160 Victimizations by Marital Status: 1991-I 153
   Table 161 Victimizations by Marital Status: 1991-II 153
   Table 162 Victims of Violence, Relationship of Offender to Victim: 1991 154
   Table 163 Victimizations: 1974-1990 155
   Table 164 Victimizations: 1987-1991 155
   Table 165 Victimizations: 1991 157
   Table 166 Victims of Crime Act Funds Allocation, Spouse Abuse and Sexual Assault: 1986
          and 1991 158
   Table 167 Victims of Crime Act Funds Allocation: 1990 and 1991 159
   Table 168 Victims of Crime Act Funds, Victims Served: 1990 159
   Table 169 Victims of Larceny, Characteristics: 1987-1991 160
   Table 170 Victims of Rape 161
   Table 171 Victims of Rape, America Versus Europe 162
   Table 172 Victims of Violence Committed by Intimates: 1987-1992 162
   Table 173 Victims of Violence, Characteristics: 1987-1991 163
   Table 174 Victims of Violence, Involvement of Alcohol-I 165
   Table 175 Victims of Violence, Involvement of Alcohol-II 166
   Table 176 Victims of Violence, Police Action: 1987-1991 168
   Table 177 Victims of Violence, Reasons for Reporting Crime: 1987-1991 169
   Table 178 Victims of Violence, Relationship of Offender to Victim: 1987-1991-I 170
   Table 179 Victims of Violence, Relationship of Offender to Victim: 1987-1991-II 170
   Table 180 Victims of Violence, Selected Countries 171
   Table 181 Victims of Violent Crimes, Characteristics: 1987-1991 173
   Table 182 Victims, Characteristics: 1987-1991 174
   Table 183 Victims, Race: 1987-1991 176
   Table 184 Victims, Weapons Present and Injuries Sustained: 1987-1991 177
   Table 185 Violence Against Women 178
   Table 186 Violence Against Women Worldwide 179
   Table 187 Violence Toward Spouse 180

CHAPTER 4 - DOMESTIC LIFE 181
Allocation of Time 181
   Table 188 Contribution of Housework to Worldwide Gross Domestic Product 181
   Table 189 Help with the Chores 183
   Table 190 Time Spent Getting Water in Developing Countries 183
   Table 191 Time Spent on Activities Worldwide-I 184
   Table 192 Time Spent on Activities Worldwide-II 186
   Table 193 Time Spent on Housework Worldwide 188
Children 189
   Table 194 Adoption and Black Children 189
   Table 195 Adoption Odds 189
   Table 196 Adoption Placements: 1970-1988 190
   Table 197 Adoption Vs. Abortion 191
   Table 198 Adoption: 1970-1982 192
   Table 199 Children in Substitute Care: 1986-1989 194
   Table 200 Out-of-Wedlock Children: 1970-1988 195
   Table 201 Two-Parent Families with Children: 1987-1992 195

CHAPTER 4 - DOMESTIC LIFE continued:
    Table 202   With Whom Did Children Live?: 1960-1990 196
  Displaced Homemakers 196
    Table 203   Profile of Displaced Homemakers: 1990 196
  Families 197
    Table 204   Female-Headed Families: 1980-1993 197
    Table 205   Married Couple Families with Children: 1980-1993 198
    Table 206   Profile of American Families: 1990 199
    Table 207   Types of Asian and Pacific Islander Families: 1990 and 1993 200
    Table 208   Types of Black and White Families: 1980-1993 201
    Table 209   Types of Black Families: 1970-1992 202
    Table 210   Types of Families: 1960-1993 202
    Table 211   Types of Families: 1970-1992 203
    Table 212   Types of Hispanic Families: 1993 204
  Living Arrangements 205
    Table 213   Fewest People in the Household Worldwide 205
    Table 214   Homeless Adults 206
    Table 215   Households Headed by Women Worldwide 207
    Table 216   Households: 2000-2010 208
    Table 217   Living Alone: 1970-1993 209
    Table 218   Living Arrangements by Presence of Children: 1980-1993 210
    Table 219   Living Arrangements by Type of Household: 1993 211
    Table 220   Living Arrangements of People 15 Years Old and Over: 1993 212
    Table 221   Living Arrangements of the Elderly 213
    Table 222   Living Arrangements of the Elderly by Race/Ethnicity 214
    Table 223   Living Arrangements of Young Adults: 1970-1993 215
    Table 224   Most People in the Household Worldwide 216
    Table 225   Reasons for Leaving Home: 1920-1980s 217
    Table 226   Urban Population in Latin America and the Caribbean 218
    Table 227   Urban Population in Sub-Saharan Africa 219
    Table 228   Urban Population in the Middle East and North Africa 220
    Table 229   Women Living Alone: 2000-2010 220
  Marriage and Divorce 221
    Table 230   Divorce: Reasons 221
    Table 231   What Women Look for in Marriage 222
  Mothers 223
    Table 232   Characteristics of Mothers Who Are Single by Choice 223
    Table 233   Distribution of Household Tasks 223
    Table 234   Single Mothers: 2000-2010 224
    Table 235   Spanking Beliefs and Practices 224
    Table 236   Time Spent on Household Tasks and Children 225
    Table 237   Time Spent Taking Care of Household and Children 226

CHAPTER 5 - EDUCATION 227
  Computers 227
    Table 238   Computer Knowledge Scores: 1992 227
    Table 239   International Comparison, Computer Knowledge Scores: 1992 228
    Table 240   Opportunity to Learn About Computers: 1992 229
    Table 241   Out-Of-School Computer Access: 1992 229
    Table 242   Out-Of-School Computer Types: 1992 230

CHAPTER 5 - EDUCATION continued:

Table 243	Sent Messages to Another Computer: 1992	230
Table 244	Took a Programming Course: 1992	231
Degrees		231
Table 245	Associates' Degrees by Field of Study: 1991-1992	231
Table 246	Associates' Degrees Conferred: 1991 and 1992	232
Table 247	Bachelors' Degrees by Field of Study: 1991-1992	233
Table 248	Bachelors' Degrees Conferred: 1991 and 1992	234
Table 249	Degrees by Race/Ethnicity: 1991-1992	235
Table 250	Degrees Conferred: 1991 and 1992	235
Table 251	Doctoral Degrees by Field of Study: 1991-1992	236
Table 252	Doctors' Degrees by Race/Ethnicity: 1978-1993	237
Table 253	Doctors' Degrees Conferred: 1991 and 1992	238
Table 254	Doctors' Degrees: 1992-2003	239
Table 255	First-Professional Degrees by Field and Race/Ethnicity: 1991-1992	239
Table 256	First-Professional Degrees by Field of Study: 1991-1992	241
Table 257	First-Professional Degrees Conferred: 1991 and 1992	242
Table 258	First-Professional Degrees: 1992-2003	243
Table 259	Masters' Degrees by Field of Study: 1991-1992	244
Table 260	Masters' Degrees Conferred: 1991 and 1992	245
Table 261	Mathematics Degrees, Trends: 1978-1991	246
Table 262	Physics Degrees Granted: 1992-1993	246
Table 263	Science Degrees, Trends: 1978-1991	247
Table 264	Time to Complete Baccalaureate Degree: 1977-1990	247
Educational Attainment		248
Table 265	Educational Attainment by Race/Ethnicity: 1990	248
Table 266	Educational Attainment of Persons Aged 25 and Over: 1991	249
Table 267	Illiteracy in Africa: 1970-1992	249
Table 268	Illiteracy in Asia	251
Table 269	Illiteracy in Asia: 1970-1992	252
Table 270	Illiteracy in Developed Countries	253
Table 271	Illiteracy in Europe: 1970-1992	254
Table 272	Illiteracy in Latin America and the Caribbean	255
Table 273	Illiteracy in Latin America/Caribbean: 1970-1992	256
Table 274	Illiteracy in North Africa and the Middle East	257
Table 275	Illiteracy in Oceania: 1970-1992	258
Table 276	Illiteracy in Sub-Saharan Africa	258
Table 277	Illiteracy in the Near East: 1970-1992	260
Table 278	International Comparisons of Educational Attainment: 1991	261
Table 279	Persistence and Degree Attainment	261
Enrollment		262
Table 280	African School Enrollment Preceding the First Level	262
Table 281	African School Enrollment at the First Level	263
Table 282	African School Enrollment at the Second Level	265
Table 283	African School Enrollment at the Third Level	267
Table 284	African School Enrollment in Vocational Education	269
Table 285	Asian School Enrollment Preceding the First Level	271
Table 286	Asian School Enrollment at the First Level	272
Table 287	Asian School Enrollment at the Second Level	274
Table 288	Asian School Enrollment at the Third Level	275

CHAPTER 5 - EDUCATION continued:

Table 289	Asian School Enrollment in Vocational Education	277
Table 290	College Enrollment by Race/Ethnicity: 1990-1992	279
Table 291	College Enrollment by State: 1993-1994	280
Table 292	College Enrollment of Older Students: 1992	281
Table 293	College Enrollment: 1993	282
Table 294	Enrollment Status of the Population, Enrolled: 1993	283
Table 295	Enrollment Status of the Population, Not Enrolled: 1993	286
Table 296	European School Enrollment Preceding the First Level	289
Table 297	European School Enrollment at the First Level	290
Table 298	European School Enrollment at the Second Level	291
Table 299	European School Enrollment at the Third Level	293
Table 300	European School Enrollment in Vocational Education	294
Table 301	Graduate Physics Students: 1991-1992	296
Table 302	Latin American/Caribbean School Enrollment Preceding the First Level	296
Table 303	Latin America/Caribbean School Enrollment at the First Level	298
Table 304	Latin American/Caribbean School Enrollment at the Second Level	299
Table 305	Latin American/Caribbean School Enrollment at the Third Level	301
Table 306	Latin American/Caribbean School Enrollment in Vocational Education	302
Table 307	North American School Enrollment Preceding the First Level	304
Table 308	North American School Enrollment at the First Level	304
Table 309	North American School Enrollment at the Second Level	305
Table 310	North American School Enrollment at the Third Level	305
Table 311	Nursery School Enrollment: 1968-1993	306
Table 312	Oceanian School Enrollment Preceding the First Level	307
Table 313	Oceanian School Enrollment at the First Level	308
Table 314	Oceanian School Enrollment at the Second Level	309
Table 315	Oceanian School Enrollment at the Third Level	310
Table 316	Oceanian School Enrollment in Vocational Education	311
Table 317	Secondary and Postsecondary Enrollment in G-7 Countries: 1988	312
Table 318	Seminary Enrollment: 1972-1992	312
High School		313
Table 319	ACT Students' Aspirations	313
Table 320	Alcohol Use by High School Seniors: 1987-1992	314
Table 321	Course Taking in Core Subject Areas: 1982-1992	315
Table 322	High School Dropouts by Race/Ethnicity: 1978-1993	316
Table 323	High School Dropouts, Reasons: 1992	316
Table 324	High School Dropouts: 1991	318
Table 325	High School Dropouts: 1993	318
Table 326	High School Programs: 1972-1992	319
Table 327	Mathematics Advanced Placement Examinations: 1986-1993	319
Table 328	Science Advanced Placement Examinations: 1986-1993	320
Table 329	Students' Aspirations	321
Table 330	Students' Occupational Expectations	321
Higher Education		322
Table 331	Medical School Admissions: 1994	322
Table 332	Time to Complete Doctorate: 1993	323
Table 333	Vocational Education	323
Sexual Harassment at School		325
Table 334	Frequency of Harassment	325

CHAPTER 5 - EDUCATION continued:
Table 335   Reaction of Victim: Tell Her Parents? 326
Table 336   Reactions of School Administration 327
Table 337   Reactions of Victim 328
Table 338   Reporting Harassment: Does It Make a Difference? 329
Table 339   Types of Harassment Experienced 329
Table 340   Types of Harassment Experienced by Age 330
Table 341   Types of Harassment Experienced by Race 331
Table 342   Types of Harassment Experienced by Type of School 332
Table 343   Where Does Harassment Happen? 333
Table 344   Who Are the Harassers? 334
Teachers 335
Table 345   Teaching Hours Per Year in 16 Countries 335
Table 346   Teachers Who Leave Teaching 336
Test Scores 337
Table 347   ACT Test Scores by Race/Ethnicity: 1994 337
Table 348   ACT Test Scores: 1994 338
Table 349   LSAT Scores 338
Table 350   Mathematics Proficiency: 1992 339
Table 351   National Merit Scholarship Competition: 1988-1993 339
Table 352   Reading Proficiency: 1992 340
Table 353   SAT Score Averages: 1994 341
Table 354   SAT Scores: 1987 and 1994 342
Table 355   SAT Trends: 1988-1994 343
Table 356   Science Proficiency: 1970-1990 344

CHAPTER 6 - HEALTH AND MEDICAL CARE 345
Abortions 345
Table 357   Abortions in Romania 345
AIDS 346
Table 358   AIDS Attributed to IV Drug Use: 1988 346
Alcohol and Drugs 348
Table 359   Alcohol Problems and a History of Abuse 348
Table 360   Alcohol Use and Abuse 349
Table 361   Alcohol and Self-Destructive Behavior 351
Table 362   Alcohol and Tranquilizers 353
Table 363   Drinking During Pregnancy: 1979-1993 354
Table 364   Drinking Problems 354
Table 365   Drinking to Get Drunk 355
Table 366   Drug Facts 356
Table 367   Relationship Between Eating Disorders and Alcoholism 357
Cancer 358
Table 368   Breast Cancer by Race-I 358
Table 369   Breast Cancer by Race-II 361
Table 370   Breast Cancer Incidence: 1973-1990 362
Table 371   Breast Cancer Risk Linked to Childbearing 363
Table 372   Cancer Incidence Rates: 1973-1990 364
Table 373   Cancer Incidence: 1975-1991 365
Table 374   Cancer Survival Rates 366
Table 375   Cancer Survival Rates by Race: 1974-1989 366

CHAPTER 6 - HEALTH AND MEDICAL CARE continued:

Table 376 Lung Cancer Incidence: 1973-1990 367
Cigarette Smoking 368
Table 377 Profile of Cigarette Smokers 368
Table 378 Smokers: 1965-1991 368
Table 379 Smoking and Elderly Women 369
Table 380 Smoking in Asia and the Near East 370
Table 381 Smoking in Europe 371
Table 382 Smoking in Latin America and the Caribbean 372
Table 383 Smoking in North America 373
Table 384 Smoking in Oceania 373
Table 385 Smoking in Sub-Saharan Africa 374
Table 386 Smoking in the Middle East and North Africa 374
Clitoridectomy 375
Table 387 Female Genital Mutilation in Africa 375
Conditions 376
Table 388 Acute Conditions: 1992 376
Table 389 Alzheimer's Disease 377
Table 390 Alzheimer's Disease Linked to Down's Syndrome 378
Table 391 Chronic Conditions: 1992 378
Table 392 Disability Status: 1990 379
Table 393 High Cholesterol: 1960-1991 380
Table 394 Injuries: 1970-1991 381
Table 395 Injuries: 1992 382
Table 396 Sexually Transmitted Diseases Among Teenagers 382
Table 397 Sexually Transmitted Diseases Worldwide-I 383
Table 398 Sexually Transmitted Diseases Worldwide-II 385
Contraception 385
Table 399 Effectiveness of the Female Condom 385
Dietary and Health Practices 386
Table 400 Benefits of Olive Oil 386
Table 401 Calcium Intake 388
Table 402 Daily Nutrient Intake 388
Table 403 Dietary Consumption and Perceived Consumption 389
Table 404 Dieting, Bulimia, and Substance Abuse 390
Table 405 Protein Intake 390
Table 406 Teenage Girls and Exercise 391
Table 407 Thinking About Food: 1994 392
Health Care Coverage 393
Table 408 Coverage and Death Rates 393
Table 409 Coverage and Risk of Dying 394
Table 410 Coverage for Persons Aged 25 to 64 394
Table 411 Coverage: 1990-1992 395
Table 412 Health Service Usage by Insurance Status 396
Health Care Personnel/Institution Contacts 397
Table 413 Hospital Utilization: 1970-1992 397
Table 414 Physician and Dental Visits: 1970-1992 398
HIV/AIDS 399
Table 415 AIDS Cases and the Drug Epidemic 399
Table 416 AIDS Cases by Transmission Category 400

CHAPTER 6 - HEALTH AND MEDICAL CARE continued:
    Table 417 AIDS Cases Reported: 1981-1992 400
    Table 418 AIDS Tests for Pregnant Women 401
    Table 419 AIDS Virus Infections Worldwide: 1989 401
    Table 420 Characteristics of Women at Risk for HIV Infection 402
    Table 421 HIV Positive Prison Inmates: 1991 403
    Table 422 HIV Prevalence in 14 Countries 404
    Table 423 HIV Risk Among Drug-Injecting Lesbians and Bisexual Women 405
    Table 424 Maternal-Infant HIV Transmission 406
  Mental Health 407
    Table 425 Behaviors Associated with a History of Childhood Sexual Abuse 407
    Table 426 Effects of Incest 408
  Operations and Other Procedures 409
    Table 427 Medical Device Implants: 1988 409
    Table 428 Prenatal Ultrasound's Effect on Perinatal Outcome 410
    Table 429 Procedures Performed at Short-Stay Hosptials: 1980-1992 411
  Pregnancy and Infant Health 412
    Table 430 Ectopic Pregnancies Increase: 1970-1992 412
    Table 431 Risk of Late Childbearing 412
    Table 432 Substance-Exposed Infants 414
  Weight 415
    Table 433 Weight Guidelines for Persons Aged 40 and Over 415
    Table 434 Weight Guidelines: 1985-1990 416

CHAPTER 7 - INCOME, SPENDING, AND WEALTH 417
  Income 417
    Table 435 Family and Household Income: 1990 417
    Table 436 Higher Education Assistance: 1990-1991 418
    Table 437 Income and Risk of Dying 420
    Table 438 Income by Race/Ethnicity: 1989 420
    Table 439 Married-Couple Families, Income by Race: 1967-1990 421
    Table 440 Median Income of Full-Time Workers: 1989 422
    Table 441 Supplemental Security Income and Older Women 422
    Table 442 Teenagers' Allowances and Income 423
    Table 443 Welfare Benefits: Recipients and Cost 424
  Spending 426
    Table 444 "Barbie" Dolls 426
    Table 445 Buying Groceries 427
    Table 446 Charges for Cesarean Delivery: 1993 428
    Table 447 Charges for Vaginal Delivery: 1993 429
    Table 448 Charitable Contributions Asked for and Given 430
    Table 449 Charitable Contributions: 1987-1993 430
    Table 450 Child Care Expenditures 431
    Table 451 College Athletic Scholarships: 1993-1994 432
    Table 452 Cost of Earning a Doctorate: 1993 438
    Table 453 Cost of Postsecondary Schooling: 1990-1991 439
    Table 454 Cost to Government of Teenage Births: 1990 440
    Table 455 Doctorate Recipients' Sources of Support: 1993 440
    Table 456 Expenditures of Renters by Government Assistance Category 441
    Table 457 Expenditures, With Children, With and Without a Husband: 1993 443

CHAPTER 7 - INCOME, SPENDING, AND WEALTH continued:

Table 458   Federal Grants for WIC Program by State: 1990 444
Table 459   Government Spending for Teenage Mothers: 1990 446
Table 460   Medical Costs for the Uninsured Midlife Woman 447
Table 461   Purchases of Athletic Footwear 447
Table 462   Shrinking Pantyhose Market 448
Table 463   Spending on Sporting Goods and Equipment 449
Table 464   What Price a Good Jacket? 449

Wages and Salaries 450
Table 465   African Agricultural Wages 450
Table 466   African Construction Wages 450
Table 467   African Manufacturing Wages 451
Table 468   African Mining and Quarrying Wages 452
Table 469   African Transport, Storage, and Communication Wages 452
Table 470   Artists' Earnings: 1989 453
Table 471   Asian Agricultural Wages 454
Table 472   Asian Construction Wages 454
Table 473   Asian Manufacturing Wages 455
Table 474   Asian Mining and Quarrying Wages 457
Table 475   Asian Transport, Storage, and Communication Wages 457
Table 476   Choreographers' Income 459
Table 477   Contribution to Household Income: 1995 459
Table 478   Earnings by Age and Race/Ethnicity: 1994 460
Table 479   Earnings by Educational Attainment: 1991 461
Table 480   Earnings by Educational Attainment: 1994 462
Table 481   Earnings by Occupation: 1991 463
Table 482   Earnings by Union Membership Status 464
Table 483   Earnings in 20 Leading Occupations: 1991 465
Table 484   Earnings in Selected Occupations: 1983-1991 466
Table 485   Earnings of Employed Black Women 467
Table 486   Earnings of Special Libraries Association Members: 1976-1994 467
Table 487   Effect of Education on Hourly Earnings 468
Table 488   Effect of Work Experience on Wages 469
Table 489   European Agricultural Wages 469
Table 490   European Construction Wages 470
Table 491   European Manufacturing Wages 472
Table 492   European Mining and Quarrying Wages 474
Table 493   European Transport, Storage, and Communication Wages 475
Table 494   Faculty Salaries by Field: 1993-1994 476
Table 495   Faculty Salaries in Higher Education: 1982-1993 478
Table 496   Growth of Full-Time Equivalent Wages: 1979-1987 479
Table 497   Income of Displaced Workers: 1994 480
Table 498   Latin American/Caribbean Agricultural Wages 480
Table 499   Latin American/Caribbean Construction Wages 481
Table 500   Latin American/Caribbean Manufacturing Wages 481
Table 501   Latin American/Caribbean Mining and Quarrying Wages 482
Table 502   Latin American/Caribbean Transport, Storage, and Communication Wages . . . 482
Table 503   Librarians' Salaries 483
Table 504   Library Directors' Salaries 483
Table 505   Male-Female Earnings Ratio: 1980-1991 484

CHAPTER 7 - INCOME, SPENDING, AND WEALTH continued:

Table 506   Median Earnings by Educational Attainment: 1990 484
Table 507   Nonphysician Professionals' Income 485
Table 508   Oceanian Construction Wages 486
Table 509   Oceanian Manufacturing Wages 486
Table 510   Oceanian Mining and Quarrying Wages 487
Table 511   Oceanian Transport, Storage, and Communication Wages 487
Table 512   Physics Bachelors' Starting Salaries: 1990 488
Table 513   Salaries by Occupation: 1994 488
Table 514   Salaries in State and Local Government 491
Table 515   Salaries of Chemical Engineers: 1980-1993 492
Table 516   Salaries of Doctors of Physics: 1992 493
Table 517   Salaries of Federal White Collar Workers 494
Table 518   Teachers' Salaries: 1993-1994 495
Table 519   Wage Gap: 1990 496
Table 520   Weekly Earnings by Educational Attainment and Race: 1994 497
Table 521   Weekly Earnings by Educational Attainment: 1994 498
Table 522   Weekly Earnings by Occupation: 1994 500
Table 523   Weekly Earnings of Full-Time Workers: 1993 and 1994 502

Wealth and Poverty 504
Table 524   Displaced Homemakers' Median Income by Age and Race: 1990 504
Table 525   Displaced Homemakers' Median Income by Education and Race: 1990 504
Table 526   Displaced Homemakers' Poverty Status: 1990-I 505
Table 527   Displaced Homemakers' Poverty Status: 1990-II 506
Table 528   Distribution of Household Wealth 507
Table 529   Elderly People in Poverty 508
Table 530   Income of Older Women 508
Table 531   Participation in Major Assistance Programs: 1988 510
Table 532   Poverty Rates for Persons and Families 511
Table 533   Poverty Status of Female Householders: 1989 512
Table 534   Single Mothers' Median Income by Age and Race: 1990 513
Table 535   Single Mothers' Median Income by Education and Race: 1990 513
Table 536   Single Mothers' Poverty Status: 1990-I 514
Table 537   Single Mothers' Poverty Status: 1990-II 515

CHAPTER 8 - LABOR, EMPLOYMENT, AND OCCUPATIONS 516

Employment 516
Table 538   Changes in Industry Employment Following Recession: 1990-1992 516
Table 539   Changes in Industry Employment Since 1969 517
Table 540   Changing Jobs: 1965-1991 517
Table 541   Employment of Women in Africa: 1990 518
Table 542   Employment of Women in Asia and the Pacific: 1990 519
Table 543   Employment of Women in Developed Regions: 1990 520
Table 544   Employment of Women in Latin America/Caribbean: 1990 521
Table 545   Informal Employment Sector in Six Countries 522
Table 546   Job Loss Attributed to Race or Sex 523
Table 547   Labor Force Distribution in Six Countries 524
Table 548   Multiple Jobholders: 1980-1989 524
Table 549   Part-Time Employment: 1980-1991 525
Table 550   Skilled Trades 526

CHAPTER 8 - LABOR, EMPLOYMENT, AND OCCUPATIONS continued:

Labor and Laborers 526
   Table 551   Black Women in the Labor Force 526
   Table 552   Child Care Constraints on Employment 527
   Table 553   Education and Business Experience Trends: 1965-1990 528
   Table 554   Employment Participation in the Private Sector 529
   Table 555   Hispanic Women in the Labor Force 530
   Table 556   Job Promotion Characteristics 530
   Table 557   Job Promotions 531
   Table 558   Labor Force by Race/Ethnicity: 1975-2005 533
   Table 559   Labor Force in Africa by Status in Employment: 1980-1987 534
   Table 560   Labor Force in Asia 535
   Table 561   Labor Force in Asia and the Pacific by Status in Employment: 1980-1987 536
   Table 562   Labor Force in Developed Regions by Status in Employment: 1980-1987 537
   Table 563   Labor Force in Europe 538
   Table 564   Labor Force in Latin America/Caribbean by Status in Employment: 1980-1987 . 539
   Table 565   Labor Force Participation Rates: 1965-1993 541
   Table 566   Labor Force: 2000-2050 542
   Table 567   Projections of Women in the Labor Force 543
   Table 568   Union Membership: 1984-1991 544
   Table 569   Welfare Mothers and Work 544
   Table 570   What If You Lost Your Job? 545
   Table 571   Women in the Labor Force: 1950-2000 546
   Table 572   Work Experience of Married Mothers by Race/Ethnicity: 1992 546
   Table 573   Work Experience of Married Mothers: 1992 547
   Table 574   Work Experience of Married Parents by Race/Ethnicity: 1992 548
   Table 575   Work Experience Trends of Married Mothers: 1970-1992 549
   Table 576   Work Experience: 1992 550
   Table 577   Worker Training: 1983-1991 551
   Table 578   Workers in the Informal Sector Worldwide 551
   Table 579   Working While Attending College: 1989-1990 553
Occupations 553
   Table 580   African University Teachers 553
   Table 581   Architects: 1994 555
   Table 582   Artists in Detail: 1970-1990 555
   Table 583   Artists: 1970-1990 557
   Table 584   Asian University Teachers 558
   Table 585   College Professors Worldwide 559
   Table 586   College Professors, Trends in Employment: 1993-1994 560
   Table 587   College Professors: 1987 561
   Table 588   Distribution of Employment by Major Industry Group: 1993 561
   Table 589   Distribution of Employment by Work Disability Status: 1988 562
   Table 590   Distribution of Occupations: 1993 563
   Table 591   Elementary and Secondary Public School Employment 563
   Table 592   European University Teachers 564
   Table 593   Federal Government Employment Projections 565
   Table 594   Federal Government Executive Branch Employment 566
   Table 595   Federal Government Executive Branch Employment Distribution 566
   Table 596   Food Service Managers and Supervisors 567
   Table 597   Food Service Workers 567

CHAPTER 8 - LABOR, EMPLOYMENT, AND OCCUPATIONS continued:

Table 598   Latin American/Caribbean University Teachers 568
Table 599   North American University Teachers 569
Table 600   Occupation of Employed Females by Race/Ethnicity: 1990-II 570
Table 601   Occupation of Employed Persons by Race/Ethnicity: 1990-I 571
Table 602   Occupational Outlook: 1990-2005 573
Table 603   Occupations of Hispanic Women: 1992 574
Table 604   Oceanian University Teachers 575
Table 605   Physicians: 1970-1992 575
Table 606   Physics and Chemistry Teachers: 1989-1990 576
Table 607   Physics Faculty: 1993-1994 576
Table 608   Professionals in the Private Sector 578
Table 609   Profile of Physics Teachers 579
Table 610   Registered Nurses 580
Table 611   Scientific and Engineering Faculty: 1991 582
Table 612   Secretaries 583
Table 613   Sisters Teaching in Catholic Schools: 1991 and 1992 584
Table 614   State and Local Government Executive Branch Employment 585
Table 615   Teachers: 1978-2003 585
Table 616   Tenure Status of Faculty in Higher Education 586
Table 617   Wait Staff at America's Best Restaurants 586

CHAPTER 9 - THE MILITARY 588
Operations Desert Storm/Desert Shield 588
Table 618   Active-Duty and Deployed Personnel by Rank: 1992 588
Table 619   Active-Duty and Deployed Personnel: 1992 589
Table 620   Deployed Personnel - I 590
Table 621   Deployed Personnel - II 591
Table 622   Deployed Personnel - III 592
Table 623   Deployed Personnel - IV 593
Performance 595
Table 624   Persian Gulf Deployment: Conditions 595
Table 625   Persian Gulf Deployment: Women's Performance 596
Table 626   Pilot Training Performance 598
Personnel 599
Table 627   Active Duty Forces by Rank: 1990-I 599
Table 628   Active Duty Forces by Rank: 1990-II 600
Table 629   Active-Duty Personnel by Branch: 1993 601
Table 630   Active-Duty Personnel: 1991 602
Table 631   Occupations of Active Duty Military Personnel 603
Table 632   Veteran Status by Race/Ethnicity: 1990 604
Sexual Harassment 605
Table 633   Harassment at the Academy: 1988-1993 605
Table 634   Harassment at the Academy: 1990-1991 606
Table 635   Harassment at the Academy: Don't Report It? 607
Table 636   Harassment at the Academy: Report It? 608
Table 637   Harassment at the Academy: Resulting Stress 609

CHAPTER 10 - POPULATION AND VITAL STATISTICS 610

CHAPTER 10 - POPULATION AND VITAL STATISTICS continued:

Abortions . . . .
Table 638   Abortions and Fetal Losses by Age of Woman: 1988 610
Table 639   Abortions and Fetal Losses: 1976-1988 610
Table 640   Abortions and Teenagers 611
Table 641   Abortions by Race: 1975-1992 612
Table 642   Abortions Worldwide 613
Table 643   Abortions, Characteristics: 1980-1990 614
Table 644   Abortions, Locations 616
Table 645   Abortions, Risks 617
Table 646   Fewest Legally Induced Abortions Worldwide 618
Table 647   Most Legally Induced Abortions Worldwide 619
Table 648   Legally Induced Abortions in Africa 620
Table 649   Legally Induced Abortions in Africa by Age of Woman 620
Table 650   Legally Induced Abortions in Asia 621
Table 651   Legally Induced Abortions in Asia by Age of Woman 621
Table 652   Legally Induced Abortions in Europe 622
Table 653   Legally Induced Abortions in Europe by Age of Woman 623
Table 654   Legally Induced Abortions in North America 624
Table 655   Legally Induced Abortions in North America by Age of Woman 627
Table 656   Legally Induced Abortions in Oceania 627
Table 657   Legally Induced Abortions in Oceania by Age of Woman 628
Table 658   Legally Induced Abortions in South America 629
Table 659   Legally Induced Abortions in South America by Age of Woman 629
Table 660   Post-Abortion Reaction 630
Births 630
Table 661   Asian and Near Eastern Births: 1994 631
Table 662   Birth Rate Projections by Race and Age Group: 1993 and 2010 631
Table 663   Births to Teenage Mothers by Hispanic Origin and Race: 1991 632
Table 664   Births to Teenage Mothers: 1980 and 1985-1991 633
Table 665   Births to Unmarried Teenage Mothers: 1980 and 1985-1991 634
Table 666   Births to Unmarried Women Worldwide 635
Table 667   Births to Unmarried Women: 1970-1991 636
Table 668   Births to Unmarried Women: 1980-1992 638
Table 669   Cesarean Section Deliveries: 1970-1992 639
Table 670   European Births: 1994 640
Table 671   Latin American/Caribbean Births: 1994 641
Table 672   Live Births by Mother's Medical Risk Factor and Race: 1991 643
Table 673   Live Births by Mother's Smoking Status: 1991 644
Table 674   Live Births by Obstetric Procedures: 1991 646
Table 675   Live Births by Race and Hispanic Origin: 1990-1991 647
Table 676   Live Births by Race of Child and Age of Mother: 1970-1991 649
Table 677   Live Births: 1970 to 1993 650
Table 678   Location of Births and Birth Weights: 1970-1991 651
Table 679   Multiple Births: 1985-1991 652
Table 680   Multiple Births: 1991 653
Table 681   North African Births: 1994 653
Table 682   North American Births: 1994 654
Table 683   Oceanian Births: 1994 655
Table 684   Sub-Saharan Africa Births: 1994 655
656

CHAPTER 10 - POPULATION AND VITAL STATISTICS continued: 658
    Table 685   World Births: 1994 659
Contraception 659
    Table 686   Contraceptive Use in Asia and the Near East 659
    Table 687   Contraceptive Use in Asia and the Near East by Age of Woman 660
    Table 688   Contraceptive Use in Europe 662
    Table 689   Contraceptive Use in Europe by Age of Woman 663
    Table 690   Contraceptive Use in Latin America and the Caribbean 664
    Table 691   Contraceptive Use in Latin America and the Caribbean by Age of Woman 665
    Table 692   Contraceptive Use in North Africa 667
    Table 693   Contraceptive Use in North Africa by Age of Woman 668
    Table 694   Contraceptive Use in North America 668
    Table 695   Contraceptive Use in North America by Age of Woman 669
    Table 696   Contraceptive Use in Oceania 669
    Table 697   Contraceptive Use in Oceania by Age of Woman 670
    Table 698   Contraceptive Use in Sub-Saharan Africa 671
    Table 699   Contraceptive Use in Sub-Saharan Africa by Age of Woman 673
    Table 700   Contraceptive Use in the Soviet Union 674
    Table 701   Contraceptive Use: 1982-1988 675
    Table 702   Effectiveness of Contraceptive Methods 677
    Table 703   Fewest Women Using Contraception Worldwide 677
    Table 704   Most Women Using Contraception Worldwide 678
    Table 705   Norplant Use by Teenagers 679
    Table 706   Religious Affiliation and Contraceptive Use 680
    Table 707   Teenage Contraceptive Use 680
    Table 708   Types of Contraception Used 681
    Table 709   Types of Contraception Used by Race: 1990 682
    Table 710   Types of Contraception Used: 1990 683
Deaths 683
    Table 711   Accident and Violence Deaths: 1980-1991 683
    Table 712   African Deaths by Age-I 684
    Table 713   African Deaths by Age-II 686
    Table 714   AIDS Deaths Among Americans 25 to 44 Years Old: 1995 687
    Table 715   AIDS Deaths: 1982-1992 688
    Table 716   Asian and Near Eastern Maternal Mortality Rates: 1980-1990 689
    Table 717   Asian Deaths by Age-I 690
    Table 718   Asian Deaths by Age-II 692
    Table 719   Breast Cancer Deaths: 1973-1990 695
    Table 720   Cancer Deaths: 1970-1991 696
    Table 721   Death Rates by Education and Income Level: 1986 698
    Table 722   Deaths by Age: 1970-1992 699
    Table 723   Deaths by Race and Cause: 1988 700
    Table 724   Deaths by Race: 1970-1991 701
    Table 725   European Deaths by Age-I 702
    Table 726   European Deaths by Age-II 706
    Table 727   European Maternal Mortality Rates: 1980-1990 711
    Table 728   Firearm Deaths to Age 34: 1991 712
    Table 729   Heart Disease Deaths: 1970-1991 713
    Table 730   High Maternal Mortality Rates Worldwide 714
    Table 731   High Mortality Rates Among Young Girls Worldwide 715

CHAPTER 10 - POPULATION AND VITAL STATISTICS continued:

Table 732	Infant Deaths: 1970-1993	716
Table 733	Latin America/Caribbean Deaths by Age-I	717
Table 734	Latin America/Caribbean Deaths by Age-II	722
Table 735	Latin America/Caribbean Maternal Mortality Rates: 1980-1990	726
Table 736	Leading Causes of Death by Age: 1991	727
Table 737	Lung Cancer Deaths: 1973-1990	730
Table 738	Maternal and Infant Deaths: 1970-1991	731
Table 739	Middle Eastern Deaths by Age-I	731
Table 740	Middle Eastern Deaths by Age-II	732
Table 741	Middle East/North African Maternal Mortality Rates: 1980-1990	733
Table 742	North American Deaths by Age-I	734
Table 743	North American Deaths by Age-II	734
Table 744	North American Maternal Mortality Rates: 1980-1990	735
Table 745	Oceanian Deaths by Age-I	736
Table 746	Oceanian Deaths by Age-II	737
Table 747	Oceanian Maternal Mortality Rates: 1980-1990	739
Table 748	Sub-Saharan Africa Maternal Mortality Rates: 1980-1990	740
Table 749	Suicide Rates: 1980-1991	741
Table 750	Suicides: 1970-1991	741
Table 751	Traffic Accident Deaths: 1975-1990	742
Table 752	Traffic Accident Deaths: 1990	743
Fertility		744
Table 753	Asian and Near Eastern Fertility Rates: 1995-2020	744
Table 754	European Fertility Rates: 1995-2020	745
Table 755	Fertility Rates and Race of Child: 1970-1991	747
Table 756	Latin American/Caribbean Fertility Rates: 1995-2020	748
Table 757	North African Fertility Rates: 1995-2020	749
Table 758	North American Fertility Rates: 1995-2020	750
Table 759	Oceanian Fertility Rates: 1995-2020	751
Table 760	Sub-Saharan African Fertility Rates: 1995-2020	752
Table 761	World's Largest Fertility Decline: 1985 to 1994	753
Table 762	Yugoslavian and Soviet Union Fertility Rates: 1995-2020	754
Fetal and Infant Deaths		755
Table 763	Female Infant Mortality in Asia	755
Table 764	Infant Mortality in Asia and the Near East: 1994	756
Table 765	Infant Mortality in Developed Countries: 1993	758
Table 766	Infant Mortality in Europe: 1994	759
Table 767	Infant Mortality in Latin America/Caribbean: 1994	760
Table 768	Infant Mortality in North Africa: 1994	762
Table 769	Infant Mortality in North America: 1994	762
Table 770	Infant Mortality in Oceania: 1994	763
Table 771	Infant Mortality in Sub-Saharan Africa: 1994	764
Table 772	Infant Mortality in Yugoslavia and the Soviet Union: 1994	766
Life Expectancy		767
Table 773	Expectation of Life at Birth and Other Ages: 1979-1991	767
Table 774	Expectation of Life at Birth: 1970-1992	768
Table 775	Expectation of Life at Birth: 1995-2010	768
Table 776	Expectation of Life by Age in 1990	769
Table 777	Expectation of Life in 1993	771

CHAPTER 10 - POPULATION AND VITAL STATISTICS continued:

Table 778   Expectation of Life in Asia and the Near East: 1994 772
Table 779   Expectation of Life in Europe: 1994 773
Table 780   Expectation of Life in Latin America/Caribbean: 1994 775
Table 781   Expectation of Life in North Africa: 1994 776
Table 782   Expectation of Life in North America: 1994 777
Table 783   Expectation of Life in Oceania: 1994 778
Table 784   Expectation of Life in Sub-Saharan Africa: 1994 779
Table 785   Expectation of Life in Yugoslavia and the Soviet Union: 1994 781
Marital Status 782
Table 786   Asian and Near Eastern Married Women: 1990-2000 782
Table 787   European Married Women: 1990-2000 783
Table 788   Latin American/Caribbean Married Women: 1990-2000 784
Table 789   Marital Status by Age: 1990 Census-I 786
Table 790   Marital Status by Age: 1990 Census-II 787
Table 791   Marital Status by Race and Hispanic Origin: 1970-1993 788
Table 792   Marital Status of the African Population 789
Table 793   Marital Status of the Asian and Near Eastern Population 790
Table 794   Marital Status of the European Population 790
Table 795   Marital Status of the Latin American/Caribbean Population 792
Table 796   Marital Status of the North American Population 792
Table 797   Marital Status of the Oceanian Population 793
Table 798   Never Married: 1970 and 1992 793
Table 799   North African Married Women: 1990-2000 794
Table 800   North American Married Women: 1990-2000 795
Table 801   Oceanian Married Women: 1990-2000 795
Table 802   Sub-Saharan African Married Women: 1990-2000 796
Table 803   Yugoslavian and Soviet Union Married Women: 1990-2000 797
Marriages and Divorces 799
Table 804   African Divorces 799
Table 805   African Marriages by Age-I 799
Table 806   African Marriages by Age-II 800
Table 807   African Marriages: 1987-1991 802
Table 808   Age at Marriage and Previous Marital Status: 1980-1988 802
Table 809   Asian Divorces 803
Table 810   Asian Marriages by Age-I 804
Table 811   Asian Marriages by Age-II 807
Table 812   Asian Marriages: 1987-1991 810
Table 813   Average Age at Marriage Worldwide 811
Table 814   Breakups of Two-Parent Families 813
Table 815   Divorce Rates in 5 Countries: 1920-1985 813
Table 816   European Divorces 814
Table 817   European Marriages by Age-I 815
Table 818   European Marriages by Age-II 820
Table 819   European Marriages: 1987-1991 824
Table 820   Ever Divorced: 1975 and 1990 825
Table 821   Ever Married: 1975 and 1990 826
Table 822   Lowest Divorce Rates Worldwide 826
Table 823   Highest Divorce Rates Worldwide 827
Table 824   Latin American/Caribbean Divorces 828

CHAPTER 10 - POPULATION AND VITAL STATISTICS continued:

Table 825   Latin American/Caribbean Marriages by Age-I 829
Table 826   Latin American/Caribbean Marriages by Age-II 831
Table 827   Latin American/Caribbean Marriages: 1987-1991 834
Table 828   Least Marrying Countries 835
Table 829   Most Marrying Countries 836
Table 830   Marriage Experience: 1975-1990-I 837
Table 831   Marriage Experience: 1975-1990-II 838
Table 832   Marriage Rates and Age of Bride and Groom: 1970-1988 839
Table 833   Marriages and Divorces: 1970-1993 839
Table 834   Middle Eastern Marriages: 1987-1990 840
Table 835   North American Divorces 841
Table 836   North American Marriages by Age-I 841
Table 837   North American Marriages by Age-II 842
Table 838   North American Marriages: 1987-1991 842
Table 839   Oceanian Divorces 843
Table 840   Oceanian Marriages by Age-I 843
Table 841   Oceanian Marriages by Age-I 844
Table 842   Oceanian Marriages: 1987-1991 845
Table 843   Will Divorce: 1990 846
Table 844   Will Divorce Again: 1990 847
Population 848
Table 845   Asian and Near Eastern Young and Elderly Population: 1990 848
Table 846   Childless Women: 1992 849
Table 847   Children Ever Born: 1992 851
Table 848   Developed Countries' Young and Elderly Population: 1990 852
Table 849   Elderly Population Worldwide 854
Table 850   Elderly Population, Characteristics: 1980-1993 855
Table 851   Elderly Population: 1980-1992 856
Table 852   Latin American/Caribbean Young and Elderly Population: 1990 857
Table 853   Middle East/North African Young and Elderly Population: 1990 858
Table 854   Most Females in Population Worldwide 859
Table 855   Ratio of Elderly Males to Females: 1990 859
Table 856   Ratio of Females to Males Worldwide 860
Table 857   Ratio of Females to Males Worldwide: Fewest Men 861
Table 858   Ratio of Females to Males Worldwide: Most Men 862
Table 859   Ratio of Males to Females in Asia 863
Table 860   Ratio of Males to Females: 1970-1990 864
Table 861   Resident Population by Age: 1970-1990-I 864
Table 862   Resident Population by Age: 1970-1990-II 865
Table 863   Sub-Saharan African Young and Elderly Population: 1990 865
Table 864   Urban and Rural Populations by Age: 1990 867
Population Estimates and Projections 868
Table 865   Asian Population: 2000 868
Table 866   Developed Countries' Population: 2000 869
Table 867   Elderly Population: 2000 870
Table 868   Estimates of the World's Population: 1990 871
Table 869   Hispanic and Non-Hispanic Populations: 1995-2050 872
Table 870   Latin America/Caribbean Population: 2000 873
Table 871   Middle East/North African Population: 2000 874

CHAPTER 10 - POPULATION AND VITAL STATISTICS continued:
    Table 872 Resident Population by Age and Race: 1992-I 874
    Table 873 Resident Population by Age and Race: 1992-II 875
    Table 874 Resident Population by Age: 1993-2050 876
    Table 875 Resident Population by Hispanic Origin: 1992-I 877
    Table 876 Resident Population by Hispanic Origin: 1992-II 878
    Table 877 Resident Population by Race: 1995-2050 879
    Table 878 Sub-Saharan African Population: 2000 880

CHAPTER 11 - PUBLIC LIFE 882
Politics and Government 882
    Table 879 Appointments to Civilian Positions by President Bush 882
    Table 880 Appointments to Civilian Positions by President Reagan 883
    Table 881 Gender Gap in 1990 and 1992 Elections 883
    Table 882 Heads of Government Worldwide 885
    Table 883 Ministerial Positions Worldwide 886
    Table 884 Parliamentary Representation Worldwide 887
    Table 885 Political Party Identification: 1952-1986 889
    Table 886 Political Party Identification: 1970-1988 890
    Table 887 Voter Turnout by Race and Origin: 1984-1992 891
    Table 888 Voter Turnout: 1964-1984 891
    Table 889 Voter Turnout: 1980-1992 892
    Table 890 Votes for Representatives: 1984-1994 893
    Table 891 Women in Elective Offices: 1975-1995 894
    Table 892 Women in State Legislatures, Best and Worst States: 1995 895
    Table 893 Women in State Legislatures: 1969-1995 896
    Table 894 Women in Statewide Elective Offices: 1995 897
    Table 895 Women in the U.S. Congress: 1979-1995 897
    Table 896 Women of Color in Elective Office: 1995 898
Volunteers 899
    Table 897 Asked to Volunteer and Did So 899
    Table 898 Involvement in Church, School, Community 899
    Table 899 Mother Volunteered 900
    Table 900 Volunteers: 1988-1994 901

CHAPTER 12 - RELIGION 902
Catholic Sisters/Missionaries 902
    Table 901 Catholic Missionaries Overseas: 1992 902
    Table 902 Catholic Missionary Sisters: 1980-1992 903
    Table 903 Number of Canadian Catholic Sisters: 1991 903
    Table 904 Number of Catholic Sisters by State: 1992 904
    Table 905 Number of Catholic Sisters: 1992 and 1993 906
Religious Practices, Preferences, and Attitudes 906
    Table 906 African Denominations and Membership 906
    Table 907 Asian Denominations and Membership 907
    Table 908 Catholic Marriages Performed: 1992 908
    Table 909 European Denominations and Membership 910
    Table 910 Latin America/Caribbean Denominations and Membership 911
    Table 911 Oceanian Denominations and Membership 913
    Table 912 Religious Preferences of Women Entering College: 1994 914

CHAPTER 12 - RELIGION continued:
    Table 913   The Churches' Stands on Abortion 915
   Women Clergy 919
    Table 914   African-American Pastors 919

CHAPTER 13 - SEXUALITY 920
   Sexual Practices, Preferences, and Attitudes 920
    Table 915   Achieving Orgasm 920
    Table 916   Are One-Night Stands Degrading? 921
    Table 917   Attraction 922
    Table 918   Caution in Sex 922
    Table 919   Cohabitation 923
    Table 920   Frequency of Achieving Orgasm 924
    Table 921   Frequency of Homosexual Activity 924
    Table 922   Frequency of Masturbation 925
    Table 923   Frequency of Sexual Activity 926
    Table 924   Group Sex 926
    Table 925   Number of Sex Partners 927
    Table 926   Number of Sex Partners by Age and Race 928
    Table 927   Partners of the Same Sex 929
    Table 928   Premarital Sex 929
    Table 929   Sex Ever or in the Last Three Months: 1982-1988 930
    Table 930   Sexual Self-Assessment 931
    Table 931   Simultaneous Orgasm 932
    Table 932   Variety of Sex Techniques 933
   Teenagers 934
    Table 933   Sex Ever, Teenagers by Race/Ethnicity and Poverty Level: 1982-1988 934
    Table 934   Teenage Sexual Activity 934

CHAPTER 14 - SPORTS AND RECREATION 936
   Exercise 936
    Table 935   Exercise Activities 936
   General Participation 937
    Table 936   Sports Participation: 1992 937
    Table 937   Tennis 939
    Table 938   Tennis Players' Other Activities 940
   Girl Scouts 940
    Table 939   Profiles of Girl Scouts 940
   High School 944
    Table 940   Favorite Sports 944
    Table 941   High School Athletics Participation: 1993-1994 944
    Table 942   Sports Participation: 1971-1994 946
   Leisure 947
    Table 943   Activities of College-Age Women-I 947
    Table 944   Activities of College-Age Women-II 948
    Table 945   Attendance at Arts Activities: 1982-1992 948
    Table 946   Attendance at Arts Activities: 1992-I 949
    Table 947   Attendance at Arts Activities: 1992-II 949
    Table 948   Cable Network Preferences 950
    Table 949   Desire to Attend More Arts Performances: 1992 951

CHAPTER 14 - SPORTS AND RECREATION continued:

Table 950	Lessons in Arts Activities: 1992	952
Table 951	Listening to Broadcast and Recorded Media: 1982-1992-I	952
Table 952	Listening to Broadcast and Recorded Media: 1982-1992-II	953
Table 953	Listening to Broadcast and Recorded Media: 1992-I	953
Table 954	Listening to Broadcast and Recorded Media: 1992-II	954
Table 955	Magazines, Newspapers, Television, and Online Data Services: 1993	954
Table 956	Media Exposure: 1993	955
Table 957	Musical Preferences: 1992	956
Table 958	Not Enough Leisure Time	957
Table 959	Participation in Arts Activities: 1992-I	957
Table 960	Participation in Arts Activities: 1992-II	958
Table 961	Participation in Leisure Activities: 1992	958
Table 962	Radio Format Preferences	959
Table 963	Radio Network Preferences	960
Table 964	Subscribers to Online Services	961
Table 965	Television and Teenagers	961
The Economics of Sports		962
Table 966	Sports Business	962

List of Sources Consulted	965
Subject and Geographic Index	985

PREFACE

Strong interest in the field of women's studies continues to be seen in government, the media, and academia, as well as among business marketers, and interest in the topic has lately expanded to encompass women around the world. Students, researchers, government officials, journalists, and the concerned public are hungry for information of all kinds on the topic of women. The need for easy-to-use statistics on any subject from multiple sources is particularly acute. *Statistical Record of Women*, 2nd Edition seeks to address these needs by bringing together actual statistical data on the lives and status of women throughout the world from a wide variety of sources —government and nongovernment, U.S. and international, published and unpublished—in a single accessible and affordable compilation.

MULTIPLICITY OF SOURCES

The data arranged herein have been collected from periodical literature, government documents, reports and studies from associations, companies, institutions, research centers, organizations, and other materials that provide statistical information on women regularly or incidentally. Coverage is approximately 60% U.S. and 40% international. In short, *Statistical Record of Women Worldwide*, 2nd Edition is not a repackaging of U.S. Census Bureau information; rather, it is a compilation of data from many sources illustrating the condition of women around the world.

COMPARATIVE AND HISTORICAL DATA

Because statistical data are more meaningful when comparisons can be made, data for men, data by race/ethnicity, and data for girls are presented in this book when feasible. Further, to underscore progress or its lack in the improvement of the lot of women, U.S. data are sometimes presented in a historical context; due to space limitations, however, such data generally go back no further than 1970. Space constraints usually preclude presentation of international data in a historical context as well. Some forecast data are presented.

COVERAGE OF TOPICS NATIONALLY AND INTERNATIONALLY

When consulting this volume, the reader will note that some topics are covered in more detail than others. This is a reflection of the general availability of the published data. There is no shortage of data on topics such as labor, population, education, and health; religion and sexuality, however, are areas for which data are not so plentiful. When the Census Bureau proposed to include a question about religious affiliation in the 1970 census, a storm of protest arose, asserting that such a question was a violation of the constitutional guarantee of freedom of religion. And information about sexuality, when it does exist, can be unreliable.

Because data collection methods and accuracy vary from country to country, international coverage in this book is for the most part limited to data collected and standardized by international sources rather than by individual foreign national sources. (In this respect, it is interesting to note that as late as 1990, only 75 of the World Health Organization's 164 member states were able to measure maternal mortality, although maternal mortality accounted for the largest or near-largest proportion of deaths among women of reproductive age in most of the developing world.

GEOGRAPHIC SCOPE OF THIS VOLUME

The geographic scope of this book ranges from individual cities to states and the United States as a whole, from major world areas to individual countries. Individual countries and U.S. cities and states are indexed in the "Subject and Geographic Index" at the end of this book.

ARRANGEMENT OF CHAPTERS

The status of a woman in a society is often defined in terms of her level of income, employment, education, health and fertility, and the roles she plays in the family and society. With this in mind, chapters in this book are divided into such topics as Income, Spending, and Wealth; Labor, Employment, and Occupations; Education; Health and Medical Care; Domestic Life; and Public Life. Other topics include Crime, Law Enforcement, and Legal Justice; Business and Economics; The Military; Population and Vital Statistics; Religion; Sexuality; and Sports and Recreation. Within each chapter are subheadings that group tables together under broad subjects. Each table has a sequential entry number above a brief headline outlining its scope. Subject access is facilitated by a comprehensive "Table of Contents," which lists each table within a chapter, and by a detailed "Subject and Geographic Index." For a detailed explanation, refer to the How to Use This Book section.

ACKNOWLEDGMENTS

The editor gratefully acknowledges the assistance of proofreader Ann Lane and research assistant Zohre Raein Frouzan. Thanks to all those sources who provided materials for inclusion in this book. And thanks to Anna Sheets at Gale Research Inc. and Gary Alampi at Editorial Code and Data for their encouragement and assistance.

HOW TO USE THIS BOOK

Entries in the *Statistical Record of Women Worldwide* are arranged into 14 chapters, as outlined on the Contents pages. Within each chapter, tables are arranged under broad subject headings and are assigned a sequential entry number. A sample entry illustrating and explaining the types of information typically provided in an entry is shown below.

Access to entries is facilitated by the alphabetical Subject and Geographic Index appearing at the end of this volume. An explanation of this index follows the sample entry.

SAMPLE ENTRY

The boldfaced number next to each portion of the sample entry designates an item of information that might be included in an entry. Each item is explained in the paragraph below preceded by the corresponding number in the sample entry.

1. Sequential Entry Number. The entries in this volume are numbered sequentially, beginning with the first entry in Attitudes and Opinions and ending with the last entry in Sports and Recreation. Both the sequential entry number and the page number are used in the Subject and Geographic Index (the entry number is surrounded by brackets) to refer to an entry.

2. Headline. A brief headline outlines the scope of the table.

3. Explanatory Note. An explanation of table details such as the universe included. May also include information provided in the table's source document that is relevant to the information presented in the table but may not be included there or that helps clarify the information provided in the table.

4. Legend. Defines who or what are to be enumerated below.

5. Data. Statistical information appears here, usually in the form of percentages or numbers (this is clearly indicated on the table). In a few cases, where data does not easily lend itself to the tabular format, summaries of data are provided in text form.

6. Source Notes. Here appears a description of the source from which this book's editor took the data. A fuller description of the source is provided in the List of Sources Consulted at the end of the book.

7. Primary Source. Here appears a description of where the data that is described in the Source Notes was obtained.

Other information that might appear after the Primary Source includes general notes about the table, other information that is available in the cited source, footnotes from the cited source, and references to related reading on the topic.

Sample Entry

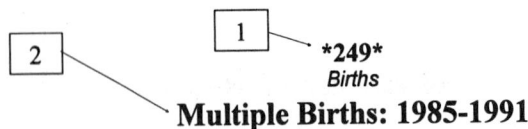

249
Births

Multiple Births: 1985-1991

This table gives data about multiple births by age of the mother in 1985 and 1991. Incidence of plural births increases with the age of the mother, and the rate reached 3.4 for white women and 3.6 for black women aged 35 to 39 in 1991. Multiple birth rates were 14% higher in 1991than in 1985 for women of all races and ages combined. The rages increased in each age group, with the largest rise among women between 40 and 44 years of age.

[Rate per 1,000 total live births.]

Age of mother	1985			1991		
	All plural deliveries	Twin births	Triplet/other high order	All plural deliveries	Twin births	Triplet/other high order
Total	21.0	20.5	0.5	23.9	23.1	0.8
Under 15	9.6	9.3	0.3	11.6	11.3	0.2
15-19	13.2	13.1	0.1	14.6	14.4	0.2
20-24	18.7	18.3	0.4	19.8	19.4	0.4
25-29	22.3	21.6	0.7	24.5	23.7	0.8
30-34	26.2	25.5	0.7	29.9	28.4	1.4
35-39	27.0	26.3	0.7	33.5	31.8	1.7
40-44	21.0	20.5	0.6	26.8	26.3	0.5
45-49	18.9	18.8	--	20.5	20.5	--

Source: "Birth Rates by Plurality and Age of Mother United States, 1985 and 1991," *Statistical Bulletin,* 75(3), July-September 1994, Table 2, p. 31. Primary sources: National Center for Health Statistics; computations by the Health and Safety Education Division, Medical Department, Metropolitan Life Insurance Company.

SUBJECT AND GEOGRAPHIC INDEX

A comprehensive Subject and Geographic Index is provided at the end of this volume. The Subject and Geographic Index indexes general table topics as well as "line items" within tables for every table in the book. Unless otherwise specified, the index items relate to women. Subject terms refer to the United States only unless modified by "worldwide" or by a country name. Tables listed under "United States" feature the United States and are international in scope. Here it should be noted that the source conventions for naming countries were used in the presentation of data. Therefore, some tables refer to Burma while others refer to Myanmar, the name by which Burma is now known. In such cases, appropriate "See also" references are provided.

LIST OF SOURCES CONSULTED

Here appears detailed information and sometimes ordering information about the source from which the data for this book were collected.

CONCLUSION

While censuses of population have been conducted for at least five thousand years, it is only since about 1970 that there has existed the technology enabling the collection of detailed information specifically on women. The collection and interpretation of such a vast amount of data are always subject to error. Particularly in the case of international statistics, the contributions of women to the family, society, and socioeconomic development are often grossly underestimated and sometimes completely disregarded in official statistics. The rationale for the exclusion of whole areas of productive activity, such as the fruits of subsistence farming (which still comprises most of the world's farming activity and is primarily the work of women) is summarized in the 1953 revision of the United Nations' System of National Accounts thus: "primary production and the consumption of their own produce by nonprimary producers is of little or no importance." Data on female labor force participation in developing countries is affected by variables such as male respondents being less likely to report female economic activity, and by male interviewers making assumptions about female respondents (that they are housewives, for example). So, these statistics about women should in many cases be approached as general guidelines to what is known about the lives and status of women and girls worldwide.

Statistical
Record
OF Women
Worldwide

Chapter 1
ATTITUDES AND OPINIONS

Abortion

★ 1 ★

Is Abortion Murder?

The table below shows the responses of women and men to a survey question about whether they consider abortion to be murder.

Response	Women, total	Career women	Home-makers	Men
N =	1,411	639	281	1,343
Abortion is murder.				
Strongly agree	15%	12%	15%	14%
Agree	15%	13%	14%	16%
No opinion	15%	15%	23%	18%
Disagree	26%	26%	29%	32%
Strongly disagree	29%	34%	19%	20%
Strongly agree + agree	30%	25%	29%	30%
Disagree + strongly disagree	55%	60%	48%	52%

Source: "Abortion Is Murder," Samuel S. Janus, PhD, and Cynthia L. Janus, MD, *The Janus Report on Sexual Behavior*, (New York: John Wiley & Sons, Inc., 1993), Table 3.6, p. 61. Between 1988 and 1992, the authors distributed 4,550 questionnaires to subjects at a variety of sites. The sample design was planned to conform to the population distribution of the United States in the areas of sex, age, region, income, education, and marital status. Returned questionnaires totaled 3,260. Of these, 495 were discarded. Satisfactorily completed questionnaires totaled 2,765: 1,418 women and 1,347 men. In this table, women have been further designated as career women or homemakers.

★ 2 ★

Abortion

Southerners' Views on Abortion

This table presents the answers of Southerners who were asked, "Do you think abortion should be legal under all circumstances, legal only under certain circumstancs, or illegal under all circumstances?" The Southern states are Alabama, Arkansas, Florida, Georgia, Kentucky, Louisiana, Mississippi, North Carolina, South Carolina, Tennessee, Texas, and Virginia.

Group	Legal under all	Legal under some	Illegal under all
Total	27%	50%	18%
Male	27%	49%	18%
Female	27%	51%	19%

Source: Selected from Rosita M. Thomas, *Abortion: National and State Public Opinion Polls,* CRS Report for Congress, 89-591 GOV, October 24, 1989, p. CRS-63. Primary source: Baxter, Tom, "Survey Shows South Is Torn Over Abortion," *The Atlanta Journal-Constitution,* July 28, 1989, p. A1, A6. The results of the Atlanta Journal-Constitution Southern Poll are based on telephone interviews with 1,403 adults in 12 Southern and border states. The survey was conducted between July 20-24, 1989. According to the release, "one can say with 95 percent certainty that the survey results represent the views of all adults in the 12 Southern and border states within plus or minus 3 percentage points." For results based on subgroups the margin of error is larger.

★ 3 ★

Abortion

Views on Abortion-I

This table presents some of the views of 2,406 women surveyed by the *Los Angeles Times* in 1989 on various aspects of the abortion question.

Question	Yes	No	Not sure	Refused
Candidate's Stand on Abortion				
Is the abortion issue so important to you that you would switch your vote from your original choice and vote for somebody else because you disagreed on abortion, or not?	32%	59%	8%	1%
Do you think a political candidate's position on abortion... is an important factor in deciding whether or not to vote for that candidate?	44%	51%	4%	1%

[Continued]

★3★

Views on Abortion-I
[Continued]

Question	Yes	No	Not sure	Refused
Fewer Abortions if Made Illegal? Do you think that making abortion illegal will reduce the number of abortions in the United States, or not?	31%	62%	6%	1%
Is Adoption the Solution? Do you think the solution to abortion is adoption, or not?	54%	35%	10%	1%

Source: Selected from Rosita M. Thomas, *Abortion: National and State Public Opinion Polls*, CRS Report for Congress, 89-591 GOV, October 24, 1989, pp. CRS44-CRS60. Primary source: The Los Angeles Times Poll. The results are based on a telephone survey across the nation, including the states of Alaska and Hawaii, with a sample of 2,406 women, 18 years of age or older, contacted during the period March 3-10, 1989. The margin of error is plus or minus 4 percentage points.

★4★

Abortion

Views on Abortion-II

This table presents some of the views of 2,406 women surveyed by the *Los Angeles Times* in 1989 on various aspects of the abortion question.

Question	Not aware	Favor strongly	Favor somewhat	In-different	Oppose somewhat	Oppose strongly	Not sure	Refused
What Is Your Stand? Generally speaking... are you in favor of abortion, or are you opposed to it, or are you indifferent on the subject, or haven't you heard enough about it yet to say?	3%	17%	17%	18%	13%	27%	4%	1%
Roe vs. Wade are you in favor of the Supreme Court decision which permits a woman to get an abortion from a doctor at any time within the first three months of her pregnancy, or are you opposed to that, or are you indifferent on the subject...	5%	27%	19%	10%	11%	24%	3%	1%

[Continued]

★4★

Views on Abortion-II
[Continued]

Question	Not aware	Favor strongly	Favor somewhat	In-different	Oppose somewhat	Oppose strongly	Not sure	Refused
Public Funds for Abortions?								
are you in favor of using public funds for abortions when the mother cannot afford it...	2%	17%	21%	3%	20%	32%	5%	0%
Nationwide Standards?								
are you in favor of wiping out nationwide standards about abortion and permitting each state to decide whether abortions are legal within its boundaries...	2%	15%	19%	5%	18%	32%	8%	1%
Amend Constitution?								
are you in favor of an amendment to the United States Constitution that would prohibit abortions...	2%	20%	8%	2%	21%	42%	5%	0%
RU-486								
A new abortion pill, called RU-486, has been developed in France that can be purchased at a drugstore with a doctor's prescription and is 95 percent effective during the first seven weeks of pregnancy. Generally speaking, would you be in favor of such a pill if it were available here in America...	6%	18%	14%	3%	14%	39%	6%	0%
Public Funds for Adoption?								
If abortion were to become illegal again, would you be in favor of using public funds to support the adoption of the babies that would result from the policy...	1%	36%	27%	1%	12%	16%	6%	1%

Source: Selected from Rosita M. Thomas, *Abortion: National and State Public Opinion Polls*, CRS Report for Congress, 89-591 GOV, October 24, 1989, pp. CRS44-CRS60. Primary source: The Los Angeles Times Poll. The results are based on a telephone survey across the nation, including the states of Alaska and Hawaii, with a sample of 2,406 women, 18 years of age or older, contacted during the period March 3-10, 1989. The margin of error is plus or minus 4 percentage points.

★ 5 ★

Abortion

Views on Abortion-III

This table presents some of the views of 2,406 women surveyed by the *Los Angeles Times* in 1989 on various aspects of the abortion question.

Question	Yes	No	Not sure	Refused
What if Baby Deformed?				
Please tell me whether or not you think it should be possible for a pregnant woman to obtain a legal abortion if there is a strong chance of serious defect in the baby.	74%	17%	8%	1%
Mother Wants No More Children				
Should a pregnant woman be able to get a legal abortion, or not, if she is married and does not want any more children?	36%	54%	9%	1%
What if Health Is Endangered?				
How about when a woman's health is seriously endangered by pregnancy? Do you think it should, or should not, be possible for a woman to obtain a legal abortion in that case?	88%	6%	5%	1%
What if Family Is Poor?				
Should a pregnant woman be able to obtain a legal abortion if the family has a very low income and cannot afford any more children, or not?	41%	49%	9%	1%
What About Rape or Incest?				
If a woman became pregnant as the result of rape or incest, should it be possible for a woman to obtain a legal abortion, or not?	84%	10%	6%	0%
Matrimony Not Desired				
If an unmarried woman who is pregnant does not want to marry the man, should she be able to get a legal abortion, or not?	40%	51%	8%	1%

[Continued]

★5★

Views on Abortion-III
[Continued]

Question	Yes	No	Not sure	Refused
Any Reason at all?				
Do you think a pregnant woman should, or should not, be able to get a legal abortion no matter what the reason?	34%	57%	8%	1%

Source: Selected from Rosita M. Thomas, *Abortion: National and State Public Opinion Polls*, CRS Report for Congress, 89-591 GOV, October 24, 1989, pp. CRS44-CRS60. Primary source: The Los Angeles Times Poll. The results are based on a telephone survey across the nation, including the states of Alaska and Hawaii, with a sample of 2,406 women, 18 years of age or older, contacted during the period March 3-10, 1989. The margin of error is plus or minus 4 percentage points.

★6★

Abortion

Views on Abortion-IV

This table presents some of the views of 2,406 women surveyed by the *Los Angeles Times* in 1989 on various aspects of the abortion question.

Question/response	Percent
Who Should Be Punished?	
If abortion were to become illegal again, who do you think should be punished for breaking the law? Do you think the woman should be punished, or the father of the child, or the doctor who performed the abortion, or somebody else, or do you think no one should be punished for breaking the law?	
No one	22%
Woman	9%
Father	1%
Doctor	34%
Someone else	3%
Not sure	12%
Refused	2%
Everyone	17%

Source: Selected from Rosita M. Thomas, *Abortion: National and State Public Opinion Polls*, CRS Report for Congress, 89-591 GOV, October 24, 1989, pp. CRS44-CRS60. Primary source: The Los Angeles Times Poll. The results are based on a telephone survey across the nation, including the states of Alaska and Hawaii, with a sample of 2,406 women, 18 years of age or older, contacted during the period March 3-10, 1989. The margin of error is plus or minus 4 percentage points.

★7★

Abortion

Views on Abortion-V

This table presents some of the views of 2,406 women surveyed by the *Los Angeles Times* in 1989 on various aspects of the abortion question.

Question/response	Percent
Who Should Pay for Abortion?	
Who do you think ought to pay the expenses of an abortion? Should the government pay, or medical insurance...	
Both father and mother	18%
Government	4%
Insurance	10%
Agency[1]	0%
Church	0%
Mother	27%
Father	24%
Mother's relatives	1%
Someone else	2%
Not sure	11%
Refused	3%

Source: Selected from Rosita M. Thomas, *Abortion: National and State Public Opinion Polls,* CRS Report for Congress, 89-591 GOV, October 24, 1989, pp. CRS44-CRS60. Primary source: The Los Angeles Times Poll. The results are based on a telephone survey across the nation, including the states of Alaska and Hawaii, with a sample of 2,406 women, 18 years of age or older, contacted during the period March 3-10, 1989. The margin of error is plus or minus 4 percentage points. *Note:* 1. "Some private agency..."

★8★

Abortion

Views on Abortion-VI

This table presents some of the views of 2,406 women surveyed by the *Los Angeles Times* in 1989 on various aspects of the abortion question.

Question/response	Percent
Morality of Abortion	
Do you believe abortion is morally right or morally wrong? Are you completely convinced about that, or do you sometimes have doubts?	
Not aware	1%

[Continued]

★ 8 ★

Views on Abortion-VI
[Continued]

Question/response	Percent
Convinced/right	12%
Doubt/right	10%
Indifferent	4%
Doubt/wrong	24%
Convinced/wrong	37%
Not sure	11%
Refused	1%

Source: Selected from Rosita M. Thomas, *Abortion: National and State Public Opinion Polls*, CRS Report for Congress, 89-591 GOV, October 24, 1989, pp. CRS44-CRS60. Primary source: The Los Angeles Times Poll. The results are based on a telephone survey across the nation, including the states of Alaska and Hawaii, with a sample of 2,406 women, 18 years of age or older, contacted during the period March 3-10, 1989. The margin of error is plus or minus 4 percentage points.

★ 9 ★
Abortion

Views on Abortion-VII

This table presents some of the views of 2,406 women surveyed by the *Los Angeles Times* in 1989 on various aspects of the abortion question.

Question	Agree strongly	Agree somewhat	Disagree somewhat	Disagree strongly	Not sure	Refused
Permission for Minors?						
Minors should have to get their parents' permission before they get an abortion.	64%	17%	6%	8%	4%	1%
Is Abortion Murder?						
Abortion is murder.	42%	16%	15%	19%	7%	1%
Abortion a Woman's Decision						
I personally feel that abortion is morally wrong, but I also feel that whether or not to have an abortion is a decision that has to be made by every woman for herself.	49%	25%	9%	12%	4%	1%

[Continued]

★ 9 ★

Views on Abortion-VII
[Continued]

Question	Agree strongly	Agree somewhat	Disagree somewhat	Disagree strongly	Not sure	Refused
I am in favor of abortion because every woman has the right to control her own body.	34%	17%	14%	30%	4%	1%

Source: Selected from Rosita M. Thomas, *Abortion: National and State Public Opinion Polls*, CRS Report for Congress, 89-591 GOV, October 24, 1989, pp. CRS44-CRS60. Primary source: The Los Angeles Times Poll. The results are based on a telephone survey across the nation, including the states of Alaska and Hawaii, with a sample of 2,406 women, 18 years of age or older, contacted during the period March 3-10, 1989. The margin of error is plus or minus 4 percentage points.

★ 10 ★

Abortion

Views on Abortion-VIII

This table presents some of the views of 2,406 women surveyed by the *Los Angeles Times* in 1989 on various aspects of the abortion question.

Question	Percent
When Does Life Begin?	
Do you believe that life begins at conception, or at birth, or somewhere in-between, or haven't you heard enough about that yet to say?	
Not aware	10%
Conception	41%
In-between	27%
Birth	15%
Not sure	6%
Refused	1%

[Continued]

★ 10 ★

Views on Abortion-VIII
[Continued]

Question	Percent
Perspectives on Abortion	
There are a number of different ways to think about abortion: Some people think of abortion mainly as a moral or religious question, having to do mainly with what is right or wrong... Some pople think of abortion mainly as a way to shape the future of a woman and her child, of rescuing them perhaps from grief and economic distress... Some people think of abortion mainly as a human right that guarantees a woman control over her own body... And some people think of abortion mainly as a realistic solution, a necessary evil for a personal dilemma. What is your opinion about abortion? Do you see it mainly as a...	
Moral	39%
Rescue	6%
Human right	25%
Realism	18%
Other	2%
Not sure	9%
Refused	1%
Roe versus Wade	
In 1973, the U.S. Supreme Court decided that state laws which made it illegal for a woman to have an abortion up to three months of pregnancy were unconstitutional, and that the decision on whether or not a woman should have an abortion up to three months of pregnancy should be left to the woman and her doctor to decide. In general, do you favor or oppose the U.S. Supreme Court decision...	
Favor	56%

[Continued]

★ 10 ★

Views on Abortion-VIII
[Continued]

Question	Percent
Oppose	42%
Not sure	2%

Source: Selected from Rosita M. Thomas, *Abortion: National and State Public Opinion Polls,* CRS Report for Congress, 89-591 GOV, October 24, 1989, pp. CRS44-CRS60. Primary source: The Los Angeles Times Poll. The results are based on a telephone survey across the nation, including the states of Alaska and Hawaii, with a sample of 2,406 women, 18 years of age or older, contacted during the period March 3-10, 1989. The margin of error is plus or minus 4 percentage points.

Economy

★ 11 ★

Which Tax Is the Worst?

This table shows responses of men and women to a public opinion survey asking the question, "Which do you think is the worst tax, that is, the least fair: Federal income tax, Social Security tax, state income tax, State sales tax, local property tax?" The sample for the poll was 1,003 adults aged 18 and over.

Characteristic of respondent	Federal Income tax	Social Security tax	State Income tax	State sales tax	Local Property tax	Don't know/ No answer
Total public	27.2%	12.4%	7.4%	13.6%	28.4%	11.0%
Male	28.9%	12.0%	7.9%	11.9%	28.5%	10.8%
Female	25.6%	12.8%	6.9%	15.2%	28.3%	11.2%
Total head of household	28.3%	12.6%	6.7%	13.3%	29.0%	10.1%
Male head	29.5%	11.1%	7.1%	12.2%	30.5%	9.5%
Female head	27.2%	13.9%	6.3%	14.2%	27.7%	10.7%

Source: Selected from "Which Do You Think is the Worst Tax - That is, the Least Fair: Federal Income Tax, Social Security Tax, State Income Tax, State Sales Tax, Local Property Tax?" Advisory Commission on Intergovernmental Relations, Washington, DC, 1994, *Changing Public Attitudes on Governments and Taxes,* Table A1, p. 11.

Home, Family, Community

★ 12 ★

Do You Feel Your Contributions Are Valued?

According to a survey based on interviews with 1,502 women aged 18 to 55, two-thirds of whom were employed outside the home at least part time, more working women feel their taking care of their responsibilities at home is valued than do women in general. Among the findings of the survey was that 88% of all women agree that it is their responsibility to care for their families. This table shows the responses of all women and working women to the question: "How much do you think others value you for taking care of your responsibilities at home?"

Response	All women	Working women
How much to you think others value you for taking care of your responsibilities at home?		
Very much	59%	62%
Somewhat	35%	33%
Not at all	5%	4%
Other	1%	1%

Source: Jacquelynn Boyle, "Job important, but majority of female workers put family first," *Detroit Free Press*, May 11, 1995, pp. 1A,8A. Tamar Lewin, "Study Says More Women Earn Half Their Household Income," *The New York Times*, May 11, 1995, p. A13 Y. Primary source: Whirlpool Foundation survey by Louis Harris and Associates, New York, of 1,502 U.S. women 18-55 years old interviewed November-December 1994; margin of error is plus or minus 2 percentage points.

★ 13 ★

Home, Family, Community

Gift Preferences

This table shows selected gifts, ranked by preference scores, for men and women aged 18 and older, in 1993.

[Based on scale of 1 being least preferred and 5 being most.]

Rank and Gift	Total	Men	Women
1. Money	4.20	4.24	4.17
2. Travel	3.80	3.81	3.79
3. Clothing	3.42	3.19	3.64
4. Audio/video	3.27	3.56	2.98
5. Books	3.17	3.03	3.31
6. Photographs	2.99	2.71	3.28

[Continued]

★ 13 ★

Gift Preferences
[Continued]

Rank and Gift	Total	Men	Women
7. Home accessories	2.98	2.75	3.20
8. Jewelry	2.94	2.46	3.41
9. Flowers or plants	2.77	2.17	3.37
10. Kitchen gadgets/ appliances	2.73	2.50	2.96
11. Sports equipment	2.69	3.30	2.08
12. Fragrance	2.66	2.34	2.97
13. Tools	2.61	3.35	1.87
14. Magazine subscription	2.29	2.42	2.15
15. Food or candy	2.28	2.21	2.34
16. Games	2.25	2.37	2.14

Source: "The Year Ahead," *American Demographics*, December 1993, pp. 42-52, p. 48, table entitled "What We Want: Money and Travel Are Everyone's Most Wanted Gifts." Primary source: Discovery Research Group/Present Perfect Survey.

★ 14 ★

Home, Family, Community

Is It Necessary to Delay Marriage for Financial Security?

This table shows the responses of college-educated and non-college-educated women to the question: "Is it necessary in today's economy to delay marriage or having children so you can get on a sound financial footing?

Description	Yes	No	Don't know
College-educated women	80%	16%	4%
Women without college	65%	30%	4%

Source: Jeanne May, "Career first, most agree, then a family," *Detroit Free Press*, May 17, 1995, pp. 1+. Primary source: Free Press/WXYZ-TV survey of 18- to 35-year-olds in Wayne, Oakland and Macomb counties, conducted April 9-17 by EPIC/MRA of Lansing. Some responses do not total 100 percent because of rounding.

★ 15 ★

Home, Family, Community

Modern Families

Author Shere Hite collected responses from more than 3,000 people mainly from Western countries for an analysis of the modern family. A prepublication excerpt from her book, *The Hite Report on the Family: Growing Up Under Patriarchy*, appeared in *Ms.* magazine. This table summarizes some of the points from that prepublication excerpt.

Item	Number/percent
Childrens' view: My parents seem completely asexual.	83%
Views of girls from single-parent families:	
It was a positive experience.	49%
I did not like it.	20%
Mixed feelings.	31%
Life experiences of boys from mom-only families:	
Formed "strong, lasting ties with women."	80%
By comparison, boys from two-parent families.	40%

Source: Selected from "Bringing Democracy Home," *Ms.*, March/April 1995, pp. 55-61. Excerpted from *The Hite Report on the Family: Growing Up Under Patriarchy*, Grove Press, 1994.

★ 16 ★

Home, Family, Community

Single or Married Life the Best?

The table below shows the responses of single women and men to a survey question about whether or not they considered the singles' life the most gratifying life-style. More women than men do not find the single life gratifying. The authors suggest womens' awareness of their "biological clock" and their lower incomes as possible reasons.

Responses	Women	Men
N =	438	377
Singles' life is the most gratifying.		
Strongly agree	6%	8%
Agree	15%	21%
No opinion	19%	25%
Disagree	52%	42%
Strongly disagree	8%	4%

[Continued]

★ 16 ★

Single or Married Life the Best?
[Continued]

Responses	Women	Men
Strongly agree + Agree	21%	29%
Disagree + Strongly disagree	60%	46%

Source: "The Singles' Life Is the Most Gratifying Life-Style," Samuel S. Janus, PhD, and Cynthia L. Janus, MD, *The Janus Report on Sexual Behavior*, (New York: John Wiley & Sons, Inc., 1993), Table 5.3, p. 146. Between 1988 and 1992, the authors distributed 4,550 questionnaires to subjects at a variety of sites. The sample design was planned to conform to the population distribution of the United States in the areas of sex, age, region, income, education, and marital status. Returned questionnaires totaled 3,260. Of these, 495 were discarded. Satisfactorily completed questionnaires totaled 2,765: 1,418 women and 1,347 men.

★ 17 ★

Home, Family, Community

Use of Husband's Last Name

This table shows the percent of currently married women who did not use their husband's last name in 1993. According to researchers, "Achiever" women, such as Hillary Rodham Clinton, are more likely to use a last name different from their spouse's.

Characteristic	Percent
All currently married women	10%
Education	
High school graduate	5%
Some college	8%
Associate degree	9%
Bachelor's degree	15%
Post-grad. degree	21%
Age of householder	
Less than 30	14%
30 to 39	14%
40 to 49	10%
50 to 59	5%
60 and older	5%
Household Income	
Less than $12,500	10%
$12,500-$24,999	7%
$25,000-$39,999	7%

[Continued]

★ 17 ★

Use of Husband's Last Name
[Continued]

Characteristic	Percent
$40,000-$59,999	9%
$60,000 and more	13%

Source: "Why Hillary Chooses Rodham Clinton," *American Demographics*, March 1994, p. 9, table entitled "I Do, But Not With Your Name." Primary source: NFO Research, Inc. for American Demographics.

★ 18 ★

Home, Family, Community

What Makes You Feel Successful at Home?

This table shows the responses of women and men to the question, "What makes you feel successful at home?"[1].

Response	Women	Men
What makes you feel successful at home?		
Good family relationships	26%	27%
Well-adjusted, healthy kids	22%	8%
Getting everything done	20%	13%
Care for spouse, kids	18%	7%
Clean, orderly home	15%	2%
Money to afford things	5%	20%
Time for myself	2%	5%

Source: Jacquelynn Boyle, "Job important, but majority of female workers put family first," *Detroit Free Press*, May 11, 1995, pp. 1A,8A. Tamar Lewin, "Study Says More Women Earn Half Their Household Income," *The New York Times*, May 11, 1995, p. A13 Y. Primary source: Whirlpool Foundation survey by Louis Harris and Associates, New York, of 1,502 U.S. women 18-55 years old interviewed November-December 1994; margin of error is plus or minus 2 percentage points. Men's responses from a companion Harris survey of 460 American men taken around the same time; margin of error is plus or minus 3 percentage points. *Note:* 1. Most popular responses.

International Opinion Polls

★ 19 ★

British Women on Health

This table shows the responses of British men and women to statements about women's health. The date was February 1992. The sample size was 2,077.

Statement	Agree		Disagree	
	Men	Women	Men	Women
Women with painful periods should seek relief.	81%	94%	2%	2%
Women with period problems should see their doctor.	81%	92%	2%	3%
Women with period problems are best off in the company of other women when they have their periods.	30%	26%	30%	53%
Women's periods make men's life a misery.	24%	23%	47%	62%
Women make too much fuss about having periods.	12%	23%	54%	62%

Source: Selected from Elizabeth Hann Hastings and Philip K. Hastings, eds., *Index to International Public Opinion, 1992-1993*, 1994, p. 171.

★ 20 ★

International Opinion Polls

British Women on Sexual Harassment at Work-I

This table shows the percentages of British men and women who responded "very/fairly serious" to statements about sexual harassment in the work place. The questions were asked in May 1992 of 989 full- or part-time workers.

Questions and responses	Very/fairly serious		
	Total	Men	Women
I am going to read out a number of things that some people have said constitute sexual harassment when men do them to women at work. I'd like you to tell me how serious an example of sexual harassment each is, if at all.			
Telling a women colleague that your sexual fantasies involve her.	89%	89%	90%
Flirting and making playful grabs for women colleagues.	87%	86%	88%
Touching or kissing a woman colleague.	86%	84%	88%
Telling sexual jokes that belittle women.	72%	71%	74%
Hugging or patting a woman colleague for doing her job.	62%	60%	64%
Touching a woman colleague when explaining things to her.	62%	62%	63%
Expecting women to get the coffee and run errands.	48%	42%	57%
Pinning up girlie calendars.	39%	37%	42%
Commenting on the sexual attractiveness of women colleagues.	34%	32%	37%
Calling a woman colleague "love" or "dear."	8%	7%	9%

Source: Selected from Elizabeth Hann Hastings and Philip K. Hastings, eds., *Index to International Public Opinion, 1992-1993*, 1994, p. 496.

★ 21 ★

International Opinion Polls

British Women on Sexual Harassment at Work-II

This table shows the responses of British men and women to a question about the reasons why they believe sexual harassment occurs at work. The questions were asked in May 1992 of 989 full- or part-time workers.

Question and responses	Total	Men	Women
Now looking through this list, which of these would you say are the main, or most common, reasons why sexual harassment occurs at work?			
Men not understanding what women find offensive.	52%	50%	54%
Men who see women as sex objects.	44%	40%	49%
Women not making their objections clear before a problem gets worse.	35%	31%	39%
Men not taking women's roles at work seriously.	32%	28%	38%
Women wearing provocative clothes.	30%	29%	32%
Women flirting with male colleagues.	28%	28%	29%
Men resenting women for taking "men's" jobs.	23%	16%	32%
An inevitable result of men's sexual urges.	15%	15%	14%
None of these.	--	1%	--

Source: Selected from Elizabeth Hann Hastings and Philip K. Hastings, eds., *Index to International Public Opinion, 1992-1993,* 1994, p. 496.

★ 22 ★

International Opinion Polls

British Women on the Battle of the Sexes

This table shows some highlights of a London *Mail* poll of 1,000 women, as reported in the *Detroit News*.

Item	Number/Percent
Working women who said they had suffered sexual harassment at work	50%
Percentage of women who believe the "New Man" who considers women his equals is a myth	50%
Percentage of women who said they do all the housework	64%
Percentage of women who cook all the meals	65%
Percentage of women who thought their own sons showed even more sexual prejudice than their fathers	30%

Source: "We're No. 2 in the battle of the sexes, British women say in poll," *Detroit News*, June 25, 1995, p. 5A.

★ 23 ★

International Opinion Polls

Canadian Women on Women's Status

This table shows the responses of Canadian men and women to two questions about women's status. The date of the first question was June 1992 and the sample size was 1,024. The date of the second question was February 1993 and the sample size was 1,041.

Statement	Support/ Yes	Don't sup-port/No	No opinion/ Don't know
Do you support the goals of the feminist movement or not?			
Men	61%	27%	12%

[Continued]

★ 23 ★

Canadian Women on Women's Status
[Continued]

Statement	Support/ Yes	Don't sup- port/No	No opinion/ Don't know
Women	58%	30%	12%
In your opinion, do women in Canada get as good a break as men?			
Men	47%	49%	4%
Women	34%	63%	3%

Source: Selected from Elizabeth Hann Hastings and Philip K. Hastings, eds., *Index to International Public Opinion, 1992-1993,* 1994, p. 494.

★ 24 ★

International Opinion Polls

Canadian Women on Working Mothers

This table shows the responses of Canadian men and women to the question: "There are more married women with families in the working world than ever before. Do you think this has a harmful effect on family life or not?" The question was asked in December 1992 of a sample size of 1,011 people.

Gender	Harmful	Not harmful	Don't know
Male	54%	42%	4%
Female	51%	44%	5%

Source: Selected from Elizabeth Hann Hastings and Philip K. Hastings, eds., *Index to International Public Opinion, 1992-1993,* 1994, pp. 249-250.

★ 25 ★
International Opinion Polls

German Women on Equal Rights

This table shows the responses of German men and women to the statement: "As you see it, have equal rights for women in everyday life been introduced as a general rule, in most instances, partially,...?" The question was asked in April 1992. The sample size was 1,001.

Gender	Generally	In most cases	Partially	Frequently not	Usually not	No answer
Men	7%	31%	39%	16%	7%	--
Women	4%	20%	43%	20%	9%	2%

Source: Selected from Elizabeth Hann Hastings and Philip K. Hastings, eds., *Index to International Public Opinion, 1992-1993*, 1994, p. 495.

★ 26 ★
International Opinion Polls

German Women on Politics

This table shows the responses of German men and women to the statement: "There were demands recently that half of all seats in the parliaments and half of all cabinet rank ministries should be held by women, thus guaranteeing that the same number of women hold these positions as men do. Which of the following opinions do you tend to agree with?" (Opinions below.) The question was asked in September 1992. The sample size was 2,156.

Opinion	Percent agreeing		
	Total	Men	Women
It is not the gender that is important, but only personal qualifications.	43%	51%	35%
If the distribution in the general population between men and women is 50-50, the same ratio should apply to the Bundestag and cabinets.	36%	27%	43%

Source: Selected from Elizabeth Hann Hastings and Philip K. Hastings, eds., *Index to International Public Opinion, 1992-1993*, 1994, p. 495.

★ 27 ★

International Opinion Polls

German Women on Work

This table shows the responses of East and West German working women to the question, "What are your reasons for working? The date was April 1992. The sample size was 2,644 working women in West Germany and 1,711 working women in East Germany.

Response	West Germany	East Germany
To earn my own money and be independent.	63%	64%
To have contacts with others.	41%	64%
To achieve something, use my abilities.	40%	57%
To be able to afford myself.	39%	64%
Because I love my job.	36%	53%
I need to get away from housework.	31%	38%
I need to contribute to family income.	23%	43%
To be recognized, to be somebody.	14%	19%

Source: Selected from Elizabeth Hann Hastings and Philip K. Hastings, eds., *Index to International Public Opinion, 1992-1993*, 1994, p. 495.

★ 28 ★

International Opinion Polls

German Women on Working Women-I

This table shows the responses of West German men and women and East German women to the question: "Recently someone said, 'Women have only one choice, either to raise children or to have a career. If a woman wants one of the two, she has to go without the other.' Would you say this is true or not?" The question was asked in April 1992 of a sample size of 2,666 West Germans and 1,711 East Germans.

| Response | West Germany | | | | East Germany Women |
| | Total | | Women | | |
	1986	1992	1986	1992	1992
True	58%	55%	57%	57%	44%
False	32%	35%	35%	33%	45%
Undecided	10%	10%	8%	10%	11%

Source: Selected from Elizabeth Hann Hastings and Philip K. Hastings, eds., *Index to International Public Opinion, 1992-1993,* 1994, pp. 250.

★ 29 ★

International Opinion Polls

German Women on Working Women-II

This table shows the responses of East and West German men and women to the question: "Perhaps you know that one has to make a decision for what is more important. If you had to choose between a career and a family, what would you put in first place?" The question was asked in April 1992 of a sample size of 2,644 West Germans and 1,711 East Germans.

Response	Total	Total women	Working women	Men
Career				
West Germany	11%	7%	11%	16%
East Germany	13%	9%	11%	18%
Family				
West germany	62%	70%	58%	51%
East Germany	58%	66%	61%	48%
Undecided				
West Germany	27%	23%	31%	33%
East Germany	29%	25%	28%	34%

Source: Selected from Elizabeth Hann Hastings and Philip K. Hastings, eds., *Index to International Public Opinion, 1992-1993,* 1994, pp. 250.

★ 30 ★
International Opinion Polls

Japanese Women on Children

This table shows the responses of Japanese married couples (wives 16-49 years old) to questions about children. The questions were asked in March 1992 of a sample of 2,389 married couples.

| Question | Wife's Response | | Husband |
	1992	1990	1992
Ideally, how many children do you want to have?			
None	1%	--	2%
One	3%	3%	2%
Two	41%	37%	36%
Three	46%	47%	45%
Four	8%	8%	6%
More than four	1%	1%	3%
No answer	1%	4%	7%
Asked of those who have children: How many more children do you want?			
No more	71%	72%	68%
One more	19%	15%	16%
Two more	7%	6%	8%
Three more	1%	1%	2%
Four more	--	--	--
More than four	--	--	--
No answer	3%	5%	6%
Asked of wives who do not want any more children: Why do you not want any more children? Choose up to two from the answers below.			
It costs a lot to raise children.	38%	30%	
It is physically tiring to take care of children.	11%	--	
It takes constant care to bring up children (e.g., entrance exams and training).	16%	--	
Fewer children would be better for my work.	4%	4%	
Fewer children better for enjoying life.	2%	6%	
Our house is too small.	10%	8%	

[Continued]

★ 30 ★

Japanese Women on Children
[Continued]

Question	Wife's Response		Husband
	1992	1990	1992
Household economy is not good because of housing loan etc.	5%	5%	
The future of children is insecure because of the lack of resources and environmental problems.	10%	9%	
Already have had as many as I want.	33%	32%	
Other	18%	30%	
No answer	3%	7%	
Asked of wives who do not want any more children: If the government takes the measures below, will you change your mind and want to have more children?			
If the amount of pension is increased according to the number of children.			
Yes	8%	7%	
No	72%	73%	
Don't know	18%	14%	
No answer	3%	7%	
If parental leave is introduced to lighten women's burden of caring for family member.			
Yes	11%		
No	66%		
Don't know	20%		
No answer	3%		
What do you think the government should do about the decrease in the number of children in our families?			
Should take measures to increase number of births.	34%	18%	35%

[Continued]

★ 30 ★

Japanese Women on Children
[Continued]

Question	Wife's Response		Husband
	1992	1990	1992
Improper for government to encourage increase in births, since to have a child or not is a personal matter.	61%	78%	57%
Asked of wives only: Is your family "couple-centered" or "child(ren)-centered?"			
Couple-centered	20%		
Child(ren)-centered	42%		
Difficult to say	38%		
No answer	1%		

Source: Selected from Elizabeth Hann Hastings and Philip K. Hastings, eds., *Index to International Public Opinion, 1992-1993*, 1994, pp. 245-46.

★ 31 ★

International Opinion Polls

Japanese Women on Reasons to Work

This table shows the responses of Japanese married couples (wives 16-49 years old) to questions about working wives. The questions were asked in March 1992 of a sample of 2,389 married couples.

Question/Response	1992	1990
Asked of working wives: What are the main reasons you are working? Choose up to two from the answers below.		
Money for children's education.	30%	27%
To pay house mortgage.	9%	10%
Family business.	18%	20%
To use my abilities.	10%	9%
To be financially independent.	14%	10%
I have extra time after raising children.	13%	15%
My husband's income is low.	18%	16%
My job is important to my life.	14%	13%

[Continued]

★ 31 ★

Japanese Women on Reasons to Work
[Continued]

Question/Response	1992	1990
To widen my social view.	22%	21%
Asked of husbands: Are you for or against the idea of your wife's working?		
For	54%	
Against but can't stop it	23%	
Against	16%	
No answer	8%	
If "Against" wife's working : What is the main reason for that?		
We are financially OK.	7%	
Wives should be at home taking good care of the family.	54%	
Working mothers do not take good care of children.	34%	
It is not respectable for my wife to work outside.	1%	

Source: Selected from Elizabeth Hann Hastings and Philip K. Hastings, eds., *Index to International Public Opinion, 1992-1993*, 1994, pp. 251.

★ 32 ★

International Opinion Polls

Japanese Women on Work

This table shows the responses of Japanese working women to the question: "What is your working history so far? Choose one from the following." The question was asked in November 1991. Sample size was 2,137; the question was asked of the unspecified number of respondents who were working women.

Response	Percent
Have kept a job (including changing jobs) since I started working, without becoming a full time homemaker.	40%
Once quit a job and became a homemaker, but have started working again.	48%

[Continued]

★ 32 ★

Japanese Women on Work

[Continued]

Response	Percent
Became a homemaker without working experience, but am now working.	11%
Other.	2%

Source: Selected from Elizabeth Hann Hastings and Philip K. Hastings, eds., *Index to International Public Opinion, 1992-1993,* 1994, p. 497.

Major Concerns

★ 33 ★

Biggest Worries

According to a survey based on interviews with 1,502 women aged 18 to 55, two-thirds of whom were employed outside the home at least part time, the biggest worries are lack of family time and crime. More money would improve the lives of a third of the respondents. This table shows their responses to the questions, "What's your biggest worry?" and "What one change would imrpove your life."[1].

Response	Percent
What's your biggest worry?	
Lack of family time	26%
Crime	25%
Quality of schools	18%
Quality of child care	8%
Care for elderly relative	7%
Fast pace of life	6%
What one change would improve your life?	
More money	34%
Better job	13%
More time	10%
More education	8%
Family situation	5%

[Continued]

★ 33 ★

Biggest Worries

[Continued]

Response	Percent
Neighborhood	4%
Different man	1%

Source: Jacquelynn Boyle, "Job important, but majority of female workers put family first," *Detroit Free Press*, May 11, 1995, pp. 1A,8A. Tamar Lewin, "Study Says More Women Earn Half Their Household Income," *The New York Times*, May 11, 1995, p. A13 Y. Primary source: Whirlpool Foundation survey by Louis Harris and Associates, New York, of 1,502 U.S. women 18-55 years old interviewed November-December 1994; margin of error is plus or minus 2 percentage points. *Note:* 1. Most popular responses.

★ 34 ★

Major Concerns

What Are Major Economic Worries?

The Ms. Foundation for Women and the Center for Policy Alternatives collaborated on a project involving six focus groups and a nationwide poll to find out what were the concerns of all women and to identify those that were specific to certain groups of women. This table shows the responses of women, especially women of color and women who identified themselves as blue-collar, to questions about their ability to get and keep a job. Women around the country expressed concern that either they or their husbands would be laid off. The Women's Voices Poll found that more than 50% of women believe that economic concerns are the nation's greatest problem.

Economic worry	
Making ends meet	36%
Lose job	32%
Become sole support	28%
Can't pay rent	22%

Source: Womens Voices: A Polling Report, A Joint Project of the Ms. Foundation for Women and Center for Policy Alternatives, p. 19.

★ 35 ★
Major Concerns
What Are Women's Top Concerns?

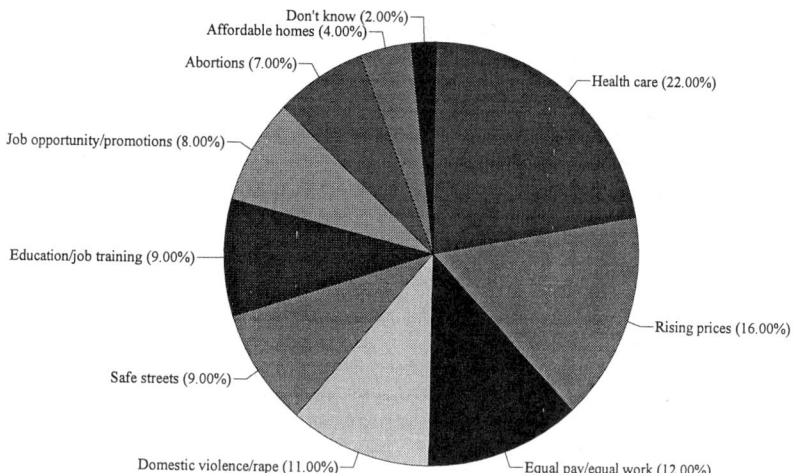

The Ms. Foundation for Women and the Center for Policy Alternatives collaborated on a project involving six focus groups and a nationwide poll to find out what were the concerns of all women and to identify those that were specific to certain groups of women. This table shows those areas that women identified as necessary to meet their basic needs. *Fifty-one percent* of all women surveyed reported feeling that they had fallen behind economically over the last year. *Eighty-six percent* of women surveyed want guaranteed health insurance provided for everyone regardless of ability to pay for it.

Concern	Percent
Health care	22%
Rising prices	16%
Equal pay/equal work	12%
Domestic violence/rape	11%
Safe streets	9%
Education/job training	9%
Job opportunity/promotions	8%
Abortions	7%
Affordable homes	4%
Don't know	2%

Source: Womens Voices: A Polling Report, A Joint Project of the Ms. Foundation for Women and Center for Policy Alternatives, p. 13.

Politics and Government

★ 36 ★

Approval Ratings of President Reagan

This table shows the differences between men and women in approval ratings of President Reagan at various years during his term. Women were less supportive than men of the Reagan administration at the national level and among every major population sub-group. While 49% of college-educated men supported Mr. Reagan, only 42% of college-educated women did. Sixty-two percent of Republican women supported Mr. Reagan, compared to 74% of Republican men. In households where the chief wage-earner was employed in business or the professions, 45% of women approved compared to 52% of men. Thirty percent of women in blue-collar occupations approved compared to 35% of men. Sixteen percent of black men approved, compared to 6% of black women.

Year	Avg. percent approving during year		
	Men	Women	% difference
1985	53%	47%	6 points
1986	68%	59%	9 points
1987-1988[1]	53%	44%	9 points

Source: "Differences Between Men and Women in Approval Ratings of President Reagan, 1985-1987," Jennifer D. Williams, *CRS Report for Congress: The "Gender Gap": Differences Between Men and Women in Political Attitudes and Voting Behavior in the 1980s*, September 28, 1989, Table 2, p. CRS-10. Primary sources: Average approval ratings for 1985 are from four Gallup Polls for which sample sizes were published, enabling an average to be computed by the Congressional Research Service. Averages for 1986 and 1987-1988 are from: George Gallup, "Reagan's Public Standing Unaffected by 1987's Momentous Events." Gallup Poll Press Release, Feb. 28, 1988, p. 5. *Note:* 1. Average approval ratings for 1987 and January 1988.

★ 37 ★

Politics and Government

Approval Ratings of Presidents

This table shows the differences between men and women in approval ratings of presidents Eisenhower through Reagan. The author of the *CRS Report for Congress* says, "Before 1980, most studies of political attitudes and voting behavior found few differences between the sexes. Since that year, however, notable differences—known as the 'gender gap'—have been observed.

President	Avg. percent approving during term		
	Men	Women	% difference
Reagan (1981 through mid-1984)	54%	45%	9 points
Reagan (1981 through Sept. 1988)	56%	48%	8 points
Carter	46%	47%	1 point
Ford	45%	46%	1 point
Nixon	50%	47%	3 points
Johnson	56%	54%	2 points
Kennedy	70%	70%	0 points
Eisenhower	63%	65%	2 points

Source: "Differences Between Men and Women in Approval Ratings of Presidents Eisenhower Through Reagan," Jennifer D. Williams, *CRS Report for Congress: The "Gender Gap": Differences Between Men and Women in Political Attitudes and Voting Behavior in the 1980s*, September 28, 1989, Table 1, p. CRS-9. Primary sources: George Gallup, "Reagan's Strong Job Rating Unchanged Since November." Gallup Poll Press Release, Aug. 5, 1984, p. 2. George Gallup and Alec., "Reagan Regaining Public's Confidence." Gallup Poll Press Release, Oct. 9, 1988, p. 2.

★ 38 ★

Politics and Government

Dissatisfaction with Major Political Parties

This table shows the percentage of men and women who said they agreed with the following statement: "Some people say we should have a third major political party in this country in addition to the Democrats and Republicans." The percentage of men and women who said they voted for Ross Perot, an independent candidate for President in 1992, is also shown. The poll was said to depict an "embittered and cynical" electorate.

Gender	Should have a 3d major political party	Said they voted for Perot in 1992
Total	53%	14%
Male	58%	17%
Female	47%	11%

Source: Richard L. Berke, "U.S. Voters Focus on Selves, Poll Says," *The New York Times,* September 21, 1994." Primary source: From a survey by the Times Mirror Center for People and the Press. Telephone interviews were conducted July 12-27, 1994, with 3,800 epople age 18 and older. Margin of error: plus or minus two percentage points.

★ 39 ★

Politics and Government

Opinions on Political Issues: 1981-1983

This table shows the differences between men and women in opinions on political issues from 1981-1983.

Question	Men	Women	Difference[1]
War and Peace Issues			
"How likely do you think it is that a third world war using nuclear weapons will break out in the next twenty years...?" (Harris, March 1983)			
Very likely	24%	33%	15.5
Somewhat likely	32%	38%	
Not very likely at all	42%	26%	
"[If increasing aid and military advisors] did not stop them, would you support sending U.S. combat troops to fight the rebels [in El Salvador]?" (CBS/NY Times, June 1983)			
Favor	42%	24%	-14.0
Oppose	52%	62%	

[Continued]

★ 39 ★

Opinions on Political Issues: 1981-1983
[Continued]

Question	Men	Women	Difference[1]
"U.S. Marines went to Lebanon as part of an international peace-keeping force to try to prevent fighting there. Do you approve or disapprove of the Government's sending troops to Lebanon for that purpose?" (CBS/ NY Times			
September 1983			
Approve	47%	28%	-16.0
Disapprove	46%	59%	
October 26-27, 1983			
Approve	55%	41%	-12.0
Disapprove	38%	48%	
ERA and Abortion			
"Do you favor or oppose the Equal Rights Amendment... the constitutional amendment concerning women?" (CBS/NY Times, June 1982)			
Favor	53%	51%	-1.0
Oppose	35%	35%	
"Do you think abortions should be legal under any circumstances, legal under only certain circumstances, or illegal in all circumstances?" (Gallup, June 1983)			
Legal (all)	24%	22%	-1.0
Legal (certain)	57%	58%	
Illegal (all)	16%	17%	
Environment			
"Protecting the environment is so important that requirements and standards cannot be too high and continuing environmental improvements must be made regardless of cost." (CBS/NY Times)			
September 1981			
Agree	41%	48%	7.0[2]
April 1983			
Agree	58%	58%	0

[Continued]

★ 39 ★

Opinions on Political Issues: 1981-1983
[Continued]

Question	Men	Women	Difference[1]
Most Important Problem			
"What do you think is the most important problem facing the country today?" (CBS/NY Times, January 1983)			
Unemployment	31%	41%	10.0[3]
Budget deficit	27%	17%	-10.0
Inflation	8%	15%	7.0
Social security	10%	11%	1.0
Foreign competition	6%	3%	-3.0
U.S. military strength	7%	4%	-3.0
Interest rates	7%	3%	-4.0

Source: Selected from "Differences Between Men and Women in Opinions on Issues, 1981-1983" Jennifer D. Williams, *CRS Report for Congress: The "Gender Gap": Differences Between Men and Women in Political Attitudes and Voting Behavior in the 1980s,* September 28, 1989, Table 5, p. CRS-27. Primary sources: Public opinion polls conducted between September 1981 and October 1983 by CBS/*NY Times,* Gallup, and Harris. *Notes:* 1. A positive number indicates that women were more likely than men to give a positive response; a negative number means that women were more likely to choose the negative alternative. Difference = [(% women positive minus % men positive) minus (% women negative minus % men negative)] / 2. 2. Difference = % women agreeing minus % men agreeing. 3. Difference = % women who chose the problem minues % of men who did so.

★ 40 ★

Politics and Government

Opinions on Political Issues: 1986-1988

This table shows the differences between men and women in opinions on political issues from 1986-1988. As in the earlier part of the 1980s, the sexes had different opinions on war and peace issues. Women were more pessimistic about the likelihood of nuclear war. Women were more inclined to feel that defense spending was not beneficial to the domestic economy. Women were also more critical than men of the country's military presence in the Persian Gulf War.

Question	Men	Women	Difference[1]
War and Peace Issues			
"How likely is it that we in the United States will get into a nuclear war within the next twenty-five years...?" (Marttila and Kiley, Inc., March 1988)			
Very likely	9%	12%	10.5
Fairly likely	18%	25%	
Fairly unlikely	34%	33%	
Very unlikely	37%	27%	

[Continued]

★ 40 ★

Opinions on Political Issues: 1986-1988
[Continued]

Question	Men	Women	Difference[1]
"Would you generally agree or disagree with this statement: The amount of money we are spending on defense is hurting our country's economic well being." (Marttila and Kiley, Inc., March 1988)			
Agree	50%	60%	10.5
Disagree	47%	36%	
"Do you approve or disapprove of the American military presence in the Persian Gulf?" (Gallup, November 1987)			
Approve	68%	45%	-16.5
Disapprove	25%	35%	
Defense versus Economy			
"...of these two issues, which do you think is more important: maintaining a strong national defense or handling the nation's economic problems?" (NBC, September 1988)			
Strong defense	37%	27%	-9.0[2]
Economic problems	50%	58%	
Defense versus Environment			
"...which of these two issues do you think is more important: maintaining a strong national defense or handling the nation's environmental problems?" (NBC, September 1988)			
Strong defense	52%	43%	-8.5[2]
Environmental problems	35%	43%	
Women's Issues			
"If your party nominated a woman for President, would you vote for her if she were qualified for the job?" (Gallup, August 1987)			
Yes	81%	83%	2.0[3]

[Continued]

★ 40 ★

Opinions on Political Issues: 1986-1988
[Continued]

Question	Men	Women	Difference[1]
"Do you think that private clubs should or should not have the right to exclude prospective members on the basis of their sex?" (Gallup, July 1987)			
Should	39%	25%	-12.5
Should not	58%	69%	
"The U.S. Supreme Court has ruled that a woman may go to a doctor to end pregnancy at any time during the first three months of pregnancy. Do you favor or oppose this ruling?" (Gallup, February 1986)			
Favor	45%	45%	-1.5
Oppose	43%	46%	
Most important problem			
"What do you think is the most important problem facing this country today...?" [Respondents were given the choices listed below and could name other problems if they wished.] (LA Times, May 1987)			
Federal budget deficit	43%	32%	-11.0[4]
Farm problems	14%	10%	-4.0
Inflation	8%	15%	7.0
Nuclear arms control	20%	21%	1.0
Moral decline	23%	30%	7.0
Balance of foreign trade	23%	10%	-13.0
Iran-Contra affair	11%	19%	8.0
Unemployment	16%	26%	10.0
Other	12%	9%	-3.0

Source: Selected from "Differences Between Men and Women in Opinions on Issues, 1986-1988," Jennifer D. Williams, *CRS Report for Congress: The "Gender Gap": Differences Between Men and Women in Political Attitudes and Voting Behavior in the 1980s*, September 28, 1989, Table 6, p. CRS-31. Primary sources: Public opinion polls conducted between February 1986 and September 1988 by Gallup, *LA Times*, Marttila and Kiley, Inc., and NBC. *Notes:* 1. A positive number indicates that women were more likely than men to give a positive response; a negative number means that women were more likely to choose the negative alternative. Difference = [(% women positive minus % men positive) minus (% women negative minus % men negative)] / 2. 2. Difference = [(% women choosing the first problem minus % men choosing the first problem) minus (% women choosing the second problem minus % men choosing the second problem)] / 2. 3. Difference = % women answering "yes" minus % men answering "yes." 4. Difference = % women who chose the problem minus % of men who did so.

★ 41 ★

Politics and Government

Opinions on Political Issues: 1990-1992

This table shows the differences between men's and women's opinions on contemporary issues, according to recent polls.

Question	Women	Men
War and Peace		
Do you approve or disapprove of the United States' decision to send U.S. troops to Saudi Arabia as a defense against Iraq? (Gallup, January 1991)		
Approve	54%	78%
Do you feel that the U.S. and its allies should have continued fighting until Saddam Hussein was removed from power, or not? (Gallup, April 1991)		
Should have continued	48%	65%
How likely do you think we are to get into a nuclear war within the next ten years – very likely, fairly likely, fairly unlikely, or very unlikely? (Gallup, October 1991)		
Very or fairly likely	35%	20%
Do you think it was a good thing or a bad thing that the atomic bomb was developed? (Gallup, July 1990)		
Good thing	27%	47%
Use of Force in Nonmilitary Situations		
Are you in favor of the death penalty for persons convicted of murder? (Gallup, June 1991)		
Yes	72%	81%
Would you favor or oppose a ban on the sale of all handguns, except those that are issued to law-envorcement officers? (New York Times/ CBS News Poll, March 1992)		
Favor	49%	31%

[Continued]

★ 41 ★

Opinions on Political Issues: 1990-1992
[Continued]

Question	Women	Men
Environmental Protection and Nuclear Safety		
All in all, which of the following best describes how you feel about the environmental problems facing the earth? Life on earth will continue without major environmental disruptions only: If we take additional, immediate, and drastic action concerning the environment; (or) if we take some additional actions concerning the environment; (or) if we take just about the same actions we have been taking on the environment. (Gallup, April 1991)		
Immediate drastic action	61%	53%
Some people think we should built more nuclear power plants because they don't burn coal or oil, which create air pollution. Others think that we should not build any more nuclear power plants because of the threat of accident or radiation. Which do you agree with? (NBC Poll, July 1990)		
Should build	24%	46%
Health and Social Welfare		
If you had a say in making up the federal budget this year, for which would you like to see spending increased, decreased or kept the same? (Times Mirror Center, October 1990)		
Social Security? Increased	69%	57%
Improving the nation's health care? Increased	83%	76%
Reducing drug addiction? Increased	77%	68%
Programs for the homeless? Increased	72%	63%
With which of the following statements do you agree? The government should help the needy even if that means more debt?		
Agree	55%	48%

[Continued]

★ 41 ★

Opinions on Political Issues: 1990-1992
[Continued]

Question	Women	Men
The government should guarantee all food and shelter?		
Agree	68%	57%
Do you think all employers, regardless of size, should or should not be required to provide health insurance for their employees? (NBC Poll, 12/91)		
Agree	74%	58%
Racial Equality and Civil Rights		
Generally speaking, do you think that companies should be required to hire about the same proportion of blacks and other minorities as live in the surrounding community? (Gallup, June 1991)		
Should be required	52%	37%
Do you think that "affirmative action" for blacks and women always means quotas, or do you think it is possible to have affirmative action without quotas? (CBS/New York Times, 9/91)		
Means quotas	17%	25%
Equal Opportunity		
Some people say that the United States continues to need a strong women's movement to push for changes that benefit women. Do you agree or disagree? (CBS/New York Times, July 1989)		
Agree	65%	51%
Do you feel that women in this country have equal job opportunities with men or not? (Gallup, February 1990)		
Yes	37%	46%

Source: Center for the American Woman and Politics (CAWP), Eagleton Institute of Politics, Rutgers University, *Fact Sheet.* Primary sources: Public opinion polls.

★ 42 ★

Politics and Government

Opinions on Political Parties: 1987-1988

This table shows the differences between men's and women's opinions about which political parties are better able to handle inflation, unemployment, and national security.

Question	Men	Women	Difference[1]
"[Which political party is better at] reducing unemployment?" (NBC/ Wall Street Journal, January 1988)			
Republican	35%	28%	-5.0
Democratic	45%	48%	
"[Which political party is better at] keeping inflation down?" (NBC/ Wall Street Journal, January 1988)			
Republican	53%	39%	-11.5
Democratic	24%	33%	
"[Which political party is better at] maintaining U.S. security?" (NBC/Wall Street Journal, January 1988)			
Republican	54%	40%	-10.5
Democratic	23%	30%	
"Looking ahead for the next few years, which political party do you think would be more likely to keep the United States out of World War III?" (Gallup, December 1987)			
Republican	36%	30%	-5.0
Democratic	38%	42%	
"Which political party will do a better job of keeping the country prosperous?" (Gallup, December 1987)			
Republican	46%	36%	-5.5
Democratic	37%	38%	

Source: Selected from "Differences Between Men and Women in Party Evaluations, 1987-1988," Jennifer D. Williams, *CRS Report for Congress: The "Gender Gap": Differences Between Men and Women in Political Attitudes and Voting Behavior in the 1980s*, September 28, 1989, Table 8, p. CRS-41. Primary sources: Public opinion polls conducted in December 1987 by Gallup and January 1988 by NBC/*Wall Street Journal. A positive number indicates that women were more likely than men to select the Republican party as better able to handle the problem; a negative number means that women were more likely to choose the Democratic Party. Difference = [(% women Republican minus % men Republican) minus (% women Democratic minus % men Democratic)] / 2.*

★ 43 ★

Politics and Government

What Is a Top Priority for Government?

The Ms. Foundation for Women and the Center for Policy Alternatives collaborated on a project involving six focus groups and a nationwide poll to find out what were the concerns of all women and to identify those that were specific to certain groups of women. This table shows the cumulative responses of all women who agree that the item is a top priority or is very important for government. Along with health care and pay equity, women still consider discrimination in pay and promotion their top concerns.

Concern	
Guarantee health care	86%
Pass laws/equal pay	78%
Discrimination laws	74%
Increase minimum wage	66%
Help parents/day care	69%
Violence prevention	68%
Keep abortion legal	53%
Require/family leave	69%
Increase funds/women's education	68%
Tax credit/child care	63%
Fund job training	66%
After school programs	58%
Tax credit/homemakers	47%
More child support	47%

Source: Womens Voices: A Polling Report, A Joint Project of the Ms. Foundation for Women and Center for Policy Alternatives, p. 14.

★ 44 ★

Politics and Government

Which Level of Government Is the Least Effective?

This table shows responses of men and women to a public opinion survey asking the question, "From which level of government do you feel you get the least for your money—Federal, State, or Local?" Sample size was 1,003 adults aged 18 and over.

Characteristic of respondent	Federal	State	Local	Don't know/ No answer
Total public	46.1%	21.2%	19.3%	13.3%
Male	51.9%	20.3%	16.6%	11.2%
Female	40.7%	22.1%	21.9%	15.4%
Total head of household	47.2%	21.1%	18.8%	12.8%
Male head	54.7%	19.1%	16.5%	9.7%
Female head	40.8%	22.8%	20.8%	15.5%

Source: Selected from "From Which Level of Government Do You Feel You Get the Least for Your Money-Federal, State, or Local?" Advisory Commission on Intergovernmental Relations, Washington, DC, 1994, *Changing Public Attitudes on Governments and Taxes,* Table A2, p. 12.

★ 45 ★

Politics and Government

Would the Country Be Better Off with Women Leaders?

The Ms. Foundation for Women and the Center for Policy Alternatives collaborated on a project involving six focus groups and a nationwide poll to find out what were the concerns of all women and to identify those that were specific to certain groups of women. This table shows the responses of groups of women to the question, "Would the country be better off if half the leadership were women?

Characteristic	Yes
Q. Would the country be better off if half the leadership were women?	
All women	
Better off	74%
Much better off	27%
College-educated women	
Much better off	35%

[Continued]

★ 45 ★

Would the Country Be Better Off with Women Leaders?
[Continued]

Characteristic	Yes
City dwellers Much better off	35%
Latina Much better off	38%
College-educated Latina Much better off	56%
College-educated African American women Much better off	45%

Source: Womens Voices: A Polling Report, A Joint Project of the Ms. Foundation for Women and Center for Policy Alternatives, p. 29.

Religion

★ 46 ★

Sisters on the Sisterhood and Morality

The *Los Angeles Times* surveyed 1,041 nuns to determine their views on abortion and other issues, their expectations about their profession and their level of job satisfaction. One-quarter of the sample was over age 75, and 11% were under the age of 45. The Jesuit magazine *America* analyzed the survey data. This table shows some of the findings.

Statement	Agree
Percent of nuns who are "very satisfied" with their lives.	60%
Percent of nuns who are "satisfied" with their lvies.	29%
Percent who would "definitely" choose to become a nun if given the opportunity again.	74%
Percent of nuns who would "probably" choose to become a nun if given the opportunity again.	19%

[Continued]

★ 46 ★

Sisters on the Sisterhood and Morality
[Continued]

Statement	Agree
Percent of nuns who agree the sisterhood exceeds their expectations.	64%
Percent of nuns who agree the sisterhood is worse than they had expected.	5%
Percent of nuns who say it is "very unlikely" they would leave the sisterhood.	94%
Percent of nuns who "definitely" would seek ordination if the church permitted women priests.	2%
Percent of those aged 36-45	36%
Percent of nuns who describe their religious beliefs and moral doctrine as	
Liberal	38%
Moderate	39%
Conservative	24%
"Is there any one group or type of person in the United States who particularly needs better ministry or more attention from the church than it's getting?"	
Children and youth	22%
Percent who support the rights of the laity to disagree with church teaching and still be considered faithful Catholics.	70%
Percent who reported counseling individuals to act in contradiction to church teaching.	14%
Percent who agree that euthanasia is always a sin.	81%
Percent who agree that suicide is always a sin.	74%
Percent who believe abortion, premarital sex and homosexual sex are always a sin.	62%

[Continued]

★ 46 ★

Sisters on the Sisterhood and Morality
[Continued]

Statement	Agree
Percent who believe surrogate motherhood is always a sin.	51%
Percent who condemn pro-choice politicans.	46%
Percent who condemn masturbation.	39%
Percent who condemn the use of condoms against AIDS.	35%
Percent who endorse the church doctrine on birth control.	31%
Percent who believe the church is in "excellent" or "good" condition.	47%
Percent who believe the church is getting better.	35%
Percent who approve of the job performance of Pope John Paul II.	71%
Think he is "too conservative."	50%
Percent who believe that at least some of the changes brought about by Vatican II have helped the church.	61%
Percent who favor	
Married priests	70%
Ordination for women	60%
Election of bishops	58%
Rights for dissenting theologians	56%
Allowing priests to run for office	49%
Declaring sexism a sin	73%

Source: Elizabeth Durkin and Julie Durkin Montague, "Surveying U.S. Nuns," *America*, 172(4), February 11, 1995, pp. 11+. Related reading, Francis X. Clines, "As Nuns Grow Fewer, Sisters Find their Rewards Expanding," *New York Times*, February 23, 1995, p. B 8 Y. According to the article, from 1965 to 1995, the number of U.S. nuns declined by half, to fewer than 100,000. Ninety-seven percent of U.S. nuns are 40 or older, and the median age is 65 and rising.

★ 47 ★

Religion

Women Pastors?

This table shows the responses of African American clergy to the question: "Do you approve or disapprove of a woman as pastor of a church?" Only 3.7% of African American clergy in 2,150 churches are female.

Characteristic	Approve	Disapprove
Female clergy	81.5%	18.5%
Male clergy	50.8%	49.2%

Source: Kate DeSmet, "The Pain of the Woman Pastor," *The Detroit News and Free Press*, February 5, 1995, p. A1, A10. Primary source: C. Eric Lincoln and Lawrence H. Mamiya, *The Black Church in the African American Experience* (Duke University Press, 1990).

Sex Roles

★ 48 ★

Teenagers and Sex Roles

This table shows the responses of 1,055 teenagers aged 13 to 17 to various questions about sex roles. The poll showed that boys are significantly more traditional in their expectations of the family life they will have as adults than girls are. Seventy-one percent of the respondents had mothers employed outside the home.

Statement/Response	All	Girls	Boys
In today's society, there are more advantages in:			
Being a man	35%	37%	32%
Being a woman	7%	8%	6%
It's the same	55%	52%	59%
Do most girls you know think of boys as:			
Equals	50%	57%	41%
Better than themselves	49%	42%	56%
Do most boys you know think of girls as:			
Equals	36%	34%	39%
Lesser than themselves	61%	63%	59%

[Continued]

★ 48 ★

Teenagers and Sex Roles
[Continued]

Statement/Response	All	Girls	Boys
How likely is it that you will get married?			
Very likely	63%	65%	62%
Somewhat likely	32%	29%	34%
Not at all likely	4%	6%	3%
How likely is it that you will have children?			
Very likely	55%	57%	53%
Somewhat likely	38%	35%	41%
Not at all likely	6%	7%	4%
Could you have a happy life or would you feel you missed part of what you need to be happy if:			
You don't get married?			
Missed	32%	26%	38%
Still happy	67%	73%	61%
You don't have children?			
Missed	48%	49%	47%
Still happy	51%	50%	52%
You get divorced?			
Missed	30%	22%	37%
Still happy	68%	77%	60%
GIRLS			
When you get married, do you expect to:			
Stay at home	X	7%	X
Work	X	86%	X
BOYS			
When you get married, do you expect your wife to:			
Work	X	X	58%
Stay at home	X	X	19%

Source: Tamar Levin, "Traditional Family Favored by Boys, Not Girls, Poll Says, *The New York Times,* July 11, 1994, pp. 1+. Primary source: Based on nationwide telephone interviews with 1,055 teenagers aged 13 to 17 conducted May 26-June 1, 1994 by *The New York Times* and CBS News.

★ 49 ★

Sex Roles

Traditional Sex Roles in Modern Society

The table below shows the responses of women and men, by age, to a survey question about the place of traditional sex roles in modern society. Traditionalists believe in maintaining traditional sex roles, while Feminists advocate change. Men 65 years and older had the highest rate of Feminist responses, and men aged 51 to 64 were second. Following interviews with respondents, the authors concluded that these men, who were often the fathers and grandfathers of career women, saw little value in Traditionalist sex roles. Women aged 27 to 50, the age group that deals with the pressures of family life, were most opposed to Traditionalist roles. Overall, however, the Feminist perspective was in the minority.

Response	Ages (Years)									
	18 to 26		27 to 38		39 to 50		51 to 64		65+	
	F	M	F	M	F	M	F	M	F	M
N =	274	255	382	356	299	284	234	229	223	216
Traditional sex roles have no place.										
a. Strongly agree	7%	6%	9%	3%	9%	6%	3%	8%	4%	11%
b. Agree	24%	21%	32%	24%	32%	18%	22%	24%	35%	28%
c. No opinion	16%	19%	10%	14%	10%	14%	6%	16%	13%	15%
d. Disagree	47%	42%	45%	51%	43%	54%	58%	42%	42%	36%
e. Strongly disagree	6%	12%	4%	8%	6%	8%	11%	10%	6%	10%
Feminist (lines a + b)	31%	27%	41%	27%	41%	24%	25%	32%	39%	39%
Traditionalist (lines d + e)	53%	54%	49%	59%	49%	62%	69%	52%	48%	46%

Source: "Traditional Sex Roles Have No Place in Modern Society," Samuel S. Janus, PhD, and Cynthia L. Janus, MD, *The Janus Report on Sexual Behavior*, (New York: John Wiley & Sons, Inc., 1993), Table 2.7, p. 38. Between 1988 and 1992, the authors distributed 4,550 questionnaires to subjects at a variety of sites. The sample design was planned to conform to the population distribution of the United States in the areas of sex, age, region, income, education, and marital status. Returned questionnaires totaled 3,260. Of these, 495 were discarded. Satisfactorily completed questionnaires totaled 2,765: 1,418 women and 1,347 men.

Sexual Harassment

★ 50 ★

What Should Be Done About It?

More than 4,200 girls completed and returned questionnaires for a survey sponsored by the Wellesley College Center for Research on Women and the NOW Legal Defense and Education Fund, published in *Seventeen* magazine in September 1992. Respondents were asked what their schools should do about sexual harassment at school.

[N=2,002 girls responding.]

Response	Percent of respondents
What Should Schools Do?	
Adopt/enforce a school-wide policy to prevent sexual harassment	26%
Take action against the harasser	34%
Punishment (no action specified)	13%
Verbal warning or reprimand	5%
Notify harasser's parents	3%
Suspend harasser (if a student)	14%
Expel harasser (if a student)	7%
Dismiss harasser (if teacher/staff)	1%
Press charges, arrest harasser	3%
Force harasser to get counseling	2%
Force harasser to apologize	0.9%
Make harasser pay a fine	0.3%
Education/increase awareness	47%
Education for students on harassment	21%
Education for teachers/administrators	14%
Education for entire school community	17%
Offer self-defense classes	0.2%
Encourage discussion in school	5%
Security	6%
Have increased adult supervision	5%
Install hall cameras	0.7%

[Continued]

★ 50 ★

What Should Be Done About It?
[Continued]

Response	Percent of respondents
Supportive environment for those who have been harassed	18%
Teach and encourage students to speak up about harassment	5%
Believe students when they speak up	4%
Establish peer support groups for victims of harassment	2%
Have counselors available for victims	7%
Keep bathroom stalls and other areas clean from degrading graffiti	1%
Take other action	26%
Schools cannot do anything about sexual harassment	3%

Source: "What Should Schools Do About Sexual Harassment?" NOW Legal Defense and Education Fund and Wellesley College Center for Research on Women, *Secrets in Public: Sexual Harassment in Our Schools: A Report on the Results of a Seventeen Magazine Survey,* March 1993, Table G, p. 14. These are readers' spontaneously generated responses to an open-ended question, and thus the percentages are a conservative estimate of the support for various options.

Work

★ 51 ★

Commitment to a Job by Minority Status

This table shows the responses of minority and nonminority women employees of the Federal Government to various statements about job commitment and future plans. Survey data showed that minority women were promoted less often than nonminority women, even though both groups had about the same amount of education, devoted the same amount of time to their jobs, relocated as often, and took about the same number of leaves of absence.

Statement	To some or a great extent	
	Minority women	Nonminority women
I am willing to devote whatever time is necessary to my job in order to advance my career.	86%	75%
I am very committed to my job.	96%	95%
I am always enthusiastic about my job.	89%	90%
Percent who are planning to apply for promotion within the next three to five years.	74%	70%

Source: "Percent of female survey participants responding to statements about job commitment and future plans, by minority and nonminority status," *A Question of Equity: Women and the Glass Ceiling in the Federal Government*, U.S. Merit Systems Protection Board, October 1992, Table 13, p. 34.

★ 52 ★

Work

Employee Ratings of Female Managers: 1995

A human resource consulting firm conducted a study of the management and leadership skills of male and female managers. The study included 1,059 managers (676 males, 383 females) at all levels from 211 organizations. Each manager's skills were assessed by him/herself, his/her employees, and his/her boss. Employees rated female managers higher than male managers in 19 of 20 skill areas. Men were not rated higher by their employees in any skill area. Bosses rated female managers higher than male managers in 18 of 20 skill areas. Men were not rated higher by bosses in any area. On self ratings, women scored themselves higher in 14 skill areas. Men scored themselves higher in only 3 areas: Technical Expertise, Strategy, and Self Confidence. Bosses judged men even with women in Technical Expertise.

[M = Men; W = Women; N = No; Y = Yes.]

MLPI Factors[1]	Employee ratings		Boss ratings		Self ratings	
	Higher rated	Statistically significant[2]	Higher rated	Statistically significant[2]	Higher rated	Statistically significant[2]
Goal setting	W	Y[3]	W	Y[3]	W	N
Planning	W	Y[4]	W	Y[4]	W	N
Technical expertise	W	N	X	N	M	N
Performance standards	W	Y[3]	W	Y[4]	W	Y[4]
Coaching	W	Y[3]	W	Y[4]	W	Y[4]
Evaluating performance	W	Y[4]	W	Y[4]	W	Y[4]
Facilitating change	W	Y[4]	W	Y[4]	W	Y[4]
Delegation	W	N	W	N	X	N
Recognition	W	Y[4]	W	Y[4]	W	Y[4]
Approachable	W	Y[3]	W	Y[4]	W	Y[3]
Directive	W	Y[3]	W	Y[4]	W	Y[3]
Participative	W	Y[3]	W	Y[4]	W	N
Strategy	W	Y[3]	W	N	M	N
Communication	W	Y[4]	W	Y[4]	X	N
Teamwork	W	Y[3]	W	Y[4]	W	Y[3]
Empowering employees	W	Y[4]	W	Y[4]	W	Y[3]
Trust	W	N	W	Y[4]	W	Y[3]
Resourcefulness	W	Y[4]	W	Y[4]	W	Y[3]
Self confidence	X	N	W	N	M	N
Decisiveness	W	Y[4]	W	Y[3]	W	N

Source: "Study Reveals Gender Differences in Management and Leadership Skills (Table of Results)", Lawrence A. Pfaff and Associates, 1995. *Notes:* 1. Management-Leadership Practices Inventory (MLPI), a 360-degree feedback inventory that uses 85 items to measure 20 skill areas. 2. Significance level indicates the probability that the measured difference would occur at random in a population this size. The commonly accepted standard is to consider differences as statistically significant when the probability is 5% or less. 3. Probability is 5% or less. 4. Probability is 1% or less.

★ 53 ★
Work

How Is A Career Advanced?

This table shows the responses of employees of the Federal Government to questions about the effect of various items on their career advancement. A questionnaire was administered in the fall of 1991 to a sample of about 13,000 full-time, permanent, white-collar Federal employees. Some 8,408 surveys were returned (4,827 from men, 3,443 from women, and 138 from gender not specified). All respondents were very aware of the importance of work experience and education in career advancement. Men were more likely than women to say that formal educational qualifications helped them.

| Item | Percent responding: | | | | | |
| | Helped a lot | | Helped a little | | No effect | |
	Women	Men	Women	Men	Women	Men
Formal educational qualifications	44%	50%	30%	31%	15%	15%
Previous work experience	60%	58%	24%	26%	13%	15%
My performance or "track" record	79%	67%	16%	23%	3%	9%
Opportunity to act in a position(s) prior to appointment	44%	30%	27%	29%	27%	38%
Completion of specialized or technical training	44%	38%	35%	35%	20%	27%
Completion of formal developmental program or managerial training	26%	15%	31%	34%	42%	50%
Developmental assignments	42%	26%	37%	39%	20%	33%
Having a senior person/mentor looking out for my interests	28%	12%	37%	32%	31%	52%
Social/informal contacts with managers in the organization	8%	6%	32%	27%	53%	61%
Social/informal contacts with personnel office staff	4%	2%	19%	12%	72%	83%
Contacts through professional association or other formal network	8%	5%	24%	19%	67%	74%
Recommendations of friends or acquaintances who knew the selecting official	17%	10%	30%	24%	51%	65%
Having friends or acquaintances on the staff of the organization(s) where I applied	11%	7%	30%	22%	58%	70%

Source: "Responses of survey respondents about the effect of various items on their career advancement, by sex," *A Question of Equity: Women and the Glass Ceiling in the Federal Government,* U.S. Merit Systems Protection Board, October 1992, table 10, p. 23.

★ 54 ★

Work

Is It Important to Work Close to Home?

This table shows the responses of women and men to a question about working close to home.

Characteristic	Extremely	Very	Important	Not
How important is it to you to work close to home?				
All	49%	32%	13%	6%
Full-timers	47%	32%	13%	6%
Part-timers	51%	38%	9%	2%
Women	54%	29%	11%	4%
Men	43%	35%	14%	7%
Two parents working full-time	47%	32%	15%	6%
Holding two jobs	56%	25%	14%	3%
Working 60+ hours	39%	25%	16%	18%

Source: Doron Levin, "Nowadays, a getaway is often the highway," *Detroit Free Press*, March 2, 1995, pp. 1+. Primary source: February surveys of 1,000 Michigan residents by EPIC-MRA of Lansing for the Free Press and WXYZ-TV. Margin of error for entire sample is 4 percentage points; margins are larger for smaller groups within the survey. Figures may not total 100 percent because of rounding. Also in source: Responses to the question, "How long does it take you to get to work?" Black people were more likely than white people to spend more time commuting, a result of more jobs moving out to suburbs. People with a one-way commute of an hour or more were most likely to come from homes where only one person had a job. Part-time workers made the shortest daily trips.

★ 55 ★

Work

Perceptions About Work

This table shows the responses of employees of the Federal Government to various questions about women in the workplace. The suggestion is made that whether or not the women's perceptions stem from real differences in the way they are treated by colleagues, their perceptions should be taken seriously.

Statement	Percent agreeing	
	Women	Men
In general, in my organization...		
A woman must perform better than a man to be promoted.	55%	9%

[Continued]

★ 55 ★

Perceptions About Work
[Continued]

Statement	Percent agreeing	
	Women	Men
Standards are higher for women than men.	45%	5%
The viewpoint of a woman is often not heard at a meeting until it is repeated by a man.	41%	6%
Women and men are respected equally.	30%	51%

Source: "Perceptions of Female and Male Survey Respondents," *A Question of Equity: Women and the Glass Ceiling in the Federal Government,* U.S. Merit Systems Protection Board, October 1992, Figure 8, p. 31.

★ 56 ★
Work

Perceptions About Work by Minority Status

This table shows the percentages of minority and nonminority female employees of the Federal Government disagreeing with various questions about equitable treatment in the workplace. Minority women are just as likely to perceive discrimination based on gender as nonminority women, but a significant portion also perceive discrimination based on their race of national origin.

Statement	Minority women	Nonminority women
Percent Disagreeing: In general, in my organization:		
Women and men are respected equally.	60%	51%
People are promoted based on their competence.	35%	20%
Percent responding "to little or no extent": In general, I think that managers in my organization believe:		
People should be rewarded based on their performance, regardless of whether they are men or women.	25%	16%

[Continued]

★ 56 ★

Perceptions About Work by Minority Status
[Continued]

Statement	Minority women	Nonminority women
Women and men can perform the same work equally well.	32%	25%
In general, in my organization...		
A woman must perform better than a man to be promoted.	55%	9%
Standards are higher for women than men.	45%	5%
The viewpoint of a woman is often not heard at a meeting until it is repeated by a man.	41%	6%
Women and men are respected equally.	30%	51%

Source: "Percent of female survey respondents disagreeing with statements about equitable treatment in the workplace, by minority and nonminority status," *A Question of Equity: Women and the Glass Ceiling in the Federal Government,* U.S. Merit Systems Protection Board, October 1992, Table 14, p. 35.

★ 57 ★
Work

Responsible for Improving Own Job Performance?

This table shows the percentage of adult workers who strongly agreed that workers should be expected to think up better ways to do their jobs.

Sex	Percent
Male	25%
Female	21%

Source: Selected from "Perceived Responsibility for Improving Job Performance," *The National Education Goals Report: Volume One: The National Report,* National Education Goals Panel, 1993, Exhibit 84, p. 128. Primary Source: Cornell University, 1992.

★ 58 ★
Work

What Are the Biggest Problems at Work?

The Ms. Foundation for Women and the Center for Policy Alternatives collaborated on a project involving six focus groups and a nationwide poll to find out what were the concerns of all women and to identify those that were specific to certain groups of women. When they were asked what was the biggest problem facing women at work, *30%* gave an answer relating to the combination of work and family. This table shows responses to questions about the biggest problems facing "most women" and "you personally" at work.

Concern	Most women	You personally
Combining work/family	30%	22%
Discriminating/hiring	20%	13%
Low pay	19%	25%
Sexual harassment	9%	6%
Poor health benefits	6%	10%
Poor retirement benefits	5%	6%
Education/job training	3%	5%
None/Don't know	3%	9%
All	4%	3%

Source: Womens Voices: A Polling Report, A Joint Project of the Ms. Foundation for Women and Center for Policy Alternatives, p. 16.

★ 59 ★
Work

What Do People Want from Work?

This table shows the responses of 1,000 Michigan residents to a survey question asking, "What's important from work?"

Response	Women	Men
Low stress	53%	36%
Helping others	60%	48%
Daytime hours	60%	49%
Flexible hours	48%	35%
Good conditions	70%	54%

Source: Vickie Elmer and Michael Betzold, "Men and Women Both Say They Want More," *Detroit Free Press*, February 27, 1995, p. 1+. Primary source: February surveys of 1,000 Michigan residents for Free Press/WXYZ-TV by EPIC-MRA, Lansing.

★ 60 ★
Work

What Do Working Women Want More Time For?

This table shows the responses of working women with children at home to a question about what they want more time for.

Response	Percent
Work	18%
Religion	36%
Sleep	52%
Housework	56%
Family	63%
Fitness	72%
Themselves	79%

Source: Selected from Cassandra Spratling, "Mom's Many Jobs Keep House Running," *Detroit Free Press*, February 28, 1995, p. 8A. Primary source: February surveys of 1,000 residents, ages 30-55, by EPIC-MRA of Lansing for the Free Pressn and WXYZ-TV. Margin of error is plus or minus 4 percentage points.

★ 61 ★
Work

What Do You Like Best About Your Job?

Working Women Count! was formed in May 1994 by the U.S. Department of Labor's Women's Bureau to ask working women about their jobs. A questionnaire was distributed by more than 1,600 entities (including *Essence, Ms., Working Mother,* and *Working Woman* magazines), and more than 250,000 women responded. (Their responses are tallied here under the heading "Popular.") In addition, the Women's Bureau conducted a telephone survey with a scientifically selected, national random sample of women. (Their responses appear under the heading "Scientific.") For this table, respondents were asked to choose 3 things from a list of 11 possibilities that they like most about their jobs. The same five issues appeared in the top half of both lists, but the top three choices differed. Women in the scientific sample focused on their relationships with other workers and their need for flexibility. Women in the popular sample focused on their pay and benefits.

Like best	Scientific	Popular
Enjoy co-workers	43.0%(#1)	25.8%
Hours are flexible	39.0%(#2)	31.2%
Like what I do	38.2%(#3)	41.4%(#2)
Get paid well	35.2%	33.3%(#3)
Good benefits	32.3%	48.0%(#1)

Source: "What Do You Like Best About Your Job?," *Working Women Count! A Report to the Nation,* Women's Bureau, 1994, p. 17.

★ 62 ★

Work

What Is Important About Your Job?

In February 1995, 550 Michigan residents were asked, "What's extremely important about your job?" This table shows the responses of women with full- and part-time jobs compared to men. In the same survey, 44% of respondents declared that the ideal situation for a modern American family was to have one parent working and the other parent at home. Twenty-four percent responded that the ideal situation was to have one parent working full-time and the other working part-time.

Response	All	Women with full-time job	Women with part-time job	Men
Benefits	75%	75%	64%	73%
Pay	69%	67%	60%	70%
Working conditions	63%	68%	62%	54%
Interesting work	61%	65%	60%	59%
Learning new things	57%	62%	58%	52%
Daytime hours	55%	61%	49%	49%
Helping others	54%	61%	55%	48%
Being on my own	53%	51%	57%	52%
Recognition	50%	53%	51%	47%
Vacation time	47%	62%	42%	41%
Low stress	45%	53%	42%	36%
Improves society	43%	45%	42%	41%
People contact	43%	47%	49%	42%
Flexible hours	42%	62%	49%	35%

Source: February survey of 550 residents of Wayne, Oakland, and Macomb (MI) counties by EPIC-MRA of Lansing. Reported in the *Detroit Free Press*, March 1, 1995, p. 8A. Margin of error for entire sample is 4 percentage points; larger for smaller groups within the survey.

★ 63 ★

Work

What Makes You Feel Successful at Work?

According to a survey based on interviews with 1,502 women aged 18 to 55, two-thirds of whom were employed outside the home at least part time, doing quality work makes more than half of them feel successful at work. This table shows their responses to the question, "What makes you feel successful at work?"[1].

Response	Percent
What makes you feel successful at work?[1]	
Doing quality work	51%

[Continued]

★ 63 ★

What Makes You Feel Successful at Work?
[Continued]

Response	Percent
Getting a lot done	16%
Recognition	12%
Money	7%
Promotions	4%

Source: Jacquelynn Boyle, "Job important, but majority of female workers put family first," *Detroit Free Press*, May 11, 1995, pp. 1A,8A. Tamar Lewin, "Study Says More Women Earn Half Their Household Income," *The New York Times*, May 11, 1995, p. A13 Y. Primary source: Whirlpool Foundation survey by Louis Harris and Associates, New York, of 1,502 U.S. women 18-55 years old interviewed November-December 1994; margin of error is plus or minus 2 percentage points. *Note:* 1. Most popular responses.

★ 64 ★
Work

What Problems Do You Have at Work?

Working Women Count! was formed in May 1994 by the U.S. Department of Labor's Women's Bureau to ask working women about their jobs. A questionnaire was distributed by more than 1,600 entities (including *Essence, Ms., Working Mother,* and *Working Woman* magazines), and more than 250,000 women responded. (Their responses are tallied here under the heading "Popular.") In addition, the Women's Bureau conducted a telephone survey with a scientifically selected, national random sample of women. (Their responses appear under the heading "Scientific.") For this table, respondents were asked to rate each of 10 possible problems in terms of their seriousness. The number one problem women complained about was "too much stress." Differences in income affected the extent to which women saw pay and benefit levels as a problem. Of women who made less than $25,000 a year, 55% did not think they were paid what their job was worth. Of women earning more than $50,000 a year, 34% felt that way.

Problem	Scientific	Popular
Too much stress	58.5%(#1)	57.9%(#1)
Getting paid what job is worth	48.9%(#2)	55.3%(#2)
Getting better benefits	43.8%(#3)	36.3%(#3)

Source: "Serious Problems on the Job," *Working Women Count! A Report to the Nation,* Women's Bureau, 1994, p. 19.

★ 65 ★
Work

What Would You Like to See Changed in Your Workplace?

Working Women Count! was formed in May 1994 by the U.S. Department of Labor's Women's Bureau to ask working women about their jobs. A questionnaire was distributed by more than 1,600 entities (including *Essence, Ms., Working Mother,* and *Working Woman* magazines), and more than 250,000 women responded. (Their responses are tallied here under the heading "Popular.") In addition, the Women's Bureau conducted a telephone survey with a scientifically selected, national random sample of women. (Their responses appear under the heading "Scientific.") For this table, respondents were asked to rate their priorities on a scale of 10 to 0 (most important to least important) from a list of 10 possible items. Health care and pay scales were the top two priorities for change.

Priorities	Scientific	Popular
Health care insurance for all	65.4%(#1)	64.2%(#2)
Improving pay scales	64.5%(#2)	72.7%(#1)
On-the-job training	51.8%	60.5%
Insuring equal opportunity	51.3%	62.5%
More responsibility for how they do their job	50.9%	54.4%
Paid leave	48.4%	50.5%

Source: "Serious Problems on the Job," *Working Women Count! A Report to the Nation,* Women's Bureau, 1994, p. 19.

★ 66 ★

Work

Why Was a Promotion Denied?

This table shows the responses of employees of the Federal Government to questions about how important they believe not being "part of the group" was when they were denied a promotional opportunity or developmental assignment. Survey participants were asked to agree or disagree with the statement: "Those who participate in social activities (e.g., sports, card games, after-work cocktails) are more likely to be promoted than those who don't." The responses indicate that a substantial minority of both men and women believe that exclusion from a particular group or network can hinder their promotion potential.

Importance in being---	Percent responding:			
	Somewhat/very important		Little or no importance	
	Women	Men	Women	Men
Denied a promotion	37%	44%	56%	50%
Denied a developmental opportunity	41%	41%	52%	50%

Source: "How important survey respondents believe not being "part of the group" was when they were denied a promotional opportunity or developmental assignment, by sex," *A Question of Equity: Women and the Glass Ceiling in the Federal Government*, U.S. Merit Systems Protection Board, October 1992, table 11, p. 26. Not shown are those responding "Don't know."

★ 67 ★

Work

Will Present Job Skills be Useful in Five Years?

This table shows the percentage of adult workers who reported that their present job skills will be useful in five years.

Sex	Percent
Male	60%
Female	54%

Source: Selected from "Perceived Usefulness of Skills in the Future," *The National Education Goals Report: Volume One: The National Report*, National Education Goals Panel, 1993, Exhibit 83, p. 127. Primary Source: Cornell University, 1992.

★ 68 ★
Work

Women Executives on Work-I

This table shows the responses of 400 women executives in companies having $100 million in sales annually to the questions: "How would you rate large corporations generally as places for women executives such as yourself to work? How would you rate your own company as a place for women such as yourself to work?" The question was asked in April 1992.

Response	Corporations generally	Own company
Excellent	8%	35%
Pretty good	60%	49%
Only fair	28%	16%
Poor	1%	1%
Not sure	4%	--

Source: Selected from Elizabeth Hann Hastings and Philip K. Hastings, eds., *Index to International Public Opinion, 1992-1993,* 1994, pp. 498-499.

★ 69 ★
Work

Women Executives on Work-II

This table shows the responses of 400 women executives in companies having $100 million in sales annually to various questions about the workplace. The questions were asked in April 1992.

Question	Percent
Do you prefer to work for a man or a woman, or doesn't it make any difference to you?	
A man	12%
A woman	2%
Makes no difference	83%
Not sure	3%
Compared with five years ago, how do you think large companies are doing in relation to the hiring and promotion of women executives?	
Much better	16%
Somewhat better	48%
The same	29%
Somewhat worse	5%
Much worse	1%

[Continued]

★ 69 ★

Women Executives on Work-II
[Continued]

Question	Percent
Not sure	2%
In your company today, would you say that women have the same chance as equally-qualified men to be promoted to senior management positions, or not?	
Same chance to be promoted	46%
Not same chance	53%
Not sure	1%
If women get promoted to senior management positions, do you think they will be paid a higher salary, a lower salary, or the same salary as men in those positions?	
Paid higher salary	--
Lower salary	63%
Same salary	36%
Not sure	1%

Source: Selected from Elizabeth Hann Hastings and Philip K. Hastings, eds., *Index to International Public Opinion, 1992-1993*, 1994, pp. 498-499.

★ 70 ★
Work

Women Executives on Work-III

This table shows the responses of 400 women executives in companies having $100 million in sales annually to the question: "Would you say the following are obstacles to success for women executives at your company, or not?" The questions were asked in April 1992.

Item	Is an obstacle	Is not an obstacle	Not sure
A glass ceiling or a point beyond which women never seem to advance.	56%	41%	4%
The tendency to put women in token positions without any real power or operating responsibility.	23%	77%	--

[Continued]

★ 70 ★

Women Executives on Work-III
[Continued]

Item	Is an obstacle	Is not an obstacle	Not sure
A male-dominated corporate culture.	70%	30%	--

Source: Selected from Elizabeth Hann Hastings and Philip K. Hastings, eds., *Index to International Public Opinion, 1992-1993*, 1994, pp. 498-499.

★ 71 ★
Work

Women Executives on Work-IV

This table shows the responses of 400 women executives in companies having $100 million in sales annually to questions about women in the workplace. The questions were asked in April 1992.

Item	Agree	Disagree	Not sure
Do you agree or disagree with each of the following strategies?			
Women executives should not make waves but do a good job and expect equal recognition and promotion.	34%	63%	3%
Women should build networks with other women to help each other.	83%	15%	2%
Women should demand that their companies have specific written policies for the hiring and promotion of women executives.	34%	64%	2%
Women should take legal action including filing law suits or regulatory complaints when they see evidence of discrimination.	76%	20%	4%

Source: Selected from Elizabeth Hann Hastings and Philip K. Hastings, eds., *Index to International Public Opinion, 1992-1993*, 1994, pp. 498-499.

★ 72 ★
Work

Women Executives on Work-V

This table shows the responses of 400 women executives in companies having $100 million in sales annually to questions about women in the workplace. The questions were asked in April 1992.

Item	Percent
If your company had to choose between two equally qualified candidates for a promotion – a man and a woman – who do you thing would get the job, the man or the woman?	
Man	51%
Woman	13%
Not sure	37%
In five years' time, how many senior women executives do you think there will be at your company?	
Many more women executives	5%
Somewhat more	59%
Somewhat fewer	3%
Many fewer	1%
The same number	31%
Not sure	2%
Which one of the four following statements best describes how large American companies are doing in relation to hiring and promotion of women executives?	
They are still making real improvements.	39%
The rate of progress has slowed down.	52%
There are no longer any improvements.	5%
Things are getting worse.	2%
Not sure.	3%

[Continued]

★ 72 ★

Women Executives on Work-V
[Continued]

Item	Percent
Have you personally ever been the victim of what you consider to be sexual harassment, or not?	
Yes	27%
No	73%
Not sure	--
(If "Yes"): Did you report this to your employer or not?	
Yes, reported	25%
No, did not report	75%
Not sure	--
(If did not report): Why not?	
Handled situation myself	21%
Would hurt my career	17%
Would do no good	17%
Was employer/most senior employer	16%
Long time ago/wasn't an issue	10%
Would not be believed	9%
Was young/teenager	9%
Fear of repercussions	9%
Tolerated/expected it	7%
Ignorance	5%
Embarrassed	4%
All others	2%
Not sure	5%

Source: Selected from Elizabeth Hann Hastings and Philip K. Hastings, eds., *Index to International Public Opinion, 1992-1993*, 1994, pp. 498-499.

★ 73 ★

Work

Would You Work If You Didn't Have To?

According to a survey based on interviews with 1,502 women aged 18 to 55, two-thirds of whom were employed outside the home at least part time, a majority of women would work or volunteer even if they had enough money to live comfortably. This table shows the responses of women to the question: "If you had enough money to live comfortably, would you work?" For this question, women's responses were compared to those of a group of 460 men.

Response	All women	Working women	Men
If you had enough money to live comfortably, would you work?			
Full-time	15%	16%	33%
Part-time	33%	38%	28%
Volunteer work	20%	21%	17%
Be a homemaker	31%	24%	21%

Source: Jacquelynn Boyle, "Job important, but majority of female workers put family first," *Detroit Free Press*, May 11, 1995, pp. 1A,8A. Tamar Lewin, "Study Says More Women Earn Half Their Household Income," *The New York Times*, May 11, 1995, p. A13 Y. Primary source: Whirlpool Foundation survey by Louis Harris and Associates, New York, of 1,502 U.S. women 18-55 years old interviewed November-December 1994; margin of error is plus or minus 2 percentage points.

Young Women

★ 74 ★

Political Views of Women Entering College: 1994-I

This table shows how women entering college in 1994 described their political views. The percentage of all students who described themselves as middle-of-the-road increased, while the numbers who described themselves as conservative or liberal/far left decreased. For this survey, the national population included 2,700 institutions. The data are based on responses from 237,777 freshmen entering 461 two- and four-year institutions in 1994.

Political Views	Type of Institution				
	All institutions	All 2-year colleges	All 4-year colleges	All universities	All black colleges
Far left	1.8%	2.0%	1.9%	1.5%	4.3%
Liberal	25.5%	21.1%	26.2%	30.2%	31.9%
Middle of the road	54.5%	60.6%	52.5%	49.8%	49.4%
Conservative	17.4%	15.7%	18.5%	17.7%	13.2%
Far right	0.8%	0.6%	0.9%	0.7%	1.2%

Source: Selected from "Weighted National Norms for Freshman Women, Fall 1994: Political Views" Astin, A.W. et al., *The American Freshman: National Norms for Fall 1994*, 1994, p. 58.

★ 75 ★

Young Women

Political Views of Women Entering College: 1994-II

This table shows the percentages of women entering college in 1994 who reported agreeing strongly or somewhat with various statements. Men differed from women on the question of sex being OK if the people like each other (mens responses: 56.2%, 57.7%, 54.8%, 56.3% 64.3%). Men's responses to the statement that married women are best in the home were 30.8%, 33.1%, 31.3%, 26.9%, 40.0%. Men felt more strongly that homosexual relations should be prohibited (45.4%, 52.0%, 44.7%, 37.6%, 48.9%). Regarding the statement that a man is not entitled to sex on a date, the percentages of men who agreed strongly or somewhat were 83.9%, 81.2%, 84.2%, 87.0%, and 75.5%. Men did not feel as strongly that the federal government should do more to control handguns. For this survey, the national population included 2,700 institutions. The data are based on responses from 237,777 freshmen entering 461 two- and four-year institutions in 1994.

Statement	Type of Institution				
	All institutions	All 2-year colleges	All 4-year colleges	All universities	All black colleges
Agrees strongly or somewhat:					
government not protecting consumer	74.7%	77.0%	74.7%	71.3%	81.0%
government not controlling pollution	87.8%	88.2%	87.6%	87.9%	86.9%
raise taxes to reduce deficit	22.7%	18.3%	23.3%	27.6%	17.9%
too much concern for criminals	71.3%	71.9%	71.0%	71.2%	59.8%

[Continued]

★ 75 ★

Political Views of Women Entering College: 1994-II
[Continued]

Statement	Type of Institution				
	All institutions	All 2-year colleges	All 4-year colleges	All universities	All black colleges
abortion should be legal	60.3%	56.7%	59.2%	67.4%	67.6%
abolish death penalty	22.1%	19.5%	23.9%	22.5%	38.4%
sex OK if people like each other	32.1%	33.2%	31.0%	32.6%	28.2%
married women best in home	20.1%	24.1%	19.3%	15.9%	30.2%
marijuana should be legalized	28.3%	25.8%	27.9%	32.7%	28.2%
prohibit homosexual relations	24.0%	29.0%	23.7%	17.7%	29.1%
employers can require drug tests	82.5%	83.7%	82.6%	80.7%	87.4%
control AIDS by mandatory tests	63.2%	68.6%	61.5%	58.8%	66.7%
man not entitled to sex on date	94.3%	92.6%	94.7%	95.8%	90.7%
federal government do more control handgun	89.2%	88.0%	89.4%	90.3%	93.8%
national health care plan needed	74.3%	76.9%	73.9%	71.4%	87.0%
racial discrimination no longer problem	13.7%	16.9%	12.5%	11.2%	7.7%
discourage energy consumption	74.1%	71.1%	74.4%	77.9%	64.6%
individual can do little to change society	28.3%	33.6%	26.4%	24.2%	32.5%
wealthy should pay more taxes	68.3%	70.0%	68.8%	65.1%	71.7%
prohibit racist/sexist speech	66.6%	70.0%	67.0%	60.9%	65.5%
de-emphasize college sports	31.7%	34.2%	31.8%	27.8%	33.9%
disobey laws that violate values	31.7%	30.9%	32.8%	30.8%	35.5%

Source: Selected from "Weighted National Norms for Freshman Women, Fall 1994: Agrees Strongly or Somewhat," Astin, A.W. et al., *The American Freshman: National Norms for Fall 1994*, 1994, p. 58.

★ 76 ★
Young Women

Self Esteem: Black Girls and White Girls

This table shows some highlights of a study on the differences between the ways black and white girls view their bodies. The study, which was to be published in the journal *Human Organization* in spring 1995, was described by *Newsweek* magazine in their April 24, 1995 issue.

Item	Number/Percent
White Girls	
Percentage of white girls dissatisfied with their body	90%
Percentage of white girls who dieted in the last year	62%

[Continued]

★ 76 ★

Self Esteem: Black Girls and White Girls
[Continued]

Item	Number/Percent
White girls' definition of the perfect body: Height Wcight	5'7" 100-110 lbs.
Black Girls	
Percentage of black girls satisfied with their bodies	70%
Percentage of black girls who said women get more beautiful as they age	65%
Percentage of black girls who defined beauty as "the right attitude"	65%
Percentage of black girls who say it's better to be a little overweight than underweight	64%
Percentage of black girls who reported dieting in the last year	51%

Source: Michele Ingrassia, "The Body of the Beholder," *Newsweek*, April 24, 1995, pp. 66+.

★ 77 ★
Young Women

Self-Assessments of Women Entering College: 1994

This table shows the percentages of entering college freshmen women who rated themselves above average or in the top 10% in various categories. For this survey, the national population included 2,700 institutions. The data are based on responses from 237,777 freshmen entering 461 two- and four-year institutions in 1994.

Attribute	Type of Institution				
	All institutions	All 2-year colleges	All 4-year colleges	All universities	All black colleges
I am above average or in the top 10% in:					
academic ability	51.3%	27.6%	58.0%	72.1%	45.5%
artistic ability	22.2%	16.5%	23.4%	27.9%	14.7%
competitiveness	41.4%	30.9%	43.9%	51.6%	42.2%

[Continued]

★ 77 ★

Self-Assessments of Women Entering College: 1994
[Continued]

Attribute	Type of Institution				
	All institutions	All 2-year colleges	All 4-year colleges	All universities	All black colleges
cooperativeness	70.6%	63.3%	73.1%	76.2%	69.5%
creativity	42.1%	33.0%	44.7%	49.8%	42.3%
drive to achieve	64.0%	51.4%	67.7%	75.0%	72.0%
emotional health	47.2%	37.6%	49.6%	56.1%	50.6%
leadership ability	47.6%	34.9%	51.3%	58.6%	53.5%
mathematical ability	31.7%	19.7%	34.5%	43.1%	30.0%
physical appearance	34.9%	30.2%	36.0%	39.5%	59.6%
physical health	43.6%	35.6%	45.3%	51.6%	52.0%
popularity	29.7%	22.7%	30.6%	37.8%	37.4%
public speaking ability	27.8%	17.6%	30.8%	36.5%	34.2%
self-confidence (intellectual)	43.5%	29.7%	47.7%	55.1%	62.9%
self-confidence (social)	40.7%	33.1%	42.7%	47.7%	59.2%
sensitivity to criticism	25.0%	22.0%	26.0%	27.5%	25.1%
stubborness	41.3%	38.3%	41.9%	44.2%	33.5%
understanding of others	73.4%	66.0%	76.3%	78.3%	72.6%
writing ability	39.9%	27.9%	43.6%	49.9%	40.9%

Source: Selected from "Weighted National Norms for Freshman Women, Fall 1994: Student Rated Self Above Average or Top 10% in" Astin, A.W. et al., *The American Freshman: National Norms for Fall 1994*, 1994, p. 47.

★ 78 ★

Young Women

Student Satisfaction with the Local High School: 1994

This table shows female student satisfaction with various aspects of the local high school. Respondents are the 260,818 females who took the ACT Assessment and graduated in the spring of 1994.

Aspect of local high school	Satisfied. No change necess.	Pretty much neutral.	Dissatisfied. Need improve.	No experience.
Classroom instruction.	53%	26%	13%	1%
Number and variety of course offerings.	48%	17%	27%	1%
Grading practices and policies.	50%	26%	15%	1%
Number and kinds of tests given.	47%	34%	12%	1%

[Continued]

★ 78 ★

Student Satisfaction with the Local High School: 1994
[Continued]

Aspect of local high school	Satisfied. No change necess.	Pretty much neutral.	Dissatisfied. Need improve.	No experience.
Guidance services provided by total school.	45%	20%	25%	3%
School rules, regulations, & policies.	35%	25%	32%	1%
Library or learning center.	51%	25%	16%	2%
Laboratory facilities.	42%	27%	19%	4%
Provisions for special help in reading, math, etc.	33%	21%	15%	24%
Provisions for academically outstanding students.	50%	20%	13%	9%
Adequacy of progress in career education & planning.	35%	25%	25%	7%

Source: Selected from "Student Satisfaction with Various Aspects of the Local High School," *ACT High School Profile Report HS Graduating Class 1994: National Report for Females,* p. 5.

★ 79 ★
Young Women

Which Values Are Important?

This table shows the percentage of high school seniors in 1972 and 1992 who believed each value to be "very important." Values changed during the 20-year period. High school women in the 1990s see a different future from those in the 1970s. They plan to seek more education and are more likely to expect to obtain professional jobs. Although children and family are still considered important, women in the 1990s tend to hold values that are increasingly similar to men's.

Values	All seniors		Males		Females	
	1972	1992	1972	1992	1972	1992
Being successful in work	84.5%	89.3%	86.2%	89.0%	82.8%	89.6%
Marrying and having happy family	81.7%	79.0%	78.5%	75.7%	84.9%	82.3%
Having lots of money	17.8%	37.4%	25.9%	45.3%	9.8%	29.4%
Having strong friendships	79.2%	79.9%	80.4%	79.8%	78.0%	80.1%

[Continued]

★ 79 ★

Which Values Are Important?
[Continued]

Values	All seniors		Males		Females	
	1972	1992	1972	1992	1972	1992
Being able to find steady work	77.8%	87.9%	82.1%	87.1%	73.5%	88.6%
Being able to give children better opportunities	66.8%	75.5%	66.8%	74.5%	66.9%	76.5%
Living close to parents and relatives	7.7%	16.9%	7.1%	15.2%	8.3%	18.7%
Working to correct social and economic inequalities	26.9%	20.3%	22.4%	17.0%	31.3%	23.6%

Source: "Percentage of high school seniors in 1972 and 1992 who believed each value to be 'very important,' by gender," U.S. Department of Education, National Center for Education Statistics, *Statistics in Brief,* November 1993, "High School Seniors Look to the Future, 1972 and 1992," NCES 93-473, Table 3, p. 4. Primary source: U.S. Department of Education, National Center for Education Statistics, National Longitudinal Study, 1972 (Base Year); National Education Longitudinal Study of 1988 (NELS:88) 1992 Second Followup. Percentages may not add to 100 due to rounding.

Chapter 2
BUSINESS AND ECONOMICS

★ 80 ★

Asian/Pacific Islander Industry Leaders-I

This and the following table show Asian and Pacific Islander (API) executives, administrators, and managers (EAM) of private for-profit companies by ethnicity and educational attainment in 1990. The total API population with college degrees was 1,597,381. Seventy-seven percent of the total API population had less than a Bachelor's degree. The number of API males with a Bachelor's who are executives, administrators, and managers is nearly double the number of females. This table only includes BS professional degrees.

Ethnicity	Total with Bachelor's		EAM with Bachelor's		EAM percent of total	
	Male	Female	Male	Female	Male	Female
Total API Population	506,811	571,925	44,175	23,397	8.7%	4.1%
Chinese	124,622	138,199	9,925	7,382	8.0%	5.3%
Filipino	109,125	182,696	5,736	6,082	5.3%	3.3%
Japanese	82,885	80,828	15,262	3,835	18.4%	4.7%
Asian Indian	71,255	64,232	5,587	2,429	7.8%	3.8%
Korean	52,075	58,028	4,475	2,045	8.6%	3.5%
Vietnamese	27,729	16,502	496	495	1.8%	3.0%
Hawaiian	5,263	4,574	414	266	8.0%	5.8%
Other S.E. Asian	11,203	8,564	566	246	5.1%	2.9%
Other API	22,704	17,302	1,714	617	7.5%	3.6%

Source: "National Asian & Pacific Islander American Executives, Administrators, and Managers of Private-for-Profit Companies by Ethnicity, Educational Attainment, and Sex, 1990," *Good for Business: Making Full Use of the Nation's Human Capital*, Washington, D.C., Glass Ceiling Commission, March 1995, Table 7, p. 108. Primary sources: 1990 Bureau of the Census, PUMS File 95% Confidence Interval; 1994 Asian/Pacific Islander Data Consortium, ACCIS San Francisco, CA.

★ 81 ★

Corporate Officers/Executives

Asian/Pacific Islander Industry Leaders-II

This and the preceding table show Asian and Pacific Islander (API) executives, administrators, and managers (EAM) of private for-profit companies by ethnicity and educational attainment in 1990. The total API population with college degrees was 1,597,381. Seventy-seven percent of the total API population had less than a Bachelor's degree. Doctorates and Associate college degrees are excluded.

Ethnicity	Total with Masters/Prof.		EAM with Masters/Prof.		EAM percent of total	
	Male	Female	Male	Female	Male	Female
Total API Population	321,164	197,481	26,043	7,627	8.1%	3.9%
Chinese	105,297	65,033	7,935	3,102	7.5%	4.8%
Filipino	29,422	34,471	1,475	1,198	5.0%	3.5%
Japanese	33,028	22,164	3,608	844	10.9%	3.8%
Asian Indian	87,718	41,863	8,882	1,430	10.1%	3.4%
Korean	32,309	16,749	1,660	527	5.1%	3.1%
Vietnamese	8,792	3,707	439	158	5.0%	4.3%
Hawaiian	1,596	1,595	114	38	7.1%	2.4%
Other S.E. Asian	5,645	3,735	347	31	6.1%	0.8%
Other API	17,357	8,173	1,583	299	9.1%	3.7%

Source: "National Asian & Pacific Islander American Executives, Administrators, and Managers of Private-for-Profit Companies by Ethnicity, Educational Attainment, and Sex, 1990," *Good for Business: Making Full Use of the Nation's Human Capital*, Washington, D.C., Glass Ceiling Commission, March 1995, Table 7, p. 108. Primary sources: 1990 Bureau of the Census, PUMS File 95% Confidence Interval; 1994 Asian/Pacific Islander Data Consortium, ACCIS San Francisco, CA.

★ 82 ★

Corporate Officers/Executives

Asian/Pacific Islander Industry Leaders by Industry

This table shows the number and percentage of Asian and Pacific Islander (API) executives, administrators, and managers (EAM) of private for-profit companies by industry in the top four industries in 1990. Number and percent of total API male/female working-age population 16 years and over with specified degree are shown.

Gender/Degree/Industry	Number	Percent
Female Population with Bachelor's Degrees		
Professional & Related Svcs.	4,959	21.2%
FIRE[1]	4,917	21.0%
Manufacturing	3,626	15.5%
Retail Trade	2,698	11.5%
Male Population with Bachelor's Degrees		
Manufacturing	12,019	27.2%

[Continued]

★ 82 ★

Asian/Pacific Islander Industry Leaders by Industry
[Continued]

Gender/Degree/Industry	Number	Percent
FIRE[1]	6,562	14.9%
Retail Trade	6,209	14.1%
Other Industries	5,461	12.4%
Female Population with Master's Degrees		
Professional & Related Svcs.	1,936	25.4%
FIRE[1]	1,620	21.2%
Manufacturing	1,603	21.0%
Wholesale Trade	614	8.1%
Male Population with Master's Degrees		
Manufacturing	9,210	35.4%
FIRE[1]	3,618	13.9%
Professional & Related Svcs.	2,643	10.1%
Retail Trade	2,395	9.2%

Source: "Asian & Pacific Islander American Executives, Administrators, and Managers of Private-for-Profit Companies: Top Four Industries, 1990," *Good for Business: Making Full Use of the Nation's Human Capital*, Washington, D.C., Glass Ceiling Commission, March 1995, Table 8, p. 110. Primary sources: 1990 Bureau of the Census, PUMS File 95% Confidence Interval; 1994 Asian/Pacific Islander Data Consortium, ACCIS San Francisco, CA. *Note:* 1. Finance, Insurance, and Real Estate.

★ 83 ★

Corporate Officers/Executives

Asian/Pacific Islander Industry Leaders' Income-I

This table shows mean salary income of the U.S. born Asian and Pacific Islander (API) population of executives, administrators, and managers of private for-profit companies in 1989 by educational attainment.

Ethnicity/ Sex	Total Dollars	Total Number	Educational Attainment			
			Less than BA/BS	BA/BS	MA/MS	Doctoral
Total API Population	$35,338	46,604				
Chinese	$38,806	10,602	$30,850	$36,132	$63,793	$66,809
Male			$35,072	$41,506	$69,553	$78,992
Female			$25,194	$30,487	$55,590	$45,781
Filipino	$26,759	6,948	$24,472	$30,370	$38,861	$60,080
Male			$27,883	$38,129	$40,614	0
Female			$20,611	$22,433	$36,157	$60,080
Japanese	$39,113	20,394	$31,249	$44,067	$55,336	$83,020
Male			$34,867	$51,611	$62,967	$83,020
Female			$26,910	$29,410	$34,228	0

[Continued]

★ 83 ★

Asian/Pacific Islander Industry Leaders' Income-I

[Continued]

Ethnicity/ Sex	Total Dollars	Total Number	Educational Attainment			
			Less than BA/BS	BA/BS	MA/MS	Doctoral
Asian Indian	$28,813	811	$11,743	$19,762	$58,356	$72,345
Male			$10,540	$6,500	$65,329	$72,345
Female			$13,094	$22,103	$350	0
Korean	$34,991	1,248	$24,160	$31,714	$83,050	$19,000
Male			$32,377	$36,333	$96,591	0
Female			$20,597	$27,253	$31,758	$19,000
Vietnamese	$25,424	139	$15,612	$28,726	0	0
Male			$15,612	0	0	0
Female			0	$28,726	0	0
Hawaiian	$27,938	4,795	$26,471	$30,074	$62,010	0
Male			$29,644	$34,786	$46,546	0
Female			$23,720	$23,272	$100,263	0
Other S.E. Asian	$3,310	50	$3,310	0	0	0
Male			$2,500	0	0	0
Female			$3,727	0	0	0
Other API	$29,162	1,617	$25,031	$32,873	$35,952	$31,579
Male			$27,112	$37,878	$38,000	$31,579
Female			$22,919	$29,155	$33,392	0

Source: "National U.S. Born Asian & Pacific Islander American Population Executives, Administrators, and Managers of Private-for-Profit Companies. Mean Salary Income in 1989 by Ethnicity, Educational Attainment, and Sex (in dollars)," *Good for Business: Making Full Use of the Nation's Human Capital*, Washington, D.C., Glass Ceiling Commission, March 1995, Table 12, p. 117. Total number of U.S. born EAMs from "National U.S. Born Asian & Pacific Islander American Executives, Administrators, and Managers of Private-for-Profit Companies, Number of Cases by Ethnicity, Educational Attainment, and Sex," Table 14, p. 119. Primary sources: 1990 Bureau of the Census, PUMS File 95% Confidence Interval; 1994 Asian/Pacific Islander Data Consortium, ACCIS San Francisco, CA.

★ 84 ★

Corporate Officers/Executives

Asian/Pacific Islander Industry Leaders' Income-II

This table shows mean salary income of the foreign-born Asian and Pacific Islander (API) population of U.S. executives, administrators, and managers of private for-profit companies in 1989 by educational attainment.

Ethnicity/ Sex	Total	Educational Attainment			
		Less than BA/BS	BA/BS	MA/MS	Doctoral
Total API Population	$40,338				
Chinese	$37,111	$24,458	$36,328	$53,775	$70,746
Male		$27,199	$41,165	$57,416	$70,101
Female		$20,670	$28,650	$42,892	$76,995

[Continued]

★ 84 ★

Asian/Pacific Islander Industry Leaders' Income-II
[Continued]

Ethnicity/ Sex	Total	Educational Attainment			
		Less than BA/BS	BA/BS	MA/MS	Doctoral
Filipino	$30,798	$23,566	$34,087	$42,551	$81,563
Male		$24,787	$39,381	$51,947	$81,563
Female		$22,239	$29,243	$30,798	0
Japanese	$65,099	$42,689	$76,131	$71,954	$78,549
Male		$51,048	$80,057	$75,055	$87,337
Female		$24,664	$35,759	$49,234	$13,268
Asian Indian	$46,265	$22,565	$40,189	$59,348	$84,177
Male		$25,386	$45,574	$63,325	$89,112
Female		$17,011	$25,572	$31,974	$29,371
Korean	$31,754	$22,619	$38,160	$43,547	$88,540
Male		$24,886	$43,243	$47,573	$88,540
Female		$19,475	$25,506	$27,445	0
Vietnamese	$28,556	$23,330	$35,284	$55,810	$70,000
Male		$26,584	$44,503	$63,294	$70,000
Female		$18,763	$24,066	$34,041	0
Hawaiian	$27,456	$24,243	$53,500	$28,000	0
Male		$25,500	$53,500	$28,000	0
Female		$24,077	0	0	0
Other S.E. Asian	$26,198	$23,289	$26,283	$37,802	$78,500
Male		$26,354	$26,960	$36,677	$78,500
Female		$18,908	$24,066	$66,000	0
Other API	$31,444	$22,119	$38,975	$42,608	$44,650
Male		$23,518	$40,687	$45,238	$44,650
Female		$19,583	$30,146	$23,095	0

Source: "National Foreign Born Asian & Pacific Islander American Population Executives, Administrators, and Managers of Private-for-Profit Companies. Mean Salary Income in 1989 by Ethnicity, Educational Attainment, and Sex (in dollars)," *Good for Business: Making Full Use of the Nation's Human Capital,* Washington, D.C., Glass Ceiling Commission, March 1995, Table 13, p. 118. Primary sources: 1990 Bureau of the Census, PUMS File 95% Confidence Interval; 1994 Asian/Pacific Islander Data Consortium, ACCIS San Francisco, CA.

★ 85 ★

Corporate Officers/Executives

Executive Suites at Major Corporations

This table shows statistics about women in executive suites in major Michigan corporations, as listed in each company's 1993 annual report. The *Detroit Free Press* article noted that in its 1994 reorganization, Ford Motor Company named 32 executives to new jobs in its new global structure. None of the new executives was a woman.

Company	Total	Women
Ameritech	18	2
Chrysler Corp.	36	0
Comerica Inc.	20	1
Detroit Edison Co.	16	1
Ford Motor Co.	72	2
General Motors Corp.	58	3
Gerber Products Co.	12	1
Kelly Services Inc.	10	2
Knight-Ridder Inc.	27	4
NBD Inc.	39	2
Whirlpool Corp.	23	0

Source: Vickie Elmer, "Women Are Missing in Ford Reorganization," *Detroit Free Press*, April 26, 1994, p. 1E. Primary source: Free Press research.

★ 86 ★

Corporate Officers/Executives

Heads of Billion-Dollar Businesses

This table lists some of the women who run major divisions of large U.S. industrial and service corporations and shows the size of the operation.

Name, age, title, company or division	Size of operation
Jill E. Barad, 43 President and CEO Mattel	$3.2 billion
Brenda Barnes, 41 CEO Pepsi-Cola N.A.	$6.0 billion
Rose Marie Bravo, 44 President Saks Fifth Avenue	$1.4 billion

[Continued]

★ 86 ★

Heads of Billion-Dollar Businesses
[Continued]

Name, age, title, company or division	Size of operation
Maxine Clark, 46 President Payless Shoesource, The May Company	$2.1 billion
Susan Falk, 43 President Express, The Limited	$1.4 billion
Ann M. Fudge, 44 President Maxwell House Coffee	$1.5 billion
Kris Gibney, 46 Vice president Pharmaceutical Services Caremark International	$1.5 billion
Christina A. Gold, 48 President Avon U.S.A.	$1.5 billion
Pamela McConathy Goodman, 39 President Lerner New York, The Limited	$1.0 billion
Lois D. Juliber, 46 President Colgate North America	$1.6 billion
Karen L. Katen, 46 VP and general manager U.S. Pharmaceuticals, Pfizer	$3.2 billion
Sherry Lansing, 50 Chairwoman Paramount Motion Picture Group, Viacom	$1.0 billion[1]
Loida N. Lewis, 52 Chairman and chief exec. TLC Beatrice Holdings	$1.8 billion

[Continued]

★ 86 ★

Heads of Billion-Dollar Businesses
[Continued]

Name, age, title, company or division	Size of operation
Ellen R. Marram, 48 President The Seagram Beverage Group	$1.5 billion
Grace Nichols, 48 President Victoria's Secret Stores, The Limited	$1.2 billion
Patricia F. Russo, 42 President AT&T Global Business Communications Systems	$4.0 billion
Carolyn M. Ticknor, 48 General Manager Laser Jet Printer Group, Hewlett-Packard	$5.0 billion[2]

Source: Judith H. Dobrzynski, "Way Beyond the Glass Ceiling: Billion-Dollar Command Now, a C.E.O. Chair Next?" *The New York Times,* May 11, 1995, p. C1, C8, chart entitled "At the Helms of Billion-Dollar Businesses." *Notes:* 1. Furman Seiz estimate. 2. Goldman Sachs estimate.

★ 87 ★

Corporate Officers/Executives

Hispanic Origin Industry Leaders by Industry

This table shows the number and percent distribution of Hispanic origin executives, administrators, and managers (EAM) of private sector companies by industry in 1990. This group is compared to white executives, administrators, and managers.

[Percentages are for industry. Based on a sampling of households.]

Industry/Gender	Mexican Amer.	Puerto Rican	Cuban	Other Hispanic	White	Total
Manufacturing						
Male	112 (0.9%)	21 (0.2%)	9 (0.1%)	50 (0.4%)	12,413 (98.5%)	12,605
Female	55 (1.7%	17 (0.5%)	5 (0.2%)	25 (0.8%)	3,179 (96.9%)	3,272
Transportation						
Male	50 (1.3%)	7 (0.2%)	4 (0.8%)	15 (0.4%)	3,724 (98.0%)	3,799
Female	24 (1.7%)	5 (0.4%)	4 (0.3%)	12 (0.9%)	1,374 (96.8%)	1,419
Wholesale						
Male	24 (1.0%)	1 (0.0%)	6 (0.3%)	11 (0.5%)	2,366 (98.3%)	2,408
Female	17 (1.9%)	4 (0.4%)	2 (0.2%)	5 (0.6%)	884 (96.9%)	912

[Continued]

★ 87 ★

Hispanic Origin Industry Leaders by Industry
[Continued]

Industry/Gender	Mexican Amer.	Puerto Rican	Cuban	Other Hispanic	White	Total
Retail						
Male	120 (2.1%)	11 (0.2%)	3 (0.1%)	33 (0.6%)	5,548 (97.1%)	5,715
Female	113 (2.8%)	8 (0.2%)	3 (0.1%)	18 (0.5%)	3,865 (96.59%)	4,007
Business						
Male	53 (1.6%)	8 (0.3%)	3 (0.1%)	20 (0.6%)	3,172 (97.4%)	3,256
Female	21 (1.4%)	3 (0.2%)	5 (0.3%)	11 (0.7%)	1,459 (97.3%)	1,499
Finance						
Male	65 (1.4%)	16 (0.2%)	6 (0.1%)	22 (0.6%)	4,531 (97.7%)	4,640
Female	95 (2.2%)	15 (0.4%)	3 (0.1%)	19 (0.4%)	4,126 (96.9%)	4,258
Professional						
Male	47 (1.0%)	10 (0.2%)	5 (0.1%)	27 (0.6%)	4,548 (98.1%)	4,637
Female	112 (1.3%)	19 (0.3%)	6 (0.1%)	29 (0.5%)	5,951 (97.1%)	6,127
Total						
Male	471 (1.3%)	74 (0.2%)	36 (0.1%	178 (0.5%)	36,403 (98.0%)	37,162
Female	447 (2.1%)	71 (0.3%)	30 (0.1%)	119 (0.6%)	20,829 (96.9%)	21,496

Source: "Distribution and Representation of Private Sector Executive, Administrative, and Managerial Occupations in the U.S. by Industry, Hispanic Subgroup, and Gender," *Good for Business: Making Full Use of the Nation's Human Capital*, Washington, D.C., Glass Ceiling Commission, March 1995, Table 16, p. 130. Primary sources: 1990 Bureau of the Census, PUMS File 95% Confidence Interval; compiled by Tomas Rivera Center Research Staff.

★ 88 ★

Corporate Officers/Executives

Hispanic Origin Industry Leaders' Income

This table shows the mean wage income of Mexican American and white managers and Puerto Rican and white managers, by state, in private for-profit industry, selected states.

Industry/ Gender	California Mex. American	California White	Texas Mexican American	Texas White	Illinois Mex. American	Illinois White	New York Puerto Rican	New York White	Illinois Puerto Rican	Illinois White
Manufacturing										
Male	$41,456	$58,666	$30,821	$56,616	$49,998	$64,223	$45,853	$62,403	$25,300	$64,223
Female	$26,296	$31,662	$23,449	$29,883	$29,849	$33,500	$31,448	$37,160	$21,333	$33,500
Transportation										
Male	$33,353	$50,677	$30,948	$51,716	$34,295	$51,486	$35,096	$55,671	$33,000	$51,486
Female	$32,791	$32,933	$24,926	$31,968	$37,671	$32,471	$31,857	$36,081	$36,500	$32,471
Wholesale										
Male	$41,967	$58,283	$32,871	$57,216	$33,657	$60,450	$37,654	$67,696	$80,000	$60,450
Female	$25,686	$29,125	$18,037	$28,340	--	$30,425	$16,000	$36,998	--	$30,425
Retail										
Male	$24,213	$36,439	$19,740	$37,700	$32,346	$39,743	$27,837	$40,820	$24,667	$39,743
Female	$15,527	$18,461	$13,150	$20,188	$17,802	$20,184	$18,403	$22,942	$24,721	$20,184

[Continued]

★ 88 ★

Hispanic Origin Industry Leaders' Income
[Continued]

Industry/ Gender	California Mex. American	California White	Texas Mexican American	Texas White	Illinois Mex. American	Illinois White	New York Puerto Rican	New York White	Illinois Puerto Rican	Illinois White
Business										
Male	$27,998	$45,468	$21,809	$44,327	$28,750	$50,946	$70,257	$54,503	$29,000	$50,946
Female	$24,725	$29,037	$18,783	$26,772	$24,743	$32,221	$29,330	$37,628	$23,000	$32,221
Finance										
Male	$36,894	$59,240	$32,061	$55,769	$40,200	$67,531	$40,368	$70,000	$13,800	$67,531
Female	$23,332	$29,467	$19,940	$23,860	$28,218	$30,712	$29,268	$37,704	$10,000	$30,712
Professional										
Male	$32,180	$51,024	$32,769	$50,841	$28,605	$52,795	$35,375	$52,340	$29,000	$52,795
Female	$22,357	$26,773	$19,029	$24,294	$27,976	$28,028	$24,826	$30,931	$19,443	$28,028

Source: "Comparison of the Mean Wage Income of Mexican American and White Managers by State, Private-For-Profit Industry, Gender, and Hispanic Subgroup," and Comparison of the Mean Wage Income of Puerto Rican and White Managers by State, Private-For-Profit Industry, Gender, and Hispanic Subgroup," *Good for Business: Making Full Use of the Nation's Human Capital*, Washington, D.C., Glass Ceiling Commission, March 1995, Tables 17a and 17b, pp. 132-133. Primary sources: 1990 Bureau of the Census, Public Use Microdata (5%) Sample; 95% Confidence Interval. Compiled by Tomas Rivera Center Research Staff. The number of cases used to determine mean wages is in some instances as few as one. Sample sizes from a 5% file are expectedly small. Data is provided for all cases regardless of sample size.

★ 89 ★

Corporate Officers/Executives

Income of Business Executives and Managers

This table shows the average earnings of U.S. business executives and managers by race and gender, based on 1990 census data.

[NA Not available.]

Industry	White		Black	
	Males	Females	Males	Females
Business services	$45,560	$29,037	$36,338	$29,037
Finance, real estate, insurance	$59,240	$29,336	$34,299	$32,286
Manufacturing	$58,366	$31,662	$48,152	$38,055
Retail	$36,439	$23,540	$22,592	$21,863
Transportation	$50,677	$38,768	$39,275	$39,275
Wholesale	$58,283	$29,125	$25,819	NA
Other profession	$51,024	$26,773	$22,808	$21,124

Source: Marla Dickerson, "Set-asides could be first to get federal ax," *The Detroit News*, April 2, 1995, p. 11A, table entitled "Who Are Our Industry Leaders?" Primary source: U.S. Labor Department's Glass Ceiling Commission.

★ 90 ★

Corporate Officers/Executives

Industry Leaders by Educational Attainment

This table shows the percentage of all white male, white female, black male, and black female executives, administrators, and managers (EAM) by educational attainment.

	Educational attainment			
	< HS	4 yrs HS	1-3 yrs college	4+yrs college
All white male EAMs	3.5%	22.0%	21.3%	53.1%
All white female EAMs	2.8%	35.4%	25.8%	36.1%
All black male EAMs	5.8%	19.6%	23.7%	51.3%
All black female EAMs	3.5%	22.8%	25.4%	48.0%

Source: Selected from "Executive, Administrative, and Managerial Occupations by Race, Educational Attainment, and Sex, 1990" *Good for Business: Making Full Use of the Nation's Human Capital,* Washington, D.C., Glass Ceiling Commission, March 1995, Table 1, p. 75.

★ 91 ★

Corporate Officers/Executives

Industry Leaders by Major Industry Category

This table shows the percentage breakdown of executive, administrative, and managerial occupations for major industry categories by race/ethnicity and gender, 1990. Black women held 2.2% of these jobs in all private sector industries (4.6% in the public and private sectors combined). In a 1990 *Business Week* profile of the chief executives of the 1,000 most valuable publicly held U.S. companies, it was concluded that the critical career path for senior management positions is finance, marketing, or operations. Black men and women are underrepresented in these positions, as they are in executive, administrative, and managerial occupations in every single industry category.

Industry	Percent in Occupations							
	White		Black		Hispanic		Asian	
	M	F	M	F	M	F	M	F
Banking	44.8%	37.6%	2.6%	2.6%	3.4%	5.0%	1.8%	2.6%
Business Services	51.6%	32.8%	3.5%	0.5%	5.2%	3.2%	1.7%	1.2%
Communication	47.6%	36.6%	3.7%	4.9%	3.3%	1.8%	1.6%	1.6%
Construction	74.6%	15.6%	1.9%	0.3%	1.7%	0.9%	0.3%	0.3%
Education/Elementary	35.4%	45.3%	3.5%	4.3%	2.7%	5.5%	0.8%	0.8%
Education/College	38.4%	48.3%	1.6%	4.5%	0.8%	2.9%	1.6%	0.8%
Entertainment	50.2%	38.1%	2.5%	1.0%	4.1%	1.5%	1.5%	--
Health Services	16.2%	66.7%	1.3%	2.5%	1.6%	4.4%	--	0.9%
Hospitals	29.9%	50.2%	2.1%	4.6%	4.6%	4.6%	1.7%	1.7%
Insurance	44.0%	40.7%	3.2%	3.0%	2.0%	4.2%	0.5%	1.7%

[Continued]

★ 91 ★

Industry Leaders by Major Industry Category
[Continued]

Industry	Percent in Occupations							
	White		Black		Hispanic		Asian	
	M	F	M	F	M	F	M	F
Manufacturing	62.9%	23.3%	1.6%	0.9%	2.8%	2.0%	2.3%	0.9%
Personal Services	41.3%	40.4%	3.4%	2.5%	4.3%	2.8%	2.5%	1.9%
Public Administration	47.5%	31.9%	3.6%	4.8%	5.2%	3.6%	0.6%	1.3%
Retail	41.7%	39.1%	2.3%	2.6%	4.6%	4.3%	3.5%	1.7%
Social Services	16.4%	65.6%	3.1%	7.2%	1.0%	3.6%	0.5%	0.5%
Transportation	58.4%	25.6%	2.4%	1.0%	6.1%	3.4%	1.7%	0.3%
Utilities	71.9%	17.2%	3.1%	0.8%	3.1%	0.7%	--	0.8%
Wholesale	53.4%	36.2%	1.2%	0.3%	2.7%	2.1%	2.4%	1.8%
Other Professions	52.8%	37.8%	1.2%	1.6%	1.9%	1.9%	1.9%	1.5%
Total (All Private Sector Industries)	49.4%	35.9%	2.3%	2.2%	3.5%	3.1%	1.7%	1.2%
Total Employed (Public and Private Sector Industries)	39.8%	36.3%	3.9%	4.6%	6.4%	5.0%	1.5%	1.3%

Source: "Executive, Administrative, and Managerial Occupations for Major Industry Categories, by Race and Sex, 1990," *Good for Business: Making Full Use of the Nation's Human Capital*, Washington, D.C., Glass Ceiling Commission, March 1995, Table 3, p. 79. Primary sources: 1990 Bureau of the Census, PUMS File 95% Confidence Interval; *The Impact of the Glass Ceiling on African American Men and Women*; Congressional Black Caucus Foundation's Institute for Policy Research and Education. Data does not always add up to 100.0 percent due to rounding errors.

★ 92 ★

Corporate Officers/Executives

Industry Leaders by Race/Ethnicity

This table shows the percentage breakdown of executives, managers, and administrators in private-industry fields by race/ethnicty. The U.S. population mix is whites, 75.3%; Hispanics, 9.0%; Blacks, 12.0%; and Asian/Pacific Islanders, 2.9%.

Industry and Race/ethnicity	Men	Women	Total
Business services			
Whites	51.6%	32.8%	84.4%
Hispanics	5.2%	3.2%	8.4%
Blacks	3.5%	0.5%	4.0%
Asians	1.7%	1.2%	2.9%
Finance			
Whites	44.8%	37.6%	82.4%

[Continued]

★ 92 ★

Industry Leaders by Race/Ethnicity
[Continued]

Industry and Race/ethnicity	Men	Women	Total
Hispanics	3.4%	5.0%	8.4%
Blacks	2.6%	2.6%	5.2%
Asians	1.8%	2.6%	4.4%
Insurance			
Whites	44.0%	40.7%	84.7%
Hispanics	2.0%	4.2%	6.2%
Blacks	3.2%	3.0%	6.2%
Asians	0.5%	1.7%	2.2%
Communications			
Whites	47.6%	36.6%	84.2%
Hispanics	3.3%	1.8%	5.1%
Blacks	3.7%	4.9%	8.6%
Asians	1.6%	1.6%	3.2%
Retail Trade			
Whites	41.7%	39.1%	80.8%
Hispanics	2.8%	2.0%	4.8%
Blacks	2.3%	2.6%	4.9%
Asians	3.5%	1.7%	5.2%
Transportation			
Whites	58.4%	25.6%	84.0%
Hispanics	6.1%	3.4%	9.5%
Blacks	2.4%	1.0%	3.4%
Asians	1.7%	0.3%	2.0%
Utilities			
Whites	71.9%	17.2%	89.1%
Hispanics	3.1%	0.7%	3.9%
Blacks	3.1%	0.8%	3.9%
Asians	0.0%	0.8%	0.8%
Wholesale Trade			
Whites	53.4%	36.2%	89.6%
Hispanics	2.7%	2.1%	4.8%
Blacks	1.2%	0.3%	1.5%
Asians	2.4%	1.8%	4.2%

Source: Marla Dickerson, "Set-asides could be first to get federal ax," *The Detroit News*, April 2, 1995, p. 11A, table entitled "Who Are Our Industry Leaders?" Primary source: U.S. Labor Department's Glass Ceiling Commission. Percentage may not total 100 because of rounding or because not all racial/ethnic groups are shown. Hispanics can be of any race. Whites counted in this report are non-Hispanic.

★ 93 ★
Corporate Officers/Executives

Industry Leaders by Race/Ethnicity and Educational Attainment

This table shows the percentage breakdown of persons in executive, administrative, and managerial occupations in the private sector by race, educational attainment, and sex in 1990. Black women are underrepresented in these positions for each educational level. Black and white women continue to be underrepresented in these positions whether they have a college degree or not. White men are overrepresented at the top regardless of educational level.

Item	Percent in Occupations			
	White		Black	
	M	F	M	F
Education				
Less than high school diploma	63.5%	28.9%	4.6%	3.0%
4 years of high school	49.5%	46.1%	1.9%	2.5%
1 to 3 years of college	55.2%	38.8%	2.7%	3.2%
4 or more years of college	67.5%	26.6%	2.9%	3.0%
Total Executives, Administrators, and Managers (Blacks and whites only)	59.8%	34.7%	2.6%	2.9%
Total Employed (Percent of blacks and whites employed in ALL occupations)	47.7%	38.5%	5.0%	5.2%

Source: "Executive, Administrative, and Managerial Occupations by Race (Blacks and Whites Only), Educational Attainment, and Sex, 1990," *Good for Business: Making Full Use of the Nation's Human Capital*, Washington, D.C., Glass Ceiling Commission, March 1995, Table 1, p. 75. Primary sources: 1990 Bureau of the Census, PUMS File 95% Confidence Interval; *The Impact of the Glass Ceiling on African American Men and Women*; Congressional Black Caucus Foundation's Institute for Policy Research and Education.

★ 94 ★

Corporate Officers/Executives

Industry Leaders' Income by Educational Attainment and Race

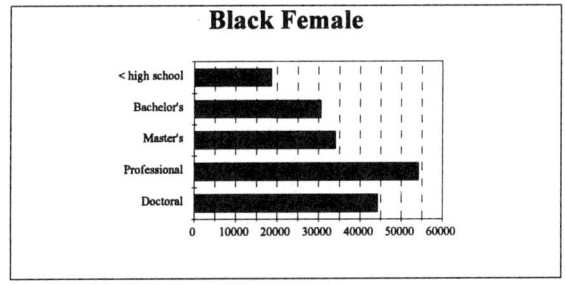

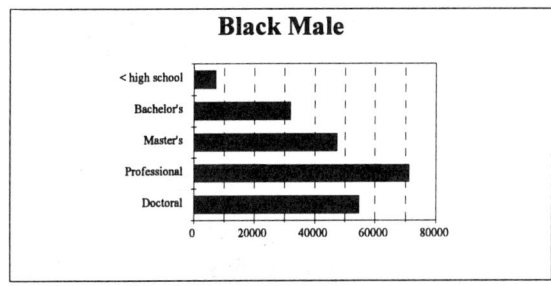

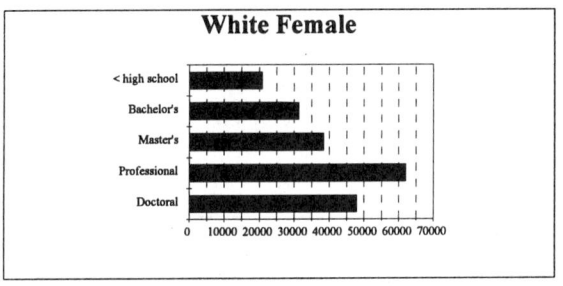

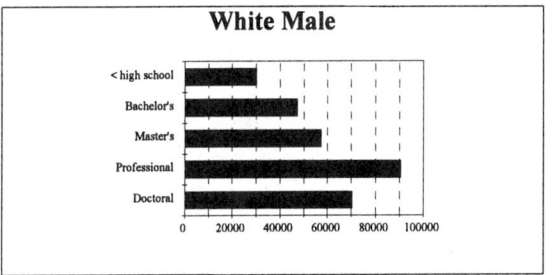

This table shows income of black and white males and females in executive, administrative, and managerial occupations by educational attainment. Figures are for private sector employees only. Private sector refers to Business Services, Communications, Construction, Entertainment, Manufacturing, Public Administration, and Utilities industries. Even when one succeeds in obtaining such a position, black men, white women, and black women earn subsantially less than do white men.

Gender/ Race	Doctoral Degree	Professional Degree	Master's Degree	Bachelor's Degree	4 or More yrs. college	1 to 3 yrs. college	4 years of high school	Less than high school	Less than Bachelor's
Black Female	$44,230	$54,171	$34,006	$30,584	$32,452	$24,262	$22,732	$18,629	$23,291
Black Male	$54,741	$71,114	$47,234	$32,001	$40,939	$26,027	$25,534	$7,203	$23,947
White Female	$47,876	$61,995	$38,391	$31,338	$32,332	$25,195	$22,015	$20,876	$23,230
White Male	$70,414	$90,610	$57,371	$47,181	$50,052	$38,588	$33,074	$30,275	$34,862

Source: "Executive, Administrative, and Managerial Occupations by Race, Education Attainment, Income, and Gender," *Good for Business: Making Full Use of the Nation's Human Capital*, Washington, D.C., Glass Ceiling Commission, March 1995, Table 4, p. 81. Primary sources: 1990 Bureau of the Census, PUMS File 95% Confidence Interval; *The Impact of the Glass Ceiling on African American Men and Women*; Congressional Black Caucus Foundation's Institute for Policy Research and Education.

★ 95 ★

Corporate Officers/Executives

Industry Leaders' Income by Industry and Race

This table shows mean income of black and white males and females in executive, administrative, and managerial occupations by selected industry.

[Private sector only.]

Industry	Mean Income			
	White		Black	
	M	F	M	F
Business Services	$45,560	$29,037	$36,338	$29,037
Finance, Real Estate,				
Insurance	$59,240	$29,366	$34,299	$32,286
Manufacturing	$58,366	$31,662	$48,152	$38,055
Retail	$36,439	$23,540	$22,592	$21,863
Transportation	$50,677	$38,768	$39,275	$39,275
Wholesale	$58,283	$29,125	$25,819	--
Other Profession	$51,024	$26,773	$22,808	$21,124

Source: "Executive, Administrative, and Managerial Occupations by Race, Selected Industry, Mean Income, and Sex," *Good for Business: Making Full Use of the Nation's Human Capital,* Washington, D.C., Glass Ceiling Commission, March 1995, Table 5, p. 82. Primary sources: 1990 Bureau of the Census, PUMS File 95% Confidence Interval; *The Impact of the Glass Ceiling on African American Men and Women;* Congressional Black Caucus Foundation's Institute for Policy Research and Education.

★ 96 ★

Corporate Officers/Executives

Industry Leaders' Income Disparities by Race/Ethnicity

This table shows the mean income of non-Hispanic white males and females with bachelor's or master's degrees in executive, administrative, and managerial occupations by race/ethnicity, in 1990. Their mean income is then used as the base, with the white non-Hispanic mean incomes, male and female, as the comparatives. The only group to fare better than the white non-Hispanic male population was the Japanese male population. However, the figures include people who worked in the United States on assignment from Japan-based parent firms who were compensated on par with salaries according to the cost-of-living in Japan.

Race/ Ethnicity	Bachelor's Degree		Master's Degree	
	Male	Female	Male	Female
Non-Hispanic White	$47,181	$31,338	$57,371	$38,391
African American	($15,180)	($754)	($10,137)	($4,385)
Chinese	($5,924)	($2,032)	$1,481	$7,292
Filipino	($7,992)	($3,045)	($7,204)	($7,160)
Japanese	$22,406	($373)	$13,071	$1,533
Asian Indian	($1,872)	($6,906)	$5,997	($6,970)
Korean	($4,400)	($5,559)	($5,801)	($10,576)

[Continued]

★ 96 ★

Industry Leaders' Income Disparities by Race/Ethnicity
[Continued]

Race/ Ethnicity	Bachelor's Degree		Master's Degree	
	Male	Female	Male	Female
Vietnamese	($2,678)	($6,267)	$5,923	($4,350)
Other S.E. Asian	($20,221)	($6,679)	($20,694)	[1]
Hawaiian	($11,252)	($8,066)	($14,079)	[1]
Other A/PI	($6,853)	($1,688)	($12,734)	($11,695)

Source: "National Mean Income Disparities-Race/Ethnicity by Gender of Executives, Administrators, and Managers of Private-for-Profit Companies with Bachelor's or Master's Degrees: 1990 Census," *Good for Business: Making Full Use of the Nation's Human Capital*, Washington, D.C., Glass Ceiling Commission, March 1995, p. 162. *Note:* 1. Results very unreliable due to extremely small sample size.

★ 97 ★

Corporate Officers/Executives

Industry Leaders' Occupational Achievement Compared to Education

This table shows the percentage breakdown of racial groups in executive, administrative, and managerial occupations (blacks and whites only) by educational level. It then shows ratios: the percent of blacks and whites, males and females, in top corporate positions compared to their representation in the particular educational category. By this reckoning, white men with less than a high school diploma have 68% more of executive, administrative, and managerial positions than should be expected at this educational level, all things being equal.

Item	White		Black	
	M	F	M	F
Educational Level of Racial Groups				
Less than high school diploma	37.7%	42.0%	7.5%	8.8%
4 years of high school	38.4%	47.6%	5.1%	6.1%
1 to 3 years of college	41.0%	53.2%	4.4%	6.0%
4 or more years of college	48.3%	39.9%	2.7%	3.4%
Ratios: Percentage in Top Positions/Percentage in Educational Category				
Less than high school diploma	1.68	0.68	0.61	0.34
4 years of high school	1.30	0.97	0.37	0.41

[Continued]

★ 97 ★

Industry Leaders' Occupational Achievement
Compared to Education
[Continued]

Item	White		Black	
	M	F	M	F
1 to 3 years of college	1.35	0.73	0.61	0.53
4 or more years of college	1.40	0.67	1.07	0.88

Source: "Percent of Educational Level of Racial Groups Compared to Percent of Racial Groups in Executive, Administrative, and Managerial Occupations, 1990," *Good for Business: Making Full Use of the Nation's Human Capital*, Washington, D.C., Glass Ceiling Commission, March 1995, Table 2, p. 76. Primary sources: 1990 Bureau of the Census, PUMS File 95% Confidence Interval; *The Impact of the Glass Ceiling on African American Men and Women*; Congressional Black Caucus Foundation's Institute for Policy Research and Education.

Legal Matters

★ 98 ★

Breast Implant Settlement Approved

In 1994 U.S. District Judge Sam Pointer granted final approval of a $4.25 billion agreement to compensate women who claimed silicone breast implants made them ill. This agreement was the largest product liability settlement in U.S. history to that time.[1] This table delineates some of the points of the settlement.

Item	Number/Percent
Number of U.S. manufacturers of silicone breast implants involved in the lawsuit, approx.	60
Dow Corning Corporation's share of the settlement, the largest	$2 billion
Initial payment due from all companies by mid-October, 1994	$900 million
Number of women who made claims against silicone implant manufacturers	>90,500
Women from other countries	500
Number of women who rejected the settlement, approx.	15,000

[Continued]

★ 98 ★

Breast Implant Settlement Approved
[Continued]

Item	Number/Percent
Lowest amount due to American women with certain diseases, depending on age and health, under terms of settlement	$105,000
Highest amount due to American women with certain diseases, depending on age and health, under terms of settlement	$1.4 million
Amount judge promised to limit lawyers' fees and administrative costs to	$1 billion

Source: "$4.2 Billion Implant Settlement Is Approved," *The New York Times*, September 2, 1994, p. A16 Y. *Note:* 1. Previous high was $3 billion in an asbestos exposure case.

Sales of Contraceptives

★ 99 ★

The Market for Norplant

Norplant, a birth control device that is implanted under the skin and lasts for five years, went on the U.S. market in February 1991 after 30 years of development and testing. By 1992, 1% of women aged 15 to 44 who used contraceptives chose Norplant. However, Norplant faces an onslaught of lawsuits brought by many of the same lawyers who won a $4 billion settlement against the makers of silicone breast implants. While its maker, Wyeth-Ayerst Laboratories, says it has no plans to take Norplant off the market, it also says that negative publicity has affected sales of the product. This table shows some statistics about Norplant sales.

Item	Number/Percent
Sales of Norplant devices per day:	
Upon introduction	800
Following negative publicity	60
Total sales in 1992 of health care and food products by Norplant's manufacturer:	$7.9 billion
Norplant's share	$141 million
What a Norplant device sells for:	$365

[Continued]

★ 99 ★

The Market for Norplant
[Continued]

Item	Number/Percent
Congressional estimate of what it costs to make and market Norplant:	$16
Plus a royalty paid to the Population Council, which developed and tested Norplant	$14.60
Number of lawsuits filed against American Home Products and its Wyeth-Ayerst division, makers of Norplant:	
1991-1993	20
1994	180
Amount of silicone in	
Norplant	0.75 grams
Breast implants	250-500 grams

Source: Gina Kolata, "Will the Lawyers Kill Off Norplant," *The New York Times*, May 28, 1995, p. 3.

Shopping

★ 100 ★

Getting a Second Opinion

This table shows the percent of adults aged 18 and older who say they would seek independent information about getting the best deal when shopping for selected products and services.

Product or service	Men	Women
Air fares	49%	62%
Checking accounts	54%	69%
Eyeglasses	51%	64%
Food purchases at market	52%	67%
Home purchase	78%	80%
Investments	79%	79%
Long-distance telephone service	44%	57%
Mortgage loan	74%	76%

[Continued]

★ 100 ★

Getting a Second Opinion
[Continued]

Product or service	Men	Women
New car	80%	85%
Nonprescription drugs	48%	61%

Source: Selected from "Waiting for a New TV," *American Demographics,* July 1994, pp. 16-17, p. 17, table entitled "Mr. Know-It-All." Primary source: Opinion Research Corporation, Princeton, NJ.

The Media

★ 101 ★

Media Reviews of Mystery Writers

Sisters in Crime offers these statistics on women mystery writers.

Sisters in Crime was formed in 1986 "to combat discrimination against women in the mystery field, educate publishers and the general public as to inequalities in the treatment of female authors, and to raise the level of awareness of their contribution to the field." To that end, the following statistics were collected:

1. Of the 88 mysteries reviewed by the *New York Times* in 1985, only **14 (16%)** were written by women.

2. In other major publications, **15% was a typical figure.**

3. A second count in 1992 of 20 publications showed that more than **30%** of books reviewed were written by women.

Source: Selected from "An Introduction to Sisters in Crime" (membership application pamphlet).

★ 102 ★

The Media

Smoking Linked to Advertising

The New York Times reports on a study to be published in *The Journal of the American Medical Association* linking an increase in smoking by teenaged girls in the late 1960s and early 1970s to "soaring sales of widely advertised cigarettes for women." The study's authors contend that their findings provide strong evidence that advertising, in spite of the tobacco industry's assertions otherwise, lures young people into starting to smoke. Advertising campaigns for Virginia Slims, Silva Thins, and Eve cigarettes were linked to increases in the start of smoking by young women. A spokesman for the tobacco industry attributed the increase in smoking by young girls in the late 1960s to the women's liberation movement, "the time when bra-burning women were abandoning traditional roles." This table shows some of the results of the study and other figures cited in the newspaper article.

Item	Number/percent
Increase in smoking during the six-year period from 1967 to 1973 for:	
12-year-old girls	110%
13-year-old girls	55%
14-year-old girls	70%
15-year-old girls	75%
16-year-old girls	55%
17-year-old girls	35%
Sales of "women's" cigarettes in peak year 1975	$16 billion
Estimate of the number of packs of cigarettes that are sold to persons under 18 each year	1 billion

Source: Jane E. Brody, "Study Links Ads to 60's-Era Smoking, *The New York Times*, February 23, 1994, p. B6 Y. Primary source: Dr. John P. Pierce/University of California, San Diego. Based on national health surveys conducted among 102,626 adults who had been regular smokers at some point in their lives.

★ 103 ★

The Media

Top Online Services

This table shows the top 16 consumer online services and the number of subscribers on December 31, 1994, and December 31, 1993, with percent change. Number 16, **Women's Wire**, was not a contender in 1993.

Online Service	Subscribers		
	12/31/94	12/31/93	Change
CompuServe Information Svc.	2,660,000	1,600,000	66.3%
America Online	1,500,000	531,000	182.5%
Prodigy	1,200,000	1,000,000	20.0%
ZiffNet	260,000	200,000	30.0%
Telescan	143,000	80,000	78.8%
GEnie	120,000	100,000	20.0%
Delphi	100,000	85,000	17.6%
The ImagiNation Network	57,000	30,000	90.0%
Reuters Money Network	31,000	24,000	29.2%
Access Atlanta	16,000	X	X
Hawaii FYI	13,197	10,200	29.4%
The WELL	11,000	10,000	10.0%
101 Online	7,500	7,000	7.1%
StarText	4,300	3,600	19.4%
SeniorNet	2,500	1,700	47.1%
Women's Wire	1,300	X	X

Source: Selected from "Electronic Information Report Year End Online Subscriber Survey," *Electronic Information Report*, March 17, 1995, p. 6. See the table in **Sports and Recreation** entitled "Subscribers to Online Services" for the percentages of women and men who subscribe to online services.

Women Business Owners

★ 104 ★

Women-Owned Businesses: 1990 and 1994

This table shows figures in millions and percentages relating to women-owned businesses.

[Numbers in millions.]

Item	Total
Firms owned by women	
1990	5.4
1994	7.7
Percent change	+42.6%
Number of employees	
1990	11.0
1994	15.5
Percent change	+40.9%
Still in business since 1991	
All U.S. businesses	66.6%
Women-owned businesses	72.2%
Low credit risk	
All U.S. businesses	56.0%
Women-owned businesses	59.5%
Low risk of failure	
All U.S. businesses	86.3%
Women-owned businesses	85.3%

Source: Selected from Vickie Elmer, "Firms Run by Women Thrive," *Detroit Free Press*, April 12, 1995, pp. 1+. Primary source: Dun & Bradstreet Information Services and the National Foundation for Women Business Owners.

Chapter 3
CRIME, LAW ENFORCEMENT, AND LEGAL JUSTICE

Crime and Criminals

★ 105 ★

Arrestees' Age and Race: 1988

This table shows the age and race of females who were arrested in 1988 in major U.S. cities. Blacks were the largest racial group for both male and female arrestees in most cities. Hispanic arrestees predominated in San Antonio. White arrestees were the largest racial group in Phoenix, Portland, and San Diego.

City and State	Age					Race			
	15-20	21-25	26-30	31-35	36+	Black	White	Hispanic	Other
Birmingham, AL	14%	21%	27%	21%	17%	60%	38%	0%	2%
Chicago, IL	14%	24%	32%	17%	12%	83%	14%	3%	1%
Dallas, TX	14%	33%	26%	14%	14%	52%	46%	2%	- -
Detroit, MI	11%	28%	30%	18%	13%	63%	37%	0%	0%
Kansas City, MO	16%	40%	21%	12%	10%	80%	20%	0%	0%
Los Angeles, CA	8%	28%	27%	18%	19%	42%	29%	26%	2%
New Orleans, LA	15%	27%	26%	14%	18%	79%	18%	2%	- -
New York, NY	12%	31%	28%	16%	13%	55%	19%	25%	1%
Philadelphia, PA	12%	26%	24%	16%	23%	68%	21%	11%	0%
Phoenix, AZ	12%	31%	26%	16%	14%	17%	57%	19%	7%
Portland, OR	15%	23%	27%	20%	14%	33%	58%	2%	6%
St. Louis, MO	12%	24%	21%	12%	31%	69%	31%	0%	0%
San Antonio, TX	17%	14%	33%	16%	21%	15%	34%	50%	0%
San Diego, CA	12%	22%	28%	20%	18%	31%	48%	16%	4%

Source: "Age and Race of Female Arrestees," DUF: 1988 Drug Use Forecasting Annual Report, National Institute of Justice, March 1990, p. 21. Note: - - represents less than 1%.

★ 106 ★

Crime and Criminals

Arrestees' Offenses: 1988-I

This table shows the charges at arrest against females who were arrested in 1988 in major U.S. cities.

City and State	Charge at Arrest									
	Assault	Burglary	Destruction of property	Drug sale/possession[1]	Family offense	Fight/bench warrant	Fraud/forgery	Homicide/manslaughter	Larceny/theft	Probation/parole violation
Birmingham, AL	0%	4%	4%	15%	0%	0%	15%	2%	35%	12%
Chicago, IL	7%	2%	3%	31%	3%	5%	1%	0%	7%	1%
Dallas, TX	10%	1%	- -	12%	- -	0%	6%	0%	25%	2%
Detroit, MI	1%	1%	2%	7%	4%	1%	6%	4%	6%	2%
Indianapolis, IN	11%	2%	0%	0%	0%	22%	0%	2%	35%	0%
Kansas City, MO	9%	0%	2%	2%	2%	0%	6%	2%	24%	7%
Los Angeles, CA	6%	9%	2%	19%	3%	2%	5%	- -	16%	0%
New Orleans, LA	11%	- -	3%	12%	- -	6%	4%	- -	28%	1%
New York, NY	8%	3%	- -	23%	- -	0%	1%	0%	24%	0%
Philadelphia, PA	11%	4%	- -	24%	0%	4%	4%	- -	29%	0%
Phoenix, AZ	6%	6%	1%	9%	3%	2%	8%	- -	24%	3%
Portland, OR	8%	4%	- -	15%	- -	5%	10%	- -	20%	4%
St. Louis, MO	5%	2%	2%	4%	0%	4%	1%	0%	24%	1%
San Antonio, TX	6%	- -	0%	5%	0%	4%	8%	0%	29%	- -
San Diego, CA	2%	10%	0%	43%	2%	4%	3%	0%	9%	2%

Source: Selected from "Distribution of Charges in Male and Female Arrestees," *DUF: 1988 Drug Use Forecasting Annual Report,* National Institute of Justice, March 1990, p. 24-25. - - represents less than 1%. *Note:* 1. Drug sale and possession charges were undersampled.

★ 107 ★

Crime and Criminals

Arrestees' Offenses: 1988-II

This table shows the charges at arrest against females who were arrested in 1988 in major U.S. cities.

City and State	Charge at Arrest								
	Prostitution	Public peace disturbance[1]	Robbery	Sex Offense	Stolen Property	Stolen Vehicle	Traffic Offenses	Weapons	Other
Birmingham, AL	0%	0%	2%	0%	2%	0%	0%	0%	9%
Chicago, IL	29%	2%	3%	0%	1%	1%	0%	2%	2%
Dallas, TX	17%	4%	1%	0%	--	2%	11%	2%	5%
Detroit, MI	25%	23%	0%	1%	0%	1%	0%	1%	15%
Indianapolis, IN	4%	9%	0%	2%	0%	2%	0%	0%	11%
Kansas City, MO	12%	4%	3%	0%	0%	1%	10%	6%	10%
Los Angeles, CA	21%	3%	2%	--	1%	2%	0%	--	8%
New Orleans, LA	9%	12%	--	1%	2%	--	0%	3%	4%

[Continued]

★ 107 ★

Arrestees' Offenses: 1988-II

[Continued]

City and State	Charge at Arrest								
	Prostitution	Public peace disturbance[1]	Robbery	Sex Offense	Stolen Property	Stolen Vehicle	Traffic Offenses	Weapons	Other
New York, NY	20%	4%	6%	0%	1%	2%	0%	0%	7%
Philadelphia, PA	4%	2%	5%	--	--	2%	0%	1%	8%
Phoenix, AZ	11%	9%	--	1%	2%	1%	4%	--	8%
Portland, OR	19%	4%	2%	--	--	2%	0%	1%	4%
St. Louis, MO	14%	21%	0%	0%	0%	1%	9%	6%	6%
San Antonio, TX	4%	6%	2%	--	0%	0%	21%	--	13%
San Diego, CA	7%	3%	--	0%	2%	3%	6%	--	3%

Source: Selected from "Distribution of Charges in Male and Female Arrestees," *DUF: 1988 Drug Use Forecasting Annual Report*, National Institute of Justice, March 1990, p. 24-25. —represents less than 1%. *Note:* 1. Includes trespassing, criminal mischief, reckless endangerment.

★ 108 ★

Crime and Criminals

Arrestees' School Dropout History: 1988

The National Institute of Justice's Drug Use Forecasting Program covered 20 cities in 1988. It is designed to provide cities with an estimate of drug use among arrestees and information for detecting changes in drug use trends. This table shows the percentage of females who admitted that they had completed less than 12 grades of school, by race and Hispanic origin.

City and State	Black N = 1,533	White N = 1,169	Hispanic N = 438
San Antonio, TX	- -	42%	74%
Kansas City, MO	51%	- -	- -
St. Louis, MO	52%	38%	- -
Philadelphia, PA	56%	42%	- -
Dallas, TX	46%	49%	- -
New Orleans, LA	48%	44%	- -
New York, NY	57%	54%	64%
Indianapolis, IN	36%	64%	- -
Chicago, IL	48%	- -	- -
Detroit, MI	54%	67%	- -
Portland, OR	51%	65%	- -
Birmingham, AL	52%	55%	- -
Los Angeles, CA	29%	42%	72%
Phoenix, AZ	47%	50%	74%
San Diego, CA	31%	46%	71%

Source: "School Dropout Among Arrestees," *DUF: 1988 Drug Use Forecasting Annual Report*, National Institute of Justice, March 1990, p. 19. - - represents less than 20 cases.

★ 109 ★

Crime and Criminals

Convicted Felons: 1992

This table shows percentages of men and women convicted of felonies by State courts in 1992 by offense. Although men made up almost 50% of the adult U.S. population, they comprised 87% of persons convicted of a felony and 93% of persons convicted of a violent felony.

Most serious conviction offense	Percent of convicted felons		
	Total	Sex	
		Male	Female
All offenses	100%	87%	13%
Violent offenses	100%	93%	7%
Murder[1]	100%	90%	10%
Rape	100%	98%	2%
Robbery	100%	94%	6%
Aggravated assault	100%	90%	10%
Other violent[2]	100%	93%	7%
Property offenses	100%	83%	17%
Burglary	100%	95%	5%
Larceny[3]	100%	81%	19%
Fraud[4]	100%	62%	38%
Drug offenses	100%	85%	15%
Possession	100%	83%	17%
Trafficking	100%	86%	14%
Weapons offenses	100%	96%	4%
Other offenses[5]	100%	90%	10%

Source: Selected from "Demographic characteristics of persons convicted of felonies by State courts, 1992," Patrick A. Langan, Ph.D., and Helen A. Graziadei, *Felony Sentences in State Courts, 1992,* U.S. Department of Justice, Bureau of Justice Statistics Bulletin, January 1995, NCJ-151167, Table 5, p. 5. *R Data on sex were available for 781,681. *Notes:* 1. Includes nonnegligent manslaughter. 2. Includes offenses such as negligent manslaughter, sexual assault, and kidnaping. 3. Includes motor vehicle theft. 4. Includes forgery and embezzlement. 5. Composed of nonviolent offenses such as receiving stolen property and vandalism.

★ 110 ★
Crime and Criminals

Correctional Institution Population: 1992

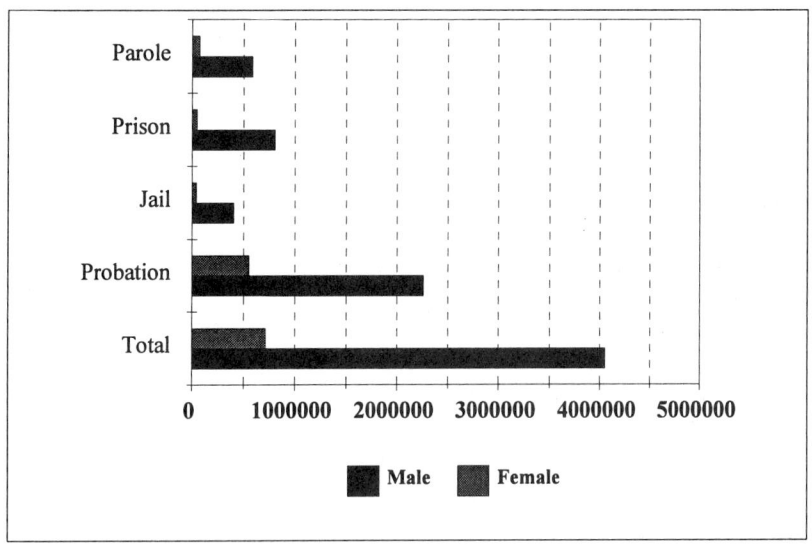

This table shows the number of males and females who were in local jails or prisons or on probation or parole in 1992. The total U.S. adult resident population 18 years or older on July 1, 1992, was 188,898,000 (90,574,000 males and 98,324,000 females). The percent under correctional care or in custody was 2.5% (4.4% males and 0.7% females).

Location	Total[1]	Male	Female
Total	4,763,200	4,050,900	712,300
Probation[2]	2,811,600	2,257,900	553,700
Jail	441,800	401,100	40,700
Prison	851,200	804,200	47,100
Parole[2]	658,600	587,700	70,800

Source: Selected from "Estimated number of adults on probation, in jail, in prison, or on parole and their percent of the adult population, by sex and race, 1992," Tracy L. Snell, *Correctional Populations in the United States, 1992,* U.S. Department of Justice, Bureau of Justice Statistics, table 1.2, p. 5. *R Detail may not add to total because of rounding. In cases where sex or race was unknown or not reported, percentages were applied based on known cases. *Notes:* 1. A small number of individuals have multiple correctional statuses; consequently, the total number of persons under correctional supervision is an overestimate. 2. The estimated total number of adults on probation, on parole, and in prison on December 31, 1992, were revised by the authors and differ from those reported in other tables in the source.

★ 111 ★

Crime and Criminals

Jail Inmates' Criminal History: 1983 and 1989

This table shows the criminal history of jail inmates, by sex, in 1989 and 1983. Female inmates were more likely than male inmates to be first-time offenders.

Criminal history	% of jail inmates, 1989		% of jail inmates, 1983	
	Female	Male	Female	Male
Total	100.0%	100.0%	100.0%	100.0%
No previous sentence	31.3%	21.5%	30.9%	19.3%
Current violent offense	6.2%	6.7%	7.9%	7.8%
Current nonviolent offense	25.1%	14.8%	23.0%	11.5%
Violent recidivists	16.2%	31.4%	20.7%	37.8%
Current and prior violent	2.2%	8.1%	5.4%	11.5%
Current violent only	6.2%	10.9%	8.1%	12.5%
Prior violent only	7.8%	12.4%	7.2%	13.8%
Nonviolent recidivists	52.4%	47.1%	48.4%	42.8%
Prior minor public-order offenses only	4.1%	3.4%	8.1%	4.1%
Other prior offenses	48.3%	43.7%	40.3%	38.7%
Number of inmates	35,333	340,249	15,034	200,241

Source: "Criminal history of jail inmates, by sex, 1989 and 1983," Tracy L. Snell, "Women in Jail 1989," *Bureau of Justice Statistics Special Report*, March 1992, Table 8, p. 6. Excludes an estimated 19,971 inmates in 1989 and 8,277 in 1983 for whom current offense and prior probation/incarceration offenses were unknown.

★ 112 ★

Crime and Criminals

Jail Inmates' Employment and Income Source: 1989

This table compares pre-arrest employment, income source, and pre-arrest monthly income of female and male inmates in 1989. Females were less likely than male inmates to have been employed at the time of their arrest. Females were far more likely than males to report receiving welfare income and to report receiving income from illegal sources (17.5% compared to 11.4%).

Characteristic	Percent of female inmates			% male inmates Total
	Free less than 1 year	Free at least 1 year	Total	
Pre-arrest employment				
Employed	26.1%	40.3%	38.0%	68.2%
Full time	16.8%	29.2%	27.2%	56.6%
Part time	9.3%	11.1%	10.8%	11.5%

[Continued]

★ 112 ★

Jail Inmates' Employment and Income Source: 1989
[Continued]

Characteristic	Percent of female inmates			% male inmates Total
	Free less than 1 year	Free at least 1 year	Total	
Unemployed	74.0%	59.7%	62.0%	31.7%
Looking	26.6%	28.7%	28.4%	20.4%
Not looking	47.4%	31.0%	33.7%	11.5%
Income source[1]				
Wages/salaries	38.6%	61.6%	58.0%	84.7%
Family or friend	28.4%	31.6%	31.1%	20.7%
Welfare	27.9%	30.1%	29.8%	7.7%
Illegal income	34.3%	14.4%	17.5%	11.4%
Social Security	7.2%	7.3%	7.3%	5.4%
Unemployment	0.3%	2.9%	2.5%	4.5%
Educational grants/ scholarships	2.6%	2.1%	2.2%	2.0%
Other	2.9%	3.9%	3.7%	3.2%
Pre-arrest monthly income				
Less than $500[2]	47.0%	57.4%	55.7%	42.3%
$500-$999	27.9%	21.1%	22.2%	25.0%
$1,000 or more	25.0%	21.5%	22.1%	32.7%
Number of inmates	5,774	29,586	35,360	341,662

Source: "Pre-arrest employment and income of jail inmates, by sex, 1989," Tracy L. Snell, "Women in Jail 1989," *Bureau of Justice Statistics Special Report*, March 1992, Table 2, p. 3. Data exclude inmates free less than 1 month. Detail may not add to total because of rounding. *Notes:* 1. Percents add to more than 100% because inmates may have had more than one source of income. 2. Includes inmates reporting no income.

★ 113 ★

Crime and Criminals

Jail Inmates' Offenses: 1989

This table shows the most serious offense of jail inmates in 1989 and 1983. The change for females between 1983 and 1989 was dramatic. Over the six years, the proportion of accused or convicted drug offenders rose and the proportions of property and violent offenders fell. While about 1 of every 8 female inmates were in jail for a drug offense in 1983, by 1989 the total had risen to nearly 1 of every 3. Female inmates were far more likely than male inmates to be in jail for a drug offense.

Most serious offense	Percent of prison inmates			
	1989		1983	
	Female	Male	Female	Male
All offenses	100.0%	100.0%	100.0%	100.0%
Violent offenses	13.2%	23.5%	21.3%	31.4%
Murder[1]	1.8%	2.9%	3.8%	4.1%
Negligent manslaughter	0.4%	0.5%	1.5%	0.6%
Kidnaping	1.1%	0.7%	0.6%	1.4%
Rape	0.0%	0.9%	0.1%	1.6%
Other sexual assault	0.2%	2.8%	0.2%	2.2%
Robbery	3.9%	7.0%	6.2%	11.5%
Assault	5.2%	7.4%	8.1%	3.7%
Other violent[2]	0.6%	1.1%	0.7%	1.3%
Property offenses	31.9%	29.9%	42.7%	38.3%
Burglary	4.0%	11.4%	5.1%	15.0%
Larceny/theft	12.9%	7.4%	18.4%	11.2%
Motor vehicle theft	0.9%	3.0%	0.7%	2.5%
Arson	0.6%	0.7%	0.6%	0.9%
Fraud	11.6%	3.2%	15.2%	4.2%
Stolen property	1.4%	2.5%	1.7%	2.6%
Other property[3]	0.5%	1.7%	1.0%	2.0%
Drug offenses	33.6%	21.9%	13.1%	9.0%
Possession	14.9%	9.2%	7.1%	4.6%
Trafficking	16.9%	11.5%	4.6%	4.0%
Other/Unspecified	1.9%	1.2%	1.4%	0.5%
Public-order offenses	19.0%	23.2%	22.0%	20.5%
Weapons	1.4%	2.0%	1.1%	2.4%
Obstruction of justice	3.6%	2.8%	3.1%	1.9%
Traffic	1.3%	2.8%	1.3%	2.2%
Driving while intoxicated[4]	3.6%	9.3%	5.2%	7.1%
Drunkenness/morals[5]	5.3%	1.3%	8.3%	3.0%
Violation of parole/probation[6]	3.6%	3.0%	2.0%	2.3%
Other public-order[7]	0.2%	2.0%	0.9%	1.7%

[Continued]

★ 113 ★

Jail Inmates' Offenses: 1989
[Continued]

Most serious offense	Percent of prison inmates			
	1989		1983	
	Female	Male	Female	Male
Other offenses[8]	2.2%	1.5%	0.9%	0.8%
Number of inmates	35,625	344,535	15,259	204,314

Source: "Most serious offense of jail inmates, by sex, 1989 and 1983," Tracy L. Snell, "Women in Jail 1989," *Bureau of Justice Statistics Special Report*, March 1992, Table 3, p. 4. Excludes an estimated 15,393 inmates in 1989 and 3,979 inmates in 1983 because their offense was unknown. Detail may not add to total because of rounding. *Notes:* 1. Includes nonnegligent manslaughter. 2. Includes blackmail, extortion, hit-and-run driving with bodily injury, child abuse, and criminal endangerment. 3. Includes destruction of property, vandalism, hit-and-run driving without bodily injury, trespassing, and possession of burglary tools. 4. Includes driving while intoxicated and driving under the influence of drugs or alcohol. 5. Includes drunkenness, vagrancy, disorderly conduct, unlawful assembly, morals, and commercialized vice. 6. Includes parole or probation violations, escape, AWOL, and flight to avoid prosecution. 7. Includes rioting, abandonment, non-support, immigration violations, invasion of privacy, liquor law violations, tax evasion, and bribery. 8. Includes juvenile offenses and unspecified offenses.

★ 114 ★

Crime and Criminals

Jail Inmates' Prior Sentences: 1989

This table shows the prior sentences of jail inmates, by sex, in 1989. Criminal records of women were slightly shorter than those of men.

Prior sentence	Percent of jail inmates	
	Female	Male
None	33.1%	22.4%
Juvenile	4.5%	7.9%
Adult only	47.6%	45.9%
Both	14.8%	23.7%
Number of times		
0	33.1%	22.4%
1	20.4%	20.6%
2	14.5%	16.7%
3-5	18.9%	22.9%
6-10	7.9%	11.0%
11 or more	5.1%	6.3%
Number of inmates	35,822	342,532

Source: "Prior sentences of jail inmates, by sex, 1989," Tracy L. Snell, "Women in Jail 1989," *Bureau of Justice Statistics Special Report*, March 1992, Table 9, p. 104. Excludes an estimated 17,200 inmates for whom data on prior sentences to probation or incarceration were unknown. Detail may not add to total because of rounding.

★ 115 ★

Crime and Criminals

Jail Inmates' Use of Jail Time: 1989

This table shows how inmates sentenced to jail occupied their time. Female inmates reported spending nearly 17 hours daily in their cells or housing units and about an hour outside their cells doing exercise. Male inmates reported spending fewer hours in their cells and more time exercising.

Characteristic of work assignment	Inmates sentenced to jail	
	Female	Male
Percent of inmates with work assignments		
Total[1]	43.8%	58.9%
Inside the jail	37.7%	41.1%
Outside the jail	8.1%	23.2%
Average hours per day spent working	4.2	5.9
Inmates assigned work, by type of work[1,2]		
Janitorial	39.2%	23.3%
Maintenance	5.4%	28.5%
Goods production/farming	4.2%	5.9%
Food preparation	18.0%	25.5%
Hospital, infirmary or other medical services	4.6%	0.2%
Laundry	9.8%	5.0%
Other services (library, stockroom, store, office help, etc.)	12.9%	7.7%
Other	10.5%	12.7%

Source: Tracy L. Snell, "Women in Jail 1989," *Bureau of Justice Statistics Special Report*, March 1992, p. 8. *Notes:* 1. Detail may add to more than total because inmates may have had work assignment both inside and outside the facility or more than one work assignment. 2. Based on inmates with work assignments.

★ 116 ★
Crime and Criminals

Jail Inmates: 1983 and 1989

This table compares characteristics of female and male jail inmates in 1983 and 1989. Over that period, women increased in number from 15,769 to 37,383. Nearly half of the increase was the result of more women being held for drug violations. Females in jail in 1989 were slightly better educated than they had been in 1983 and slightly better educated than male inmates. They were less likely than male inmates to have been employed at the time of their arrest.

Characteristic	Percent of female inmates		Percent of male inmates	
	1989	1983	1989	1983
Race/ Hispanic origin				
White non-Hispanic	37.8%	41.8%	38.7%	46.9%
Black non-Hispanic	43.4%	42.2%	41.5%	37.1%
Hispanic	16.3%	12.7%	17.5%	14.3%
Other[1]	2.5%	3.2%	2.3%	1.7%
Age				
17 or younger	0.7%	0.9%	1.6%	1.3%
18-24	27.2%	36.8%	33.2%	40.7%
25-34	51.2%	44.3%	42.1%	38.2%
35-44	15.6%	12.4%	16.9%	12.4%
45-54	3.9%	4.3%	4.6%	4.9%
55 or older	1.3%	1.3%	1.7%	2.4%
Median age	28	26	28	26
Marital status				
Married	16.2%	19.3%	19.3%	21.1%
Widowed	3.8%	3.9%	0.7%	1.2%
Divorced	17.2%	18.0%	14.9%	15.6%
Separated	14.0%	14.5%	7.6%	7.4%
Never married	48.9%	44.4%	57.5%	54.8%
Education[2]				
8th grade or less	11.9%	13.7%	16.0%	17.9%
Some high school	37.6%	39.2%	38.2%	41.5%
High school grad.	34.9%	32.3%	33.0%	28.9%
Some college or more	15.7%	14.7%	12.8%	11.6%
Median grade completed	11	11	11	11
Number of inmates	37,383	15,566	358,171	206,537

Source: "Characteristics of jail inmates, by sex, 1989 and 1983," Tracy L. Snell, "Women in Jail 1989," *Bureau of Justice Statistics Special Report*, March 1992, Table 1, p. 3. Detail may not add to total because of rounding. *Notes:* 1. Includes Asians, Pacific Islanders, American Indians, Alaska Natives, and other racial groups. 2. Based on highest grade completed.

★ 117 ★

Crime and Criminals

Mothers in Prison: 1991

This table shows characteristics of women in prison in 1991 who had children. An estimated 25,700 female inmates had more than 56,000 children under age 18. Male inmates were somewhat less likely to have children.

Characteristic	Percent of female inmates				% male inmates
	All[1]	White	Black	Hispanic	All[1]
Have children					
No	21.9%	26.1%	20.4%	17.8%	36.1%
Yes	78.1%	73.9%	79.6%	82.2%	63.9%
Under age 18	66.6%	61.6%	69.0%	71.6%	56.1%
Adult only	11.4%	12.3%	10.6%	10.6%	7.6%
Number of inmates	38,658	13,983	17,754	5,521	669,732
Number of children under age 18[2]					
1	37.3%	40.7%	37.0%	31.2%	43.2%
2	29.9%	30.8%	28.4%	33.3%	28.9%
3	18.1%	17.5%	18.2%	19.8%	15.2%
4	8.5%	6.5%	9.0%	10.0%	6.8%
5 or more	6.1%	4.5%	7.4%	5.7%	5.9%
Lived with child(ren) under 18 before entering prison[2]					
No	28.3%	31.3%	24.5%	34.3%	47.1%
Yes	71.7%	68.7%	75.5%	65.7%	52.9%
Where child(ren) under 18 live(s) now[2,3]					
Father/mother	25.4%	35.2%	18.7%	24.4%	89.7%
Grandparents	50.6%	40.6%	56.7%	54.9%	9.9%
Other relatives	20.3%	14.7%	23.7%	22.8%	2.9%
Friends	4.1%	5.7%	2.7%	4.2%	0.4%
Foster home	8.6%	12.6%	5.8%	6.5%	1.7%
Agency or institution	2.1%	2.1%	1.8%	2.1%	0.5%
Alone	2.0%	1.9%	2.3%	1.5%	1.1%

Source: "Children of State prison inmates, by race and sex of inmates, 1991," Tracy L. Snell, "Survey of State Prison Inmates, 1991: Women in Prison," *Bureau of Justice Statistics Special Report*, March 1994, Table 9, p. 6. Female prison inmates had an estimated total of 56,123 children under age 18, and male inmates had 770,841 minor children. *Notes:* 1. Includes Asians, Pacific Islanders, American Indians, Alaska Natives, and other racial groups. 2. Percents are based on those inmates with children under age 18. 3. Percents add to more than 100% because inmates with more than one child may have provided multiple responses.

★ 118 ★
Crime and Criminals

Offenders, Characteristics: 1987-1991

This table shows the sex, age, and alcohol or drug use of single offenders who victimized females, as reported by the victim, by type of violent crime, 1987-1991.

Characteristic of single violent offender against women	Percent of single-offender victimizations				
	Total	Rape	Robbery	Aggravated assault	Simple assault
Sex					
Total	100%	100%	100%	100%	100%
Male	75%	98%	87%	76%	71%
Female	23%	1%[1]	12%	22%	28%
Not ascertained	2%	1%	1%	2%	1%
Age					
Total	100%	100%	100%	100%	100%
Under 18	15%	5%	10%	14%	18%
Under 21	11%	9%	14%	11%	10%
Over 21	70%	81%	70%	70%	69%
Not ascertained	4%	5%	6%	5%	3%
Alcohol/drug use					
Total	100%	100%	100%	100%	100%
Yes	37%	45%	31%	45%	35%
No	26%	18%	18%	21%	29%
Not ascertained	37%	36%	50%	33%	35%
Type of drug[1]					
Total	100%	100%	100%	100%	100%
Alcohol	53%	65%	30%	53%	58%
Drugs	19%	14%	37%	19%	15%
Both	20%	15%	19%	20%	20%
Not ascertained	8%	6%	14%	8%	7%

Source: "Perceived sex, age, and alcohol/drug use of single offenders who victimized females, by type of violent crime, 1987-91," Ronet Bachman, Ph.D. *Violence against Women: A National Crime Victimization Survey Report,* January 1994, U.S. Department of Justice, Table 7, p. 5. Detail may not add to 100% because of rounding. *Notes:* 1. Estimate is based on 10 or fewer sample cases. 2. Based on those cases reporting alcohol/drug use by offender.

★ 119 ★

Crime and Criminals

Prisoners of State or Federal Authorities: 1993

This table gives statistics about women under the jurisdiction of State or Federal authorities at yearend 1993. The number of female inmates increased at a faster rate during 1993 (9.6%) than the number of male inmates (893,516 at 7.2%). The rate of incarceration for sentenced males (679 per 100,000 males in the resident population) was almost 18 times higher than that for sentenced females (38 per 100,000).

[NA Not available.]

Jurisdiction	Number of female inmates	Percent of all inmates	Percent change in female inmate population 1992-1993	Incarceration rate, 1993[1]
U.S. total	55,365	5.8%	9.6%	38
Federal	6,891	7.7%	7.7%	4
State	48,474	5.6%	9.9%	34
States with at least 500 female inmates				
California	7,580	6.3%	12.3%	43
Texas[2]	4,015	5.6%	61.4%	NA
New York	3,528	5.5%	0.8%	37
Florida	2,696	5.1%	3.7%	38
Ohio	2,584	6.4%	6.8%	45
Michigan	1,801	4.6%	-2.2%	37
Georgia	1,760	6.3%	21.0%	47
Illinois	1,688	4.9%	15.9%	28
Oklahoma	1,582	9.6%	13.0%	95
Virginia	1,219	5.3%	4.8%	36
Pennsylvania	1,194	4.6%	8.0%	19
New Jersey	1,134	4.8%	3.6%	28
Alabama	1,131	6.1%	2.7%	50
North Carolina	1,119	5.1%	17.8%	30
Louisiana	1,119	5.0%	9.5%	47
South Carolina	1,105	5.9%	-2.0%	52
Arizona	1,037	5.8%	3.6%	49
Connecticut	994	7.3%	40.0%	38
Maryland	976	4.8%	2.3%	33
Missouri	920	5.7%	NA	34
Indiana	778	5.4%	5.4%	26
District of Columbia	687	6.3%	-4.6%	119
Washington	666	6.4%	7.8%	25
Massachusetts	622	6.2%	10.3%	12
Mississippi	589	5.8%	16.6%	39

[Continued]

★ 119 ★

Prisoners of State or Federal Authorities: 1993
[Continued]

Jurisdiction	Number of female inmates	Percent of all inmates	Percent change in female in-mate population 1992-1993	Incarceration rate, 1993[1]
Kentucky	545	5.2%	0.0%	28
Colorado	542	5.7%	2.8%	30
Tennessee	521	4.1%	-1.3%	20

Source: Darrell K. Gilliard and Allan J. Beck, "Prisoners in 1993," *Bureau of Justice Statistics Bulletin*, June 1994, Table 6, p. 5, "Women under the jurisdiction of State or Federal correctional authorities, yearend 1993." *Notes:* 1. The number of female prisoners with sentences of more than 1 year per 100,000 female residents on December 31, 1993. 2. Excludes 3,363 local jail backups.

★ 120 ★

Crime and Criminals

Prisoners Sentenced to Death, State and Race: 1993

This table shows the number of women and the number of black women under sentence of death at the end of 1993 by state.

State	Women under death sentence 12/31/93		
	Total	White	Black
Total	35	24	11
Alabama	4	2	2
California	4	3	1
Florida	4	3	1
Illinois	4	2	2
Oklahoma	4	3	1
Pennsylvania	3	1	2
Texas	3	2	1
Missouri	2	2	0
North Carolina	2	2	0
Arizona	1	1	0
Idaho	1	1	0
Mississippi	1	1	0
Nevada	1	0	1
Tennessee	1	1	0

Source: U.S. Department of Justice, Bureau of Justice Statistics Bulletin, *Capital Punishment 1993*, December 1994, NCJ-150042, p. 8.

★ 121 ★

Crime and Criminals

Prisoners Sentenced to Death: 1993

This table shows the number of prisoners under sentence of death at the end of 1993, and the number of admissions and number of removals of prisoners during that year. Between January 1 and December 31, 1993, 30 State prison systems and the Federal prison system reported receiving 282 prisoners under sentence of death. All had been convicted of murder. By sex and race, 141 were white men, 129 were black men, 1 was an Asian man, 3 were Hispanic men classified as "Other race" in Pennsylvania, **5 were white women, and 1 was a black woman.** No women were executed during 1993.

Characteristic	Under sentence of death, 1993		
	Yearend	Admissions	Removals
Total number under sentence of death	2,716	282	145
Sex			
Female	1.3%	2.1%	3.4%
Male	98.7%	97.9%	96.6%

Source: "Demographic characteristics of prisoners under sentence of death, 1993," U.S. Department of Justice, Bureau of Justice Statistics Bulletin, *Capital Punishment 1993*, December 1994, NCJ-150042, Table 6, p. 9. Also in source: data by race, Hispanic origin, education, and marital status.

★ 122 ★

Crime and Criminals

Sentenced Prisoners: 1980-1992

This table shows the number of sentenced prisoners in State or Federal prisons, by race, from 1980 through 1992. Sentenced prisoners are those with a sentence of more than one year. The number of sentenced prisoners rose more than 530,000 between 1980 and 1992. The number of white females grew 275% and the number of black females 278%. The growth in the number of black male prisoners accounted for nearly half of the total increase during this period.

	All[1]	Male		Female	
		White	Black	White	Black
1980	315,974	159,500	140,600	5,900	6,300
1981	353,673	178,200	156,100	6,900	7,200
1982	395,516	199,400	174,900	8,000	8,200
1983	419,346	210,700	185,900	8,700	8,500
1984	443,398	223,500	194,600	9,500	9,400
1985	480,568	242,700	210,500	10,800	10,200
1986	522,084	258,900	232,000	12,400	11,800
1987	560,812	277,200	249,700	13,700	12,600
1988	603,732	292,200	274,300	15,500	14,200

[Continued]

★ 122 ★

Sentenced Prisoners: 1980-1992

[Continued]

	All[1]	Male		Female	
		White	Black	White	Black
1989	680,907	322,100	313,700	18,400	18,300
1990	739,980	346,700	344,300	20,000	20,100
1991	789,610	363,600	372,200	20,900	22,200
1992	847,271	388,000	401,700	22,100	23,800

Source: Darrell K. Gilliard and Allan J. Beck, "Prisoners in 1993," *Bureau of Justice Statistics Bulletin,* June 1994, Table 13, p. 9, "Number of sentenced prisoners in State or Federal prisons, by sex and race, 1980-92." Primary sources: *Prisoners,* 1980-84, BJS reports; *Correctional Populations in the United States,* 1985-91, BJS reports; National Prisoner Statistics-1, 1992. The numbers for sex and race were estimated and rounded to the nearest 100. For men and women, the total number of sentenced prisoners was multiplied by the proportion of black or white of the total population in each group. The reported racial distribution was used to estimate unreported data. *Note:* 1. Includes sentenced prisoners of other races.

★ 123 ★

Crime and Criminals

Sentences of Jail Inmates: 1989

This table shows the sentences of jail inmates, by sex, in 1989. About one-half of the female inmates were sentenced, and more than three-quarters of these women expected to serve their sentences in a local jail. Women and men sentenced to jail received similar sentences, but women sentenced to State or Federal prison received shorter sentences than men. This difference is explained in part by the larger percentage of male violent offenders awaiting transfer to prison.

Sentence length and conditions	Sentenced jail inmates	
	Female	Male
Location where sentence to be served		
Jail	77.0%	76.1%
Prison	15.4%	11.6%
Unknown	7.6%	12.3%
Maximum sentence length (months)		
Sentenced to jail		
Median	6	6
Mean	18	18
Awaiting transfer to State or Federal prison (months)		
Median	60	72

[Continued]

★ 123 ★

Sentences of Jail Inmates: 1989
[Continued]

Sentence length and conditions	Sentenced jail inmates	
	Female	Male
Mean	72	103
Special conditions		
Any condition or restriction	35.8%	26.8%
Restitution	9.2%	5.5%
Community service	7.7%	3.0%
Drug treatment	13.7%	4.5%
Alcohol treatment	7.2%	6.4%
Psychiatric/psychological counseling	1.3%	1.9%
Regular employment	6.1%	2.4%
House arrest	1.6%	1.0%
Other	15.5%	13.0%
Number of inmates	16,375	147,281

Source: "Sentence length and special sentencing conditions of jail inmates, by sex, 1989," Tracy L. Snell, "Women in Jail 1989," *Bureau of Justice Statistics Special Report*, March 1992, Table 6, p. 5. Data include only those inmates who were new court commitments with a valid sentence length. Detail may add to more than 100% because an inmate may have received more than one special sentencing condition.

★ 124 ★

Crime and Criminals

State Prison Inmates' Abuse History and Types of Crimes: 1991

This table shows the types of offenses committed by imprisoned females who reported having suffered abuse before being imprisoned. Victims of abuse were more likely to be in prison for a violent offense. They were less likely to be in prison for a drug or property offense. Half of the violent female inmates who had been abused were sentenced for homicide, compared to two-fifths of other violent female inmates.

Offense	% of female inmates who experienced	
	Prior abuse[1]	No prior abuse
Most serious offense		
Violent	41.7%	25.0%
Property	25.3%	31.4%
Drug	25.3%	38.5%
Public-order	6.9%	4.6%
Other	0.7%	0.5%

[Continued]

★ 124 ★

State Prison Inmates' Abuse History and Types of Crimes: 1991

[Continued]

Offense	% of female inmates who experienced	
	Prior abuse[1]	No prior abuse
Number of inmates	16,385	21,439
Violent offense		
Homicide	50.8%	41.9%
Sexual assault	6.1%	3.9%
Robbery	20.1%	29.4%
Assault	18.0%	20.7%
Other violent	5.0%	4.2%
Number of inmates	6,827	5,369

Source: Tracy L. Snell, "Survey of State Prison Inmates, 1991: Women in Prison," *Bureau of Justice Statistics Special Report*, March 1994, p. 6. Sexual abuse includes fondling, incest, molestation, sodomy, rape, and other types of sexual assault. *Note:* 1. Those who experienced abuse prior to current incarceration.

★ 125 ★

Crime and Criminals

State Prison Inmates' Abuse History: 1991

This table shows how state prison inmates responded to questions about a history of prior physical or sexual abuse. More than 4 in 10 women reported having been abused at least once before their current admission to prison.

Item	Percent of State prison inmates		
	Total	Female	Male
Ever physically or sexually abused before current incarceration:			
No	86.1%	56.8%	87.8%
Yes	13.9%	43.2%	12.2%
Before age 18	11.9%	31.7%	10.7%
After age 18	4.2%	24.5%	3.0%
Physically	11.3%	33.5%	10.0%
Sexually	6.8%	33.9%	5.3%
Number of inmates	700,475	38,109	662,367
Relationship of abuser to inmate[1]:			
Intimate	11.2%	49.8%	3.0%

[Continued]

★ 125 ★

State Prison Inmates' Abuse History: 1991
[Continued]

Item	Percent of State prison inmates		
	Total	Female	Male
Spouse/ex-spouse	6.1%	30.5%	1.0%
Boyfriend/girlfriend	6.6%	27.6%	2.2%
Relative	68.1%	56.1%	70.6%
Parent/guardian	53.7%	37.7%	57.1%
Other relative	22.6%	26.5%	21.7%
Friend/acquaintance	22.8%	20.1%	23.4%
Someone else	21.2%	19.6%	21.6%
Refusal to answer	1.1%	1.3%	1.1%

Source: "Prior physical or sexual abuse of State prison inmates, by sex, 1991," Tracy L. Snell, "Survey of State Prison Inmates, 1991: Women in Prison," *Bureau of Justice Statistics Special Report*, March 1994, Table 8, p. 5. Sexual abuse includes fondling, incest, molestation, sodomy, rape, and other types of sexual assault. Detail adds to more than total because some inmates were abused both before and after age 18 or were both sexually and physically abused; inmates may also have reported more than one abuser. *Note:* 1. Based on those inmates who were abused and knew their abuser.

★ 126 ★

Crime and Criminals

State Prison Inmates' Abuse Types: 1991

This table shows the types of abuse suffered by female prison inmates who reported prior abuse, 1991. An estimated 50% of the women who reported abuse said they experienced the abuse at the hands of an intimate, compared to only 3% of men.

Type of abuse	% of female inmates who were abused
Physical only	21.2%
Sexual only	21.9%
Both	56.9%
Type of sexual abuse	
Total	78.8%
Completed rape	55.8%
Attempted rape	13.0%
Other sexual abuse	10.0%
Refusal	0.8%

Source: Tracy L. Snell, "Survey of State Prison Inmates, 1991: Women in Prison," *Bureau of Justice Statistics Special Report*, March 1994, p. 6. Sexual abuse includes fondling, incest, molestation, sodomy, rape, and other types of sexual assault.

★ 127 ★

Crime and Criminals

State Prison Inmates' Criminal History: 1991

This table shows the criminal history of State prison inmates, by sex, in 1991. Female inmates in general had not been previously sentenced to imprisonment or probation as were male inmates.

Criminal history	Female	Male
No previous sentence	28.2%	18.7%
Current violent offense	15.8%	12.5%
Current nonviolent offense	12.4%	6.2%
Violent recidivists	25.7%	50.2%
Current and prior violent	6.9%	17.9%
Current violent only	10.8%	19.3%
Prior violent only	8.0%	13.0%
Nonviolent recidivists	46.1%	31.1%
Prior minor public-order offenses only	2.1%	1.2%
Other prior offenses	44.0%	29.9%
Number of inmates	38,158	660,007

Source: "Criminal history of State prison inmates, by sex, 1991," Tracy L. Snell, "Survey of State Prison Inmates, 1991: Women in Prison," *Bureau of Justice Statistics Special Report*, March 1994, Table 4, p. 4. Excludes an estimated 13,477 inmates for whom current offense and prior probation/incarceration offenses were unknown.

★ 128 ★

Crime and Criminals

State Prison Inmates' Family Characteristics: 1991

This table shows the family structure, incarceration history of family members, and history of parental abuse of alcohol or drugs, as reported by State prison inmates in 1991. More than half the women in prison had grown up in a household without the presence of both parents. About 42% lived in a single-parent household, and another 16% lived with neither parent. Female prison inmates were nearly twice as likely to have grown up in a single-parent household compared to the general population. When most of the 1991 inmates were between the ages of 10 and 18, in 1975, 80% of the 66.1 million children in the nation's households were living with both parents. Women in prison were more likely than men in prison to have had at least one family member who had also been incarcerated. A third of female inmates said that a parent or guardian abused drugs or alcohol.

Characteristic	Percent of female inmates				% of male inmates
	All[1]	White	Black	Hispanic	All[1]
Person(s) lived with most of the time while growing up:					
Both parents	42.0%	55.1%	31.9%	40.3%	43.1%
Mother only	38.9%	29.3%	46.1%	41.0%	39.2%
Father only	3.4%	3.7%	3.0%	3.8%	4.0%
Grandparents	9.3%	6.1%	11.3%	10.3%	7.6%
Other relatives	3.0%	1.1%	4.7%	2.8%	3.0%
Friends	0.4%	0.4%	0.4%	0.5%	0.4%
Foster home	1.8%	2.7%	1.5%	0.8%	1.5%
Agency or institution	0.8%	1.1%	0.6%	0.2%	0.8%
Other	0.5%	0.5%	0.5%	0.2%	0.5%
Ever lived in a foster home, agency, or institution while growing up:					
No	82.8%	78.9%	85.9%	85.6%	82.7%
Yes	17.2%	21.1%	14.1%	14.4%	17.3%
Family member ever incarcerated:					
No	53.4%	61.1%	47.3%	53.0%	63.1%
Yes[2]	46.6%	38.9%	52.7%	47.0%	36.9%
Spouse	1.8%	3.1%	1.1%	1.4%	0.2%
Mother	4.0%	3.5%	4.5%	3.6%	1.5%
Father	7.8%	10.9%	5.4%	6.7%	6.3%
Brother	35.1%	26.1%	42.0%	35.9%	30.9%
Sister	10.0%	5.6%	12.4%	14.6%	4.2%

[Continued]

★ 128 ★

State Prison Inmates' Family Characteristics: 1991
[Continued]

Characteristic	Percent of female inmates				% of male inmates
	All[1]	White	Black	Hispanic	All[1]
Child	1.6%	1.3%	1.6%	2.3%	0.2%
Parent/guardian abused alcohol or drugs:					
No	66.4%	57.7%	74.0%	67.1%	73.5%
Yes	33.6%	42.3%	26.0%	32.9%	26.5%
Alcohol only	26.3%	32.7%	20.7%	25.4%	21.9%
Drugs only	1.6%	1.0%	2.0%	2.2%	0.8%
Both	5.7%	8.6%	3.2%	5.2%	3.6%
Number of inmates	38,630	13,969	17,739	5,521	669,578

Source: "Family structure, incarceration of family members, and parental abuse of alcohol or drugs reported by State prison inmates, 1991," Tracy L. Snell, "Survey of State Prison Inmates, 1991: Women in Prison," *Bureau of Justice Statistics Special Report*, March 1994, Table 7, p. 5. Excludes 3,435 inmates for whom information on family history was missing. *Notes:* 1. Includes Asians, Pacific Islanders, American Indians, Alaska Natives, and other racial groups. 2. Detail adds to more than total because more than one family member may have been incarcerated.

★ 129 ★

Crime and Criminals

State Prison Inmates' Offenses by Drug Use History: 1991

This table shows the most serious offense of State prison inmates in 1991 by drug use history. The crimes committed by female inmates who used drugs differed from those who did not use drugs. Users were less likely than nonusers to be serving a sentence for a violent offense.

Most serious offense	Used drugs in the month before current offense		Under the influence of drugs at time of offense		Committed offense to get money to buy drugs	
	Yes	No	Yes	No	Yes	No
Violent offenses	25.0%	40.8%	24.3%	37.0%	17.1%	37.0%
Homicide[1]	8.8%	22.5%	8.5%	19.0%	2.2%	19.3%
Sexual assault[2]	0.4%	3.0%	0.3%	2.4%	0.0%	2.2%
Robbery	9.6%	5.7%	10.7%	6.1%	13.2%	6.0%
Assault	5.2%	7.3%	3.7%	7.6%	1.5%	7.7%
Other violent	0.9%	2.2%	1.0%	1.8%	0.3%	1.9%
Property offenses	30.0%	27.1%	30.6%	27.6%	42.6%	24.4%
Burglary	5.7%	3.2%	5.4%	4.1%	7.2%	3.7%
Larceny/theft	12.9%	8.9%	13.9%	9.5%	21.9%	7.8%
Fraud	8.8%	12.0%	9.0%	11.0%	11.9%	9.6%
Other property	2.6%	3.1%	2.4%	3.1%	1.5%	3.3%

[Continued]

★ 129 ★

State Prison Inmates' Offenses by Drug Use History: 1991
[Continued]

Most serious offense	Used drugs in the month before current offense		Under the influence of drugs at time of offense		Committed offense to get money to buy drugs	
	Yes	No	Yes	No	Yes	No
Drug offenses	39.0%	25.7%	39.6%	28.8%	36.0%	31.8%
Possession	15.4%	7.5%	15.8%	9.3%	11.2%	11.9%
Trafficking	21.9%	17.4%	21.7%	18.7%	23.3%	18.7%
Other drug	1.7%	0.7%	2.1%	0.8%	1.4%	1.2%
Public-order offenses	5.5%	5.8%	5.2%	5.9%	3.9%	6.1%
Weapons	0.6%	0.4%	0.5%	0.4%	0.3%	0.5%
Other public-order	4.9%	5.4%	4.7%	5.5%	3.7%	5.6%
Other offenses	0.5%	0.7%	0.3%	0.8%	0.4%	0.7%
Number of inmates	20,758	17,639	13,827	24,220	9,098	28,812

Source: "Most serious offense of female State prison inmates, by drug use history, 1991," Tracy L. Snell, "Survey of State Prison Inmates, 1991: Women in Prison," *Bureau of Justice Statistics Special Report*, March 1994, Table 13, p. 8. *Notes:* 1. Includes murder, negligent manslaughter, and nonnegligent manslaughter. 2. Includes rape and other sexual assault.

★ 130 ★
Crime and Criminals

State Prison Inmates' Offenses: 1986 and 1991

This table shows the most serious offense of State prison inmates in 1986 and 1991. During that period, the percentage of women in prison for drug offenses increased from 12.0% to 32.8%, while the percentage in prison for property offenses declined. Women imprisoned for violent offenses represented about 3 in 10 female inmates in 1991, a decrease from 4 in 10 in 1986. However, the **number** of women sentenced for a violent offense rose from 8,045 to 12,400. Murder was the most prevalent violent offense.

Most serious offense	Percent of prison inmates			
	1991		1986	
	Female	Male	Female	Male
All offenses	100.0%	100.0%	100.0%	100.0%
Violent offenses	32.2%	47.4%	40.7%	55.2%
Murder[1]	11.7%	10.5%	13.0%	11.2%
Negligent manslaughter	3.4%	1.7%	6.8%	3.0%
Kidnaping	0.4%	1.2%	0.9%	1.7%
Rape	0.4%	3.7%	0.2%	4.5%
Other sexual assault	1.3%	6.2%	0.9%	4.7%
Robbery	7.8%	15.2%	10.6%	21.3%
Assault	6.2%	8.3%	7.1%	8.1%
Other violent[2]	1.1%	0.5%	1.2%	0.8%

[Continued]

★ 130 ★

State Prison Inmates' Offenses: 1986 and 1991
[Continued]

Most serious offense	Percent of prison inmates			
	1991		1986	
	Female	Male	Female	Male
Property offenses	28.7%	24.6%	41.2%	30.5%
Burglary	4.5%	12.9%	5.9%	17.0%
Larceny/theft	11.1%	4.5%	14.7%	5.6%
Motor vehicle theft	0.7%	2.3%	0.5%	1.4%
Arson	1.0%	0.7%	1.2%	0.7%
Fraud	10.2%	2.4%	17.0%	3.2%
Stolen property	1.0%	1.4%	1.6%	2.0%
Other property[3]	0.1%	0.5%	0.4%	0.5%
Drug offenses	32.8%	20.7%	12.0%	8.4%
Possession	11.8%	7.3%	4.0%	2.9%
Trafficking	19.8%	13.0%	7.3%	5.3%
Other/Unspecified	1.3%	0.4%	0.7%	0.2%
Public-order offenses	5.7%	7.0%	5.1%	5.2%
Weapons	0.5%	1.9%	0.9%	1.5%
Other public-order[4]	5.1%	5.1%	4.3%	3.7%
Other offenses	0.6%	0.4%	0.9%	0.7%
Number of inmates	38,462	665,719	19,761	430,151

Source: "Most serious offense of State prison inmates, by sex, 1991 and 1986," Tracy L. Snell, "Survey of State Prison Inmates, 1991: Women in Prison," *Bureau of Justice Statistics Special Report*, March 1994, Table 2, p. 3. Excludes an estimated 7,462 inmates in 1991 and 505 inmates in 1986 for whom offense was unknown. Detail may not add to total because of rounding. *Notes:* 1. Includes nonnegligent manslaughter. 2. Includes blackmail, extortion, hit-and-run driving with bodily injury, child abuse, and criminal endangerment. 3. Includes destruction of property, vandalism, hit-and-run driving without bodily injury, trespassing, and possession of burglary tools. 4. Includes escape from custody, driving while intoxicated, offenses against morals and decency, and commercialized vice.

★ 131 ★

Crime and Criminals

State Prison Inmates' Prior Sentences: 1991

This table shows the prior sentences of State prison inmates, by sex, in 1991. Female inmates generally had records of less violent past convictions than did males. About 28% of women reported no previous sentences to prison or probation, compared to 19% of men. Four in ten women had a history of violence, compared to more than 6 in 10 men.

Prior sentence	Female	Male
None	28.9%	19.6%
Juvenile	3.5%	8.4%
Adult only	50.7%	40.6%
Both	17.0%	31.4%
Number of times		
0	28.9%	19.6%
1	22.0%	19.2%
2	14.9%	16.3%
3-5	20.1%	26.2%
6-10	9.1%	12.7%
11 or more	5.1%	6.1%
Number of inmates	38,038	661,021

Source: "Prior sentences of State prison inmates, by sex, 1991," Tracy L. Snell, "Survey of State Prison Inmates, 1991: Women in Prison," *Bureau of Justice Statistics Special Report*, March 1994, Table 5, p. 4. Excludes an estimated 12,584 inmates for whom data on prior sentences to probation or incarceration were unknown.

★ 132 ★

Crime and Criminals

State Prison Inmates' Sentences: 1991

This table shows the maximum sentences of State prison inmates, by most serious offense and by sex, in 1991. Female prisoners had shorter maximum sentences than men. Half the women had maximum sentences of 60 months or less, compared to sentences of 120 months or less for half the men. Women received sentences that were 48 months shorter on average than those of men (excluding sentences to life or death). An estimated 7% of women and 9% of men received sentences to life or death.

Most serious offense	Maximum sentence length					
	Female inmates			Male inmates		
	Number	Median (months)	Mean (months)	Number	Median (months)	Mean (months)
All offenses	37,429	60	105	653,292	120	153
Violent offenses	12,118	180	178	310,946	180	217
Murder	4,432	840	310	69,405	Life	386

[Continued]

★ 132 ★

State Prison Inmates' Sentences: 1991
[Continued]

Most serious offense	Maximum sentence length					
	Female inmates			Male inmates		
	Number	Median (months)	Mean (months)	Number	Median (months)	Mean (months)
Negligent man-slaughter	1,309	120	158	11,333	156	188
Sexual assault[1]	[2]	[2]	[2]	65,223	180	211
Robbery	2,913	120	145	99,730	144	201
Assault	2,309	72	109	54,004	120	160
Property offenses	10,743	44	74	160,702	72	116
Burglary	1,747	60	81	84,490	96	142
Larceny/theft	4,140	36	53	29,125	48	74
Fraud	3,836	60	92	15,660	60	100
Drug offenses	12,264	54	79	134,539	60	97
Possession	4,410	36	64	47,515	56	82
Trafficking	7,379	60	89	84,310	72	106
Public-order offenses	2,075	36	60	44,515	48	84

Source: "Total maximum sentence length of State prison inmates, by most serious offense and sex, 1991," Tracy L. Snell, "Survey of State Prison Inmates, 1991: Women in Prison," *Bureau of Justice Statistics Special Report*, March 1994, Table 6, p. 4. Excludes an estimated 1,367 female inmates and 19,555 male inmates for whom current offense or sentence length was unknown. Sentence length refers to the total maximum sentence for all inmates, including consecutive sentences for inmates with multiple offenses. Suspended sentences were excluded from the total. *Notes:* 1. Includes rape and other sexual assault. 2. Too few cases to mention.

★ 133 ★

Crime and Criminals

State Prison Inmates: 1986 and 1991

This table compares characteristics of State prison inmates in 1991 and 1986. The total State prison population grew 58% between those years, and the number of women in prison increased 75%. Women in State prisons in 1991 were most likely to be black, aged 25 to 34, unemployed at the time of arrest, high school graduates, holders of a GED or with some college, and never married. Compared to 1986, the 1991 female prison population had more Hispanics, women older than 25, and women who had completed high school.

Characteristic	Percent of female inmates		Percent of male inmates	
	1991	1986	1991	1986
Race/ Hispanic origin				
White non-Hispanic	36.2%	39.7%	35.4%	39.5%
Black non-Hispanic	46.0%	46.0%	45.5%	45.2%

[Continued]

★ 133 ★

State Prison Inmates: 1986 and 1991
[Continued]

Characteristic	Percent of female inmates		Percent of male inmates	
	1991	1986	1991	1986
Hispanic	14.2%	11.7%	16.8%	12.7%
Other[1]	3.6%	2.5%	2.3%	2.5%
Age				
17 or younger	0.1%	0.2%	0.7%	0.5%
18-24	16.3%	22.3%	21.6%	26.9%
25-34	50.4%	50.5%	45.5%	45.5%
35-44	25.5%	19.6%	22.6%	19.4%
45-54	6.1%	5.5%	6.6%	5.2%
55 or older	1.7%	1.8%	3.2%	2.5%
Median age	31	29	30	29
Marital status				
Married	17.3%	20.1%	18.1%	20.4%
Widowed	5.9%	6.7%	1.6%	1.6%
Divorced	19.1%	20.5%	18.4%	18.0%
Separated	12.5%	11.0%	5.9%	5.8%
Never married	45.1%	41.7%	55.9%	54.3%
Education[2]				
8th grade or less	16.0%	16.5%	19.6%	20.9%
Some high school	45.8%	49.7%	46.2%	50.6%
High school grad.	22.7%	19.1%	21.9%	17.7%
Some college or more	15.5%	14.8%	12.3%	10.8%
Pre-arrest employment				
Employed	46.7%	47.1%	68.5%	70.1%
Full time	35.7%	37.1%	56.5%	58.4%
Part time	11.0%	10.0%	12.0%	11.7%
Unemployed	53.3%	52.9%	31.5%	30.0%
Looking	19.2%	22.0%	16.2%	17.8%
Not looking	34.1%	30.9%	15.3%	12.2%
Number of inmates	38,796	19,812	672,847	430,604

Source: "Characteristics of State prison inmates, by sex, 1991 and 1986," Tracy L. Snell, "Survey of State Prison Inmates, 1991: Women in Prison," *Bureau of Justice Statistics Special Report*, March 1994, Table 1, p. 2. In 1991, data were missing on marital status for 1.1% of cases, on education for 0.8%, and on prearrest employment for 0.7%. In 1986, data were missing for race and Hispanic origin for 0.4% of cases, on marital status for 0.1%, on education for 0.4%, and on prearrest employment for 0.5% *Notes:* 1. Includes Asians, Pacific Islanders, American Indians, Alaska Natives, and other racial groups. 2. Based on highest grade completed.

Drugs

★ 134 ★

Arrestees' Alcohol and Marijuana Use: 1988

The National Institute of Justice's Drug Use Forecasting Program covered 20 cities in 1988. It is designed to provide cities with an estimate of drug use among arrestees and information for detecting changes in drug use trends. This table shows the percentage of females who admitted ever using alcohol and marijuana by various characteristics. The median age of onset for alcohol use was 15 to 17 years, about one year older than for males. More than 60% of female arrestees in each city reported having tried marijuana.

City and State	Alcohol					Marijuana				
	Ever used	Median age of 1st use	If used, ever dependent	Used in last 30 days	Used in last 48 hours	Ever used	Median age of 1st use	If used, ever dependent	Used in last 30 days	Used in last 48 hours
Birmingham, AL	96%	16	8%	48%	25%	83%	16	2%	31%	14%
Chicago, IL	92%	15	20%	62%	56%	83%	15	15%	40%	29%
Dallas, TX	94%	16	9%	59%	42%	79%	16	5%	26%	15%
Detroit, MI	92%	15	23%	68%	47%	91%	15	12%	36%	18%
Kansas City, MO	91%	16	12%	63%	43%	79%	16	2%	25%	12%
Los Angeles, CA	93%	16	16%	56%	43%	78%	15	12%	25%	18%
New Orleans, LA	89%	17	4%	60%	46%	63%	16	4%	23%	15%
New York, NY	90%	16	5%	50%	26%	80%	15	2%	26%	10%
Philadelphia, PA	87%	16	13%	58%	44%	71%	16	10%	38%	25%
Phoenix, AZ	91%	16	15%	56%	38%	70%	15	8%	30%	19%
Portland, OR	96%	15	10%	62%	50%	90%	15	4%	38%	26%
St. Louis, MO	88%	17	8%	48%	28%	63%	17	10%	21%	16%
San Antonio, TX	95%	17	6%	62%	47%	60%	16	3%	19%	12%
San Diego, CA	97%	16	17%	57%	42%	82%	15	3%	36%	18%

Source: "Female Arrestees: Self-Reported Alcohol and Marijuana Use," *DUF: 1988 Drug Use Forecasting Annual Report*, National Institute of Justice, March 1990, p. 15.

★ 135 ★

Drugs

Arrestees' Cocaine and Crack Use: 1988

The National Institute of Justice's Drug Use Forecasting Program covered 20 cities in 1988. It is designed to provide cities with an estimate of drug use among arrestees and information for detecting changes in drug use trends. This table shows the percentage of females who admitted ever using cocaine and crack by various characteristics. Twenty-two percent of all persons who reported ever using cocaine reported dependence on it. Between 16% and 62% of females reported cocaine use in the last month. The median age of onset of crack use was not reported because of its relatively recent emergence.

City and State	Cocaine					Crack			
	Ever used	Median age of 1st use	If used, ever de-pendent	Used in last 30 days	Used in last 48 hours	Ever used	Median age of 1st use	If used, ever de-pendent	Used in last 48 hours
Birmingham, AL	54%	21	25%	31%	23%	23%	25%	17%	10%
Chicago, IL	83%	20	50%	62%	53%	9%	33%	4%	2%
Dallas, TX	47%	20	23%	22%	17%	16%	22%	6%	5%
Detroit, MI	49%	19	30%	22%	10%	68%	46%	47%	27%
Kansas City, MO	43%	22	38%	21%	16%	27%	61%	19%	13%
Los Angeles, CA	60%	20	28%	26%	21%	39%	41%	22%	17%
New Orleans, LA	39%	22	24%	21%	13%	3%	1	1%	1%
New York, NY	67%	19	18%	36%	21%	45%	34%	32%	27%
Philadelphia, PA	59%	21	43%	44%	38%	20%	54%	18%	12%
Phoenix, AZ	54%	20	25%	26%	16%	10%	13%	3%	2
Portland, OR	75%	20	25%	37%	29%	22%	24%	10%	5%
St. Louis, MO	41%	22	24%	22%	15%	10%	1	5%	2%
San Antonio, TX	35%	20	10%	16%	11%	7%	1	3%	2%
San Diego, CA	64%	21	32%	36%	28%	28%	28%	14%	5%

Source: "Female Arrestees: Self-Reported Cocaine and Crack Use," *DUF: 1988 Drug Use Forecasting Annual Report,* National Institute of Justice, March 1990, p. 17. *Notes:* 1. Less than 20 cases. 2. Less than 1%.

★ 136 ★

Drugs

Arrestees' Cocaine Use: 1991

This table shows the percentage of female booked arrestees who tested positive by urinalysis for cocaine during the period January through December 1991 by city.

City	Percent posi-tive cocaine	Percent positive by age					Percent positive by race		
		15-20	21-25	26-30	31-35	36+	Black	White	Hispanic
Atlanta, GA	66%	35%	64%	83%	77%	56%	68%	59%	1
Birmingham, AL	44%	26%	36%	50%	52%	41%	53%	30%	1
Cleveland, OH	76%	50%	70%	84%	83%	76%	78%	67%	1
Dallas, TX	45%	28%	35%	53%	48%	58%	51%	37%	39%
Denver, CO	41%	24%	33%	54%	55%	32%	60%	32%	34%

[Continued]

★ 136 ★

Arrestees' Cocaine Use: 1991
[Continued]

City	Percent positive cocaine	Percent positive by age					Percent positive by race		
		15-20	21-25	26-30	31-35	36+	Black	White	Hispanic
Detroit, MI	62%	25%	63%	67%	66%	65%	61%	67%	1
Ft. Lauderdale, FL	55%	33%	49%	62%	69%	47%	63%	48%	1
Houston, TX	52%	28%	53%	61%	58%	44%	59%	51%	25%
Indianapolis, IN	26%	11%	18%	31%	34%	30%	40%	12%	1
Kansas City, MO	56%	15%	62%	70%	56%	46%	62%	42%	1
Los Angeles, MO	62%	38%	48%	69%	72%	63%	73%	55%	49%
New York, NY (Manhattan)	66%	28%	62%	73%	83%	61%	64%	69%	68%
New Orleans, LA	42%	12%	36%	55%	61%	37%	43%	38%	1
Philadelphia, PA	64%	38%	63%	71%	76%	56%	68%	40%	60%
Phoenix, AZ	45%	42%	42%	49%	48%	40%	72%	39%	38%
Portland, OR	40%	32%	33%	41%	42%	49%	54%	35%	1
St. Louis, MO	47%	34%	44%	62%	47%	44%	50%	38%	1
San Antonio, TX	25%	9%	29%	33%	22%	33%	43%	19%	23%
San Diego, CA	40%	31%	32%	45%	49%	37%	72%	28%	39%
San Jose, CA	30%	18%	31%	39%	29%	26%	63%	20%	25%
Washington, DC	68%	33%	47%	81%	82%	70%	70%	59%	1

Source: Selected from "Cocaine Use by Male and Female Booked Arrestees," National Institute of Justice, Research in Brief, *Drug Use Forecasting 1991 Annual Report*, p. 8. Primary source: National Institute of Justice/Drug Use Forecasting Program. *Note:* 1. Less than 20 cases.

★ 137 ★

Drugs

Arrestees' Drug Use By Type of Drug: 1988

The National Institute of Justice's Drug Use Forecasting Program covered 20 cities in 1988. It is designed to provide cities with an estimate of drug use among arrestees and information for detecting changes in drug use trends. This table shows the percentage of females who reported drug use within the last 24 to 48 hours before arrest, and the percentage who tested positive by urinalysis, for marijuana, cocaine, and heroin. Female arrestees were more likely than male arrestees to self-report recent use of marijuana (which can be detected by urinalysis up to several weeks after use). Female arrestees underreported recent cocaine use, but less so than males. Self reports of heroin use more closely approximated urinalysis findings.

City and State	Marijuana		Cocaine		Heroin	
	Self-report	Urinalysis	Self-report	Urinalysis	Self-report	Urinalysis
Birmingham, AL	14%	15%	23%	38%	0%	14%
Chicago, IL	29%	33%	53%	70%	20%	21%
Dallas, TX	15%	25%	18%	48%	5%	9%
Detroit, MI	18%	26%	30%	71%	9%	20%
Kansas City, MO	12%	16%	25%	57%	2%	6%
Los Angeles, CA	18%	22%	34%	61%	15%	22%
New Orleans, LA	15%	25%	13%	40%	2%	7%

[Continued]

★ 137 ★

Arrestees' Drug Use By Type of Drug: 1988
[Continued]

City and State	Marijuana Self-report	Marijuana Urinalysis	Cocaine Self-report	Cocaine Urinalysis	Heroin Self-report	Heroin Urinalysis
New York, NY	10%	19%	44%	75%	18%	26%
Philadelphia, PA	25%	21%	39%	63%	6%	18%
Phoenix, AZ	19%	31%	16%	36%	9%	12%
Portland, OR	26%	38%	30%	54%	18%	25%
St. Louis, MO	16%	15%	16%	31%	2%	7%
San Antonio, TX	12%	18%	12%	26%	14%	20%
San Diego, CA	18%	20%	32%	50%	17%	21%

Source: "Female Arrestees: Drug Use by Self-Report and Urinalysis," *DUF: 1988 Drug Use Forecasting Annual Report*, National Institute of Justice, March 1990, p. 13. Also in source: Statistics for multiple drug use by arrestees. —represents less than 20 cases. No data was available for females in Cleveland, Fort Lauderdale, Houston, Indianapolis, Miami, and Omaha.

★ 138 ★
Drugs

Arrestees' Drug Use: 1988

The National Institute of Justice's Drug Use Forecasting Program covered 20 cities in 1988. It is designed to provide cities with an estimate of drug use among arrestees and information for detecting changes in drug use trends. This table shows the percentage of males and females whose urinalysis tested positive for any drug during the period January through December 1988. The table also shows the percentages who tested positive by age and by race.

City and State	Positive	15-20	21-25	26-30	31-35	36+	Black	White	Hispanic	Other
Birmingham, AL										
Males	72%	58%	75%	86%	69%	62%	74%	69%	--	--
Females	65%	--	--	--	--	--	58%	75%	--	--
Chicago, IL										
Males	80%	70%	83%	84%	88%	74%	82%	71%	72%	--
Females	77%	--	84%	82%	--	--	77%	--	--	--
Dallas, TX										
Males	66%	57%	66%	77%	77%	52%	69%	63%	49%	--
Females	65%	66%	61%	76%	60%	55%	63%	68%	--	--
Detroit, MI										
Males	68%	63%	68%	69%	65%	75%	70%	57%	--	--
Females	81%	--	84%	82%	--	--	81%	82%	--	--
Kansas City, MO										
Males	54%	41%	66%	59%	62%	--	61%	42%	--	--

[Continued]

132

★ 138 ★

Arrestees' Drug Use: 1988
[Continued]

City and State	Positive	Percent positive by age					Percent postive by race			
		15-20	21-25	26-30	31-35	36+	Black	White	Hispanic	Other
Females	70%	--	67%	--	--	--	74%	--	--	--
Los Angeles, CA										
Males	75%	65%	74%	83%	80%	72%	82%	72%	74%	24%
Females	76%	67%	75%	84%	78%	69%	88%	77%	59%	--
New Orleans, LA										
Males	70%	66%	76%	78%	74%	58%	73%	54%	--	--
Females	55%	32%	53%	65%	71%	48%	54%	59%	--	--
New York, NY										
Males	83%	70%	87%	93%	86%	74%	86%	82%	81%	--
Females	80%	70%	80%	83%	85%	77%	83%	79%	74%	--
Philadelphia, PA										
Males	81%	82%	83%	85%	90%	59%	82%	69%	87%	--
Females	79%	--	76%	90%	85%	68%	80%	85%	--	--
Phoenix, AZ										
Males	63%	74%	68%	67%	67%	41%	75%	60%	64%	47%
Females	60%	57%	58%	71%	69%	40%	84%	60%	49%	45%
Portland, OR										
Males	74%	75%	80%	77%	78%	63%	83%	70%	74%	66%
Females	78%	69%	80%	79%	88%	71%	86%	75%	--	70%
St. Louis, MO										
Males	56%	41%	62%	70%	57%	48%	55%	56%	--	--
Females	44%	--	--	--	--	28%	56%	21%	--	--
San Antonio, TX										
Males	63%	58%	73%	64%	60%	58%	62%	53%	68%	--
Females	51%	--	--	63%	--	36%	--	58%	38%	--
San Diego, CA										
Males	82%	72%	86%	86%	86%	72%	85%	83%	79%	--
Females	79%	88%	89%	78%	84%	55%	89%	78%	62%	--

Source: "Any Drug Use by Male and Female Arrestees," *DUF: 1988 Drug Use Forecasting Annual Report*, National Institute of Justice, March 1990, p. 4. Also in source: Statistics for multiple drug use by arrestees. —represents less than 20 cases. No data was available for females in Cleveland, Fort Lauderdale, Houston, Indianapolis, Miami, and Omaha.

★ 139 ★

Drugs

Arrestees' Use of Injected Drugs: 1988

The National Institute of Justice's Drug Use Forecasting Program covered 20 cities in 1988. It is designed to provide cities with an estimate of drug use among arrestees and information for detecting changes in drug use trends. This table shows the percentage of males and females who admitted ever injecting drugs and the percentage of injectors who admitted currently sharing needles.

City and State	Ever injected	Currently share needles
Birmingham, AL		
Males	28%	20%
Females	33%	--
Chicago, IL		
Males	18%	24%
Females	35%	25%
Dallas, TX		
Males	22%	34%
Females	31%	30%
Detroit, MI		
Males	18%	21%
Females	32%	21%
Kansas City, MO		
Males	20%	8%
Females	15%	30%
Los Angeles, CA		
Males	27%	44%
Females	33%	35%
New Orleans, LA		
Males	15%	33%
Females	21%	27%
New York, NY		
Males	24%	29%
Females	30%	17%
Philadelphia, PA		
Males	19%	30%
Females	20%	18%
Phoenix, AZ		
Males	29%	26%

[Continued]

★ 139 ★

Arrestees' Use of Injected Drugs: 1988
[Continued]

City and State	Ever injected	Currently share needles
Females	33%	36%
Portland, OR		
Males	36%	26%
Females	47%	26%
St. Louis, MO		
Males	18%	23%
Females	22%	12%
San Antonio, TX		
Males	34%	35%
Females	26%	39%
San Diego, CA		
Males	34%	28%
Females	38%	30%

Source: Selected from "Injection in Arestees and CDC Estimates of AIDS," *DUF: 1988 Drug Use Forecasting Annual Report*, National Institute of Justice, March 1990, p. 9. —represents less than 20 cases. No data was available for females in Cleveland, Fort Lauderdale, Houston, Indianapolis, Miami, and Omaha.

★ 140 ★
Drugs

Jail Inmates' Drug Use: 1989

This table shows the drug use history of convicted jail inmates in 1989. Female inmates used more drugs and used them more frequently than did males. Women were also more likely than men to have used a major drug in the month before their current offense.

Drug use	Percent of inmates	
	Female	Male
Any drug[1]		
Ever used	83.6%	77.4%
Ever used on a regular basis	70.0%	56.8%
Used in the month before current offense	55.1%	42.7%
Used daily in the month before current offense	40.1%	28.6%

[Continued]

★ 140 ★

Jail Inmates' Drug Use: 1989
[Continued]

Drug use	Percent of inmates	
	Female	Male
Under the influence at time of current offense	37.5%	25.9%
Major drug[2]		
Ever used	70.7%	54.5%
Ever used on a regular basis	56.7%	35.4%
Used in the month before current offense	43.9%	25.9%
Used daily in the month before current offense	31.8%	15.7%
Under the influence at time of current offense	31.3%	16.8%
Number of inmates	21,782	196,620

Source: "Drug use history of convicted jail inmates, by sex, 1989," Tracy L. Snell, "Women in Jail 1989," *Bureau of Justice Statistics Special Report*, March 1992, Table 12, p. 7. *Notes:* 1. Includes cocaine, heroin, PCP, LSD, methadone, marijuana or hashish, amphetamines, barbiturates, methaqualone, and all other drugs. 2. Includes only cocaine, heroin, PCP, LSD, and methadone.

★ 141 ★
Drugs

Prison Inmates' Drug Use: 1986 and 1991

Ths table shows drugs used in the month before their offense and the percentage of female prison inmates who were under the influence of drugs at the time of the offense for which they were imprisoned, in 1991 and 1986. Women in prison in 1991 used more drugs and used them more frequently than men. Nearly 1 in 4 female inmates reported committing their offense in order to get money to buy drugs. Compared to women in prison in 1986, higher percentages of female inmates in 1991 reported using drugs in the month before their offense.

[NA Not available.]

Type of drug	Used in the month before the offense		Under the influence at the time of the offense	
	1991	1986	1991	1986
Any drug	53.9%	50.0%	36.3%	33.9%
Marijuana	20.5%	30.5%	4.6%	8.5%
Cocaine/crack[2]	36.5%	23.3%	22.6%	12.1%
Cocaine	26.2%	23.3%	14.2%	12.1%
Crack	19.1%	NA	10.1%	NA
Heroin/opiate	15.9%	17.9%	11.3%	12.9%
Heroin	14.8%	17.2%	10.8%	12.3%
Other opiates	3.4%	2.1%	1.0%	1.0%
Stimulants[2]	7.6%	7.8%	2.8%	4.0%
Amphetamines	4.6%	7.8%	0.9%	4.0%
Methamphetamines	5.1%	NA	2.2%	NA
Depressants	5.0%	9.1%	1.4%	4.5%
Barbiturates	4.8%	9.0%	1.3%	3.9%
Methaqualone	0.8%	3.0%	0.1%	0.7%
Hallucinogens	2.2%	3.5%	1.1%	1.5%
LSD	1.0%	1.6%	0.4%	0.4%
PCP	1.5%	2.2%	0.7%	1.1%

Source: "Drug use by female State prison inmates, by type of drug, 1991 and 1986," Tracy L. Snell, "Survey of State Prison Inmates, 1991: Women in Prison," *Bureau of Justice Statistics Special Report*, March 1994, Table 12, p. 8. Detail may add to more than total because inmates may have been using more than one drug.

Juveniles

★ 142 ★

Child Rape Victims, Relationship to Offender: 1992

This table shows the relationship between the victim and the offender in cases of child rape, as reported by the victims and the rapists. Information was gathered from two sources: interviews with rape victims reported to law enforcement agencies in 1991 in three States (Alabama, North Dakota, and South Carolina) and 1991 interviews with rapists confined in State prisons. The older the victim, the less likely that victim and offender were family members and the more likely they were strangers to one another.

Age of victim	Victim-offender relationship			
	Total	Family member	Acquaintance/friend[1]	Stranger
Source: Victims in 3 States				
Under 12	100%	46%	50%	4%
12-17	100%	20%	65%	15%
18 or older	100%	12%	55%	33%
Source: Imprisoned rapists				
Under 12[2]	100%	70%	24%	6%
12-17	100%	36%	45%	19%
18 or older	100%	8%	45%	47%

Source: Patrick A. Langan, Ph.D., and Caroline Wolf Harlow, Ph.D., *Child Rape Victims, 1992,* U.S. Department of Justice Crime Data Brief, June 1994, NCJ-147001, p. 2. Primary source: Tabulated from data described in *Using NIBRS Data to Analyze Violent Crime,* BJS technical report, NCJ-144785, October 1993; BJS, *Survey of State Prison Inmates, 1991,* NCJ-136949, March 1993. *Notes:* 1. Includes other nonfamily relationships. 2. May include some 12-year-olds.

★ 143 ★
Juveniles

Child Rape Victims: 1992

This table shows the number of female child victims of forcible rape, by age and State, and the cumulative percent of female victims under age 18 and 18 or older, in 1992. According to the FBI, 109,062 forcible rapes of females were reported to law enforcement agencies in 1992. The Bureau of Justice Statistics asked for data on victims' ages. Thirty-six States reported that they did not keep such statistics. The 15 States in this table responded with information on 26,427 female victims, nearly one-fourth of the national total. Twelve States reported in enough detail to distinguish juvenile from adult rape victims. Their 20,824 victims made up 20% of the national total. In those 12 states, 51% of female rape victims were juveniles under the age of 18. That age group of females made up 25% of the 1992 U.S. female population. The Bureau of Justice Statistics found that one in five rape victims under age 12 is raped by her father.

[Blanks indicate detail was not reported.]

State	Number of female victims of forc.rape[1]	Cumulative percent of female victims of forcible rape									
		under age 10	under age 11	under age 12	under age 13	under age 14	under age 15	under age 16	under age 17	under age 18	18 or older
Alabama	1,404	4%	6%	7%	10%	17%	24%	30%	35%	38%	62%
Arkansas	986	9%				24%	24%			44%	56%
Delaware	783	22%			29%		50%	61%	66%	71%	29%
District of Columbia	205			5%				22%	28%	32%	68%
Florida	7,280		14%							46%	54%
Idaho	221	5%			9%		20%	24%	29%	35%	65%
Kansas	1,013	1%					12%				
Michigan	4,731	25%	28%	31%	35%	41%	49%	58%	64%	68%	32%
Nebraska	290		6%					31%		42%	58%
North Carolina	2,397		5%					20%			
North Dakota	124		25%	30%	35%	44%	48%	50%	52%	57%	43%
Pennsylvania	2,996		9%		14%		25%	32%	37%	42%	58%
Rhode Island	490					49%				70%	30%
South Carolina	2,193	9%			16%				40%		
Wisconsin	1,314	4%	6%	8%	10%	14%	22%	29%	37%	42%	58%

Source: Patrick A. Langan, Ph.D., and Caroline Wolf Harlow, Ph.D., *Child Rape Victims, 1992*, U.S. Department of Justice Crime Data Brief, June 1994, NCJ-147001, p. 1. Related reading: "Report Cites Heavy Toll of Rapes on Young," *The New York Times* National Report, June 23, 1994, p. A8 Y. *Note:* 1. Excludes victims with unknown age.

★ 144 ★

Juveniles

Dating Violence Among High School Students

Students from three high schools in the Midwest were surveyed to find out about their experiences with sexual, physical, and verbal dating violence. Responses were received from 631 suburban, rural, and inner-city students. This table shows the responses, total and by sex. The highest incidence of dating violence was found in the suburban school, the second highest in the inner-city school, and the third highest in the rural school.

Sex	Sexual Violence	Physical Violence	Sexual and/ or Physical	Any violence Verbal, sexual and/or physical
Total	10.5%	12.0%	17.7%	28.0%
Male	4.4%	7.8%	9.9%	23.5%
Female	15.7%	15.7%	24.6%	32.0%

Source: Libby Bergman, "Dating Violence among High School Students," *Social Work*, Vol. 37, No. 1, January 1992, Figure 2, "Proportion of Students Reporting Dating Violence," p. 23.

★ 145 ★

Juveniles

Incest and Paternal Caregiving

Some statistics on the relationship between a biological father's involvement in caretaking and its influence on the incidence of incest.

Incestuous fathers were studied. One closely observed phenomenon was paternal absence from home during the child's early life. A sample of Navy fathers was included and compared to the civilian sample. It was found that there was no significant difference in the amount of time incestuous and nonincestuous fathers were separated from the daughter in the first 4 years of her life. Other findings:

1. Fifty-four percent of incestuous fathers had experienced severe abuse at the hands of their own fathers, as compared to 25% of the nonincestuous fathers. **Abuse by their mothers nearly tripled the odds of men incestuously abusing a daughter.**

2. Sixty-five percent of incestuous fathers had been rejected or neglected by their fathers, compared to 29% of nonincestuous fathers. Paternal rejection increased the odds of being an incestuous father more than four times, **as did rejection by the mother.**

[Continued]

★ 145 ★

Incest and Paternal Caregiving
[Continued]

3. Sixty-nine percent of incestuous fathers were sexually victimized during their childhood, compared to 28% of nonincestuous fathers. Fathers who had been sexually abused during their childhood were more than five times as likely as nonabused fathers to incestuously abuse a daughter.

4. Incestuous fathers were more likely to have initiated sexual abuse of a child or rape of an adult during their young or teenage years. These men were nearly four times more likely to become incestuous fathers.

5. Men who were dissatisfied with their marriages were five times more likely to incestuously abuse a daughter.

6. There was more than double the risk of incest among fathers who reported little involvement in care of their daughter during her early years. However, it was also found that being the sole caregiver for a daughter for at least 30 consecutive days was found to increase the risk of later incestuous abuse. The authors found that fathers actively involved in the care of a daughter (as opposed to being sole caretakers) appeared to be at lower risk for incest.

Source: Selected from Linda Meyer Williams and David Finkelhor, "Paternal Caregiving and Incest: A Test of a Biosocial Model," *American Journal of Orthopsychiatry,* 65(1), January 1995. Distributed by Family Research Laboratory, University of New Hampshire, 126 Horton Social Science Center, Durham, NH 03824; telephone (603)862-2342; FAX (603)862-1122 e-mail: williams@christa.unh.edu.

★ 146 ★

Juveniles

Juvenile Delinquency Trends: 1986-1991

This table compares trends in delinquency of male and female juveniles under the age of 18 for the period from 1987 to 1991.

Item and years	Females	Males
Robbery arrests, increase 1987-1991	88%	49%
Property Crime Index arrests, 1987-1991	14%	7%
All youth arrests, 1991	23%	77%
Violent Crime Index arrests	12%	88%
Property Crime Index arrests	22%	78%
Increase in volume of juvenile court cases, 1986-1990	10%	10%
Growth in person offense cases, 1986-1990	32%	29%

[Continued]

★ 146 ★

Juvenile Delinquency Trends: 1986-1991
[Continued]

Item and years	Females	Males
Growth in property cases, 1986-1990	13%	7%
Delinquency cases processed, 1990	19%	81%
Person offense	19%	81%
Property offense	19%	81%
Drug offense	13%	87%
Cases involving detention during court processing, 1990	17%	24%
Increase in admissions to juvenile custody facilities, 1978-1988	18%	18%

Source: "Female delinquency" U.S. Department of Justice, Office of Juvenile Justice and Delinquency Prevention, *Comprehensive Strategy for Serious, Violent, and Chronic Juvenile Offenders*, Program Summary, June 1994, p. 30.

★ 147 ★
Juveniles

Juvenile Prostitution

A few statistics on juvenile prostitution, defined by the National Center on Child Abuse and Neglect as "the use of, or participation by, children under the age of majority in sexual acts with adults or other minors where no force is present."

Item	Number/Percent
Estimate of number of juvenile prostitutes practicing annually.	100-300,000
Percentage of these juvenile prostitutes who are "throwaways," encouraged or forced to leave home by their families.	75%

Source: Selected from *Juvenile Prostitution*, National Victims Resource Center "Fact Sheet." Primary sources: *Sexual Abuse of Children: Selected Readings*. National Center on Child Abuse and Neglect and Department of Health and Human Services. November 1980. H.A. Davidson and G.A. Loken. *Child Pornography and Prostitution: Background and Legal Analysis*. National Center for Missing and Exploited Children and the National Obscenity Enforcement Unit, U.S. Department of Justice. 1987. M.I. Cohen. *Identifying and Combating Juvenile Prostitution - A Manual for Action*. National Association of Counties. 1987.

★ 148 ★

Juveniles

Juveniles in Custody: 1991

This table shows the total number, and the number of male and female juveniles who were in custody in public juvenile facilities on one-day counts, by reason for custody, in 1991. Admissions to juvenile detention and corrections facilities are increasing. This has resulted in crowded facilities, institutional violence, and suicidal behavior. Admissions began rising in 1984 and reached an all-time high in 1990.

Public facilities	Total N = 57,661	Females N = 6,379	Males N = 51,282
Delinquent Offenses	95%	80.7%	97.3%
Violent	19%	10.3%	20.5%
Other personal	12%	9.4%	12.1%
Serious property	24%	17.1%	24.4%
Other property	12%	12.9%	12.5%
Alcohol offenses	1%	1.0%	1.0%
Drug-related offenses	10%	5.3%	10.4%
Public order offenses	4%	5.4%	4.4%
Probation/parole violation	8%	12.9%	7.2%
Other	5%	6.4%	4.8%
Status offenses	3%	12.9%	1.8%
Nonoffenders	1%	4.2%	0.7%
Voluntary commitments	1%	2.2%	0.2%

Source: "U.S. Juveniles in Custody in Public Juvenile Facilities 1-Day Counts by Reason for Custody and Sex, 1991," U.S. Department of Justice, Office of Juvenile Justice and Delinquency Prevention, *Comprehensive Strategy for Serious, Violent, and Chronic Juvenile Offenders*, Program Summary, June 1994, Figure 2, p. 3. Offense categories include the following offenses: **Violent:** murder, nonnegligent manslaughter, forcible rape, robbery, aggravated assault. **Other personal:** negligent manslaughter, assault, sexual assault. **Serious property:** burglary, arson, larceny-theft, motor vehicle theft. **Other property:** vandalism, forgery, counterfeiting, fraud, stolen property, unauthorized vehicle use. **Public order:** alcohol offenses, drug-related offenses, public order offenses. **Status:** offenses not considered crimes if committed by adults. **Nonoffenders:** dependency, neglect, abuse, emotional disturbance, retardation, other.

★ 149 ★
Juveniles

Juveniles' Use of Drugs: 1992-I

This table shows the thirty-day prevalence of use of various types of drugs by eighth, tenth, and twelfth graders in 1992 (that is, the percentages of students who reported using the particular drug within the last 30 days). While males in three population groups (seniors in high school, college students, and young adults) are more likely to use most illicit drugs, female use of stimulants and tranquilizers in high school is at the same level or higher. There are fewer sex differences in the use of drugs in the eighth and tenth grade samples. This may be because the girls tend to date older boys in age groups more likely to use drugs.

Sex	Marijuana			Inhalants[1,2]			Hallucinogens[2]			LSD		
	8th	10th	12th	8th	10th	12th	8th	10th	12th	8th	10th	12th
Total	3.7%	8.1%	11.9%	4.7%	2.7%	2.3%	1.1%	1.8%	2.1%	0.9%	1.6%	2.0%
Sex												
Male	3.8%	9.0%	13.4%	4.4%	2.9%	3.0%	1.1%	2.1%	2.9%	0.9%	1.9%	2.7%
Female	3.5%	7.1%	10.2%	4.9%	2.6%	1.6%	1.0%	1.4%	1.4%	0.9%	1.3%	1.3%

Source: Selected from "Thirty-Day Prevalence of Use of Various Types of Drugs by Subgroups Eighth, Tenth, and Twelfth Graders, 1992," U.S. Department of Health and Human Services, National Institute on drug Abuse, *National Survey Results on Drug Use from the Monitoring the Future Study, 1975-1992*, Volume 1, Secondary School Students, Table 8, pp. 57-58. Also in source, data by college plans, region, population density, and parental education. Approximate numbers are: total eighth grade, 18,600 (8,800 males and 9,300 females); total tenth grade, 14,800 (7,000 males and 7,400 females); total twelfth, 15,800 (7,400 males and 7,900 females). *Notes:* 1. 12th grade only: Data based on five questionnaire forms. Numbers are five-sixths of total numbers of students indicated. 2. Unadjusted for known underreporting of certain drugs. See source for details.

★ 150 ★
Juveniles

Juveniles' Use of Drugs: 1992-II

This table shows the thirty-day prevalence of use of various types of drugs by eighth, tenth, and twelfth graders in 1992 (that is, the percentages of students who reported using the particular drug within the last 30 days).

Sex	Cocaine			Crack			Other cocaine[1]			Heroin		
	8th	10th	12th	8th	10th	12th	8th	10th	12th	8th	10th	12th
Total	0.7%	0.7%	1.3%	0.5%	0.4%	0.6%	0.5%	0.6%	1.0%	0.4%	0.2%	0.3%
Sex												
Male	0.6%	0.8%	1.5%	0.4%	0.4%	0.8%	0.4%	0.6%	1.2%	0.4%	0.3%	0.5%
Female	0.8%	0.6%	0.9%	0.5%	0.4%	0.4%	0.6%	0.5%	0.7%	0.3%	0.2%	0.2%

Source: Selected from "Thirty-Day Prevalence of Use of Various Types of Drugs by Subgroups Eighth, Tenth, and Twelfth Graders, 1992," U.S. Department of Health and Human Services, National Institute on drug Abuse, *National Survey Results on Drug Use from the Monitoring the Future Study, 1975-1992*, Volume 1, Secondary School Students, Table 8, pp. 57-58. Also in source, data by college plans, region, population density, and parental education. Approximate numbers are: total eighth grade, 18,600 (8,800 males and 9,300 females); total tenth grade, 14,800 (7,000 males and 7,400 females); total twelfth, 15,800 (7,400 males and 7,900 females). For "other cocaine" category, the numbers are four-sixths of the numbers indicated here. *Note:* 1. 12th grade only: data based on four questionnarie forms.

★ 151 ★

Juveniles

Juveniles' Use of Drugs: 1992-III

This table shows the thirty-day prevalence of use of various types of drugs by eighth, tenth, and twelfth graders in 1992 (that is, the percentages of students who reported using the particular drug within the last 30 days).

[NA means not available.]

Sex	Stimulants[1]			Barbiturates[1]			Tranquilizers[1]			Alcohol		
	8th	10th	12th	8th	10th	12th	8th	10th	12th	8th	10th	12th
Total	3.3%	3.6%	2.8%	NA	NA	1.1%	0.8%	1.5%	1.0%	26.1%	39.9%	51.3%
Sex												
Male	2.5%	3.0%	2.9%	NA	NA	1.2%	0.5%	1.1%	1.0%	26.3%	41.6%	55.8%
Female	4.0%	4.1%	2.5%	NA	NA	0.9%	1.0%	1.8%	1.1%	25.9%	38.3%	46.8%

Source: Selected from "Thirty-Day Prevalence of Use of Various Types of Drugs by Subgroups Eighth, Tenth, and Twelfth Graders, 1992," U.S. Department of Health and Human Services, National Institute on drug Abuse, *National Survey Results on Drug Use from the Monitoring the Future Study, 1975-1992*, Volume 1, Secondary School Students, Table 8, pp. 57-58. Also in source, data by college plans, region, population density, and parental education. Approximate numbers are: total eighth grade, 18,600 (8,800 males and 9,300 females); total tenth grade, 14,800 (7,000 males and 7,400 females); total twelfth, 15,800 (7,400 males and 7,900 females). *Note:* 1. Only drug use not under doctor's orders is included.

★ 152 ★

Juveniles

Juveniles' Use of Drugs: 1992-IV

This table shows the thirty-day prevalence of use of various types of drugs by eighth, tenth, and twelfth graders in 1992 (that is, the percentages of students who reported using the particular drug within the last 30 days).

Sex	Been Drunk[1]			Cigarettes			Smokeless Tobacco[2]			Steroids[1]		
	8th	10th	12th	8th	10th	12th	8th	10th	12th	8th	10th	12th
Total	7.5%	18.1%	29.9%	15.5%	21.5%	27.8%	7.0%	9.6%	11.4%	0.5%	0.6%	0.6%
Sex												
Male	7.4%	18.6%	35.2%	14.9%	20.6%	29.2%	12.5%	18.1%	20.8%	0.9%	1.0%	1.1%
Female	7.6%	17.5%	24.5%	15.9%	22.2%	26.1%	2.0%	1.8%	2.0%	0.2%	0.1%	0.1%

Source: Selected from "Thirty-Day Prevalence of Use of Various Types of Drugs by Subgroups Eighth, Tenth, and Twelfth Graders, 1992," U.S. Department of Health and Human Services, National Institute on drug Abuse, *National Survey Results on Drug Use from the Monitoring the Future Study, 1975-1992*, Volume 1, Secondary School Students, Table 8, pp. 57-58. Also in source, data by college plans, region, population density, and parental education. Approximate numbers are: total eighth grade, 18,600 (8,800 males and 9,300 females); total tenth grade, 14,800 (7,000 males and 7,400 females); total twelfth, 15,800 (7,400 males and 7,900 females). *Notes:* 1. 12th grade only: Data based on two questionnaire forms. Numbers are two-sixths of numbers of students indicated. 2. Data based on one questionnaire form. Number is one-sixth of number indicated for 12th grade. Number is one-half of number indicated for 8th and 10th grades.

★ 153 ★

Juveniles

Victimizations at School

This table shows characteristics of students who reported at least one victimization at school. The National Crime Victimization Survey collected responses during the first half of 1989. The data represent an estimated 21.6 million students, ages 12 to 19.

Student characteristic	Total no. of students	Reporting victimization at school		
		Total	Violent	Property
Sex				
Female	10,387,776	9%	2%	8%
Male	11,166,316	9%	2%	7%
Race				
White	17,306,626	9%	2%	7%
Black	3,449,488	8%	2%	7%
Other	797,978	10%	2%[2]	8%
Hispanic origin				
Hispanic	2,026,968	7%	3%	5%
Non-Hispanic	19,452,697	9%	2%	8%
Not ascertained	74,428	3%[2]	[1]	3%[2]
Age				
12	3,220,891	9%	2%	7%
13	3,318,714	10%	2%	8%
14	3,264,574	11%	2%	9%
15	3,214,109	9%	3%	7%
16	3,275,002	9%	2%	7%
17	3,273,628	8%	1%	7%
18	1,755,825	5%	1%[2]	4%
19	231,348	2%[2]	[1]	2%[2]

Source: Selected from "Students reporting at least one victimization at school, by personal and family characteristics," U.S. Department of Justice, Bureau of Justice Statistics, *School Crime: A National Crime Victimization Survey Report*, Table 1, p. 1. Also in source, data by number of times family moved in last 5 years, family income, and place of residence. *Notes:* 1. Less than 0.5%. 2. Estimate is based on 10 or fewer sample cases.

★ 154 ★

Juveniles

Victims of Childhood Sexual Abuse, Recall

One hundred twenty-nine women with documented histories of child sexual abuse were interviewed to answer the question: "Do people actually forget traumatic events such as child sexual abuse, and if so, how common is such forgetting?" Some findings: Thirty-eight percent of women did not recall the abuse that had been reported 17 years before. Women who were younger at the time of the abuse, and those who had been molested by someone they knew, were more likely to have no memory of the abuse. Most of the girls (87) in the sample were at least 7 years old at the time of the abuse. This table shows characteristics of the abuse and of the victims from that age group.

Characteristic of victim/abuse	Percent who remembered	Percent with no recall
Age 7 or older at time of abuse	72%	28%
Physical force used	69%	31%
Penetration	64%	36%
Genital trauma	51%	49%
Perpetrator was stranger	82%	18%
Perpetrator was family member	53%	47%

Source: Selected from Linda Meyer Williams, "Recall of Childhood Trauma: A Prospective Study of Women's Memories of Child Sexual Abuse," *Journal of Consulting and Clinical Psychology*, 1994, Vol. 62, No. 6, pp. 1167-1176. Table 1, p. 1172, "Characteristics of Abuse and No Recall of Child Sexual Victimization." Correspondence concerning this article should be directed to Linda Meyer Williams, Family Research Laboratory, University of New Hampshire, 126 Horton Social Science Center, Durham, NH 03824; telephone (603)862-2342; FAX (603)862-1122 e-mail: williams@christa.unh.edu.

★ 155 ★
Juveniles

Sexually Molested as a Child

The table below shows the responses of women and men to a survey question about whether they were sexually molested as children. Nearly one-quarter of of all women responding said they had been sexually molested as children.

Responses	Women, total	Career women	Home-makers	Men
N =	1,371	631	269	1,318
I was sexually molested as a child.				
Yes	23%	28%	18%	11%
No	77%	72%	82%	89%
Of "Yes" responses:				
N =	318	--	--	142
Who was the molester?				
Adult stranger	21%	--	--	33%
Relative	62%	--	--	44%
Person in authority position	17%	--	--	23%
How often?				
Once	41%	--	--	42%
Often	39%	--	--	44%
Ongoing	20%	--	--	14%
Was the incident(s) reported to authorities?				
Yes	12%	--	--	12%
No	88%	--	--	88%
Any arrest?				
Yes	5%	--	--	12%
No	95%	--	--	88%

[Continued]

★ 155 ★

Sexually Molested as a Child
[Continued]

Responses	Women, total	Career women	Home- makers	Men
Any convictions?				
Yes	3%	--	--	9%
No	97%	--	--	91%

Source: "I Was Sexually Molested as a Child," Samuel S. Janus, PhD, and Cynthia L. Janus, MD, *The Janus Report on Sexual Behavior,* (New York: John Wiley & Sons, Inc., 1993), Table 3.18, p. 73. Between 1988 and 1992, the authors distributed 4,550 questionnaires to subjects at a variety of sites. The sample design was planned to conform to the population distribution of the United States in the areas of sex, age, region, income, education, and marital status. Returned questionnaires totaled 3,260. Of these, 495 were discarded. Satisfactorily completed questionnaires totaled 2,765: 1,418 women and 1,347 men. In this table, women have been further designated as career women or homemakers.

Law Enforcement

★ 156 ★

Resolution of EEOC Complaints: 1993

Title VII of the Civil Rights Act of 1964 prohibits discrimination in the workplace on the basis of race, color, sex, religion, or national origin. In 1993, the Equal Employment Opportunity Commission received 53,078 complaints under Title VII. The complaints filed in 1993 represented about 60% of all complaints on file with the commission. This table shows what happened to those cases. Between 1989 and 1994, the commission received 54,908 sexual harassment complaints. Seventy-three percent (34,471 cases) were rejected for insufficient evidence or were closed for other reasons. An additional 7,899 cases were "left adrift in the growing backlog of the unresolved." Only 991 sexual harassment cases reached the threshold of a lawsuit.

Resolution	Percent
Not resolved in workers' favor	73%
Case closed for administrative reasons	23%
Agency finds insufficient evidence of discrimination	50%
Case resolved in workers' favor	14%
Found that worker has "reasonable cause" to sue	2%

[Continued]

★ 156 ★

Resolution of EEOC Complaints: 1993
[Continued]

Resolution	Percent
Worker received payment or other settlement without formal finding of discrimination	12%
Backlog	13%

Source: Peter T. Kilborn, "In Rare Move, Agency Acts Swiftly in a Sexual Harassment Case," *The New York Times*, January 10, 1995, p. C18 Y. Primary source: EEOC.

Victims

★ 157 ★

Battered Women

Some statistics on male violence against women.

The American Psychological Association's Committee on Women in Psychology reviewed research on "the prevalence, causes, and impact of several different forms of violence against women..." Some highlights from this review are:

1. Between **21% and 34%** of all women in the United States will be physically assaulted by an intimate adult partner.

2. **Fifty-two percent** of women murdered in the United States during the first half of the 1980s were victims of partner homicide.

3. Between **14% and 25%** of all adult women have "endured rape according to its legal definition, which includes acts involving nonconsensual sexual perpetration obtained by physical force, by threat of bodily harm, or when the victim is incapable of giving consent..."

4. **Fifty percent** of working women can expect to be sexually harassed at some point during their working lives.

Source: Selected from Lisa A. Goodman, Mary P. Koss, et al., "Male Violence Against Women: Current Research and Future Directions," *American Psychologist*, Vol. 48, No. 10, pp. 1054-1058, October 1993. The authors comprise the American Psychological Association's Committee on Women in Psychology's Task Force on Male Violence Against Women. Senator Joseph Biden also contributed to the report. Direct correspondence concerning the article to Lisa A. Goodman, Department of Psychology, University of Maryland, College Park, MD 20742-4411. Related reading: Daniel Goleman, "An Elusive Picture of Violent Men Who Kill Mates," *The New York Times* National, January 15, 1995, p. 13.

★ 158 ★

Victims

Jail Inmates' Victims: 1989

This table shows the sex, race, and age of victims of convicted violent jail inmates, by sex of inmate, 1989. Most women reported victimizing either someone close to them or someone they knew. About half the women and men in jail following conviction for a violent crime had victimized a female.

Victim	% of convicted inmates	
characteristic	Female	Male
SEX		
Male	50.4%	50.7%
Female	48.5%	40.7%
Both	1.1%	8.6%
RACE		
White	57.0%	65.7%
Black	39.0%	28.3%
Other	4.0%	2.4%
Mixed	0.0%	3.6%
AGE		
Minor	13.5%	22.7%
Adult	85.6%	75.2%
Both	0.9%	2.1%
VICTIM/OFFENDER		
RELATIONSHIP		
Close	31.4%	22.9%
Relative	16.0%	16.1%
Intimate	15.4%	6.8%
Known	30.1%	32.9%
Well-known	16.8%	13.1%
Casual	13.3%	19.8%
Stranger	38.4%	44.1%
Number of inmates	1,850	31,816

Source: "Characteristics of victims of convicted violent jail inmates, by sex of inmates, 1989," Tracy L. Snell, "Women in Jail 1989," *Bureau of Justice Statistics Special Report*, March 1992, Table 11, p. 7. *Spouse* includes common-law spouse. *Offspring* includes grandchild and step-child. *Parent* includes grandparent and step-parent. *Sibling* includes step-sibling. *Other* includes cousin, in-law, extended family members, and other family members. Detail percentages may not add to total because of rounding.

★ 159 ★
Victims

Murder Victims and Defendants: 1988

This table shows the sex, race, and age of murder victims and defendants, by the family relationship of murder victims and defendants. More than half of all murders committed in the United States occur in 75 counties (out of a total of more than 3,000 counties). The data for this table were compiled from a sample of 33 counties out of the 75. Sixteen percent of murder victims had a family relationship to at least one defendant in the case, and the most frequent specific relationship was that of spouse. Thirteen percent of defendants had a family relationship to at least one of the victims in a murder case. Husbands and wives were the most likely to be involved in family murders. Spouses were 4 in 10 of all defendants and victims involved in a family murder. Husbands killed wives more frequently than wives killed husbands, but the predominance of husbands as defendants varied by race. In black murders, wives were about as likely as husbands to be charged with murder of their spouse. Of the 283 black-on-black spouse killings, 53% of assailants were husbands, compared to 62% of the 218 white-on-white spouse killings. In all 11 Asian, Native American, Pacific Islander, or Alaska Native spouse murders, the husband killed the wife.

[Murder victims = 8,063; defendants = 9,576.]

Relationship of victim to assailant	All	Sex		Race			Age				
		Male	Female	White	Black	Other	Under 12	12-19	20-29	30-59	60+
Victims											
All	100%	77.8%	22.2%	43.5%	54.2%	2.3%	4.8%	10.9%	35.6%	41.8%	7.0%
Nonfamily	100%	82.2%	17.8%	44.4%	53.3%	2.3%	2.1%	12.2%	38.5%	41.1%	6.1%
Family	100%	55.5%	44.5%	39.0%	58.6%	2.4%	18.8%	3.9%	20.3%	45.3%	11.6%
Spouse	100%	40.2%	59.8%	41.2%	56.4%	2.4%	0%	0%	27.9%	65.0%	7.1%
Offspring	100%	55.8%	44.2%	32.6%	65.6%	1.8%	78.5%	10.9%	7.7%	3.0%	0%
Parent	100%	57.2%	42.8%	54.8%	45.2%	0%	0%	0%	9%	56.7%	42.4%
Sibling	100%	73.0%	27.0%	33.5%	64.5%	2.0%	8.7%	2.0%	43.3%	42.6%	3.3%
Other	100%	74.9%	25.1%	34.1%	61.0%	4.9%	4.6%	8.2%	19.1%	47.5%	20.6%
Defendants											
All	100%	89.5%	10.5%	36.2%	61.9%	1.8%	0.1%	21.8%	42.5%	31.4%	4.2%
Nonfamily	100%	93.2%	6.8%	35.7%	62.6%	1.8%	0.1%	23.1%	44.5%	28.4%	3.8%
Family	100%	65.5%	34.5%	39.7%	58.0%	2.3%	0%	13.0%	29.7%	50.5%	6.8%
Spouse	100%	59.3%	40.7%	41.8%	56.1%	2.2%	0%	0.9%	21.9%	66.1%	11.1%
Offspring	100%	45.4%	54.6%	34.5%	64.5%	1.0%	0%	17.2%	36.4%	40.3%	6.0%
Parent	100%	81.6%	18.4%	49.8%	50.2%	0%	0%	38.2%	30.7%	29.4%	1.7%
Sibling	100%	84.9%	15.1%	32.2%	65.8%	2.0%	0%	16.9%	36.7%	46.4%	0%
Other	100%	83.5%	16.5%	38.1%	56.1%	5.9%	0%	18.0%	35.9%	41.3%	4.9%

Source: "Sex, race, and age, by the family relationship of murder victims and defendants, 1988," John M. Dawson and Patrick A. Langan, Ph.D., "Murder in Families," *Bureau of Justice Statistics Special Report*, July 1994, Table 2, p. 3. *Spouse* includes common-law spouse. *Offspring* includes grandchild and step-child. *Parent* includes grandparent and step-parent. *Sibling* includes step-sibling. *Other* includes cousin, in-law, extended family members, and other family members. Detail percentages may not add to total because of rounding.

★ 160 ★
Victims

Victimizations by Marital Status: 1991-I

This table shows the victimization rates for persons age 12 and over, by marital status of victims, in 1991.

[Rate per 1,000 persons age 12 or older.]

Sex and marital status	Total population	Crimes of violence	Completed violent crimes	Attempted violent crimes	Rape	Robbery		
						Total	With injury	Without injury
Female								
Never married	28,341,740	43.0	18.0	25.0	3.1	6.4	2.4	4.1
Married	54,656,280	11.1	3.7	7.4	0.3[1]	1.5	0.2[1]	1.3
Widowed	11,323,860	5.9	2.1[1]	3.9	0.2[1]	1.6[1]	0.8[1]	0.8[1]
Divorced or separated	11,883,130	45.0	20.9	24.0	3.9	7.6	2.9	4.7
Male								
Never married	32,351,190	79.7	30.3	49.4	0.2[1]	14.5	5.0	9.5
Married	56,241,990	18.5	5.7	12.7	0.2[1]	3.7	1.1	2.7
Widowed	2,151,010	7.8[1]	5.0[1]	2.8[1]	0.0[1]	3.9[1]	1.7[1]	2.2[1]
Divorced or separated	8,038,370	43.8	16.8	27.0	0.3[1]	9.9	3.8	6.2

Source: "Victimization rates for persons age 12 and over, by sex and marital status of victims and type of crime," U.S. Department of Justice, Bureau of Justice Statistics, *Criminal Victimization in the United States, 1991,* Table 13, p. 31. Detail may not add to total shown because of rounding. Excludes data on persons whose marital status was not ascertained. *Note:* 1. Estimate is based on about 10 or fewer sample cases.

★ 161 ★
Victims

Victimizations by Marital Status: 1991-II

This table shows the victimization rates for persons age 12 and over, by marital status of victims, in 1991.

[Rate per 1,000 persons age 12 or older.]

Sex and marital status	Assault			Crimes of theft	Completed theft	Attempted theft	Personal larceny	
	Total	Aggra-vated	Simple				With contact	Without contact
Female								
Never married	33.5	8.0	25.4	90.3	84.2	6.1	3.4	86.9
Married	9.3	2.4	6.9	44.4	41.2	3.2	1.5	42.8
Widowed	4.2	1.9[1]	2.3[1]	21.8	20.3	1.6[1]	4.5	17.3
Divorced or separated	33.4	7.7	25.7	73.9	69.7	4.3	4.1	69.9
Male								
Never married	65.0	24.0	41.0	97.4	91.9	5.5	3.5	93.9
Married	14.5	4.7	9.8	43.2	39.7	3.5	0.9	42.4

[Continued]

★ 161 ★

Victimizations by Marital Status: 1991-II

[Continued]

Sex and marital status	Assault			Crimes of theft	Com- pleted theft	At- tempted theft	Personal larceny	
	Total	Aggra- vated	Simple				With contact	Without contact
Widowed	3.9[1]	3.9[1]	0.0[1]	23.4	22.5	0.9[1]	5.0[1]	18.5
Divorced or separated	33.6	10.6	22.9	95.2	89.5	5.7	3.9	91.3

Source: "Victimization rates for persons age 12 and over, by sex and marital status of victims and type of crime," U.S. Department of Justice, Bureau of Justice Statistics, *Criminal Victimization in the United States, 1991*, Table 13, p. 31. Detail may not add to total shown because of rounding. Excludes data on persons whose marital status was not ascertained. *Note:* 1. Estimate is based on about 10 or fewer sample cases.

★ 162 ★
Victims

Victims of Violence, Relationship of Offender to Victim: 1991

This table shows the relationship of violent offenders to their victims in 1991. Nearly two-thirds of the women in prison for a violent offense had victimized a relative, intimate, or someone else they knew. Another third of the women had victimized a stranger, compared to half the men. Women who were in prison for homicide were almost twice as likely to have killed a husband, ex-husband, or boyfriend as a relative.

Relationship	% of violent State Prison inmates	
	Female	Male
Total	100.0%	100.0%
Close	35.7%	16.3%
Intimate	19.9%	6.8%
Relataive	15.9%	9.6%
Known	29.2%	33.2%
Well known	14.1%	14.6%
Acquaintance	10.8%	12.0%
By sight only	4.3%	6.5%
Strangers	35.1%	50.5%
Number of inmates	11,800	299,380

Source: "Relationship of violent offenders to their victims, by sex, 1991," Tracy L. Snell, "Survey of State Prison Inmates, 1991: Women in Prison," *Bureau of Justice Statistics Special Report*, March 1994, Table 3, p. 3. Excludes an estimated 16,778 inmates who did not report their relationship to the victim. Detail may not add to total because of rounding.

★ 163 ★

Victims

Victimizations: 1974-1990

This table shows the percent change in assaults, violent crime, and murder against women and men at various ages, between 1974 and 1990.

Crime and Age	Increase/decrease	
	Male	Female
Assaults, ages 20-24	-11.8%	+48.1%
Violent crime, ages 12-24	-6.0%	+18.0%
Violent crime, ages 20-24	-12.4%	+32.7%
Murders, age 65 and older	-5.6%	+29.9%

Source: U.S. Senate, Committee on the Judiciary, *One Hundred First Congress Second Session on Legislation to Reduce the Growing Problem of Violent Crime Against Women,* June 20, 1990, Part 1, Serial No. J-101-80, pp. 13-16.

★ 164 ★

Victims

Victimizations: 1987-1991

This table shows the average annual rate per 1,000 persons and average annual number of personal crime victimizations, by sex of victim, from 1987 to 1991. Women were less likely than men to become victims of violent crime, except for rape.

[Annual rate per 1,000 persons.]

Type of crime	Male	Female
Average annual rate of crime victimizations per 1,000 persons		
Crimes of violence	40.5	24.8
Rape	0.2	1.3
Completed	0.1	0.6
Attempted	0.1	0.7
Robbery	7.4	4.0
Completed	4.6	3.0
Attempted	2.7	1.0
Assault		
Aggravated	12.4	5.1
Simple	20.4	14.3

[Continued]

★ 164 ★

Victimizations: 1987-1991
[Continued]

Type of crime	Male	Female
Crimes of theft	71.6	64.2
Personal larceny		
With contact	2.3	3.1
Without contact	69.3	61.1
Average annual number of victimizations		
Crimes of violence	3,926,415	2,600,607
Rape	17,859	132,172
Completed	7,268	58,614
Attempted	10,590	73,558
Robbery	719,865	426,975
Completed	449,302	316,187
Attempted	270,562	106,788
Assault		
Aggravated	1,207,673	543,153
Simple	1,981,016	1,498,305
Crimes of theft	6,943,990	6,712,738
Personal larceny		
With contact	222,104	314,882
Without contact	6,721,886	6,397,855

Source: "Average annual rate per 1,000 persons and average annual number of personal crime victimizations, by sex of victim, 1987-91," Ronet Bachman, Ph.D.,, *Violence against Women: A National Crime Victimization Survey Report,* January 1994, U.S. Department of Justice, Table 1, p. 2. Detail may not add to total shown because of rounding.

★ 165 ★
Victims

Victimizations: 1991

This table shows the victimization rates for persons age 12 and over, by type of crime and sex of victims, in 1991. Rates of violent crime and theft victimizations were significantly higher for males than for females.

[Annual rate per 1,000 persons age 12 or older.]

Type of crime	Both sexes	Male	Female
All personal crimes	92.3	105.1	80.4
Crimes of violence	31.3	40.3	22.9
Completed	11.9	14.7	9.3
Attempted	19.4	25.6	13.5
Rape	0.8	0.2[1]	1.4
Completed	0.3	0.0[1]	0.6
Attempted	0.5	0.2[1]	0.8
Robbery	5.6	7.8	3.5
Completed	3.7	4.9	2.5
With injury	1.3	1.7	0.8
From serious assault	0.6	1.1	0.2[1]
From minor assault	0.6	0.6	0.6
Without injury	2.4	3.2	1.7
Attempted	1.9	2.9	1.0
With injury	0.6	0.9	0.4
From serious assault	0.3	0.5	0.1[1]
From minor assault	0.3	0.3	0.3
Without injury	1.3	2.0	0.6
Assault	24.9	32.4	17.9
Aggravated	7.8	11.5	4.4
Completed with injury	2.9	4.3	1.6
Attempted with weapon	4.9	7.2	2.9
Simple	17.0	20.9	13.4
Completed with injury	5.0	5.4	4.6
Attempted with weapon	12.0	15.5	8.8
Crimes of theft	61.0	64.8	57.5
Completed	56.9	60.5	53.6
Attempted	4.1	4.3	3.9
Personal larceny with contact	2.3	2.1	2.6
Purse snatching	0.7	0.1[1]	1.2
Pocket picking	1.7	2.0	1.4
Personal larceny without contact	58.7	62.7	54.9
Completed	54.7	58.5	51.3
Less than $50	21.2	20.9	21.6
$50 or more	30.7	35.2	26.6
Amount not available	2.7	2.4	3.1

[Continued]

★ 165 ★

Victimizations: 1991
[Continued]

Type of crime	Both sexes	Male	Female
Attempted	4.0	4.3	3.6
Population age 12 and over	205,344,910	98,929,210	106,415,700

Source: "Victimization rates for persons age 12 and over, by type of crime and sex of victims," U.S. Department of Justice, Bureau of Justice Statistics, *Criminal Victimization in the United States, 1991,* Table 3, p. 22. Detail may not add to total shown because of rounding. *Note:* 1. Estimate is based on about 10 or fewer sample cases.

★ 166 ★

Victims

Victims of Crime Act Funds Allocation, Spouse Abuse and Sexual Assault: 1986 and 1991

This table shows the distribution of Victims of Crime Act Assistance Funds for child abuse, spouse abuse, and sexual assault in 1986 and 1991.

[In millions of dollars.]

Type of crime	VOCA Assistance Funds	
	FY 1986	FY 1991
Child Abuse	$6.869	$12.835
Spouse Abuse	$11.932	$22.722
Sexual Assault	$8.26	$13.948

Source: "Distribution of VOCA Assistance Funds: Child Abuse/Spouse Abuse/Sexual Assault," U.S. Department of Justice, Office for Victims of Crime, *Report to Congress June 1994,* Figure 13, p. 34.

★ 167 ★

Victims

Victims of Crime Act Funds Allocation: 1990 and 1991

The Victims of Crime Act (VOCA) of 1984 provided funding to support essential assistance services to crime victims. As violent crime increased throughout the 1980s, Congress amended VOCA in 1988. One amendment required states to give special consideration to "previously underserved" victims of violent crime. This table shows how state grantees allocated 1990 and 1991 VOCA assistance awards for services by types of crimes. The 1988 VOCA Program Guidelines required each state to allocate at least 40% of each year's VOCA victim assistance grant to provide services to victims of sexual assault, domestic violence, child abuse, and previously underserved victims of violent crime, as identified by the state. States have most often identified victims of homicide, driving under the influence or driving while intoxicated (DUI/DWI) crashes, and physical assault as "previously underserved" victim populations.

Type of crime	VOCA Assistance Funds FY 1991		FY 1990	
	Percent	Amount	Percent	Amount
Domestic violence	35.2%	$22,630,810	35.0%	$22,722,100
Sexual assault	21.8%	$14,034,750	21.5%	$13,948,190
Child abuse	21.3%	$13,699,530	19.8%	$12,835,040
Undesignated crime	14.1%	$9,040,334	12.1%	$7,823,693
DWI/DUI	2.2%	$1,444,410	2.4%	$1,580,960
Homicide	3.7%	$2,403,092	4.2%	$2,745,788
Assault	1.6%	$1,037,902	2.3%	$1,515,001

Source: "Distribution of VOCA Assistance Funds by Type of Crime FY 1990-1991," U.S. Department of Justice, Office for Victims of Crime, *Report to Congress June 1994*, Figures 14 and 15, p. 34. 1.2% ($770,590) of VOCA assistance funds were awarded in 1990 to adults molested as children.

★ 168 ★

Victims

Victims of Crime Act Funds, Victims Served: 1990

This table shows the number and percent of primary victims served by the Victims of Crime Act, by type of victimization, in fiscal year 1990. The total number of primary victims served was 6,980.

Type of crime	Victims Served	
	Number	Percent
Domestic violence	4,463	63.9%
Child victim (physical)	929	13.3%
Child victim (sex)	518	7.4%
Survivors (homicide)	126	1.8%
Survivors (incest)	126	1.8%
Adult sex assault	110	1.6%

[Continued]

★ 168 ★

Victims of Crime Act Funds, Victims Served: 1990
[Continued]

Type of crime	Victims Served	
	Number	Percent
DWI/DUI	78	1.1%
Other	630	9.0%

Source: "Number of Primary Victims Served by Type of Victimization FY 1990=Total 6,980," U.S. Department of Justice, Office for Victims of Crime, *Report to Congress June 1994*, Figure 19, p. 43.

★ 169 ★
Victims

Victims of Larceny, Characteristics: 1987-1991

This table shows the average annual rate of personal larceny involving contact per 1,000 females age 12 or older, by various demographic characteristics of the victim, from 1987 through 1991.

[Annual rate per 1,000 persons age 12 or older.]

Victim characteristic	Rate
Total	3.1
Race	
White	2.6
Black	5.0
Other	4.5
Ethnicity	
Hispanic	5.8
Non-Hispanic	2.7
Age	
12-19	1.3
20-24	4.1
25-34	3.2
35-49	2.2
50-64	2.7
65 or over	3.2
Education	
Some high school or less	2.9
High school graduate	2.0
Some college	3.0
College graduate or more	5.1
Family income	
Less than $9,999	4.3

[Continued]

★ 169 ★

Victims of Larceny, Characteristics: 1987-1991

[Continued]

Victim characteristic	Rate
$10,000-$19,999	2.9
$20,000-$29,999	2.7
$30,000-$49,999	2.1
$50,000 or more	2.9
Marital status	
Never married	4.1
Married	1.9
Widowed	3.6
Divorced/separated	4.3
Location of residence	
Central city	6.4
Suburban	1.9
Rural	0.5

Source: "Average annual rate of personal larceny involving contact per 1,000 females age 12 or older, by demographic characteristics, 1987-91," Ronet Bachman, Ph.D.,, *Violence against Women: A National Crime Victimization Survey Report,* January 1994, U.S. Department of Justice, Table 4, p. 4. Also in source: Characteristics of personal larceny, such as value of property taken, location of incident, whether incident took place in daylight or dark, etc.

★ 170 ★

Victims

Victims of Rape

Some statistics about rape in America according to *A Life Without Fear.*

1. **One out of every four college women will be sexually assaulted.**

2. **One out of every eight women in America has been raped.**

3. Each year, **683,000 rapes occur in America, one every 46 seconds.**

4. **Twenty-nine percent of all rape victims are under the age of 11.** Thirty-two percent of all rape victims are between the ages of 11 and 17.

5. **Eighty-four percent of rape victims do not report the crime to police. Sixty-nine percent fear being blamed by others for causing the rape.**

6. Eight out of ten women know their attacker.

Source: Selected from Laura C. Martin, *A Life Without Fear: A Guide to Preventing Sexual Assault,* 1992.

★ 171 ★

Victims

Victims of Rape, America Versus Europe

This table shows how many times lower the rape rate was in various foreign countries than it was in the United States in 1990.

Country	Times lower than U.S. rate
Portugal	20
Japan	26
England	15
France	8
Italy	23
Greece	46

Source: Selected from *Fighting Crime in America: An Agenda for the 1990's,* A Majority Staff Report Prepared for the Use of the Committee on the Judiciary, United States Senate, March 12, 1991.

★ 172 ★

Victims

Victims of Violence Committed by Intimates: 1987-1992

This table shows the number of single-offender victimizations by intimates, the rate per 1,000 population, and the percent of all victimizations committed by intimates, for the years 1987-1992. During that period, the rate of violent victimizations committed by intimates varied little from the average annual rate of 5 per 1,000 for females and 0.5 per 1,000 for males.

Item and year	Females	Males
Number of single-offender victim-izations by intimates		
1987	405,640	31,685
1988	585,261	55,877
1989	586,137	52,816
1990	531,179	26,737
1991	585,385	62,004
1992	593,546	49,038
Rate per 1,000 population		
1987	4.0	0.3
1988	5.5	0.6
1989	5.6	0.5
1990	5.0	0.2
1991	5.5	0.6
1992	5.5	0.5

[Continued]

★ 172 ★

Victims of Violence Committed by Intimates: 1987-1992
[Continued]

Item and year	Females	Males
Percent of all victimizations committed by intimates		
1987	27.0%	1.6%
1988	26.6%	2.1%
1989	28.1%	2.0%
1990	26.9%	1.1%
1991	27.4%	2.2%
1992	27.4%	2.2%

Source: U.S. Department of Justice, Bureau of Justice Statistics Selected Findings, *Domestic Violence: Violence Between Intimates*, November 1994, NCJ-149259, p. 3.

★ 173 ★
Victims

Victims of Violence, Characteristics: 1987-1991

This table shows the average annual rate of single-offender violent victimizations per 1,000 females, by victim-offender relationship and demographic characteristics, 1987-1991. While white and black women experienced about the same rate of violence committed against them by intimates and other relatives, black women were far more likely to suffer violence at the hands of acquaintances or strangers. Poor, less educated women were more likely to be victimized by intimates than were women who had higher family incomes and had graduated from college.

Characteristic	Rate of single-offender violent victimizations per 1,000 females in categories of victim-offender relationship			
	Intimate	Other relative	Acquaintance	Stranger
Total	5.4	1.1	7.6	5.4
Race				
White	5.4	1.2	7.2	5.1
Black	5.8	1.3	10.5	7.4
Other	3.6	0.7[1]	6.2	5.3
Ethnicity				
Hispanic	5.5	1.3	6.3	7.2
Non-Hispanic	5.4	1.1	7.7	5.3
Age				
12-19	5.8	2.3	21.7	8.0
20-24	15.5	1.5	14.3	11.6
25-34	8.8	1.1	7.3	6.5
35-49	4.0	1.2	5.2	4.6
50-64	0.9	0.4	1.9	2.6
65 or over	0.0[1]	0.2	0.7	1.1

[Continued]

★ 173 ★

Victims of Violence, Characteristics: 1987-1991
[Continued]

Characteristic	Rate of single-offender violent victimizations per 1,000 females in categories of victim-offender relationship			
	Intimate	Other relative	Acquaintance	Stranger
Education				
Some high school or less	5.3	1.7	11.8	4.9
High school graduate	6.1	0.7	5.3	4.2
Some college	6.4	1.2	6.8	8.0
College graduate or more	2.5	0.5	6.0	6.0
Family income				
Less than $9,999	11.4	2.0	12.7	7.7
$10,000-$19,999	6.7	1.4	7.9	5.8
$20,000-$29,999	5.9	0.9	7.8	4.6
$30,000-$49,999	2.7	0.7	5.8	4.4
$50,000 or more	1.6	0.5	4.6	4.2
Marital status				
Never married	7.1	1.7	16.6	10.0
Married	1.5	0.5	3.2	3.0
Widowed	0.7[1]	0.5	1.4	2.1
Divorced/separated	16.7	2.6	12.6	8.8
Location of residence				
Central city	6.5	1.1	9.5	8.8
Suburban	4.6	1.0	6.4	4.6
Rural	5.6	1.4	7.2	2.3

Source: "Average annual rate of single-offender violent victimizations per 1,000 females, by victim-offender relationship and demographic characteristics, 1987-91," Ronet Bachman, Ph.D.,, *Violence against Women: A National Crime Victimization Survey Report*, January 1994, U.S. Department of Justice, Table 11, p. 7. *Note:* 1. Estimate is based on 10 or fewer sample cases.

★ 174 ★

Victims

Victims of Violence, Involvement of Alcohol-I

The *Journal of Studies on Alcohol* reports on a study conducted to examine how spousal violence and women's alcoholism problems were related. Forty-five alcoholic women from local treatment agencies and Alcoholics Anonymous groups were compared to 40 non-alcoholic women selected randomly from households. It was found that alcoholic women had higher levels of "spouse-to-woman negative verbal interaction, moderate violence and severe violence." The journal article states that few studies have examined the victim's alcohol use in the context of violence. It also briefly summarizes other research on violence among married couples. Some highlights of the authors' study and the other research mentioned are summarized here.

1. In a random sample of 2,143 families in the United States, Straus et al.[1] found that 28% of marital couples experienced violence during the relationship.

2. Makepeace[2] reported in 1986 that one-fifth of college women sampled reported courtship violence.

3. Roscoe and Benaske[3] reported in 1985 that 50% of women in shelters in Michigan experienced courtship violence.

4. Kantor and Straus[4] reported in 1986 that 46% of severely assaulted women reported being drunk at least once during the survey year, compared to 36% of minor violence victims and 16% of nonvictimized women.

5. Lehmann and Krupp[5] reported that 72% of abused women admitted to a domestic violence center reported that their mates had a drinking problem and became abusive when drinking.

6. Kantor and Strauss[6] reported in 1986 that 70% of husbands who had severely assaulted their wives stated that they had been drunk at least once during the survey year, compared to 50% of husbands who had moderately assaulted their wives and 31% of husbands who did not assault their wives.

Some of the differences found between the samples of alcoholic versus what the authors refer to as household women:

7. The average age of the alcoholic sample was 39.44 years compared to the household women average age of 30.98 years.

8. Forty-one percent of the alcoholic sample derived most of their income from entitlements or unemployment compensation, compared to 10% of the household women.

9. The alcoholic sample reported a greater number of changes experienced in their childhood family (1.49 compared to 0.78). The changes were defined as parental divorce or separation, death in the family, and mother's or father's remarriage.

10. Seventy-one percent of alcoholic women reported having at least one alcoholic parent, compared to 23% of household women.

[Continued]

★ 174 ★

Victims of Violence, Involvement of Alcohol-I
[Continued]

11. Fifty-five percent of alcoholic women had spouses with alcohol problems, compared to 10% of household women.

Source: Selected from Brenda A. Miller, Ph.D., William R. Downs, Ph.D., and Dawn M. Gondoli, "Spousal Violence among Alcoholic Women as Compared to a Random Household Sample of Women," *Journal of Studies on Alcohol*, Vol. 50, No. 6, 1989, pp. 533-540. An earlier version of this article was presented at the 38th annual meeting of the American Society of Criminology, Atlanta, Georgia, October 1986. *Notes:* 1. Straus, M.A., Gelles, R.J., and Steinmetz, S.K. Behind Closed Doors: Violence in the American Family, New York: Doubleday & Co., Inc., 1980. 2. Makepeace, J.M. Gender differences in courtship violence victimization. Fam. Relat. 35: 383-388, 1986. 3. Roscoe, B., and Benaske, N. Courtship violence experienced by abused wives: Similarities in patterns of abuse. Fam. elat. 34: 419-424, 1985. 4. Kantor, G.K., and Straus, M.A. Substance abuse as a precipitant of family violence victimization. Amer. J. Drug Alcohol Abuse 15: 173-189, 1989. 5. Lehmann, N. and Krupp, S.L. Incidence of alcohol-related domestic violence: An assessment. Alcohol Hlth Res World 3 (No. 2): 23-27, 39, 1983/84. 6. Straus, M.A. and Gelles, R.J. Societal change and change in family violence from 1975 to 1985 as revealed by two national surveys. J. Marriage Fam. 48: 465-479, 1986.

★ 175 ★
Victims

Victims of Violence, Involvement of Alcohol-II

The *Journal of Studies on Alcohol* reports on a study conducted to examine how spousal violence and women's alcoholism problems were related. Forty-five alcoholic women from local treatment agencies and Alcoholics Anonymous groups were compared to 40 non-alcoholic women selected randomly from households. It was found that alcoholic women had higher levels of "spouse-to-woman negative verbal interaction, moderate violence and severe violence." This table shows the responses of the alcoholic women and what the authors refer to as the household women to questions about levels of conflict with spouses.

Response	Alcoholic	Household
Discuss issue calmly	80%	97%
Insulted or swore at women	80%	44%
Insulted or swore at women in sexual manner	40%	3%
Sulked or refused to talk	91%	69%
Stomped out	87%	64%
Cried	47%	23%
Said or did something to spite woman	87%	49%
Threatened abandonment	50%	13%
Threatened to hit or throw something	51%	13%

[Continued]

★ 175 ★

Victims of Violence, Involvement of Alcohol-II
[Continued]

Response	Alcoholic	Household
Threw, smashed, hit or kicked something	58%	26%
Threw something at women	29%	8%
Pushed or grabbed woman	60%	13%
Slapped woman	44%	5%
Kicked, hit, or hit with fist	27%	5%
Hit with object	27%	5%
Beaten up	24%	5%
Threatened life in some manner	26%	6%
Threatened with knife or gun	20%	5%
Used knife or gun	9%	0%

Source: Selected from Brenda A. Miller, Ph.D., William R. Downs, Ph.D., and Dawn M. Gondoli, "Spousal Violence among Alcoholic Women as Compared to a Random Household Sample of Women," *Journal of Studies on Alcohol*, Vol. 50, No. 6, 1989, pp. 533-540. An earlier version of this article was presented at the 38th annual meeting of the American Society of Criminology, Atlanta, Georgia, October 1986.

★ 176 ★
Victims

Victims of Violence, Police Action: 1987-1991

This table shows the percent distribution of single-offender victimizations against females where police came to the victim, by police response time and victim-offender relationship, 1987-1991. The table also shows the percent distribution of single-offender victimizations against females where police came to the crime scene, by police action and victim-offender relationship, 1987-1991. Police responded to more than three-quarters of reports by coming to the crime scene. Police were more likely to respond quickly if the offender was a stranger. While police took a report in more than two-thirds of incidents regardless of the relationship of the victim to the offender, they weere more likely to take a formal report if the offender was a stranger. The police were more likely to search the crime scene for evidence when the perpetrator was a stranger.

| Response | Percent of female victims of violence | | | | |
| | Total | Victim-offender relationship | | | |
		Intimate	Other relative	Acquaintance	Stranger
For those who indicated police visited crime scene, response time was[1]	100%	100%	100%	100%	100%
Within 5 minutes	28%	25%	24%	24%	36%
Within 10 minutes	28%	28%	33%	28%	28%
Within 1 hour	35%	37%	35%	38%	28%
Within 1 day	4%	4%	6%	6%	4%
Longer or don't know	5%	5%	2%	4%	4%
Type of response[2]					
Took report	72%	69%	67%	70%	77%
Took evidence for case	5%	2%	2%	3%	9%
Promised police surveillance	5%	4%	4%	5%	5%
Searched	15%	7%	8%	10%	29%

Source: "Percent distribution of single-offender violent victimizations where police came to female victim, by police response time and victim-offender relationship, 1987-91," and "Percent distribution of single-offender violent victimizations against females where police came to crime scene, by police action and victim-offender relationship, 1987-91," Ronet Bachman, Ph.D.,, *Violence against Women: A National Crime Victimization Survey Report,* January 1994, U.S. Department of Justice, Tables 17 and 18, p. 10. See table entitled, "Victims, Reasons for Reporting Crime to Police" for percentages of victims who reported violent crime to police. *Notes:* 1. Detail may not add to 100% because of rounding and because some respondents who called police did not respond to the question. 2. Because this is a multiple response question, totals to not sum to 100%.

★ 177 ★

Victims

Victims of Violence, Reasons for Reporting Crime: 1987-1991

This table shows the percent of female victims who reported single-offender violent crimes to police and the most important reason why the crime was or was not reported, by victim-offender relationship, 1987-1991. Although the percentage of female victims who reported their victimizations to police did not depend on their relationship to the offender, the reasons given for not reporting an incident did. Female victims who knew the perpetrator most often did not report the incident because they believed it was a personal matter. When a crime committed by a stranger was not reported, it was most often because the victim felt the incident was minor. Nearly six times as many women who were victimized by intimates as those victimized by strangers did not report the incident to the police because of fear of reprisal.

| Whether reported and reasons why or why not | Percent of female victims of violence | | | | |
| | Total | Victim-offender relationship | | | |
		Intimate	Other relative	Acquaintance	Stranger
Reported to police	52%	56%	58%	45%	55%
Most important reason for NOT reporting					
Total	100%	100%	100%	100%	100%
Private or personal matter	39%	33%	43%	48%	20%
It was a minor incident	20%	6%	8%	17%	28%
Police couldn't do anything	3%	1%[1]	0%	1%	12%
Police wouldn't do anything	10%	13%	3%	7%	11%
Didn't want to get offender in trouble	5%	9%	15%	3%	1%[1]
Afraid of reprisal from offender	7%	18%	11%	6%	3%
Other	16%	20%	20%	18%	25%
Most important reason for reporting					
Total	100%	100%	100%	100%	100%
To stop or prevent this from happening to me or to others	22%	28%	28%	20%	15%
To recover loss-insurance	4%	2%	1%[1]	3%	8%
To punish offender	46%	50%	40%	46%	43%
It was my duty	4%	2%	0%	3%	7%

Source: "Percent of female victims reporting single-offender violent crime to police and the most important reason for reporting or not reporting, by victim-offender relationship, 1987-91," Ronet Bachman, Ph.D.,, *Violence against Women: A National Crime Victimization Survey Report*, January 1994, U.S. Department of Justice, Table 15, p. 9. Detail may not add to 100% because of rounding. *Note:* 1. Estimate is based on 10 or fewer sample cases.

★ 178 ★
Victims

Victims of Violence, Relationship of Offender to Victim: 1987-1991-I

This table shows the average annual number and average annual rate per 1,000 population of single-offender violent victimizations for the years 1987-1991. Females experienced more than 10 times as many incidents of violence by an intimate annually than males. While women are less likely to become victims of violent crime than men, they are more likely to be victimized by intimates such as husbands or boyfriends.

[Rate is per 1,000 population.]

Victim-offender relationship	Sex of victim	
	Female	Male
Annual number		
Intimate	572,032	48,983
Other relative	117,201	75,587
Acquaintance	796,067	1,268,506
Stranger	571,114	1,182,307
Annual rate		
Intimate	5.0	0.5
Other relative	1.0	0.7
Acquaintance	8.0	13.0
Stranger	5.0	12.0

Source: "Average annual number of single-offender violent victimizations, 1987-91," and "Average annual rate per 1,000 population of single-offender violent victimizations, 1987-91," U.S. Department of Justice, Bureau of Justice Statistics Selected Findings, *Domestic Violence: Violence Between Intimates,* November 1994, NCJ-149259, p. 2. Primary source: BJS, *Violence Against Women: A National Crime Victimization Survey Report,* 1994.

★ 179 ★
Victims

Victims of Violence, Relationship of Offender to Victim: 1987-1991-II

This table shows the percent of all victims of violence who were female, by victim-offender relationship, for the years 1987-1991.

Victim-offender relationship	Female percent. of all victims
Intimate	
Spouse	93%
Boyfriend/girlfriend	91%
Ex-spouse	89%

[Continued]

★ 179 ★

Victims of Violence, Relationship of Offender to Victim: 1987-1991-II
[Continued]

Victim-offender relationship	Female percent. of all victims
Other relatives	
Child	78%
Brother/sister	59%
Other relative	57%
Parent	52%
Unspecified	28%
Other known offender	38%
Stranger	32%

Source: U.S. Department of Justice, Bureau of Justice Statistics Selected Findings, *Domestic Violence: Violence Between Intimates*, November 1994, NCJ-149259, p. 2. Primary source: *Highlights from 20 Years of Surveying Crime Victims: The National Crime Victimization Survey, 1973-92*, 1993.

★ 180 ★
Victims

Victims of Violence, Selected Countries

This table gives numbers on crimes against women around the world.

Country and item	Number
U.S. women using emergency medical services for injuries related to battering, annually	1,000,000
Canadian girls who will be sexually assaulted before reaching age 17	1 in 4
Indian women burned to death by husbands and in-laws seeking higher dowries, annually	5,000
Estimates of how many of Thailand's 2,000,000 prostitutes are children	800,000
Estimates of how many of Thailand's prostitutes are HIV-positive	> 40%

[Continued]

★ 180 ★

Victims of Violence, Selected Countries
[Continued]

Country and item	Number
Estimate of how many women in Kenya have undergone circumcision	> 6,000,000
Estimate of how many circumcised Kenyan females die from bleeding or infection	15%
Estimate of how many women in Africa now living have undergone circumcision	100,000,000
Estimate of how many girls and women are circumcised in Africa annually	2,000,000
Number of African countries where female circumcision is common	26
Incidence rate of female circumcision in Somalia	90%
Incidence rate of female circumcision in Mali	75%
Ratio of females to every 1,000 males in India in 1991, attributed to selective abortion, female infanticide, withholding of medical care and food from females, and violence	929

Source: Selected from "Crimes Against Women," by Anne Reifenberg, *Dallas Morning News.* Reprinted in the *Detroit Free Press*, June 13, 1993, p. 1F +.

★ 181 ★
Victims

Victims of Violent Crimes, Characteristics: 1987-1991

This table shows the average annual rate for crimes of violence per 1,000 females age 12 or older, by various demographic characteristics of the victim, from 1987 through 1991. Black females were more than twice as likely to experience a robbery as white females. Hispanic females were more likely to experience a robbery, but all females were equally likely to experience other violent crimes. Women age 20-24 were the most likely to be victims of all kinds of violent crimes.

[Annual rate per 1,000 persons age 12 or older.]

Victim characteristic	Total	Rape	Robbery	Aggravated assault	Simple assault
Total		1.3	4.0	5.1	14.3
Race					
White	23.8	1.1	3.4	4.8	14.4
Black	32.3	2.0	8.7	7.6	13.8
Other	23.2	1.3	3.9	4.8	13.0
Ethnicity					
Hispanic	29.3	1.1	6.6	7.0	14.6
Non-Hispanic	24.4	1.2	3.8	5.0	14.3
Age					
12-19	31.1	1.8	3.4	6.1	19.5
20-24	52.1	3.1	7.6	10.9	30.3
25-34	28.5	1.5	5.3	5.9	15.7
35-49	18.5	0.7	3.1	4.0	10.7
50-64	7.8	0.2	2.1	1.6	3.8
65 or over	3.5	0.1[1]	1.3	0.9	1.2
Education					
Some high school or less	31.8	1.5	4.5	7.1	18.6
High school graduate	20.0	1.1	3.5	4.1	11.3
Some college	28.1	1.6	4.6	6.1	15.8
College graduate or more	18.2	1.0	3.6	2.8	10.9
Family income					
Less than $9,999	42.9	2.4	7.4	10.1	22.9
$10,000-$19,999	27.3	1.4	4.6	5.7	15.6
$20,000-$29,999	23.6	1.0	3.0	5.0	14.5
$30,000-$49,999	17.3	1.0	2.2	3.0	11.3
$50,000 or more	15.1	0.5	2.1	2.8	9.5
Marital status					
Never married	46.6	2.9	7.3	9.1	27.0
Married	11.1	0.3	1.8	2.7	6.3
Widowed	6.8	0.3	2.1	1.6	2.6
Divorced/separated	55.2	2.8	8.8	11.0	32.5

[Continued]

★ 181 ★

Victims of Violent Crimes, Characteristics: 1987-1991
[Continued]

Victim characteristic	Total	Rape	Robbery	Aggravated assault	Simple assault
Location of residence					
Central city	34.4	2.0	7.6	7.3	17.3
Suburban	20.6	0.9	2.6	4.1	12.9
Rural	20.1	0.9	1.9	4.3	12.8

Source: "Average annual rate for crimes of violence per 1,000 females age 12 or older, by demographic characteristics, 1987-91," Ronet Bachman, Ph.D., *Violence against Women: A National Crime Victimization Survey Report*, January 1994, U.S. Department of Justice, Table 3, p. 3. *Note:* 1. Estimate is based on 10 or fewer sample cases.

★ 182 ★
Victims

Victims, Characteristics: 1987-1991

This table shows the average annual rate of personal crimes per 1,000 persons age 12 or older for females and males, by various demographic characteristics of the victim, from 1987 through 1991. Black and Hispanic females were more likely to experience a crime of violence than were white and non-Hispanic females. Non-Hispanic females and males were victims of higher rates of theft crimes than were female and male Hispanics. White females had higher theft victimization rates than black females, but the reverse was true for males. Younger females and males were more likely than older persons to experience violent and theft victimizations. Females and males with lower incomes experienced more crimes of violence than did females and males with higher family incomes.

[Annual rate per 1,000 persons age 12 or older.]

Victim characteristic	Male		Female	
	Crimes of violence	Crimes of theft	Crimes of violence	Crimes of theft
Total	40.5	71.6	24.8	64.2
Race				
White	38.6	71.0	23.8	65.2
Black	55.9	76.7	32.3	58.8
Other	38.7	71.8	23.2	57.8
Ethnicity				
Hispanic	49.5	67.8	29.3	60.3
Non-Hispanic	39.7	71.9	24.4	64.4
Age				
12-19	97.1	114.0	31.1	64.1
20-24	87.3	126.2	52.1	108.6
25-34	43.8	85.8	28.5	63.9
35-49	24.9	61.2	18.5	63.1

[Continued]

★ 182 ★

Victims, Characteristics: 1987-1991
[Continued]

Victim characteristic	Male		Female	
	Crimes of violence	Crimes of theft	Crimes of violence	Crimes of theft
50-64	10.8	40.1	7.8	37.0
65 or over	5.0	20.1	3.5	19.5
Education				
Some high school or less	54.2	66.2	31.8	58.8
High school graduate	33.4	58.7	20.0	47.9
Some college	48.5	92.7	28.1	82.9
College graduate or more	22.9	78.4	18.2	86.8
Family income				
Less than $9,999	69.0	79.5	42.9	59.5
$10,000-$19,999	45.3	65.2	27.3	59.5
$20,000-$29,999	37.9	69.3	23.6	63.8
$30,000-$49,999	32.5	70.5	17.3	65.2
$50,000 or more	28.8	76.6	15.1	77.7
Marital status				
Never married	78.8	110.6	46.6	101.1
Married	18.5	47.9	11.1	49.4
Widowed	12.7	33.5	6.8	24.8
Divorced/separated	51.1	95.3	55.2	62.1
Location of residence				
Central city	55.9	90.2	34.4	79.1
Suburban	36.1	71.1	20.6	65.1
Rural	29.1	47.9	20.1	41.1

Source: "Average annual rate of personal crimes per 1,000 persons age 12 or older for males and females, by demographic characteristics, 1987-91," Ronet Bachman, Ph.D., *Violence against Women: A National Crime Victimization Survey Report*, January 1994, U.S. Department of Justice, Table 2, p. 2.

★ 183 ★
Victims

Victims, Race: 1987-1991

This table shows the race of female victims of a single violent offender, by the type of crime and the race of the offender as reported by the victim, 1987-1991. Violent crime against women tended to be intra-racial. Robbery of white females was the victimization most often inter-racial, and the victim was just as likely to have been victimized by a black robber as a white robber.

| Type of crime and race of victim | Percent of single-offender violent victimizations | | | | |
| | Total | Perceived race of offender | | | |
		White	Black	Other	Not known or ascertained
Crimes of violence					
White	100%	80%	13%	5%	2%
Black	100%	4%	89%	6%	1%[1]
Rape					
White	100%	78%	15%	4%	3%
Black	100%	1%[1]	98%	0%[1]	5%[1]
Robbery					
White	100%	40%	43%	12%	5%
Black	100%	5%	88%	5%	2%
Aggravated assault					
White	100%	83%	8%	7%	1%[1]
Black	100%	12%	83%	5%	1%[1]
Simple assault					
White	100%	87%	5%	6%	1%[1]
Black	100%	5%	89%	5%	1%[1]

Source: "Race of female victims of a single violent offender, by the type of crime and perceived race of the offender, 1987-91," Ronet Bachman, Ph.D., *Violence against Women: A National Crime Victimization Survey Report,* January 1994, U.S. Department of Justice, Table 8, p. 6. Detail may not add to 100% because of rounding. *Note:* 1. Estimate is based on 10 or fewer sample cases.

★ 184 ★
Victims

Victims, Weapons Present and Injuries Sustained: 1987-1991

This table shows the percent of single-offender violent crime victimizations where a weapon was present, and the percent that resulted in injuries, medical care, and hospital care, by victim-offender relationship, 1987-1991. A woman who was victimized by a stranger was more likely to face an armed offender than was a woman victimized by an intimate, relative, or acquaintance. Guns were the weapon of choice of strangers. Knives or other sharp instruments were chosen by intimates and other relatives. When the offender was an intimate, women were nearly twice as likely to be injured and were more likely to require medical care.

Item	Percent of female victims of violence				
	Total	Victim-offender relationship			
		Intimate	Other relative	Acquain-tance	Stranger
Weapon present	27%	18%	22%	21%	33%
Type of weapon used					
Total	100%	100%	100%	100%	100%
Guns	30%	34%	19%	23%	38%
Knives/sharp instruments	34%	40%	41%	36%	35%
Blunt objects	18%	12%	16%	20%	14%
Other weapons	18%	15%	24%	22%	13%
Injury	34%	59%	48%	31%	27%
Serious	3%	3%	3%	3%	2%
Minor	31%	56%	45%	28%	25%
Received medical care	19%	27%	20%	14%	14%
Rece	9%	15%	10%	8%	8%

Source: "Percent of single-offender violent crime victimizations where weapon was present, by victim-offender relationship, 1987-1991," and "Percent of single-offender violent crime victimizations resulting in injuries, medical care, and hospital care for female victims, by victim-offender relationship, 1987-1991," Ronet Bachman, Ph.D., *Violence against Women: A National Crime Victimization Survey Report*, January 1994, U.S. Department of Justice, Tables 13 and 14, p. 8. Serious injuries include gunshot or knife wounds, broken bones, loss of teeth, internal injuries, loss of consciousness, and undetermined injuries requiring 2 or more days of hospitalization. Minor injuries include bruises, black eyes, cuts, scratches, swelling, and undetermined injuries requiring less than 2 days of hospitalization. Medical care refers to any care or treatment given for injuries by a medical provider, a nonmedical person, or by the victim herself.

★ 185 ★

Victims

Violence Against Women

Some national statistics on violence against women.

1. Domestice violence is the **number one** cause of injury to women between the ages of 15 and 44 in the U.S., surpassing injuries caused by automobile accidents, muggings, and rapes combined.

2. **One in eight** women will be raped during their lifetime. There are more than **683,000** forcible rapes of American women annually.

3. **Every fifteen seconds**, an American woman is beaten.

4. A minimum of **2.5 million** American women annually experience violence.

5. More than **two-thirds** of incidents of violence against women are committed by someone they know.

6. About **1,500** American women (**4 per day**) are killed each year by their partners.

7. There are almost three times as many animal shelters in this country as there are shelters for battered women and their children.

8. Battered women are more likely to miscarry or give birth to low-birth-weight babies.

9. Domestic violence costs between **$5 billion and $10 billion** annually in health care costs, lost wages, litigation and imprisonment of batterers and juveniles who commit crimes because of their abusive home life.

10. Nearly **one-third** of survivors of rape develop Post-Traumatic Stress Disorder. They are **13 times** more likely to have serious alcohol problems. They are **26 times** more likely to have major drug problems.

11. More than **one-half** of homeless women are escaping domestic violence.

Source: "The Consequences of Violence Against Women," The Ryka ROSE Foundation, *What Every Woman Needs to Know About Violence Against Women,* pamphlet. Primary sources: 1. Surgeon General, United States, 1992. 2. National Victim Center, 1992. 3. Federal Bureau of Investigation, 1991. 4. U.S. Department of Justice, 1994. 5. U.S. Department of Justice. 6. Federal Bureau of Investigation, 1992. 7. U.S. Senate Judiciary Hearings, 1990. 8. March of Dimes, 1992. 9. Dr. Richard Gelles, American Medical News, 1992. 10. National Victim Center. 11. U.S. Senate Judiciary Committee.

★ 186 ★

Victims

Violence Against Women Worldwide

This table presents statistics on violence against women compiled by the United Nations Secretariat's Division for the Advancement of Women in the mid-1980s.

Item	Number/Percent
Austria	
Percentage of 1,500 divorce cases in 1985 where domestic violence against the wife was cited as a contributing factor:	59%
Of those instances, percentage of wives who called the police in response to battering:	
Working-class wives	38%
Middle-class wives	13%
Upper-class wives	4%
Colombia	
Number of 1,170 cases of bodily injury in 1982 and 1983 determined to be due to conjugal violence	1 of 5
Percentage of cases hospitalized who were battered women	94%
India	
Registered cases of dowry deaths:	
1985	999
1986	1,319
1987	1,786
Kuwait	
Responses of 153 Kuwaiti women to a survey about violence:	
Ever been assaulted?	33%
Percent who had friends or relatives who were victims of assault.	80%
Thailand	
Percent of malnourished children at a Bangkok rehabilitation center treated in the first half of 1985 who were from families where the "mother was regularly beaten by her spouse."	25%

[Continued]

★ 186 ★

Violence Against Women Worldwide
[Continued]

Item	Number/Percent
Percent of married women in Bangkok's largest slum and construction sites who were regularly beaten by their spouses:	> 50%

Source: Selected from *The World's Women: Trends and Statistics 1970-1990*, United Nations, 1991, p. 19.

★ 187 ★
Victims

Violence Toward Spouse

Some national statistics on domestic violence.

1. In 1985, more than **1,300** women were killed by a husband or boyfriend. This was **30%** of the total murders of females. **Six percent** of male homicide victims were killed by wives or girlfriends.

2. About **37%** of pregnant women are physically abused.

3. **Four million** women are severely beaten annually.

4. More than **one-third** of assaults against women involve punching, kicking, choking, beating up, or using a weapon such as a gun or a knife.

5. Between **one-fifth** and **one-third** of all women will be physically assaulted by their mate during their lifetime.

6. The rate of injuries to women from beatings exceeds the rate incurred in automobile accidents and muggings combined.

7. About **95%** of battering victims are women.

8. **Twenty-one percent** of all women who make use of hospital emergency surgery services are battered women.

Source: "National Statistics on Domestic Violence," Nancy Kilgore, *Every Eighteen Seconds: A Journey Through Domestic Violence*, 1992, pp.79-80. Primary sources: 1. Federal Bureau of Investigation. (1986). *Uniform Crime Reports: Crime in the United States*, 1985. Washington, DC: U.S. Department of Justice. 2. Helton A, McFarlane, J, Anderson E. "Battered and pregnant: A prevalence study." *Am J Public Health*, 1987: 77: 1337-1993. 3. Langan P, Innes CA. *Preventing Domestic Violence Against Women*. Washington, DC: U.S. 4. Department of Justice, Bureau of Justice Statistics: 1986. 5. Frieze I H, Browne A: "Violence in marriage." In: Ohlin L, Tonry M, eds. *Family Violence: Crime and Justice*, a Review of Research. Chicago, Ill: University of Chicago Press; 1989: 163-218. 6. McClear SV, Anwar RA. "The role of the emergency physician in the prevention of domestic violence." *Ann Emerg Med*. 1987: 16: 1155-1161) 7. Bureau of Justice Statistics, "Report to the Nation on Crime and Justice: The Data," Washington, DC: Office of Justice Programs, U.S. Department of Justice, October 1983. 8. Stark, E. *Wife abuse in the medical setting: an introduction for health personnel*. (Monograph ser. No 7) Rockville, MD, National Clearinghouse on Domestic Violence, April 1981).

Chapter 4

DOMESTIC LIFE

Allocation of Time

★ 188 ★

Contribution of Housework to Worldwide Gross Domestic Product

This table gives estimates of how much would be added to the gross domestic product if women's unpaid housework were included. Footnotes describe the sponsoring organization or researcher who made the estimates.

Country	Year	Value of unpaid housework as % of GDP
All women **Developed regions**		
Canada[1]	1961	27%
	1971	28%
Denmark[2]	1949	50%
Finland[3]	1979	31%
France[4]	1975	24%
Norway[5]	1972	41%
	1981	28%
United States[6]	1929	25%
	1960	29%
	1970	27%
	1975	30%
	1980[8]	23%
Developing regions		
India[7]	1970	33%

[Continued]

★ 188 ★

Contribution of Housework to Worldwide Gross Domestic Product
[Continued]

Country	Year	Value of unpaid housework as % of GDP
Pakistan[8]	1975	35%
Philippines[9]	1982	11%
Houswives not economically active		
Chile[10]	1981	15%
Japan[11]	1955	11%
	1970	9%
Venezuela[12]	1982	22%

Source: "Estimates of addition to GDP if women's unpaid housework were included," *The World's Women: Trends and Statistics 1970-1990*, United Nations, 1991, Table 6.17, p. 95. Primary source: Compiled by Luisella Goldschmidt-Clermont as consultant to the United Nations Secretariat, based on the sources outlined in the footnotes below. Methods of valuation based on equivalent market wages or services were used except in the case of Japan, where overall average female wage was used. *Notes:* 1. H.J. Adler and D. Hawrylshyn, "Estimates of the value of household work, Canada, 1961 and 1971," *Review of Income and Wealth* (New Haven, USA, December 1978). 2. Statistics Department, "Nationalproduktet og national-indkomsten 1946-1949," in *Statistiske Meddelelser* (Copenhagen), Series 4, Vol. 140, Fasc. 2 (1951). 3. Ministry of Social Affairs and Health, Research Department, 1980-86, *Housework Study*, Parts I to XIV, Sepcial Social Studies, Official Statistics of Finland (Helsinki, 1980/86). 4. A. Chadeau and A. Fouquet, "Peut-on measurer le travail domestique?" *Economie et statistique* (Paris), No. 136 (1981); A. Chadeau, "Measuring household production, conceptual issues and results for France," report to the Second ECE/INSTRAW, Joint Meeting on Statistics of Women, CES/AC.60/44 (Geneva, 1989). 5. A.L. Brathaug and A.B. Dahle, 1989, "Verdiskapning i husholdningene," paper presented at the seminar "Kvinner og okonomi," held at Bergen 5-7 October 1989. 6. S. Kuznets, *National Income and Its Composition, 1919-1938*, Publication No. 40, 2 vols. (New York, National Bureau of Economic Research, 1941); M. Murphy, "The value of non-market household production: opportunity cost vs market cost estimates," *Review of Income and Wealth* (New Haven, USA, September 1978); M. Weinrobe, "Household production and national production: an improvement of the record," *Review of Income and Wealth* (New Haven, USA, March 1974); J. Peskin, "The value of household work in the 1980s," in *Proceedings* of the Social Statistics Section of the American Statistical Association Meeting, held at Toronto, Canada, 15-18 August 1983. 7. M. Mukherjee, "Contributions to and use of social product by women," in *Tyranny of the Household*, D. Jain and N. Banerjee, eds. (Delhi, Shakti Books/Vikas). 8. T. Alauddin, "Contribution of housewives to GNP: a case study of Pakistan," M.S. thesis (Vanderbilt University, Nashville, USA, 1980). Data from one or a small number of major cities only. 9. National Commission on the Role of Filipino Women, "Quantification of housework," NCRFW monograph No. 4 (Manila, 1985). 10. V.L. Pardo and N.P. Cruz, "La duena de casa en sus actividades de trabajo; su valoracion en el mercado y dentro del hogar," Documento Serie Investigacion, No. 59 (Santiago, Universidad de Chile, Departamento de Economia, 1983). Data from one or a small number of major cities only. 11. Economic Council, Net National Welfare Measurement Committee, *Measuring Net National Welfare in Japan* (Tokyo, 1973). 12. T.H. Valecillos et al., "Division del trabajo, distribucion personal del tiempo diario y valor economico, del trabajo realizado en los hogares Venezolanos" (Caracas, Banco Central de Venezuela, 1983). Data from one or a small number of major cities only.

★ 189 ★

Allocation of Time

Help with the Chores

This table presents some statistics on housework, reported on in the St. Louis *Post-Dispatch*. The article quotes Peggy Guest, who teaches Psychology of Women at Washington University: "So many women still feel they're responsible for the way the house looks."

Item	Number/Percent
Report on University of Missouri researcher David Demo's findings, released 9/93:	
Average number of hours spent on housework:	
Women who worked more than 30 hours a week on a job outside the home:	40-44 hours
Men	13 hours
Mother's contribution of time needed for household tasks in all types of families:	68-95%
Women's contribution to yard work:	31%

Source: Selected from Florence Shinkle, "The Chore Wars," *Post-Dispatch*, January 30, 1994, pp. 1C+.

★ 190 ★

Allocation of Time

Time Spent Getting Water in Developing Countries

This table shows the number of hours per week spent drawing and carrying water by women in selected developing countries.

Country	Hours per week
Africa	
Botswana	
rural areas	5.5
Burkina Faso	
Zimtenga region	4.4
Cote d'Ivoire	
rural farmers	4.4
Ghana	
northern farms	4.5

[Continued]

★ 190 ★

Time Spent Getting Water in Developing Countries
[Continued]

Country	Hours per week
Kenya	
villages	
dry season	4.2
wet season	2.2
Mozambique	
villages	
dry season	15.3
wet season	2.9
Senegal	
farming village	17.5
Asia	
India	
Baroda region	7.0
Nepal	
villages	
girls aged 5-9	1.5
girls aged 10-14	4.9
girls aged 15+	4.7
Pakistan	
village survey	3.5

Source: "Women in many developing regions must spend hours each week drawing and carrying water," *The World's Women: Trends and Statistics 1970-1990*, United Nations, 1991, Table 5.6, p. 75. Primary source: Compiled by the Statistical Office of the United Nations Secretariat from local survey studies and reports.

★ 191 ★

Allocation of Time

Time Spent on Activities Worldwide-I

This table shows hours per week spent on economic activity, unpaid housework, child care, and personal care and free time, by men and women in selected countries, latest available year.

[NA Not available.]

Country	Year	Economic activity		Unpaid housework						Personal care and free time	
				Household chores		Child care		Total			
		Women	Men	Women	Men	Women	Men	Women	Men	Women	Men
North America and Australia											
Australia[1]	1987	16.9	35.5	27.2	13.8	5.8	1.6	33.0	15.3	118	117
Canada[2]	1986	17.5	32.9	24.6	12.1	4.3	1.4	28.9	13.5	121	121

[Continued]

★ 191 ★

Time Spent on Activities Worldwide-I
[Continued]

Country	Year	Economic activity		Unpaid housework						Personal care and free time	
				Household chores		Child care		Total			
		Women	Men	Women	Men	Women	Men	Women	Men	Women	Men
United States[3]	1986	24.5	41.3	29.9	17.4	2.0	0.8	31.9	18.1	112	109
Western Europe											
Belgium[4]	1966	19.3	50.8	34.7	6.0	3.6	0.8	38.4	6.9	110	111
Finland[5]	1979	21.8	30.0	22.5	10.8	3.0	0.9	25.6	11.7	122	125
France[6]	1965	21.7	51.8	35.0	9.9	7.6	1.3	42.6	11.3	104	105
Germany Fed. Rep. of Germany[7]	1965	13.3	42.4	39.3	10.2	4.9	0.9	44.2	11.1	111	115
Netherlands[8]	1980	7.1	23.9	27.9	7.4	5.5	1.5	33.4	8.8	130	135
Norway[9]	1981	17.1	34.2	25.1	7.1	4.8	2.0	29.8	9.2	121	125
United Kingdom[10]	1984	14.1	26.8	26.4	10.3	3.6	1.1	30.0	11.4	124	130
Eastern Europe and USSR											
Bulgaria[11]	1988	37.7	46.9	29.3	14.3	4.3	1.1	33.7	15.3	97	106
Czechoslovakia[12]	1965	29.8	44.4	36.0	12.7	4.7	2.5	40.7	15.1	97	109
Hungary[13]	1976	26.7	41.5	30.2	10.9	3.0	1.4	33.3	12.3	108	114
Poland[14]	1984	24.9	42.2	30.5	7.7	4.4	2.0	34.9	9.7	108	116
Yugoslavia[15]	1965	19.5	49.5	37.0	8.1	3.8	1.4	40.7	9.5	108	109
USSR[16]	1986	38.5	49.0	25.7	14.6	4.4	1.5	30.1	16.1	99	103
Latin America											
Guatemala[17]	1977	29.4	56.7	39.9	6.3	9.8	4.6	49.7	10.9	89	101
Peru[18]	1966	15.1	52.1	36.0	5.6	4.5	0.5	40.5	6.1	112	110
Venezuela[19]	1983	15.5	42.2	28.2	3.0	4.0	0.7	32.2	3.7	120	122

[Continued]

★ 191 ★

Time Spent on Activities Worldwide-I
[Continued]

Country	Year	Economic activity		Unpaid housework						Personal care and free time	
				Household chores		Child care		Total			
		Women	Men	Women	Men	Women	Men	Women	Men	Women	Men
Asia											
Indonesia Java[20]	1973	41.3	55.3	28.9	3.0	7.2	2.6	36.1	5.6	NA	NA
Nepal[21]	1979	32.3	40.7	38.5	10.8	4.8	1.1	43.3	11.9	NA	NA

Source: Selected from "Indicators on time use," *The World's Women: Trends and Statistics 1970-1990*, United Nations, 1991, Table 7, p. 101. Primary source: Compiled by Andrew Harvey as consultant to the United Nations Secretariat, from national reports and studies outlined in the footnotes below. *Notes:* 1. Time Use Pilot Survey, 1987, Australian Bureau of Statistics. 2. General Social Survey—Time Use Study, 1986, Statistics Canada. 3. Study of Americans' Use of Time, 1986, Survey Research Center (University of Maryland). 4. Multinational Time-Budget Project, 1965, Sociological Institute (Free University of Brussels). 5. Time Use Study, 1987, Central Statistical Office of Finland. 6. 1985/86 Time Use Survey. 7. Multinational Time-Budget Project, 1965, Institute for Comparative Social Research (University of Cologne); Multinational Time-Budget Project-- Osnabruck, 19675, Institute for Social Research (Dortmund); Multinational Time-Budget Project, 1965, Hoyerswerda, and Time-Budget Study, 1972, Institute for Living Standard and Consumption, University of Economic Sciences (Berlin); Time Use Study, 1974, 1980, and 1985, State Central Administration of Statistics (Berlin). Pre-unification. 8. National Time Use Survey, 1980, Social and Cultural Planning Bureau. 9. Time Budget Survey, 1980/81, Central Bureau of Statistics. 10. National Time Use Study, 1975, British Broadcasting Corporation. 11. Time Use in Bulgaria, 1985, Institute of Sociology; Time Use in Bulgaria, 1988, Central Statistical Office. 12. Multinational Time-Budget Project, 1965, Sociological Laboratory (Polytechnical Institute, Prague); Survey on Family Budget Statistics. 13. Time-Budget Survey, 1976/77, Central Statistical Office. 14. Time-Budget Survey of Working People in Poland, 1984, Central Statistical Office. 15. Multinational Time-Budget Project, 1965, Institute of Sociology (Belgrade); Multinational Time-Budget Project—Maribor and Surroundings, 1965; Institute of Philosophy and Sociology, University of Ljubljana. 16. Time Use in Pskov, 1986, USSR Academy of Sciences. 17. Family Time Use in Four Villages in Highland Guatemala, 1977, James Loucky. 18. Multinational Time-Budget Project, 1966, Political and Social Science Institute (Catholic University of Louvain), Rudolf Rezsohazy. 19. Division of Labour, Time Diary and Economic Value of Work Performed in Households in Venezuela, Central Bank of Venezuela, 1982. 20. Time Use of Adults and Children in 20 Households in Java, 1972/73, Moni Nag, B.N.F. White, and R.C. Peet. 21. Status of Women Project, 1978, Tribhuvan University; Time Use of Adults and Children in Rural Nepal, 1980, Moni Nag, B.N.F. White, and R.C. Peet, Agricultural Development Council.

★ 192 ★
Allocation of Time

Time Spent on Activities Worldwide-II

This table shows hours per week spent on specific household tasks by men and women in selected countries, latest available year.

[NA Not available.]

Country	Year	Unpaid housework (Percent share of women and men)									
		Preparing meals		Child care		Shopping		Other housework		Total	
		Women	Men	Women	Men	Women	Men	Women	Men	Women	Men
North America and Australia											
Australia[1]	1987	76%	24%	78%	22%	60%	40%	53%	47%	68%	32%
Canada[2]	1986	81%	19%	76%	24%	58%	42%	67%	33%	68%	32%
United States[3]	1986	78%	22%	73%	28%	60%	40%	61%	39%	64%	36%
Western Europe											
Belgium[4]	1966	94%	6%	81%	19%	76%	24%	83%	17%	85%	15%
Finland[5]	1979	82%	18%	77%	23%	57%	43%	54%	46%	69%	31%

[Continued]

★ 192 ★

Time Spent on Activities Worldwide-II
[Continued]

| Country | Year | Unpaid housework (Percent share of women and men) | | | | | | | | | |
| | | Preparing meals | | Child care | | Shopping | | Other housework | | Total | |
		Women	Men	Women	Men	Women	Men	Women	Men	Women	Men
France[6]	1965	87%	13%	85%	15%	70%	30%	76%	24%	79%	21%
Germany											
Fed. Rep. of Germany[7]	1965	94%	6%	84%	16%	75%	25%	74%	26%	80%	20%
(Former) Ger. Dem. Rep.	1966	80%	20%	75%	25%	67%	33%	75%	25%	75%	25%
Netherlands[8]	1980	80%	20%	79%	21%	63%	37%	86%	14%	79%	21%
Norway[9]	1981	81%	19%	70%	30%	57%	43%	82%	18%	76%	24%
United Kingdom[10]	1984	74%	26%	76%	24%	60%	40%	76%	24%	72%	28%
Eastern Europe and USSR											
Bulgaria[11]	1988	88%	12%	81%	19%	70%	30%	58%	42%	69%	31%
Czechoslovakia[12]	1965	85%	15%	66%	34%	70%	30%	69%	31%	73%	27%
Hungary[13]	1976	90%	10%	68%	32%	65%	35%	64%	36%	73%	27%
Poland[14]	1984	90%	10%	69%	31%	70%	30%	76%	24%	78%	22%
Yugoslavia[15]	1965	94%	6%	73%	27%	63%	37%	80%	20%	81%	19%
USSR[16]	1986	75%	25%	75%	25%	62%	38%	59%	41%	65%	35%
Latin America											
Guatemala[17]	1977	99%	1%	68%	32%	58%	42%	73%	27%	82%	18%
Peru[18]	1966	94%	6%	90%	10%	69%	31%	86%	14%	87%	13%
Venezuela[19]	1983	98%	2%	85%	15%	70%	30%	87%	13%	90%	10%

[Continued]

★ 192 ★

Time Spent on Activities Worldwide-II

[Continued]

Country	Year	Unpaid housework (Percent share of women and men)									
		Preparing meals		Child care		Shopping		Other housework		Total	
		Women	Men	Women	Men	Women	Men	Women	Men	Women	Men
Asia											
Indonesia											
Java[20]	1973	96%	4%	74%	26%	88%	13%	80%	20%	87%	13%
Nepal	1979	88%	12%	81%	19%	41%	59%	76%	24%	78%	22%

Source: Selected from "Indicators on time use," *The World's Women: Trends and Statistics 1970-1990*, United Nations, 1991, Table 7, p. 101. Primary source: Compiled by Andrew Harvey as consultant to the United Nations Secretariat, from national reports and studies outlined in the footnotes below. *Notes:* 1. Time Use Pilot Survey, 1987, Australian Bureau of Statistics. 2. General Social Survey—Time Use Study, 1986, Statistics Canada. 3. Study of Americans' Use of Time, 1986, Survey Research Center (University of Maryland). 4. Multinational Time-Budget Project, 1965, Sociological Institute (Free University of Brussels). 5. Time Use Study, 1987, Central Statistical Office of Finland. 6. 1985/86 Time Use Survey. 7. Multinational Time-Budget Project, 1965, Institute for Comparative Social Research (University of Cologne); Multinational Time-Budget Project-- Osnabruck, 19675, Institute for Social Research (Dortmund); Multinational Time-Budget Project, 1965, Hoyerswerda, and Time-Budget Study, 1972, Institute for Living Standard and Consumption, University of Economic Sciences (Berlin); Time Use Study, 1974, 1980, and 1985, State Central Administration of Statistics (Berlin). Pre-unification. 8. National Time Use Survey, 1980, Social and Cultural Planning Bureau. 9. Time Budget Survey, 1980/81, Central Bureau of Statistics. 10. National Time Use Study, 1975, British Broadcasting Corporation. 11. Time Use in Bulgaria, 1985, Institute of Sociology; Time Use in Bulgaria, 1988, Central Statistical Office. 12. Multinational Time-Budget Project, 1965, Sociological Laboratory (Polytechnic Institute, Prague); Survey on Family Budget Statistics. 13. Time-Budget Survey, 1976/77, Central Statistical Office. 14. Time-Budget Survey of Working People in Poland, 1984, Central Statistical Office. 15. Multinational Time-Budget Project, 1965, Institute of Sociology (Belgrade); Multinational Time-Budget Project—Maribor and Surroundings, 1965; Institute of Philosophy and Sociology, University of Ljubljana. 16. Time Use in Pskov, 1986, USSR Academy of Sciences. 17. Family Time Use in Four Villages in Highland Guatemala, 1977, James Loucky. 18. Multinational Time-Budget Project, 1966, Political and Social Science Institute (Catholic University of Louvain), Rudolf Rezsohazy. 19. Division of Labour, Time Diary and Economic Value of Work Performed in Households in Venezuela, Central Bank of Venezuela, 1982. 20. Time Use of Adults and Children in 20 Households in Java, 1972/73, Moni Nag, B.N.F. White, and R.C. Peet. 21. Status of Women Project, 1978, Tribhuvan University; Time Use of Adults and Children in Rural Nepal, 1980, Moni Nag, B.N.F. White, and R.C. Peet, Agricultural Development Council.

★ 193 ★

Allocation of Time

Time Spent on Housework Worldwide

This table shows the number of hours per week spent on economic activity and on unpaid housework by men and women in developed regions of the world since 1976. When unpaid housework is taken into account, women in most regions spend at least as much time working as men do.

Region	Economic activity		Unpaid housework		Total working time	
	Women	Men	Women	Men	Women	Men
North America and Australia	19	35	30	15	49	50
Japan	27	52	29	3	57	55
Western Europe	18	34	31	11	49	44
Eastern Europe and USSR	37	48	33	15	70	63

Source: Selected from "Since 1975, both women and men have spent less time in total work in most of the developed regions," *The World's Women: Trends and Statistics 1970-1990*, United Nations, 1991, Table 6.2, p. 82. Primary source: Data are averages from a small number of studies in each region, compiled by the Statistical Office of the United Nations Secretariat.

Children

★ 194 ★

Adoption and Black Children

This table gives statistics on the large number of black children waiting to be adopted. The *Ebony* article describes an increasing number of unmarried black women who are choosing to adopt children, despite the fact that "their marital status [is] questioned by case workers who believe that single women are less capable of parenting than married couples."

Item	Number/Percent
Number of children of all races available for adoption, 1992	100,000
Number who are black	50,000
Boys	35,000
Number of black children in foster care	250,000

Source: Selected from Karima A. Haynes, "Latest Trend in Motherhood: Single Black Women Who Adopt," *Ebony,* 49(7), May 1994, pp. 68-72.

★ 195 ★
Children

Adoption Odds

The New York Times reports on a National Center for Health Statistics (NCHS) Study on adoption. This table gives statistics on various aspects of adoption gleaned by the reporter from that study and elsewhere.

Item	Number/Percent
Number of women who sought adoption in 1988 per NCHS survey	200,000
Number of women seeking to adopt according to the National Committee for Adoption	2,000,000
Percent of infertile women ever seeking to adopt per NCHS survey	17%
Percent of white, married women who were infertile, had no living children, and were 30 to 44 years old who had ever sought to adopt	<50%

[Continued]

★ 195 ★

Adoption Odds
[Continued]

Item	Number/Percent
Average fee to adopt a child (not including legal costs and preparation to receive the child)	$8,500

Source: Philip J. Hilts, "New Study Challenges Estimates on Odds of Adopting a Child," *The New York Times*, December 10, 1990, p. B10. The survey used personal interviews with 8,450 women aged 15 to 44 on the topics of fertility, infertility, and adoption. Dr. William L. Pierce, president of the National Committee for Adoption, called the survey figure of 200,000 women who sought adoption in 1988 "incredibly understated." The estimate of the National Committee for Adoption on the number of women seeking to adopt was based on the number of women who had sought help for infertility problems and the assumption that most of them would want to adopt.

★ 196 ★
Children

Adoption Placements: 1970-1988

This table gives statistics on babies placed for adoption and on the percentage of children conceived out of wedlock who were born to married women before 1973, from 1973-1981, and 1982-1988. Data from the 1982 and 1988 cycles of the National Survey of Family Growth (NSFG) were analyzed. The data showed that unmarried white women were far less likely than they were in the early 1970s to place their children for adoption. Black women showed low levels of relinquishment of children for adoption throughout this entire period, and relinquishment by Hispanic women "may be virtually nonexistent." When the NSFG data were analyzed, it was concluded that a woman still in school was more likely to place a child for adoption. Other factors positively associated with placing a child for adoption were well-educated mothers, mothers with no labor force experience, and mothers who were older. It was suggested that the decline in adoption among whites may be a result of the destigmatization of raising a child out of wedlock. The figures in this table show that the proportion of children conceived out of wedlock whose parents had married by the time the children were born fell from 48% before 1973 to 24% in 1982-1988.

Item/race	Before 1973	1973-1981	1982-1988
Among children ever born to never-married women, percentage who were relinquished for adoption, by race, according to year of birth[1]			
All women	8.7%	4.1%	2.0%
Black	1.5%	0.2%	1.1%
White	19.3%	7.6%	3.2%

[Continued]

★ 196 ★

Adoption Placements: 1970-1988
[Continued]

Item/race	Before 1973	1973-1981	1982-1988
Percentage of children conceived out of wedlock who were born to married women, by race, according to year of birth[2]			
All women	47.7%	30.0%	23.7%
Black	20.9%	10.1%	6.9%
White	64.2%	43.3%	37.7%

Source: Selected from Christine A. Bachrach, Kathy Shepherd Stolley, and Kathryn A. London, "Relinquishment of Premarital Births: Evidence from National Survey Data," *Family Planning Perspectives,* 24(1), January/February 1992, pp. 27+, Table 1, p. 29, entitled "Among children born to never-married women, percentage who were relinquished for adoption, by race, according to year of birth," and Table 2, p. 30, entitled "Percentage of children conceived out of wedlock who were born to married women, by race, according to year of birth." *Notes:* 1. Percentages are based on combined data from the 1982 and 1988 NSFG and refer to premarital births that had occurred to women who were 15-44 years of age at either survey. 2. Percentages are based on combined data from the 1982 and 1988 NSFG and refer to premaritally conceived births occurring to women who were 15-44 years of age at either survey.

★ 197 ★

Children

Adoption Vs. Abortion

This table gives statistics on abortion and adoption. The author makes the point that if abortion were banned, there would be another 1.5 million babies born annually in this country. Adoption professionals disagree on whether or not the adoption system could handle this increase. Many of these children would be born to poor minority women. Most adoptive couples are white, and many states discourage transracial adoptions.

Item	Number/Percent
According to the U.S. National Center for Health Statistics, the number of abortions per 2.5 live births	1
Alan Guttmacher Institute estimate of annual number of unwanted pregnancies	3,000,000
Terminated by abortion	50%
Unwanted babies born	1,500,000
Alan Guttmacher Institute estimate of annual number of unwanted babies born annually that are placed for adoption	25,000

[Continued]

★ 197 ★

Adoption Vs. Abortion
[Continued]

Item	Number/Percent
National Committee for Adoption estimate of qualified couples waiting to adopt, in millions	1-2
Potential families per child placed for adoption	40

Source: T.R. Reid, "Abortion and the Adoption Option: What the Numbers Show About Women's Choices," *Washington Post*, Health Section, August 15, 1989, pp. 6-7.

★ 198 ★

Children

Adoption: 1970-1982

This table gives statistics pertinent to the placement of babies for adoption in the 1970s and 1980s. Unmarried white women are much more likely to do so than are black or Hispanic women. In the study of adoption carried out by Christine Bachrach of the National Center for Health Statistics, it was found that adopted children have fared better in a material sense than children who remained with their unmarried mothers. Unmarried women who placed their babies for adoption were less likely to be receiving public assistance.

Item	Number/Percent
Annual number of unrelated adoptions, 1970	89,000
Annual number of unrelated adoptions, 1975	48,000
Births among unmarried white women, 1976	197,100
Births among unmarried white women, 1982	355,180
Of all babies placed for adoption by women aged 15-44 in 1982,	
Percent born to never-married women	88%
Percent born to ever-married women who were single at the time of the baby's birth	6%
Percent born to women who were married	6%

[Continued]

★ 198 ★

Adoption: 1970-1982
[Continued]

Item	Number/Percent
Of babies born to single women, Percent born to white women who were placed for adoption	12%
Percent born to black women who were placed for adoption	< 1%
Percent of single women who had kept their babies who were receiving some form of public assistance	45%
Percent of premaritally pregnant women who were married before giving birth who were receiving some form of public assistance at time of birth	22%
Percent of women who placed their babies for adoption who were receiving some form of public assistance	26%
Percent of unmarried women who raised their babies who had completed high school	61%
Percent of married mothers who raised their babies who had completed high school	73%
Percent of women who placed their babies for adoption who had completed high school	80%
Percent of ever-married women aged 15-44 who had adopted a child, according to 1973 and 1982 NSFG data	2%
Non-contraceptively sterile women	6%
Fecund women	< 1%
Unrelated adopted children who were living below the poverty level, 1982	2%
Percent of children who remained with their never-married mothers who were living below the poverty level, 1982	62%

[Continued]

★ 198 ★

Adoption: 1970-1982
[Continued]

Item	Number/Percent
Percent of adopted children who were living in families with incomes at least three times the poverty level	54%
Percent of children who remained with their never-married mothers who lived in families with incomes at least three times the poverty level	8%

Source: Selected from "Unmarried White Women Are Those Most Likely to Place Children for Adoption, NSFG Data Show," *Family Planning Perspectives,* 19(1), January/February 1987.

★ 199 ★
Children

Children in Substitute Care: 1986-1989

This table shows the number of children in substitute care by gender in 1986, 1987, 1988, and 1989. Information was gathered through the Voluntary Cooperative Information System (VCIS) from public child welfare agencies in the 50 states, the District of Columbia, and Puerto Rico.

[No. of states reporting four-year trend = 23.]

Year	Female	Male	Unknown/Not reported	Total
1989				
Trend national estimate	186,395	195,818	339	382,552
Reporting states total	114,834	120,639	209	235,682
Percent	48.7%	51.2%	0.1%	100.0%
1988				
Trend national estimate	169,531	174,240	346	344,177
Reporting states total	101,812	104,640	208	206,660
Percent	49.3%	50.6%	0.1%	100.0%
1987				
Trend national estimate	145,811	154,301	315	300,428
Reporting states total	87,366	92,453	189	180,008
Percent	48.5%	51.4%	0.1%	100.0%
1986				
Trend national estimate	136,823	143,946	280	281,049
Reporting states total	79,128	83,247	162	162,537
Percent	48.7%	51.2%	0.1%	100.0%

Source: Selected from "Children in Substitute Care, Classified by Gender, VCIS Survey 1986-1989," Caliber Associates in conjunction with MAXIMUS, Inc., *Analysis of 1989 Child Welfare Data,* Exhibit III-10, p. 23. Primary source: VCIS survey, Part I, question 7.

★ 200 ★
Children

Out-of-Wedlock Children: 1970-1988

This table shows the percentage of black and white babies who were born out-of-wedlock in 1970, 1980, and 1988. Single black women are more likely to have a child than single white women. The disparity is greatest among teenagers. In 1988, unmarried white teenagers age 15 to 17 bore 17 births per 1,000 girls, while unmarried black teenagers bore 74 births per 1,000 girls.

Race	1970	1980	1988
Blacks	38%	55%	64%
Whites	6%	11%	18%

Source: Selected from William P. O'Hare, Kelvin M. Pollard, Taynia L. Mann et al., "African Americans in the 1990s," *Population Bulletin*, Washington, D.C., Population Reference Bureau, July 1991, p. 11, Figure 2, "Babies Born Out-Of-Wedlock, by Race, 1970, 1980, and 1988." Primary source: National Center for Health Statistics, *Monthly Vital Statistics Report* 39, no. 4, supplement (1990), table 18; and *Vital Statistics of the United States 1987* (Washington, D.C.: GPO, 1989), table 1-31.

★ 201 ★
Children

Two-Parent Families with Children: 1987-1992

This table shows the total number of two-parent families with children under age 18, in thousands, for the years 1987-1992. It also shows the earner status of father and mother. The "traditional" family in which the husband but not the wife is an earner was less prevalent in 1992 than in 1987. There was an increase during the period in two-parent families in which the father was not an earner, probably the result of the poor conditions in the labor market during the period.

[Numbers in thousands.]

Year	Total two-parent families	Father earner, not mother		Father and mother earners		Father not earner	
		Number	Percent of total	Number	Percent of total	Number	Percent of total
1987	24,635	6,557	26.6%	17,120	69.5%	958	3.9%
1988	24,751	6,474	26.2%	17,321	70.0%	956	3.9%
1989	24,552	6,336	25.8%	17,299	70.5%	917	3.7%
1990	24,435	6,360	26.0%	17,200	70.4%	875	3.6%
1991	24,460	6,020	24.6%	17,377	71.0%	1,063	4.3%
1992	24,746	6,281	25.4%	17,285	69.8%	1,180	4.8%

Source: Howard V. Hayghe, "Are women leaving the labor force?" *Monthly Labor Review*, July 1994, pp. 37-39, Table 2, p. 39, "Two-parent families with children under age 18, by earner status of father and mother, 1987-92." Father not earner includes families in which mother and/or other family members are earners, or in which there are no earners.

★ 202 ★

Children

With Whom Did Children Live?: 1960-1990

This table shows how the living arrangements of children changed between 1960 and 1990. According to the author, "The United States is becoming an increasingly fatherless society... Today, a child can reasonably expect not" to grow up with his or her father.

Item	1960	1980	1990
U.S. kids living with...			
Father and mother	80.6%	62.3%	57.7%
Mother only	7.7%	18.0%	21.6%
Father only	1.0%	1.7%	3.1%
Father and stepmother	0.8%	1.1%	0.9%
Mother and stepfather	5.9%	8.4%	10.4%
Neither parent	3.9%	5.8%	4.3%

Source: David Blankenhorn, "Life Without Father," excerpted from *Fatherless America: Confronting Our Most Urgent Social Problems* in *Detroit News and Free Press USA Weekend,* February 24-26, 1995, p. 7. Primary source: *America's Children* by Donald Hernandez; U.S. Census Bureau. Because the statistics are from separate sources, they don't total 100%.

Displaced Homemakers

★ 203 ★

Profile of Displaced Homemakers: 1990

This table presents demographic information on displaced homemakers. Displaced homemakers are women whose main activity has been homemaking and who have lost their main source of income because of divorce, separation, widowhood, a spouse's disability or long-term unemployment, or lost eligibility for public assistance. In 1990 there were 17.8 million displaced homemakers in the United States.

Item	Number/Percent
Age	
Under 35 years	13%
35-44 years	9%
45-54 years	8%
55-64 years	12%

[Continued]

★ 203 ★

Profile of Displaced Homemakers: 1990

[Continued]

Item	Number/Percent
65 and over	59%
Race	
White	76%
Black	14%
Hispanic	4%
Native American	1%
Asian	2%
Other races	3%
By Age of Youngest Child	
0-2 years	23%
3-5 years	20%
6-12 years	36%
13-17 years	22%

Source: Selected from *Women Work, Poverty Persists: A Status Report on Displaced Homemakers & Single Mothers in the United States*, Women Work!, Washington, D.C., May 1990, pp. 11-13. Primary source: 1990 census.

Families

★ 204 ★

Female-Headed Families: 1980-1993

This table shows characteristics by race and Hispanic origin of female family householders with no spouse present, 1980 to 1993. The term "family" refers to a group of two or more persons related by birth, marriage, or adoption and residing together in a household. A "household" comprises all persons who occupy a "housing unit," that is, a house, an apartment or other group of rooms, or a single room that constitutes "separate living quarters."

[Householders 15 years old and over in thousands, as of March.]

Characteristic	White			Black			Hispanic Origin[1]		
	1980	1990	1993	1980	1990	1993	1980	1990	1993
Female Family Householder	6,052	7,306	7,848	2,495	3,275	3,680	610	1,116	1,238
Marital status									
Never married	11%	15%	17%	27%	39%	43%	23%	27%	31%
Married, spouse absent	17%	16%	16%	29%	21%	20%	32%	29%	26%
Widowed	33%	26%	23%	22%	17%	15%	15%	16%	14%

[Continued]

★ 204 ★

Female-Headed Families: 1980-1993
[Continued]

Characteristic	White			Black			Hispanic Origin[1]		
	1980	1990	1993	1980	1990	1993	1980	1990	1993
Divorced	40%	43%	44%	22%	23%	22%	30%	29%	28%
Presence of children under 18									
No own children	41%	43%	42%	28%	32%	34%	25%	33%	33%
With own children	59%	58%	58%	72%	68%	66%	75%	67%	67%

Source: Female Family Householders with No Spouse Present—Characteristics, by Race and Hispanic Origin: 1980 to 1993," U.S. Bureau of the Census, *Statistical Abstract of the United States 1994*, Table 76, p. 64. Primary source: U.S. Bureau of the Census, *Current Population Reports*, P20-477 and earlier reports. Based on Current Population Survey. *Note:* 1. May be of any race.

★ 205 ★

Families

Married Couple Families with Children: 1980-1993

This table shows characteristics of married couple family households with children, 1980 to 1993. The term "family" refers to a group of two or more persons related by birth, marriage, or adoption and residing together in a household. A "household" comprises all persons who occupy a "housing unit," that is, a house, an apartment or other group of rooms, or a single room that constitutes "separate living quarters."

[As of June. Numbers in thousands. - Represents or rounds to zero.]

Type of family	Number (1,000)			Percent distribution		
	1980	1985	1990	1980	1985	1990
Total	24,091	23,868	25,314	100.0%	100.0%	100.0%
Biological[1]	19,037	18,470	19,253	79.0%	77.4%	76.1%
Adoptive[2]	429	303	345	1.8%	1.3%	1.4%
Biological mother-stepfather[3]	1,818	2,207	2,619	7.5%	9.2%	10.3%
Biological father-stepmother[4]	171	180	152	0.7%	0.8%	0.6%
Joint biological-step[5]	1,862	2,038	2,475	7.7%	8.5%	9.8%
Joint biological-adoptive[6]	429	223	324	1.8%	0.9%	1.3%
Joint step-adoptive[7]	12	15	8	-	0.1%	-

[Continued]

★ 205 ★

Married Couple Families with Children: 1980-1993
[Continued]

Type of family	Number (1,000)			Percent distribution		
	1980	1985	1990	1980	1985	1990
Joint bio-step-adoptive[8]	25	29	-	0.1%	0.1%	-
Unknown[9]	309	403	137	1.3%	1.7%	0.5%

Source: "Married Couple Family Households with Children: 1980 to 1993," U.S. Bureau of the Census, *Statistical Abstract of the United States 1994*, Table 78, p. 65. Primary source: U.S. Bureau of the Census, *Current Population Reports*, P23-180. Covers only those married-couple families with at least one "own child" under age 18 living in their household. "Own children" are children of the householder and/or the householder's spouse. Each child who was the biological child of one of the parents but not of the other parent was classified as a stepchild. If one spouse adopted the biological child of the other spouse, the child was still considered to be a stepchild. Children who were the biological children of both parents were classified as biological children, while all "own" children who were not biological children of either of their parents were classified as adoptive children. Based on Current Population Survey. *Notes:* 1. All the own children were biological children of both parents. 2. All the own children were adoptive children of both parents. 3. All the own children were biological children of the mother and stepchildren of the father. 4. All the own children were biological children of the father and stepchildren of the mother. 5. At least one child was a biological child of both parents, at least one was a biological child of one parent and a stepchild of the other parent, and no other type of child was present; or a stepchild of each parent and no other type of child was present. 6. At least one child was a biological child of both parents, at least one was an adopted child of both parents, and no other type of child was present. 7. At least one child was a biological child of one parent and a stepchild of the other parent, at least one was an adopted child of both parents, and no other type of child was present. 8. At least one child was a biological child of both parents, at least one was the biological child of one parent and the stepchild of the other, and at least one was an adopted child of both parents. 9. At least one child had at least one parent for whom the nature of the relationship could not be designated.

★ 206 ★
Families

Profile of American Families: 1990

This table presents a profile of the American family in 1990. In 1970, more than 40% of the American population lived in a two-parent family with children. Today, only 25% do.

[Number of families in thousands.]

Family type	Number of families	With children under age 18
All races		
Married-couple families	52,317	46.9%
Female householder	10,890	60.6%
Male householder	2,884	40.0%
White		
Married-couple families	46,981	45.9%
Female householder	7,306	57.5%
Male householder	2,303	40.8%
Black		
Married-couple families	3,750	52.6%
Female householder	3,275	68.2%

[Continued]

★ 206 ★

Profile of American Families: 1990
[Continued]

Family type	Number of families	With children under age 18
Male householder	446	38.8%
Hispanic Origin		
Married-couple families	3,395	64.5%
Female householder	1,116	66.8%
Male householder	329	35.9%

Source: "Women in the U.S. Work Force," *Womens Voices: A Polling Report,* A Joint Project of the Ms. Foundation for Women and Center for Policy Alternatives, p. 26.

★ 207 ★

Families

Types of Asian and Pacific Islander Families: 1990 and 1993

This table gives numbers and percent distribution of Asian and Pacific Islander families for the years 1990 and 1993. The term "family" refers to a group of two or more persons related by birth, marriage, or adoption and residing together in a household.

[As of March.]

Characteristic	Number (thousands)		Percent distribution	
	1990	1993	1990	1993
Total persons	6,679	7,285	100.0%	100.0%
Family type				
Total families	1,531	1,662	100.0%	100.0%
Married couple	1,256	1,335	82.1%	80.3%
Female householder, no spouse present	188	232	12.3%	14.0%
Male householder, no spouse present	86	95	5.6%	5.7%
Families below poverty level	182	200	11.9%	12.0%
Persons below poverty level	939	912	14.1%	12.5%

Source: Selected from "Social and Economic Characteristics of the Asian and Pacific Islander Populations: 1990 and 1993," U.S. Bureau of the Census, *Statistical Abstract of the United States 1994,* Table 50, p. 49. Primary source: U.S. Bureau of the Census, *Current Population Reports,* P20-459; and unpublished data. Excludes members of Armed Forces except those living off post or with their families on post. Based on Current Population Survey.

★ 208 ★
Families

Types of Black and White Families: 1980-1993

This table gives numbers and percent distribution of white and black families and family income for the years 1980, 1990, and 1993. The term "family" refers to a group of two or more persons related by birth, marriage, or adoption and residing together in a household.

[As of March. X means Not applicable.]

| Characteristic | Number (thousands) | | | | | | Percent distribution | | | |
| | White | | | Black | | | White | | Black | |
	1980	1990	1993	1980	1990	1993	1980	1993	1980	1993
Total persons	191,905	206,983	211,955	26,033	30,392	32,036	100.0%	100.0%	100.0%	100.0%
Family type										
Total families	52,243	56,590	57,858	6,184	7,470	7,888	100.0%	100.0%	100.0%	100.0%
With own children[1]	26,474	26,718	27,334	3,820	4,378	4,560	50.7%	47.2%	61.8%	57.8%
Married couple	44,751	46,981	47,601	3,433	3,750	3,748	85.7%	82.3%	55.5%	47.5%
With own children[1]	22,415	21,579	21,684	1,927	1,972	1,945	42.9%	37.5%	31.2%	24.7%
Female householder, no spouse present	6,052	7,306	7,848	2,495	3,275	3,680	11.6%	13.6%	40.3%	46.7%
With own children[1]	3,558	4,199	4,552	1,793	2,232	2,434	6.8%	7.9%	29.0%	30.9%
Male householder, no spouse present	1,441	2,303	2,409	256	446	460	2.8%	4.2%	4.1%	5.8%
With own children[1]	500	939	1,098	99	173	182	1.0%	1.9%	1.6%	2.3%
Family Income in Previous Year in Constant (1992) Dollars										
Less than $5,000	952	1,240	1,547	424	691	888	1.8%	2.7%	6.9%	11.3%
$5,000 to $9,999	2,213	2,370	2,608	899	968	1,186	4.2%	4.5%	14.5%	15.0%
$10,000 to $14,999	3,239	3,567	3,842	803	968	933	6.2%	6.6%	13.0%	11.8%
$15,000 to $24,999	8,222	8,145	8,780	1,356	1,383	1,480	15.7%	15.2%	21.9%	18.8%
$25,000 to $34,999	8,416	8,377	8,826	861	1,021	1,028	16.1%	15.3%	13.9%	13.0%
$35,000 to $49,999	12,199	11,590	11,571	956	1,110	1,104	23.4%	20.0%	15.5%	14.0%
$50,000 or more	17,002	21,303	20,685	886	1,329	1,269	32.5%	35.8%	14.3%	16.1%
Median income	$38,751	$40,704	$38,909	$21,944	$22,866	$21,161	X	X	X	X
Families below poverty level	3,581	4,409	5,160	1,722	2,077	2,435	6.9%	8.9%	27.8%	30.9%
Persons below povery level	17,214	20,785	24,523	8,050	9,302	10,613	9.0%	11.6%	31.0%	33.3%

Source: Selected from "Social and Economic Characteristics of the White and Black Populations: 1980 to 1993," U.S. Bureau of the Census, *Statistical Abstract of the United States 1994,* Table 49, p. 48. Primary source: U.S. Bureau of the Census, *Current Population Reports,* P20-471, and earlier reports; P60-184 and P60-185; and unpublished data. Excludes members of Armed Forces except those living off post or with their families on post. Based on Current Population Survey. *Note:* 1. Civilian under 18 years.

★ 209 ★
Families

Types of Black Families: 1970-1992

This table shows types of black families in 1970, 1980, and 1992.

Type	1992	1980	1970
Married-couple families	47.1%	55.5%	68.1%
Female householder, no spouse present	46.4%	40.2%	28.3%
Male householder, no spouse present	6.5%	4.3%	3.7%

Source: Selected from U.S. Bureau of the Census, *Population Profile of the United States: 1993,* Special Studies Series P23-185, Figure 34, p. 35, "Black Families by Type: 1970 to 1992."

★ 210 ★
Families

Types of Families: 1960-1993

This table gives numbers relating to all families for the years 1960 to 1993. The term "family" refers to a group of two or more persons related by birth, marriage, or adoption and residing together in a household. A subfamily consists of a married couple and their children, if any, or one parent with one or more never-married children under 18 years old living in a household. A related subfamily is related to, but does not include, the householder. Members of a related subfamily are also members of the family with whom they live. The number of related subfamilies, therefore, is not included in the count of families. An unrelated subfamily may include persons such as guests, lodgers, or resident employees and their spouses and/ or children; none of whom is related to the householder.

[In thousands. As of March. B means base less than 75,000.]

Type of unit	1960	1970	1975	1980	1985	1990	1992	1993	Percent change		
									1970-80	1980-90	1990-93
Families	45,111	51,586	55,712	59,550	62,706	66,090	67,173	68,144	15%	11%	3%
Average size	3.67	3.58	3.42	3.29	3.23	3.17	3.17	3.16	X	X	X
Married couple	39,329	44,755	46,971	49,112	50,350	52,317	52,457	53,171	10%	7%	2%
Male house- holder[1]	1,275	1,239	1,499	1,733	2,228	2,884	3,025	3,026	40%	66%	5%
Female householder[1]	4,507	5,591	7,242	8,705	10,129	10,890	11,692	11,947	56%	25%	10%
Unrelated sub- families	207	130	149	360	526	534	669	708	177%	48%	33%
Married couple	75	27	20	20	46	68	92	83	B	B	B
Male reference person[1]	47	11	14	36	85	45	55	68	B	B	B

[Continued]

★ 210 ★

Types of Families: 1960-1993
[Continued]

Type of unit	1960	1970	1975	1980	1985	1990	1992	1993	Percent change		
									1970-80	1980-90	1990-93
Female reference person[1]	85	91	115	304	395	421	523	557	234%	39%	32%
Related subfamilies	1,514	1,150	1,349	1,150	2,228	2,403	2,559	2,671	[2]	109%	11%
Married couple	871	617	576	582	719	871	963	945	-6%	50%	8%
Father-child[1]	115	48	69	54	116	153	134	170	B	B	11%
Mother-child[1]	528	484	705	512	1,392	1,378	1,462	1,556	6%	169%	13%

Source: Selected from "Households, Families, Subfamilies, Married Couples, and Unrelated Individuals: 1960 to 1993," U.S. Bureau of the Census, *Statistical Abstract of the United States 1994*, Table 66, p. 58. Primary source: U.S. Bureau of the Census, *Current Population Reports*, P20-477. Includes members of Armed Forces living off post or with their families on post, but excludes all other members of Armed Forces. Based on Current Population Survey. X means Not applicable. *Notes:* 1. No spouse present. 2. Represents or rounds to zero.

★ 211 ★
Families

Types of Families: 1970-1992

This table shows types of households as a percent of total households in 1970, 1980, and 1992. The term "household" refers to the people occupying a housing unit, rather than the physical structure in which they live. Households can be families or nonfamilies. A family household is made up of at least two persons related by birth, marriage, or adoption. Household composition has changed significantly since 1970. While most households are family households, they do not account for as large a share of the total as they once did. The proportion of households represented by families has dropped from 81% in 1970 to 70% in 1992.

Type	Percent of total households		
	1992	1980	1970
Married couples with children[1]	25.5%	30.9%	40.3%
Married couples, no children[1]	29.3%	29.9%	30.3%
Other families with children[1]	8.7%	7.5%	5.0%
Other families, no children[1]	6.7%	5.4%	5.6%
Men living alone	10.0%	8.6%	5.6%
Women living alone	15.0%	14.0%	11.5%
Other nonfamily households	4.7%	3.6%	1.7%

Source: Selected from U.S. Bureau of the Census, *Population Profile of the United States: 1993*, Special Studies Series P23-185, Figure 15, p. 16, "Household Composition: 1970 to 1992." *Note:* 1. Own children under 18.

★ 212 ★
Families

Types of Hispanic Families: 1993

This table gives numbers and percent distribution of Hispanic families and family income in 1993. The term "family" refers to a group of two or more persons related by birth, marriage, or adoption and residing together in a household.

[As of March. X means Not applicable.]

Characteristic	Number (thousands)						Percent distribution					
	Hispan-ic, total	Mexi-can	Puerto Rican	Cuban	Cent. & S. American	Other Hispanic	Hispan-ic, total	Mexi-can	Puerto Rican	Cuban	Cent. & S. American	Other Hispanic
Total persons	22,752	14,628	2,402	1,071	3,052	1,598	100.0%	100.0%	100.0%	100.0%	100.0%	100.0%
Family type												
Total families	5,318	3,210	653	309	751	395	100.0%	100.0%	100.0%	100.0%	100.0%	100.0%
Married couple	3,674	2,320	349	235	510	261	69.1%	72.3%	53.4%	76.1%	67.9%	66.0%
Female householder, no spouse present	1,238	622	264	56	186	110	23.3%	19.4%	40.5%	18.2%	24.7%	27.7%
Male householder, no spouse present	407	269	40	18	56	25	7.7%	8.4%	6.2%	5.7%	7.4%	6.3%
Family Income in 1992												
Less than $5,000	320	178	60	14	45	23	6.0%	5.5%	9.2%	4.5%	6.0%	5.8%
$5,000 to $9,999	620	338	123	23	85	50	11.7%	10.5%	18.8%	7.4%	11.3%	12.7%
$10,000 to $14,999	671	423	70	29	116	32	12.6%	13.2%	10.7%	9.4%	15.4%	8.1%
$15,000 to $24,999	1,152	740	140	61	142	71	21.7%	23.1%	21.4%	19.7%	18.9%	18.0%
$25,000 to $34,999	865	550	89	47	124	53	16.3%	17.1%	13.6%	15.2%	16.5%	13.4%
$35,000 to $49,999	802	503	77	50	104	66	15.1%	15.7%	11.8%	16.2%	13.8%	16.7%
$50,000 or more	889	478	96	85	133	98	16.7%	14.9%	14.7%	27.5%	17.7%	24.8%
Median income	$23,912	$23,714	$20,301	$31,015	$23,649	$28,562	X	X	X	X	X	X
Families below poverty level	1,395	847	212	47	203	86	26.2%	26.4%	32.5%	15.4%	27.0%	21.7%
Persons below poverty level	6,655	4,404	874	194	815	368	29.3%	30.1%	36.5%	18.1%	26.7%	23.1%

Source: Selected from "Social and Economic Characteristics of the Hispanic Population: 1993," U.S. Bureau of the Census, *Statistical Abstract of the United States 1994,* Table 53, p. 51. Primary source: U.S. Bureau of the Census, *Current Population Reports*, P20-475. Excludes members of Armed Forces except those living off post or with their families on post. Based on Current Population Survey.

Living Arrangements

★ 213 ★

Fewest People in the Household Worldwide

This table shows the size of the family or household in the 13 countries with the fewest people in the family or household in 1988. International comparability of data is limited by the different definitions of what makes up a household.

[H = household. F = Family.]

Country	Size of family or household
Belgium	F 2.7
Bermuda	H 2.7
France	H 2.7
West Germany	F 2.7
United Kingdom	H 2.7
Netherlands	H 2.6
United States	F 2.6
Switzerland	H 2.5
Norway	F 2.4
Sweden	H 2.4
Monaco	H 2.3
Denmark	F 2.0
Greenland	F 2.0

Source: Selected from George Kurian, *The New Book of World Rankings*, Facts on File, Inc., New York, 1991, pp. 30-31, table entitled "Average household size." Primary source: *U.N. Demographic Yearbook.*

★ 214 ★

Living Arrangements

Homeless Adults

This table presents statistics on characteristics of homeless adults in cities of population over 100,000. The majority of adult homeless individuals is male, but only 12% of homeless adults in homeless families are male. The average homeless individual has been homeless for a median of 12 months, the average homeless family 4.5 months. Homeless men are more likely to have earned income; homeless women are more likely to collect means-tested benefits. Thirty-seven percent of homeless persons report eating one meal a day or less and 36% report going at least 1 day a week without any nourishment.

[In weighted percentages. NA=Not available.]

Characteristic	Homeless adults		
	Individuals	In families	Total
Total	77%	8%	85%[1]
Male	88%	12%	81%
Female	12%	88%	19%
Marital status			
Married	9%	23%	10%
Divorced/separated	30%	25%	29%
Widowed	6%	6%	5%
Never married	56%	47%	55%
Monthly cash income			
Mean	$146	$301	NA
Median	$64	$300	NA
Receiving benefits			
Food Stamps	15%	50%	NA
AFDC	1%	33%	NA
General assistance	10%	33%	NA

Source: Selected from "Characteristics of Homeless Adults in Cities of Population over 100,000," U.S. House of Representatives, Committee on Ways and Means, *1991 Green Book*, May 7, 1991, Table 80, pp. 1070-71. Primary source: All data from a study done by the Urban Institute on 1,704 service-using homeless persons. *Note:* 1. The remaining 15% are children in homeless families.

★ 215 ★

Living Arrangements

Households Headed by Women Worldwide

This table shows the countries of the world where more than 20% of
households were headed by women in the early 1980s. Because of data
collection methods in most countries, women are not usually listed as heads
of households unless they are living alone or there is no adult male in the
household. Therefore, women's household responsibilities tend to be
understated. In the developed regions of the world, female-headed
households usually consist of women living alone, while in the developing
regions of the world, most female-headed households include children.

Country	Households headed by women
Developed regions	
Australia	25%
Austria	31%
Belgium	21%
Canada	25%
Czechoslovakia	23%
France	22%
Luxembourg	23%
New Zealand	24%
Norway	38%
Poland	27%
Sweden	27%
Switzerland	25%
United Kingdom	25%
United States	31%
Africa	
Botswana	45%
Congo	21%
Ghana	27%
Malawi	29%
Reunion	25%
Rwanda	25%
Sudan	22%
Zambia	28%
Latin America/Caribbean	
Barbados	44%
Chile	22%
Cuba	28%
Dominica	38%
El Salvador	22%

[Continued]

★ 215 ★

Households Headed by Women Worldwide
[Continued]

Country	Households headed by women
French Guiana	31%
Grenada	45%
Guadeloupe	34%
Guyana	24%
Honduras	22%
Jamaica	34%
Martinique	35%
Netherlands Antilles	30%
Panama	22%
Peru	23%
Puerto Rico	25%
Saint Kitts and Nevis	46%
Saint Lucia	39%
St. Vincent and the Grenadines	42%
Trinidad and Tobago	25%
Uruguay	21%
Venezuela	22%
Asia and Pacific	
Hong Kong	24%

Source: "Where more than 20 per cent of households are headed by women," *The World's Women: Trends and Statistics 1970-1990*, United Nations, 1991, Table 1.12, p. 18. Primary source: Statistical Office of the United Nations Secretariat.

★ 216 ★

Living Arrangements

Households: 2000-2010

This table shows numbers in thousands and percent of all households by type in 2000, 2005, and 2010. Percent change is shown for 1990-2000 and 2000-2010. *American Demographics* projects slow growth because only a small group, the youngest "baby busters," will be forming new households, and the children of "baby boomers" will begin to form new households.

[Numbers in thousands.]

Type of household	2000		2005	2010		Change, 1990-2000	Change 2000-2010
	Number	Percent	Number	Number	Percent		
All households	110,140	100.0%	111,039	117,696	100.0%	18.0%	6.9%
Families	77,705	70.6%	76,100	80,193	68.1%	17.6%	3.2%
Married couples	60,969	55.4%	58,269	61,266	52.1%	16.5%	0.5%

[Continued]

★ 216 ★

Households: 2000-2010
[Continued]

Type of household	2000		2005	2010		Change, 1990-2000	Change 2000-2010
	Number	Percent	Number	Number	Percent		
with children < 18[1]	24,286	22.1%	23,807	23,433	19.9%	-1.0%	-3.5%
with children 18+ only	5,318	4.8%	6,108	6,884	5.8%	-15.0%	29.4%
with no children	31,365	28.5%	28,354	30,950	26.3%	45.7%	-1.3%
Single fathers	1,523	1.4%	1,598	1,660	1.4%	32.1%	9.0%
Single mothers	7,473	6.8%	7,607	7,779	6.6%	13.25	4.1%
Other families	7,741	7.0%	8,626	9,488	8.1%	28.5%	22.6%
Nonfamilies	32,434	29.4%	34,940	37,503	31.9%	15.6%	18.0%
Men living alone	10,898	9.9%	11,751	12,577	10.7%	20.4%	15.4%
Women living alone	16,278	14.8%	17,397	18,578	15.8%	16.7%	14.1%
Other nonfamilies	5,258	4.8%	5,792	6,347	5.4%	23.5%	20.7%

Source: "The Future of Households," *American Demographics*, December 1993, pp. 27-40, selected from p. 29, table entitled "Households to 2010." *Note:* 1. Includes those with children both younger than 18 and 18 and older.

★ 217 ★

Living Arrangements

Living Alone: 1970-1993

This table gives the total number and percent distribution of persons and females living alone from 1970 to 1993, by age.

[Numbers in thousands, as of March.]

Sex and Age	Number of persons (1,000)					Percent Distribution				
	1970	1980	1985	1990	1993	1970	1980	1985	1990	1993
Both sexes	10,851	18,296	20,602	22,999	23,642	100%	100%	100%	100%	100%
15 to 24 yrs[1]	556	1,726	1,324	1,210	1,186	5%	9%	6%	5%	5%
25 to 34 yrs	1,604[2]	4,729[2]	3,905	3,972	3,735	15%[2]	26%[2]	19%	17%	16%
35 to 44 yrs	[2]	[2]	2,322	3,138	3,286	[2]	[2]	11%	14%	14%
45 to 64 yrs old	3,622	4,514	4,939	5,502	6,081	33%	25%	24%	24%	26%
65 to 74 yrs	2,815	3,851	4,130	4,350	4,330	26%	21%	20%	19%	18%
75 yrs +	2,256	3,477	3,982	4,825	5,025	21%	19%	19%	21%	21%
Female	7,319	11,330	12,680	13,950	14,206	68%	62%	62%	61%	60%
15 to 24 yrs[1]	282	779	573	536	521	3%	4%	3%	2%	2%
25 to 34 yrs	671	1,809	1,598	1,578	145	6%[2]	10%[2]	8%	7%	6%
35 to 44 yrs	[2]	[2]	916	1,303	1,313	[2]	[2]	4%	6%	6%
45 to 64 yrs	2,470	2,901	3,095	3,300	3,559	23%	16%	15%	14%	15%
65 to 74 yrs	2,204	3,076	3,262	3,309	3,284	20%	17%	16%	14%	14%

[Continued]

★ 217 ★

Living Alone: 1970-1993

[Continued]

Sex and Age	Number of persons (1,000)					Percent Distribution				
	1970	1980	1985	1990	1993	1970	1980	1985	1990	1993
75 yrs +	1,693	2,766	3,236	3,924	4,078	16%	15%	16%	17%	17%
Male	3,532	6,966	7,922	9,049	9,436	33%	38%	39%	39%	40%

Source: Selected from "Persons Living Alone, by Sex and Age: 1970 to 1993," U.S. Bureau of the Census, *Statistical Abstract of the United States, 1994,* Table 83, p. 68. Primary source: U.S. Bureau of the Census, *Current Population Reports,* P20-450, and earlier reports; and unpublished data. Based on Current Population Survey. *Notes:* 1. In 1970, persons 14 to 24 years old. 2. Data for persons 35 to 44 years old included with persons 25 to 34 years old.

★ 218 ★

Living Arrangements

Living Arrangements by Presence of Children: 1980-1993

This table gives total number of households in thousands in 1980, 1990, and 1993; percent distribution in 1980 and 1993; persons in households and persons per household 1993, by type of household and presence of children. Living arrangements refer to residence in households or in group quarters. A "household" comprises all persons who occupy a "housing unit," that is, a house, an apartment or other group of rooms, or a single room that constitutes "separate living quarters." A person living alone or a group of unrelated persons sharing the same housing unit is also counted as a household.

[As of March. Numbers in thousands.]

Type of house-hold and presence of children	Households					Persons in households '93		Persons per household, 1993
	Number (1,000)			Percent distribution				
	1980	1990	1993	1980	1993	Number	Distribution	
Total households	80,776	93,347	96,391	100%	100%	253,924	100%	2.63
Family households	59,550	66,090	68,144	74%	71%	218,965	86%	3.21
With own children < 18	31,022	32,289	33,257	38%	35%	130,542	51%	3.93
Without own children under 18	28,528	33,801	34,887	35%	36%	88,423	35%	2.53
Married couple family	49,112	52,317	53,171	61%	55%	172,268	68%	3.24
With own children < 18	24,961	24,537	24,707	31%	26%	102,581	40%	4.15
Without own children under 18	24,151	27,780	28,464	30%	30%	69,687	27%	2.45
Male householder, no spouse present	1,733	2,884	3,026	2%	3%	9,395	4%	3.11
With own children < 18	616	1,153	1,324	1%	1%	4,396	2%	3.32
Without own children under 18	1,117	1,731	1,702	1%	2%	4,999	2%	2.94
Female householder, no spouse present	8,705	10,890	11,947	11%	12%	37,302	15%	3.12
With own children < 18	5,445	6,599	7,226	7%	7%	23,565	9%	3.26
Without own children under 18	3,261	4,290	4,721	4%	5%	13,737	5%	2.91

[Continued]

★ 218 ★

Living Arrangements by Presence of Children: 1980-1993
[Continued]

Type of house-hold and presence of children	Households					Persons in households '93		Persons per household, 1993
	Number (1,000)			Percent distribution				
	1980	1990	1993	1980	1993	Number	Distribution	
Nonfamily households	21,226	27,257	28,247	26%	29%	34,959	14%	1.24
Living alone	18,296	22,999	23,642	23%	25%	23,642	9%	1.00
Male householder	8,807	11,606	12,254	11%	13%	16,448	6%	1.34
Living alone	6,966	9,049	9,436	9%	10%	9,436	4%	1.00
Female householder	12,419	15,651	15,993	15%	17%	18,511	7%	1.16
Living alone	11,330	13,950	14,206	14%	15%	14,206	6%	1.00

Source: Selected from "Households, 1980 to 1993, and Persons in Households, 1993, by Type of Household and Presence of Children," *Statistical Abstract of the United States, 1994,* Table 67, p. 59. Primary source: U.S. Bureau of the Census, *Current Population Reports,* P20-477, and earlier reports. Based on Current Population Survey.

★ 219 ★

Living Arrangements

Living Arrangements by Type of Household: 1993

This table gives total number of households and type of households in 1993 and the percent distribution by type of household. Living arrangements refer to residence in households or in group quarters. A "household" comprises all persons who occupy a "housing unit," that is, a house, an apartment or other group of rooms, or a single room that constitutes "separate living quarters." A person living alone or a group of unrelated persons sharing the same housing unit is also counted as a household.

[As of March. Numbers in thousands. X is Not applicable.]

Characteristic	Number of households (1,000)					Percent distribution				
	Total	Family households			Non-family households	Total	Family households			Non-family households
		Total[1]	Married couple	Female householder[2]			Total[1]	Married couple	Female householder[2]	
Total	96,391	68,144	53,171	11,947	28,247	100%	100%	100%	100%	100%
Age of householder										
15 to 24 years	5,022	2,751	1,463	1,005	2,271	5%	4%	3%	8%	8%
25 to 29 years	8,614	5,932	4,210	1,342	2,682	9%	9%	8%	11%	9%
30 to 34 years	11,127	8,444	6,444	1,604	2,682	12%	12%	12%	13%	9%
35 to 44 years	21,718	17,569	13,521	3,269	4,148	23%	26%	25%	27%	15%
45 to 54 years	16,575	13,070	10,550	1,956	3,506	17%	19%	20%	16%	12%
55 to 64 years	12,438	9,117	7,674	1,179	3,321	13%	13%	14%	10%	12%
65 to 74 years	11,834	7,350	6,223	913	4,484	12%	11%	12%	8%	16%
75 years and over	9,061	3,911	3,083	679	5,151	9%	6%	6%	6%	18%
Marital status of householder										
Never married	14,652	4,117	X	3,037	10,534	15%	6%	X	25%	37%
Married, spouse present	53,171	53,171	53,171	X	X	55%	78%	100%	X	X
Married, spouse absent	4,425	2,494	X	2,064	1,931	5%	4%	X	17%	7%
Widowed	11,621	2,856	X	2,418	8,765	12%	4%	X	20%	31%
Divorced	12,523	5,506	X	4,427	7,017	13%	8%	X	37%	25%

[Continued]

★ 219 ★

Living Arrangements by Type of Household: 1993
[Continued]

Characteristic	Number of households (1,000)					Percent distribution				
	Total	Family households			Non-family households	Total	Family households			Non-family households
		Total[1]	Married couple	Female householder[2]			Total[1]	Married couple	Female householder[2]	
Tenure										
Owner occupied	62,220	48,807	41,928	5,237	13,413	65%	72%	79%	44%	47%
Renter occupied	34,171	19,336	11,243	6,710	14,835	35%	28%	21%	56%	53%

Source: Selected from "Household Characteristics, by Type of Household," *Statistical Abstract of the United States, 1994,* Table 68, p. 59. Primary source: U.S. Bureau of the Census, *Current Population Reports,* P60-184 and unpublished data. Based on Current Population Survey. *Notes:* 1. Includes male householder, no spouse present. 2. No spouse present.

★ 220 ★

Living Arrangements

Living Arrangements of People 15 Years Old and Over: 1993

This table gives the total population for persons and females aged 15 years and over, and living arrangements in percent for all races and females, white persons and females, and black persons and females.

[In thousands, as of March.]

Age and Sex	All Races[2]					White Persons Living			Black Persons Living		
	Total	Living				Alone	With spouse	With other relatives	Alone	With spouse	With other relatives
		Alone	With spouse	With other relatives	With non-relatives						
Total	197,254	12%	55%	26%	7%	12%	58%	23%	13%	33%	48%
15 to 19 yrs	16,627	1%	3%	93%	4%	1%	3%	92%	[1]	[1]	97%
20 to 24 yrs	17,802	6%	23%	56%	16%	6%	25%	52%	6%	11%	75%
25 to 34 yrs	41,864	9%	56%	24%	11%	9%	60%	20%	10%	32%	49%
35 to 44 yrs	40,342	8%	69%	17%	6%	8%	72%	14%	10%	44%	39%
45 to 54 yrs	28,503	11%	73%	12%	4%	10%	76%	10%	14%	51%	28%
55 to 64 yrs	21,247	14%	71%	11%	4%	14%	74%	9%	21%	47%	26%
65 yrs +	30,870	30%	55%	13%	2%	30%	56%	11%	33%	39%	25%
65 to 74 yrs	18,362	24%	64%	11%	2%	23%	66%	9%	30%	46%	22%
75 yrs +	12,508	40%	42%	16%	2%	41%	43%	14%	40%	25%	32%
Female	102,400	14%	53%	28%	5%	14%	56%	24%	13%	30%	53%
15 to 19 yrs	8,202	1%	4%	91%	4%	1%	5%	90%	[1]	1%	97%
20 to 24 yrs	9,016	5%	28%	52%	15%	5%	31%	48%	6%	14%	74%
25 to 34 yrs	21,007	7%	60%	25%	8%	7%	64%	20%	7%	31%	56%
35 to 44 yrs	20,438	6%	69%	21%	4%	6%	73%	17%	7%	39%	51%
45 to 54 yrs	14,655	11%	70%	17%	3%	11%	72%	14%	14%	45%	36%
55 to 64 yrs	11,042	18%	66%	14%	2%	17%	69%	11%	26%	39%	33%
65 yrs +	18,038	41%	41%	17%	2%	41%	42%	15%	39%	26%	32%
65 to 74 yrs	10,249	32%	52%	14%	1%	32%	54%	12%	36%	35%	28%

[Continued]

★ 220 ★

Living Arrangements of People 15 Years Old and Over: 1993
[Continued]

Age and Sex	Total	All Races[2]				White Persons Living			Black Persons Living		
		Living									
		Alone	With spouse	With other relatives	With non-relatives	Alone	With spouse	With other relatives	Alone	With spouse	With other relatives
75 yrs +	7,790	52%	25%	20%	2%	54%	26%	18%	44%	14%	39%
Male	94,854	10%	57%	25%	8%	10%	60%	22%	12%	37%	41%

Source: Selected from "Living Arrangements of Persons 15 Years Old and Over, by Selected Characteristics: 1993," U.S. Bureau of the Census, *Statistical Abstract of the United States, 1994,* Table 63, p. 57. Primary source: U.S. Bureau of the Census, unpublished data. Based on Current Population Survey which includes members of Armed Forces living off post or with families on post, but excludes other Armed forces. *Notes:* 1. Represents or rounds to zero. 2. Includes other races not shown separately.

★ 221 ★

Living Arrangements

Living Arrangements of the Elderly

This table shows the living arrangements of men and women aged 65 to 74 and aged 75 and older in 1991. While three out of four men aged 65 and older lived with their wife, fewer than half of older women lived with their husband. Most older women live alone.

Arrangement and age	Men	Women
Ages 65 to 74		
Alone	13%	34%
With spouse	79%	51%
With other relatives	6%	13%
With nonrelatives	2%	2%
Age 75 and over		
Alone	21%	53%
With spouse	66%	24%
With other relatives	11%	20%
With nonrelatives	3%	3%

Source: Selected from Dennis A. Ahlburg and Carol J. DeVita, *New Realities of the American Family,* Population Bulletin, Vol. 47, No. 2, August 1992, Figure 3, p. 10, "Living Arrangements of the Elderly, 1991." Primary source: U.S. Bureau of the Census, *Current Population Reports* P-20, no. 461.

★ 222 ★

Living Arrangements

Living Arrangements of the Elderly by Race/Ethnicity

This table shows statistics compiled by the American Association of Retired Persons about older women of color.

Item	Number/Percent
Older women living alone, 1992:	
Hispanic origin	25%
Black	40%
White	42%
Older women (age 65+) living alone in 1992 who were poor:	
Black	58%
Hispanic origin	50%
White	23%
Percentage of older women living alone who spent between 70% and 90% of their income on housing in 1991:	
Hispanic origin	11%
All older women	5%
Percentage of older women living alone who spent half or more of their income on housing in 1991:	
Hispanic origin	30%
Black	24%
All older women	20%

Source: Selected from "Facts About Older Women: Housing and Living Arrangements," AARP *Fact Sheet.*

★ 223 ★

Living Arrangements

Living Arrangements of Young Adults: 1970-1993

This table gives total population figures by age for all persons and females 18 to 24 years old and 25 to 34 years old, and percent distribution of that population by living arrangement. Living arrangements refer to residence in households or in group quarters. A "household" comprises all persons who occupy a "housing unit," that is, a house, an apartment or other group of rooms, or a single room that constitutes "separate living quarters." A person living alone or a group of unrelated persons sharing the same housing unit is also counted as a household.

[1970 and 1980 as of April. Beginning 1985 as of March.]

Living arrange-ments and sex	Persons 18 to 24 years old					Persons 25 to 34 years old				
	1970	1980	1985	1990	1993	1970	1980	1985	1990	1993
Total (1,000)	22,357	29,122	27,844	25,310	24,309	24,566	36,796	40,857	43,240	41,863
Percent distribution										
Child of householder[1]	47%	48%	54%	53%	53%	8%	9%	11%	12%	12%
Family householder										
or spouse	38%	29%	24%	22%	22%	83%	72%	66%	65%	63%
Nonfamily householder	5%	10%	8%	9%	9%	5%	12%	13%	13%	13%
Other	10%	13%	14%	16%	16%	4%	7%	9%	11%	12%
Female (1,000)	11,959	14,844	14,149	12,860	12,260	12,637	18,689	20,673	21,779	21,007
Percent distribution										
Child of householder[1]	41%	43%	48%	48%	47%	7%	7%	8%	8%	9%
Family householder										
or spouse	45%	36%	32%	30%	29%	86%	78%	76%	73%	72%
Nonfamily householder	4%	8%	7%	8%	8%	4%	9%	10%	10%	10%
Other	10%	13%	13%	15%	16%	4%	6%	7%	9%	10%

Source: Selected from "Living Arrangements of Young Adults: 1970 to 1993," U.S. Bureau of the Census, *Statistical Abstract of the United States, 1994,* Table 64, p. 57. Primary source: U.S. Bureau of the Census, *1970* and *1980 Census of Population,* PC92)- 4B and *Current Population Reports,* P20-410 and P20-450; and unpublished data. Beginning 1985, based on Current Population Survey. *Note:* 1. Includes unmarried college students living in dormitories.

★ 224 ★

Living Arrangements

Most People in the Household Worldwide

This table shows the size of the family or household in the 11 countries with the most people in the family or household in 1988. International comparability of data is limited by the different definitions of what makes up a household. Family units tend to be largest on small islands. Families are also largest in countries where large families are encouraged, such as in Muslim nations.

[H = household. F = Family.]

Country	Size of family or household
Nauru	H 8.0
Trust Territory of the Pacific Islands	H 8.0
Western Samoa	F 7.8
Kuwait	H 7.2
American Samoa	H 7.1
Micronesia, Fed. States of	H 7.0
Iraq	H 6.9
Jordan	H 6.9
Nicaragua	H 6.9
Bahrain	H 6.7
Pakistan	H 6.7

Source: Selected from "Average household size," George Kurian, *The New Book of World Rankings*, Facts on File, Inc., New York, 1991, pp. 37-38. Primary source: *U.N. Demographic Yearbook.*

★ 225 ★

Living Arrangements

Reasons for Leaving Home: 1920-1980s

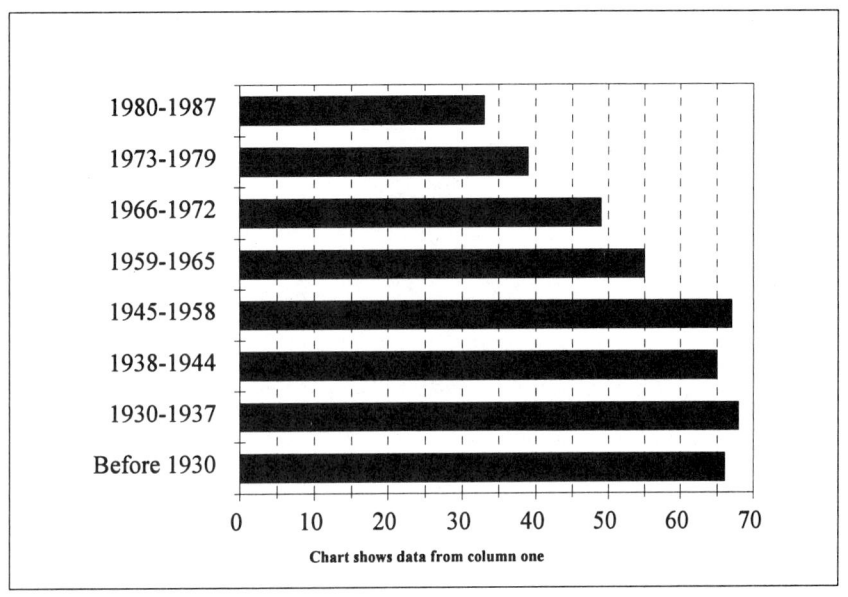

This table shows women's reasons for leaving home from the 1920s to the 1980s. It is apparent that marriage is no longer the main reason for leaving home. Nest-leaving cohorts left home the year they reached age 18. About 25% of the cohort had not left home by 1987-1988.The most common answers in the "other" category were "to get a job" and "to live on my own." "Military" represented less than 3% for any cohort.

Year	Marriage	School	Other
Before 1930	66%	11%	23%
1930-1937	68%	10%	22%
1938-1944	65%	12%	23%
1945-1958	67%	17%	16%
1959-1965	55%	23%	21%
1966-1972	49%	28%	22%
1973-1979	39%	27%	33%
1980-1987	33%	28%	39%

Source: "Women's Reasons for Leaving Home, 1920s to 1980s," *Population Bulletin: Leaving and Returning Home in 20th Century America*, Population Reference Bureau, Inc., Vol. 48, No. 4, March 1994, Figure 4, p. 15. Primary source: Authors' analysis of the National Survey of Families and Households. Percentages may not add to 100 because of rounding.

★ 226 ★

Living Arrangements

Urban Population in Latin America and the Caribbean

This table shows the percentages of women who lived in urban areas in Latin America and the Caribbean. Data are for the latest available year.

Country	Women in urban areas
Latin America and the Caribbean	
Argentina	85%
Bahamas, The	76%
Bolivia	50%
Brazil[1]	72%
Chile	85%
Colombia	70%
Costa Rica	46%
Cuba	73%
Ecuador[2]	53%
El Salvador	41%
Guatemala	38%
Guyana	23%
Haiti	28%
Honduras	41%
Jamaica	43%
Mexico	67%
Nicaragua	56%
Panama	54%
Paraguay	44%
Peru[1]	68%
Puerto Rico	68%
Saint Kitts and Nevis	36%
Trinidad and Tobago	48%
Uruguay[3]	86%
Venezuela[1]	84%
Virgin Islands	

Source: Selected from "Indicators on housing, human settlements and environment," *The World's Women: Trends and Statistics 1970-1990,* United Nations, 1991, Table 6, p. 77. Primary source: Compiled by the Statistical Office of the United Nations Secretariat from local survey studies and reports. *Notes:* 1. Excluding Indian jungle population. 2. Excluding nomadic Indian tribes. 3. 1975/76.

★ 227 ★

Living Arrangements

Urban Population in Sub-Saharan Africa

This table shows the percentages of women who lived in urban areas in Sub-Saharan Africa. Data are for the latest available year. During the early 1980s, between 70 and 90 percent of Africa's rural population lacked access to safe water. Even in urban areas, 33% of the population lacks access to safe water.

Country	Women in urban areas
Sub-Saharan Africa	
Benin	31%
Botswana	20%
Burundi	4%
Cameroon	27%
Central African Republic[1]	35%
Comoros	23%
Congo	35%
Ethiopia	11%
Gabon	33%
Guinea	18%
Kenya	14%
Lesotho	5%
Liberia	31%
Madagascar[1]	17%
Malawi	8%
Mali[1]	17%
Mauritania	21%
Mauritius	41%
Mozambique	12%
Namibia	43%
Nigeria	19%
Rwanda	4%
Senegal[1]	34%
Seychelles	38%
South Africa	55%
Sudan	19%
Tanzania	13%
Uganda	11%
Zaire	17%
Zambia	39%
Zimbabwe	22%

Source: Selected from "Indicators on housing, human settlements and environment," *The World's Women: Trends and Statistics 1970-1990,* United Nations, 1991, Table 6, p. 77. Primary source: Compiled by the Statistical Office of the United Nations Secretariat from local survey studies and reports. *Note:* 1. 1975/76.

Living Arrangements

Urban Population in the Middle East and North Africa

This table shows the percentages of women who lived in urban areas in the Middle East and North Africa. Data are for the latest available year.

Country	Women in urban areas
Middle East/North Africa	
Algeria	61%
Egypt	44%
Iran[1]	46%
Iraq	67%
Jordan	59%
Lebanon	76%
Morocco	43%
Syria	
Syrian Arab Republic[2]	49%
Tunisia	53%
Turkey	43%
United Arab Emirates	84%
Yemen[3]	35%

Source: Selected from "Indicators on housing, human settlements and environment," *The World's Women: Trends and Statistics 1970-1990*, United Nations, 1991, Table 6, p. 77. Primary source: Compiled by the Statistical Office of the United Nations Secretariat from local survey studies and reports. *Notes:* 1. 1975-76. 2. Excluding Jammu and Kashmir, the final status of which had not yet been fully determined, Junagardh, Manavadar, Gilgit and Baltistan. 3. Data refer to the former Democratic Yemen only.

Living Arrangements

Women Living Alone: 2000-2010

This table shows projected numbers in thousands and projected percentages of women living alone, by age of householder, in 2000 and 2010, and the projected percent change, 1990-2000 and 2000-2010.

[Numbers in thousands.]

Age	2000		2005	2010		Change, 1990-2000	Change 2000-2010
	Number	Percent	Number	Number	Percent		
All single women living alone	16,278	100.0%	17,397	18,578	100.0%	16.7%	14.1%
Younger than 25	495	3.0%	502	488	2.6%	-7.7%	-1.3%
25 to 34	1,351	8.3%	1,257	1,224	6.6%	-14.4%	-9.4%
35 to 44	1,757	10.8%	1,756	1,682	9.1%	34.8%	-4.2%

[Continued]

★ 229 ★

Women Living Alone: 2000-2010

[Continued]

Age	2000		2005	2010		Change,	Change
	Number	Percent	Number	Number	Percent	1990-2000	2000-2010
45 to 54	2,310	14.2%	2,700	2,940	15.8%	83.95	27.3%
55 to 64	2,016	12.4%	2,422	2,805	15.1%	-1.4%	39.2%
65 to 74	3,389	20.8%	3,427	3,924	21.1%	2.4%	15.8%
75 and older	4,962	30.5%	5,332	5,515	29.7%	26.4%	11.1%

Source: "The Future of Households," *American Demographics*, December 1993, pp. 27-40, selected from p. 39, table entitled "Single Women to 2010."

Marriage and Divorce

★ 230 ★

Divorce: Reasons

The table below shows the responses of divorced women and men to a survey question about the primary reason they divorced. According to the authors, a major reason for divorce was to be found in one or another of the elements of the sexual relationship. On the other hand, if the sexual relationship was good, a couple would find ways to negotiate nonsexual differences.

Responses	Women	Men
N =	127	122
The one primary reason I am divorced was...		
Sex	5%	17%
Money	7%	7%
Rejection	13%	12%
Children	1%	1%
Emotional problems	27%	31%
Extramarital affairs	22%	11%
Open marriage[1]	2%	1%
Other	23%	20%

Source: "If Divorced, the One Primary Reason Was:," Samuel S. Janus, PhD, and Cynthia L. Janus, MD, *The Janus Report on Sexual Behavior*, (New York: John Wiley & Sons, Inc., 1993), Table 6.19, p. 195. Between 1988 and 1992, the authors distributed 4,550 questionnaires to subjects at a variety of sites. The sample design was planned to conform to the population distribution of the United States in the areas of sex, age, region, income, education, and marital status. Returned questionnaires totaled 3,260. Of these, 495 were discarded. Satisfactorily completed questionnaires totaled 2,765: 1,418 women and 1,347 men. *Note:* 1. Sexual experience outside of the marriage.

★ 231 ★

Marriage and Divorce

What Women Look for in Marriage

Sixty-nine couples ranging in age from 44 to 92 years old and married an average of 41 years were studied. The separate effects of giving, receiving, and reciprocity on spouses' marital satisfaction were examined. It was found that perceptions of social support received from the spouse are more strongly related to the marital satisfaction and general well-being of wives than husbands. Linda Acitelli, an author of the report, is quoted in a newspaper article as saying, "Being married is important to men, whereas the quality of marriage is important to women."[1] This table shows the means and standard deviations of perceptions of social support, health, and well-being. For example, on average, spouses reported both giving to and receiving from their partners 4 of 6 types of social support. While there were no significant differences between husbands and wives in their mean scores on the giving, receiving, or perceived reciprocity scales, there was a tendency for husbands to report more giving and receiving than wives did.

Variable	Husbands		Wives	
	M	SD	M	SD
Receiving	4.48	1.75	4.03	2.15
Giving	4.52	1.96	4.03	2.07
Perceived reciprocity	3.89	2.19	3.36	2.18
Actual reciprocity	3.31	2.12	3.31	2.12
Well-being (standardized)	.03	.71	-.05	.87
Health	3.05	2.38	2.94	2.30
Length of marriage	41.16	14.72	41.16	14.72

Source: Linda K. Acitelli and Toni C. Antonucci, "Gender Differences in the Link Between Marital Support and Satisfaction in Older Couples," *Journal of Personality and Social Psychology,* 1994, Vol. 67, No. 4, pp. 688-698, Table 1, p. 691, "Means and Standard Deviations of Perceptions of Social Support, Health, and Well-Being." Address correspondence to Linda K. Acitelli, 5081 Institute for Social Research, P.O. Box 1248, Ann Arbor, MI 48106-1248. *Note:* 1. *Detroit Free Press,* October 18, 1994, p. 2B.

Mothers

★ 232 ★

Characteristics of Mothers Who Are Single by Choice

Statistics on single mothers compiled by the group Single Mothers by Choice, a national organization.

According to the organization Single Mothers by Choice, more than **170,000** single women over the age of 30 gave birth in 1990, the most recent year for which statistics were available. Between 1980 and 1990, the birth rate for white unmarried mothers aged 30-34 increased **120%**. During that period the rate for black unmarried women in that age group was up **28%**. For unmarried white women aged 35-39 years, the birth rate increased by **78%**, and for white women aged 40-44 years, the rate was up **38%**.

Most members of Single Mothers by Choice (SMC) are in their mid-thirties, with a median annual income of **$42,000**, compared to the 1991 median income of the average man of $23,000.

Source: Single Mothers by Choice, 1995 newsletter excerpted from *Single Mothers by Choice: A Guidebook for Single Women Who Are Considering or Have Chosen Motherhood*. Jane Mattes. Random House, 1994. Primary sources: U.S. Public Health Service; *US News & World Report*.

★ 233 ★

Mothers

Distribution of Household Tasks

This table shows the percentage of time contributed by children, husbands, and wives to various household tasks. Husbands and children substitute for one another in performing these tasks, according to the authors. So, for example, if there is a teenage daughter in the house, the father's workload is lessened, but the mother's workload remains the same.

Task	Children	Husband	Wife	Nonfamily
Laundry	10%	7%	81%	2%
Shopping	3%	19%	78%	--
Cooking	7%	15%	77%	1%
Cleaning	19%	12%	66%	3%
Dishwashing	26%	13%	60%	1%
Paperwork	1%	29%	70%	--
Child care	4%	32%	63%	2%
Yardwork	9%	49%	40%	2%

Source: Selected from Dennis A. Ahlburg and Carol J. DeVita, *New Realities of the American Family*, Population Bulletin, Vol. 47, No. 2, August 1992, Figure 11, p. 27, "Distribution of Household Tasks by Family Members, mid-1980s. Primary source: Goldscheider and Waite, *New Families, No Families?*, 1991, using National Longitudinal Surveys of Young Women and Mature Women.

★ 234 ★

Mothers

Single Mothers: 2000-2010

This table shows numbers in thousands and percent of single-mother households, by age of householder, projected for 2000 and 2010. It shows the projected percent change between 1990-2000 and 2000-2010. Teen birth rates have been rising, expecially for 18- and 19-year-olds. This age group will grow in the near future, because the oldest children of "baby boomers" turned 17 in 1994. So, the number of single mothers under the age of 25 could grow by more than 50% between 1990 and 2010.

[Numbers in thousands.]

Age	2000		2005	2010		Change, 1990-2000	Change 2000-2010
	Number	Percent	Number	Number	Percent		
All single mothers	7,473	100.0%	7,607	7,779	100.0%	13.2%	4.1%
Younger than 25	931	12.5%	1,091	1,234	15.9%	18.4%	32.5%
25 to 34	2,605	34.9%	2,637	2,834	36.4%	-0.7%	8.8%
35 to 44	2,966	39.7%	2,852	2,675	34.4%	26.7%	-9.8%
45 to 54	851	11.4%	891	879	11.3%	20.4%	3.3%
55 to 64	93	1.2%	109	127	1.6%	-6.0%	36.6%
65 to 74	17	0.2%	17	20	0.3%	-43.9%	13.9%
75 and older	9	0.1%	10	10	0.1%	7.7%	16.8%

Source: "The Future of Households," *American Demographics*, December 1993, pp. 27-40, selected from p. 37, table entitled "Single Mothers to 2010."

★ 235 ★

Mothers

Spanking Beliefs and Practices

A study of 204 mothers with children younger than 4 was conducted at two New York sites to determine maternal beliefs and practices of spanking infants and toddlers. This table shows mothers' beliefs regarding spanking. Among other findings of the study: 42% of mothers said they had spanked their child in the past week; 11% said they had spanked their child more than once a day.

Is It Okay to...?	Never	Rarely	Usually/ Always	Total Yes
Spank a child less than 1 year old	81%	16%	3%	19%
Spank a child 1 to 3 years old	26%	50%	24%	74%
Spank so that it leaves a mark	92%	6%	2%	8%

[Continued]

★ 235 ★

Spanking Beliefs and Practices

[Continued]

Is It Okay to...?	Never	Rarely	Usually/Always	Total Yes
Spank with something other than a hand	81%	12%	7%	19%
Spank somewhere besides buttocks	57%	31%	12%	33%

Source: Selected from Rebecca R.S. Socolar, M.D., and Ruth E.K. Stein, M.D., "Spanking Infants and Toddlers: Maternal Belief and Practice," *Pediatrics,* Vol. 95, No. 1, January 1995, Table 4, p. 108, "Mother's Belief: Is It Okay to...?" Address reprint requests to Rebecca R.S. Socolar, M.D., C.B. #7225, Community Pediatrics, University of North Carolina, Chapel Hill, NC 27599-7225.

★ 236 ★

Mothers

Time Spent on Household Tasks and Children

This table shows the adjusted mean time spent (in hours per week) on specific household tasks and child care, by married homemakers and by married women working part time and full time. Figures are also shown for males by the employment status of their wives.

| | Wife's Employment Status | | | | | |
| | Women | | | Men | | |
	Homemaker	Part time	Full time	Homemaker	Part time	Full time
Meal preparation	9.7	8.0	5.0	1.2	1.5	2.1
Meal cleanup	3.7	2.8	1.4	0.6	0.3	0.5
Chores	.03	0.1	.01	0.2	.04	0.1
Clean inside	6.4	6.2	3.1	0.6	1.3	0.6
Clean outside	0.5	1.0	0.7	3.0	1.9	2.2
Misc. chores	1.2	1.0	0.2	1.1	1.5	0.8
Repair	1.3	0.6	0.4	2.3	2.2	1.1
Garden	1.1	0.5	X	0.5	0.7	0.9
Paperwork	0.9	0.1	0.1	0.4	0.2	0.4
Shop	3.9	4.6	2.2	2.0	1.7	1.7
Acquiring services	3.2	3.3	1.8	2.6	2.7	2.7
Errands	.05	0.2	.04	.07	.02	0.2
Routine child care	5.5	3.6	2.3	1.4	1.7	1.0
Help child	0.6	0.4	0.2	.05	0.2	.04
Play with child	1.3	0.8	0.2	0.6	0.6	0.4
Help others	2.0	1.4	0.4	1.2	2.0	1.7

Source: Selected from Beth Anne Shelton, "The Distribution of Household Tasks: Does Wife's Employment Status Make a Difference?" *Journal of Family Issues,* Vol. 11, No. 2, June 1990, pp. 115-135, Table 3, p. 125, "Adjusted Mean Time Spent (in hours per week) on Household Tasks and Child Care, by Wife's Employment Status and Gender." Primary source: Data used are from the 1980-1981 Study of Time Use, collected by the Institute for Social Research (Juster, Hill, Stafford, & Parsons, 1983).

★ 237 ★

Mothers

Time Spent Taking Care of Household and Children

This table shows the adjusted mean time spent (in hours per week) on household labor and child care, by married homemakers and by married women working part time and full time. Figures are also shown for husbands whose wives were full-time homemakers and husbands whose wives worked part time and full time. There was an association between wives' employment status and time spent on these activities, but there was no such association for husbands. Employed women spent less time on household labor and child-care related tasks. Those employed full time spent less time than those employed part-time. Time spent by husbands on housework and child care did not vary in any systematic way depending on wives' employment status.

| | Wife's Employment Status | | | | | |
| | Women | | | Men | | |
	Homemaker	Part time	Full time	Homemaker	Part time	Full time
Preschool-age children in household						
Household labor	33.4	30.3	15.0	9.4	13.1	8.2
Child care	19.1	10.2	5.2	4.8	5.2	2.8
School-age children in household						
Household labor	35.6	28.7	18.9	12.5	12.3	11.7
Child care	3.5	3.3	2.7	1.7	1.9	1.1
No children in household						
Household labor	31.0	32.9	14.6	14.7	13.3	13.6
Child care	X	X	X	X	X	X
All households						
Household labor	35.6	28.7	18.9	11.6	14.0	12.1
Child care	7.0	3.7	2.1	2.1	1.8	1.0

Source: Selected from Beth Anne Shelton, "The Distribution of Household Tasks: Does Wife's Employment Status Make a Difference?" *Journal of Family Issues,* Vol. 11, No. 2, June 1990, pp. 115-135, Table 2, p. 124, "Adjusted Mean Time Spent (in hours per week) in Household Labor and Child Care, by Wife's Employment Status and Gender." Primary source: Data used are from the 1980-1981 Study of Time Use, collected by the Institute for Social Research (Juster, Hill, Stafford, & Parsons, 1983).

Chapter 5
EDUCATION

★ 238 ★

Computer Knowledge Scores: 1992

This table shows the percent correct for U.S. 8th and 11th grade students on the Functional Information Technology Test (FITT), by sex and home computer type. FITT is an international test of practical computer knowledge.

Student characteristics	8th Graders			11th Graders		
	Percent correct	Jackknifed std. error	Number	Percent correct	Jackknifed std. error	Number
Sex						
Male	72.21	1.00	1,395	58.59	1.05	1,842
Female	68.80	.71	1,606	57.89	.99	1,946
Total	70.42	.81	3,001	58.23	.95	3,788
Home Computer						
Apple II	68.48	1.36	377	57.45	1.30	574
Macintosh	74.63	1.69	177	60.80	1.89	149
IBM PC or compatible	76.62	.82	805	64.75	1.47	707
Other	71.30	1.66	415	59.44	1.17	495
Don't know	66.03	.93	363	55.02	1.19	538
None	64.86	1.18	912	55.50	.86	1,324
Total	70.02	.83	3,049	58.15	.84	3,788

Source: Selected from "Practical Computer Knowledge Scores (Percent Correct on FITT) and Jackknifed Standard Errors for U.S. 8th Grade Students by Sex, Race, and Home Computer Type, 1992," and Practical Computer Knowledge Scores (Percent Correct on FITT) and Jackknifed Standard Errors for U.S. 11th Grade Students by Sex, Race, and Home Computer Type, 1992," Ronald E. Anderson (ed.), *Computers in American Schools 1992: An Overview*, A National Report from the International IEA Computers in Education Study, University of Minnesota, tables 3.2 a and 3.2 b, pp. 37 and 39. Primary source: IEA Computers in Education Study, United States (1992). Related reading: Barbara Kantrowitz, "Men, Women & Computers," *Newsweek*, May 16, 1994, pp. 48-55.

★ 239 ★

Computers

International Comparison, Computer Knowledge Scores: 1992

This table shows the total percent correct for U.S. 8th and 11th grade students on the Functional Information Technology Test (FITT), by sex, and the total scores for other countries administering the test. FITT is an international test of practical computer knowledge. American students show smaller gender gaps in computer knowledge than do the countries shown here.

Country	Female Mean	Male Mean	Male Minus Female Score
Grade 8			
Austria	66	72	-6
Germany	65	72	-7
Japan	45	53	-8
Netherlands	65	69	-4
United States	60	62	-1
Grade 11			
Austria	81	90	-9
Japan	62	68	-6
United States	70	73	-3

Source: "Practical Computer Knowledge (Percent Correct on FITT) Scores for All U.S. 8th and 11th Grade Students by Sex, Total Difference by Sex, and Country, 1992," Ronald E. Anderson (ed.), *Computers in American Schools 1992: An Overview*, A National Report from the International IEA Computers in Education Study, University of Minnesota, table 3.4, p. 43. Primary source: International IEA Computers in Education Study (Pelgrum & Plomp 1993).

★ 240 ★

Computers

Opportunity to Learn About Computers: 1992

This table shows the percentage of U.S. students who were ever taught a "tool-equivalent" computer course by gender and race. This type of course-equivalent involves running programs, using word processors, and using databases or spreadsheets. There are no large differences in opportunity; slightly more females than males reported more instruction in the 11th grade.

Gender	Grade 5	Grade 8	Grade 11
	N=3,947	N=3,491	N=2,951
Female	20%	46%	50%
Male	24%	45%	45%

Source: Selected from "Percent of U.S. Students Ever Taught a "Tool-Equivalent" Computer Course by Gender, Race, and Region within Grade Level, 1992" Ronald E. Anderson (ed.), *Computers in American Schools 1992: An Overview*, A National Report from the International IEA Computers in Education Study, University of Minnesota, table 6.4, p. 78. Primary source: IEA Computers in Education Study, United States (1992).

★ 241 ★

Computers

Out-Of-School Computer Access: 1992

This table shows the percentage of U.S. students who reported out-of-school computer access, a computer in the home, and mean hours of non-computer use during 1992.

Gender	Any access outside school (this year)	Computer in the home	Hours per week using non-school computer	
			Mean	SD
Grade 5				
Female	82%	37%	2.2	4.3
Male	83%	40%	2.9	6.2
Grade 8				
Female	82%	45%	1.7	3.1
Male	83%	51%	2.7	4.8
Grade 11				
Female	79%	46%	1.7	3.1
Male	81%	57%	3.0	5.7

Source: Selected from "Percent of U.S. Students Who Report Out-of-School Computer Access, a Computer in the Home, and Mean Hours of Non-School Computer Use during 1992 by Sex and Socioeconomic Status within Grade Level," Ronald E. Anderson (ed.), *Computers in American Schools 1992: An Overview*, A National Report from the International IEA Computers in Education Study, University of Minnesota, table 7.3, p. 88. Primary source: IEA Computers in Education Study, United States (1992).

★ 242 ★

Computers

Out-Of-School Computer Types: 1992

This table shows the percentage of U.S. students with out-of-school computer access during 1992 by the type of computer they most often used.

Gender and grade	Type of computer					
	None, no access	Apple II	Macintosh	IBM	Other	Don't know
Grade 5						
Female	37%	20%	3%	12%	8%	20%
Male	38%	20%	4%	17%	11%	12%
Grade 8						
Female	16%	21%	5%	23%	12%	23%
Male	19%	19%	5%	31%	16%	10%
Grade 11						
Female	10%	17%	9%	34%	12%	19%
Male	12%	14%	9%	40%	18%	7%

Source: Selected from "Percent of U.S. Students with Out-of-School Computer Access during 1992 by Type of Computer Most Often Used, Sex, and Socioeconomic Status within Grade Level" Ronald E. Anderson (ed.), *Computers in American Schools 1992: An Overview*, A National Report from the International IEA Computers in Education Study, University of Minnesota, table 7.5, p. 93. Primary source: IEA Computers in Education Study, United States (1992).

★ 243 ★

Computers

Sent Messages to Another Computer: 1992

This table shows the percentage of U.S. students ever taught to send messages to another computer. Schools linked up with the Internet were relatively uncommon in 1992.

Gender	Grade 5	Grade 8	Grade 11
Female	12%	20%	15%
Male	19%	28%	24%

Source: Selected from "Percent of U.S. Students Ever Taught to "Send Messages to Another Computer" by Gender, Race, and Region within Grade Level, 1992," Ronald E. Anderson (ed.), *Computers in American Schools 1992: An Overview*, A National Report from the International IEA Computers in Education Study, University of Minnesota, table 6.6, p. 80. Sample sizes are 3,947, 3,491, and 2,951 in 5th, 8th, and 11th grade, respectively. Primary source: IEA Computers in Education Study, United States (1992).

★ 244 ★

Computers

Took a Programming Course: 1992

This table shows the percentage of U.S. students who said they took a programming course this year or last year by gender.

Gender	BASIC			Pascal		
	5th	8th	11th	5th	8th	11th
Female	27%	35%	18%	12%	12%	6%
Male	31%	38%	22%	15%	18%	11%

Source: Selected from "Percent of U.S. Students Who Said They Ever Took a Programming Course This Year or Last Year by Gender, Race, and Region within Grade Level, 1992," Ronald E. Anderson (ed.), *Computers in American Schools 1992: An Overview*, A National Report from the International IEA Computers in Education Study, University of Minnesota, table 6.5, p. 79. Sample sizes are 3,947, 3,491, and 2,951 in 5th, 8th, and 11th grade, respectively. Primary source: IEA Computers in Education Study, United States (1992).

Degrees

★ 245 ★

Associates' Degrees by Field of Study: 1991-1992

This table shows the total number of associates' degrees conferred by field of study to men and women in academic year 1991-1992.

Field of Study	Men	Women	Total	5-year change
Agriculture and natural resources	3,576	1,675	5,251	-4%
Architecture and related programs	106	337	443	-73%
Area, ethnic, and cultural studies	9	20	29	+107%
Biological/life sciences	564	797	1,361	+52%
Business management	30,274	71,953	102,227	-11%
Communications	890	996	1,886	+19%
Communications technologies	1,145	649	1,794	-8%
Computer and information sciences	4,565	4,725	9,290	+2%
Education	3,708	6,559	10,267	+40%
Engineering	2,341	344	2,685	-41%
Engineering-related technologies	32,104	3,757	35,861	-17%
English language and literature	348	671	1,019	+101%
Foreign languages and literatures	128	305	433	+2%
Health professions	10,805	68,648	79,453	+27%
Home economics	687	5,749	6,436	-12%

[Continued]

★ 245 ★

Associates' Degrees by Field of Study: 1991-1992
[Continued]

Field of Study	Men	Women	Total	5-year change
Law and legal studies	907	6,146	7,053	+182%
Liberal/general studies	62,817	91,777	154,594	+39%
Library science	18	85	103	-12%
Mathematics	464	280	744	+12%
Multi/interdisciplinary studies	3,782	4,059	7,841	+17%
Parks, recreation, leisure, and fitness studies	369	251	620	+8%
Philosophy and religion	43	17	60	-40%
Physical sciences	1,205	861	2,066	+3%
Precision production trades	7,133	1,872	9,005	+13%
Protective services	11,241	3,876	15,117	+27%
Psychology	338	871	1,209	+19%
Public administration and services	639	2,523	3,162	+40%
ROTC and military technologies	156	16	172	+244%
Social sciences and history	1,400	1,760	3,160	+22%
Theological studies	280	216	496	-17%
Transportation and material moving	1,978	440	2,418	+87%
Visual and performing arts	4,803	7,085	11,888	+37%
Other and unclassified by field	18,658	7,430	26,088	--
All fields	207,481	296,750	504,231	+16%

Source: Selected from "Earned Degrees Conferred 1991-92," *The Chronicle of Higher Education Almanac,* September 1, 1994, p. 31. Primary source: U.S. Department of Education.

★ 246 ★

Degrees

Associates' Degrees Conferred: 1991 and 1992

This table shows the total number of associates' degrees conferred by institutions of higher education, numbers by public and private institutions, and the numbers by sex, for academic years 1990-1991 and 1991-1992.

Item	Associate's Degrees				Percent change
	1990-1991		1991-1992		
	Number	Percent	Number	Percent	
All institutions	481,720	100.0%	504,231	100.0%	4.7%
Public	398,055	82.6%	420,265	83.3%	5.6%
Private	83,665	17.4%	83,966	16.7%	0.4%

[Continued]

★ 246 ★

Associates' Degrees Conferred: 1991 and 1992
[Continued]

Item	Associate's Degrees				
	1990-1991		1991-1992		Percent
	Number	Percent	Number	Percent	change
Men	198,634	41.2%	207,481	41.1%	4.5%
Women	283,086	58.8%	296,750	58.9%	4.8%

Source: Selected from "Degrees conferred by institutions of higher education, by level of degree, control of institution, race/ethnicity and sex of recipient: 50 states and the District of Columbia: 1990-91 and 1991-92," U.S. Department of Education, National Center for Education Statistics, *Degrees and Other Awards Conferred by Institutions of Higher Education: 1991-92*, NCES 94-053, Table A-1, p. V. Primary source: U.S. Department of Education, National Center for Education Statistics, Integrated Postsecondary Education Data System, "Completions" survey, 1990-91 and 1991-92 and "Consolidated" survey 1991 and 1992.

★ 247 ★

Degrees

Bachelors' Degrees by Field of Study: 1991-1992

This table shows the total number of bachelors' degrees conferred by field of study to men and women in academic year 1991-1992.

Field of Study	Men	Women	Total	5-year change
Agriculture and natural resources	9,869	5,255	15,124	+1%
Architecture and related programs	5,805	2,948	8,753	-2%
Area, ethnic, and cultural studies	1,907	3,435	5,342	+56%
Biological/life sciences	20,798	22,143	42,941	+13%
Business management	135,440	121,163	256,603	+7%
Communications	21,150	33,107	54,257	+23%
Communications technologies	347	373	720	-48%
Computer and information sciences	17,510	7,047	24,557	-38%
Education	22,686	85,320	108,006	+24%
Engineering	51,768	9,438	61,206	-17%
Engineering-related technologies	14,948	1,387	16,335	-14%
English language and literature	18,536	36,415	54,951	+51%
Foreign languages and literatures	3,985	9,918	13,903	+26%
Health professions	10,189	51,531	61,720	-2%
Home economics	1,687	13,211	14,898	+3%
Law and legal studies	701	1,443	2,144	+82%
Liberal/general studies	12,784	19,390	32,174	+36%
Library science	8	89	97	-29%
Mathematics	7,888	6,895	14,783	-13%
Multi/interdisciplinary studies	8,628	12,019	20,647	+48%
Parks, recreation, leisure, and fitness studies	4,144	4,302	8,446	+98%
Philosophy and religion	4,752	2,774	7,526	+26%

[Continued]

★ 247 ★

Bachelors' Degrees by Field of Study: 1991-1992
[Continued]

Field of Study	Men	Women	Total	5-year change
Physical sciences	11,431	5,529	16,960	-15%
Precision production trades	280	98	378	-17%
Protective services	11,659	7,196	18,855	+46%
Psychology	17,031	46,482	63,513	+48%
Public administration and services	3,479	12,508	15,987	+30%
ROTC and military technologies	158	26	184	-52%
Social sciences and history	73,001	60,973	133,974	+39%
Theological studies	3,552	1,177	4,729	-17%
Transportation and material moving	3,239	359	3,598	+118%
Visual and performing arts	17,616	28,906	46,522	+27%
Other and unclassified by field	3,835	2,885	6,720	--
All fields	520,811	615,742	1,136,553	+15%

Source: Selected from "Earned Degrees Conferred 1991-92," *The Chronicle of Higher Education Almanac,* September 1, 1994, p. 31. Primary source: U.S. Department of Education.

★ 248 ★
Degrees

Bachelors' Degrees Conferred: 1991 and 1992

This table shows the total number of bachelors' degrees conferred by institutions of higher education, numbers by public and private institutions, and the numbers by sex, for academic years 1990-1991 and 1991-1992.

Item	Bachelor's Degrees				Percent change
	1990-1991		1991-1992		
	Number	Percent	Number	Percent	
All institutions	1,094,538	100.0%	1,136,553	100.0%	3.8%
Public	724,062	66.2%	759,475	66.8%	4.9%
Private	370,476	33.8%	377,078	33.2%	1.8%
Men	504,045	46.1%	520,811	45.8%	3.3%
Women	590,493	53.9%	615,742	54.2%	4.3%

Source: Selected from "Degrees conferred by institutions of higher education, by level of degree, control of institution, race/ethnicity and sex of recipient: 50 states and the District of Columbia: 1990-91 and 1991-92," U.S. Department of Education, National Center for Education Statistics, *Degrees and Other Awards Conferred by Institutions of Higher Education: 1991-92*, NCES 94-053, Table A-1, p. V. Primary source: U.S. Department of Education, National Center for Education Statistics, Integrated Postsecondary Education Data System, "Completions" survey, 1990-91 and 1991-92 and "Consolidated" survey 1991 and 1992.

★ 249 ★

Degrees

Degrees by Race/Ethnicity: 1991-1992

This table shows the total number of degrees conferred by institutions of higher education by level of degree, and numbers by sex and race-ethnicity, for the academic years 1991-1992.

Level of degree/ sex of recipient	Total	White, non-Hispanic	Black non-Hispanic	Hispanic	Asian or Pacific Isl.	Amer Ind/ Alaska Nat.	Nonresident alien	Race/ethnicity unknown
Associates' degrees	504,231	388,038	38,673	26,118	15,158	3,873	7,989	19,614
Men	207,481	155,557	13,559	10,890	6,897	1,420	3,418	13,078
Women	296,750	232,481	25,114	15,228	8,261	2,453	4,571	6,536
Bachelors' degrees	1,136,553	921,432	71,223	40,251	46,459	5,128	28,467	22,189
Men	520,811	422,510	26,503	17,772	23,139	2,151	17,070	10,949
Women	615,742	498,922	44,720	22,479	23,320	2,977	11,397	11,240
Masters' degrees	352,838	257,052	17,379	9,050	12,289	1,221	39,644	15,504
Men	161,842	110,793	5,788	3,989	6,819	501	26,235	7,424
Women	190,996	146,259	11,591	5,061	5,470	720	13,409	8,080
Doctors' degrees	40,659	25,301	1,202	798	1,545	118	10,649	976
Men	25,557	14,377	565	447	1,046	65	8,398	622
Women	15,102	10,924	637	351	499	53	2,251	354
First-professional degrees	74,146	59,866	3,568	2,820	4,757	294	1,342	1,155
Men	45,071	37,087	1,620	1,668	2,728	157	948	690
Women	59,075	22,779	1,948	1,152	2,029	137	394	465

Source: Selected from "Degrees conferred by institutions of higher education, by race/ethnicity, level of degree, and sex of recipient: 50 states and the District of Columbia: 1991-92," U.S. Department of Education, National Center for Education Statistics, *Degrees and Other Awards Conferred by Institutions of Higher Education: 1991-92,* NCES 94-053, Table 2, p. 9. Primary source: U.S. Department of Education, National Center for Education Statistics, Integrated Postsecondary Education Data System, "Completions" survey, 1991-92 and "Consolidated" survey 1992. Totals include 4,768 associates'; 1,404 bachelors'; 699 masters'; 70 doctors'; and 314 first-professional degrees for which race/ethnicity was not reported.

★ 250 ★

Degrees

Degrees Conferred: 1991 and 1992

This table shows the total number of degrees conferred by institutions of higher education, numbers by public and private institutions, and the numbers by sex, for academic years 1990-1991 and 1991-1992. Degrees include associates', bachelors', masters', doctors', and first-professional.

Item	Total Degrees				Percent change
	1990-1991		1991-1992		
	Number	Percent	Number	Percent	
All institutions	2,024,668	100.0%	2,108,427	100.0%	4.1%
Public	1,370,409	67.7%	1,439,324	68.3%	5.0%
Private	654,259	32.3%	669,103	31.7%	2.3%

[Continued]

★ 250 ★

Degrees Conferred: 1991 and 1992

[Continued]

| Item | Total Degrees | | | | |
| | 1990-1991 | | 1991-1992 | | Percent change |
	Number	Percent	Number	Percent	
Men	927,763	45.8%	960,762	45.6%	3.6%
Women	1,096,905	54.2%	1,147,665	54.4%	4.6%

Source: Selected from "Degrees conferred by institutions of higher education, by level of degree, control of institution, race/ethnicity and sex of recipient: 50 states and the District of Columbia: 1990-91 and 1991-92," U.S. Department of Education, National Center for Education Statistics, *Degrees and Other Awards Conferred by Institutions of Higher Education: 1991-92*, NCES 94-053, Table A-1, p. V. Primary source: U.S. Department of Education, National Center for Education Statistics, Integrated Postsecondary Education Data System, "Completions" survey, 1990-91 and 1991-92 and "Consolidated" survey 1991 and 1992.

★ 251 ★

Degrees

Doctoral Degrees by Field of Study: 1991-1992

This table shows the total number of doctoral degrees conferred by field of study to men and women in academic year 1991-1992.

Field of Study	Men	Women	Total	5-year change
Agriculture and natural resources	963	251	1,214	+16%
Architecture and related programs	93	39	132	+43%
Area, ethnic, and cultural studies	90	65	155	+16%
Biological/life sciences	2,620	1,623	4,243	+24%
Business management	953	289	1,242	+17%
Communications	131	121	252	-8%
Communications technologies	1	2	3	+50%
Computer and information sciences	669	103	772	+106%
Education	2,783	4,081	6,864	+7%
Engineering	4,961	527	5,488	+44%
Engineering-related technologies	11	0	11	-35%
English language and literature	537	736	1,273	+32%
Foreign languages and literatures	378	472	850	+29%
Health professions	698	963	1,661	+37%
Home economics	71	222	293	-1%
Law and legal studies	50	18	68	-43%
Liberal/general studies	30	37	67	+20%
Library science	16	34	50	-12%
Mathematics	851	231	1,082	+43%
Multi/interdisciplinary studies	144	87	231	-6%
Parks, recreation, leisure, and fitness studies	41	20	61	+91%
Philosophy and religion	365	110	475	+13%

[Continued]

★ 251 ★

Doctoral Degrees by Field of Study: 1991-1992
[Continued]

Field of Study	Men	Women	Total	5-year change
Physical sciences	3,429	962	4,391	+20%
Precision production trades	0	0	0	0
Protective services	13	11	24	+33%
Psychology	1,359	2,014	3,373	-5%
Public administration and services	204	228	432	+9%
ROTC and military technologies	0	0	0	0
Social sciences and history	2,126	1,092	3,218	+10%
Theological studies	1,077	182	1,259	+2%
Transportation and material moving	0	0	0	0
Visual and performing arts	504	402	906	+14%
Other and unclassified by field	389	180	569	--
All fields	25,557	15,102	40,659	+19%

Source: Selected from "Earned Degrees Conferred 1991-92," *The Chronicle of Higher Education Almanac,*
September 1, 1994, p. 31. Primary source: U.S. Department of Education.

★ 252 ★

Degrees

Doctors' Degrees by Race/Ethnicity: 1978-1993

This table shows the number of women receiving doctorates, and the number who were U.S. citizens, by race/ethnicity, from 1978 through 1993.

Race/ ethnicity	1978	1983	1984	1985	1986	1987	1988	1989	1990	1991	1992	1993
TOTAL WOMEN	8,322	10,533	10,699	10,744	11,305	11,428	11,818	12,512	13,106	13,870	14,420	15,108
U.S. Citizens	7,355	9,239	9,297	9,147	9,446	9,408	9,565	10,004	10,740	11,183	11,475	11,902
Total known race/ ethnicity	7,704	10,021	10,149	10,114	10,492	10,543	10,940	11,545	12,532	13,408	13,986	14,699
U.S. Citizens	6,956	9,063	9,120	8,990	9,315	9,256	9,455	9,902	10,626	11,046	11,367	11,840
Native Americans	10	31	20	56	41	53	42	45	45	58	70	59
U.S. Citizens	10	31	20	56	41	53	42	45	44	56	67	59
Asians	422	582	614	697	687	777	935	1,027	1,261	1,646	1,854	2,048
U.S. Citizens	103	180	174	187	183	173	200	185	214	305	309	337
Blacks	481	549	591	589	563	517	566	562	618	674	656	767
U.S. Citizens	449	509	526	533	500	451	499	494	547	586	569	666

[Continued]

★ 252 ★

Doctors' Degrees by Race/Ethnicity: 1978-1993
[Continued]

Race/	Year of Doctorate											
ethnicity	1978	1983	1984	1985	1986	1987	1988	1989	1990	1991	1992	1993
Hispanics	212	334	296	354	391	377	370	400	468	513	542	557
U.S. Citizens	156	251	221	261	270	285	274	274	341	361	368	412
Whites	6,579	8,525	8,628	8,418	8,810	8,819	9,027	9,511	10,140	10,517	10,864	11,268
U.S. Citizens	6,238	8,092	8,179	7,953	8,321	8,294	8,440	8,904	9,480	9,738	10,054	10,366
Unknown Race/												
Ethnicity	618	512	550	630	813	885	878	967	574	462	434	409
U.S. Citizens	399	176	177	157	131	152	110	102	114	137	108	62

Source: Selected from "Doctorates: Women," Thurgood, D.H., and J.E. Clarke, 1995, *Summary Report 1993: Doctorate Recipients from United States Universities,* Table B-2, p. 80. Primary source: National Research Council, Survey of Earned Doctorates.

★ 253 ★

Degrees

Doctors' Degrees Conferred: 1991 and 1992

This table shows the total number of doctors' degrees conferred by institutions of higher education, numbers by public and private institutions, and the numbers by sex, for academic years 1990-1991 and 1991-1992.

Item	Doctor's Degrees				Percent
	1990-1991		1991-1992		change
	Number	Percent	Number	Percent	
All institutions	39,294	100.0%	40,659	100.0%	3.5%
Public	25,681	65.4%	26,820	66.0%	4.4%
Private	13,613	34.6%	13,839	34.0%	1.7%
Men	24,756	63.0%	25,557	62.9%	3.2%
Women	14,538	37.0%	15,102	37.1%	3.9%

Source: Selected from "Degrees conferred by institutions of higher education, by level of degree, control of institution, race/ethnicity and sex of recipient: 50 states and the District of Columbia: 1990-91 and 1991-92," U.S. Department of Education, National Center for Education Statistics, *Degrees and Other Awards Conferred by Institutions of Higher Education: 1991-92,* NCES 94-053, Table A-1, p. V. Primary source: U.S. Department of Education, National Center for Education Statistics, Integrated Postsecondary Education Data System, "Completions" survey, 1990-91 and 1991-92 and "Consolidated" survey 1991 and 1992.

★ 254 ★

Degrees

Doctors' Degrees: 1992-2003

This table shows the middle-level projection series for doctor's degrees by sex of recipient, 1992 to 2003. Women received 54% of all college degrees conferred in 1992 and this share is expected to remain the same into the following decade. Women, though, are earning growing shares of certain types of degrees, such as doctorates.

Year ending	Total	Men	Women
1992	39,800	24,500	15,300
1993	40,500	24,800	15,700
1994	40,900	24,700	16,200
1995	40,900	24,200	16,700
1996	41,100	23,900	17,200
1997	41,300	23,700	17,600
1998	41,400	23,400	18,000
1999	41,900	23,400	18,500
2000	41,600	22,700	18,900
2001	41,600	22,300	19,300
2002	41,700	22,000	19,700
2003	41,800	21,700	20,100

Source: Selected from "Doctor's degrees, by sex of recipient, with alternative projections, 50 States and D.C., 1977-78 to 2002-2003," National Center for Education Statistics, *Projections of Education Statistics to 2003*, Table 30, p. 61. Primary source: U.S. Department of Education, National Center for Education Statistics, "Degrees and Other Formal Awards Conferred" survey; Integrated Postsecondary Education Data System (IPEDS), "Completions" survey; and "National Higher Education Statistics: Fall 1991," *Early Estimates*.

★ 255 ★

Degrees

First-Professional Degrees by Field and Race/Ethnicity: 1991-1992

This table shows the total number of first-professional degrees conferred by institutions of higher education, numbers by field for public and private institutions, and the numbers by sex and race/ethnicity, for academic year 1991-1992.

Field of study, sex of recipient	Total	White, non-Hispanic	Black non-Hispanic	Hispanic	Asian or Pacific Isl.	Amer Ind/ Alaska Nat.	Nonresident alien	Race/ethnicity unknown
Total, all fields	74,146	59,866	3,568	2,820	4,757	294	1,342	1,185
Men	45,071	37,087	1,620	1,668	2,728	157	948	690
Women	29,075	22,779	1,948	1,152	2,029	137	394	495
Chiropractic (D.C., D.C.M.)	2,694	2,311	35	63	81	27	172	5
Men	2,012	1,717	27	53	63	15	134	3
Women	682	594	8	10	18	12	38	2
Dentistry (D.D.S., D.M.D.)	3,593	2,346	174	236	520	15	203	87
Men	2,431	1,647	94	169	316	13	132	60

[Continued]

★ 255 ★

First-Professional Degrees by Field and Race/Ethnicity: 1991-1992

[Continued]

Field of study, sex of recipient	Total	White, non-Hispanic	Black non-Hispanic	Hispanic	Asian or Pacific Isl.	Amer Ind/ Alaska Nat.	Nonresident alien	Race/ethnicity unknown
Women	1,162	699	80	67	204	2	71	27
Medicine (M.D.)	15,243	11,384	829	623	1,785	65	203	354
Men	9,796	7,495	386	401	1,122	33	144	215
Women	5,447	3,889	443	222	663	32	59	139
Optometry (O.D.)	1,232	964	34	44	142	7	31	10
Men	676	564	7	20	56	4	19	6
Women	556	400	27	24	86	3	12	4
Osteopathic Medicine (D.O.)	1,326	1,097	55	57	98	5	8	6
Men	887	745	21	41	67	2	5	6
Women	439	352	34	16	31	3	3	0
Pharmacy (B.Pharm., Pharm.D.)	1,339	926	65	42	219	4	66	17
Men	493	350	22	22	62	1	30	6
Women	846	576	43	20	157	3	36	11
Podiatry (D.P.M., D.P.,Pod.D.)	504	394	44	22	32	2	8	2
Men	359	286	28	13	22	2	6	2
Women	145	108	16	9	10	0	2	0
Veterinary Medicine (D.V.M.)	2,044	1,863	51	59	32	9	5	25
Men	850	780	19	23	10	6	2	10
Women	1,194	1,083	32	36	22	3	3	15
Law (LL.B.,J.D.)	38,848	33,225	1,875	1,448	1,228	149	259	664
Men	22,260	19,501	753	768	629	74	162	373
Women	16,588	13,724	1,122	680	599	75	97	291
Divinity/Ministry (B.D.,M.Div.)	4,950	3,958	334	120	233	8	283	11
Men	3,731	2,962	220	96	199	5	243	6
Women	1,219	996	114	24	34	3	40	5
Rabbinical & Talmudic Stu. (M.H.L./Rav)	301	293	0	2	0	0	6	0
Men	294	286	0	2	0	0	6	0
Women	7	7	0	0	0	0	0	0
Other/undefined field	2,072	1,150	72	104	387	3	98	4
Men	1,282	754	43	60	182	2	65	3
Women	790	351	29	44	205	1	33	1

Source: Selected from "First-professional degrees conferred by institutions of higher education, by race/ethnicity, field of study, and sex of recipient: 50 states and the District of Columbia: 1991-92," U.S. Department of Education, National Center for Education Statistics, *Degrees and Other Awards Conferred by Institutions of Higher Education: 1991-92,* NCES 94-053, Table 2b, p. 11. Primary source: U.S. Department of Education, National Center for Education Statistics, Integrated Postsecondary Education Data System, "Completions" survey, 1991-92 and "Consolidated" survey 1992. Totals include 12 Dentistry; 3 Divinity/Ministry; and 299 Other/undefined field degrees for which race/ethnicity was not reported.

★ 256 ★
Degrees

First-Professional Degrees by Field of Study: 1991-1992

This table shows the total number of first-professional degrees conferred by institutions of higher education, numbers by field for public and private institutions, and the numbers by sex, for academic year 1991-1992.

Field of study, sex of recipient	Total	Public	Private		
			Total	Nonprofit	For-profit
Total, all fields	74,146	29,366	44,780	44,363	417
Men	45,071	17,338	27,733	27,496	237
Women	29,075	12,028	17,047	16,867	180
Chiropractic (D.C., D.C.M.)	2,694	0	2,694	2,694	0
Men	2,012	0	2,012	2,012	0
Women	682	0	682	682	0
Dentistry (D.D.S., D.M.D.)	3,593	2,200	1,393	1,393	0
Men	2,431	1,505	926	926	0
Women	1,162	695	467	467	0
Medicine (M.D.)	15,243	9,259	5,984	5,984	0
Men	9,796	5,908	3,888	3,888	0
Women	5,447	3,351	2,096	2,096	0
Optometry (O.D.)	1,232	595	637	637	0
Men	676	309	367	367	0
Women	556	286	270	270	0
Osteopathic Medicine (D.O.)	1,326	416	910	910	0
Men	887	290	597	597	0
Women	439	126	313	313	0
Pharmacy (B.Pharm., Pharm.D.)	1,339	852	487	487	0
Men	493	316	177	177	0
Women	846	536	310	310	0
Podiatry (D.P.M., D.P.,Pod.D.)	504	0	504	504	0
Men	359	0	359	359	0
Women	145	0	145	145	0
Veterinary Medicine (D.V.M.)	2,044	1,831	213	213	0
Men	850	782	68	68	0
Women	1,194	1,049	145	145	0
Law (LL.B.,J.D.)	38,848	14,097	24,751	24,340	411
Men	22,260	8,160	14,100	13,866	234

[Continued]

★ 256 ★

First-Professional Degrees by Field of Study: 1991-1992
[Continued]

Field of study, sex of recipient	Total	Public	Private		
			Total	Nonprofit	For-profit
Women	16,588	5,937	10,651	10,474	177
Divinity/Ministry					
(B.D.,M.Div.)	4,950	0	4,950	4,950	0
Men	3,731	0	3,731	3,731	0
Women	1,219	0	1,219	1,219	0
Rabbinical & Talmudic Stu.					
(M.H.L./Rav)	301	0	301	301	0
Men	294	0	294	294	0
Women	7	0	7	7	0
Other/undefined field	2,072	116	1,956	1,950	6
Men	1,282	68	1,214	1,211	3
Women	790	48	742	739	3

Source: Selected from "First-professional degrees conferred by institutions of higher education, by control of institution, field of study, and sex of recipient: 50 states and the District of Columbia: 1991-92," U.S. Department of Education, National Center for Education Statistics, *Degrees and Other Awards Conferred by Institutions of Higher Education: 1991-92*, NCES 94-053, Table 1a, p. 8. Primary source: U.S. Department of Education, National Center for Education Statistics, Integrated Postsecondary Education Data System, "Completions" survey, 1991-92 and "Consolidated" survey 1992.

★ 257 ★

Degrees

First-Professional Degrees Conferred: 1991 and 1992

This table shows the total number of first-professional degrees conferred by institutions of higher education, numbers by public and private institutions, and the numbers by sex, for academic years 1990-1991 and 1991-1992.

Item	First-professional Degrees				
	1990-1991		1991-1992		Percent change
	Number	Percent	Number	Percent	
All institutions	71,948	100.0%	74,146	100.0%	3.1%
Public	29,554	41.1%	29,366	39.6%	-0.6%
Private	42,394	58.9%	44,780	60.4%	5.6%

[Continued]

★ 257 ★

First-Professional Degrees Conferred: 1991 and 1992
[Continued]

| Item | First-professional Degrees | | | | Percent change |
| | 1990-1991 | | 1991-1992 | | |
	Number	Percent	Number	Percent	
Men	43,846	60.9%	45,071	60.8%	2.8%
Women	28,102	39.1%	29,075	39.2%	3.5%

Source: Selected from "Degrees conferred by institutions of higher education, by level of degree, control of institution, race/ethnicity and sex of recipient: 50 states and the District of Columbia: 1990-91 and 1991-92," U.S. Department of Education, National Center for Education Statistics, *Degrees and Other Awards Conferred by Institutions of Higher Education: 1991-92*, NCES 94-053, Table A-1, p. V. Primary source: U.S. Department of Education, National Center for Education Statistics, Integrated Postsecondary Education Data System, "Completions" survey, 1990-91 and 1991-92 and "Consolidated" survey 1991 and 1992.

★ 258 ★
Degrees

First-Professional Degrees: 1992-2003

This table shows the middle-level projection series for first-professional degrees by sex of recipient, 1992 to 2003. Women received 54% of all college degrees conferred in 1992 and this share is expected to remain the same into the following decade. Women's proportion of first-professional degrees rose from 21% in 1977-78 to 38% in 1990-91. By 2002-2003, women's proportion is expected to be 41%.

Year ending	Total	Men	Women
1992	77,000	45,000	32,000
1993	81,000	46,700	34,300
1994	84,600	48,000	36,600
1995	85,700	49,100	36,600
1996	85,200	49,100	36,100
1997	85,700	49,800	35,900
1998	85,400	49,800	35,600
1999	86,200	50,400	35,800
2000	86,600	50,800	35,800
2001	87,300	51,500	35,800
2002	87,300	51,500	35,800
2003	88,000	52,200	35,800

Source: Selected from "First-professional degrees, by sex of recipient, with alternative projections, 50 States and D.C., 1977-78 to 2002-2003," National Center for Education Statistics, *Projections of Education Statistics to 2003*, Table 31, p. 62. Primary source: U.S. Department of Education, National Center for Education Statistics, "Degrees and Other Formal Awards Conferred" survey; Integrated Postsecondary Education Data System (IPEDS), "Completions" survey; and "National Higher Education Statistics: Fall 1991," *Early Estimates*.

★ 259 ★
Degrees

Masters' Degrees by Field of Study: 1991-1992

This table shows the total number of masters' degrees conferred by field of study to men and women in academic year 1991-1992.

Field of Study	Men	Women	Total	5-year change
Agriculture and natural resources	2,413	1,322	3,735	+6%
Architecture and related programs	2,271	1,369	3,640	+15%
Area, ethnic, and cultural studies	688	697	1,385	+60%
Biological/life sciences	2,301	2,484	4,785	-3%
Business management	54,705	29,937	84,642	+26%
Communications	1,537	2,643	4,180	+15%
Communications technologies	155	129	284	+5%
Computer and information sciences	6,884	2,646	9,530	+12%
Education	21,244	71,424	92,668	+25%
Engineering	21,327	3,656	24,983	+13%
Engineering-related technologies	816	178	994	+56%
English language and literature	2,513	4,937	7,450	+36%
Foreign languages and literatures	971	1,955	2,926	+23%
Health professions	4,691	18,374	23,065	+25%
Home economics	409	2,003	2,412	+17%
Law and legal studies	1,597	772	2,369	+22%
Liberal/general studies	870	1,524	2,394	+51%
Library science	992	3,901	4,893	+29%
Mathematics	2,452	1,559	4,011	+8%
Multi/interdisciplinary studies	995	1,131	2,126	-14%
Parks, recreation, leisure, and fitness studies	650	708	1,358	+143%
Philosophy and religion	731	415	1,146	+3%
Physical sciences	3,909	1,465	5,374	-4%
Precision production trades	0	0	0	0
Protective services	797	452	1,249	+23%
Psychology	2,988	7,227	10,215	+7%
Public administration and services	5,769	13,474	19,243	+17%
ROTC and military technologies	0	0	0	-100%
Social sciences and history	7,237	5,465	12,702	+21%
Theological studies	3,199	1,986	5,185	+4%
Transportation and material moving	354	31	385	-11%
Visual and performing arts	4,078	5,275	9,353	+10%

[Continued]

★ 259 ★

Masters' Degrees by Field of Study: 1991-1992
[Continued]

Field of Study	Men	Women	Total	5-year change
Other and unclassified by field	2,299	1,857	4,156	--
All fields	161,842	190,996	352,838	+22%

Source: Selected from "Earned Degrees Conferred 1991-92," *The Chronicle of Higher Education Almanac,* September 1, 1994, p. 31. Primary source: U.S. Department of Education.

★ 260 ★
Degrees

Masters' Degrees Conferred: 1991 and 1992

This table shows the total number of masters' degrees conferred by institutions of higher education, numbers by public and private institutions, and the numbers by sex, for academic years 1990-1991 and 1991-1992.

Item	Master's Degrees				Percent change
	1990-1991		1991-1992		
	Number	Percent	Number	Percent	
All institutions	337,168	100.0%	352,838	100.0%	4.6%
Public	193,057	57.3%	203,398	57.6%	5.4%
Private	144,111	42.7%	149,440	42.4%	3.7%
Men	156,482	46.4%	161,842	45.9%	3.4%
Women	180,686	53.6%	190,996	54.1%	5.7%

Source: Selected from "Degrees conferred by institutions of higher education, by level of degree, control of institution, race/ethnicity and sex of recipient: 50 states and the District of Columbia: 1990-91 and 1991-92," U.S. Department of Education, National Center for Education Statistics, *Degrees and Other Awards Conferred by Institutions of Higher Education: 1991-92,* NCES 94-053, Table A-1, p. V. Primary source: U.S. Department of Education, National Center for Education Statistics, Integrated Postsecondary Education Data System, "Completions" survey, 1990-91 and 1991-92 and "Consolidated" survey 1991 and 1992.

★ 261 ★

Degrees

Mathematics Degrees, Trends: 1978-1991

This table shows the number of mathematics degrees earned by sex in 1978-1979 and 1990-1991 and the percent change. The combined number of undergraduate and graduate degrees earned increased 5% for males and 35% for females during that period.

Sex	Undergraduate			Graduate			Combined graduate & undergraduate		
	1978-1979	1990-1991	% change	1978-1979	1990-1991	% change	1978-1979	1990-1991	% change
Total	11,536	14,206	23%	3,177	3,067	-3%	14,713	17,273	17%
Male	6,698	7,430	11%	2,116	1,850	-13%	8,814	9,280	5%
Female	4,838	6,776	40%	1,061	1,217	15%	5,899	7,993	35%

Source: Selected from "Trends in Mathematics Degrees Earned, by Sex," *The National Education Goals Report: Volume One: The National Report*, National Education Goals Panel, 1993, Exhibit 68, p. 104. Primary Source: National Science Foundation, various years, and National Research Council, 1992.

★ 262 ★

Degrees

Physics Degrees Granted: 1992-1993

This table shows the total number of physics degrees granted at the end of academic year 1992-1993, by type of degree, sex, minority group status, and citizenship.

Type of degree and sex	Total number of degrees	Black		Hispanic		Oriental		Asian Indian		Arab		Other
		U.S.	Foreign	U.S.	Foreign	U.S.	Foreign	U.S.	Foreign	U.S.	Foreign	Foreign
Bachelor's												
Men	4,096	142	9	63	9	135	74	32	50	12	6	31
Women	704	51	1	10	3	32	4	5	12	2	2	10
Master's enroute												
Men	769	9	1	4	8	22	159	6	36	2	10	75
Women	151	6	X	2	X	5	30	1	16	X	1	9
Terminal master's												
Men	745	36	3	6	5	9	137	3	22	2	9	48
Women	132	19	2	1	2	6	35	1	13	X	2	7
Doctoral												
Men	1,199	8	5	13	28	30	322	4	51	5	17	135
Women	170	X	X	1	1	6	62	X	10	2	1	12

Source: Selected from "Enrollments and Degrees Report," American Institute of Physics, *AIP Report*, Pub. No. R-151.31, November 1994, table VII, p. 9, "Number of physics degrees granted by sex, minority group status, and citizenship, 1992-93." The minority data presented in this table are underreported and represents lower limits.

★ 263 ★

Degrees

Science Degrees, Trends: 1978-1991

This table shows the number of science degrees earned by sex in 1978-1979 and 1990-1991 and the percent change. The combined number of undergraduate and graduate degrees earned by females increased 13% versus a 9% decrease for males.

Sex	Undergraduate			Graduate			Combined graduate & undergraduate		
	1978-1979	1990-1991	% change	1978-1979	1990-1991	% change	1978-1979	1990-1991	% change
Total	413,979	408,982	-1%	97,460	103,610	6%	511,439	512,592	<1%
Male	230,704	210,843	-9%	59,055	52,087	-12%	289,759	262,930	-9%
Female	183,275	198,139	8%	38,405	51,523	34%	221,680	249,662	13%

Source: Selected from "Trends in Science Degrees Earned, by Sex," *The National Education Goals Report: Volume One: The National Report,* National Education Goals Panel, 1993, Exhibit 67, p. 104. Primary Source: National Science Foundation, various years, and National Research Council, 1992.

★ 264 ★

Degrees

Time to Complete Baccalaureate Degree: 1977-1990

This table shows how many years it took people to complete a baccalaureate degree in 1977, 1986, and 1990. Most baccalaureate programs can be completed within 4 years of entering. Taking long to graduate may result from delaying entrance, changing schools or majors, stopping out, or taking reduced course loads for financial, academic, or social reasons. In 1990, the percentage of students completing college within 4 years was larger for females than for males.

Year of college graudation	Total				Male				Female			
	4 or fewer years	5 or fewer years	6 or fewer years	More than 6 years	4 or fewer years	5 or fewer years	6 or fewer years	More than 6 years	4 or fewer years	5 or fewer years	6 or fewer years	More than 6 years
1977	45.4%	67.2%	75.3%	24.7%	39.2%	61.8%	71.1%	28.9%	52.8%	73.8%	80.5%	19.5%
1986	34.5%	60.2%	70.8%	29.2%	30.8%	57.4%	69.8%	30.2%	38.2%	62.9%	71.8%	28.2%
1990	31.1%	57.2%	68.4%	31.6%	26.6%	54.3%	67.6%	32.4%	35.1%	59.8%	69.1%	30.9%

Source: "Percentage of college graduates completing the baccalaureate degree within various years of graduating from high school, by sex: Year of college graduation 1977, 1986, and 1990," U.S. Department of Education, National Center for Education Statistics, Indicator of the Month, October 1993, *Time to complete baccalaureate degree,* NCES 93-641. Primary source: U.S. Department of Education, National Center for Education Statistics, Recent College Graduate surveys.

Educational Attainment

★ 265 ★

Educational Attainment by Race/Ethnicity: 1990

This table shows the educational attainment of the female population aged 25 years and over, by race and Hispanic origin, as reported in the 1990 census.

[Amer Ind/Esk/Aleut refers to American Indian or Alaskan native.]

Educational attainment	All persons	Race					Hispanic or. (any race)	White, not of Hisp. origin
		White	Black	Amer Ind/ Esk/Aleut	Asian or Pac Isl	Other race		
Females, 25 years +	83,654,171	69,252,013	9,257,807	562,703	2,282,675	2,298,973	5,657,519	66,108,006
Less than 5th grade	2,161,459	1,200,562	363,978	26,399	192,850	377,670	760,704	836,966
5th to 8th grade	6,546,831	5,018,665	857,047	51,569	165,589	453,961	989,986	4,512,548
9th to 12th grade, no diploma	12,360,377	9,404,264	2,131,892	117,140	235,312	471,769	1,085,425	8,834,508
High school graduate (includes equivalency)	26,850,606	23,179,568	2,559,021	163,733	464,698	483,586	1,275,286	22,434,508
Some college, no degree	15,520,115	13,060,799	1,738,237	118,641	316,915	285,523	794,048	12,587,768
Associate degree, occupational program	2,920,672	2,473,486	284,688	21,071	88,196	53,231	140,882	2,392,632
Associate degree, academic program	2,538,505	2,142,909	239,853	15,626	92,715	47,402	140,303	2,056,521
Bachelor's degree	10,015,766	8,661,760	717,007	32,661	515,986	88,352	316,611	8,452,135
Master's degree	3,581,055	3,109,749	296,503	11,565	139,879	23,359	98,201	3,039,111
Professional school deg.	857,999	740,400	50,116	3,104	52,911	11,468	42,677	711,806
Doctorate degree	300,786	259,851	19,465	1,194	17,624	2,652	13,396	249,503

Source: Selected from "School Enrollment and Educational Attainment by Race and Hispanic Origin: 1990," U.S. Bureau of the Census, 1990 Census of Population, *Social and Economic Characteristics, United States*, 1990 CP-2-1, Table 42, p. 42.

★ 266 ★

Educational Attainment

Educational Attainment of Persons Aged 25 and Over: 1991

This table shows the highest level of education attained by persons 25 years and over as of March 1991. Since 1970 the college gains of young adult women outstripped those of young adult men so that by 1991 there was little difference in the proportions of men and women 25 to 29 years old with 4 or more years of college.

Sex	High school 4 years	College 1 to 3 years	College 4 years +	Total high school grad +
Total	38.6%	18.4%	21.4%	78.4%
Male	36.0%	18.2%	24.3%	78.5%
Female	41.0%	18.6%	18.8%	78.3%

Source: Selected from U.S. Bureau of the Census, *Population Profile of the United States: 1993*, Special Studies Series P23-185, Figure 14, p. 15, "Educational Attainment of Persons 25 Years and Over, by Sex, Race, Hispanic Origin, and Age: March 1991."

★ 267 ★

Educational Attainment

Illiteracy in Africa: 1970-1992

This table shows the percentage of the total population age 15+ who were illiterate in 1970-1975 and 1980-1985. It gives the most recent estimate of illiteracy for the period 1987-1992. The percentages of females aged 15+ who were illiterate are also shown. The countries for which no information was available are not shown here.

[NA Not available.]

Country	Percent of population age 15+			Percent of females age 15+		
	1970-1975	1980-1985	Most recent est. 1987-92	1970-1975	1980-1985	Most recent est. 1987-92
Africa						
Algeria	74%	51%	43%	NA	65%	55%
Angola	NA	64%	58%	NA	77%	72%
Benin	NA	81%	77%	NA	88%	84%
Botswana	59%	30%	26%	NA	40%	35%
Burkina Faso	91%	86%	82%	NA	94%	91%
Burundi	NA	58%	50%	NA	68%	60%
Cameroon	NA	52%	46%	NA	64%	57%
Cape Verde	63%	53%	NA	NA	NA	NA
Central African Republic	NA	69%	62%	NA	81%	75%
Chad	NA	77%	70%	NA	88%	82%
Comoros	NA	52%	NA	NA	NA	NA

[Continued]

★ 267 ★

Illiteracy in Africa: 1970-1992
[Continued]

Country	Percent of population age 15+			Percent of females age 15+		
	1970-1975	1980-1985	Most recent est. 1987-92	1970-1975	1980-1985	Most recent est. 1987-92
Congo	NA	48%	43%	NA	62%	56%
Cote d'Ivoire	NA	51%	46%	NA	66%	60%
Egypt						
Arab Rep. of	NA	55%	52%	NA	71%	66%
Equatorial Guinea	NA	55%	50%	NA	69%	63%
Ethiopia	96%	38%	NA	NA	NA	NA
Gabon	NA	44%	39%	NA	57%	52%
Gambia	NA	80%	73%	NA	90%	84%
Ghana	70%	47%	40%	NA	58%	49%
Guinea	NA	83%	76%	NA	92%	87%
Guinea-Bissau	NA	70%	64%	NA	82%	76%
Kenya	NA	35%	31%	NA	47%	42%
Lesotho	NA	26%	NA	NA	16%	NA
Liberia	80%	68%	61%	NA	79%	71%
Libya	61%	44%	36%	NA	60%	50%
Madagascar	NA	23%	20%	NA	32%	27%
Malawi	NA	59%	NA	NA	69%	NA
Mali	NA	77%	68%	NA	85%	76%
Mauritania	NA	73%	66%	NA	84%	79%
Mauritius	NA	17%	NA	NA	23%	NA
Morocco	79%	58%	51%	NA	71%	62%
Mozambique	NA	72%	67%	NA	84%	79%
Niger	NA	79%	72%	NA	89%	83%
Nigeria	NA	57%	49%	NA	69%	61%
Reunion	NA	21%	NA	NA	NA	NA
Rwanda	NA	55%	50%	NA	68%	63%
Sao Tome and Principe	NA	43%	33%	NA	NA	NA
Senegal	NA	68%	62%	NA	81%	75%
Seychelles	42%	NA	NA	NA	NA	NA
Sierra Leone	NA	87%	79%	NA	94%	89%
Somalia	NA	83%	76%	NA	91%	86%
Sudan	NA	76%	73%	NA	90%	88%
Swaziland	NA	32%	NA	NA	34%	NA
Togo	84%	62%	57%	NA	75%	69%
Tunisia	62%	42%	35%	NA	53%	44%
Uganda	NA	57%	46%	NA	71%	55%
Zaire	NA	34%	28%	NA	47%	39%

[Continued]

★ 267 ★

Illiteracy in Africa: 1970-1992
[Continued]

Country	Percent of population age 15+			Percent of females age 15+		
	1970-1975	1980-1985	Most recent est. 1987-92	1970-1975	1980-1985	Most recent est. 1987-92
Zambia	NA	33%	27%	NA	41%	35%
Zimbabwe	NA	38%	33%	NA	45%	40%

Source: Selected from *Social Indicators of Development 1994*, World Bank, 1994, pp. 3+. Primary source: World Bank International Economics Department, April 1994.

★ 268 ★

Educational Attainment

Illiteracy in Asia

This table shows the percentage of all adults and of males and females who are illiterate in selected Asian countries. Information on adult literacy may not always be comparable. UNESCO defines literacy as the ability to read and write simple sentences. In some countries, people who have never attended school are considered illiterate. With very few exceptions, illiteracy is higher among females. Of the one billion illiterate people expected to exist by the year 2000, three-quarters of them will live in China, India, Indonesia, Pakistan, and Bangladesh.

[NA Not available.]

Country	Percent illiterate		
	Total	Male	Female
Asia, excluding Near East			
Afghanistan	76.0%	NA	NA
Bangladesh	70.8%	60.3%	82.0%
Cambodia	25.0%	NA	NA
China	34.5%	20.8%	48.9%
Hong Kong	12.0%	NA	NA
India	59.2%	45.2%	74.3%
Indonesia	32.7%	22.5%	42.3%
Iran	49.0%	NA	NA
Laos	16.1%	8.0%	24.2%
Malaysia	30.4%	20.4%	40.3%
Nepal	79.4%	68.3%	90.8%
Pakistan	73.8%	64.0%	84.8%
Philippines	16.7%	16.1%	17.2%
Singapore	17.1%	8.4%	26.0%
Sri Lanka	13.2%	8.7%	18.0%
Thailand	12.0%	7.7%	16.0%

[Continued]

★ 268 ★

Illiteracy in Asia
[Continued]

Country	Percent illiterate		
	Total	Male	Female
Near East			
Iraq	10.7%	9.8%	12.5%
Israel	8.2%	5.0%	11.3%
Jordan	25.0%	NA	NA
Kuwait	25.5%	21.8%	31.2%
Lebanon	22.0%	NA	NA
Oman	70.0%	NA	NA
Qatar	24.3%	23.2%	27.5%
Saudi Arabia	48.9%	28.9%	69.2%
Syria	40.0%	NA	NA
Turkey	25.8%	14.1%	37.5%
Yemen (South)	58.0%	NA	NA

Source: "Literacy," *The Economist book of vital world statistics: a complete guide to the world in figures*, The Economist Books Ltd., London, 1990, pp. 210-211.

★ 269 ★

Educational Attainment

Illiteracy in Asia: 1970-1992

This table shows the percentage of the total population age 15+ who were illiterate in 1970-1975 and 1980-1985. It gives the most recent estimate of illiteracy for the period 1987-1992. The percentages of females aged 15+ who were illiterate are also shown. The countries for which no information was available are not shown here.

[NA Not available.]

Country	Percent of population age 15+			Percent of females age 15+		
	1970-1975	1980-1985	Most recent est. 1987-92	1970-1975	1980-1985	Most recent est. 1987-92
Asia						
Afghanistan	NA	76%	71%	NA	91%	86%
Bangladesh	74%	68%	65%	NA	81%	78%
Bhutan	NA	68%	62%	NA	81%	75%
Brunei	36%	22%	NA	NA	NA	NA
Cambodia	NA	71%	30%	NA	83%	35%
China	NA	32%	27%	NA	45%	38%
Hong Kong	23%	12%	NA	NA	19%	NA
India	66%	56%	52%	NA	71%	66%
Indonesia	43%	28%	23%	NA	37%	32%
Iran Islamic Rep. of	NA	52%	46%	NA	64%	57%

[Continued]

★ 269 ★

Illiteracy in Asia: 1970-1992
[Continued]

Country	Percent of population age 15+			Percent of females age 15+		
	1970-1975	1980-1985	Most recent est. 1987-92	1970-1975	1980-1985	Most recent est. 1987-92
Japan	1	1	1	1	1	1
Korea						
Rep. of	12%	5%	4%	NA	9%	7%
Laos						
Lao People's						
Dem. Rep.	65%	56%	NA	NA	24%	NA
Macau	21%	NA	NA	NA	NA	NA
Malaysia	42%	26%	22%	NA	35%	30%
Myanmar	29%	22%	19%	NA	31%	28%
Nepal	81%	78%	74%	NA	89%	87%
Pakistan	79%	69%	65%	NA	82%	79%
Philippines	17%	12%	10%	NA	13%	11%
Singapore	31%	14%	NA	NA	21%	NA
Sri Lanka	22%	13%	12%	NA	19%	17%
Thailand	21%	9%	7%	NA	13%	10%
Viet Nam	NA	16%	12%	NA	20%	16%

Source: Selected from *Social Indicators of Development 1994*, World Bank, 1994, pp. 3+. Primary source: World Bank International Economics Department, April 1994. *Note:* 1. According to UNESCO, illiteracy is less than 5%.

★ 270 ★

Educational Attainment

Illiteracy in Developed Countries

This table shows the percentage of all adults and of males and females who are illiterate in selected developed countries. Information on adult literacy may not always be comparable. UNESCO defines literacy as the ability to read and write simple sentences. In some countries, people who have never attended school are considered illiterate.

[NA Not available.]

Country	Percent illiterate		
	Total	Male	Female
Developed Countries			
Greece	9.5%	3.9%	14.7%
Hungary	1.1%	0.7%	1.5%
Israel	8.2%	5.0%	11.3%
Italy	3.0%	2.1%	3.7%
Portugal	16.0%	11.2%	20.3%
Spain	7.1%	4.0%	9.9%

[Continued]

★ 270 ★

Illiteracy in Developed Countries

[Continued]

Country	Percent illiterate		
	Total	Male	Female
United States	4.0%	NA	NA
Yugoslavia	10.4%	4.5%	16.1%

Source: "Literacy," *The Economist book of vital world statistics: a complete guide to the world in figures,* The Economist Books Ltd., London, 1990, pp. 210-211.

★ 271 ★

Educational Attainment

Illiteracy in Europe: 1970-1992

This table shows the percentage of the total population age 15+ who were illiterate in 1970-1975 and 1980-1985. It gives the most recent estimate of illiteracy for the period 1987-1992. The percentages of females aged 15+ who were illiterate are also shown. The countries for which no information was available are not shown here. In most European countries, illiteracy is now less than 5%.

[NA Not available.]

Country	Percent of population age 15+			Percent of females age 15+		
	1970-1975	1980-1985	Most recent est. 1987-92	1970-1975	1980-1985	Most recent est. 1987-92
Europe						
Greece	16%	9%	7%	NA	14%	11%
Hungary	2%	1%	NA	NA	NA	NA
Italy	6%	4%	1	NA	5%	1
Malta	NA	16%	NA	NA	18%	NA
Poland	2%	NA	NA	NA	NA	NA
Portugal	29%	18%	15%	NA	23%	19%
Spain	8%	6%	5%	NA	8%	7%

Source: Selected from *Social Indicators of Development 1994*, World Bank, 1994, pp. 3+. Primary source: World Bank International Economics Department, April 1994. *Note:* 1. According to UNESCO, illiteracy is less than 5%.

★ 272 ★

Educational Attainment

Illiteracy in Latin America and the Caribbean

This table shows the percentage of all adults and of males and females who are illiterate in selected Latin American and Caribbean countries. Information on adult literacy may not always be comparable. UNESCO defines literacy as the ability to read and write simple sentences. In some countries, people who have never attended school are considered illiterate. With very few exceptions, illiteracy is higher among females.

[NA Not available.]

Country	Percent illiterate		
	Total	Male	Female
Latin America and the Caribbean			
Argentina	6.1%	5.7%	6.4%
Bolivia	25.0%	NA	NA
Brazil	22.2%	20.9%	23.4%
Chile	8.9%	8.5%	9.2%
Colombia	14.8%	13.6%	16.1%
Costa Rica	7.4%	7.3%	7.4%
Cuba	3.8%	3.8%	3.8%
Dominican Republic	31.4%	31.8%	30.9%
Ecuador	19.8%[1]	15.8%	23.8%
El Salvador	30.2%	26.9%	33.2%
Guatemala	45.0%	NA	NA
Haiti	65.2%	62.7%	67.5%
Honduras	40.5%	39.3%	41.6%
Mexico	9.7%	7.7%	11.7%
Netherlands Antilles	6.2%	5.8%	6.6%
Nicaragua	12.0%	NA	NA
Panama	11.8%	11.0%	12.3%
Paraguay	12.5%	9.7%	15.2%
Peru	18.1%[2]	9.9%	26.1%
Puerto Rico	10.9%	10.3%	11.5%
Trinidad and Tobago	5.1%	3.5%	6.6%
Uruguay	5.0%	5.6%	4.5%
Venezuela	15.3%[2]	13.5%	17.0%

Source: "Literacy," *The Economist book of vital world statistics: a complete guide to the world in figures,* The Economist Books Ltd., London, 1990, pp. 210-211. *Notes:* 1. Estimate. 2. Excluding Indian jungle population.

★ 273 ★

Educational Attainment

Illiteracy in Latin America/Caribbean: 1970-1992

This table shows the percentage of the total population age 15+ who were illiterate in 1970-1975 and 1980-1985. It gives the most recent estimate of illiteracy for the period 1987-1992. The percentages of females aged 15+ who were illiterate are also shown. The countries for which no information was available are not shown here.

[NA Not available.]

Country	Percent of population age 15+			Percent of females age 15+		
	1970-1975	1980-1985	Most recent est. 1987-92	1970-1975	1980-1985	Most recent est. 1987-92
Latin America and the Caribbean						
Argentina	7%	5%	5%	NA	6%	5%
Barbados	1%	NA	NA	NA	NA	NA
Belize	9%	NA	NA	NA	NA	NA
Bolivia	NA	28%	23%	NA	36%	29%
Brazil	34%	22%	19%	NA	23%	20%
Chile	11%	8%	7%	NA	8%	7%
Colombia	19%	15%	13%	NA	16%	14%
Costa Rica	12%	8%	7%	NA	8%	7%
Cuba	NA	8%	6%	NA	9%	7%
Dominica	6%	NA	NA	NA	NA	NA
Dominican Republic	33%	20%	17%	NA	22%	18%
Ecuador	26%	17%	14%	NA	20%	16%
El Salvador	43%	31%	27%	NA	35%	30%
French Guiana	NA	17%	NA	NA	NA	NA
Grenada	2%	NA	NA	NA	NA	NA
Guadeloupe	NA	10%	NA	NA	NA	NA
Guatemala	54%	48%	45%	NA	56%	53%
Guyana	8%	5%	4%	NA	6%	5%
Haiti	79%	52%	47%	NA	58%	53%
Honduras	43%	32%	27%	NA	35%	29%
Jamaica	4%	2%	[1]	NA	2%	[1]
Martinique	NA	7%	NA	NA	NA	NA
Mexico	26%	15%	13%	NA	18%	15%
Nicaragua	43%	13%	NA	NA	NA	NA
Panama	22%	14%	12%	NA	14%	12%
Paraguay	20%	12%	10%	NA	14%	12%
Peru	28%	18%	15%	NA	26%	21%
Puerto Rico	12%	11%	NA	NA	NA	NA
Saint Kitts and Nevis	2%	NA	NA	NA	NA	NA
Saint Lucia	18%	NA	NA	NA	NA	NA
Saint Vincent	4%	NA	NA	NA	NA	NA
Suriname	NA	7%	5%	NA	8%	5%
Trinidad and Tobago	8%	4%	NA	NA	5%	NA

[Continued]

★ 273 ★

Illiteracy in Latin America/Caribbean: 1970-1992
[Continued]

Country	Percent of population age 15+			Percent of females age 15+		
	1970-1975	1980-1985	Most recent est. 1987-92	1970-1975	1980-1985	Most recent est. 1987-92
Uruguay	6%	5%	4%	NA	5%	4%
Venezuela	24%	14%	7%	NA	12%	14%

Source: Selected from *Social Indicators of Development 1994*, World Bank, 1994, pp. 3+. Primary source: World Bank International Economics Department, April 1994. *Note:* 1. According to UNESCO, illiteracy is less than 5%.

★ 274 ★

Educational Attainment

Illiteracy in North Africa and the Middle East

This table shows the percentage of all adults and of males and females who are illiterate in selected North African and Middle Eastern countries. Information on adult literacy may not always be comparable. UNESCO defines literacy as the ability to read and write simple sentences. In some countries, people who have never attended school are considered illiterate. With very few exceptions, illiteracy is higher among females.

[NA Not available.]

Country	Percent illiterate		
	Total	Male	Female
Middle East/North Africa			
Algeria	55.3%	42.7%	68.3%
Bahrain	22.3%	15.1%	29.6%
Egypt	56.5%	43.2%	71.0%
Iran	49.0%	NA	NA
Iraq	10.7%	9.8%	12.5%
Jordan	25.0%	NA	NA
Kuwait	25.5%	21.8%	31.2%
Lebanon	22.0%	NA	NA
Libya	25.0%	NA	NA
Malta	15.9%	14.0%	17.7%
Morocco	66.0%	NA	NA
Oman	70.0%	NA	NA
Saudi Arabia	48.9%	28.9%	69.2%
Syria	40.0%	NA	NA
Tunisia	49.3%	39.5%	59.4%
Turkey	25.8%	14.1%	37.5%
Yemen (South)	58.0%	NA	NA

Source: "Literacy," *The Economist book of vital world statistics: a complete guide to the world in figures*, The Economist Books Ltd., London, 1990, pp. 210-211.

★ 275 ★

Educational Attainment

Illiteracy in Oceania: 1970-1992

This table shows the percentage of the total population age 15+ who were illiterate in 1970-1975 and 1980-1985. It gives the most recent estimate of illiteracy for the period 1987-1992. The percentages of females aged 15+ who were illiterate are also shown. The countries for which no information was available are not shown here.

[NA Not available.]

Country	Percent of population age 15+			Percent of females age 15+		
	1970-1975	1980-1985	Most recent est. 1987-92	1970-1975	1980-1985	Most recent est. 1987-92
Oceania						
Fiji	NA	15%	NA	NA	19%	NA
Papua New Guinea	68%	53%	48%	NA	68%	62%
Western Samoa	2%	NA	NA	NA	NA	NA

Source: Selected from *Social Indicators of Development 1994*, World Bank, 1994, pp. 3+. Primary source: World Bank International Economics Department, April 1994. *Note:* 1. According to UNESCO, illiteracy is less than 5%.

★ 276 ★

Educational Attainment

Illiteracy in Sub-Saharan Africa

This table shows the percentage of all adults and of males and females who are illiterate in selected African countries. Information on adult literacy may not always be comparable. UNESCO defines literacy as the ability to read and write simple sentences. In some countries, people who have never attended school are considered illiterate. With very few exceptions, illiteracy is higher among females.

[NA Not available.]

Country	Percent illiterate		
	Total	Male	Female
Sub-Saharan Africa			
Angola	59.0%	51.0%	68.0%[1]
Benin	73.0%	NA	NA
Botswana	29.0%	NA	NA
Burkina Faso	86.0%	NA	NA
Burundi	66.2%	57.2%	74.3%
Central African Republic	49.0%	NA	NA
Chad	74.0%	NA	NA
Congo	37.1%	28.6%	44.6%
Cote d'Ivoire	58.0%	NA	NA
Ethiopia	37.6%	NA	NA

[Continued]

★ 276 ★

Illiteracy in Sub-Saharan Africa
[Continued]

Country	Percent illiterate		
	Total	Male	Female
Gabon	38.0%	NA	NA
Ghana	46.0%	NA	NA
Guinea	71.0%	NA	NA
Kenya	40.0%	NA	NA
Lesotho	27.0%	NA	NA
Liberia	65.0%	NA	NA
Madagascar	32.0%	NA	NA
Malawi	58.0%	NA	NA
Mali	83.0%	NA	NA
Mauritania	83.0%	NA	NA
Mozambique	72.8%	56.0%	87.8%
Niger	86.0%	NA	NA
Nigeria	57.0%	NA	NA
Rwanda	53.0%	NA	NA
Senegal	72.0%	NA	NA
Sierra Leone	70.0%	NA	NA
Somalia	88.0%	NA	NA
Sudan	77.0%	NA	NA
Togo	68.6%	53.3%	81.5%
Uganda	42.0%	NA	NA
Zaire	38.0%	NA	NA
Zambia	24.0%	NA	NA
Zimbabwe	26.0%	NA	NA

Source: "Literacy," *The Economist book of vital world statistics: a complete guide to the world in figures*, The Economist Books Ltd., London, 1990, pp. 210-211. *Note:* 1. Estimate.

★ 277 ★

Educational Attainment

Illiteracy in the Near East: 1970-1992

This table shows the percentage of the total population age 15+ who were illiterate in 1970-1975 and 1980-1985. It gives the most recent estimate of illiteracy for the period 1987-1992. The percentages of females aged 15+ who were illiterate are also shown. The countries for which no information was available are not shown here.

[NA Not available.]

Country	Percent of population age 15+			Percent of females age 15+		
	1970-1975	1980-1985	Most recent est. 1987-92	1970-1975	1980-1985	Most recent est. 1987-92
Near East						
Bahrain	60%	27%	23%	NA	37%	31%
Iraq	NA	48%	40%	NA	59%	51%
Israel	12%	5%	NA	NA	7%	NA
Jordan	NA	26%	20%	NA	38%	30%
Kuwait	40%	29%	27%	NA	37%	33%
Lebanon	NA	23%	20%	NA	31%	27%
Qatar	NA	24%	NA	NA	28%	NA
Saudi Arabia	NA	42%	38%	NA	58%	52%
Syria						
Syrian Arab Rep.	60%	41%	36%	NA	57%	49%
Turkey	40%	24%	19%	NA	36%	29%
United Arab Emirates	47%	NA	NA	NA	NA	NA
Yemen						
Rep. of	NA	68%	62%	NA	80%	74%

Source: Selected from *Social Indicators of Development 1994*, World Bank, 1994, pp. 3+. Primary source: World Bank International Economics Department, April 1994.

★ 278 ★

Educational Attainment

International Comparisons of Educational Attainment: 1991

This table shows the percentage of the population in large industrialized countries who have completed secondary and higher education, by age, in 1991. The United States has the most educated population compared to other large industrialized countries. Young women in this country were more likely to have completed higher education (4 years of college or more) than were women or men in other countries (with the exception of men in Japan).

Country	25-64 years old Both sexes		25-34 years old					
			Both sexes		Male		Female	
	Secondary	Higher	Secondary	Higher	Secondary	Higher	Secondary	Higher
United States	83.3%	23.6%	86.1%	23.7%	85.7%	23.5%	86.5%	23.8%
Japan[1]	69.7%	13.3%	90.6%	22.9%	89.3%	34.2%	91.8%	11.5%
Germany	81.8%	11.2%	89.3%	11.5%	91.7%	12.7%	86.7%	10.3%
United Kingdom	65.3%	9.6%	79.2%	11.7%	80.7%	13.6%	77.6%	9.8%
France	50.5%	9.7%	65.9%	11.6%	67.3%	11.7%	65.4%	11.5%
Italy	28.2%	6.1%	43.1%	6.6%	42.3%	6.7%	43.8%	6.4%
Canada	75.7%	16.7%	86.0%	17.5%	84.6%	18.0%	87.3%	17.1%

Source: "Percentage of population in large industrialized countries who have completed secondary and higher education, by age, sex, and country: 1991," U.S. Department of Education, National Center for Education Statistics, Indicator of the Month, December 1993, "International Compariesons of Educational Attainment." Primary source: Organization for Economic Co-operation and Development, Center for Educational Research and Innovation, International Indicators Project. In the United States, completing secondary education is defined as completing high school; completing higher education is defined as completing 4 or more years of college. *Note:* 1. 1989 data.

★ 279 ★

Educational Attainment

Persistence and Degree Attainment

A group of students who began postsecondary educational careers during academic year 1989-1990 was followed to determine what percentage persisted until a degree was attained. This table shows the percentages of men and women who left by June 1990, by June 1991, and after June 1991. It also shows the percentages who were still enrolled in spring 1992 and the percentages who attained any certificate, license, or award by spring 1992. Females were less likely than males to leave postsecondary education during their first year.

Gender	Left school			Still enrolled	Attained
	By 6/90	7/90-6/91	After 6/91		
Male	23%	10%	11%	42%	14%
Female	19%	10%	10%	39%	21%

Source: Selected from "Persistence and attainment percentages by spring 1992 for postsecondary students who began in AY 1989-90," U.S. Department of Education, National Center for Education Statistics, Beginning Postsecondary Students Longitudinal Study 1992 Followup (BPS: 90/92), *Persistence and Attainment in Postsecondary Education for Beginning AY 1989-90 Students as of Spring 1992,* NCES 94-477, November 1993, Table 1, p. 1. Details may not add to 100% due to rounding.

Enrollment

★ 280 ★

African School Enrollment Preceding the First Level

This table shows the total number of pupils enrolled and the percentage who were female in selected African countries, in the latest year for which data on female enrollment is available. Education preceding the first level refers to kindergartens, nursery schools, and infant classes attached to schools at higher levels.

[NA Not available.]

Country or area	Year	Pupils enrolled	Percent female
Africa			
Angola[1]	1990	164,146	34%
Benin	1985	11,302	45%
Burkina Faso	1989	7,655	51%
Burundi	1988	2,381	49%
Cameroon	1990	93,771	50%
Cape Verde	1986	4,523	NA
Central African Republic	1986	11,450	39%
Comoros	1980	17,778	48%
Congo	1985	5,595	49%
Cote d'Ivoire	1991	11,217	48%
Djibouti	1992	218	65%
Egypt	1990	198,742	49%
Ethiopia	1991	58,444	50%
Gabon	1991	950	51%
Gambia	1991	13,118	NA
Ghana	1989	323,406	48%
Guinea-Bissau[2]	1988	754	49%
Kenya	1990	850,000	53%
Liberia	1980	80,215	42%
Libya			
Libyan Arab Jamahiriya	1985	15,028	48%
Mauritius	1982	10,617	49%
Morocco	1991	788,326	29%
Mozambique[1]	1986	45,100	46%
Namibia	1990	5,649	53%
Niger	1990	9,434	48%
Reunion	1985	37,694	49%
Rwanda	1987	8,000	NA
St. Helena	1985	88	68%

[Continued]

★ 280 ★

African School Enrollment Preceding the First Level

[Continued]

Country or area	Year	Pupils enrolled	Percent female
Sao Tome and Principe	1989	3,446	51%
Senegal	1989	15,964	51%
Seychelles	1991	3,257	50%
Somalia	1985	1,558	57%
Sudan[3]	1990	283,126	35%
Swaziland	1990	12,000	65%
Togo	1990	10,949	49%
Tunisia	1991	58,488	NA

Source: Selected from "Education preceding the first level," United Nations, *Statistical Yearbook 1992,* New York, 1994, Table 10, pp. 55+. Primary source: United Nations Educational, Scientific and Cultural Organization (Paris). *Notes:* 1. Data refer to initiation classes where pupils learn Portuguese. 2. Data refer to "Sector autonomo Bissau" only. 3. Data include Koranic schools "khalwas" which accept pupils of all ages.

★ 281 ★

Enrollment

African School Enrollment at the First Level

This table shows the total number of pupils enrolled and the percentage who were female in selected African countries, in the latest year for which data on female enrollment is available. The purpose of education at the first level is to provide basic instruction in the tools of learning, for example at elementary and primary schools. Its length may vary from 4 to 9 years.

[NA Not available.]

Country or area	Year	Pupils enrolled	Percent female
Africa			
Algeria	1990	4,189,152	45%
Angola	1990	990,155	48%
Benin	1985	444,163	34%[1]
Botswana	1992	308,840	51%
Burkina Faso	1991	530,013	39%
Burundi	1991	631,039	45%
Cameroon	1990	1,964,146	46%
Cape Verde	1989	67,761	49%
Central African Republic	1989	323,661	39%
Chad	1991	591,417	32%
Comoros	1987	64,737	44%
Congo	1990	502,918	46%
Cote d'Ivoire	1991	1,447,785	42%

[Continued]

★ 281 ★

African School Enrollment at the First Level
[Continued]

Country or area	Year	Pupils enrolled	Percent female
Djibouti	1992	30,589	43%
Egypt	1990	6,964,306	44%
Equatorial Guinea	1983	61,532	NA
Ethiopia	1991	2,063,636	42%
Gabon	1991	210,000	50%
Gambia	1991	90,645	41%
Ghana	1990	1,945,422	45%
Guinea	1990	346,807	32%
Guinea Bissau	1988	79,035	36%
Kenya	1990	5,392,319	49%
Lesotho	1990	351,632	55%
Liberia	1984	132,889	35%[2]
Libya Libyan Arab Jamahiriya	1991	1,238,986	48%
Madagascar	1990	1,570,721	49%
Malawi	1990	1,400,682	45%
Mali	1991	375,131	37%
Mauritania	1991	188,580	43%
Mauritius	1991	135,233	49%
Morocco	1991	2,578,566	40%
Mozambique	1992	1,199,847	42%
Namibia	1990	313,528	52%
Niger	1990	368,732	36%
Nigeria	1991	13,776,854	44%
Reunion	1985	73,985	48%
Rwanda	1990	1,100,437	50%
St. Helena	1985	582	55%
Sao Tome and Principe	1989	19,822	47%
Senegal	1985	583,890	40%[3]
Seychelles	1991	14,669	49%
Sierra Leone	1990	367,426	41%
Somalia	1985	196,496	34%
Sudan	1990	2,042,743	43%
Swaziland	1991	172,908	50%
Tanzania United Rep. of[5]	1991	3,512,347	49%
Togo	1990	651,962	39%
Tunisia	1991	1,426,215	46%
Uganda[4]	1980	1,292,377	43%

[Continued]

★ 281 ★

African School Enrollment at the First Level

[Continued]

Country or area	Year	Pupils enrolled	Percent female
Zaire	1987	4,356,516	42%
Zambia	1985	1,348,318	47%
Zimbabwe	1992	2,301,642	50%

Source: Selected from "Education at the first level," United Nations, *Statistical Yearbook 1992,* New York, 1994, Table 11, pp. 65+. Primary source: United Nations Educational, Scientific and Cultural Organization (Paris). *Notes:* 1. Enrollment in 1991 (public education only) was 505,970. Percent female not available. 2. Enrollment in 1986 (public education only) was 80,048. Percent female not available. 3. Enrollment in 1990 was 708,448. Percent female not available. 4. Data refer to government-maintained and aided schools only. Enrollment in 1988 was 2,632,764. Percent female not available. 5. Data refer to Tanzania mainland only.

★ 282 ★

Enrollment

African School Enrollment at the Second Level

This table shows the total number of pupils enrolled and the percentage who were female in selected African countries, latest available year. Education at the second level is based upon at least four years of previous instruction at the first level and provides general or specialized instruction or both. Second level education may refer to middle and secondary schools, high schools, teachers' training schools at this level, or schools of a vocational or technical nature.

[NA Not available.]

Country or area	Year	Pupils enrolled	Percent female
Africa			
Algeria	1990	2,175,580	43%
Angola	1990	186,449	NA
Benin	1986	102,171	29%
Botswana	1991	78,804	54%
Burkina Faso	1991	105,542	NA
Burundi	1991	48,398	38%
Cameroon	1990	500,272	41%
Cape Verde	1989	3,866	50%
Central African Rep.	1989	49,147	29%
Chad	1989	58,570	18%
Comoros	1986	21,168	40%
Congo	1990	183,023	42%
Cote d'Ivoire	1980	221,940	30%
Djibouti	1992	9,740	43%
Egypt	1990	5,507,257	43%
Equatorial Guinea	1975	4,523	17%

[Continued]

★ 282 ★

African School Enrollment at the Second Level
[Continued]

Country or area	Year	Pupils enrolled	Percent female
Ethiopia	1988	882,243	NA
Gabon	1985	44,124	42%
Gambia	1991	21,766	35%
Ghana	1989	829,518	39%
Guinea	1990	85,942	24%
Guinea-Bissau	1988	6,330	32%
Kenya	1988	563,440	41%
Lesotho	1985	37,343	60%
Liberia	1980	54,623	28%
Libya			
Libyan Arab Jamahiriya	1991	215,508	56%
Madagascar	1990	340,191	49%
Malawi	1990	32,275	34%
Mali	1990	78,523	32%
Mauritania	1991	39,821	34%
Mauritius	1990	79,229	50%
Morocco	1991	1,168,918	41%
Mozambique	1991	162,486	37%
Namibia	1990	62,976	55%
Niger	1990	76,758	29%
Nigeria	1991	3,123,277	42%
Reunion	1986	69,585	53%
Rwanda	1990	70,400	43%
St. Helena	1985	513	49%
Sao Tome and Principe	1986	5,255	NA
Senegal	1985	130,338	33%[2]
Seychelles	1991	4,495	48%
Sierra Leone	1990	102,474	37%
Somalia	1985	45,686	35%
Sudan	1990	731,624	43%
Swaziland	1985	31,109	NA
Tanzania			
United Rep. of[1]	1991	183,109	43%
Togo	1990	125,545	25%
Tunisia	1991	589,674	44%
Uganda	1975	55,263	26%[3]
Zaire	1987	1,066,351	32%

[Continued]

★ 282 ★

African School Enrollment at the Second Level
[Continued]

Country or area	Year	Pupils enrolled	Percent female
Zambia	1980	102,019	35%
Zimbabwe	1991	710,619	44%

Source: Selected from "Education at the second level," United Nations, *Statistical Yearbook 1992*, New York, 1994, Table 12, pp. 78+. Primary source: United Nations Educational, Scientific and Cultural Organization (Paris). *Notes:* 1. Data refer to Tanzania Mainland only. 2. Enrollment in 1989 was 181,170. Percent female not available. 3. Enrollment in 1988 was 260,069. Percent female not available. 4. Enrollment in 1985 was 140,743. Percent female not available.

★ 283 ★
Enrollment

African School Enrollment at the Third Level

This table shows the total number of pupils enrolled in all third-level institutions and in universities and equivalent institutions in selected African countries. It shows the percentage who were female, in the latest year for which data on female enrollment is available. Education at the third level requires as a minimum condition of admission the successful completion of education at the second level or proof of equivalent knowledge or experience. The types of institutions in which third level education may be obtained include universities, teacher-training institutions, and technical institutions.

[NA Not available.]

Country or area	All institutions			Universities and equivalent institutions		
	Year	Students	% Female	Year	Students	% Female
Africa						
Algeria[1]	1985	132,057	31%[2]	1985	132,057	31%[2]
Angola	1990	6,534	NA	1990	6,534	NA
Benin	1990	10,873	13%	1975	2,102	15%
Botswana	1980	1,078	35%[3]	1990	3,365[3]	44%[3]
Burkino Faso	1990	5,422	23%	1990	5,086	22%
Burundi	1991	3,830	26%	1991	3,830	26%
Cameroon	1990	33,177	NA	1975	7,191	15%
Central African Republic	1985	2,651	11%	1991	3,783	15%
Chad	1984	1,643	9%	1984	1,470	9%
Comoros	1989	248	15%	NA	NA	NA
Congo	1991	12,045	19%	1991	12,045	19%
Cote d'Ivoire	1975[1]	7,174	17%	1984	11,300	21%
Egypt[4]	1990	708,417	35%	1990	600,680	35%
Ethiopia	1990	34,076	18%	1991[5]	20,948	16%
Gabon	1975	1,014	20%	1991	3,000	28%
Ghana	1975	9,079	16%	1990	9,609	22%
Guinea	1985	8,801	14%	1988	6,245	10%
Guinea-Bissau	1988	404	6%	NA	NA	NA
Kenya	1985	21,756	26%	1990	35,421	28%

[Continued]

★ 283 ★

African School Enrollment at the Third Level
[Continued]

Country or area	All institutions			Universities and equivalent institutions		
	Year	Students	% Female	Year	Students	% Female
Lesotho	1991	4,165	53%	1991	3,060	61%
Liberia	1987	5,095	23%	1987	4,855	24%
Libya Libyan Arab Jamahiriya	1991	72,899	46%	1991	72,899	46%
Madagascar	1990	35,824	45%	1990	35,824	45%
Malawi	1989	5,594	28%	1989	2,685	21%
Mali	1990	6,703	14%	1990	6,703	14%
Mauritania	1991	5,850	15%	1991	5,580	14%
Mauritius	1985	1,161	36%	1990	1,658	32%
Morocco[6]	1990	221,217	36%	1990	206,725	37%
Mozambique	1987	2,335	22%	1987	2,335	22%
Namibia	1991	4,157	64%	1991	1,496	65%
Niger	1989	4,506	15%	1989	4,506	15%
Nigeria	1985	266,679	27%[7]	1989	180,871	27%
Rwanda	1989	3,389	19%	1989	2,489	21%
St. Helena	1980	36	25%	NA	NA	NA
Senegal	1980	13,626	18%	1989	16,764	22%
Seychelles	1980	144	89%	NA	NA	NA
Sierra Leone	1975	1,642	16%[8]	1985	2,386	19%
Somalia	1986	15,672	20%	1986	15,672	20%
Sudan	1989	60,134	40%	1989	54,558	41%
Swaziland	1991	3,224	47%	1991	1,689	44%
Tanzania United Rep. of	1985	4,863[2,3]	15%[2,3]	1985	3,414[2,3]	16%[2,3]
Togo	1989	7,826	13%	1989	7,732	13%
Tunisia	1991	76,097	41%	1991	76,097	41%
Uganda	1990	17,578	28%	1990	7,618	25%
Zaire	1988	61,422	NA	1988	27,166	NA
Zambia	1990	15,343	NA	1986	4,857	17%
Zimbabwe	1992	61,553	27%	1992	9,048	26%

Source: Selected from "Education at the third level," United Nations, *Statistical Yearbook 1992*, New York, 1994, Table 13, pp. 91+. Primary source: United Nations Educational, Scientific and Cultural Organization (Paris). *Notes:* 1. Data refer to institutions under the Ministry of Education. 2. Excluding post-graduate students. 3. Full time only. 4. Excluding private higher institutions. 5. Not including Asmara University and Kotebe college. 6. 1990 data incomplete. 7. Enrollment in all third-level institutions was 335,824 in 1989. Percent female not available. 8. Enrollment in all third-level institutions was 4,742 in 1990. Percent female not available.

★ 284 ★
Enrollment

African School Enrollment in Vocational Education

This table shows the total number of pupils enrolled and the percentage who were female in selected African countries, in the latest year for which data on female enrollment is available. Vocational education refers to education provided in secondary schools that aim at preparing students directly for a trade or occupation other than teaching.

[NA Not available.]

Country or area	Year	Pupils enrolled	Percent female
Africa			
Algeria	1990	153,360	31%
Angola	1990	10,934	NA
Benin	1986	6,115	40%
Botswana	1991	3,609	31%
Burkina Faso	1991	8,022	45%
Burundi	1991	6,174	35%
Cameroon	1990	90,028	42%
Cape Verde	1989	588	36%
Central African Rep.	1989	3,514	42%
Chad	1989	2,802	24%
Comoros	1986	302	26%
Congo	1990	12,278	47%
Cote d'Ivoire	1986	25,328[1]	39%[1]
Djibouti	1992	1,545	66%
Egypt	1991	1,110,184	43%
Equatorial Guinea	1975	370	NA
Ethiopia	1988	4,101	NA
Gabon	1985	8,656	31%
Gambia	1984	1,107	38%
Ghana	1989	20,777[3]	15%[3]
Guinea	1990	8,202	27%
Guinea-Bissau	1988	649	9%
Kenya	1988	8,880	24%
Lesotho	1985	1,263	52%
Liberia	1980	2,322	27%
Libya			
Libyan Arab Jamahiriya	1991	37,157	64%
Madagascar	1990	17,033	41%
Malawi	1990	780	8%
Mali	1990	10,518	26%
Mauritania	1991	1,030	14%
Mauritius	1990	1,119	32%
Morocco	1991	17,147[4]	37%[4]
Mozambique	1991	9,729	19%

[Continued]

★ 284 ★

African School Enrollment in Vocational Education
[Continued]

Country or area	Year	Pupils enrolled	Percent female
Namibia	1990	1,175	29%
Niger	1990	843	9%
Nigeria	1990	113,556	45%
Reunion	1986	17,759	43%
Rwanda	1990	39,849	44%
St. Helena	1980	32	13%
Sao Tome and Principe	1989	101	33%
Senegal	1989	5,658	30%
Seychelles	1991	1,302	42%
Sierra Leone	1990	5,425	52%
Somalia	1985	5,933	23%
Sudan	1990	30,332	22%
Swaziland	1985	395	15%
Togo	1990	8,392	26%
Tunisia	1991	20,503	39%
Uganda	1975	3,296	3%[5]
Zaire	1987	291,743	35%
Zambia	1980	2,506	26%[6]
Zimbabwe	1980	734	100%[7]

Source: Selected from "Education at the second level," United Nations, *Statistical Yearbook 1992,* New York, 1994, Table 12, pp. 78+. Primary source: United Nations Educational, Scientific and Cultural Organization (Paris). *Notes:* 1. Data refer to schools attached to Ministry of Education only. 2. Data refer to Tanzania Mainland only. 3. Data refer to public education only. 4. Data exclude professional schools. 5. Enrollment in 1988 was 6,556. Percent female not available. 6. Enrollment in 1990 was 3,313. Percent female not available. 7. Enrollment in 1985 was 292. Percent female not available.

★ 285 ★

Enrollment

Asian School Enrollment Preceding the First Level

This table shows the total number of pupils enrolled and the percentage who were female in selected Asian countries, in the latest year for which data on female enrollment is available. Education preceding the first level refers to kindergartens, nursery schools, and infant classes attached to schools at higher levels.

[NA Not available.]

Country or area	Year	Pupils enrolled	Percent female
Asia			
Afghanistan	1988	19,660	49%
Bahrain	1991	10,161	49%
Bangladesh	1988	2,317,181	45%
Brunei Darussalam	1991	9,278	48%
China	1991	22,092,900	47%
Cyprus[1]	1990	23,694	48%
Hong Kong	1985	229,089	48%
India	1990	1,510,090	46%
Indonesia	1976	579,876	55%[2]
Iran			
Islamic Rep. of	1991	252,513	48%
Iraq	1990	86,508	48%
Israel	1980	269,506	47%[3]
Japan	1991	1,977,611	49%
Jordan	1991	49,422	46%
Korea			
Dem. People's Rep.	1987	728,000	48%
Republic of	1992	450,882	48%
Kuwait[4]	1991	39,246	49%
Laos			
Lao People's Dem. Rep.	1991	25,675	53%
Lebanon	1988	131,217	48%
Malaysia	1991	372,767	49%
Maldives	1992	3,298	48%
Mongolia	1991	95,715	NA
Nepal	1984	16,864	41%
Oman	1991	4,223	44%
Palestine			
Gaza Strip	1991	24,203	46%
Philippines[5]	1985	189,654	52%
Qatar	1991	5,684	46%
Saudi Arabia	1990	67,069	45%
Singapore	1989	17,858	47%

[Continued]

★ 285 ★

Asian School Enrollment Preceding the First Level
[Continued]

Country or area	Year	Pupils enrolled	Percent female
Syria			
Syrian Arab Rep.	1991	86,006	46%
Thailand	1980	367,313	49%[6]
Turkey	1991	132,724	47%
United Arab Emirates	1991	49,064	48%
Viet Nam	1985	1,701,681	52%
Yemen[7]	1989	11,500	49%

Source: Selected from "Education preceding the first level," United Nations, *Statistical Yearbook 1992*, New York, 1994, Table 10, pp. 55+. Primary source: United Nations Educational, Scientific and Cultural Organization (Paris). *Notes:* 1. Not including Turkish schools. 2. Enrollment in 1989 was 1,544,541. Percent female not available. 3. Enrollment in 1990 was 329,050. Percent female not available. 4. The school year 1991-1992 was exceptionally organized from February 1992 to August 1992 instead of the usual duration September to June. 5. Enrollment in 1990 was 397,364. Percent female not available. 6. Enrollment in 1989 was 1,224,259. Percent female not available. 7. Data refer to former Democratic Yemen only.

★ 286 ★

Enrollment

Asian School Enrollment at the First Level

This table shows the total number of pupils enrolled and the percentage who were female in selected Asian countries, in the latest year for which data on female enrollment is available. The purpose of education at the first level is to provide basic instruction in the tools of learning, for example at elementary and primary schools. Its length may vary from 4 to 9 years.

[NA Not available.]

Country or area	Year	Pupils enrolled	Percent female
Asia			
Afghanistan	1989	726,287	33%
Bahrain	1991	66,694	49%
Bangladesh	1990	11,939,949	45%
Bhutan	1988	55,340	37%
Brunei Darussalam	1991	38,933	47%
China	1991	121,641,500	46%
Cyprus[1]	1990	62,962	48%
Hong Kong	1985	534,903	48%
India	1990	99,118,320	41%
Indonesia	1989	29,933,790	48%
Iran			
Islamic Rep. of	1991	9,787,593	47%

[Continued]

★ 286 ★

Asian School Enrollment at the First Level
[Continued]

Country or area	Year	Pupils enrolled	Percent female
Iraq	1990	3,328,212	44%
Israel	1990	724,502	49%
Japan	1991	9,157,429	49%
Jordan[2]	1991	981,255	49%
Korea			
Dem. People's Rep.	1987	1,543,000	49%
Republic of	1992	4,560,128	48%
Kuwait[3]	1991	114,641	49%
Laos			
Lao People's Dem. Rep.	1991	580,792	44%
Lebanon[2]	1988	346,534	48%
Malaysia	1991	2,540,623	49%
Maldives	1992	45,333	49%
Mongolia	1990	166,200	50%
Myanmar	1985	4,710,616	48%
Nepal	1988	2,108,739	32%
Oman	1991	277,370	47%
Pakistan[4]	1990	8,855,997	34%
Palestine			
Gaza Strip	1991	127,257	NA
Philippines	1985	8,925,959	49%[5]
Qatar	1991	48,785	47%
Saudi Arabia	1990	1,876,916	46%
Singapore	1989	257,833	47%
Sri Lanka	1991	2,112,723	48%
Syria			
Syrian Arab Republic[2]	1991	2,539,081	47%
Thailand	1990	6,464,853	49%
Turkey	1991	6,878,923	47%
United Arab Emirates	1991	231,674	48%
Viet Nam	1985	8,125,836	48%
Yemen[6]	1990	1,291,372	24%

Source: Selected from "Education at the first level," United Nations, *Statistical Yearbook 1992*, New York, 1994, Table 11, pp. 65+. Primary source: United Nations Educational, Scientific and Cultural Organization (Paris). *Notes:* 1. Excluding Turkish schools. 2. Data refer to grades 1 to 10. Including UNRWA schools. 3. The school year 1991-1992 was exceptionally organized from February 1992 to August 1992 instead of the usual duration September to June. 4. Including education preceding the first level. 5. Enrollment in 1991 was 10,558,105. Percent female not available. 6. Excluding former Democratic Yemen.

★ 287 ★

Enrollment

Asian School Enrollment at the Second Level

This table shows the total number of pupils enrolled and the percentage who were female in selected Asian countries, in the latest year for which data on female enrollment is available. Education at the second level is based upon at least four years of previous instruction at the first level and provides general or specialized instruction or both. Second level education may refer to middle and secondary schools, high schools, teachers' training schools at this level, or schools of a vocational or technical nature.

[NA Not available.]

Country or area	Year	Pupils enrolled	Percent female
Asia			
Afghanistan	1975	93,497	11%[1]
Bahrain	1991	48,600	50%
Bangladesh	1990	3,592,995	33%
Brunei Darussalam	1991	25,699	50%
China	1990	52,267,900	43%
Cyprus[2]	1990	44,614	49%
Hong Kong	1987	458,444	49%
India	1985	44,484,544	33%
Indonesia	1989	11,243,323	45%
Iran			
Islamic Rep. of	1991	5,619,057	42%
Iraq	1988	1,166,859	38%
Israel	1990	309,098	51%
Japan	1989	11,143,930	49%
Jordan[3]	1991	109,429	49%
Korea			
Rep. of	1992	4,484,422	48%
Kuwait[4]	1991	167,195	49%
Laos			
Lao People's			
Dem. Rep.	1991	125,702	39%
Lebanon[3]	1980	287,310	NA
Malaysia	1991	1,482,530	50%
Maldives	1992	16,087	49%
Mongolia	1980	245,600	NA
Myanmar	1987	1,358,788	NA
Nepal	1988	612,943	27%
Oman	1991	119,497	45%
Pakistan	1990	3,983,462	29%
Palestine			
Gaza Strip	1991	73,940	NA
Philippines	1985	3,214,159	50%

[Continued]

★ 287 ★

Asian School Enrollment at the Second Level
[Continued]

Country or area	Year	Pupils enrolled	Percent female
Qatar	1991	31,120	50%
Saudi Arabia	1990	892,585	44%
Singapore	1980	180,817	50%
Sri Lanka	1976	1,088,089	51%
Syria			
Syrian Arab Rep.[3]	1991	902,819	42%
Thailand	1990	2,397,262	48%
Turkey	1991	3,987,423	38%
United Arab Emirates	1991	118,011	51%
Viet Nam	1976	3,200,912	49%
Yemen[5]	1990	420,697	15%

Source: Selected from "Education at the second level," United Nations, *Statistical Yearbook 1992*, New York, 1994, Table 12, pp. 78+. Primary source: United Nations Educational, Scientific and Cultural Organization (Paris). *Notes:* 1. Enrollment in 1980 was 136,898. Percent female not available. 2. Not including Turkish schools. From 1985, data on commercial schools are included with general education. 3. Including UNRWA schools. 4. The school year 1991-1992 was exceptionally organized from February 1992 to August 1992 instead of the usual duration September to June. 5. Excluding former Democratic Yemen.

★ 288 ★

Enrollment

Asian School Enrollment at the Third Level

This table shows the total number of pupils enrolled in all third-level institutions and in universities and equivalent institutions in selected Asian countries. It shows the percentage who were female, latest available year. Education at the third level requires as a minimum condition of admission the successful completion of education at the second level or proof of equivalent knowledge or experience. The types of institutions in which third level education may be obtained include universities, teacher-training institutions, and technical institutions.

[NA Not available.]

Country or area	All institutions			Universities and equivalent institutions		
	Year	Students	% Female	Year	Students	% Female
Asia						
Afghanistan	1990	24,333	31%	1990	9,367	42%
Armenia	1990	68,400	NA	NA	NA	NA
Azerbaijan	1991	107,900	NA	NA	NA	NA
Bahrain	1990	6,868	56%	1990	6,194	54%
Bangladesh	1990	434,309	16%	1990	51,775	20%
Bhutan	1980	322	22%	1984	220	20%
Brunei Darussalam	1987	945	51%	1987	747	55%
China[1]	1990	2,146,853	33%	1985	3,194	48%
Cyprus	1990	6,554	52%	NA	NA	NA

[Continued]

★ 288 ★

Asian School Enrollment at the Third Level
[Continued]

Country or area	All institutions			Universities and equivalent institutions		
	Year	Students	% Female	Year	Students	% Female
Georgia	1990	103,900	NA	NA	NA	NA
Hong Kong	1984	76,844	35%	1984	14,436	35%
India	1985	4,470,844	30%	NA	NA	NA
Indonesia	1984	980,162	32%	1984	852,104	32%
Iran Islamic Rep. of	1985[2]	184,442	29%	1991	256,212	29%
Iraq	1988	209,818	38%	1980	81,782	32%
Israel[3]	1990	119,124	49%	1990	71,190	51%
Japan[4]	1985	2,347,463	35%	1985	1,932,785	24%
Jordan	1991	84,226	48%	1991	46,068	43%
Kazakhstan	1990	287,400	NA	NA	NA	NA
Korea Dem. People's Rep.	1987	390,000	34%	1987	325,000	29%
Republic of	1991	1,761,775	33%	1991	1,159,463	29%
Kuwait	1991	23,686	60%	1991	15,313	70%
Kyrgyzstan	1990	58,800	NA	NA	NA	NA
Laos Lao People's Dem. Rep.	1989	4,730	32%	1989	3,425	42%
Lebanon	1991	85,495	48%	1991	85,495	48%
Malaysia	1990	121,412	45%	1990	57,059	45%
Mongolia	1981[5]	38,200	63%	1981[5]	18,700	57%
Myanmar	1987	202,381	NA	NA	NA	NA
Nepal	1991	110,239	24%	1991	110,239	24%
Oman	1991	7,322	49%	1991	3,615	53%
Pakistan	1989	304,922	28%	1989	243,574	24%
Palestine Gaza Strip	1991	4,711	44%	1991	2,215	40%
Philippines	1991	1,656,815	59%	1980	1,143,702	54%
Qatar	1989	6,469	71%	1989	6,371	71%
Saudi Arabia	1990	153,967	43%	1990	128,538	46%
Singapore	1983	35,192	42%	1983	14,179	49%
Sri Lanka	1985	59,377	40%	1990	38,424	40%
Syria Syrian Arab Rep.	1991[6]	183,079	37%	1985	135,191	32%
Tajikistan	1990	68,800	NA	NA	NA	NA
Thailand	1975[7]	130,965	40%	1975[7]	78,229	43%
Turkey	1991	810,781	34%	1991	444,018	37%
Turkmenistan	1990	41,800	NA	NA	NA	NA
United Arab Emirates	1991	10,405	75%	1991	8,668	78%

[Continued]

★ 288 ★

Asian School Enrollment at the Third Level
[Continued]

Country or area	All institutions			Universities and equivalent institutions		
	Year	Students	% Female	Year	Students	% Female
Uzbekistan	1990	340,900	NA	NA	NA	NA
Viet Nam	1980[8]	114,701	24%	1980	114,701	24%
Yemen[9]	1980	4,519	11%	1980	4,519	11%

Source: Selected from "Education at the third level," United Nations, *Statistical Yearbook 1992*, New York, 1994, Table 13, pp. 91+. Primary source: United Nations Educational, Scientific and Cultural Organization (Paris). *Notes:* 1. Full time only. 2. Public education only. 3. Data exclude open University. 4. Including correspondence courses. 5. Enrollment in all third-level institutions was 28,209 in 1991. Enrollment in universities and equivalent institutions in 1991 was 13,223. Percent female not available. 6. Excluding teacher training. 7. Enrollment in all third-level institutions was 952,012 in 1989. Enrollment in universities and equivalent institutions in 1989 was 197,539. Percent female not available. 8. Including correspondence courses. 9. Excluding former Democratic Yemen. Enrollment in all third-level institutions was 23,457 in 1988. Enrollment in universities and equivalent institutions in 1988 was 23,457. Percent female not available.

★ 289 ★

Enrollment

Asian School Enrollment in Vocational Education

This table shows the total number of pupils enrolled and the percentage who were female in selected Asian countries, in the latest year for which data on female enrollment is available. Vocational education refers to education provided in secondary schools that aim at preparing students directly for a trade or occupation other than teaching.

[NA Not available.]

Country or area	Year	Pupils enrolled	Percent female
Asia			
Afghanistan	1975	5,960	11%
Bahrain	1991	6,615	26%
Bangladesh	1990	25,791	8%
Brunei Darussalam	1991	1,188	36%
China	1991	4,771,500	44%
Cyprus[1]	1991	3,172	17%
Hong Kong	1987	45,943	32%
India	1985	677,164	30%
Indonesia	1989	1,349,050	42%
Iran Islamic Rep. of	1991	260,576	20%
Iraq	1988	160,278	29%
Israel	1990	115,076	45%
Japan	1989	1,450,704	47%
Jordan	1991	25,499	37%
Korea Rep. of	1992	835,598[2]	53%[2]

[Continued]

★ 289 ★

Asian School Enrollment in Vocational Education
[Continued]

Country or area	Year	Pupils enrolled	Percent female
Kuwait[3]	1991	498	27%
Laos			
Lao People's Dem. Rep.	1991	3,703	34%
Lebanon[4]	1986	31,045	40%
Malaysia	1991	32,219	26%
Maldives	1992	154	3%
Mongolia	1991	17,961	NA
Myanmar	1987	15,631	NA
Nepal	1976	16,815	NA
Oman	1991	2,680	5%
Pakistan	1985	51,426	14%
Palestine			
Gaza Strip	1991	997	NA
Qatar	1991	843	NA
Saudi Arabia	1990	24,815	17%
Singapore	1980	9,391	23%
Sri Lanka	1976	4,778	33%
Syria			
Syrian Arab Rep.[4]	1991	53,289	38%
Thailand	1990	444,218	43%
Turkey	1991	976,916	35%
United Arab Emirates	1991	893	NA
Viet Nam	1976	66,553	35%[5]
Yemen[6]	1990	5,068	9%

Source: Selected from "Education at the second level," United Nations, *Statistical Yearbook 1992*, New York, 1994, Table 12, pp. 78+. Primary source: United Nations Educational, Scientific and Cultural Organization (Paris). *Notes:* 1. Not including Turkish schools. 2. Including part-time education. 3. The school year 1991-1992 was exceptionally organized from February 1992 to August 1992 instead of the usual duration September to June. 4. Including UNRWA schools. 5. Enrollment in 1990 was 188,989. Percent female not available. 6. Excluding former Democratic Yemen.

★ 290 ★

Enrollment

College Enrollment by Race/Ethnicity: 1990-1992

This table shows the total number of women enrolled in institutions of higher education by race/ethnicity from the fall of 1990 through the fall of 1992. Male enrollment in all institutions was 6,283,909 (1990); 6,501,844 (1991); and 6,526,089 (1992).

Level of study and race/ethnicity	Number			Percent distribution		
	1990	1991	1992	1990	1991	1992
All institutions	7,534,728	7,857,109	7,965,137	100.0%	100.0%	100.0%
White, non-Hispanic	5,861,475	6,027,568	5,987,581	77.8%	76.7%	75.2%
Black, non-Hispanic	762,341	818,381	856,394	10.1%	10.4%	10.8%
Hispanic	428,529	476,027	527,052	5.7%	6.1%	6.6%
Asian or Pacific Isl.	277,540	312,035	354,494	3.7%	4.0%	4.3%
American Ind/Alaskan Native	59,664	66,097	68,794	0.8%	0.8%	0.9%
Nonresident alien	145,179	157,001	179,822	1.9%	2.0%	2.3%
4-year institutions	4,527,414	4,607,119	4,655,650	60.1%	58.6%	58.5%
White, non-Hispanic	3,586,864	3,607,936	3,596,325	47.6%	45.9%	45.2%
Black, non-Hispanic	436,980	458,255	477,430	5.8%	5.8%	6.0%
Hispanic	193,437	206,560	223,294	2.6%	2.6%	2.8%
Asian or Pacific Isl.	169,864	183,536	197,729	2.3%	2.3%	2.5%
American Ind/Alaskan Native	27,323	29,289	31,118	0.4%	0.4%	0.4%
Nonresident alien	112,946	121,543	129,754	1.5%	1.5%	1.6%
2-year institutions	3,007,314	3,249,990	3,309,487	39.9%	41.4%	41.5%
White, non-Hispanic	2,274,611	2,419,632	2,391,256	30.2%	30.8%	30.0%
Black, non-Hispanic	325,361	360,126	378,964	4.3%	4.6%	4.8%
Hispanic	235,092	269,467	303,758	3.1%	3.4%	3.8%
Asian or Pacific Isl.	107,676	128,499	147,765	1.4%	1.6%	1.9%
Amer Ind/Alaska Native	32,341	36,808	37,676	0.4%	0.5%	0.5%
Nonresident alien	32,233	35,458	50,068	0.4%	0.5%	0.6%

Source: "Female enrollment in institutions of higher education in 50 states and the District of Columbia, by level of institution and race/ethnicity: Fall 1990 through fall 1992," U.S. Department of Education, National Center for Education Statistics, *Trends in Enrollment in Higher Education, by Racial/Ethnic Category: Fall 1982 Through Fall 1992*, NCES 94-104, March 1994, Table 2b, p. 6. Primary source: U.S. Department of Education, National Center for Education Statistics, Integrated Postsecondary Education Data System "Fall Enrollment" surveys for 1990, 1991, and 1992. Data for 1990 and 1991 may differ from that in prior NCES publications due to corrections and the addition of late data. Detail may not sum to total due to rounding.

College Enrollment by State: 1993-1994

This table shows the percentage of students enrolled in college who were female, in academic year 1993-1994, by state.

State	Female
Alabama	55.0%
Alaska	59.1%
Arizona	54.1%
Arkansas	57.1%
California	54.4%
Colorado	53.4%
Connecticut	55.8%
Delaware	57.0%
District of Columbia	53.2%
Florida	55.5%
Georgia	55.5%
Hawaii	54.6%
Idaho	54.6%
Illinois	55.0%
Indiana	53.7%
Iowa	53.9%
Kansas	55.1%
Kentucky	58.4%
Louisiana	57.0%
Maine	58.2%
Maryland	57.0%
Massachusetts	55.4%
Michigan	55.4%
Minnesota	54.8%
Mississippi	56.0%
Missouri	54.7%
Montana	53.3%
Nebraska	54.4%
Nevada	55.4%
New Hampshire	56.0%
New Jersey	55.7%
New Mexico	56.1%
New York	56.2%
North Carolina	56.2%
North Dakota	49.6%
Ohio	54.1%
Oklahoma	54.4%

[Continued]

★ 291 ★

College Enrollment by State: 1993-1994
[Continued]

State	Female
Oregon	52.8%
Pennsylvania	54.3%
Rhode Island	55.1%
South Carolina	57.0%
South Dakota	55.6%
Tennessee	55.0%
Texas	53.7%
Utah	49.2%
Vermont	57.1%
Virginia	55.8%
Washington	55.4%
West Virginia	55.4%
Wisconsin	55.3%
Wyoming	56.7%

Source: Selected from "The States," *The Chronicle of Higher Education Almanac*, September 1, 1994, p. 46+.

★ 292 ★
Enrollment

College Enrollment of Older Students: 1992

This table shows characteristics of the population aged 35 and older who were enrolled in college in 1992. Women were two-thirds of the number, up from 53.4% in 1972, the first year in which the Census Bureau surveyed older students. Anne Cronin suggests the incentive may be the money. The 1990 census found that college graduates earn an average of $2,116 per month, compared to $1,077 per month for persons with only a high school diploma.

Characteristic	Percent
35 and older enrolled in college, 1992	
Age	
35 to 44	68.6%
45 to 54	23.2%
55 and older	8.2%
Sex	
Male	33.4%
Female	66.6%
Enrollment	
Full-time	29.0%

[Continued]

★ 292 ★

College Enrollment of Older Students: 1992
[Continued]

Characteristic	Percent
Part-time	71.0%
Program	
2-year	33.7%
4-year	31.8%
Graduate school	34.4%

Source: Anne Cronin, "When the Juniors Are Senior," *The New York Times*, August 17, 1994, p. B7 Y. Primary source: Census Bureau.

★ 293 ★

Enrollment

College Enrollment: 1993

This table gives characteristics of the college population for the academic year 1993-1994. Women accounted for 54.5% of all college students in 1993, continuing the majority position they have occupied since 1979. In 1973, women made up only 43.7% of all college students. In the ten years prior to 1993, enrollment among persons ages 25 and older increased. Much of the older student enrollment was enrollment by women. Among all college students, women were more likely than men to be enrolled in two-year colleges and public colleges and universities.

[Numbers in thousands.]

Characteristic	Total population	Enrolled in college	Type of college			Enrolled full-time	Public school	Percent employed		
			2-year	4-year	Grad. school			Total	Full-time	Part-time
Total	201,242	13,898	4,196	7,311	2,391	64.9%	78.5%	59.7%	30.8%	28.9%
Male	96,581	6,324	1,748	3,446	1,130	69.4%	77.3%	59.7%	31.1%	28.6%
Female	104,660	7,574	2,448	3,865	1,261	61.1%	79.5%	59.7%	30.6%	29.1%

Source: Selected from "Characteristics of the College Population: October 1993," U.S. Bureau of the Census, *Current Population Reports*, P20-479, Table G, p. xvii.

★ 294 ★
Enrollment

Enrollment Status of the Population, Enrolled: 1993

This table gives numbers in thousands and percents relating to the population 3 years old and over enrolled in school in October 1993, by age, totals and females, race, and Hispanic origin.

[Numbers in thousands.]

Age, sex, race, and Hispanic origin	Population	Enrolled in school					
		Total		Below college level[1]		In college	
		Number	Percent	Number	Percent	Number	Percent
ALL RACES							
Both sexes, 3 yrs. +	243,232	65,363	26.9%	51,465	21.2%	13,898	5.7%
3 to 34 years old	121,026	62,730	51.8%	51,320	42.4%	11,409	9.4%
3 and 4 years old	8,097	3,275	40.4%	3,275	40.4%	X	X
5 and 6 years old	7,651	7,298	95.4%	7,298	95.4%	X	X
7 to 9 years old	11,273	11,211	99.5%	11,211	99.5%	X	X
10 to 13 years old	14,969	14,899	99.5%	14,899	99.5%	X	X
14 and 15 years old	7,092	7,011	98.9%	7,008	98.8%	4	0.1%
16 and 17 years old	6,745	6,339	94.0%	6,220	92.2%	119	1.8%
18 and 19 years old	6,594	4,063	61.6%	1,137	17.2%	2,926	44.4%
20 and 21 years old	6,575	2,810	42.7%	76	1.2%	2,734	41.6%
22 to 24 years old	10,931	2,579	23.6%	45	0.4%	2,533	23.2%
25 to 29 years old	19,046	1,942	10.2%	75	0.4%	1,867	9.8%
30 to 34 years old	22,053	1,303	5.9%	76	0.3%	1,227	5.6%
35 years old and over	122,206	2,634	2.2%	145	0.1%	2,488	2.0%
Female, 3 years old +	125,145	32,475	26.0%	24,901	19.9%	7,574	6.1%
3 to 34 years old	60,275	30,767	51.0%	24,808	41.2%	5,958	9.9%
3 and 4 years old	3,938	1,548	39.3%	1,548	39.3%	X	X
5 and 6 years old	3,724	3,547	95.2%	3,547	95.2%	X	X
7 to 9 years old	5,491	5,457	99.4%	5,457	99.4%	X	X
10 to 13 years old	7,332	7,295	99.5%	7,295	99.5%	X	X
14 and 15 years old	3,451	3,407	98.7%	3,403	98.6%	4	0.1%
16 and 17 years old	3,288	3,054	92.9%	2,986	90.8%	67	2.1%
18 and 19 years old	3,265	2,014	61.7%	425	13.0%	1,588	48.7%
20 and 21 years old	3,383	1,452	42.9%	29	0.9%	1,422	42.0%
22 to 24 years old	5,554	1,210	21.8%	21	0.4%	1,189	21.4%
25 to 29 years old	9,684	1,043	10.8%	48	0.5%	995	10.3%
30 to 34 years old	11,165	741	6.6%	48	0.4%	693	6.2%
35 years old and over	64,870	1,708	2.6%	92	0.1%	1,616	2.5%
WHITE							
Both sexes, 3 yrs. +	203,169	52,152	25.7%	40,719	20.0%	11,434	5.6%
3 to 34 years old	97,821	49,985	51.1%	40,619	41.5%	9,366	9.6%
3 and 4 years old	6,326	2,581	40.8%	2,581	40.8%	X	X
5 and 6 years old	6,059	5,784	95.5%	5,784	95.5%	X	X
7 to 9 years old	8,955	8,911	99.5%	8,911	99.5%	X	X
10 to 13 years old	11,889	11,828	99.5%	11,828	99.5%	X	X
14 and 15 years old	5,633	5,572	98.9%	5,568	98.9%	4	0.1%
16 and 17 years old	5,380	5,060	94.1%	4,966	92.3%	94	1.8%
18 and 19 years old	5,252	3,242	61.7%	787	15.0%	2,456	46.8%
20 and 21 years old	5,214	2,295	44.0%	52	1.0%	2,243	43.0%

[Continued]

★ 294 ★

Enrollment Status of the Population, Enrolled: 1993
[Continued]

| Age, sex, race, and Hispanic origin | Population | Enrolled in school | | | | | |
| | | Total | | Below college level[1] | | In college | |
		Number	Percent	Number	Percent	Number	Percent
22 to 24 years old	8,964	2,091	23.3%	27	0.3%	2,064	23.0%
25 to 29 years old	15,709	1,537	9.8%	47	0.3%	1,490	9.5%
30 to 34 years old	18,440	1,083	5.9%	67	0.4%	1,015	5.5%
35 years old and over	105,348	2,167	2.1%	100	0.1%	2,068	2.0%
Female							
3 years old +	103,945	25,923	24.9%	19,711	19.0%	6,212	6.0%
3 to 34 years old	48,435	24,511	50.6%	19,655	40.6%	4,855	10.0%
3 and 4 years old	3,085	1,231	39.9%	1,231	39.9%	X	X
5 and 6 years old	2,955	2,830	95.8%	2,830	95.8%	X	X
7 to 9 years old	4,361	4,338	99.5%	4,338	99.5%	X	X
10 to 13 years old	5,792	5,762	99.5%	5,762	99.5%	X	X
14 and 15 years old	2,744	2,714	98.9%	2,710	98.8%	4	0.1%
16 and 17 years old	2,627	2,442	93.0%	2,389	90.9%	53	2.0%
18 and 19 years old	2,611	1,642	62.9%	289	11.1%	1,353	51.8%
20 and 21 years old	2,644	1,143	43.3%	20	0.8%	1,123	42.5%
22 to 24 years old	4,535	990	21.8%	16	0.4%	974	21.5%
25 to 29 years old	7,876	821	10.4%	30	0.4%	791	10.0%
30 to 34 years old	9,207	599	6.5%	40	0.4%	558	6.1%
35 years old and over	55,510	1,413	2.6%	56	0.1%	1,357	2.4%
BLACK							
Both sexes, 3 yrs. +	30,197	9,791	32.4%	8,245	27.3%	1,545	5.1%
3 to 34 years old	17,667	9,470	53.6%	8,209	46.5%	1,261	7.1%
3 and 4 years old	1,320	526	39.8%	526	39.8%	X	X
5 and 6 years old	1,205	1,139	94.6%	1,139	94.6%	X	X
7 to 9 years old	1,724	1,706	99.0%	1,706	99.0%	X	X
10 to 13 years old	2,379	2,375	99.8%	2,375	99.8%	X	X
14 and 15 years old	1,128	1,111	98.5%	1,111	98.5%	X	X
16 and 17 years old	1,081	1,024	94.7%	1,011	93.6%	13	1.2%
18 and 19 years old	1,040	600	57.7%	289	27.8%	311	30.0%
20 and 21 years old	1,027	308	30.0%	11	1.0%	297	29.0%
22 to 24 years old	1,449	262	18.1%	8	0.6%	253	17.5%
25 to 29 years old	2,590	269	10.4%	24	0.9%	245	9.5%
30 to 34 years old	2,725	149	5.5%	8	0.3%	141	5.2%
35 years old and over	12,530	321	2.6%	37	0.3%	284	2.3%
Female							
3 years old +	16,099	4,891	30.4%	3,983	24.7%	909	5.6%
3 to 34 years old	9,072	4,678	51.6%	3,951	43.6%	727	8.0%
3 and 4 years old	631	239	37.8%	239	37.8%	X	X
5 and 6 years old	578	532	92.1%	532	92.1%	X	X
7 to 9 years old	858	847	98.7%	847	98.7%	X	X
10 to 13 years old	1,166	1,162	99.7%	1,162	99.7%	X	X
14 and 15 years old	558	547	97.9%	547	97.9%	X	X

[Continued]

★ 294 ★

Enrollment Status of the Population, Enrolled: 1993
[Continued]

Age, sex, race, and Hispanic origin	Population	Enrolled in school					
		Total		Below college level[1]		In college	
		Number	Percent	Number	Percent	Number	Percent
16 and 17 years old	533	498	93.4%	489	91.8%	8	1.6%
18 and 19 years old	523	272	51.9%	109	20.8%	163	31.2%
20 and 21 years old	558	196	35.1%	5	0.9%	191	34.2%
22 to 24 years old	776	130	16.7%	X	X	130	16.7%
25 to 29 years old	1,388	145	10.5%	16	1.2%	129	9.3%
30 to 34 years old	1,504	112	7.5%	7	0.4%	106	7.0%
35 years old and over	7,027	213	3.0%	31	0.4%	182	2.6%
HISPANIC ORIGIN[2]							
Both sexes, 3 yrs. +	21,672	6,839	31.6%	5,843	27.0%	995	4.6%
3 to 34 years old	13,674	6,689	48.9%	5,823	42.6%	867	6.3%
3 and 4 years old	1,024	275	26.8%	275	26.8%	X	X
5 and 6 years old	900	844	93.8%	844	93.8%	X	X
7 to 9 years old	1,357	1,352	99.6%	1,352	99.6%	X	X
10 to 13 years old	1,653	1,639	99.2%	1,639	99.2%	X	X
14 and 15 years old	813	793	97.6%	793	97.6%	X	X
16 and 17 years old	823	727	88.3%	712	86.5%	15	1.8%
18 and 19 years old	710	355	50.0%	160	22.6%	195	27.4%
20 and 21 years old	816	260	31.8%	19	2.3%	241	29.6%
22 to 24 years old	1,246	170	13.7%	4	0.3%	166	13.4%
25 to 29 years old	2,069	159	7.7%	10	0.5%	149	7.2%
30 to 34 years old	2,264	116	5.1%	16	0.7%	100	4.4%
35 years old and over	7,999	149	1.9%	21	0.3%	129	1.6%
Female							
3 years old +	10,843	3,425	31.6%	2,872	26.5%	553	5.1%
3 to 34 years old	6,591	3,332	50.6%	2,857	43.4%	475	7.2%
3 and 4 years old	471	126	26.7%	126	26.7%	X	X
5 and 6 years old	486	457	93.9%	457	93.9%	X	X
7 to 9 years old	651	647	99.4%	647	99.4%	X	X
10 to 13 years old	814	810	99.6%	810	99.6%	X	X
14 and 15 years old	405	398	98.2%	398	98.2%	X	X
16 and 17 years old	375	328	87.4%	319	85.1%	9	2.3%
18 and 19 years old	385	200	51.9%	74	19.3%	126	32.6%
20 and 21 years old	405	130	32.0%	6	1.6%	123	30.4%
22 to 24 years old	628	91	14.5%	4	0.6%	87	13.9%
25 to 29 years old	978	100	0.2%	7	0.7%	93	9.5%
30 to 34 years old	992	47	4.8%	9	1.0%	38	3.8%
35 years old and over	4,252	93	2.2%	15	0.4%	78	1.8%

Source: Selected from "Enrollment Status of the Population 3 Years Old and Over, by Age, Sex, Race, Hispanic Origin, and Selected Educational Characteristics: October 1993," U.S. Bureau of the Census, *Current Population Reports*, P20-479, Table 1, pp. 1+. *R *Notes:* 1. Includes nursery school, kindergarten, and grades 1 to 12. 2. May be of any race.

★ 295 ★

Enrollment

Enrollment Status of the Population, Not Enrolled: 1993

This table gives numbers in thousands and percents relating to the population 3 years old and over NOT enrolled in school in October 1993, by age, totals and females, race, and Hispanic origin.

[Numbers in thousands.]

Age, sex, race, and Hispanic origin	Population	Not enrolled in school					
		Total		High school graduate		Not high school graduate	
		Number	Percent	Number	Percent	Number	Percent
ALL RACES							
Both sexes, 3 yrs. +	243,232	177,869	73.1%	138,997	57.2%	38,872	16.0%
3 to 34 years old	121,026	58,296	48.2%	44,617	36.9%	13,679	11.3%
3 and 4 years old	8,097	4,822	59.6%	X	X	4,822	59.6%
5 and 6 years old	7,651	353	4.6%	X	X	353	4.6%
7 to 9 years old	11,273	63	0.6%	X	X	63	0.6%
10 to 13 years old	14,969	69	0.5%	X	X	69	0.5%
14 and 15 years old	7,092	80	1.1%	4	0.1%	76	1.1%
16 and 17 years old	6,745	406	6.0%	80	1.2%	326	4.8%
18 and 19 years old	6,594	2,531	38.4%	1,753	26.6%	778	11.8%
20 and 21 years old	6,575	3,765	57.3%	2,885	43.9%	880	13.4%
22 to 24 years old	10,931	8,352	76.4%	6,941	63.5%	1,412	12.9%
25 to 29 years old	19,046	17,104	89.8%	14,798	77.7%	2,306	12.1%
30 to 34 years old	22,053	20,750	94.1%	18,157	82.3%	2,593	11.8%
35 years old and over	122,206	119,572	97.8%	94,379	77.2%	25,193	20.6%
Female, 3 years old +	125,145	92,671	74.1%	72,329	57.8%	20,342	16.3%
3 to 34 years old	60,275	29,509	49.0%	22,866	37.9%	6,642	11.0%
3 and 4 years old	3,938	2,390	60.7%	X	X	2,390	60.7%
5 and 6 years old	3,724	177	4.8%	X	X	177	4.8%
7 to 9 years old	5,491	34	0.6%	X	X	34	0.6%
10 to 13 years old	7,332	37	0.5%	X	X	37	0.5%
14 and 15 years old	3,451	44	1.3%	4	0.1%	40	1.2%
16 and 17 years old	3,288	234	7.1%	48	1.5%	186	5.7%
18 and 19 years old	3,265	1,251	38.3%	877	26.9%	375	11.5%
20 and 21 years old	3,383	1,931	57.1%	1,495	44.2%	436	12.9%
22 to 24 years old	5,554	4,344	78.2%	3,661	65.9%	683	12.3%
25 to 29 years old	9,684	8,641	89.2%	7,568	78.2%	1,073	11.1%
30 to 34 years old	11,165	10,424	93.4%	9,214	82.5%	1,210	10.8%
35 years old and over	64,870	63,162	97.4%	49,463	76.3%	13,699	21.1%
WHITE							
Both sexes, 3 yrs. +	203,169	151,016	74.3%	120,146	59.1%	30,870	15.2%
3 to 34 years old	97,821	47,836	48.9%	37,114	37.9%	10,722	11.0%
3 and 4 years old	6,326	3,745	59.2%	X	X	3,745	59.2%
5 and 6 years old	6,059	274	4.5%	X	X	274	4.5%
7 to 9 years old	8,955	44	0.5%	X	X	44	0.5%
10 to 13 years old	11,889	61	0.5%	X	X	61	0.5%
14 and 15 years old	5,633	61	1.1%	X	X	61	0.5%
16 and 17 years old	5,380	320	6.0%	67	1.3%	253	4.7%
18 and 19 years old	5,252	2,010	38.3%	1,382	26.3%	628	12.0%
20 and 21 years old	5,214	2,919	56.0%	2,264	43.4%	655	12.6%

[Continued]

★ 295 ★

Enrollment Status of the Population, Not Enrolled: 1993
[Continued]

Age, sex, race, and Hispanic origin	Population	Not enrolled in school					
		Total		High school graduate		Not high school graduate	
		Number	Percent	Number	Percent	Number	Percent
22 to 24 years old	8,964	6,873	76.7%	5,787	64.6%	1,086	12.1%
25 to 29 years old	15,709	14,172	90.2%	12,297	78.3%	1,875	11.9%
30 to 34 years old	18,440	17,357	94.1%	15,318	83.1%	2,040	11.1%
35 years old and over	105,348	103,180	97.9%	83,032	78.8%	20,148	19.1%
Female							
3 years old +	103,945	78,022	75.1%	62,117	59.8%	15,905	15.3%
3 to 34 years old	48,435	23,925	49.4%	18,838	38.9%	5,087	10.5%
3 and 4 years old	3,085	1,855	60.1%	X	X	1,855	60.1%
5 and 6 years old	2,955	125	4.2%	X	X	125	4.2%
7 to 9 years old	4,361	23	0.5%	X	X	23	0.5%
10 to 13 years old	5,792	30	0.5%	X	X	30	0.5%
14 and 15 years old	2,744	30	1.1%	X	X	30	1.1%
16 and 17 years old	2,627	185	7.1%	39	1.5%	146	5.6%
18 and 19 years old	2,611	969	37.1%	679	26.0%	290	11.1%
20 and 21 years old	2,644	1,500	56.8%	1,169	44.2%	332	12.5%
22 to 24 years old	4,535	3,544	78.2%	3,041	67.1%	503	11.1%
25 to 29 years old	7,876	7,055	89.6%	6,199	78.7%	857	10.9%
30 to 34 years old	9,207	8,608	93.5%	7,712	83.8%	896	9.7%
35 years old and over	55,510	54,097	97.5%	43,279	78.0%	10,818	19.5%
BLACK							
Both sexes, 3 yrs. +	30,197	20,407	67.6%	14,090	46.7%	6,317	20.9%
3 to 34 years old	17,667	8,197	46.4%	5,918	33.5%	2,280	12.9%
3 and 4 years old	1,320	794	60.2%	X	X	794	60.2%
5 and 6 years old	1,205	65	5.4%	X	X	65	5.4%
7 to 9 years old	1,724	17	1.0%	X	X	17	1.0%
10 to 13 years old	2,379	4	0.2%	X	X	4	0.2%
14 and 15 years old	1,128	17	1.5%	4	0.4%	13	1.2%
16 and 17 years old	1,081	57	5.3%	7	0.7%	50	4.6%
18 and 19 years old	1,040	440	42.3%	306	29.5%	133	12.8%
20 and 21 years old	1,027	719	70.0%	524	51.0%	195	19.0%
22 to 24 years old	1,449	1,187	81.9%	938	64.7%	250	17.2%
25 to 29 years old	2,590	2,321	89.6%	1,975	76.2%	346	13.4%
30 to 34 years old	2,725	2,576	94.5%	2,164	79.4%	412	15.1%
35 years old and over	12,530	12,209	97.4%	8,172	65.2%	4,038	32.2%
Female							
3 years old +	16,099	11,208	69.6%	7,720	48.0%	3,488	21.7%
3 to 34 years old	9,072	4,934	48.4%	3,176	35.0%	1,218	13.4%
3 and 4 years old	631	393	62.2%	X	X	393	62.2%
5 and 6 years old	578	46	7.9%	X	X	46	7.9%
7 to 9 years old	858	11	1.3%	X	X	11	1.3%
10 to 13 years old	1,166	4	0.3%	X	X	4	0.3%
14 and 15 years old	558	12	2.1%	4	0.7%	7	1.3%

[Continued]

★ 295 ★

Enrollment Status of the Population, Not Enrolled: 1993
[Continued]

Age, sex, race, and Hispanic origin	Population	Not enrolled in school					
		Total		High school graduate		Not high school graduate	
		Number	Percent	Number	Percent	Number	Percent
16 and 17 years old	533	35	6.6%	4	0.8%	31	5.8%
18 and 19 years old	523	251	48.1%	172	32.8%	80	15.3%
20 and 21 years old	558	362	64.9%	272	48.8%	90	16.1%
22 to 24 years old	776	646	83.3%	497	64.0%	149	19.3%
25 to 29 years old	1,388	1,243	89.5%	1,076	77.6%	166	12.0%
30 to 34 years old	1,504	1,392	92.6%	1,150	76.5%	242	16.1%
35 years old and over	7,027	6,814	97.0%	4,544	64.7%	2,270	32.3%
HISPANIC ORIGIN[2]							
Both sexes, 3 yrs. +	21,672	14,834	68.4%	7,428	34.3%	7,405	34.2%
3 to 34 years old	13,674	6,984	51.1%	3,475	25.4%	3,509	25.7%
3 and 4 years old	1,024	749	73.2%	X	X	749	73.2%
5 and 6 years old	900	56	6.2%	X	X	56	6.2%
7 to 9 years old	1,357	6	0.4%	X	X	6	0.4%
10 to 13 years old	1,653	13	0.8%	X	X	13	0.8%
14 and 15 years old	813	20	2.4%	X	X	20	2.4%
16 and 17 years old	823	96	11.7%	15	1.8%	82	9.9%
18 and 19 years old	710	355	50.0%	155	21.8%	201	28.3%
20 and 21 years old	816	556	68.2%	320	39.2%	236	29.0%
22 to 24 years old	1,246	1,076	86.3%	605	48.6%	470	37.8%
25 to 29 years old	2,069	1,909	92.3%	1,114	53.9%	795	38.5%
30 to 34 years old	2,264	2,148	94.9%	1,267	56.0%	881	38.9%
35 years old and over	7,999	7,849	98.1%	3,953	49.4%	3,896	48.7%
Female							
3 years old +	10,843	7,418	68.4%	3,721	34.3%	3,697	34.1%
3 to 34 years old	6,591	3,259	49.4%	1,654	25.1%	1,605	24.4%
3 and 4 years old	471	346	73.3%	X	X	346	73.3%
5 and 6 years old	486	30	6.1%	X	X	30	6.1%
7 to 9 years old	651	4	0.6%	X	X	4	0.6%
10 to 13 years old	814	4	0.4%	X	X	4	0.4%
14 and 15 years old	405	7	1.8%	X	X	7	1.8%
16 and 17 years old	375	47	12.6%	3	0.9%	44	11.8%
18 and 19 years old	385	185	48.1%	89	23.2%	96	25.0%
20 and 21 years old	405	275	68.0%	158	39.0%	118	29.0%
22 to 24 years old	628	537	85.5%	312	49.7%	225	35.8%
25 to 29 years old	978	879	89.8%	528	54.0%	351	35.8%
30 to 34 years old	992	945	95.2%	563	56.7%	382	38.5%
35 years old and over	4,252	4,159	97.8%	2,068	48.6%	2,092	49.2%

Source: Selected from "Enrollment Status of the Population 3 Years Old and Over, by Age, Sex, Race, Hispanic Origin, and Selected Educational Characteristics: October 1993," U.S. Bureau of the Census, *Current Population Reports*, P20-479, Table 1, pp. 1+. *R *Notes:* 1. Includes nursery school, kindergarten, and grades 1 to 12. 2. May be of any race.

★ 296 ★
Enrollment

European School Enrollment Preceding the First Level

This table shows the total number of pupils enrolled and the percentage who were female in selected European countries, in the latest year for which data on female enrollment is available. Education preceding the first level refers to kindergartens, nursery schools, and infant classes attached to schools at higher levels.

[NA Not available.]

Country or area	Year	Pupils enrolled	Percent female
Europe			
Albania	1990	130,007	NA
Austria	1991	197,186	49%
Belarus	1991	460,100	NA
Belgium	1991	398,005	49%
Bulgaria	1991	258,995	49%
(Former) Czechoslovakia	1991	512,503	NA
Denmark	1990	51,583	49%
Finland	1991	37,047	NA
France	1989	2,535,955	49%
Germany			
Fed. Rep. of	1990	1,755,944	48%
Former G. Dem Rep.	1989	747,140	NA
Gibraltar[1]	1984	150	35%
Greece	1989	141,756	49%
Hungary	1991	394,091	48%
Iceland	1985	4,528	49%
Ireland	1990	127,512	48%
Italy	1991	1,552,255	49%
Luxembourg	1980	7,621	49%
Malta	1990	11,313	47%
Monaco	1991	962	47%
Netherlands	1990	360,880	49%
Norway	1991	155,153	NA
Poland	1991	1,098,279	NA
Portugal	1990	181,450	48%
Romania	1991	742,232	50%
San Marino	1991	750	46%
Slovenia	1990	78,611	NA
Spain	1985	1,127,348	49%
Sweden	1991	220,307	NA
Switzerland	1991	141,160	49%
Ukraine	1991	1,875,000	NA

[Continued]

★ 296 ★

European School Enrollment Preceding the First Level
[Continued]

Country or area	Year	Pupils enrolled	Percent female
United Kingdom	1990	792,700	49%
(Former) USSR	1990	12,609,000	49%
Yugoslavia	1991	261,988	48%
Yugoslavia, SFR	1990	423,899	48%

Source: Selected from "Education preceding the first level," United Nations, *Statistical Yearbook 1992*, New York, 1994, Table 10, pp. 55+. Primary source: United Nations Educational, Scientific and Cultural Organization (Paris). *Note:* 1. Data refer to public education only.

★ 297 ★
Enrollment

European School Enrollment at the First Level

This table shows the total number of pupils enrolled and the percentage who were female in selected European countries, in the latest year for which data on female enrollment is available. The purpose of education at the first level is to provide basic instruction in the tools of learning, for example at elementary and primary schools. Its length may vary from 4 to 9 years.

[NA Not available.]

Country or area	Year	Pupils enrolled	Percent female
Europe			
Albania	1990	551,294	48%
Austria	1991	378,676	49%
Belarus	1991	897,000	NA
Belgium	1991	711,521	49%
Bulgaria	1991	920,694	48%
(Former) Czechoslovakia	1991	1,898,470	49%
Denmark	1990	340,267	49%
Finland	1991	392,695	49%
France	1990	4,149,143	48%
Germany			
Fed. Rep. of	1990	2,561,267	49%
former G. Dem Rep.	1989	957,675	48%
Gibraltar	1984	2,830	48%
Greece	1989	834,688	48%
Hungary	1991	1,081,213	49%
Iceland	1985	24,603	49%
Ireland	1990	416,747	49%
Italy	1991	3,004,264	49%

[Continued]

★ 297 ★

European School Enrollment at the First Level
[Continued]

Country or area	Year	Pupils enrolled	Percent female
Luxembourg	1990	23,465	51%
Malta	1990	36,899	48%
Monaco	1991	1,761	49%
Netherlands	1990	1,082,022	50%
Norway	1991	308,516	49%
Poland	1991	5,218,323	49%
Portugal	1990	1,019,794	48%
Romania	1991	2,608,914	49%
San Marino	1991	1,200	48%
Spain	1989	2,961,953	48%
Sweden	1991	584,203	49%
Switzerland	1991	414,129	49%
Ukraine	1991	4,033,000	NA
United Kingdom	1990	4,532,500	49%
(Former) USSR	1990	25,633,000	49%
Yugoslavia	1991	470,669	49%
Yugoslavia, SFR	1990	1,392,789	48%

Source: Selected from "Education at the first level," United Nations, *Statistical Yearbook 1992*, New York, 1994, Table 11, pp. 65+. Primary source: United Nations Educational, Scientific and Cultural Organization (Paris).

★ 298 ★
Enrollment

European School Enrollment at the Second Level

This table shows the total number of pupils enrolled and the percentage who were female in selected European countries, in the latest year for which data on female enrollment is available. Education at the second level is based upon at least four years of previous instruction at the first level and provides general or specialized instruction or both. Second level education may refer to middle and secondary schools, high schools, teachers' training schools at this level, or schools of a vocational or technical nature.

[NA Not available.]

Country or area	Year	Pupils enrolled	Percent female
Europe			
Albania	1990	205,774	45%
Austria	1991	756,385	47%
Belarus	1991	691,300	NA
Belgium	1991	765,672	49%

[Continued]

★ 298 ★

European School Enrollment at the Second Level
[Continued]

Country or area	Year	Pupils enrolled	Percent female
Bulgaria	1991	383,825	50%
(Former) Czechoslovakia	1991	848,721	50%
Denmark	1990	464,555	49%
Finland	1991	446,207	54%
France	1991	5,614,894	50%
Germany			
Fed. Rep. of	1990	5,972,607	48%
former G. Dem. Rep.	1989	1,406,374	48%
Gibraltar	1984	1,806	49%
Greece	1989	843,732	48%
Hungary	1991	525,151	49%
Iceland	1985	27,559	47%
Ireland	1990	345,941	51%
Italy	1991	5,010,467	49%
Luxembourg	1987	22,496	49%
Malta	1990	32,544	47%
Monaco	1991	2,858	49%
Netherlands	1991	1,178,857	48%
Norway	1991	367,395	49%
Poland	1991	1,965,021	50%
Portugal	1990	670,035	53%
Romania	1991	1,208,630	49%
San Marino	1991	1,158	49%
Spain	1988	4,845,905	50%
Sweden	1991	585,527	50%
Switzerland	1991	562,465	47%
Ukraine	1991	3,354,400	NA
United Kingdom	1990	4,335,600	50%
(Former) USSR	1990	21,090,000	NA
Yugoslavia	1991	816,143	49%
Yugoslavia, SFR	1990	2,344,331	48%

Source: Selected from "Education at the second level," United Nations, *Statistical Yearbook 1992*, New York, 1994, Table 12, pp. 78+. Primary source: United Nations Educational, Scientific and Cultural Organization (Paris).

★ 299 ★
Enrollment

European School Enrollment at the Third Level

This table shows the total number of pupils enrolled in all third-level institutions and in universities and equivalent institutions in selected European countries. It shows the percentage who were female, latest available year. Education at the third level requires as a minimum condition of admission the successful completion of education at the second level or proof of equivalent knowledge or experience. The types of institutions in which third level education may be obtained include universities, teacher-training institutions, and technical institutions.

[NA Not available.]

Country or area	All institutions			Universities and equivalent institutions		
	Year	Students	% Female	Year	Students	% Female
Europe						
Albania[1]	1990	22,059	52%	1990	22,059	52%
Austria	1991	216,529	46%	1991	201,615	44%
Belarus[1]	1991	187,400	53%	NA	NA	NA
Belgium	1989	271,007	48%	1989	108,480	44%
Bulgaria[1]	1991	185,914	53%	1991	156,242	51%
(Former) Czechoslovakia	1991	177,110	46%	1991	177,110	46%
Denmark[2]	1990	142,968	52%	1990	120,125	51%
Estonia	1990	25,900	NA	NA	NA	NA
Finland	1991	173,702[3]	53%[3]	1991	115,358[3]	52%[3]
France[4]	1991	1,840,307	54%	1991	1,246,898	55%
Germany						
Federal Rep. of	1990	1,799,394	40%	1990	1,578,592	38%
Former G. Dem. Rep.[11]	1988	438,930	52%	1988	156,296	45%
Greece	1989	194,419	50%	1989	117,260	53%
Hungary[1]	1991	107,079	50%	1991	71,452	49%
Iceland	1991	6,161	59%	NA	NA	NA
Ireland	1990	90,296	46%	1990	47,955	51%
Italy	1991	1,533,202	50%	1991	1,522,824	49%
Latvia	1990	46,000	NA	NA	NA	NA
Lithuania	1990	65,600	NA	NA	NA	NA
Luxembourg[5]	1985	759	34%	NA	NA	NA
Malta	1990	3,123	44%	1990	3,123	44%
Moldova						
Republic of	1990	54,700	NA	NA	NA	NA
Netherlands	1988	478,869	44%	1988	190,448	41%
Norway	1991	154,180	53%	1991	68,249	52%
Poland[1]	1991	535,656	57%	1991	434,796	52%
Portugal	1990	185,762	56%	1990	128,468	56%
Romania[1]	1985	159,798	45%	1985	159,798	45%
Russia						
Russian Federation	1991	2,823,900	NA	NA	NA	NA
Slovakia	1991	36,504	NA	NA	NA	NA

[Continued]

★ 299 ★

European School Enrollment at the Third Level
[Continued]

Country or area	All institutions			Universities and equivalent institutions		
	Year	Students	% Female	Year	Students	% Female
Spain	1989	1,169,141	51%	1989	1,083,766	51%
Sweden	1991	207,265	54%	NA	NA	NA
Switzerland	1991	143,067	35%	1991	89,031	40%
Ukraine[1]	1990	889,574	50%	NA	NA	NA
United Kingdom	1990	1,258,188	48%	1990	428,858	44%
(Former) USSR	1990	5,253,088	49%	NA	NA	NA
Yugoslavia	1991	133,331	52%		106,361	52%
Yugoslavia SFR	1990	327,092	51%	1990	285,094	50%

Source: Selected from "Education at the third level," United Nations, *Statistical Yearbook 1992*, New York, 1994, Table 13, pp. 91+. Primary source: United Nations Educational, Scientific and Cultural Organization (Paris). *Notes:* 1. Including evening and corresponding courses. 2. Data refer to students enrolled in higher institutions under the authority of the Holy See. 3. Full time only. 4. The total number of students (all institutions) is overestimated due to some students enrolled at institutions, considered here as non-university being enrolled also at the universities. 5. Data refer to students enrolled in institutions located in Luxembourg. At university level, the majority of the students pursue their studies in the following countries: Austria, Belgium, France, Federal Republic of Germany, and Switzerland.

★ 300 ★

Enrollment

European School Enrollment in Vocational Education

This table shows the total number of pupils enrolled and the percentage who were female in selected European countries, in the latest year for which data on female enrollment is available. Vocational education refers to education provided in secondary schools that aim at preparing students directly for a trade or occupation other than teaching.

[NA Not available.]

Country or area	Year	Pupils enrolled	Percent female
Europe			
Albania	1990	135,935	39%
Austria	1991	303,604	44%
Belarus	1991	111,100	NA
Belgium	1985	374,335	47%
Bulgaria	1991	233,528	38%
(Former) Czechoslovakia	1991	367,652	41%
Denmark[1]	1990	147,807	44%
Finland	1991	130,341	55%
France	1991	1,325,008	45%
Germany			
Fed. Rep. of	1990	2,016,029	45%
Former G. Dem. Rep.	1989	314,190	41%

[Continued]

★ 300 ★

European School Enrollment in Vocational Education
[Continued]

Country or area	Year	Pupils enrolled	Percent female
Gibraltar	1984	57	7%
Greece	1989	130,738	32%
Hungary	1991	390,908	43%
Iceland	1985	7,165	35%
Ireland	1990	24,464	64%
Italy	1991	1,926,642	44%
Luxembourg	1987	14,790	46%
Malta	1990	6,653	22%
Monaco	1991	475	36%
Netherlands	1991	505,589	44%
Norway	1991	118,056	45%
Poland	1991	1,446,221	42%
Portugal	1990	32,274	36%
Romania[2]	1991	946,856	44%
San Marino	1991	137	26%
Spain	1988	1,234,045	51%
Sweden	1991	212,395	46%
Switzerland	1991	209,927	42%
Ukraine	1991	528,700	NA
(Former) USSR	1990	2,852,000	NA
United Kingdom	1990	480,400	54%
Yugoslavia	1991	272,149	45%
Yugoslavia, SFR	1990	780,071	45%

Source: Selected from "Education at the second level," United Nations, *Statistical Yearbook 1992,* New York, 1994, Table 12, pp. 78+. Primary source: United Nations Educational, Scientific and Cultural Organization (Paris). *Notes:* 1. Data include apprenticeship training. 2. Data include evening classes.

★ 301 ★

Enrollment

Graduate Physics Students: 1991-1992

This table compares percentages of minority U.S. and foreign graduate physics students in the class of 1991-1992. The total population of graduate students was 14,534.

Sex	Black		Native American	Hispanic		Asian Indian		Oriental		Arab	
	U.S.	Foreign		U.S.	Foreign	U.S.	Foreign	U.S.	Foreign	U.S.	Foreign
Female	22%	14%	6%	12%	18%	20%	22%	17%	18%	12%	15%
Male	78%	86%	94%	88%	82%	80%	78%	83%	82%	88%	85%

Source: Selected from "1991-92 Graduate Student Survey, American Institute of Physics, *AIP Report*, Pub. No. R-207.25, October 1993, table II, p. 3, "A comparison of the characteristics of U.S. minorities with those of foreign graduate physics students, 1991-92." Primary source: Data were derived from the survey of Enrollments and Degrees.

★ 302 ★

Enrollment

Latin American/Caribbean School Enrollment Preceding the First Level

This table shows the total number of pupils enrolled and the percentage who were female in Latin America and the Caribbean, in the latest year for which data on female enrollment is available. Education preceding the first level refers to kindergartens, nursery schools, and infant classes attached to schools at higher levels.

[NA Not available.]

Country or area	Year	Pupils enrolled	Percent female
Latin America and the Caribbean			
Argentina	1985	693,259	50%
Barbados	1982	3,052	49%
Belize	1991	4,756	51%
Bolivia	1990	121,132	49%
Brazil[3]	1980	1,335,317	49%
British Virgin Islands	1984	226	49%
Chile	1991	205,283	49%
Colombia	1985	285,286	50%
Costa Rica	1991	52,040	49%
Cuba	1980	123,741	49%
Dominica	1991	2,000	52%
Dominican Republic	1989	22,237[1]	48%[1]
Ecuador	1987	108,348	50%
El Salvador	1991	83,865	51%

[Continued]

★ 302 ★

Latin American/Caribbean School Enrollment Preceding the First Level
[Continued]

Country or area	Year	Pupils enrolled	Percent female
French Guiana	1990	7,231	NA
Grenada	1987	3,584	51%
Guadeloupe	1991	20,408	49%
Guatemala	1991	145,719	48%
Guyana	1988	26,080	49%
Haiti[2]	1990	230,391	48%
Honduras	1991	60,137	51%
Jamaica	1990	133,687	50%
Martinique	1991	20,435	50%
Mexico	1991	2,791,550	50%
Montserrat[1]	1981	278	45%
Netherlands Antilles	1982	8,707	50%
Nicaragua	1991	68,657	51%
Panama	1985	27,501	50%
Paraguay	1991	39,358	50%
Peru	1985	342,779	50%
Saint Kitts and Nevis	1988	1,618	52%
Saint Lucia	1989	4,500	NA
Saint Vincent and the Grenadines	1990	2,492	52%
Suriname	1988	18,449	49%
Trinidad and Tobago	1990	1,429	51%
Uruguay	1985	55,092	50%
Venezuela	1991	674,644	49%
Virgin Islands	1985	2,656	NA

Source: Selected from "Education preceding the first level," United Nations, *Statistical Yearbook 1992*, New York, 1994, Table 10, pp. 55+. Primary source: United Nations Educational, Scientific and Cultural Organization (Paris). *Notes:* 1. Data refer to public education only. 2. Data refer to infant classes. 3. Enrollment in 1991 was 3,798,200. Percent female not available.

★ 303 ★

Enrollment

Latin America/Caribbean School Enrollment at the First Level

This table shows the total number of pupils enrolled and the percentage who were female in selected Latin America and Caribbean countries, in the latest year for which data on female enrollment is available. The purpose of education at the first level is to provide basic instruction in the tools of learning, for example at elementary and primary schools. Its length may vary from 4 to 9 years.

[NA Not available.]

Country or area	Year	Pupils enrolled	Percent female
Latin America and the Caribbean			
Antigua and Barbuda	1991	9,298	49%
Argentina	1985	4,589,291	49%
Bahamas	1985	32,848	49%
Barbados	1991	26,662	49%
Belize	1991	44,645	48%
Bolivia	1990	1,278,775	47%
Brazil	1991	28,742,471	NA[1]
British Virgin Islands	1984	2,069	48%
Chile	1991	2,033,982	49%
Colombia	1991	4,310,970	50%
Costa Rica	1991	453,297	49%
Cuba	1991	917,889	48%
Dominica	1991	12,120	49%
Dominican Republic[2,3]	1989	1,032,055	49%
Ecuador	1985	1,738,549	49%
El Salvador	1991	1,000,671	50%
Falkland Islands Malvinas	1980	223	58%
French Guiana	1990	14,256	NA
Grenada	1980	18,076	48%
Guadeloupe	1991	38,255	49%
Guatemala	1991	1,249,413	46%
Guyana	1988	118,015	49%
Haiti	1990	555,433	48%
Honduras	1991	908,446	50%
Jamaica	1990	323,378	50%
Martinique	1991	32,747	48%
Mexico	1991	14,396,375	49%
Montserrat	1981	1,725	50%
Netherlands Antilles	1982	32,380	49%
Nicaragua	1991	674,045	51%

[Continued]

★ 303 ★

Latin America/Caribbean School Enrollment at the First Level
[Continued]

Country or area	Year	Pupils enrolled	Percent female
Panama	1985	340,135	48%
Paraguay	1991	720,983	48%
Peru	1985	3,711,592	48%
Saint Kitts and Nevis	1991	7,236	48%
Saint Lucia	1989	33,148	48%
Saint Vincent and the Grenadines	1990	22,030	49%
Suriname	1988	65,798	49%
Trinidad and Tobago[4]	1990	193,992	49%
Turks and Caicos Islands[2]	1984	1,429	49%
Uruguay	1990	346,416	49%
Venezuela[5]	1991	4,190,047	50%
Virgin Islands[2]	1985	20,548	NA

Source: Selected from "Education at the first level," United Nations, *Statistical Yearbook 1992*, New York, 1994, Table 11, pp. 65+. Primary source: United Nations Educational, Scientific and Cultural Organization (Paris). *Notes:* 1. Enrollment in 1980 was 22,598,254. Percent female was 49%. 2. Data refer to public education only. 3. Data include intermediate education (grades 7 and 8 of "tradicional" education. 4. Data refer to government-maintained and aided schools only. 5. Data refer to grades 1 to 9.

★ 304 ★

Enrollment

Latin American/Caribbean School Enrollment at the Second Level

This table shows the total number of pupils enrolled and the percentage who were female in selected Latin American and Caribbean countries, in the latest year for which data on female enrollment is available. Education at the second level is based upon at least four years of previous instruction at the first level and provides general or specialized instruction or both. Second level education may refer to middle and secondary schools, high schools, teachers' training schools at this level, or schools of a vocational or technical nature.

[NA Not available.]

Country or area	Year	Pupils enrolled	Percent female
Latin America and the Caribbean			
Antigua and Barbuda	1991	5,845	50%
Argentina	1988	1,974,119	52%
Bahamas	1985	27,604	52%
Barbados	1989	24,004	47%
Belize	1990	7,904	53%

[Continued]

★ 304 ★

Latin American/Caribbean School Enrollment at the Second Level
[Continued]

Country or area	Year	Pupils enrolled	Percent female
Bolivia	1990	219,232	46%
Brazil	1980	2,819,182	54%[1]
British Virgin Islands	1983	1,323	58%
Chile	1991	699,455	51%
Colombia	1991	2,377,947	54%
Costa Rica	1991	139,303	50%
Cuba	1991	912,165	53%
Dominica	1985	7,370	54%
Dominican Republic	1985	463,511	NA
Ecuador	1987	771,928	50%
El Salvador	1991	94,268	55%
Falkland Islands	1980	90	56%
French Guiana	1975	5,534	52%[2]
Grenada	1980	8,626	59%[3]
Guadeloupe	1990	49,846	53%
Guatemala	1980	171,903	45%[4]
Guyana	1986	76,012	51%
Haiti	1985	143,758	NA
Honduras	1991	194,083	55%
Jamaica	1990	225,240	52%
Martinique	1991	46,373	52%
Mexico	1991	6,704,188	49%
Montserrat	1980	887	NA
Nicaragua	1990	168,888	58%
Panama	1985	184,536	52%
Paraguay	1991	169,167	51%
Peru	1985	1,427,261	47%
Saint Kitts and Nevis	1991	4,396	51%
Saint Lucia	1985	6,833	61%
Saint Vincent and the Grenadines	1990	10,719	55%
Suriname	1988	34,248	54%
Trinidad and Tobago	1988	99,741	50%
Turks and Caicos Islands	1984	707	NA
Uruguay[5]	1980	148,294	53%

[Continued]

★ 304 ★

Latin American/Caribbean School Enrollment at the Second Level
[Continued]

Country or area	Year	Pupils enrolled	Percent female
Venezuela	1991	289,430	57%
Virgin Islands	1985	7,948	NA

Source: Selected from "Education at the second level," United Nations, *Statistical Yearbook 1992,* New York, 1994, Table 12, pp. 78+. Primary source: United Nations Educational, Scientific and Cultural Organization (Paris). *Notes:* 1. Enrollment in 1991 was 3,558,946. Percent female not available. 2. Enrollment in 1990 was 10,722. Percent female not available. 3. Enrollment in 1987 was 6,497. Percent female not available. 4. Enrollment in 1987 was 241,053. Percent female not available. 5. Enrollment in 1991 was 276,482. Percent female not available.

★ 305 ★
Enrollment

Latin American/Caribbean School Enrollment at the Third Level

This table shows the total number of pupils enrolled in all third level institutions and in universities and equivalent institutions in selected Latin American and Caribbean countries. It shows the percentage who were female, latest available year. Education at the third level requires as a minimum condition of admission the successful completion of education at the second level or proof of equivalent knowledge or experience. The types of institutions in which third level education may be obtained include universities, teacher-training institutions, and technical institutions.

[NA Not available.]

Country or area	All institutions			Universities and equivalent institutions		
	Year	Students	% Female	Year	Students	% Female
Latin America/Caribbean						
Argentina	1985	846,145	53%	1985	664,200	46%
Bahamas	1987	5,305	68%	NA	NA	NA
Barbados	1989	4,242	60%	1989	1,901	57%
Bolivia	NA	NA	NA	1991	109,503	NA
Brazil	1991	1,565,056	53%[1]	1991	1,565,056	53%
Chile	1985	197,437	43%	1980	120,168	40%[5]
Colombia[6]	1989	474,787	52%	1989	410,396	51%
Costa Rica[2]	1991	80,442	NA	1991	61,364	NA
Cuba	1990	242,434	57%	1990	242,434	57%
Dominica	1991[3]	658	55%	NA	NA	NA
Dominican Republic	1985	123,748	NA	NA	NA	NA
Ecuador	1990	206,541	NA	1980	264,136	37%
El Salvador	1990	78,211	33%	1990	66,092	31%
Guatemala[4]	1975	22,881	23%	1975	22,881	23%
Haiti	1985	6,288	26%	1985	4,471	29%
Guyana	1989	4,665	43%	1989	2,192	49%
Honduras	1980	25,825	38%	1990	39,324	43%

[Continued]

★ 305 ★

Latin American/Caribbean School Enrollment at the Third Level
[Continued]

Country or area	All institutions			Universities and equivalent institutions		
	Year	Students	% Female	Year	Students	% Female
Jamaica	1990	16,018	NA	1990	6,083	62%
Mexico	1980	929,865	33%	1990	1,252,027	43%
Nicaragua	1990	30,733	52%	1990	29,780	52%
Panama	1985	55,303	58%	1985	55,303	58%
Paraguay	1990	32,884	NA	1990	29,447	46%
Peru	1980	306,353	35%[7]	1980	246,510	35%[7]
Puerto Rico	1980	131,184	59%	1975	91,254	53%
Suriname	1990	4,319	53%	1990	2,373	44%
Saint Kitts and Nevis	1991	325	54%	NA	NA	NA
Saint Lucia	1987	389	54%	NA	NA	NA
Saint Vincent and the Grenadines	1989	677	68%	NA	NA	NA
Trinidad and Tobago	1985	6,282	40%	1990	4,090	49%
Uruguay	1991	73,660	NA	1987	61,450	57%
Venezuela	1985	443,064	41%[8]	1985	347,618	NA
Virgin Islands	1990	2,466	75%	1990	2,466	75%

Source: Selected from "Education at the third level," United Nations, *Statistical Yearbook 1992*, New York, 1994, Table 13, pp. 91+. Primary source: United Nations Educational, Scientific and Cultural Organization (Paris). *Notes:* 1. Excluding post-graduate students. 2. Data refer only to institutions recognized by the National Council for Higher Education. 3. Excluding teacher training. 4. Data refer to the University of San Carlos only. Enrollment in both categories was 51,860 in 1986. Percent female not available. 5. Enrollment in all third-level institutions was 286,926 in 1991. Enrollment in universities and equivalent institutions was 213,058 in 1991. Percent female not available. 6. Data on universities include the Open university. 7. Enrollment in all third-level institutions was 743,569 in 1990. Enrollment n universities and equivalent institutions was 504,700 in 1990. Percent female not available. 8. Enrollment in all third-level institutions was 550,030 in 1990. Percent female not available.

★ 306 ★

Enrollment

Latin American/Caribbean School Enrollment in Vocational Education

This table shows the total number of pupils enrolled and the percentage who were female in selected Latin American and Caribbean countries, in the latest year for which data on female enrollment is available. Vocational education refers to education provided in secondary schools that aim at preparing students directly for a trade or occupation other than teaching.

[NA Not available.]

Country or area	Year	Pupils enrolled	Percent female
Latin America and the Caribbean			
Argentina	1988	1,162,863	43%
Belize	1990	105	4%

[Continued]

★ 306 ★

Latin American/Caribbean School Enrollment in Vocational Education
[Continued]

Country or area	Year	Pupils enrolled	Percent female
British Virgin Islands	1983	309	66%
Chile	1991	262,563	48%
Colombia	1991	510,726	59%
Costa Rica	1991	30,959	48%
Cuba	1991	293,408	48%
Dominica	1985	259	36%
Dominican Republic	1985	21,156	NA
Ecuador	1987	260,850	55%
El Salvador	1991	65,640	56%
French Guiana	1975	1,536	46%
Guadeloupe	1990	10,638	49%
Guatemala	1980	29,768	39%
Guyana	1986	2,594	25%
Haiti	1985	3,469	NA
Honduras	1991	58,566	56%
Jamaica[1]	1985	8,690	50%
Martinique	1991	13,866	34%
Mexico	1991	818,202	54%
Montserrat	1975	53	45%
Netherlands Antilles	1982	10,088	42%
Nicaragua	1990	15,332	54%
Panama	1985	49,154	54%
Paraguay	1991	11,680	44%
Peru	1980	51,368	40%
Saint Lucia	1985	594	100%
Saint Vincent and the Grenadines	1990	296	71%
Suriname	1988	9,292	40%
Trinidad and Tobago	1988	829	32%
Uruguay	1991	45,027	49%
Venezuela	1991	51,013	54%

Source: Selected from "Education at the second level," United Nations, *Statistical Yearbook 1992*, New York, 1994, Table 12, pp. 78+. Primary source: United Nations Educational, Scientific and Cultural Organization (Paris). *Note:* 1. Data refer to public education only.

★ 307 ★

Enrollment

North American School Enrollment Preceding the First Level

This table shows the total number of pupils enrolled and the percentage who were female in North America, in the latest year for which data on female enrollment is available. Education preceding the first level refers to kindergartens, nursery schools, and infant classes attached to schools at higher levels.

[NA Not available.]

Country or area	Year	Pupils enrolled	Percent female
North America			
Bermuda	1984	1,287	49%
Canada	1990	485,000	49%
Saint Pierre and Miquelon	1986	373	44%
United States	1989	6,745,146	48%

Source: Selected from "Education preceding the first level," United Nations, *Statistical Yearbook 1992*, New York, 1994, Table 10, pp. 55+. Primary source: United Nations Educational, Scientific and Cultural Organization (Paris). *Note:* 1.

★ 308 ★

Enrollment

North American School Enrollment at the First Level

This table shows the total number of pupils enrolled and the percentage who were female in selected North American countries, in the latest year for which data on female enrollment is available. The purpose of education at the first level is to provide basic instruction in the tools of learning, for example at elementary and primary schools. Its length may vary from 4 to 9 years.

[NA Not available.]

Country or area	Year	Pupils enrolled	Percent female
North America			
Bermuda	1984	5,398	50%
Canada	1990	2,371,558	48%
Saint Pierre and Miquelon	1985	558	47%
United States[1]	1989	28,973,069	49%

Source: Selected from "Education at the first level," United Nations, *Statistical Yearbook 1992*, New York, 1994, Table 11, pp. 65+. Primary source: United Nations Educational, Scientific and Cultural Organization (Paris). *Note:* 1. Grades 1 to 8.

★ 309 ★

Enrollment

North American School Enrollment at the Second Level

This table shows the total number of pupils enrolled and the percentage who were female in selected North American countries, in the latest year for which data on female enrollment is available. Education at the second level is based upon at least four years of previous instruction at the first level and provides general or specialized instruction or both. Second level education may refer to middle and secondary schools, high schools, teachers' training schools at this level, or schools of a vocational or technical nature.

[NA Not available.]

Country or area	Year	Pupils enrolled	Percent female
North America			
Canada	1990	2,292,735	49%
Saint Pierre and Miquelon	1986	800	53%
United States	1989	12,583,484	49%

Source: Selected from "Education at the second level," United Nations, *Statistical Yearbook 1992*, New York, 1994, Table 12, pp. 78+. Primary source: United Nations Educational, Scientific and Cultural Organization (Paris).

★ 310 ★

Enrollment

North American School Enrollment at the Third Level

This table shows the total number of pupils enrolled in all third-level institutions and in universities and equivalent institutions in selected North American countries. It shows the percentage who were female, latest available year. Education at the third level requires as a minimum condition of admission the successful completion of education at the second level or proof of equivalent knowledge or experience. The types of institutions in which third level education may be obtained include universities, teacher-training institutions, and technical institutions.

[NA Not available.]

Country or area	All institutions			Universities and equivalent institutions		
	Year	Students	% Female	Year	Students	% Female
North America						
Bermuda	1980	608	51%	NA	NA	NA
Canada	1991	1,942,814	54%	1991	867,352	55%
United States	1985	12,247,055	52%	1985	7,715,978	51%

Source: Selected from "Education at the third level," United Nations, *Statistical Yearbook 1992*, New York, 1994, Table 13, pp. 91+. Primary source: United Nations Educational, Scientific and Cultural Organization (Paris).

★ 311 ★

Enrollment

Nursery School Enrollment: 1968-1993

This table gives nursery school enrollment figures, totals and figures by labor force status and education of the mother, for the years 1993, 1983, 1973, and 1968, for children 3 and 4 years old. About 40.4% of children in this age group were enrolled in preprimary school in the fall of 1993. Children of mothers in the labor force were much more likely than other children to attend full day. Increased educational attainment of mothers can be associated with their increased labor force participation rate and increased nursery school enrollment of their children.

[Numbers in thousands.]

Characteristic	1993	1983	1973	1968
Children, 3 and 4 yrs.				
All races	8,097	6,986	7,000	7,803
Enrolled in nursery school	2,732	2,160	1,242	738
Percent enrolled	33.7%	30.9%	17.7%	9.5%
By Labor Force				
Status of Mother				
Mother in labor force	4,374	3,514	2,527	2,413
Enrolled in nursery school	1,620	1,216	520	282
Percent enrolled	37.0%	34.6%	20.6%	11.7%
Full-day	705	496	286	142
Percent full-day	43.5%	40.8%	55.0%	50.4%
Mother not in labor force	3,138	3,278	4,337	5,288
Enrolled in nursery school	949	899	705	451
Percent enrolled	30.2%	27.4%	16.3%	8.5%
Full-day	193	124	64	61
Percent full-day	20.3%	13.8%	9.1%	13.5%
By Education of				
Mother				
All children with mother	7,512	6,792	6,864	7,701
Not high school graduate	1,258	1,612	1,911	2,710
High school graduate	2,657	3,047	3,213	3,527
Some college	2,138	1,157	1,036	884
Bachelor's or higher	1,459	975	705	582
Enrolled in nursery school	2,569	2,115	1,225	733
Not high school graduate	212	247	165	114
High school graduate	779	842	463	301
Some college	837	493	294	153
Bachelor's or higher	741	532	304	164
Percent enrolled	34.2%	31.1%	17.8%	9.5%
Not high school graduate	16.9%	15.3%	8.6%	4.2%
High school graduate	29.3%	27.6%	14.4%	8.5%

[Continued]

★ 311 ★

Nursery School Enrollment: 1968-1993
[Continued]

Characteristic	1993	1983	1973	1968
Some college	39.1%	42.6%	28.4%	17.3%
Bachelor's or higher	50.8%	54.6%	43.1%	28.2%

Source: Selected from "Nursery School Enrollment, by Full-day and Public School Attendance, Race, Hispanic Origin, and Education and Labor Force Status of Mother, for Children 3 and 4 Years Old: 1993, 1983, 1973, and 1986," U.S. Bureau of the Census, *Current Population Reports*, P20-479, Table C, p. ix.

★ 312 ★
Enrollment

Oceanian School Enrollment Preceding the First Level

This table shows the total number of pupils enrolled and the percentage who were female in selected Oceanian countries, in the latest year for which data on female enrollment is available. Education preceding the first level refers to kindergartens, nursery schools, and infant classes attached to schools at higher levels.

[NA Not available.]

Country or area	Year	Pupils enrolled	Percent female
Oceania			
American Samoa	1985	2,001	47%
Australia[1]	1991	180,809	49%
Cook Islands	1988	360	NA
Fiji	1991	7,506	50%
French Polynesia	1992	16,472	48%
Guam	1983	2,892	43%
Nauru	1985	383	49%

Source: Selected from "Education preceding the first level," United Nations, *Statistical Yearbook 1992*, New York, 1994, Table 10, pp. 55+. Primary source: United Nations Educational, Scientific and Cultural Organization (Paris). *Note:* 1. Data refer only to preprimary classes in primary schools.

★ 313 ★

Enrollment

Oceanian School Enrollment at the First Level

This table shows the total number of pupils enrolled and the percentage who were female in selected Oceanian countries, in the latest year for which data on female enrollment is available. The purpose of education at the first level is to provide basic instruction in the tools of learning, for example at elementary and primary schools. Its length may vary from 4 to 9 years.

[NA Not available.]

Country or area	Year	Pupils enrolled	Percent female
Oceania			
American Samoa	1991	7,884	48%
Australia	1991	1,605,720	49%
Cook Islands	1988	2,376	NA
Fiji	1991	144,924	49%
French Polynesia	1992	29,622	48%
Guam	1988	15,516	NA
Kiribati	1992	16,020	49%
Nauru	1985	1,451	47%
New Caledonia	1991	22,325	48%
New Zealand	1990	314,487	49%
Niue[1]	1988	453	49%
Pacific Islands			
Palau[2]	1975	30,285	48%
Papua New Guinea	1990	415,195	44%
Samoa	1989	37,833	48%
Solomon Islands	1991	60,259	45%
Tokelau	1991	361	50%
Tonga	1990	16,522	48%
Tuvalu[3]	1990	1,485	48%
Vanuatu[3]	1992	26,267	47%

Source: Selected from "Education at the first level," United Nations, *Statistical Yearbook 1992*, New York, 1994, Table 11, pp. 65+. Primary source: United Nations Educational, Scientific and Cultural Organization (Paris). *Notes:* 1. Grades 1 to 7. 2. Including data for Federated States of Micronesia, Marshall Islands, and Northern Marianna Islands. 3. Data refer to public education only.

★ 314 ★

Enrollment

Oceanian School Enrollment at the Second Level

This table shows the total number of pupils enrolled and the percentage who were female in selected Oceanian countries, in the latest year for which data on female enrollment is available. Education at the second level is based upon at least four years of previous instruction at the first level and provides general or specialized instruction or both. Second level education may refer to middle and secondary schools, high schools, teachers' training schools at this level, or schools of a vocational or technical nature.

[NA Not available.]

Country or area	Year	Pupils enrolled	Percent female
Oceania			
American Samoa	1991	3,643	46%
Australia	1991	1,288,691	50%
Fiji	1985	45,093	50%
French Polynesia	1992	22,261	54%
Guam	1988	16,017	NA
Kiribati	1992	3,357	52%
Nauru	1985	482	50%
New Caledonia	1991	21,908	52%
New Zealand	1990	335,456	50%
Niue	1988	194	45%
Pacific Islands (Paulau)[2]	1975	7,951	44%
Papua New Guinea	1990	65,643	38%
Samoa	1980	19,785	49%
Solomon Islands	1986	6,615	38%
Tokelau	1983	488	50%
Tonga	1990	14,749	48%
Tuvalu	1990	345	52%
Vanuatu	1980	2,426	42%

Source: Selected from "Education at the second level," United Nations, *Statistical Yearbook 1992*, New York, 1994, Table 12, pp. 78+. Primary source: United Nations Educational, Scientific and Cultural Organization (Paris). *Note:* 1. Inc. Fed. States of Microneisa, Marshall Is., No. Mariana Is.

★ 315 ★
Enrollment

Oceanian School Enrollment at the Third Level

This table shows the total number of pupils enrolled in all third-level institutions and in universities and equivalent institutions in selected Oceanian countries. It shows the percentage who were female, latest available year. Education at the third level requires as a minimum condition of admission the successful completion of education at the second level or proof of equivalent knowledge or experience. The types of institutions in which third level education may be obtained include universities, teacher-training institutions, and technical institutions.

[NA Not available.]

Country or area	All institutions			Universities and equivalent institutions		
	Year	Students	% Female	Year	Students	% Female
Oceania						
American Samoa	1988	909	54%	NA	NA	NA
Australia	1991	534,538	53%	1991	534,530	53%
Cook Islands	1980	360	45%	1980	303	44%
Fiji[1]	1985	2,313	38%	1985	1,932	37%
French Polynesia	1991	301	50%	NA	NA	NA
Guam	1980	3,217	55%	1988	4,257	59%
New Caledonia	1985	761	44%	NA	NA	NA
New Zealand[2]	1991	128,078	53%	1991	72,381	50%
Pacific Islands (Palau)[3]	1980	2,129	24%	NA	NA	NA
Papua New Guinea	1986	6,397	24%	1986	3,413	17%
Samoa[4]	1983	562	47%	1983	136	50%
Tonga	1985	705	56%	1985	85	22%

Source: Selected from "Education at the third level," United Nations, *Statistical Yearbook 1992*, New York, 1994, Table 13, pp. 91+. Primary source: United Nations Educational, Scientific and Cultural Organization (Paris). *Notes:* 1. Enrollments in 1991 were 7,908 and 3,621. Percent female NA. 2. Including correspondence courses. 3. Including data for Federated States of Micronesia, Marshall Islands, and Northern Mariana Islands. 4. Data exclude school of agriculture.

★ 316 ★

Enrollment

Oceanian School Enrollment in Vocational Education

This table shows the total number of pupils enrolled and the percentage who were female in selected Oceanian countries, in the latest year for which data on female enrollment is available. Vocational education refers to education provided in secondary schools that aim at preparing students directly for a trade or occupation other than teaching.

[NA Not available.]

Country or area	Year	Pupils enrolled	Percent female
Oceania			
American Samoa	1991	160	4%
Fiji	1985	3,588	48%[1]
French Polynesia	1992	3,628	48%
Kiribati	1992	234	42%
Nauru	1985	17	47%
New Caledonia	1991	7,019	45%
New Zealand	1990	5,690	59%
Papua New Guinea	1990	7,614	35%
Samoa	1980	264	41%
Solomon Islands	1986	1,144	37%
Tokelau	1983	380	50%
Tonga	1990	662	44%
Tuvalu	1990	31	NA
Vanuatu	1992	444	32%

Source: Selected from "Education at the second level," United Nations, *Statistical Yearbook 1992*, New York, 1994, Table 12, pp. 78+. Primary source: United Nations Educational, Scientific and Cultural Organization (Paris). *Note:* 1. Enrollment in 1991 was 5,992. Percent female not available.

★ 317 ★

Enrollment

Secondary and Postsecondary Enrollment in G-7 Countries: 1988

This table shows selected enrollment and graduation characteristics at upper secondary and postsecondary levels in educational systems in G-7 countries in 1988. G-7 countries are the most highly industrialized and developed in the world.

[NA Not available.]

| Country | Number of upper secondary full-time enrollees per 100 individuals in age[1,2] | | | | | | | | | Number graduating secondary per 100 in age group[3] | No. enrolling in post-secondary per 100 in age group[4] |
| | All upper secondary | | | General | | | Voc-tech education and apprenticeship | | | | |
	Total	Male	Female	Total	Male	Female	Total	Male	Female		
Canada[5]	97.8	96.6	99.1	NA	NA	NA	NA	NA	NA	67.9	NA
France[5]	84.9	82.8	87.1	37.1	30.6	43.8	47.8	52.2	43.3	84.5	36.4
Germany (West)[6]	118.1	123.5	112.5	24.0	23.6	24.5	94.1	99.9	88.0	112.1	28.7
Italy[7]	60.2	59.2	61.3	19.1	14.0	24.3	41.2	45.3	36.9	43.2	28.3
Japan[5]	94.0	92.4	95.7	67.5	64.9	70.1	26.6	27.3	25.8	89.5	51.4
United Kingdom[8]	76.9	74.7	79.2	63.0	62.2	63.9	13.5	12.1	15.0	65.1	21.2
United States[5]	90.2	88.0	92.6	NA	NA	NA	NA	NA	NA	73.7	69.5

Source: "Selected enrollment and graduation characteristics at upper secondary and postsecondary levels in educational systems in G-7 countries: 1988," National Center for Education Statistics, Research and Development Report, *Vocational Education in G-7 Countries: Profiles and Data*, September 1994, Table 3.1, p. 76. Primary source: Organization for Economic Cooperation and Development, Center for Educational Research and Innovation, *Education at a Glance* (Paris: OECD, 1992), 75, 77, 97. *Notes:* 1. Upper secondary age group varies from country to country; it may begin at age 14, 15, or 16, and the duration may be 3,4, or 5 years. 2. May overestimate percentage of population in age range enrolled, since some students may be older or younger than the secondary age range. 3. Includes 17- or 18-year-olds. In the case of Germany, many graduates are older than 18, the reference age. 4. University or nonuniversity 18- or 19-year-olds. 5. Upper secondary theoretical starting age is 15; duration is 3 years. 6. Upper secondary theoretical starting age is 16; duration is 3 years. Some students are outside the normal enrollment age range; including, in particular, older students who previously completed a general secondary program and returned to enroll in a vocational program. The result overestimates the size of the upper secondary population relative to the size of the normal age range for upper secondary enrollment. 7. Upper secondary theoretical starting age is 14; duration is 5 years. 8. Upper secondary theoretical starting age is 14; duration is 4 years.

★ 318 ★

Enrollment

Seminary Enrollment: 1972-1992

Number of women seminary students, annual precent change, and percentage of total enrollment, 1972-1992. Collection of data on women seminary students began in 1972. Then, women made up only 10.2% of total enrollment. By 1992 they made up 31.1% of the student body.

Year	Number of women	Annual change	% of total enrollment
1972	3,358	--	10.2%
1973	4,021	+19.7%	11.8%
1974	5,255	+30.7%	14.3%
1975	6,505	+23.8%	15.9%
1976	7,349	+13.0%	17.1%
1977	8,371	+13.9%	18.5%
1978	8,972	+7.2%	19.3%
1979	10,204	+13.7%	21.1%
1980	10,830	+6.1%	21.8%
1981	11,683	+7.9%	23.1%

[Continued]

★ 318 ★

Seminary Enrollment: 1972-1992
[Continued]

Year	Number of women	Annual change	% of total enrollment
1982	12,473	+6.8%	23.7%
1983	13,451	+7.8%	24.4%
1984	14,142	+5.1%	25.0%
1985	14,572	+3.0%	25.8%
1986	14,864	+2.0%	26.4%
1987	15,310	+3.0%	27.0%
1988	16,344	+6.8%	29.3%
1989	16,461	+0.7%	29.3%
1990	17,571	+6.7%	29.7%
1991	18,384	+4.6%	30.6%
1992	19,653	+6.9%	31.1%

Source: "Women Enrollment," *Yearbook of American & Canadian Churches 1993*, Table 4, p. 263.

High School

★ 319 ★

ACT Students' Aspirations

This table shows the percentage distribution of planned educational majors and vocational choices of the 494,761 females who took the ACT Assessment and graduated in 1994.

Planned major or vocational choice	Planned Educational Major				Educational major	1st voc. choice
	Number of students	Avg. ACT Composite	Certainty			
			Very	Fairly		
Agric & Ag Tech	4,634	20.3	41%	47%	1%	1%
Arch & Env Design	7,079	20.7	39%	46%	2%	2%
Business & Mgmt	52,083	20.1	40%	47%	11%	11%
Business & Office	8,456	17.6	36%	50%	2%	2%
Marketing & Distrib	4,566	18.7	33%	49%	1%	1%
Comm & Comm Tech	20,640	21.1	37%	48%	4%	5%
Comm & Personal Svcs	14,129	18.4	45%	43%	3%	4%
Computer & Info Sci	5,910	18.4	43%	47%	1%	1%
Cross-Disc Studies	627	23.8	22%	48%	0%	0%
Education	33,659	20.2	50%	41%	7%	8%
Teacher Education	20,480	20.5	47%	43%	4%	5%
Engineering (Pre)	13,180	23.3	38%	48%	3%	3%
Engineering Tech	1,543	21.0	36%	48%	0%	0%

[Continued]

★ 319 ★

ACT Students' Aspirations
[Continued]

Planned major or vocational choice	Planned Educational Major				Educational major	1st voc. choice
	Number of students	Avg. ACT Composite	Certainty			
			Very	Fairly		
Foreign Languages	2,583	23.1	37%	47%	1%	0%
Health Sciences	120,409	20.3	56%	37%	26%	27%
Home Economics	5,123	18.4	40%	45%	1%	1%
Letters	3,956	24.3	32%	49%	1%	1%
Mathematics	1,915	24.1	30%	51%	0%	0%
Phil, Relig & Theol	1,544	22.0	45%	41%	0%	0%
Sciences (Bio & Phy)	21,917	23.2	38%	48%	5%	3%
Social Sciences	55,415	21.3	43%	46%	12%	12%
Trade & Industrial	777	20.0	45%	43%	0%	0%
Visual & Perf Arts	19,922	21.0	46%	42%	4%	4%
Undecided	41,116	20.7	6%	11%	9%	8%
No response	33,098					

Source: Selected from "Percentage Distribution of Planned Educational Majors & Vocational Choices," *ACT High School Profile Report HS Graduating Class 1994: National Report for Females*, p. 10.

★ 320 ★

High School

Alcohol Use by High School Seniors: 1987-1992

This table shows the percentages of male and female high school seniors who reported alcohol use by selected characteristics. The top four substances used by high school seniors are alcohol, cigarettes, marijuana/hashish, and all other illicit drugs combined. Alcohol drinking is widespread among high school seniors.

Characteristic	"Ever" in lifetime use	Use in last year	Daily use in 30 days	Binge[1]
1991				
Total	88.0%	77.7%	3.6%	29.8%
Female	87.9%	76.2%	1.6%	21.2%
Male	88.2%	79.0%	5.3%	37.8%

[Continued]

★ 320 ★

Alcohol Use by High School Seniors: 1987-1992
[Continued]

Characteristic	"Ever" in lifetime use	Use in last year	Daily use in 30 days	Binge[1]
1987	92.2%	85.7%	4.8%	35.7%
1992[2]	87.5%	76.8%	3.4%	27.9%
Percent change 1987-1992	-5.1%	-10.4%	-29.2%	-21.8%

Source: Selected from "Trends in Drug and Alcohol Use by Youth in the U.S.A.," *Statistical Bulletin*, Vol. 74, No. 3, Jul-Sep 1993, Table 1, p. 21, "Alcohol Use by Selected Demographic Characteristics of 1991 U.S. High School Seniors and Consumption Changes, 1987-1992." Primary source: Smoking, Drinking and Illicit Drug Use Among American Secondary School Students, College Students, and Young Adults, 1975-1991, National Institute of Drug Abuse, 1992 and unpublished data from the 1992 survey. *Notes:* 1. Five or more drinks in a row in the past two weeks. 2. Unpublished data.

★ 321 ★

High School

Course Taking in Core Subject Areas: 1982-1992

In 1983, the report entitled *A Nation At Risk* recommended that all students seeking a high school diploma be required to enroll in the "New Basics," a core curriculum composed of 4 units of English, 3 units of science, 3 units of social studies, 3 units of mathematics, and 0.5 units of computer science. This table shows the percentage of high school graduates who earned these recommended units (not including the 0.5 units of computer science) in 1982, 1987, 1990, and 1992.

Characteristic	1982	1987	1990	1992	Percentage point change			
					1982-87	1987-90	1990-92	1982-92
Total	12.7%	28.6%	39.9%	46.8%	15.9%	11.3%	6.9%	34.1%
Male	13.7%	30.1%	40.6%	46.5%	16.5%	10.5%	5.9%	32.8%
Female	11.8%	27.2%	39.2%	47.2%	15.4%	12.0%	8.0%	35.4%

Source: "Percentage of high school graduates who earned the recommended units in core courses, by selected student characteristics: 1982, 1987, 1990, and 1992," U.S. Department of Education, National Center for Education Statistics, Indicator of the Month, June 1994, "High school course taking in the core subject areas." Primary source: U.S. Department of Education, National Center for Education Statistics, High School and Beyond Transcript Study, 1987 and 1990 NAEP High School Transcript Studies, National Education Longitudinal Study Transcripts, 1992. The panel's recommendation of 0.5 units of computer science was not included here.

★ 322 ★

High School

High School Dropouts by Race/Ethnicity: 1978-1993

This table shows the event dropout rate by race-ethnicity in 1993. Event dropout rates measure the proportion of individuals who dropped out of school over a specified time interval, such as a 12-month period.

Year	White, non-Hispanic		Black, non-Hispanic		Hispanic	
	Male	Female	Male	Female	Male	Female
1978	6.4%	5.1%	11.0%	9.5%	15.9%	8.5%
1980	5.7%	4.8%	7.7%	8.7%	17.6%	6.7%
1982	4.9%	4.6%	8.9%	6.6%	9.5%	8.8%
1984	4.8%	4.1%	6.0%	5.5%	12.3%	10.2%
1986	3.8%	3.7%	5.1%	5.7%	12.4%	11.3%
1988[1]	4.3%	4.1%	6.3%	5.6%	12.3%	8.2%
1990[1]	3.5%	3.1%	4.2%	5.7%	8.7%	7.2%
1992[1,2]	3.5%	4.0%	3.3%	6.7%	7.6%	9.0%
1993[1,2]	4.1%	3.7%	6.4%	5.3%	5.1%	8.0%

Source: Selected from "Event dropout and retention rates, grades 10-12, ages 15-24, by sex and race-ethnicity: October 1978 through October 1993," National Center for Education Statistics, *Dropout Rates in the United States: 1993*, NCES 94-669, September 1994, Table 5, p. 12. Primary source: U.S. Department of Commerce, Bureau of The Census, Current Population Survey, October (various years), and unpublished data. Some figures are revised from those previously published. *Notes:* 1. Numbers for these years reflect new editing procedures instituted by the Bureau of the Census for cases with missing data on school enrollment items. 2. Numbers for these years reflect new wording of the educational attainment item in the CPS.

★ 323 ★

High School

High School Dropouts, Reasons: 1992

This table shows the percentage of 10th- to 12th-grade dropouts who reported that various reasons for dropping out of school applied to them, by race-ethnicity, 1992.

[NA Not applicable.]

Reasons for dropping out	Total	Sex		Hispanic	Black, non-Hispanic	White, non-Hispanic
		Male	Female			
School-related:						
Did not like school	42.9%	43.6%	42.2%	48.0%	28.8%	45.5%
Could not get along with teachers	22.8%	24.6%	21.1%	24.6%	27.8%	21.5%
Could not get along with students	14.5%	17.7%	11.6%	15.6%	18.4%	13.6%
Did not feel safe at school	6.0%	7.0%	5.1%	8.3%	8.5%	4.8%
Felt I didn't belong	24.2%	25.8%	22.7%	16.0%	25.9%	26.6%

[Continued]

★ 323 ★

High School Dropouts, Reasons: 1992
[Continued]

Reasons for dropping out	Total	Sex		Hispanic	Black, non-Hispanic	White, non-Hispanic
		Male	Female			
Could not keep up with schoolwork	31.3%	32.7%	29.9%	35.0%	25.6%	30.3%
Was failing school	38.7%	43.4%	34.5%	40.6%	39.5%	36.6%
Changed school and did not like new school	10.6%	10.5%	10.7%	12.3%	9.1%	10.2%
Was suspended/expelled from school	15.5%	21.6%	10.0%	10.1%	24.4%	15.4%
Job-related:						
Could not work and go to school at same time	22.8%	26.9%	19.1%	20.4%	15.4%	24.6%
Found a job	28.5%	35.9%	21.8%	34.1%	19.1%	27.5%
Family-related:						
Had to support family	11.2%	10.4%	11.9%	15.8%	11.8%	9.9%
Wanted to have family	7.5%	6.4%	8.4%	9.1%	4.6%	8.2%
Was pregnant[1]	26.8%	NA	26.8%	30.6%	34.5%	25.6%
Became parent	14.7%	7.7%	21.0%	19.6%	21.0%	12.4%
Got married	12.1%	3.7%	19.7%	13.4%	2.0%	15.1%
Had to care for family member	11.9%	9.5%	14.0%	8.5%	14.7%	10.7%
Other:						
Wanted to travel	8.1%	8.2%	8.0%	6.6%	7.3%	7.1%
Friends dropped out	8.0%	8.5%	7.5%	7.6%	6.7%	8.6%
Had a drug and/or alcohol problem	4.4%	6.1%	2.8%	1.8%	2.1%	5.9%

Source: "Percentage of NELS:88 10th- to 12th-grade dropouts who reported that various reasons for dropping out of school applied to them, by sex and race-ethnicity: 1992," National Center for Education Statistics, *Dropout Rates in the United States: 1993,* NCES 94-669, September 1994, Table 19, p. 38. Primary source: U.S. Department of Education, National Center for Education Statistics, National Education Longitudinal Study of 1988 Second Followup Survey, 1992, unpublished data. *Note:* 1. Females only.

★ 324 ★

High School

High School Dropouts: 1991

This table shows the number in thousands and the percentage of all students in the 10th, 11th, or 12th grade that dropped out of school during the one-year period from October 1990 to October 1991. This dropout rate is considerably lower than the level of 5.9% reported 10 years earlier.

[Numbers in thousands.]

Sex	Number	Percent
Total	348	4.0%
Male	167	3.8%
Female	180	4.3%

Source: Selected from U.S. Bureau of the Census, *Population Profile of the United States: 1993*, Special Studies Series P23-185, Figure 12, p. 13, "Annual High School Dropout Rate: October 1991.

★ 325 ★

High School

High School Dropouts: 1993

This table shows the event dropout rate, school retention rate, number of dropouts, and the percentage of dropouts who were male and female, in 1993. Event dropout rates measure the proportion of individuals who dropped out of school over a specified time interval, such as a 12-month period. So, in 1993, 4.5% of all high school students 15 through 24 years old dropped out of grades 10 through 12. The school retention rate of 95.5% is the proportion of 15- through 24-year-old students remaining in school from 1992 to 1993.

Characteristics	Event drop-out rate	School reten-rate	Number of dropouts	Percent of all dropouts
Total	4.5%	95.5%	381,000	100.0%
Male	4.6%	95.4%	199,000	52.2%
Female	4.3%	95.7%	182,000	47.8%

Source: Selected from "Event dropout and retention rates and number and distribution of dropouts from grades 10-12, ages 15-24, by sex, race-ethnicity, income, region, and metropolitan status: October 1993" U.S. Department of Education, National Center for Education Statistics, *Dropout Rates in the United States: 1993*, NCES 94-669, September 1994, Table 2, p. 6. Primary source: U.S. Department of Commerce, Bureau of The Census, Current Population Survey, October 1993, unpublished data. Percentages may not add to 100 due to rounding.

★ 326 ★
High School

High School Programs: 1972-1992

This table shows the percentage of high school seniors who reported being enrolled in academic/college preparatory programs, general programs, and vocational programs in 1972, 1980, and 1992. The percentage of female students enrolled in academic or college preparatory programs increased 5% over the twenty-year period, compared to a decrease of 2% for males.

	Academic/College Prep.			General			Vocational		
	1972	1980	1992	1972	1980	1992	1970	1980	1992
Males	49%	39%	47%	33%	38%	41%	18%	23%	12%
Females	44%	38%	49%	30%	36%	39%	26%	26%	12%

Source: Selected from "High School Programs Attended," *The National Education Goals Report: Volume One: The National Report*, National Education Goals Panel, 1993, Exhibit 52, p. 82. Primary Source: National Center for Education Statistics, 1993.

★ 327 ★
High School

Mathematics Advanced Placement Examinations: 1986-1993

This table shows numbers of advanced placement mathematics (calculus AB and BC) examinations taken in 1986 and 1993 and the percent change. During that period, the total number of advanced placement calculus examinations taken nearly doubled. Rates of increase were greater for females than for males, but males still took many more exams.

Sex	1986	1993	% change
Total	50,804	97,003	91%
Male	31,332	54,529	74%
Female	19,472	42,474	118%

Source: Selected from "Trends in Advanced Placement Mathematics Examinations, by Sex," *The National Education Goals Report: Volume One: The National Report*, National Education Goals Panel, 1993, Exhibit 63, p. 100. Primary Source: The College Board, various years.

★ 328 ★

High School

Science Advanced Placement Examinations: 1986-1993

This table shows numbers of advanced placement science examinations taken in 1986 and 1993 and the percent change. Males took more than 1-1/2 times as many chemistry exams and nearly 3 times as many physics exams as females did in 1993. Females narrowed the gap and surpassed males in the number of biology exams taken.

Type of exam and sex	1986	1993	% change
Biology			
Total	25,548	41,839	64%
Male	12,830	19,344	51%
Female	12,718	22,495	77%
Chemistry			
Total	14,950	27,330	83%
Male	10,367	16,684	61%
Female	4,583	10,646	132%
Physics			
Total	10,902	24,922	129%
Male	8,808	18,134	106%
Female	2,094	6,788	224%

Source: Selected from "Trends in Advanced Placement Science Examinations, by Sex," *The National Education Goals Report: Volume One: The National Report,* National Education Goals Panel, 1993, Exhibit 62, p. 99. Primary Source: The College Board, various years.

★ 329 ★

High School

Students' Aspirations

This table shows the percentage of high school seniors in 1972 and 1992 who expected to attend various types of postsecondary institutions. There was a dramatic difference between female students in 1972 and in 1992 with reference to graduate school compared to vocational training.

Highest level of schooling expected	All seniors		Males		Females	
	1972	1992	1972	1992	1972	1992
High school	18.9%	5.3%	15.5%	6.7%	22.2%	3.9%
Vocational school	18.0%	10.8%	17.4%	11.8%	18.6%	9.9%
College	50.4%	50.6%	50.8%	50.4%	50.1%	50.8%
Graduate/professional	12.6%	33.3%	16.3%	31.1%	9.1%	35.4%

Source: "Percentage of high school seniors in 1972 and 1992 who expected to attend various types of postsecondary institutions, by gender," U.S. Department of Education, National Center for Education Statistics, *Statistics in Brief,* November 1993, "High School Seniors Look to the Future, 1972 and 1992," NCES 93-473, Table 1, p. 3. Primary source: U.S. Department of Education, National Center for Education Statistics, National Longitudinal Study, 1972 (Base Year); National Education Longitudinal Study of 1988 (NELS:88) 1992 Second Followup. Percentages may not add to 100 due to rounding.

★ 330 ★

High School

Students' Occupational Expectations

This table shows the percentage of high school seniors in 1972 and 1992 who expected to be employed in various occupations. Although the majority of women in both 1972 and 1992 expected to be in the labor force, the type of work they anticipated changed. More than a quarter of female seniors in 1972 expected to be employed in clerical occupations. In 1992, only 5.7% expected to hold a clerical position. In 1972, fewer than 1% of women expected to own a business. This percentage increased to 4.8% in 1992.

Occupations	All seniors		Males		Females	
	1972	1992	1972	1992	1972	1992
Clerical	14.2%	3.5%	1.9%	1.2%	25.5%	5.7%
Craftsman/trade	7.5%	2.8%	15.1%	5.3%	0.5%	0.3%
Farming	1.6%	1.0%	2.7%	1.6%	0.6%	0.4%
Homemaker	3.1%	1.2%	0.0%	0.1%	5.9%	2.2%
Laborer	2.5%	0.8%	4.9%	1.4%	0.3%	0.1%
Manager	3.1%	6.0%	5.1%	6.6%	1.3%	5.4%
Military	2.4%	3.2%	4.1%	5.6%	0.8%	0.8%
Operative	2.3%	1.2%	3.9%	2.1%	0.8%	0.2%
Professional	45.4%	59.0%	41.8%	49.3%	48.8%	68.8%
Proprietor	1.8%	6.7%	3.2%	8.7%	0.5%	4.8%

[Continued]

★ 330 ★

Students' Occupational Expectations
[Continued]

Occupations	All seniors		Males		Females	
	1972	1992	1972	1992	1972	1992
Protective services	2.2%	4.1%	4.2%	6.9%	0.4%	1.4%
Sales	3.0%	1.9%	2.7%	2.3%	3.3%	1.5%
Service	4.2%	2.6%	1.6%	0.6%	6.7%	4.6%
Technical	6.6%	6.0%	8.8%	8.4%	4.6%	3.7%

Source: "Percentage of high school seniors in 1972 and 1992 who expected to be employed in various occupations, by gender," U.S. Department of Education, National Center for Education Statistics, *Statistics in Brief*, November 1993, "High School Seniors Look to the Future, 1972 and 1992," NCES 93-473, Table 2, p. 3. Primary source: U.S. Department of Education, National Center for Education Statistics, National Longitudinal Study, 1972 (Base Year); National Education Longitudinal Study of 1988 (NELS:88) 1992 Second Followup. Percentages may not add to 100 due to rounding.

Higher Education

★ 331 ★

Medical School Admissions: 1994

The *Detroit Free Press* reported on a historic event—for the first time in history, women outnumbered men among first-year medical students at 18 of the country's 126 medical schools. This table shows some statistics relating to women in medical school, as reported in the article. Robert Gifford, an associate dean at Yale School of Medicine, is quoted as saying: "I can't tell you how much better it is. It is a much more civil place to be."

Institution	Number/Percent
Women's share of first-year medical students, 1994:	
Yale School of Medicine	56%
Harvard University	53%
Johns Hopkins	53%
Michigan State University College of Human Medicine	52%
Wayne State University Medical School	44%
University of Michigan Medical School	40%

Source: "Top med schools undergo transformation, *Detroit Free Press*, May 31, 1995, p. 5A.

★ 332 ★

Higher Education

Time to Complete Doctorate: 1993

This table shows the median years[1] to a doctorate from a baccalaureate award, by field of study, in 1993.

Sex	All fields	Physical science[4]	Engineering	Life sciences	Social sciences	Human-ities	Educa-tion	Prof./Other
Registered time from baccalaureate[2]								
All Ph.D.s	7.1	6.5	6.3	6.8	7.5	8.3	8.2	7.5
Men	6.9	6.5	6.3	6.8	7.4	8.2	8.1	7.4
Women	7.5	6.5	6.4	6.9	7.5	8.4	8.2	7.7
Total time from baccalaureate[3]								
All Ph.D.s	10.5	8.3	8.8	9.4	10.4	11.9	19.2	13.3
Men	9.9	8.3	8.9	9.2	10.3	11.7	18.4	12.4
Women	12.2	8.1	8.0	9.7	10.7	12.0	19.7	15.2

Source: Selected from "Median Years to Doctorate from Baccalaureate Award, by Demographic Group and Broad Field, 1993," Thurgood, D.H., and J.E. Clarke, 1995, *Summary Report 1993: Doctorate Recipients from United States Universities*, Table 10, p. 28. Primary source: National Research Council, Survey of Earned Doctorates. *Notes:* 1. Medians are based on the number of individuals who provided complete information about their postbaccalaureate education. 2. Registered time gauges the amount of time actually enrolled in graduate school, including master's degrees and enrollment in nondegree programs. 3. Total time measures the number of years elapsed between receipt of the baccalaureate and the Ph.D. 4. Includes mathematics and computer sciences.

★ 333 ★

Higher Education

Vocational Education

This table presents statistics on vocational education, especially as they may be of interest to midlife and older women.

Item	Number
Women aged 45 and over in the work force, 1990:	15.9 million
Percentage of all women 45 and over in the work force, 1990:	38%
Women in Vocational Ed.	
Students at public vocational institutions who are women	56%
Students at proprietary schools who are women:	65%

[Continued]

★ 333 ★

Vocational Education
[Continued]

Item	Number
Women 25 and older enrolled in vocational school:	1.9 million
Men 25 and over enrolled in vocational school:	1.6 million
Women 45 and older enrolled in vocational school:	533,000
Percent of enrollees 25 and over	15.5%
Percent of population 25 and over	26.6%
Age between 45 and 54	60%
Age between 55 and 64	27%
Age 65 and over	13%
Enrollees in 11 responding states aged 45 or older who were in programs for single parents and displaced homemakers (1989)	20%
Percent of all working women employed in nontraditional jobs (1988)	9%
Earnings of women in non-traditional jobs compared to women in traditional occupations	20-30% higher

Source: Selected from "Vocational Education: A Resource for Midlife and Older Women," American Association of Retired Persons Fact Sheet. Primary sources: Herz, Diane. Unpublished data, Bureau of Labor Statistics, September 1991. Goodwin, Postsecondary Vocational Education. National Assessment of Vocational Education, 1989. U.S. Bureau of Labor Statistics. October 1990 school enrollment supplements to the Current Population Survey (CPS). National Displaced Homemakers Network, unpublished survey data, 1989. "Women and Nontraditional Work." National Commission on Working Women of Wider Opportunities for Women, 1989.

Sexual Harassment at School

★ 334 ★

Frequency of Harassment

This table shows how often sexual harassment was experienced by girls and young women at school. More than 4,200 girls completed and returned questionnaires for a survey sponsored by the Wellesley College Center for Research on Women and the NOW Legal Defense and Education Fund, published in *Seventeen* magazine in September 1992. Of the 2,001 respondents who said they had experienced harassment at school, 39% said it occurred on a daily basis during the last year.

[N = 1,982 girls experiencing harassment more than once.]

Frequency of harassment	Number of occurrences	Proportion of sample
Once/twice a year	215	11%
Once a month or so	422	21%
Once a week	574	29%
Every day	771	39%

Source: "Frequency of Harassment," NOW Legal Defense and Education Fund and Wellesley College Center for Research on Women, *Secrets in Public: Sexual Harassment in Our Schools: A Report on the Results of a Seventeen Magazine Survey*, March 1993, Table B, p. 5.

★ 335 ★

Sexual Harassment at School

Reaction of Victim: Tell Her Parents?

This table shows the percentage of victims of sexual harassment at school who told their parents about the incident, depending on whether they were harassed by another student or by a teacher, administrator, or staff member. More than 4,200 girls completed and returned questionnaires for a survey sponsored by the Wellesley College Center for Research on Women and the NOW Legal Defense and Education Fund, published in *Seventeen* magazine in September 1992.

Decision	Harasser	
	Student	Teacher, admin-istrator, staff
Told a parent	17%	39%
Did not tell a parent	83%	61%
N	1,862	71

Source: "Whether Girls Told Their Parents, by Who Harassed Them," NOW Legal Defense and Education Fund and Wellesley College Center for Research on Women, *Secrets in Public: Sexual Harassment in Our Schools: A Report on the Results of a Seventeen Magazine Survey,* March 1993, Table 10, p. 24.

★ 336 ★

Sexual Harassment at School

Reactions of School Administration

More than 4,200 girls completed and returned questionnaires for a survey sponsored by the Wellesley College Center for Research on Women and the NOW Legal Defense and Education Fund, published in *Seventeen* magazine in September 1992. Respondents were asked what their schools do about sexual harassment. Only 8% of schools enforced a school-wide policy, 2% held workshops or assemblies, 3% provided educational materials, and 5% provided trained peer counselors or mediators. Eighty-two percent of schools reportedly do nothing. Schools were less likely to respond when the harasser was an adult. Nothing happened to the harasser in 45% of reported incidents. Schools were less likely to do something when the harasser was a teacher. This table shows what happened to the harasser when something was actually done. Treatment was different for student and adult harassers. This table includes only incidents in which the student told a teacher or administrator about the harassment. In addition, this table includes only schools without a policy or program against harassment, because readers reported too few cases of adult harassment in schools with policies to allow a comparison.

[N = 1,999 girls reporting reactions.]

Treatment	Harasser	
	Student	Teacher, Administrator, Staff
Harasser was reprimanded, expelled, fired, or resigned	53%	24%
Nothing happened to harasser	47%	77%
N	253	17

Source: "Differential Treatment of Student and Adult Harassers" NOW Legal Defense and Education Fund and Wellesley College Center for Research on Women, *Secrets in Public: Sexual Harassment in Our Schools: A Report on the Results of a Seventeen Magazine Survey,* March 1993, Table F, p. 12.

★ 337 ★

Sexual Harassment at School

Reactions of Victim

This table shows the responses of girls who were harassed at school to a question about how they reacted when harassed. More than 4,200 girls completed and returned questionnaires for a survey sponsored by the Wellesley College Center for Research on Women and the NOW Legal Defense and Education Fund, published in *Seventeen* magazine in September 1992. Ways of dealing with harassment depended on the status of the harasser and the nature of the incident. When harassed by teachers, administrators, or school staff, girls were more likely to do nothing or to walk away. When physically threatened or assaulted, girls were more likely to use physical force.

[N = 1,999 girls reporting reactions.]

Reaction	Number	Proportion of incidents
Did nothing	262	13%
Walked away from the harasser	799	40%
Told harasser to stop	1,293	65%
Resisted with physical force	690	35%

Source: "How Girls Reacted When Harassed," NOW Legal Defense and Education Fund and Wellesley College Center for Research on Women, *Secrets in Public: Sexual Harassment in Our Schools: A Report on the Results of a Seventeen Magazine Survey,* March 1993, Table E, p. 8. Percents do not add up to 100 since respondents may have reacted in more than one way.

★ 338 ★

Sexual Harassment at School

Reporting Harassment: Does It Make a Difference?

This table shows what happened when girls reported sexual harassment at school, depending on whom they told. More than 4,200 girls completed and returned questionnaires for a survey sponsored by the Wellesley College Center for Research on Women and the NOW Legal Defense and Education Fund, published in *Seventeen* magazine in September 1992.

Outcome	Told no one	Told someone	Told Teacher/ administrator	Didn't tell teacher/admin.
School did nothing	95%	79%	45%	91%
Harasser was reprimanded, suspended, expelled, fired, or resigned	5%	21%	55%	9%
N	469	1,456	334	1,591

Source: "Does Telling Someone Make a Difference?," NOW Legal Defense and Education Fund and Wellesley College Center for Research on Women, *Secrets in Public: Sexual Harassment in Our Schools: A Report on the Results of a Seventeen Magazine Survey,* March 1993, Table 12, p. 25.

★ 339 ★

Sexual Harassment at School

Types of Harassment Experienced

This table shows the types of sexual harassment experienced by girls and young women at school. More than 4,200 girls completed and returned questionnaires for a survey sponsored by the Wellesley College Center for Research on Women and the NOW Legal Defense and Education Fund, published in *Seventeen* magazine in September 1992.

[N = 2,001 girls experiencing harassment.]

Type of harassment	Number of occurrences	Proportion of sample
Touched, pinched, or grabbed	1,651	83%
Leaned over or cornered	931	47%
Received sexual notes or pictures	559	28%
Received suggestive gestures, looks, comments, or jokes	1,786	89%

[Continued]

★ 339 ★

Types of Harassment Experienced
[Continued]

Type of harassment	Number of occurrences	Proportion of sample
Pressured to do something sexual	546	27%
Forced to do something sexual	205	10%
Other form of harassment	131	7%

Source: "Types of Harassment," NOW Legal Defense and Education Fund and Wellesley College Center for Research on Women, *Secrets in Public: Sexual Harassment in Our Schools: A Report on the Results of a Seventeen Magazine Survey,* March 1993, Table A, p. 4. Percents do not add to 100 because readers could indicate more than one type of harassment.

★ 340 ★

Sexual Harassment at School

Types of Harassment Experienced by Age

This table shows the types of sexual harassment experienced by girls and young women at school by age of the respondent. More than 4,200 girls completed and returned questionnaires for a survey sponsored by the Wellesley College Center for Research on Women and the NOW Legal Defense and Education Fund, published in *Seventeen* magazine in September 1992.

Type of harassment	Age of Harassed Student		
	9-12	13-16	17-19
Touched, pinched, or grabbed	77%	83%	81%
Leaned over or cornered	38%	48%	45%
Received sexual notes or pictures	27%	28%	29%
Received sexual gestures or comments	86%	90%	81%
Pressured to do something sexual	20%	29%	21%

[Continued]

★ 340 ★

Types of Harassment Experienced by Age

[Continued]

Type of harassment	Age of Harassed Student		
	9-12	13-16	17-19
Forced to do something sexual	9%	10%	15%
N	272	1,593	113

Source: Selected from "Age of Respondent and Types of Harassment," NOW Legal Defense and Education Fund and Wellesley College Center for Research on Women, *Secrets in Public: Sexual Harassment in Our Schools: A Report on the Results of a Seventeen Magazine Survey,* March 1993, Table 4, p. 21. Percents will not add to 100% because respondents could report more than one type of harassment in the past year.

★ 341 ★

Sexual Harassment at School

Types of Harassment Experienced by Race

This table shows the types of sexual harassment experienced by girls and young women at school by racial or ethnic background of the respondent. More than 4,200 girls completed and returned questionnaires for a survey sponsored by the Wellesley College Center for Research on Women and the NOW Legal Defense and Education Fund, published in *Seventeen* magazine in September 1992.

Type of harassment	Racial/Ethnic Background			
	White	African-American	Latina	Asian
Touched, pinched, or grabbed	82%	95%	81%	88%
Leaned over or cornered	47%	35%	46%	39%
Received sexual notes or pictures	28%	30%	25%	21%
Received sexual gestures or comments	90%	65%	85%	88%
Pressured to do something sexual	27%	30%	25%	15%

[Continued]

★ 341 ★

Types of Harassment Experienced by Race
[Continued]

Type of harassment	Racial/Ethnic Background			
	White	African-American	Latina	Asian
Forced to do something sexual	10%	11%	12%	6%
N	1,715	37	67	33

Source: Selected from "Race of Respondents and Types of Harassment," NOW Legal Defense and Education Fund and Wellesley College Center for Research on Women, *Secrets in Public: Sexual Harassment in Our Schools: A Report on the Results of a Seventeen Magazine Survey,* March 1993, Table 3, p. 21. Percents will not add to 100% because respondents could report more than one type of harassment in the past year.

★ 342 ★

Sexual Harassment at School

Types of Harassment Experienced by Type of School

This table shows the types of sexual harassment experienced by girls and young women at school by type of school. More than 4,200 girls completed and returned questionnaires for a survey sponsored by the Wellesley College Center for Research on Women and the NOW Legal Defense and Education Fund, published in *Seventeen* magazine in September 1992.

Type of harassment	Type of School			
	Public	Private	Parochial	Vocational
Touched, pinched, or grabbed	83%	76%	76%	71%
Leaned over or cornered	46%	46%	41%	57%
Received sexual notes or pictures	28%	22%	29%	21%
Received sexual gestures or comments	89%	88%	92%	86%
Pressured to do something sexual	27%	27%	25%	14%

[Continued]

★ 342 ★

Types of Harassment Experienced by Type of School
[Continued]

Type of harassment	Type of School			
	Public	Private	Parochial	Vocational
Forced to do something sexual	10%	9%	18%	14%
N	1,774	123	63	14

Source: "Type of School and Types of Harassment," NOW Legal Defense and Education Fund and Wellesley College Center for Research on Women, *Secrets in Public: Sexual Harassment in Our Schools: A Report on the Results of a Seventeen Magazine Survey,* March 1993, Table 2, p. 20. Differences between types of schools are not statistically significant. Percents will not add to 100% because respondents could report more than one type of harassment in the past year.

★ 343 ★

Sexual Harassment at School

Where Does Harassment Happen?

This table shows the responses of girls who were harassed at school to a question about where the harassment happens. More than 4,200 girls completed and returned questionnaires for a survey sponsored by the Wellesley College Center for Research on Women and the NOW Legal Defense and Education Fund, published in *Seventeen* magazine in September 1992. Sexual harassment is a public event, occurring most often in the classroom or halls and in the presence of others.

[N = 1,995 girls reporting location of harassment.]

Location	Class-room	Hall	Parking lot/field	Activity not at school	Multiple locations	Other
In public (others present)	94%	76%	69%	71%	90%	84%
In private (no one else present)	6%	24%	31%	29%	10%	16%
Number of incidents	456	352	108	55	869	155
Proportion of all incidents	23%	18%	6%	3%	44%	7%

Source: "Where Harassment Happens," NOW Legal Defense and Education Fund and Wellesley College Center for Research on Women, *Secrets in Public: Sexual Harassment in Our Schools: A Report on the Results of a Seventeen Magazine Survey,* March 1993, Table D, p. 7. Incidents occurring in "multiple locations" usually occurred in classrooms and/or halls, plus other locations.

★ 344 ★

Sexual Harassment at School

Who Are the Harassers?

This table shows the responses of girls who were harassed at school to a question about who committed the most serious offense in the past year. More than 4,200 girls completed and returned questionnaires for a survey sponsored by the Wellesley College Center for Research on Women and the NOW Legal Defense and Education Fund, published in *Seventeen* magazine in September 1992. Girls are most often harassed by other students. Most harassers are male.

[N = 2,002 harassers.]

Harasser	Number	Proportion of all harassers	Proportion who are male
Students	1,929	96%	97%
Administrators	8	0.4%	100%
Teachers or counselors	58	3%	98%
Other school staff	7	0.3%	100%

Source: "Who the Harassers Are," NOW Legal Defense and Education Fund and Wellesley College Center for Research on Women, *Secrets in Public: Sexual Harassment in Our Schools: A Report on the Results of a Seventeen Magazine Survey,* March 1993, Table C, p. 6.

Teachers

★ 345 ★

Teaching Hours Per Year in 16 Countries

This table shows the number of hours spent teaching per year by teachers in 16 countries. Many Americans believe the reason students in other countries outscore American students is because those countries have longer school years and teachers spend more time teaching. In fact, according to a survey by the Organization for Economic Cooperation and Development (OECD), American teachers spend hundreds of hours more in the classroom than teachers in other countries.

[NA Not available.]

Country	Teaching hours per year		
	Primary	Lower Sec.	Upper Sec.
Austria	780	747	664
Belgium	840	720	660
Finland	874	798	760
France	944	632	NA
Germany	790	761	673
Ireland	951	792	792
Italy	748	612	612
Netherlands	1,000	954	954
New Zealand	790	897	813
Norway	749	666	627
Portugal	882	648	612
Spain	900	900	630
Sweden	624	576	528
Turkey	900	1,080	1,080
United Kingdom	NA	669	NA
United States	1,093	1,042	1,019
Mean	858	781	745

Source: Albert Shanker, "Less Is More," *The New York Times,* May 28, 1995, p. E7. Primary Source: OECD.

★ 346 ★
Teachers

Teachers Who Leave Teaching

This table shows the reasons given for leaving teaching by selected school characteristics, 1992. These were the reasons given by those saying "very" or "fairly" likely they will leave teaching within the next five years. A representative sample of U.S. public school teachers was surveyed by Louis Harris and Associates, Inc. Of the surveyed teachers, 78% were female, 93% were white, and nearly 60% taught in elementary school.

Percent saying a major problem was:	School Level			Minority Students			Low-income Students			Most important reason
	Elementary	Junior/ Middle	High	All or Many	Some	Few or None	All or Many	Some	Few or None	
Lack of parental support for students	32%	41%	51%	53%	36%	30%	50%	36%	23%	18%
Need/want more money	30%	22%	32%	34%	24%	29%	31%	26%	38%	16%
Lack of support from school administration	26%	35%	27%	37%	24%	25%	39%	27%	10%	18%
Students' social problems make teaching too difficult	23%	18%	33%	36%	21%	18%	32%	22%	13%	7%
Not fully prepared to teach students with different ethnic/ cultural background	3%	6%	6%	8%	3%	4%	5%	6%	3%	1%
Teaching is boring/ less satisfying	4%	4%	6%	9%	3%	3%	6%	6%	1	3%

Source: Selected from "Expectations and Ideals of the American Teachers, 1992," *Statistical Bulletin*, Vol. 74, No. 3, Jul-Sep 1993, Table 3, p. 16, "Reasons for Leaving Teaching by Selected School Characteristics, United States, 1992." Primary source: The Metropolitan Life Survey of the American Teacher, 1992. *Note:* 1. Represents zero.

Test Scores

★347★

ACT Test Scores by Race/Ethnicity: 1994

This table shows average (mean) ACT scores by ethnic group for females in 1994. Composite scores for males are also given.

Area	Black	Amer Ind/ Alaska Nat	White	Mex Amer/ Chicano	Asian Am/ Pac Isldr	P Rican/ Hispanic
Total Group	N = 48,893	N = 6,084	N = 346,574	N = 16,716	N = 14,277	N = 8,980
English	16.8	17.9	21.4	17.8	20.8	18.8
Usage/Mech	8.1	8.8	10.9	8.7	10.6	9.3
Rhet Skills	8.6	9.1	11.0	9.1	10.7	9.6
Mathematics	16.7	17.6	20.0	17.9	22.5	18.6
Pre/Elem-Alg	8.2	8.8	10.4	9.0	11.7	9.4
Alg/Crd-Geom	8.4	8.7	10.0	8.9	11.4	9.3
Plane Geom/Trig	8.1	8.8	10.2	9.0	11.6	9.4
Reading	17.4	19.0	22.2	18.6	21.7	19.7
Soc Stu/Sci	8.3	9.2	10.8	8.8	10.6	9.4
Arts/Literature	9.0	10.0	11.9	9.9	11.5	10.5
Sci Reasoning	17.3	18.7	21.0	18.4	21.0	19.0
Composite	17.2	18.4	21.3	18.3	21.6	19.1
Composite (Males)	16.8	18.6	21.6	18.7	21.8	19.5

Source: Selected from "Average ACT Scores by Academic Preparation for Different Ethnic Groups," *ACT High School Profile Report HS Graduating Class 1994: National Report for Females* and *National Report for Males*, p 4.

ACT Test Scores: 1994

This table shows mean ACT scores for females in 1994. Mean scores for males are also given.

Area	Females	Males
English	20.7	19.8
Mathematics	19.6	20.8
Reading	21.4	21.1
Sci Reasoning	20.4	21.6
Composite	20.7	20.9

Source: Selected from "Mean ACT Scores and Standard Deviations for Males and Females," *ACT High School Profile Report HS Graduating Class 1994: National Report for Females* and *National Report for Males*, p. 8.

LSAT Scores

This table shows mean Law School Admission Test (LSAT) scores for men and women in 1991.

Sex	LSAT Mean
Male	32.87
Female	31.95

Source: Selected from "Mean LSAT Scores by Selected Subgroup," *FairTest Examiner*, Vol. 8, No. 4, Fall 1994, p. 12. Primary source: Most recent data released by LSAS. Scores based on 10-48 scale.

★ 350 ★

Test Scores

Mathematics Proficiency: 1992

This table shows the percentage of 12th graders who scored proficient and above on the National Assessment of Educational Progress mathematics assessment in 1990 and 1992.

Sex	Proficient and above	
	1990	1992
Male	16%	18%
Female	10%	14%

Source: Selected from "Mathematics Achievement—Grade 12," *The National Education Goals Report: Volume One: The National Report,* National Education Goals Panel, 1993, Exhibit 33, p. 60. Primary Source: National Center for Education Statistics, 1993.

★ 351 ★

Test Scores

National Merit Scholarship Competition: 1988-1993

In 1993, FairTest, The National Center for Fair & Open Testing filed a complaint with the U.S. Department of Education's Office for Civil Rights, charging the Educational Testing Service (ETS) and the College Entrance Examination Board (College Board) with violating equal education laws by designing, administering, and co-sponsoring a biased testing process that is used by the National Merit Scholarship Corporation to determine eligibility for more than $35 million in college tuition aid each year. It is claimed that the test denies girls an equal opportunity to compete for and receive the awards. Annually, more than three-fifths of the scholarships go to boys. FairTest's Office for Civil Rights prepared the chart shown here, which shows how reliance on PSAT/NMSQT scores as the sole factor in selecting National Merit Semifinalists introduces gender discrimination into the process.

[NA Not available.]

H.S. Grad. Class	Test-Takers[1]		Semifinalists[2]		Winners[3]	
	Girls	Boys	Girls	Boys	Girls	Boys
1988	54.7%	45.3%	36.0%	60.1%	38.2%	61.8%
1989	54.8%	45.2%	31.4%	62.9%	35.8%	64.2%
1990	54.8%	45.2%	35.8%	57.8%	40.4%	59.6%
1991	54.9%	45.1%	37.3%	59.2%	39.2%	60.8%
1992	55.1%	44.9%	37.3%	59.0%	40.3%	59.7%

[Continued]

★ 351 ★

National Merit Scholarship Competition: 1988-1993
[Continued]

H.S. Grad. Class	Test-Takers[1]		Semifinalists[2]		Winners[3]	
	Girls	Boys	Girls	Boys	Girls	Boys
1993	55.3%	44.7%	35.3%	60.8%	35.3%	60.8%[4]
1994	55.8%	44.2%	38.6%	57.1%	NA	NA

Source: "Flawed Selection Test Again Cheats Girls Out of National Merit Scholarships," *FairTest Examiner,* Vol 8, No. 2, Spring 1994, pp. 1, 4, table entitled "National Merit Scholarship Competition Gender Summary." Gender was determined by name. In cases of ambiguity, the name was classified as unknown. *Notes:* 1. From PSAT/NMSQT Summary Reports. 2. From FairTest gender identification of Semifinalists' names. Percentages do not add up to 100 because some students' genders could not be determined from their names. 3. From National Merit Scholarship Corporation Annual Reports. 4. "1993 National Merit Semifinalists," *FairTest Examiner,* Vol. 7, No. 4, Winter 1993-94, p. 1+.

★ 352 ★
Test Scores

Reading Proficiency: 1992

This table shows average reading proficiency and achievement levels by gender, grades 4, 8, and 12, on the National Assessment of Educational Progress (NAEP), 1992 Reading Assessment. Females had higher average reading proficiency than males at all three grades.

	Percentage of students	Average proficiency	Percentage of students at or above			Below Basic
			Advanced	Proficient	Basic	
Grade 4						
Male	51%(0.6)	214(1.2)	4%(0.6)	22%(1.2)	54%(1.7)	46%(1.7)
Female	49%(0.6)	222(1.0)	6%(0.7)	28%(1.5)	64%(1.3)	36%(1.3)
Grade 8						
Male	51%(0.7)	254(1.1)	1%(0.3)	22%(1.2)	63%(1.2)	37%(1.2)
Female	49%(0.7)	267(1.0)	3%(0.5)	33%(1.4)	75%(1.1)	25%(1.1)
Grade 12						
Male	49%(0.6)	286(0.7)	2%(0.3)	31%(1.1)	70%(1.1)	30%(1.1)
Female	51%(0.6)	296(0.7)	4%(0.4)	42%(1.2)	80%(0.9)	20%(0.9)

Source: "Average Reading Proficiency and Achievement Levels by Gender, Grades 4, 8, and 12, 1992 Reading Assessment," National Center for Education Statistics, *NAEP 1992 Reading Report Card for the Nation and the States,* September 1993, table 3.4, p. 105. Primary source: National Assessment of Educational Progress (NAEP), 1992 Reading Assessment. The standard errors of estimated percentages and proficiences appear in parentheses. It can be said with 95 percent certainty for each population of interest, the value for the whole population is within plus or minus two standard errors of the estimate for the sample. In comparing two estimates, one must use the standard error of the difference.

★ 353 ★
Test Scores

SAT Score Averages: 1994

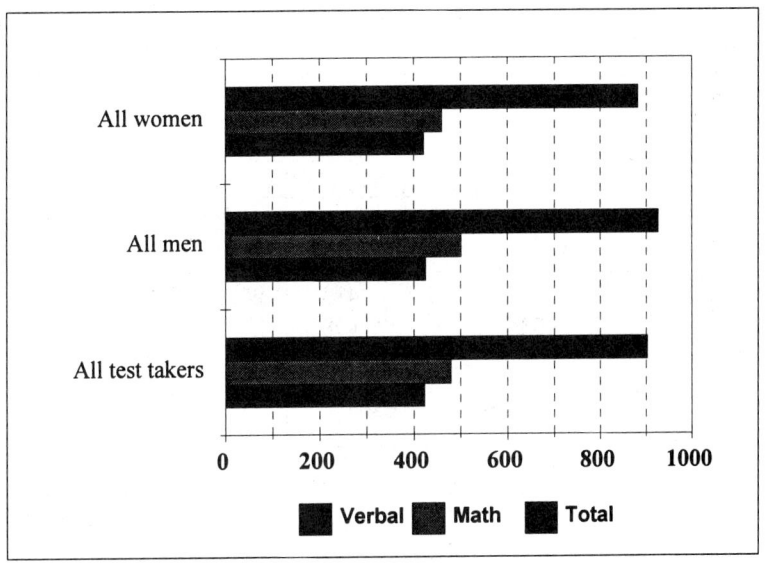

This table shows average verbal, math, and total SAT scores in 1994. According to the National Center for Fair & Open Testing, "Despite an eight-point narrowing of the gender gap, the SAT continues to discriminate against young women and members of most minority groups. Among this year's graduates, college-bound males still scored 45 points higher on the SAT's 400-1600 point scale than college-bound females, even though girls earn higher grades than boys in both high school and college when matched for identical courses."

Sex	Verbal	Math	Total
All test takers	423	479	902
All men	425	501	926
All women	421	460	881

Source: Selected from "1994 SAT Score Averages," *FairTest Examiner*, Vol. 8, No. 4, Fall 1994, p. 10. Primary source: *College Bound Seniors 1994*, College Board.

★ 354 ★

Test Scores

SAT Scores: 1987 and 1994

This table shows SAT scores in 1994 by race/ethnicity. Donald A. Stewart, president of the College Board, which oversees the tests, said upon releasing the scores: "Since 1987, women have narrowed the male-female gaps in S.A.T. scores by six points for math and verbal, even though they are the majority of S.A.T. takers and come from families with less income and education than men—factors which tend to depress scores." Black women improved their test scores more than any other group.

Race/ Ethnicity	1987				1994			
	Verbal		Mathematics		Verbal		Mathematics	
	Men	Women	Men	Women	Men	Women	Men	Women
American Indian	396	391	452	413	397	395	459	425
Asian American	408	403	543	498	417	414	557	514
Black	354	349	391	367	348	354	399	381
Mexican American	387	373	449	402	375	368	448	410
Puerto Rican	366	355	423	380	371	365	432	395
Other Hispanic	393	382	459	408	389	379	462	414
White	452	442	514	466	445	441	519	475
Other	415	396	485	428	426	424	505	459
National averages	435	425	500	453	425	421	501	460

Source: "Gender Gap Continues to Close in S.A.T.'s," *The New York Times*, August 25, 1994, p. A8 Y. Primary Source: College Board.

★ 355 ★

Test Scores

SAT Trends: 1988-1994

This table shows trends on exams in the SAT series. Each figure represents the difference between the average score of males and females on the two parts of the PSAT and SAT. Males have scored higher on both parts of each test since 1972. The National Center for Fair & Open Testing alleges discrimination against females on these tests. A new series of SAT exams was administered for the first time in the 1993-1994 school year. On the October 1993 PSAT/NMSQT, the first exam in the revised series, the difference between boys and girls declined by only one-tenth of a point for Math and one-half of a point for Verbal when compared with the 1992 data. A study reported in the journal *Education*[3] concluded that the timed nature of the test was a major contributor to the gender gap. Researchers administered sample SAT Math exams to high school algebra and pre-calculus students in both timed and untimed settings. When test-takers were allowed to use as much time as they needed, girls' scores increased greatly, but boys' did not change. Boys still received higher scores, but the gender gap narrowed significantly.

[NA Not available.]

H.S. Grad Class	PSAT/NMSQT			SAT		
	Math	Verbal	Total	Math	Verbal	Total
1995[1]	3.8	0.2	4.0	NA	NA	NA
1994	3.9	0.7	4.6	NA	NA	NA
1993	3.5	1.5	5.0	45	8	53
1992	4.2	1.2	5.4	43	9	52
1991	3.9	1.3	5.2	44	8	52
1990	3.7	0.7	4.4	44	10	54
1989	4.1	1.3	5.4	46	13	59
1988	4.1	1.3	5.4	43	13	56

Source: "'New' SAT Still Shows Gender Bias," *FairTest Examiner*, Vol. 8, No. 3, Summer 1994, p. 1,4, Table entitled "The SAT Gender Gap." *Notes:* 1. First administration of "new" series of exams. 2. See preceding table for scores. 3. L. Diane Miller, Charles E. Mitchell, and Marilyn Van Ausdall, "Evaluating Achievement in Mathematics: Exploring the Gender Biases of Timed Testing," *Education*, Vol. 114, No. 3, Spring 1994.

★ 356 ★

Test Scores

Science Proficiency: 1970-1990

This table shows average science proficiency (scale score, ranging from 0 to 500) by age and sex, 1970-1990. In 1990, similar scores were achieved by 9-year-old boys and girls, but 17-year-old males had significantly higher average proficiency scores than did 17-year-old females.

Year	Age 9		Age 13		Age 17	
	Male	Female	Male	Female	Male	Female
1970	228	223	257	253	314[1]	297[1]
1973	223[1]	218[1]	252[1]	247[2]	304[1,2]	288[2]
1977	222[1,2]	218[1,2]	251[1,2]	244[1,2]	297[2]	282[2]
1982	221[1]	221[1]	256	245[1,2]	292[2]	275[1,2]
1986	227	221[1]	256	247[2]	295[2]	282[2]
1990	230	227	259	252	296[2]	285[2]

Source: "Average science proficiency (scale score), by age and sex: 1970-1990," *The Condition of Education 1993* (Washington, D.C., National Center for Education Statistics, 1993), p. 46. Primary Source: National Assessment of Educational Progress, *Trends in Academic Progress: Achievement of American Students in Science, 1969-70 to 1990, Mathematics, 1973 to 1990, Reading, 1971 to 1990, Writing, 1984 to 1990,* 1991. *Notes:* 1. Statistically significant difference from 1990. 2. Statistically significant difference from 1970 for all except Hispanics. Statistically significant difference from 1977 for Hispanics.

Chapter 6
HEALTH AND MEDICAL CARE

Abortions

★ 357 ★

Abortions in Romania

This table presents some statistics on abortions in Romania. Under the dictatorship of Nicolae Ceausescu, contraception was banned and abortions were allowed only for mothers of more than 5 children. The intention was to push the population from 23 million to 30 million by the end of this century. Despite these efforts, abortion and abortion-related mortality rates rose.

Item	Number/Percent
Estimated number of clandestine abortions performed annually in Romania:	1.2 million
Number of abortions performed annually in the United States:	1.6 million
Number of times more people in the U.S. than in Romania:	11
Number of failed abortions at Bucharest Municipal Hospital in 1989:	3,000
Number of women in Bucharest who die each year due to "botched" abortions:	> 1,000

Source: Selected from Jodi Jacobson, "The Global Politics of Abortion," *Utne Reader*, March/ April 1991, pp. 55-59.

AIDS

★ 358 ★

AIDS Attributed to IV Drug Use: 1988

This table shows the percentage of AIDS cases attributed by the Centers for Disease Control to intravenous drug use and the AIDS annual incidence rates in major U.S. metropolitan areas.

City and State	Due to IV drug use[1]	Total annual incid. rates[2]
Birmingham, AL		
Males	25%	
Females	...	8.6
Chicago, IL		
Males	13%	
Females	36%	14.3
Dallas, TX		
Males	15%	
Females	...	21.0
Detroit, MI		
Males	30%	
Females	61%	7.3
Kansas City, MO		
Males	11%	
Females	...	15.8
Los Angeles, CA		
Males	12%	
Females	22%	22.7
New Orleans, LA		
Males	15%	
Females	26%	17.4
New York, NY		
Males	37%	
Females	62%	70.5
Philadelphia, PA		
Males	19%	
Females	38%	14.2
Phoenix, AZ		
Males	19%	

[Continued]

★ 358 ★

AIDS Attributed to IV Drug Use: 1988
[Continued]

City and State	Due to IV drug use[1]	Total annual incid. rates[2]
Females	23%	8.9
Portland, OR		
Males	13%	
Females	...	11.3
St. Louis, MO		
Males	9%	
Females	...	7.1
San Antonio, TX		
Males	17%	
Females	...	19.0
San Diego, CA		
Males	13%	
Females	32%	19.5

Source: Selected from "Injection in Arestees and CDC Estimates of AIDS," *DUF: 1988 Drug Use Forecasting Annual Report*, National Institute of Justice, March 1990, p. 9. ... represents less than 20 cases. No data was available for females in Cleveland, Fort Lauderdale, Houston, Indianapolis, Miami, and Omaha. *Notes:* 1. For males, includes IV drug users and homosexual IV drug users. 2. AIDS annual incidence rates per 100,000 population, by metropolitan areas with 500,000 or more population, reported February 1988 through January 1989.

Alcohol and Drugs

★ 359 ★

Alcohol Problems and a History of Abuse

Eighty-eight consecutive new women patients were surveyed in an adult psychiatric inpatient unit that did not have a program for the treatment of alcoholics. The women who reported a history of physical and/or sexual abuse scored higher on the Michigan Alcoholism Screening Test (MAST) than did those women with no such history. This table shows some of the results of the survey.

Item	Number/Percent
Number of patients who were diagnosed with alcohol abuse or dependence by a psychiatrist	20
Number of patients who reported a history of alcohol problems measured by scores of 7 or more on the MAST	33
Percent	38%
Percent in a general population of adults	7%
MAST scores of 7 or more by abuse history:	
Both physical and sexual abuse	61%
Physical abuse only	73%
Sexual abuse only	33%
No reported abuse history	21%

Source: Selected from Chester Swett, M.D., and Margaret Halpert, B.A., "High Rates of Alcohol Problems and History of Physical and Sexual Abuse Among Women Inpatients," *American Journal of Drug and Alcohol Abuse* 202(2), pp. 263-272, 1994. Address correspondence to Chester Swett, M.D., Dartmouth Medical School, New Hampshire Hospital, 105 Pleasant Street, Concord, NH 03301.

★ 360 ★

Alcohol and Drugs

Alcohol Use and Abuse

A report prepared in 1991 for the U.S. Congress discussed alcohol use and abuse by women. This table summarizes some of the points made in the report.

Item	Number/Percent
Estimated number of alcohol-abusing and dependent individuals nationwide	15.1 million
Women	4.6 million
Percentage of research subjects on alcoholism between 1970 and 1984 who were women:	8%
Recent National Institute on Alcohol Abuse and Alcoholism research grants including women as research subjects (N=217)	85%
Only women as subjects	15.7%
Between 50 and 99% women	30.4%
From 1 to 49% women	21.2%
No women	15.2%
Problem drinkers seeking assistance in traditional drinking centers nationwide:	
Women	25.4%
Men	75%
Ratio of female to male alcoholics	30:70
Results from the 1988 National Household Survey on Drug Abuse[1,2]	
Current drinkers:	
Males	60.6%
Females	46.7%
Percentage of women who were multi-drug addicts who grew up in families where one or two parents were addicted to alcohol:[3]	87%
Fetal Alcohol Syndrome (FAS)	
Estimates of prevalence per 1,000 live births:	
European and U.S. studies	1-3
Australian, European, and U.S. studies	1.9

[Continued]

★ 360 ★

Alcohol Use and Abuse
[Continued]

Item	Number/Percent
Percentage of offspring of alcohol-abusing women who showed adverse effects that could be attributed to prenatal alcohol exposure:[4]	50%
Average IQ of FAS patients[5]	66
Native American Women and FAS	
Estimate of the number of the 10 leading causes of death among the Native American population that are directly or indirectly related to the effects of alcohol abuse[6]	50%
Number of Native American women who die from alcohol-related cirrhosis of the liver for every two Native American men	1
Rank of FAS among Native American birth defects during the 1980s	3
Overall rate of Native American mothers who produced FAS children per 1,000 women of childbearing age	6.1
Percentage of Native American mothers who had produced one FAS affected child who also produced others	25%

Source: Selected from Edith Fairman Cooper, "Alcohol Use and Abuse by Women," *CRS Report for Congress*, 91-680 SPF, September 13, 1991. *Notes:* 1. Completed by 8,814 individuals. 2. U.S. Dept. of Health and Human Services. Public Health Service. Alcohol, Drug Abuse, and Mental Health Admin. National Institute on Drug Abuse. National Household Survey on Drug Abuse. Main Findings 1988. Washington, U.S. Govt. Print. Off., 1990. DHHS Publication No. (ADM) 90-1682. 135 p. With appendices. 3. Worth, Dooley. American Women and Polydrug Abuse. In Alcohol and Drugs are Women's Issues, v. 1., p. 7. 4. U.S. Dept. of Health and Human Services, Seventh Special Report to the U.S. Congress on Alcohol and Health, p. 140. 5. Weeks, Maureen (for Sen. John Binkley). Economic Impact of Fetal Alcohol Syndrome in Alaska. Senate Advisory Council. Alaska State Legislature. Juneau, Alaska, Feb. 1989. p. 2. 6. National Clearinghouse for Alcohol and Drug Information. Alcohol Topics: Research Review—Alcohol and Native Americans. Sept. 1985. p. RPO 307.

★ 361 ★

Alcohol and Drugs

Alcohol and Self-Destructive Behavior

Mary-Ellen Fortini and Carol Lederhaus Popkin at North Carolina's Department of Human Resources reviewed some of the available literature on alcohol consumption and its relationship to injuries in women. This table presents statistics from some of the studies they cite.

Item	Number/Percent
Women Drivers	
Women's percentage of all drivers	48.6%
Women's percentage of travel time	35.2%
Women's involvement in police-	
reported crashes	37.9%
Fatal crashes[1]	23.9%
Drinking and Driving	
Alcohol-related crashes as	
percentage of all crashes	50-55%
Percentage of fatally injured white	
females aged 21-24 with Blood Alcohol	
Counts (BAC) greater than or equal to 0.10,	
1974-1988	35%
non-white females aged 21-24	14%
Percentage of fatally injured white	
females aged 55 and over with BAC greater	
than or equal to 0.10, 1974-188	8%
non-white females aged 55 and over	36%
BAC levels of fatally injured women	
drivers, 1974-1988:	
White women, aged 21-24	0.085
Non-white women, aged 21-24	0.030
White women, aged 55 and over	0.015
Non-white women, aged 55 and over	0.065
Decline in alcohol-related fatal	
crash involvement rates per 100,000	
licensed drivers, 1982-1992:	
Women	16%
Men	21%
Increase or decrease in involvement rates	
for alcohol-related crashes among persons	
aged 21-24 from mid-1970s to mid-1980s	
in North Carolina:[2]	
Females	+93%

[Continued]

★ 361 ★

Alcohol and Self-Destructive Behavior
[Continued]

Item	Number/Percent
Males	-7%
Percentage of persons involved in motor vehicle crashes with positive BACs:	
Women	38%
Men	49%
Alcohol-Related Injuries/Fatalities	
In the 66% of unintentional fatal injuries that were tested for blood alcohol in Oklahoma, percentage that were found to be alcohol-related:[3]	49%
In the 90% of homicide victims in Oklahoma who were tested for blood alcohol, percentage who were alcohol positive:	52%
Of the 73% of suicide victims in Oklahoma who were tested for blood alcohol, percentage who were alcohol-related:	40%
Percentage of all victims of these alcohol-related injuries/fatalities with blood alcohol levels over 0.10%:	
Females	60%
Males	70%
In a study of 1,467 women and 3,779 men admitted to a Level I trauma center for trauma-related injuries, percentage with positive BACs:[4]	
Women	22.9%
Men	40.3%

Source: Selected from Mary-Ellen Fortin and Carol Lederhaus Popkin, "Alcohol-Related Injuries Among Women," *Drug and Alcohol Abuse Reviews, Vol. 7: Alcohol, Cocaine, and Accidents,* R.R. Watson (ed.), 1995, Humana Press Inc., Totawa, NJ. *Notes:* 1. E.C. Cerrelli (1992) *Crash Data and Rates for Age-Sex Groups of Drivers, 1990.* National Highway Traffic Safety Administration Department of Transportation Research Note, Washington DC. 2. C.L. Popkin (1991) Drinking and driving by young females. *Accident anal. Prev.* 23, 37-44. 3. R.A. Goodman, G.R. Istre, F.B. Jordan et al., Alcohol and fatal injuries in Oklahoma. *J Stud. Alcohol* 52, 156-161. 4. C.A. Soderstrom and P. Dischinger (1993) (personal communication) Preliminary findings of patients admitted to R. Adams Cowley Shock Trauma Center, Baltimore, MD.

★ 362 ★

Alcohol and Drugs

Alcohol and Tranquilizers

Some national statistics on women and substance use.

1. It is estimated that of the 15.1 million people who abuse alcohol or are dependent on alcohol, **4.6 million** are women.

2. African American women are more likely to have abstained from alcohol (**66.9%**) during the month preceding their interview than were white women (**52.6%**).

3. Women account for nearly **one-half** of deaths from cirrhosis among the American Indian population, although their consumption of alcohol is relatively low.

4. In 1989, emergency room visits as a result of Valium abuse were **4.1%** for women compared to 2.5 percent for men.

5. More than **4.8 million (8%)** of the **60.1 million women** of childbearing age (15-44 years) have used an illicit drug in the past month. A little more than **500,000 (0.9%)** used cocaine and **3.9 million (6.5%)** used marijuana in the past month.

6. Estimates indicate that the number of American women who drink has increased significantly over the last 40 years. As many as **16%** of young, employed women may consume from three to five drinks per day.

7. More than **80%** of cases of AIDS in women are associated with IV drug use.

Source: Selected from "A Snapshot of Women and Substance Use," from *Impact: A Newsletter of Chemical Health in Minnesota*, Vol. 10, No. 3, Spring 1992, p. 2. Primary source: Office for Substance Abuse Prevention, *Prevention Resource Guide: Women*, 1992.

★ 363 ★

Alcohol and Drugs

Drinking During Pregnancy: 1979-1993

This table gives statistics concerning babies born with health problems because their mothers drank alcohol during pregnancy. Federal government researchers who released the report did not know whether the reported increase in the percentage of babies born with health problems was a result of improved diagnosis by doctors or an increase in the number of pregnant women who drank.

Item	Number/percent
Rate per 10,000 births of babies born with health problems because of maternal drinking during pregnancy:	
1979	1
1993	6.7
Number of births, 1979-1993	9.4 million
Number of cases of infant health problems due to maternal drinking, 1979-1993	2,032

Source: "Use of Alcohol Linked to Rise in Fetal Illness," *The New York Times*, April 7, 1995, p. A13 Y. Primary source: Centers for Disease Control and Prevention.

★ 364 ★

Alcohol and Drugs

Drinking Problems

This table gives statistics on problems due to drinking experienced by college students. The authors cite numerous studies. Among the findings: The drinks of choice among females are spirits (43%), beer (41%), and wine (6%). A higher percentage of college men are likely to drink, to drink more often, to consume more, and to have more drinking problems than women.

[Men, N=1,319. Women, N=2,104.]

Problem	Men	Women
Hangover	90.4%	84.5%
Vomited	85.6%	77.6%
Drove car after drinking	84.2%	67.8%
Drove car after knowing had too much to drink	70.8%	54.2%
Drove car while drinking	71.4%	48.5%
Came to class after drinking	29.8%	16.8%
Cut class because of drinking	26.3%	16.4%
Missed class because of drinking	44.6%	35.9%
Stopped for DWI	4.8%	1.6%
Criticized for drinking too much	28.5%	18.1%

[Continued]

★ 364 ★

Drinking Problems
[Continued]

Problem	Men	Women
Had trouble with the law	19.5%	5.9%
Lost job	0.6%	0.5%[1]
Received lower grade	16.8%	9.4%
Problems with school adminis-tration	7.6%	3.6%
Gotten into fight	37.4%	17.3%
Thought have drinking problem	23.4%	13.7%
Damaged property	40.4%	10.7%
Heavy drinking[2]	37.8%	17.4%

Source: Selected from Ruth C. Engs and David J. Hanson, "Gender Differences in Drinking Patterns and Problems Among College Students: A Review of the Literature," *Journal of Alcohol and Drug Education*, Vol. 35(2), Winter 1990, pp. 36-47; p. 42, Table 1, entitled "Problems Due to Drinking Ever Experienced Among Drinkers by Sex, in Percent." Primary source: Parts of the article appeared in the authors' chapter "College Students' Drinking Patterns and problems" in *Alcohol Policies and Practices on College and University Campuses* (NASPA) publications. *Notes:* 1. Difference not statistically significant. All other differences significant at .001 level of confidence. 2. Heavy drinking defined as consuming six or more drinks at one sitting at least once a week.

★ 365 ★

Alcohol and Drugs

Drinking to Get Drunk

The New York Times reports on a Columbia University study on drinking by college students. The study showed that the number of college women who drank abusively more than tripled between 1979 and 1993. This table shows some of the results of the study.

Item	Number/Percent
Percent of all students who reported engaging in binge drinking (consuming 5 or more drinks at a time:	
College students	42%
Non-students	33%
Percent of college women who reported drinking to get drunk:	
1979	10%
1993	35%
Percentage of reported campus rapes in which alcohol had been used by either the assailant, the victim, or both	90%

[Continued]

★ 365 ★

Drinking to Get Drunk
[Continued]

Item	Number/Percent
Percentage of college women in whom a sexually transmitted disease like herpes or AIDS was diagnosed who were drunk at the time of incurring the infection	60%

Source: William Celis 3d, "More College Women Drinking to Get Drunk," *The New York Times*, June 8, 1994, p. B8 Y. Primary sources: Center on Addiction and Substance Abuse at Columbia University; Core Alcohol and Drug Survey.

★ 366 ★

Alcohol and Drugs

Drug Facts

This table gives statistics on women and drug abuse, based on 1992 data.

Item	Number/Percent
Number of women who have used drugs at least once in lifetime	8.8 million
Women of childbearing age, approx.	4.4 million
Number of women who had used an illicit drug at least once in the past month	4.3 million
Number of women who have used cocaine at least once	600,000
Number of women who had used cocaine in the past month	420,000
Number of women who had used inhalants in the past month	350,000
Number of women who have used marijuana at least once	5.6 million
Number of women who had used marijuana at least once in the past month	> 3 million
Number of women who have taken prescription drugs non-medically during the last year	3.7 million
During the past month	1.3 million

[Continued]

★ 366 ★

Drug Facts
[Continued]

Item	Number/Percent
Number of AIDS cases among women that are drug-related	28,000
Percent	70%
Number of women who need treatment for drug abuse	> 4 million
Percent of female drug users who had been sexually abused by the age of 16	70%

Source: Selected from "Women & Drug Abuse: You and Your Community Can Help," National Institute on Drug Abuse, p. 7, and *NIDA Capsules.*

★ 367 ★

Alcohol and Drugs

Relationship Between Eating Disorders and Alcoholism

A study was done to examine the co-prevalence and characteristics of the eating disorders anorexia nervosa (AN) and bulimia nervosa (BN) among two populations of adult women: those seeking treatment for alcoholism and those referred to a specialized eating disorders program. This table shows some of the results of the study and other studies reported on in the article.

Item	Number/Percent
Number of females with alcohol problems who met psychometric cut-off scores for eating disorder (N=73)	22
Percent	30.1%
Number of females with eating disorders who gave psychometric evidence of alcohol dependence (N=96)	25
Percent	26.9%
Percentage of 105 AN patients reported on in 1979 who showed a prevalence rate for alcohol abuse and dependence[1]	6.7%
Percentage of BN women who revealed alcohol abuse prevalence in controlled studies[2]	48.6%
Alcohol dependence	22.9%
Percentage of female referrals to an alcoholism treatment unit who gave a history of BN (20 consecutive referrals)[3]	25%
AN	10%

[Continued]

★ 367 ★

Relationship Between Eating Disorders and Alcoholism
[Continued]

Item	Number/Percent
In a survey of 27 female alcoholics, percentage who reported binge eating[4]	40%
In a study of 31 women in treatment for alcoholism using self-report questionnaires, percentage who revealed a "probable" diagnosis of AN	7%
BN	7%
Variants of BN[5]	14%

Source: Selected from David S. Goldbloom, Claudio A. Naranjo, Karen E. Bremner et al., "Eating disorders and alcohol abuse in women," *British Journal of Addiction* (1992) 87, pp. 913-920. Address correspondence to David S. Goldbloom, Eaton 8N-219, The Toronto Hospital, 200 Elizabeth Street, Toronto, Ontario, Canada M5G 2C4. *Notes:* 1. Eckert, E.D., Goldberg, S.C., Halmi, K.A., et al. (1979) Alcoholism in anorexia nervosa, in Pickens, R.W. and Heston, L.L., (Eds) *Psychiatric Factors in Drug Abuse*, p. 267 (New York, Grune and Stratton). 2. Bulik, C.M. (1987) Drug and alcohol abuse by bulimic women and their families, *American Journal of Psychiatry*, 144, pp. 1604-1606. 3. Beary, M.D., Lacey, J.H., and Merry, J. (1986) Alcoholism and eating disorders in women of fertile age, *British Journal of Addiction*, 81, pp. 685-689. 4. Lacey, J.H., and Moureli, E. (1986) Bulimic alcoholics: Some features of a clinical subgroup, *British Journal of Addiction*, 81, pp. 389-393. 5. Peveler, R., and Fairburn, C. (1990) Eating disorders in women who abuse alcohol, *British Journal of Addiction*, 85, pp. 1633-1638.

Cancer

★ 368 ★

Breast Cancer by Race-I

A study of 963 newly diagnosed invasive breast cancer tumors was done at Louisiana State Medical Center. Tumors from black women were more likely to have several microscopic features in their tissues associated with a poor diagnosis. The black/white difference in survival for women with breast cancer has been observed in the United States since the 1950s. The 5-year relative survival rates for all stages combined were 62% in blacks and 79% in whites for the period 1983-1988. Studies have suggested that socio-economic status is the main determinant of survival differences. Other studies suggest that black patients are less likely to have aggressive therapies and cancer-directed treatments. Another explanation is limited access to health care among black women. This table shows some characteristics of the invasive breast cancer patients in the study.

Variables	Black (n = 506)		White (n = 457)	
	Number	Percent[1]	Number	Percent
Age at diagnosis				
20-49 years	203	40.1%	177	38.7%
50-64 years	174	34.4%	166	36.3%
65-79 years	129	25.5%	114	25.0%

[Continued]

★ 368 ★

Breast Cancer by Race-I
[Continued]

Variables	Black (n = 506)		White (n = 457)	
	Number	Percent[1]	Number	Percent
Clinical factors				
Stage I	100	19.8%	165	36.1%
Stage II (no)	113	22.3%	72	15.8%
Stage II (n1)	143	28.3%	134	29.3%
Stage III	111	21.9%	61	13.4%
Stage IV	39	7.7%	25	5.5%
Primary Tumor (T)				
T-1	147	29.1%	217	47.7%
T-2	233	46.1%	168	36.9%
T-3	60	11.9%	37	8.1%
T-4	65	12.9%	33	7.3%
Unknown	2	(0.0)[2]	1	(0.0)
No. of positive nodes				
0	230	50.9%	253	58.6%
1-3	132	29.2%	113	26.2%
4-9	43	9.5%	34	7.9%
>10	47	10.4%	32	7.4%
Unknown	25	(5.5)	54	(10.7)
Metastases				
No	467	92.3%	432	94.5%
Yes	39	7.7%	25	5.5%
Socio-demographic factors				
Marital Status				
Married	211	42.1%	291	64.0%
Widow	118	23.6%	86	18.9%
Separated/ divorced	127	25.4%	52	11.4%
Never married	45	9.0%	26	5.7%
Unknown	5	(1.0)	2	(0.4)
Education				
<12 years	172	41.4%	54	13.9%
12 years	118	28.4%	129	33.1%
>12 years	126	30.3%	207	53.1%
Occupation				
Housewives	59	14.4%	146	37.4%
Manager/prof.	62	15.1%	106	27.2%
Technical sales/ administration	84	20.5%	99	25.4%

[Continued]

★ 368 ★

Breast Cancer by Race-I
[Continued]

Variables	Black (n = 506)		White (n = 457)	
	Number	Percent[1]	Number	Percent
Service	154	37.6%	24	6.2%
Others	51	12.4%	15	3.9%
Lifestyle				
Alcohol consumption				
Nondrinker	200	49.9%	105	27.6%
<0.5 drinks/day	99	24.7%	149	39.2%
0.5-1.9 drinks/day	65	16.2%	78	20.5%
2 or more drinks/day	37	9.2%	48	12.6%
Smoking				
Never	212	51.2%	200	51.2%
Ex-smoker	121	29.2%	137	35.0%
Current smoker	81	19.6%	54	13.8%
Reproductive experience				
Parity				
0	94	20.8%	88	20.9%
1-2	183	40.4%	190	45.1%
3-4	97	21.4%	121	28.7%
5 or more	79	17.4%	22	5.2%
Age at first pregnancy				
Never pregnant	110	23.6%	97	22.5%
Under 20	176	37.8%	63	14.6%
20 or older	180	38.6%	271	62.9%
Access to health care				
Usual source				
None	82	19.8%	50	17.1%
Public clinic	42	10.1%	2	2.1%
Private	291	70.1%	339	80.8%
Health insurance				
None	58	13.9%	8	2.1%
Public (Medicare and Medicaid)	113	27.1%	18	4.6%
Private	246	59.0%	365	93.4%

Source: Selected from Vivien W. Chen, Pelayo Correa et al., "Histological Characteristics of Breast Carcinoma in Blacks and Whites," *Cancer Epidemiology, Biomarkers & Prevention*, Vol. 3, March 1994, pp. 127-135, Table 2, p. 130, "Distributions of selected characteristics among invasive breast cancer patients by race," Requests for reprints should be addressed to Vivien W. Chen, Dept. of Pathology, Louisiana State University Medical Center, 1901 Perdido St., New Orleans, LA 70112. *Notes:* 1. Percent of known response. 2. Items in parentheses indicate the percentage of total.

★ 369 ★

Cancer

Breast Cancer by Race-II

A study was done on 1,130 women (612 blacks and 518 whites) aged 20 to 79 years who were diagnosed with primary invasive breast cancer. It was found that the risk of dying was 2.2 times greater for blacks than whites. About 75% of the racial difference in survival was explained by prognostic factors (stage and tumor pathology). Sociodemographic variables appeared to have to do with racial differences in stage at diagnosis. This may change with improved access to and use of screening for black women. This table shows some characteristics of the invasive breast cancer patients in th study.

Characteristic	Black (n = 612)		White (n = 518)	
	Number	Percent	Number	Percent
Age				
20-49 years	241	39.4%	202	39.0%
50-64 years	204	33.3%	187	36.1%
65-79 years	167	27.3%	129	24.9%
Marital status				
Married/living as				
married	252	41.9%	321	62.0%
Widowed	152	25.3%	100	19.3%
Divorced/separated	142	23.6%	64	12.4%
Never married	56	9.3%	29	5.6%
Occupation				
Manager/prof.	73	11.9%	135	26.1%
Homemaker	33	5.4%	92	17.8%
Technical/sales/				
administration	100	16.3%	139	26.8%
Skilled labor	145	23.7%	54	10.4%
Unskilled labor	135	22.1%	19	3.7%
Usual source of				
health care				
Private	338	55.2%	381	73.6%
Public	96	16.0%	12	2.3%
None	55	9.0%	47	9.1%
Health insurance				
Any private	285	46.6%	411	79.3%
Public only	142	23.2%	20	3.9%
None	66	10.8%	9	1.7%
Tumor stage				
T1	180	30.0%	247	48.8%
T2	273	45.5%	187	37.0%
T3	67	11.2%	38	7.5%
T4	80	13.3%	34	6.7%
Positive nodes				
0	261	42.7%	284	54.8%

[Continued]

★ 369 ★

Breast Cancer by Race-II
[Continued]

Characteristic	Black (n = 612)		White (n = 518)	
	Number	Percent	Number	Percent
1-3	145	23.7%	120	23.2%
4-9	49	8.0%	37	7.1%
More than 10	50	8.2%	34	6.6%

Source: Selected from J. William Eley, M.D., MPH; Holly A. Hill, M.D., PhD., et al., "Tumor Biologic Factors and Breast Cancer Prognosis Among White, Hispanic, and Black Women in the United States," JAMA, Vol 272(12), September 28, 1994, pp. 947-954, table 1, p. 948, "Distribution of Selected Characteristics by Race Among Women Enrolled in the Black White Cancer Survival Study Who Were Diagnosed with Invasive Breast Cancer," Requests for reprints should be addressed to J. William Eley, M.D., Division of Epidemiology, Emory University School of Public Health, Atlanta, GA 30322.

★ 370 ★
Cancer

Breast Cancer Incidence: 1973-1990

This table shows age-adjusted incidence rates per 100,000 population of breast cancer by race for the years 1973-1990. Although breast cancer incidence is aboout 20% higher in white women than in black women, breast cancer fatality is higher for black women. Age-adjusted incidence rates rose 32% between 1980 and 1988 but then leveled off. This is attributed to the increase in the early 1980s to greater use of mammograms by asymptomatic women. Five-year survival rates for breast cancer rose by about 4% in the 1980s and by 1994 had reached 79% for all breast cancer patients and 93% for patients when diagnosed in an early stage.

[Incidence rate per 100,000 population, age adjusted.]

Year	All races	White	Black
1973	82.4	83.9	68.8
1974	94.5	96.0	78.6
1975	87.7	89.5	78.3
1976	85.2	87.3	70.4
1977	83.8	85.6	71.5
1978	83.9	86.1	71.2
1979	85.3	87.1	72.5
1980	85.0	87.1	74.0
1981	88.5	91.3	77.3
1982	89.0	91.7	76.8
1983	93.0	95.5	85.7
1984	96.6	99.6	83.7
1985	103.4	106.1	92.2
1986	106.0	108.7	93.8
1987	112.3	116.7	90.3
1988	109.6	113.3	97.7

[Continued]

★ 370 ★

Breast Cancer Incidence: 1973-1990
[Continued]

Year	All races	White	Black
1989	105.5	109.1	87.8
1990	108.8	112.7	95.8

Source: Selected from "Age-Adjusted Breast Cancer Incidence and Mortality Rates, Among Women, by Race, United States, 1973-1990," *Statistical Bulletin* 75(3), Jul-Sep 1994, Table 3, p. 25. Primary source: National Cancer Institute, *Cancer Statistics Review, 1973-1990,* 1993. Adjusted on basis of age distribution of the U.S. total population, 1970.

★ 371 ★
Cancer

Breast Cancer Risk Linked to Childbearing

Researchers tested the hypothesis that a woman's risk of breast cancer increases for a time after pregnancy but then falls to a level below that of women who have not given birth. A total of 12,666 Swedish women with breast cancer were compared with 62,121 age-matched control subjects. This table summarizes some of the results of the study.

Item	Number/Percent
Risk of breast cancer faced by a 35-year-old woman who has just given birth compared to a woman the same age who has not given birth	+41%
That mother's risk by age 59 compared to her counterpart	-21%
Risk of breast cancer faced by a 35-year-old woman who gave birth at age 25 compared to a woman the same age without children	+8%
That mother's risk by age 59 compared to her counterpart	-29%
Risk of breast cancer faced by a 30-year-old woman who gave birth at age 20 compared to a woman the same age without children	+2%

[Continued]

★ 371 ★

Breast Cancer Risk Linked to Childbearing
[Continued]

Item	Number/Percent
That mother's risk by age 59 compared to her counterpart	-32%

Source: Daniel Q. Haney, "Risk of breast cancer linked to childbearing," *Detroit Free Press*, July 7, 1994, p. 1. Primary source: Mats Lambe, M.D., Chung-Cheng Hsieh, D.Sc., Dimitrios Trichopoulos, M.D., "Transient Increase in the Risk of Breast Cancer After Giving Birth," *The New England Journal of Medicine*, Vol. 331, 1994, pp. 5-9. Address reprint requests to Dr. Lambe at the Department of Social Medicine, University Hospital, S-751 85 Uppsala, Sweden.

★ 372 ★

Cancer

Cancer Incidence Rates: 1973-1990

This table shows age-adjusted cancer incidence rates for selected cancer sites for white and black females, selected years 1973-1990.

Race and Site	Number of new cases per 100,000 population[1]									Estimated ann % change[2]
	1973	1975	1980	1985	1986	1987	1988	1989	1990	
White Female										
All sites	293.7	309.7	309.9	341.4	339.5	350.2	346.5	344.3	348.1	0.9%
Colon and rectum	41.6	42.9	44.6	45.8	42.9	41.0	40.0	40.7	39.7	-0.3%
Colon	30.2	30.8	32.9	33.8	32.1	30.1	29.3	29.9	29.7	-0.2%
Rectum	11.4	12.0	11.8	11.9	10.8	10.9	10.7	10.8	10.0	-0.6%
Pancreas	7.4	7.1	7.3	8.1	7.8	7.5	7.6	7.4	7.6	0.2%
Lung and bronchus	17.8	21.9	28.3	35.9	37.7	39.6	41.4	40.6	41.5	4.9%
Melanoma of skin	5.8	6.9	9.1	10.2	10.6	11.0	10.3	10.7	10.4	3.5%
Breast	83.9	89.5	87.1	106.1	108.7	116.7	113.3	109.1	112.7	1.8%
Cervix uteri	12.8	11.1	9.1	7.6	8.0	7.4	7.9	8.2	8.3	-2.6%
Corpus uteri	29.4	33.7	25.3	23.1	22.3	22.6	21.3	22.0	22.7	-2.5%
Ovary	14.6	14.4	13.9	15.0	13.5	14.6	15.5	16.0	15.7	0.4%
Non-Hodgkin's lymphoma	7.5	8.4	9.2	11.3	11.1	11.4	12.1	11.7	12.4	2.8%
Black Female										
All sites	282.8	296.0	304.3	322.7	328.2	326.2	334.4	320.5	334.4	1.0%
Colon and rectum	41.1	43.4	49.4	45.8	47.2	47.8	45.9	44.4	48.8	0.9%
Colon	29.5	32.8	40.9	36.0	36.7	37.1	36.4	34.1	38.3	1.3%
Rectum	11.6	10.6	8.5	9.9	10.5	10.7	9.5	10.2	10.5	-0.0%
Pancreas	11.6	11.8	13.0	11.3	13.0	14.8	14.2	11.1	10.6	0.5%
Lung and bronchus	20.9	20.6	34.0	40.8	43.3	38.9	42.6	45.0	45.3	4.9%
Breast	68.8	78.3	74.0	92.2	93.8	90.3	97.7	87.8	95.8	1.9%
Cervix uteri	29.7	27.9	19.0	15.9	15.2	15.0	15.3	12.9	13.3	-4.5%
Corpus uteri	15.0	17.2	14.1	15.1	14.2	13.8	14.0	16.5	14.5	-0.2%

[Continued]

★ 372 ★

Cancer Incidence Rates: 1973-1990
[Continued]

Race and Site	Number of new cases per 100,000 population[1]									Estimated ann % change[2]
	1973	1975	1980	1985	1986	1987	1988	1989	1990	
Ovary	10.5	10.1	10.0	10.0	9.1	10.0	10.6	10.7	10.4	0.2%
Non-Hodgkin's lymphoma	5.5	4.1	6.2	6.8	6.8	8.0	7.2	7.8	8.5	3.9%

Source: Selected from "Age-adjusted cancer incidence rates for selected cancer sites, according to sex and race: Selected geographic areas, selected years 1973-90," U.S. Department of Health and Human Services, *Health United States 1992*, Table 59, p. 97. Primary source: National Cancer Institute, National Institutes of Health, Cancer Statistics Review, 1973-1990, NIH Pub. No. 93-2789. U.S. Department of Health and Human Services. Public Health Service, Bethesda, MD., 1993. *Notes:* 1. Age adjusted by the direct method to the 1970 U.S. population. 2. The estimated annual percent change has been calculated by fitting a linear regression model to the natural logarithm of the year rates from 1973-90.

★ 373 ★
Cancer

Cancer Incidence: 1975-1991

This table shows statistics on the changes in cancer incidence and mortality among women for the periods 1975-1979 and 1987-1991. The analysis suggested that while more cancers were being diagnosed, people treated for cancer were living longer. During the time span studied, cancer incidence adjusted for age rose by 12.4% among women. Increased rates of breast and lung cancer accounted for most of the rise in the incidence of cancer among women.

Type of Cancer	Incidence per 100,000	% change, '75-'79 to '87-'91	Mortality per 100,000	% change, '75-'79 to '87-'91
Breast	113.2	30.1%	27.2	1.9%
Lung	41.5	65.3%	30.95	75.6%
Melanoma	10.9	41.6%	1.7	6.3%
Non-Hodgkin's lymphoma	12	34.8%	5.2	26.8%
Kidney	6.1	38.6%	2.3	15.0%
Brain & nervous system	5.7	16.3%	3.7	8.8%
Thyroid	6.4	12.3%	0.3	-40.0%
Skin cancer, except melanoma	0.8	100.0%	0.4	0%
Larynx	1.7	21.4%	0.5	25.0%
Liver	1.5	25%	1.7	13.3%

Source: Jane E. Brody, "Cancer Cases Are Up, But the Future Isn't Bleak," *The New York Times*, February 1, 1995, p. B6 Y. Primary source: *Journal of the National Cancer Institute*.

★ 374 ★
Cancer

Cancer Survival Rates

This table shows five-year survival rates for three major cancer sites affecting women and diagnosed between 1983 and 1989.

[NA Not applicable.]

Cancer Site	5-year survival rate		
	Total	Men	Women
Lung	13.2%	11.8%	15.7%
Breast	NA	NA	79.3%
Colorectal	58.4%	58.9%	57.8%

Source: Selected from "Five-Year Survival Rates (Percent) for Four Major Cancer Sites Diagnosed Between 1983 and 1989, United States," *Statistical Bulletin* 75(3), Jul-Sep 1994, Figure C, p. 23. Primary source: National Cancer Institute, *Cancer Statistics Review, 1973-1990*, 1993.

★ 375 ★
Cancer

Cancer Survival Rates by Race: 1974-1989

This table shows five-year cancer survival rates for selected sites by race for various years between 1974 and 1989. The rate is the ratio of the observed survival rate for the patient group to the expected survival rate for persons in the general population similar to the patient group with respect to age, sex, race, and calendar year of observation. It estimates the chance of surviving the effects of cancer.

Cancer Site	All races				White				Black			
	1974-76	1977-79	1980-82	1983-89	1974-76	1977-79	1980-82	1983-89	1974-76	1977-79	1980-82	1983-89
Female												
All sites	56.7	56.0	55.9	57.9	57.5	56.8	56.7	59.1	46.7	46.2	45.5	44.7
Colon	50.6	53.6	55.0	58.1	50.7	53.7	55.2	59.1	46.9	49.5	50.5	49.2
Rectum	49.4	50.8	53.9	57.0	49.7	51.4	54.6	57.7	49.3	38.5	40.3	47.5
Pancreas	2.1	2.6	3.4	3.9	2.1	2.3	3.0	3.7	3.1	4.8	5.9	5.1
Lung and bronchus	15.6	17.0	15.9	15.7	15.8	17.0	16.0	16.0	12.9	16.9	15.4	13.0
Melanoma of skin	84.7	85.8	87.5	88.4	84.8	86.1	87.5	88.5	X	X	X	73.3
Breast	74.3	74.5	76.1	79.3	74.9	75.2	76.9	80.5	62.8	62.5	65.6	64.1
Cervix uteri	68.5	67.8	66.8	66.8	69.3	68.9	67.5	69.1	63.4	61.9	60.3	57.0
Corpus uteri	87.8	84.9	81.4	82.9	88.7	86.2	82.7	84.6	60.6	57.8	53.8	55.5
Ovary	36.5	38.1	38.8	40.6	36.3	37.5	38.7	40.2	40.1	39.8	37.3	40.2
Non-Hodgkin's lymphoma	47.3	50.5	52.5	53.9	47.4	50.4	52.6	54.5	54.1	58.9	54.7	46.5

Source: Selected from "Five-year relative cancer survival rates for selected sites, according to race and sex: Selected geographic areas, 1974-76, 1977-79, 1980-82, and 1983-89," U.S. Department of Health and Human Services, *Health United States 1992*, Table 60, p. 98. Primary source: National Cancer Institute, National Institutes of Health, Cancer Statistics Review, 1973-1989. NIH Pub. No. 92-2789. U.S. Department of Health and Human Services. Public Health Service. Bethesda, MD., 1992; National Cancer Institute, Division of Cancer Prevention and Control: Unpublished data. Data are based on the Surveillance, Epidemiology, and End Results Program's population-based registries in Atlanta, Detroit, Seattle-Puget Sound, San Francisco-Oakland, Connecticut, Iowa, New Mexico, Utah, and Hawaii. Rates are based on followup of patients through 1990.

★ 376 ★
Cancer

Lung Cancer Incidence: 1973-1990

This table shows age-adjusted incidence rates per 100,000 population of lung cancer by race and sex for the years 1973-1990. Lung cancer incidence rates among women continue to rise, and in 1986, lung cancer became the leading cause of cancer deaths among women.

[Incidence rate per 100,000 population, age adjusted.]

Year	All Races			White			Black		
	Total	Men	Women	Total	Men	Women	Total	Men	Women
1973	42.5	73.2	18.2	41.5	72.2	17.8	59.0	105.1	20.9
1974	43.9	74.5	19.9	43.3	73.9	19.9	59.0	102.3	21.6
1975	45.4	76.2	21.6	45.1	75.7	21.9	56.6	101.2	20.6
1976	47.9	79.4	23.8	47.2	78.4	23.8	62.4	110.4	25.2
1977	49.0	80.8	24.8	48.2	79.8	24.6	64.2	109.1	28.7
1978	50.2	81.9	26.2	49.7	81.0	26.5	65.0	113.3	27.2
1979	50.9	81.4	27.8	50.4	80.5	28.0	65.5	111.4	29.7
1980	52.3	84.3	28.2	51.1	82.0	28.3	76.1	131.2	34.0
1981	53.9	84.5	30.9	53.4	83.3	31.3	73.3	126.3	33.0
1982	54.9	85.0	32.5	54.5	83.5	33.4	71.2	123.9	31.2
1983	55.0	84.1	33.3	54.4	81.9	34.4	75.9	131.0	34.6
1984	56.9	86.5	34.7	55.6	84.0	34.8	82.9	140.4	39.9
1985	56.2	83.9	35.4	55.5	81.9	35.9	79.5	131.7	40.8
1986	57.0	83.6	37.1	56.3	81.7	37.7	81.6	134.3	43.3
1987	58.4	85.0	38.5	58.3	83.9	39.6	74.6	123.7	38.9
1988	58.5	83.0	40.3	58.4	81.6	41.4	77.6	125.8	42.6
1989	57.6	81.6	39.7	57.3	80.1	40.6	76.9	121.0	45.0
1990	57.3	79.6	40.7	57.2	78.6	41.5	74.7	116.0	45.3

Source: Selected from "Age-Adjusted Lung Cancer Incidence and Mortality Rates, by Race and Sex, United States, 1973-1990," *Statistical Bulletin* 75(3), Jul-Sep 1994, Table 1, p. 20. Primary source: National Cancer Institute, *Cancer Statistics Review, 1973-1990,* 1993. Adjusted on basis of age distribution of the U.S. total population, 1970.

Cigarette Smoking

★ 377 ★

Profile of Cigarette Smokers

Based on a 1989 telephone survey of 2,017 Minnesota women, this profile of young (aged 18-30) female cigarette smokers emerged.

[N=2,017 .]

Characteristic	Percent
Women smokers were more likely to be...	
Separated, divorced, or widowed	60%
High school education or less	59%
Vocational/business college students	45%
Blue collar workers	50%
Not working for pay	44%

Source: "Prevalence of Cigarette Use High Among Pregnant Women in Rural Minnesota," *Impact: A Newsletter of Chemical Health in Minnesota*, Vol 10, No. 3, Spring 1992, p. 4. Primary source: 1989 Adult Women's Survey on Tobacco Use: Results of a Telephone Survey on the Tobacco-Related Knowledge, Attitudes, and Behaviors of 2,107 Minnesota Women Aged 18-30. Minnesota Department of Health, 1990.

★ 378 ★

Cigarette Smoking

Smokers: 1965-1991

This table shows the percentage of women, by race, who are current smokers. A current smoker has smoked at least 100 cigarettes and now smokes. This includes occasional smokers.

Age and Race	1965	1974	1979	1983	1985	1987	1988	1990	1991
Total smokers, 18 years old and over	42.4%	37.1%	33.5%	32.1%	30.1%	28.8%	28.1%	25.5%	25.6%
Female, total	33.9%	32.1%	29.9%	29.5%	27.9%	26.5%	25.7%	22.8%	23.5%
18 to 24 years	38.1%	34.1%	33.8%	35.5%	30.4%	26.1%	26.3%	22.5%	22.4%
25 to 34 years	43.7%	38.8%	33.7%	32.6%	32.0%	31.8%	31.3%	28.2%	28.4%
35 to 44 years	43.7%	39.8%	37.0%	33.8%	31.5%	29.6%	27.8%	24.8%	27.6%

[Continued]

★ 378 ★

Smokers: 1965-1991
[Continued]

Age and Race	1965	1974	1979	1983	1985	1987	1988	1990	1991
45 to 64 years	32.0%	33.4%	30.7%	31.0%	29.9%	28.6%	27.7%	24.8%	24.6%
65 years and over	9.6%	12.0%	13.2%	13.1%	13.5%	13.7%	12.8%	11.5%	12.0%
White female, total	34.0%	31.7%	30.1%	29.4%	27.7%	26.7%	25.7%	23.4%	23.7%
18 to 24 years	38.4%	34.0%	34.5%	36.5%	31.8%	27.8%	27.5%	25.4%	25.1%
25 to 34 years	43.4%	38.6%	34.1%	32.2%	32.0%	31.9%	31.0%	28.5%	28.4%
35 to 44 years	43.9%	39.3%	37.2%	34.8%	31.0%	29.2%	28.3%	25.0%	27.0%
45 to 64 years	32.7%	33.0%	30.6%	30.6%	29.7%	29.0%	27.7%	25.4%	25.3%
65 years and over	9.8%	12.3%	13.8%	13.2%	13.3%	13.9%	12.6%	11.5%	12.1%
Black female, total	33.7%	36.4%	31.1%	32.2%	31.0%	28.0%	27.8%	21.2%	24.4%
18 to 24 years	37.1%	35.6%	31.8%	32.0%	23.7%	20.4%	21.8%	10.0%	11.8%
25 to 34 years	47.8%	42.2%	35.2%	38.0%	36.2%	35.8%	37.2%	29.1%	32.4%
35 to 44 years	42.8%	46.4%	37.7%	32.7%	40.2%	35.3%	27.6%	25.5%	35.3%
45 to 64 years	25.7%	38.9%	34.2%	36.3%	33.4%	28.4%	29.5%	22.6%	23.4%
65 years and over	7.1%	8.9%	8.5%	13.1%	14.5%	11.7%	14.8%	11.1%	9.6%

Source: Selected from "Current Cigarette Smoking," U.S. Bureau of the Census, *Statistical Abstract of the United States 1994*, Table 212, p. 143. Primary source: U.S. National Center for Health Statistics, *Health, United States, 1992.*

★ 379 ★

Cigarette Smoking

Smoking and Elderly Women

This table gives statistics related to current and lifetime smoking and alcohol use and their effects on physical function in an older population. Participants were 9,704 white women over the age of 65. The authors found that women who currently smoked had poorer muscle strength, agility, and balance than did their nonsmoking contemporaries. Moderate drinkers, those who averaged fewer than 14 drinks a week, did better on 11 of 12 physical tasks than did their nondrinking counterparts.

Item	Number/Percent
Smokers Number of performance tests of muscle strength, agility and coordination, gait and balance, and self-reported functional status	12
Number of performance tests on which women who never smoked performed better than women who currently smoked (all except grip strength)	11

[Continued]

★ 379 ★

Smoking and Elderly Women
[Continued]

Item	Number/Percent
This decrease in function 50% to 100% as great as an increase in age of	5 years
Drinkers	
Number of performance tests on which women who drank moderately performed better than women who didn't drink	11

Source: Selected from Heidi D. Nelson, MD, MPH, Michael C. Nevitt, PhD, Jean C. Scott, DrPh, et al., "Smoking, Alcohol, and Neuromuscular and Physical Function of Older Women," *JAMA The Journal of the American Medical Association*, Vol 272(23), December 21, 1994, pp. 1825-1831. Reprint requests to Division of General Internal Medicine, Oregon Health Sciences University, 3181 SW Sam Jackson Park Rd, L475, Portland, OR 97201-3098 (Dr. Nelson).

★ 380 ★

Cigarette Smoking

Smoking in Asia and the Near East

This table shows the percentage of adult females in Asia and the Near East who smoke.

Country	Adult females who smoke
Asia, excluding Near East	
Bangladesh	20%
China	8%
Hong Kong	4%
India	3%
Indonesia	5%
Japan	14%
Korea	
Republic of	7%
Malaysia	4%
Nepal	58%
Pakistan	6%
Papua New Guinea	80%
Singapore	3%
Sri Lanka	2%
Thailand	13%
Vietnam	2%

[Continued]

★ 380 ★

Smoking in Asia and the Near East
[Continued]

Country	Adult females who smoke
Near East	
Iraq	6%
Israel	25%
Kuwait	12%
Turkey	50%

Source: Selected from "Indicators on health and child-bearing," *The World's Women: Trends and Statistics 1970-1990*, United Nations, 1991, Table 5, p. 69. Primary source: *World Health Statistics Quarterly*, 41 (Geneva, 1988); and unpublished data from Pan American Health Organization.

★ 381 ★

Cigarette Smoking

Smoking in Europe

This table shows the percentage of adult females in Europe who smoke.

Country	Adult females who smoke
Europe	
Austria	22%
Belgium	21%
Czech Republic	
Czechoslovakia	14%
Denmark	38%
Finland	17%
France	26%
Germany[1]	
Federal Rep. of Germany	29%
Greece	13%
Hungary	25%
Ireland	32%
Italy	18%
Netherlands	33%
Norway	32%
Poland	29%
Portugal	10%
Romania	13%
Spain	27%
Sweden	30%
Switzerland	29%

[Continued]

★ 381 ★

Smoking in Europe
[Continued]

Country	Adult females who smoke
USSR	11%
United Kingdom	32%
Yugoslavia	10%

Source: Selected from "Indicators on health and child-bearing," *The World's Women: Trends and Statistics 1970-1990*, United Nations, 1991, Table 5, p. 69. Primary source: *World Health Statistics Quarterly*, 41 (Geneva, 1988); and unpublished data from Pan American Health Organization. *Note:* 1. Data are pre-unification.

★ 382 ★

Cigarette Smoking

Smoking in Latin America and the Caribbean

This table shows the percentage of adult females in Latin America and the Caribbean who smoke. Latin America and the Caribbean have the highest proprotion of the world's female smokers.

Country	Adult females who smoke
Latin America and the Caribbean	
Argentina	18%
Bolivia	61%
Brazil	53%
Chile	18%
Colombia	31%
Guatemala	10%
Guyana	4%
Mexico	44%
Peru[1]	7%
Trinidad and Tobago	5%
Uruguay	45%
Venezuela	67%

Source: Selected from "Indicators on health and child-bearing," *The World's Women: Trends and Statistics 1970-1990*, United Nations, 1991, Table 5, p. 68. Primary source: *World Health Statistics Quarterly*, 41 (Geneva, 1988); and unpublished data from Pan American Health Organization. *Note:* 1. Data refer to 1970s.

★ 383 ★

Cigarette Smoking

Smoking in North America

This table shows the percentage of adult females in North America who smoke.

Country	Adult females who smoke
North America	
Canada	28%
United States	24%

Source: Selected from "Indicators on health and child-bearing," *The World's Women: Trends and Statistics 1970-1990*, United Nations, 1991, Table 5, p. 69. Primary source: *World Health Statistics Quarterly*, 41 (Geneva, 1988); and unpublished data from Pan American Health Organization.

★ 384 ★

Cigarette Smoking

Smoking in Oceania

This table shows the percentage of adult females in Oceania who smoke.

Country	Adult females who smoke
Oceania	
Australia	30%
Fiji[1]	44%
French Polynesia[2]	46%
Kiribati	70%
New Caledonia[3]	22%
New Zealand	29%
Papua New Guinea	80%
Tonga	38%

Source: Selected from "Indicators on health and child-bearing," *The World's Women: Trends and Statistics 1970-1990*, United Nations, 1991, Table 5, p. 69. Primary source: *World Health Statistics Quarterly*, 41 (Geneva, 1988); and unpublished data from Pan American Health Organization. *Notes:* 1. Melanesian population only. 2. Maori population only. 3. Data refer to 1970s.

★ 385 ★

Cigarette Smoking

Smoking in Sub-Saharan Africa

This table shows the percentage of adult females in Sub-Saharan Africa who smoke. Africa has the lowest proportion of the world's women smokers.

Country	Adult females who smoke
Sub-Saharan Africa	
Cote d'Ivoire[1]	1%
Egypt	2%
Ghana[1]	1%
Mauritius	7%
Nigeria	3%
Senegal	35%
Swaziland	72%
Zambia	7%

Source: Selected from "Indicators on health and child-bearing," *The World's Women: Trends and Statistics 1970-1990,* United Nations, 1991, Table 5, p. 67. Primary source: *World Health Statistics Quarterly,* 41 (Geneva, 1988); and unpublished data from Pan American Health Organization. *Note:* 1. Data refer to 1970s.

★ 386 ★

Cigarette Smoking

Smoking in the Middle East and North Africa

This table shows the percentage of adult females in the Middle East and North Africa who smoke.

Country	Adult females who smoke
Middle East/North Africa	
Egypt	2%
Iraq	6%
Kuwait	12%
Tunisia	6%
Turkey	50%

Source: Selected from "Indicators on health and child-bearing," *The World's Women: Trends and Statistics 1970-1990,* United Nations, 1991, Table 5, p. 69. Primary source: *World Health Statistics Quarterly,* 41 (Geneva, 1988); and unpublished data from Pan American Health Organization.

Clitoridectomy

★387★

Female Genital Mutilation in Africa

This table shows estimated prevalence rates and actual number of currently living women upon whom female genital mutilation (FGM) has been committed in Africa. There is no country-by-country data collection on this practice. Fran Hosken, an American, collected anecdotal estimates, which were published in 1992. Global estimates of FGM that appear elsewhere are derived from her estimates. The estimated prevalence rates here were developed from reviews of national surveys, small studies, country reports, and Fran Hosken.

Country	Prevalence	Actual number
Benin[1]	50%	1,200,000
Burkina[1]	70%	3,290,000
Central African Republic[1]	50%	750,000
Chad	60%	1,530,000
Cote d'Ivoire[1]	60%	3,750,000
Djibouti	98%	196,000
Egypt	50%	13,625,000
Ethiopia and Eritrea	90%	23,940,000
Gambia[1]	60%	270,000
Ghana	30%	2,325,000
Ghana	30%	2,325,000
Guinea[1]	50%	1,875,000
Guinea Bissau[1]	50%	250,000
Kenya	50%	6,300,000
Liberia[1]	60%	810,000
Mali[1]	75%	3,112,500
Mauritania[1]	25%	262,500
Niger[1]	20%	800,000
Nigeria	50%	30,625,000
Senegal	20%	750,000
Sierra Leone	90%	1,935,000
Somalia	98%	3,773,000
Sudan (North)	89%	9,220,400
Tanzania	10%	1,345,000
Togo[1]	50%	950,000
Uganda[1]	5%	467,500

[Continued]

★ 387 ★

Female Genital Mutilation in Africa
[Continued]

Country	Prevalence	Actual number
Zaire[1]	5%	945,000
Total	X	114,296,900

Source: Nahid Toubia, *Female Genital Mutilation: A Call for Global Action*, Women, Ink, 1993, p. 25. For further information contact Nahid Toubia, (212) 477-3318. Primary source: Fran Hosken, *WIN News*, Vol 18, No. 4, Autumn 1992. Related reading: A.M. Rosenthal, "The Possible Dream," *The New York Times*, June 13, 1995, p. A11 Y. *Note:* 1. Anecdotal information only; no published studies.

Conditions

★ 388 ★

Acute Conditions: 1992

This table shows numbers of acute conditions in millions and the rate per 100 population, by type of condition, for 1992.

[Number in millions. NA Not available.]

Characteristic	Number of conditions (millions)					Rate per 100 population				
	Infective and parasitic	Respiratory		Digestive system	Injuries	Infective and parasitic	Respiratory		Digestive system	Injuries
		Common cold	Influenza				Common cold	Influenza		
1992, total	56.2	64.6	107.3	17.6	59.6	22.4	25.7	42.7	7.0	23.7
Male	23.4	28.3	47.6	8.7	32.8	19.1	23.2	39.0	7.1	26.8
Female	32.9	36.3	59.7	8.9	26.8	25.4	28.1	46.2	6.9	20.7

Source: Selected from "Acute Conditions, by Type: 1970 to 1992," U.S. Bureau of the Census, *Statistical Abstract of the United States 1994*, Table 207, p. 140. Primary sources: U.S. National Center for Health Statistics, *Vital and Health Statistics*, series 10, No. 189, and earlier reports; and unpublished data. Covers civilian noninstitutional population. Estimates include only acute conditions which were medically attended or caused at least 1 day of restricted activity. Based on National Health Interview Survey.

★ 389 ★

Conditions

Alzheimer's Disease

This table presents statistics cited in the *Detroit Free Press* about a study to be released in the May 4, 1995, issue of the *Journal of the American Medical Association* on Alzheimer's disease risk. The study did not address the issue of whether women have a greater tendency toward Alzheimer's, but the issue is of particular significance to women because they live longer on average.

Item	Number/Percent
Life expectancy in 1994	
Males	72
Females	79
Chance of developing Alzheimer's disease for a baby born in 1994 who survives to an average life expectancy	
Boys	1 in 16
Girls	1 in 6
Number of people who will develop Alzheimer's by age 90	1 in 2
Percent of population who will develop Alzheimer's	
by age 70	4.7%
by age 80	18.2%
by age 90	49.6%

Source: "People who live longer face greater Alzheimer's risk," *Detroit Free Press*, May 3, 1995, p. 5A.

★ 390 ★

Conditions

Alzheimer's Disease Linked to Down's Syndrome

Nearly all Down's syndrome patients who live into their 40's develop Alzheimer's disease. Researchers postulated that a shared genetic susceptibility to Down's syndrome (DS) and Alzheimer's disease (AD) would be associated with an increased frequency of AD among mothers, but not fathers, of persons with DS. They also postulated that the shared susceptibility could involve an accelerated aging process, leading to the birth of a child with DS to a relatively young mother and to an increased risk of dementia in the mother and her relatives. They suggest that it is possible that a woman who gives birth to a child with DS before she is 35 is biologically older than her chronological age. Families of 96 adults with DS and of 80 adults with other forms of mental retardation were interviewed. This table shows some of the results. In other words, there was shown to be an increase in risk of dementia among mothers of DS children. The risk for mothers who were 35 or younger when their DS children were born was 5 times that of control mothers (mothers of children with other forms of retardation). There was no increase in risk of dementia among mothers who were older than 35 at the time of the DS child's birth.

Characteristics	All parents	Demented	Cumulative risk to age 85 (SE)	Rate ratio (95% CI)
Mothers				
Children with DS	95	17	0 27(0 076)	2 6(0 9-7 3)
< age 35 at birth	58	13	0 39(0 109)	4 9(1 6-15 4)
> age 35 at birth	37	4	0 09(0 062)	0 8(0 2-3 4)
Controls (with other				
forms of retardation)	77	5	0 10(0 048)	1 0

Source: Selected from Nicole Schupf, Deborah Kapell, Joseph H. Lee, et al., "Increased risk of Alzheimer's disease in mothers of adults with Down's syndrome," *The Lancet,* Vol 344, August 6, 1994, pp. 353-56, p. 354, Table 2, entitled "Cumulative incidence and rate ratio of dementia in parents of DS probands and of control probands (with other forms of mental retardation." Address correspondence to Dr. Nicole Schupf, Laboratory of Epidemiology, NYS Institute for Basic Research in Developmental Disabilities, 1050 Forest Hill Road, Staten Island, NY 10314.

★ 391 ★

Conditions

Chronic Conditions: 1992

This table shows number of chronic conditions in thousands and the rate per 1,000 population, by type of condition and age, in 1992.

[Number in thousands. Rate per 1,000 persons.]

Chronic Condition	Conditions (1,000)	Rate per 1,000 persons							
		Male				Female			
		Under 45	45-64 years	65 to 74 years	75 years+	Under 45	45-64 years	65 to 74 years	75 years+
Arthritis	33,317	26.1	199.2	364.8	417.2	42.2	315.9	508.7	611.2
Dermatitis, incl.									
eczema	10,146	32.6	32.1	33.5	37.9	48.6	50.1	49.0	24.8
Trouble with-									
Dry (itching skin)	5,383	14.5	19.8	25.4	35.3	20.7	31.5	34.3	49.1

[Continued]

★ 391 ★

Chronic Conditions: 1992
[Continued]

| Chronic Condition | Conditions (1,000) | Rate per 1,000 persons | | | | | | | |
| | | Male | | | | Female | | | |
		Under 45	45-64 years	65 to 74 years	75 years +	Under 45	45-64 years	65 to 74 years	75 years +
Ingrown nails	6,273	21.6	26.1	28.3	29.0[1]	17.0	35.9	47.2	75.7
Corns & calluses	4,433	6.5	24.3	13.9[1]	44.4	11.2	41.4	51.2	58.9
Visual impairments	8,976	31.1	66.0	96.6	131.9	14.5	33.1	49.6	99.4
Cataracts	6,721	2.5	18.7	112.5	193.2	1.7[1]	32.3	137.1	245.2
Hearing impairments	23,777	44.3	216.2	322.3	452.7	30.4	96.9	204.3	392.9
Tinnitus	7,779	11.4	75.2	95.5	113.7	13.5	45.1	77.1	84.6
Deformities or ortho-pedic impairments	31,605	102.1	181.8	154.9	185.8	100.5	167.4	167.1	243.0
Ulcer	4,408	11.1	23.2	38.4	31.8[1]	13.4	29.5	34.0	26.9
Hernia of abdominal cavity	5,228	11.5	39.0	61.5	64.8	6.5	34.1	57.4	67.5
Frequent indigestion	6,374	19.0	37.9	56.0	34.4	16.9	42.0	43.4	35.7
Frequent constipation	4,296	4.8	12.6	24.9	40.9	16.0	28.2	40.9	88.8
Diabetes	7,417	6.1	52.5	119.6	96.8	9.0	59.2	109.2	110.2
Migraine	10,627	26.0	18.4	15.3[1]	8.4[1]	60.8	80.6	35.4	21.7
Heart conditions	21,584	25.7	150.8	334.7	408.5	32.9	120.3	220.6	401.2
High blood pressure (hypertension)	27,816	37.5	231.0	341.4	314.7	30.2	222.1	377.7	374.3
Varicose veins of lower extremities	7,281	5.3	26.7	34.3	56.3	24.2	76.9	84.4	101.0
Hemorrhoids	9,562	19.0	77.3	63.9	56.7	30.5	65.6	51.6	68.9
Chronic bronchitis	13,494	41.0	43.6	76.6	40.1	58.0	71.9	80.0	65.9
Asthma	12,375	50.7	32.4	28.9	35.7	53.5	56.6	55.9	32.8
Hay fever, allergic rhinitis without asthma	25,698	102.4	98.2	61.5	63.7	109.2	104.8	103.0	90.5
Chronic sinusitis	36,659	108.5	152.7	123.9	120.2	155.0	219.3	185.4	183.6

Source: Selected from "Prevalence of Selected Chronic Conditions, by Age and Sex: 1992," U.S. Bureau of the Census, *Statistical Abstract of the United States 1994,* Table 208, p. 140. Primary sources: U.S. National Center for Health Statistics, *Vital and Health Statistics,* series 10, No. 189, and earlier reports; and unpublished data. Covers civilian noninstitutional population. Conditions classified according to ninth revision of International Classification of Diseases. Based on National Health Interview Survey. *Note:* 1. Figure does not meet standards of reliability or precision.

★ 392 ★
Conditions

Disability Status: 1990

This table gives figures relating to the disability status of the female population aged 16 to 64 years. It tells whether they have a disability and whether or not they are in the labor force, as reported in the 1990 census.

Disability status	Total
Females 16 to 64 years	80,654,515
With a mobility or self-care limitation	3,792,873
with a mobility limitation	1,886,716
in labor force	377,913
with a self-care limitation	2,746,467

[Continued]

★ 392 ★

Disability Status: 1990
[Continued]

Disability status	Total
With a work disability	6,120,550
in labor force	1,959,588
prevented from working	3,435,036
No work disability	74,533,965
in labor force	52,950,611

Source: Selected from "Age, Sex, Ability to Speak English, and Disability: 1990," U.S. Bureau of the Census, 1990 Census of Population, *Social and Economic Characteristics, United States, 1990* CP-2-1, Table 15, p. 15.

★ 393 ★

Conditions

High Cholesterol: 1960-1991

This table shows the percentage of women 20 years old and over with high serum cholesterol levels, by race and Hispanic origin, for various years beginning in 1960 through 1991. It also shows mean serum cholesterol levels. High serum cholesterol is defined as greater than or equal to 240 mg/dl (6.20 mmol/L). Risk levels have been defined by the National Cholesterol Education Program expert Panel on Detection, Evaluation and Treatment of High Blood Cholesterol in Adults, November 1987).[4]

[X means Not available.]

Age, race, and Hispanic origin[1]	Percent of population with high serum cholesterol				Mean serum cholesterol level, Mg/dL			
	1960-1962	1971-1974	1976-1980[2]	1988-1991	1960-1962	1971-1974	1976-1980[2]	1988-1991
Female, 20-74 years, age adjusted[3]	34.5%	28.2%	27.6%	20.2%	222	215	214	205
White female	35.1%	28.1%	28.0%	20.3%	223	215	214	205
Black female	30.7%	29.2%	24.9%	20.7%	216	217	213	205
White, non-Hispanic female	X	X	28.3%	20.0%	X	X	214	205
Black, non-Hispanic female	X	X	24.9%	20.7%	X	X	214	205
Mexican-American female	X	X	20.0%	19.4%	X	X	207	205
Female, 20-74 years, crude	36.3%	29.6%	28.5%	20.3%	225	217	215	205
White female	37.5%	29.8%	29.2%	20.8%	227	217	216	206
Black female	29.9%	28.8%	23.7%	18.1%	216	216	212	201
White, non-Hispanic female	X	X	29.8%	20.9%	X	X	216	206
Black, non-Hispanic female	X	X	23.7%	18.2%	X	X	212	200
Mexican-American female	X	X	16.5%	15.6%	X	X	202	200
Female, by age								
20-34 years	12.4%	10.9%	9.8%	8.3%	194	191	189	185
35-44 years	23.1%	19.3%	20.7%	11.7%	214	207	207	195
45-54 years	46.9%	38.7%	40.5%	25.2%	237	232	232	217
55-64 years	70.1%	53.1%	52.9%	40.4%	262	245	249	237

[Continued]

★ 393 ★

High Cholesterol: 1960-1991

[Continued]

Age, race, and Hispanic origin[1]	Percent of population with high serum cholesterol				Mean serum cholesterol level, Mg/dL			
	1960-1962	1971-1974	1976-1980[2]	1988-1991	1960-1962	1971-1974	1976-1980[2]	1988-1991
65-74 years	68.5%	57.7%	51.6%	43.2%	266	250	246	234
75 years and over	X	X	X	39.2%	X	X	X	230

Source: Selected from "Persons 20 years of age and over with high serum cholesterol levels and mean serum cholesterol levels, according to sex, age, race, and Hispanic origin: United States, 1960-62, 1971-74, 1976-80, and 1988-91," U.S. Department of Health and Human Services, *Health United States 1992*, Table 72, p. 111. Primary source: Centers for Disease Control and Prevention, National Center for Health Statistics, Division of Health Examination Statistics. Data are based on physical examinations of a sample of the civilian noninstitutionalized population. *Notes:* 1. The race groups, white and black, include persons of both Hispanic and non-Hispanic origin. Conversely, persons of Hispanic origin may be of any race. 2. Data for Mexican-Americans are for 1982-84. 3. Age-adjusted by the direct method to the 1980 U.S. resident population using the following 5 age groups: 20-34 years, 35-44 years, 45-54 years, 55-64 years, and 65-74 years. 4. *Archives of Internal Medicine*: January 1988, 148: 36-69).

★ 394 ★

Conditions

Injuries: 1970-1991

This table shows the number of persons injured in millions and the rate per 100 population for the years 1970 to 1991.

[Persons injured in millions.]

Year	Persons injured		Rate per 100 population	
	Male	Female	Male	Female
1970	31.8	24.2	33.0	23.3
1975	93.4	32.5	39.1	30.0
1980	39.0	29.1	37.1	25.8
1983	33.0	28.1	29.8	23.7
1984	33.7	27.4	30.1	22.9
1985	34.6	28.0	30.6	23.1
1986	34.0	28.4	29.8	23.3
1987	33.6	28.4	29.1	23.1
1988	32.4	26.8	27.7	21.6
1989	31.7	26.3	26.9	20.9
1990	33.6	26.6	28.1	21.0
1991	32.2	27.5	26.7	21.5

Source: Selected from "Persons Injured, by Sex: 1970 to 1992," U.S. Bureau of the Census, *Statistical Abstract of the United States 1994*, Table 198, p. 135. Primary sources: U.S. National Center for Health Statistics, *Vital and Health Statistics*, series 10, No. 189, and earlier reports; and unpublished data. Covers civilian noninstitutional population and comprises incidents leading to restricted activity and/or medical attention. Beginning 1982, data not strictly comparable with other years.

★ 395 ★

Conditions

Injuries: 1992

This table shows the number of persons injured in millions and the rate per 100 population, by age, in 1992. It also shows figures by type of injury.

Age and Type	Persons injured			Rate per 100 population		
	Total	Male	Female	Total	Male	Female
1992, total[1]	59.6	32.8	26.8	23.7	26.8	20.7
Under 5 years	4.8	2.6	2.2	24.5	26.3	22.6
5 to 17 years	13.4	8.2	5.2	28.6	34.2	22.7
18 to 44 years	27.7	16.7	11.1	26.3	32.1	20.6
45 years and over	13.6	5.2	8.4	17.1	14.5	19.4
Fractures[2]	7.8	4.6	3.2	3.1	3.7	2.5
Sprains and strains	13.8	7.0	6.8	5.5	5.8	5.2
Open wounds & lacerations	12.4	7.8	4.6	4.9	6.4	3.5
Contusions[3]	10.7	6.1	4.6	4.2	5.0	3.6
Other	15.0	7.3	7.6	5.9	6.0	5.9

Source: Selected from "Persons Injured, by Sex: 1970 to 1992," U.S. Bureau of the Census, *Statistical Abstract of the United States 1994,* Table 198, p. 135. Primary sources: U.S. National Center for Health Statistics, *Vital and Health Statistics,* series 10, No. 189, and earlier reports; and unpublished data. Covers civilian noninstitutional population and comprises incidents leading to restricted activity and/or medical attention. *Notes:* 1. Includes unknown place of accident not shown separately. 2. Includes dislocations. 3. Includes superficial injuries.

★ 396 ★

Conditions

Sexually Transmitted Diseases Among Teenagers

Some statistics about teenagers and sexually transmitted diseases (STD), gathered by The Alan Guttmacher Institute. It is reported that infectious syphilis rates have more than doubled among teenagers since the mid-1980s, and that infertility, cancer, and HIV infection can result from an STD. Teenage women have the highest rate of hospitalization for acute pelvic inflammatory disease, which is most often caused by untreated gonorrhea or chlamydia.

Item	Number/Percent
Number of teenagers who acquire an STD annually	3,000,000
Chances of a teenage woman acquiring an STD in a single act of unprotected sex with an infected partner:	
HIV	1%
Genital herpes	30%
Gonorrhea	50%

[Continued]

★ 396 ★

Sexually Transmitted Diseases Among Teenagers
[Continued]

Item	Number/Percent
Percents of sexually active teenage women tested in different settings for STDs who have been found to have chlamydia	10% to 29%

Source: Selected from "Teenage Reproductive Health in the United States," The Alan Guttmacher Institute, *Facts In Brief.*

★ 397 ★
Conditions

Sexually Transmitted Diseases Worldwide-I

This table presents some statistics on sexually transmitted diseases in developing countries. The author claims that STDs take a greater toll on women's lives than does AIDS in men, women, and children combined. She asserts that the cure, contraception, is cheap but neglected. In Africa, infertility is epidemic among poor rural females. Their husbands migrate to urban areas to work, carry STDs from one prostitute to another then back home to their wives. In Sub-Saharan Africa, traditional healers prescribe sex with virgins to cure men with STDs.

Item	Number/Percent
Estimate of the percentage of female infertility in developing countries that is due to STDs	70%
Estimated number of deaths among women each year worldwide due to STDs	750,000
Illnesses	75 million
Projected number of deaths by 2000	> 1.5 million
Estimated number of these deaths annually due to sexually transmitted papillomavirus	Nearly 50%
Estimated number of new STDs transmitted each year	250 million
Chlamydia	50 million
Human papillomavirus	30 million
HIV (April-December 1991)	1 million
Percentage of 650 rural women examined in the Indian state of Maharashtra who had one or more gynecological and sexual diseases:	92%
Average number of infections per woman	3.6
Percentage of those women who had ever had a gynecological exam	< 8%

[Continued]

★ 397 ★

Sexually Transmitted Diseases Worldwide-I
[Continued]

Item	Number/Percent
Percentage of 509 non-pregnant women aged 20 to 60 in two rural Egyptian villages who had reproductive tract infections	50%
Percentage of 3,000 Bangladesh women who reported symptoms of reproductive tract infections	22%
Percentage of Mexican women who seek state-sponsored birth control without the knowledge of their spouses	60%
Number of facilities for the diagnosis and treatment of STDs in Kenya	2
Number of STD clinics in Ibadan, Nigeria (pop. 2 million)	1
Maternal infections with chlamydia, gonorrhea, or herpes that are transferred to infants at birth	25 to 50%
Cost of preventing the most common adverse outcomes associated with gonorrhea transfer	$1.40
Cost of preventing the most common adverse outcomes associated with syphilis transfer	$12
Percentage of ectopic pregnancies due to reproductive infections in developing countries:	80%

Source: Selected from Jodi L. Jacobson, "The Other Epidemic," *World Watch*, May/June 1992, pp. 10-17.

★ 398 ★
Conditions

Sexually Transmitted Diseases Worldwide-II

This table gives the number of new sexually transmitted infections worldwide in 1990.

[Number in millions.]

Infection	Number
Trichomoniasis	120
Chlamydia	50
Human Papillomavirus	30
Gonorrhea	25
Herpes	20
Syphilis	4
Chancroid	2
HIV	1

Source: Selected from Jodi L. Jacobson, "The Other Epidemic," *World Watch*, May/June 1992, pp. 10-17, p. 10, Table 2: "Number of New Sexually Transmitted Infections Worldwide, 1990." Primary source: World Health Organization.

Contraception

★ 399 ★

Effectiveness of the Female Condom

A study was conducted to determine the effectiveness of the female condom and to provide information about the device to the U.S. Food and Drug Administration. A clinical trial was conducted at sites in the United States and Latin America on a total of 328 subjects in monogamous relationships who agreed to use the condom as their only means of contraception for six months. This table shows cumulative rates of discontinuation of use of the female condom by reason for discontinuation. Twenty-two U.S. subjects and 17 Latin American subjects became pregnant, yielding 6-month gross cumulative accidental pregnancy rates of 12.4 and 22.2. With perfect (consistent and correct) use of the female condom, the 6-month accidental pregnancy rates were 2.6 and 9.5. The researchers concluded that the female condom was as effective as other barrier methods of contraception.

[U.S. Subgroup N = 221. Latin American Subgroup N = 107.]

Reason for Discontinuation	U.S. Subgroup		Latin American subgroup	
	Rate[1]	SE	Rate[1]	SE
Accidental pregnancy	12.4	2.55	22.2	5.34
Personal reasons	21.0	2.99	33.4	5.61
Planned pregnancy	0.5	0.58	6.4	3.44
Medical reasons	2.5	1.28	3.8	2.74

[Continued]

★ 399 ★

Effectiveness of the Female Condom
[Continued]

Reason for Discontinuation	U.S. Subgroup		Latin American subgroup	
	Rate[1]	SE	Rate[1]	SE
Lost to follow-up	2.5	1.29	6.0	3.35
Total discontinuation[2]	34.5	3.18	56.2	4.79

Source: Gaston Farr, MA, Henry Gabelnick, PhD, Kim Sturgen et al., "Contraceptive Efficacy and Acceptability of the Female Condom," *American Journal of Public Health*, Vol. 84, No. 12, December 1994, pp. 1960-1964, Table 3, p. 1962, "Gross Cumulative 6-Month Life-Table Rates of Discontinuation for the Efficacy Population (n = 328)." *Notes:* 1. Per 100 women. 2. Discontinuation for any of the reasons listed above.

Dietary and Health Practices

★ 400 ★

Benefits of Olive Oil

The New York Times reported on a survey in Greece of 820 women with breast cancer and 1,548 women who were free of cancer to see whether diet had any effect on protection against cancer. This table shows some of the results of that study and other studies on the benefits of vegetables in the diet as reported in the *Times*.

Item	Number/Percent
Greek Study	
Risk of breast cancer among women who ate the most vegetables compared to those who ate the fewest vegetables	-48%
Risk of breast cancer among women who ate the most fruits compared to those who ate the fewest fruits	-32%
Risk of breast cancer among women who consumed olive oil more than once a day compared to women who did not consume olive oil daily[1]	-25%
Average amount of saturated fats in the North American diet, coming from animal products, daily	30 grams

[Continued]

★ 400 ★

Benefits of Olive Oil
[Continued]

Item	Number/Percent
Amount of calories derived from mostly saturated fat in the daily diet of the average American woman	35%
Amount of calories derived from mostly monounsaturated fat in the daily diet of the average Greek woman	42%
Breast cancer rates in Mediterranean countries, where olive oil, a mono-unsaturated fat, is widely used, compared to the United States	-50%
Amount by which American women might reduce their breast cancer risk if they consumed more olive oil	50%
Previous Studies	
Amount by which a woman's ovarian cancer risk is reduced for every 10 grams of vegetable fiber added to her daily diet	37%
Amount by which a woman's ovarian cancer risk is raised for every 10 grams of saturated fat added to her daily diet	20%

Source: Jane E. Brody, "New evidence on the Benefits of Olive Oil," *The New York Times*, January 18, 1995, p. B8 Y. Primary source: The Greek study was to have been published in the January 18 issue of *The Journal of the National Cancer Institute. Note:* 1. This protective effect found mainly among women past menopause.

★ 401 ★

Dietary and Health Practices

Calcium Intake

This table gives optimal calcium requirements recommended by the National Institutes of Health Consensus panel for women between the ages of 25 and 50 and women over 50 and over 65. *JAMA* reports that in women 65 years of age and older, calcium intake of less than 600 milligrams a day is common. Calcium insufficiency can lead to an accelerated rate of age-related bone loss in older women.

Age Group	Optimal daily intake, mg
Women 25-50 years	1000

Over 50 (postmenopausal)
  On estrogens
  Not on estrogens
	1000
	1500

Over 65	1500
Pregnant and nursing	1200-1500

Source: "Optimal Calcium Intake," *Journal of the American Medical Association (JAMA)* 272(24), December 28, 1994, pp. 1942-1948, p. 1943, table entitled "Optimal Calcium Requirements Recommended by the National Institutes of Health Consensus Panel."

★ 402 ★

Dietary and Health Practices

Daily Nutrient Intake

This table shows the specific daily nutrient intake by women. Data were gathered from 2,000 households for the National Live Stock and Meat Board.

Diet	Calories (kcal)	Total fat (g)	Saturated fat (g)	Monounsaturated fat (g)	Polyunsaturated fat (g)	Cholesterol (mg)	Protein (g)	Iron (mg)	Zinc (mg)	Carbohydrates (g)	Sodium (mg)
Adult Females											
Total Diet	1447.4	58.4	20.6	21.6	11.6	225.3	58.8	10.6	8.6	174.3	2631.9
Meat group	360.0	22.4	7.5	9.6	3.1	158.2	32.4	2.9	4.5	5.5	768.8
Meats	212.4	14.6	5.5	6.5	1.2	65.7	18.2	1.7	3.2	0.8	509.9
Beef	105.2	6.8	2.6	2.9	0.3	34.5	10.1	1.0	2.2	0.3	151.6
Pork	37.2	2.4	0.8	1.1	0.3	11.7	3.6	0.2	0.4	0.1	132.0
Lamb	1.8	0.1	0.1	[1]	[1]	0.6	0.2	[1]	[1]	[1]	0.9
Veal	1.0	0.1	[1]	[1]	[1]	0.5	0.1	[1]	[1]	[1]	1.3
Processed meats	54.5	4.7	1.7	2.2	0.5	10.2	2.5	0.2	0.3	0.3	186.6
Variety/other meats	12.7	0.6	0.2	0.2	0.1	8.2	1.7	0.3	0.3	0.1	37.5
Poultry	66.7	3.4	1.0	1.3	0.8	25.5	8.0	0.4	0.6	0.6	99.2
Fish/Seafood	26.4	1.1	0.2	0.4	0.4	10.3	3.1	0.2	0.2	0.9	59.8
Eggs/Dry Beans/Nuts	54.5	3.3	0.9	1.4	0.8	56.8	3.1	0.5	0.4	3.2	99.9
Bread Group	453.5	12.1	3.4	4.7	3.0	27.8	11.1	5.2	1.8	75.9	852.1

[Continued]

★ 402 ★

Daily Nutrient Intake
[Continued]

Diet	Calories (kcal)	Total fat (g)	Saturated fat (g)	Monounsatur-ated fat (g)	Polyunsatur-ated fat (g)	Cholesterol (mg)	Protein (g)	Iron (mg)	Zinc (mg)	Carbohy-drates (g)	Sodium (mg)
Milk Group	165.1	8.3	5.0	2.5	0.4	27.5	9.0	0.3	1.1	14.0	258.0
Fruit Group	77.3	0.5	0.1	0.1	0.1	0.1	0.9	0.3	0.1	18.8	4.3
Vegetable Group	144.1	5.0	1.3	1.7	1.7	4.6	3.7	1.4	0.6	23.0	488.2
Fats/Oils/Sweets	233.6	10.0	3.2	3.0	3.2	7.1	1.3	0.4	0.3	34.0	226.8

Source: Selected from "Specific Daily Nutrient Intake by Women and Men," *Eating in America Today: A Dietary Pattern and Intake Report/Edition II (EAT II)*, commissioned by the National Live Stock and Meat Board, p. 36. Nutrient intake data were calculated by MRCA Information Services, Inc. Nutrient Intake Database (NID). The NID uses the "1987-88 USDA Nutrient Database for Food Intake" Survey Release 5 for determining nutrient intake. For recently introduced foods or foods not included, the USDA database was supplemented with manufacturers' information. *Note:* 1. .05 or less.

★ 403 ★

Dietary and Health Practices

Dietary Consumption and Perceived Consumption

This table shows what adult females actually eat by food group and how much they think they eat. Data were gathered from 2,000 households for the National Live Stock and Meat Board.

Food Group	Servings		
	Actual consumption	Perceived consumption	Recommended consumption
Fats, oils, sweets	3.2	1.8	use sparingly
Milk, yogurt, cheese	1.0	2.3	2-3
Meat, fish, dry beans etc.	1.9	2.8	2-3
Vegetables	2.0	2.4	3-5
Fruits	1.0	2.3	2-4
Bread, cereal, rice, pasta	4.6	2.7	6-11

Source: "Women's and Men's Diets Compared to the Pyramid," *Eating in America Today: A Dietary Pattern and Intake Report/Edition II (EAT II)*, commissioned by the National Live Stock and Meat Board, p. 5. Primary source: MRCA Information Services.

★ 404 ★

Dietary and Health Practices

Dieting, Bulimia, and Substance Abuse

Researchers distributed a self-administered questionnaire that was completed by 1,796 women prior to their freshman year in college. Respondents were divided into categories of dieting: nondieters, casual, intense, severe, at-risk, or bulimic dieters. Only 13.8% of the women were nondieters. Bulimia nervosa criteria were met by 1.6% of the women. The relationship between dieting severity and the frequency and intensity of alcohol use and the frequency of marijuana and cigarette use was assessed. Bulimic and at-risk dieters were found to be similar in their alcohol and drug use. Researchers concluded that dieting-related attitudes and behaviors in young women may be related to increased susceptibility to alcohol and drug abuse. This table shows the prevalence of drinking alcohol and smoking cigarettes and marijuana in the past month by dieting-severity categories for the women in the study.

Dieting-Severity Categories	Prevalence in last month		
	Alcohol	Smoking	Marijuana
Bulimic	72.0%	20.7%	14.8%
At-Risk	71.7%	18.6%	9.7%
Severe	65.0%	11.8%	7.2%
Intense	61.8%	15.7%	5.3%
Casual	57.7%	9.5%	5.4%
Nondieting	43.9%	4.9%	6.8%

Source: Selected from "Prevalence of Drinking Alcohol, Bivariate Odds Ratios and 95% Confidence Intervals for Past Month's Drinking," "Prevalence of Smoking in Past Month, Bivariate Odds Ratios and 95% Confidence Intervals," and "Prevalence of Marijuana Use in Past Month, Bivariate Odds Ratios and 95% Confidence Intervals," Dean Krahn, Candace Kurth, Mark Demitrack et al., "The Relationship of Dieting Severity and Bulimic Behaviors to Alcohol and Other Drug Use in Young Women," *Journal of Substance Abuse*, 4, 341-353 (1992), Table 2, p. 345, Table 3, p. 347, and Table 4, p. 348. Correspondence and requests for reprints should be sent to Dean Krahn, William S. Middleton Memorial veterans Hospital, 2500 Overlook Terrace, Madison, WI 53705.

★ 405 ★

Dietary and Health Practices

Protein Intake

This table gives statistics about American adults' protein intake. Data were gathered from 2,000 households for the National Live Stock and Meat Board.

Item	Number/Percent
Average daily protein consumption:	
Men	79 grams
Women	59 grams
Number of calories gotten from protein daily:	
Men	17%

[Continued]

★ 405 ★

Protein Intake
[Continued]

Item	Number/Percent
Women	16%
Recommended intake	10-20%
Amount of protein gotten from the Meat Group daily:	
Men	46 grams
Women	32 grams
Amount of protein gotten from the Milk and Bread groups daily, combined:	
Men	26 grams
Women	20 grams

Source: Selected from "Study Measures Protein Intake," *Eating in America Today: A Dietary Pattern and Intake Report/Edition II (EAT II),* December 1994 news release from a study commissioned by the National Live Stock and Meat Board. Primary source: MRCA Information Services.

★ 406 ★
Dietary and Health Practices

Teenage Girls and Exercise

The New York Times reports on the national increase in inactivity among all age groups, and the fact that it seems especially pronounced among teen-age girls. The article cites a number of studies to support this contention. This table shows some of the figures cited. The study also found a correlation between economic class and lack of exercise. Black girls and children who lived in poor neighborhoods were at greatest risk from lack of exercise.

Item	Number/Percent
Centers for Disease Control and Prevention (CDC) estimate of percentage of teenagers who exercise vigorously on a regular basis:	
Girls	25%
Boys	50%
In a CDC 1990 survey of 11,000 students, percentage of ninth-graders who participated in 20 minutes of vigorous activity 3 times a week:	
Girls	35%
Boys	53%
Percentage of twelfth-graders:	
Girls	25%

[Continued]

★ 406 ★

Teenage Girls and Exercise
[Continued]

Item	Number/Percent
Boys	50%
Percentage of female high school students who went to a gym class every day:	19%
CDC report on the percentage of female high school seniors who smoked every day, often using cigarettes as a weight control tool (1993):	18%

Source: Selected from Jennifer Steinhauer, "Teen-Age Girls Talk Back on Exercise," *The New York Times*, January 4, 1995, p. B1-B4 Y.

★ 407 ★

Dietary and Health Practices

Thinking About Food: 1994

This table shows the percent of adults aged 18 and older who agreed with selected statements about food in 1994.

Food belief	Women			Men		
	18-34 yrs.	35-54 yrs.	55+	18-34 yrs.	35-54 yrs.	55+
Eating out						
Order nutritious food	82%	91%	85%	72%	82%	78%
Look for low-fat food	35%	46%	56%	24%	38%	42%
Attitudes						
Prefer broiled to fried foods	55%	70%	72%	43%	51%	58%
Eat anything anytime	41%	40%	47%	58%	54%	46%
Nutritious foods don't taste good	26%	33%	42%	30%	27%	27%
Self-described "meat-and-potatoes" person	35%	32%	34%	62%	56%	40%
Tired of nutrition news	36%	42%	54%	44%	42%	55%

Source: "Thoughts of Food," *The Numbers News*, March 1995, p. 2. Primary source: National Restaurant Association, from *Table Service Restaurant Trends*. National Restaurant Association, 1200 17th Street, NW, Washington, DC 20036; telephone (800)424-5156.

Health Care Coverage

★ 408 ★

Coverage and Death Rates

This table shows age-adjusted death rates per 10,000 person-years and the ratio of death rates in health insurance categories relative to those with employer insurance. In the study there were 147,779 persons aged 25 to 64 years who contributed more than 600,000 person-years for analysis of mortality by health insurance. Death rates in this sample were high for those with Medicare, probably reflecting the nature of the Medicare population at these ages (that is, eligibility for Medicare under age 65 years is related to documented end-stage renal disease or long-term disability). The next highest death rates were in the Medicaid populations. Those with no health insurance had higher mortality than those with employer health insurance.

Health Insurance	White Men		White Women		Black Men		Black Women	
	Rate	Ratio[1]	Rate	Ratio[1]	Rate	Ratio[1]	Rate	Ratio[1]
Employer	36	1.0	21	1.0	52	1.0	35	1.0
Medicare	135	3.8	74	3.5	153	2.9	85	2.4
Medicaid	126	3.5	54	2.6	145	2.8	84	2.4
Military	56	1.6	20	1.0	116	2.2	[2]	[2]
Other	38	1.1	25	1.2	66	1.3	58	1.7
None	56	1.6	36	1.7	85	1.6	39	1.1

Source: Selected from Paul D. Sorlie, PhD, Norman J. Johnson, PhD, Eric Backlund, MS, et al., "Mortality in the Uninsured Compared with that in Persons with Public and Private Health Insurance," *Arch Intern Med,* Vol. 154, November 14, 1994, pp. 2409-2416, Table 2, p. 2411, "Age-Adjusted Death Rates per 10,000, Confidence Intervals, and Ratios[1] by Health Insurance, Sex, and Race for Persons Aged 25 to 64 Years in the NLMS." The NLMS is a study of mortality occurring during the years 1979 through 1987 in combined samples of the noninstitutionalized U.S. population. Address correspondence to National Heart, Lung, and Blood Institute, Federal Bldg., Room 3A10, Bethesda, MD 20892 (Dr. Sorlie). *Notes:* 1. Ratio of age-adjusted death rate in insurance groups relative to employer group. 2. Less than 10 deaths in this category.

★ 409 ★

Health Care Coverage

Coverage and Risk of Dying

This table shows the risk of mortality for those with each health insurance plan shown relative to those with employer-provided health insurance, for persons aged 25 to 64 years. Compared with persons with employer-based insurance, people with Medicare or Medicaid had higher death rates after adjustment for income differences. Men, but not women, with military insurance had higher death rates. After adjustment for differences in income, those with no insurance had higher death rates than those with employer-based insurance in three of the four sex-race groups.

[RR = Relative risk.]

Health Insurance	White Men RR	White Women RR	Black Men RR	Black Women RR
Employer	1.0	1.0	1.0	1.0
Medicare	2.7	2.9	2.7	1.6
Medicaid	2.4	2.1	2.4	1.9
Military	1.6	1.1	2.1	[1]
Other	1.0	1.1	1.4	1.5
None	1.2	1.5	1.5	0.8

Source: Selected from Paul D. Sorlie, PhD, Norman J. Johnson, PhD, Eric Backlund, MS, et al., "Mortality in the Uninsured Compared with that in Persons with Public and Private Health Insurance," *Arch Intern Med*, Vol. 154, November 14, 1994, pp. 2409-2416, Table 4, p. 2413, "Risk of Mortality for Those with Each Health Insurance Plan Relative to Those with Employer-Provided Health Insruance, Adjusted for Age and Income, for Persons Aged 25 to 64 Years in the NLMS." The NLMS is a study of mortality occurring during the years 1979 through 1987 in combined samples of the noninstitutionalized U.S. population. Relative risk was estimated by Cox proportional hazards model. Address correspondence to National Heart, Lung, and Blood Institute, Federal Bldg., Room 3A10, Bethesda, MD 20892 (Dr. Sorlie). *Note:* 1. Less than 10 deaths in this category.

★ 410 ★

Health Care Coverage

Coverage for Persons Aged 25 to 64

This table shows the distribution of health insurance coverage for men and women aged 25 to 64 years, by race, in the National Longitudinal Mortality Study. Data from that survey were used to show that persons with no insurance or with Medicare and Medicaid had higher mortality rates than those with employer-provided insurance.

Provider	Men		Women	
	White	Black	White	Black
Employer	72.3%	62.1%	68.5%	54.1%
Medicare	2.1%	3.4%	1.7%	3.3%
Medicaid	1.8%	5.4%	4.2%	17.9%
Military	3.1%	4.8%	2.4%	1.6%
Other	8.8%	4.5%	11.1%	5.2%

[Continued]

★ 410 ★

Coverage for Persons Aged 25 to 64
[Continued]

Provider	Men		Women	
	White	Black	White	Black
None	12.0%	19.8%	12.0%	17.9%
No. of persons	65,326	5,766	68,983	7,704

Source: Selected from Paul D. Sorlie, PhD, Norman J. Johnson, PhD, Eric Backlund, MS, et al., "Mortality in the Uninsured Compared with that in Persons with Public and Private Health Insurance," *Arch Intern Med*, Vol. 154, November 14, 1994, pp. 2409-2416, Table 1, p. 2410, "Distribution of Health Insurance Coverage for Men and Women Aged 25 to 64 Years by Race in the NLMS." The NLMS is a study of mortality occurring during the years 1979 through 1987 in combined samples of the noninstitutionalized U.S. population. Address correspondence to National Heart, Lung, and Blood Institute, Federal Bldg., Room 3A10, Bethesda, MD 20892 (Dr. Sorlie).

★ 411 ★

Health Care Coverage

Coverage: 1990-1992

This table shows statistics on percentages of people who were covered by health insurance over time up to a 32-month period. Between 1990 and 1992, 75% of all people had continuous health insurance coverage over the entire 32-month period. Twenty-five percent lacked health insurance for at least 1 month. Women were more likely than men to have continuous health insurance coverage. They are more likely than men to live in families with incomes below poverty,[1] and are more likely to take part in means-tested assistance programs [2]like Medicaid. Another factor is age. More women are 65 years old and over and nearly everyone in that age group is covered by Medicare.

Health insurance coverage	Both sexes	Male	Female
All persons (thousands)	235,811	113,681	122,131
Percent	100.0%	100.0%	100.0%
Percent distribution			
Covered by private or government health insurance:			
Less than 32 months	25.3%	26.6%	24.0%
No months	3.8%	4.3%	3.3%
1 to 6 months	2.4%	2.7%	2.2%
7 to 12 months	3.0%	3.1%	2.9%
13 to 18 months	2.7%	2.8%	2.6%
19 to 24 months	4.8%	4.7%	4.8%
25 to 30 months	7.5%	7.8%	7.1%
31 months	1.1%	1.1%	1.1%
32 months	74.7%	73.4%	76.0%
Covered by private health insurance:			
Less than 32 months	35.4%	34.8%	35.9%

[Continued]

★ 411 ★

Coverage: 1990-1992
[Continued]

Health insurance coverage	Both sexes	Male	Female
No months	11.6%	10.7%	12.4%
1 to 6 months	3.6%	3.7%	3.6%
7 to 12 months	3.7%	3.7%	3.7%
13 to 18 months	2.7%	2.8%	2.6%
19 to 24 months	4.9%	4.9%	4.9%
25 to 30 months	7.9%	8.0%	7.7%
31 months	1.0%	1.0%	0.9%
32 months	64.6%	65.2%	64.1%
Covered by Medicaid:			
Less than 32 months	95.3%	96.7%	94.1%
No months	87.7%	90.3%	85.3%
1 to 6 months	2.5%	2.2%	2.8%
7 to 12 months	1.8%	1.4%	2.1%
13 to 18 months	0.9%	0.7%	1.1%
19 to 24 months	1.1%	1.0%	1.3%
25 to 30 months	1.1%	1.0%	1.2%
31 months	-	-	-
32 months	4.7%	3.3%	5.9%

Source: Selected from "All Persons, by Sex, Race, Hispanic Origin, and Health Insurance Coverage: 1990 to 1992," U.S. Bureau of the Census, Current Population Reports, P70-37, Table B, p. 5. *Notes:* 1. In 1992 the official poverty rate was 12.7% for males and 16.3% for females. 2. From the 1990 Survey of Income and Program Participation panel file, 20.7% of all females participated in means-tested public assistance programs, compared with 15.9% of all males.

★ 412 ★

Health Care Coverage

Health Service Usage by Insurance Status

This table shows the percentage of midlife women who use various medical services by whether they are insured or uninsured.

[Midlife are persons aged 45 to 64.]

Type of service	Uninsured	Insured
Physician services	60.8%	83.3%
Hospital outpatient	10.8%	26.1%
Hospital stay	6.0%	11.9%
Prescribed medicine	58.6%	73.5%
Home health care	0.6%	2.7%
At least one service	76.3%	91.9%

Source: "Midlife Women Who Use Services by Insurance Status," American Association of Retired Persons Fact Sheet, *Health Insurance Status of Midlife Women*, Chart 9, p. 6. Primary source: 1987 National Medical Expenditure Survey. Projected forward using medical CPI.

Health Care Personnel/Institution Contacts

★ 413 ★

Hospital Utilization: 1970-1992

This table shows the number of patients discharged in thousands, the total, male, and female patients discharged per 1,000 persons[1], the total, and male and female days of care per 1,000 persons, and the average stay, for the years 1970-1992.

[Patients discharged in thousands.]

Selected characteristic	Patients discharged	Patients discharged per 1,000 persons[1]			Days of care per 1,000 persons[1]			Average stay (days)		
		Total	Male	Female	Total	Male	Female	Total	Male	Female
1970	29,127	144	118	169	1,122	982	1,251	8.0	8.7	7.6
1980	37,832	168	139	194	1,217	1,068	1,356	7.3	7.7	7.0
1985	35,056	148	124	171	954	849	1,053	6.5	6.9	6.2
1986	34,256	143	121	164	913	817	1,003	6.4	6.9	6.1
1987	33,387	138	116	159	889	806	968	6.4	6.9	6.1
1988[2]	31,146	128	107	147	834	757	907	6.5	7.1	6.2
1989[2]	30,947	126	105	145	815	741	884	6.5	7.0	6.1
1990[2]	30,788	124	102	144	792	704	875	6.4	6.9	6.1
1991[2]	31,098	124	103	144	795	715	869	6.4	7.0	6.0
1992,[2] total	30,951	122	101	142	751	680	818	6.2	6.7	5.8
Age:										
Under 1 year	822	206	232	179	1,292	1,531	1,041	6.3	6.6	5.8
1 to 4 years	806	52	58	46	185	200	170	3.6	3.5	3.7
5 to 14 years	904	25	26	24	117	120	114	4.7	4.6	4.8
15 to 24 years	3,287	93	40	146	333	220	448	3.6	5.5	3.1
25 to 34 years	4,615	110	53	166	461	346	574	4.2	6.5	3.5
35 to 44 years	3,325	84	69	99	443	410	475	5.3	6.0	4.8
45 to 64 years	6,329	131	135	128	827	863	794	6.3	6.4	6.2
65 to 74 years	4,883	265	293	242	2,041	2,240	1,885	7.7	7.6	7.8
75 years and over	5,981	433	470	412	3,748	3,929	3,648	8.7	8.4	8.9

Source: Selected from "Hospital Utilization Rates: 1970 to 1992," U.S. Bureau of the Census, *Statistical Abstract of the United States 1994*, Table 185, p. 128. Primary source: U.S. National Center for Health Statistics, *Vital and Health Statistics*, series 13; and unpublished data. *Notes:* 1. Based on Bureau of the Census estimated civilian population as of July 1. Estimates for 1980-90 do not reflect revisions based on the 1990 Census of Population. 2. Comparisons beginning 1988 with data for earlier years should be made with caution as estimates of change may reflect improvements in the design rather than true changes in hospital use.

★ 414 ★

Health Care Personnel/Institution Contacts

Physician and Dental Visits: 1970-1992

This table shows the total visits in millions paid by males and females to physicians and dentists and the number of visits per year for various years ranging from 1970-1992.

[Total visits in millions.]

Type of visit and year	Total visits		Visits per person per year	
	Male	Female	Male	Female
Physicians				
1970	396	531	4.1	5.1
1980	426	610	4.0	5.4
1983	470	694	4.3	5.8
1985	498	733	4.4	6.1
1986	515	756	4.5	6.2
1987	523	765	4.5	6.2
1988	530	774	4.5	6.2
1989	552	771	4.7	6.1
1990	558	806	4.7	6.4
1991	589	842	4.9	6.6
1992	624	889	5.1	6.9
Dentists				
1970	133	171	1.4	1.7
1980	158	207	1.5	1.8
1983	183	239	1.6	2.0
1986	210	256	1.9	2.2
1989	221	271	1.9	2.2

Source: Selected from "Physician and Dental Contacts, by Patient Characteristics: 1970 to 1992," U.S. Bureau of the Census, *Statistical Abstract of the United States 1994,* Table 174, p. 122. Primary source: U.S. National Center for Health Statistics, *Vital and Health Statistics,* series 10, No. 189, and earlier reports; and unpublished data.

HIV/AIDS

★ 415 ★

AIDS Cases and the Drug Epidemic

This table shows statistics presented in *The New York Times*, based on an unpublished analysis by researchers at the Federal Centers for Disease Control and Prevention, on the relationship of the AIDS epidemic to the drug epidemic.

Item	Number/Percent
Fraction of the 40,000 new infections with HIV in 1994 that were among drug addicts	Nearly 3/4
Of those newly diagnosed with AIDS in 1993, percent who were:	
gay men	About 1/2
intravenous drug users	Nearly 1/4
Of those infected with HIV in 1994, fraction who were:	
gay men	1/4
drug users who shared needles	About 1/2
heterosexually transmitted	About 1/4
Percent of people getting HIV infections through heterosexual transmission who were women (1994)	70-80%

Source: Gina Kolata, "New Picture of Who Will Get AIDS Is Crammed with Addicts," *The New York Times*, February 28, 1995, p. B6 Y. Primary source: Centers for Disease Control and Prevention.

★ 416 ★

HIV/AIDS

AIDS Cases by Transmission Category

This table shows the number of AIDS cases reported for females age 13 and over and their percent distribution by means of transmission of AIDS, for the years 1985 through 1992.

[Based on reporting by State health departments.]

Transmission category	Percent distribution	Number, by year of report								
		All years[1]	1985	1986	1987	1988	1989	1990	1991	1992
Female AIDS cases	100.0%	25,928	526	962	1,684	3,040	3,374	4,552	5,378	5,940
Injecting drug use	49.8%	12,925	284	477	840	1,630	1,771	2,260	2,683	2,701
Hemophilia, coagulation disorder	0.2%	43	1	4	4	4	6	9	8	3
Born in Caribbean/ African countries	3.4%	885	31	56	74	108	130	111	167	170
Heterosexual contact[2]	31.8%	8,236	116	276	486	861	1,003	1,499	1,826	2,092
Sex with injecting drug user	20.7%	5,374	82	193	330	634	694	1,019	1,160	1,207
Transfusion[3]	7.1%	1,848	60	105	217	322	284	324	239	263
Undetermined[4]	7.7%	1,991	34	44	63	115	180	349	455	711

Source: Selected from "Acquired immunodeficiency syndrome (AIDS) cases, according to race, Hispanic origin, sex, and transmission category for persons 13 years of age and over at diagnosis: United States, 1985-92," U.S. Department of Health and Human Services, *Health United States 1992*, Table 55, p. 91-92. Primary source: Centers for Disease Control and Prevention, National Center for Infectious Diseases, Division of HIV/AIDS. *Notes:* 1. Includes cases prior to 1985. 2. Includes persons who have had heterosexual contact with a person with human immunodeficiency virus (HIV) infection or at risk of HIV infection. 3. Receipt of blood transfusion, blood components, or tissue. 4. Includes persons for whom risk information is incomplete (because of death, refusal to be interviewed, or loss to followup), persons still under investigation, and interviewed persons for whom no specific risk is identified.

★ 417 ★

HIV/AIDS

AIDS Cases Reported: 1981-1992

This table shows the number of AIDS cases reported and their percent distribution by sex for the years 1981 through 1992.

[Provisional figures.]

Characteristic	Number of Cases									Percent distribution	
	Total	1981-1986	1986	1987	1988	1989	1990	1991	1992	1981-1985	1992
Total	244,939	15,564	13,147	21,088	30,719	33,595	41,653	43,701	45,472	100.0%	100.0%
Male	217,141	14,466	12,099	19,256	27,435	29,942	36,770	38,013	39,160	92.9%	86.1%
Female	27,798	1,098	1,048	1,832	3,264	3,653	4,883	5,688	6,312	7.1%	13.9%

Source: Selected from "AIDS Cases Reported, by Patient Characteristic: 1981 to 1992," U.S. Bureau of the Census, *Statistical Abstract of the United States 1994*, Table 206, p. 139. Primary source: U.S. Centers for Disease Control and Prevention, Atlanta, GA; unpublished data.

★ 418 ★

HIV/AIDS

AIDS Tests for Pregnant Women

The U.S. Government proposed in February 1995 that doctors counsel all pregnant women about AIDS and urged that they be tested for the AIDS virus. The figures in this table were cited as reasons.

Item	Number/Percent
Number of women who become pregnant each year	4,000,000
Number infected with HIV	7,000
Estimate of number of hetero-sexual women of childbearing age who have HIV	80,000
Cost of HIV test	$25
Number of babies born each year with HIV	2,000

Source: "AIDS Tests Urged for All Pregnant Women," *The New York Times*, February 23, 1995, p. A11 Y. Primary source: Centers for Disease Control and Prevention.

★ 419 ★

HIV/AIDS

AIDS Virus Infections Worldwide: 1989

This table shows estimates of the numbers of persons infected with AIDS in 1989.

Country	Estimated number infected persons		
	Total	Ratio of f to m	Infected females
Northern America, western Europe, Australia and New Zealand; some Latin America and Caribbean	< 3 million	1 to 9	0.3 million
Sub-Saharan Africa; some Latin America and Caribbean	> 3 million	About 1 to 1	> 1.5 million

[Continued]

★ 419 ★

AIDS Virus Infections Worldwide: 1989
[Continued]

Country	Estimated number infected persons		
	Total	Ratio of f to m	Infected females
Eastern Europe; northern Africa and eastern Mediterranean; Asia and Pacific	0.1 million	1 to 2	33,000
Total	6 million+	1 to 3	2 million+

Source: Selected from "Estimated numbers of infected persons," *The World's Women: Trends and Statistics 1970-1990*, United Nations, 1991, Table 4.12 A., p. 63. Primary source: World Health Organization, Global Programme on AIDS, Surveillance, Forcasting and Impact Assessment Unit, 1989 and 1990.

★ 420 ★

HIV/AIDS

Characteristics of Women at Risk for HIV Infection

The National AIDS Demonstration Research (NADR) program, coordinated by the National Institute on Drug Abuse, was launched in 1987 to "test the efficacy of strategies for reaching and intervening with two populations at significant risk for contracting and transmitting HIV—injection drug users (IDUs) and the sexual partners of IDUs." By March 28, 1990, data had been collected from 5,192 women. This table shows some of the characteristics of these women.

Characteristics	IDUs N=3,272	non-IDUs N=1,913
Age		
29	36%	58%
30-39	52%	32%
40	13%	10%
Ethnicity		
White	33%	11%
Black	48%	66%
Hispanic	19%	23%
Children Under 18		
Living with parents	35%	48%
Not living with parents	45%	35%
Daily non-injection drug use		
Cocaine	25%	26%
Alcohol	28%	19%
Marijuana	15%	13%

[Continued]

★ 420 ★

Characteristics of Women at Risk for HIV Infection
[Continued]

Characteristics	IDUs N=3,272	non-IDUs N=1,913
Trade sex for drugs/money		
Yes	42%	30%
No	58%	70%
STDs in past six months		
Yes	11%	11%
No	89%	89%
Ever in formal drug treatment		
Yes	65%	25%
No	35%	73%

Source: "Characteristics of Women at Risk for HIV Infection (in Percentages," Gloria Weissman and the National AIDS Research Consortium (NARC), "AIDS Prevention for Women at Risk: Experience from a National Demonstration Research Program," *The Journal of Primary Prevention*, Vol 12(1), 1991, pp. 49-63, Table I, p. 57. Address correspondence to Gloria Weissman, National Institute on Drug Abuse, 5600 Fishers Lane, Room 9A42, Rockville, MD 29857.

★ 421 ★

HIV/AIDS

HIV Positive Prison Inmates: 1991

This table shows the percentage of State prison inmates who tested positive for the human immunodeficiency virus (HIV) in 1991 and the percentage of HIV positive inmates who had ever used a needle. Women were more likely than men to test positive (3.3% compared to 2.1% of men).

Group	Percent of inmates who tested HIV positive	
	All	Ever used a needle
Female	3.3%	6.7%
White	1.9%	3.9%
Black	3.5%	8.3%
Hispanic	6.8%	11.6%
Male	2.1%	4.7%

Source: Tracy L. Snell, "Survey of State Prison Inmates, 1991: Women in Prison," *Bureau of Justice Statistics Special Report*, March 1994, p. 9. Female includes Asians, Pacific Islanders, American Indians, Alaska Natives, and other racial groups.

★ 422 ★

HIV/AIDS

HIV Prevalence in 14 Countries

Nearly 211,000 AIDS cases were reported to the World Health Organization (WHO) from Sub-Saharan Africa by the end of 1992. WHO estimated that a cumulative total of 1.75 million people in the region had developed AIDS. In mid-1993, WHO estimated that more than 8 million people in Sub-Saharan Africa were HIV infected. This represents more than half of all HIV infections in the world. HIV infections in Sub-Saharan Africa occur through heterosexual contact. In order to track HIV infection around the world, the U.S. Bureau of the Census maintains an HIV/AIDS Surveillance Data Base. It contains a compilation of aggregate data from HIV seroprevalence studies in developing countries. The data base is updated biannually into a summary table, which lists the most recent and best available study of seroprevalence levels for high- and low-risk populations in urban and rural areas.[1] It was determined that a reasonable cut-off point for selection of countries to be included in the data base would be those with 5% HIV prevalence among their low-risk urban populations. A total of 14 countries met the 5% criterion. All but one of those countries was in Africa (Haiti was the exception). This table shows the HIV seroprevalence levels for these 14 countries at the beginning of the study and later. This information is being developed in an effort to understand the dynamics of AIDS epidemics and to anticipate their future course.

[NA Data not available.]

| Country | Urban pregnant women | | | | Rural adults | | Estimated total country Percent |
| | Earlier | | Later | | | | |
	Year[2]	Percent	Year[2]	Percent	Year[2]	Percent	
Burkina	1986	1.7%	1991	6.0%	1989	3.8%	3.9%
Burundi	1986	16.3%	1988	17.5%	1988	6.0%	8.3%
Central African Republic	1986	4.7%	1989	8.0%	1988	3.0%	3.8%
Congo	1990	7.7%	1991	9.0%	1989	3.5%	3.8%
Cote d'Ivoire	1987	8.0%	1991	10.5%	1989	2.8%	3.7%
Haiti	1986	8.4%	1988	10.3%	1986	3.0%	4.1%
Kenya	1991	13.0%	1992	15.0%	1989	3.2%	4.5%
Malawi	1989	20.1%	1990	22.8%	1989	4.0%	7.8%
Rwanda	1989	23.2%	1990	26.2%	1990	10.2%	13.7%
Tanzania	1988	10.6%	1991	16.3%	1987	4.5%	5.5%
Uganda	1985	10.7%	1992	29.5%	1989	13.4%	15.9%
Zaire	1985	6.9%	1988	8.0%	1988	2.2%	2.9%
Zambia	1987	11.6%	1990	24.5%	1990	15.0%	17.4%
Zimbabwe	NA	NA	1990	18.0%	1990	12.8%	13.8%

Source: "Empirical Seroprevalence Data for Selected Countries by Urban/Rural Residence," U.S. Bureau of the Census, *World Population Profile: 1994*, 1994, Table B-1, p. B-6. Primary source: Urban and rural data from HIV/AIDS Surveillance Data Base, Center for International Research, U.S. Bureau of the Census, 1993. *Notes:* 1. High risk includes samples of commercial sex workers and their clients, sexually-transmitted disease patients, or other persons with known risk factors. Low risk includes samples of pregnant women, volunteer blood donors, or others with no known risk factors. 2. Data pertain to varying months of the years indicated.

★ 423 ★

HIV/AIDS

HIV Risk Among Drug-Injecting Lesbians and Bisexual Women

Data on the HIV risks of lesbian/bisexual injection-drug users (IDUs) is limited, according to the authors of a study in *AIDS & Public Policy Journal* (1992). The Association for Women's AIDS Research and Education (AWARE) is a research program that has been assessing HIV infection risk from drug use and sexual behavior in San Francisco and Alameda counties. Since 1988, 711 women have participated in the project. This table shows some of the characteristics of these women.

Item	Number/Percent
Demographics	
Race/Ethnicity	
Of the 711 women who participated in the study between 1988-1992, percent who are:	
Black	69%
White	21%
Latina	6%
Other	4%
Age	
Under age 25	17%
Between 25 and 35	56%
More than 35	27%
Percentage of the women in the study who have used drugs, including alcohol, during the three years prior to entry in the program[1]	99.7%
Injected drugs	41%
Crack cocaine	32%
Sexual Behaviors	
Self-descriptions:	
Exclusively heterosexual	76%
Exclusively homosexual	3%
A combination	21%
HIV Risk Practices	
Of the 329 women who had had one or more female sexual partners since 1980, percent who had injected drugs during that time period	76%

[Continued]

★ 423 ★

HIV Risk Among Drug-Injecting Lesbians and Bisexual Women

[Continued]

Item	Number/Percent
No female partners	42%
Of the women who had had at least one female sexual partner in the three years prior to entry to the program, percent who had engaged in anal intercourse with a male partner	33%
No female partners	19%
Percent of self-identified lesbians who were HIV seropositive	15%
Self-identified bisexuals	13%
Self-identified heterosexual	11%

Source: Selected from Rebecca M. Young, Gloria Weissman, and Judith B. Cohen, "Assessing Risk in the Absence of Information: HIV Risk Among Women Injection-Drug Users Who Have Sex with Women," *AIDS & Public Policy Journal*, Fall 1992, Vol. 7, No. 3, pp. 175-183. *Note:* 1. With most reporting more than one kind of drug use.

★ 424 ★

HIV/AIDS

Maternal-Infant HIV Transmission

The New York Times reported on a Federal study on AIDS in babies "whose results were so stunning that it was halted prematurely and its results were announced...to great fanfare." The study involved 477 pregnant women infected with HIV. Half of the women were given the AIDS drug AZT and the other half received a placebo. This table shows some of the results of the study and cites other statistics from *The New York Times* article.

Item	Number/Percent
Percent of babies born to women who took AZT who were infected with HIV	8.3%
Percent of babies born to women who took the placebo who were infected with HIV	25.5%
Number of times per day during the last 6 months of pregnancy a woman must take AZT to prevent her baby from being infected with HIV	5

[Continued]

★ 424 ★

Maternal-Infant HIV Transmission

[Continued]

Item	Number/Percent
Federal health officials' estimate of the number of HIV-infected babies born in the U.S. annually	1,000-2,000

Source: Gina Kolata, "Debate on Infant AIDS vs. Mother's Rights," *The New York Times,* November 3, 1994, p. A13 Y. Primary source: Edward M. Connor, M.D., Rhoda S. Sperling, M.D., Richard Gelber, PhD., et al., "Reduction of Maternal-Infant Transmission of Human Immunodeficiency Virus Type 1 with Zidovudine Treatment, *The New England Journal of Medicine,* 331(18), November 3, 1994, pp. 1173-1179. Address reprint requests to Dr. Connor at MedImmune, Inc., 35 W. Watkins Mill Rd., Gaithersburg, MD 20878.

Mental Health

★ 425 ★

Behaviors Associated with a History of Childhood Sexual Abuse

The authors of this study report that estimates indicate the possibility that 30% of adults have experienced sexual assault in childhood. Subjects were enrolled in a study to investigate the causes of transmission of HIV. The investigators identified current behaviors affecting the risk of HIV infection that were associated with a history of early sexual abuse. Of the 186 individuals enrolled, about 28% of the women and 15% of the men reported a history of childhood sexual assault. This table shows behaviors associated with a history of childhood sexual abuse that place the individuals at risk for HIV infection. Survivors were four times more likely to report having engaged in prostitution.

Behavior	Childhood Sexual Abuse							
	Women			Men			Overall	
	Yes (N=29)	No (N=54)	Prev. Ratio	Yes (N=12)	No (N=69)	Prev. Ratio	Prev. ratio (MH)[1]	90% confidence interval
Prostitution	6	4	2.8	4	3	7.6	4.0	(2.0,8.0)
IV drug use[2]	8	13	1.2	6	32	1.2	1.2	(.78,1.8)
Average yearly sexual partners (more than 2 vs 2 or fewer)	15	16	1.7	10	24	2.4	2.0	(1.4,2.8)
Never/rarely use condom in last year[3]	21	36	1.0	5	41	0.8	1.0	(.76,1.2)
Sex with strangers[4]	23	28	1.5	10	52	1.2	1.4	(1.1,1.6)

[Continued]

★ 425 ★

Behaviors Associated with a History of Childhood Sexual Abuse
[Continued]

Behavior	Childhood Sexual Abuse							
	Women			Men			Overall	
	Yes (N=29)	No (N=54)	Prev. Ratio	Yes (N=12)	No (N=69)	Prev. Ratio	Prev. ratio (MH)[1]	90% confidence interval
Education (less than high school vs high school or more)	9	5	3.4	2	15	0.8	1.9	(1.0,3.5)
Pregnancy before 18 years old	18	13	2.6	X	X	X	2.6	(1.6,4.1)

Source: Selected from Sally Zierler, DrPH, Lisa Feingold, MSPH, Deborah Laufer, MSPH, et al., "Adult Survivors of Childhood Sexual Abuse and Subsequent Risk of HIV Infection," *American Journal of Public Health,* May 1991, Vol. 81(5), pp. 572-575, p. 574, Table 3, "Behaviors Associated with a History of Childhood Sexual Abuse." Address reprint requests to Sally Zierler, DrPH, Department of Community Health, Brown University, Box G-A405, Providence, RI 02912. *Notes:* 1. Mantel-Haenszel estimates of prevalence ratios pooled over gender strata. 2. One woman and one man with history of child sexual abuse were deleted from analysis because temporal sequence of age of sexual abuse and age of IV drug use not specified. 3. Four sexually inactive individuals deleted from analysis. 4. Eight individuals deleted due to missing data.

★ 426 ★

Mental Health

Effects of Incest

A group of 57 girls aged 8 to 14 years was studied. All were from dysfunctional families and half had experienced incest. The Child Behaviour Check List (CBCL)[1], the Piers-Harris Self-Esteem measure[2] and the Harter and Pike Self-Competence Scale[3] were completed, as were questionnaires. The children were interviewed and their dossiers analyzed. There were no differences between the two samples on the CBCL, but the girls who had experienced incest showed greatly lowered self-esteem, troubled relations with their mothers, more sexualized attitudes and behaviors, and more inward-turned aggression than girls from equally dysfunctional families who had not experienced incest. This table shows the mean scores of the two groups.

[T = tendency, NS = Not significant.]

Measures	Group I (Incest)	Group C (Comparison)	Level of Significance
Global CBCL	>63	>63	NS
Self-Esteem			
Harter & Pike	81.07	88.27	[4]
Piers Harris	47.92	53.93	[4]
Children interview	17.28	19.21	T
Dossiers	1.14	1.65	[5]
Sexualization			
Children interview	9.83	9.03	NS
Clinician's questionnaire	16.93	14.55	[4]
Dossiers	2.29	0.55	[5]
Aggressivity			
Children interview	7.96	5.83	[4]
Clinician's questionnaire	6.68	5.93	[4]

[Continued]

★ 426 ★

Effects of Incest
[Continued]

Measures	Group I (Incest)	Group C (Comparison)	Level of Significance
Dossiers	2.21	0.52	5
Mother-Daughter Relationship			
Harter & Pike	13.68	16.03	4
Children interview	2.55	3.59	5

Source: Jean-Pierre Hotte and Sandra Rafman, "The Specific Effects of Incest on Prepubertal Girls from Dysfunctional Families," *Child Abuse & Neglect*, Vol 16, pp. 273-283, 1992, p. 280, Table 1, "Mean Scores of Group 1 and Group C on Global and Specific Measures." Requests for reprints may be sent to Jean-Pierre Hotte, Carrefour des Jeunes de Montreal, 4675 rue Belanger est. Montreal, Quebec, Canada, HIT, IC2. *Notes:* 1. Achenbach, T.M. and Edelbrock, C.S. (1979). The Child Behavior Profile II: Boys aged 12-16 and girls aged 6-11. *Journal of Consulting and Clinical Psychology*, 47: 223-233. 2. Piers, E.U. (1984). *Piers-Harris Self-Concept Scale* (revised manual). Los Angeles: Western Psychological Services. 3. Harter, S., and Pike, R. (1984). The Pictorial Scale of Perceived Competence and Social Acceptance for Young Children, *Child Development*, 55, pp. 1969-1982. 4. p < .05. 5. p < .001.

Operations and Other Procedures

★ 427 ★

Medical Device Implants: 1988

This table shows the percentage of males and females who had various types of medical devices implanted in 1988.

[Numbers in thousands, except percent.]

Device	Total	Percent distribution	
		Male	Female
Artificial joints[1]	1,625	39.9%	60.1%
Hip joints	816	37.5%	62.4%
Knee joints	521	41.8%	58.2%
Fixation devices[2]	4,890	57.2%	42.8%
Head	351	57.3%	42.7%
Torso	563	62.7%	37.5%
Upper extremities	646	70.4%	29.7%
Lower extremities	2,690	52.8%	47.2%
Other	622	57.9%	42.1%
Other devices:			
Ear vent tubes	1,494	39.9%	61.1%
Silicone implants	620	8.2%	91.8%
Breast implants	544	2.0%[3]	98.0%
Shunt or catheter	321	50.5%	49.2%
Dental implants	275	56.4%	43.6%

[Continued]

★ 427 ★

Medical Device Implants: 1988
[Continued]

Device	Total	Percent distribution	
		Male	Female
Heart valve	279	52.3%	47.8%
Pacemaker	460	50.4%	49.6%
Eye lens	3,765	37.6%	62.4%

Source: Selected from "Medical Device Implants, by Age, Sex, and Race: 1988," U.S. Bureau of the Census, *Statistical Abstract of the United States 1994*, Table 216, p. 145. Primary source: U.S. National Center for Health Statistics, *National Health Interview Survey*, 1988; unpublished data. *Notes:* 1. Includes other devices not shown separately. 2. Includes sites unknown. Each device represents a single body part regardless of the number of pins, screws, nails, wires, rods, or plates. 3. Figure does not meet standards of reliability or precision.

★ 428 ★

Operations and Other Procedures

Prenatal Ultrasound's Effect on Perinatal Outcome

A six-year, $7 million study was done on 15,151 women at low risk for perinatal problems to find out whether ultrasound screening decreased the frequency of adverse perinatal outcomes. It was found that ultrasound screening did not improve the outcome of pregnancies for low-risk women, and the authors said the results indicated that ultrasound should be used more selectively. This table shows some of the results of the study.

Item	Number/Percent
Fetal defects at birth among women who received routine ultrasound at 15 to 22 weeks and again at 31 to 35 weeks	5%
Fetal defects at birth among women who received no ultra-sound screening	4.9%
Gestational age at which more than half of fetal defects were detected, at or after...	24 weeks
Estimated amount of money wasted on excessive ultra-sound screening annually	$1 billion
Estimated percentage of women at risk of complications from pregnancy	40%

[Continued]

★ 428 ★

Prenatal Ultrasound's Effect on Perinatal Outcome
[Continued]

Item	Number/Percent
Estimated savings annually if screening were limited to those women at risk of complications	$500 million

Source: Selected from Bernard G. Ewigman, M.D., James P. crane, M.D., Frederic D. Frigoletto, M.D., et al., "Effect of Prenatal Ultrasound Screening on Prenatal Outcome," *The New England Journal of Medicine,* Vol. 329(12), September 16, 1993, pp. 821-7). Address reprint requests to Dr. Ewigman at MA303 Health Sciences Center, Department of Family and Community Medicine, University of Missouri Health Sciences Center, 1 Hospital Dr., Columbia, MO 65212.

★ 429 ★

Operations and Other Procedures

Procedures Performed at Short-Stay Hosptials: 1980-1992

This table shows the types of surgical procedures performed on female patients discharged from short-stay hospitals in the years 1980 through 1992.

[Number of procedures in thousands.]

Type of procedure	Number of procedures (1,000)				Rate per 1,000 population[2]			
	1980	1985	1990[1]	1992[1]	1980	1985	1990[1]	1992[1]
Surgical procedures, total[3,4]	24,494	24,799	23,051	23,253	108.6	104.6	92.4	91.7
Female								
Total[3,4]	15,989	15,994	14,513	14,607	137.1	130.6	113.0	112.0
Procedures to assist delivery[4]	2,391	2,494	2,491	2,441	20.5	20.4	19.4	18.7
Cesarean section	619	877	945	921	5.3	7.2	7.4	7.1
Repair of current obstetric laceration	355	548	795	790	3.0	4.5	6.2	6.1
Hysterectomy	649	670	591	580	5.6	5.5	4.6	4.4
Diagnostic and other non-surgical procedures, total[4,5]	6,918	11,961	17,455	19,381	30.7	50.5	70.0	76.5
Female								
Total[4,5]	3,532	6,072	10,077	11,231	30.3	49.6	78.5	86.1
Diagnostic ultrasound	204	756	941	871	1.7	6.2	7.3	6.7
CAT scan[7]	154	707	770	658	1.3	5.8	6.0	5.0

Source: Selected from "Procedures for Inpatients Discharged from Short-Stay Hospitals: 1980 to 1992," U.S. Bureau of the Census, *Statistical Abstract of the United States 1994,* Table 188, p. 130. *R Primary source: U.S. National Center for Health Statistics, *Vital and Health Statistics,* series 13; and unpublished data. Excludes newborn infants and discharges from Federal hospitals. *Notes:* 1. Comparisons beginning 1988 with data for earlier years should be made with caution as estimates of change may reflect improvements in the design rather than true changes in hospital use. 2. Based on Bureau of the Census estimated civilian population as of July 1. Population estimates for the 1980s do not reflect revised estimates based on the 1990 Census of Population. 3. Includes other types of surgical procedures not shown separately. 4. Beginning in 1989, the definition of some surgical and diagnostic and other nonsurgical procedures was revised, causing a discontinuity in the trends for some totals. 5. Includes other nonsurgical procedures not shown separately. 6. Using contrast material. 7. Computerized axial tomography.

Pregnancy and Infant Health

★ 430 ★

Ectopic Pregnancies Increase: 1970-1992

Ectopic pregnancy is the development of the fetus outside the uterus. The Federal Centers for Disease Control and Prevention announced in January 1995 that this condition had increased sixfold between 1970 and 1992 because of sexually transmitted diseases. This table reports some statistics on ectopic pregnancy.

Item	Number/Percent
Estimated rate of ectopic pregnancies per 1,000 reported pregnancies, 1970:	4.5
Number of women	17,800
Estimated rate of ectopic pregnancies per 1,000 reported pregnancies, 1992:	19.7
Number of women	108,800

Source: Selected from "Ectopic Pregnancies Reported on the Rise," *Detroit Free Press*, January 27, 1995, p. 3. Primary source: Federal Centers for Disease Control and Prevention.

★ 431 ★

Pregnancy and Infant Health

Risk of Late Childbearing

Researchers compared pregnancy and delivery complications of first births in women 35 years and older with women 25-29 years old. Although the risk of complications was found to be somewhat greater than in younger women, older women and their newborns were not found to be at greater risk of dying. This table compares labor and newborn characteristics of 1,054 women aged 25-29 giving birth for the first time to 890 women aged 35 and over also giving birth for the first time.

Item	Women 25-29	Women 35+
Labor characteristics		
Labor		
Spontaneous	81.2%	74.0%
Induced	15.2%	17.2%
None	3.6%	8.9%

[Continued]

★ 431 ★

Risk of Late Childbearing
[Continued]

Item	Women 25-29	Women 35+
Anesthesia for vaginal delivery[1]		
Local	78.1%	70.1%
Spinal	8.8%	10.4%
Epidural	8.1%	13.2%
Pudendal	3.9%	4.2%
None	1.0%	2.2%
Oxytocin	34.9%	42.9%
Meconium	19.5%	20.6%
Presentation		
Vertex	93.6%	90.6%
Other	6.4%	9.4%
Mode of delivery		
Vaginal		
Spontaneous	60.1%	42.1%
Forceps	11.7%	12.4%
Vacuum	0.8%	1.8%
Cesarean	27.5%	43.7%
Indications for cesareans (percentage of births)		
CPD, dystocia	15.2%	20.7%
Breech	5.3%	8.9%
Fetal distress	4.6%	8.7%
Other[2]	2.5%	5.5%
Newborn characteristics		
Gestational age (weeks) (mean)	39.59	39.02
Birth weight (g) (mean)	3393	3277
Low birth weight	6.4%	10.9%
Preterm delivery[3]	6.1%	12.5%
Postterm delivery[3]	10.3%	8.5%
Small for gestational age	4.9%	7.2%
Large for gestational age	16.1%	17.2%
Infant anomalies	5.2%	6.1%
Abnormal karyotypes	0.2%	0.9%
Perinatal death	0.9%	1.5%
Birth trauma	0.6%	0.4%

[Continued]

★ 431 ★

Risk of Late Childbearing
[Continued]

Item	Women 25-29	Women 35+
NICU admission	6.7%	10.6%
NICU stay (days)	12.3	16.3

Source: Jason Kahn, "With care, later pregnancies seen as safe," *Detroit Free Press,* January 10, 1995, p. 5A. Primary source: Michael Prysak, PhD, Robert P. Lorenz, MD, and Anne Kisly, "Pregnancy Outcome in Nulliparous Women 35 Years and Older," *Obstetrics & Gynecology,* 85(1), January 1995, pp. 65-70, p. 68, Table 3, "Labor Characteristics," and Table 4, "Newborn Characteristics." *Notes:* 1. N=764 for the control group, 501 for the case group. 2. Other indications included herpes, preeclampsia with unfavorable cervix, maternal exhaustion, or postterm (no labor) with unfavorable cervix. 3. Based on gestational age less than 37 weeks for preterm delivery, gestational age greater than or equal to 42 weeks for postterm delivery.

★ 432 ★

Pregnancy and Infant Health

Substance-Exposed Infants

Deanna Gomby and Patricia Shiono of the Center for the Future of Children responded to "reports of a rising tide of illegal drug use during pregnancy" by reviewing 27 reports on the topic published during or after 1980. They also made their own estimates of likely substance exposure rates for women aged 12-34 based on National Institute on Drug Abuse data. This table shows some of the results of their study.

Item	Number/Percent
Estimated number of U.S. newborns who may have been cocaine-exposed, annually	2-3%
Estimated number of U.S. newborns who may have been marijuana-exposed, annually	3-12%
Estimated number of U.S. newborns who may have been exposed to cigarettes, annually	38%
Estimated number of U.S. newborns who may have been exposed to alcohol, annually	73%

Source: Selected from Deanna Gomby, Ph.D., and Patricia Shiono, Ph.D., "Estimating the Number of Substance-Exposed Infants," *The Future of Children,* a publication of the Center for the Future of Children, Spring 1991.

Weight

★ 433 ★

Weight Guidelines for Persons Aged 40 and Over

This table shows a weight chart devised by Dr. Reubin Andres, clinical director at the National Institute on Aging. Dr. Andres studied insurance industry data from 4 million people up to age 70 and found that the lowest death rates among older people occurred at heavier weights. From this he concluded that "the best weight for survival is heavier, but we don't really know why." There is no distinction between the sexes, and Dr. Andres says the best weights for survival are about the same for men and women.

Height	Age		
	40-49	50-59	60-69
4'10"	99-127	107-135	115-142
4'11"	103-131	111-139	119-147
5'0"	106-135	114-143	123-152
5'1"	110-140	118-148	127-157
5'2"	113-144	122-153	131-163
5'3"	117-149	126-158	135-168
5'4"	121-154	130-163	140-173
5'5"	125-159	134-168	144-179
5'6"	129-164	138-174	148-184
5'7"	133-169	143-179	153-190
5'8"	137-174	147-184	158-196
5'9"	141-179	151-190	162-201
5'10"	145-184	156-195	167-207
5'11"	149-190	160-201	172-213
6'0"	153-195	165-207	177-219
6'1"	157-200	169-213	182-225

Source: "A little extra weight may help you live longer," *Better Homes and Gardens*, June 1995, pp. 62-64, table entitled "How Much Do You Weigh?"

★ 434 ★

Weight

Weight Guidelines: 1985-1990

This table shows desirable body weight ranges issued by the U.S. Departments of Agriculture and Health and Human Services in 1985 and 1990. In 1990 men and women were grouped together and broken down by age, suggesting that it was desirable for women over the age of 35 to gain weight. However, *The New York Times* article in which this table appeared cites a 14-year study of nearly 116,000 women by researchers from the Harvard School of Public Health and Harvard Medical School. The study found that weight gains of as little as 11 to 18 pounds in adult life resulted in a 25% greater chance of suffering or dying of a heart attack compared with that faced by women who gained less than 11 pounds after the age of 18. With each increment of weight, coronary risk rose—to a 60% increase for weight gains of 18 to 25 pounds, and to a 200 to 300% increase for weight gains above 25 pounds. The findings from the study were to be published in the February 8, 1995, issue of *The Journal of the American Medical Association*.

[X Not shown.]

Height	1985		1990	
	Men	Women	Age 19-34	Age 35+
4'10"	X	92-121	X	X
4'11"	X	95-124	X	X
5'0"	X	98-127	97-128	108-138
5'1"	105-134	101-130	101-132	111-143
5'2"	108-137	104-134	104-137	115-148
5'3"	111-141	107-138	107-141	119-152
5'4"	114-145	110-142	111-146	122-157
5'5"	117-149	114-146	114-150	126-162
5'6"	121-154	118-150	118-155	130-167
5'7"	125-159	122-154	121-160	134-172
5'8"	129-163	126-159	125-164	138-178
5'9"	133-167	130-164	129-169	142-183
5'10"	137-172	134-169	132-174	146-188
5'll"	141-177	X	136-179	151-194
6'0"	145-182	X	140-184	155-199
6'1"	149-187	X	144-189	159-205
6'2"	153-192	X	148-195	164-210
6'3"	157-197	X	152-200	168-216

Source: Jane E. Brody, "Study Rebuts 'Acceptable' Midlife Weight Gain," *The New York Times,* February 8, 1995, p. B7.

Chapter 7
INCOME, SPENDING, AND WEALTH

Income

★ 435 ★

Family and Household Income: 1990

This table shows the median annual income of U.S. families and households, by race and Hispanic origin and type of family/household, 1990. White families, no matter what their structure, are better off than minority families.

Type of family/ household	All	White	Black	Hispanic
All families	$35,400	$36,900	$21,400	$23,400
Married couples	$39,900	$40,300	$33,800	$28,000
No children	$38,300	$38,700	$30,100	$30,200
With children	$41,300	$41,700	$35,700	$27,500
Female-headed	$17,000	$19,500	$12,100	$11,900
No children	$27,000	$28,900	$21,300	$22,300
With children	$13,100	$14,900	$10,300	$10,100
Elderly (age 65+) household				
Married couple	$25,500	$26,100	$17,200	$18,800
Male alone	$12,900	$13,400	$7,200	$9,700
Female alone	$9,500	$9,900	$5,600	$6,300

Source: Selected from Dennis A. Ahlburg and Carol J. DeVita, *New Realities of the American Family,* Population Bulletin, Vol. 47, No. 2, August 1992, Table 7, p. 34, "Median Annual Income of U.S. Families and Households, 1990." Primary source: U.S. Bureau of the Census, *Current Population Reports* P-60, no. 174, and custom tabulations by Decision Demographics.

★ 436 ★

Income

Higher Education Assistance: 1990-1991

This table shows average aid received for postsecondary education by males and females for school year 1990-1991. The average overall aid package among persons who received any financial aid at all was $2,919. The single largest aid amount was that based on loans, at $3,155. Women were more likely than men to have received aid from a Pell Grant or from a loan, while men were more likely to have gotten aid from a veterans' program or their employer. The maximum Pell Grant award in 1991 was $2,300.

[Numbers in thousands.]

Type of aid	Male	Female
All students	9,439	11,120
All aid recipients		
Number	4,773	5,687
Percent	51%	51%
Mean	$2,953	$2,891
Std. error	148	125
Pell Grant		
Number	1,008	1,873
Percent	11%	17%
Mean	$1,439	$1,341
Std. error	86	50
Percent of total aid		
Mean	45%	53%
Std. error	3%	2%
GI Bill or VEAP		
Number	314	102
Percent	3%	1%
Mean	$2,761	1
Std. error	325	1
Percent of total aid		
Mean	81%	1
Std. error	4%	1
SEOG or college work study		
Number	392	498
Percent	4%	4%
Mean	$1,422	$1,580
Std. error	223	162
Percent of total aid		
Mean	36%	32%
Std. error	4%	3%
Loan		
Number	1,256	1,766
Percent	13%	16%
Mean	$2,979	$3,280

[Continued]

★ 436 ★

Higher Education Assistance: 1990-1991
[Continued]

Type of aid	Male	Female
Std. error	156	140
Percent of total aid		
Mean	67%	66%
Std. error	2%	2%
Employer assistance or Job Training Partnership Act		
Number	1,875	1,742
Percent	20%	16%
Mean	$1,077	$875
Std. error	99	89
Percent of total aid		
Mean	96%	93%
Std. error	1%	1%
Fellowship, scholarship or tuition reduction		
Number	1,079	1,357
Percent	11%	12%
Mean	$2,971	$2,068
Std. error	369	190
Percent of total aid		
Mean	60%	58%
Std. error	3%	3%
Other aid		
Number	1,195	1,593
Percent	13%	14%
Mean	$1,886	$1,787
Std. error	180	162
Percent of total aid		
Mean	53%	55%
Std. error	3%	2%

Source: Selected from "Average Aid Received and Number of Recipients by Social and Demographic Characteristics: 1990-1991," *Dollars for Scholars: Postsecondary Costs and Financing, 1990-1991,* U.S. Bureau of the Census, Current Population Reports, P70-39, Table 4, p. 22. Also in source: data by race, Hispanic origin, monthly family income, and for dependent and independent students. *Note:* 1. Base is less than 200,000.

★ 437 ★

Income

Income and Risk of Dying

This table shows the risk of death for each income group relative to those with income less than $5,000 per year. Mortality declined with increasing income. The risk of death for women in the highest income group was 70% of that for women in the lowest income group.

[RR = Relative risk.]

Family income (annual)	Men RR	Women RR
Less than $5,000	1.0	1.0
$5,000-$9,999	1.0	0.7
$10,000-$14,999	0.9	0.5
$15,000-$19,999	0.7	0.6
$20,000-$24,999	0.6	0.5
$25,000-$49,999	0.5	0.5
More than $50,000	0.4	0.4

Source: Selected from Paul D. Sorlie, PhD, Norman J. Johnson, PhD, Eric Backlund, MS, et al., "Mortality in the Uninsured Compared with that in Persons with Public and Private Health Insurance," *Arch Intern Med*, Vol. 154, November 14, 1994, pp. 2409-2416, Table 5, p. 2413, "Age-Adjusted Risk of Death for Each Income Group Relative to Those with Income Less than $5000 Without and With Adjustment for Health Insurance, in White Men and Women Aged 25 to 64 Years in the NLMS." The NLMS is a study of mortality occurring during the years 1979 through 1987 in combined samples of the noninstitutionalized U.S. population. Address correspondence to National Heart, Lung, and Blood Institute, Federal Bldg., Room 3A10, Bethesda, MD 20892 (Dr. Sorlie).

★ 438 ★

Income

Income by Race/Ethnicity: 1989

This table shows the income of female householders and females 15 years and over with income in 1989, by race/ethnicity, reported for the 1990 census. It also shows the median income in dollars of females and males 15 years and over, those with income and those who work full-time, year-round.

[Amer Ind/Esk/Aleut refers to American Indian or Alaskan native.]

Income	All persons	Race					Hispanic or. (any race)	White, not of Hisp. origin
		White	Black	Amer Ind/ Esk/Aleut	Asian or Pac Isl	Other race		
Female householder, no husband present	10,381,654	6,540,382	3,045,283	121,370	185,926	488,693	1,029,646	6,058,841
Less than $5,000	1,530,177	679,291	696,002	28,076	20,848	105,960	206,345	592,849
$5,000 to $9,999	1,636,764	883,985	582,809	29,368	23,576	117,,026	224,843	789,442
$10,000 to $14,999	1,379,635	844,016	424,271	18,718	20,000	72,630	151,134	773,575
$15,000 to $24,999	2,286,235	1,531,229	603,978	23,312	34,272	93,444	202,370	1,432,881
$25,000 to $49,999	2,718,497	1,973,670	591,036	18,180	54,590	81,021	194,382	1,870,903
$50,000 or more	830,346	628,191	147,187	3,716	32,640	18,612	50,572	599,191

[Continued]

★ 438 ★

Income by Race/Ethnicity: 1989
[Continued]

Income	All persons	Race					Hispanic or. (any race)	White, not of Hisp. origin
		White	Black	Amer Ind/ Esk/Aleut	Asian or Pac Isl	Other race		
Females 15 years and over, with income	84,560,106	69,613,017	9,965,635	587,568	2,125,535	2,268,351	5,473,121	66,627,911
Median income	$10,371	$10,652	$8,825	$7,310	$11,986	$7,876	$8,354	$10,474
Percent year-round full-time workers	33.9%	33.6%	35.0%	29.5%	40.6%	31.9%	33.4%	33.6%
Median income	$19,570	$19,916	$18,005	$16,680	$21,335	$15,362	$16,307	$20,048
Males 15 years and over, with income	86,674,947	72,504,525	8,337,527	605,578	2,285,437	2,941,880	6,688,401	68,980,277
Median income	$20,409	$21,695	$12,950	$12,180	$19,396	$12,493	$13,501	$22,065
Percent year-round full-time workers	53.0%	54.2%	44.9%	40.9%	52.4%	47.5%	48.7%	54.4%
Median income	$29,237	$30,468	$21,647	$22,080	$30,075	$18,627	$20,316	$30,764

Source: Selected from "Income in 1989 of Households, Families, and Persons, by Race and Hispanic Origin: 1990," U.S. Bureau of the Census, 1990 Census of Population, *Social and Economic Characteristics, United States,* 1990 CP-2-1, Table 48, p. 48.

★ 439 ★

Income

Married-Couple Families, Income by Race: 1967-1990

This table shows the median income in 1990 dollars of married-couple black and white families in 1967 and 1990. When both husband and wife work, black married-couple families have a real median income closer to that of comparable white families than they did in 1967. After adjusting for inflation, black married-couple families with wives in the paid labor force had income in 1990 representing $85 for every $100 of comparable white families. This compares to $72 for every $100 in 1967. In 1967, one-half of wives in black married-couple families were in the paid labor force; by 1990, the proportion had increased to two-thirds. However, the proportion of black families that are married couples has declined from 68% to 48% during that period.

Type of family/race	1967	1990
Husband and Wife Earner		
Black	$28,700	$40,040
White	$40,000	$47,250

[Continued]

★ 439 ★

Married-Couple Families, Income by Race: 1967-1990

[Continued]

Type of family/race	1967	1990
Husband Only Earner		
Black	$18,370	$20,330
White	$30,460	$30,780

Source: "Generation-Long Portrait of Black Families," *Census and You,* Vol 27, No. 11, November 1992, p. 1, table entitled "Black Married-Couple Families, Husband and Wife Both Working, Have Made Gains Since the Sixties." Primary source: U.S. Bureau of the Census, *The Black Population in the United States: March 1991.*

★ 440 ★

Income

Median Income of Full-Time Workers: 1989

This table shows the median income in 1989 of year-round full-time workers in urban and rural areas.

Urban/Rural	Male	Female
United States	$29,237	$19,570
Urban	$30,302	$20,461
Rural	$26,338	$16,473

Source: Selected from "Summary of Occupation, Income, and Poverty Characteristics: 1990," U.S. Bureau of the Census, 1990 Census of Population, *Social and Economic Characteristics, United States,* 1990 CP-2-1, Table 3, p. 3.

★ 441 ★

Income

Supplemental Security Income and Older Women

This table gives statistics about Supplemental Security Income (SSI) as it relates to women. The SSI program was established in 1972 to help the poor aged, blind, and disabled meet their basic needs. It was designed to supplement the income of those who do not qualify for Social Security benfits or whose benefits are not adequate for subsistence.

Item	Number/Percent
Maximum SSI benefit for an individual	$458
Percent of poverty line	75%
Maximum SS benefit for a couple	$687
Percent of poverty line	90%

[Continued]

★ 441 ★

Supplemental Security Income and Older Women
[Continued]

Item	Number/Percent
Percent of SSI recipients who are women	60%
Percent of those women who are also receiving Social Security benefits	64%
Number of older women who are eligible for SSI benefits who are not receiving them	> 1 million
Federal entitlement spending represented by SSI	3%
Total federal spending on SSI	1.6%

Source: "Supplemental Security Income and Older Women," *OWL Fact Sheet*, Older Women's League.

★ 442 ★

Income

Teenagers' Allowances and Income

This table shows average weekly incomes in constant 1993 dollars in 1988 and 1993 of teenagers by age and type of income. Girls earn more and have higher allowances than boys.

Sex and age	1993	1988	Percent change
Girls, 13 to 15			
Total income	$37.20	$39.28	-6.3%
Allowance	$19.35	$19.09	1.4%
Earnings	$17.85	$20.19	-11.6%
Boys, 13 to 15			
Total income	$32.00	$35.99	-11.1%
Allowance	$16.15	$17.39	-7.1%
Earnings	$15.85	$18.61	-14.8%
Girls, 16 to 19			
Total income	$82.45	$86.50	-4.7%
Allowance	$32.45	$33.79	-4.0%
Earnings	$50.00	$52.70	-5.1%
Boys, 16 to 19			
Total income	$75.35	$82.96	-9.2%
Allowance	$30.15	$32.39	-6.9%
Earnings	$45.20	$50.57	-10.6%

Source: "Why Teens Have Less Green," *American Demographics*, July 1994, p. 9, table entitled "Girls Make and Take More." Primary source: The Rand Youth Poll, New York, NY, 41st nationwide survey of 2,630 boys and girls aged 13 to 19.

★ 443 ★

Income

Welfare Benefits: Recipients and Cost

This table shows who receives welfare and who stays on welfare.

Item	Number/percent
Who Receives Welfare	
Number of families on AFDC	5,000,000
Percentage of recipients who are:	
Children	67%
White	38.9%
Black	37.2%
Hispanic	17.8%
Average family size	2.9 people
Average monthly benefit	$373
Average monthly benefit in 1970 (1993 dollars)	$676
Highest maximum benefit in the 48 contiguous states:[1]	
New York	$703
Lowest maximum benefit:	
Mississippi	$120
Total Federal spending (billions)	$13.8
Total Federal and state spending (billions)	$25.2
Average cost for each American taxpayer[2]	$156
Percentage of AFDC mothers...	
under 18[3]	1.2%
under 20	7.6%
older than 40	11.8%
who first became mothers at age 19 or younger[4]	51.4%
with part-time job	4.2%
with full-time job	2.2%
in school or training	16.7%
Who Stays on Welfare	
Typical time on AFDC after first enrolling:[5]	
Less than 3 years	30%
3 to 4 years	20%
5 to 7 years	19%

[Continued]

★ 443 ★

Welfare Benefits: Recipients and Cost
[Continued]

Item	Number/percent
8 years or more	30%
At a particular point in time, how long people have been on AFDC[5]	
Less than 3 years	7%
3 to 4 years	11%
5 to 7 years	17%
8 years or more	65%
Odds that an adult going on AFDC will be there 10 years later:	
White	1 in 5
Black	1 in 3
Main reasons families go on welfare:	
Divorce or separation	45%
Unmarried mother has child	30%
Earnings of single mother fall	12%
Main reasons families leave welfare rolls:	
Marriage	35%
Earnings of single mother increase	21%
Rise in other benefits	14%
Percentage of children on AFDC by race:	
White, 1973	6.5%
White, 1992	6.2%
Black, 1973	42.7%
Black, 1992	35.1%
Percentage of poor children not receiving AFDC	40%
Other Benefits	
Percentage of AFDC families in public housing	9.2%
Percentage who get Federal rent subsidies	12.1%
Unmarried mothers above poverty line who get child support from father	43%

[Continued]

★ 443 ★

Welfare Benefits: Recipients and Cost
[Continued]

Item	Number/percent
Amount in child support collected for each enforcement dollar spent	$3.98
Maximum monthly food stamp allotment: Family of 3	$295
Average monthly food stamp allotment: Family of 3	$68
Percentage of families receiving food stamps:	
1975	7.6%
1993	10.4%

Source: David E. Rosenbaum, "Notebook: Welfare: Who Gets It? How Much Does It Cost?" *The New York Times*, March 23, 1995, p. A11 Y. Unless otherwise specified, the statistics are for 1993, and the source is the 1994 Green Book, a compilation of data by the House Ways and Means Committee mostly from Government reports but occasionally from private academic surveys. *Notes:* 1. Excludes Alaska and Hawaii because of the high costs of living in those states. 2. Based on an estimated 162 million payers of Federal income tax. 3. Source: Department of Health and Human Services, 1992 data. 4. Tabulation by Kristin A. Moore of Child Trends Inc., based on 1990 data. 5. Based on a 1983 study by Mary Jo Bane and David T. Elwood under contract with the Department of Health and Human Services.

Spending

★ 444 ★

"Barbie" Dolls

This table presents some statistics about the *Barbie* doll.

Item	Number/Percent
Number of countries in which Barbie is sold	140
Number of Barbie dolls sold every second	2
Number of Barbie dolls owned by the average American girl between the ages of 3 and 10	8

[Continued]

★ 444 ★

"Barbie" Dolls
[Continued]

Item	Number/Percent
Barbie sales in 1993	$1 billion
Ratio of Barbies to Kens	8:1

Source: Selected from Amy M. Spindler, "Bless Her Pointy Little Feet," *The New York Times Book Review*, February 5, 1995, p. 22. Primary sources: M.G. Lord, *Forever Barbie: The Unauthorized Biography of a Real Doll*, New York: William Morrow & Company; Ruth Handler with Jacqueline Shannon, *Dream Doll: The Ruth Handler Story*, Stamford CT: Longmeadow Press.

★ 445 ★

Spending

Buying Groceries

This table shows the percentage of men and women who say selected methods of paying are most convenient when buying groceries.

Method of payment	Men	Women
Check	42%	52%
Cash	51%	41%
Credit card	5%	3%

Source: "Need Cash? Ask a Guy," *The Numbers News*, February 1995, p. 3, table entitled "Percent of adults aged 18 and older who say selected methods are most convenient when purchasing groceries, by sex, 1994." Primary source: Data collected by The Gallup Organization for the Financial Stationers Association.

★ 446 ★

Spending

Charges for Cesarean Delivery: 1993

This table shows the number of cesarean deliveries charged to the Metropolitan Life Insurance Company in 1993, their percentage of all births, and the average charges for an uncomplicated cesarean delivery, by geographic area. By comparison, the charge was $6,430 for women having an uncomplicated vaginal delivery.

Geographic Area	Number of of cases	Percent of all births[1]	Average Costs				
			Total hospital & physician	Hospital Charge			Physician Charge
				Total	Room & board[2]	Ancillary[2]	
United States	9,994	21.3%	$11,000	$6,930	$2,380	$4,550	$4,070
New England	319	17.8%	$11,540	$7,060	$2,890	$4,170	$4,480
Middle Atlantic	1,271	20.3%	$13,040	$7,580	$3,500	$4,080	$5,460
East North Central	1,617	19.0%	$10,230	$6,750	$2,490	$4,260	$3,480
West North Central	619	20.3%	$9,670	$6,520	$2,120	$4,400	$3,150
South Atlantic	1,927	23.6%	$11,190	$6,760	$1,940	$4,820	$4,430
East South Central	519	23.6%	$8,770	$5,850	$1,620	$4,230	$2,920
West South Central	2,004	27.3%	$9,880	$6,290	$1,930	$4,360	$3,590
Mountain	431	16.3%	$10,920	$7,110	$2,190	$4,920	$3,810
Pacific	1,287	18.7%	$12,890	$8,350	$2,870	$5,480	$4,540

Source: Selected from Margaret Mushinski, "Average Charges for Uncomplicated Cesarean and Vaginal Deliveries, United States, 1993, *Statistical Bulletin*, Vol 75(4), Oct-Dec 1994, p.29, table 1, "Percent of All Births and Average Charges for an Uncomplicated Cesarean Delivery, Metropolitan Life Insurance Company Group Health Claims, 1993." Also in source: data by state. Primary source: Claims data from Metropolitan Life Insurance Company merged and edited by Corporate Health Strategies, Inc. Analyses and computations by the Health and Safety Education Division, Medical Department, Metropolitan Life Insurance Company. *Notes:* 1. Percentages include complicated deliveries. 2. Estimated on basis of 1986 distribution of total hospital charges.

★ 447 ★

Spending

Charges for Vaginal Delivery: 1993

This table shows the number of vaginal deliveries charged to the Metropolitan Life Insurance Company in 1993 and the average costs for an uncomplicated vaginal delivery, by geographic area.

Geographic Area	Number of cases	Average Costs				
		Total hospital and physician	Hospital charge			Physician charge
			Total	Room & board[1]	Ancillary[1]	
United States	29,438	$6,430	$3,690	$1,350	$2,340	$2,740
New England	1,269	$6,920	$3,760	$1,530	$2,230	$3,160
Middle Atlantic	4,331	$8,350	$4,370	$2,040	$2,330	$3,980
East North Central	5,853	$5,910	$3,600	$1,390	$2,210	$2,310
West North Central	2,081	$4,640	$3,490	$1,220	$2,270	$2,150
South Atlantic	5,170	$6,490	$3,550	$1,090	$2,460	$2,940
East South Central	1,292	$5,500	$3,310	$900	$2,410	$2,190
West South Central	4,002	$5,720	$3,380	$1,000	$2,380	$2,340
Mountain	1,788	$5,530	$3,240	$1,120	$2,120	$2,290
Pacific	3,652	$6,720	$3,980	$1,470	$2,510	$2,740

Source: Selected from Margaret Mushinski, "Average Charges for Uncomplicated Cesarean and Vaginal Deliveries, United States, 1993, *Statistical Bulletin,* Vol 75(4), Oct-Dec 1994, p.33, Table 2, "Average Charges for an Uncomplicated Vaginal Delivery, Metropolitan Life Insurance Company Group Health Claims, 1993." Also in source: data by state. Primary source: Claims data from Metropolitan Life Insurance Company merged and edited by Corporate Health Strategies, Inc. Analyses and computations by the Health and Safety Education Division, Medical Department, Metropolitan Life Insurance Company. *Note:* 1. Estimated on basis of 1986 distribution of total hospital charges.

★ 448 ★

Spending

Charitable Contributions Asked for and Given

This table shows the percentage of respondents to a survey who reported that they were asked to contribute money or other property to charitable organizations in the past year and the percentage who actually contributed. It was concluded that "For the most part, people give when they are asked." Information was obtained from in-home personal interviews conducted by The Gallup Organization from April 22 to May 15, 1994, with a representative national sample of 1,509 adult Americans aged 18 or older. The very wealthy (those with incomes above $200,000) were not targeted.

Characteristic	Asked to contribute	Did contribute	Not asked to contribute	Did contribute
Total	76.9%	84.1%	21.9%	38.1%
Male	75.5%	82.4%	23.6%	33.5%
Female	78.2%	85.7%	20.3%	43.0%

Source: Selected from "Respondents who were asked to contribute money or other property to charitable organizations in the past year and actual giving behavior: 1993," *Giving and Volunteering in the United States*, Independent Sector, 1994, Table 4.9, p. 76. Respondents who did not answer or did not know were not considered in this table.

★ 449 ★

Spending

Charitable Contributions: 1987-1993

This table shows the percentage of respondents to a survey who made charitable contributions, the average donation, and its percentage of total household income, various years. Information was obtained from in-home personal interviews conducted by The Gallup Organization from April 22 to May 15, 1994, with a representative national sample of 1,509 adult Americans aged 18 or older. The very wealthy (those with incomes above $200,000) were not targeted.

Gender	1993 Contributions			1991 Contributions			1989 Contributions			1987 Contributions		
	Percent of all respondents	Average	Percent of hsld income	Percent of all respondents	Average	Percent of hsld income	Percent of all respondents	Average	Percent of hsld income	Percent of all respondents	Average	Percent of hsld income
All	73.4%	$880	2.1%	72.2%	$899	2.2%	75.1%	$978	2.5%	71.1%	$790	1.9%
Male	70.3%	$996	2.2%	70.0%	$1,057	2.4%	71.9%	$1,294	3.1%	68.9%	$888	2.1%
Female	76.2%	$781	2.0%	74.2%	$763	2.0%	78.1%	$683	1.8%	73.1%	$700	1.8%

Source: Selected from "Demographic characteristics of givers: 1991 and 1993," and "Demographic characteristics of givers: 1987 and 1989," *Giving and Volunteering in the United States*, Independent Sector, 1994, Tables 1.9 and 1.10, pp. 39-40.

★ 450 ★

Spending

Child Care Expenditures

This table shows average weekly and hourly expenditures in 1988 dollars on child care and average number of hours per week of child care used, by age of child. The data are from two sources: the 1988 National Longitudinal Survey of Youth (Youth Survey) and the 1983 National Longitudinal Survey of Young Women (Young Women Survey. The Youth Survey provides information on a sample of 6,283 young women who were 14 to 22 years old in 1979 and who have been interviewed annually since 1979.[1] The Young Woman Survey obtains information from regular interviews of a cohort of women who were 14 to 24 years in 1968.[2] Both surveys are used because both asked participants a variety of questions about child care. Together, the surveys allow the examination of a wide range of mothers. According to the organization *9 to 5*, low-income parents spend 23% of family income on child care, compared with 5% for higher-income families.[3].

[Figures in 1988 dollars.]

	Youth Survey (women ages 23-31)			Young Women Survey (women ages 29-39)		
	Avg. weekly expenditures	Avg. no. of hours per week	Avg. hourly expenditures	Avg. weekly expenditures	Avg. no. of hours per week	Avg. hourly expenditures
Total	$61.51	39.38	$1.56	$44.46	24.69	$1.80
Age of youngest child:						
Birth to 1 year	$59.51	43.73	$1.36	$63.48	35.55	$1.79
2-4 years	$71.46	40.19	$1.78	$52.59	34.28	$1.53
5 years and over	$49.03	35.42	$1.38	$37.63	20.46	$1.84
Marital status:						
Married, spouse present	$64.36	38.54	$1.67	$46.58	24.97	$1.87
Other	$55.11	41.03	$1.34	$36.61	23.79	$1.54
Net family income:						
(in 1988 dollars)						
$0-$14,999	$44.11	39.69	$1.11	$32.84	23.05	$1.42
$15,000-$24,999	$43.11	40.31	$1.07	$42.08	23.76	$1.77
$25,000-$49,999	$66.12	38.17	$1.73	$44.28	24.38	$1.82
$50,000 and more	$83.99	44.06	$1.91	$53.33	28.33	$1.88

Source: Jonathan R. Veum and Philip M. Gleason, "Child care: arrangements and costs," *Monthly Labor Review*, October 1991, pp. 10-17, Table 5, p. 15, "Weekly and hourly expenditures on child care and the number of hours per week used by women in the National Longitudinal Survey who use paid child care." *Notes:* 1. In 1988, the sample, which includes an overrepresentation of blacks, Hispanics, and economically disadvantaged whites, had 10,466 respondents. 2. The original sample, in which there was an overrepresentation of blacks, included 5,553 young women; in 1983, 68.7% of them were still being interviewed. 3. *9 to 5 Profile of Working Women*, 1994-1995 edition.

★ 451 ★
Spending

College Athletic Scholarships: 1993-1994

This table shows the total amount of money spent on athletic scholarships by NCAA Division I institutions in 1993-1994 who responded to a survey. It shows the percentage share that went to women and the percentage share that went to men. A survey conducted by the NCAA more than two years before this survey was undertaken by *The Chronicle of Higher Education* showed that male athletes received the majority of scholarships. *The Chronicle's* survey showed that little had changed.

| Institution | Athletes | | Spending on athletic scholarships | | |
	Percent men	Percent women	Total	Men	Women
Alabama State U	76.8%	23.2%	$501,785	77.5%	22.5%
Alcorn State U	80.0%	20.0%	$624,166	81.5%	18.5%
American U	48.1%	51.9%	$1,708,234	50.3%	49.7%
Appalachian State U	73.7%	26.3%	$931,170	77.3%	22.7%
Auburn U	67.4%	32.6%	$1,898,185	58.7%	41.3%
Austin Peay State U	75.3%	24.7%	$788,874	70.4%	29.6%
Ball State U	61.3%	38.7%	$1,616,547	64.4%	35.6%
Bethune-Cookman C	62.4%	37.6%	$864,558	78.2%	21.8%
Boise State U	70.1%	29.9%	$1,114,063	62.7%	37.3%
Boston C	67.6%	32.4%	$4,826,387	68.1%	31.9%
Bowling Green State U	65.0%	35.0%	$2,187,076	70.8%	29.2%
Bradley U	57.0%	43.0%	$1,147,664	50.0%	50.0%
Brigham Young U	72.9%	27.1%	$1,430,232	67.7%	32.3%
California State U Fresno	72.8%	27.2%	$1,438,739	69.1%	30.9%
California State U Fullerton	57.9%	42.1%	$592,156	54.0%	46.0%
California State U Long Beach	60.7%	39.3%	$570,484	47.5%	52.5%
California State U Northridge	68.6%	31.4%	$617,849	63.0%	37.0%
California State U Sacramento	71.1%	28.9%	$531,403	60.5%	39.5%
Campbell U	57.3%	42.7%	$919,911	53.5%	46.5%
Canisius C	72.0%	28.0%	$776,705	51.6%	48.4%
Centenary C (La)	54.5%	45.4%	$803,642	57.1%	42.9%
Central CT State U	74.5%	25.5%	$581,931	50.1%	49.9%
Charleston Southern U	67.6%	32.4%	$1,009,511	59.4%	40.6%
Chicago State U	54.3%	45.7%	$518,696	52.5%	47.5%
Clemson U	76.9%	23.1%	$2,490,059	73.0%	27.0%
Cleveland State U	57.0%	43.0%	$821,395	54.0%	46.0%
Coastal Carolina U	60.8%	39.2%	$953,154	54.6%	45.4%
C of Charleston	51.9%	48.1%	$598,341	57.8%	42.2%
C of the Holy Cross	60.0%	40.0%	$1,483,872	69.9%	30.1%
C of William and Mary	62.9%	37.1%	$2,051,800	64.5%	35.5%
Coppin State C	50.0%	50.0%	$428,001	63.6%	36.4%

[Continued]

★451★

College Athletic Scholarships: 1993-1994
[Continued]

Institution	Athletes		Spending on athletic scholarships		
	Percent men	Percent women	Total	Men	Women
Creighton U	54.0%	46.0%	$1,029,181	49.5%	50.5%
Davidson C	61.8%	38.2%	$590,258	53.0%	47.0%
Delaware State U	70.4%	29.6%	$820,309	76.5%	23.5%
DePaul U	55.4%	44.6%	$1,449,548	43.8%	56.2%
Drake U	69.8%	30.2%	$1,682,085	44.7%	55.3%
Drexel U	67.7%	32.3%	$1,482,845	57.1%	42.9%
Duquesne U	65.6%	34.4%	$1,207,100	52.4%	47.6%
East Carolina U	64.5%	35.5%	$1,495,044	77.6%	22.4%
East TN State U	73.9%	26.1%	$1,096,330	72.4%	27.6%
Eastern Illinois U	72.5%	27.5%	$832,174	73.5%	26.5%
Eastern Kentucky U	68.9%	31.1%	$1,000,941	66.8%	33.2%
Eastern Michigan U	74.5%	25.5%	$1,699,750	63.1%	36.9%
Eastern Washington U	60.4%	39.6%	$922,294	64.6%	35.4%
Fairfield U	60.2%	39.8%	$875,470	51.4%	48.6%
Florida A&M U	65.2%	34.8%	$882,480	77.1%	22.9%
Florida International U	58.8%	41.2%	$1,019,440	52.1%	47.9%
Florida State U	69.6%	30.4%	$1,800,540	62.0%	38.0%
Fordham U	69.0%	31.0%	$2,569,125	73.2%	26.8%
Furman U	72.6%	27.4%	$2,142,893	71.0%	29.0%
George Mason U	60.2%	39.8%	$1,608,736	55.2%	44.8%
Georgetown U	62.8%	37.2%	$1,931,594	52.3%	47.7%
George Washington U	52.9%	47.1%	$3,283,600	46.7%	53.3%
GA. Inst. of Technology	72.8%	27.2%	$2,152,225	76.0%	24.0%
Georgia Southern U	70.5%	29.5%	$802,353	69.8%	30.2%
Georgia State U	66.7%	33.3%	$691,503	48.8%	51.2%
Gonzaga U	56.8%	43.2%	$870,750	51.5%	48.5%
Grambling State U	77.5%	22.5%	$893,960	70.8%	29.2%
Hofstra U	68.2%	31.8%	$1,250,000	55.4%	44.6%
Howard U	77.4%	22.6%	$2,046,278	72.9%	27.1%
Idaho State U	69.3%	30.7%	$1,079,977	65.3%	34.7%
Illinois State U	66.6%	33.4%	$1,293,632	60.8%	39.2%
Indiana State U	68.1%	31.9%	$1,347,583	65.8%	34.2%
Indiana U	65.2%	34.8%	$2,751,300[1]	63.8%	36.2%
Iona C	73.8%	26.2%	$998,655	56.7%	44.3%
Iowa State U	67.9%	32.1%	$2,184,099	65.8%	34.2%
Jackson State U	75.7%	24.3%	$739,664	78.0%	22.0%
Jacksonville U	62.9%	37.1%	$737,400	63.5%	36.5%
James Madison U	61.5%	38.5%	$1,963,691	62.7%	37.3%
Kansas State U	74.4%	25.6%	$1,518,151	71.6%	28.2%

[Continued]

★ 451 ★

College Athletic Scholarships: 1993-1994
[Continued]

Institution	Athletes		Spending on athletic scholarships		
	Percent men	Percent women	Total	Men	Women
Liberty U	74.1%	25.9%	$2,087,000	72.7%	27.3%
Long Island U-					
Brooklyn Center	54.3%	45.7%	$1,133,270	59.5%	40.5%
Louisiana State U	72.1%	27.9%	$1,846,173	61.7%	38.3%
Louisiana Tech U	77.1%	22.9%	$917,309	76.2%	23.8%
Loyola C (MD)	49.8%	50.2%	$1,281,352	54.1%	45.9%
Loyola Marymount U	55.5%	44.5%	$1,202,315	51.7%	48.3%
Loyola U of Chicago	52.6%	47.4%	$1,120,000	48.6%	51.4%
Manhattan C	51.1%	48.9%	$1,371,634	49.9%	50.1%
Marist C	67.4%	32.6%	$948,493	56.9%	43.1%
Marquette U	58.8%	41.2%	$1,013,350	50.2%	49.8%
Marshall U	75.8%	24.2%	$1,234,373	73.7%	26.3%
McNeese State U	73.0%	27.0%	$923,594	72.3%	27.7%
Mercer U	57.1%	42.9%	$1,043,487	51.8%	48.2%
Miami U	71.7%	28.3%	$2,278,527	67.4%	32.6%
Middle TN State U	71.2%	28.8%	$1,017,288	73.2%	26.8%
Mississippi State U	78.3%	21.7%	$1,251,583	71.8%	39.2%
Mississippi Valley State U	79.1%	20.9%	$461,692	81.8%	18.2%
Monmouth C (NJ)	70.1%	29.9%	$899,342	52.9%	47.1%
Montana State U	67.3%	32.7%	$1,197,172	67.9%	32.1%
Morehead State U	71.8%	28.2%	$759,819	71.2%	28.8%
Morgan State U	68.8%	31.2%	$1,031,478	75.0%	25.0%
Mount Saint Mary's C	61.7%	38.3%	$909,074	53.9%	46.1%
Murray State U	78.9%	21.1%	$1,081,652	79.7%	20.3%
New Mexico State U	70.3%	29.7%	$1,369,863	69.9%	30.1%
Niagara U	51.8%	48.2%	$749,679	46.7%	53.3%
Nicholis State U	78.6%	21.4%	$745,843	73.7%	26.3%
North Carolina State U	77.5%	22.5%	$2,314,860	68.9%	31.1%
Northeast Louisiana U	68.4%	31.6%	$863,000	71.7%	28.3%
Northeastern Illinois U	56.9%	43.1%	$386,700	44.8%	55.2%
Northeastern U	66.2%	33.8%	$3,874,512	68.9%	31.1%
Northern Arizona U	66.7%	33.3%	$1,422,796	66.2%	33.8%
Northwestern State U					
of Louisiana	71.7%	28.3%	$693,350	70.7%	29.3%
Ohio State U	68.6%	31.4%	$3,335,968	58.0%	42.0%
Oklahoma State U	75.7%	24.3%	$1,320,235	73.3%	26.7%
Old Dominion U	57.8%	42.1%	$1,112,400	54.4%	45.6%
Oral Roberts U	53.7%	46.3%	$1,219,692	50.7%	49.3%
Oregon State U	61.5%	38.5%	$1,642,540	67.1%	32.9%
Pennsylvania State U	66.4%	33.6%	$3,422,470	66.2%	33.8%

[Continued]

★ 451 ★

College Athletic Scholarships: 1993-1994
[Continued]

Institution	Athletes		Spending on athletic scholarships		
	Percent men	Percent women	Total	Men	Women
Prairie View A&M U	72.7%	27.3%	$41,474	35.4%	64.6%
Providence C	55.9%	44.1%	$2,133,928	54.9%	45.1%
Purdue U	69.0%	31.0%	$2,456,206	71.2%	28.8%
Radford U	53.3%	46.7%	$805,744	51.3%	48.7%
Rider U	61.7%	38.3%	$1,389,185	52.6%	47.4%
Robert Morris C (PA)	51.8%	48.2%	$809,811	49.6%	50.4%
Rutgers U	65.7%	34.3%	$2,081,550	74.4%	25.6%
Saint Bonaventure U	53.1%	46.9%	$947,008	51.0%	49.0%
Saint Francis C (NY)	57.1%	42.9%	$603,029	54.7%	45.3%
Saint Francis C (PA)	65.0%	35.0%	$732,334	52.0%	48.0%
Saint Joseph's U	52.2%	47.8%	$1,281,000	50.9%	49.1%
Saint Mary's C of CA	72.8%	27.2%	$1,278,612	61.0%	39.0%
Saint Peter's C	63.9%	36.1%	$847,481	49.6%	50.4%
Samford U	71.1%	28.9%	$1,581,885	72.3%	27.7%
Sam Houston State U	71.2%	28.8%	$738,733	68.9%	31.1%
San Diego State U	65.9%	34.1%	$1,189,142	71.8%	28.2%
San Jose State U	65.9%	34.1%	$1,180,096	66.6%	33.4%
Santa Clara U	41.2%	58.8%	$1,260,676	50.8%	49.2%
Seton Hall U	63.0%	37.0%	$1,994,597	51.3%	48.7%
Siena C	64.1%	35.9%	$748,195	49.2%	50.8%
South Carolina State U	66.5%	33.5%	$515,255	72.2%	27.8%
Southeast MO State U	65.0%	35.0%	$949,991	67.5%	32.5%
Southeastern LA U	55.4%	44.6%	$354,101	47.9%	52.1%
Southern Utah U	69.5%	30.5%	$480,592	62.9%	37.1%
Southwest MO State U	70.2%	29.8%	$1,437,522	64.2%	35.8%
Southwest Texas State U	69.0%	31.0%	$995,724	66.2%	33.8%
Stanford U	63.4%	36.6%	$4,839,738	67.9%	32.1%
Stephen F. Austin State U	73.8%	26.2%	$851,490	71.6%	28.4%
Stetson U	46.7%	53.3%	$994,402	52.3%	47.7%
Syracuse U	67.6%	32.4%	$4,317,880	73.7%	26.3%
Tennessee State U	65.4%	34.6%	$711,237	79.5%	20.5%
TN Technological U	68.0%	32.0%	$910,262	75.2%	24.8%
Texas A&M U	65.6%	34.4%	$1,433,031	60.2%	39.8%
Texas Southern U	73.9%	26.1%	$677,929	77.4%	22.6%
Texas Tech U	77.2%	22.8%	$1,383,682	70.7%	29.3%
Towson State U	62.8%	37.2%	$1,081,344	62.2%	37.8%
Tulane U	69.6%	30.4%	$4,235,365	75.6%	24.4%
U of Akron	73.2%	26.8%	$1,739,185	76.4%	23.6%
U of Alabama Birmingham	77.4%	22.6%	$774,000	56.2%	43.8%
U of Arizona	68.8%	31.2%	$3,132,265	59.4%	40.6%
U of AK Fayetteville	73.6%	26.4%	$1,631,077	72.5%	27.5%

[Continued]

★ 451 ★

College Athletic Scholarships: 1993-1994
[Continued]

Institution	Athletes		Spending on athletic scholarships		
	Percent men	Percent women	Total	Men	Women
U of AK Little Rock	63.3%	36.7%	$782,737	64.4%	35.6%
U of CA Berkeley	67.4%	32.6%	$2,562,303	67.0%	33.0%
U of CA Irvine	56.7%	43.3%	$537,024	50.1%	49.9%
U of CA Los Angeles	65.5%	34.5%	$2,728,365	63.8%	36.2%
U of CA Santa Barbara	63.2%	36.8%	$786,618	48.1%	51.9%
U of Cincinnati	77.1%	22.9%	$2,067,000	78.4%	21.6%
U of Connecticut	61.1%	38.9%	$2,256,634	66.5%	33.5%
U of Dayton	71.2%	28.8%	$869,850	50.9%	49.1%
U of Detroit Mercy	55.2%	44.8%	$1,088,500	50.0%	50.0%
U of Evansville	66.7%	33.3%	$1,096,710	51.9%	48.1%
U of Florida	68.4%	31.6%	$1,614,559	68.0%	32.0%
U of Georgia	66.0%	34.0%	$1,941,040	60.0%	40.0%
U of Hawaii	74.1%	25.9%	$1,675,257	65.6%	34.4%
U of Idaho	63.5%	36.5%	$1,090,303	68.2%	31.8%
U of Illinois Chicago	58.1%	41.9%	$1,235,876	59.1%	40.9%
U of Illinois Urbana Champaign	72.1%	27.9%	$2,366,673	65.8%	34.2%
U of Iowa	68.3%	31.7%	$2,449,741	60.0%	40.0%
U of Kansas	70.0%	30.0%	$2,091,589	64.4%	35.6%
U of Kentucky	66.7%	33.3%	$1,933,442	63.4%	36.6%
U of Louisville	69.3%	30.7%	$1,895,191	70.1%	29.9%
U of Maine	66.9%	33.1%	$1,666,977	76.6%	23.4%
U of Maryland Baltimore County	51.3%	48.7%	$754,778	55.4%	44.6%
U of Maryland College Park	65.1%	34.9%	$2,698,712	69.2%	30.8%
U of Maryland Eastern Shore	55.6%	44.4%	$367,678	47.0%	53.0%
U of Massachusetts Amherst	65.8%	34.2%	$2,472,062	61.5%	38.5%
U of Memphis	76.8%	23.2%	$1,386,926	74.2%	25.8%
U of Michigan	62.5%	37.5%	$5,237,220	61.4%	38.6%
U of Minnesota Twin Cities	62.7%	37.3%	$2,691,928	68.7%	31.3%
U of Mississippi	75.9%	24.1%	$1,342,011	70.6%	29.4%
U of MO Columbia	65.8%	34.2%	$1,828,649	65.8%	34.2%
U of MO Kansas City	50.3%	49.7%	$787,672	51.3%	48.7%
U of Montana	64.4%	35.6%	$1,061,277	69.6%	30.4%
U of Nebraska Lincoln	70.2%	29.8%	$1,887,050	63.0%	37.0%
U of Nevada Las Vegas	70.8%	28.2%	$2,334,650	67.4%	32.6%

[Continued]

★ 451 ★

College Athletic Scholarships: 1993-1994
[Continued]

Institution	Athletes		Spending on athletic scholarships		
	Percent men	Percent women	Total	Men	Women
U of Nevada Reno	68.3%	31.7%	$1,572,915	71.8%	28.2%
U of New Hampshire	60.0%	40.0%	$2,182,337	67.7%	32.3%
U of New Mexico	70.1%	29.9%	$2,215,480	70.2%	29.8%
U of New Orleans	58.6%	41.4%	$663,393	55.7%	44.3%
U of NC Asheville	57.3%	42.7%	$550,376	56.0%	44.0%
U of NC Chapel Hill	63.1%	36.9%	$2,781,746	61.9%	38.1%
U of NC Charlotte	61.3%	38.7%	$690,000	57.4%	42.6%
U of NC Greensboro	58.4%	41.6%	$700,420	49.1%	50.9%
U of NC Wilmington	58.7%	41.3%	$667,799	57.2%	42.8%
U of North Texas	70.8%	29.2%	$876,235	71.3%	28.7%
U of Northern Iowa	67.6%	32.4%	$984,504	69.6%	30.4%
U of Notre Dame	70.5%	29.5%	$4,385,570	67.7%	32.3%
U of Oklahoma	70.4%	29.6%	$1,618,651	66.6%	33.4%
U of Oregon	69.4%	30.6%	$1,899,777	65.5%	34.5%
U of the Pacific	68.4%	31.6%	$3,288,267	67.6%	32.3%
U of Pittsburgh	78.2%	21.8%	$2,450,246	71.9%	28.1%
U of Portland	56.5%	43.5%	$1,120,125	52.2%	47.8%
U of Rhode Island	63.1%	36.9%	$2,098,650	66.8%	33.2%
U of San Diego	61.8%	38.2%	$1,500,300	49.5%	50.5%
U of San Francisco	52.0%	48.0%	$1,378,494	53.8%	46.2%
U of South Alabama	68.7%	31.3%	$637,403	59.6%	40.4%
U of South Carolina	66.6%	33.4%	$1,836,602	63.8%	36.2%
U of South Florida	53.7%	46.3%	$820,828	47.9%	52.1%
U of Southern CA	67.0%	33.0%	$4,655,152	66.7%	33.3%
U of Southern MS	80.6%	19.4%	$1,156,809	76.0%	24.0%
U of Southwestern LA	79.7%	20.3%	$765,544	72.4%	27.6%
U of TN Chattanooga	72.9%	27.1%	$1,190,931	78.3%	21.7%
U of TN Knoxville	71.4%	28.6%	$1,841,846	70.3%	29.7%
U of TN Martin	67.1%	32.9%	$807,760	78.6%	21.4%
U of TX Arlington	57.6%	42.4%	$642,692	49.4%	50.6%
U of TX Austin	69.8%	30.2%	$1,324,073	66.8%	33.2%
U of TX El Paso	71.3%	28.7%	$1,291,149	72.8%	27.2%
U of TX Pan American	70.1%	29.9%	$452,178	60.0%	40.0%
U of Toledo	66.2%	33.8%	$1,825,897	65.3%	34.7%
U of Tulsa	68.7%	31.3%	$2,420,920	73.3%	26.7%
U of Utah	67.1%	32.9%	$1,736,264	67.6%	32.4%
U of Vermont	52.7%	47.3%	$1,417,504	51.6%	48.4%
U of Virginia	64.7%	35.3%	$3,026,095	67.6%	32.4%
U of Washington	56.0%	44.0%	$2,959,952	58.6%	41.4%
U of WI Green Bay	43.5%	56.5%	$715,648	45.6%	54.4%
U of WI Madison	66.0%	34.0%	$2,484,906	70.7%	29.3%

[Continued]

★ 451 ★

College Athletic Scholarships: 1993-1994
[Continued]

Institution	Athletes Percent men	Athletes Percent women	Spending on athletic scholarships Total	Men	Women
U of WI Milwaukee	59.9%	40.1%	$706,995	54.5%	45.5%
U of Wyoming	74.9%	25.1%	$1,550,661	73.1%	26.9%
Utah State U	69.3%	30.7%	$1,215,504	71.4%	28.6%
Valparaiso U	66.8%	33.2%	$994,736	51.4%	48.6%
Villanova U	66.6%	33.4%	$2,932,746	70.0%	30.0%
VA Commonwealth U	63.6%	36.4%	$1,041,474	52.7%	47.3%
VA Polytechnic Institute and State U	73.7%	26.3%	$2,160,459	78.1%	21.9%
Wagner C	67.1%	32.9%	$1,160,073	54.6%	45.4%
Washington State U	52.8%	47.2%	$2,063,153	59.0%	41.0%
Weber State U	65.8%	34.2%	$765,596	72.3%	27.7%
West Virginia U	76.7%	23.3%	$2,039,391	74.1%	25.9%
Western Carolina U	74.1%	25.9%	$662,262	75.2%	24.8%
Western Illinois U	70.4%	29.6%	$905,350	66.2%	33.8%
Western Kentucky U	74.9%	25.1%	$985,279	75.5%	24.5%
Western Michigan U	72.4%	27.6%	$1,690,745	69.9%	30.1%
Wichita State U	61.2%	38.8%	$811,937	45.5%	54.5%
Wright State U	55.5%	44.5%	$962,633	50.9%	49.1%
Xavier U (Ohio)	57.1%	42.9%	$1,013,652	53.0%	47.0%
Youngstown State U	71.2%	28.8%	$981,025	70.8%	29.2%
Division I average	66.4%	33.6%	$1,463,524	64.3%	35.7%

Source: Debra E. Blum, "Slow Progress on Equity: Survey of Division I colleges shows little has changed for female athletes," *The Chronicle of Higher Education*, October 26, 1994, p. A45+. *Note:* 1. Estimate.

★ 452 ★
Spending

Cost of Earning a Doctorate: 1993

This table shows the median level of debt related to the education of doctorate recipients in 1993.

Gender	All Ph.D.s	Responses to debt status	Percent with debt	Median dollars[1]
All Ph.D.s	39,754	36,861	47.6%	$10,500
Men	24,646	22,777	47.8%	$10,500
Women	15,108	14,084	47.4%	$10,600

Source: Selected from "Median Level of Debt Related to the Education of Doctorate Recipients, 1993," Thurgood, D.H., and J.E. Clarke, 1995, *Summary Report 1993: Doctorate Recipients from United States Universities*, Table 112, p. 30. Primary source: National Research Council, Survey of Earned Doctorates. "All Ph.D.s" includes recipients whose debt status is unknown; percentages are based on the number with "responses to debt status." *Note:* 1. Rounded to nearest hundred dollars.

★ 453 ★

Spending

Cost of Postsecondary Schooling: 1990-1991

This table shows average postsecondary schooling costs by level of enrollment and gender for school year 1990-1991.

Characteristic and gender	Total	College yrs. 1 to 2	College yrs. 3 to 4	College yrs. 5+	Voc tech/bus school/other
Female					
Total cost					
Mean	$2,560	$2,627	$3,559	$2,552	$1,098
Std. error	79	132	174	177	106
Tuition and fees					
Mean	$1,621	$1,587	$2,083	$1,788	$898
Std. error	53	87	117	127	88
Books and supplies					
Mean	$283	$301	$385	$267	$128
Std. error	10	12	23	22	22
Room and board					
Mean	$3,221	$3,309	$3,446	$2,927	[1]
Std. error	112	155	162	381	[1]
Male					
Total cost					
Mean	$2,762	$2,871	$4,130	$2,812	$1,036
Std. error	96	165	207	212	134
Tuition and fees					
Mean	$1,686	$1,775	$2,290	$1,879	$720
Std. error	62	107	133	143	94
Books and supplies					
Mean	$296	$318	$416	$323	$107
Std. error	12	19	26	36	16
Room and board					
Mean	$3,125	$3,075	$3,481	$2,935	$2,043
Std. error	110	151	169	353	378

Source: Selected from "Average Postsecondary Schooling Costs by Level of Enrollment, Sex, Race/Ethnicity, Family Income and Dependency Status: 1990-1991," *Dollars for Scholars: Postsecondary Costs and Financing, 1990-1991*, U.S. Bureau of the Census, Current Population Reports, P70-39, Table 2, p. 17. *Note:* 1. Base is less than 200,000.

★ 454 ★

Spending

Cost to Government of Teenage Births: 1990

This table shows the projected average 20-year cost to support *each* family begun by a teenager in 1990 and the potential savings associated with delaying these births.[1,3]

Age	No. of first births[2]	Family cost[3]	Avg. single potential savings[4]
Under 15	11,006	$23,094	$9,237
15-17	154,244	$23,050	$9,219
18-19	228,869	$14,581	$5,834
TOTAL	394,119	$18,133	$7,253

Source: "1990 Single Birth Cost," *Teenage Pregnancy and Too-Early Childbearing: Public Costs, Personal Consequences,* The Center for Population Options, 6th Edition, 1992, Table III, p. 6. *Notes:* 1. Based on AFDC, Medicaid, and Food Stamp expenditures. 2. 1989 natality statistics were the latest available. 3. Cost is expressed in 1990 "present value" dollars, which means that this is the amount that would have to be set aside in 1990 to cover the 20-year cost of the average family begun by a first birth to a teen in 1990, after taking into consideration inflation and the future earning power of a dollar invested in 1990. 4. Calculated at 40% of full cost.

★ 455 ★

Spending

Doctorate Recipients' Sources of Support: 1993

This table shows the primary sources of support for doctorate recipients in 1993.

Primary source of support	All Ph.D.s	Men	Women
All fields	26,260	16,227	10,033
Personal	36.8%	29.9%	48.0%
University	51.0%	56.7%	41.7%
Federal	5.5%	5.4%	5.8%
Other	6.7%	8.0%	4.5%

Source: Selected from "Primary Sources of Support for Doctorate Recipients, by Broad Field and Demographic Group, 1993," Thurgood, D.H., and J.E. Clarke, 1995, *Summary Report 1993: Doctorate Recipients from United States Universities,* Table 11, p. 29. Primary source: National Research Council, Survey of Earned Doctorates. Numbers represent those Ph.D.s with known primary support; percentages are based on these numbers. The overall nonresponse rate to "primary" source of support was 33.9% in 1993. "Personal" includes loans as well as own earnings and contributions from the spouse/family. Federally funded research assistantships (RAs) are grouped under "University" because not all recipients of such support are aware of the actual source of funding. "Other" support includes U.S. nationally competitive fellowships, business/employer funds, foreign government, state government, and other nonspecified sources. Also in source: figures by broad field.

★ 456 ★
Spending

Expenditures of Renters by Government Assistance Category

This table shows average annual income and average total quarterly expenditures for three groups of renters: those receiving government assistance; those not receiving assistance; and those ineligible for assistance. About 40% of all renters receiving assistance are single parents, compared to 13% of eligible renters who do not receive assistance and 6% of ineligible renters. Thirty-two percent of households receiving assistance are headed by a black reference person. The average household size of renters receiving assistance is 2.6 persons, compared to 2.3 persons in households of renters who are eligible but not receiving assistance. On average, both eligible groups spend less than one-half of the amount spent by ineligible renters. The largest portion of the total budget of renters in both eligible groups goes to rent and utilities.

Variable	Eligible for assistance		Ineligible for assistance
	Receiving assistance	Not receiving assistance	
Mean quarterly rental assistance	$918.49	$0.00	$0.00
Mean annual income before taxes	$7,723.82	$9,646.48	$25,387.15
Wages and salary:			
Mean	$2,418	$6,506	$21,118
Percent reporting	39.0%	56.7%	82.7%
Percent of total income	31.3%	67.4%	83.2%
Self-employment and farm income:[2]			
Mean	$74.11	$214.67	$1,325.81
Percent reporting	1.6%	3.5%	9.1%
Percent of total income	1.0%	2.2%	5.2%
Social Security and retirement income:[3]			
Mean	$1,689.98	$1,503.02	$1,111.32
Percent reporting	29.6%	22.7%	12.0%
Percent of total income	21.9%	15.6%	4.4%
Assistance income:[4]			
Mean	$3,485.18	$1,242.24	$683.28
Percent reporting	71.3%	33.3%	18.6%
Percent of total income	45.1%	12.9%	2.7%
Dividend and interest income:			
Mean	$12.66	$144.73	$418.22
Percent reporting	7.6%	13.3%	29.7%
Percent of total income	0.2%	1.5%	1.6%
Other types of income:[5]			
Mean	$43.73	$39.68	$730.52
Percent reporting	4.1%	1.7%	2.9%
Percent of total income	0.6%	0.4%	0.3%

[Continued]

★ 456 ★

Expenditures of Renters by Government Assistance Category
[Continued]

Variable	Eligible for assistance		Ineligible for assistance
	Receiving assistance	Not receiving assistance	
Total quarterly expenditures[6]			
Food:			
Mean	$658.35	$604.56	$1,023.78
Percent reporting	99.2%	99.4%	99.9%
Budget share	29.3%	25.2%	17.6%
Alcohol and tobacco:			
Mean	$80.84	$88.64	$173.16
Percent reporting	56.1%	56.6%	76.7%
Budget share	3.6%	3.7%	3.0%
Rent and utilities:			
Mean	$663.54	$1,012.19	$1,630.49
Percent reporting	99.6%	99.3%	99.9%
Budget share	29.5%	42.2%	28.0%
Household operations and furnishings:			
Mean	$112.74	$60.54	$323.88
Percent reporting	68.0%	54.8%	80.6%
Budget share	5.0%	2.5%	5.6%
Apparel and services:			
Mean	$152.44	$113.86	$359.54
Percent reporting	90.8%	83.5%	95.2%
Budget share	6.8%	4.7%	6.2%
Transportation:			
Mean	$232.03	$272.16	$1,180.29
Percent reporting	77.8%	83.8%	98.3%
Budget share	10.3%	11.3%	20.3%
Health and personal care:			
Mean	$134.87	$118.84	$323.31
Percent reporting	74.3%	78.5%	95.0%
Budget share	6.0%	4.9%	5.5%
Entertainment:			
Mean	$100.07	$70.92	$321.12
Percent reporting	74.5%	67.6%	93.7%
Budget share	4.5%	3.0%	5.5%
Other expenditures:[7]			
Mean	$91.39	$57.26	$370.89

[Continued]

★ 456 ★

Expenditures of Renters by Government Assistance Category
[Continued]

Variable	Eligible for assistance		Ineligible for assistance
	Receiving assistance	Not receiving assistance	
Percent reporting	65.1%	66.9%	92.6%
Budget share	4.1%	2.4%	6.4%

Source: Robert Cage, "How does rental assistance influence spending behavior," *Monthly Labor Review*, May 1994, Table 3, "Weighted income and expenditure statistics for renters, by category of assistance, Consumer Expenditure Survey, 1988-90[1]." *Notes:* 1. Sample size of all renters was 24,855. Those in public housing (n = 868), those not reporting amount of assistance (n = 553), and those reporting assistance other than governmental (n = 1,363) were removed. 2. Self-employment and farm income includes all earnings from self-employment, both farm and nonfarm. 3. Social Security and retirement income includes Social Security income and income from pensions or annuities from private companies, the Federal Government, or individual retirement accounts. 4. Assistance income includes unemployment compensation, workers' compensation, veterans' payments, public assistance, supplemental security income, food stamps, and other financial assistance. 5. Other types of income include money received from care of foster children, cash scholarships, and stipends not based on working. 6. Total quarterly expenditures equal Bureau of Labor Statistics published definition, minus personal insurance and pensions and vehicle monthly payment, instead of purchases and interest. 7. Other expenditures include expenditures for reading and education, miscellaneous expenditures, cash contributions, and other housing expenditures.

★ 457 ★
Spending

Expenditures, With Children, With and Without a Husband: 1993

This table shows average annual expenditures and characteristics of consumer units, from the Consumer Expenditure Survey, 1993.

[Units in thousands.]

Item	Husband and wife consumer units			One parent, at at least one child under 18
	Total husband & units	Husband & wife only	Husband & wife with children	
Number of consumer units	52,516	21,179	27,330	7,022
Consumer unit characteristics:				
Income before taxes	$46,614	$41,473	$50,615	$19,458
Averages:				
Age of reference person	48.0	57.0	41.0	34.9
Number of persons in unit	3.2	2.0	3.9	2.9
Number of earners	1.7	1.2	2.0	0.9
Number of vehicles	2.6	2.3	2.7	1.0
Percent homeowner	79%	82%	77%	31%
Average annual expenditures	$39,771	$34,566	$43,644	$20,937
Food	$5,641	$4,632	$6,258	$4,043
Food at home	$3,515	$2,780	$3,896	$2,926
Food away from home	$2,126	$1,852	$2,362	$1,117
Alcoholic beverages	$288	$288	$297	$124

[Continued]

★ 457 ★

Expenditures, With Children, With and Without a Husband: 1993
[Continued]

Item	Husband and wife consumer units			One parent, at at least one child under 18
	Total husband & units	Husband & wife only	Husband & wife with children	
Housing	$11,952	$10,181	$13,292	$7,656
Apparel and services	$2,150	$1,767	$2,424	$1,434
Transportation	$7,453	$6,363	$8,169	$2,728
Health care	$2,323	$2,648	$2,102	$885
Entertainment	$2,178	$1,805	$2,526	$1,038
Personal care products and services	$505	$460	$533	$275
Reading	$204	$213	$202	$90
Education	$588	$321	$815	$259
Tobacco products and smoking supplies	$299	$236	$329	$230
Miscellaneous	$865	$768	$916	$513
Cash contributions	$1,265	$1,542	$1,107	$260
Personal insurance and pensions	$4,061	$3,342	$4,673	$1,404
Life and other personal insurance	$581	$508	$650	$211
Pensions and Social Security	$3,481	$2,834	$4,024	$1,193

Source: Selected from "Composition of consumer unit: Average annual expenditures and characteristics, Consumer Expenditure Survey, 1993," *Consumer Expenditures in 1993*, U.S. Department of Labor, Bureau of Labor Statistics, Report 885, December 1994, Table 5, p. 10.

★ 458 ★

Spending

Federal Grants for WIC Program by State: 1990

This table shows the amount granted to each state for the Women, Infants, and Children Special Supplemental Food Program in 1990. States are shown in order from the state receiving the most to the state receiving the least. The state's percentage of the national total outlay of $2,111,431,000 is also shown.

State	Grant	% of total
California	$193,289,000	9.15%
New York	$165,965,000	7.86%
Texas	$149,360,000	7.07%
Ohio	$86,882,000	4.11%
Florida	$84,949,000	4.02%
Illinois	$84,580,000	4.01%

[Continued]

★ 458 ★

Federal Grants for WIC Program by State: 1990
[Continued]

State	Grant	% of total
Pennsylvania	$79,267,000	3.75%
Michigan	$70,703,000	3.35%
Georgia	$65,794,000	3.12%
North Carolina	$65,598,000	3.11%
Louisiana	$57,819,000	2.74%
New Jersey	$45,046,000	2.13%
Missouri	$43,520,000	2.06%
Tennessee	$41,368,000	1.96%
Mississippi	$40,923,000	1.94%
Alabama	$40,900,000	1.94%
Virginia	$40,806,000	1.93%
South Carolina	$40,749,000	1.93%
Kentucky	$40,390,000	1.91%
Indiana	$38,043,000	1.80%
Arizona	$36,760,000	1.74%
Massachusetts	$33,612,000	1.59%
Oklahoma	$32,471,000	1.54%
Wisconsin	$31,835,000	1.51%
Minnesota	$31,772,000	1.50%
Connecticut	$29,720,000	1.41%
Washington	$28,324,000	1.34%
Arkansas	$27,943,000	1.32%
Maryland	$26,449,000	1.25%
Oregon	$21,798,000	1.03%
Colorado	$21,434,000	1.02%
Iowa	$21,164,000	1.00%
Utah	$21,002,000	0.99%
West Virginia	$18,371,000	0.87%
Kansas	$17,789,000	0.84%
New Mexico	$17,715,000	0.84%
Nebraska	$11,882,000	0.56%
Hawaii	$10,945,000	0.52%
Maine	$10,891,000	0.52%
Idaho	$10,733,000	0.51%
South Dakota	$9,457,000	0.45%
Rhode Island	$8,395,000	0.40%
Montana	$7,831,000	0.37%
Nevada	$7,749,000	0.37%
New Hampshire	$7,681,000	0.36%

[Continued]

★ 458 ★

Federal Grants for WIC Program by State: 1990

[Continued]

State	Grant	% of total
North Dakota	$7,516,000	0.36%
Vermont	$6,753,000	0.32%
Alaska	$6,190,000	0.29%
Delaware	$5,089,000	0.24%
Wyoming	$4,870,000	0.23%
District of Columbia	$6,783,000	0.32%
Puerto Rico	$87,567,000	4.15%

Source: "Federal Grants to State and Local Governments for WIC Program in 1990," *State Rankings,* 1992, p. 431. Primary source: U.S. Bureau of the Census, "Federal Expenditures by State for FY 1990," (April 1991).

★ 459 ★

Spending

Government Spending for Teenage Mothers: 1990

This table shows the single year public cost for all families started by a teen birth and the potential savings associated with delaying these births.

[In billions of dollars.]

Funding Source	Total outlay for AFDC recipients	Attributable to teenage childbearing[1]	Potential savings[2]
Aid to Families with Dependent Children	$21.20	$11.23	$4.49
Food Stamps	$7.50	$3.98	$1.56
Medicaid	$18.57	$9.84	$3.94
TOTAL		$25.05	$10.02

Source: "1990 Single Year Cost," *Teenage Pregnancy and Too-Early Childbearing: Public Costs, Personal Consequences,* The Center for Population Options, 6th Edition, 1992, Table 1, p. 5. *Notes:* 1. Based on the assumption that families begun by a teen birth consume 53% of these funding sources. 2. Calculated at 40% of full cost.

★ 460 ★

Spending

Medical Costs for the Uninsured Midlife Woman

This table shows average out-of-pocket costs for medical expenditures for uninsured midlife women and men by type of service.

[Midlife are persons aged 45 to 64.]

Type of service	Men	Women
Hospital stay	$1,262	$3,024
Physician visits	$132	$212
Outpatient	$41	$599
Home health	$53	$387
Prescription drugs	$180	$219

Source: "Average Out-Of-Pocket Costs for Uninsured Midlife Women and Men by Type of Service," American Association of Retired Persons Fact Sheet, *Health Insurance Status of Midlife Women,* Chart 7, p. 5. Primary source: 1987 National Medical Expenditure Survey. Projected forward using medical CPI.

★ 461 ★

Spending

Purchases of Athletic Footwear

This table shows the amount of money spent on women's athletic footwear between 1982 and 1992. Athletic footwear is footwear made for sports and fitness activities.

[In billions of dollars.]

Year	Billions
1982	$1.16
1984	$1.45
1986	$2.37
1988	$3.55
1990	$4.69
1992	$4.68

Source: "Retail Dollars Sales," *The U.S. Athletic Footwear Market Today,* Athletic Footwear Association, 1993, p. 2.

★ 462 ★

Spending

Shrinking Pantyhose Market

This table presents some statistics about pantyhose and high-heeled shoes. According to *American Demographics*, the Sara Lee Corporation, makers of L'Eggs and Hanes Hosiery, experienced a 5% worldwide decline in hosiery sales in the last 3 months of 1992 and an 8% decline in the first quarter of 1993. A more casual lifestyle is blamed for the decline.

Item	Number/Percent
Percentage of women who wore pantyhose "nearly every day," 1992:	26%
Executive and professional women	49%
White-collar workers	43%
Blue-collar workers	22%
Homemakers	11%
Percentage of women who bought at least one pair of pantyhose in the last 6 months:	
1986	82%
1993	75%
Women's complaints about pantyhose:	
They rip too easily	39%
They are hard to put on	31%
They bind at the waist	17%
They itch	12%
Percentage of women who wore high-heeled shoes at least twice a week:	
1985	38%
1992	26%
Percentage of women working in professional jobs who bought a new pair of dress shoes in the last year:	
1986	57%
1993	30%

Source: Deborah Bosanko, "The Pantyhose Market Is in a Bind," *American Demographics*, April 1994, p. 17.

★ 463 ★

Spending

Spending on Sporting Goods and Equipment

This table shows the total amount of money spent on sporting goods and equipment in 1992 in millions and the percentages of males and females who used the equipment.

[Projected sales in millions.]

Item	Projected sales	Male	Female
Athletic and sport clothing	$10,101.1	48.8%	51.2%
Athletic footwear	$6,242.0	48.8%	51.2%
Athletic and sport equipment	$12,815.8	48.8%	51.2%

Source: Selected from *The Sporting Goods Market in 1993,* National Sporting Goods Association, 1993, all pages.

★ 464 ★

Spending

What Price a Good Jacket?

Consumer Reports tested women's and men's jackets purchased in spring 1994. The results showed that a good women's jacket is usually expensive, while a good men's jacket need not be. This table shows the top five rated women's jackets in order of quality and their prices.

Brand	Price
Calvin Klein	$380
Francess & Rita	$218
Ralph Lauren	$510
Ellen Tracy	
(Linda Allard)	$395
Brooks Brothers	$295

Source: "How to Buy a Jacket," *Consumer Reports*, March 1995, pp. 134+.

Wages and Salaries

★ 465 ★

African Agricultural Wages

This table shows earnings in agriculture in selected African countries for the years 1987-1992.

Country	Time period	Currency	1987	1988	1989	1990	1991	1992
Africa								
Botswana[1]	Month	Pula						
Total			92.56	98.62	129.40	161.00	212.00	166.00
Male			NA	NA	NA	NA	217.00	164.00
Female			NA	NA	NA	NA	198.00	168.00
Egypt[2]	Week	Pounds						
Total			25	25	29	34	NA	NA
Male			26	25	29	32	NA	NA
Female			22	22	26	34	NA	NA
Kenya[3]	Month	Shillings						
Total			794.3	933.9	990.8	1,084.9	1,225.4	NA
Male			864.4	1,009.6	1,051.2	1,148.4	1,291.5	NA
Female			553.0	691.6	791.9	882.5	1,012.1	NA
Swaziland|4	Month	Emalengeni						
Male			631	1,146	NA	NA	NA	NA
Female			120	811	NA	NA	NA	NA

Source: Selected from "Wages in agriculture," *Year Book of Labour Statistics,* International Labour Office, Geneva, 1994, Table 21, pp. 807+. *Notes:* 1. Citizens only; employees. September of each year, except 1991-1992, which is March. 2. Establishments with 10 or more persons employed. October of each year. 3. Employees. Including the value of payments in kind. June of each year. 4. June of each year. Skilled wage earners. Including forestry.

★ 466 ★

Wages and Salaries

African Construction Wages

This table shows earnings in construction in three African countries for the years 1987-1991. Later data was not available.

Country	Time period	Currency	1987	1988	1989	1990	1991
Africa							
Egypt[1]	Week	Pounds					
Total			40	45	51	55	NA
Male			41	45	51	55	NA

[Continued]

★ 466 ★

African Construction Wages
[Continued]

Country	Time period	Currency	1987	1988	1989	1990	1991
Female			32	44	47	50	NA
Kenya²	Month	Shillings					
Total			1,593.0	1,736.0	1,976.3	2,262.7	2,622.0
Male			1,619.9	1,749.4	2,006.4	2,292.5	2,650.1
Female			1,298.0	1,505.2	1,664.5	1,754.5	2,160.0
Swaziland³	Month	Emalangeni					
Male			169	180	181	NA	NA
Female			137	131	128	NA	NA

Source: Selected from "Wages in construction," *Year Book of Labour Statistics,* International Labour Office, Geneva, 1994, Table 19, pp. 790+. *Notes:* 1. Establishments with 10 or more persons employed. October of each year. 2. Employees. Including the value of payments in kind. June of each year. 3. June of each year. Unskilled wage earners.

★ 467 ★

Wages and Salaries

African Manufacturing Wages

This table shows earnings in manufacturing in selected African countries for the years 1987-1991. Later figures were not available.

Country	Time period	Currency	1987	1988	1989	1990	1991
Africa							
Egypt¹							
Total¹	Week	Pounds¹	38	41	46	54	NA
Men¹			39	43	48	56	NA
Women¹			28	31	34	38	NA
Kenya²							
Total²	Month	Shillings	2,293.8	2,469.7	2,797.5	3,064.6	3,324.2
Men²			2,376.7	2,576.0	2,890.9	3,159.8	3,430.1
Women²			1,551.1	1,751.7	2,001.7	2,317.7	2,515.8
Swaziland							
Skilled wage earners	Month	Emalengeni					
Males			1,032	941	1,040	NA	NA
Females			577	404	561	NA	NA
Unskilled wage earners							
Males			234	218	257	NA	NA
Females			192	170	207	NA	NA

Source: Selected from "Wages in manufacturing," *Year Book of Labour Statistics,* International Labour Office, Geneva, 1994, Table 17, pp. 710+. *Notes:* 1. Establishments with 10 mor more persons employed. October of each year. 2. Employees. Including the value of payments in kind. June of each year. .

★ 468 ★

Wages and Salaries

African Mining and Quarrying Wages

This table shows earnings in mining and quarrying in three African countries for the years 1987-1991.

Country	Time period	Currency	1987	1988	1989	1990	1991
Africa							
Egypt[1]	Week	Pounds					
Total			59	NA	86	NA	NA
Male			59	NA	86	NA	NA
Female			75	NA	96	NA	NA
Kenya[2]	Month	Shillings					
Total			1,807.1	1,841.3	2,171.5	2,315.2	2,550.8
Male			1,825.4	1,991.7	2,136.5	2,264.6	2,476.1
Female			969.9	2,231.1	2.329.9	2,509.1	2,843.9
Swaziland[3]	Month	Emalangeni					
Male			299	302	330	NA	NA
Female			238	243	307	NA	NA

Source: Selected from "Wages in mining and quarrying," *Year Book of Labour Statistics,* International Labour Office, Geneva, 1994, Table 18, pp. 782+. *Notes:* 1. Establishments with 10 or more persons employed. October of each year. 2. Employees. Including the value of payments in kind. June of each year. 3. June of each year. Unskilled wage earners.

★ 469 ★

Wages and Salaries

African Transport, Storage, and Communication Wages

This table shows earnings in transport, storage, and communication in selected African countries for the years 1987-1991. Later data was not available.

Country	Time period	Currency	1987	1988	1989	1990	1991
Africa							
Egypt[1]	Week	Pounds					
Total			36	46	50	53	NA
Male			36	46	49	53	NA
Female			41	50	55	55	NA
Kenya[2]	Month	Shillings					
Total			3,208.4	3,669.7	3,968.7	4,276.9	4,714.5
Male			3,017.0	3,827.1	4,060.4	4,358.2	4,805.5
Female			4,935.0	2,557.5	3,370.3	3,745.9	4,150.6

[Continued]

★ 469 ★

African Transport, Storage, and Communication Wages
[Continued]

Country	Time period	Currency	1987	1988	1989	1990	1991
Swaziland³	Month	Emalangeni					
Male			183	201	198	NA	NA
Female			NA	137	162	NA	NA

Source: Selected from "Wages in transport, storage and communication," *Year Book of Labour Statistics,* International Labour Office, Geneva, 1994, Table 20, pp. 799+. *Notes:* 1. Establishments with 10 or more persons employed. October of each year. 2. Employees. Including the value of payments in kind. June of each year. 3. June of each year. Unskilled wage earners.

★ 470 ★

Wages and Salaries

Artists' Earnings: 1989

This table shows the total number of artists who were full-year, full-time earners in the year before the 1990 census and shows median earnings in 1989, by gender.

Worked full time, full year, 1989	Male		Female	
	Number	Med. earnings	Number	Med. earnings
Actors/directors	36,822	$32,077	21,257	$28,032
Announcers	24,571	$21,424	5,305	$19,325
Architects	107,245	$40,110	14,300	$29,451
Authors	28,890	$33,837	20,481	$25,101
Dancers[1]	1,273	$16,623	3,445	$15,623
Designers	197,675	$32,549	164,067	$20,394
Musicians/composers	36,143	$22,988	9,730	$18,653
Painters	60,433	$24,320	49,595	$18,762
Photographers	66,562	$25,456	19,428	$17,381
Teachers, art	3,304	$34,982	2,254	$25,316
Other artists	21,629	$25,310	14,855	$19,193
Total artists	584,547	$31,124	324,717	$20,825
Other professionals	5,484,889	$40,095	3,928,275	$27,580
Labor force	45,249,794	$28,522	28,456,430	$19,086

Source: Selected from *Trends in Artist Occupations 1970-1990,* prepared by Diane C. Ellis and John C. Beresford, National Endowment for the Arts Research Division Report #29, August 1994, Table 29, p. A-45, "Earnings in year before the census of artists by sex, for artists with some earnings who worked 50 to 52 weeks, and 35 to 99 hours per week, United States: 1980 and 1990." Includes armed forces in households for 1990. *Note:* 1. Median earnings not useful because of small sample size.

★ 471 ★

Wages and Salaries

Asian Agricultural Wages

This table shows earnings in agriculture in selected Asian countries for the years 1987-1993.

Country	Time period	Currency	1987	1988	1989	1990	1991	1992	1993
Asia									
Cyprus[1]	Week	Pounds							
Total			49.63	53.29	56.75	63.14	72.00	78.35	91.10
Male			65.12	74.51	75.17	85.17	97.77	99.71	113.64
Female			41.89	43.26	47.23	51.75	58.68	65.66	71.84
Japan[2]	Day	Yen							
Male			6,245	6,374	6,539	6,711	6,995	7,408	NA
Female			4,783	4,869	4,995	5,126	5,305	5,602	NA
Korea									
Republic of[3]	Day	Won							
Male			10,568	12,275	15,162	18,563	NA	NA	NA
Female			7,699	8,855	10,666	13,224	NA	NA	NA
Singapore[4]	Month	Dollars							
Total			643.92	704.77	704.99	733.44	NA	NA	NA
Male			NA	721.86	710.65	751.88	NA	NA	NA
Female			NA	648.74	687.42	682.62	NA	NA	NA
Sri Lanka[5]	Day	Rupees							
Male			25.23	35.71	41.48	51.25	51.11	70.99	76.22
Female			23.45	34.64	39.48	47.25	51.01	63.17	67.28

Source: Selected from "Wages in agriculture," *Year Book of Labour Statistics,* International Labour Office, Geneva, 1994, Table 21, pp. 807+. *Notes:* 1. Wage earners. Adults. October of each year. 2. Year ending in March of the year indicated. Casual day workers. 3. Including the value of payments in kind. Agricultural workers. 4. Establishments employing 25 or more employees. August of each year. 5. Agricultural workers. Tea plantations. March and September of each year.

★ 472 ★

Wages and Salaries

Asian Construction Wages

This table shows earnings in construction in selected Asian countries for the years 1987-1993.

Country	Time period	Currency	1987	1988	1989	1990	1991	1992	1993
Asia									
Cyprus[1]	Week	Pounds							
Total			71.61	77.43	86.26	95.96	102.98	109.47	122.56
Male			72.69	78.20	87.19	97.18	104.21	111.06	126.23
Female			47.35	51.29	55.97	62.44	74.21	72.72	83.13

[Continued]

★ 472 ★

Asian Construction Wages
[Continued]

Country	Time period	Currency	1987	1988	1989	1990	1991	1992	1993
Japan[2]	Month	Yen							
Total			331,368	348,360	373,211	401,560	424,579	437,381	444,452
Male			359,091	376,860	404,326	436,081	459,764	NA	NA
Female			170,213	179,714	189,874	204,342	226,531	NA	NA
Korea, Rep. of[6]	Month	Won							
Total			453	504	594	745	885	1,020	1,155
Male			481	536	632	797	940	1,081	1,223
Female			227	252	301	380	461	545	589
Myanmar[3]	Month	Kyats							
Male			307.14	567.96	748.73	NA	778.25	912.77	NA
Female			266.21	529.56	778.29	NA	816.29	904.69	NA
Singapore[4]	Month	Dollars							
Total			926.3	1,005.0	1,127.5	1,274.8	1,425.9	1,624.1	1,713.3
Male			NA	NA	1,167.8	1,321.2	1,484.4	1,701.3	1,796.0
Female			NA	NA	952.9	1,081.6	1,195.0	1,332.1	1,413.3
Thailand[5]	Month	Baht							
Total			NA	NA	3,324	3,790	4,454	5,270	NA
Male			NA	NA	3,594	NA	NA	NA	NA
Female			NA	NA	2,715	NA	NA	NA	NA

Source: Selected from "Wages in construction," *Year Book of Labour Statistics,* International Labour Office, Geneva, 1994, Table 19, pp. 790+. *Notes:* 1. Including family allowances and the value of payments in kind. Adults. 2. Employees. Including family allowances and mid- and end-of-year bonuses. Sample design revised in 1985. 3. Employees. March and September of each year. 4. Social security statistics. Employees. 5. Employees. 6. Figures in thousands. Including family allowances and the value of payments in kind. Employees. 1993 data classified according to ISIC, Rev. 3.

★ 473 ★

Wages and Salaries

Asian Manufacturing Wages

This table shows earnings in manufacturing in selected Asian countries for the years 1987-1993.

Country	Time period	Currency	1987	1988	1989	1990	1991	1992	1993
Asia									
Cyprus[1]	Week	Pounds							
Total			58.06	61.85	68.02	74.23	80.34	88.98	101.03
Men			76.69	80.55	89.39	98.75	105.61	116.37	134.17
Women			44.32	47.66	52.11	56.84	62.97	69.93	75.85
Hong Kong	Day	Dollars							
Total			119.40	136.90	157.00	179.50	200.70	218.60	241.70
Men			143.30	166.10	191.70	224.50	249.90	274.80	313.80
Women			108.20	123.70	140.30	155.80	173.60	189.60	206.80

[Continued]

★ 473 ★

Asian Manufacturing Wages
[Continued]

Country	Time period	Currency	1987	1988	1989	1990	1991	1992	1993
Japan[2]	Month	Yen							
Total			313,170	318,663	336,648	352,020	368,011	372,594	371,356
Men			381,138	393,804	414,981	436,135	450,336	454,482	NA
Women			163,944	164,673	173,097	180,253	193,112	198,058	NA
Korea, Republic of	Month	Won							
Total[3]			329	393	492	591	690	799	885[8]
Men			413	491	609	724	843	964	1,056
Women			208	250	307	364	428	497	551
Macau[4]	Month	Patacas							
Total			NA	NA	1,859	2,058	2,232	2,509	NA
Men			NA	NA	NA	NA	NA	3,321	NA
Women			NA	NA	NA	NA	NA	2,222	NA
Myanmar[5]	Month	Kyats							
Men			325.74	533.08	729.52	NA	631.91	880.52	NA
Women			261.09	496.92	705.60	NA	670.90	866.82	NA
Singapore[6]	Month	Dollars							
Total			1,008.8	1,115.9	1,242.9	1,395.0	1,551.8	1,686.2	1,817.8
Men			NA	NA	1,623.0	1,797.5	1,970.1	2,127.4	2,266.2
Women			NA	NA	876.2	983.3	1,096.8	1,190.7	1,294.5
Sri Lanka	Hour	Rupees							
Total			5.96	6.63	7.51	9.49	11.20	11.83	13.65
Men			6.39	6.91	8.16	9.80	11.69	12.26	14.08
Women			4.55	4.76	5.36	8.86	9.35	10.44	12.65
Thailand[7]	Month	Baht							
Total			NA	NA	2,995	3,366	3,734	4,016	NA
Men			NA	NA	3,726	NA	NA	NA	NA
			NA	NA	2,453	NA	NA	NA	NA

Source: Selected from "Wages in manufacturing," *Year Book of Labour Statistics,* International Labour Office, Geneva, 1994, Table 17, pp. 710+. *Notes:* 1. October of each year. Including family allowances and the value of payments in kind. Adults. 2. Employees. Including family allowances and mid- and end-of-year bonuses. 3. Employees. Figures in thousands. Including family allowances and the value of payments in kind. 4. Employees. Labor force sample survey. 5. Employees. 6. Social security statistics. Employees. 7. Employees. 8. Data classified according to ISIC, Rev. 3.

★ 474 ★

Wages and Salaries

Asian Mining and Quarrying Wages

This table shows earnings in mining and quarrying in selected Asian countries for the years 1987-1993.

Country	Time period	Currency	1987	1988	1989	1990	1991	1992	1993
Asia									
Cyprus[1]	Week	Pounds							
Total			93.17	108.75	100.29	114.34	125.63	144.01	171.92
Male			93.90	109.36	101.16	115.41	126.95	145.00	172.63
Female			50.70	61.12	48.76	56.12	61.83	75.45	80.08
Japan[2]	Month	Yen							
Total			346,241	344,329	359,359	379,777	417,826	433,125	429,280
Male			365,405	359,635	375,430	398,339	442,719	NA	NA
Female			191,300	187,999	199,667	211,663	235,407	NA	NA
Korea, Rep. of[3]	Month	Won							
Total			385	447	530	605	711	860	980[4]
Male			396	457	543	619	733	882	1,014[4]
Female			184	222	268	328	367	457	519[4]
Myanmar[5]	Month	Kyats							
Male			256.87	424.66	733.45	NA	722.85	831.85	NA
Female			381.47	510.78	804.05	NA	780.46	891.62	NA
Thailand	Month	Baht							
Total			NA	NA	3,247	4,336	3,883	5,147	NA
Male			NA	NA	3,377	NA	NA	NA	NA
Female			NA	NA	2,358	NA	NA	NA	NA

Source: Selected from "Wages in mining and quarrying," *Year Book of Labour Statistics,* International Labour Office, Geneva, 1994, Table 18, pp. 782+.
Notes: 1. October of each year. Including family allowances and the value of payments in kind. Adults. 2. Employees. Including family allowances and mid- and end-of-year bonuses. 3. Employees. Figures in thousands. Including family allowances and the value of payments in kind. 4. Data classified according to ISIC, Rev. 3. 5. Employees. Metal mining.

★ 475 ★

Wages and Salaries

Asian Transport, Storage, and Communication Wages

This table shows earnings in transport, storage, and communication in selected Asian countries for the years 1987-1993.

Country	Time period	Currency	1987	1988	1989	1990	1991	1992	1993
Asia									
Cyprus[1]	Week	Pounds							
Total			81.11	85.06	91.45	96.76	100.97	119.50	122.04

[Continued]

★ 475 ★

Asian Transport, Storage, and Communication Wages
[Continued]

Country	Time period	Currency	1987	1988	1989	1990	1991	1992	1993
Male			83.99	88.60	95.45	100.21	104.52	121.44	125.80
Female			56.09	59.31	62.89	70.95	72.45	99.98	89.03
Japan[2]	Month	Yen							
Total			369,410	377,449	395,349	413,077	422,216	430,949	439,653
Male			382,812	390,949	409,985	432,230	447,106	NA	NA
Female			255,139	267,531	272,224	267,344	281,743	NA	NA
Korea									
Rep. of[3]	Month	Won							
Total			410	461	522	584	699	778	863
Male			428	480	536	594	715	796	881
Female			293	324	410	504	577	636	719
Myanmar[4]	Month	Kyats							
Male			282.54	584.90	625.70	NA	525.54	792.39	NA
Female			345.85	637.28	728.05	NA	817.46	966.59	NA
Singapore[5]	Month	Dollars							
Total			1,304.6	1,373.3	1,488.1	1,609.9	1,677.1	1,887.8	1,973.4
Male			NA	NA	1,558.8	1,686.7	1,761.9	2,032.4	2,122.0
Female			NA	NA	1,290.3	1,406.9	1,460.5	1,565.3	1,650.9
Thailand[6]	Month	Baht							
Total			NA	NA	3,999	3,986	4,940	5,906	NA
Male			NA	NA	3,951	NA	NA	NA	NA
Female			NA	NA	4,108	NA	NA	NA	NA

Source: Selected from "Wages in transport, storage and communication" *Year Book of Labour Statistics*, International Labour Office, Geneva, 1994, Table 20, pp. 799+. *Notes:* 1. Including family allowances and the value of payments in kind. Adults. October of each year. 2. Employees. Including family allowances and mid- and end-of-year bonuses. Sample design revised in 1985. 3. Employees. Figures in thousands. Including family allowances and the value of payments in kind. Data for 1993 classified according to ISIC, Rev. 3. 4. Employees. Excluding storage and communication; including sea transport. March and September of each year. 5. Social security statistics. Employees. 6. Employees.

★ 476 ★
Wages and Salaries

Choreographers' Income

This table shows the average income from choreography for men and women, including grants and excluding grants. Grants to men average about 50% more than grants to women. Data came from more than 500 choreographers who completed mail questionnaires and more than 200 telephone interviews. The female respondents were more highly educated than the males and were about as experienced. When all differences in the characteristics of the men and women surveyed were considered, women made $3,804 less from choreography.

Item	Men	Women
Choreography income, including grants	$9,328	$4,784
Choreography income, excluding grants	$7,233	$3,339

Source: Selected from *Dancemakers*, prepared by Dick Netzer and Ellen Parker based on a survey conducted by Alyce Dissette and Richard J. Orend, National Endowment for the Arts, Research Report #28, October 1993, p. 59.

★ 477 ★
Wages and Salaries

Contribution to Household Income: 1995

According to a survey based on interviews with 1,502 women aged 18 to 55, two-thirds of whom were employed outside the home at least part time, more than half of working women provide at least half of their household income. The figure was 39% in 1987. According to an economist at the Bureau of Labor Statistics, in 1993 women earned more than men in 23% of the married-couple families where both spouses worked. This table shows womens' responses to the question: "How much of your household income do you provide?"

Response	Percent
How much of your household income do you provide?	
All	18%
Half or more	55%
More than half	11%
Half	26%
Less than half	44%

Source: Jacquelynn Boyle, "Job important, but majority of female workers put family first," *Detroit Free Press*, May 11, 1995, pp. 1A,8A. Tamar Lewin, "Study Says More Women Earn Half Their Household Income," *The New York Times*, May 11, 1995, p. A13 Y. Primary source: Whirlpool Foundation survey by Louis Harris and Associates, New York, of 1,502 U.S. women 18-55 years old interviewed November-December 1994; margin of error is plus or minus 2 percentage points.

★ 478 ★

Wages and Salaries

Earnings by Age and Race/Ethnicity: 1994

This table shows median usual weekly earnings of full-time wage and salary workers by age, race, Hispanic origin, and gender, fourth quarter 1994 averages. The highest-earning 10% of men had weekly earnings of $1,126 or more, while the highest 10% of women earned $840 or more.

[Workers in thousands.]

Age, race, Hispanic origin	Total		Men		Women	
	Workers	Med. earnings	Workers	Med. earnings	Workers	Med. earnings
Total						
16 years and over	88,247	$472	50,478	$531	37,769	$403
25 years and over	78,322	$503	44,776	$581	33,547	$424
55 years and over	8,561	$496	4,953	$591	3,609	$392
White						
16 years and over	73,926	$489	43,019	$559	30,907	$411
16 to 24 years	8,357	$298	4,831	$306	3,526	$286
25 years and over	65,569	$520	$38,188	$600	27,381	$435
25 to 54 years	58,160	$521	33,842	$599	24,318	$438
55 years and over	7,409	$508	4,346	$610	3,064	$405
Black						
16 years and over	10,553	$383	5,308	$406	5,245	$362
16 to 24 years	1,142	$264	621	$281	520	$242
25 years and over	9,412	$402	4,687	$431	4,725	$378
25 to 54 years	8,562	$403	4,252	$428	4,310	$383
55 years and over	850	$387	435	$460	415	$343
Hispanic origin						
16 years and over	8,616	$327	5,464	$349	3,152	$303
16 to 24 years	1,444	$247	1,007	$260	437	$224
25 years and over	7,172	$361	4,457	$388	2,715	$323
25 to 54 years	6,604	$365	4,097	$387	2,506	$329
55 years and over	569	$324	360	$390	209	$281

Source: **Selected from** "Median usual weekly earnings of full-time wage and salary workers by age, race, Hispanic origin, and sex, fourth quarter 1994 averages, not seasonally adjusted," U.S. Department of Labor *News*, USDL 95-43, Table 2.

★ 479 ★
Wages and Salaries

Earnings by Educational Attainment: 1991

This table shows the percentage difference between the median annual earnings of wage and salary workers who are high school graduates and workers with other levels of educational attainment, by sex, race/ethnicity, type of worker, and age, in 1991. Generally speaking, the earnings advantage of college graduates was greater for females than for males. That is, the percentage difference between earnings of college graduates and high school graduates was greater for females. The earnings advantage of having a bachelor's degree was more than double the earnings advantage of having attended only some college. For example, among white female workers 25-34 years old, the earnings of college graduates were 88% greater than those of high school graduates, and the earnings of those with some college were 32% greater than those of high school graduates.

[Parentheses are used to indicate negative numbers.]

Type of workers/ educational attainment	Male				Female			
	Total	White	Black	Hispanic	Total	White	Black	Hispanic
Ages 25 to 34								
All workers								
Grades 9 to 11	(35%)	(30%)	(32%)	(16%)	(40%)	(37%)	(47%)	(42%)
Some college	12%	13%	14%	26%	30%	32%	31%	24%
Bachelor's degree	54%	47%	62%	62%	88%	88%	93%	71%
Full-time, full-year workers								
Grades 9 to 11	(20%)	(15%)	(22%)	(14%)	(29%)	(29%)	(34%)	[1]
Some college	18%	13%	25%	35%	18%	19%	16%	18%
Bachelor's degree	57%	49%	65%	81%	56%	55%	46%	49%
Ages 45 to 54								
All workers								
Grades 9 to 11	(27%)	(27%)	(29%)	[1]	(20%)	(21%)	(11%)	[1]
Some college	22%	17%	23%	43%	28%	26%	54%	[1]
Bachelor's degree	62%	56%	47%	[1]	93%	93%	99%	[1]
Full-time, full-year workers								
Grades 9 to 11	(29%)	(24%)	(32%)	[1]	(22%)	(25%)	(15%)	[1]
Some college	16%	14%	25%	[1]	24%	22%	42%	18%
Bachelor's degree	52%	53%	40%	[1]	68%	68%	68%	[1]

Source: "Percentage difference between median annual earnings of wage and salary workers who are high school graduates and workers with other levels of educational attainment, by sex, race/ethnicity, type of worker, and age: 1991," U.S. Department of Education, National Center for Education Statistics, Indicator of the Month, March 1994, "Annual earnings of young adults." Primary source: U.S. Department of Commerce, Bureau of the Census, March Current Population Survey, 1992. Grades 9 to 11 includes those who attended grade 12 but did not receive a diploma. High school includes those who received an equivalency certificate. Some college includes those who have received an associate's degree. Bachelor's degree includes those who received advanced degrees. Included in the total but not shown separately are workers of other races, primarily Asians and American Indians. *Note:* 1. Too few sample observations for a reliable estimate.

★ 480 ★

Wages and Salaries

Earnings by Educational Attainment: 1994

This table shows quartiles and selected deciles of usual weekly earnings of full-time male and female wage and salary workers, fourth quarter 1994 averages, by eductional attainment. According to the organization *9 to 5*, on average, a woman with some college experience earns less than a man without a high school diploma.[1].

[Workers in thousands.]

Educational attainment	Number of of workers	Upper limit of:				
		1st decile	1st quartile	2nd quartile	3rd quartile	9th decile
Women, 25 years and over	33,547	$214	$294	$424	$621	$869
Less than a high school diploma	2,740	$157	$197	$256	$342	$455
High school grad, no college	11,415	$200	$266	$357	$489	$636
Some college or associate degree	10,077	$231	$305	$420	$583	$756
College graduates, total	9,315	$334	$463	$644	$891	$1,169
Bachelor's degree only	6,303	$315	$427	$596	$817	$1,037
Advanced degree	3,012	$407	$585	$774	$1,020	$1,350
Men, 25 years and over	44,776	$275	$386	$581	$830	$1,156
Less than a high school diploma	5,282	$191	$251	$334	$494	$654
High school grad, no college	14,747	$268	$358	$502	$696	$904
Some college or associate degree	11,634	$298	$408	$588	$786	$1,018
College graduates, total	13,112	$393	$587	$824	$1,157	$1,581
Bachelor's degree only	8,810	$377	$545	$761	$1,056	$1,452
Advanced degree	4,302	$452	$679	$960	$1,369	$1,881

Source: Selected from "Quartiles and selected deciles of usual weekly earnings of full-time wage and salary workers by selected characteristics, fourth quarter 1994 averages, not seasonally adjusted," U.S. Department of Labor *News*, USDL 95-43, Table 4. Ten percent of all full-time wage and salary workers earn less than the upper limit of the first decile; 25% earn less than the upper limit of the first quartile; 50% earn less than the upper limit of the second quartile, or median; 75% earn less than the upper limit of the third quartile; and 90% earn less than the upper limit of the ninth decile. *Note:* 1. *9 to 5 Profile of Working Women*, 1994-95 edition.

★ 481 ★

Wages and Salaries

Earnings by Occupation: 1991

This table shows women's employment percentage by occupation and the median weekly earnings of both sexes in the occupation. Among skilled blue-collar occupations, women tend to be overrepresented in low-paying jobs and underrepresented in high-paying jobs. According to an analysis conducted by the U.S. Bureau of Labor Statistics, there is an inverse relationship between industries that employ a large proportion of women and industries that pay well. For example, health services ranked second highest in terms of female employment but ranked 36th out of 50 industries in terms of earnings level. Coal mining ranked lowest in the proportion of women employed, but it ranked highest in earnings level[1].

Occupational group	% women employed in occupation	Median wkly. earnings (both sexes)
All occupations	45.6%	$430
Exec., admin., & managerial	40.6%	$627
Personnel & labor relations mgrs.	57.6%	$752
Mktg., advertising, & p.r. mgrs.	30.6%	$784
Financial managers	44.7%	$743
Purchasing managers	33.9%	$784
Management-related occupations	50.8%	$576
Management analysts	31.4%	$717
Personnel/trng/labor rel. spec.	60.8%	$592
Professional specialty	51.6%	$634
Engineers	8.2%	$847
Teachers, elementary school	85.9%	$537
Technicians	49.4%	$508
Health record technologists & technicians	93.9%	$338
Computer programmers	34.0%	$662
Electrical/electronic techs.	13.6%	$544
Sales occupations	48.8%	$418
Apparel sales workers	79.9%	$246
Radio, TV, hifi, & appliance sales	30.0%	$379
Cashiers	80.0%	$278
Administrative support	79.8%	$365
Secretaries, stenos, typists	98.5%	$357
Service occupations	64.6%	$280
Hairdressers & cosmetologists	90.2%	$263
Waiters & waitresses	81.6%	$218
Precision production, craft, & repair	8.6%	$483

[Continued]

★ 481 ★

Earnings by Occupation: 1991
[Continued]

Occupational group	% women employed in occupation	Median wkly. earnings (both sexes)
Electrical/electronic equip. repair	9.6%	$591
Construction trades	1.8%	$483
Textile, apparel, & furnishings machine workers (e.g. dressmakers)	59.5%	$295
Operators, fabricators, laborers	25.2%	$351
Textile sewing machine operators	89.2%	$215
Welders & cutters	4.1%	$424

Source: Linda Levine, Pay Equity Legislation in the 102d Congress, CRS Report for Congress, updated January 6, 1993 (archived), Table 2, p. CRS-6, "Women's Employment Pattern by Occupation and Earnings by Occupation (Both Sexes), 1991." Primary source: U.S. Bureau of Labor Statistics. Note: 1. CRS Report 90-99 E, Women at Work: Where and for How Much?

★ 482 ★

Wages and Salaries

Earnings by Union Membership Status

This table shows the median weekly earnings of full-time wage and salary workers, by union membership status, from 1984 through 1991. Union membership has provided women with higher median weekly earnings commpared to nonunion women workers.

Year	Members of unions		Nonunion	
	Women	Men	Women	Men
1984	$326	$444	$251	$362
1985	$350	$465	$262	$383
1986	$368	$482	$274	$394
1987	$388	$494	$288	$406
1988	$403	$506	$300	$416
1989	$417	$527	$312	$430
1990	$448	$542	$326	$457
1991	$467	$568	$348	$473

Source: "Median weekly earnings of full-time wage and salary workers, by union membership status, 1984-91," 1993 Handbook on Women Workers: Trends & Issues, U.S. Department of Labor, Women's Bureau, 1994, Table 13, p. 9. Primary source: U.S. Department of Labor, Bureau of Labor Statistics, Employment and Earnings, January 1986, 1988, 1990, and 1992.

★ 483 ★

Wages and Salaries

Earnings in 20 Leading Occupations: 1991

This table shows women's median weekly earnings in the 20 leading occupations of employed women, 1991 annual averages. Eleven of these 20 occupations are known as traditionally "female" jobs. That is, throughout history they have been performed primarily by women. Fourteen of the 20 leading occupations for women offer median weekly earnings below the $368 average for all women employed full time in 1991.

Occupation	Number of women	Percent women	Women's med. wkly. earnings
Total	53,284	45.6%	$368
Secretaries[1,4]	3,755	99.0%	$359
Managers and administrators, n.e.c.[2]	2,660	33.6%	$481
Cashiers[1,4]	2,023	80.9%	$214
Bookkeepers, accounting and auditing clerks[1,4]	1,750	91.5%	$341
Registered nurses[1]	1,623	94.8%	$630
Nursing aides, orderlies, and attendants[1,4]	1,344	89.2%	$263
Elementary school teachers[1]	1,309	85.9%	$522
Sales supervisors and proprietors[4]	1,284	34.3%	$361
Waiters and waitresses[1,4]	1,105	81.6%	$205
Sales workers, other commodities[3,4]	1,034	71.1%	$243
Child care workers[1,4]	933	96.0%	$216
Machine operators, assorted materials[4]	865	33.1%	$284
Receptionists[1,4]	850	97.1%	$295
Administrative support occupations, n.e.c.[2]	841	79.4%	$374
Cooks, except short order[4]	834	46.9%	$219
Accountants and auditors	745	51.5%	$501
Hairdressers and cosmetologists[1,4]	672	90.2%	$252
Secondary school teachers	668	54.7%	$543
Janitors and cleaners[4]	657	30.9%	$251
General office clerks[1,4]	619	80.9%	$333

Source: "20 leading occupations of employed women, 1991 annual averages," *1993 Handbook on Women Workers: Trends & Issues*, U.S. Department of Labor, Women's Bureau, 1994, Table 12, p. 18. Primary source: U.S. Department of Labor, Bureau of Labor Statistics, *Employment and Earnings*, January 1992. *Notes:* 1. Traditionally considered a "female" occupation. 2. Not elsewhere classified. 3. Includes food, drugs, health, and other commodities. 4. 1991 median weekly earnings below total for all women ($368).

★ 484 ★

Wages and Salaries

Earnings in Selected Occupations: 1983-1991

This table shows the ratio of median weekly earnings for women and men and the ratio of women's employment to total employment in selected occupations in 1991 and 1983.

Occupational class	Women to men earnings rat.		Women to total employ. rat	
	1991	1983	1991	1983
Total, all occupations	74.0%	66.7%	42.6%	40.4%
Executive/managerial	66.5%	64.0%	43.4%	34.2%
Financial managers	58.7%	63.8%	44.5%	38.7%
Marketing/pr managers	65.5%	60.1%	29.0%	21.0%
Misc. managers	62.1%	58.4%	37.3%	28.7%
Underwriters/financial officers	67.5%	65.0%	51.3%	42.6%
Health diagnosing occup.	61.2%	79.7%	27.2%	24.0%
Physicians	53.9%	81.6%	26.6%	22.8%
Sales occupations	59.5%	52.4%	42.1%	39.0%
Sales supervisors/ proprietors	65.8%	61.6%	35.1%	28.5%
Securities/financial services sales	65.7%	NA	32.8%	26.8%
General ofc. supervisors	67.4%	64.5%	67.6%	65.3%
Insurance adjusters/ investigators	68.0%	65.0%	79.8%	66.7%
Precision production occup.	62.4%	61.3%	20.4%	18.9%
Machine operators, exc. precis.	65.7%	62.1%	39.6%	41.6%
Metal/plastic machine operators	67.6%	72.1%	16.9%	16.5%
Productin inspectors/examiners	66.5%	56.3%	54.3%	53.1%

Source: "Ratio of median weekly earnings for women and men and ratio of women's employment to total employment, selected occupations, 1991 and 1983," *1993 Handbook on Women Workers: Trends & Issues*, U.S. Department of Labor, Women's Bureau, 1994, Table 12, p. 18. Primary source: U.S. Department of Labor, Bureau of Labor Statistics, unpublished Table 5: Median weekly earnings of wage and salary workers who usually work full time, by detailed (3-digit census code) occupations and sex, 1983 and 1991 annual averages.

★ 485 ★

Wages and Salaries

Earnings of Employed Black Women

This table shows the median earnings of year-round, full-time black women workers from 1980-1991. It also shows the equivalent in 1990 dollars. Black women accounted for only 5.3% of all women employed in 1991 in high-paying occupations like lawyers, engineers, mathematical and computer scientists, teachers in colleges and universities, managers in health and medicine, registered nurses, education administrators, physicians, computer programmers, and educational and vocational counselors. The median weekly earnings ranged from $595 to $821 in those occupations.

Year	Med. earnings	In 1990 dollars
1980	$10,672	$16,948
1981	$11,199	$16,245
1982	$12,132	$16,586
1983	$12,690	$16,652
1984	$13,720	$17,259
1985	$14,308	$17,380
1986	$14,734	$17,571
1987	$16,002	$18,411
1988	$16,538	$18,271
1989	$17,389	$18,329
1990	$18,040	$18,040
$1991	$18,720	$17,964

Source: "Total money earnings of year-round, full-time black women workers, 1980-91," *1993 Handbook on Women Workers: Trends and Issues*, U.S. Department of Labor, Women's Bureau, 1994, Table 4, p. 51. Primary source: U.S. Department of Commerce, Bureau of the Census, *Money Income of Households, Families, and Persons in the United States: 1980-1986, Money Income and Poverty Status in the United States: 1988-89,* and *Money Income of Households, Families, and Persons in the United States: 1990 and 1991.*

★ 486 ★

Wages and Salaries

Earnings of Special Libraries Association Members: 1976-1994

This table shows median annual earnings of Special Libraries Association members for survey years 1976 to 1994 and the percentage increase over 1976 median earnings.

Survey year	Female		Male	
	Median	Over 1976	Median	Over 1976
1976	$14,700	--	$18,100	--
1979	$17,400	18%	$19,000	5%
1982	$22,500	53%	$26,000	43%
1985	$26,980	84%	$30,400	68%
1988	$31,580	115%	$35,000	93%

[Continued]

★ 486 ★

Earnings of Special Libraries Association Members: 1976-1994

[Continued]

Survey year	Female		Male	
	Median	Over 1976	Median	Over 1976
1990	$35,000	138%	$38,000	110%
1992	$39,000	165%	$41,368	129%
1994	$40,000	172%	$42,000	132%

Source: "Change in Earnings by Gender in United States," *SLA Biennial Salary Survey 1995*, Special Libraries Association, Washington, D.C. 1976 and 1979 data reflect combined figures for U.S. and Canada.

★ 487 ★

Wages and Salaries

Effect of Education on Hourly Earnings

This table shows the index of relative hourly earnings by education level for the years 1975-1990. Since at least 1949, the hourly wages of those with at least some college education have increased faster than the wages of high school graduates.

[Index, 12 years of completed schooling = 100.]

Year	Years of Education						
	1-4	5-8	9-11	12	13-15	16	17+
1975	74.0	80.3	85.0	100.0	112.0	120.6	127.6
1976	75.5	80.5	86.5	100.0	111.7	127.1	143.1
1977	74.1	78.1	86.3	100.0	112.0	127.1	150.7
1978	78.5	80.6	84.3	100.0	110.2	120.3	139.2
1979	73.4	79.4	87.4	100.0	111.3	131.6	145.6
1980	84.2	80.3	87.4	100.0	113.8	132.5	140.2
1981	68.2	81.8	85.2	100.0	115.1	128.5	151.4
1982	62.4	78.4	86.7	100.0	113.1	133.0	149.1
1983	62.4	78.2	85.1	100.0	115.7	133.7	158.4
1984	78.3	79.0	86.4	100.0	117.6	138.0	163.6
1985	67.6	77.1	86.7	100.0	116.1	142.9	165.7
1986	78.3	77.6	83.2	100.0	116.5	145.2	173.7
1987	66.1	73.1	85.6	100.0	118.4	139.9	172.2
1988	66.2	74.4	84.5	100.0	120.5	152.0	175.7
1989	70.0	75.3	83.2	100.0	118.6	155.6	167.1
1990	73.4	73.0	83.7	100.0	118.0	152.8	171.2

Source: Selected from "Index of relative hourly earnings of women by education level, 1949-90," U.S. Department of Labor, Bureau of Labor Statistics, *Labor Composition and U.S. Productivity Growth, 1984-90*, Bulletin 2426, December 1993, Table 13, p. 16.

★ 488 ★

Wages and Salaries

Effect of Work Experience on Wages

This table shows the percent change in wages that resulted from an additional year of work experience, for selected years, 1949-1990. The percent change is measured as the percentage difference in hourly wages between a worker with a given number of years of work experience and 1 year less of experience, for example, the percentage change in hourly wages between 4 and 5 years of work experience. The payoff to additional experience has risen for workers at low and intermediate levels of experience. Most of the increase has occurred since 1970.

Year	Years of work experience					
	1	5	10	15	25	30
Women						
1949	2.8%	2.2%	1.4%	0.6%	-0.9%	-1.6%
1959	2.7%	2.3%	1.7%	1.1%	-0.1%	-0.7%
1970	3.2%	2.4%	1.5%	0.5%	-1.3%	-2.2%
1975	5.0%	3.8%	2.2%	0.6%	-2.4%	-3.9%
1980	4.9%	3.7%	2.2%	0.6%	-2.3%	-3.8%
1985	6.4%	4.8%	2.9%	0.9%	-2.8%	-4.6%
1990	6.7%	5.0%	2.9%	0.8%	-3.2%	-5.1%
Men						
1949	5.3%	4.4%	3.3%	2.2%	-0.1%	-1.1%
1959	5.9%	4.9%	3.7%	2.5%	0.1%	-1.1%
1970	5.4%	4.5%	3.3%	2.1%	-0.2%	-1.3%
1975	7.9%	6.4%	4.7%	2.9%	-0.5%	-2.1%
1980	7.7%	6.3%	4.7%	3.0%	-0.2%	-1.7%
1985	8.4%	6.9%	5.2%	3.5%	-0.2%	-1.5%
1990	7.0%	5.9%	4.5%	3.1%	0.4%	-1.0%

Source: "Percent change in wages due to an additional year of work experience, men and women, selected years, 1949-90," U.S. Department of Labor, Bureau of Labor Statistics, *Labor Composition and U.S. Productivity Growth, 1984-90*, Bulletin 2426, December 1993, Table 14, p. 16.

★ 489 ★

Wages and Salaries

European Agricultural Wages

This table shows earnings in agriculture selected European countries for the years 1987-1993.

Country	Time period	Currency	1987	1988	1989	1990	1991	1992	1993
Europe									
Belgium[1]	Hour	Francs							
Male			NA	234.0	NA	NA	NA	NA	NA
Female			NA	215.0	NA	NA	NA	NA	NA

[Continued]

★ 489 ★

European Agricultural Wages
[Continued]

Country	Time period	Currency	1987	1988	1989	1990	1991	1992	1993
Finland[2]	Hour	Markkaa							
Total			25.90	27.60	30.70	33.21	37.19	37.96	NA
Male			26.52	28.00	31.33	34.37	38.10	38.88	NA
Female			23.71	26.18	28.58	29.86	33.15	33.51	NA
Latvia[3]	Month	Lats							
Total			NA	NA	NA	1.41	2.38	17.80	39.06
Male			NA	NA	NA	NA	NA	17.77	NA
Female			NA	NA	NA	NA	NA	17.28	NA
Switzerland[4]	Hour	Francs							
Male			15.63	16.14	16.99	18.08	19.35	20.19	NA
Female			12.36	13.06	13.82	14.64	15.71	16.56	NA
Sweden[5]	Hour	Kronor							
Total			58.23	64.81	69.59	NA	84.49	89.16	NA
Male			58.60	65.30	70.40	NA	85.58	90.17	NA
Female			56.22	62.01	65.93	NA	74.15	84.82	NA
Turkey[6]	Day	Liras							
Total			NA	7,323.5	11,161	28,947	47,283	86,085	154,478
Male			NA	7,511.0	11,171	29,299	47,549	86,469	154,939
Female			NA	5,231.5	10,571	24,764	44,065	81,617	154,563
United Kingdom[7]	Week	Pounds							
Total			133.40	149.70	158.00	175.60	187.60	198.70	207.00
Male			135.10	154.20	162.00	179.50	192.50	203.10	211.70
Female			111.80	109.00	118.70	134.30	142.10	152.60	157.60

Source: Selected from "Wages in agriculture," *Year Book of Labour Statistics,* International Labour Office, Geneva, 1994, Table 21, pp. 807+.
Notes: 1. Biennial survey. Agricultural workers. 2. Agriculture and livestock production. 3. October of each year. Figures under "Total" are employees, including juveniles. "Male" and "Female" are adult employees. 3. State sector. Employees. Prior to 1993: roubles; 1 lat = 200 roubles. 4. October of each year. Horticulture, including family allowances. Adults. 5. Adults. Second quarter of each year. Agriculture and livestock productin. Including holidays and sick-leave payments and the value of payments in kind. 6. Agriculture, hunting and forestry. September of each year. Insurance statistics; employees. 7. Agriculture and livestock production; excluding Northern Ireland. April of each year. Adults.

★ 490 ★

Wages and Salaries

European Construction Wages

This table shows earnings in construction in selected European countries for the years 1987-1993.

Country	Time period	Currency	1987	1988	1989	1990	1991	1992	1993
Europe									
Belgium[1]	Month	Francs							
Total			67,582	71,041	74,555	79,073	83,979	87,439	NA

[Continued]

★ 490 ★

European Construction Wages
[Continued]

Country	Time period	Currency	1987	1988	1989	1990	1991	1992	1993
Male			73,147	76,931	80,524	85,390	90,532	94,248	NA
Female			46,675	48,910	52,132	55,343	59,361	61,858	NA
Finland	Hour	Markkaa							
Total			44.95	48.74	52.88	57.58	59.72	58.34	NA
Male			45.52	49.34	53.54	58.32	60.42	58.94	NA
Female			31.50	34.20	37.13	40.39	43.10	43.38	NA
France[2]	Hour	Francs							
Total			39.96	38.85	40.73	43.04	45.87	47.08	48.18
Male			40.02	38.94	40.82	43.14	45.85	47.13	48.29
Female			NA	31.98	35.03	35.27	40.40	40.61	40.68
Gibraltar[3]	Week	Pounds							
Total			155.01	163.64	206.81	215.47	251.98	238.91	NA
Male			155.39	164.57	208.89	216.74	253.51	239.62	NA
Female			139.40	120.59	128.32	160.20	177.85	213.74	NA
Luxembourg[4]	Month	Francs							
Total			75,289	76,394	82,282	87,260	92,125[4]	NA	NA
Male			84,895	88,242	94,680	100,348	104,770[4]	NA	NA
Female			50,037	50,805	55,665	59,984	64,131[4]	NA	NA
Portugal	Hour	Escudos							
Total			NA	NA	247	290	338	384	420
Male			NA	NA	248	290	339	385	421
Female			NA	NA	214	NA	270	327	379
Sweden[5]	Hour	Kronor							
Total			74.32	82.19	93.01	101.79	106.63	110.15	NA
Male			74.47	82.34	93.18	102.00	106.63	110.31	NA
Female			63.76	71.39	82.84	83.24	95.62	90.60	NA
Turkey[6]	Day	Liras							
Total			NA	7,589.0	16,291	30,630	57,204	91,920	136,637
Male			NA	7,640.0	16,963	30,708	57,081	85,215	136,530
Female			NA	7,417.0	16,282	26,006	62,213	92,640	141,079

Source: Selected from "Wages in construction," *Year Book of Labour Statistics,* International Labour Office, Geneva, 1994, Table 19, pp. 790+. *Notes:* 1. October of each year. Salaried employees. 2. October of each year. Beginning April 1985: revised series. Methodology again revised 1988; data not strictly comparable. 3. October of each year. 4. October of each year, except 1991, April. Wage earners. 5. Adults. Second quarter of each year. Including holidays and sick-leave payments and the value of payments in kind. 6. September of each year. Insurance statistics; employees.

★ 491 ★

Wages and Salaries

European Manufacturing Wages

This table shows earnings in manufacturing in selected European countries for the years 1987-1993.

Country	Time period	Currency	1987	1988	1989	1990	1991	1992	1993
Europe									
Belgium[1]	Hour	Francs							
Total			302.24	309.78	327.13	342.40	363.12	379.62	NA
Male			321.22	329.30	348.21	364.04	385.65	403.78	NA
Female			239.90	245.25	257.64	271.23	287.68	300.20	NA
Czechoslovakia[2]	Month	Koruny							
Total			3,112	3,172	3,239	3,325	3,882	4,565	5,717
Male			3,560	3,628	3,705	3,803	4,440	5,221	6,539
Female			2,416	2,463	2,515	2,582	3,014	3,544	4,439
Denmark[3]	Hour	Kroner							
Total			86.76	92.06	95.95	99.94	104.62	108.26	NA
Male			90.18	95.56	99.64	103.76	108.51	112.24	NA
Female			75.92	80.70	84.33	87.81	92.05	95.44	NA
Finland[4]	Hour	Markkaa							
Total			36.48	39.74	43.45	47.65	50.68	52.25	NA
Male			39.18	42.61	46.65	51.07	53.90	55.40	NA
Female			30.28	32.90	35.82	39.50	42.09	43.38	NA
France	Hour	Francs							
Total			40.97	41.79[16]	43.43	45.46	47.47	49.36	50.63
Male			43.39	44.40[16]	46.23	48.38	50.47	52.43	53.68
Female			34.35	35.14[16]	36.29	38.17	39.69	41.23	42.46
Germany[5]	Hour	Mark							
Total			17.53	18.33	19.10	20.07	21.31	22.52	23.79
Male			18.62	19.45	20.25	21.29	22.55	23.76	25.00
Female			13.60	14.19	14.74	15.48	16.50	17.50	18.46
Germany[6]	Hour	Mark							
Total			NA	NA	NA	NA	9.44	11.89	13.90
Male			NA	NA	NA	NA	9.74	12.25	14.40
Female			NA	NA	NA	NA	8.39	10.47	11.88
Gibraltar	Week	Pound							
Total			152.74	190.57	190.07	238.51	214.13	239.36	NA
Male			158.66	203.27	194.26	247.70	254.43	254.50	NA
Female			118.63	121.98	137.14	151.73	148.75	161.71	NA
Greece[7]	Hour	Drachma							
Total			388.20	459.70	554.00	661.30	772.10	878.20	970.80
Male			430.20	509.20	614.50	733.80	854.70	967.50	1,063.6
Female			333.70	397.40	481.00	575.30	673.20	765.30	851.40

[Continued]

★ 491 ★

European Manufacturing Wages
[Continued]

Country	Time period	Currency	1987	1988	1989	1990	1991	1992	1993
Ireland[8]	Hour	Pounds							
Total			4.70	4.90	5.10	5.35	5.62	5.90	NA
Male			5.33	5.53	5.74	6.01	6.30	6.59	NA
Female			3.59	3.81	3.98	4.16	4.40	4.66	NA
Latvia[9]	Month	Lats							
Total			NA	NA	NA	1.55	3.16	22.09	48.69[17]
Male			NA	NA	NA	NA	NA	23.51	NA
Female			NA	NA	NA	NA	NA	20.17	NA
Luxembourg	Month	Francs							
Total			101,653	104,768	112,273	118,556	125,555	NA	NA
Male			109,561	113,309	122,207	129,207	136,207	NA	NA
Female			60,172	63,289	66,793	72,152	76,207	NA	NA
Netherlands[10]	Hour	Guilders							
Total			19.87	20.29	20.75	21.54	22.28	22.67	NA
Male			20.99	21.49	21.94	22.75	23.52	23.89	NA
Female			15.58	16.07	16.49	17.14	17.75	18.29	NA
Norway[11]	Hour	Kroner							
Total			78.64	82.99	87.25	92.45	97.35	100.42	103.15
Male			81.00	85.36	89.48	94.63	99.51	102.66	105.42
Female			67.83	71.98	76.47	81.79	86.67	89.20	91.80
Portugal	Hour	Escudos							
Total			NA	NA	281	324	370	419	436
Male			NA	NA	320	368	419	480	485
Female			NA	NA	222	254	295	326	390
Switzerland[12]	Hour	Francs							
Male			20.51	21.26	22.08	23.38	25.00	26.18	NA
Female			13.81	14.34	14.96	15.87	17.01	17.84	NA
Sweden[13]	Hour	Kronor							
Total			67.04	72.21	79.30	87.33	91.69	98.34	NA
Male			68.48	73.77	81.14	89.46	93.83	100.68	NA
Female			61.67	66.39	72.59	79.51	83.66	90.09	NA
Turkey[14]	Day	Liras							
Total			NA	8,461.1	17,821	30,582	61,620	88,144	135,236
Male			NA	8,642.9	18,679	31,231	62,140	91,204	138,746
Female			NA	6,877.3	13,830	25,299	56,660	84,558	122,721
United Kingdom[15]	Hour	Pounds							
Total			4.13	4.41	4.76	5.20	5.62	5.98	6.19

[Continued]

★ 491 ★

European Manufacturing Wages
[Continued]

Country	Time period	Currency	1987	1988	1989	1990	1991	1992	1993
Male			4.38	4.69	5.06	5.51	5.98	6.35	6.56
Female			2.97	3.16	3.42	3.77	4.06	4.34	4.52

Source: Selected from "Wages in manufacturing," *Year Book of Labour Statistics,* International Labour Office, Geneva, 1994, Table 17, pp. 710+. *Notes:* 1. Wage earners. October of each year. 2. State industry. 3. Third quarter of each year. Adults. 4. Including mining, quarrying, and electricity. 5. The series relates to the territory of the Federal Republic of Germany before October 3, 1990. Including family allowances paid directly by the employers. 6. 5 new Lander and Berlin (East). 7. Establishments with 10 or more persons employed. Wage earners. 8. September of each year. 9. State sector. Employees. 10. "Total" includes juveniles. "Male" and "Female" adults. 11. Adults. Including the value of payments in kind. 12. October of each year. Adults. Including family allowances. 13. Adults. Second quarter of each year. Including holidays and sick-leave payments nad the value of payments in kind. 14. September of each year. Insurance statistics; employees. 15. Including quarrying. Full-time workers on adult rates of pay. April; excluding Northern Ireland. 1. Methodology revised; data not strictly comparable. 1. Prior to 1993: roubles; 1 lat = 200 roubles.

★ 492 ★

Wages and Salaries

European Mining and Quarrying Wages

This table shows earnings in mining and quarrying in selected European countries for the years 1987-1993.

Country	Time period	Currency	1987	1988	1989	1990	1991	1992	1993
Europe									
Belgium[1]	Month	Francs							
Total			67,084	69,215	73,567	86,068	90,345	99,760	NA
Male			67,490	69,665	74,216	86,918	91,165	104,828	NA
Female			57,173	58,224	57,749	65,330	70,318	75,064	NA
Czechoslovakia[2]	Month	Koruny							
Total			4,442	4,506	4,524	4,404	5,067	NA	NA
Male			4,725	4,793	4,812	4,685	5,390	NA	NA
Female			2,733	2,772	2,783	2,709	3,117	NA	NA
Czech Republic	Month	Koruny							
Total			NA	NA	NA	4,550	5,299	6,258	7,635
Male			NA	NA	NA	4,840	5,637	6,657	8,122
Female			NA	NA	NA	2,799	3,260	3,850	4,697
Finland[3]	Hour	Markkaa							
Total			44.42	47.80	52.26	57.97	61.17	62.03	NA
Male			45.79	49.23	53.90	59.40	62.52	63.13	NA
Female			28.35	31.11	34.76	40.12	42.63	44.12	NA
France	Hour	Francs							
Total			NA	46.74	48.97	49.49	52.54	54.73	55.79
Male			NA	47.67	50.13	50.43	53.41	55.82	56.73
Female			NA	34.74	35.32	37.39	38.44	40.66	41.35
Ireland[4]	Hour	Pounds							
Total			5.35	5.88	5.94	6.24	7.01	7.54	NA

[Continued]

★ 492 ★

European Mining and Quarrying Wages
[Continued]

Country	Time period	Currency	1987	1988	1989	1990	1991	1992	1993
Male			5.41	5.96	6.01	6.30	7.08	7.58	NA
Female			3.36	NA	NA	NA	NA	NA	NA
Sweden[5]	Hour	Kronor							
Total			76.66	82.88	88.42	100.06	107.76	116.64	NA
Male			77.18	83.66	89.17	100.89	108.76	117.45	NA
Female			70.42	73.10	77.82	87.54	92.21	101.83	NA
Turkey[6]	Day	Liras							
Total			NA	8,649.0	20,778	34,595	70,675	108,924	156,027
Male			NA	8,635.4	20,838	34,746	70,876	108,723	152,810
Female			NA	9,217.4	18,597	27,672	60,287	78,432	131,059

Source: Selected from "Wages in mining and quarrying," *Year Book of Labour Statistics,* International Labour Office, Geneva, 1994, Table 18, pp. 782+. *Notes:* 1. Wage earners. October of each year. 2. State industry. 3. Metal mining. 4. September of each year. Including juveniles under "Total." Adults under "Male" and "Female." 5. Adults. Second quarter of each year. Including holidays and sick-leave payments and the value of payments in kind. 6. Insurance statistics; employees.

★ 493 ★

Wages and Salaries

European Transport, Storage, and Communication Wages

This table shows earnings in transport, storage, and communication in selected European countries for the years 1987-1993.

Country	Time period	Currency	1987	1988	1989	1990	1991	1992	1993
Europe									
Gibraltar[1]	Week	Pounds							
Total			155.47	185.16	196.91	198.52	199.80	235.50	NA
Male			163.71	193.47	196.91	198.52	204.22	240.06	NA
Female			87.98	96.19	151.89	150.37	162.85	245.72	NA
Netherlands[2]	Hour	Guilders							
Total			18.70	19.04	19.42	20.06	20.93	21.69	NA
Male			19.24	19.63	20.06	20.73	21.57	22.29	NA
Female			16.51	16.81	17.23	17.68	18.76	19.64	NA
Norway[3]	Hour	Kroner							
Total			72.48	77.23	80.37	84.01	89.05	90.64	92.63
Male			72.93	77.70	80.84	84.45	89.56	91.20	93.12
Female			63.79	68.65	72.18	76.12	81.08	83.59	85.72
Portugal	Hour	Escudos							
Total			NA	NA	482	498	557	682	695
Male			NA	NA	482	503	563	683	702
Female			NA	NA	437	445	490	NA	612

[Continued]

★ 493 ★

European Transport, Storage, and Communication Wages
[Continued]

Country	Time period	Currency	1987	1988	1989	1990	1991	1992	1993
Switzerland[4]	Hour	Francs							
Male			21.34	21.83	22.80	24.91	26.97	28.27	NA
Female			19.94	20.45	21.40	22.63	24.67	25.80	NA
Sweden[5]	Hour	Kronor							
Total			63.41	67.33	73.06	NA	90.93	97.29	NA
Male			63.47	67.37	73.14	NA	91.03	97.53	NA
Female			57.94	63.72	67.79	NA	89.80	94.32	NA
Turkey[6]	Day	Liras							
Total			NA	9,219.7	21,808	33,537	66,496	93,816	146,943
Male			NA	9,342.3	22,077	34,119	68,183	90,762	149,719
Female			NA	8,459.0	19,621	26,901	52,296	81,229	115,858
United Kingdom[7]	Hour	Pounds							
Total			4.25	4.46	4.83	5.17	5.68	5.96	6.21
Male			4.28	4.50	4.86	5.20	5.71	5.99	6.23
Female			3.57	3.75	4.20	4.59	5.21	5.46	5.74

Source: Selected from "Wages in transport, storage and communication," *Year Book of Labour Statistics*, International Labour Office, Geneva, 1994, Table 20, pp. 799+. *Notes:* 1. October of each year. 2. October of each year. Figures under "Total" are employees, including juveniles. "Male" and "Female" are adult employees. 3. Private land transport. Including the value of payments in kind. Adults. 4. October of each year. Including family allowances. Adults. 5. Adults. Second quarter of each year. Including holidays and sick-leave payments and the value of payments in kind. 6. Excluding storage and communication. September of each year. Insurance statistics; employees. 7. Full-time workers on adult rates of pay. April; excluding Northern Ireland.

★ 494 ★

Wages and Salaries

Faculty Salaries by Field: 1993-1994

This table shows average faculty salaries by rank in selected fields at public four-year institutions for academic year 1993-1994.

[NA Not available.]

Field	Professor	Associate professor	Assistant professor[1]	New assistant professor	Instructor	All ranks
Accounting	$65,633	$55,131	$49,557	$53,874	$30,838	$54,293
Anthropology	$57,237	$44,420	$35,695	$32,954	NA	$47,739
Business and management, general	$62,702	$52,823	$48,326	$48,402	$32,134	$53,430
Business management & administrative svcs.	$63,702	$52,236	$48,309	$49,118	$29,969	$53,185
Business marketing	$63,399	$52,822	$48,727	$47,218	$30,833	$53,842
Chemistry, general	$58,064	$43,410	$35,661	$33,272	$28,119	$48,699
Communications	$54,027	$42,677	$35,009	$34,538	$27,206	$40,676
Computer & info. sci.	$64,421	$51,588	$45,093	$43,612	$30,563	$51,370

[Continued]

★ 494 ★

Faculty Salaries by Field: 1993-1994
[Continued]

Field	Professor	Associate professor	Assistant professor[1]	New assistant professor	Instructor	All ranks
Economics, general	$61,509	$49,145	$42,816	$42,046	$31,010	$52,030
Education	$53,463	$42,473	$35,136	$34,549	$27,427	$42,870
Engineering	$68,097	$53,805	$46,007	$44,648	$33,212	$57,396
English language & literature	$53,460	$42,228	$33,312	$31,667	$24,234	$41,397
Foreign languages & literatures	$55,769	$43,083	$34,085	$31,874	$26,245	$42,322
History, general	$55,357	$43,232	$33,484	$32,623	$27,465	$46,373
Life sciences	$56,391	$44,717	$36,946	$34,861	$27,160	$47,474
Mathematics	$58,869	$44,891	$36,084	$34,773	$26,225	$45,602
Music, general	$52,271	$40,692	$32,558	$30,960	$27,205	$42,000
Nursing	$53,005	$42,929	$35,548	$34,747	$30,526	$38,334
Philosophy & religion	$58,386	$43,136	$33,546	$31,955	$26,644	$47,515
Physical sciences	$56,797	$42,851	$35,926	$32,671	$26,281	$46,867
Physics, general	$61,006	$46,391	$37,717	$34,821	$27,455	$51,959
Political science, general	$57,523	$43,697	$34,782	$33,069	$28,028	$46,692
Psychology	$56,259	$43,649	$34,817	$33,013	$28,525	$46,546
Social sciences, general	$55,917	$45,198	$35,153	$31,992	$26,044	$45,863
Social work	$57,931	$46,060	$36,290	$33,056	$32,326	$44,589
Sociology	$53,551	$42,732	$34,368	$32,583	$28,542	$44,632
Special education, general	$52,900	$42,042	$34,925	$33,304	$27,200	$42,850
Teacher education	$51,834	$41,642	$35,202	$34,344	$27,388	$41,241
Visual and performing arts	$51,427	$40,033	$33,108	$30,810	$25,848	$41,152

Source: Selected from "Average Faculty Salaries by Rank in Selected Fields at Four-Year Institutions, 1993-94," *The Chronicle of Higher Education Almanac*, September 1, 1994, p. 36. Primary source: College and University Personnel Association. Figures are based on reports covering 88,733 faculty members at 307 public four-year institutions and 47,071 faculty members at 490 private four-year institutions. The sample includes mostly baccalaureate and comprehensive colleges and universities, and largely excludes doctorate-granting institutions. The figures cover full-time faculty members on 9- or 10-month contracts. Also in source: figures for private institutions. *Notes:* 1. Includes data for new assistant professors. 2. Includes data for new assistant professors.

★ 495 ★
Wages and Salaries

Faculty Salaries in Higher Education: 1982-1993

This table shows average salaries by sex in constant 1992-93 dollars of full-time instructional faculty in institutions of higher education, by academic rank, for academic years 1982-1984 through 1992-1993.

[Salaries in constant 1992-1993 dollars.]

Academic year and sex	All ranks	Professor	Associate professor	Assistant professor	Instructor	Lecturer	No academic rank
1982-83							
Total	$39,619	$51,755	$39,158	$32,060	$25,643	$29,391	$37,193
Men	$41,718	$52,272	$39,611	$32,822	$26,481	$31,019	$38,600
Women	$33,889	$47,368	$37,539	$30,722	$24,904	$27,605	$34,743
1984-85							
Total	$41,028	$53,555	$40,352	$33,241	$26,367	$30,096	$37,122
Men	$43,366	$54,264	$40,954	$34,133	$27,333	$31,744	$38,443
Women	$34,956	$48,274	$38,428	$31,768	$25,525	$28,304	$34,940
1985-86							
Total	$42,426	$55,361	$41,634	$34,417	$27,398	$31,133	$38,099
Men	$44,917	$56,101	$42,270	$35,487	$28,413	$33,056	$39,643
Women	$36,118	$50,101	$39,686	$32,700	$26,506	$29,172	$35,588
1987-88							
Total	$44,166	$57,875	$43,346	$35,815	$27,963	$31,960	$38,795
Men	$46,890	$58,730	$44,074	$37,016	$29,091	$34,022	$40,290
Women	$37,525	$52,131	$41,251	$33,958	$27,020	$29,983	$36,424
1989-90							
Total	$45,048	$59,277	$44,216	$36,692	$28,095	$32,540	$38,790
Men	$48,000	$60,220	$45,045	$37,918	$29,108	$34,978	$40,386
Women	$38,369	$53,500	$42,057	$34,897	$27,298	$30,301	$36,512
1990-91[1]							
Total	$44,876	$59,110	$44,076	$36,648	$28,024	$32,032	$38,735
Men	$47,962	$60,184	$44,954	$37,926	$29,149	$34,655	$35,361
Women	$38,187	$52,925	$41,857	$34,828	$27,175	$29,918	$36,376
1991-92							
Total	$45,221	$59,227	$44,270	$36,862	$31,881	$31,407	$38,964
Men	$48,311	$60,321	$45,183	$38,123	$34,401	$33,869	$40,653

[Continued]

★ 495 ★

Faculty Salaries in Higher Education: 1982-1993
[Continued]

Academic year and sex	All ranks	Professor	Associate professor	Assistant professor	Instructor	Lecturer	No academic rank
Women	$38,706	$53,233	$42,039	$35,127	$29,775	$29,441	$36,735
1992-93							
Total	$44,714	$58,789	$43,945	$36,625	$28,501	$30,529	$37,771
Men	$47,865	$59,974	$44,855	$37,841	$29,584	$32,486	$39,365
Women	$38,386	$52,757	$41,863	$35,033	$27,702	$28,920	$35,792

Source: "Average salaries in constant 1992-93 dollars of full-time instructional faculty on 9- and 10-month contracts in institutions of higher education, by academic rank and sex: 50 states and the District of Columbia, 1982-83 through 1992-93," U.S. Department of Education, National Center for Education Statistics, *Salaries of Full-Time Instructional Faculty on 9- and 10-Month Contracts in Institutions of Higher Education, 1982-83 Through 1992-93*, NCES 93-475, December 1993, Table 3, p. 7. Primary source: U.S. Department of Education, National Center for Education Statistics, IPEDS "Salaries, Tenure, and Fringe Benefits of Full-Time Instructional Faculty" 1987-88, and 1989-90 through 1992-93 surveys and HEGIS "Salaries, Tenure, and Fringe Benefits of Full-Time Instructional Faculty" surveys 1982-83 through 1985-86. Data for the 1983-84 academic year were not edited and could not be analyzed. Data were not collected for the 1986-87 and 1988-89 academic years. *Note:* 1. Data revised from previously published data.

★ 496 ★

Wages and Salaries

Growth of Full-Time Equivalent Wages: 1979-1987

This table shows the full-time equivalent wage growth of workers, by age and race, between 1979 and 1987. For all young workers (ages 16-34), earnings were 7.2% less in 1987 than they were in 1979. Wages increased slightly for white women but fell for black women. The decline is attributed to a rapid shift to low-wage work.

Age group and year	All	Black women	Black men	White women	White men
Age 16-24					
1979	$11,170	$9,899	$10,643	$10,526	$12,316
1987	$9,778	$8,060	$8,914	$9,455	$10,400
Age 25-34					
1979	$18,317	$13,500	$18,139	$15,198	$22,808
1987	$17,000	$13,000	$14,222	$15,392	$20,500

Source: Selected from Ray Marshall, *The State of Families, 3: Losing Direction*, Family Service America, 1991, pp. 45-46, Figures 4.6 and 4.7, "Full-time Equivalent Wage Growth of Young Workers, Aged 25-34, 1979-1987," and "Full-time Equivalent Wage Growth of Young Workers, Aged 16-24, 1979-1987." Primary source: Adapted from Lawrence Mishel and David Frankel, *The State of Working America* (Washington, DC: Economic Policy Institute, 1990), p. 212.

★ 497 ★

Wages and Salaries

Income of Displaced Workers: 1994

This table shows the median weekly earnings of displaced full-time wage and salary workers on their lost jobs and on jobs held in February 1994. The incidence of job loss beginning with the recession in the early 1990s was especially high among manufacturing workers, but nonmanufacturing industries and the finance, insurance, and real estate industry were also hard hit. About three-quarters of those displaced from full-time jobs in 1991 and 1992 had found new jobs by the time they were surveyed in 1994. Earnings declined 7% for women and 9% for men between the lost and current job. However, men continued to have higher pay than women. And men displaced from full-time wage and salary jobs were more likely than their female counterparts to be reemployed in another full-time job.

[Numbers in thousands, except percent and dollars.]

Gender	Displaced full-time wage and salary workers[1]	Reemployed in full-time wage and salary jobs in February 1994							
		Total	Earnings relative to those of lost job				Median weekly earnings on[2]		
			20% or more below	Below, but within 20%	Equal or above but within 20%	20% or more above	Lost job	Job held in February 1994	Percent change
Men, 20 years and older	1,595	1,029	30.8%	14.9%	27.2%	27.0%	$576	$523	-9.2%
Women, 20 years and older	924	486	31.9%	18.3%	21.8%	28.0%	$413	$384	-7.0%

Source: Jennifer M. Gardner, "Worker displacement: a decade of change," *Monthly Labor Review*, April 1995, pp. 45-50; selected from Table 4, p. 49, "Median weekly earnings of displaced full-time wage and salary workers on their lost jobs and on jobs held in February 1994 by age, sex, race, and Hispanic origin." Data refer to persons who had 3 or more years of tenure on a full-time wage and salary job they had lost or left between January 1991 and December 1992 because their plant or company closed or moved, there was insufficient work for them to do, or their positions or shifts were abolished. Figures were not available for women by race and Hispanic origin because the base was less than 75,000.

★ 498 ★

Wages and Salaries

Latin American/Caribbean Agricultural Wages

This table shows earnings in agriculture in the two Latin American countries for which information was available for the years 1987-1993.

Country	Time period	Currency	1987	1988	1989	1990	1991	1992	1993
Latin America/Caribbean									
Costa Rica[1]	Month	Colones							
Total			7,769	9,241	10,973	13,539	16,521	22,503	NA
Male			7,907	9,416	10,991	13,651	16,507	22,630	NA
Female			6,314	7,391	10,782	12,246	16,661	21,115	NA
Paraguay[2]	Month	Guaranies							
Total			NA	75,735	115,438	91,408	168,817	184,756	230,589
Male			NA	77,376	117,845	91,513	167,854	182,428	229,252
Female			NA	60,858	93,979	89,873	178,910	207,172	243,430

Source: Selected from "Wages in agriculture," *Year Book of Labour Statistics*, International Labour Office, Geneva, 1994, Table 21, pp. 807+. *Notes:* 1. Employees. Labor force sample survey. July of each year. 2. Employees.

★ 499 ★

Wages and Salaries

Latin American/Caribbean Construction Wages

This table shows earnings in construction in the two Latin American countries for which information was available for the years 1987-1993.

Country	Time period	Currency	1987	1988	1989	1990	1991	1992	1993
Latin America/Caribbean									
Costa Rica[1]	Month	Colones							
Total			13,440	15,277	15,918	21,736	23,373	29,345	NA
Male			13,462	15,294	15,808	21,552	23,319	29,294	NA
Female			10,598	14,522	25,329	32,011	26,474	32,382	NA
Paraguay[2]	Month	Guaranies							
Total			NA	220,400	269,416	337,175	610,681	438,475	607,045
Male			NA	222,892	296,953	340,896	620,931	428,524	601,669
Female			NA	161,833	170,054	247,777	334,607	626,675	700,093

Source: Selected from "Wages in construction," *Year Book of Labour Statistics,* International Labour Office, Geneva, 1994, Table 19, pp. 790+. *Notes:* 1. Employees. Labour force sample survey. July of each year. Beginning 1987, methodology revised. 2. Employees.

★ 500 ★

Wages and Salaries

Latin American/Caribbean Manufacturing Wages

This table shows earnings in manufacturing in selected Latin American and Caribbean countries for the years 1987-1993.

Country	Time period	Currency	1987	1988	1989	1990	1991	1992	1993
Latin America/Caribbean									
Costa Rica[1]	Month	Colones							
Total[1]			13,211	14,658	16,784	20,037	27,229	32,948	NA
Men[1]			14,207	16,573	18,534	21,887	30,152	36,427	NA
Women[1]			11,021	11,102	13,505	16,262	21,733	26,282	NA
El Salvador	Hour	Colones							
Total			3.18	3.21	3.27	3.27	NA	NA	NA
Men			3.34	3.34	3.36	3.37	NA	NA	NA
Women			3.02	3.02	3.05	3.17	NA	NA	NA
Paraguay	Month	Guaranies							
Total			NA	115,897	177,464	220,548	273,537	298,682	380,096
Men			NA	118,473	170,222	234,234	292,787	342,552	407,117
Women			NA	105,252	212,743	155,744	196,738	177,754	298,952

Source: Selected from "Wages in manufacturing," *Year Book of Labour Statistics,* International Labour Office, Geneva, 1994, Table 17, pp. 710+. *Note:* 1. Employees. Labor force sample survey. July of each year.

★ 501 ★

Wages and Salaries

Latin American/Caribbean Mining and Quarrying Wages

This table shows earnings in mining and quarrying in two Latin American countries for the years 1987-1993.

Country	Time period	Currency	1987	1988	1989	1990	1991	1992	1993
Latin America/Caribbean									
Costa Rica[1]	Month	Colones							
Total			9,632	18,273	17,929	18,165	16,382	NA	NA
Male			9,633	18,489	18,178	18,513	16,949	NA	NA
Female			NA	10,989	10,989	13,187	8,000	NA	NA
Paraguay	Month	Guaranies							
Total			NA	129,152	150,005	177,763	241,415	258,148	317,823
Male			NA	131,251	141,205	166,138	236,260	257,189	332,242
Female			NA	112,464	219,366[2]	565,277[2]	359,196[2]	276,347[2]	260,834

Source: Selected from "Wages in mining and quarrying," *Year Book of Labour Statistics,* International Labour Office, Geneva, 1994, Table 18, pp. 782+. *Notes:* 1. Employees. Labor force sample survey. July of each year. 2. According to source document.

★ 502 ★

Wages and Salaries

Latin American/Caribbean Transport, Storage, and Communication Wages

This table shows earnings in transport, storage, and communication in the two Latin American countries for which information was available for the years 1987-1993.

Country	Time period	Currency	1987	1988	1989	1990	1991	1992	1993
Latin America/Caribbean									
Costa Rica[1]	Month	Colones							
Total			15,834	18,231	21,020	25,853	32,712	37,597	NA
Male			16,132	17,718	21,232	25,815	32,604	36,917	NA
Female			13,474	21,627	18,842	26,254	34,471	42,693	NA
Paraguay[2]	Month	Guaranies							
Total			NA	115,077	159,281	173,336	256,287	291,596	339,796
Male			NA	112,631	154,992	169,719	250,819	285,249	341,549
Female			NA	132,635	189,778	199,786	297,466	340,865	327,134

Source: Selected from "Wages in transport, storage and communication," *Year Book of Labour Statistics,* International Labour Office, Geneva, 1994, Table 20, pp. 799+. *Notes:* 1. Employees. Labour force sample survey. July of each year. Beginning 1987, methodology revised. 2. Employees.

★ 503 ★

Wages and Salaries

Librarians' Salaries

This table shows the distribution of beginning professional librarians' salaries by the sex of the library's director. This data was collected to determine if there was a financial advantage to working in a library headed by a male director. There did not appear to be a significant difference, but it was found that the only beginning librarians making more than $40,000 worked for women.

Salary range	Male Directors		Female Directors	
	Number	Percent	Number	Percent
$16,000-$19,999	12	6%	9	5%
$20,000-$21,999	23	12%	31	17%
$22,000-$23,999	36	18%	42	23%
$24,000-$25,999	42	21%	22	12%
$26,000-$27,999	38	19%	40	22%
$28,000-$29,999	20	10%	14	8%
$30,000-$34,999	23	12%	20	11%
$35,000-$39,999	2	1%	3	2%
Over $40,000	0	0	21	12%

Source: Selected from Kay Jones Muther, "Sex, Salaries, and Library Support: A New Look," *Wilson Library Bulletin*, April 1995, pp. 37-40, p. 40, table entitled "Distribution of Beginning Professionals' Salaraies by Sex of Director."

★ 504 ★

Wages and Salaries

Library Directors' Salaries

This table shows median salaries by sex and by size of population served for library directors in 1987 and 1994. It shows dollar difference and percent difference between male and female directors' salaries.

[NA Not available.]

Category	1987				1994			
	Male	Female	Difference	Percent diff.	Male	Female	Difference	Percent diff.
Median Salaries								
A[1]	$41,876	$39,733	$2,143	5%	$59,585	$57,774	$1,811	3%
B[2]	$45,463	$44,221	$1,242	3%	$71,927	$68,989	$2,968	4%
C[3]	$60,843	$53,153	$7,690	14%	$82,252	$75,494	$6,758	9%
D[4]	$58,257	$61,157	-$2,900	-5%	$79,292	$90,626	-$11,334	-14%

Source: Selected from Kay Jones Muther, "Sex, Salaries, and Library Support: A New Look," *Wilson Library Bulletin*, April 1995, pp. 37-40, p. 39, Tables 6 and 7, entitled "Directors' Median Salaries by Sex and by Size of Population Served," and "Directors' Median Salaray Increases by Sex." *Notes:* 1. Serving populations of 100,000 to 199,999 in 1987, and 100,000 to 249,999 in 1994. 2. Serving populations of 250,000 to 499,999 in 1994. 3. Serving populations of 500,000 to 1,000,000 in 1994. 4. Serving populations over 1 million.

★ 505 ★

Wages and Salaries

Male-Female Earnings Ratio: 1980-1991

This table shows women's earnings as a proportion of men's earnings. The first column shows the ratio among persons aged 15 or older employed year-round, full-time (median annual earnings data). The second column shows the ratio among wage and salary workers aged 16 or older employed full time (median weekly earnings data).

[Numbers in thousands.]

Year	I[1]	II[2]
1991	69.9	74.0
1990	71.6	71.8
1989	68.6	70.1
1988	66.0	70.2
1987	65.2	70.0
1986	64.3	69.2
1985	64.6	68.2
1984	63.7	67.8
1983	63.6	66.7
1982	61.7	65.4
1981	59.2	64.6
1980	60.2	64.4

Source: Linda Levine, *Pay Equity Legislation in the 102d Congress*, CRS Report for Congress, updated January 6, 1993 (archived), Table 1, p. CRS-3, "Male-Female Earnings Ratio According to Three Data Series." Data relate to full-time workers for reasons of comparability between the sexes, as far more women than men are employed part-time voluntarily. A comparison between all female and workers would thus upwardly bias the wage gap because of women's greater willingness to work fewer hours a week. If the wage gap were calculated for *all* workers aged 16 or older, women employed part- and full-time earned 66% as much as men employed part- and full-time in 1991, according to data from the U.S. Bureau of Labor Statistics. *Notes:* 1. Data from the U.S. Census Bureau. 2. Data from the U.S. Bureau of Labor Statistics.

★ 506 ★

Wages and Salaries

Median Earnings by Educational Attainment: 1990

This table shows the median earnings of men and women over the age of 25 by race/ethnicity and educational attainment in 1990. In 1990, the median annual earnings of all women were $12,250, not sufficient to support a family of four above the federal povery line. Men's median earnings were $21,522.

Gender/Race/ Ethnicity	1-3 yrs. high school	4 yrs. of high school	1-3 yrs. college	4 or more yrs. of college
All Men	$16,181	$22,378	$27,308	$37,230
All Women	$8,936	$12,412	$16,284	$23,861
Hispanic Men	$15,129	$18,230	$27,308	$32,245

[Continued]

★ 506 ★

Median Earnings by Educational Attainment: 1990
[Continued]

Gender/Race/ Ethnicity	1-3 yrs. high school	4 yrs. of high school	1-3 yrs. college	4 or more yrs. of college
Hispanic Women	$9,250	$11,830	$16,284	$21,857
Black Men	$12,396	$17,181	$22,095	$30,282
Black Women	$8,685	$12,675	$16,496	$25,874
White Men	$16,926	$23,557	$28,392	$37,996
White Women	$9,015	$12,368	$16,270	$23,598

Source: "Median Earnings of Men and Women in 1990," *Women's Voices: A Joint Project* (Policy Guide), Ms. Foundation for Women, September 1992, p. 6. Primary source: U.S. Bureau of the Census. Data for Asian and Native Americans not available.

★ 507 ★
Wages and Salaries

Nonphysician Professionals' Income

This table shows 1992 incomes and percent increases over 1991 level for advanced practice nurses, physical therapists, and physician assistants.

Title	1992 income	Over 1991
Nurse anesthetist	$77,462	7.7%
Nurse midwife	$51,411	6.9%
Nurse practitioner	$42,500	5.7%
Physical therapist	$47,746	13.9%
Physician assistant	$43,407	1.7%

Source: Selected from "Nonphysician Professionals Define Their Roles," *Statistical Bulletin*, Vol 75(2), Apr-Jun 1994, p. 19. Primary source: Neel, J.R., "Extending the extenders," *Physician's Weekly*, X(48): December 27, 1993.

★ 508 ★

Wages and Salaries

Oceanian Construction Wages

This table shows earnings in construction in two Oceanian countries for the years 1987-1993.

Country	Time period	Currency	1987	1988	1989	1990	1991	1992	1993
Oceania									
Australia[1]	Hour	Dollars[1]							
Total			112.0	119.1	127.2	132.9	136.5	137.1	138.7
Male			112.0	118.9	127.1	132.8	136.3	136.9	138.5
Female			112.9	121.4	128.3	133.7	139.7	140.2	141.9
New Zealand	Hour	Dollars							
Total			10.82	11.74	12.19	12.85	13.26	13.31	13.25
Male			10.92	11.84	12.26	12.93	13.33	13.39	13.33
Female			9.54	10.48	11.13	11.73	12.22	12.26	12.19

Source: Selected from "Wages in construction," *Year Book of Labour Statistics,* International Labour Office, Geneva, 1994, Table 19, pp. 790+. *Note:* 1. Index of hourly award rates of pay (June 1985=100). Adult full time.

★ 509 ★

Wages and Salaries

Oceanian Manufacturing Wages

This table shows earnings in manufacturing in selected Oceanian countries for the years 1987-1993.

Country	Time period	Currency	1987	1988	1989	1990	1991	1992	1993
Oceania									
Australia[1]	Hour	Dollars							
Total			NA	NA	NA	12.89	13.27	13.68	14.02
Male			NA	NA	NA	13.45	13.77	14.19	14.58
Female			NA	NA	NA	11.09	11.66	12.02	12.37
New Zealand[2]	Hour	Dollars							
Total			10.95	11.99	12.62	13.43	13.88	14.12	14.20
Male			11.87	12.89	13.51	14.37	14.84	15.02	15.08
Female			8.61	9.61	10.17	10.77	11.18	11.55	11.63

Source: Selected from "Wages in manufacturing," *Year Book of Labour Statistics,* International Labour Office, Geneva, 1994, Table 17, pp. 710+. *Notes:* 1. Full-time adult non-managerial employees. November of each year. Including the value of payments in kind. 2. Employees. Establishments with the equivalent of more than 2 full-time paid employees.

★ 510 ★

Wages and Salaries

Oceanian Mining and Quarrying Wages

This table shows earnings in mining and quarrying in selected Oceanian countries for the years 1987-1993.

Country	Time period	Currency	1987	1988	1989	1990	1991	1992	1993
Oceania									
Australia[1]	Hour	Dollars							
Total			16.61	16.80	18.45	18.83	20.69	21.49	23.88
Male			16.96	17.19	18.82	19.27	21.39	21.91	24.39
Female			11.71	12.81	13.77	13.87	14.73	15.96	17.91
New Zealand[2]	Hour	Dollars							
Total			13.68	14.69	14.71	15.51	16.72	17.17	17.08
Male			14.01	15.01	14.93	15.70	17.01	17.46	17.33
Female			10.83	12.05	12.43	13.72	14.33	14.77	14.81

Source: Selected from "Wages in mining and quarrying," *Year Book of Labour Statistics,* International Labour Office, Geneva, 1994, Table 18, pp. 782+. *Notes:* 1. Full-time adult non-managerial employees. 1987-1989 are May of each year; other figures are November of each year. 1987-1989 include the value of payments in kind. 2. Employees. Establishments with the equivalent of more than 2 full-time paid employees.

★ 511 ★

Wages and Salaries

Oceanian Transport, Storage, and Communication Wages

This table shows earnings in transport, storage, and communication in two Oceanian countries for the years 1987-1993.

Country	Time period	Currency	1987	1988	1989	1990	1991	1992	1993
Oceania									
Australia[1]	Hour	Dollars							
Total			NA	NA	NA	13.93	14.51	15.49	16.02
Male			NA	NA	NA	14.21	14.85	15.79	16.30
Female			NA	NA	NA	12.74	13.08	14.27	14.70
New Zealand	Hour	Dollars							
Total			11.44	12.72	13.99	15.44	15.99	16.35	16.35
Male			12.14	13.55	15.03	16.51	17.11	17.42	17.33
Female			9.82	10.85	11.76	13.14	13.65	14.05	14.25

Source: Selected from "Wages in transport, storage, and communication," *Year Book of Labour Statistics,* International Labour Office, Geneva, 1994, Table 20, pp. 799+. *Note:* 1. May of each year. Full-time adult non-managerial employees.

★ 512 ★

Wages and Salaries

Physics Bachelors' Starting Salaries: 1990

This table divides industry into three parts and separates the starting salaries reported by men and women holders of bachelor's degrees in physics, class of 1992. Figures are also given for degree holders who obtained employment in high schools, colleges or universities, and government. The highest median salary was reported by women whose positions involved the manufacture of technical products.

[Men = 283 reported salaries. Women = 56 reported salaries.]

Type of employer	Men		Women		Total	
	Distribution by employer	Median monthly salary	Distribution by employer	Median monthly salary	Distribution by employer	Median monthly salary
Industry						
Manufacturing						
Technical products	18%	$2,500	10%	$2,890	16%	$2,500
Other products	3%	[1]	5%	[1]	4%	$1,875
Service	22%	$2,310	26%	$2,020	23%	$2,250
High school[2]	10%	$2,350	15%	$2,230	11%	$2,330
College or university	5%	$2,020	4%	[1]	5%	$2,020
Government						
Civilian	7%	$2,040	18%	$2,080	9%	$2,080
Military	32%	$1,960	18%	$1,750	29%	$1,920
Other	3%	[1]	4%	[1]	3%	$1,920
Total	100%	$2,085	100%	$2,030	100%	$2,085

Source: "1991-92 Survey of Physics and Astronomy Bachelor's Degree Recipients," American Institute of Physics, *AIP Report*, Pub. No. R-211.24, March 1993, table IX, p. 6, "Starting salaries of physics bachelors in the U.S., class of 1992," *Notes:* 1. Insufficient data. 2. The high school salaries were calculated by dividing the annual salary by the number of months in the school year.

★ 513 ★

Wages and Salaries

Salaries by Occupation: 1994

This table is excerpted from the fifteenth annual *Working Woman* magazine salary survey. It shows salaries by occupation.

Occupation	Women	Men	Total
Auditors, accountants	$26,936	$36,816	$31,200
Advertising			
CEO	$400,000	$450,000	$440,000

[Continued]

★ 513 ★

Salaries by Occupation: 1994
[Continued]

Occupation	Women	Men	Total
Sr. VP/Acct. Mgr.			
(10-12 yrs.)	$115,000	$115-121,000	$118,000
Director	$83,000	$92,000	$90,000
Colleges & Universities			
Dean, Law	$149,500	$130,000	$133,164
CEO, System	$130,973	$154,340	$149,750
CEO, Single Institution	$120,300	$142,326	$138,600
Chief Academic Officer	$112,000	$120,000	$119,000
Dean, Arts & Sciences	$98,500	$100,478	$99,468
Chief Admissions Officer	$56,715	$63,000	$60,259
FACULTY			
Professor			
Private	$59,970	$70,180	$68,690
Public	$52,900	$59,240	$58,370
Assoc. Prof.			
Private	$44,410	$48,070	$46,910
Public	$41,840	$44,810	$44,070
Asst. Prof.			
Private	$36,390	$40,300	$38,610
Public	$35,310	$38,110	$37,000
Instructor			
Private	$27,750	$29,340	$28,290
Public	$27,010	$28,670	$27,750
All computer programmers	$31,616	$37,596	$35,620
Engineering			
All engineers:			
Under 30	$39,132	$37,693	$37,994
30-39	$50,721	$52,880	$52,654
40-49	$60,120	$66,138	$65,896
50+	$62,574	$75,237	$75,044
All ages	$48,555	$59,750	$58,933
Federal Government			
General Attorney	$60,153	$69,057	$66,163
Economist	$48,484	$59,407	$56,715
Engineer/Architect	$40,418	$49,958	$48,790
Computer Specialist	$41,131	$47,836	$45,266
Accountant	$39,880	$49,005	$45,219
Nurse	$42,928	$42,819	$42,916
Personnel Management/			
Industrial Relations	$32,071	$43,388	$35,578

[Continued]

★ 513 ★

Salaries by Occupation: 1994
[Continued]

Occupation	Women	Men	Total
Financial Services			
Financial Managers	$31,876	$51,064	$39,728
Securities and Financial-Services Salespeople	$27,560	$51,272	$40,300
Underwriters, Financial Officers	$26,208	$41,912	$34,008
Human Resources			
All personnel, training and labor relations specialists	$29,120	$39,572	$31,720
Insurance			
Insurance salespeople	$23,504	$35,308	$30,108
Law			
Lawyers	$47,684	$61,100	$56,420
Medicine			
Orthopedic surgeon	$152,841	$286,654	$283,029
Ophthalmologist	$155,618	$213,374	$207,339
Obstetrician/ Gynecologist	$180,800	$202,956	$198,726
General Surgeon	$150,108	$190,269	$188,379
Psychiatrist	$110,270	$117,879	$117,129
Internist	$90,916	$117,251	$112,704
Pediatrician	$88,149	$117,693	$109,601
Family Practitioner	$85,000	$107,778	$105,536
Magazine Publishing (4-10 years)			
EDITORIAL			
Management	$67,553	$72,570	$70,423
Editor-in-Chief	$37,409	$41,137	$38,783
Managing Editor	$37,029	$39,337	$37,733
Senior Editor	$37,554	$41,552	$39,915
PRODUCTION			
Production Director	$45,355	$51,714	$48,900
Production Manager	$33,538	$37,560	$34,800
Nursing			
Registered Nurses	$34,476	$32,916	$34,424
Physical Therapy			
Physical therapy staff	$25,895	$28,221	$26,198
Self-employed	$52,765	$63,931	$55,955

[Continued]

★ 513 ★

Salaries by Occupation: 1994
[Continued]

Occupation	Women	Men	Total
Pharmacy			
Chain	$49,000	$51,600	$51,000
Hospital	$48,200	$51,100	$50,300
Independent store	$44,000	$45,600	$45,300
Public Relations			
Senior Manager	$54,677	$78,525	X
Supervisor	$41,707	$59,627	X
Account Executive	$30,036	$33,908	X
Sales Management			
Sales Representative			
Commodities	$24,596	$34,268	$32,032
Finance, Bus. Services	$25,272	$36,296	$30,420
Real Estate	$24,908	$34,632	$27,612
Advertising	$24,960	$29,744	$26,416

Source: Diane Harris, et al., "Does Your Pay Measure Up," *Working Woman,* January 1994, pp. 26+. Primary sources: College and University Administration: 1992-93 median salaries for institutions offering doctoral programs. Faculty: 1992-93 average salaries for all institutions with academic ranks. (Sources: College and University Personnel; American Association of University Professors.) Computers: Source Services Corp; Bureau of Labor Statistics. Engineering: National Society of Professional Engineers; Society of Women Engineers. Federal Government: U.S. Office of Personnel Management. Financial Services: Kling Personnel Associates; Securities Industry Association; Bureau of Labor Statistics. Human Resources: William Mercer; Bureau of Labor Statistics. Insurance: Life Office Management Associations; Bureau of Labor Statistics. Law: Altman Well Pensa; Bureau of Labor Statistics. Medicine: Medical Group Mgt. Association. Magazine publishing: *Folio* magazine. Nursing: National Association for Health Care Recruitment; BLS. Physical therapy: American Physical Therapy Association. Pharmacy: *Drug Topics* magazine. Public Relations: Public Relations Society of America. Sales Management: Administrative Management Society Foundation; BLS.

★ 514 ★

Wages and Salaries

Salaries in State and Local Government

This table shows the average annual salaries of total, administrative and professional employees in state and local government in 1974 and 1991. The 5.4 million full-time employees in that sector had a median annual salary of $25,523 in 1991. Figures are also given by race/ethnicity.

Gender and Job Category	Year	Total, All Groups	Individual Population Group				
			White	Black	Hispanic	Asians, Pac. Islanders	Amer. Ind., Alask. Native
Total, All Jobs							
Men	1974	$10,269	$10,586	$8,676	$8,756	$13,329	$9,474
Women		$7,523	$7,562	$7,380	$7,034	$9,546	$7,122
Men	1991	$28,395	$29,269	$24,117	$27,019	$35,452	$25,449

[Continued]

★ 514 ★

Salaries in State and Local Government
[Continued]

Gender and Job Category	Year	Total, All Groups	Individual Population Group				
			White	Black	Hispanic	Asians, Pac. Islanders	Amer. Ind., Alask. Native
Women		$22,669	$22,885	$21,672	$22,180	$30,434	$21,461
Officials and Administrators							
Men	1974	$15,039	$15,070	$14,572	$13,879	$18,426	$13,596
Women		$11,747	$11,595	$13,065	$11,160	$13,717	$10,250
Men	1991	$43,666	$43,654	$43,256	$43,750	$46,169	$41,850
Women		$37,019	$36,443	$39,502	$37,039	$44,913	$34,696
Professionals							
Men	1974	$13,289	$13,334	$12,210	$12,508	$16,232	$12,497
Women		$10,935	$10,847	$11,239	$10,958	$12,134	$10,809
Men	1991	$35,926	$36,214	$31,546	$34,711	$41,717	$32,574
Women		$30,778	$30,655	$29,818	$30,805	$38,388	$28,367

Source: "Salaries of Full-Time Employees in State and Local Government," U.S. Equal Employment Opportunity Commission, *Indicators of Equal Employment Opportunity-Status and Trends*, September 1993, p. 48. Primary source: Equal Employment Opportunity Commission, State and Local Government Information (EEO-4) Reports. Data for total men and women in 1974 include salaries of a small number of "other" minorities, not shown separately.

★ 515 ★

Wages and Salaries

Salaries of Chemical Engineers: 1980-1993

This table shows median and mean salaries of chemical engineers by year of bachelor's degree and gender, for the years 1980-1993. Salaries are reported to the American Institute of Chemical Engineers (AIChE), which conducts a salary survey among its members from time to time. There are comparatively few female members of AIChE, but the number is growing. Women accounted for about 1 in 5 of persons earning their bachelor's degrees in chemical engineering in the 1980s and about 1 in 3 in the 1990s. The survey notes that women chemical engineers in Great Britain in the 25-29 age range earn $2,235 less per year than men.

Year of Bachelor's Degree	Women			Men		
	Number of respondents	Median	Mean	Number of respondents	Median	Mean
1993	34	$39,600	$36,638	46	$37,900	$35,952
1992	35	$40,000	$39,317	72	$41,200	$42,297
1991	29	$42,700	$40,838	67	$44,000	$43,013
1990	22	$45,000	$43,595	45	$44,500	$42,109
1989	37	$44,000	$54,281	55	$47,200	$47,282
1988	22	$48,000	$46,636	60	$45,850	$46,120

[Continued]

★ 515 ★

Salaries of Chemical Engineers: 1980-1993
[Continued]

Year of Bachelor's Degree	Women			Men		
	Number of respondents	Median	Mean	Number of respondents	Median	Mean
1987	16	$50,650	$50,394	83	$50,000	$57,306
1986	32	$48,550	$55,150	103	$50,500	$57,759
1985	28	$55,050	$54,275	96	$52,700	$56,761
1984	29	$52,700	$50,359	111	$54,600	$55,359
1983	19	$55,600	$57,437	114	$57,100	$62,163
1982	14	$55,100	$56,593	90	$58,400	$58,864
1981	17	$56,800	$60,429	119	$62,300	$62,050
1980	11	$63,300	$62,391	120	$62,000	$63,948

Source: Selected from "Salary by year of bachelor's degree and gender," *AIChE 1994 Salary Survey Report*, 1994, Table 12, p. 87.

★ 516 ★

Wages and Salaries

Salaries of Doctors of Physics: 1992

This table shows 1992 mean salaries of Physics PhDs and their mean ages, by employment sectors and gender, as reported to the American Institute of Physics. Among full-time employed society members, women made up only 8% of PhD recipients, 16% of masters' degree recipients, and 11% of bachelors' degree recipients. Both men and women are mainly employed in universities, followed by industry and government.

[Salaries in thousands of dollars.]

Employment Sector	Reported mean salary	Adjusted mean salary[2]	Mean age
Industry			
Male	$78.9	$69.2	45
Female	$66.4	$66.4	39
Government			
Male	$67.8	$58.0	48

[Continued]

★ 516 ★

Salaries of Doctors of Physics: 1992

[Continued]

Employment Sector	Reported mean salary	Adjusted mean salary[2]	Mean age
Female	$53.7	$53.7	42
FFR&DC[3]			
Male	$73.4	$66.8	46
Female	$61.2	$61.2	39

Source: "1992 reported and adjusted salaries by selected employment sectors and gender, PhDs,"[1] Jean M. Curtin and Raymond Y. Chu, *1992 Salaries: Society Membership Survey,* American Institute of Physics, Table 19, p. 20. *Notes:* 1. Postdoctorates excluded. 2. Salaries adjusted from mean salaries by years from degree. 3. FFR&DC=Federally Funded Research and Development Centers.

★ 517 ★

Wages and Salaries

Salaries of Federal White Collar Workers

This table shows the average annual salaries of total, administrative and professional employees in Federal Government positions around the world in 1991 (excluding non-Postal employees). Figures are also given by race/ethnicity.

Gender and Job Category	Total, All Groups	Individual Population Group				
		White	Black	Hispanic	Asians, Pac. Islanders	Amer. Ind., Alask. Native
Total, All Jobs						
Men	$41,220	$42,736	$32,607	$34,825	$40,727	$34,929
Women	$28,461	$29,383	$26,265	$26,726	$30,540	$24,982
Administrators						
Men	$44,477	$45,234	$40,844	$39,821	$40,130	$42,606
Women	$36,859	$37,317	$36,123	$34,409	$35,287	$34,237
Professionals						
Men	$49,830	$50,440	$44,698	$45,012	$48,444	$43,308
Women	$40,130	$40,300	$38,996	$38,147	$42,768	$36,723

Source: "Average Annual Salaries of Federal Civilian White Collar Employees," U.S. Equal Employment Opportunity Commission, *Indicators of Equal Employment Opportunity-Status and Trends,* September 1993, p. 50. Primary source: U.S. Office of Personnel Management, Central Personnel Data File (CPDF), 1991.

★ 518 ★
Wages and Salaries

Teachers' Salaries: 1993-1994

This table shows the average salaries of public school teachers in 1993-1994 by state. It also shows the number of teachers and the percent who were men.

State	Avg. salary	Teachers	% Men
United States	$35,723	2,505,004	26.9%
Connecticut	$49,910	34,660	28.5%
Alaska[1]	$46,581	7,094	32.9%
New York	$45,772	188,500	29.9%
New Jersey	$44,693	84,568	26.7%
District of			
Columbia	$42,543	6,450	21.7%
Michigan[1]	$42,500	83,972	34.2%
Pennsylvania	$42,411	101,301	34.4%
Massachusetts	$40,852	58,893	37.9%
California[1]	$40,289	218,496	29.5%
Maryland	$39,463	44,169	23.9%
Illinois	$39,387	110,620	28.7%
Rhode Island	$39,261	9,917	27.8%
Oregon	$37,590	27,195	34.8%
Delaware	$37,469	6,381	26.4%
Hawaii	$36,564	10,427	22.4%
Minnesota	$36,146	46,588	34.1%
Wisconsin	$35,990	51,011	33.6%
Washington	$35,855	45,438	33.3%
Indiana	$35,711	54,989	30.6%
Ohio	$35,684	103,180	29.0%
Vermont	$34,517	7,357	30.2%[1]
New Hampshire	$34,121	11,971	26.5%
Nevada	$33,955	12,396	26.1%
Kansas	$33,919	30,281	32.1%[1]
Colorado	$33,826	33,661	29.0%
Virginia	$33,063	68,859[1]	18.4%[1]
Florida	$31,944	112,283	22.4%
Arizona	$31,800	36,459	29.1%[1]
Kentucky	$31,640	38,100	21.6%
Maine	$30,996	15,090	30.7%
Wyoming	$30,952	6,675	34.5%
Iowa	$30,760	31,695	31.8%
West Virginia	$30,549	20,900	26.9%
Georgia	$30,527	75,602	16.6%
Texas	$30,519	223,126	21.9%

[Continued]

★ 518 ★

Teachers' Salaries: 1993-1994
[Continued]

State	Avg. salary	Teachers	% Men
Tennessee	$30,514	47,000	21.5%
Missouri	$30,324	54,544	23.0%
North Carolina	$29,727	68,744	19.0%
South Carolina	$29,566	37,538	16.6%
Nebraska	$29,564	19,330	29.1%
Alabama	$28,705	42,515	20.4%
Montana	$28,200	9,950	34.0%
Utah	$28,056	19,972	30.2%
New Mexico	$27,922	17,758	26.5%
Arkansas	$27,873	26,236	22.0%
Idaho	$27,756	12,006	30.8%
Oklahoma	$27,009	39,080	25.5%
Louisiana	$26,285	46,837	18.2%
North Dakota	$25,506	7,755	30.8%
Mississippi	$25,153	28,551	17.9%
South Dakota	$25,059	8,884	28.3%

Source: "Average Salaries of Public School Teachers, 1993-94," "Number of Teachers in Public Elementary and Secondary Schools, 1993-94," and "Percent of Public School Teachers Who Are Men, 1993-94," National Education Association Research, *Estimates* data bank. *Note:* 1. Data estimated by NEA.

★ 519 ★

Wages and Salaries

Wage Gap: 1990

This table shows the median annual earnings of men and women full-time workers aged 15 and over by race/ethnicity. It also shows the wage gap of women with men of the same ethnicity and with men of all ethnicities.

[Wage gap is amount earned by women compared to $1.00 earned by men.]

Race/ Ethnicity	Women	Men	Wage gap with men of same ethnicity	Wage gap with men of all ethnicities
All ethnic backgrounds	$19,822	$27,678	X	71.6 cents
White	$20,048	$28,881	69.4 cents	72.4 cents
Black	$18,040	$21,114	85.4 cents	65.1 cents
Hispanic	$15,672	$19,136	81.8 cents	56.6 cents

Source: "The Wage Gap: 1990 Median Annual Earnings, Full-Time Workers 15 and Over," *Women's Voices: A Joint Project* (Policy Guide), Ms. Foundation for Women, September 1992, p. 6.

★ 520 ★
Wages and Salaries

Weekly Earnings by Educational Attainment and Race: 1994

Total number of workers, quartiles, and selected deciles of usual weekly earnings of full-time wage and salary workers by sex, race, and educational attainment, 1994 annual averages. (See notes below table for a discussion of quartiles and deciles.) Earnings are before taxes and other deductions and include any overtime pay, taxes, commissions, or tips usually received. The median is the amount that divides a given earnings distribution into two equal groups, one having earnings above the median and the other having earnings below the median.

[Number of workers in thousands.]

Characteristic	Number of workers	Upper limit of:				
		First decile	First quartile	Second quartile (median)	Third quartile	Ninth decile
Sex, Race, and Educational Attainment						
White men						
Total, 25 years and over	37,624	$280	$400	$595	$855	$1,189
Less than high school diploma	4,177	$196	$258	$351	$499	$671
High school grad, no college	12,401	$275	$372	$511	$702	$914
Some college or associate deg.	9,801	$303	$424	$603	$812	$1,056
College graduates, total	11,245	$407	$593	$845	$1,173	$1,666
Bachelor's degree only	7,367	$386	$553	$772	$1,087	$1,500
Advanced degree	3,878	$477	$690	$974	$1,385	$1,910
White women						
Total, 25 years and over	26,981	$220	$301	$434	$623	$867
Less than high school diploma	1,988	$153	$199	$260	$342	$449
High school grad, no college	9,325	$203	$271	$361	$490	$635
Some college or associate deg.	7,917	$238	$315	$431	$588	$764
College graduates, total	7,750	$337	$475	$643	$869	$1,148
Bachelor's degree only	5,114	$313	$434	$594	$787	$1,013
Advanced degree	2,637	$426	$585	$760	$1,005	$1,346
Black men						
Total, 25 years and over	4,504	$224	$296	$425	$625	$871
Less than high school diploma	660	$187	$234	$320	$457	$592
High school grad, no college	1,729	$217	$281	$383	$556	$738
Some college or associate deg.	1,286	$244	$314	$457	$637	$854
College graduates, total	830	$303	$434	$644	$899	$1,185
Bachelor's degree only	617	$297	$417	$613	$848	$1,134
Advanced degree	213	$339	$539	$762	$1,031	$1,321

[Continued]

★ 520 ★

Weekly Earnings by Educational Attainment and Race: 1994
[Continued]

Characteristic	Number of workers	Upper limit of:				
		First decile	First quartile	Second quartile (median)	Third quartile	Ninth decile
Black women						
Total, 25 years and over	4,574	$190	$254	$361	$521	$739
Less than high school diploma	439	$149	$192	$248	$331	$422
High school grad, no college	1,664	$182	$229	$304	$419	$552
Some college or associate deg.	1,541	$203	$280	$383	$519	$700
College graduates, total	929	$302	$410	$587	$801	$1,019
Bachelor's degree only	683	$288	$386	$518	$729	$940
Advanced degree	246	$403	$571	$728	$952	$1,221

Source: Selected from "Quartiles and selected deciles of usual weekly warnings of full-time wage and salary workers by selected characteristics, 1994 annual averages," *News,* U.S. Department of Labor, Bureau of Labor Statistics, USDL 95-43, February 9, 1995, Table 8. Ten percent of all full-time wage and salary workers earn less than the upper limit of the first decile; 25 percent earn less than the upper limit of the first quartile; 50 percent earn less than the upper limit of the second quartile, or median; 75 percent earn less than the upper limit of the third quartile; and 90 percent earn less than the upper limit of the ninth decile. Detail for the above race and Hispanic-origin groups will not sum to totals because data for the "other races" group are not presented and Hispanics are included in both the white and black population groups.

★ 521 ★

Wages and Salaries

Weekly Earnings by Educational Attainment: 1994

Total number of workers, quartiles, and selected deciles of usual weekly earnings of full-time wage and salary workers by sex, race, Hispanic origin, and educational attainment, fourth quarter, 1994. (See notes below table for a discussion of quartiles and deciles.) Earnings are before taxes and other deductions and include any overtime pay, taxes, commissions, or tips usually received. The median is the amount that divides a given earnings distribution into two equal groups, one having earnings above the median and the other having earnings below the median. The highest-earning 10% of men had weekly earnings of $1,126 or more, while the highest-earning 10% of women earned $840 or more.

[Number of workers in thousands.]

Characteristic	Number of workers	Upper limit of:				
		First decile	First quartile	Second quartile (median)	Third quartile	Ninth decile
Sex, Race, and Hispanic Origin						
Total, 16 years and over	88,247	$224	$310	$472	$713	$1,005
Men	50,478	$247	$346	$531	$789	$1,126
Women	37,769	$203	$280	$403	$599	$840
White	73,926	$231	$319	$489	$734	$1,034
Men	43,019	$258	$365	$559	$817	$1,151

[Continued]

★ 521 ★

Weekly Earnings by Educational Attainment: 1994
[Continued]

Characteristic	Number of workers	Upper limit of:				
		First decile	First quartile	Second quartile (median)	Third quartile	Ninth decile
Women	30,907	$208	$286	$411	$609	$857
Black	10,553	$195	$267	$383	$579	$789
Men	5,308	$210	$284	$406	$607	$817
Women	5,245	$184	$249	$362	$517	$750
Hispanic	8,616	$182	$237	$327	$507	$753
Men	5,464	$191	$253	$349	$532	$769
Women	3,152	$169	$216	$303	$469	$678
Educational Attainment						
Total, 25 years and over	78,322	$240	$333	$503	$745	$1,042
Less than high school diploma	8,021	$179	$225	$305	$437	$601
High school grad, no college	26,162	$228	$304	$428	$607	$806
Some college or associate deg.	21,711	$260	$348	$496	$701	$924
Advanced degree	22,427	$362	$517	$744	$1,034	$1,450
Bachelor's degree only	15,113	$343	$481	$684	$953	$1,289
Advanced degree	7,314	$429	$621	$871	$1,215	$1,670
Men, 25 years and over	44,776	$275	$386	$581	$830	$1,156
Less than high school diploma	5,282	$191	$251	$334	$494	$654
High school grad, no college	14,747	$268	$358	$502	$696	$904
Some college or associate deg.	11,634	$298	$408	$588	$786	$1,018
College grads, total	13,112	$393	$587	$824	$1,157	$1,581
Bachelor's degree only	8,810	$377	$545	$761	$1,056	$1,452
Advanced degree	4,302	$452	$679	$960	$1,369	$1,881
Women, 25 years and over	33,547	$214	$294	$424	$621	$869
Less than high school diploma	2,740	$157	$197	$256	$342	$455
High school grad, no college	11,415	$200	$266	$357	$489	$636
Some college or associate deg.	10,077	$231	$305	$420	$583	$756
College graduates, total	9,315	$334	$463	$644	$891	$1,169
Bachelor's degree only	6,303	$315	$427	$596	$817	$1,307
Advanced degree	3,012	$407	$585	$774	$1,020	$1,350

Source: Selected from "Quartiles and selected deciles of usual weekly warnings of full-time wage and salary workers by selected characteristics, fourth quarter 1994 averages, not seasonally adjusted," *News*, U.S. Department of Labor, Bureau of Labor Statistics, USDL 95-43, February 9, 1995, Table 4. Ten percent of all full-time wage and salary workers earn less than the upper limit of the first decile; 25 percent earn less than the upper limit of the first quartile; 50 percent earn less than the upper limit of the second quartile, or median; 75 percent earn less than the upper limit of the third quartile; and 90 percent earn less than the upper limit of the ninth decile. Detail for the above race and Hispanic-origin groups will not sum to totals because data for the "other races" group are not presented and Hispanics are included in both the white and black population groups.

★ 522 ★
Wages and Salaries
Weekly Earnings by Occupation: 1994

Total number of workers and median usual weekly earnings of full-time wage and salary workers by occupation and gender, fourth quarter, 1994. Earnings are before taxes and other deductions and include any overtime pay, taxes, commissions, or tips usually received. The median is the amount that divides a given earnings distribution into two equal groups, one having earnings above the median and the other having earnings below the median.

[Number of workers in thousands.]

Occupation and sex	Number of workers	Median weekly earnings
Total		
Managerial and professional specialty	25,827	$692
Executive, administrative, managerial	12,639	$665
Professional specialty	13,188	$717
Technical, sales, and admin. support	25,655	$420
Technicians and related support	3,152	$535
Sales occupations	8,540	$433
Admin. support, incl. clerical	13,964	$396
Service occupations	9,498	$301
Private household	333	$181
Protective service	2,042	$517
Other service	7,123	$277
Precision production, craft, repair	10,815	$513
Mechanics and repairers	3,701	$533
Construction trades	3,477	$497
Other	3,637	$508
Operators, fabricators, laborers	14,996	$379
Machine operators, assemblers, and inspectors	7,127	$368
Transportation and material moving occupations	4,068	$459
Handlers, equipment cleaners, helpers, and laborers	3,804	$317
Farming, forestry, and fishing	1,456	$287
Women		
Managerial and professional specialty	12,406	$602
Executive, administrative, managerial	5,662	$553
Professional specialty	6,744	$631

[Continued]

★ 522 ★

Weekly Earnings by Occupation: 1994
[Continued]

Occupation and sex	Number of workers	Median weekly earnings
Technical, sales, and admin. support	16,023	$376
Technicians and related support	1,515	$464
Sales occupations	3,784	$317
Admin. support, incl. clerical	10,724	$378
Service occupations	4,593	$257
Private household	319	$175
Protective service	249	$445
Other service	4,025	$257
Precision production, craft, repair	994	$380
Mechanics and repairers	182	$591
Construction trades	58	[1]
Other	754	$347
Operators, fabricators, laborers	3,569	$293
Machine operators, assemblers, and inspectors	2,634	$291
Transportation and material moving occupations	251	$342
Handlers, equipment cleaners, helpers, and laborers	684	$283
Farming, forestry, and fishing	183	$242
Men		
Managerial and professional specialty	13,421	$805
Executive, administrative, managerial	6,976	$798
Professional specialty	6,444	$810
Technical, sales, and admin. support	9,632	$560
Technicians and related support	1,637	$624
Sales occupations	4,755	$567
Admin. support, incl. clerical	3,239	$497
Service occupations	4,905	$359
Private household	15	[1]
Protective service	1,793	$533
Other service	3,098	$303
Precision production, craft, repair	9,821	$524
Mechanics and repairers	3,519	$530
Construction trades	3,419	$499
Other	2,883	$559

[Continued]

★ 522 ★

Weekly Earnings by Occupation: 1994
[Continued]

Occupation and sex	Number of workers	Median weekly earnings
Operators, fabricators, laborers	11,427	$413
Machine operators, assemblers, and inspectors	4,490	$427
Transportation and material moving occupations	3,817	$467
Handlers, equipment cleaners, helpers, and laborers	3,120	$330
Farming, forestry, and fishing	1,273	$295

Source: Selected from "Median usual weekly earnings of full-time wage and salary workers by occupation and sex, quarterly averages, not seasonally adjusted," *News*, U.S. Department of Labor, Bureau of Labor Statistics, USDL 95-43, February 9, 1995, Table 3. *Note:* 1. Data not shown where base is less than 100,000.

★ 523 ★

Wages and Salaries

Weekly Earnings of Full-Time Workers: 1993 and 1994

Total number of workers and median usual weekly earnings of full-time wage and salary workers by gender, age, and race or Hispanic origin, fourth quarter, 1993 and 1994. Earnings are before taxes and other deductions and include any overtime pay, taxes, commissions, or tips usually received. The median is the amount that divides a given earnings distribution into two equal groups, one having earnings above the median and the other having earnings below the median. Median weekly earnings for women who worked full time were $403, which is 75.9% of the $531 earned by men. White women earned 73.5% of what men earned. The female-male ratio was higher among blacks (89.2%) and Hispanics (86.8%). Racial differences were less among women than men, as black women's median earnings ($362) were 88.1% of that of white women ($411), compared to black men, who earned 72.6% of the median for white men.

[Number of workers in thousands.]

Characteristic	Number of workers		Median weekly earnings			
	IV 1993	IV 1994	In current dollars		Constant (1982) dollars	
			IV-1993	IV-1994	IV-1993	IV-1994
Sex and Age						
Total, 16 years and over	85,795	88,247	$471	$472	$312	$304
Women						
16 years and over	37,014	37,769	$400	$403	$265	$260
16 to 24 years	4,048	4,223	$281	$279	$186	$180
25 years and over	32,965	33,547	$417	$424	$276	$273
Men						
16 years and over	48,781	50,478	$520	$531	$344	$343

[Continued]

★ 523 ★

Weekly Earnings of Full-Time Workers: 1993 and 1994
[Continued]

Characteristic	Number of workers		Median weekly earnings			
	IV 1993	IV 1994	In current dollars		Constant (1982) dollars	
			IV-1993	IV-1994	IV-1993	IV-1994
16 to 24 years	5,302	5,702	$293	$303	$194	$195
25 years and over	43,479	44,776	$567	$581	$375	$375
Race, Hispanic Origin, Sex						
White	72,777	73,926	$485	$489	$321	$315
Women	30,621	30,907	$408	$411	$270	$265
Men	42,157	43,019	$544	$559	$360	$361
Black	9,933	10,553	$367	$383	$243	$247
Women	5,037	5,245	$352	$362	$233	$233
Men	4,895	5,308	$382	$406	$253	$262
Hispanic origin	7,223	8,616	$334	$327	$221	$211
Women	2,583	3,152	$315	$303	$209	$195
Men	4,640	5,464	$351	$349	$232	$225

Source: "Median usual weekly earnings of full-time wage and salary workers by selected characteristics, quarterly averages, not seasonally adjusted," *News,* U.S. Department of Labor, Bureau of Labor Statistics, USDL 95-43, February 9, 1995, Table 1. Detail for the above race and Hispanic-origin groups will not sum to totals because data for the "other races" group are not presented and Hispanics are included in both the white and black population groups.

Wealth and Poverty

★ 524 ★

Displaced Homemakers' Median Income by Age and Race: 1990

This table shows the median personal income of displaced homemakers by race and age. Personal income includes both earned and cash benefits. The median annual personal income for all displaced homemakers was $6,766. Displaced homemakers are women whose main activity has been homemaking and who have lost their main source of income because of divorce, separation, widowhood, a spouse's disability or long-term unemployment, or lost eligibility for public assistance. In 1990 there were 17.8 million displaced homemakers in the United States.

Race/ ethnicity	25-34 years	35-44 years	45-54 years	55-64 years	65+ years
White	$5,486	$7,015	$6,766	$7,958	$8,019
Black	$4,090	$4,557	$4,201	$4,515	$5,027
Hispanic	$3,756	$4,745	$4,067	$4,033	$5,014
Native Amer.	$4,432	$4,735	$4,381	$4,692	$5,768
Asian	$1,652	$5,620	$4,225	$2,598	$4,955

Source: Selected from *Women Work, Poverty Persists: A Status Report on Displaced Homemakers & Single Mothers in the United States*, Women Work!, Washington, D.C., May 1990, Appendix 8, "Displaced Homemakers: Personal Median Income by Age and Race."

★ 525 ★
Wealth and Poverty

Displaced Homemakers' Median Income by Education and Race: 1990

This table shows the median personal income of displaced homemakers by education and race. Personal income includes both earned and cash benefits. White displaced homemakers benefit more from education than do other women.

Years of education	White	Black	Hispanic	Native American	Asian
0-8 years	$6,058	$4,244	$3,096	$4,266	$4,030
8-11 years	$6,566	$4,275	$4,120	$4,362	$3,900
High school grad.	$8,173	$4,778	$4,898	$5,035	$4,725
Some college	$9,709	$5,891	$5,905	$5,957	$5,479
College grad.	$14,922	$10,032	$7,073	$7,499	$5,614

Source: Selected from *Women Work, Poverty Persists: A Status Report on Displaced Homemakers & Single Mothers in the United States*, Women Work!, Washington, D.C., May 1990, Appendix 8, "Displaced Homemakers: Personal Median Income by Education and Race."

★ 526 ★

Wealth and Poverty

Displaced Homemakers' Poverty Status: 1990-I

This table presents statistics related to the poverty and near poverty status of displaced homemakers by race and age, ages 15-34 years. Displaced homemakers are women whose main activity has been homemaking and who have lost their main source of income because of divorce, separation, widowhood, a spouse's disability or long-term unemployment, or lost eligibility for public assistance. In 1990 there were 17.8 million displaced homemakers in the United States. Poverty is measured by households or families, not individuals. Displaced homemakers who are the primary heads of family households have a poverty rate of 42%, with another 13% living in near poverty. By comparison, the poverty rate for all adult U.S. householders in 1990 was 11%. Black, Hispanic, Native Americans, and some subgroups of Asian displaced homemakers have poverty rates about two times higher than white displaced homemakers. The figures in this table were arrived at using the 1990 poverty threshold for a three-person family or household with two children, which was $10,530. Persons living near poverty have incomes between 100% and 150% of the poverty level (here that means $15,795).

Race/ ethnicity	15-19 years		20-24 years		25-34 years	
	Number	Percent	Number	Percent	Number	Percent
White						
Below poverty	8,492	69.64%	83,102	80.61%	395,199	68.37%
100-150% of poverty	1,431	11.74%	10,204	9.90%	75,053	12.98%
Poor and near poor	9,923	81.38%	93,306	90.51%	470,252	81.36%
Total	12,194	X	103,087	X	578,018	X
Black						
Below poverty	2,561	73.32%	23,413	85.81%	169,576	81.79%
100-150% of poverty	330	9.45%	1,974	7.23%	17,619	8.50%
Poor and near poor	2,891	82.77%	25,387	93.04%	187,195	90.28%
Total	3,493	X	27,286	X	207,338	X
Hispanic						
Below poverty	1,070	78.68%	8,268	84.28%	47,330	80.12%
100-150% of poverty	137	10.07%	869	8.86%	5,495	9.30%
Poor and near poor	1,207	88.75%	9,137	93.14%	52,825	89.42%
Total	1,360	X	9,810	X	59,074	X
Native American						
Below poverty	222	80.73%	2,103	85.49%	12,895	81.45%
100-150% of poverty	29	10.55%	231	9.39%	1,526	9.64%
Poor and near poor	251	91.27%	2,334	94.88%	14,421	91.09%
Total	275	X	2,460	X	15,831	X
All Asians						
Below poverty	85	61.15%	1,315	72.77%	9,851	66.50%
100-150% of poverty	23	16.55%	241	13.34%	1,776	11.99%
Poor and near poor	108	77.70%	1,556	86.11%	11,627	78.49%
Total	139	X	1,807	X	14,814	X
All Races						
Below poverty	13,462	72.16%	128,168	82.07%	685,906	73.20%
100-150% of poverty	2,067	11.08%	14,546	9.31%	106,967	11.42%

[Continued]

505

★ 526 ★

Displaced Homemakers' Poverty Status: 1990-I
[Continued]

Race/ ethnicity	15-19 years		20-24 years		25-34 years	
	Number	Percent	Number	Percent	Number	Percent
Poor and near poor	15,529	83.24%	142,714	91.39%	792,873	84.62%
Total	18,655	X	156,167	X	936,976	X

Source: Selected from *Women Work, Poverty Persists: A Status Report on Displaced Homemakers & Single Mothers in the United States,* Women Work!, Washington, D.C., May 1990, Appendix 6, "Displaced Homemakers Poverty & Near Poverty by Race & Age."

★ 527 ★

Wealth and Poverty

Displaced Homemakers' Poverty Status: 1990-II

This table presents statistics related to the poverty and near poverty status of displaced homemakers by race and age, ages 35-65+ years.

Race/ ethnicity	35-44 years		45-54 years		55-64 years		65 + years	
	Number	Percent	Number	Percent	Number	Percent	Number	Percent
White								
Below poverty	324,104	47.38%	237,510	36.95%	377,008	30.14%	1,501,146	22.26%
100-150% of poverty	103,957	15.20%	90,391	14.06%	190,970	15.27%	1,581,415	23.45%
Poor and near poor	428,061	62.58%	327,901	51.01%	567,978	45.41%	3,082,561	45.70%
Total	683,992	X	642,866	X	1,250,776	X	6,744,776	X
Black								
Below poverty	186,471	67.82%	144,407	57.08%	175,633	52.89%	398,014	48.68%
100-150% of poverty	34,428	12.52%	36,038	14.24%	50,899	15.33%	178,798	21.87%
Poor and near poor	220,899	80.35%	180,445	71.32%	226,532	68.21%	576,812	70.54%
Total	274,933	X	253,005	X	332,091	X	817,670	X
Hispanic								
Below poverty	45,978	67.44%	27,705	51.19%	29,925	46.76%	66,444	42.81%
100-150% of poverty	8,772	12.87%	8,082	14.93%	10,930	17.08%	35,577	22.92%
Poor and near poor	54,750	80.31%	35,787	66.13%	40,855	63.83%	102,021	65.73%
Total	68,176	X	54,118	X	64,002	X	155,221	X
Native American								
Below poverty	12,204	69.08%	7,986	58.48%	8,585	54.41%	14,929	44.46%
100-150% of poverty	2,361	13.36%	2,225	16.29%	2,645	16.76%	7,803	23.24%
Poor and near poor	14,565	82.44%	10,211	74.77%	11,230	71.18%	22,732	67.71%
Total	17,667	X	13,656	X	15,777	X	33,575	X
All Asians								
Below poverty	14,000	57.50%	8,834	44.36%	7,031	30.81%	13,861	26.69%
100-150% of poverty	3,258	13.38%	2,936	14.74%	2,869	12.57%	12.140	23.38%
Poor and near poor	17,258	70.88%	11,770	59.11%	9,900	43.38%	26,001	50.07%
Total	24,349	X	19.913	X	22,824	X	51,928	X

[Continued]

★ 527 ★

Displaced Homemakers' Poverty Status: 1990-II
[Continued]

Race/ ethnicity	35-44 years		45-54 years		55-64 years		65 + years	
	Number	Percent	Number	Percent	Number	Percent	Number	Percent
All Races								
Below poverty	628,313	55.38%	452,081	43.90%	620,145	35.87%	2,022,797	25.71%
100-150% of poverty	162,168	14.29%	147,096	14.29%	265,667	15.37%	1,832,011	23.29%
Poor and near poor	790,481	69.67%	599,177	58.1%	885,812	51.23%	3,854,808	49.00%
Total	1,134,605	X	1,029,701	X	1,729,028	X	7,864,468	X

Source: Selected from *Women Work, Poverty Persists: A Status Report on Displaced Homemakers & Single Mothers in the United States,* Women Work!, Washington, D.C., May 1990, Appendix 6, "Displaced Homemakers Poverty & Near Poverty by Race & Age."

★ 528 ★

Wealth and Poverty

Distribution of Household Wealth

This table shows the distribution of median net worth among various types of households in 1984. More than half of all families in 1983 had negative or zero financial assets.

Type of household	Black	White	Black/white ratio
All	$3,397	$39,135	.09
Married couples	$13,061	$54,184	.24
Female head	$671	$22,500	.03
Male head	$3,022	$11,826	.26

Source: Selected from Ray Marshall, *The State of Families, 3: Losing Direction,* Family Service America, 1991, p. 49.

★ 529 ★

Wealth and Poverty

Elderly People in Poverty

This table shows the percent of people aged 65 and over who were in poverty in 1990 by age, sex, race, and ethnicity.

Age	White		Black		Hispanic origin	
	Men	Women	Men	Women	Men	Women
65 to 74 years	5%	10%	25%	34%	18%	23%
75 years and over	8%	17%	34%	44%	20%	30%

Source: Selected from "Our Nation's Elderly—A Portrait," *Census and You,* December 1992, p. 6, table entitled "Poverty Rates for Elderly Differ by Age, Sex, Race, and Ethnicity. Primary source: *Sixty-Five Plus in America,* P-23, No. 178.

★ 530 ★

Wealth and Poverty

Income of Older Women

This table presents statistics about income and poverty of older women, reported by the American Association of Retired Persons.

Item	Number/Percent
Median income, age	
65 and older, 1992:	
Men	$14,548
Women	$8,189
Difference	56%
White women	$8,579
Black women	$6,220
Hispanic women	$5,968
Black women aged 65+	
in 1992 who:	
Received less than $5,000	32%
Had annual incomes under	
$10,000	80%
Median annual income for	
all widows aged 65+ in 1992:	$9,281
White women	$9,732
Black women	$6,589
Hispanic women	$6,518

[Continued]

★ 530 ★

Income of Older Women
[Continued]

Item	Number/Percent
Median income of persons aged 55-64 employed full-time, year-round, 1992:	
Men	$31,904
Women	$21,250
Aged 65+	
Women	$17,848
Men	$27,356
Average monthly Social Security benefit, 1992:	
Women who receive 50% of their husband's worker benefit	$366
Women who receive benefits as retired workers	$562
Social Security's share as income source for older unmarried women:	
One-third of unmarried women aged 65+ who received SS	90%
One-sixth of unmarried women aged 65+ who received SS	100%
Women aged 65+ in 1992 who received pension income based on previous employment:	
Percent	22%
Annual average amount	$5,432
Men aged 65+ in 1992 who received pension income based on previous employment:	
Percent	49%
Average annual amount	$10,031

Source: "Facts About Older Women: Income and Poverty," American Association of Retired Persons *Fact Sheet.* Primary sources: U.S. Bureau of the Census, Current Population Reports, Series P-60-184, *Money Income of Households, Families, and Persons in the United States: 1992*; unpublished data from U.S. Bureau of the Census; Social Security Administration, U.S. Department of Health and Human Services, *Social Security Bulletin Annual Statistical Supplement, 1993*; Grad, Susan, Social Security Administration, Office of Research and Statistics, SSA Publication No. 13-11871, *Income of the Population 55 or Older, 1990.*

★ 531 ★

Wealth and Poverty

Participation in Major Assistance Programs: 1988

This table shows the percentage of persons who participated in major government assistance programs (Aid to Families with Dependent Children, Supplemental Security Income, food stamps, public or subsidized housing, and Medicaid) in 1988. Females were more likely than males to participate; the proportion of persons who participated for at least 1 month was more than 3 percentage points higher for women than men.

Participant	Rate
All persons	14.2%
Persons in married-couple families	8.7%
Persons in female-householder families	41.5%
White	10.5%
Black	38.5%
Hispanic origin (of any race)	27.3%

Source: Selected from U.S. Bureau of the Census, *Population Profile of the United States: 1993*, Special Studies Series P23-185, Figure 30, p. 31, "Program Participation Rates in Major Assistance Programs for Persons with Selected Characteristics: 1988."

★ 532 ★

Wealth and Poverty

Poverty Rates for Persons and Families

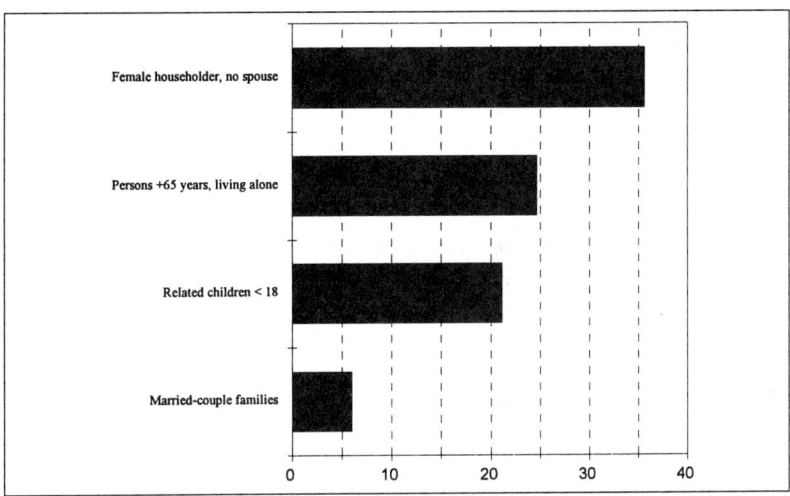

This table shows the percentage of persons and various types of families that were in poverty in 1991.

Type	In Poverty
Married-couple families	6.0%
Related children < 18	21.1%
Persons 65 years and over, living alone	24.6%
Female householder, no spouse present	35.6%

Source: Selected from U.S. Bureau of the Census, *Population Profile of the United States: 1993,* Special Studies Series P23-185, Figure 28, p. 29, "Poverty Rates for Persons and Families with Selected Characteristics: 1991."

★ 533 ★

Wealth and Poverty

Poverty Status of Female Householders: 1989

This table shows total numbers of female householders with no husband present in 1989 and those who had income below the poverty level in 1989, by race/ethnicity, as reported for the 1990 census.

[Amer Ind/Esk/Aleut refers to American Indian or Alaskan native.]

Income level in 1989	All persons	Race					Hispanic or. (any race)	White, not of Hisp. origin
		White	Black	Amer Ind/ Esk/Aleut	Asian or Pac Isl	Other race		
ALL INCOME LEVELS								
Female householder,								
no husband present	10,381,654	6,540,382	3,045,283	121,370	185,926	488,693	1,029,646	6,415,256
With related children under 18	6,783,155	3,868,218	2,315,622	95,111	111,206	392,598	782,487	3,870,845
With related children under 5	2,532,331	1,245,846	1,023,650	42,989	37,058	182,788	345,235	1,260,399
Householder worked in 1989	6,889,101	4,520,231	1,899,466	73,683	127,662	268,059	596,021	4,494,482
Householder worked year round full-time in 1989	3,876,706	2,640,115	1,005,228	32,741	73,571	125,051	296,656	2,627,999
Householder high school graduate or higher	7,088,336	4,815,394	1,875,252	75,312	128,201	194,177	461,745	4,808,024
Householder 65 years and over	1,549,529	1,167,361	321,013	12,115	18,962	30,078	84,741	1,095,393
With public assistance income in 1989	2,541,129	1,180,751	1,078,071	47,625	41,385	193,297	366,937	1,169,372
With Social Security income in 1989	2,380,686	1,748,397	522,774	20,903	28,903	59,709	151,265	1,659,943
INCOME IN 1989 BELOW POVERTY LEVEL								
Female householder,								
no husband present	3,230,201	1,517,746	1,356,384	61,131	47,873	247,067	470,419	1,517,708
With related children under 18	2,866,941	1,327,810	1,216,660	55,054	39,608	227,809	428,177	1,330,290
With related children under 5	1,452,618	636,307	645,676	29,124	17,660	123,851	226,184	639,943
Householder worked in 1989	1,403,435	727,287	549,447	26,600	16,518	83,583	166,736	746,303
Householder worked year round full-time in 1989	248,472	115,458	110,452	3,922	2,467	16,173	32,943	122,591
Householder high school graduate or higher	1,721,637	902,046	686,327	32,129	24,192	76,943	157,238	938,748
Householder 65 years and over	215,978	104,759	96,037	4,531	2,111	8,540	21,428	103,323
With public assistance income in 1989	1,642,582	692,869	755,527	34,480	21,009	138,697	251,953	694,564
With Social Security income in 1989	390,389	188,630	171,162	7,631	2,967	19,999	43,205	189,180
Mean income deficit	$5,764	$5,068	$6,453	$5,922	$5,786	$6,215	$6,176	$5,155

Source: Selected from "Poverty Status in 1989 of Families and Persons by Race and Hispanic Origin: 1990," U.S. Bureau of the Census, 1990 Census of Population, *Social and Economic Characteristics, United States*, 1990 CP-2-1, Table 49, p. 49.

★ 534 ★

Wealth and Poverty

Single Mothers' Median Income by Age and Race: 1990

This table shows the median personal income of single mothers by race and age. Personal income includes both earned and cash benefits.

Age	White	Black	Hispanic	Nat. Amer.	Asian
15-19	$1,635	$600	$425	$1,000	$875
20-24	$5,674	$4,299	$4,849	$4,749	$6,099
25-34	$10,949	$7,349	$7,824	$7,074	$10,449
35-44	$17,649	$11,374	$9,999	$9,799	$14,799
45-54	$17,299	$9,324	$8,299	$8,049	$12,324
55-64	$15,399	$6,099	$5,649	$5,474	$7,274
65+	$8,024	$5,300	$4,949	$6,599	$6,149

Source: Selected from *Women Work, Poverty Persists: A Status Report on Displaced Homemakers & Single Mothers in the United States*, Women Work!, Washington, D.C., May 1990, Appendix 8, "Single Mothers: Personal Median Income by Age and Race."

★ 535 ★

Wealth and Poverty

Single Mothers' Median Income by Education and Race: 1990

This table shows the median personal income of single mothers by education and race. Personal income includes both earned and cash benefits. Nearly three out of four single mothers have income from wages, which reflects the high rate of their labor force participation.

Race/ ethnicity	0-8 years	8-11 years	HS grad	Some college	College grad
White	$4,795	$5,749	$11,215	$14,830	$22,999
Black	$3,979	$4,143	$7,082	$10,999	$18,710
Hispanic	$5,352	$5,089	$8,508	$11,984	$18,007
Native Amer.	$4,065	$4,429	$6,882	$9,216	$15,053
Asian	$6,829	$6,841	$9,952	$13,528	$20,999

Source: Selected from *Women Work, Poverty Persists: A Status Report on Displaced Homemakers & Single Mothers in the United States*, Women Work!, Washington, D.C., May 1990, Appendix 8, "Single Mothers: Personal Median Income by Education and Race."

★ 536 ★

Wealth and Poverty

Single Mothers' Poverty Status: 1990-I

This table presents statistics related to the poverty and near poverty status of single mothers by race and age, ages 15-34 years. Poverty is measured by households or families, not individuals. Forty-four percent of single mothers are poor and another 14% are near-poor. By comparison, the poverty rate for all adult U.S. householders in 1990 was 11%. The figures in this table were arrived at using the 1990 poverty threshold for a three-person family or household with two children, which was $10,530. Persons living near poverty have incomes between 100% and 150% of the poverty level (here that means $15,795). The poorest age group of single mothers are teen mothers, 86% of whom are poor.

Race/ ethnicity	15-19 years		20-24 years		25-34 years	
	Number	Percent	Number	Percent	Number	Percent
White						
Below poverty	28,627	84.47%	172,026	68.89%	513,130	42.92%
100-150% of poverty	2,861	8.44%	36,682	14,69%	188,790	15.79%
Poor and near poor	31,488	92.91%	208,708	83.57%	701,920	58.71%
Total	33,891	X	249,727	X	1,195,533	X
Black						
Below poverty	25,686	88.23%	165,490	78.34%	502,735	60.54%
100-150% of poverty	1,708	5.87%	21,749	10.30%	112,174	13.51%
Poor and near poor	27,394	94.10%	187,239	88.63%	614,909	74.05%
Total	29,112	X	211,248	X	830,382	X
Hispanic						
Below poverty	4,166	86.85%	22,103	73.13%	77,875	59.74%
100-150% of poverty	345	7.19%	3,780	12.51%	18,358	14.08%
Poor and near poor	4,511	94.04%	25,883	85.63%	96,233	73.83%
Total	4,797	X	30,226	X	130,349	X
Native American						
Below poverty	1,435	87.98%	7,311	76.64%	22,204	64.32%
100-150% of poverty	88	5.40%	1,156	12.12%	5,011	14.52%
Poor and near poor	1,523	93.38%	8,467	88.76%	27,215	78.84%
Total	1,631	X	9,539	X	34,519	X
All Asians						
Below poverty	803	74.15%	3,568	66.69%	12,165	48.06%
100-150% of poverty	82	7.57%	706	13.20%	3,150	12.44%
Poor and near poor	885	81.72%	4,274	79.89%	15,315	60.50%
Total	1,083	X	5,350	X	25,313	X
All Races						
Below poverty	66,341	86.30%	400,604	73.44%	1,221,992	51.81%
100-150% of poverty	5,455	7.10%	68,499	12.56%	345,391	14.64%
Poor and near poor	71,796	93.40%	469,103	86.00%	1,567,383	66.45%
Total	76,870	X	545,467	X	2,358,680	X

Source: Selected from *Women Work, Poverty Persists: A Status Report on Displaced Homemakers & Single Mothers in the United States,* Women Work!, Washington, D.C., May 1990, Appendix 7, "Single Mothers Poverty & Near Poverty by Race & Age."

★ 537 ★

Wealth and Poverty

Single Mothers' Poverty Status: 1990-II

This table presents statistics related to the poverty and near poverty status of single mothers by race and age, ages 35 to 65+ years. Poverty is measured by households or families, not individuals. More than half of single mothers aged 55 and older are poor. These are often grandmothers, aunts, and other relatives, who are raising young children without adequate resources to do so.

Race/ ethnicity	35-44 years		45-54 years		55-64 years		65+ years	
	Number	Percent	Number	Percent	Number	Percent	Number	Percent
White								
Below poverty	297,883	22.84%	73,001	20.18%	18,753	31.71%	13,769	36.14%
100-150% of poverty	169,073	12.96%	42,197	11.66%	9,278	15.69%	7,400	19.42%
Poor and near poor	466,956	35.81%	115,198	31.84%	28,031	47.40%	21,169	55.56%
Total	1,304,144	X	361,778	X	59,139	X	38,101	X
Black								
Below poverty	269,206	42.61%	81,243	43.29%	34,263	54.48%	29,190	62.88%
100-150% of poverty	89,456	14.16%	27,485	14.64%	9,783	15.56%	7,479	16.11%
Poor and near poor	358,662	56.77%	108,728	57.93%	44,046	70.04%	36,669	78.99%
Total	631,728	X	187,692	X	62,886	X	46,421	X
Hispanic								
Below poverty	57,605	46.23%	17,835	41.63%	5,331	49.93%	2,887	60.87%
100-150% of poverty	19,015	15.26%	7,044	16.44%	1,785	16.72%	628	13.24%
Poor and near poor	76,620	61.49%	24,879	58.07%	7,116	66.64%	3,515	74.11%
Total	124,610	X	42,844	X	10,678	X	4,743	X
Native American								
Below poverty	13,183	48.37%	3,987	46.68%	1,488	56.66%	1,110	64.50%
100-150% of poverty	4,344	15.94%	1,393	16.31%	463	17.63%	245	14.24%
Poor and near poor	17,527	64.31%	5,380	62.99%	1,951	74.30%	1,355	78.73%
Total	27,252	X	8,541	X	2,626	X	1,721	X
All Asians								
Below poverty	14,046	32.43%	5,719	29.76%	1,266	33.64%	663	42.39%
100-150% of poverty	5,741	13.26%	2,577	13.41%	524	13.93%	293	18.73%
Poor and near poor	19,787	45.69%	8,296	43.17%	1,790	47.57%	956	61.13%
Total	43,306	X	19,218	X	3,763	X	1,564	X
All Races								
Below poverty	713,485	31.73%	200,641	30.40%	66,269	44.51%	49,835	51.76%
100-150% of poverty	307,062	13.66%	87,805	13.30%	23,490	15.78%	16,697	17.34%
Poor and near poor	1,020,547	45.38%	288,446	43.70%	89,759	60.29%	66,532	69.11%
Total	2,248,714	X	660,036	X	148,872	X	96,276	X

Source: Selected from *Women Work, Poverty Persists: A Status Report on Displaced Homemakers & Single Mothers in the United States*, Women Work!, Washington, D.C., May 1990, Appendix 7, "Single Mothers Poverty & Near Poverty by Race & Age."

Chapter 8
LABOR, EMPLOYMENT, AND OCCUPATIONS

Employment

★ 538 ★

Changes in Industry Employment Following Recession: 1990-1992

This table shows gains and losses in nonfarm employment by industry from the peak in employment just before the recession of 1990-1991 to the low point. Men accounted for the vast majority of jobs that were cut in connection with that recession. It was expected that when employment returned to prerecession level, men would regain most of the lost jobs. This proved not to be so.

[Numbers in thousands, seasonally adjusted.]

Division	Changes in employment		
	Both sexes	Women	Men
Total nonfarm	-1,844	+124	-1,968
Goods-producing sector	-1,784	-370	-1,414
Mining	-66	-1	-65
Construction	-681	-42	-639
Manufacturing	-1,037	-327	-710
Service-producing sector	-60	+494	-554
Transportation, communication, and utilities	-83	-29	-54
Wholesale trade	-148	-42	-106
Retail trade	-366	-158	-208
Finance, insurance, and real estate	-136	-50	-86
Services	+700	+640	+60
Government	-27	+133	-160

Source: William Goodman, "Women and jobs in recoveries: 1970-93," *Monthly Labor Review*, July 1994, pp. 28-36, Table 1, p. 30, "Peak-to-trough changes in employment by sex and industry, June 1990-February 1992."

★ 539 ★

Employment

Changes in Industry Employment Since 1969

This table shows gender shifts in employment by industry sector over the 25-year period between January 1969 and January 1994.

Division and year	Women	Men
Goods-producing sector		
1969	24.1%	75.9%
1994	27.8%	72.2%
Service-producing sector		
1969	42.7%	57.3%
1994	53.8%	46.2%

Source: William Goodman, "Women and jobs in recoveries: 1970-93," *Monthly Labor Review*, July 1994, pp. 28-36, Chart 2, p. 32, "Gender shifts in employment of industry sectors over 25 years."

★ 540 ★

Employment

Changing Jobs: 1965-1991

This table shows the percentage of employed women and men who changed jobs within the last year in 1965-1966 and in 1990-1991, by age.

Age	Rate in 1990-1991	Rate in 1965-1966
Women		
25 to 34	12.3%	8.5%
35 to 44	8.1%	5.3%
45 to 54	5.5%	4.7%
Men		
25 to 34	11.6%	13.8%
35 to 44	6.3%	7.4%
45 to 54	4.5%	5.2%

Source: "Career Hopping," *American Demogrpahics*, December 1993, p. 6, table entitled "The Occupational Divide." Primary source: Bureau of Labor Statistics.

★ 541 ★

Employment

Employment of Women in Africa: 1990

This table shows the number of women who were economically active in 1990, the percentages of men and women who were economically active in 1990, the average annual growth rate between 1970 and 1990, women as a percentage of the total economically active population, and the number of females per 100 males who were economically active by occupational group during the 1980s.

[Numbers in thousands, except percent. NA Not available.]

Country	Economically active population aged 15 years and over						Occupational groups (F/ 100 M), 1980s			
	Women econ. active, 1990	Estimate econ. activ. rate		Avg. ann. growth 1970-1990		Women as % total, '90	Admin/mgrl workers	Clerical,sales, service work	Product'n, trans, labor	Agric.,hunt, forestry
		Women, 1990	Men, 1990	Women	Men					
Africa										
Algeria	543	8%	75%	6.0%	3.4%	9%	NA	NA	NA	NA
Angola	1,462	52%	87%	2.1%	2.6%	39%	NA	NA	NA	NA
Benin	986	77%	89%	2.1%	2.2%	48%	NA	NA	NA	NA
Botswana	152	42%	85%	2.2%	4.4%	36%	56	197	29	105
Burkina Faso	1,742	77%	93%	1.7%	2.1%	46%	NA	NA	NA	NA
Burundi	1,201	78%	93%	1.4%	1.9%	48%	NA	NA	NA	NA
Cameroon	1,344	41%	87%	1.3%	2.2%	33%	6	26	9	82
Cape Verde	40	33%	90%	3.3%	2.0%	31%	NA	NA	NA	NA
Central African Republic	584	68%	88%	1.1%	1.8%	46%	NA	NA	NA	NA
Chad	387	23%	90%	1.4%	2.0%	21%	NA	NA	NA	NA
Comoros	85	59%	91%	2.6%	3.1%	40%	0	17	14	38
Congo	292	51%	84%	2.0%	2.2%	39%	NA	NA	NA	NA
Cote d'Ivoire	1,459	48%	88%	2.2%	3.0%	34%	NA	NA	NA	NA
Egypt	1,359	9%	80%	4.6%	2.4%	10%	16	23	6	26
Equatorial Guinea	69	52%	84%	1.1%	1.6%	40%	NA	NA	NA	NA
Ethiopia	7,188	52%	89%	1.7%	2.3%	37%	NA	NA	NA	NA
Gabon	193	47%	82%	0.5%	1.0%	37%	NA	NA	NA	NA
Gambia	121	58%	90%	1.4%	1.9%	40%	17	48	7	118
Ghana	2,224	51%	80%	2.3%	2.8%	40%	10	292	81	90
Guinea	1,128	57%	90%	1.5%	2.0%	40%	NA	NA	NA	NA
Guinea-Bissau	172	57%	90%	2.4%	2.7%	41%	NA	NA	NA	NA
Kenya	3,527	58%	90%	3.3%	3.9%	40%	NA	NA	NA	NA
Lesotho	340	65%	91%	1.5%	2.5%	44%	NA	NA	NA	NA
Liberia	253	37%	88%	2.2%	2.6%	30%	NA	NA	NA	NA
Libya Libyan Arab Jamahiriya	95	9%	77%	5.9%	3.6%	9%	NA	NA	NA	NA
Madagascar	1,799	55%	89%	1.9%	2.3%	39%	NA	NA	NA	NA
Malawi	1,303	57%	89%	2.1%	2.9%	41%	NA	NA	NA	NA
Mali	408	16%	90%	1.8%	2.2%	16%	NA	NA	NA	NA
Mauritania	140	24%	87%	2.6%	2.4%	22%	NA	NA	NA	NA
Mauritius	117	29%	84%	4.2%	2.4%	27%	17	53	55	45
Morocco	1,480	19%	81%	5.8%	3.1%	20%	34[1]	26[2]	30	19
Mozambique	3,655	79%	91%	2.7%	3.3%	48%	NA	NA	NA	NA
Namibia	122	24%	83%	2.5%	2.3%	23%	NA	NA	NA	NA
Niger	1,512	79%	93%	1.9%	2.4%	47%	NA	NA	NA	NA
Nigeria	13,624	46%	88%	2.6%	3.2%	35%	NA	NA	NA	NA
Reunion	80	38%	77%	5.8%	2.3%	34%	NA	NA	NA	NA
Rwanda	1,500	79%	93%	2.7%	3.2%	47%	NA	NA	NA	NA
Sao Tome and Principe	NA	NA	NA	NA	NA	NA	10	85	7	56
Senegal	1,112	53%	86%	2.4%	2.9%	39%	NA	NA	NA	NA
Seychelles	NA	NA	NA	NA	NA	NA	13	142	17	20
Sierra Leone	451	38%	84%	0.8%	1.4%	32%	NA	NA	NA	NA
Somalia	762	53%	88%	2.5%	3.0%	39%	NA	NA	NA	NA
South Africa	4,429	40%	75%	2.5%	1.9%	36%	21	163	14	37
Sudan	1,668	24%	87%	3.3%	2.8%	22%	NA	NA	NA	NA
Swaziland	110	53%	87%	1.8%	2.6%	39%	NA	NA	NA	NA
Togo	455	47%	88%	1.9%	2.5%	36%	9	206	61	78
Tunisia	635	26%	78%	7.3%	2.8%	25%	27[1]	22[2]	28	25
Uganda	2,974	62%	92%	2.5%	3.0%	41%	NA	NA	NA	NA
Tanzania	5,452	77%	89%	2.6%	3.2%	48%	NA	NA	NA	NA
Zaire	4,350	45%	85%	1.4%	2.8%	35%	NA	NA	NA	NA

[Continued]

★ 541 ★

Employment of Women in Africa: 1990
[Continued]

| Country | Economically active population aged 15 years and over | | | | | | Occupational groups (F/ 100 M), 1980s | | | |
| | Women econ. active, 1990 | Estimate econ. activ. rate | | Avg. ann. growth 1970-1990 | | Women as % total, '90 | Admin/mgrl workers | Clerical,sales, service work | Product'n, trans, labor | Agric.,hunt, forestry |
		Women, 1990	Men, 1990	Women	Men					
Zambia	699	33%	87%	3.5%	3.0%	28%	12	44	6	69
Zimbabwe	1,214	44%	88%	2.5%	3.2%	34%	17	57	16	98

Source: Selected from "Indicators on women's economic activity," *The World's Women: Trends and Statistics 1970-1990*, United Nations, 1991, Table 8, p. 104. Primary sources: International Labour Office, *Economically Active Population—Estimates, 1950-1980, Projections, 1985-2025*, six volumes (Geneva, 1986); International Labour Office, *Year Book of Labour Statistics* (Geneva, various years). *Notes:* 1. Administrative and managerial workers and clerical and related workers combined. 2. Sales and service workers only.

★ 542 ★

Employment

Employment of Women in Asia and the Pacific: 1990

This table shows the number of women who were economically active in 1990, the percentages of men and women who were economically active in 1990, the average annual growth rate between 1970 and 1990, women as a percentage of the total economically active population, and the number of females per 100 males who were economically active by occupational group during the 1980s.

[Numbers in thousands, except percent. NA Not available.]

| Country | Economically active population aged 15 years and over | | | | | | Occupational groups (F/100 M), 1980s | | | |
| | Women econ. active, '90 | Estimate econ. activ. rate | | Avg. ann. growth 1970-1990 | | Women as % total, '90 | Admin/mgrl workers | Clerical,sales, service work | Product'n, trans, labor | Agric.,hunt, forestry |
		Women, 1990	Men, 1990	Women	Men					
Asia and Pacific										
Afghanistan	502	8%	86%	3.7%	2.1%	9%	NA	NA	NA	NA
Bahrain	23	18%	88%	13.0%	6.5%	11%	4	20	0.5	0.2
Bangladesh	2,206	7%	87%	4.4%	2.5%	7%	2	29	20	1
Bhutan	197	43%	89%	1.5%	2.1%	31%	NA	NA	NA	NA
Brunei	NA	NA	NA	NA	NA	NA	6	60	4	23
Cambodia	1,409	52%	86%	1.0%	1.5%	38%	NA	NA	NA	NA
China	283,433	70%	87%	2.8%	2.4%	43	12	71	55	88
Cyprus	115	44%	82%	1.5%	1.1%	35%	7	84	35	86
East Timor	36	15%	89%	3.0%	1.4%	14%	NA	NA	NA	NA
Fiji	52	22%	86%	5.7%	2.2%	20%	10	71	10	13
French Polynesia	NA	NA	NA	NA	NA	NA	8	101	20	26
Guam	15[1]	50%[1]	76%[1]	4.2%	-0.8%	41%[1]	NA	NA	NA	NA
Hong Kong	1,037	48%	84%	3.2%	3.4%	33%	13	78	43	51
India	76,570	29%	84%	1.2%	2.3%	25%	2	11	15	31
Indonesia	21,628	37%	83%	2.6%	2.3%	31%	7	86	36	55
Iran										
Islamic Rep. of	2,589	17%	80%	5.2%	3.2%	18%	NA	NA	NA	NA
Iraq	1,043	21%	77%	10.3%	3.3%	21%	NA	NA	NA	NA
Israel	608	37%	75%	3.2%	2.3%	34%	16	125	16	19
Jordan	99	9%	77%	5.2%	2.6%	10%	NA	NA	NA	NA
Korea										
D. People's R.	4,787	64%	81%	3.1%	2.9%	46%	NA	NA	NA	NA
Republic of	6,303	40%	78%	2.9%	2.6%	34%	3	92	45	83
Kuwait	120	24%	85%	10.0%	5.9%	14%	4	43	0.2	0.4
Laos										
Lao People's Dem. Rep.	955	71%	88%	1.6%	2.0%	44%	NA	NA	NA	NA
Lebanon	249	25%	72%	3.8%	1.2%	27%	NA	NA	NA	NA
Malaysia	2,463	44%	82%	4.2%	3.1%	35%	9	49	28	61
Maldives	NA	NA	NA	NA	NA	NA	11	19	57	11
Mongolia	468	72%	87%	3.0%	2.9%	46%	NA	NA	NA	NA
Myanmar	6,375	48%	85%	2.0%	2.4%	36%	NA	NA	NA	NA
Nepal	2,253	43%	87%	1.8%	2.2%	32%	NA	NA	NA	NA
Oman	34	9%	84%	5.8%	4.1%	9%	NA	NA	NA	NA
Pakistan	3,983	13%	86%	4.7%	2.9%	12%	NA	NA	NA	NA
Papua New Guinea	663	58%	87%	1.8%	2.4%	38%	NA	NA	NA	NA
Philippines	6,843	36%	81%	2.4%	2.8%	31%	34	163	28	33
Qatar	13	17%	93%	13.7%	6.6%	7%	NA	NA	NA	NA
Samoa	NA	NA	NA	NA	NA	NA	24	81	10	3
Saudi Arabia	282	9%	84%	6.9%	4.8%	7%	NA	NA	NA	NA

[Continued]

★ 542 ★

Employment of Women in Asia and the Pacific: 1990
[Continued]

| Country | Economically active population aged 15 years and over | | | | | | Occupational groups (F/100 M), 1980s | | | |
| | Women econ. active, '90 | Estimate econ. activ. rate | | Avg. ann. growth 1970-1990 | | Women as % total, '90 | Admin/mgrl workers | Clerical,sales, service work | Product'n, trans, labor | Agric.,hunt, forestry |
		Women, 1990	Men, 1990	Women	Men					
Singapore	417	40%	83%	4.1%	2.5%	32%	28	114	40	23
Sri Lanka	1,691	29%	80%	2.45	1.9%	27%	7	35	31	51
Syria										
Syrian Arab Republic	488	15%	78%	5.8%	3.4%	16%	49	7	4	34
Thailand	12,754	68%	85%	2.6%	3.1%	45%	26	126	43	93
Tonga	5[2]	18%[2]	69%[2]	8.1%	0.3%	21%[2]	16	96	14	1
Turkey	7,762	45%	84%	1.7%	2.6%	34%	3	14	9	109
United Arab Emirates	48	18%	92%	13.2%	11.0%	6%	1	9	0.1	0.1
Vietnam	15,040	70%	86%	2.6%	2.8%	47%	NA	NA	NA	NA
Yemen	303	10%	84%	5.25	1.75	12%	NA	NA	NA	NA

Source: Selected from "Indicators on women's economic activity," *The World's Women: Trends and Statistics 1970-1990*, United Nations, 1991, Table 8, p. 104. Primary sources: International Labour Office, *Economically Active Population—Estimates, 1950-1980, Projections, 1985-2025*, six volumes (Geneva, 1986); International Labour Office, *Year Book of Labour Statistics* (Geneva, various years). *Notes:* 1. 1988. 2. 1986.

★ 543 ★

Employment

Employment of Women in Developed Regions: 1990

This table shows the number of women who were economically active in 1990, the percentages of men and women who were economically active in 1990, the average annual growth rate between 1970 and 1990, women as a percentage of the total economically active population, and the number of females per 100 males who were economically active by occupational group during the 1980s.

[Numbers in thousands, except percent. NA Not available.]

| Country | Economically active population aged 15 years and over | | | | | | Occupational groups (F/ 100 M), 1980s | | | |
| | Women econ. active, '90 | Estimate econ. activ. rate | | Avg. ann. growth 1970-1990 | | Women as % total, '90 | Admin/mgrl workers | Clerical,sales, service work | Product'n, trans, labor | Agric.,hunt, forestry |
		Women, 1990	Men, 1990	Women	Men					
Developed Countries										
Albania	653	59%	83%	3.1%	2.8%	41%	NA	NA	NA	NA
Australia	3,037	46%	77%	3.0%	1.5%	38%	42	138	28	30
Austria	1,432	44%	74%	0.9%	0.6%	40%	14	194	17	87
Belgium	1,400	33%	70%	1.2%	0.5%	34%	15	102	16	28
Bulgaria	2,075	57%	68%	0.3%	-0.1%	46%	41	352	54	117
Canada	5,313	49%	78%	3.2%	1.6%	40%	54	178	17	25
Czechoslovakia	3,908	62%	76%	1.0%	0.4%	47%	NA	NA	NA	NA
Denmark	1,272	58%	76%	2.0%	0.2%	45%	16	183	29	17
Finland	1,200	57%	70%	1.1%	0.4%	47%	24	282	24	56
France	10,132	45%	71%	1.3%	0.5%	40%	10	164	18	48
Germany										
Federal Rep.										
of Germany	10,915	41%	75%	0.6%	0.4%	37%	20	140	18	82
former German										
Dem. Rep.	4,396	62%	83%	0.5%	0.7%	45%	NA	NA	NA	NA
Greece	1,024	25%	73%	0.9%	0.6%	27%	18	72	21	80
Hungary	2,372	53%	72%	0.4%	-0.6%	45%	NA	NA	NA	NA
Iceland	58	60%	82%	3.2%	1.5%	43%	NA	NA	NA	NA
Ireland	435	32%	77%	2.0%	1.2%	29%	19	103	17	7
Italy	7,450	30%	69%	1.1%	0.3%	32%	60	45	60	4
Japan	23,557	46%	79%	0.6%	0.9%	38%	8	99	41	91
Luxembourg	50	32%	72%	1.8%	0.5%	32%	6	135	6	48
Malta	35	22%	78%	2.1%	1.4%	24%	NA	NA	NA	NA
Netherlands	1,900	31%	71%	2.2%	1.0%	31%	14	127	9	27
New Zealand	548	40%	77%	2.7%	1.4%	35%	21	178	20	39
Norway	875	50%	75%	3.1%	0.5%	41%	28	252	18	38
Poland	8,983	60%	77%	0.7%	0.6%	46%	NA	NA	NA	NA
Portugal	1,734	40%	80%	3.9%	0.9%	37%	17	108	34	101
Romania	5,495	60%	72%	0.7%	0.1%	46%	NA	NA	NA	NA
Spain	3,534	22%	73%	2.2%	0.7%	24%	6	96	15	33

[Continued]

★ 543 ★

Employment of Women in Developed Regions: 1990

[Continued]

Country	Economically active population aged 15 years and over						Occupational groups (F/ 100 M), 1980s			
	Women econ. active, '90	Estimate econ. activ. rate		Avg. ann. growth 1970-1990		Women as % total, '90	Admin/mgrl workers	Clerical,sales, service work	Product'n, trans, labor	Agric.,hunt, forestry
		Women, 1990	Men, 1990	Women	Men					
Sweden	1,927	55%	71%	1.9%	0.0%	45%	191[1]	145[2]	23	34
Switzerland	1,175	43%	79%	0.9%	0.1%	37%	6	136	17	36
USSR	70,411	60%	75%	0.9%	1.4%	48%	NA	NA	NA	NA
United Kingdom	10,724	46%	77%	0.8%	0.2%	39%	29	225	18	18
United States	50,531	50%	77%	2.4%	1.3%	41%	61	183	23	19
Yugoslavia	4,217	45%	74%	1.2%	0.7%	39%	15	138	23	88

Source: Selected from "Indicators on women's economic activity," *The World's Women: Trends and Statistics 1970-1990*, United Nations, 1991, Table 8, p. 104. Primary sources: International Labour Office, *Economically Active Population—Estimates, 1950-1980, Projections, 1985-2025*, six volumes (Geneva, 1986); International Labour Office, *Year Book of Labour Statistics* (Geneva, various years). *Notes:* 1. Administrative and managerial workers and clerical and related workers combined. 2. Sales and service workers only.

★ 544 ★

Employment

Employment of Women in Latin America/Caribbean: 1990

This table shows the number of women who were economically active in 1990, the percentages of men and women who were economically active in 1990, the average annual growth rate between 1970 and 1990, women as a percentage of the total economically active population, and the number of females per 100 males who were economically active by occupational group during the 1980s.

[Numbers in thousands, except percent. NA Not available.]

Country	Economically active population aged 15 years and over						Occupational groups (F/ 100 M), 1980s			
	Women econ. active, '90	Estimate econ. activ. rate		Avg. ann. growth 1970-1990		Women as % total, '90	Admin/mgrl workers	Clerical,sales, service work	Product'n, trans, labor	Agric.,hunt, forestry
		Women, 1990	Men, 1990	Women	Men					
Latin America and the Caribbean										
Argentina	3,233	28%	75%	1.8%	0.9%	28%	NA	NA	NA	NA
Barbados	64	61%	78%	2.9%	1.4%	47%	45	165	35	63
Belize	NA	NA	NA	NA	NA	NA	14	89	14	3
Bolivia	559	27%	83%	3.5%	2.3%	25%	NA	NA	NA	NA
Brazil	14,886	30%	81%	4.3%	2.6%	28%	NA	NA	NA	NA
Chile	1,352	29%	75%	3.7%	2.0%	28%	22	113	16	8
Colombia	2,249	22%	79%	3.0%	2.7%	22%	27	117	26	20
Costa Rica	222	24%	84%	4.6%	3.3%	22%	29	95	25	5
Cuba	1,413	36%	74%	5.5%	1.8%	32%	NA	NA	NA	NA
Dominica	NA	NA	NA	NA	NA	NA	32	184	18	22
Dominican Republic	322	15%	85%	5.0%	3.1%	15%	27	112	16	11
Ecuador	623	19%	82%	4.0%	2.9%	19%	18	79	13	8
El Salvador	531	29%	86%	4.3%	3.0%	25%	19	188	32	22
French Guiana	NA	NA	NA	NA	NA	NA	21	151	13	55
Guadeloupe	69	53%	73%	2.4%	1.4%	44%	NA	NA	NA	NA
Guatemala	412	16%	84%	3.8%	2.5%	16%	19	93	14	2
Guyana	96	28%	84%	4.2%	3.0%	25%	15	75	10	10
Haiti	1,208	56%	83%	1.1%	2.1%	41%	50	542	46	34
Honduras	293	21%	86%	5.2%	3.3%	20%	NA	NA	NA	NA
Jamaica	571	68%	83%	3.3%	2.6%	46%	NA	182	29	50
Martinique	68	52%	73%	2.8%	1.2%	44%	NA	NA	NA	NA
Mexico	8,195	30%	82%	6.2%	3.3%	27%	18	70	20	14
Netherlands Antilles	32%[1]	44%[1]	67%[1]	1.4%	-0.4%	42%[1]	16	135	5	11
Nicaragua	295	28%	83%	4.8%	3.2%	26%	NA	NA	NA	NA
Panama	236	30%	79%	3.2%	2.6%	27%	29	144	13	3
Paraguay	287	23%	88%	3.3%	3.4%	21%	58[2]	98[3]	21	5
Peru	1,702	25%	79%	4.2%	2.9%	24%	9	60	13	17
Puerto Rico	365	26%	69%	2.7%	2.1%	29%	34	119	32	3
Saint Kitts and Nevis	NA	NA	NA	NA	NA	NA	16	167	34	43
Saint Lucia	NA	NA	NA	NA	NA	NA	23	211	22	30

[Continued]

★ 544 ★

Employment of Women in Latin America/Caribbean: 1990

[Continued]

| Country | Economically active population aged 15 years and over | | | | | | Occupational groups (F/ 100 M), 1980s | | | |
| | Women econ. active, '90 | Estimate econ. activ. rate | | Avg. ann. growth 1970-1990 | | Women as % total, '90 | Admin/mgrl workers | Clerical,sales, service work | Product'n, trans, labor | Agric.,hunt, forestry |
		Women, 1990	Men, 1990	Women	Men					
Saint Vincent and the Grenadines	NA	NA	NA	NA	NA	NA	25	152	24	30
Suriname	42	31%	73%	2.4%	1.2%	31%	NA	NA	NA	NA
Trinidad and Tobago	151	34%	81%	2.3%	2.3%	30%	196[2]	105[3]	13	28
Uruguay	378	32%	75%	1.4%	0.2%	31%	33	111	22	7
Venezuela	1,893	31%	81%	5.7%	3.7%	28%	17	86	11	4
Virgin Islands	NA	NA	NA	NA	NA	NA	64	203	20	4

Source: Selected from "Indicators on women's economic activity," *The World's Women: Trends and Statistics 1970-1990*, United Nations, 1991, Table 8, p. 104. Primary sources: International Labour Office, *Economically Active Population—Estimates, 1950-1980, Projections, 1985-2025*, six volumes (Geneva, 1986); International Labour Office, *Year Book of Labour Statistics* (Geneva, various years). *Notes:* 1. 1986. 2. Administrative and managerial workers and clerical and related workers combined. 3. Sales and service workers only.

★ 545 ★

Employment

Informal Employment Sector in Six Countries

This table shows (1)the distribution of gross domestic product and of women in the labor force in total industry production outside of agriculture and mining; (2)the estimated percentage of production in industry groups that is informal; and (3)the estimated percentage of informal production in each industry group that is produced by women. Data is for six countries singled out for special study by the United Nations in 1988-1989. The informal sector involves home-based activities like beer brewing, tailoring, or soap making, performed by poor women who are shut out of public and private wage employment because of the monopoly by men. The columns under "Total" refer to (1)the percentage of women in the labor force working outside of agriculture and mining; (2)the estimated percentage of total production outside of agriculture and mining that is informal; and (3)the estimated percentage of this informal production produced by women.

| Area and country | Industry (exc. mining) | | | Transport | | | Services (exc. transport) | | | Total[1] | | |
	Percent of female labor force[1]	Percent of production informal	Percent of informal female	Percent of female labor force[1]	Percent of production informal	Percent of informal female	Percent of female labor force[1]	Percent of production informal	Percent of informal female	Percent of female labor force[2]	Percent of production informal	Percent of informal female
Sub-Saharan Africa												
Congo (1984)	10.3%	44.0%	9.95	2.0%	13.4%	1.3%	87.9%	41.9%	60.4%	26.8%	37.9%	39.3%
Gambia (1983)	5.6%	45.0%	10.9%	2.0%	18.0%	2.2%	92.2%	36.4%	30.6%	14.5%	35.8%	25.0%
Zambia (1986)	15.0%	41.3%	41.4%	0.9%	6.8%	10.8%	84.1%	48.4%	67.7%	17.3%	41.7%	53.3%
Latin America												
Venezuela												
1983	15.4%	21.3%	25.3%	2.3%	44.8%	1.4%	82.3%	26.4%	27.4%	97.3%	27.0%	20.5%
1987	18.7%	13.6%	37.6%	1.8%	43.6%	1.6%	79.4%	20.0%	26.7%	97.6%	20.2%	29.2%
Southeastern Asia												
Indonesia (1980)	27.4%	44.1%	45.4%	0.3%	44.6%	0.8%	71.6%	59.1%	46.8%	45.8%	52.5%	43.0%
Malaysia (1986)	30.6%	13.1%	53.7%	1.6%	20.5%	2.8%	67.7%	22.7%	42.6%	67.2%	18.6%	43.2%

Source: "Contribution of women in the informal sector to industry and services production," *The World's Women: Trends and Statistics 1970-1990*, United Nations, 1991, Table B, p. 93. Primary source: "Compendium of statistics on women in the informal sector" (United Nations), INSTRAW, and Statistical Office of the United Nations Secretariat. *Notes:* 1. Excluding agriculture and mining. 2. Female labor force in industry, transport and services as percent of total female labor force in all branches of the economy.

★ 546 ★

Employment

Job Loss Attributed to Race or Sex

Working Women Count! was formed in May 1994 by the U.S. Department of Labor's Women's Bureau to ask working women about their jobs. A questionnaire was distributed by more than 1,600 entities (including *Essence, Ms., Working Mother,* and *Working Woman* magazines), and more than 250,000 women responded. In addition, the Women's Bureau conducted a telephone survey with a scientifically selected, national random sample of women. Respondents were asked whether they had ever lost a job or promotion because of their sex or race. The data showed that women of color experienced this at nearly twice the rate that white women did. However, both groups of women considered "insuring equal opportunity" as a high priority for change in the workplace. This table shows demographic characteristics for these two items.

Characteristics	Have lost job because of race or sex	High priority: Insuring equal opportunity
Age		
Under 25	12.8%	52.4%
25-54	17.9%	53.1%
55 and over	6.8%	36.9%
Race/ ethnicity		
White	14.2%	49.5%
Black	28.0%	61.0%
Hispanic	23.0%	52.5%
Hours worked		
Part-time (<35)	14.1%	43.4%
Full-time (35+)	18.8%	48.5%
Occupations		
Professional/ managerial	18.7%	47.7%
Technical	20.0%	50.0%
Low-wage white collar	14.1%	52.3%
Low-wage blue collar	17.0%	54.7%

Source: "Equal Opportunity Issues," *Working Women Count! A Report to the Nation,* Women's Bureau, 1994, p. 35. The following occupations are included in each category: Professional/ managerial: Executives or managers and professionals. Technical: technicians. Low-wage white collar; clerical, sales, and services. Low-wage blue collar: Operators/fabricators, craft/repair, and transportation.

★ 547 ★

Employment

Labor Force Distribution in Six Countries

This table shows the percentage distribution of gross domestic product and of men and women in the labor force among four industry groups in six countries singled out for special study by the United Nations in 1988-1989. It was found that economically active women in these countries were concentrated in low-productivity agricultural or service industries. The groups of economic activities shown are mutually exclusive and comprise all economic activities. Percentages of GDP, female labor force, and male labor force each total 100% for each country.

Area and country	Agriculture			Mining			Industry, (excl. mining), transport			Services (excl. transport)		
	Percent of GDP	Percent of labor force		Percent of GDP	Percent of labor force		Percent of GDP	Percent of labor force		Percent of GDP	Percent of labor force	
		Women	Men		Women	Men		Women	Men		Women	Men
Sub-Saharan Africa												
Congo (1984)	7.3%	72.9%	35.7%	45.8%	0.3%	2.2%	21.9%	3.2%	28.3%	25.1%	23.3%	33.7%
Gambia (1983)	33.3%	85.5%	63.5%	X	X	X	17.9%	1.1%	11.5%	48.1%	13.4%	25.0%
Zambia (1986)	14.0%	72.7%	57.4%	21.05	0.2%	4.1%	35.5%	4.3%	15.2%	29.5%	22.8%	23.5%
Latin America												
Venezuela												
1983	6.8%	2.4%	20.5%	16.3%	0.3%	1.9%	35.6%	17.2%	36.5%	41.3%	80.1%	41.2%
1987	6.35	2.0%	19.0%	10.1%	0.4%	1.2%	37.3%	20.1%	38.2%	46.4%	77.5%	41.6%
Southeastern Asia												
Indonesia												
1980	24.8%	53.8%	57.0%	25.7%	0.4%	0.9%	22.1%	12.8%	16.5%	27.5%	33.1%	25.6%
1985	23.7%	53.6%	55.3%	16.3%	0.3%	0.9%	26.5%	12.0%	18.0%	33.6%	34.1%	25.8%
Malaysia (1986)	26.2%	32.5%	29.7%	10.8%	0.3%	0.9%	30.8%	21.7%	28.7%	32.3%	45.6%	40.6%

Source: "Distribution of GDP and female and male labour force by type of economic activity," *The World's Women: Trends and Statistics 1970-1990*, United Nations, 1991, Table A, p. 93. Primary source: Data are averages from a small number of studies in each region, compiled by the Statistical Office of the United Nations Secretariat.

★ 548 ★

Employment

Multiple Jobholders: 1980-1989

This table shows the total number of employed women aged 16 and over who were multiple jobholders in May 1980 and May 1989, by age. Women are much more likely than men to work two part-time jobs, and they do so primarily for economic reasons—to meet regular household expenses or to pay off debts.

[Numbers in thousands.]

Age	May 1980		May 1989	
	Number	Percent	Number	Percent
Total, 16+	1,549	100.0%	3,109	100.0%
16-19	112	7.2%	132	4.2%
20-24	258	16.7%	399	12.8%
25-34	507	32.7%	957	30.8%
35-44	320	20.7%	914	29.4%
45-54	233	15.0%	494	15.9%

[Continued]

★ 548 ★

Multiple Jobholders: 1980-1989
[Continued]

Age	May 1980		May 1989	
	Number	Percent	Number	Percent
55-64	107	6.9%	181	5.8%
65+	13	0.8%	33	1.1%

Source: "Female multiple jobholders by age, May 1980 and May 1989," *1993 Handbook on Women Workers: Trends & Issues*, U.S. Department of Labor, Women's Bureau, 1994, Table 4, p. 145. Primary source: U.S. Department of Labor, Bureau of Labor Statistics, *Montly Labor Review*, May 1982 and July 1990.

★ 549 ★

Employment

Part-Time Employment: 1980-1991

This table shows the total number of employed women in thousands and the percentage who were working part-time.

[Numbers in thousands.]

Year	Total employed women	Percent part time
1980	42,117	22.9%
1981	43,000	22.7%
1982	43,256	22.9%
1983	44,047	22.3%
1984	45,915	21.9%
1985	47,259	21.7%
1986	48,706	26.4%
1987	50,334	26.1%
1988	51,696	25.7%
1989	53,027	25.5%
1990	53,479	25.2%
1991	53,284	25.6%

Source: "Employment of women, 1980-91," *1993 Handbook on Women Workers: Trends & Issues*, U.S. Department of Labor, Women's Bureau, 1994, Table 7, p. 6. Primary source: U.S. Department of Labor, Bureau of Labor Statistics, *Employment and Earnings*, January 1981-1992.

★ 550 ★

Employment

Skilled Trades

Eighty percent of women are in jobs traditionally held by women, many of which are low paying. Employment in skilled trades offers potentially higher wages, better fringe benefits, a wider variety of work schedules, more job security, more opportunities for advancement, and the potential for improving the economic status of women and minorities. The Women's Bureau of the U.S. Department of Labor reports the statistics noted here about employment in skilled trades.

Item	Number/Percent
Number of apprentices in more than 41,000 apprenticeship programs registered with the Bureau of Apprenticeship and Training or State apprenticeship agencies, FY 1992:	262,704
Women	19,917
Percent women	7.6%
Women's participation in registered apprenticeships:	
1973	0.7%
1983	6.6%
1990	7.1%

Source: 1993 Handbook on Women Workers: Trends & Issues, U.S. Department of Labor, Women's Bureau, 1994, pp. 220-221.

Labor and Laborers

★ 551 ★

Black Women in the Labor Force

This table shows employment of black women age 16 and older, by age and years of school completed, in 1991. The more years of schooling, the higher the labor force participation rate.

[Numbers in thousands.]

Age	Total	8 yrs. or less of school	1-3 years of high school	4 years of high school	1-3 years of college	4 or more years of college
16 and older	5,994	228	758	2,606	1,438	964
16 to 19	231	6	103	98	24	0
20 to 24	639	5	47	321	211	55
25 to 34	1,815	15	144	790	533	334
35 to 44	1,688	32	164	743	406	342

[Continued]

★ 551 ★

Black Women in the Labor Force
[Continued]

Age	Total	8 yrs. or less of school	1-3 years of high school	4 years of high school	1-3 years of college	4 or more years of college
45 to 54	987	55	157	429	188	158
55 to 64	503	78	112	185	65	62
65 and older	132	37	31	40	11	14

Source: "Employment of black women age 16 years and older, by age and years of school completed, 1991," *1993 Handbook on Women Workers: Trends and Issues*, U.S. Department of Labor, Women's Bureau, 1994, Table 3, p. 51. Primary source: U.S. Department of Labor, Bureau of Labor Statistics, unpublished tabulations from the Current Population Survey, 1991 annual averages.

★ 552 ★
Labor and Laborers

Child Care Constraints on Employment

This table shows the percentage of mothers or spouses who lost work within the last four weeks or the last year because of child-care problems. It also shows the percentage of mothers who dropped out of the labor force because of child-care problems. The data are from two sources: the 1988 National Longitudinal Survey of Youth (Youth Survey) and the 1983 National Longitudinal Survey of Young Women (Young Women Survey). The Youth Survey provides information on a sample of 6,283 young women who were 14 to 22 years old in 1979 and who have been interviewed annually since 1979.[1] The Young Woman Survey obtains information from regular interviews of a cohort of women who were 14 to 24 years in 1968.[2] Both surveys are used because both asked participants a variety of questions about child care. Together, the surveys allow the examination of a wide range of mothers. The figures in this table suggest that young women lose employment because they cannot find satisfactory child care.

Characteristics	Mother/spouse lost work in last 4 weeks	Mother lost work in last year	Mother dropped out of labor force
Total	3.7%	21.7%	2.3%
Age of youngest child:			
Birth to 1 year	5.3%	18.4%	3.0%
2-4 years	2.8%	27.0%	2.0%
5 years and over	3.4%	20.4%	2.0%
Marital status:			
Married, spouse present	3.7%	27.8%	2.5%
Other	3.6%	18.1%	1.9%
Net family income (in 1988 dollars)			
$0-$14,999	3.7%	16.3%	4.2%
$15,000-$24,999	3.4%	18.6%	2.6%

[Continued]

★ 552 ★

Child Care Constraints on Employment
[Continued]

Characteristics	Mother/spouse lost work in last 4 weeks	Mother lost work in last year	Mother dropped out of labor force
$25,000-$49,999	3.1%	24.6%	1.6%
$50,000 and more	4.7%	27.7%	0.3%

Source: Jonathan R. Veum and Philip M. Gleason, "Child care: arrangements and costs," *Monthly Labor Review,* October 1991, pp. 10-17, Table 6, p. 16, "Child-care related constraints on women's employment." *Notes:* 1. In 1988, the sample, which includes an overrepresentation of blacks, Hispanics, and economically disadvantaged whites, had 10,466 respondents. 2. The original sample, in which there was an overrepresentation of blacks, included 5,553 young women; in 1983, 68.7% of them were still being interviewed. 3. From the Youth Survey: Mother (23-31). 4. From the Young Women Survey: Mother (29-39).

★ 553 ★

Labor and Laborers

Education and Business Experience Trends: 1965-1990

This table presents trends in two important characteristics of the work force since 1965. There has been a steady and persistent increase in the average level of educational attainment. The level of work experience rose between 1948 and 1958 and then began to decline in an irregular fashion until about 1979. Since then, the level of work experience for men has remained fairly constant, while the work experience of women has increased about half a year.

Year	Education		Experience	
	Men	Women	Men	Women
1965	10.9	10.9	19.6	13.5
1966	10.9	11.0	19.6	13.4
1967	11.1	11.0	19.6	13.2
1968	11.2	11.2	19.6	13.1
1969	11.4	11.4	19.5	13.0
1970	11.5	11.5	19.4	13.1
1971	11.6	11.5	19.2	12.9
1972	11.8	11.6	18.7	12.5
1973	11.9	11.8	18.4	12.5
1974	12.1	11.9	18.5	12.2
1975	12.1	12.0	18.4	12.0
1976	12.2	12.0	18.1	11.8
1977	12.3	12.1	18.0	11.8
1978	12.4	12.2	17.8	11.6
1979	12.4	12.3	17.5	11.6
1980	12.5	12.4	17.6	11.7
1981	12.6	12.5	17.6	11.6
1982	12.8	12.6	17.7	11.7
1983	12.9	12.7	17.6	11.7

[Continued]

★ 553 ★

Education and Business Experience Trends: 1965-1990

[Continued]

Year	Education		Experience	
	Men	Women	Men	Women
1984	12.9	12.8	17.6	11.7
1985	12.9	12.8	17.5	11.7
1986	12.9	12.9	17.6	11.7
1987	13.0	12.9	17.5	11.8
1988	13.0	12.9	17.6	12.0
1989	13.0	13.0	17.7	12.0
1990	13.0	13.0	17.8	12.1

Source: Selected from "Average years of completed schooling and experience of working men and women in private business," U.S. Department of Labor, Bureau of Labor Statistics, *Labor Composition and U.S. Productivity Growth, 1984-90*, Bulletin 2426, December 1993, Table 1, p. 4. Averages are calculated by weighting educational attainment or work experience by the hours of workers.

★ 554 ★

Labor and Laborers

Employment Participation in the Private Sector

This table shows employment participation rates of women by race/ethnicity in all jobs in the private sector in 1966, 1978, and 1992. Data is collected from all private employers with 100 or more employess and Federal government contractors with 50 or more employees, and is estimated to cover about half of all private sector payroll employment.

Gender	Year	Total, all groups	White	Minorities				
				Total	Black	Hispanic	Asian/PacIsl	AmerInd/AK Nat
Total, both	1966	100.0%	88.8%	11.2%	8.2%	2.5%	0.3%	0.2%
men and	1978	100.0%	82.1%	17.9%	11.2%	5.0%	1.3%	0.4%
women	1992	100.0%	77.2%	22.8%	12.3%	7.1%	3.0%	0.5%
Men	1966	68.8%	60.9%	7.8%	5.7%	1.8%	0.2%	0.1%
	1978	60.0%	49.9%	10.1%	6.1%	3.1%	0.7%	0.3%
	1992	53.1%	41.5%	11.6%	5.8%	4.1%	1.5%	0.3%
Women	1966	31.2%	27.8%	3.4%	2.4%	0.8%	0.1%	0.1%
	1978	40.0%	32.2%	7.8%	5.1%	1.9%	0.6%	0.1%
	1992	46.9%	35.7%	11.2%	6.6%	3.0%	1.5%	0.2%

Source: "Private Sector Employment Participation Rate by Population Group, U.S. Summary, 1966, 1978 and 1992," U.S. Equal Employment Opportunity Commission, *Indicators of Equal Employment Opportunity-Status and Trends*, September 1993, p. 6. Primary source: Equal Employment Opportunity Commission, Employer Information (EEO-1) Reports.

★ 555 ★
Labor and Laborers

Hispanic Women in the Labor Force

This table describes Hispanic women 16 years of age and over who were in the labor force, 1991 annual averages. The population of Hispanic women aged 16 and older increased 52% between 1980 and 1991. In 1991 there were 3.9 million Hispanic women in the labor force. The Bureau of Labor Statistics projects that number will increase to 6 million by the year 2000.

[Numbers in thousands.]

Population	All His- panic women	Mexican- or. women	Puerto Rican- or. women	Cuban-origin women
Civilian noninsti- tutional population	7,442	4,310	926	435
Civilian labor force	3,890	2,220	425	229
Percent of population	52.3%	51.5%	45.9%	52.8%
Employed	3,521	1,997	380	210
Unemployed	368	223	46	20
Unemployment rate	9.5	10.0	10.7	8.6

Source: "Hispanic Women age 16 years and older in the labor force, 1991 annual averages," *1993 Handbook on Women Workers: Trends and Issues*, U.S. Department of Labor Women's Bureau, 1994, Table 5, p. 52.

★ 556 ★
Labor and Laborers

Job Promotion Characteristics

This table presents information on various qualitative aspects of a promotion (what the promotion involved) among women aged 37-48 in 1991 who had received a job promotion within the past year.

Characteristics	More pay	More challeng- ing work	More authority over other wkrs	More responsibility
Total	87.4%	73.0%	54.0%	81.8%
Race				
White	87.0%	73.6%	54.6%	82.6%
Black or other	90.1%	69.0%	49.8%	76.2%
Marital status				
Married	88.4%	71.6%	54.1%	80.8%
Single	85.4%	75.8%	53.6%	83.8%
Education				
High school dropout	79.1%	74.9%	46.8%	82.4%
High school grad.	89.9%	78.4%	50.8%	83.3%

[Continued]

★ 556 ★

Job Promotion Characteristics
[Continued]

Characteristics	More pay	More challeng-ing work	More authority over other wkrs	More responsibility
Some college	79.3%	76.1%	62.8%	87.8%
College graduate	93.5%	59.8%	54.2%	73.3%
Employment status				
Full time	89.0%	73.1%	56.3%	82.9%
Part time	77.9%	72.4%	40.1%	75.5%
Number employed at plant or office				
Less than 10	87.8%	71.5%	54.4%	81.3%
10-24	86.1%	73.1%	54.8%	82.6%
25-99	88.9%	73.0%	53.6%	78.7%
100-499	83.6%	76.6%	55.9%	84.5%
500 or more	92.5%	69.4%	48.7%	83.3%
Occupation				
Professional, technical	85.5%	75.9%	60.4%	84.3%
Manager	93.7%	80.3%	81.5%	93.8%
Clerical, sales	86.7%	66.6%	41.0%	74.7%
Craft worker, blue-collar supervisor, laborer	92.1%	73.6%	41.2%	73.5%
Service	76.3%	74.2%	43.3%	87.7%

Source: "Characteristics of a promotion among women age 37-48 in 1991 who received a job promotion within the past year (in percent)," *Work and Family: Promotions Among Women*, Data from the National Longitudinal Surveys, U.S. Department of Labor, Bureau of Labor Statistics, Report 868, March 1994, Table 2, p. 2. Primary source: National Longitudinal Survey of Young Women.

★ 557 ★

Labor and Laborers

Job Promotions

This table shows the percent of working women aged 37-48 in 1991 who received a job promotion within the last year by various characteristics of the woman. Nearly 14% of working women were promoted. There were essentially no differences in promotion probabilities by race and only small differences by marital status, with single women slightly more likely to be promoted than married women.

Characteristics	Percent promoted
Total	13.9%
Race	
White	13.9%
Black or other	13.7%

[Continued]

★ 557 ★

Job Promotions
[Continued]

Characteristics	Percent promoted
Marital status	
Married	13.6%
Single	14.5%
Education	
High school dropout	10.9%
High school grad.	14.7%
Some college	14.6%
College graduate	13.3%
Employment status	
Full time	15.6%
Part time	8.5%
Number employed at plant or office	
Less than 10	11.2%
10-24	14.4%
25-99	13.5%
100-499	17.2%
500 or more	16.5%
Occupation	
Professional, technical	13.9%
Manager	20.6%
Clerical, sales	13.3%
Craft worker, blue-collar supervisor, laborer	13.2%
Service	9.4%

Source: "Percent of working women age 37-48 in 1991 who received a job promotion within the past year," *Work and Family: Promotions Among Women*, Data from the National Longitudinal Surveys, U.S. Department of Labor, Bureau of Labor Statistics, Report 868, March 1994, Table 1, p. 2. Primary source: National Longitudinal Survey of Young Women.

★ 558 ★

Labor and Laborers

Labor Force by Race/Ethnicity: 1975-2005

This table shows the civilian labor force 16 years and older, by sex, race, and Hispanic origin, 1975 and 1990, and projection to 2005. Female labor force participation will increase in all racial groups. Women of Hispanic origin and Asian and other women will have the biggest increase—nearly 80%.

[Numbers in thousands.]

Gender/race ethnicity	1975	1990	2005	Percent change 1990-2005
Total	93,775	124,787	150,732	20.8%
Women	37,475	56,554	71,394	26.2%
Men	56,299	68,234	79,338	16.3%
White	82,831	107,177	125,785	17.4%
Women	32,508	47,879	58,934	23.1%
Men	50,324	59,298	66,851	12.7%
Black	9,263	113,493	17,766	31.7%
Women	4,247	6,785	9,062	33.6%
Men	5,106	6,708	8,704	29.8%
Hispanic origin	[1]	9,576	16,790	75.3%
Women	[1]	3,821	6,888	80.3%
Men	[1]	5,755	9,902	72.1%
Asian and other	1,643	4,116	7,181	74.5%
Women	712	1,890	3,398	79.8%
Men	931	2,226	3,783	69.9%

Source: "Civilian labor force 16 years and older, by sex, race, and Hispanic origin, 1975 and 1990, and projection to 2005," *1993 Handbook on Women Workers: Trends & Issues,* U.S. Department of Labor, Women's Bureau, 1994, Table 1, p. 231. Primary source: U.S. Bureau of Labor Statistics, *Monthly Labor Review,* November 1991. *Note:* 1. Comparable data on Hispanics not available before 1980.

★ 559 ★

Labor and Laborers

Labor Force in Africa by Status in Employment: 1980-1987

This table shows the classification of all economically active people as employers, employees, or unpaid family workers for the period 1980-1987. It also shows the percentage who were female. An employer or own-account worker is a person who operates his or her own economic enterprise or is engaged independently in a profession or trade. An employee works for a public or private employer and is paid in wages, salary, commission, tips, piece-rates or in-kind. An unpaid family worker works without pay in a business operated by a related person who lives in the same household.

[NA Not available.]

| Country | Labor force by status in employment | | | | | |
| | Employers/own-account | | Employees | | Unpaid family | |
	% of total	% female	% of total	% female	% of total	% female
Africa						
Algeria	17%[1]	1%[1]	47%[1]	8%[1]	2%[1]	2%[1]
Botswana	2%	63%	33%	40%	39%	57%
Burundi	36%[1]	28%[1]	6%[1]	9%[1]	59%[1]	73%[1]
Cameroon	60%	37%	15%	9%	18%	68%
Comoros	48%	25%	26%	24%	0%	..
Egypt	27%	10%	51%	14%	17%	41%
Ghana	68%	56%	16%	24%	12%	63%
Lesotho	8%[1]	38%[1]	50%[1]	15%[1]	37%[1]	52%[1]
Malawi	80%[1]	55%[1]	18%[1]	9%[1]	0.3%[1]	50%[1]
Mali	46%[1]	5%[1]	4%[1]	11%[1]	43%[1]	30%[1]
Morocco	27%	11%	41%	18%	18%	31%
Nigeria	56%	37%	28%	18%	9%	42%
Reunion	10%	13%	56%	39%	1%	35%
Rwanda	39%[1]	33%[1]	7%[1]	15%[1]	54%[1]	70%[1]
Sao Tome and Principe	16%	26%	79%	32%	0.1%	54%
Seychelles	11%	15%	77%	38%	0.3%	60%
South Africa	4%	18%	89%	31%	0%	..
Togo	70%	48%	10%	15%	11%	54%
Tunisia	22%	26%	58%	14%	6%	77%
Zambia	23%	34%	43%	24%	4%	72%

Source: Selected from "Indicators on the economy and women's work," *The World's Women: Trends and Statistics 1970-1990*, United Nations, 1991, Table 9, p. 198. Primary sources: *National Accounts Statistics: Analysis of Main Aggregates, 1987* (United Nations); National Accounts Database of the Statistical Office of the United Nations Secretariat; International Lbour Office, *Year Book of Labour Statistics* (Geneva, various years). *Note:* 1. 1975-79.

★ 560 ★

Labor and Laborers

Labor Force in Asia

This table shows the percent economically active among population aged 15 years and over, by gender, for selected Asian countries for the latest available year. Women aged 15 and over were most likely to be in the labor force if they lived in Mainland China, Mongolia, and Thailand. However, in most countries women's participation rates tend to be underreported, primarily because of the failure to count women in subsistence agriculture and other areas of the informal sector.

| Country | Year | Economically active | |
		Women	Men
China			
Mainland	1990	73%	85%
Mongolia	1989	71%	82%
Thailand	1989	71%	87%
Vietnam	1989	62%	82%
Singapore	1990	50%	79%
Philippines	1990	48%	82%
South Korea	1988	45%	72%
Sri Lanka	1990	45%	78%
Indonesia	1985	44%	82%
Hong Kong	1990	37%	62%
Fiji	1986	23%	86%
Maldives	1990	20%	77%
Pakistan	1990-91	11%	85%
Bangladesh	1985-86	10%	89%

Source: "In Most Countries, Women's Labor Force Participation Lags Far Behind Men's," U.S. Bureau of the Census, *Statistical Brief: Statistical Indicators on Women: An Asian Perspective,* November 1993, p. 4.

★ 561 ★
Labor and Laborers

Labor Force in Asia and the Pacific by Status in Employment: 1980-1987

This table shows the classification of all economically active people as employers, employees, or unpaid family workers for the period 1980-1987. It also shows the percentage who were female. An employer or own-account worker is a person who operates his or her own economic enterprise or is engaged independently in a profession or trade. An employee works for a public or private employer and is paid in wages, salary, commission, tips, piece-rates or in-kind. An unpaid family worker works without pay in a business operated by a related person who lives in the same household.

[NA Not available.]

Country	Labor force by status in employment					
	Employers/own-account		Employees		Unpaid family	
	% of total	% female	% of total	% female	% of total	% female
Asia and the Pacific						
Bahrain	9%	1%	86%	12%	0.1%	8%
Bangladesh	38%	4%	44%	14%	16%	6%
Brunei	7%	19%	88%	23%	0.6%	55%
Cyprus	24%	31%	71%	35%	2%	83%
Fiji	34%	10%	42%	26%	16%	20%
French Polynesia	15%	22%	72%	33%	5%	47%
Hong Kong	12%	20%	85%	38%	2%	90%
India	9%	9%	17%	12%	4%	23%
Indonesia	44%	26%	25%	30%	28%	67%
Iran Islamic Rep. of	31%[1]	5%[1]	48%[1]	12%[1]	10%[1]	49%[1]
Iraq	25%[1]	7%[1]	60%[1]	8%[1]	11%[1]	88%[1]
Israel	18%	24%	74%	42%	1%	74%
Jordan	23%[1]	1%[1]	67%[1]	9%[1]	0.8%[1]	4%[1]
Korea D. People's R.	33%[1]	27%[1]	40%[1]	29%[1]	24%[1]	69%[1]
Republic of	30%	30%	54%	36%	13%	83%
Malaysia	29%	29%	54%	31%	10%	54%
Maldives	49%	26%	39%	14%	6%	37%
Nepal	86%	36%	9%	15%	3%	55%
New Caledonia	15%	22%	72%	33%	5%	47%
Pakistan	45%	2%	26%	5%	26%	7%
Philippines	36%	295	40%	37%	15%	52%
Samoa	21%	5%	43%	30%	35%	3%
Singapore	13%	19%	80%	40%	2%	68%
Sri Lanka	24%	20%	50%	30%	11%	52%
Syria Syrian Arab Republic	33%	4%	55%	12%	10%	54%
Thailand	30%	27%	24%	38%	43%	65%
Tonga	33%[1]	1%[1]	33%[1]	24%[1]	13%[1]	4%[1]
Turkey	23%	7%	32%	15%	41%	70%

[Continued]

★ 561 ★

Labor Force in Asia and the Pacific by Status in Employment: 1980-1987

[Continued]

Country	Labor force by status in employment					
	Employers/own-account		Employees		Unpaid family	
	% of total	% female	% of total	% female	% of total	% female
United Arab Emirates	7%	1%	93%	5%	0.1%	9%
Yemen[2]	45%[1]	NA	34%[1]	NA	19%[1]	NA

Source: Selected from "Indicators on the economy and women's work," *The World's Women: Trends and Statistics 1970-1990,* United Nations, 1991, Table 9, p. 198. Primary sources: *National Accounts Statistics: Analysis of Main Aggregates, 1987* (United Nations); National Accounts Database of the Statistical Office of the United Nations Secretariat; International Lbour Office, *Year Book of Labour Statistics* (Geneva, various years). *Notes:* 1. 1975-79. 2. Data refer to the former Yemen Arab Republic only.

★ 562 ★

Labor and Laborers

Labor Force in Developed Regions by Status in Employment: 1980-1987

This table shows the classification of all economically active people as employers, employees, or unpaid family workers for the period 1980-1987. It also shows the percentage who were female. An employer or own-account worker is a person who operates his or her own economic enterprise or is engaged independently in a profession or trade. An employee works for a public or private employer and is paid in wages, salary, commission, tips, piece-rates or in-kind. An unpaid family worker works without pay in a business operated by a related person who lives in the same household.

[NA Not available.]

Country	Labor force by status in employment					
	Employers/own-account		Employees		Unpaid family	
	% of total	% female	% of total	% female	% of total	% female
Developed Countries						
Australia	14%	30%	77%	41%	0.8%	59%
Austria	10%	31%	86%	39%	4%	77%
Belgium	12%	26%	72%	38%	3%	78%
Bulgaria	0.3%	27%	98%	47%	0%	..
Canada	9%	33%	90%	44%	0.7%	78%
Czechoslovakia	0.1%	39%	91%	47%	8%	48%
Denmark	9%	17%	89%	47%	2%	97%
Finland	14%	37%	85%	49%	1%	39%
France	11%	22%	75%	43%	3%	82%
Germany Federal Rep. of	9%	21%	88%	40%	3%	87%
Greece	33%	17%	46%	32%	14%	79%
Hungary	4%	34%	81%	46%	2%	89%
Iceland	14%[1]	NA	85%[1]	NA	0%[1]	NA
Ireland	18%	10%	71%	37%	2%	35%
Italy	21%	23%	62%	35%	4%	65%
Japan	15%	31%	73%	36%	9%	83%

[Continued]

★ 562 ★

Labor Force in Developed Regions by Status in Employment: 1980-1987
[Continued]

| Country | Labor force by status in employment | | | | | |
| | Employers/own-account | | Employees | | Unpaid family | |
	% of total	% female	% of total	% female	% of total	% female
Luxembourg	9%	27%	85%	34%	2%	85%
Malta	16%	15%	80%	29%	0%	..
Netherlands	9%	29%	79%	35%	2%	83%
New Zealand	16%	25%	76%	43%	1%	75%
Norway	9%	20%	87%	46%	2%	67%
Poland	13%[1]	32%[1]	74%[1]	43%[1]	12%[1]	76%[1]
Portugal	25%	43%	64%	39%	5%	58%
Spain	18%	24%	65%	30%	5%	59%
Sweden	9%	25%	89%	50%	0.4%	74%
Switzerland	10%	14%	90%	39%	0%	..
United Kingdom	10%	25%	79%	45%	0%	..
United States	8%	31%	91%	45%	0.3%	76%
Yugoslavia	17%	30%	66%	35%	10%	72%

Source: Selected from "Indicators on the economy and women's work," *The World's Women: Trends and Statistics 1970-1990*, United Nations, 1991, Table 9, p. 198. Primary sources: *National Accounts Statistics: Analysis of Main Aggregates, 1987* (United Nations); National Accounts Database of the Statistical Office of the United Nations Secretariat; International Labour Office, *Year Book of Labour Statistics* (Geneva, various years). *Note:* 1. 1975-79.

★ 563 ★

Labor and Laborers

Labor Force in Europe

This table shows the total labor force and the percentage of the work force that was female in 1990 in Europe. The highest shares of economically active women were in Eastern Europe and the USSR.

Country	Total labor force	Percent female
Albania	1,591,000	41.2%
Austria	3,570,000	40.0%
Belgium	4,157,000	33.7%
Czechoslovakia	8,386,000	47.0%
Denmark	2,852,000	44.6%
East Germany	9,670,000	45.5%
Finland	2,552,000	47.0%
France	25,404,000	39.9%
Greece	3,852,000	26.7%
Hungary	5,276,000	44.9%
Iceland	136,000	42.6%
Ireland	1,481,000	29.4%

[Continued]

★ 563 ★

Labor Force in Europe

[Continued]

Country	Total labor force	Percent female
Italy	23,339,000	31.9%
Luxembourg	155,000	31.6%
Malta	146,000	23.3%
Netherlands	6,153,000	30.9%
Norway	2,128,000	41.2%
Poland	19,704,000	45.6%
Portugal	4,740,000	36.7%
Romania	11,825,000	46.4%
Spain	14,456,000	24.4%
Sweden	4,319,000	44.6%
Switzerland	3,212,000	36.6%
United Kingdom	27,766,000	38.6%
USSR	146,634,000	48.0%
West Germany	29,311,000	37.2%
Yugoslavia	10,858,000	38.9%

Source: "Percentage of the Work Force that Is Female, 1990," *Market Europe*, Vol. 1, No. 3, October 1990, p. 2. Primary Source: Economically Active Population, 1950-2025, Vol. IV, International Labor Office, Geneva.

★ 564 ★

Labor and Laborers

Labor Force in Latin America/Caribbean by Status in Employment: 1980-1987

This table shows the classification of all economically active people as employers, employees, or unpaid family workers for the period 1980-1987. It also shows the percentage who were female. An employer or own-account worker is a person who operates his or her own economic enterprise or is engaged independently in a profession or trade. An employee works for a public or private employer and is paid in wages, salary, commission, tips, piece-rates or in-kind. An unpaid family worker works without pay in a business operated by a related person who lives in the same household.

[NA Not available.]

Country	Labor force by status in employment					
	Employers/own-account		Employees		Unpaid family	
	% of total	% female	% of total	% female	% of total	% female
Latin America and the Caribbean						
Argentina	25%	NA	71%	NA	3%	NA
Bahamas, The	10%	33%	81%	44%	0.5%	68%
Barbados	9%	34%	75%	45%	1%	23%
Bolivia	49%[1]	19%[1]	38%[1]	24%[1]	9%[1]	38%[1]
Brazil	26%	17%	65%	31%	7%	35%

[Continued]

★ 564 ★

Labor Force in Latin America/Caribbean by Status in Employment: 1980-1987
[Continued]

| Country | Labor force by status in employment | | | | | |
| | Employers/own-account | | Employees | | Unpaid family | |
	% of total	% female	% of total	% female	% of total	% female
Chile	24%	21%	64%	33%	4%	33%
Colombia	28%	31%	61%	43%	2%	70%
Costa Rica	23%	18%	71%	31%	5%	18%
Cuba	5%	7%	94%	33%	0.2%	5%
Dominica	29%	23%	50%	38%	2%	34%
Dominican Republic	36%	20%	51%	35%	3%	43%
Ecuador	37%	15%	48%	25%	6%	20%
El Salvador	28%	43%	59%	32%	11%	25%
French Guiana	15%	24%	61%	36%	3%	72%
Guadeloupe	19%	25%	54%	46%	0.5%	52%
Guatemala	31%	25%	47%	24%	16%	22%
Haiti	52%	36%	14%	42%	9%	35%
Martinique	12%	22%	57%	49%	0.3%	53%
Mexico	27%	25%	44%	27%	5%	35%
Panama	26%	14%	65%	38%	4%	15%
Paraguay	43%	15%	38%	20%	9%	11%
Peru	49%	17%	45%	20%	6%	55%
Puerto Rico	13%	13%	85%	41%	0.8%	75%
Suriname	11%	19%	78%	29%	2%	56%
Trinidad and Tobago	19%	25%	73%	33%	5%	50%
Uruguay	23%	25%	71%	35%	2%	40%
Venezuela	26%	19%	63%	32%	3%	30%
Virgin Islands	7%	25%	86%	47%	0.3%	66%

Source: Selected from "Indicators on the economy and women's work," *The World's Women: Trends and Statistics 1970-1990*, United Nations, 1991, Table 9, p. 198. Primary sources: *National Accounts Statistics: Analysis of Main Aggregates, 1987* (United Nations); National Accounts Database of the Statistical Office of the United Nations Secretariat; International Labour Office, *Year Book of Labour Statistics* (Geneva, various years). *Note:* 1. 1975-79.

★ 565 ★
Labor and Laborers

Labor Force Participation Rates: 1965-1993

This table shows the labor force participation rates of women by age, annual averages, 1965-1993. The participation rates of women rose consistently from 1965 to 1989. Between 1989 and 1991 the trend was interrupted, increased again in 1992, and flattened out in 1993. Some speculated that women were leaving the labor force to care for their children or to become homemakers. The Bureau of Labor Statistics attributed the 1989-1991 interruption to three factors: the business cycle; a rise in births; and changes in the erratic participation trends of 16- to 24-year-old women, especially teenagers.

Year	Total, 16 years+	16 to 19 years	20 to 24 years	25 to 34 years	35 to 44 years	45 to 54 years	55 years and older
1965	39.3%	38.0%	49.9%	38.5%	46.1%	50.9%	24.6%
1966	40.3%	41.4%	51.5%	39.8%	46.8%	51.7%	24.8%
1967	41.1%	41.6%	53.3%	41.9%	48.1%	51.8%	25.0%
1968	41.6%	43.2%	56.7%	43.7%	49.9%	53.8%	25.0%
1969	42.7%	41.9%	54.5%	42.6%	48.9%	52.3%	25.5%
1970	43.3%	44.0%	57.7%	45.0%	51.1%	54.4%	25.3%
1971	43.4%	43.4%	57.7%	45.6%	51.6%	54.3%	25.1%
1972	43.9%	45.8%	59.1%	47.8%	52.0%	53.9%	24.5%
1973	44.7%	47.8%	61.1%	50.4%	53.3%	53.7%	23.8%
1974	45.7%	49.1%	63.1%	52.6%	54.7%	54.6%	23.0%
1975	46.3%	49.1%	64.1%	54.9%	55.8%	54.6%	23.1%
1976	47.3%	49.8%	65.0%	57.3%	57.8%	55.0%	23.0%
1977	48.4%	51.2%	66.5%	59.7%	59.6%	55.8%	22.9%
1978	50.0%	53.7%	68.3%	62.2%	61.6%	57.1%	23.1%
1979	50.9%	54.2%	69.0%	63.9%	63.6%	58.3%	23.2%
1980	51.5%	52.9%	68.9%	65.5%	65.5%	59.9%	22.8%
1981	52.1%	51.8%	69.6%	66.7%	66.8%	61.1%	22.7%
1982	52.6%	51.4%	69.8%	68.0%	68.0%	61.6%	22.7%
1983	52.9%	50.8%	69.9%	69.0%	68.7%	61.9%	22.4%
1984	53.6%	51.8%	70.4%	69.8%	70.1%	62.9%	22.2%
1985	54.5%	52.1%	71.8%	70.9%	71.8%	64.4%	22.0%
1986	55.3%	53.0%	72.4%	71.6%	73.1%	65.9%	22.1%
1987	56.0%	53.3%	73.0%	72.4%	74.5%	67.1%	22.0%
1988	56.6%	53.6%	72.7%	72.7%	75.2%	69.0%	22.3%
1989	57.4%	53.9%	72.4%	73.5%	76.0%	70.5%	23.0%
1990	57.5%	51.8%	71.6%	73.6%	76.5%	71.2%	23.0%
1991	57.3%	50.2%	70.4%	73.3%	76.6%	72.0%	22.8%
1992	57.8%	49.2%	71.2%	74.1%	76.8%	72.7%	23.0%
1993	57.9%	49.9%	71.3%	73.6%	76.7%	73.5%	23.0%

Source: Howard V. Hayghe, "Are women leaving the labor force?" *Monthly Labor Review*, July 1994, pp. 37-39, Table 1, p. 38, "Labor force participation rates of women by age, annual averages, 1965-93." See also: "Women's labor force growth appears stalled," *Issues in Labor Statistics*, Summary 92-2 (Bureau of Labor Statistics, January 1992. *I Labor force participation rates.

★ 566 ★

Labor and Laborers

Labor Force: 2000-2050

This table shows projections of the civilian noninstitutional population and labor force participation rates, by age and sex, for the year 2000. It also shows population projections for 2030, and 2050.[1] The percentage of the population that is middle-aged (35-54) is expected to peak around the turn of the century. This group made up 33.9% of the population in 1987 and will make up 42.5% of the population in 2000. Thereafter, the percentage of this group will fall to 33.6% of the population in 2030 and 31.9% in 2050. The percentage of the population that is 65 and over is projected to increase, rising from 16.7% of the population in 1987 to 17.4% in 2000, 27.9% in 2030, and 29% in 2050. At the same time, the proportion of young adults (20-34) will be falling.

[Numbers in thousands.]

| Gender | 2000 | | | | | 2030 | | 2050 | |
| | Population | | Labor force | | LF partici-pation rate | Population | | Population | |
	Level	Percent	Level	Percent		Level	Percent	Level	Percent
Women									
20 and over	99,341	52.3%	61,260	47.2%	61.7%	116,592	52.3%	117,017	52.5%
20-34	26,952	14.2%	21,884	16.8%	81.0%	26,270	11.8%	25,947	11.7%
35-54	40,745	21.5%	32,658	25.1%	80.2%	38,016	17.0%	36,038	16.2%
55-64	12,518	6.6%	5,732	4.4%	45.8%	17,738	7.9%	18,636	8.4%
65-74	9,808	5.2%	885	0.7%	9.0%	18,620	8.3%	16,296	7.3%
75 and over	9,318	4.9%	141	0.1%	1.5%	15,948	7.1%	20,100	9.0%
Men									
20 and over	90,481	47.7%	68,635	52.8%	75.9%	106,550	47.7%	105,682	47.5%
20-34	25,698	13.5%	23,564	18.1%	91.7%	24,995	11.2%	24,639	11.1%
35-54	39,560	20.8%	36,465	28.1%	92.2%	37,028	16.6%	35,054	15.7%
55-64	11,448	6.0%	7,238	5.6%	63.2%	16,917	7.6%	17,782	8.0%
65-74	8,073	4.3%	1,122	0.9%	13.9%	16,660	7.5%	14,675	6.6%
75 and over	5,702	3.0%	246	0.2%	4.3%	10,950	4.9%	13,532	6.1%

Source: Gail McCallion, *A Demogrpahic Portrait of Older Workers*, CRS Report for Congress, September 27, 1988, Table 1, p. CRS-2, "Civilian Noninstitutional Population, Labor Force and Participation Rates by Age and Sex, Actual 1987 and Moderate Growth Projections for 2000, 2030, and 2050." Primary source: U.S. Bureau of Labor Statistics. Projections 2000. Bulletin 2302. pp. 93-95. Unpublished U.S. Bureau of Labor data. *Note:* 1. Labor force projections for 2030 and 2050 were not available.

★ 567 ★

Labor and Laborers

Projections of Women in the Labor Force

This table shows the projected number of women in the labor force in 2005 by age, the projected change in number by age from 1992-2005, and the projected annual growth from 1992-2005. Statistics are also shown by race and Hispanic origin. By 2005 nearly 72 million women are projected to be in the labor force, representing about 63% of the civilian female population age 16 and over. The median age is projected to be 40.5 years. Fastest growth is expected to be among workers aged 45-54 and 55-64. By 2005, about 35% of all working women will be in those age groups.

[Numbers in thousands.]

Age/Race/ Hispanic origin	Number 2005	Change 1992-2005	Annual growth 1992-2005
Age			
16-19	4,222	1,018	2.1%
20-24	7,169	708	0.8%
25-34	14,839	-909	-0.5%
35-44	18,643	3,202	1.5%
45-54	17,354	7,064	4.1%
55-64	7,825	2,656	3.2%
65 and over	1,747	262	1.3%
Race/Origin[1]			
White	58,840	10,144	1.5%
Black	9,040	2,041	2.0%
Asian and others	3,918	1,815	4.9%
Hispanic origin	6,953	2,913	4.3%

Source: Selected from Robert H. Vatter, "Women in the Labor Force," *Statistical Bulletin,* Vol 75(3), Jul-Sep 1994, pp. 2-10, Table 2, p. 9, "Projected Changing Nature of Women in the Labor Force, United States, 1992-2005." Primary source: Bureau of Labor Statistics, *The American Work Force: 1992-2005.* Washington, DC: U.S. Department of Labor, Bulletin 2452, April 1994. *Note:* 1. Persons of Hispanic origin may be of any race.

★ 568 ★

Labor and Laborers

Union Membership: 1984-1991

This table shows total union employment, the number of women union members, and the percentage of union membership that is women. As the nation shifts from a manufacturing economy to a service economy, where women represent 60% of workers, it is speculated that the increased participation of women in labor organizations may help reverse the recent trend of overall declining union membership.

[Numbers in thousands.]

Year	Total union employment	Women union members	Percent women
1984	17,340	5,829	33.6%
1985	16,996	5,732	33.7%
1986	16,975	5,802	34.2%
1987	16,913	5,842	34.5%
1988	17,002	5,982	35.2%
1989	16,960	6,141	36.2%
1990	16,740	6,175	36.9%
1991	16,568	6,138	37.0%

Source: "Employed women by union affiliation, 1984-91," *1993 Handbook on Women Workers: Trends & Issues*, U.S. Department of Labor, Women's Bureau, 1994, Table 12, p. 9. Primary source: U.S. Department of Labor, Bureau of Labor Statistics, *Employment and Earnings*, January 1986, 1988, 1990, and 1992.

★ 569 ★

Labor and Laborers

Welfare Mothers and Work

This table presents some statistics regarding welfare mothers who attempt to find and hold jobs.

Item	Number/Percent
Percent of women coming on the welfare rolls who left within two years.	64%
Percentage of those who left and then returned.	66%
Within a year	45%
"Work" given as the reason for leaving the welfare rolls.	46%
Left for work and then returned:	
Within a year	40%
Within 5 years	66%

[Continued]

★ 569 ★

Welfare Mothers and Work
[Continued]

Item	Number/Percent
Left for work and stayed off welfare for at least 24 months	30%
Welfare Cyclers[1]	
Percentage of women who began a welfare spell who fit the welfare cycler category.	40%
Number of checks collected in a five-year period.	>24
Long-term users of welfare (i.e., collecting checks continuously for five years)	18%
Long-term users of welfare as percentage of all people on welfare	66%

Source: Selected from Jason DeParle, "Welfare Mothers Find Jobs Easy to Get but Hard to Hold," *The New York Times,* October 24, 1994, pp. 1+; and "Welfare to Work: Breaking the Cycle of Dependency," *Research Bulletin,* Malcolm Wiener Center for Social Policy, Fall 1993, pp. 1, 8. Primary source: LaDonna A. Pavetti, "The Dynamics of Welfare and Work: Exploring the Process by Which Women Work Their Way Off Welfare," dissertation paper for the Malcolm Wiener Center for Social Policy. Available from the Center as Dissertation Series #D-93-1. Malcolm Wiener Center for Social Policy, telephone (617)495-1461. *Note:* 1. Persons who go on and off the welfare rolls repeatedly.

★ 570 ★

Labor and Laborers

What If You Lost Your Job?

This table shows the responses of 1,000 Michigan residents to a survey question asking, "If you lost your job today, how easy would it be to find comparable work?"

Response	Women	Men
Easy	67%	57%
Difficult	27%	38%
Wouldn't look	6%	5%
Those doing nothing to prepare for a possible job change:	46%	42%
Could maintain life-style without my paycheck for:		
A week or less	23%	10%

[Continued]

★ 570 ★

What If You Lost Your Job?

[Continued]

Response	Women	Men
2-5 weeks	27%	30%
6-12 weeks	22%	21%

Source: Vickie Elmer and Michael Betzold, "Men and Women Both Say They Want More," *Detroit Free Press*, February 27, 1995, p. 1+. Primary source: February surveys of 1,000 Michigan residents for Free Press/WXYZ-TV by EPIC-MRA, Lansing.

★ 571 ★

Labor and Laborers

Women in the Labor Force: 1950-2000

This table shows the percentage of women, by age, who were or are projected to be in the U.S. work force, from 1950-2000.

Age	1950	1960	1970	1980	1990	2000
16-19	41%	39.3%	44%	52.9%	51.8%	59.6%
20-24	46%	46.1%	57.7%	68.9%	71.6%	77.9%
25-34	34%	36%	45%	65.5%	73.6%	82.4%
35-44	39.1%	43.4%	51.1%	65.5%	76.5%	84.9%
45-54	37.9%	49.9%	54.4%	59.9%	71.2%	76.5%
55-64	27%	37.2%	43%	41.3%	45.3%	49%
65 and over	9.7%	10.8%	9.7%	8.1%	8.7%	7.6%

Source: "Women in the U.S. Work Force," *Womens Voices: A Polling Report*, A Joint Project of the Ms. Foundation for Women and Center for Policy Alternatives, p. 19.

★ 572 ★

Labor and Laborers

Work Experience of Married Mothers by Race/Ethnicity: 1992

This table shows the work experience of married mothers in 1992 by the age of her youngest child. Data are given for white, black, and Hispanic origin married mothers. Hispanic mothers are less likely to work during a year than their white or black counterparts.

[Numbers in thousands.]

Work experience	White				Black				Hispanic origin			
	Total	With children 6 to 17 only	With children under 6		Total	With children 6 to 17 only	With children under 6		Total	With children 6 to 17 only	With children under 6	
			Total	Under 3			Total	Under 3			Total	Under 3
Married mothers, total	21,702	11,207	10,495	6,341	1,863	992	871	495	2,441	1,082	1,359	837
Worked in 1992	15,758	8,786	6,972	4,205	1,481	819	663	357	1,407	704	704	404
As percent of total	72.6%	78.4%	66.4%	66.3%	79.5%	82.6%	76.1%	72.1%	57.6%	65.1%	51.8%	48.3%
Percent of married mothers who:												
Worked full year in 1992[1]	47.3%	55.0%	39.1%	36.0%	55.4%	59.8%	50.2%	41.9%	36.2%	45.7%	28.6%	25.2%

[Continued]

★ 572 ★

Work Experience of Married Mothers by Race/Ethnicity: 1992
[Continued]

Work experience	White				Black				Hispanic origin			
	Total	With children 6 to 17 only	With children under 6		Total	With children 6 to 17 only	With children under 6		Total	With children 6 to 17 only	With children under 6	
			Total	Under 3			Total	Under 3			Total	Under 3
Full time[2]	35.6%	41.7%	29.1%	26.9%	49.1%	52.6%	44.9%	36.0%	29.5%	37.6%	23.2%	20.4%
Part time[2]	11.7%	13.3%	10.0%	9.1%	6.3%	7.2%	5.3%	5.9%	6.7%	8.0%	5.5%	4.8%
Worked part year in 1992[3]	25.2%	23.4%	27.4%	30.4%	24.2%	22.5%	25.9%	30.2%	21.4%	19.3%	23.2%	23.2%
Full time[2]	11.5%	10.9%	12.3%	14.7%	15.3%	15.1%	15.6%	19.6%	13.6%	12.0%	14.8%	15.6%
Part time[2]	13.7%	12.5%	15.1%	15.7%	8.9%	7.4%	10.3%	10.6%	7.8%	7.3%	8.4%	7.6%
Did not work in 1992	27.4%	21.6%	33.6%	33.7%	20.5%	17.4%	23.9%	27.9%	42.4%	35.0%	48.2%	51.6%

Source: Howard V. Hayghe and Suzanne M. Bianchi, "Married mothers' work patterns: the job-family compromise," *Monthly Labor Review*, June 1994, pp. 24-30, Table 3, p. 26, "Work experience of married mothers in 1992 by race and Hispanic origin: age of youngest child, March 1993." Detail for race and Hispanic-origin groups do not sum to totals because data for the "other races" group are not presented and Hispanics are included in both the white and black population groups. *Notes:* 1. Fifty to 52 weeks. 2. Full time is defined as 35 hours a week or more. Part time is less than 35 hours. 3. One to 49 weeks.

★ 573 ★

Labor and Laborers

Work Experience of Married Mothers: 1992

This table shows the work experience of married mothers in 1992 by the age of her youngest child. The work patterns of many married mothers differ by the child care needs of their children.

[Numbers in thousands.]

Work experience	With children 6 to 17, none younger	With children under 6	
		Total	Under 3
Married mothers, total	12,764	11,942	7,168
Worked in 1992	10,004	8,013	4,776
As percent of total	78.4%	67.2%	66.6%
Percent of married mothers who:			
Worked full year in 1992[1]	55.2%	40.0%	36.3%
Full time[2]	42.6%	30.6%	27.7%
Part time[2]	12.6%	9.4%	8.6%
Worked part year in 1992[3]	23.1%	27.1%	30.4%
Full time[2]	11.2%	12.7%	15.2%
40 to 49 weeks	4.2%	4.6%	5.6%
27 to 39 weeks	2.7%	2.8%	3.4%
1 to 26 weeks	4.3%	5.3%	6.2%
Part time[2]	11.9%	14.4%	15.2%
40 to 49 weeks	3.6%	3.1%	3.1%
27 to 39 weeks	2.8%	2.7%	2.8%

[Continued]

★ 573 ★

Work Experience of Married Mothers: 1992
[Continued]

Work experience	With children 6 to 17, none younger	With children under 6	
		Total	Under 3
1 to 26 weeks	5.5%	8.6%	9.4%
Did not work in 1992	21.6%	32.9%	33.4%

Source: Howard V. Hayghe and Suzanne M. Bianchi, "Married mothers' work patterns: the job-family compromise," *Monthly Labor Review*, June 1994, pp. 24-30, Table 2, p. 25, "Work experience of married mothers in 1992 by age of youngest child, March 1993." *Notes:* 1. Fifty to 52 weeks. 2. Full time is defined as 35 hours a week or more. Part time is less than 35 hours. 3. One to 49 weeks.

★ 574 ★

Labor and Laborers

Work Experience of Married Parents by Race/Ethnicity: 1992

This table shows the work experience of fathers and mothers in two-parent families in 1992 by age of youngest child, race, and Hispanic origin. In 7 out of 10 of the 24.7 million two-parent families, both mother and father worked at some time during 1992. The proportion was higher among families in which the youngest child was 6 to 17 years old.

[Numbers in thousands.]

Parents' work experience	Total	With children 6 to 17, none younger	With children under 6	White	Black	Hispanic origin
Two-parent families, number	24,706	12,764	11,942	21,702	1,863	2,441
Percent in which:						
Both parents worked during year	70.1%	74.8%	65.0%	70.0%	74.1%	54.1%
Father only worked during year	25.1%	19.6%	31.0%	25.8%	16.6%	38.8%
Mother only worked during year	2.2%	3.5%	2.1%	2.6%	5.4%	3.6%
Two-parent families, percent	100.0%	100.0%	100.0%	100.0%	100.0%	100.0%
Father worked year round[1] full time[2]	78.1%	78.4%	77.7%	78.8%	71.7%	67.3%
Mother worked year round[1] full time[2]	29.5%	34.3%	24.3%	28.6%	38.0%	21.3%
Mother worked less than year round full time[3]	28.2%	27.8%	28.6%	29.2%	21.8%	17.9%
Mother did not work	20.4%	16.2%	24.9%	21.0%	11.9%	28.0%
Father worked less than year round full time[3]	17.2%	16.1%	18.3%	17.0%	19.1%	25.6%
Mother worked year round[1] full time[2]	5.7%	6.3%	5.1%	5.5%	7.8%	6.5%
Mother worked less than year round full time[3]	6.7%	6.4%	7.0%	6.7%	6.6%	8.4%
Mother did not work	4.7%	3.4%	6.2%	4.8%	4.7%	10.8%

[Continued]

★ 574 ★

Work Experience of Married Parents by Race/Ethnicity: 1992
[Continued]

Parents' work experience	Total	With children 6 to 17, none younger	With children under 6	White	Black	Hispanic origin
Father did not work	4.8%	5.5%	4.0%	4.2%	9.2%	7.1%
Mother worked year round[1] full time[2]	1.6%	2.0%	1.2%	1.5%	3.2%	1.8%
Mother worked less than year round full time[3]	1.2%	1.5%	0.9%	1.1%	2.1%	1.8%
Mother did not work	1.9%	2.0%	1.9%	1.6%	3.8%	3.6%

Source: Howard V. Hayghe and Suzanne M. Bianchi, "Married mothers' work patterns: the job-family compromise," *Monthly Labor Review*, June 1994, pp. 24-30, Table 4, p. 27, "Work experience of fathers and mothers in two-parent families in 1992 by age of youngest child, race and Hispanic origin, March 1993." Detail for race and Hispanic-origin groups do not sum to totals because data for the "other races" group are not presented and Hispanics are included in both the white and black population groups. *Notes:* 1. Fifty to 52 weeks. 2. Full time is defined as 35 hours a week or more. Part time is less than 35 hours. 3. Worked 1 to 49 weeks, either full or part time.

★ 575 ★

Labor and Laborers

Work Experience Trends of Married Mothers: 1970-1992

This table shows trends in the work experience of black and white married mothers with children under 18 and with children under 6 for selected years between 1970 and 1992. There was a dramatic gain in the proportion of married mothers who were year round full-time workers. In 1970, little more than half of married mothers worked at all during the year. By 1992, nearly 3 out of 4 did so.

[Numbers in thousands.]

Year and Race	With children under 18					With children under 6				
	Population	Percent who worked during year			Percent who did not work during year	Population	Percent who worked during year			Precent who did not work during year
		Total	Year round full time[1]	Other[2]			Total	Year round full time[1]	Other[2]	
Total										
1970	24,602	51.3%	16.4%	34.9%	48.7%	11,919	44.4%	9.6%	34.8%	55.6%
1975	25,361	53.7%	18.1%	35.7%	46.3%	11,819	47.0%	11.9%	35.2%	53.0%
1980	25,217	63.4%	23.7%	39.7%	36.6%	11,725	58.1%	17.7%	40.4%	41.9%
1985	25,003	73.9%	31.3%	42.6%	27.1%	12,217	63.0%	22.7%	40.3%	37.0%
1990	24,393	72.8%	34.0%	38.7%	27.2%	12,099	67.9%	28.0%	39.9%	32.1%
1991	24,416	73.5%	35.7%	37.9%	26.5%	11,925	67.6%	28.8%	38.7%	32.4%
1992	24,706	72.9%	36.8%	36.1%	27.1%	11,942	67.1%	30.6%	36.5%	32.9%
White										
1970	22,512	50.2%	15.4%	34.7%	49.8%	10,723	42.8%	8.4%	34.4%	57.2%
1975	22,893	52.8%	17.0%	35.8%	47.2%	10,531	45.9%	10.8%	35.1%	54.1%
1980	22,541	62.8%	22.3%	40.5%	37.2%	10,405	57.1%	16.1%	41.0%	42.9%
1985	22,056	67.3%	27.0%	40.3%	32.7%	10,808	62.2%	20.9%	41.3%	37.8%
1990	21,504	72.7%	32.4%	40.3%	27.3%	10,686	67.7%	26.4%	41.3%	32.3%
1991	21,488	73.4%	34.4%	39.1%	26.6%	10,501	67.3%	27.4%	39.9%	32.7%
1992	21,702	72.6%	35.6%	37.0%	27.4%	10,495	66.4%	29.1%	37.3%	33.6%
Black										
1970	1,910	64.2%	27.2%	37.0%	35.8%	1,049	60.6%	21.1%	39.5%	39.4%
1975	1,971	64.5%	29.8%	34.7%	35.5%	981	59.5%	22.5%	37.0%	40.5%
1980	1,924	69.8%	36.5%	33.3%	30.2%	899	69.7%	32.3%	37.4%	30.3%
1985	1,965	76.1%	45.0%	31.0%	23.9%	926	73.5%	39.1%	34.4%	26.5%
1990	1,846	78.9%	48.9%	30.0%	21.1%	908	77.3%	44.6%	32.7%	22.7%

[Continued]

★ 575 ★

Work Experience Trends of Married Mothers: 1970-1992

[Continued]

Year and Race	With children under 18					With children under 6				
	Population	Percent who worked during year			Percent who did not work during year	Population	Percent who worked during year			Precent who did not work during year
		Total	Year round full time[1]	Other[2]			Total	Year round full time[1]	Other[2]	
1991	1,870	78.4%	48.7%	29.7%	21.7%	884	76.7%	43.3%	33.4%	23.3%
1992	1,863	79.5%	49.1%	30.4%	20.5%	871	76.1%	44.9%	31.2%	23.9%

Source: Howard V. Hayghe and Suzanne M. Bianchi, "Married mothers' work patterns: the job-family compromise," *Monthly Labor Review*, June 1994, pp. 24-30, selected from Table 5, p. 28, "Work experience trends of married mothers by age of youngest child and race, selected years 1970-92." Also in source: data by mothers with children 6 to 17, none younger. *Notes:* 1. Worked full time (35 hours or more a week) 50 to 52 weeks. 2. Worked either full or part time (less than 35 hours a week) for 1 to 49 weeks.

★ 576 ★

Labor and Laborers

Work Experience: 1992

This table shows the work experience of persons in 1992 by selected characteristics. Nearly 75% of all married mothers worked at some time during that year. Thirty-seven percent worked year round full time. Eighty-five percent of women with no children had work experience, and 54% were year-round full-time workers.

[Numbers in thousands.]

Work experience	Parents		Persons 20 to 54 years old		
			Women with no children < 18	Men	
	Married mothers	All fathers		Total	With no children < 18
Total	24,706	26,182	30,616	62,625	36,443
Worked in 1992	18,018	24,784	26,007	57,282	32,498
As percent of total	72.9%	94.7%	84.9%	91.5%	89.2%
Percent of total who:					
Worked full year in 1992[1]	47.9%	77.9%	63.5%	69.2%	62.9%
Full time[2]	36.8%	76.1%	54.1%	65.6%	58.0%
Part time[2]	11.1%	1.8%	9.4%	3.6%	4.9%
Worked part year in 1992[3]	25.1%	16.8%	21.5%	22.2%	26.2%
Full time[2]	12.0%	14.5%	12.8%	17.4%	19.4%
40 to 49 weeks	4.4%	6.6%	4.9%	6.9%	7.0%
27 to 39 weeks	2.8%	3.6%	2.9%	4.1%	4.5%
1 to 26 weeks	4.8%	4.3%	5.0%	6.4%	7.9%
Part time[2]	13.1%	2.3%	8.7%	4.8%	6.8%
40 to 49 weeks	3.4%	0.6%	2.7%	1.2%	1.6%
27 to 39 weeks	2.7%	0.5%	1.8%	0.9%	1.4%

[Continued]

★ 576 ★

Work Experience: 1992
[Continued]

Work experience	Parents		Persons 20 to 54 years old		
	Married mothers	All fathers	Women with no children < 18	Men	
				Total	With no children < 18
1 to 26 weeks	7.0%	1.2%	4.2%	2.7%	3.8%
Did not work in 1992	27.1%	5.3%	15.1%	8.6%	10.8%

Source: Howard V. Hayghe and Suzanne M. Bianchi, "Married mothers' work patterns: the job-family compromise," *Monthly Labor Review*, June 1994, pp. 24-30, Table 1, p. 25, "Work experience of persons in 1992 by selected characteristics, March 1993," Based on the fact that nearly all parents are 20 to 54 years old, data for men and women 20 to 54 years old with no children under 18 were constructed by subtracting parents from estimates for all 20- to 54-year-olds. *Notes:* 1. Fifty to 52 weeks. 2. Full time is defined as 35 hours a week or more. Part time is less than 35 hours. 3. One to 49 weeks.

★ 577 ★
Labor and Laborers

Worker Training: 1983-1991

This table shows the percentage of adult workers who took training to improve their current job skills in 1983 and 1991. White collar workers, college graduates, and workers in mid-career were most likely to pursue further training.

Sex	1983	1991
Male	35%	40%
Female	34%	41%

Source: Selected from "Worker Training," *The National Education Goals Report: Volume One: The National Report*, National Education Goals Panel, 1993, Exhibit 89, p. 133. Primary Source: Bureau of Labor Statistics, 1992.

★ 578 ★
Labor and Laborers

Workers in the Informal Sector Worldwide

This table presents some statistics on the informal job sector worldwide. In some countries, more women participate in the informal economy than in the regular work force.

Item	Number/Percent
Official statistics on the labor force population in India: Women Men	 14% 52%

[Continued]

★ 578 ★

Workers in the Informal Sector Worldwide
[Continued]

Item	Number/Percent
Percentage of working women in India found to be employed in the informal sector in a 1988 survey:	90%
International Labor Organization estimates of the contribution of the "shadow economy" to GDP in Africa, Asia, and Latin America:	5-35%
Estimate of the percentage of the urban working population in the informal sector in developing countries:	50%+
Amount by which women's rates of enrollment in secondary schools lag behind men's in selected countries:	
Bangladesh	56%
Malawi	40%
Togo	68%
Number of manufacturing jobs per 100 people in selected countries:	
Algeria	2.3
Egypt	3.6
United States	9.2
Japan	11.9

Source: Selected from Ann Misch, "Lost in the Shadow Economy," *World Watch*, March/April 1992, pp. 18-25.

★ 579 ★

Labor and Laborers

Working While Attending College: 1989-1990

This table shows the percentage distribution of undergraduates' employment status while enrolled in postsecondary education during school year 1989-1990. Women were more likely than men not to work while enrolled in school. If they did work, they were less likely than men to work full time.

Gender	Not working while enrolled	Work 1-15 hours/week	Work 16-24 hours/week	Work 25-34 hours/week	Work 35 or hours/week
Total	22.8%	9.9%	13.1%	14.3%	39.9%
Male	18.9%	8.6%	11.9%	14.0%	46.7%
Female	24.8%	11.1%	14.2%	14.9%	35.0%

Source: Selected from "Percentage distribution of undergraduates' employment status while enrolled in postsecondary education, by selected characteristics: 1989-90," U.S. Department of Education, National Center for Education Statistics, Statistical Analysis Report, NCES 94-311, September 1994, *Undergraduates Who Work While Enrolled in Postsecondary Education, 1989-90*, Table 2.8, p. 22.

Occupations

★ 580 ★

African University Teachers

This table shows the total number of teachers in all third-level institutions and in universities and equivalent institutions in selected African countries for which data was available. It shows the percentage who were female, latest available year. Education at the third level requires as a minimum condition of admission the successful completion of education at the second level or proof of equivalent knowledge or experience. The types of institutions in which third level education may be obtained include universities, teacher-training institutions, and technical institutions.

[NA Not available.]

Country or area	All institutions			Universities and equivalent institutions		
	Year	Teachers	% Female	Year	Teachers	% Female
Africa						
Burkina Faso	1975	166	13%	1975	166	13%
Burundi	1991	492	11%	1991	492	11%
Central African Republic	1985	489	8%	1991	139[1]	11%[1]
Chad	1984	141	8%	1984	104	5%
Comoros	1989	32	31%	NA	NA	NA
Congo	1991	1,159	8%	1991	1,159	8%
Egypt[2]	1985	31,903	NA	1990	34,553	29%
Ethiopia	1990	1,690	8%	1991[3]	1,440	5%

[Continued]

★ 580 ★

African University Teachers
[Continued]

Country or area	All institutions			Universities and equivalent institutions		
	Year	Teachers	% Female	Year	Teachers	% Female
Guinea	1985	1,107	4%	1988	805	3%
Lesotho	1991	469	10%	1991	297	10%
Liberia	1987	472	18%	1987	444	20%
Madagascar	1990	939	27%	1990	939	27%
Mauritius	1990	414	20%	1990	274	15%
Morocco[4]	NA	NA	NA	1985	5,310	17%
Mozambique	1987	368	26%	1987	368	26%
Namibia	1991	331	50%	1991	141	50%
Niger	1986	349	13%	1986	349	13%
Nigeria	1989	19,601	NA	1989	11,936	10%
Rwanda	1989	464	5%	1989	469	6%
St. Helena	1980	9	44%	NA	NA	NA
Senegal	1980	1,084	NA	1985	701	13%
Seychelles	1980	28	57%	1976	NA	15%
Sierra Leone	1975	289	13%	1975	289	13%
Sudan	1989	2,522	16%	1989	1,933	12%
Swaziland	1991	452	40%	1991	240	30%
Tanzania United Rep. of	1989	1,206	NA	1981	893	3%
Togo	1980	297[5]	12%[5]	1986	268	12%
Tunisia	1990	4,550	22%	1990	4,550	22%
Uganda	1975	617	9%	1975	444	7%
Zimbabwe	1992	3,076	NA	1992	976	16%

Source: Selected from "Education at the third level," United Nations, *Statistical Yearbook 1992*, New York, 1994, Table 13, pp. 91+. Primary source: United Nations Educational, Scientific and Cultural Organization (Paris). *Notes:* 1. Full time only. 2. Teaching staff after 1985 excludes Al Azhar University. Since 1988, excludes private higher institutions. 3. In 1991, not including Asmara University and Kotebe college. 4. Data on female teachers refer to University only. In 1990, data on other third level institutions are incomplete. 5. Excluding teacher training.

★ 581 ★

Occupations

Architects: 1994

This table shows some statistics relating to women in architecture.

Item	Number/Percent
U.S. population, 1990	
Men	48.8%
Women	51.2%
All U.S. architects[1]	
Men	84.9%
Women	15.1%
Amount of money that men with 15 years experience earn more than comparably experienced women architects, annually	$10,000
Female tenured architectural faculty in U.S. universities	8.7%
Percentage of female architecture students who complete their degrees	26%

Source: Selected from Sheri Olson, "Architecture Doesn't Look Much Like America," *Architectural Record*, November 1994, p. 25. Primary sources: American Institute of Architecture; 1990 and 1993 U.S. censuses. *Note:* 1. Includes related professions such as landscape architects.

★ 582 ★

Occupations

Artists in Detail: 1970-1990

This table shows numbers of artists by occupation, by gender, for the years 1970, 1980, and 1990.

Occupation/year	Number			Percent distribution		
	Total	Male	Female	Total	Male	Female
Actors & directors						
1990	109,573	67,787	41,786	100.0%	61.9%	38.1%
1980	67,180	44,049	23,131	100.0%	65.6%	34.4%
1970	40,201	26,339	13,826	100.0%	65.5%	34.5%
Announcers						
1990	60,269	47,752	12,517	100.0%	79.2%	20.8%
1980	46,986	38,392	8,594	100.0%	81.7%	18.3%
1970	25,942	24,291	1,651	100.0%	93.6%	6.4%

[Continued]

★ 582 ★

Artists in Detail: 1970-1990
[Continued]

Occupation/year	Number			Percent distribution		
	Total	Male	Female	Total	Male	Female
Architects						
1990	156,874	133,212	23,662	100.0%	84.9%	15.1%
1980	107,693	98,743	8,950	100.0%	91.7%	8.3%
1970	53,670	51,534	2,136	100.0%	96.0%	4.0%
Authors						
1990	106,730	53,863	52,867	100.0%	50.5%	49.5%
1980	45,748	25,409	20,339	100.0%	55.5%	44.5%
1970	27,752	19,578	8,174	100.0%	70.5%	29.5%
Dancers						
1990	21,913	5,097	16,816	100.0%	23.3%	76.7%
1980	13,194	3,350	9,844	100.0%	25.4%	74.6%
1970	7,404	1,381	6,023	100.0%	18.7%	81.3%
Designers						
1990	596,802	265,299	331,503	100.0%	44.5%	55.5%
1980	338,374	169,604	168,770	100.0%	50.1%	49.9%
1970	232,890	148,572	84,318	100.0%	63.8%	36.2%
Musicians & composers						
1990	148,020	99,409	48,611	100.0%	67.2%	32.8%
1980	140,556	99,065	41,491	100.0%	70.5%	29.5%
1970	99,533	64,767	34,766	100.0%	65.1%	34.9%
Painters, sculptors, craft-artists, and artists printmakers						
1990	212,762	101,067	111,695	100.0%	47.5%	52.5%
1980	153,162	79,445	73,717	100.0%	51.9%	48.1%
1970	86,849	52,827	34,022	100.0%	60.8%	39.2%
Photographers						
1990	143,520	100,169	43,351	100.0%	69.8%	30.2%
1980	94,762	72,496	22,266	100.0%	76.5%	23.5%
1970	67,588	57,597	9,991	100.0%	85.2%	14.8%
Teachers of art, drama, and music						
1990	21,393	10,591	10,802	100.0%	49.5%	50.5%
1980	28,385	14,718	13,667	100.0%	51.9%	48.1%
1970	42,000	25,310	16,690	100.0%	60.3%	39.7%
Other artists						
1990	93,421	46,865	46,556	100.0%	50.2%	49.8%

[Continued]

★ 582 ★

Artists in Detail: 1970-1990
[Continued]

Occupation/year	Number			Percent distribution		
	Total	Male	Female	Total	Male	Female
1980	49,653	29,356	20,297	100.0%	59.1%	40.9%
1970	53,131	37,742	15,389	100.0%	71.0%	29.0%
Total artists						
1990	1,671,277	931,111	740,166	100.0%	55.7%	44.3%
1980	1,085,693	674,627	411,066	100.0%	62.1%	37.9%
1970	736,960	509,938	227,022	100.0%	69.2%	30.8%

Source: Selected from *Trends in Artist Occupations 1970-1990*, prepared by Diane C. Ellis and John C. Beresford, National Endowment for the Arts Research Division Report #29, August 1994, Table 20, p. A-34, "Detailed artist occupations by sex, race, and Hispanic [origin], United States: 1990, 1980, and 1970," and Table 21, p. A-35, "Percent distribution of artist occupations by sex, race, and Hispanic [origin], United States: 1990, 1980, and 1970." There was a 1980 to 1990 decrease in the number of teachers who specified subject taught and an increase in the number of teachers who did not specify the subject taught.

★ 583 ★

Occupations

Artists: 1970-1990

This table shows numbers of artists and percentages, by gender, for the years 1970, 1980, and 1990.

Gender	Number			Percent			Percent change		
	1990	1980	1970	1990	1980	1970	1970-1990	1980-1990	1970-1980
Total	1,671,277	1,085,693	736,960	100.0%	100.0%	100.0%	126.8%	53.9%	47.3%
Male	931,111	674,627	509,938	55.7%	62.1%	69.2%	82.6%	38.0%	32.3%
Female	740,166	411,066	227,022	44.3%	37.9%	30.8%	226.0%	80.1%	81.1%

Source: Selected from *Trends in Artist Occupations 1970-1990*, prepared by Diane C. Ellis and John C. Beresford, National Endowment for the Arts Research Division Report #29, August 1994, Table 19, p. A-32, "All artists, professional occupations, and the labor force by sex, race, Hispanic [origin], age, and years of school completed for the United States: 1990, 1980, and 1970."

★ 584 ★

Occupations

Asian University Teachers

This table shows the total number of teachers in all third-level institutions and in universities and equivalent institutions in selected Asian countries for which data was available. It shows the percentage who were female, latest available year. Education at the third level requires as a minimum condition of admission the successful completion of education at the second level or proof of equivalent knowledge or experience. The types of institutions in which third level education may be obtained include universities, teacher-training institutions, and technical institutions.

[NA Not available.]

Country or area	All institutions			Universities and equivalent institutions		
	Year	Teachers	% Female	Year	Teachers	% Female
Asia						
Afghanistan	1990	1,342	24%	1990	444	22%
Bahrain	1990	557	29%	1990	464	20%
Bangladesh	1990	22,447	13%	1990	2,959	12%
Bhutan	1980	37	27%	1980	15	20%
Brunei Darussalam	1987	174	14%	1987	130	18%
China[1]	1990	394,567	29%	1985	343	31%
Cyprus	1985	343	31%	NA	NA	NA
Hong Kong	1984	5,928	24%	1984	1,569	18%
India	1985	302,843	21%	NA	NA	NA
Indonesia	1984	75,589	18%	NA	NA	NA
Iran						
Islamic Rep. of	1991	25,208	17%	1991	19,564	19%
Iraq	1988	11,072	25%	1980	4,627	16%
Israel	NA	NA	NA	1980	10,237	32%
Japan[2]	1985	243,507	14%	1985	191,533	10%
Jordan	1991	3,753	18%	1991	2,123	12%
Korea						
Dem. People's Rep.	1987	27,000	19%	1987	23,000	17%
Rep. of	1991	77,458	20%	1991	60,671	22%
Kuwait	1980	1,151	23%	1980	608	10%
Laos						
Lao People's Dem. Rep.	1989	698	19%	1989	476	25%
Lebanon	1991	5,400	24%	1991	5,400	24%
Malaysia	1985	8,213	22%	1985	4,718	24%
Mongolia	1981	2,400	38%	1981	1,300	31%
Nepal	1980	2,918	16%	1980	2,918	16%
Pakistan	1985	7,805	17%	1985	7,744	17%
Palestine						
Gaza Strip	1991	217	8%	1991	104	17%
Philippines	1980	43,770	53%	1985	50,821	NA
Qatar	1989	451	25%	1989	451	25%

[Continued]

★ 584 ★

Asian University Teachers
[Continued]

Country or area	All institutions			Universities and equivalent institutions		
	Year	Teachers	% Female	Year	Teachers	% Female
Saudi Arabia	1990	13,260	25%	1990	10,143	27%
Singapore	1983	3,141	21%	1983	1,613	20%
Sri Lanka	1975	2,000	17%	1990	2,013	30%
Syria						
Syrian Arab Rep.	NA	NA	NA	1985	4,504	17%
Thailand	1975	9,070	56%	1975	9,070	56%
Turkey	1991	35,123	32%	1991	33,455	32%
United Arab Emirates	1991	1,082	14%	1991	728	9%
Viet Nam[2]	1980	17,242	22%	1980	17,242	22%
Yemen[3]	1980	157	4%	1980	157	4%

Source: Selected from "Education at the third level," United Nations, *Statistical Yearbook 1992*, New York, 1994, Table 13, pp. 91+. Primary source: United Nations Educational, Scientific and Cultural Organization (Paris). *Notes:* 1. Full time only. 2. Including correspondence classes. 3. Excluding former Democratic Yemen.

★ 585 ★

Occupations

College Professors Worldwide

This table shows the percentages of college professors who are males and females in selected foreign countries.

Country	Male	Female
Australia	65%	35%
Brazil	61%	39%
Chile	67%	33%
England	77%	23%
Germany[1]	83%	17%
Hong Kong	75%	25%
Israel	72%	28%
Japan	92%	8%
Mexico	64%	36%
Netherlands	78%	22%
Russia	74%	27%
South Korea	87%	13%

[Continued]

★ 585 ★

College Professors Worldwide
[Continued]

Country	Male	Female
Sweden	74%	26%
United States	70%	30%

Source: Selected from "Carnegie Foundation International Survey of Attitudes and Characteristics of Faculty Members," *The Chronicle of Higher Education Almanac,* September 1, 1994, p. 45. Primary source: "The Academic Profession: An International Perspective," published by the Carnegie Foundation for the Advancement of Teaching. The figures are from a survey of 20,000 faculty members in 13 countries and Hong Kong. It was conducted by the Carnegie Foundation for the Advancement of Teaching from 1991 to 1993. The participating nations were chosen because they had university systems that were relatively comparable. Because of rounding or multiple responses, figures may not add to 100%. *Note:* 1. Includes only institutions in the former West Germany.

★ 586 ★

Occupations

College Professors, Trends in Employment: 1993-1994

This table shows college administrators' views on female faculty employment trends, as reported in 1993-1994. The proportion of institutions reporting changes in the number of female faculty members from 1992-1993 to 1993-1994 are shown.

[Res./ Doctoral refers to Research/Doctoral institutions.]

Proportions reporting changes in number of	All	Public institutions				Private institutions		
		All	2-year	Comprehensive	Res./Doctoral	All	Colleges[1]	Res./Doctoral
Women faculty members								
Net gain	58%	56%	55%	50%	72%	62%	62%	65%
No net change	36%	38%	40%	39%	19%	33%	34%	26%
Net loss	6%	7%	5%	11%	9%	5%	4%	10%

Source: Selected from "Administrators' Views on Faculty Employment Trends, 1993-94," *The Chronicle of Higher Education Almanac,* September 1, 1994, p. 44. Primary source: "Campus Trends, 1994," published by American Council on Education. The figures are based on responses to a survey sent to senior administrators at 508 colleges and universities in the winter of 1994. The response rate was 80%. Because of rounding or multiple responses, figures may not add to 100%. *Note:* 1. Includes liberal-arts and comprehensive institutions.

★ 587 ★
Occupations

College Professors: 1987

This table shows the total number of full-time college professors by type of institution and gives percentages of men and women.

	All	Research		Doctoral		Comprehensive		Liberal Arts	2-Year		Medical	Other
		Public	Private	Public	Private	Public	Private	All	Public	Private		
Total	489,000	96,000	39,000	36,000	15,000	93,000	35,000	39,000	91,000	4,000	25,000	15,000
Men	72.7%	79.3%	80.5%	74.5%	77.3%	71.1%	72.5%	70.9%	62.1%	64.2%	75.7%	78.7%
Women	27.3%	20.7%	19.5%	25.5%	22.7%	28.9%	27.5%	29.1%	37.9%	35.8%	24.3%	21.3%

Source: Selected from "Characteristics of Full-Time College Professors, 1987" *The Chronicle of Higher Education Almanac*, September 1, 1994, p. 33. Primary source: U.S. Department of Education.

★ 588 ★
Occupations

Distribution of Employment by Major Industry Group: 1993

This table shows the percent of all women employed in each major industry group in 1993, and shows women as a percent of employment in the industry.

Industry	Percent of all women employment	Women as percent of industry employment
Agriculture and mining	1.4%	19.9%
Construction	1.1%	8.6%
Manufacturing	11.6%	32.3%
Transportation and utilities	4.4%	28.5%
Wholesale trade	2.4%	28.9%
Retail trade	18.8%	50.8%
Finance, insurance, real estate	8.5%	58.6%
Services	47.3%	61.7%
Public administration	4.5%	42.9%

Source: Selected from Robert H. Vatter, "Women in the Labor Force," *Statistical Bulletin*, Vol 75(3), Jul-Sep 1994, pp. 2-10, Table 1, p. 8, "Employment of Women by Major Industry Groups, United States, 1993." Primary source: Basic data from *Employment and Earnings*, U.S. Department of Labor, Bureau of Labor Statistics, January 1994. Analyses and computations by Health and Safety Education Division, Medical Department, Metropolitan Life Insurance Company.

★ 589 ★

Occupations

Distribution of Employment by Work Disability Status: 1988

This table shows the differences in employment distribution of women with and without disabilities in 1988. More disabled working women were employed in 1988 than ten years previously, and they were more likely to be employed full time. Disabled women workers earned 38% less than nondisabled women workers in 1987. They had mean earnings of $8,075, while women workers with no work disabilities had mean earnings of $13,000. Black women with work disabilities had earnings of $6,432. Women of Hispanic origin with work disabilities earned $7,559.

Occupations	Persons with work disabilities					No work disabilities	
	Men	Women				Men	Women
		Total	White	Black	Hispanic		
Managerial and professional specialty	18.2%	16.0%	17.7%	7.5%	13.3%	26.3%	25.6%
Technical, sales and administrative support	17.5%	39.5%	41.2%	28.3%	28.5%	19.9%	45.3%
Service	12.5%	27.3%	23.7%	47.7%	31.8%	9.2%	17.0%
Farming, forestry and fishing	4.6%	1.4%	1.5%	0.8%	2.9%	3.7%	0.8%
Precision production, crafts and repair	19.6%	2.2%	2.4%	0.5%	4.6%	19.8%	2.2%
Operators, fabricators and laborers	27.4%	13.3%	13.2%	14.9%	18.6%	20.9%	8.7%

Source: "Occupations of Employed Persons by Work Disability Status and Sex, 16 to 64 Years of Age, 1988," U.S. Department of Labor, Women's Bureau, *Facts on Working Women*, No. 92.2, March 1992, Table I, p. 3.

★ 590 ★

Occupations

Distribution of Occupations: 1993

This table shows the percent distribution of occupations among employed men and women aged 20 and over in 1993.

Occupation	Women	Men
Technical, sales, administrative	42.7%	20.6%
Managerial and professional	29.5%	27.1%
Services	17.0%	9.4%
Other	10.8%	42.9%

Source: Selected from Robert H. Vatter, "Women in the Labor Force," *Statistical Bulletin*, Vol 75(3), Jul-Sep 1994, pp. 2-10, Figure D, p. 7, entitled "Percent Distribution of Occupations Among Employed Civilians Age 20 and Over, by Sex, United States, 1993. Primary source: Basic data from *Employment and Earnings*, U.S. Department of Labor, Bureau of Labor Statistics, January 1994. Analyses and computations by Health and Safety Education Division, Medical Department, Metropolitan Life Insurance Company.

★ 591 ★

Occupations

Elementary and Secondary Public School Employment

This table shows the full-time participation rates of women for five of the most important occupations in elementary and secondary schools for academic years 1975-76 and 1992-93. These occupations account for more than half of the total full-time employment in the sector. Data were provided for the 1992-1993 school year by nearly 4,500 school districts with an enrollment of more than 34 million students.

Job category	School Year	Women
Officials and Administrators	1975-76	15.1%
	1992-93	38.4%
Principals	1975-76	12.8%
	1992-93	37.3%
Assistant Principals	1975-76	21.1%
	1992-93	43.6%
Elementary Class-room Teachers	1975-76	83.3%
	1992-93	86.9%

[Continued]

★ 591 ★

Elementary and Secondary Public School Employment
[Continued]

Job category	School Year	Women
Secondary Class-room Teachers	1975-76	45.9%
	1992-93	55.0%

Source: "Full-time employment participation rates of minorities and women in elementary and secondary school districts, U.S. summary, 1975-76 and 1992-93 school years," U.S. Equal Employment Opportunity Commission, *Indicators of Equal Employment Opportunity-Status and Trends,* September 1993, p. 30. Primary source: Equal Employment Opportunity Commission, Elementary-Secondary Staff Information (EEO-5) Reports.

★ 592 ★

Occupations

European University Teachers

This table shows the total number of teachers in all third-level institutions and in universities and equivalent institutions in selected European countries for which data was available. It shows the percentage who were female, latest available year. Education at the third level requires as a minimum condition of admission the successful completion of education at the second level or proof of equivalent knowledge or experience. The types of institutions in which third level education may be obtained include universities, teacher-training institutions, and technical institutions.

[NA Not available.]

Country or area	All institutions			Universities and equivalent institutions		
	Year	Teachers	% Female	Year	Teachers	% Female
Europe						
Albania[1]	1990	1,806	28%	1990	1,806	28%
Austria	1991	15,201	25%	1991	13,315[2]	23%[2]
Bulgaria[1]	1990	23,663	40%	1991	20,940	37%
(Former) Czechoslovakia	1991	23,952	29%	1991	23,952	29%
France[3]	NA	NA	NA	1991	50,331	28%
Germany						
Fed. Rep. of	1990	208,881	24%	1990	163,140	20%
former G. Dem. Rep.[11]	1980	38,699	27%	1988	30,921	28%
Greece	1989	13,451	32%	1989	8,104	29%
Holy See	1991	1,584	8%	1991	1,584	8%
Hungary[1]	1991	17,477	32%	1991	13,036	29%
Luxembourg	1985	366	11%	NA	NA	NA
Malta	1990	252	11%	1990	252	11%
Norway	1990	9,504	39%	1990	4,516	21%
Poland[1]	NA	NA	NA	1985	57,280	35%
Portugal[4]	1985	12,476	37%	1985	7,614	32%
Romania[1]	1985	12,961	29%	1985	12,961	29%
Spain	1989	59,135	29%	1989	58,310	29%

[Continued]

★ 592 ★

European University Teachers
[Continued]

Country or area	All institutions			Universities and equivalent institutions		
	Year	Teachers	% Female	Year	Teachers	% Female
Switzerland	NA	NA	NA	1991	7,344	12%
United Kingdom	1990	86,200	21%	1990	36,500	19%
(Former) USSR	1975	317,152	37%	NA	NA	NA
Yugoslavia	1991	11,647	30%	1991	9,617	31%
Yugoslavia SFR	1990	27,042	30%	1990	24,150	30%

Source: Selected from "Education at the third level," United Nations, *Statistical Yearbook 1992*, New York, 1994, Table 13, pp. 91+. Primary source: United Nations Educational, Scientific and Cultural Organization (Paris). *Notes:* 1. Including evening and corresponding courses. 2. Full time only. 3. Public universities only. 4. In 1985, excluding the University of Porto.

★ 593 ★

Occupations

Federal Government Employment Projections

This table shows the percentage of each grade held by women in professional and administrative jobs in the Federal Government in 1990 and projected for 1992-2017.

Year	GS-5	GS-7	GS-9	GS-11	GS-12	GS-13	GS-14	GS-15	SES[1]	Total
1990	55%	55%	54%	44%	31%	22%	16%	13%	11%	34%
1992	54%	53%	55%	46%	33%	24%	18%	14%	12%	35%
1997	54%	54%	55%	48%	36%	29%	24%	19%	16%	38%
2002	54%	54%	55%	49%	39%	32%	28%	24%	20%	39%
2007	54%	54%	56%	49%	40%	34%	32%	28%	24%	41%
2012	54%	54%	56%	49%	40%	36%	34%	31%	27%	42%
2017	54%	54%	56%	49%	41%	36%	35%	34%	30%	42%

Source: "Percentage of each grade held by women in Professional and Administrative jobs, 1990 and Projected 1992-2017," *A Question of Equity: Women and the Glass Ceiling in the Federal Government*, U.S. Merit Systems Protection Board, October 1992, table 2, p. 11. *Note:* 1. Senior Executive Service.

★ 594 ★

Occupations

Federal Government Executive Branch Employment

This table shows the distribution of general schedule and equivalent executive branch employment by grade, race, ethnic origin, and gender, as of September 30, 1990. Women and minorities are underrepresented in the higher grades of the Executive Branch of the Federal Government. These statistics cover more than 9 of 10 Federal civilian non-Postal Executive Branch employees.

Grade level	Percent employed				
	Women	Blacks	Hispanics	Asians & Pac. Isl.	American Ind./ Alask. Natives
Grade 1 through Grade 15 (average)	50.2%	16.5%	5.0%	3.3%	1.7%
Grade 12	29.1%	9.7%	3.7%	3.5%	0.9%
Grade 13	21.8%	7.6%	2.9%	2.9%	0.8%
Grade 14	16.3%	5.7%	2.3%	2.3%	0.7%
Grade 15	13.2%	4.0%	2.3%	4.0%	0.5%
Total Executives	11.1%	4.7%	1.5%	0.9%	0.6%

Source: Linda Levine, *The "Glass Ceiling:" Access of Women and Minorities to Management Positions*, CRS Report for Congress, August 19, 1991, Table 2, p. CRS-11, "Distribution of General Schedule and Equivalent Executive Branch Employment by Grade, Race, Ethnic Origin, and Sex (as of September 30, 1990)." Employment Pattern by Occupation and Earnings by Occupation (Both Sexes), 1991." Primary source: Office of Personnel Management, Central Personnel Data File.

★ 595 ★

Occupations

Federal Government Executive Branch Employment Distribution

This table shows the distribution of white-collar and administrative positions in the Federal Executive Branch by Race, ethnic origin, and gender as of September 30, 1990.

Occupational group	Percent employed				
	Women	Blacks	Hispanics	Asians & Pac. Isl.	American Ind./ Alask. Natives
All white collar	49.7%	15.9%	5.0%	3.2%	1.7%
Administrative	38.3%	12.3%	4.6%	2.1%	1.2%

Source: Linda Levine, *The "Glass Ceiling:" Access of Women and Minorities to Management Positions*, CRS Report for Congress, August 19, 1991, Table 3, CRS-12, "Distribution of White-Collar and Administrative Positions in the Federal Executive Branch by Race, Ethnic Origin, and Sex (as of September 30, 1990)." Employment Pattern by Occupation and Earnings by Occupation (Both Sexes), 1991." Primary source: Office of Personnel Management, Central Personnel Data File.

★ 596 ★

Occupations

Food Service Managers and Supervisors

This table profiles "typical" foodservice and lodging managers compared to supervisors in food-preparation and service occupations.

Occupation	% of Total
Foodservice and lodging managers:	
Male	57%
White	85%
Age 35 or older	53%
Supervisor in food-preparation and service occupations:	
Female	68%
White	85%
Under age 35	90%

Source: Selected from "Foodservice managers and supervisors," National Restaurant Association, *Restaurants USA*, August 1994, p. 41, extracted from the report *Foodservice Employee Profile: 1993. Note:* 1. Persons age 16 and older.

★ 597 ★

Occupations

Food Service Workers

This table profiles women employed in food service occupations in 1993.

Occupation	Women as per-cent of total
All employed persons[1]	46%
Food preparation and service occupations	58%
Supervisors, food-preparation and service occupations	68%
Bartenders	53%
Waiters and waitresses	80%
Cooks	44%
Food-counter, fountain, and related occupations (fast food)	69%
Kitchen workers, food-preparation workers	75%
Waiters/waitresses assistants (buspersons)	44%

[Continued]

★ 597 ★

Food Service Workers
[Continued]

Occupation	Women as per- cent of total
Miscellaneous food-preparation occupations	47%

Source: Selected from "Proportion of Women, African-Americans and Hispanics Employed in Foodservice Occupations, 1993," National Restaurant Association, *Restaurants USA*, August 1994, p. 40, extracted from the report *Foodservice Employee Profile: 1993*. Primary source: U.S. Department of Labor, Bureau of Labor Statistics. *Note:* 1. Persons age 16 and older.

★ 598 ★

Occupations

Latin American/Caribbean University Teachers

This table shows the total number of teachers in all third-level institutions and in universities and equivalent institutions in selected Latin American and Caribbean countries for which data was available. It shows the percentage who were female, latest available year. Education at the third level requires as a minimum condition of admission the successful completion of education at the second level or proof of equivalent knowledge or experience. The types of institutions in which third level education may be obtained include universities, teacher-training institutions, and technical institutions.

[NA Not available.]

Country or area	All institutions			Universities and equivalent institutions		
	Year	Teachers	% Female	Year	Teachers	% Female
Latin America/Caribbean						
Argentina	1985	70,699	46%	1985	44,038	32%
Bahamas	1987	249	48%	NA	NA	NA
Barbados	1980	317	28%	1980	140	23%
Brazil	1991	133,135	38%	1991	133,135	38%
Colombia[2]	1989	51,725	25%	1989	43,248	24%
Cuba	1990	24,668	44%	1990	24,668	44%
Dominica[3]	1991	40	33%	NA	NA	NA
El Salvador	1990	4,216	26%	1990	3,452	26%
Guatemala	1980	4,024	NA	1980	4,024	NA
Guyana	1985	527	23%	1987	390	17%
Haiti	1985	654	37%	1985	479	17%
Jamaica	NA	NA	NA	1985	295	29%
Mexico	1990	134,424	NA	1980	72,742	NA
Nicaragua	1990	2,289	NA	1990	2,180	NA
Panama	1991	3,308	NA	1991	3,308	NA
Peru	1975	11,598	14%	1980	14,384	16%
Saint Kitts and Nevis	1991	38	42%	NA	NA	NA
Saint Lucia	1987	62	34%	NA	NA	NA

[Continued]

★ 598 ★

Latin American/Caribbean University Teachers
[Continued]

Country or area	All institutions			Universities and equivalent institutions		
	Year	Teachers	% Female	Year	Teachers	% Female
Saint Vincent and the Grenadines	1989	96	53%	NA	NA	NA
Virgin Islands	1990	226	41%	1990	226	41%

Source: Selected from "Education at the third level," United Nations, *Statistical Yearbook 1992*, New York, 1994, Table 13, pp. 91+. Primary source: United Nations Educational, Scientific and Cultural Organization (Paris). *Notes:* 1. Full time only. 2. Data include the Open university; teaching posts only. 3. Excluding teacher training.

★ 599 ★

Occupations

North American University Teachers

This table shows the total number of teachers in all third-level institutions and in universities and equivalent institutions in selected North American countries for which data was available. It shows the percentage who were female, latest available year. Education at the third level requires as a minimum condition of admission the successful completion of education at the second level or proof of equivalent knowledge or experience. The types of institutions in which third level education may be obtained include universities, teacher-training institutions, and technical institutions.

[NA Not available.]

Country or area	All institutions			Universities and equivalent institutions		
	Year	Teachers	% Female	Year	Teachers	% Female
North America						
Bermuda	1982	110	36%	NA	NA	NA
Canada	1991	67,122	28%	1991	36,800	21%
United States	1980	395,992[1]	26%[1]	1980	305,982[1]	24%[1]

Source: Selected from "Education at the third level," United Nations, *Statistical Yearbook 1992*, New York, 1994, Table 13, pp. 91+. Primary source: United Nations Educational, Scientific and Cultural Organization (Paris). *Note:* 1. Full time only.

★ 600 ★

Occupations

Occupation of Employed Females by Race/Ethnicity: 1990-II

This table shows the occupations of all employed females 16 years and over, by race and Hispanic origin, as reported in the 1990 census.

[Amer Ind/Esk/Aleut refers to American Indian or Alaskan native.]

Occupation	All persons	Race					Hispanic origin (of any race)	White, not of Hispanic origin
		White	Black	Amer Ind/ Esk/Aleut	Asian or Pac Isl	Other race		
EMPLOYED FEMALES 16 YRS+	52,976,623	43,515,117	6,015,288	340,042	1,590,897	1,515,279	3,669,186	41,499,763
Managerial and professional specialty occupations	14,752,659	12,741,104	1,283,844	73,848	448,538	205,325	623,927	12,348,409
Executive, administrative, and managerial occupations	5,993,163	5,202,033	484,659	31,884	179,835	94,752	278,720	5,028,901
Officials and administrators, public administration	251,316	201,382	38,849	2,820	4,454	3,811	11,588	194,171
Management and related occup.	2,156,867	1,835,280	192,955	10,586	82,290	35,756	103,345	1,771,995
Professional specialty occup.	8,759,496	7,539,071	799,185	41,964	268,703	110,573	345,207	7,319,508
Engineers and natural scientists	551,261	461,596	42,566	1,980	38,787	6,332	21,209	447,566
Engineers	151,962	125,956	11,185	541	12,264	2,016	6,190	121,964
Health diagnosing occupations	171,791	137,721	9,596	423	22,310	1,741	7,727	132,394
Health assessment and treating	2,163,863	1,835,159	188,300	8,654	94,913	18,837	61,812	1,815,016
Teachers, librarians, counselors	3,977,806	3,440,715	392,151	20,144	70,241	54,555	169,075	3,331,338
Teachers, elem. & second. schools	2,946,061	2,541,887	308,959	14,472	38,662	42,081	128,741	2,459,000
Technical, sales, and adminis- trative support occupations	23,120,191	19,454,638	2,330,616	134,493	636,528	563,916	1,434,647	18,638,286
Health technologists & technicians	1,133,078	920,524	148,650	7,017	35,757	21,130	55,644	889,284
Technologists & technicians, exc. health	832,879	688,505	76,882	4,297	48,025	15,170	41,899	663,359
Sales occupaations	6,584,290	5,633,355	551,297	38,479	197,333	163,826	417,587	5,394,135
Supervisors & proprietors, sales occup.	1,155,921	1,025,665	68,822	6,098	35,101	20,235	56,425	991,276
Sales reps, commodities and finance	1,314,555	1,192,130	67,358	4,753	31,043	19,271	59,102	1,154,046
Other sales occupations	4,113,814	3,415,560	415,117	27,628	131,189	124,320	302,060	3,248,813
Cashiers	1,995,673	1,562,480	268,886	16,528	71,840	75,939	171,625	1,473,643
Adminis. support occup., incl. clerical	14,569,944	12,212,254	1,553,787	84,700	355,413	363,790	919,517	11,691,508
Computer equipment operators	394,508	316,845	54,886	2,378	11,366	9,033	23,351	303,446
Secretaries, stenographers, & typists	4,490,363	3,909,921	380,866	24,934	78,838	95,804	250,655	3,764,243
Financial records processing occup.	2,062,414	1,837,858	123,890	10,443	52,787	37,436	102,477	1,776,315
Mail & message distributing occup.	368,423	258,492	83,180	2,288	14,313	10,150	22,607	247,099
Service occupations	8,929,509	6,701,294	1,508,458	79,643	259,244	380,870	863,229	6,254,384
Private household occupations	494,920	296,628	130,525	3,556	12,698	51,513	114,019	238,248
Protective service occupations	310,463	224,472	71,413	2,643	3,923	8,012	20,185	213,290
Police and firefighters	66,355	48,652	14,615	652	699	1,737	4,581	45,958
Service occup, exc. protect. & household	8,124,126	6,180,194	1,306,520	73,444	242,623	321,345	729,025	5,802,846
Food service occupations	3,062,435	2,507,545	325,529	26,436	106,592	96,333	223,035	2,387,604
Cleaning & building svc. occup.	1,278,437	814,051	308,521	13,895	.40,319	101,651	212,298	710,772
Farming, forestry, & fishing	449,506	383,374	21,048	3,740	8,330	33,014	59,747	357,362
Farm operators and managers	149,675	143,343	2,089	772	1,586	1,885	3,646	141,648
Farm workers & related occup.	290,041	232,000	18,074	2,662	6,561	30,744	55,354	208,059
Precision production, craft, and repair occupations	1,235,327	957,420	143,560	10,609	65,307	58,431	128,792	890,922
Mechanics and repairers	175,669	139,398	25,220	1,332	4,492	5,227	11,970	132,964
Construction trades	131,124	110,834	11,938	1,550	2,178	4,624	9,876	105,794
Precision production occupations	923,593	703,036	105,934	7,648	58,598	48,377	106,538	648,197

[Continued]

★ 600 ★

Occupation of Employed Females by Race/Ethnicity: 1990-II

[Continued]

Occupation	All persons	Race					Hispanic origin (of any race)	White, not of Hispanic origin
		White	Black	Amer Ind/ Esk/Aleut	Asian or Pac Isl	Other race		
Operators, fabricators, and laborers	4,489,431	3,277,287	727,762	37,709	172,950	273,723	558,844	3,010,400
Machine operators & tenders, except precision	2,018,059	1,410,339	355,868	15,613	96,039	140,200	283,994	1,276,251
Fabricators, assemblers, inspectors, and samplers	1,082,797	782,067	174,765	9,008	47,664	69,293	140,821	714,412
Transportation occupations	426,426	345,352	63,642	4,650	3,688	9,094	22,356	333,025
Motor vehicle operators	419,603	340,356	62,240	4,538	3,541	8,928	21,943	328,241
Material moving equip. operators	46,995	35,735	8,228	605	507	1,920	4,332	33,544
Handlers, equipment cleaners, helpers, and laborers	915,154	703,794	125,259	7,833	25,052	53,216	107,341	653,168
Construction laborers	36,177	28,614	4,294	497	562	2,210	4,257	26,708
Freight, stock, material hndlrs.	359,459	294,616	41,876	2,819	8,021	12,127	27,511	280,178

Source: Selected from "Occupation of Employed Persons by Race and Hispanic Origin: 1990," U.S. Bureau of the Census, 1990 Census of Population, *Social and Economic Characteristics, United States,* 1990 CP-2-1, Table 45, p. 45.

★ 601 ★

Occupations

Occupation of Employed Persons by Race/Ethnicity: 1990-I

This table shows the occupations of all employed persons 16 years and over, by race and Hispanic origin, as reported in the 1990 census.

[Amer Ind/Esk/Aleut refers to American Indian or Alaskan native.]

Occupation	All persons	Race					Hispanic origin (of any race)	White, not of Hispanic origin
		White	Black	Amer Ind/ Esk/Aleut	Asian or Pac Isl	Other race		
EMPLOYED PERSONS 16 YRS+	115,681,202	96,237,561	11,407,803	728,953	3,411,586	3,895,299	8,981,516	91,447,312
Managerial and professional specialty occupations	30,533,582	26,877,354	2,066,054	133,555	1,045,160	411,459	1,262,178	26,072,188
Executive, administrative, and managerial occupations	14,227,916	12,651,035	875,835	62,825	428,273	209,948	627,693	12,254,816
Officials and administrators, public administration	578,334	484,939	68,142	6,345	10,748	8,160	25,469	468,576
Management and related occup.	4,140,575	3,606,211	303,762	17,191	149,459	63,952	189,088	3,488,813
Professional specialty occup.	16,305,666	14,226,319	1,190,219	70,730	616,887	201,511	634,485	13,817,372
Engineers and natural scientists	3,000,976	2,635,125	126,864	9,274	201,193	28,520	96,970	2,569,523
Engineers	1,672,559	1,475,994	58,041	4,865	117,858	15,801	52,479	1,440,584
Health diagnosing occupations	869,543	754,907	28,401	1,467	77,501	7,267	35,277	728,482
Health assessment and treating	2,482,553	2,124,802	213,393	10,064	110,659	23,635	76,252	2,077,587
Teachers, librarians, counselors	5,713,591	4,963,417	512,599	28,766	131,237	77,572	238,263	4,809,953
Teachers, elem. & second. schools	3,861,446	3,358,038	380,073	19,080	49,959	54,296	165,455	3,251,700
Technical, sales, and administrative support occupations	36,718,398	31,121,238	3,354,120	195,096	1,134,130	913,814	2,321,918	29,799,821
Health technologists & technicians	1,397,189	1,123,408	182,904	8,853	52,383	29,641	77,782	1,079,681
Technologists & technicians, exc. health	2,860,046	2,445,404	190,994	14,113	155,867	53,668	143,367	2,361,025
Sales occupaations	13,634,686	11,984,176	875,576	63,582	400,985	310,367	808,785	11,511,646
Supervisors & proprietors, sales occup.	3,352,054	3,012,184	153,862	13,853	109,710	62,445	172,723	2,907,048

[Continued]

★ 601 ★

Occupation of Employed Persons by Race/Ethnicity: 1990-I
[Continued]

Occupation	All persons	Race					Hispanic origin (of any race)	White, not of Hispanic origin
		White	Black	Amer Ind/ Esk/Aleut	Asian or Pac Isl	Other race		
Sales reps, commodities and finance	3,941,568	3,649,726	151,055	11,351	78,905	50,531	157,289	3,547,155
Other sales occupations	6,341,064	5,322,266	570,659	38,378	212,370	197,391	478,773	5,057,443
Cashiers	2,533,,639	1,976,839	327,343	20,049	105,851	103,557	232,840	1,856,694
Adminis. support occup., incl. clerical	18,826,477	15,568,250	2,104,646	108,548	524,895	520,138	1,291,984	14,847,469
Computer equipment operators	640,982	511,106	86,759	3,554	23,640	15,923	40,615	488,214
Secretaries, stenographers, & typists	4,582,070	3,980,228	393,893	25,649	83,460	98,840	258,327	3,830,459
Financial records processing occup.	2,315,205	2,043,830	147,273	11,484	67,517	45,101	123,119	1,970,166
Mail & message distributing occup.	990,423	715,310	197,530	5,198	41,046	31,339	73,208	677,075
Service occupations	15,295,917	11,354,441	2,522,099	134,744	504,688	779,945	1,719,992	10,481,292
Private household occupations	521,154	312,888	136,283	3,856	14,044	54,083	119,588	251,678
Protective service occupations	1,992,852	1,580,054	312,808	17,198	29,083	53,709	134,930	1,504,544
Police and firefighters	732,609	624,642	78,005	5,930	7,596	16,436	43,644	598,591
Service occup, exc. protect. & household	12,781,911	9,461,499	2,073,008	113,690	461,561	672,153	1,465,474	8,725,070
Food service occupations	5,167,308	3,981,476	609,088	42,233	250,384	284,127	608,350	3,675,719
Cleaning & building svc. occup.	3,127,932	2,113,844	660,057	32,043	86,854	235,134	491,540	1,876,092
Farming, forestry, & fishing	2,839,010	2,370,802	166,079	24,405	40,718	237,006	446,133	2,168,116
Farm operators and managers	1,066,944	1,022,746	16,660	4,255	7,679	15,604	33,300	1,005,516
Farm workers & related occup.	1,590,184	1,194,090	133,366	15,449	30,175	217,104	403,200	1,013,742
Precision production, craft, and repair occupations	13,097,963	11,257,116	930,011	99,782	273,473	537,581	1,177,553	10,648,470
Mechanics and repairers	4,080,305	3,554,246	286,565	27,650	74,673	137,171	315,039	3,385,520
Construction trades	4,793,935	4,174,722	310,992	42,638	56,341	209,242	452,936	3,942,128
Precision production occupations	4,047,043	3,368,249	324,809	27,530	141,794	184,661	395,605	3,168,249
Operators, fabricators, and laborers	17,196,332	13,256,610	2,369,440	141,371	413,417	1,015,494	2,053,742	12,277,425
Machine operators & tenders, except precision	4,981,876	3,706,366	721,735	35,625	169,521	348,629	684,988	3,389,822
Fabricators, assemblers, inspectors, and samplers	2,922,321	2,235,775	382,571	24,645	95,890	183,440	362,199	2,066,445
Transportation occupations	3,760,910	3,030,438	511,246	28,763	50,674	139,789	314,362	2,867,043
Motor vehicle operators	3,580,137	2,870,272	495,739	27,380	49,126	137,620	307,684	2,711,162
Material moving equip. operators	968,091	785,824	120,269	10,715	8,046	43,237	87,111	743,694
Handlers, equipment cleaners, helpers, and laborers	4,563,134	3,498,207	633,619	41,623	89,286	300,399	605,082	3,210,421
Construction laborers	948,540	727,176	116,549	10,986	11,419	82,410	162,235	651,253
Freight, stock, material hndlrs.	1,576,991	1,244,126	221,599	12,327	31,370	67,569	145,346	1,170,890

Source: Selected from "Occupation of Employed Persons by Race and Hispanic Origin: 1990," U.S. Bureau of the Census, 1990 Census of Population, *Social and Economic Characteristics, United States*, 1990 CP-2-1, Table 45, p. 45.

★ 602 ★

Occupations

Occupational Outlook: 1990-2005

This table shows the fastest growing occupations predicted for the years between 1990 and 2005. The three fastest growing major occupational groups are executive, administrative and managerial; professional specialites; and technicians and related support. In 1990 women represented 45% of all workers in these three groups. The three groups are expected to grow by 7.7 million jobs. More and more women are entering these professions each year. Between 1983 and 1990, women accounted for an additional 303,000 accountants and auditors, 132,000 computer systems analysts and scientists, 80,000 financial managers, 56,000 lawyers, 29,000 physicians, and 24,000 electrical and electronic engineers.

[Numbers in thousands.]

Occupation	Employment		Change in Employment	
	1990	2005	Number	Percent
Home health aides	287	550	263	91.7%
Paralegals	90	167	77	85.2%
Systems analysts and computer scientists	463	829	366	78.9%
Personal and home care aides	103	183	79	76.7%
Physical therapists	88	155	67	76.0%
Medical assistants	165	287	122	73.9%
Operations research analysts	57	100	42	73.2%
Human services workers	145	249	103	71.2%
Radiologis technologists and technicians	149	252	103	69.5%
Medical secretaries	232	390	158	68.3%

Source: "The Gastest Growing Occupations, 1990-2005," U.S. Department of Labor Women's Bureau, *Facts on Working Women*, No. 92-1, January 1992, Table 3. Primary source: U.S. Department of Labor, Bureau of Labor Statistics, *Monthly Labor Review*, November 1991.

★ 603 ★

Occupations

Occupations of Hispanic Women: 1992

This table shows the occupations of Hispanic females compared to non-Hispanic females in March 1992. Hispanic females were more likely to be engaged as operators, fabricators, and laborers or in service occupations than non-Hispanic females. Hispanic females were more likely than Hispanic males to be in managerial and professional specialty occupations (16% and 11% respectively) and in technical, sales, and administrative support occupations (40% and 16% respectively).

[Percent of employed females 16 years and over.]

Occupation	Hispanic	Non-Hispanic
Managerial and professional specialty	16.4%	28.2%
Technical, sales, and administrative support	39.6%	44.8%
Service occupations	24.8%	17.0%
Farming, forestry, and fishing	1.7%	0.8%
Precision production, craft, and repair	2.9%	1.9%
Operators, fabricators, and laborers	14.6%	7.2%

Source: "Occupations of Females: March 1992," *Hispanic Americans Today,* U.S. Bureau of the Census, Current Population Reports, P23-183, figure 24, p. 17.

★ 604 ★

Occupations

Oceanian University Teachers

This table shows the total number of teachers in all third-level institutions and in universities and equivalent institutions in selected Oceanian countries for which data was available. It shows the percentage who were female, latest available year. Education at the third level requires as a minimum condition of admission the successful completion of education at the second level or proof of equivalent knowledge or experience. The types of institutions in which third level education may be obtained include universities, teacher-training institutions, and technical institutions.

[NA Not available.]

Country or area	All institutions			Universities and equivalent institutions		
	Year	Teachers	% Female	Year	Teachers	% Female
Oceania						
Australia	1991	28,671[1]	33%[1]	1991	28,671[1]	33%[1]
Cook Islands	1980	41	24%	1980	32	25%
Fiji	1991	277	33%	1991	213	25%
French Polynesia	1980	14	7%	NA	NA	NA
Guam	NA	NA	NA	1988	202	34%
New Caledonia	1980	97	48%	NA	NA	NA
New Zealand[2]	1991	11,291	39%	1991	4,623	24%
Papua New Guinea	1986	902	21%	1986	400	14%
Samoa[3]	1983	37	30%	1983	11	NA
Tonga	NA	NA	NA	1985	17	18%

Source: Selected from "Education at the third level," United Nations, *Statistical Yearbook 1992*, New York, 1994, Table 13, pp. 91+. Primary source: United Nations Educational, Scientific and Cultural Organization (Paris). *Notes:* 1. Full time only. 2. Including correspondence courses. 3. Excluding school of agriculture.

★ 605 ★

Occupations

Physicians: 1970-1992

This table shows the number of doctors of medicine and the number who were women, in thousands, from 1970-1992.

[Numbers in thousands. NA Not available.]

Gender	1970	1980	1985	1988	1989	1990	1992
Doctors of medicine, total	334.0	467.7	552.7	585.6	600.8	615.4	653.1
Female	21.4	44.7	71.9	NA	NA	93.3	107.0

Source: Selected from "Physicians, by Selected Activity: 1970 to 1992," U.S. Bureau of the Census, *Statistical Abstract of the United States 1994*, Table 171, p. 121. Primary source: American Medical Association, Chicago, IL, *Physician Characteristics and Distribution in the U.S.*, annual.

★ 606 ★

Occupations

Physics and Chemistry Teachers: 1989-1990

This table shows what proportion of various high school teacher groups were women acccording to the 1989-90 AIP High School Physics and Chemistry Teacher Survey. Although women make up the majority of all teachers and about half of all high school teachers, they make up less than one-quarter of physics and about one-third of chemistry teachers and high school science teachers.

Item	Women
All primary/secondary teachers	71%
Secondary teachers only	50%
Secondary science teachers only	33%
Chemistry teachers	35%
Physics teachers	22%

Source: Selected from Michael Neuschatz and Lori Alpert, *AIP Report: Physics in the High Schools II*, American Institute of Physics, Pub. No. R-390, April 1994, p. 13, Figure 7, "Proportion of Women Among Various Teacher Groups." Primary source: 1989-90 AIP High School Physics & Chemistry Teacher Survey; State Data on Teacher Supply, Demand, and Qualifications (Council of Chief State School Officers), p. 14.

★ 607 ★

Occupations

Physics Faculty: 1993-1994

This table shows the percent of faculty positions in physics that were held by women by rank held and type of department where employed. Women represented 6% of the physics faculty, up from 3% in 1985. Of the estimated 8,200 physics faculty at all ranks (excluding postdoctorates), about 495 were women. Sixty-six percent of PhD-granting departments had women professors on the faculty, compared to 45% in 1985.

Rank	Type of Department			
	PhD	Masters	Bachelors	Overall
Full	3%	4%	2%	3%
Associate	7%	6%	9%	8%
Assistant	10%	16%	15%	12%
Other ranks	6%	8%	20%	8%
Percent of departments with women at any rank	66%	43%	29%	41%

[Continued]

★ 607 ★

Physics Faculty: 1993-1994
[Continued]

Rank	Type of Department			
	PhD	Masters	Bachelors	Overall
Total number of women faculty	257	54	184	495

Source: Selected from "1993-94 Academic Workforce Report," American Institute of Physics, *AIP Report*, Pub. No. R-392.1, December 1994, table 2, p. 3, "Percent of Faculty Positions in Physics that Were Held by Women, 1993-94."

★ 608 ★

Occupations

Professionals in the Private Sector

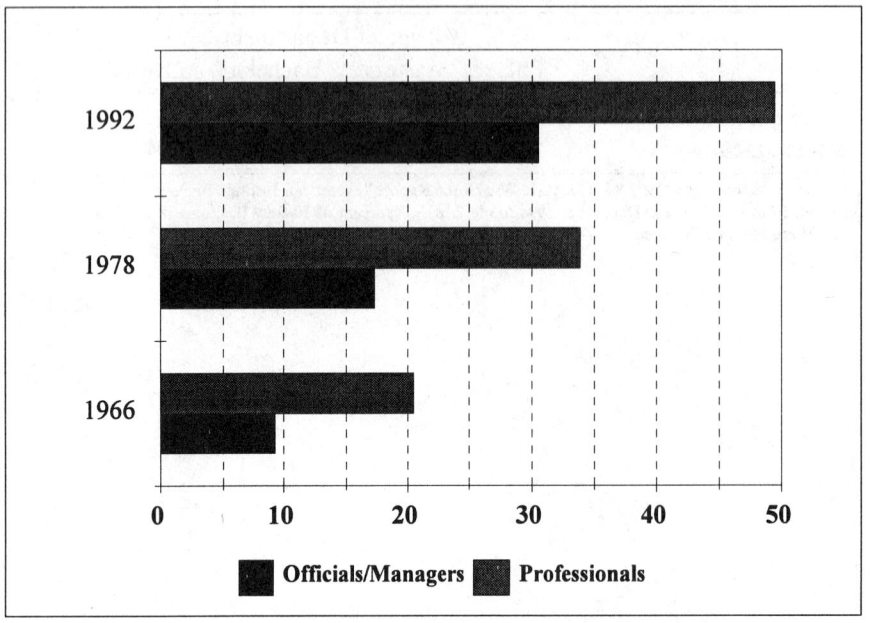

This table shows employment participation rates of women in managerial and professional jobs in the private sector in 1966, 1978, and 1992. Employment in these categories is a critical indicator of equal employment opportunity progress. These are the higher paying jobs with increased advancement opportunities.

Job category	Year	Women
Officials and	1966	9.3%
Managers	1978	17.3%
	1992	30.5%
Professionals	1966	20.5%
	1978	33.9%
	1992	49.4%

Source: Selected from "Private Sector Employment Participation Rates of Whites, Minorities, and Women in Managerial and Professional Jobs, U.S. Summary, 1966, 1978 and 1992," U.S. Equal Employment Opportunity Commission, *Indicators of Equal Employment Opportunity-Status and Trends,* September 1993, p. 14. Primary source: Equal Employment Opportunity Commission, Employer Information (EEO-1) Reports. The "Professionals" job definition was changed in 1967. The participation rates from that year were used to make the rates comparable to the 1978 and 1992 rates.

★ 609 ★

Occupations

Profile of Physics Teachers

This table shows various characteristics of high school physics teachers. Female physics teachers are more prevalent in the South than are male physics teachers. They tend to be younger and have less seniority. This study suggests that younger teachers tend to have a greater attrition rate than teachers further along in their careers. More women than men said they planned to leave teaching prior to retirement.

Item	Female (22%)	Male (78%)
Median base salary	$24,000	$30,000
School type:		
Public	75%	85%
Secular private	5%	5%
Mainstream relig.	18%	7%
Fundamentalist	2%	3%
Region:		
North+West	74%	88%
South	26%	12%
Years teaching high school:		
1-5	29%	16%
6-10	21%	13%
11-20	34%	32%
21+	16%	39%
Of all physics teachers, percent who feel unprepared to teach:		
Basic physics	6%	1%
Recent physics developments	50%	31%
Physics labs	35%	17%
Applications to everyday life	24%	8%
Percent of teachers earning:		
Physics or physics education degree	13%	31%
Any grad. degree	55%	64%
Median age	40	44
Median years teaching physics	5	10

Source: Selected from Michael Neuschatz and Lori Alpert, *AIP Report: Physics in the High Schools II*, American Institute of Physics, Pub. No. R-390, April 1994, p. 14, Table 4, "Gender by Selected Variables."

★ 610 ★

Occupations

Registered Nurses

This table presents statistics about licensed registered nurses.

Item	Number/Percent
Licensed Registered Nurses, March 1992	
Number	2,239,816
Percent actively employed	
in nursing	83%
Full time	69%
Percent who were women	96%
Members of racial or	
ethnic minorities	9%
Age	
Average age, 1992	43.1
Average age at graduation	
from associate degree prog.	29.2
Average age at graduation	
from baccalaureate prog.	24.2
Average age at graduation	
from hospital diploma prog.	22.3
Proportion under 30, 1980	25%
Proportion under 30, 1992	11%
Proportion projected to be	
over age 40 by 2000	66%
Ratio of employed LPNs	
per 100,000 population	726
Physicians per 100,000	255
Practice settings[1]	
Hospitals	1,232,717
Percent	66.7%
Nursing homes	128,983
Percent	7.0%
Community/public health[2]	250,004
Percent	13.5%
Ambulatory care	144,110
percent	7.8%
Nursing education	36,514
Other[3]	56,263
Percent	3.0%

[Continued]

★ 610 ★

Registered Nurses
[Continued]

Item	Number/Percent
Educational background	
Diploma from hospital	
training school	30%
Associate degree	31%
Baccalaureate degree	31%
Master's or doctoral	
in nursing or related field	8%
Income	
Average, full-time RN	$37,738
Average annual increase of	
RNs since 1977	50,000
Advanced Practice	
Nurses, 1992[4]	
Nurse practitioners	
Graduates	1,535
In practice	42,624
Certified nurse-midwives	
Graduates	110
In practice	4,235
Nurse anesthetists	
Graduates	160
In practice	21,776
Clinical nurse specialists	
Graduates	3,321
In practice	50,352
Projections	
Projected increase in number	
of positions, 1992-2005	42%
Projected number of positions	
available for associate degree	
nurses, 2000	848,000
Projected number of associate	
degree nurses, 2000	692,000
Projected number of positions	
available for baccalaureate	
degree nurses, 2000	1,019,000
Projected number of baccalaureate	
degree nurses, 2000	591,000
Percentage of RNs in educational	
programs leading to BSN degree, 1992	61%

[Continued]

★ 610 ★

Registered Nurses
[Continued]

Item	Number/Percent
Projected number of masters- and doctoral-prepared full-time RNs needed by 2000	392,000
Projected supply, 2000	185,000
Projected shortage of primary care physicians by 2020	80,000

Source: Selected from Linda H. Aiken, PhD, Marne E. Gwyther, BA, and Christopher R. Friese, "The Registered Nurse Workforce: Infrastructure for Health Care Reform," *Statistical Bulletin*, Vol 76(1), Jan-Mar 1995, pp. 2-9. *Notes:* 1. Source: *National Sample Survey of Registered Nurses*, Public Health Service, 1994. 2. Includes school and occupational health settings. 3. Includes private duty nursing, insurance companies, and jails. 4. Advanced Practice Nurses are nurse practitioners, nurse midwives, nurse anesthetists, and clinical nurse specialists with post-RN graduate clinical training. They are qualified to conduct health assessments, diagnose and treat a range of common acute and chronic illnesses, and manage normal maternity care among other duties. Nurse-midwives attended about 4% of births in 1992; nurse anesthetists were involved in providing an estimated 65% of all anesthesia services.

★ 611 ★

Occupations

Scientific and Engineering Faculty: 1991

This table shows the total number of persons and women employed as doctoral scientists and engineers in educational institutions in 1991.

Field	Total	Women	% Women
All fields	206,225	42,235	20%
Biological science	44,726	11,652	26%
Environmental science	5,508	692	13%
Computer science	2,494	336	13%
Chemistry	14,834	1,639	11%
Mathematics	12,248	1,063	9%
Physics/Astronomy	14,534	808	6%
Engineering	22,947	936	4%

Source: "Employed Women Doctoral Scientists & Engineers in Educational Institutions, 1991," CPST *Professional Women & Minorities*, 1994. Postdocs are included in all the data, thus the figures cited may overstate the number of women in educational institutions, since women have a higher representation as postdocs.

★612★

Occupations

Secretaries

This table presents statistics on secretaries, as reported in *American Demographics* to mark Secretaries Week. According to the National Restaurant Association, Secretaries Week is one of the ten most common occasions for dining out.

Item	Number/Percent
Number of greeting cards exchanged on Secretaries day, nearly	2 million
Number of secretaries, stenographers, and typists, U.S., 1992	4.2 million
American women working as secretaries, stenographers, or typists, 1992	7%
Median salary, full-time, year-round secretaries, stenographers, typists, 1992	$21,000
Secretaries who work full time	64%
All women with earnings working full time	53%
Results of a survey of Professional Secretaries International members:	
Taken to lunch/dinner on Secretaries Day	77%
Wanted to be taken to lunch/dinner	7%
Frustrated by lack of computer training	50%
Say computer training would benefit them	62%
Used word processing software:	
1992	95%
1987	71%
Used database software	
1992	46%
1987	23%
Used graphics programs	
1992	41%
1987	10%
Desktop publishing part of job	
1992	19%
1987	6%
Have computer at home	45%
Are involved with computer equipment purchases at work	60%

Source: Judith Waldrop, "More than a typist," *American Demographics*, April 1994, p. 4.

★ 613 ★

Occupations

Sisters Teaching in Catholic Schools: 1991 and 1992

Total number of teachers and number of sisters teaching in Catholic educational institutions and programs as of January 1, 1991 and 1992.

Item and year	Number
Teachers in Catholic educational institutions	
1991 Total	162,761
Lay persons	140,635
Priests	3,071
Brothers	1,917
Scholastics	124
Sisters	17,014
1992 Total	164,661
Lay persons	144,354
Priests	2,738
Brothers	1,756
Scholastics	78
Sisters	15,735

Source: Selected from "Summary of School Statistics," *1993 Catholic Almanac*, p. 533, and *1994 Catholic Almanac*, p. 533. Primary sources: *The Official Catholic Directory, 1992*, and *The Official Catholic Directory, 1993*.

★ 614 ★

Occupations

State and Local Government Executive Branch Employment

This table shows full-time employment participation rates of women in state and local government administrative and professional jobs in 1974 and 1991. Employment in these categories is a critical indicator of equal employment opportunity progress. These are the higher paying jobs involving managerial and policy functions and responsibilities.

Job category	Year	Women
Officials and Administrators	1974	18.0%
	1991	30.4%
Professionals	1974	38.4%
	1991	50.4%

Source: Selected from "State and Local Government Full-Time Employment Participation Rates of Whites, Minorities and Women in Administrative and Professional Jobs, U.S. Summary, 1974 and 1991," U.S. Equal Employment Opportunity Commission, *Indicators of Equal Employment Opportunity-Status and Trends*, September 1993, p. 16. Primary source: Equal Employment Opportunity Commission, State and Local Government Information (EEO-4) Reports.

★ 615 ★

Occupations

Teachers: 1978-2003

This table shows the average annual rate of change in the number of elementary and secondary school teachers from 1978-1991 and gives middle alternative projections for 1991 to 2003. The number of classroom teachers in elementary and secondary schools decreased from 2.48 million in 1978 to 2.44 million in 1981. Then the number increased steadily to about 2.79 million in 1991. Under the middle alternative, the number of classroom teachers is projected to increase to 3.35 million by 2003.

Type of school	1978-1985	1985-1991	Projected	
			1991-1997	1997-2003
Total	0.4%	1.5%	1.8%	1.3%
Elementary	1.1%	2.4%	1.4%	1.1%
Secondary	-0.5%	0.2%	2.6%	1.5%
Public	-0.0%	1.6%	1.9%	1.3%
Private	3.4%	0.6%	1.7%	1.2%

Source: "Average annual rate of change (in percent)," National Center for Education Statistics, *Projections of Education Statistics to 2003*, p. 63.

★ 616 ★

Occupations

Tenure Status of Faculty in Higher Education

This table shows the tenure status of women full-time faculty in higher education in academic years 1975-1976 and 1991-1992. Whether faculty has tenure is an indication of how they are viewed by the institutions for which they work. It also indicates the degree of job stability.

Tenure Status	Academic Year	Women
Tenured	1975-76	38.4%
	1991-92	37.1%
Non-Tenured On-Track	1975-76	36.0%
	1991-92	26.6%
Other Non-Tenured	1975-76	25.5%
	1991-92	36.2%

Source: "Tenure Status Full-Time Faculty in Higher Education," U.S. Equal Employment Opportunity Commission, *Indicators of Equal Employment Opportunity-Status and Trends,* September 1993, p. 34. Primary source: Equal Employment Opportunity Commission, Higher Education Staff Information (EEO-6) Reports.

★ 617 ★

Occupations

Wait Staff at America's Best Restaurants

Researchers in a study commissioned by the National Bureau of Economic Research sent men and women with similar, fictitious resumes to apply for waiter/waitress jobs at 65 Philadelphia restaurants. At the "high-end" restaurants, 12 job offers were made—10 of them to men. At the "cheap" restaurants, 9 out of 11 job offers went to women. The researchers estimated that wait staff in the expensive restaurants earned almost $19 per hour in wages and tips, while wait staff in the "cheap" restaurants earned a little over $11. This table shows the ratio of male to female servers at some of America's best restaurants.

Restaurant/ City	Male to Female Ratio
Olives, Boston	3:3
Le Francais, Chicago	9:1
The Riviera, Dallas	8:0
Patina, Los Angeles	4:2
Bouley, New York	28:6

[Continued]

★ 617 ★

Wait Staff at America's Best Restaurants
[Continued]

Restaurant/ City	Male to Female Ratio
Le Bec-Fin, Philadelphia	20:8
Masa's, San Francisco Bay area	8:0
Inn at Little Washington, Washington, D.C. area	11:6

Source: "Waiting for Table Scraps: Restaurants: High class still means men only," *Newsweek,* April 10, 1995, p. 67, table entitled "Big Tab? Bet You'll Tip a Guy."

Chapter 9
THE MILITARY

Operations Desert Storm/Desert Shield

★ 618 ★

Active-Duty and Deployed Personnel by Rank: 1992

This table shows a comparison of total active duty personnel and active duty personnel deployed for Operations Desert Shield and Desert Storm by rank, race, or Hispanic origin, and gender. Among all racial groups, for both officer and enlisted ranks, a smaller percentage of women were deployed than were present among active duty personnel.

Gender, Rank, Race or Origin	Active duty personnel		Active duty deployed personnel	
	Officers	Enlisted	Officers	Enlisted
Women				
White	9.4%	6.2%	5.7%	2.7%
Black	1.6%	3.7%	1.2%	2.5%
Hispanic	0.3%	0.5%	0%	0.2%
Other	0.5%	0.4%	0.3%	0.3%
Men				
White	78.1%	61.2%	81.0%	61.3%
Black	5.5%	19.2%	6.8%	23.5%
Hispanic	1.8%	4.6%	2.1%	5.1%
Other	2.6%	4.0%	2.7%	4.5%

Source: Selected from "Composition of Active Duty and Active Duty Deployed Personnel by Rank, Race or Hispanic Origin, and Gender for the Services Combined," U.S. General Accounting Office, *Operation Desert Storm: Race and Gender Comparison of Deployed Forces with all Active Duty Forces,* June 1992, Table 3, p. 4. Columns may not add to 100% due to rounding.

★ 619 ★

Operations Desert Storm/Desert Shield

Active-Duty and Deployed Personnel: 1992

This table shows a comparison of total active duty forces and forces deployed for Operations Desert Shield and Desert Storm by race and gender. The difference in the proportion of women deployed versus the total active force is attributed to combat exclusion restrictions that reduce the number of women assigned to units and job categories most likely to be included in a hostile deployment.

Characteristic	Total active duty	Deployed active duty
N =	2,038,341	467,159
Race		
Black	21%[1]	24%[1]
Hispanic	5%	5%
Other	4%	5%
White	70%[1]	66%[1]
Total	100%	100%
Gender		
Men	89%	94%
Women	11%	6%
Total[2]	100%	100%
Women		
Black	3%[1]	2%[1]
Hispanic	0%	0%
Other	0%	0%
White	7%[1]	3%[1]

Source: Selected from "Composition of Total Active Duty Personnel and Deployed Active Duty Personnel by Race or Hispanic Origin and by Gender," U.S. General Accounting Office, *Operation Desert Storm: Race and Gender Comparison of Deployed Forces with all Active Duty Forces,* June 1992, Table 1, p. 2. *Notes:* 1. This figure does not include personnel of Hispanic origin. 2. Totals may not add to 100% due to rounding.

★ 620 ★

Operations Desert Storm/Desert Shield

Deployed Personnel - I

This table shows the number and percent of active duty personnel as of February/March 1991 who were deployed for Operations Desert Storm and Desert Shield, by branch of military service, by race or Hispanic origin, and by gender.

Race or Origin, Gender	Services combined	Army	Air Force	Navy	Marine Corps
Total	467,159	246,682	50,571	98,652	71,254
Race					
Black	112,570	74,973	6,569	18,214	12,814
Hispanic	23,206	10,264	1,589	6,227	5,126
Other	21,571	11,134	1,297	6,852	2,288
White	309,812	150,311	41,116	67,359	51,026
Gender					
Women	27,066	19,590	2,978	3,400	1,098
Men	440,093	227,092	47,593	95,252	70,156
Women, Race/ Origin					
Black	10,957	9,325	550	826	256
Hispanic	954	577	72	226	79
Other	1,235	934	85	171	45
White	13,920	8,754	2,271	2,177	718
Percentages					
Race					
Black	24%	30%	13%	18%	18%
Hispanic	5%	4%	3%	6%	7%
Other	5%	5%	3%	7%	3%
White	66%	61%	81%	68%	72%
Gender					
Women	6%	8%	6%	3%	1%
Men	94%	92%	94%	96%	98%
Women, Race/ Origin					
Black	2%	4%	1%	1%	0%
Hispanic	0%	0%	0%	0%	0%

[Continued]

★ 620 ★

Deployed Personnel - I
[Continued]

Race or Origin, Gender	Services combined	Army	Air Force	Navy	Marine Corps
Other	0%	0%	0%	0%	0%
White	3%	3%	4%	2%	1%

Source: Selected from "Composition of Active Duty Deployed Personnel by Race or Hispanic Origin and by Gender (as of February/March 1991)," U.S. General Accounting Office, *Operation Desert Storm: Race and Gender Comparison of Deployed Forces with All Active Duty Forces,*" Tables II.1 and II.2, pp. 14-15. Percentage totals within each subgroup may not add to 100% due to rounding.

★ 621 ★
Operations Desert Storm/Desert Shield

Deployed Personnel - II

This table shows total active duty military personnel and deployed active duty personnel for Operations Desert Shield and Desert Storm in their combat or combat support status, by race or Hispanic origin, and by gender. Combat personnel are those assigned to a combat or combat-related occupation not open to women. Some noncombat positions are included in these Defense Manpower Data Center categories, accounting for the small percentages of women included in the data under the "combat" heading. Combat support personnel are those involved in all other occupations.

Race/Origin, Gender	Active duty forces			Deployed forces		
	Combat	Support	Total	Combat	Support	Total
Total	582,415	1,455,926	2,038,341	226,792	240,367	467,159
Race/Hispanic Origin						
Black	110,543	310,730	421,273	45,698	66,872	112,570
Hispanic	32,167	63,082	95,249	13,405	9,801	23,206
Other	25,186	63,167	88,353	9,992	11,579	21,571
White	414,519	1,018,947	1,433,466	157,697	152,115	309,812
Gender						
Women	7,531	216,462	223,993	1,548	25,518	27,066
Men	574,884	1,239,464	1,814,348	225,244	214,849	440,093
Race/Hispanic Origin, Gender						
Black women	1,960	67,448	69,408	321	10,636	10,957
Black men	108,583	243,282	351,865	45,377	56,236	101,613
Hispanic women	491	8,811	9,302	94	860	954

[Continued]

★ 621 ★

Deployed Personnel - II
[Continued]

Race/Origin, Gender	Active duty forces			Deployed forces		
	Combat	Support	Total	Combat	Support	Total
Hispanic men	31,676	54,271	85,947	13,311	8,941	22,252
Other women	301	8,608	8,909	63	1,172	1,235
Other men	24,885	54,559	79,444	9,929	10,407	20,336
White women	4,779	131,595	136,374	1,070	12,850	13,920
White men	409,740	887,352	1,297,092	156,627	139,265	295,892

Source: Selected from "Composition of Total Active Duty and of Active Duty Deployed Forces in Combat or Combat Support Positions for the Services Combined by Race or Hispanic Origin and by Gender (as of February/March 1991)," U.S. General Accounting Office, *Operation Desert Storm: Race and Gender Comparison of Deployed Forces with All Active Duty Forces,*" Table IV.1, p. 17. Data for black and white personnel do not include personnel of Hispanic origin. Personnel with unknown race are included in total numbers but not in race categories; this may cause the service data by race not to equal the service total.

★ 622 ★

Operations Desert Storm/Desert Shield

Deployed Personnel - III

This table shows total active duty and deployed active duty officer personnel for Operations Desert Shield and Desert Storm in their combat or combat support status, by race or Hispanic origin, and by gender. Combat personnel are those assigned to a combat or combat-related occupation not open to women. Some non-combat positions are included in these Defense Manpower Data Center categories, accounting for the small percentages of women included in the data under the "combat" heading. Combat support personnel are those involved in all other occupations.

Race/Origin, Gender	Active duty officers			Deployed officers		
	Combat	Support	Total	Combat	Support	Total
Total	75,804	219,764	295,568	23,253	25,985	49,238
Race/Hispanic Origin						
Black	4,862	16,105	20,967	1,460	2,475	3,935
Hispanic	1,483	4,742	6,225	517	576	1,093
Other	2,007	7,016	9,023	615	828	1,443
White	67,410	191,204	258,614	20,645	22,010	42,655
Gender						
Women	1,144	33,451	34,595	266	3,319	3,585
Men	74,660	186,313	260,973	22,987	22,666	45,653

[Continued]

★ 622 ★

Deployed Personnel - III
[Continued]

Race/Origin, Gender	Active duty officers			Deployed officers		
	Combat	Support	Total	Combat	Support	Total
Race/Hispanic Origin, Gender						
Black women	146	4,480	4,626	32	545	577
Black men	4,716	11,625	16,341	1,428	1,930	3,358
Hispanic women	29	737	766	6	72	78
Hispanic men	1,454	4,005	5,459	511	504	1,015
Other women	38	1,351	1,389	10	117	127
Other men	1,969	5,665	7,634	605	711	1,316
White women	930	26,794	27,724	218	2,577	2,795
White men	66,480	164,410	230,890	20,427	19,433	39,860

Source: Selected from "Composition of Total Active Duty and of Active Duty Deployed Officer Personnel in Combat or Combat Support Positions for the Services Combined by Race or Hispanic Origin and by Gender (as of February/March 1991)," U.S. General Accounting Office, *Operation Desert Storm: Race and Gender Comparison of Deployed Forces with All Active Duty Forces,*" Table IV.2, p. 19. *R Data for black and white personnel do not include personnel of Hispanic origin. Personnel with unknown race are included in total numbers but not in race categories; this may cause the service data by race not to equal the service total.

★ 623 ★

Operations Desert Storm/Desert Shield

Deployed Personnel - IV

This table shows total active duty and deployed active duty enlisted personnel for Operations Desert Shield and Desert Storm in their combat or combat support status, by race or Hispanic origin, and by gender. Combat personnel are those assigned to a combat or combat-related occupation not open to women. Some non-combat positions are included in these Defense Manpower Data Center categories, accounting for the small percentages of women included in the data under the "combat" heading. Combat support personnel are those involved in all other occupations.

Race/Origin, Gender	Active duty enlisted forces			Deployed enlisted forces		
	Combat	Support	Total	Combat	Support	Total
Total	506,611	1,236,162	1,742,773	203,539	214,385	417,921
Race/Hispanic Origin						
Black	105,681	294,625	400,306	44,238	64,397	108,635
Hispanic	30,684	58,340	89,024	12,888	9,225	22,113
Other	23,043	55,006	78,049	9,339	10,564	19,903
White	347,109	827,743	1,174,852	137,052	130,105	267,157

[Continued]

★ 623 ★

Deployed Personnel - IV
[Continued]

Race/Origin, Gender	Active duty enlisted forces			Deployed enlisted forces		
	Combat	Support	Total	Combat	Support	Total
Gender						
Women	6,387	183,011	189,398	1,282	22,199	23,481
Men	500,224	1,053,151	1,553,375	202,257	192,183	394,440
Race/Hispanic Origin, Gender						
Black women	1,814	62,968	64,782	289	10,091	10,380
Black men	103,867	231,657	335,524	43,949	54,306	98,255
Hispanic women	462	8,074	8,536	88	788	876
Hispanic men	30,222	50,266	80,488	12,800	8,437	21,237
Other women	261	7,095	7,356	53	1,032	1,085
Other men	22,782	47,911	70,693	9,286	9,532	18,818
White women	3,849	104,801	108,650	852	10,273	11,125
White men	343,260	722,942	1,066,202	136,200	119,832	256,032

Source: Selected from "Composition of Total Active Duty and of Active Duty Deployed Enlisted Personnel in Combat or Combat Support Positions for the Services Combined by Race or Hispanic Origin and by Gender (as of February/March 1991)," U.S. General Accounting Office, *Operation Desert Storm: Race and Gender Comparison of Deployed Forces with All Active Duty Forces,*" Table IV.3, p. 21. *R Data for black and white personnel do not include personnel of Hispanic origin. Personnel with unknown race are included in total numbers but not in race categories; this may cause the service data by race not to equal the service total.

Performance

★ 624 ★

Persian Gulf Deployment: Conditions

The authors visited 10 military units, which had both men and women assigned to them, after their return from deployment to the Persian Gulf War. Discussions were held with 47 groups about encampment conditions. The men and women endured the same physical conditions during the deployment. It was found that both women and men preferred more privacy than was available, and that although both women and men considered the wartime stress to be significant, it was not considered to be a gender-based problem.

Housing condition	Percent of 47 groups	Percent of men's groups	Percent of women's groups
No housing for part or all of deployment	30%	35%	24%
Tent for part or all of deployment	91%	92%	90%
Semipermanent structure/ part or all of deployment	43%	42%	43%
Permanent structure for part or all of deployment	30%	38%	19%
Other type for part or all of deployment	4%	4%	5%
Number of types of housing lived in			
One type	19%	19%	19%
Two types	32%	19%	48%
Three types	28%	38%	14%
Four types	13%	15%	9%
Women and men shared housing at least part of deployment	55%	58%	52%
Sharing was temporary	28%	31%	24%
Sharing was not temporary	30%	35%	24%
Sharing caused problems	25%	27%	24%
Sharing did not cause problems	30%	27%	33%

[Continued]

★ 624 ★

Persian Gulf Deployment: Conditions
[Continued]

Housing condition	Percent of 47 groups	Percent of men's groups	Percent of women's groups
Women and men did not share housing during deployment	62%	69%	52%

Source: "Housing Facilities and Conditions Described by the 47 Army, Air Force, and Marine Corps Discussion Groups," U.S. General Accounting Office, *Women in the Military: Deployment in the Persian Gulf War,* July 1993, Table 3.1, p. 31. There was no recorded information for 4 of the 47 groups.

★ 625 ★

Performance

Persian Gulf Deployment: Women's Performance

The authors visited 10 military units, which had both men and women assigned to them, after their return from deployment to the Persian Gulf War. Discussions were held with 63 groups; 59 were included in the data base. Of those, 32 were men's groups, 27 were women's groups, 16 were officer groups, 22 were non-commissioned officer groups, and 21 were enlisted personnel groups. This table shows women's and men's group assessments of women's performance and group participant expectations for women's performance.

Item	No. responding	
	Women's groups	Men's groups
Assessments of women's actual job performance		
Women performed as well as or better than men	15	26
Women did not perform as well as men	6	14
Group patterns of assessments		
All positive assessments	11	13
Both positive and negative assessments	4	13
All negative assessments	2	1
No assessments expressed	10	5

[Continued]

★ 625 ★

Persian Gulf Deployment: Women's Performance
[Continued]

Item	No. responding	
	Women's groups	Men's groups
Expectations for women's performance		
Women should/would perform as well as or better than men	8	12
Women should/would not perform as well as men	9	12
Group patterns of expectations		
All positive expectations	3	6
Both positive and negative expectations	5	6
All negative expectations	4	6
No expectations expressed	15	14

Source: "Group Participant Assessments of Women's Performance," and "Group Participant Expectations for Women's Performance," U.S. General Accounting Office, *Women in the Military: Deployment in the Persian Gulf War,* July 1993, Tables 2.2 and 2.3, p. 21. .

★ 626 ★

Performance

Pilot Training Performance

A study done in 1988 reported that male pilot candidates successfully completed Undergraduate Pilot Training (UPT) at a significantly higher rate than did female pilot candidates.[1] Another study suggested that most of the difference in UPT performance could be attributed to differences on pre-UPT performance indicators. When male and female pilot candidates were matched on their level of pre-UPT performance composites, both sexes commissioned through either Reserve Officer Training School (ROTC) or Officer Training School (OTS) performed equally well in UPT. (Results for Air Force Academy pilot candidates were mixed.) The subjects in the study included 11,625 male and 347 female UPT students who completed pilot training between October 1978 and September 1987. The table presented here is a composite of several tables in that study.

Item	Male	Female
UPT Graduation Percent by Source of Commission:		
Air Force Academy	86.8%	74.6%
ROTC	72.0%	64.9%
Officer Training School	75.7%	63.8%
Total	77.8%	68.6%
Mean UPT Ranking Index by Source of Commission:		
Air Force Academy	84.3	82.7
ROTC	83.6	83.0
Officer Training School	83.9	82.4
Total	83.9	82.8
Mean Scores on Pre-UPT Indicators by Source of Commission:		
Air Force Academy		
AFA Class	450.5	446.9
ROTC		
AFOQT[2] Pilot Composite	71.1	67.1
AFOQT[2] Navigator/ Technical Composite	64.8	64.4
Officer Training School		
AFOQT[2] Pilot Composite	76.5	59.1
AFOQT[2] Navigator/ Technical Composite	71.9	54.7

Source: Thomas R. Carretta, Ph.D., "Gender Differences in USAF Pilot Training Performance," Air Force Human Resources Laboratory Technical Report, 1990, 20 pages. Distributed by Thomas R. Carretta, AFHRL/MOEA, Brooks AFB, TX 78235. *Notes:* 1. Frederick M. Siem and Linda L. Sawin, "Comparison of Male and Female USAF Pilot Candidates," U.S. Air Force Technical Report, distributed by Thomas R. Carretta, AFHRL/MOEA, Brooks AFB, TX 78235. 2. AFOQT=Air Force Officer Qualifying Test.

Personnel

★ 627 ★

Active Duty Forces by Rank: 1990-I

This table shows the distribution of active duty forces by rank, race or Hispanic origin, and gender, for Fiscal Year 1990.

O = Officer; W = Warrant Officer; E = Enlisted

Active Duty Personnel	Race or Hispanic origin				Gender	
	White	Black	Hispanic	Other	Women	Men
O-7 to 11	1,019	33	8	8	8	1,060
O-6	13,231	351	124	267	397	13,576
O-5	30,263	1,083	363	660	1,981	30,388
O-4	47,669	3,367	936	1,256	5,846	47,382
O-3	92,157	8,772	2,446	3,244	14,657	91,962
O-2	32,580	2,988	942	1,366	5,875	32,001
O-1	27,309	2,513	886	1,385	4,856	27,237
Unknown	23	1	0	0	0	24
Total O	244,251	19,108	5,705	8,186	33,620	243,630
W-4	2,685	188	49	55	8	2,969
W-3	4,343	413	105	171	93	4,939
W-2	6,913	922	217	385	339	8,098
W-1	2,653	337	104	96	181	3,009
Unknown	0	0	0	0	0	O
Total W	16,594	1,860	475	707	621	19,015
O/W Total	260,845	20,968	6,180	8,893	34,241	262,645
E-9	11,673	2,442	382	799	186	15,110
E-8	27,925	6,453	1,344	2,337	1,138	36,921
E-7	92,167	27,785	5,934	8,216	7,395	126,707
E-6	157,284	56,690	11,568	13,543	20,465	218,620
E-5	240,211	89,261	16,376	16,025	41,052	320,821
E-4	287,128	103,568	20,103	16,930	56,654	371,075
E-3	190,073	63,232	16,051	10,600	34,111	245,845
E-2	96,052	29,947	8,837	4,977	17,630	122,183
E-1	64,958	21,450	6,625	3,467	10,282	86,218
Unknown	1	0	0	0	0	1

[Continued]

★ 627 ★

Active Duty Forces by Rank: 1990-I
[Continued]

Active Duty Personnel	Race or Hispanic origin				Gender	
	White	Black	Hispanic	Other	Women	Men
Total E	1,167,472	400,828	87,220	76,894	188,913	1,543,501
Total	1,428,317	421,796	93,400	85,787	223,154	1,806,146

Source: Selected from "Composition of Active Duty Forces by Rank, Race, or Hispanic Origin, and Gender for the Services Combined (Fiscal Year 1990)," U.S. General Accounting Office, *Operation Desert Storm: Race and Gender Comparison of Deployed Forces with All Active Duty Forces,"* Table V.1, p. 23. There were no personnel in warrant officer grades for the Air Force. Percentage totals for race/Hispanic origin, gender, and gender by race/Hispanic origin may not add to 100% due to rounding.

★ 628 ★
Personnel

Active Duty Forces by Rank: 1990-II

This table shows the distribution of active duty forces by rank and detailed race or Hispanic origin by gender, for Fiscal Year 1990.

O = Officer; W = Warrant Officer; E = Enlisted

Active Duty Personnel	Men				Women			
	White	Black	Hispanic	Other	White	Black	Hispanic	Other
O-7 to 11	1,013	31	8	8	6	2	0	0
O-6	12,907	331	114	224	324	20	10	43
O-5	28,523	963	339	563	1,740	120	24	97
O-4	42,667	2,789	838	1,088	5,002	578	98	168
O-3	80,579	6,578	2,075	2,730	11,578	2,194	371	514
O-2	27,979	2,103	828	1,091	4,601	885	114	275
O-1	23,501	1,830	773	1,133	3,808	683	113	252
Unknown	23	1	0	0	0	0	0	0
Total O	217,192	14,626	4,975	6,837	27,059	4,482	730	1,349
W-4	2,677	188	49	55	8	0	0	0
W-3	4,264	401	104	170	79	12	1	1
W-2	6,668	850	205	375	245	72	12	10
W-1	2,525	301	94	89	128	36	10	7
Unknown	0	0	0	0	0	0	0	0
Total W	16,134	1,740	452	689	460	120	23	18
O/W Total	233,326	16,366	5,427	7,526	27,519	4,602	753	1,367
E-9	11,531	2,407	375	797	142	35	7	2
E-8	27,085	6,227	1,308	2,301	840	226	36	36
E-7	87,444	25,596	5,706	7,961	4,723	2,189	228	255
E-6	145,732	49,305	10,861	12,722	11,552	7,385	707	821

[Continued]

★ 628 ★

Active Duty Forces by Rank: 1990-II
[Continued]

Active Duty Personnel	Men				Women			
	White	Black	Hispanic	Other	White	Black	Hispanic	Other
E-5	217,487	74,034	14,838	14,462	22,724	15,227	1,538	1,563
E-4	256,051	82,608	17,705	14,711	31,077	20,960	2,398	2,219
E-3	169,877	52,416	14,249	9,303	20,196	10,816	1,802	1,297
E-2	85,018	24,968	7,831	4,366	11,034	4,979	1,006	611
E-1	58,546	18,590	5,983	3,099	6,412	2,860	642	368
Unknown	1	0	0	0	0	0	0	0
Total E	1,058,772	336,151	78,856	69,722	108,700	64,677	8,364	7,171
Total	1,292,098	352,517	84,283	77,248	136,219	69,279	9,117	8,539

Source: Selected from "Composition of Active Duty Forces by Rank, Race, or Hispanic Origin, and Gender for the Services Combined (Fiscal Year 1990)," U.S. General Accounting Office, *Operation Desert Storm: Race and Gender Comparison of Deployed Forces with All Active Duty Forces*," Table V.1, p. 24. There were no personnel in warrant officer grades for the Air Force. Percentage totals for race/Hispanic origin, gender, and gender by race/Hispanic origin may not add to 100% due to rounding.

★ 629 ★

Personnel

Active-Duty Personnel by Branch: 1993

This table shows the distribution of military women by service, the number of women by service, and the percentage of enlisted personnel and officers who are women by service. The Army has the most women, but the Air Force has the highest proportion of women.

Branch	Number/Percent
Army	36.6%
Enlisted	11.2%
Officer	12.1%
Number	78,063
Navy	25.8%
Enlisted	9.7%
Officer	11.3%
Number	55,010
Marine Corps	4.1%
Enlisted	4.7%
Officer	3.5%
Number	8,813
Air Force	33.4%
Enlisted	14.4%
Officer	13.8%

[Continued]

601

★ 629 ★

Active-Duty Personnel by Branch: 1993
[Continued]

Branch	Number/Percent
Number	71,167
Total Military Women	213,053

Source: "Women on Active Duty by Branch of Service," *Military Family Demographics: Profile of the Military Community*, Military Family Resource Center, Arlington, VA, June 1993, p. 6.

★ 630 ★
Personnel

Active-Duty Personnel: 1991

This table shows the composition of active duty military personnel by race or Hispanic origin, by gender, and by branch of service as of February/March 1991.

	Services combined	Army	Air Force	Navy	Marine Corps
Total	2,038,341	740,471	527,609	570,384	199,877
Race					
Black	421,273	212,338	79,887	91,330	37,718
Hispanic	95,249	30,106	18,367	32,913	13,863
Other	88,353	34,230	17,155	30,827	6,141
White	1,433,466	463,797	412,200	415,314	142,155
Gender					
Women	223,993	83,711	74,515	56,435	9,332
Men	1,814,348	656,760	453,094	513,949	190,545
Women, Race/ Origin					
Black	69,408	36,958	16,033	13,778	2,639
Hispanic	9,302	2,485	2,371	3,785	661
Other	8,909	3,968	2,615	1,969	357
White	136,374	40,300	53,496	36,903	5,675
Percentages					
Race					
Black	21%	29%	15%	16%	19%
Hispanic	5%	4%	3%	6%	7%
Other	4%	5%	3%	5%	3%
White	70%	63%	78%	73%	71%

[Continued]

★ 630 ★

Active-Duty Personnel: 1991
[Continued]

	Services combined	Army	Air Force	Navy	Marine Corps
Gender					
Women	11%	11%	14%	10%	5%
Men	89%	89%	86%	90%	95%
Women, Race/ Origin					
Black	3%	5%	3%	2%	1%
Hispanic	0%	0%	0%	1%	0%
Other	0%	0%	0%	0%	0%
White	7%	5%	10%	6%	3%

Source: Selected from "Composition of Active Duty Personnel by Race or Hispanic Origin and by Gender (as of February/March 1991)" U.S. General Accounting Office, *Operation Desert Storm: Race and Gender Comparison of Deployed Forces with all Active Duty Forces,* June 1992, Table I.1, p. 12, and Table I.2, p. 13. Data for black and white personnel do not include personnel of Hispanic origin. Personnel with unknown race are included in total but not in race categories; this may cause the service data by race or Hispanic origin not to equal the service total.

★ 631 ★
Personnel

Occupations of Active Duty Military Personnel

This table shows the primary occupations of active duty women officers and enlisted women.

Occupation	Percent
OFFICERS	
Health care	43%
Administrative	18%
Service and supply	7%
Engineering/maintenance	7%
Intelligence	3%
Scientific/professional	2%
Other	20%
ENLISTED WOMEN	
Functional supply/ administrative	34%
Health care	15%
Communications/ intelligence	11%
Service and supply	10%

[Continued]

★ 631 ★

Occupations of Active Duty Military Personnel
[Continued]

Occupation	Percent
Electrical/mechanical equipment repair	9%
Other	21%

Source: "Primary occupations of active duty women officers" and "Primary occupations of active duty enlisted women," *1993 Handbook on Women Workers: Trends & Issues*, U.S. Department of Labor, Women's Bureau, 1994, Figures 3 and 4, pp. 23-24. Primary source: *Military Women in the Department of Defense*, Volume VIII, July 1990.

★ 632 ★
Personnel

Veteran Status by Race/Ethnicity: 1990

This table shows female civilian veterans according to the 1990 census, by race and Hispanic origin. A civilian veteran is a person 16 years old or over who had served (even for a short time) but is not now serving on active duty in the U.S. Army, Navy, Air Force, Marine Corps, or the Coast Guard, or who served as a Merchant Marine seaman during World War II.

[Amer Ind/Esk/Aleut refers to American Indian or Alaskan native.]

	All persons	Race					Hispanic origin (of any race)	White, not of Hispanic origin
		White	Black	Amer Ind/ Esk/Aleut	Asian or Pac Isl	Other race		
Female civilian veterans	1,151,044	965,525	144,352	12,072	13,549	15,546	43,879	940,072
Percent of civilian females 16 years and over	1.2%	1.2%	1.3%	1.7%	0.5%	0.5%	0.6%	1.2%

Source: Selected from "Geographic Mobility, Commuting, and Veteran Status by Race and Hispanic Origin: 1990," U.S. Bureau of the Census, 1990 Census of Population, *Social and Economic Characteristics, United States*, 1990 CP-2-1, Table 43, p. 43. Persons who served in the National Guard or military Reserves are classified as veterans only if they were ever called or ordered to active duty not counting the 4-6 months for initial training or yearly summer camps.

Sexual Harassment

★ 633 ★

Harassment at the Academy: 1988-1993

This table shows the distribution, by military academy, of the 107 total formally reported sexual misconduct cases that were identified from academic years 1988-1993. The authors had surveyed the 1,415 women at the academies and found that between 93% and 97% of them experienced some form of sexual harassment during academic year 1991. However, only 26 incidents were reported during that period. The incidents that were formally reported tend to be more serious forms of sexual misconduct. It is believed that reported sexual harassment cases represent only a small fraction of the total that actually occur.

Academic year	Naval Academy	Military Academy	Air Force Academy
1988	1	1	3
1989	3	2	10
1990	5	8	10
1991	13	9	5
1992	2	12	6
1993	2	8	7
Total	26	40	41

Source: "Academy Incidents Involving Sexual Misconduct, Academic Years 1988-93," U.S. General Accounting Office, *DOD Service Academies: More Actions Needed to Eliminate Sexual Harassment,* January 1994, Table 2.1, p. 26. At the Naval Academy, sexual misconduct is a specific conduct offense and refers to certain sexually related conduct, both consensual and nonconsensual. A conviction under this conduct offense could result in separation from the Academy. The term "sexual misconduct" is used in a more general sense in this report to include a range of behaviors that could be considered sexual harassment.

★ 634 ★

Sexual Harassment

Harassment at the Academy: 1990-1991

This table shows the percentage of military academy women who responded that they had experienced recurring sexual harassment, by form of harassment included in a General Accounting Office questionnaire, and by type of academy, during the 1990-1991 academic year.

Form of sexual harassment	Naval Academy	Military Academy	Air Force Academy
N = 1,415 Derogatory comments, jokes, nicknames, etc.	28%	63%	40%
Comments that standards have been lowered	33%	64%	38%
Comments that women don't belong	19%	45%	22%
Offensive posters, signs, graffiti, T-shirts, pictures	26%	49%	21%
Mocking gestures, whistles, catcalls, etc.	15%	51%	17%
Derogatory letters or messages	5%	12%	5%
Exclusion from social activities, informal gatherings, etc.	10%	18%	6%
Target of unwanted horseplay or hijinks	6%	16%	13%
Unwanted pressures for dates by a more senior student	4%	4%	4%
Unwanted sexual advances	4%	14%	5%

Source: "Percentage of Academy Women Reporting Having Experienced Sexual Harassment in Academic Year 1990-1991," U.S. General Accounting Office, *DOD Service Academies: More Actions Needed to Eliminate Sexual Harassment*, January 1994, Figure 2.1, Page 21. The 10 forms of harassment were derived from previous surveys of harassment conducted among federal workers by the Merit Systems Protection Board in 1980 and 1987, and a 1988 survey of active duty military personnel conducted by the Defense Manpower Data Center. Items were tailored somewhat to academy environments.

★ 635 ★

Sexual Harassment

Harassment at the Academy: Don't Report It?

Women at military academies tend to deal with sexual harassment informally. This table shows the result of a General Accounting Office questionnaire relating to student perceptions of the negative consequences of reporting sexual harassment. Generally, a higher proportion of women than men saw the negative consequences as likely or extremely likely.

Consequence	Naval Academy		Military Academy		Air Force Academy	
	Men	Women	Men	Women	Men	Women
It is likely or extremely likely...						
The victim would be viewed as a crybaby	63%	76%	83%	88%	73%	85%
The victim would be shunned by others	47%	59%	62%	64%	54%	61%
The victim would be viewed less favorably by student chain	27%	49%	51%	62%	48%	57%
The victim would be viewed less favorably by officer chain	12%	24%	26%	26%	32%	36%
The victim would receive lower military grades	24%	39%	34%	32%	37%	39%
The victim would be subjected to more of the same	17%	40%	36%	44%	30%	50%
Nothing would be done	17%	31%	14%	23%	19%	31%
The incident would be swept under the rug	8%	22%	16%	30%	18%	28%
The victim would receive more watchstanding duty	4%	5%	10%	12%	9%	10%
The victim would be transferred	9%	15%	18%	35%	14%	18%

Source: "Student Perceptions of Negative Consequences of Reporting Sexual Harassment," U.S. General Accounting Office, *DOD Service Academies: More Actions Needed to Eliminate Sexual Harassment,* January 1994, Figure 3.5, p. 37. At the Naval Academy, sexual misconduct is a specific conduct offense and refers to certain sexually related conduct, both consensual and nonconsensual. A conviction under this conduct offense could result in separation from the Academy. The term "sexual misconduct" is used in a more general sense in this report to include a range of behaviors that could be considered sexual harassment.

★ 636 ★
Sexual Harassment

Harassment at the Academy: Report It?

Women at military academies tend to deal with sexual harassment informally. This table shows the result of a General Accounting Office questionnaire relating to student perceptions of positive consequences of reporting sexual harassment. At each of the academies, the majority of women believed it was likely or extremely likely that an incident of harassment reported to the chain of command would be thoroughly investigated and the offender would be appropriately disciplined. Fewer than half the women felt that the victim would receive peer support if she reported an incident.

Consequence	Naval Academy		Military Academy		Air Force Academy	
	Men	Women	Men	Women	Men	Women
It is likely or extremely likely...						
The incident would be thoroughly investigated	73%	64%	67%	68%	64%	55%
The offender would be appropriately disciplined	76%	59%	72%	71%	69%	68%
The victim would be supported by classmates	46%	31%	36%	33%	48%	44%
The victim would be supported by company mates	38%	27%	30%	34%	36%	27%

Source: "Student Perceptions of Positive Consequences of Reporting Sexual Harassment," U.S. General Accounting Office, *DOD Service Academies: More Actions Needed to Eliminate Sexual Harassment,* January 1994, Figure 3.4, p. 35. At the Naval Academy, sexual misconduct is a specific conduct offense and refers to certain sexually related conduct, both consensual and nonconsensual. A conviction under this conduct offense could result in separation from the Academy. The term "sexual misconduct" is used in a more general sense in this report to include a range of behaviors that could be considered sexual harassment.

★ 637 ★

Sexual Harassment

Harassment at the Academy: Resulting Stress

A General Accounting Office survey on sexual harassment indicated that a correlation exists between a student's reported exposure to sexual harassment and higher levels of stress. Higher levels of stress were correlated with decreased interest in staying at the academy and making the military a career. Studies by the Merit Systems Protection Board estimated the annual cost of sexual harassment to be $189 million in 1980 and $267 million in 1988. This table shows responses to a GAO questionnaire inquiring about the relationship between sexual harassment and psychological stress among military academy students.

Amount of harassment	Percent indicating frequent symptoms of psychological stress		
	Naval Academy	Military Academy	Air Force Academy
None	12%	15%	13%
Some	16%	15%	18%
High	40%	27%	42%

Source: "Relationship Between Sexual Harassment and Psychological Stress Among Academy Students," U.S. General Accounting Office, *DOD Service Academies: More Actions Needed to Eliminate Sexual Harassment,* January 1994, Figure 4.1, p. 40. At the Naval Academy, sexual misconduct is a specific conduct offense and refers to certain sexually related conduct, both consensual and nonconsensual. A conviction under this conduct offense could result in separation from the Academy. The term sexual misconduct is used in a more general sense in this report to include a range of behaviors that could be considered sexual harassment.

Chapter 10
POPULATION AND VITAL STATISTICS

Abortions

★ 638 ★

Abortions and Fetal Losses by Age of Woman: 1988

This table shows total number of pregnancies, total number of live births, total number of induced abortions, and total number of fetal losses for 1988, by age of woman. Rates per 1,000 women aged 15 to 44 years are given.

[Numbers in thousands.]

Item	Total	Under 15 years	15 to 19 years	20 to 24 years	25 to 29 years	30 to 34 years	35 to 39 years	40 years old and over
NUMBER								
Total, all pregnancies	6,341	27	988	1,774	1,821	1,195	456	79
Live births	3,910	11	478	1,067	1,239	804	270	41
Induced abortions	1,591	14	393	520	347	197	96	24
Fetal losses	840	3	117	187	234	194	91	14
RATE PER 1,000 WOMEN								
Total, all pregnancies	109.0	3.3	110.8	185.3	166.7	109.7	47.2	9.6
Live births	67.2	1.3	53.6	111.5	113.4	73.7	27.9	5.0
Induced abortions	27.3	1.7	44.0	54.2	31.8	18.1	9.9	3.0
Fetal losses	14.4	0.3	13.2	19.6	21.5	17.8	9.4	1.7
PERCENT DIS-TRIBUTION								
Total, all pregnancies	100.0%	100.0%	100.0%	100.0%	100.0%	100.0%	100.0%	100.0%
Live births	61.7%	39.2%	48.4%	60.2%	68.1%	67.2%	59.1%	51.6%

[Continued]

★ 638 ★

Abortions and Fetal Losses by Age of Woman: 1988

[Continued]

Item	Total	Under 15 years	15 to 19 years	20 to 24 years	25 to 29 years	30 to 34 years	35 to 39 years	40 years old and over
Induced abortions	25.1%	50.5%	39.7%	29.3%	19.1%	16.5%	21.0%	30.9%
Fetal losses	13.3%	10.3%	11.9%	10.6%	12.9%	16.2%	19.9%	17.4%

Source: Selected from "Pregnancies, by Outcome, Age of Woman, and Race: 1988," U.S. Bureau of the Census, *Statistical Abstract of the United States, 1994,* table 109, p. 84. Also in source: data for white women and "other races." Primary sources: U.S. National Center for Health Statistics, *Monthly Vital Statistics Report,* vol. 41, No. 6, Supplement. **Live births:** source of data is statistics of registered births published annually by National Center for Health Statistics. **Induced abortions:** derived from published reports by the Alan Guttmacher Institute. **Fetal losses:** based on the National Survey of Family Growth conducted by NCHS.

★ 639 ★

Abortions

Abortions and Fetal Losses: 1976-1988

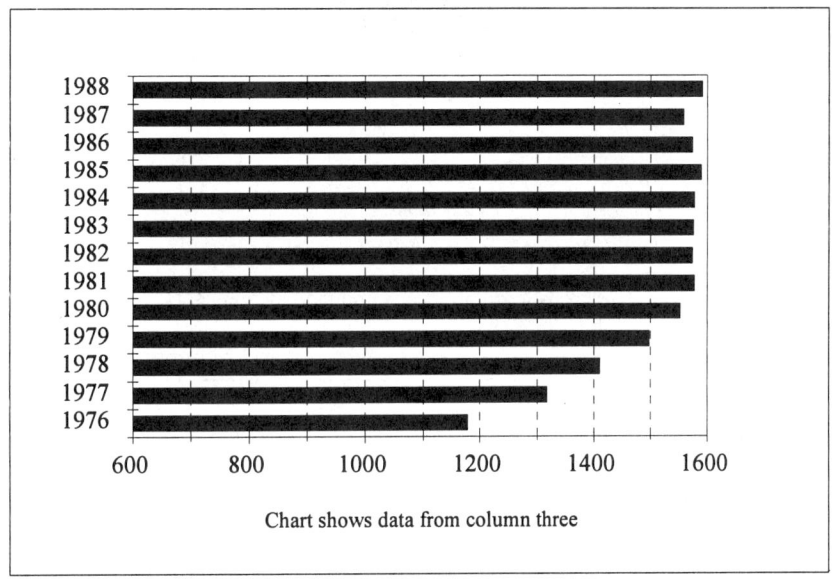

Chart shows data from column three

This table shows total number of pregnancies, total number of live births, total number of induced abortions, and total number of fetal losses for the years 1976 through 1988. Rates per 1,000 women aged 15 to 44 years are given.

[Numbers in thousands.]

Year	Number (1,000)				Rate per 1,000 women, 15 to 44 years old			
	Total	Live births	Induced abortions	Fetal losses	Total	Live births	Induced abortions	Fetal losses
1976	5,002	3,168	1,179	655	102.7	65.0	24.2	13.4
1977	5,331	3,327	1,317	687	107.0	66.8	26.4	13.8
1978	5,433	3,333	1,410	690	106.7	65.5	27.7	13.5
1979	5,714	3,494	1,498	722	109.9	67.2	28.8	13.9

[Continued]

★ 639 ★

Abortions and Fetal Losses: 1976-1988
[Continued]

Year	Number (1,000)				Rate per 1,000 women, 15 to 44 years old			
	Total	Live births	Induced abortions	Fetal losses	Total	Live births	Induced abortions	Fetal losses
1980	5,913	3,612	1,554	747	111.9	68.4	29.4	14.1
1981	5,958	3,629	1,577	751	110.7	67.4	29.3	14.0
1982	6,024	3,681	1,574	769	110.2	67.3	28.8	14.0
1983	5,975	3,639	1,575	761	108.0	65.8	28.5	13.8
1984	6,018	3,669	1,577	771	107.3	65.4	28.1	13.8
1985	6,144	3,761	1,589	795	108.2	66.2	28.0	14.0
1986	6,129	3,757	1,574	798	106.6	65.4	27.4	13.9
1987	6,183	3,809	1,559	815	106.7	65.7	26.9	14.1
1988	6,341	3,910	1,591	840	109.0	67.2	27.3	14.4

Source: "Pregnancies, Number and Outcome: 1976 to 1988," U.S. Bureau of the Census, *Statistical Abstract of the United States, 1994,* table 108, p. 83. Primary sources: U.S. National Center for Health Statistics, *Monthly Vital Statistics Report,* vol. 41, No. 6, Supplement. **Live births:** source of data is statistics of registered births published annually by National Center for Health Statistics. **Induced abortions:** derived from published reports by the Alan Guttmacher Institute. **Fetal losses:** based on the National Survey of Family Growth conducted by NCHS.

★ 640 ★

Abortions

Abortions and Teenagers

This table gives characteristics of abortions obtained by teenagers.

Item	Number
Percent of teen pregnancies that are unintended.	85%
Number of abortions obtained by teenagers, annually.	406,000
Percent of women who became pregnant as teenagers who chose abortion.	41%
Reasons for having an abortion:	
Cannot afford a baby	75%
Not mature enough to have baby	66%
Percent of unmarried teenagers under age 18 who get abortions who have never used birth control	25%

[Continued]

★ 640 ★

Abortions and Teenagers
[Continued]

Item	Number
Percent of minors who have abortions with a parent's knowledge	61%
Number of states that have mandatory parental involvement laws in effect for a minor to obtain an abortion	25
Number of states where mothers who are minors can legally place their child for adoption without parental involvement	46

Source: Facts in Brief: Abortion in the United States, The Alan Guttmacher Institute.

★ 641 ★

Abortions

Abortions by Race: 1975-1992

This table shows total number, rate, and ratio of abortions performed on women 15 to 44 years of age from 1975 to 1992. According to The Alan Guttmacher Institute, more than 50% of pregnancies are unintended, and half of these are terminated by abortion. From 1973 through 1992, more than 28 million legal abortions were carried out. Three out of 100 women aged 15 to 44 have abortions annually. Of these, 43% have had at least one previous abortion, and 49% have had a previous birth. The United States has one of the highest abortion rates among developed countries. U.S. rates of abortion and unintended pregnancy are about 5 times those of the Netherlands.[1].

[Rate per 1,000 women. Ratio per 1,000 live births.[2]]

Year	All Races				White				Black and Other			
	Women 15-44 yrs. (1,000)	Abortions			Women 15-44 yrs. (1,000)	Abortions			Women 15-44 yrs. (1,000)	Abortions		
		Number (1,000)	Rate	Ratio		Number (1,000)	Rate	Ratio		Number (1,000)	Rate	Ratio
1975	47,606	1,034	21.7	331	40,857	701	17.2	276	6,749	333	49.3	565
1978	50,920	1,410	27.7	413	43,427	969	22.3	356	7,493	440	58.7	665
1979	52,016	1,498	28.8	420	44,266	1,062	24.0	373	7,750	435	56.2	625
1980	53,048	1,554	29.3	428	44,942	1,094	24.3	376	8,106	460	56.5	642
1981	53,901	1,577	29.3	430	45,494	1,108	24.3	377	8,407	470	55.9	645
1982	54,679	1,574	28.8	428	46,049	1,095	23.8	373	8,630	479	55.5	646
1983[3]	55,340	1,575	28.5	436	46,506	1,084	23.3	376	8,834	491	55.5	670
1984	56,061	1,577	28.1	423	47,023	1,087	23.1	366	9,038	491	54.3	646
1985	56,754	1,589	28.0	422	47,512	1,076	22.6	360	9,242	513	55.5	659
1986[3]	57,483	1,574	27.4	416	48,010	1,045	21.8	350	9,473	529	55.9	661
1987	57,964	1,559	27.1	405	48,288	1,017	21.1	338	9,676	542	56.0	648
1988	58,192	1,591	27.3	401	48,325	1,026	21.2	333	9,867	565	57.3	638

[Continued]

★ 641 ★

Abortions by Race: 1975-1992
[Continued]

Year	All Races				White				Black and Other			
	Women 15-44 yrs. (1,000)	Abortions			Women 15-44 yrs. (1,000)	Abortions			Women 15-44 yrs. (1,000)	Abortions		
		Number (1,000)	Rate	Ratio		Number (1,000)	Rate	Ratio		Number (1,000)	Rate	Ratio
1989[3]	58,365	1,557	26.8	380	48,104	1,006	20.9	309	10,261	561	54.7	650
1990[3]	58,700	1,609	27.4	389	48,224	1,039	21.5	318	10,746	570	54.4	655
1991	59,076	1,557	26.3	378	NA	NA	NA	NA	NA	NA	NA	NA
1992	59,008	1,529	25.9	379	NA	NA	NA	NA	NA	NA	NA	NA

Source: "Abortions—Number, Rate, and Ratio, by Race: 1975 to 1992," U.S. Bureau of the Census, *Statistical Abstract of the United States, 1994*, table 111, p. 85. *R Primary sources: S.K. Henshaw and J. Van Vort, eds., *Abortion Factbook 1992 Edition: Readings, Trends, and State and Local Data to 1988*. The Alan Guttmacher Institute, New York, NY 1992; S.K. Henshaw and J. Van Vort, *Abortion Services in the United States, 1991 and 1992: Family Perspectives*, 26:100, 1994; and unpublished data. *Notes:* 1. *Facts in Brief: Abortion in the United States*, The Alan Guttmacher Institute. 2. Live births are those which occurred from July 1 of year shown through June 30 of the following year (to match time of conception with abortions.) Births are classified by race of child 1972-1988, and by race of mother after 1988. 3. Total numbers of abortions in 1983 and 1986 have been estimated by interpolation; 1989 and 1990 have been estimated using trends in CDC data.

★ 642 ★
Abortions

Abortions Worldwide

This table presents some statistics about abortion around the world.

Item	Number/Percent
Brazil Estimated number of abortions performed annually	4 million
Estimated amount of Brazil's Health Ministry budget for obstetrics departments that goes toward treating complications from "botched" abortions	25%
Number of hospitals in Sao Paulo that perform authorized abortions, despite the fact that nearly 15% of the 14,000 11- to 14-year-olds who become pregnant each year have been raped:	1
England and Wales	
Number of abortions performed in 1990	186,912

[Continued]

★ 642 ★

Abortions Worldwide
[Continued]

Item	Number/Percent
China	
Official number of abortions performed annually	10 million
Romania	
Number of babies terminated for every baby born, Europe's highest ratio of abortions to live births:	3
Number of abortions performed in 1991:	884,000
Estimated number of Romanian women thought to be infertile because of "botched" abortions:	1 million
Number of centers offering contraceptives:	118
Number of women seen in contraceptive centers in 1991:	146,000
Russia	
Number of abortions performed annually	> 4 million
South Africa	
Abortion requires that one doctor suggest an abortion and two others concur in writing. Percent of abortion applications that are successful:	40%
Number of legal abortions performed each year:	800-1,000
For psychiatric reasons:	77%
Turkey	
Estimate of number of abortions performed annually:	500,000
Performed in state hospitals:	20%
Cost of a state abortion	$10
Cost of a private abortion	About $100

Source: Selected from Jan Rocha et al., "A World of Conflict Over Abortion," *World Press Review*, October 1992, pp. 22-24.

★ 643 ★
Abortions

Abortions, Characteristics: 1980-1990

This table shows total abortions in thousands, percent distribution, and ratio (number of abortions per 1,000 abortions and live births). Most women obtaining abortions are young; women aged 18-19 have the highest rate. The proportion of pregnancies terminated by abortion is higher among unmarried women, women aged 40 and older, teenagers, and nonwhite women. Poor women are about 3 times more likely to have abortions. White women account for 65% of all abortions, but the nonwhite abortion rate is more than twice the white rate (57 vs. 21 per 1,000). Hispanic women are 60% more likely than non-Hispanic women to have abortions. Women who report no religious affiliation have a higher rate of abortion than do women who report some affiliation. Catholic women are about as likely to obtain an abortion as are all women nationally, while Protestants and Jews are less likely. One in 6 abortion patients in 1987 described herself as a born-again or Evangelical Christian—they are half as likely as other women to obtain an abortion. Seventy percent of women having an abortion say they intend to have children in the future. Reasons for having an abortion include: having a baby would interfere with work, school, or other responsibilities; cannot afford a child; or non-desire to be a single parent or problems in relationship with partner or husband. Among women having abortions, 1% have been advised that the fetus has a defect and another 12% fear that the fetus may have been harmed by medications or other conditions. About 16,000 women have abortions each year because they are pregnant as a result of rape or incest.[1].

Characteristic	Number (1,000)			Percent Distribution			Abortion Ratio[2]		
	1980	1985	1990[2]	1980	1985	1990[2]	1980	1985	1990[2]
Total abortions	1,554	1,589	1,609	100%	100%	100%	300	297	280
Age of woman									
Less than 15 years	15	17	13	1%	1%	1%	607	624	515
15 to 19 years old	445	399	351	29%	25%	22%	451	462	403
20 to 24 years old	549	548	532	35%	35%	33%	310	328	328
25 to 29 years old	304	336	360	20%	21%	22%	213	219	224
30 to 34 years old	153	181	216	10%	11%	13%	213	203	196
35 to 39 years old	67	87	108	4%	5%	7%	317	280	249
40 years and over	21	21	29	1%	1%	2%	461	409	354
Race of woman									
White	1,094	1,076	1,039	70%	68%	65%	274	265	241
Black and other	460	513	570	30%	32%	35%	392	397	396
Marital status of woman									
Married	320	281	284	21%	18%	18%	98	88	88
Unmarried	1,234	1,307	1,325	79%	82%	82%	649	605	527
Number of prior live births									
None	900	872	780	58%	55%	49%	365	358	316
One	305	349	396	20%	22%	25%	208	219	230
Two	216	240	280	14%	15%	17%	283	288	292

[Continued]

★ 643 ★

Abortions, Characteristics: 1980-1990
[Continued]

Characteristic	Number (1,000)			Percent Distribution			Abortion Ratio[2]		
	1980	1985	1990[2]	1980	1985	1990[2]	1980	1985	1990[2]
Three	83	85	102	5%	5%	6%	288	281	279
Four or more	51	43	50	3%	3%	3%	251	230	223

Source: Selected from "Abortions, by Selected Characteristics: 1980 to 1990," U.S. Bureau of the Census, *Statistical Abstract of the United States, 1994,* table 112, p. 85. Primary sources: Characteristics, U.S. Centers for Disease Control abortion surveillance summaries, with adjustments for changes in States reporting data to the CDC each year. Numbers, S.K. Henshaw and J. Van Vort, eds., *Abortion Factbook 1992 Edition: Readings, Trends, and State and Local Data to 1988.* The Alan Guttmacher Institute, New York, NY 1992; S.K. Henshaw and J. Van Vort, *Abortion Services in the United States, 1991 and 1992: Family Perspectives,* 26:100, 1994; and unpublished data. *Notes: 1. Facts in Brief: Abortion in the United States,* The Alan Guttmacher Institute. 2. Number of abortions per 1,000 abortions and live births. Live births are those which occurred from July 1 of year shown through June 30 of the following year (to match time of conception with abortions.) 3. Beginning 1985, data not exactly comparable with prior years because of a change in the method of calculation.

★ 644 ★

Abortions

Abortions, Locations

This table answers questions about where women have abortions.

[Rate per 1,000 women aged 15-44.]

Item	Number
Percent of abortions taking place in clinics or doctors' offices	93%
1989 cost of a first-trimester nonhospital abortion, range	$95-$1,000+
Number of abortion providers 1988	2,582
1992	2,380
Percent of U.S. counties lacking abortion providers	84%
Percent of women aged 15-44 who live in those counties	30%
Percent of abortions taking place outside of metropolitan areas	< 2%
Percent of abortion facilities providing services to women after the 12th week of pregnancy	43%

[Continued]

★ 644 ★

Abortions, Locations
[Continued]

Item	Number
States with the highest abortion rates, and rate, 1992:	
Hawaii	46
New York	46
Nevada	44
California	42
Delaware	35
District of Columbia	138
States with the lowest abortion rates, and rate, 1992:	
Utah	9
West Virginia	8
South Dakota	7
Idaho	7
Wyoming	4

Source: *Facts in Brief: Abortion in the United States*, The Alan Guttmacher Institute.

★ 645 ★
Abortions

Abortions, Risks

This table presents data on abortion risks.

[Rate per 1,000 women aged 15-44.]

Item	Number
Risk of complications	< 1%
Number of times higher is the risk of death from childbirth compared to that associated with abortion	11
Number of deaths linked to abortions increases with length of pregnancy.	
Deaths for every 5,000 abortions at 8 weeks or less:	1
Deaths for every 30,000 abortions at 16-20 weeks	1

[Continued]

★ 645 ★

Abortions, Risks
[Continued]

Item	Number
Deaths per 8,000 abortions at 21 or more weeks	1
Deaths per 100,000 legal abortions:	
1973	3.4
1987	0.4

Source: Facts in Brief: Abortion in the United States, The Alan Guttmacher Institute.

★ 646 ★

Abortions

Fewest Legally Induced Abortions Worldwide

This table shows the number of legal abortions per 1,000 live births in the 10 countries with the lowest number of legally induced abortions in 1988. In 1988 abortion was legal in 61 countries, but many abortions are performed illegally.

[Legal abortions per 1,000 live births.]

Country	Abortions per 1000 live birth
Seychelles	12.7
Hong Kong	12.0
Netherlands	11.5
Bermuda	11.0
Tunisia	9.5
Guadeloupe	8.7
Faeroe Islands	3.3
India	2.0
Chile	1.0
Greece	0.2

Source: Selected from George Kurian, *The New Book of World Rankings*, Facts on File, Inc., New York, 1991, pp. 30-31, table entitled "Legally Induced Abortions." Primary Source: Population Council.

★ 647 ★

Abortions

Most Legally Induced Abortions Worldwide

This table shows the number of legal abortions per 1,000 live births in the 10
countries with the highest number of legally induced abortions in 1988. In
1988 abortion was legal in 61 countries, but many abortions are performed
illegally. The six leading countries are communist.

[Legal abortions per 1,000 live births.]

Country	Abortions per 1000 live birth
Soviet Union	230.0
Bulgaria	107.2
Rumania	99.0
Yugoslavia	74.0
Cuba	70.8
Hungary	65.6
Czechoslovakia	52.8
Greenland	51.3
Singapore	47.1
United States	42.8

Source: Selected from George Kurian, *The New Book of World Rankings*, Facts on File, Inc., New
York, 1991, pp. 30-31, table entitled "Legally Induced Abortions." Primary Source: Population
Council.

★ 648 ★

Abortions

Legally Induced Abortions in Africa

This table shows the number of legally induced abortions performed in
Africa, the latest available year.

Country or area	Year	Number
Africa		
Botswana	1984	17
Reunion	1988	4,302
St. Helena		
excluding dependents	1990	5
Seychelles	1986	9
Tunisia	1988	23,300

Source: Selected from "Legally induced abortions, 1982-1990," United Nations, *Demographic
Yearbook*, 1991, Table 13, pp. 323-24.

★ 649 ★

Abortions

Legally Induced Abortions in Africa by Age of Woman

This table shows the number of legally induced abortions performed in two African countries by age of woman and number of previous live births of woman, latest available year.

Country or area/ year/no. previous live births	Age of woman								
	All ages	-15	15-19	20-24	25-29	30-34	35-39	40-44	Unknown
Africa									
Reunion, 1987[1]									
Total	4,140	22	574	1,303	955	683	451	134	1
0	2,931	21	513	996	613	418	270	89	--
1	939	1	49	247	268	197	138	35	--
2	133	--	3	27	40	31	25	6	--
3	28	--	--	7	4	10	5	2	--
4	3	--	--	--	1	1	1	--	--
5 plus	1	--	--	--	1	--	--	--	--
Unknown	105	--	9	26	28	26	12	2	1
Seychelles, 1985[2]									
Total	188	1	24	58	61	25	14	4	--

Source: Selected from "Legally induced abortions by age and number of previous live births of woman, latest available year," United Nations, *Demographic Yearbook*, 1991, Table 14, pp. 325-329. Numbers may not add to total because figures for 45+ are not included. *Notes:* 1. For residents only. 2. Including spontaneous abortions.

★ 650 ★

Abortions

Legally Induced Abortions in Asia

This table shows the number of legally induced abortions performed in Asia, the latest available year.

Country/Area	Year	Number
Asia		
Hong Kong	1987	17,600
India[1-6]	1990	596,345
Israel[7]	1989	15,918

[Continued]

621

★ 650 ★

Legally Induced Abortions in Asia
[Continued]

Country/Area	Year	Number
Japan[8]	1990	456,797
Singapore[1-5]	1987	21,226

Source: Selected from "Legally induced abortions, 1982-1990," United Nations, *Demographic Yearbook*, 1991, Table 13, pp. 323-24. *Notes:* 1. Continuance of pregnancy would involve risk to the life of the pregnant woman greater than if the pregnancy were terminated. 2. Continuance of pregnancy would involve risk of injury to the physical health of the pregnant woman greater than if the pregnancy were terminated. 3. Continuance of pregnancy would involve risk of injury to the mental health of the pregnant woman greater than if the pregnancy were terminated. 4. Continuance of pregnancy would involve risk of injury to mental or physical health of any existing children of the family greater than if the pregnancy were terminated. 5. There is a substantial risk that if the child were born it would suffer from such physical or mental abnormalities as to be seriously handicapped. 6. For year ending 31 March. 7. Including data for East Jerusalem and Israeli residents in certain other territories under occupation by Israeli military forces since June 1967. 8. For Japanese nationals in Japan only.

★ 651 ★
Abortions

Legally Induced Abortions in Asia by Age of Woman

This table shows the number of legally induced abortions performed in India, Israel, Japan, and Singapore by age of woman and number of previous live births to woman, latest available year.

Country or area/ year/no. previous live births	Age of woman								
	All ages	-15	15-19	20-24	25-29	30-34	35-39	40-50+	Unknown
Asia									
India, 1990[1]									
Total	596,345	2,599	41,846	131,540	167,718	102,747	43,974	7,977	97,944
Israel, 1989[2]									
Total	15,918	31	1,800	3,006	2,958	3,158	2,901	1,650	414
0	5,914	31	1,741	2,204	1,046	448	203	83	158
1	1,417	--	46	396	463	299	138	54	21
2	3,084	--	10	319	854	874	606	346	75
3	3,112	--	2	66	421	958	1,052	541	72
4	1,437	--	1	17	126	376	532	336	49
5 plus	954	--	--	4	48	203	370	290	39
Japan, 1990[3]									
Total	456,797	32,431[4]	[4]	86,367	79,205	98,232	101,705	58,735	122
Singapore, 1987									
Total	21,226	18	1,797	5,658	5,882	4,503	2,555	813	--
0	8,610	18	1,676	4,032	2,137	569	153	25	--
1	3,463	--	94	947	1,397	742	235	48	--
2	5,864	--	24	565	1,759	2,093	1,136	287	--

[Continued]

★ 651 ★

Legally Induced Abortions in Asia by Age of Woman
[Continued]

Country or area/ year/no. previous live births	Age of woman								
	All ages	-15	15-19	20-24	25-29	30-34	35-39	40-50+	Unknown
3	2,384	--	3	100	492	852	703	234	--
4 plus	905	--	--	14	97	247	328	219	--

Source: Selected from "Legally induced abortions by age and number of previous live births of woman, latest available year," United Nations, *Demographic Yearbook*, 1991, Table 14, pp. 325-329. *Notes:* 1. For year ending 31 March. 2. Birth order based on number of previous confinements (deliveries) rather than on live births. 3. For Japanese nationals in Japan only 4. 32,431 total aged under 15-19.

★ 652 ★

Abortions

Legally Induced Abortions in Europe

This table shows the number of legally induced abortions performed in Europe, the latest available year.

Country/Area	Year	Number
Europe		
Channel Islands		
Jersey	1988	313
Belarus	1988	140,900
Bulgaria	1990	144,644
Czechoslovakia[1,2,3,4]	1990	159,705
Denmark[1,2,3,4,5,]	1989	21,456
Estonia	1990	21,404
Finland[1,2,3,5,6]	1989	12,658
France[1,2,3,5]	1990	161,646
Greece[1,2,3,5,6]		
Hungary[1,2,3,4,5,]	1990	90,394
Iceland[1,2,3,5,6]	1990	714
Italy	1989	165,456
Lithuania	1990	27,504
Netherlands[1,2,3,5,6]	1985	17,300
Norway[1,2,3,4,5,]	1990	15,551
Poland[1,2,3,5,6]	1990	59,417
Sweden[1,2,3,4,5]	1990	37,489

[Continued]

★ 652 ★

Legally Induced Abortions in Europe

[Continued]

Country/Area	Year	Number
Ukraine	1988	1,080,000
United Kingdom[1,2,3,4,5,]	1990	184,092

Source: Selected from "Legally induced abortions, 1982-1990," United Nations, *Demographic Yearbook*, 1991, Table 13, pp. 323-24. *Notes:* 1. Continuance of pregnancy would involve risk to the life of the pregnant woman greater than if the pregnancy were terminated. 2. Continuance of pregnancy would involve risk of injury to the physical health of the pregnant woman greater than if the pregnancy were terminated. 3. Continuance of pregnancy would involve risk of injury to the mental health of the pregnant woman greater than if the pregnancy were terminated. 4. Continuance of pregnancy would involve risk of injury to mental or physical health of any existing children of the family greater than if the pregnancy were terminated. 5. There is a substantial risk that if the child were born it would suffer from such physical or mental abnormalities as to be seriously handicapped. 6. Other. 7. Excluding the Faeroe Islands and Greenland. 8. Based on hospital and polyclinic records. 9. For residents only.

★ 653 ★

Abortions

Legally Induced Abortions in Europe by Age of Woman

This table shows the number of legally induced abortions performed in selected European countries by age of woman and number of previous live births to woman, latest available year.

Country or area/ year/no. previous live births	Age of woman										
	All ages	-15	15-19	20-24	25-29	30-34	35-39	40-44	45-49	50 plus	Unknown
Europe											
Bulgaria, 1990											
Total	144,644	316	14,028	37,899	39,108	30,230	16,998	5,536	506	23	--
Czechoslovakia, 1990											
Total	159,705	85	13,388	36,927	41,207	33,660	25,343	8,475	595	25	--
0	22,340	85	10,157	8,328	2,270	845	467	151	34	3	--
1	33,206	--	2,897	14,531	8,438	3,929	2,531	801	71	8	--
2	75,556	--	316	12,381	24,148	19,802	14,096	4,500	307	6	--
3	22,945	--	18	1,444	5,264	7,288	6,416	2,367	143	5	--
4 plus	5,658	--	--	243	1,087	1,796	1,833	656	40	3	--
Finland, 1989[1]											
Total	12,658	24	2,146	3,342	2,478	1,796	1,620	1,106	146	2	--
0	6,423	24	2,042	2,507	1,188	373	195	89	5	2	--
1	2,196	--	82	567	546	429	329	218	25	2	--
2	2,485	--	4	206	544	609	644	428	50	2	--
3	1,120	--	1	29	156	300	333	263	38	2	--
4	289	--	--	3	21	70	93	81	21	2	--
5	67	--	--	1	1	12	23	25	5	2	--
6 plus	8	--	--	--	--	1	3	2	2	2	--
Unknown	70	--	17	29	22	2	--	--	--	--	--

[Continued]

★ 653 ★

Legally Induced Abortions in Europe by Age of Woman
[Continued]

Country or area/ year/no. previous live births	All ages	-15	15-19	20-24	25-29	30-34	35-39	40-44	45-49	50 plus	Unknown
France, 1990											
Total	161,646	16,389	2	37,301	39,287	33,115	24,033	9,902	904	50	665
Germany											
Fed. Rep. of, 1990											
Total	78,808	105	5,004	17,440	21,488	16,781	11,585	5,302	650	79	374
0	41,750	103	4,573	12,879	11,978	6,745	3,585	1,461	180	24	222
1	13,966	1	348	2,848	4,204	3,197	2,214	979	104	13	58
2	14,776	1	74	1,359	3,718	4,370	3,431	1,565	182	20	56
3	5,696	--	9	294	1,188	1,752	1,539	788	94	9	23
4	1,686	--	--	45	306	477	514	275	50	9	10
5	581	--	--	6	75	166	180	128	22	2	2
6 plus	353	--	--	9	19	74	122	106	18	2	3
Greece, 1985											
Total	180	--	16	92	69	3	--	--	--	--	--
Hungary, 1990											
Total	90,394	382	11,629	17,245	16,367	18,714	14,586	6,283	493	2	1,695
0	20,686	382	9,259	7,002	1,793	737	554	190	53	2	716
1	17,576	--	1,886	5,185	3,645	2,887	2,644	983	75	2	271
2	34,719	--	423	3,707	7,350	9,873	9,350	3,345	236	2	435
3	12,185	--	52	1,063	2,558	3,537	3,522	1,222	87	2	144
4	3,173	--	4	218	657	1,014	903	307	23	2	47
5	1,052	--	1	37	203	372	310	109	6	2	14
6 plus	992	--	4	33	160	294	303	127	13	2	58
Unknown	11	--	--	--	1	--	--	--	--	--	10
Iceland, 1990											
Total	714	2	161	194	120	107	89	36	5	--	--
0	294	2	150	102	28	7	4	1	--	--	--
1	179	--	10	77	47	30	12	3	--	--	--
2	119	--	1	12	33	36	23	11	3	--	--
3	82	--	--	3	9	23	35	10	2	--	--
4	31	--	--	--	2	8	10	11	--	--	--
5	7	--	--	--	1	3	3	--	--	--	--
6 plus	2	--	--	--	--	--	2	--	--	--	--
Italy, 1988											
Total	175,541	99	12,671	35,946	39,415	37,843	31,598	15,682	1,513	103	671
0	56,962	91	10,827	22,673	13,218	5,945	2,814	1,053	103	12	226
1	32,888	2	1,168	7,287	9,367	7,635	5,042	2,081	167	20	119
2	52,293	--	282	4,338	12,056	15,448	13,159	6,211	524	44	195
3	20,950	--	34	712	3,372	6,109	6,643	3,601	392	14	73
4	6,361	--	10	95	621	1,628	2,310	1,486	176	9	26

[Continued]

★ 653 ★

Legally Induced Abortions in Europe by Age of Woman
[Continued]

Country or area/ year/no. previous live births	All ages	-15	15-19	20-24	25-29	30-34	35-39	40-44	45-49	50 plus	Unknown
5	2,110	--	1	15	149	454	802	613	68	1	7
6 plus	1,473	--	1	13	68	249	549	512	70	3	8
Unknown	2,504	6	348	813	564	375	243	125	13	--	17
Lithuania, 1991											
Total	26,598	16	1,573	20,323	[2]	[2]	4,686	[2]	[2]	[2]	--
Netherlands, 1985											
Total	17,300	35	2,715	4,510	3,870	3,040	2,315	710	105	[2]	--
Norway, 1990											
Total	15,551	28	3,069	4,710	3,426	2,213	1,489	553	63	[2]	--
Sweden, 1990											
Total	37,489	204	6,587	9,822	8,066	5,733	4,461	2,355	261	--	--
0	15,729	173	5,526	5,994	2,697	916	305	107	11	--	--
1	6,229	2	281	1,840	1,846	1,132	735	361	32	--	--
2	7,637	--	22	635	1,922	2,059	1,873	1,008	118	--	--
3	3,404	1	2	89	606	1,002	1,070	577	57	--	--
4	925	--	--	17	142	285	263	192	26	--	--
5	207	--	--	2	17	55	81	46	6	--	--
6 plus	95	--	--	--	6	24	30	30	5	--	--
Unknown	3,263	28	756	1,245	830	260	104	34	6	--	--
United Kingdom, 1990[3]											
Total	184,092	927	40,787	58,513	40,826	23,591	13,655	5,356	401	24	12
0	106,811	910	36,862	40,660	19,233	6,182	2,281	621	49	5	8
1	28,777	3	2,948	10,411	8,014	4,263	2,257	824	56	1	--
2	29,190	--	344	5,236	8,705	7,543	5,111	2,097	144	8	2
3	11,930	--	31	1,290	3,340	3,600	2,518	1,076	73	2	--
4	3,802	--	4	213	949	1,282	881	425	44	2	2
5 plus	1,822	--	--	30	310	587	560	297	32	6	--
Unknown	1,760	14	598	673	275	134	47	16	3	--	--

Source: Selected from "Legally induced abortions by age and number of previous live births of woman, latest available year," United Nations, *Demographic Yearbook*, 1991, Table 14, pp. 325-329. *Notes:* 1. Birth order based on number of previous confinements (deliveries) rather than on live births. 2. Figure in preceding column includes this age group(s). 3. For residents only.

★654★

Abortions

Legally Induced Abortions in North America

This table shows the number of legally induced abortions performed in North America, the latest available year.

Country/Area	Year	Number
North America		
Belize	1989	822
Bermuda[1,2,3,4]	1984	92
Canada[1,2,3]	1989	70,705
Cuba	1989	151,146
Greenland[1,2,3,4,5]	1987	800
Martinique[6]	1985	1,753
Panama	1982	12
United States[6]	1987	1,354,000

Source: Selected from "Legally induced abortions, 1982-1990," United Nations, *Demographic Yearbook*, 1991, Table 13, pp. 323-24. *Notes:* 1. Continuance of pregnancy would involve risk to the life of the pregnant woman greater than if the pregnancy were terminated. 2. Continuance of pregnancy would involve risk of injury to the physical health of the pregnant woman greater than if the pregnancy were terminated. 3. Continuance of pregnancy would involve risk of injury to the mental health of the pregnant woman greater than if the pregnancy were terminated. 4. There is a substantial risk that if the child were born it would suffer from such physical or mental abnormalities as to be seriously handicapped. 5. Other. 6. Provisional.

★655★

Abortions

Legally Induced Abortions in North America by Age of Woman

This table shows the number of legally induced abortions performed in Bermuda and Canada by age of woman and number of previous live births to woman, latest available year.

Country or area/ year/no. previous live births	Age of woman										
	All ages	-15	15-19	20-24	25-29	30-34	35-39	40-44	45-49	50 plus	Unknown
North America											
Bermuda, 1984											
Total	92	3	30	21	18	14	5	--	--	1	--
0	44	3	27	9	1	3	1	--	--	--	--
1	21	--	2	6	6	6	1	--	--	--	--
2	13	--	--	3	7	2	--	--	--	1	--
3	8	--	--	2	3	1	2	--	--	--	--
4	1	--	--	--	--	--	--	--	--	--	--
5	2	--	--	--	1	1	--	--	--	--	--
Unknown	3	--	1	1	--	--	1	--	--	--	--

[Continued]

★ 655 ★

Legally Induced Abortions in North America by Age of Woman
[Continued]

Country or area/ year/no. previous live births	Age of woman										
	All ages	-15	15-19	20-24	25-29	30-34	35-39	40-44	45-49	50 plus	Unknown
Canada, 1989											
Total	70,705	374	13,578	20,121	15,181	9,425	5,202	1,417	107	6	5,294
0	35,014	344	11,215	12,624	6,709	2,750	1,139	216	15	1	1
1	12,432	2	1,270	4,186	3,659	2,047	978	274	14	1	1
2	9,677	--	187	1,685	2,841	2,717	1,748	465	32	1	1
3	3,280	--	14	376	823	1,046	760	239	22	--	--
4	835	--	2	53	222	252	208	87	13	1	--
5	225	--	--	13	36	66	69	39	2	--	--
6 plus	111	--	--	2	26	31	31	16	3	2	--
Unknown	9,128	28	890	1,182	865	516	269	81	6	--	5,291

Source: Selected from "Legally induced abortions by age and number of previous live births of woman, latest available year," United Nations, *Demographic Yearbook*, 1991, Table 14, pp. 325-329. For Canada, the birth order is based on the number of previous confinements (deliveries) rather than on live births.

★ 656 ★

Abortions

Legally Induced Abortions in Oceania

This table shows the number of legally induced abortions performed in Oceania, the latest available year.

Country/Area	Year	Number
Oceania		
New Zealand[1,2,3,4,5]	1989	10,200

Source: Selected from "Legally induced abortions, 1982-1990," United Nations, *Demographic Yearbook*, 1991, Table 13, pp. 323-24. *Notes:* 1. Continuance of pregnancy would involve risk of injury to the physical health of the pregnant woman greater than if the pregnancy were terminated. 2. Continuance of pregnancy would involve risk of injury to the mental health of the pregnant woman greater than if the pregnancy were terminated. 3. Continuance of pregnancy would involve risk of injury to mental or physical health of any existing children of the family greater than if the pregnancy were terminated. 4. There is a substantial risk that if the child were born it would suffer from such physical or mental abnormalities as to be seriously handicapped. 5. Other.

★ 657 ★
Abortions

Legally Induced Abortions in Oceania by Age of Woman

This table shows the number of legally induced abortions performed in New Zealand by age of woman and number of previous live births to woman, latest available year.

Country or area/ year/no. previous live births	All ages	-16	16-19	20-24	25-29	30-34	35-39	40-44	45-49	50 plus
Oceania										
New Zealand, 1989										
Total	10,200	500	2,050	3,009	2,454	1,518	820	287	12	--
0	5,295	50	1,871	1,973	994	315	71	21	--	--
1	1,675	--	152	637	503	249	107	27	--	--
2	1,679	--	23	305	540	436	274	98	3	--
3	976	--	4	77	295	311	210	75	4	--
4	357	--	--	14	87	134	82	40	--	--
5	143	--	--	3	26	55	42	14	3	--
6 plus	75	--	--	--	9	18	34	12	2	--

Source: Selected from "Legally induced abortions by age and number of previous live births of woman, latest available year," United Nations, *Demographic Yearbook*, 1991, Table 14, pp. 325-329.

★ 658 ★
Abortions

Legally Induced Abortions in South America

This table shows the number of legally induced abortions performed in South America, the latest available year.

Country/Area	Year	Number
South America		
Chile	1990	29
French Guiana	1984	388

Source: Selected from "Legally induced abortions, 1982-1990," United Nations, *Demographic Yearbook*, 1991, Table 13, pp. 323-24.

★ 659 ★
Abortions

Legally Induced Abortions in South America by Age of Woman

This table shows the number of legally induced abortions performed in Chile by age of woman, latest available year.

Country or area/ year/no. previous live births	Age of woman								
	All ages	-15	15-19	20-24	25-29	30-34	35-39	40-44	45-49	50 plus
South America									
Chile, 1990 Total	29	--	--	2	14	6	5	2	--	--

Source: Selected from "Legally induced abortions by age and number of previous live births of woman, latest available year," United Nations, *Demographic Yearbook*, 1991, Table 14, pp. 325-329.

★ 660 ★
Abortions

Post-Abortion Reaction

The table below shows the responses of women to a survey question about how they felt after undergoing an abortion. Very few women took pleasure in having an abortion, but very few expressed regret.

Reaction	Percent
N =	344
Relief	43%
Pleasure	4%
No reaction	8%
Sadness	29%
Guilt	10%
Regret	6%
Relief + Pleasure	47%
Sadness + Guilt + Regret	45%

Source: "Postabortion Reaction Was," Samuel S. Janus, PhD, and Cynthia L. Janus, MD, *The Janus Report on Sexual Behavior*, (New York: John Wiley & Sons, Inc., 1993), Table 7.12, p. 222. Between 1988 and 1992, the authors distributed 4,550 questionnaires to subjects at a variety of sites. The sample design was planned to conform to the population distribution of the United States in the areas of sex, age, region, income, education, and marital status. Returned questionnaires totaled 3,260. Of these, 495 were discarded. Satisfactorily completed questionnaires totaled 2,765: 1,418 women and 1,347 men.

Births

★ 661 ★

Asian and Near Eastern Births: 1994

This table shows births, births per 1,000 population, and the rate of natural increase in Asia and the Near East in 1994.

[Births in thousands. Birth rate per 1,000 population.]

Country	Births	Rate	Rate of nat. increase
Asia	82,868	25	1.6%
Asia, excluding Near East	77,792	24	1.6%
Afghanistan	735	43	2.5%
Bangladesh	4,383	35	2.3%
Bhutan	68	39	2.3%
Brunei	7	26	2.1%
Burma	1,260	28	1.9%
Cambodia	463	45	2.9%
China			
Mainland	21,547	18	1.1%
Taiwan	332	16	1.0%
Hong Kong	67	12	0.6%
India	26,171	28	1.8%
Indonesia	4,900	24	1.6%
Iran	2,785	42	3.5%
Japan	1,312	10	0.3%
Laos	203	43	2.8%
Macau	7	15	1.1%
Malaysia	549	28	2.3%
Maldives	11	44	3.6%
Mongolia	80	33	2.6%
Nepal	792	38	2.4%
North Korea	548	24	1.8%
Pakistan	5,440	42	3.0%
Philippines	1,909	27	2.0%
Singapore	47	17	1.1%
South Korea	708	16	1.0%
Sri Lanka	328	18	1.2%
Thailand	1,156	19	1.3%
Vietnam	1,983	27	1.9%

[Continued]

★ 661 ★

Asian and Near Eastern Births: 1994
[Continued]

Country	Births	Rate	Rate of nat. increase
Near East	5,076	34	2.7%
Bahrain	16	27	2.3%
Cyprus	12	17	0.9%
Gaza Strip	33	45	4.0%
Iraq	877	44	3.7%
Israel	104	21	1.4%
Jordan	154	39	3.5%
Kuwait	54	29	2.7%
Lebanon	101	28	2.1%
Oman	69	40	3.5%
Qatar	10	19	1.5%
Saudi Arabia	696	38	3.2%
Syria	650	44	3.7%
Turkey	1,615	26	2.0%
United Arab Emirates	77	28	2.5%
West Bank	47	32	2.7%
Yemen	563	51	3.6%

Source: Selected from "Population, Vital Events, and Rates, by Country or Area: 1994," U.S. Bureau of the Census, *World Population Profile: 1994,* 1994, Table 4, p. A-10. Primary source: U.S. Bureau of the Census, International Data Base.

★ 662 ★
Births

Birth Rate Projections by Race and Age Group: 1993 and 2010

This table shows the projected total fertility rate by race and Hispanic origin, projected for 1993 and 2010. The total fertility rate is the number of births that 1,000 women would have in their lifetime if, at each year of age, they experienced the birth rates occurring in the specified year. A total fertility rate of 2,110 represents "replacement level" fertility for the total population under current mortality conditions (assuming no net immigration). Also shown are projections of birth rates by race and age group. Birth rates represent live births per 1,000 women in the age group indicated. Projections are based on middle fertility assumptions.

Age group	All Races[1]		White		Black		Amer Ind, Esk, Aleut		Asian/Pacific Isl		Hispanic[2]	
	1993	2010	1993	2010	1993	2010	1993	2010	1993	2010	1993	2010
Total fertility rate	2,074	2,119	1,973	2,009	2,470	2,469	2,778	2,759	2,514	2,406	2,900	2,777
Birth rates												
10 to 14 years old	1.4	1.6	0.7	0.9	4.8	5.0	2.0	2.1	0.8	0.8	2.3	2.3
15 to 19 years old	60.5	62.4	50.4	52.9	114.4	113.8	103.9	105.2	33.7	31.6	99.6	95.8
20 to 24 years old	117.6	120.0	109.6	112.4	161.0	161.1	188.7	187.0	99.7	95.6	180.5	172.6
25 to 29 years old	118.6	120.2	117.9	118.8	112.9	113.5	141.4	141.6	160.8	153.4	149.8	143.7
30 to 34 years old	80.1	82.0	80.2	80.9	67.8	68.4	78.2	78.4	134.3	128.4	95.8	91.5

[Continued]

★ 662 ★

Birth Rate Projections by Race and Age Group: 1993 and 2010
[Continued]

Age group	All Races[1]		White		Black		Amer Ind, Esk, Aleut		Asian/Pacific Isl		Hispanic[2]	
	1993	2010	1993	2010	1993	2010	1993	2010	1993	2010	1993	2010
35 to 39 years old	31.6	31.8	31.0	30.6	28.1	27.5	34.0	33.5	61.4	57.9	43.1	40.5
40 to 44 years old	5.4	5.5	5.1	5.1	5.4	5.1	7.2	7.0	12.7	12.0	9.2	8.5
45 to 49 years old	0.2	0.3	0.2	0.2	0.3	0.3	0.4	0.4	1.3	1.2	0.6	0.5

Source: "Projected Fertility Rates, by Race and Age Group: 1993 and 2010," U.S. Bureau of the Census, *Statistical Abstract of the United States, 1994,* table 95, p. 78. Primary source: U.S. Bureau of the Census, *Current Population Reports,* P25-1104. *Notes:* 1. Includes races not shown separately. 2. Persons of Hispanic origin may be of any race.

★ 663 ★
Births

Births to Teenage Mothers by Hispanic Origin and Race: 1991

This table shows the total number of births to teenage mothers in 1991 and number of these births by Hispanic origin and race. The table also shows selected maternal and infant characteristics for teenage mothers. Birth rates for black teenagers are substantially higher than those for white teenagers, and rates for Hispanic teens are comparable to those for black teenagers. One reason for the growing level of teen childbearing is the growing proportion of teenagers who are sexually active. According to the National Survey of Family Growth, conducted by the National Center for Health Statistics, in 1990, 41% of teens aged 15-17 and 74% of older teens were sexually experienced. Contraceptive use among these teenagers often does not begin until months after sexual activity has begun. A factor in the increase in birth rates for white teenagers is that 97% of Hispanic mothers are reported as white on birth certificates. Their fertility patterns have an impact on the rates for white women. Since birth rates for Hispanic teenagers are more than twice the rates of non-Hispanic teenagers, and the number of Hispanic women aged 15-19 has increased, the increase in the white teen birth rate reflects variations in Hispanic birth rates and population changes.

Characteristic	Mothers aged 15-19 years				
	All origins[1]	Hispanic[2]	Non-Hispanic[2]		
			Total[3]	White	Black
Number of births	519,577	104,651	409,836	246,570	148,342
Birth rate (per 1,000)	62.1	106.7	56.1	43.4	118.9
Percent of births to unmarried mothers[4]	68.8%	61.2%	70.7%	57.8%	92.5%
Percent of mothers completing high school[5]	34.8%	22.0%	38.1%	40.1%	35.0%
Prenatal care:					
Start first trimester	56.6%	49.8%	58.3%	63.4%	50.4%
Late or no care[6]	10.9%	15.0%	9.9%	7.7%	13.4%

[Continued]

★ 663 ★

Births to Teenage Mothers by Hispanic Origin and Race: 1991
[Continued]

| Characteristic | Mothers aged 15-19 years | | | | |
| | All origins[1] | Hispanic[2] | Non-Hispanic[2] | | |
			Total[3]	White	Black
Percent of mothers with weight gain of <16 lbs[7]	10.7%	10.9%	10.7%	7.3%	16.7%
Percent of mothers who smoked[8]	19.7%	6.5%	21.7%	31.0%	6.6%
Percent of births of low birthweight[9]	9.3%	7.5%	9.7%	7.6%	13.4%
Percent of births preterm[10]	14.4%	13.1%	14.7%	11.3%	20.4%

Source: Selected from "Recent Trends in Teenage Childbearing in the United States," *Statistical Bulletin*, Vol. 75(4), pp. 10-17, Oct-Dec 1994, Table 2, p. 14, "Selected Maternal and Infant Characteristics for Teenage Mothers by Age, Hispanic Origin and Race, United States, 1991." Primary source: Various published reports from the National Center for Health Statistics (NCHS), 1993. *Notes:* 1. Includes origin not stated and births to residents of New Hampshire, which did not report Hispanic origin on the birth certificate. 2. Excludes births to residents of New Hampshire, which did not report Hispanic origin on the birth certificate. 3. Includes white, black, and other races. 4. For 44 states and the District of Columbia, marital status of mother is reported on the birth certificate; for 6 states, mother's marital status is inferred from other items on the birth certificate. 5. Excludes data for Washington and New York State (exclusive of New York City). 6. Care beginning in third trimester or no care. 7. Excludes data for California. 8. Excludes data for California, Indiana, New York, and South Dakota. 9. Birthweight of less than 2,500 grams (5 lb. 8 oz.). 10. Born prior to 37 completed weeks of gestation.

★ 664 ★
Births

Births to Teenage Mothers: 1980 and 1985-1991

This table shows the total number of births in 1980 through 1991 and the number of these births that were to mothers aged 15-17 and 18-19. The table also shows the birth rate and first birth rate per 1,000 women in the specified age group. Figures are given by race. More than one-half million American teenagers had babies in 1991, the highest birth rate seen in two decades for this age group. Most teenage childbearing is unintended. Negative consequences of teenage childbearing include lower educational attainment leading to lifetime poverty, and lower likelihood of receiving adequate and timely prenatal care leading to low birthweight babies and preterm births. Teen pregnancies and birth rates are much higher in this country than in most developed countries.

| Year and Race | Number of births | | | Birth rate[1] | | | First birth rate[1] | | |
	Total	15-17	18-19	Total	15-17	18-19	Total	15-17	18-19
All Races									
1980	552,161	198,222	353,939	53.0	32.5	82.1	41.4	28.5	59.7
1985	467,485	167,789	299,696	51.0	31.0	79.6	39.4	27.0	57.2
1986	461,905	168,572	293,333	50.2	30.5	79.6	38.8	26.6	57.1
1987	462,312	172,591	289,721	50.6	31.7	78.5	39.0	27.5	55.9
1988	478,353	176,624	301,729	53.0	33.6	79.9	40.5	28.9	56.6
1989	506,503	181,044	325,459	57.3	36.4	84.2	43.5	31.1	59.5

[Continued]

★ 664 ★

Births to Teenage Mothers: 1980 and 1985-1991

[Continued]

Year and Race	Number of births			Birth rate[1]			First birth rate[1]		
	Total	15-17	18-19	Total	15-17	18-19	Total	15-17	18-19
1990	521,826	183,327	338,499	59.9	37.5	88.6	45.1	31.9	62.0
1991	519,577	188,226	331,351	62.1	38.7	94.4	46.5	32.9	65.3
White									
1980	393,567	129,341	264,223	45.4	25.5	73.2	36.5	23.0	55.6
1985	324,590	107,993	216,597	43.3	24.4	70.4	34.6	21.9	52.8
1986	317,970	107,177	210,793	42.3	23.8	70.1	33.9	21.3	52.6
1987	315,464	108,592	206,872	42.5	24.6	68.9	33.9	22.0	51.5
1988	323,830	109,739	214,091	44.4	26.0	69.6	35.3	23.2	51.9
1989	340,472	111,736	228,736	47.9	28.1	72.9	38.0	25.0	54.4
1990	354,482	114,934	239,548	50.8	29.5	78.0	40.1	26.1	57.8
1991	352,359	118,809	233,550	52.8	30.7	83.5	41.5	27.1	61.5
Black									
1980	147,378	65,069	82,309	97.8	72.5	135.1	70.2	60.4	84.7
1985	130,857	55,656	75,201	95.4	69.3	132.4	68.1	57.1	83.7
1986	131,594	57,003	74,591	95.8	69.3	135.1	68.3	57.3	84.7
1987	134,050	59,361	74,689	97.6	72.1	135.8	69.0	59.0	84.0
1988	140,608	61,856	78,752	102.7	75.7	142.7	71.6	61.3	86.8
1989	150,699	63,832	86,867	111.5	81.9	151.9	76.6	65.6	91.7
1990	151,613	62,881	88,732	112.8	82.3	152.9	75.7	64.9	89.9
1991	150,956	63,571	87,385	115.5	84.1	158.6	76.6	65.9	91.2

Source: Selected from "Recent Trends in Teenage Childbearing in the United States," *Statistical Bulletin,* Vol. 75(4), pp. 10-17, Oct-Dec 1994, Table 1, p. 11, "Births and Birth Rates for Teenage Mothers Aged 15-19 by Race and Age, United States, 1980 and 1985-1991. Primary source: Various published reports from the National Center for Health Statistics (NCHS) for 1989-1991 and special computations by NCHS for 1980 to 1988. *Note:* 1. Rate per 1,000 women in specified group.

★ 665 ★

Births

Births to Unmarried Teenage Mothers: 1980 and 1985-1991

This table shows the total number of births to unmarried mothers in 1980 through 1991 and the number of these births that were to mothers aged 15-17 and 18-19. The table also shows the birth rate and first birth rate per 1,000 women in the specified age group. Figures are given by race. The majority of teenage mothers are unmarried.

Year and Race	Number of births			Birth rate[1]			Percent of total births		
	Total	15-17	18-19	Total	15-17	18-19	Total	15-17	18-19
All Races									
1980	262,777	121,900	140,877	27.6	20.6	39.0	47.6%	61.5%	39.8%
1985	270,922	118,931	151,991	31.4	22.4	45.9	58.0%	70.9%	50.7%
1986	280,720	123,491	157,229	32.3	22.8	48.0	60.8%	73.3%	53.6%
1987	292,958	130,740	162,218	33.8	24.5	48.9	63.4%	75.8%	56.0%
1988	312,499	136,137	176,362	36.4	26.4	51.5	65.3%	77.1%	58.5%

[Continued]

★ 665 ★

Births to Unmarried Teenage Mothers: 1980 and 1985-1991
[Continued]

Year and Race	Number of births			Birth rate[1]			Percent of total births		
	Total	15-17	18-19	Total	15-17	18-19	Total	15-17	18-19
1989	337,268	140,686	196,582	40.1	28.7	56.0	66.6%	77.7%	60.4%
1990	349,970	142,398	207,572	42.5	29.6	60.7	67.1%	77.7%	61.3%
1991	357,483	148,171	209,312	44.8	30.9	65.7	68.8%	78.7%	63.2%
White									
1980	130,417	58,705	71,712	16.5	12.0	24.1	33.1%	45.4%	27.1%
1985	145,457	62,673	82,784	20.8	14.5	31.2	44.8%	58.0%	38.2%
1986	153,605	65,653	87,952	21.8	14.9	33.5	48.3%	61.3%	41.7%
1987	162,039	70,118	91,921	23.2	16.2	34.5	51.4%	64.6%	44.4%
1988	173,981	72,639	101,342	25.3	17.6	36.8	53.7%	66.2%	47.3%
1989	188,253	75,108	113,145	28.0	19.3	40.2	55.3%	67.2%	49.5%
1990	199,896	78,086	121,810	30.6	20.4	44.9	56.4%	67.9%	50.8%
1991	207,035	82,823	124,212	32.8	21.8	49.6	58.8%	69.7%	53.2%
Black									
1980	126,276	60,548	65,728	87.9	68.8	118.2	85.7%	93.1%	79.9%
1985	118,058	53,229	64,829	87.6	66.8	117.9	90.2%	95.6%	86.2%
1986	119,357	54,558	64,799	88.5	67.0	121.1	90.7%	95.7%	86.9%
1987	122,502	57,044	65,458	90.9	69.9	123.0	91.4%	96.1%	87.6%
1988	129,333	59,648	69,685	96.1	73.5	130.5	92.0%	96.4%	88.5%
1989	138,718	61,372	77,346	104.5	78.9	140.9	92.0%	96.1%	89.0%
1990	139,442	60,102	79,340	106.0	78.8	143.7	92.0%	95.6%	89.4%
1991	139,325	60,817	78,508	108.5	80.4	148.7	92.3%	95.7%	89.8%

Source: Selected from "Recent Trends in Teenage Childbearing in the United States," *Statistical Bulletin*, Vol. 75(4), pp. 10-17, Oct-Dec 1994, Table 1, p. 11, "Number, Rate, and Percent of Births to Unmarried Women, for Teenage Mothers Aged 15-19 by Race and Age, United States, 1980 and 1985-1991. Primary source: Various published reports from the National Center for Health Statistics (NCHS) for 1989-1991 and special computations by NCHS for 1980 to 1988. *Notes:* 1. Rate per 1,000 women in specified group. 2. Includes white, black, and all other races.

★ 666 ★
Births

Births to Unmarried Women Worldwide

This table shows the countries of the world where the proportion of births to unmarried women is rising rapidly. Years are approximate.

Country	Births to unmarried women	
	1970	1985
Developed regions		
Australia	8%	16%
Austria	13%	22%
Bulgaria	9%	11%
Denmark	11%	43%
Finland	6%	16%

[Continued]

★ 666 ★

Births to Unmarried Women Worldwide
[Continued]

Country	Births to unmarried women	
	1970	1985
Germany		
former German Dem. Rep.	13%	34%
France	7%	20%
New Zealand	13%	25%
Norway	7%	26%
Portugal	7%	12%
Sweden	18%	46%
United Kingdom	8%	19%
United States	10%	21%
Africa		
Mauritius	3%	26%
Reunion	24%	44%
Seychelles	45%	70%
Latin America/Caribbean		
Argentina	26%	33%
Bahamas	29%	62%
Belize	44%	54%
Chile	20%	32%
Costa Rica	29%	37%
French Guiana	63%	76%
Guadeloupe	43%	57%
Martinique	51%	64%
Puerto Rico	19%	27%
Asia and Pacific		
Guam	9%	30%
Hong Kong	3%	6%
Philippines	3%	6%

Source: "The proportion of births to unmarried women is rising rapidly in many countries and regions," *The World's Women: Trends and Statistics 1970-1990*, United Nations, 1991, Table 1.9, p. 16. Primary source: Prepared by the Statistical Office of the United Nations Secretariat from *Demographic Yearbook 1975* and *1986* (UN publications, Sales Nos. E/F.76.XIII.1 and E/F.87.XIII.1).

★ 667 ★
Births

Births to Unmarried Women: 1970-1991

This table shows total live births in thousands by race of child and age of mother. The table shows the percent distribution of these births (as a percent of all births and as a percent of all births in racial groups), and it gives the rate of births to unmarried mothers per 1,000 unmarried women (never-married, widowed, and divorced). In July 1994, the Census Bureau reported that births to unmarried women rose by more than 70% between 1983 and 1993. In 1993, 6.3 million (27%) of all children under the age of 18 lived with a single parent, compared to 3.7 million in 1983. The figure was 243,000 children living with one parent who had never married in 1960. In 1993, 57% of black children were living with one parent who had never married, compared with 21% of white children, and 32% of Hispanic children.

[Total live births in thousands.]

Race of child and age of mother	1970	1980	1985	1990	1991
Total live births[1]	398.7	665.7	828.2	1,165.4	1,213.8
White	175.1	320.1	433.0	647.4	707.5
Black	215.1	325.7	365.5	472.7	463.8
Age of mother					
Under 15 years	9.5	9.0	9.4	10.7	11.0
15 to 19 years	190.4	262.8	270.9	350.0	357.5
20 to 24 years	126.7	237.3	300.4	403.9	429.1
25 to 29 years	40.6	99.6	152.0	230.0	234.6
30 to 34 years	19.1	41.0	67.3	118.2	123.9
35 years +	12.4	16.1	28.2	52.7	57.7
Percent distribution					
Total[1]	100%	100%	100%	100%	100%
Black	44%	48%	52%	56%	58%
White	54%	49%	44%	41%	38%
Under 15 years	2%	1%	1%	1%	1%
15 to 19 years	48%	40%	33%	30%	29%
20 to 24 years	32%	36%	36%	35%	35%
25 to 29 years	10%	15%	18%	20%	19%
30 to 34 years	5%	6%	8%	10%	10%
35 years +	3%	2%	3%	5%	5%
As percent of all births in racial groups					
Total[1]	11%	18%	22%	28%	30%
White	6%	11%	15%	20%	22%
Black	38%	55%	60%	65%	68%
Birth Rate[2]					
Total[1,3]	26.4	29.4	32.8	43.8	45.2
White[3]	13.9	17.6	21.8	31.8	34.6

[Continued]

★ 667 ★

Births to Unmarried Women: 1970-1991
[Continued]

Race of child and age of mother	1970	1980	1985	1990	1991
Black[3]	95.5	82.9	79.0	93.9	189.5
15 to 19 years	22.4	27.6	31.4	42.5	44.8
20 to 24 years	38.4	40.9	46.5	65.1	68.0
25 to 29 years	37.0	34.0	39.9	56.0	56.5
30 to 34 years	27.1	21.1	25.2	37.6	38.1
35 years +					

Source: "Births to Unmarried Women, by Race of Child and Age of Mother: 1970 to 1991", U.S. Bureau of the Census, *Statistical Abstract of the United States, 1994,* table 100, p. 80. Primary source: U.S. National Center for Health Statistics, *Vital Statistics of the United States,* annual; *Monthly Vital Statistics Report*; and unpublished data. Excludes births to nonresidents of United States. Data for 1970 include estimates for States in which marital status data were not reported. Beginning in 1980, marital status is inferred from a comparison of the child's and parents' surnames on the birth certificate for those States that do not report on marital status. No estimates included for misstatements on birth records or failures to register births. *Notes:* 1. Includes other races not shown separately. 2. Rate per 1,000 unmarried women (never-married, widowed, and divorced) estimated as of July 1. 3. Covers women aged 15 to 44 years.

★ 668 ★

Births

Births to Unmarried Women: 1980-1992

This table presents statistics relating to births to unmarried women that were released by the National Center for Health Statistics in June 1995.

Item	Number/Percent
Growth in births to single women between 1980 and 1992:	54%
Number of births to single women that were to teenagers:	
1980	1/2
1992	1/3
Births per 1,000 unmarried women in age group, 1980:	
15-44 years	29.4
Births per 1,000 unmarried women in age group, 1992:	
15-44 years	45.2
15-17 years	30.4
18-19 years	67.3
20-24 years	68.5
25-29 years	56.5
30-34 years	37.9

[Continued]

★ 668 ★

Births to Unmarried Women: 1980-1992
[Continued]

Item	Number/Percent
All Hispanic women	95.3
All black women	86.5
All white women	35.2
Rise in rate of births to single mothers between 1980 and 1992:	
White mothers	94%
Black mothers	7%
Number of births to single mothers in 1992:	
Teenagers	365,039
Age 20+	859,837

Source: "Births by single women up 54% from 1980 to 1992," *Detroit Free Press*, June 7, 1995, p. 4A.

★ 669 ★
Births

Cesarean Section Deliveries: 1970-1992

This table shows the total number of cesarean deliveries in thousands for years 1970 through 1992. It also gives cesarean rates by age of mother-- the number of cesarean deliveries per 100 total deliveries for the specified age. According to the Centers for Disease Control and Prevention, 22.8% of live births in 1993 were by cesarean section, a rate more than four times what it was in 1970.

[Number of deliveries in thousands.]

Age of mother	1970	1980	1985	1986	1987	1988	1989	1990	1991	1992
Number of cesarean deliveries	195	619	877	906	953	933	938	945	933	921
Rate										
Mothers, all ages	5.5	16.5	22.7	24.1	24.4	24.7	23.8	23.5	23.5	23.6
Under 20 years	3.9	14.5	16.1	18.3	18.5	19.5	18.1	16.6	18.2	17.5
20 to 24 years	4.9	15.8	21.2	21.9	22.9	20.1	21.1	21.0	21.0	21.4
25 to 29 years	5.9	16.7	22.9	25.3	23.7	26.7	24.8	23.3	24.3	23.2
30 to 34 years	7.5	18.0	26.6	26.2	28.3	28.0	26.6	27.8	26.7	27.1
35 years and over	8.3	20.6	30.7	32.6	31.6	32.1	30.3	31.4	28.4	30.1

Source: "Cesarean Section Deliveries, by Age of Mother: 1970 to 1992", U.S. Bureau of the Census, *Statistical Abstract of the United States, 1994*, table 99, p. 79. Primary source: U.S. National Center for Health Statistics, *Vital Statistics of the United States*, annual; *Monthly Vital Statistics Report*; and unpublished data. Based on data collected from the National Hospital Discharge Survey, a sample survey of hospital records of patients discharged in year shown; subject to sampling variability. Beginning 1988, comparisons with data for earlier years should be made with caution as estimates of change may reflect improvements in the 1988 design rather than true changes in hospital use.

★ 670 ★

Births

European Births: 1994

This table shows births, births per 1,000 population, and the rate of natural increase in Europe in 1994.

[Births in thousands. Birth rate per 1,000 population.]

Country	Births	Rate	Rate of nat. increase
Europe	6,278	12	0.2%
Albania	76	22	1.7%
Andorra	1	13	0.6%
Austria	91	11	0.1%
Belgium	118	12	0.1%
Bulgaria	103	12	[1]
Czech Republic	138	13	0.2%
Denmark	65	12	0.1%
Faroe Islands	1	18	1.0%
Finland	63	12	0.3%
France	759	13	0.4%
Germany	895	11	[1]
Gibraltar	[1]	15	0.7%
Greece	111	11	0.1%
Guernsey	1	13	0.3%
Hungary	129	12	[1]
Iceland	4	16	1.0%
Ireland	50	14	0.6%
Isle of Man	1	14	0.1%
Italy	627	11	0.1%
Jersey	1	13	0.3%
Liechtenstein	[1]	13	0.6%
Luxembourg	5	13	0.3%
Malta	5	14	0.6%
Monaco	[1]	11	-0.2%
Netherlands	194	13	0.4%
Norway	57	13	0.3%
Poland	520	13	0.4%
Portugal	123	12	0.2%
Romania	317	14	0.4%
San Marino	[1]	11	0.4%
Slovakia	79	15	0.5%
Spain	434	11	0.2%
Sweden	119	14	0.3%
Switzerland	86	12	0.3%
United Kingdom	778	13	0.3%

[Continued]

★ 670 ★

European Births: 1994
[Continued]

Country	Births	Rate	Rate of nat. increase
(Former) Yugoslavia[2]	327	13	0.5%
Bosnia and Herzegovina	62	13	0.7%
Croatia	53	12	[1]
Macedonia	35	11	0.1%
Serbia and Montenegro	154	11	0.1%
Slovenia	23	12	0.2%
(Former) Soviet Union	4,682	16	0.5%
BALTICS	117	14	0.3%
Estonia	23	14	0.2%
Latvia	38	14	0.1%
Lithuania	57	15	0.4%
COMMONWEALTH OF INDEPENDENT STATES	4,473	16	0.5%
Armenia	85	24	1.7%
Azerbaijan	177	23	1.6%
Belarus	137	13	0.2%
Kazakhstan	335	19	1.1%
Kyrgyzstan	124	26	1.9%
Moldova	72	16	0.6%
Russia	1,896	13	0.1%
Tajikistan	209	35	2.8%
Turkmenistan	122	30	2.3%
Ukraine	640	12	[1]
Uzbekistan	678	30	2.4%
GEORGIA	92	16	0.7%

Source: Selected from "Population, Vital Events, and Rates, by Country or Area: 1994," U.S. Bureau of the Census, *World Population Profile: 1994*, 1994, Table 4, p. A-12. Primary source: U.S. Bureau of the Census, International Data Base. *Notes:* 1. Less than 500 or between 0.05 and - 0.05%. 2. The U.S. view is that the Socialist Federal Republic of Yugoslavia has dissolved and no successor state represents its continuation. Macedonia has proclaimed independent statehood, but has not been recognized as a state by the U.S. Serbia and Montenegro have asserted the formation of a joint independent state, but this entity has not been recognized as a state by the U.S.

★ 671 ★

Births

Latin American/Caribbean Births: 1994

This table shows births, births per 1,000 population, and the rate of natural increase in Latin America and the Caribbean in 1994.

[Births in thousands. Birth rate per 1,000 population.]

Country	Births	Rate	Rate of nat. increase
Latin America/Caribbean	11,461	24	1.7%
Anguilla	1	24	1.6%
Antigua and Barbuda	1	17	1.2%
Argentina	665	20	1.1%
Aruba	1	15	0.9%
Bahamas, The	5	19	1.3%
Barbados	4	16	0.7%
Belize	7	35	2.9%
Bolivia	249	32	2.4%
Brazil	3,410	21	1.3%
British Virgin Islands	1	20	1.4%
Cayman Islands	1	15	1.0%
Chile	287	21	1.5%
Colombia	805	23	1.8%
Costa Rica	85	25	2.2%
Cuba	184	17	1.0%
Dominica	2	20	1.5%
Dominican Republic	195	25	1.9%
Ecuador	276	26	2.0%
El Salvador	189	33	2.6%
French Guiana	4	26	2.1%
Grenada	3	30	2.4%
Guadeloupe	8	18	1.2%
Guatemala	380	35	2.8%
Guyana	15	20	1.3%
Haiti	258	40	2.1%
Honduras	186	35	2.9%
Jamaica	55	22	1.6%
Martinique	7	18	1.2%
Mexico	2,505	27	2.2%
Montserrat	1	16	0.6%
Netherlands Antilles	3	17	1.1%
Nicaragua	142	35	2.8%
Panama	65	25	2.0%
Paraguay	167	32	2.8%
Peru	604	26	1.9%

[Continued]

★ 671 ★

Latin American/Caribbean Births: 1994
[Continued]

Country	Births	Rate	Rate of nat. increase
Puerto Rico	63	17	0.9%
Saint Kitts and Nevis	1	24	1.4%
Saint Lucia	3	23	1.7%
Saint Vincent and the Grenadines	2	20	1.5%
Suriname	11	25	1.9%
Trinidad and Tobago	26	20	1.3%
Turks and Caicos Islands	[1]	14	0.9%
Uruguay	57	18	0.8%
Venezuela	529	26	2.1%
Virgin Islands	2	19	1.4%

Source: Selected from "Population, Vital Events, and Rates, by Country or Area: 1994," U.S. Bureau of the Census, *World Population Profile: 1994*, 1994, Table 4, p. A-11. Primary source: U.S. Bureau of the Census, International Data Base. *Note:* 1. Less than 500 or between 0.05 and -0.05%.

★ 672 ★
Births

Live Births by Mother's Medical Risk Factor and Race: 1991

This table shows the number of live births, number of births where a medical risk factor was reported, and age and race of mother for whom the medical risk factor was reported in 1991. Rates are number of live births with specified medical risk factor per 1,000 live births in the specified group. In 1991, as in 1989 and 1990, the most frequently reported risk factors were anemia, diabetes, and pregnancy-associated hypertension. Teenage mothers have substantially elevated rates for anemia and pregnancy-associated hypertension. The rate for diabetes increases as the age of the mother advances.

Medical risk factor and race of mother	Number		Rate							Not stated
	All births[1]	Medical risk factor reported	All ages	Age of mother						
				Under 20 years	20-24 years	25-29 years	30-34 years	35-39 years	40-49 years	
All races[2]										
Anemia	4,110,907	73,970	18.8	27.9	22.5	15.7	14.4	15.1	16.2	168,710
Cardiac disease	4,110,907	14,421	3.7	2.3	2.8	3.7	4.6	5.5	6.3	168,710
Acute or chronic lung disease	4,110,907	14,465	3.7	4.4	3.5	3.2	3.7	4.5	4.8	168,710
Diabetes	4,110,907	92,345	23.4	7.9	14.9	23.3	32.1	46.9	65.8	168,710
Genital herpes[3,4]	3,634,317	28,356	8.0	5.6	6.9	7.7	9.8	11.3	11.0	95,935
Hydramnios/Oligo-hydramnios[3]	3,952,063	25,531	6.7	6.8	6.8	6.3	6.6	7.7	10.1	161,657
Hemoglobinopathy[3]	3,952,063	1,945	0.5	0.7	0.5	0.4	0.5	0.5	0.6	161,657
Hypertension, chronic	4,110,907	25,703	6.5	2.7	4.0	5.9	8.7	14.3	26.7	168,710
Hypertension, pregnancy-associated	4,110,907	107,692	27.3	32.4	27.6	25.5	25.1	29.5	35.6	168,710
Eclampsia	4,110,907	14,063	3.6	5.6	3.7	3.0	2.9	3.6	4.3	168,710

[Continued]

★ 672 ★

Live Births by Mother's Medical Risk Factor and Race: 1991
[Continued]

Medical risk factor and race of mother	Number		Rate							Not stated
	All births[1]	Medical risk factor reported	All ages	Age of mother						
				Under 20 years	20-24 years	25-29 years	30-34 years	35-39 years	40-49 years	
Incompetent cervix[3]	3,952,063	9,055	2.4	1.1	1.7	2.4	3.3	4.2	4.0	161,657
Previous infant 4,000+ grams[3]	3,952,063	38,430	10.1	1.6	6.4	10.9	15.1	18.6	22.6	161,657
Previous preterm or small-for-gestational-age infant[3]	3,952,063	44,245	11.7	5.9	11.3	11.7	13.7	15.9	17.5	161,657
Renal disease	4,110,907	8,705	2.2	3.0	2.6	1.9	1.8	2.0	1.8	168,710
Rh sensitization[5]	4,073,068	23,568	6.0	4.6	5.6	6.3	6.7	6.8	6.3	169,849
Uterine bleeding[4]	3,793,161	29,303	7.9	6.0	7.0	8.1	9.2	9.7	10.5	103,002
White										
Anemia	3,241,273	47,796	15.4	22.5	18.3	13.2	12.4	13.2	13.7	132,805
Cardiac disease	3,241,273	11,977	3.9	2.3	2.8	3.9	4.9	5.7	6.5	132,805
Acute or chronic lung disease	3,241,273	10,695	3.4	3.9	3.2	3.1	3.5	4.5	4.5	132,805
Diabetes	3,241,273	73,752	23.7	8.9	15.6	23.1	31.0	44.3	62.1	132,805
Genital herpes[3,4]	2,835,494	23,023	8.3	4.5	6.5	8.0	10.7	12.8	12.5	71,197
Hydramnios/Oligo-hydramnios[3]	3,102,783	19,320	6.5	6.5	6.6	6.1	6.4	7.3	9.5	127,153
Hemoglobinopathy[3]	3,102,783	711	0.2	0.2	0.2	0.2	0.3	0.3	X	127,153
Hypertension, chronic	3,241,273	17,966	5.8	2.3	3.7	5.2	7.4	11.8	21.9	132,805
Hypertension, pregnancy-associated	3,241,273	86,603	27.9	33.2	28.9	26.2	25.2	29.7	34.5	132,805
Eclampsia	3,241,273	10,287	3.3	5.1	3.6	2.8	2.8	3.3	4.0	132,805
Incompetent cervix[3]	3,102,783	6,953	2.3	1.2	1.6	2.2	3.1	4.2	4.1	127,153
Previous infant 4,000+ grams[3]	3,102,783	34,462	11.6	1.8	7.2	12.1	16.6	20.5	25.4	127,153
Previous preterm or small-for-gestational-age infant[3]	3,102,783	33,288	11.2	5.2	10.5	11.1	13.1	15.6	17.3	127,153
Renal disease	3,241,273	7,017	2.3	3.3	2.7	1.9	1.8	2.0	1.8	132,805
Rh sensitization[5]	3,207,599	21,173	6.9	5.5	6.4	7.1	7.5	7.7	7.2	133,845
Uterine bleeding[4]	2,973,984	24,049	8.3	6.3	7.3	8.4	9.4	10.0	10.9	76,863
Black										
Anemia	682,602	21,713	33.3	38.2	36.5	29.5	27.2	27.4	29.8	30,624
Cardiac disease	682,602	2,030	3.1	2.6	2.8	3.1	3.9	5.1	5.7	30,624
Acute or chronic lung disease	682,602	3,273	5.0	5.6	4.8	4.3	5.4	5.6	7.0	30,624
Diabetes	682,602	12,776	19.6	5.5	11.9	23.0	35.8	55.6	81.0	30,624
Genital herpes[3,4]	622,615	4,584	7.6	8.0	8.8	7.4	6.1	4.7	5.4	21,053
Hydramnios/Oligo-hydramnios[3]	665,705	5,065	8.0	7.5	7.4	7.8	8.6	10.5	14.9	29,363

[Continued]

★ 672 ★

Live Births by Mother's Medical Risk Factor and Race: 1991

[Continued]

Medical risk factor and race of mother	Number		Rate								Not stated
	All births[1]	Medical risk factor reported	All ages	Age of mother							
				Under 20 years	20-24 years	25-29 years	30-34 years	35-39 years	40-49 years		
Hemoglobinopathy[3]	665,705	1,104	1.7	1.9	1.8	1.6	1.8	1.5	X	29,363
Hypertension, chronic	682,602	6,882	10.6	3.7	5.6	10.6	19.4	35.5	67.1	30,624
Hypertension, pregnancy-associated	682,602	17,468	26.8	30.8	23.7	24.3	27.7	32.8	47.5	30,624
Eclampsia	682,602	3,251	5.0	6.7	4.3	4.2	4.5	6.2	7.4	30,624
Incompetent cervix[3]	665,705	1,829	2.9	1.0	2.2	3.7	4.8	5.6	5.2	29,363
Previous infant 4,000+ grams[3]	665,705	2,508	3.9	1.0	3.1	4.7	6.7	9.2	11.2	29,363
Previous preterm or small-for-gestational-age infant[3]	665,705	9,078	14.3	7.4	14.5	16.3	19.3	18.7	19.2	29,363
Renal disease	682,602	1,379	2.1	2.4	2.1	2.1	1.9	1.9	X	30,624
Rh sensitization[5]	679,440	1,961	3.0	2.6	3.1	3.1	3.5	2.9	3.4	30,707
Uterine bleeding[4]	639,512	4,162	6.7	5.7	6.3	6.9	8.3	8.7	8.9	22,314

Source: "Live births with selected medical risk factors and rates for selected medical risk factors, by age and race of mother: United States, 1991," National Center for Health Statistics. Advance report of maternal and infant health data from birth certificate, 1991. *Monthly Vital Statistics Report,* Vol 42, No. 11(S), May 11, 1994, Table 1, p. 14. *Notes:* 1. Total number of births to residents of areas reporting specified medical risk factor. 2. Includes races other than white and black. 3. New York City (but not New York State) reports this risk factor. 4. Texas does not report this risk factor. 5. Kansas does not report this risk factor.

★ 673 ★

Births

Live Births by Mother's Smoking Status: 1991

This table shows the number of live births and number of live births by age of mother. It also shows the smoking status of the mother. Figures are given for all races and for white and black mothers, for 46 reporting States and the District of Columbia in 1991. Smoking during pregnancy was reported by 17.8% of women who gave birth in 1991, a decline from 18.4% reported in 1989. White mothers were more likely to smoke than black mothers. Smoking is uncommon among Asian women, but maternal tobacco use was not reported on the birth certificates of California and New York, which together acccounted for 43-66% of Asian births (except Hawaiian). For Hawaiian women the rate of smoking is 19.4%. The smoking rate for American Indian mothers is 22.6%.

Smoking status and race of mother	All ages	Age of mother								
		Under 15 years	Total	15-17 years	18-19 years	20-24 years	25-29 years	30-34 years	35-39 years	40-49 years
All races[1]										
Total	3,111,544	9,720	409,564	148,200	261,364	837,451	921,862	658,395	238,127	36,425
Smoker	531,683	705	77,869	23,641	54,228	170,870	152,176	95,538	30,368	4,157
Nonsmoker	2,461,074	8,619	316,911	119,070	197,841	636,607	734,930	535,885	197,438	30,684
Not stated	118,787	396	14,784	5,489	9,295	29,974	34,756	26,972	10,321	1,584

[Continued]

★ 673 ★

Live Births by Mother's Smoking Status: 1991
[Continued]

Smoking status and race of mother	All ages	Age of mother								
		Under 15 years	Total	15-17 years	18-19 years	20-24 years	25-29 years	30-34 years	35-39 years	40-49 years
White										
Total	2,439,406	3,718	267,183	88,880	178,303	626,992	758,240	554,765	198,936	29,572
Smoker	441,529	557	67,471	20,354	47,117	143,914	124,703	77,396	24,204	3,284
Nonsmoker	1,905,945	2,982	189,974	65,147	124,827	461,149	605,622	455,041	166,159	25,018
Not stated	91,932	179	9,738	3,379	6,359	21,929	27,915	22,328	8,573	1,270
Black										
Total	563,205	5,739	130,715	55,100	75,615	184,569	130,874	78,026	28,589	4,693
Smoker	79,143	119	8,431	2,593	5,838	23,434	24,636	16,346	5,434	743
Nonsmoker	462,165	5,411	117,724	50,578	67,146	154,145	100,858	58,331	21,951	3,745
Not stated	21,897	209	4,560	1,929	2,631	6,990	5,380	3,349	1,204	205
Percent										
Smoker[1]	17.8%	7.6%	19.7%	16.6%	21.5%	21.2%	17.2%	15.1%	13.3%	11.9%
White	18.8%	15.7%	26.2%	23.8%	27.4%	23.8%	17.1%	14.5%	12.7%	11.6%
Black	14.6%	2.2%	6.7%	4.9%	8.0%	13.2%	19.6%	21.9%	19.8%	16.6%

Source: Selected from "Number of live births by smoking status of mother, percent smokers, and percent distribution by average number of cigarettes smoked by mothers per day, according to age and race of mother: Total of 46 reporting States and the District of Columbia, 1991," National Center for Health Statistics. Advance report of maternal and infant health data from birth certificate, 1991. *Monthly Vital Statistics Report*, Vol 42, No. 11(S), May 11, 1994, Table 2, p. 15. Excludes data for California, Indiana, New York, and South Dakota, which did not require reporting of tobacco use during pregnancy. *Note:* 1. Includes races other than white and black.

★ 674 ★
Births

Live Births by Obstetric Procedures: 1991

This table shows the number of live births, number of births for which a particular obstetric procedure was reported, and the age distribution of the mothers upon whom the procedure was performed, by race, in 1991. Rates are the number of live births with the specified procedure per 1,000 live births in the specified group.

Obstetric procedure and race of mother	Number		Rate								Number Not stated
	All births[1]	Obstetric procedure reported	All ages	Age of mother							
				Under 20 years	20-24 years	25-29 years	30-34 years	35-39 years	40-49 years		
All races[2]											
Amniocentesis	4,110,907	125,879	31.5	11.5	13.9	17.1	30.2	152.5	188.3		111,556
Electronic fetal monitoring	4,110,907	3,020,280	755.2	762.1	758.1	758.9	751.2	736.8	722.4		111,556
Induction of labor	4,110,907	418,346	104.6	89.5	100.9	109.5	108.7	110.7	114.4		111,556
Stimulation of labor	4,110,907	483,025	120.8	118.6	119.1	123.5	121.8	117.6	116.6		111,556

[Continued]

★674★

Live Births by Obstetric Procedures: 1991
[Continued]

Obstetric procedure and race of mother	Number		Rate							Number Not stated
	All births[1]	Obstetric procedure reported	All ages	Age of mother						
				Under 20 years	20-24 years	25-29 years	30-34 years	35-39 years	40-49 years	
Tocolysis	4,110,907	64,121	16.0	18.2	16.6	15.2	15.3	15.8	14.8	111,556
Ultrasound[3]	3,916,676	2,135,842	561.0	544.0	556.8	567.0	566.7	566.1	552.8	109,264
White										
Amniocentesis	3,241,273	107,455	34.1	12.5	14.4	17.5	31.8	162.9	204.3	85,832
Electronic fetal monitoring	3,241,273	2,402,250	761.3	768.7	764.3	765.7	757.4	742.1	729.8	85,832
Induction of labor	3,241,273	356,571	113.0	99.6	110.2	117.0	115.3	116.7	121.7	85,832
Stimulation of labor	3,241,273	393,030	124.6	123.8	123.6	126.7	124.9	120.3	121.0	85,832
Tocolysis	3,241,273	51,888	16.4	19.3	17.1	15.6	15.6	16.1	15.5	85,832
Ultrasound[3]	3,095,821	1,730,040	574.4	560.2	570.7	579.8	577.9	577.4	565.4	84,135
Black										
Amniocentesis	682,602	11,730	17.7	9.2	12.0	14.7	19.6	81.3	106.0	21,522
Electronic fetal monitoring	682,602	490,605	742.1	753.2	744.9	736.6	733.9	728.9	720.3	21,522
Induction of labor	682,602	48,026	72.6	67.9	70.1	74.4	76.8	85.5	94.1	21,522
Stimulation of labor	682,602	69,440	105.0	107.6	103.7	106.3	103.5	101.8	97.7	21,522
Tocolysis	682,602	10,038	15.2	15.9	15.3	14.6	15.1	14.9	12.8	21,522
Ultrasound[3]	639,357	317,591	513.6	508.5	513.1	512.9	521.3	520.2	517.2	21,026

Source: "Live births with selected obstetric procedures and rates for selected obstetric procedures, by age and race of mother: United States, 1991," National Cener for Health Statistics. Advance report of maternal and infant health data from birth certificate, 1991. *Monthly Vital Statistics Report*, Vol 42, No. 11(S), May 11, 1994, Table 11, p. 21. *Notes:* 1. Total number of births to residents of areas reporting specified obstetric procedure. 2. Includes races other than white and black. 3. Illinois does not report this procedure.

★ 675 ★
Births

Live Births by Race and Hispanic Origin: 1990-1991

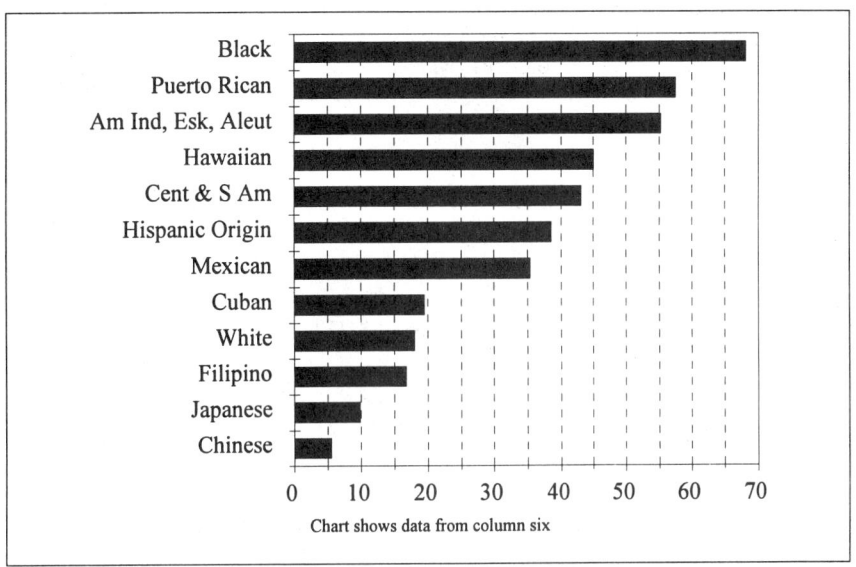

Chart shows data from column six

This table shows the total number of births in thousands by race and type of Hispanic origin; the percent of total births that were to teenage and unmarried mothers; the percent of mothers who received prenatal care; and the percent of births with low birth weight.

[Numbers in thousands. NA means Not available.]

Race and Hispanic Origin	Number of Births (1,000)		To Teenage Mothers, Percent of Total		To Unmarried Mothers, Percent of Total		Percent of mothers beginning prenatal care during--				Births with low birth weight[1]	
							1st trimester	3rd trim./none				
	1990	1991	1990	1991	1990	1991	1990	1991	1990	1991	1990	1991
Total	4,158	4,111	12.8%	12.9%	26.6%	28.0%	74.2%	76.2%	6.0%	5.8%	7.0%	7.1%
White	3,290	2,341	10.9%	11.0%	16.9%	18.0%	77.7%	79.5%	4.9%	4.7%	5.7%	5.8%
Black	684	683	23.1%	23.1%	66.7%	68.2%	60.7%	61.9%	10.9%	10.7%	13.3%	13.6%
American Indian, Eskimo, Aleut	39	39	19.5%	20.3%	53.6%	55.3%	57.9%	59.9%	12.9%	12.2%	6.1%	6.2%
Asian and Pacific Islander[2]	142	145	5.7%	5.8%	NA	NA	NA	NA	NA	NA	NA	NA
Filipino	26	26	6.1%	6.1%	15.9%	16.8%	77.1%	77.1%	4.5%	5.0%	7.3%	7.3%
Chinese	23	22	1.2%	1.1%	5.0%	5.5%	81.3%	82.3%	3.4%	3.4%	4.7%	5.1%
Japanese	9	9	2.9%	2.7%	9.6%	9.8%	87.0%	87.7%	2.9%	2.5%	6.2%	5.9%
Hawaiian	6	6	18.4%	18.1%	45.0%	45.0%	65.8%	68.1%	8.7%	7.5%	7.2%	6.7%
Hispanic Origin[3]	595	623	16.8%	17.2%	36.7%	38.5%	60.2%	61.0%	12.0%	11.0%	6.1%	6.1%
Mexican	386	411	17.7%	18.1%	33.3%	35.3%	57.8%	58.7%	13.2%	12.2%	5.5%	5.6%
Puerto Rican	59	60	21.7%	21.7%	55.9%	57.5%	63.5%	65.0%	10.6%	9.1%	9.0%	9.4%
Cuban	11	11	7.7%	7.1%	18.2%	19.5%	84.8%	85.4%	2.8%	2.4%	5.7%	5.6%
Central and South American	83	87	9.0%	9.4%	41.2%	43.1%	61.5%	63.4%	10.9%	9.5%	5.8%	5.9%

Source: Selected from "Live Births, by Race and Type of Hispanic Origin—Selected Characteristics: 1990 and 1991", U.S. Bureau of the Census, *Statistical Abstract of the United States, 1994,* table 97, p. 79. Represents registered births. Excludes births to nonresidents of the United States. Data are based on Hispanic origin of mother and beginning 1990, race of mother. Prior to 1990, data are for race of child and are not comparable. Hispanic origin data are available from only 23 States and the District of Columbia in 1985 and 48 States and DC in 1990. *Notes:* 1. Births less than 2,500 grams (5 lb.- 8 oz.) 2. Includes other races not shown separately. Hispanic persons may be of any race. Includes other types, not shown separately.

★ 676 ★

Births

Live Births by Race of Child and Age of Mother: 1970-1991

This table shows the number of live births, number of white and black babies born, and the number of male and female babies born, in thousands. Figures are given for the number of births by age of mother (in thousands). Birth rates per 1,000 population are given, total and for white and black, and male and female babies. The birth rate per 1,000 women is given for white and black babies and by age of mother. The 1981 to 1991 gain in number of males was 11,476,000 (10.3%) compared to 11,235,000 (9.5%) for females. Differential advances in mortality favoring males, as well as an increase in births late in the decade (because male births are slightly more numerous than female births) were the major contributors to this excess male growth.[1].

[Numbers in thousands.]

Item	1970	1980	1983	1984	1985	1986	1987	1988	1989	1990	1991
Live births[2]	3,731	3,612	3,639	3,669	3,761	3,757	3,809	3,910	4,041	4,158	4,111
White	3,091	2,899	2,904	2,924	2,991	2,970	2,992	3,046	3,132	3,225	3,241
Black	572	590	586	593	608	621	642	672	709	725	683
Male	1,915	1,853	1,866	1,879	1,928	1,925	1,951	2,002	2,069	2,129	2,102
Female	1,816	1,760	1,773	1,790	1,833	1,832	1,858	1,907	1,971	2,029	2,009
Males per 100 females	106	105	105	105	105	105	105	105	105	105	105
Age of mother											
Under 20 years	656	562	499	480	478	472	473	489	518	533	532
20 to 24 years	1,419	1,226	1,160	1,142	1,141	1,102	1,076	1,067	1,078	1,094	1,090
25 to 29 years	995	1,108	1,148	1,166	1,201	1,200	1,216	1,239	1,263	1,277	1,220
30 to 34 years	428	550	625	658	696	721	761	804	842	886	885
35 to 39 years	180	141	180	196	214	230	248	270	294	318	331
40 years old +	53	24	27	28	29	31	36	41	46	50	54
Birth rate per 1,000 pop.	18.4	15.9	15.6	15.6	15.8	15.6	15.7	16.0	16.4	16.7	16.3
White	17.4	14.9	14.6	14.6	14.8	14.6	14.6	14.8	15.1	15.5	15.4
Black	25.3	22.1	21.0	21.0	21.3	21.5	21.9	22.6	23.5	23.8	21.9
Birth rate per 1,000 women[3]	87.9	68.4	65.8	65.4	66.2	65.4	65.7	67.2	69.2	70.9	69.6
White[3]	84.1	64.7	62.4	62.2	63.0	61.9	62.0	63.0	64.7	66.9	67.0
Black[3]	115.4	88.1	81.7	81.4	82.2	82.4	83.8	86.6	90.4	91.9	85.2
Age of mother											
10 to 14 years	1.2	1.1	1.1	1.2	1.2	1.3	1.3	1.3	1.4	1.4	1.4
15 to 19 years	68.3	53.0	51.4	50.6	51.0	50.2	50.6	53.0	57.3	59.9	62.1
20 to 24 years	167.8	115.1	107.8	106.8	108.3	107.4	107.9	110.2	113.8	116.5	115.7
25 to 29 years	145.1	112.9	108.5	108.7	111.0	109.8	111.6	114.4	117.6	120.2	118.2
30 to 34 years	73.3	61.9	64.9	67.0	69.1	70.1	72.1	74.8	77.4	80.8	79.5
35 to 39 years	31.7	19.8	22.0	22.9	24.0	24.4	26.3	28.1	29.9	31.7	32.0

[Continued]

★ 676 ★

Live Births by Race of Child and Age of Mother: 1970-1991
[Continued]

Item	1970	1980	1983	1984	1985	1986	1987	1988	1989	1990	1991
40 to 44 years	8.1	3.9	3.9	3.9	4.0	4.1	4.4	4.8	5.2	5.5	5.5
45 to 49 years	0.5	0.2	0.2	0.2	0.2	0.2	0.2	0.2	0.2	0.2	0.2

Source: Selected from "Births and Birth Rates: 1970 to 1991," U.S. Bureau of the Census, *Statistical Abstract of the United States, 1994,* table 92, p. 76. Primary source: U.S. National Center for Health Statistics, *Vital Statistics of the United States,* annual, *Monthly Vital Statistics Report,* and unpublished data. *Notes:* 1. U.S. Bureau of the Census, *Current Population Reports,* "Population Profile of the United States 1993," p. 2. 2. Includes other races not shown separately. 3. Per 1,000 women, 15 to 44 years old in specified group. The rate for age of mother 45 to 49 years old computed by relating births to mothers 45 years old and over to women 45 to 49 years old.

★ 677 ★
Births

Live Births: 1970 to 1993

This table shows the number of live births in thousands and the rate per 1,000 population for the years 1970 through 1993. The annual number of births during 1989-1991 was the highest experienced in the United States since the peak Baby Boom years of 1954 to 1964. Many of these babies were born to baby boomer women who delayed childbearing until they were in their 30s. The 1980's were the first decade since 1900-1910 when the male population outgrew the female population. The 1981 to 1991 gain for males was 11,476,000 (10.3%) compared to 11,235,000 (9.5%) for females. Differential advances in mortality favoring males, as well as an increase in births late in the decade (because male births are slightly more numerous than female births) were the major contributors to this excess male growth.[1]

[Numbers in thousands. Rate per 1,000 population.]

Year	Number[1]	Rate
1970	3,731	18.4
1971	3,556	17.2
1972	3,258	15.6
1973	3,137	14.8
1974	3,160	14.8
1975	3,144	14.6
1976	3,168	14.6
1977	3,327	15.1
1978	3,333	15.0
1979	3,494	15.6
1980	3,612	15.9
1981	3,629	15.8
1982	3,681	15.9
1983	3,639	15.6
1984	3,669	15.6
1985	3,761	15.8
1986	3,757	15.6
1987	3,809	15.7

[Continued]

★ 677 ★

Live Births: 1970 to 1993
[Continued]

Year	Number[1]	Rate
1988	3,910	16.0
1989	4,041	16.4
1990	4,158	16.7
1991	4,111	16.3
1992	4,084	16.0
1993	4,039	15.7

Source: Selected from "Live Births, Deaths, Marriages, and Divorces: 1950 to 1992," U.S. Bureau of the Census, *Statistical Abstract of the United States, 1994*, table 90, p. 75. 1993 data are provisional statistics from *Monthly Vital Statistics Report*, 42(12), May 13, 1994, p. 1. Primary source: U.S. National Center for Health Statistics, *Vital Statistics of the United States*, annual, *Monthly Vital Statistics Report*, and unpublished data. *Notes:* 1. U.S. Bureau of the Census, *Current Population Reports*, "Population Profile of the United States 1993," p. 2. 2. Excludes births to nonresidents of the United States.

★ 678 ★
Births

Location of Births and Birth Weights: 1970-1991

This table shows numbers of attended births by place of delivery, median birth-weight totals and figures for black and white babies, and the percent of births with low birth weight, 1970 to 1991.

[Births in thousands.]

Year	Births Attended (1,000)			Median Birth Weight[3]			Percent of births with low birth weight		
	In hospital[1]	Not in hospital		Total[4]	White	Black	Total[3]	White	Black
		Physician	Midwife and other[2]						
1970	3,708	5	18	7lb-4oz	7lb-5oz	6lb-14oz	7.9%	6.8%	13.9%
1975	3,105	11	28	7lb-5oz	7lb-7oz	6lb-15 oz	7.4%	6.3%	13.1%
1980	3,576	12	24	7lb-7oz	7lb-8oz	7lb-0oz	6.8%	5.7%	12.5%
1985	3,722	10	29	7lb-7oz	7lb-9oz	7lb-0oz	6.8%	5.6%	12.4%
1986	3,720	9	27	7lb-7oz	7lb-9oz	7lb-0oz	6.8%	5.6%	12.5%
1987	3,774	8	27	7lb-7oz	7lb-9oz	7lb-0oz	6.9%	5.7%	12.7%
1988	3,872	9	28	7lb-7oz	7lb-9oz	7lb-0oz	6.9%	5.6%	13.0%
1989	3,991	13	22	7lb-7oz	7lb-8oz	6lb-15oz	7.0%	5.7%	13.2%
1990	4,110	14	21	7lb-7oz	7lb-8oz	7lb-0oz	7.0%	5.7%	13.3%
1991	4,064	46	22	7lb-7oz	7lb-8oz	6lb-159z	7.1%	5.8%	13.6%

Source: Selected from "Live Births, by Place of Delivery, Median and Low Birth Weight, and Prenatal Care: 1970 to 1991", U.S. Bureau of the Census, *Statistical Abstract of the United States, 1994*, table 98, p. 79. Primary source: U.S. National Center for Health Statistics, *Vital Statistics of the United States*, annual; *Monthly Vital Statistics Report*; and unpublished data. Represents registered births. Excludes births to nonresidents of the United States. *Notes:* 1. Includes all births in hospitals or institutions and in clinics. 2. Includes births with attendant not specified. 3. Beginning 1989, median birth weight based on race of mother; prior to 1989, based on race of child. 4. Includes other races not shown separately. 5. Through 1975, births of 2,500 grams (5 lb.- 8 oz.) or less at birth; thereafter, less than 2,500 grams.

★ 679 ★

Births

Multiple Births: 1985-1991

This table gives data about multiple births by age of the mother in 1985 and 1991. Incidence of plural births increases with the age of the mother, and the rate reached 3.4 for white women and 3.6 for black women aged 35 to 39 in 1991. Multiple birth rates were 14% higher in 1991 than in 1985 for women of all races and ages combined. The rates increased in each age group, with the larges rise among women between 40 and 44 years of age.

[Rate per 1,000 total live births.]

Age of mother	1985			1991		
	All plural deliveries	Twin births	Triplet/other high order	All plural deliveries	Twin births	Triplet/other high order
Total	21.0	20.5	0.5	23.9	23.1	0.8
Under 15	9.6	9.3	0.3	11.6	11.3	0.2
15-19	13.2	13.1	0.1	14.6	14.4	0.2
20-24	18.7	18.3	0.4	19.8	19.4	0.4
25-29	22.3	21.6	0.7	24.5	23.7	0.8
30-34	26.2	25.5	0.7	29.9	28.4	1.4
35-39	27.0	26.3	0.7	33.5	31.8	1.7
40-44	21.0	20.5	0.6	26.8	26.3	0.5
45-49	18.9	18.9	--	20.5	20.5	--

Source: "Birth Rates by Plurality and Age of Mother United States, 1985 and 1991," *Statistical Bulletin,* 75(3), July-September 1994, Table 2, p. 31. *R Primary sources: National Center for Health Statistics; computations by the Health and Safety Education Division, Medical Department, Metropolitan Life Insurance Company.

★ 680 ★

Births

Multiple Births: 1991

This table shows the total number of live births for all races and for whites and blacks; multiple births as a percent of total live births; and live twin births as a percent of total multiple births in 1991. Since the early 1970s, the number and rate of multiple births have increased steadily. Rates are higher among black women than white and are more prevalent among older women. Incidence of low birthweight babies is more frequent among multiple births. The District of Columbia, Michigan, and Massachusetts registered the highest percentage of multiple births in 1991. The lowest rates were recorded in Mexico and Wyoming.

Age of Mother	Live births			Multiple births as percent of total live births			Live twin births as percent of total multiple births		
	All races	White	Black	All races	White	Black	All races	White	Black
Total	4,110,907	3,241,273	682,602	2.4%	2.3%	2.8%	96.6%	96.2%	98.1%
Under 15 years	12,014	5,189	6,419	1.2%	1.3%	1.0%	97.8%	100.0%	95.3%
15-19 years	519,577	352,359	150,956	1.5%	1.3%	1.8%	99.0%	99.4%	98.1%
20-24 years	1,089,692	831,233	218,918	2.0%	1.8%	2.8%	98.1%	98.1%	98.1%
25-29 years	1,219,965	1,000,138	163,052	2.5%	2.4%	3.1%	96.6%	96.3%	98.0%

[Continued]

★ 680 ★

Multiple Births: 1991
[Continued]

Age of Mother	Live births			Multiple births as percent of total live births			Live twin births as percent of total multiple births		
	All races	White	Black	All races	White	Black	All races	White	Black
30-34 years	884,862	736,816	99,637	3.0%	3.0%	3.5%	95.2%	94.7%	98.5%
35-39 years	330,993	272,511	37,362	3.3%	3.4%	3.6%	95.0%	94.5%	97.1%
40-44 years	52,095	41,792	6,064	2.7%	2.7%	2.7%	98.0%	98.4%	95.7%
45-49 years	1,709	1,235	194	2.0%	1.9%	0.5%	100.0%	100.0%	100.0%

Source: "Live Births by Race of Child and Age of Mother, United States, 1991," *Statistical Bulletin,* 75(3), July-September 1994, Table 1, p. 30. Primary sources: National Center for Health Statistics; computations by the Health and Safety Education Division, Medical Department, Metropolitan Life Insurance Company.

★ 681 ★

Births

North African Births: 1994

This table shows births, births per 1,000 population, and the rate of natural increase in North Africa in 1994.

[Births in thousands. Birth rate per 1,000 population.]

Country	Births	Rate	Rate of nat. increase
North Africa	3,967	31	2.3%
Algeria	829	30	2.3%
Egypt	1,879	32	2.3%
Libya	229	45	3.7%
Morocco	816	29	2.2%
Tunisia	204	23	1.8%
Western Sahara	10	47	2.8%

Source: Selected from "Population, Vital Events, and Rates, by Country or Area: 1994," U.S. Bureau of the Census, *World Population Profile: 1994,* 1994, Table 4, p. A-10. Primary source: U.S. Bureau of the Census, International Data Base. *Note:* 1. Less than 500 or between 0.05 and - 0.05%.

★ 682 ★

Births

North American Births: 1994

This table shows births, births per 1,000 population, and the rate of natural increase in North America in 1994.

[Births in thousands. Birth rate per 1,000 population.]

Country	Births	Rate	Rate of nat. increase
North America	4,631	15	0.7%
Bermuda	1	15	0.8%
Canada	396	14	0.7%
Greenland	1	19	1.1%
Saint Pierre and Miquelon	1	13	0.7%
United States	3,963	15	0.7%

Source: Selected from "Population, Vital Events, and Rates, by Country or Area: 1994," U.S. Bureau of the Census, *World Population Profile: 1994*, 1994, Table 4, p. A-12. Primary source: U.S. Bureau of the Census, International Data Base. *Note:* 1. Less than 500 or between 0.05 and - 0.05%.

★ 683 ★

Births

Oceanian Births: 1994

This table shows births, births per 1,000 population, and the rate of natural increase in Oceania in 1994.

[Births in thousands. Birth rate per 1,000 population.]

Country	Births	Rate	Rate of nat. increase
Oceania	527	19	1.1%
American Samoa	2	37	3.3%
Australia	258	14	0.7%
Cook Islands	1	23	1.8%
Federated States of Micronesia	3	28	2.2%
Fiji	18	24	1.8%
French Polynesia	6	28	2.2%
Guam	4	26	2.2%
Kiribati	2	32	1.9%
Marshall Islands	3	46	3.9%
Nauru	1	18	1.3%
New Caledonia	4	22	1.7%
New Zealand	53	16	0.7%
Northern Mariana Islands	2	35	3.0%

[Continued]

★ 683 ★

Oceanian Births: 1994
[Continued]

Country	Births	Rate	Rate of nat. increase
Papua New Guinea	141	34	2.3%
Solomon Islands	15	39	3.4%
Tonga	3	25	1.8%
Trust Territory of the Pacific Islands (Palau)	1	23	1.6%
Tuvalu	1	26	1.7%
Vanuatu	5	32	2.3%
Wallis and Futuna	1	26	2.1%
Western Samoa	7	32	2.6%

Source: Selected from "Population, Vital Events, and Rates, by Country or Area: 1994," U.S. Bureau of the Census, *World Population Profile: 1994*, 1994, Table 4, p. A-13. Primary source: U.S. Bureau of the Census, International Data Base. *Note:* 1. Less than 500 or between 0.05 and - 0.05%.

★ 684 ★
Births

Sub-Saharan Africa Births: 1994

This table shows births, births per 1,000 population, and the rate of natural increase in Sub-Saharan Africa in 1994. Population growth rates here are the highest in the world and have been steadily increasing because of declining mortality.

[Births in thousands. Birth rate per 1,000 population.]

Country	Births	Rate	Rate of nat. increase
Sub-Saharan Africa	25,180	44	2.9%
Angola	445	45	2.7%
Benin	255	48	3.3%
Botswana	44	32	2.4%
Burkina	491	48	3.0%
Burundi	270	44	2.3%
Cameroon	532	41	2.9%
Cape Verde	20	46	3.7%
Central African Republic	133	42	2.2%
Chad	230	42	2.2%
Comoros	25	46	3.6%
Congo	99	40	2.4%
Cote d'Ivoire	665	47	3.2%
Dijibouti	18	43	2.7%
Equatorial Guinea	17	41	2.6%

[Continued]

★ 684 ★

Sub-Saharan Africa Births: 1994

[Continued]

Country	Births	Rate	Rate of nat. increase
Ethiopia	2,643	45	3.1%
Gabon	32	28	1.5%
Gambia	45	46	3.1%
Ghana	760	44	3.2%
Guinea	282	44	2.4%
Guinea-Bissau	45	41	2.4%
Kenya	1,199	42	3.1%
Lesotho	66	34	2.5%
Liberia	129	43	3.1%
Madagascar	607	45	3.2%
Malawi	491	50	2.7%
Mali	472	52	3.1%
Mauritania	104	48	3.2%
Mauritius	22	19	1.3%
Mayotte	5	49	3.8%
Mozambique	780	45	2.9%
Namibia	69	43	3.5%
Niger	494	57	3.5%
Nigeria	4,269	44	3.1%
Reunion	16	25	2.0%
Rwanda	412	49	2.8%
Saint Helena	1	10	0.3%
Sao Tome and Principe	5 ·	35	2.6%
Senegal	377	43	3.1%
Seychelles	2	22	1.5%
Sierra Leone	209	45	2.6%
Somalia	306	46	3.2%
South Africa	1,475	34	2.6%
Sudan	1,234	42	3.0%
Swaziland	40	43	3.2%
Tanzania	1,273	45	2.6%
Togo	201	47	3.6%
Uganda	979	49	2.6%
Zaire	2,065	48	3.2%
Zambia	423	46	2.8%
Zimbabwe	409	37	1.9%

Source: Selected from "Population, Vital Events, and Rates, by Country or Area: 1994," U.S. Bureau of the Census, *World Population Profile: 1994*, 1994, Table 4, p. A-9. Primary source: U.S. Bureau of the Census, International Data Base. *Note:* 1. Less than 500 or between 0.05 and - 0.05%.

★ 685 ★

Births

World Births: 1994

This table shows births in thousands and births per 1,000 population for major world regions and development categories in 1994. World population had reached 5.6 billion in 1994 and was expected to increase to 7.9 billion by the year 2020. Of these 2.3 billion new persons, more than 9 out of 10 will be added in today's developing regions—more than 1 billion in Asia alone. In 1994 the world's children aged 0 to 4 years outnumbered persons aged 60 and over. By the year 2020, the number of elderly will exceed the number of young children. Total world births are expected to continue to increase to 250 million in 2020. At the same time the world's total fertility rate will decline to 2.5 children per woman. India was the world leader in total births in 1994, with more births than the 50 Sub-Saharan African countries combined.

[Population and events in thousands.]

Region	Population	Births	Births per 1,000 pop.
World	5,642,151	139,324	25
Developing	4,401,797	122,380	28
Developed	1,240,354	16,944	14
Africa	701,327	29,148	42
Sub-Saharan Africa	571,552	25,180	44
North Africa	129,775	3,967	31
Asia	3,344,623	82,868	25
Asia, excl. Near East	3,915,443	77,792	24
Near East	149,180	5,076	34
Latin America/Caribbean	474,155	11,461	24
North America	288,952	4,361	15
Europe	508,828	6,278	12
(Former) Soviet Union	296,000	4,682	16
Baltics	8,214	117	14
Commonwealth of Independent States	282,105	4,473	16
Georgia	5,681	92	16
Oceania	28,265	527	19
Excluding China:			
World	4,451,720	117,778	26
Developing	3,211,366	100,833	31
Asia	2,154,192	61,321	28
Excl. Near East	2,005,012	56,245	28

Source: Selected from "Population, Vital Events, and Rates, by Region and Development Category: 1994," U.S. Bureau of the Census, *World Population Profile: 1994*, 1994, Table 2, p. A-3. Primary source: U.S. Bureau of the Census, International Data Base.

Contraception

★ 686 ★

Contraceptive Use in Asia and the Near East

This table shows the percent of currently married women using contraception, by method, in Asian and Near Eastern countries. Figures are shown for the latest available year. Data refer to ages 15 to 49 years unless specified otherwise.In Bangladesh, an aggressive family planning program halved the nation's birthrate between 1970 and 1990. Women drawn from villages distribute family planning materials to other village women[14].

[NA Not available. Z Less than 0.05 percent.]

Region, country or area, and year	No method	All methods	Pill	IUD	Condom	Sterilization		Other modern	Tradi-tional	Source	Remarks
						Male	Female				
Asia, excluding Near East											
Afghanistan											
1972-73	98.0%	2.0%	1.1%	0.4%	0.2%	NA	NA	0.2%	NA	Survey	1
Bangladesh											
1991	60.1%	39.9%	13.9%	1.8%	2.5%	1.2%	9.1%	2.6%	8.7%	Survey	2
China											
Mainland, 1988	28.9%	71.1%	3.5%	29.5%	1.9%	7.8%	27.2%	1.2%	NA	Survey	
Taiwan, 1985	22.0%	78.0%	NA	NA	NA	NA	NA	NA	NA	Survey	
Hong Kong											
1987	19.2%	80.8%	16.4%	4.5%	26.0%	0.9%	22.9%	4.3%	5.9%	Survey	
India											
1990	55.1%	44.9%	NA	NA	NA	X	31.3%[13]	8.6%	5.0%	Survey	1,3
Indonesia											
1991	50.3%	49.7%	14.8%	13.3%	0.8%	0.6%	2.7%	14.8%	2.6%	DHS	
Iran											
1978	77.0%	23.0%	19.8%	2.1%	NA	X	0.2%[13]	NA	0.9%	PC	1,4
Japan											
1990	42.0%	58.0%	NA	3.3%	42.9%	X	5.7%[13]	NA	14.1%	Survey	5,6
Malaysia											
1984	48.6%	51.4%	11.6%	2.0%	7.7%	0.2%	7.7%	1.0%	21.3%	Survey	7
Nepal											
1986	83.2%	16.8%	1.4%	0.3%	0.7%	6.4%	7.3%	NA	0.6%	Survey	8
Pakistan											
1990-91	88.2%	11.8%	0.7%	1.3%	2.7%	Z	3.5%	0.8%	2.8%	DHS	
Philippines											
1988	63.8%	36.2%	6.9%	2.4%	0.7%	0.4%	11.0%	0.2%	14.5%	Survey	
Singapore											
1982	25.8%	74.2%	11.6%	NA	24.3%	0.6%	22.3%	14.2%	1.2%	Survey	1
South Korea											
1988	22.7%	77.3%	2.8%	6.7%	10.2%	11.0%	37.2%	2.3%	7.1%	Survey	1
Sri Lanka											
1987	38.3%	61.7%	4.1%	2.1%	1.9%	4.9%	24.9%	2.7%	21.2%	DHS	9
Thailand											
1987	34.5%	65.5%	18.6%	6.9%	1.1%	5.7%	22.8%	8.5%	1.9%	DHS	
Vietnam											
1988	46.9%	53.2%	0.4%	33.1%	1.2%	0.3%	2.7%	NA	15.4%	Survey	

[Continued]

★ 686 ★

Contraceptive Use in Asia and the Near East
[Continued]

Region, country or area, and year	No method	All methods	Pill	IUD	Condom	Sterilization Male	Sterilization Female	Other modern	Tradi-tional	Source	Remarks
Near East											
Bahrain 1989	46.6%	53.4%	13.1%	1.7%	8.2%	NA	7.1%	0.2%	23.0%	Survey	10,11
Iraq 1989	86.3%	13.7%	4.7%	2.8%	1.0%	NA	1.4%	0.5%	3.2%	Survey	10,11
Jordan 1990	65.1%	34.9%	4.6%	15.3%	0.8%	Z	5.6%	0.6%	8.0%	DHS	
Kuwait 1987	65.4%	34.6%	24.0%	3.7%	1.5%	NA	2.0%	0.5%	2.9%	Survey	10,11
Lebanon 1971	47.0%	53.0%	13.8%	1.1%	6.9%	1.1%	NA	NA	35.0%	Survey	5
Oman 1988	91.4%	8.6%	2.4%	1.5%	1.1%	NA	2.2%	0.3%	1.1%	Survey	10,11
Qatar 1987	68.0%	32.0%	13.0%	9.0%	2.0%	NA	4.0%	NA	3.0%	Survey	11
Syria 1978	80.0%	20.0%	12.0%	1.0%	1.0%	NA	NA	1.0%	5.0%	WFS	1
Turkey 1988	36.6%	63.4%	6.2%	14.0%	7.2%	0.1%	1.7%	1.9%	32.3%	Survey	4
Yemen 1991-92	92.9%	7.1%	3.2%	1.2%	0.1%	0.1%	0.8%	0.6%	1.1%	DHS	12

Source: Selected from "Percent of Currently Married Women Using Contraception by Method: All Available Years," U.S. Bureau of the Census, *World Population Profile: 1994,* February 1994, Table 9, p. A-34. Primary sources: U.S. Bureau of the Census, International Data Base. **PC:** Population Council. Data from this source usually refer to program service statistics, sometimes with an estimate for private sector contraceptive use. Such data are often unreliable unless confirmed by an independent source such as a nationwide contraceptive prevalence or fertility survey. **Survey:** A nationwide survey conducted by a national government or independent organization, but not related to CPS, DHS, or WFS. **WFS:** World fertility survey. **DHS:** Demographic and Health survey. *Notes:* 1. Data refer to ages 15-44. 2. Data refer to ages under 56 years. 3. "Other modern" refers to all modern methods. 4. Total prevalence rate refers to currently married women, while data by method are based on exposed women. 5. Sum of data by method exceeds total prevalence rate because some women reported using more than one method. 6. Pill is included with IUD. 7. Data refer to Peninsular Malaysia only. 8. Data refer to ages 15 to 50 years. 9. Data exclude the northern and eastern provinces. 10. Data refer to nationals only. 11. Data refer to ages under 50 years. 12. Excludes breastfeeding. 13. This figure is the total percentage of males and females using sterilization as a contraceptive method. 14. John F. Burns, "Bangladesh, Still Poor, Cuts Birth Rate Sharply," *The New York Times,* September 13, 1994, p. A5 Y.

★ 687 ★

Contraception

Contraceptive Use in Asia and the Near East by Age of Woman

This table shows the percent of currently married women using contraception, by age of woman, in Asian and Near Eastern countries. Figures are shown for the latest available year.

[NA Not available.]

Region, country or area, and year	15 to 19 years	20 to 24 years	25 to 29 years	30 to 34 years	35 to 39 years	40 to 44 years	45 to 49 years	Source
Asia, excluding Near East								
Bangladesh 1991	18.7%	32.6%	45.6%	52.5%	57.0%	46.4%	29.9%	Survey

[Continued]

★ 687 ★

Contraceptive Use in Asia and the Near East by Age of Woman
[Continued]

Region, country or area, and year	15 to 19 years	20 to 24 years	25 to 29 years	30 to 34 years	35 to 39 years	40 to 44 years	45 to 49 years	Source
China								
Mainland, 1988	11.2%	38.1%	70.6%	87.6%	91.4%	84.1%	51.7%	Survey
Hong Kong								
1982	62.0%	62.0%	73.2%	82.0%	86.2%	74.2%	NA	Survey
India								
1990	NA	19.2%	43.3%	57.6%	65.2%	59.5%	NA	Survey
Indonesia								
1991	30.0%	51.0%	53.6%	56.8%	57.5%	48.3%	27.4%	DHS
Japan								
1986	100.0%	55.1%	56.7%	71.0%	73.1%	70.7%	46.9%	Survey
Malaysia								
1974	21.2%	38.2%	48.0%	44.7%	41.8%	36.5%	16.2%	WFS
Nepal								
1986	1.6%	7.8%	16.1%	26.7%	25.3%	20.5%	13.3%	Survey
Pakistan								
1990-91	2.6%	6.3%	9.6%	13.4%	20.4%	15.8%	11.8%	DHS
Philippines								
1986	9.1%	21.0%	33.1%	40.0%	40.0%	35.5%	20.0%	CPS
Singapore								
1982	60.0%	60.0%	72.4%	72.4%	79.0%	79.0%	NA	Survey
South Korea								
1988	X	45.0%[1]	65.0%	87.0%	90.0%	82.0%	NA	Survey
Sri Lanka								
1987	20.2%	42.3%	57.3%	66.8%	73.8%	71.5%	56.1%	DHS
Thailand								
1987	43.0%	56.8%	69.1%	75.0%	73.3%	69.4%	48.4%	DHS
Vietnam								
1988	5.3%	31.7%	52.2%	59.8%	68.8%	65.4%	47.1%	Survey
Near East								
Jordan								
1990	7.7%	22.3%	30.0%	41.9%	47.3%	49.3%	32.8%	DHS
Syria								
1978	9.0%	15.0%	19.0%	24.0%	31.0%	24.0%	NA	WFS
Turkey								
1988	58.4%	58.4%	82.2%	82.2%	83.9%	83.9%	71.8%	Survey
Yemen								
1991-92	1.4%	5.0%	8.5%	7.9%	9.8%	7.7%	5.0%	DHS

Source: Selected from "Percent of Currently Married Women Using Contraception by Age: All Available Years," U.S. Bureau of the Census, *World Population Profile: 1994,* February 1994, Table 10, p. A-46. Primary sources: U.S. Bureau of the Census, International Data Base. **DHS:** Demographic and health survey. **Survey:** A nationwide survey conducted by a national government or independent organization, but not related to CPS, DHS, or WFS, and not otherwise specified. **WFS:** World fertility survey. **CPS:** Contraceptive Prevalence Survey. *Note:* 1. This figure is the total percentage of women aged 15 to 24 years.

★ 688 ★
Contraception

Contraceptive Use in Europe

This table shows the percent of currently married women using contraception, by method, in Europe. Figures are shown for the latest available year. Data refer to ages 15 to 49 years unless specified otherwise.

[NA Not available. Z Less than 0.05%.]

Region, country or area, and year	No method	All methods	Pill	IUD	Condom	Sterilization Male	Sterilization Female	Other modern	Tradi- tional	Source	Remarks
Europe											
Austria											
1981-82	28.6%	71.4%	40.0%	8.4%	4.0%	0.3%	1.0%	2.6%	15.2%	Survey	1,2
Belgium											
1982-83	19.0%	81.0%	32.0%	8.0%	6.0%	NA	17.0%	Z	17.0%	Survey	3,4
Bulgaria											
1976	24.0%	76.0%	2.0%	2.0%	2.0%	1.0%	1.0%	NA	68.0%	WFS	5
Czechoslovakia											
1977	5.0%	95.0%	14.0%	18.0%	13.0%	Z	3.0%	1.0%	46.0%	WFS	6
Denmark											
1975	37.0%	63.0%	22.0%	9.0%	25.0%	NA	NA	4.0%	2.0%	WFS	5
Finland											
1977	20.0%	80.0%	11.0%	29.0%	32.0%	1.0%	4.0%	1.0%	3.0%	WFS	6,7
France											
1988	20.1%	79.9%	27.0%	24.4%	4.2%	NA	8.7%	NA	15.6%	Survey	8
Germany											
1985	22.1%	77.9%	33.7%	14.6%	5.7%	2.1%	10.3%	1.2%	10.1%	Survey	9
Hungary											
1986	26.9%	73.1%	39.3%	18.6%	3.5%	NA	NA	0.9%	10.7%	Survey	10,11
Ireland											
1973	40.1%	59.9%	NANA	NA	NA	NA	NA	NA		Survey	
Italy											
1979	22.0%	78.0%	14.0%	2.0%	13.0%	Z	1.0%	2.0%	46.0%	WFS	12
Netherlands											
1988	24.0%	76.0%	41.0%	7.0%	8.0%	11.0%	4.0%	NA	4.0%	Survey	13
Norway											
1988	24.5%	75.5%	17.8%	24.1%	14.0%	4.3%	10.4%	1.1%	10.7%	Survey	14,15
Poland											
1977	25.0%	75.0%	7.0%	2.0%	14.0%	NA	NA	3.0%	49.0%	WFS	6
Portugal											
1979-80	33.7%	66.3%	19.1%	3.6%	5.6%	0.1%	0.9%	3.5%	33.6%	WFS	
Romania											
1978	42.0%	58.0%	1.0%	Z	3.0%	NA	NA	1.0%	53.0%	WFS	16
Spain											
1985	40.6%	59.4%	15.5%	5.7%	12.2%	0.3%	4.3%	NA	21.5%	Survey	8
Sweden											
1981	22.0%	78.0%	23.0%	20.0%	25.0%	NA	2.0%	NA	7.0%	WFS	3
Switzerland											
1980	28.8%	71.2%	28.0%	10.6%	8.4%	NA	15.8%	2.1%	6.4%	Survey	1,17

[Continued]

★ 688 ★

Contraceptive Use in Europe
[Continued]

Region, country or area, and year	No method	All methods	Pill	IUD	Condom	Sterilization		Other modern	Tradi- tional	Source	Remarks
						Male	Female				
United Kingdom 1989	28.0%	72.0%	25.0%	6.0%	16.0%	12.0%	11.0%	1.0%	7.0%	Survey	10,12,14

Source: Selected from "Percent of Currently Married Women Using Contraception by Method: All Available Years," U.S. Bureau of the Census, *World Population Profile: 1994*, February 1994, Table 9, p. A-40. Primary sources: U.S. Bureau of the Census, International Data Base. Survey: A nationwide survey conducted by a national government or independent organization. **WFS:** World fertility survey. *Notes:* 1. Age range is not specified. 2. Data refer to women who married in 1974 and 1978. 3. Data refer to ages 20 to 44 years. 4. Data refer to the Flemish population only. 5. Data refer to ages 18 to 44 years. 6. Data refer to ages under 45 years. 7. Data refer to women in their first marriage. 8. Data refer to ages 18 to 49 years. 9. Data refer to Federal Republic of Germany. 10. "Other modern" methods refer to female barrier methods. 11. Data refer to ages 15 to 39 years. 12. Data refer to all women ages 18 to 44 years. 13. Data refer to ages 18 to 37 years. 14. Sum of data by method exceeds total prevalence rate because some women reported using more than one method. 15. Data refer to ages 20 to 42 years. 16. Data refer to ages 15 to 44. 17. Data refer to sample of husbands and wives.

★ 689 ★

Contraception

Contraceptive Use in Europe by Age of Woman

This table shows the percent of currently married women using contraception, by age of woman, in Europe. Figures are shown for the latest available year.

[NA Not available.]

Region, country or area, and year	15 to 19 years	20 to 24 years	25 to 29 years	30 to 34 years	35 to 39 years	40 to 44 years	45 to 49 years	Source	Remarks
Europe									
France 1988	50.0%	63.9%	72.3%	84.3%	87.1%	84.4%	73.4%	Survey	1
Hungary 1986	58.6%	57.7%	74.7%	76.7%	76.7%	NA	NA	Survey	
Italy 1979	81.0%	81.05	78.0%	78.0%	78.0%	78.0%	NA	WFS	
Norway 1977	87.0%	84.0%	83.0%	88.0%	85.0%	78.0%	NA	WFS	
Portugal 1979-80	76.8%	72.6%	77.2%	81.2%	77.5%	76.0%	69.4%	WFS	
Spain 1985	44.8%	63.9%	64.8%	68.0%	62.5%	53.1%	34.2%	Survey	1
Sweden 1981	NA	77.2%	73.0%	78.0%	80.5%	80.5%	NA	WFS	
United Kingdom 1983	66.0%	72.0%	82.0%	85.0%	88.0%	85.0%	NA	Survey	1

Source: Selected from "Percent of Currently Married Women Using Contraception by Age: All Available Years," U.S. Bureau of the Census, *World Population Profile: 1994*, February 1994, Table 10, p. A-50. Primary sources: U.S. Bureau of the Census, International Data Base. Survey: A nationwide survey conducted by a national government or independent organization, but not related to Contraceptive prevalence survey, Demographic and Health Survey, or World fertility survey, and not otherwise specified. **WFS:** World fertility survey. *Note:* 1. Rate shown for ages 15 to 19 refers to 18 to 19 years.

★ 690 ★

Contraception

Contraceptive Use in Latin America and the Caribbean

This table shows the percent of currently married women using contraception, by method, in Latin American and Caribbean countries. Figures are shown for the latest available year. Data refer to ages 15 to 49 years unless specified otherwise. Brazil, one of the six most populous countries in the world in 1994, has the world's largest Roman Catholic population. In a survey conducted there in June 1994, 88% of respondents said they don't follow church teachings on birth control. Among women aged 25 to 44, the "don't follow" group was 90%.

[NA Not available. Z Less than 0.05 percent.]

Region, country or area, and year	No method	All methods	Pill	IUD	Condom	Sterilization Male	Sterilization Female	Other modern	Tradi-tional	Source	Remarks
Latin America and the Caribbean											
Antigua and Barbuda											
1988	47.4%	52.6%	26.0%	1.0%	6.0%	NA	11.0%	6.0%	2.0%	CPS	1
Bahamas											
1988	35.1%	64.9%	33.1%	3.9%	2.5%	NA	17.2%	6.6%	1.7%	CPS	1
Barbados											
1988	45.0%	55.0%	26.2%	5.3%	7.2%	0.3%	10.4%	3.8%	1.8%	CPS	
Belize											
1991	53.3%	46.7%	14.9%	1.9%	1.9%	NA	18.7%	6.7%	2.5%	CPS	1
Bolivia											
1989	69.7%	30.3%	1.9%	4.8%	0.3%	NA	4.4%	0.8%	18.0%	DHS	
Brazil											
1986	34.2%	65.8%	25.1%	1.0%	1.7%	0.8%	26.8%	1.1%	9.3%	DHS	1
Chile											
1978	57.0%	43.0%	NA	NA	NA	NA	NA	NA	NA	SS	1
Colombia											
1990	33.9%	66.1%	14.1%	12.4%	2.9%	0.5%	20.9%	3.9%	11.5%	DHS	
Costa Rica											
1986	32.0%	68.0%	18.8%	7.3%	12.7%	0.5%	16.4%	1.8%	10.6%	Survey	
Cuba											
1987	30.0%	70.0%	10.0%	33.0%	2.0%	NA	22.0%	Z	2.0%	Survey	2
Dominica											
1987	50.2%	49.8%	16.5%	1.7%	5.6%	NA	12.6%	11.8%	1.7%	CPS	
Dominican Republic											
1991	43.6%	56.4%	9.8%	1.8%	1.2%	NA	38.5%	0.5%	4.7%	DHS	
Ecuador											
1989	47.1%	52.9%	8.6%	11.9%	1.3%	NA	18.3%	1.4%	11.3%	Survey	
El Salvador											
1988	52.9%	47.1%	7.6%	2.0%	2.4%	0.6%	29.6%	1.3%	3.4%	Survey	1
Grenada											
1985	69.0%	31.0%	8.0%	2.7%	8.6%	NA	NA	7.8%	3.9%	CPS	1
Guadeloupe											
1976	56.0%	44.0%	9.8%	3.4%	NA	X	11.6%[6]	6.3%	13.0%	WFS	
Guatemala											
1987	76.8%	23.2%	3.9%	1.8%	1.2%	0.9%	10.4%	0.9%	4.1%	DHS	1
Guyana											
1975	67.9%	32.1%	9.9%	5.8%	3.1%	X	7.9%[6]	2.3%	3.0%	WFS	1,3
Haiti											
1989	89.8%	10.2%	4.1%	0.6%	0.5%	NA	2.5%	1.7%	0.8%	CPS	
Honduras											
1987	59.4%	40.6%	13.4%	4.3%	1.8%	NA	12.6%	4.9%	3.5%	Survey	1
Jamaica											
1989	45.4%	54.6%	19.5%	1.5%	8.6%	0.1%	13.6%	8.0%	3.4%	CPS	
Martinique											
1976	49.0%	51.3%	17.3%	2.6%	4.6%	Z	11.7%	1.7%	13.5%	WFS	1

[Continued]

★ 690 ★

Contraceptive Use in Latin America and the Caribbean
[Continued]

Region, country or area, and year	No method	All methods	Pill	IUD	Condom	Sterilization Male	Sterilization Female	Other modern	Tradi-tional	Source	Remarks
Mexico											
1987	47.3%	52.7%	9.7%	10.2%	1.9%	0.8%	18.6%	3.4%	8.1%	DHS	
Montserrat											
1984	47.6%	52.4%	30.5%	11.0%	3.4%	NA	1.6%	5.6%	0.3%	CPS	1
Nicaragua											
1981	73.0%	27.0%	10.5%	2.3%	0.8%	0.1%	7.1%	2.0%	4.3%	CPS	1,4
Panama											
1984	41.8%	58.2%	11.8%	6.0%	1.6%	0.4%	32.4%	2.0%	4.0%	Survey	1
Paraguay											
1990	51.6%	48.4%	13.6%	5.7%	2.6%	NA	7.4%	6.0%	13.2%	DHS	
Peru											
1991-92	41.0%	59.0%	5.7%	13.4%	2.8%	0.1%	7.9%	2.9%	26.2%	DHS	
Puerto Rico											
1982	29.6%	70.4%	9.3%	4.1%	4.6%	4.4%	39.7%	NA	8.3%	Survey	1
Saint Kitts and Nevis											
1984	59.4%	40.6%	19.7%	3.8%	5.6%	NA	2.6%	5.3%	3.6%	CPS	1
Saint Lucia											
1988	52.3%	47.3%	18.4%	4.3%	5.8%	Z	8.6%	9.0%	1.3%	CPS	1
Saint Vincent and the Grenadines											
1988	41.7%	58.3%	24.3%	2.7%	7.4%	Z	13.1%	10.8%	Z	CPS	1
Trinidad and Tobago											
1987	47.3%	52.7%	14.0%	4.4%	11.8%	0.2%	8.2%	6.1%	7.9%	DHS	
Venezuela											
1977	39.7%	60.3%	18.8%	10.5%	5.9%	0.1%	9.4%	5.0%	10.7%	WFS	1,5

Source: Selected from "Percent of Currently Married Women Using Contraception by Method: All Available Years," U.S. Bureau of the Census, *World Population Profile: 1994*, February 1994, Table 9, p. A-37. The introductory remarks about Brazil are from James Brooke, "With Church Preaching in Vain, Brazilians Embrace Birth Control," *The New York Times*, September 2, 1994, p. A1+. Primary sources: U.S. Bureau of the Census, International Data Base. **CPS:** Contraceptive prevalence survey. **DHS:** Demographic and health survey. **PC:** Population Council. Data from this source usually refer to program service statistics, sometimes with an estimate for private sector contraceptive use. Such data are often unreliable unless confirmed by an independent source such as a nationwide contraceptive prevalence or fertility survey. **Survey:** A nationwide survey conducted by a national government or independent organization, but not related to CPS, DHS, or WFS. **WFS:** World fertility survey. *Notes:* 1. Data refer to ages 15-44. 2. "Other modern" methods refer to female barrier methods. 3. Total prevalence rate refers to currently married women, while data by method are based on exposed women. 4. Total prevalence rate refers to women in union, while data by method are based on all respondents, regardless of marital status. 5. Data refer to women exposed to the risk of pregnancy (currently married nonpregnant women who consider themselves to be fecund.) 6. This figure is the total percentage of males and females who are using sterilization as a contraceptive method.

★ 691 ★

Contraception

Contraceptive Use in Latin America and the Caribbean by Age of Woman

This table shows the percent of currently married women using contraception, by age of woman, in Latin American and Caribbean countries. Figures are shown for the latest available year.

[NA Not available.]

Region, country or area, and year	15 to 19 years	20 to 24 years	25 to 29 years	30 to 34 years	35 to 39 years	40 to 44 years	45 to 49 years	Source	Remarks
Latin America and the Caribbean									
Antigua and Barbuda									
1981	12.2%	38.1%	46.9%	45.9%	58.9%	57.9%	NA	CPS	

[Continued]

★ 691 ★

Contraceptive Use in Latin America and the Caribbean by Age of Woman
[Continued]

Region, country or area, and year	15 to 19 years	20 to 24 years	25 to 29 years	30 to 34 years	35 to 39 years	40 to 44 years	45 to 49 years	Source	Remarks
Bahamas, The									
1988	40.7%	63.4%	68.8%	64.4%	X	78.1%[3]	NA	CPS	
Barbados									
1980-81	27.7%	45.3%	53.6%	58.6%	65.1%	33.6%	NA	CPS	
Belize									
1991	26.2%	36.9%	45.6%	53.6%	54.8%	56.3%	NA	CPS	
Bolivia									
1989	16.0%	22.6%	34.3%	39.2%	36.2%	28.1%	14.8%	DHS	
Brazil									
1986	47.6%	54.1%	67.9%	73.8%	68.9%	66.5%	NA	DHS	
Colombia									
1990	36.9%	54.6%	66.5%	74.7%	76.9%	74.3%	54.0%	DHS	
Costa Rica									
1986	51.0%	60.0%	65.0%	67.0%	84.0%	78.0%	68.0%	Survey	
Dominica									
1981	32.6%	42.1%	54.1%	54.5%	69.0%	69.8%	NA	CPS	
Dominican Republic									
1991	17.4%	42.5%	55.0%	66.2%	71.3%	69.0%	55.0%	DHS	
Ecuador									
1989	25.0%	39.1%	55.2%	63.0%	61.3%	58.6%	44.8%	Survey	
El Salvador									
1988	17.1%	36.6%	51.1%	57.3%	59.4%	53.2%	NA	Survey	
Grenada									
1985	17.2%	34.9%	40.6%	49.1%	51.8%	51.8%	NA	CPS	1
Guatemala									
1987	5.4%	15.5%	21.3%	30.2%	31.1%	28.0%	NA	DHS	
Guyana									
1975	17.5%	24.5%	33.2%	43.3%	39.6%	32.6%	NA	WFS	
Haiti									
1989	5.1%	5.1%	7.1%	16.0%	13.8%	10.6%	6.5%	CPS	
Honduras									
1984	13.1%	30.3%	33.8%	44.3%	45.2%	33.2%	NA	Survey	
Jamaica									
1989	47.9%	52.5%	56.8%	58.3%	59.0%	57.3%	42.8%	CPS	
Mexico									
1987	30.2%	46.9%	54.0%	62.3%	61.3%	60.2%	34.2%	DHS	
Montserrat									
1984	49.8%	47.0%	66.0%	54.9%	X	46.7%[3]	NA	CPS	
Panama									
1984	22.6%	42.8%	57.2%	65.2%	73.8%	72.1%	NA	Survey	
Paraguay									
1990	35.4%	41.5%	52.4%	53.8%	54.9%	50.1%	34.5%	DHS	

[Continued]

★ 691 ★

Contraceptive Use in Latin America and the Caribbean by Age of Woman
[Continued]

Region, country or area, and year	15 to 19 years	20 to 24 years	25 to 29 years	30 to 34 years	35 to 39 years	40 to 44 years	45 to 49 years	Source	Remarks
Peru									
1991-92	29.1%	49.1%	59.5%	67.3%	69.9%	63.8%	42.7%	DHS	
Saint Kitts and Nevis									
1984	30.4%	41.0%	43.8%	42.2%	42.2%	50.9%	NA	CPS	
Saint Lucia									
1981	26.5%	37.1%	55.4%	46.4%	57.8%	55.0%	NA	CPS	
Saint Vincent and the Grenadines									
1981	21.4%	36.1%	46.8%	68.5%	51.8%	65.5%	NA	CPS	
Trinidad and Tobago									
1987	42.4%	55.3%	53.8%	57.1%	55.8%	52.9%	36.3%	DHS	
Venezuela									
1977	54.4%	54.4%	65.0%	65.0%	59.4%	59.4%	NA	WFS	

Source: Selected from "Percent of Currently Married Women Using Contraception by Age: All Available Years," U.S. Bureau of the Census, *World Population Profile: 1994,* February 1994, Table 10, p. A-48. Primary sources: U.S. Bureau of the Census, International Data Base. CPS: Contraceptive prevalence survey. DHS: Demographic and health survey. **Survey:** A nationwide survey conducted by a national government or independent organization, but not related to CPS, DHS, or WFS. **WFS:** World fertility survey. *Notes:* 1. Base for rates by age excludes pregnant women. 2. Rates by age refer to all women regardless of marital status. 3. This figure is the total percentage of women 35 to 44 years.

★ 692 ★

Contraception

Contraceptive Use in North Africa

This table shows the percent of currently married women using contraception, by method, in North African countries. Figures are shown for the latest available year. Prevalence rates in Africa are increasing but remain the lowest among world regions. Data refer to ages 15 to 49 years unless otherwise specified.

[NA Not available. Z Less than 0.05 percent.]

Region, country or area, and year	No method	All methods	Pill	IUD	Condom	Sterilization Male	Sterilization Female	Other modern	Tradi-tional	Source
North Africa										
Algeria										
1986-87	64.5%	35.5%	26.5%	2.1%	0.6%	Z	1.3%	0.8%	4.2%	Survey
Egypt										
1992	52.9%	47.1%	12.9%	27.9%	2.0%	NA	1.1%	0.9%	2.3%	DHS
Morocco										
1992	58.5%	41.5%	28.1%	3.2%	0.9%	NA	3.0%	0.3%	5.9%	DHS
Tunisia										
1988	50.2%	49.8%	8.8%	17.0%	1.3%	NA	11.5%	1.8%	9.4%	DHS

Source: Selected from "Percent of Currently Married Women Using Contraception by Method: All Available Years," U.S. Bureau of the Census, *World Population Profile: 1994,* February 1994, Table 9, p. A-33. Primary sources: U.S. Bureau of the Census, International Data Base. **DHS:** Demographic and health survey. **Survey:** A nationwide survey conducted by a national government or independent organization, but not related to Contraceptive prevalence survey, Demographic and Health Survey, or World fertility survey, and not otherwise specified.

★ 693 ★

Contraception

Contraceptive Use in North Africa by Age of Woman

This table shows the percent of currently married women using contraception, by age of woman, in North African countries. Figures are shown for the latest available year.

Region, country or area, and year	15 to 19 years	20 to 24 years	25 to 29 years	30 to 34 years	35 to 39 years	40 to 44 years	45 to 49 years	Source
North Africa								
Egypt 1992	13.3%	29.7%	46.0%	58.8%	59.6%	55.5%	34.5%	DHS
Morocco 1992	23.3%	35.2%	39.5%	45.4%	47.8%	47.0%	35.1%	DHS
Tunisia 1988	11.1%	34.9%	44.0%	55.0%	59.2%	61.2%	43.2%	DHS

Source: Selected from "Percent of Currently Married Women Using Contraception by Age: All Available Years," U.S. Bureau of the Census, *World Population Profile: 1994,* February 1994, Table 10, p. A-46. Primary sources: U.S. Bureau of the Census, International Data Base. DHS: Demographic and health survey.

★ 694 ★

Contraception

Contraceptive Use in North America

This table shows the percent of currently married women using contraception, by method, in Canada and the United States. Figures are shown for the latest available year. Data refer to ages 15 to 49 years unless specified otherwise.

Region, country or area, and year	No method	All methods	Pill	IUD	Condom	Sterilization Male	Sterilization Female	Other modern	Tradi-tional	Source	Remarks
North America											
Canada 1984	26.9%	73.1%	11.0%	5.8%	7.9%	12.9%	30.6%	1.5%	3.6%	Survey	1
United States 1988	25.7%	74.3%	15.1%	1.5%	10.6%	12.9%	23.4%	5.6%	5.3%	Survey	2,3

Source: Selected from "Percent of Currently Married Women Using Contraception by Method: All Available Years," U.S. Bureau of the Census, *World Population Profile: 1994,* February 1994, Table 9, p. A-40. Primary source: U.S. Bureau of the Census, International Data Base. **Survey:** A nationwide survey conducted by a national government or independent organization, but not related to Contraceptive prevalence survey, Demographic and Health Survey, or World fertility survey, and not otherwise specified. *Notes:* 1. Data refer to ages 18 to 49 years. 2. Data refer to ages 15-44. 3. "Other modern" methods refer to female barrier methods.

★ 695 ★

Contraception

Contraceptive Use in North America by Age of Woman

This table shows the percent of currently married women using contraception, by age of woman, in Canada and the United States. Figures are shown for the latest available year. Canadian data refer to women exposed to the risk of pregnancy (currently married women who consider themselves to be fecund).

Region, country or area, and year	15 to 19 years	20 to 24 years	25 to 29 years	30 to 34 years	35 to 39 years	40 to 44 years	45 to 49 years	Source
North America								
Canada								
1984	NA	61.3%	68.2%	75.4%	81.4%	78.0%	68.1%	Survey
United States								
1982	53.1%	66.6%	68.9%	70.3%	66.9%	67.8%	NA	Survey

Source: Selected from "Percent of Currently Married Women Using Contraception by Age: All Available Years," U.S. Bureau of the Census, *World Population Profile: 1994*, February 1994, Table 10, p. A-49. Primary sources: U.S. Bureau of the Census, International Data Base. **Survey:** A nationwide survey conducted by a national government or independent organization, but not related to Contraceptive prevalence survey, Demographic and Health Survey, or World fertility survey, and not otherwise specified.

★ 696 ★

Contraception

Contraceptive Use in Oceania

This table shows the percent of currently married women using contraception, by method, in Oceania. Figures are shown for the latest available year. Data refer to ages 15 to 49 years unless specified otherwise.

[NA Not available.]

Region, country or area, and year	No method	All methods	Pill	IUD	Condom	Sterilization Male	Sterilization Female	Other modern	Tradi-tional	Source	Remarks
Oceania											
American Samoa											
1979	78.0%	22.0%	NA	NA	NA	NA	NA	NA	NA	Lucas	1,2
Australia											
1986	23.9%	76.1%	24.0%	4.9%	4.4%	10.4%	27.7%	0.8%	3.9%	Survey	3,4
Cook Islands											
1983	60.0%	40.0%	NA	NA	NA	NA	NA	NA	NA	UNESCAP	5
Fiji											
1978	62.0%	38.0%	8.0%	5.0%	6.0%	NA	17.0%	2.0%	NA	SS	
Guam											
1979	93.0%	7.0%	NA	NA	NA	NA	NA	NA	NA	Lucas	1,2
Kiribati											
1982	80.6%	19.4%	NA	NA	NA	NA	NA	NA	NA	SPC	1
New Zealand											
1976	30.5%	69.5%	28.6%	4.4%	8.0%	9.1%	11.4%	NA	9.8%	Survey	5,6

[Continued]

★ 696 ★

Contraceptive Use in Oceania

[Continued]

Region, country or area, and year	No method	All methods	Pill	IUD	Condom	Sterilization		Other modern	Tradi-tional	Source	Remarks
						Male	Female				
Papua New Guinea 1980	95.5%	4.5%	NA	NA	NA	NA	NA	NA	NA	UNESCAP	
Solomon Islands 1979	77.0%	23.0%	NA	NA	NA	NA	NA	NA	NA	Lucas	1,2
Tonga 1976	54.3%	45.7%	3.1%	9.6%	10.5%	0.1%	5.0%	NA	17.4%	Survey	1
Tuvalu 1983	70.0%	30.0%	NA	NA	NA	NA	NA	NA	NA	UNESCAP	5
Vanuatu 1979	87.0%	13.0%	NA	NA	NA	NA	NA	NA	NA	Lucas	1,2
Western Samoa 1982	81.5%	18.5%	NA	NA	NA	NA	NA	NA	NA	SS	1

Source: Selected from "Percent of Currently Married Women Using Contraception by Method: All Available Years," U.S. Bureau of the Census, *World Population Profile: 1994,* February 1994, Table 9, p. A-42. Primary sources: U.S. Bureau of the Census, International Data Base. **Lucas:** David Lucas and Helen Ware, 1981, "Fertility and Family Planning in the South Pacific," Studies in Family Planning, Vol. 12, No. 3/9, p. 309. **SPC:** South Pacific Commission. **SS:** Service statistics based on number of family planning acceptors or amount of supplies distributed and assumptions about discontinuation rates. **Survey:** A nationwide survey conducted by a national government or independent organization, but not related to Contraceptive prevalence survey, Demographic and Health Survey, or World fertility survey, and not otherwise specified. **UNESCAP:** United Nations Economic and Social Commission for Asia and the Pacific. *Notes:* 1. Data refer to ages 15-44. 2. Rough estimate. 3. Data refer to ages 20 to 49 years. 4. "Other modern" methods refer to female barrier methods. 5. Age range is not specified. 6. Sum of data by method exceeds total prevalence rate because some women reported using more than one method.

★ 697 ★

Contraception

Contraceptive Use in Oceania by Age of Woman

This table shows the percent of currently married women using contraception, by age of woman, in Oceania. Figures are shown for the latest available year.

[NA Not available.]

Region, country or area, and year	15 to 19 years	20 to 24 years	25 to 29 years	30 to 34 years	35 to 39 years	40 to 44 years	45 to 49 years	Source
Oceania								
Fiji 1974	21.0%	32.3%	40.7%	49.5%	50.0%	44.9%	27.8%	WFS

Source: Selected from "Percent of Currently Married Women Using Contraception by Age: All Available Years," U.S. Bureau of the Census, *World Population Profile: 1994,* February 1994, Table 10, p. A-50. Primary sources: U.S. Bureau of the Census, International Data Base. **WFS:** World fertility survey.

★ 698 ★

Contraception

Contraceptive Use in Sub-Saharan Africa

This table shows the percent of currently married women using contraception, by method, in Sub-Saharan African countries. Figures are shown for the latest available year. Prevalence rates in Africa are increasing but remain the lowest among world regions. Data refer to ages 15 to 49 years unless otherwise specified.

[NA Not available. Z Less than 0.05 percent.]

Region, country or area, and year	No method	All methods	Pill	IUD	Condom	Sterilization Male	Sterilization Female	Other modern	Tradi-tional	Source	Remarks
Sub-Saharan Africa											
Benin											
1982	73.2%	26.8%	0.3%	0.2%	0.2%	NA	NA	NA	26.1%	WFS	1
Botswana											
1988	67.0%	33.0%	14.8%	5.6%	1.3%	0.3%	4.3%	5.4%	1.3%	DHS	
Burkina Faso											
1993	92.1%	7.9%	2.1%	0.7%	0.8%	NA	0.3%	0.2%	3.7%	DHS	
Burundi											
1987	91.3%	8.7%	0.2%	0.3%	0.1%	NA	0.1%	0.5%	7.5%	DHS	
Cameroon											
1991	83.9%	16.1%	1.2%	0.3%	0.9%	NA	1.2%	0.7%	11.8%	DHS	
Cote d'Ivoire											
1980-81	96.2%	3.8%	0.5%	0.1%	NA	NA	NA	NA	3.2%	WFS	1
Ethiopia											
1990	95.7%	4.3%	1.9%	0.3%	0.1%	Z	0.2%	Z	1.7%	Survey	
Ghana											
1988	87.1%	12.9%	1.8%	0.5%	0.3%	NA	1.0%	1.6%	7.7%	DHS	
Kenya											
1993	67.0%	33.0%	9.6%	4.3%	0.9%	NA	5.6%	7.2%	5.4%	DHS	
Lesotho											
1977	92.8%	7.2%	1.7%	0.2%	0.2%	NA	1.1%	0.3%	3.7%	WFS	1
Liberia											
1986	93.7%	6.3%	3.3%	0.6%	NA	NA	1.1%	0.5%	0.9%	DHS	
Madagascar											
1992	82.7%	17.3%	1.5%	0.6%	0.6%	Z	1.0%	1.7%	11.9%	DHS	
Malawi											
1992	87.0%	13.0%	2.2%	0.3%	1.6%	Z	1.7%	1.6%	5.6%	DHS	
Mali											
1987	95.3%	4.7%	0.9%	0.1%	Z	NA	0.1%	0.2%	3.4%	DHS	
Mauritania											
1990	96.0%	4.0%	1.0%	Z	NA	NA	NA	NA	3.0%	Survey	
Mauritius											
1991	25.0%	75.0%	21.0%	3.0%	10.0%	NA	7.0%	7.0%	27.0%	CPS	2
Namibia											
1992	71.1%	28.9%	8.3%	2.1%	0.3%	0.2%	7.4%	7.8%	2.9%	DHS	
Niger											
1992	95.6%	4.4%	1.5%	0.2%	Z	NA	0.1%	0.5%	2.2%	DHS	

[Continued]

★ 698 ★

Contraceptive Use in Sub-Saharan Africa
[Continued]

Region, country or area, and year	No method	All methods	Pill	IUD	Condom	Sterilization Male	Sterilization Female	Other modern	Tradi-tional	Source	Remarks
Nigeria 1990	94.0%	6.0%	1.2%	0.8%	0.4%	NA	0.3%	0.8%	2.5%	DHS	
Reunion 1990	27.1%	72.9%	39.9%	18.1%	2.6%	Z	5.1%	1.5%	5.8%	Survey	
Rwanda 1992	78.8%	21.2%	3.0%	0.2%	0.2%	NA	0.7%	8.7%	8.3%	DHS	
Senegal 1986	88.7%	11.3%	1.2%	0.7%	0.1%	NA	0.2%	0.2%	9.0%	DHS	
South Africa 1988	50.3%	49.7%	13.2%	5.3%	0.7%	1.4%	8.0%	19.8%	1.2%	Survey	3
Sudan 1989-90	91.3%	8.7%	3.9%	0.7%	0.1%	NA	0.8%	0.1%	3.1%	DHS	4
Swaziland 1988	80.2%	19.8%	5.5%	1.8%	0.7%	0.2%	3.2%	5.7%	2.8%	Survey	5
Tanzania 1991-92	89.6%	10.4%	3.4%	0.4%	0.7%	Z	1.6%	0.4%	3.9%	DHS	
Togo 1988	66.1%	33.9%	0.4%	0.8%	0.4%	NA	0.6%	0.8%	30.9%	DHS	
Uganda 1988-89	95.1%	4.9%	1.1%	0.2%	NA	NA	0.8%	0.4%	2.4%	DHS	
Zambia 1992	84.8%	15.2%	4.3%	0.5%	1.8%	Z	2.1%	0.2%	6.3%	DHS	
Zimbabwe 1988	56.9%	43.1%	31.1%	1.1%	1.2%	0.2%	2.3%	0.3%	6.9%	DHS	

Source: Selected from "Percent of Currently Married Women Using Contraception by Method: All Available Years," U.S. Bureau of the Census, *World Population Profile: 1994,* February 1994, Table 9, p. A-32. Primary sources: U.S. Bureau of the Census, International Data Base. **CPS:** Contraceptive prevalence survey. **DHS:** Demographic and health survey. **PC:** Population Council. Data from this source usually refer to program service statistics, sometimes with an estimate for private sector contraceptive use. Such data are often unreliable unless confirmed by an independent source such as a nationwide contraceptive prevalence or fertility survey. **SS:** Service statistics based on number of family planning acceptors or amount of supplies distributed and assumptions about discontinuation rates. See also PC. **Survey:** A nationwide survey conducted by a national government or independent organization, but not related to CPS, DHS, or WFS. **WFS:** World fertility survey. *Notes:* 1. Data refer to women exposed to the risk of pregnancy (currently married nonpregnant women who consider themselves to be fecund.) 2. Data refer to ages 15-44. 3. Data refer to ages under 50 years. 4. Data refer to North Sudan only. 5. Data refer to ever-married women and unmarried women who have had a child.

★ 699 ★
Contraception

Contraceptive Use in Sub-Saharan Africa by Age of Woman

This table shows the percent of currently married women using contraception, by age of woman, in Sub-Saharan African countries. Figures are shown for the latest available year.

[NA Not available.]

Region, country or area, and year	15 to 19 years	20 to 24 years	25 to 29 years	30 to 34 years	35 to 39 years	40 to 44 years	45 to 49 years	Source
Sub-Saharan Africa								
Benin								
1982	17.8%	25.0%	27.6%	29.0%	26.3%	27.7%	34.4%	WFS
Botswana								
1988	17.2%	25.8%	37.1%	35.6%	38.3%	36.1%	16.7%	DHS
Burkina								
1993	5.9%	8.1%	9.5%	9.9%	6.0%	7.6%	5.3%	DHS
Burundi								
1987	4.3%	9.1%	9.6%	10.2%	7.1%	8.0%	6.1%	DHS
Cameroon								
1991	18.4%	17.0%	17.2%	13.6%	17.1%	17.0%	8.6%	DHS
Cote d'Ivoire								
1980-81	2.6%	4.4%	3.4%	6.2%	2.2%	3.5%	3.4%	WFS
Ghana								
1988	4.6%	11.1%	13.2%	14.4%	15.2%	18.4%	7.7%	DHS
Kenya								
1993	10.2%	23.7%	37.6%	39.9%	36.4%	37.3%	30.6%	DHS
Lesotho								
1977	2.4%	3.9%	9.9%	10.8%	11.7%	5.5%	6.1%	WFS
Liberia								
1986	2.1%	5.4%	7.7%	8.1%	5.2%	8.3%	8.0%	DHS
Madagascar								
1992	6.5%	13.8%	18.0%	22.3%	21.7%	18.5%	11.3%	DHS
Malawi								
1992	7.3%	12.0%	14.8%	16.2%	16.4%	13.2%	6.4%	DHS
Mali								
1987	8.2%	5.5%	4.8%	5.6%	3.4%	2.0%	NA	DHS
Mauritius								
1985	54.7%	71.7%	78.4%	84.2%	85.1%	76.7%	45.0%	CPS
Namibia								
1992	20.5%	30.6%	32.3%	29.3%	32.6%	23.7%	24.6%	DHS
Niger								
1992	2.2%	5.4%	5.4%	5.4%	4.7%	3.4%	2.0%	DHS
Nigeria								
1990	1.3%	5.1%	6.0%	6.5%	8.7%	8.4%	4.6%	DHS
Rwanda								
1992	10.8%	14.4%	17.4%	25.3%	22.1%	31.0%	20.1%	DHS
Senegal								
1986	9.4%	10.9%	13.2%	13.2%	13.3%	12.4%	4.4%	DHS

[Continued]

★ 699 ★

Contraceptive Use in Sub-Saharan Africa by Age of Woman
[Continued]

Region, country or area, and year	15 to 19 years	20 to 24 years	25 to 29 years	30 to 34 years	35 to 39 years	40 to 44 years	45 to 49 years	Source
Sudan 1989-90	6.8%	6.8%	6.8%	10.3%	10.3%	10.3%	10.3%	DHS
Swaziland 1988	5.9%	18.9%	20.9%	23.3%	21.2%	16.3%	16.8%	Survey
Tanzania 1991-92	5.2%	10.1%	10.1%	13.2%	12.7%	11.0%	7.2%	DHS
Togo 1988	16.7%	33.9%	34.9%	39.0%	37.4%	37.3%	26.2%	DHS
Uganda 1988-89	1.7%	2.8%	4.3%	5.9%	8.1%	8.2%	7.9%	DHS
Zambia 1992	8.7%	13.1%	15.3%	18.3%	22.5%	17.4%	9.0%	DHS
Zimbabwe 1988	30.0%	45.8%	50.3%	50.5%	41.7%	37.2%	22.8%	DHS

Source: Selected from "Percent of Currently Married Women Using Contraception by Age: All Available Years," U.S. Bureau of the Census, *World Population Profile: 1994*, February 1994, Table 10, p. A-45. Primary sources: U.S. Bureau of the Census, International Data Base. **CPS:** Contraceptive prevalence survey. **DHS:** Demographic and health survey. **Survey:** A nationwide survey conducted by a national government or independent organization, but not related to Contraceptive prevalence survey, Demographic and Health Survey, or World fertility survey, and not otherwise specified. **WFS:** World fertility survey.

★ 700 ★

Contraception

Contraceptive Use in the Soviet Union

This table shows the percent of currently married women using contraception, by method, in the former Soviet Union. Figures are shown for the latest available year. Data refer to ages 15 to 49 years unless specified otherwise.

[NA Not available.]

Region, country or area, and year	No method	All methods	Pill	IUD	Condom	Sterilization		Other modern	Tradi- tional	Source	Remarks
						Male	Female				
(Former) Soviet Union											
BALTICS											
Estonia 1990	64.5%	35.5%	NA	NA	NA	NA	NA	NA	NA	Survey	1
Latvia 1990	68.5%	31.5%	NA	NA	NA	NA	NA	NA	NA	Survey	1
Lithuania 1990	80.5%	19.5%	NA	NA	NA	NA	NA	NA	NA	Survey	1
COMMONWEALTH OF INDEPENDENT STATES											
Armenia 1990	78.4%	21.6%	NA	NA	NA	NA	NA	NA	NA	Survey	1
Azerbaijan 1990	82.8%	17.2%	NA	NA	NA	NA	NA	NA	NA	Survey	1

[Continued]

★ 700 ★

Contraceptive Use in the Soviet Union
[Continued]

Region, country or area, and year	No method	All methods	Pill	IUD	Condom	Sterilization		Other modern	Tradi-tional	Source	Remarks
						Male	Female				
Belarus 1990	77.2%	22.8%	NA	NA	NA	NA	NA	NA	NA	Survey	1
Kazakhstan 1990	70.0%	30.0%	NA	NA	NA	NA	NA	NA	NA	Survey	1
Kyrgyzstan 1990	69.5%	30.5%	NA	NA	NA	NA	NA	NA	NA	Survey	1
Moldova 1990	78.2%	21.8%	NA	NA	NA	NA	NA	NA	NA	Survey	1
Russia 1990	68.5%	31.5%	NA	NA	NA	NA	NA	NA	NA	Survey	1
Tajikistan 1990	79.2%	20.8%	NA	NA	NA	NA	NA	NA	NA	Survey	1
Turkmenistan 1990	80.2%	19.8%	NA	NA	NA	NA	NA	NA	NA	Survey	1
Ukraine 1990	76.6%	23.4%	NA	NA	NA	NA	NA	NA	NA	Survey	1
Uzbekistan 1990	71.9%	28.1%	NA	NA	NA	NA	NA	NA	NA	Survey	1
GEORGIA 1990	82.9%	17.1%	NA	NA	NA	NA	NA	NA	NA	Survey	1

Source: Selected from "Percent of Currently Married Women Using Contraception by Method: All Available Years," U.S. Bureau of the Census, *World Population Profile: 1994,* February 1994, Table 9, p. A-41. Primary source: U.S. Bureau of the Census, International Data Base. **Survey:** A nationwide survey conducted by a national government or independent organization, but not related to Contraceptive prevalence survey, Demographic and Health Survey, or World fertility survey, and not otherwise specified. *Note:* 1. May include women over age 50 years.

★ 701 ★

Contraception

Contraceptive Use: 1982-1988

This table shows total number of women aged 15 to 44 years old in 1982 and 1988, and gives the percent distribution of these women by contraceptive method used. Figures by age, race, and marital status are given for 1988.

[Numbers in thousands.]

Contraceptive status and method	All women, total	1988								
		All women[1]	Age			Race		Marital status		
			15-24 years	25-34 years	35-44 years	White	Black	Never married	Currently married	Formerly married
All women	54,099	57,900	18,592	21,726	17,582	47,077	7,679	21,058	29,147	7,695
Percent Distribution										
Sterile	27.2%	29.7%	3.1%	27.0%	61.3%	30.5%	29.6%	5.2%	44.0%	42.6%
Surgically sterile	25.7%	28.3%	2.4%	26.0%	58.7%	29.2%	27.8%	4.3%	42.4%	40.9%
Noncontraceptively sterile[2]	6.6%	4.7%	0.2%	2.7%	12.0%	4.7%	5.7%	0.9%	6.2%	9.7%

[Continued]

★ 701 ★

Contraceptive Use: 1982-1988
[Continued]

Contraceptive status and method	All women, total	1988								
		All women[1]	Age			Race		Marital status		
			15-24 years	25-34 years	35-44 years	White	Black	Never married	Currently married	Formerly married
Contraceptively sterile[3]	19.0%	23.6%	2.2%	23.3%	46.7%	24.5%	22.1%	3.4%	36.2%	31.3%
Nonsurgically sterile[4]	1.5%	1.4%	0.7%	0.9%	2.7%	1.3%	1.8%	1.0%	1.6%	1.7%
Pregnant, postpartum	5.0%	4.8%	5.0%	7.6%	1.1%	4.8%	5.0%	2.4%	7.1%	2.5%
Seeking pregnancy	4.2%	3.8%	2.7%	5.8%	2.4%	3.7%	3.9%	1.3%	6.0%	2.0%
Other nonusers	26.9%	25.0%	45.7%	16.7%	13.5%	23.8%	26.9%	52.5%	4.8%	26.6%
Not sexually active[5]	19.5%	19.0%	37.9%	10.3%	8.5%	18.1%	16.7%	43.5%	0.3%	19.5%
Sexually active[5]	7.4%	6.5%	7.8%	6.4%	5.0%	5.7%	10.2%	9.0%	4.5%	7.1%
Nonsurgical contraceptors	36.7%	36.7%	43.5%	43.0%	21.6%	37.2%	34.6%	38.5%	38.1%	26.3%
Pill	15.6%	18.5%	29.7%	21.6%	3.0%	18.4%	21.6%	24.7%	15.1%	14.5%
IUD	4.0%	1.2%	0.1%	1.4%	2.1%	1.1%	1.7%	0.6%	1.5%	2.1%
Diaphragm	4.5%	3.5%	1.3%	4.8%	4.1%	3.8%	1.1%	2.1%	4.6%	3.0%
Condom	6.7%	8.8%	9.5%	9.1%	7.7%	9.2%	5.8%	8.2%	10.6%	3.4%
Foam	1.3%	0.6%	0.3%	0.8%	0.8%	0.6%	0.6%	0.2%	1.0%	0.5%
Rhythm[6]	2.2%	1.4%	0.6%	1.7%	1.8%	1.4%	1.2%	0.6%	2.1%	1.1%
Other methods[7]	2.5%	2.6%	2.0%	3.6%	2.2%	2.5%	2.6%	2.1%	3.2%	1.7%

Source: "Contraceptive Use by Women, 15 to 44 Years Old: 1982 and 1988," U.S. Bureau of the Census, *Statistical Abstract of the United States, 1994*, table 110, p. 84. Based on the 1982 and 1988 National Survey of Family Growth. Primary sources: U.S. National Center for Health Statistics, *Advance Data from Vital and Health Statistics*, No. 182. *Notes:* 1. Includes other races, not shown separately. 2. Persons who had sterilizing operation and who gave as one reason that they had medical problems with their female organs. 3. Includes all other sterilization operations, and sterilization of the husband or current partner. 4. Persons sterile from illness, accident, or congenital conditions. 5. Those having intercourse in the last 3 months before the survey. 6. Periodic abstinence and natural family planning. 7. Withdrawal, douche, suppository, and less frequently used methods.

★ 702 ★

Contraception

Effectiveness of Contraceptive Methods

This table shows how many women become pregnant on average in a year, depending on the type of contraception they use.

Method	Become pregnant annually
Pill	
average	6 in 100
no missed pills	1 in 1,000
Spermicides	
average	30 in 100
with ideal use	3 in 100
Condom	
average, condom packaged with spermicide	16 in 100
with perfect use	2
Diaphragm	
average	18
with perfect use	6
Periodic abstinence	
average	19
with perfect use	9

Source: Drs. Marguerite and Marshall Shearer, "Perfection counts in contraception," *Detroit Free Press*, February 19, 1995, p. 3J.

★ 703 ★

Contraception

Fewest Women Using Contraception Worldwide

This table shows the percentage of married women of childbearing age who were using contraception in 1985 in the 10 countries where the fewest women were doing so. Only 48 nation-states sanctioned and reported the use of contraceptive devices.

Country	Percent
Papua New Guinea	4%
Sierra Leone	4%
Ivory Coast	3%
Ethiopia	2%
Mali	2%

[Continued]

★ 703 ★

Fewest Women Using Contraception Worldwide
[Continued]

Country	Percent
North Yemen	2%
Mauritania	1%
Rwanda	1%
Uganda	1%
Zaire	1%

Source: Selected from George Kurian, *The New Book of World Rankings*, Facts on File, Inc., New York, 1991, pp. 30-31, table entitled "Use of Contraceptives." Primary Source: World Development Report.

★ 704 ★

Contraception

Most Women Using Contraception Worldwide

This table shows the percentage of married women of childbearing age who were using contraception in 1985 in the 10 countries where the most women were doing so. Only 48 nation-states sanctioned and reported the use of contraceptive devices.

Country	Percent
United Kingdom	83%
Belgium	81%
West Germany	78%
Netherlands	78%
Sweden	78%
Mauritius	75%
China	74%
Singapore	74%
Canada	73%
Hungary	73%

Source: Selected from George Kurian, *The New Book of World Rankings*, Facts on File, Inc., New York, 1991, pp. 30-31, table entitled "Use of Contraceptives." Primary Source: World Development Report.

★ 705 ★

Contraception

Norplant Use by Teenagers

Because there was little information available about the use of levonorgestrel implants (Norplant) by adolescent mothers, a study was done of 100 postpartum adolescents who chose a contraceptive method. Forty-eight chose Norplant, 50 chose oral contraceptives, and two chose barrier methods. The selection of Norplant was associated with higher rates of continued use and lower rates of new pregnancy and did not discourage condom use to prevent disease. This table shows some of the results of the study.

Item	Number/Percent
Factors associated with the choice of Norplant:	
Age	16.7 years
Multiparity	24 subjects
Previous use of oral contraceptives	34 subjects
Factors associated with the choice of oral contraception:	
Age	16.2 years
Multiparity	6 subjects
Previous use of oral contraception	21 subjects
Follow-up incidence of sexually transmitted diseases:	
Norplant group	42%
Oral contraceptive group	36%
Follow-up continuation of use of chosen contraceptive method:	
Norplant group	95%
Oral contraceptive group	33%
Number of pregnancies in the first postpartum year:	
Norplant group	1
Oral contraceptive group:	19

Source: Selected from Margaret Polaneczky, M.D., Gail Slap, M.D., Christine Forke, B.A., et al., "The Use of Levonorgestrel Implants (Norplant) for Contraception in Adolescent Mothers," *The New England Journal of Medicine*, 331(18), November 3, 1994, pp. 1201-6. Address reprint requests to Dr. Polaneczky at Box 392, department of Obstetrics and Gynecology, New York Hospital-Cornell Medical Center, 525 E. 68th St., New York, NY 10021.

★ 706 ★

Contraception

Religious Affiliation and Contraceptive Use

The table below shows the responses of women and men by religious affiliation to a survey question about whether they used contraception.

Response	Protestant		Catholic		Jewish		None	
	Women	Men	Women	Men	Women	Men	Women	Men
N =	483	471	344	320	150	141	150	138
Yes	63%	64%	69%	64%	69%	69%	74%	60%
No	37%	36%	31%	36%	31%	31%	26%	40%

Source: "Do You Use Contraception?" Samuel S. Janus, PhD, and Cynthia L. Janus, MD, *The Janus Report on Sexual Behavior,* (New York: John Wiley & Sons, Inc., 1993), Table 8.6, p. 233. Between 1988 and 1992, the authors distributed 4,550 questionnaires to subjects at a variety of sites. The sample design was planned to conform to the population distribution of the United States in the areas of sex, age, region, income, education, and marital status. Returned questionnaires totaled 3,260. Of these, 495 were discarded. Satisfactorily completed questionnaires totaled 2,765: 1,418 women and 1,347 men.

★ 707 ★

Contraception

Teenage Contraceptive Use

Some statistics about teenage contraceptive use, gathered by The Alan Guttmacher Institute. It is reported that single teenagers are less likely to become pregnant while using contraception than are single women in the early 20s and higher income teenagers. Those using the pill have the lowest accidental pregnancy rates.

Item	Number/Percent
Chance that a sexually active teenage woman using no contraceptive over one year will become pregnant	90%
Number of teenagers who use some type of contraception – usually a condom, the first time they have sex	2/3
Rise in contraceptive use at first intercourse among teenage women during the 1980s	48% to 65%
Rise in condom use	23% to 48%

[Continued]

★ 707 ★

Teenage Contraceptive Use
[Continued]

Item	Number/Percent
Percent of teenage women and their partners who use a contraceptive method on an ongoing basis:	
White	81%
Black	77%
Hispanic	65%
Higher income teenagers	83%
Low income teenagers	71%
Poor teenagers	78%
Percent of the 1.7 million teenagers who use the pill who also use condoms	25%

Source: Selected from "Teenage Reproductive Health in the United States," The Alan Guttmacher Institute, *Facts In Brief.*

★ 708 ★

Contraception

Types of Contraception Used

The table below shows the responses of single, married, and divorced women and men to a survey question about the type of contraception they used. Single people, especially men, were the most likely to use contraceptives. Many people listed their contraceptive as a couple (vasectomy, for example, would be listed by a man and his mate). Condoms for men and the pill for women were the most popular contraceptive methods used. In interviews with the authors, some women expressed fears about the long-term effect of use of the pill.

Type	Single		Married		Divorced	
	Women	Men	Women	Men	Women	Men
N =	441	379	805	771	127	122
Condoms	22%	60%	15%	38%	16%	41%
Birth control pill	41%	6%	15%	11%	12%	9%
Tubal ligation	4%	0%	15%	0%	26%	0%
Rhythm method	4%	4%	3%	3%	0%	0%
Abortion	2%	0%	3%	2%	2%	1%
Vasectomy	0%	3%	6%	12%	1%	10%
I.U.D.	3%	1%	2%	1%	4%	3%
Diaphragm	15%	5%	10%	8%	16%	3%
Contraceptive cream/jelly	6%	4%	5%	4%	5%	6%
None	23%	19%	42%	44%	27%	39%
No answer	4%	4%	4%	3%	5%	3%

[Continued]

★ 708 ★

Types of Contraception Used
[Continued]

Type	Single		Married		Divorced	
	Women	Men	Women	Men	Women	Men
None + No answer	27%	23%	46%	47%	32%	42%
Users (all methods)	73%	77%	54%	53%	68%	58%

Source: "Self-Identification: Type of Contraception Used," Samuel S. Janus, PhD, and Cynthia L. Janus, MD, *The Janus Report on Sexual Behavior*, (New York: John Wiley & Sons, Inc., 1993), Table 7.6, p. 217. Between 1988 and 1992, the authors distributed 4,550 questionnaires to subjects at a variety of sites. The sample design was planned to conform to the population distribution of the United States in the areas of sex, age, region, income, education, and marital status. Returned questionnaires totaled 3,260. Of these, 495 were discarded. Satisfactorily completed questionnaires totaled 2,765: 1,418 women and 1,347 men. Widowed persons and those reporting themselves were not included in this tabulation. Hysterectomy was not included because it is not a contraceptive procedure. Because many individuals use several contraceptive methods, the numbers for the methods listed total to more than 100%.

★ 709 ★

Contraception

Types of Contraception Used by Race: 1990

This table shows the types of contraceptives used by women aged 15-44 in 1990, by race. Black women rely the most on tubal ligation (female sterilization), followed by Hispanics, and then whites. The pill is most popular among Hispanics.

Type	White	Black	Hispanic
Pill	28.5%	28.5%	31.4%
Condom	17.0%	19.4%	17.1%
Male sterilization	15.5%	[1]	6.4%
Female sterilization	27.3%	41.0%	33.1%
Other	11.7%	9.8%	12.0%

Source: Selected from "Still Fumbling in the Dark," *Newsweek*, March 13, 1995, pp. 60-62, table on p. 62 entitled "Who's Using What? Primary source: National Center for Health Statistics. "Other" includes IUD, diaphragm, periodic abstinence, and other. *Note:* 1. Too few to mention.

★ 710 ★

Contraception

Types of Contraception Used: 1990

This table shows the types of contraceptives used by women aged 15-44 in 1990. Nearly 60% used contraception, and surgical sterilization was the most-used method. In 1982, it was the pill. *Newsweek* calls the survey revealing the statistics in this table "stunning," asserting that the trend of women opting for sterilization over other forms of birth control has long been associated with Third World countries.

Type	Women age 15-44
Female sterilization	29.5%
Pill	28.5%
Condom	17.7%
Male sterilization	12.6%
Diaphragm	2.8%
Periodic abstinence	2.7%
IUD	1.4%
Other methods	4.8%

Source: Selected from "Still Fumbling in the Dark," *Newsweek*, March 13, 1995, pp. 60+, table on p. 61 entitled "Options, But No Solutions." Primary source: National Center for Health Statistics.

Deaths

★ 711 ★

Accident and Violence Deaths: 1980-1991

This table shows death rates from accidents, suicide, and homicide, by sex and race, for the years 1980 to 1991.

[Rates per 100,000 population.]

Cause of death and age	White						Black					
	Male			Female			Male			Female		
	1980	1990	1991	1980	1990	1991	1980	1990	1991	1980	1990	1991
Total[1]	97.1	81.2	78.7	36.3	32.1	31.5	154.0	142.0	143.9	42.6	38.6	38.4
Motor vehicle accidents	35.9	26.1	24.4	12.8	11.4	10.8	31.1	28.1	25.6	8.3	9.4	8.7
All other accidents	30.4	23.6	23.3	14.4	12.4	12.6	46.0	32.7	34.2	18.6	13.4	13.5
Suicide	19.9	22.0	21.7	5.9	5.3	5.2	10.3	12.0	12.1	2.2	2.3	1.9
Homicide	10.9	9.0	9.3	3.2	2.8	3.0	66.6	69.2	72.0	13.5	13.5	14.2

[Continued]

★ 711 ★

Accident and Violence Deaths: 1980-1991

[Continued]

Cause of death and age	White						Black					
	Male			Female			Male			Female		
	1980	1990	1991	1980	1990	1991	1980	1990	1991	1980	1990	1991
15 to 24 years	138.6	107.3	104.2	37.3	30.5	31.2	162.0	208.0	231.9	35.0	34.9	37.0
25 to 34 years	118.4	97.4	94.2	29.0	26.0	24.7	256.9	218.1	213.8	49.4	48.1	47.7
35 to 44 years	94.1	82.3	78.5	29.2	24.4	23.5	218.1	176.6	171.8	43.2	38.5	40.0
45 to 54 years	90.8	73.5	72.9	31.8	25.3	25.2	207.3	138.5	132.4	40.2	30.7	33.1
55 to 64 years	92.3	79.5	75.6	33.8	29.4	26.6	188.5	129.9	124.7	47.3	36.1	32.5
65 years and over	163.9	150.7	147.4	87.2	80.1	79.6	215.8	175.5	182.2	102.9	81.6	78.6

Source: Selected from "Death Rates From Accidents and Violence: 1980 to 1991," U.S. Bureau of the Census, *Statistical Abstract of the United States, 1994*, table 133, p. 100. Primary source: U.S. National Center for Health Statistics, *Vital Statistics of the United States,* annual; and unpublished data. Excludes deaths of nonresidents of the United States. Beginning 1980, deaths classified according to the ninth revision of the *International Classification of Diseases.* For earlier years, classified according to the revision in use at the time. *Note:* 1. Includes persons under 15 years of age not shown separately.

★ 712 ★

Deaths

African Deaths by Age-I

This table shows the total number of deaths of men and women in Africa and deaths by age, ages under 1 year to ages 40-44, latest available year.

Country/Year	All ages	-1	1-4	5-9	10-14	15-19	20-24	25-29	30-34	35-39	40-44
Africa											
Algeria 1982 [1,2]											
Men	107,962	42,237	17,408	3,046	1,630	2,052	2,592	2,182	2,139	2,052	2,257
Women	101,065	36,867	17,250	2,909	1,565	1,946	2,156	2,066	1,876	1,785	1,775
Cape Verde 1985											
Men	1,385	462	135	21	15	23	30	21	15	8	19
Women	1,350	401	142	18	11	15	20	16	13	16	13
Egypt 1988											
Men	222,436	42,065	18,681	5,251	3,471	3,775	3,794	4,014	3,989	5,126	5,368
Women	204,582	40,772	20,861	4,367	2,715	2,842	2,795	3,082	2,870	3,852	3,389
Libya Libyan Arab Jamahiriya 1981											
Men	8,961	2,790	533	216	386	[4]	532	[4]	369	[4]	
Women	6,982	2,689	508	161	193	[4]	160	[4]	179	[4]	

[Continued]

★ 712 ★

African Deaths by Age-I
[Continued]

Country/Year	All ages	-1	1-4	5-9	10-14	15-19	20-24	25-29	30-34	35-39	40-44
Mauritius 1990											
Men	3,984	252	31	17	27	40	47	77	112	175	183
Women	2,870	182	23	10	14	33	41	42	64	48	68
Rodrigues 1990											
Men	108	17	3	1	--	2	9	1	3	2	6
Women	69	11	2	--	2	--	1	--	--	2	3
Reunion 1987 [1,3]											
Men	1,831	73	16	13	8	30	44	54	65	85	88
Women	1,243	51	14	10	6	14	20	19	27	34	50
St. Helena ex. dependents 1986											
Men	30	2	--	--	--	--	2	--	--	--	--
Women	23	1	--	--	--	--	--	--	--	--	--
Seychelles 1990											
Men	314	13	2	2	--	--	3	9	11	12	14
Women	229	8	1	3	2	1	1	4	1	4	1
Tunisia 1989											
Men	20,650	2,899	726	323	254	356	342	380	392	326	356
Women	14,271	2,252	644	241	168	176	191	226	271	226	248
Zimbabwe 1986											
Men	14,478	3,143	1,022	249	216	299	399	527	573	497	576
Women	8,545	2,832	444	219	171	232	322	335	311	305	345

Source: Selected from "Deaths by age, sex and urban/rural residence: latest available year," United Nations, *Demographic Yearbook*, 1991, Table 19, pp. 368+. *Notes:* 1. Excluding deaths of infants dying before registration of birth. 2. For Algerian population only. 3. For domicile population only. 4. The figure in the preceding column includes this age group.

★ 713 ★
Deaths

African Deaths by Age-II

This table shows the total number of deaths of men and women in Africa and deaths by age, ages 45-85+, latest available year.

Country/Year	All ages	45-49	50-54	55-59	60-64	65-69	70-74	75-79	80-84	85+	Unknown
Africa											
Algeria 1982 [1,2]											
Men	107,962	2,463	2,873	3,294	3,823	4,243	4,622	4,341	4,708	[4]	--
Women	101,065	1,795	2,096	2,427	3,180	4,002	4,924	5,075	7,371	[4]	--
Cape Verde 1985											
Men	1,385	30	38	51	41	461	[4]	[4]	[4]	[4]	15
Women	1,350	26	21	35	36	550	[4]	[4]	[4]	[4]	17
Egypt 1988											
Men	222,436	7,290	10,802	14,678	18,400	20,437	18,217	37,078	[4]	[4]	--
Women	204,582	4,830	7,545	8,529	12,831	15,930	18,398	48,974	[4]	[4]	--
Libya Libyan Arab Jamahiriya 1981											
Men	8,961	380	[4]	644	[4]	740	1,068	[4]	1,171	[4]	132
Women	6,982	250	[4]	331	[4]	600	819	[4]	984	[4]	108
Mauritius 1990											
Men	3,984	194	289	336	495	514	423	385	229	145	13
Women	2,870	82	122	152	245	316	363	378	305	382	--
Rodrigues 1990											
Men	108	3	5	5	14	9	6	8	9	5	--
Women	69	2	3	7	5	4	9	8	4	6	--
Reunion 1987 [1,3]											
Men	1,831	129	154	174	176	188	163	176	115	80	--
Women	1,243	31	40	75	93	93	150	160	159	197	--
St. Helena ex. dependents 1986											
Men	30	1	1	1	5	2	1	7	3	5	--
Women	23	--	1	1	1	4	3	3	6	3	--

[Continued]

★ 713 ★

African Deaths by Age-II
[Continued]

Country/Year	All ages	45-49	50-54	55-59	60-64	65-69	70-74	75-79	80-84	85+	Unknown
Seychelles 1990											
Men	314	15	19	31	33	31	25	32	31	31	--
Women	229	5	5	11	18	21	27	32	29	55	--
Tunisia 1989											
Men	20,650	479	778	1,116	1,417	1,770	2,049	2,407	3,099	4	1,181
Women	14,271	301	517	675	854	1,158	1,314	1,672	2,401	4	736
Zimbabwe 1986											
Men	14,478	676	932	915	1,263	1,148	894	536	317	296	--
Women	8,545	305	389	345	517	396	367	226	243	240	1

Source: Selected from "Deaths by age, sex and urban/rural residence: latest available year," United Nations, *Demographic Yearbook*, 1991, Table 19, pp. 368+.
Notes: 1. Excluding deaths of infants dying before registration of birth. 2. For Algerian population only. 3. For domicile population only. 4. The figure in the preceding column includes this age group(s).

★ 714 ★

Deaths

AIDS Deaths Among Americans 25 to 44 Years Old: 1995

This table shows statistics presented at a scientific meeting held in Washington, D.C. on January 31, 1995, as reported in *The New York Times*.

Item	Number/Percent
AIDS rank as cause of death for all Americans aged 25-44	1
AIDS rank as cause of death among women aged 25-44	4
Projected AIDS rank as cause of death among women aged 25-44 "in the next few years"	2
Number of AIDS cases reported to CDC since the disease was first recognized in 1981	440,000
Children	> 6,000

[Continued]

★ 714 ★

AIDS Deaths Among Americans 25 to 44 Years Old:
1995
[Continued]

Item	Number/Percent
Number of America's 135 largest cities in which AIDS is the leading cause of death for women	15

Source: Lawrence K. Altman, "AIDS Is Now the Leading Killer of Americans from 25 to 44," *The New York Times*, January 31, 1995, p. B8 Y. Primary source: Centers for Disease Control and Prevention. AIDS is now the leading cause of death for women in Hartford, New Haven, and Bridgeport, CT; Worcester, MS; Providence, RI; New York City, Yonkers, Elizabeth, NJ, Jersey City, Newark, Paterson, N.J.; Baltimore, Columbia, S.C., Fort Lauderdale, and Miami.

★ 715 ★
Deaths

AIDS Deaths: 1982-1992

This table shows the total number and number by sex of deaths from Acquired Immunodeficiency Syndrome for the years 1982-1992.

Characteristic	Total, 1982-92	1985	1986	1987	1988	1989	1990	1991	1992	Percent distribution Total	1982-92
Total	166,467	6,682	11,537	15,451	19,657	26,157	28,060	30,593	22,675	100%	100%
Male	148,863	6,177	10,557	13,921	17,551	23,394	24,936	27,048	20,110	89%	89%
Female	17,604	505	980	1,530	2,106	2,763	3,124	3,545	2,565	11%	11%

Source: Selected from "Acquired Immunodeficiency Syndrome (AIDS) Deaths, by Selected Characteristics: 1982 to 1992," U.S. Bureau of the Census, *Statistical Abstract of the United States, 1994*, table 130, p. 98. Also in source: deaths by age and by race/ethnicity. Primary source: U.S. Centers for Disease Control, Surveillance Report, annual. *Note:* 1. Includes deaths prior to 1982.

★ 716 ★
Deaths

Asian and Near Eastern Maternal Mortality Rates: 1980-1990

This table shows maternal deaths per 100,000 live births in Asia and the Near East for the period 1980-1990.

[Maternal deaths per 100,000 live births.]

Country	Maternal deaths per 100,000
Asia, excluding Near East	
Afghanistan[1]	690
Bangladesh	600
Bhutan	1,710
China	44
Hong Kong[2]	3
India	340
Indonesia	450
Korea	
Dem. People's Rep.	41
Republic of	14
Laos	
Lao People's Dem. Rep.	2
Malaysia	59
Mongolia	100
Myanmar	135
Nepal	830
Pakistan	400-600
Papua New Guinea	900
Philippines	93
Singapore	13
Sri Lanka	60
Thailand	81
Vietnam	140
Near East	
Bahrain	19
Israel[1]	8
Kuwait	4
Syria	
Syrian Arab Republic	280
Turkey	210

Source: Selected from "Indicators on health and child-bearing," *The World's Women: Trends and Statistics 1970-1990,* United Nations, 1991, Table 5, p. 69. Primary source: World Health Organization, "Maternal mortality rates: a tabulation of available information (second edition)," (Geneva, FHE/86.3). *Notes:* 1. 1974/75. 2. Excluding Vietnamese refugees.

★ 717 ★
Deaths

Asian Deaths by Age-I

This table shows the total number of deaths of men and women in Asia and the Near East and deaths by age, ages under 1 year to ages 40-44, latest available year.

Country/Year	All ages	-1	1-4	5-9	10-14	15-19	20-24	25-29	30-34	35-39	40-44
Asia/Near East											
Bahrain											
1990											
Men	900	134	15	12	11	19	18	40	38	31	28
Women	652	138	9	9	9	6	2	20	11	11	8
Bangladesh											
1986											
Men	643,028	217,987	93,455	24,230	11,598	9,746	9,165	9,102	8,377	6,789	11,730
Women	570,792	187,325	100,949	22,382	6,821	10,684	14,261	13,344	10,542	12,896	14,192
Brunei Darussalam											
1989											
Men	499	38	5	9	11	4	27	23	15	15	11
Women	328	24	8	1	--	7	4	9	9	15	12
Cyprus											
1989 [2]											
Men	2,450	65	11	12	3	11	35	34	19	15	32
Women	2,384	49	3	4	3	6	5	6	9	17	22
Hong Kong											
1989 [3,4]											
Men	16,264	281	48	35	42	86	157	231	282	316	413
Women	12,475	234	42	31	32	56	94	105	169	193	163
Israel											
1989 [5]											
Men	15,072	535	106	59	44	149	146	151	157	170	248
Women	13,502	466	88	45	38	56	68	71	92	106	182
Japan											
1990 [6]											
Men	443,718	3,123	1,409	844	760	3,204	3,466	2,916	3,264	5,449	9,769
Women	376,587	2,493	958	533	482	1,149	1,329	1,361	1,774	3,102	5,542
Korea											
Rep. of											
1989 [7,8]											
Men	133,846	1,092	1,543	1,492	1,102	2,825	3,357	4,437	4,991	5,609	6,725
Women	96,361	974	1,226	1,011	728	1,177	1,562	1,729	1,947	1,985	2,396

[Continued]

★ 717 ★

Asian Deaths by Age-I
[Continued]

Country/Year	All ages	-1	1-4	5-9	10-14	15-19	20-24	25-29	30-34	35-39	40-44
Macau											
1990[9]											
Men	845	36	8	6	1	8	11	21	32	22	25
Women	637	22	6	2	5	3	5	7	12	8	11
Malaysia											
1990											
Men	47,251	3,785	990	626	564	1,096	1,322	1,267	1,325	1,302	1,629
Women	35,993	2,833	857	474	359	476	547	610	659	825	1,009
Peninsular Malaysia											
1989[10]											
Men	39,321	2,838	847	493	485	796	1,032	1,020	1,026	1,044	1,217
Women	30,386	2,110	733	366	333	365	439	506	576	696	753
Sabah											
1986											
Men	3,178	615	233	66	41	74	122	142	107	107	140
Women	1,936	474	165	54	39	41	55	49	64	55	67
Sarawak											
1986											
Men	3,168	253	78	37	36	53	73	75	83	90	95
Women	2,016	173	60	26	18	34	39	41	47	46	74
Maldives											
1988											
Men	804	224	74	17	11	11	19	18	16	19	13
Women	722	175	101	28	12	19	24	37	20	16	10
Mongolia											
1989											
Men	9,400	2,600	1,100	200	--	--	200	200	200	200	200
Women	7,600	2,100	1,000	100	--	--	100	200	200	200	200
Pakistan											
1988[10]											
Men	465,735	186,977	42,427	12,299	10,808	8,807	3,942	15,611	7,263	3,581	8,567
Women	386,606	157,081	55,683	8,543	2,584	7,638	6,674	7,658	8,436	8,047	8,319
Philippines											
1988											
Men	192,044	27,335	17,488	6,111	3,155	5,047	7,329	8,158	7,737	8,059	7,665
Women	133,054	19,852	14,968	4,864	2,555	2,746	3,071	3,369	3,462	3,752	3,567

[Continued]

★ 717 ★

Asian Deaths by Age-I
[Continued]

Country/Year	All ages	-1	1-4	5-9	10-14	15-19	20-24	25-29	30-34	35-39	40-44
Qatar											
1990											
Men	572	84	20	18	9	17	20	29	27	30	36
Women	299	58	22	2	2	3	3	6	6	10	10
Singapore											
1988[3,12]											
Men	7,585	194	36	25	25	74	146	154	169	218	234
Women	6,104	173	36	25	22	34	60	85	98	145	122
Sri Lanka											
1985											
Men	59,236	5,230	1,705	833	698	1,286	2,265	2,040	1,798	2,050	2,090
Women	38,853	4,185	1,611	741	476	1,088	1,260	1,082	907	929	842
Thailand											
1990											
Men	147,887	4,507	2,665	2,094	1,798	5,159	6,947	6,809	6,708	6,588	6,837
Women	104,625	3,187	1,878	1,531	1,222	2,034	2,238	2,220	2,532	2,827	3,539

Source: Selected from "Deaths by age, sex and urban/rural residence: latest available year," United Nations, *Demographic Yearbook*, 1991, Table 19, pp. 368+. *Notes:* 1. The number in the preceding column includes this age group(s). 2. For government controlled areas. 3. Excluding deaths of unknown sex. 4. Excluding Vietnamese refugees. 5. Including data for East Jerusalem and Israeli residents in certain other territories under occupation by Israeli military forces since June 1967. 6. For Japanese nationals in Japan only. 7. Excluding alien armed forces, civilian aliens employed by armed forces, and foreign diplomatic personnel and their dependents. 8. Estimates based on the results of the continuous Demographic Sample Survey. 9. Events registered by Health Service only. 10. Excluding deaths of infants dying before registration of birth. 11. Based on the results of the Population Growth Survey. 12. Excluding non-locally domiciled military and civilian services personnel and their dependents.

★ 718 ★
Deaths

Asian Deaths by Age-II

This table shows the total number of deaths of men and women in Asia and the Near East and deaths by age, ages 45+, latest available year.

Country/Year	All ages	45-49	50-54	55-59	60-64	65-69	70-74	75-79	80-84	85+	Unknown
Asia/Near East											
Bahrain											
1990											
Men	900	38	51	54	73	68	101	169	1	1	--
Women	652	15	34	43	58	47	66	166	1	1	--
Bangladesh											
1986											
Men	643,028	12,087	21,468	20,768	35,261	33,534	33,925	83,806	1	1	--
Women	570,792	11,689	15,051	17,262	19,747	20,132	29,042	64,473	1	1	--

[Continued]

★ 718 ★

Asian Deaths by Age-II
[Continued]

Country/Year	All ages	45-49	50-54	55-59	60-64	65-69	70-74	75-79	80-84	85+	Unknown
Brunei Darussalam											
1989											
Men	499	22	22	25	31	47	57	66	42	28	1
Women	328	11	18	21	26	32	28	43	32	25	3
Cyprus											
1989 [2]											
Men	2,450	40	81	114	192	199	282	394	911	[1]	--
Women	2,384	44	49	70	108	165	286	403	1,135	[1]	--
Hong Kong											
1989 [3,4]											
Men	16,264	511	908	1,478	1,949	2,326	2,653	2,316	1,322	891	19
Women	12,475	188	376	633	908	1,293	1,716	1,988	1,780	2,468	6
Israel											
1989[5]											
Men	15,072	263	468	733	1,051	1,592	1,722	2,687	2,528	2,263	--
Women	13,502	168	278	539	811	1,223	1,648	2,591	2,377	2,655	--
Japan											
1990 [6]											
Men	443,718	14,218	20,161	32,925	42,742	42,664	51,737	69,320	67,916	67,451	380
Women	376,587	7,510	10,097	14,616	19,986	27,267	38,076	58,203	71,633	110,407	69
Korea											
Rep. of											
1989[7,8]											
Men	133,846	10,302	12,359	11,606	12,433	14,632	13,982	12,326	7,827	5,206	--
Women	96,361	3,632	4,762	5,581	6,834	9,090	11,389	13,483	12,244	14,611	--
Macau											
1990[9]											
Men	845	28	21	60	65	108	108	114	80	58	33
Women	637	4	16	27	38	60	93	85	94	130	9
Malaysia											
1990											
Men	47,251	1,917	2,842	3,370	4,123	4,570	4,996	4,676	3,650	3,078	123
Women	35,993	1,137	1,758	2,085	2,896	3,569	4,412	4,081	3,795	3,549	62
Peninsular Malaysia											
1989[10]											
Men	39,321	1,588	2,514	2,749	3,637	3,882	4,294	4,233	2,937	2,666	33
Women	30,386	981	1,463	1,715	2,305	3,207	3,683	3,932	3,164	3,011	48

[Continued]

★ 718 ★

Asian Deaths by Age-II
[Continued]

Country/Year	All ages	45-49	50-54	55-59	60-64	65-69	70-74	75-79	80-84	85+	Unknown
Sabah											
1986											
Men	3,178	141	194	200	228	194	222	136	92	86	38
Women	1,936	80	101	95	137	101	126	81	67	71	14
Sarawak											
1986											
Men	3,168	121	173	242	280	371	356	329	202	159	62
Women	2,016	72	109	151	179	240	202	214	144	110	37
Maldives											
1988											
Men	804	24	37	36	51	49	54	32	36	27	36
Women	722	21	32	36	39	38	50	16	8	10	30
Mongolia											
1989											
Men	9,400	300	400	600	600	700	1,900	[1]	[1]	[1]	--
Women	7,600	200	200	300	400	600	1,800	[1]	[1]	[1]	--
Pakistan											
1988[11]											
Men	465,735	12,327	17,750	11,240	22,314	11,608	22,584	13,975	19,016	34,639	--
Women	386,606	14,013	5,803	10,080	16,176	10,377	14,819	6,355	17,710	20,610	--
Philippines											
1988											
Men	192,044	8,767	9,670	10,108	11,292	11,391	11,723	11,920	8,570	10,516	3
Women	133,054	4,178	5,201	5,347	6,609	7,777	9,072	10,461	9,262	12,936	5
Qatar											
1990											
Men	572	24	31	42	48	20	44	17	22	29	5
Women	299	11	12	10	28	14	27	9	30	28	8
Singapore											
1988[3,12]											
Men	7,585	293	452	682	803	947	989	960	696	443	45
Women	6,104	185	270	358	463	619	796	968	788	840	17
Sri Lanka											
1985											
Men	59,236	2,700	3,279	4,153	4,462	5,171	5,479	4,499	4,484	5,000	14
Women	38,853	1,155	1,525	1,690	2,267	3,038	3,665	3,426	3,798	5,165	3

[Continued]

★ 718 ★

Asian Deaths by Age-II
[Continued]

Country/Year	All ages	45-49	50-54	55-59	60-64	65-69	70-74	75-79	80-84	85+	Unknown
Thailand											
1990											
Men	147,887	7,431	9,747	10,995	12,524	12,311	12,627	11,532	9,266	8,616	2,726
Women	104,625	4,300	5,953	6,871	8,354	8,921	10,386	10,685	11,025	13,053	1,869

Source: Selected from "Deaths by age, sex and urban/rural residence: latest available year," United Nations, *Demographic Yearbook*, 1991, Table 19, pp. 368+. *Notes:* 1. The number in the preceding column includes this age group(s). 2. For government controlled areas. 3. Excluding deaths of unknown sex. 4. Excluding Vietnamese refugees. 5. Including data for East Jerusalem and Israeli residents in certain other territories under occupation by Israeli military forces since June 1967. 6. For Japanese nationals in Japan only. 7. Excluding alien armed forces, civilian aliens employed by armed forces, and foreign diplomatic personnel and their dependents. 8. Estimates based on the results of the continuous Demographic Sample Survey. 9. Events registered by Health Service only. 10. Excluding deaths of infants dying before registration of birth. 11. Based on the results of the Population Growth Survey. 12. Excluding non-locally domiciled military and civilian services personnel and their dependents.

★ 719 ★

Deaths

Breast Cancer Deaths: 1973-1990

This table shows age-adjusted death rates per 100,000 population from breast cancer by race for the years 1973-1990. Although breast cancer incidence is aboout 20% higher in white women than in black women, breast cancer fatality is higher for black women.

[Mortality rate per 100,000 population, age adjusted.]

Year	All races	White	Black
1973	26.9	27.1	26.3
1974	26.7	26.8	26.7
1975	26.2	26.5	24.8
1976	26.5	26.8	25.2
1977	27.1	27.2	27.4
1978	26.5	26.6	26.7
1979	26.0	26.2	25.7
1980	26.4	26.6	26.4
1981	26.6	26.8	27.1
1982	26.8	26.9	28.2
1983	26.7	26.8	28.0
1984	27.3	27.3	30.0
1985	27.5	27.6	29.1
1986	27.3	27.4	29.6
1987	27.1	27.1	30.6
1988	27.5	27.4	31.4

[Continued]

★ 719 ★

Breast Cancer Deaths: 1973-1990

[Continued]

Year	All races	White	Black
1989	27.5	27.5	30.4
1990	27.5	27.4	31.7

Source: Selected from "Age-Adjusted Breast Cancer Incidence and Mortality Rates, Among Women, by Race, United States, 1973-1990," *Statistical Bulletin* 75(3), Jul-Sep 1994, Table 3, p. 25. Primary source: National Cancer Institute, *Cancer Statistics Review, 1973-1990,* 1993. Adjusted on basis of age distribution of the U.S. total population, 1970.

★ 720 ★

Deaths

Cancer Deaths: 1970-1991

This table shows death rates from cancer by sex and age for the years 1970 to 1991.

[Deaths per 100,000 population in specified age group. - represents 0.]

Age at death and selected type of cancer	Male					Female				
	1970	1980	1985	1990	1991	1970	1980	1985	1990	1991
Total U.S. rate[1]	182.1	205.3	213.4	221.3	221.5	144.4	163.6	175.7	186.0	187.5
25 to 34 years old	16.3	13.4	13.2	12.6	12.2	16.7	14.0	13.2	12.6	12.6
35 to 44 years old	53.0	44.0	42.4	38.5	38.8	65.6	53.1	49.2	48.1	47.2
45 to 54 years old	183.5	188.7	175.2	162.5	159.0	181.5	171.8	165.3	155.5	151.3
55 to 64 years old	511.8	520.8	536.9	532.9	525.7	343.2	361.7	381.8	375.2	379.1
65 to 74 years old	1,006.8	1,093.2	1,105.2	1,122.2	1,120.4	557.9	607.1	645.3	677.4	676.9
75 to 84 years old	1,588.3	1,790.5	1,839.7	1,914.4	1,898.4	891.9	903.1	937.8	1,010.3	1,202.7
85 years and over	1,720.8	2,369.5	2,451.8	2,739.9	2,753.3	1,096.7	1,255.7	1,218.4	1,372.1	1,395.2
Persons 35 to 44 years										
Respiratory, intrathoracic	17.0	12.6	10.6	9.1	8.6	6.5	6.8	5.8	5.4	5.5
Digestive organs, peritoneum	11.4	9.5	9.1	8.9	9.2	8.6	6.5	5.8	5.5	5.7
Breast	0.1	-	[2]	[2]	[2]	20.4	17.9	17.5	17.8	16.9
Genital organs	1.4	0.7	0.7	0.6	0.7	13.6	8.3	7.1	7.3	7.1
Lymphatic and hematopoietic tissues, excl. leukemia	5.6	4.3	4.6	4.5	5.1	3.2	2.4	2.3	2.1	2.2
Urinary organs	1.9	1.4	1.6	1.5	1.5	1.0	0.6	0.9	0.6	0.7
Lip, oral cavity, & pharynx	1.7	1.8	1.4	1.3	1.3	0.7	0.5	0.6	0.3	0.3
Leukemia	3.4	3.2	3.0	2.5	2.3	2.8	2.6	2.1	2.2	2.0
Persons 45 to 54 years										
Respiratory, intrathoracic	72.1	79.8	71.0	63.0	60.6	22.2	34.8	36.2	35.3	33.8
Digestive organs, peritoneum	45.9	44.3	41.9	40.4	38.2	32.5	27.8	25.9	23.3	22.3
Breast	0.4	0.2	0.3	0.3	[2]	52.6	48.1	47.1	45.4	44.3
Genital organs	3.4	3.4	3.2	2.9	3.0	34.4	24.1	20.6	19.4	18.4
Lymphatic and hematopoietic tissues, excl. leukemia	12.8	10.2	10.0	10.9	11.0	8.3	6.6	6.5	6.0	6.4

[Continued]

★ 720 ★

Cancer Deaths: 1970-1991
[Continued]

Age at death and selected type of cancer	Male					Female				
	1970	1980	1985	1990	1991	1970	1980	1985	1990	1991
Urinary organs	8.0	7.4	7.5	7.2	7.1	3.5	3.3	3.1	2.9	3.0
Lip, oral cavity, & pharynx	7.9	8.2	6.8	5.9	6.1	2.8	2.6	2.0	1.6	1.6
Leukemia	6.6	6.2	5.7	5.6	5.5	4.9	4.4	4.3	4.1	4.0
Persons 55 to 64 years										
Respiratory, intrathoracic	202.3	223.8	233.6	232.6	226.0	38.9	74.5	94.5	107.6	107.0
Digestive organs, peritoneum	139.0	129.3	130.8	124.0	125.4	86.0	79.1	75.2	69.3	70.0
Breast	0.6	0.7	0.6	0.6	0.5	77.6	80.5	84.2	78.6	79.1
Genital organs	22.8	23.5	24.6	27.9	26.8	58.2	46.8	43.1	40.1	40.3
Lymphatic and hematopoietic tissues, excl. leukemia	27.1	24.4	25.3	27.2	26.7	17.7	16.8	17.6	16.7	18.1
Urinary organs	26.4	22.9	22.5	23.5	23.2	9.4	8.9	8.6	8.8	9.6
Lip, oral cavity, & pharynx	20.1	17.9	16.0	16.2	14.7	6.2	6.0	5.4	4.7	5.3
Leukemia	15.4	14.7	14.7	14.7	14.6	9.0	9.3	9.2	8.8	9.1
Persons 65 to 74 years										
Respiratory, intrathoracic	340.7	422.0	432.5	447.3	446.0	45.6	106.1	145.3	181.7	185.8
Digestive organs, peritoneum	293.3	284.1	277.6	267.4	262.6	185.8	173.6	162.9	153.0	149.7
Breast	1.4	1.1	1.1	1.1	1.1	93.8	101.1	107.8	111.7	108.6
Genital organs	103.7	107.6	110.3	123.5	122.1	85.6	73.6	71.2	71.0	70.2
Lymphatic and hematopoietic tissues, excl. leukemia	50.3	48.1	53.2	56.8	57.9	34.6	34.4	36.6	39.5	41.1
Urinary organs	60.3	56.9	52.0	50.7	52.8	20.1	19.7	19.7	19.8	19.7
Lip, oral cavity, & pharynx	26.8	25.4	24.2	21.5	20.6	6.7	8.8	8.6	8.3	7.8
Leukemia	35.3	35.3	34.7	36.0	36.1	19.3	18.7	19.2	18.8	19.3
Persons 75 to 84 years										
Respiratory, intrathoracic	354.2	511.5	558.9	594.4	593.9	56.5	98.0	135.7	194.5	207.1
Digestive organs, peritoneum	507.5	496.6	476.1	468.0	454.1	353.3	326.3	308.7	293.3	290.0
Breast	2.7	2.1	2.3	1.6	1.7	127.4	126.4	136.2	146.3	145.1
Genital organs	299.4	315.4	321.3	358.5	363.5	104.9	95.7	92.7	95.3	94.8
Lymphatic and hematopoietic tissues, excl. leukemia	74.0	80.0	92.8	104.5	104.1	49.4	57.8	63.5	71.2	75.4
Urinary organs	112.2	112.4	106.1	107.5	103.5	44.0	37.4	36.4	38.5	38.5
Lip, oral cavity, & pharynx	36.6	31.4	27.6	26.1	25.7	10.8	10.9	9.8	11.6	11.3
Leukemia	68.3	71.5	70.0	71.9	69.7	39.6	38.5	38.0	38.8	39.8
Persons 85 years and over										
Respiratory, intrathoracic	215.3	386.3	457.3	538.0	552.1	56.5	96.3	104.2	142.8	154.4
Digestive organs, peritoneum	583.7	705.8	667.1	699.5	688.2	465.0	504.3	497.6	497.6	495.6
Breast	2.9	2.6	3.9	2.4	4.1	157.1	169.3	178.5	196.8	197.9
Genital organs	434.2	612.3	614.6	750.0	781.0	107.3	115.9	106.1	115.6	117.8
Lymphatic and hematopoietic tissues, excl. leukemia	58.1	93.2	114.8	140.5	140.7	41.7	63.0	73.7	90.0	92.8
Urinary organs	140.5	177.0	185.5	186.3	186.2	59.9	63.8	63.2	68.5	67.7

[Continued]

★ 720 ★

Cancer Deaths: 1970-1991
[Continued]

Age at death and selected type of cancer	Male					Female				
	1970	1980	1985	1990	1991	1970	1980	1985	1990	1991
Lip, oral cavity, & pharynx	47.0	40.2	32.7	37.4	31.9	19.2	16.0	16.0	17.5	17.1
Leukemia	83.3	117.1	114.8	116.0	111.7	50.9	61.1	63.9	65.0	70.0

Source: "Death Rates From Cancer, by Sex and Age: 1970 to 1991," U.S. Bureau of the Census, *Statistical Abstract of the United States, 1994,* table 132, p. 99. Primary source: U.S. National Center for Health Statistics, *Vital Statistics of the United States,* annual; and unpublished data. Excludes deaths of nonresidents of the United States. Beginning 1980, deaths classified according to the ninth revision of the *International Classification of Diseases.* For earlier years, classified according to the revision in use at the time. *Notes:* 1. Includes persons under 25 years of age and malignant neoplasms of other and unspecified sites, not shown separately. 2. Base figure to small to meet statistical standards for reliability of a derived figure.

★ 721 ★

Deaths

Death Rates by Education and Income Level: 1986

This table shows death rates among persons aged 25-64 in selected education and income groups by race and sex in 1986. Although death rates have declined since 1960, the poor and less educated have not shared in the decline. This table shows an inverse relationship between mortality and socioeconomic status.

Group	(Rate per 1,000)			
	White		Black	
	Men	Women	Men	Women
Education				
0-11 years of school	7.6	3.4	13.4	6.2
12 years of school	4.3	2.5	8.0	3.9
1-3 years of college	4.3	2.1	5.0	3.2
4 or more years college	2.8	1.8	6.0	2.2
Income				
Less than $9,000	16.0	6.5	19.5	7.6
$9,000-$14,999	10.2	3.4	10.8	4.5
$15,000-$18,999	5.7	3.3	9.8	3.7
$19,000-$24,999	4.6	3.0	4.7	2.8
$25,000 or more	2.4	1.6	3.6	2.3

Source: Selected from "The Widening Gap Between Socioeconomic Status and Mortality," *Statistical Bulletin,* Vol. 75(2), pp. 31-35, Apr-Jun 1994, Table p. 33, "Death Rates Among Persons Aged 25-64 in Selected Education and Income Groups, by Race and Sex,[1] 1986." Primary source: 1986 National Mortality Followback Survey and the 1986 National Health Interview Survey. *Note:* 1. Adjusted on basis of age distribution of U.S. population, 1940.

★ 722 ★
Deaths

Deaths by Age: 1970-1992

This table shows death rates (number of deaths per 100,000 population in specified group) by age and race for the years 1970 to 1992.

Sex, year, and race	All ages[1]	Under 1 year	1-4 years	5-14 years	15-24 years	25-34 years	35-44 years	45-54 years	55-64 years	65-74 years	75-84 years	85 years and over
Female[2]												
1970	808	1,864	75	32	68	102	231	517	1,099	2,580	6,678	15,518
1980	785	1,142	55	24	58	76	159	413	934	2,145	5,440	14,747
1990	812	856	41	19	49	74	138	343	879	1,991	4,883	14,274
1991[3]	811	804	43	18	50	74	139	339	873	1,977	4,801	14,067
1992[3]	807	808	38	17	48	70	143	323	872	1,966	4,728	13,839
White												
1970	813	1,615	66	30	62	84	193	463	1,015	2,471	6,699	15,980
1980	806	963	49	23	56	65	138	373	876	2,067	5,402	14,980
1990	847	690	36	18	46	62	117	309	823	1,924	4,839	14,401
1991[3]	848	659	38	17	47	62	117	306	822	1,909	4,733	14,188
1992[3]	843	653	33	16	43	57	118	291	814	1,911	4,686	13,919
Black												
1970	829	3,369	129	44	112	231	533	1,044	1,986	3,861	6,692	10,707
1980	733	2,124	84	31	71	150	324	768	1,561	3,057	6,212	12,367
1990	748	1,736	68	28	69	160	299	639	1,453	2,866	5,688	13,310
1991[3]	745	1,581	71	26	73	159	304	633	1,400	2,854	5,707	13,259
1992[3]	741	1,601	63	26	72	155	318	619	1,458	2,700	5,529	13,719
Male[2]												
1970	1,090	2,410	93	51	189	215	403	959	2,283	4,874	10,010	17,822
1980	977	1,429	73	37	172	196	299	767	1,815	4,105	8,817	18,801
1990	918	1,083	52	29	147	204	310	610	1,553	3,492	7,889	18,057
1991[3]	912	1,024	52	29	148	204	312	605	1,525	3,439	7,689	17,800
1992[3]	902	919	47	278	145	200	325	587	1,482	3,360	7,538	17,656
White												
1970	1,087	2,113	84	48	171	177	344	883	2,203	4,810	10,099	18,552
1980	983	1,230	66	35	167	171	257	699	1,729	4,036	8,830	19,097
1990	931	896	46	26	131	176	268	549	1,467	3,398	7,845	18,268
1991[3]	926	861	46	27	128	176	269	545	1,444	3,350	7,642	18,021
1992[3]	917	755	43	26	124	173	285	531	1,396	3,271	7,479	17,866
Black												
1970	1,187	4,299	151	67	321	560	957	1,778	3,257	5,803	9,455	12,222
1980	1,034	2,587	111	47	209	407	690	1,480	2,873	5,131	9,232	16,099
1990	1,008	2,112	86	41	252	431	700	1,261	2,618	4,946	9,130	16,955
1991[3]	999	1,957	88	42	278	426	702	1,257	2,534	4,851	9,013	16,664
1992[3]	980	1,830	68	41	271	413	683	1,186	2,512	4,761	9,035	17,014

Source: "Death Rates, by Age, Sex, and Race: 1970 to 1992," U.S. Bureau of the Census, *Statistical Abstract of the United States, 1994*, table 118, p. 89. Primary source: U.S. National Center for Health Statistics, *Vital Statistics of the United States*, annual; and *Monthly Vital Statistics Report*. Excludes deaths of nonresidents of the United States and fetal deaths. *Notes:* 1. Includes unknown age. 2. Includes other races not shown separately. 3. Includes deaths of nonresidents. Based on a 10% sample of deaths.

★ 723 ★
Deaths

Deaths by Race and Cause: 1988

This table shows the ratio of black to white death rates for both sexes, males, and females, for the 15 major causes of death, 1988. Blacks are more likely than whites to die from 13 of the 15 major causes of death. In 1988, diabetes ranked as the fourth leading cause of death for black women. The death rate from AIDS is three times higher for blacks than for whites, and the prevalence of the virus that causes AIDS is expected to spread faster among blacks in the future. Non-Hispanic blacks accounted for a majority of AIDS-related deaths among children under age 13 and women in 1988.

Cause of Death	Black to white ratio		
	Both sexes	Males	Females
Heart disease	1.4	1.3	1.6
Cancer	1.3	1.4	1.2
Stroke	1.9	1.9	1.8
Accidents	1.3	1.4	1.2
Chronic lung disease	0.8	0.9	0.7
Pneumonia, flu	1.4	1.6	1.3
Diabetes	2.4	2.1	2.6
Suicide	0.6	0.6	0.5
Cirrhosis, chronic liver disease	1.7	1.7	1.9
Kidney diseases	2.8	2.6	3.1
Atherosclerosis	1.1	1.2	1.1
Homicide	6.4	7.6	4.5
Septicemia	2.6	2.7	2.6
Conditions of newborns	2.7	3.1	3.2
AIDS	3.4	3.2	8.9

Source: Selected from William P. O'Hare, Kelvin M. Pollard, Taynia L. Mann et al., "African Americans in the 1990s," *Population Bulletin*, Washington, D.C., Population Reference Bureau, July 1991, p. 14, Table 6, "Ratio of Black to White Death Rates for the 15 Major Causes of Death, 1988." Primary source: National Center for Health Statistics, *Monthly Vital Statistics Report* 39, no. 7, supplement (1990); and unpublished data.

★ 724 ★

Deaths

Deaths by Race: 1970-1991

This table shows total number of deaths and figures by sex and race, death rates per 1,000 population in the specified group, and age-adjusted death rates for the years 1970-1991.

[Numbers in thousands. Rates per 1,000 population for specified group.]

Sex and Race	1970	1980	1982	1983	1984	1985	1986	1987	1988	1989	1990	1991
Deaths[1]	1,921	1,990	1,975	2,019	2,039	2,086	2,105	2,123	2,168	2,150	2,148	2,170
Male	1,078	1,075	1,056	1,072	1,077	1,098	1,104	1,108	1,126	1,114	1,113	1,122
Female	843	915	918	947	963	989	1,001	1,015	1,042	1,036	1,035	1,048
White	1,682	1,739	1,729	1,766	1,782	1,819	1,831	1,843	1,877	1,854	1,853	1,869
Male	942	934	919	932	935	950	953	953	965	951	951	956
Female	740	805	810	834	847	869	879	890	911	903	902	912
Black	226	233	227	233	236	244	250	255	264	268	266	270
Male	128	130	126	128	129	134	137	140	144	146	145	147
Female	98	103	101	105	107	111	113	115	120	121	120	122
Death rates[1]	9.5	8.8	8.5	8.6	8.6	8.8	8.8	8.8	8.8	8.7	8.6	8.6
Male[1]	10.9	9.8	9.4	9.4	9.4	9.5	9.4	9.4	9.5	9.3	9.2	9.1
Female	8.1	7.9	7.7	7.9	7.9	8.1	8.1	8.2	8.3	8.2	8.1	8.1
White	9.5	8.9	8.7	8.9	8.9	9.0	9.0	9.0	9.1	8.9	8.9	8.9
Male	10.9	9.8	8.5	9.6	9.5	9.6	9.6	9.5	9.6	9.4	9.3	9.3
Female	8.1	8.1	8.0	8.2	8.2	8.4	8.4	8.5	8.7	8.5	8.5	8.5
Black	10.0	8.8	8.2	8.4	8.4	8.5	8.6	8.7	8.9	8.9	8.8	8.6
Male	11.9	10.3	9.7	9.7	9.7	9.9	10.0	10.1	10.3	10.3	10.1	10.0
Female	8.3	7.3	7.0	7.2	7.2	7.3	7.4	7.5	7.6	7.6	7.5	7.4
Age-adjusted death rates[1]	7.1	5.9	5.5	5.5	5.5	5.5	5.4	5.4	5.4	5.3	5.2	5.1
Male[1]	9.3	7.8	7.3	7.3	7.2	7.2	7.2	7.1	7.1	6.9	6.8	6.7
Female[1]	5.3	4.3	4.1	4.1	4.1	4.1	4.1	4.0	4.1	4.0	3.9	3.9
White	6.8	5.6	5.3	5.3	5.3	5.2	5.2	5.1	5.1	5.0	4.9	4.9
Male	8.9	7.5	7.1	7.0	6.9	6.9	6.8	6.7	6.7	6.5	6.4	6.3
Female	5.0	4.1	3.9	3.9	3.9	3.9	3.9	3.8	3.9	3.8	3.7	3.7
Black	10.4	8.4	7.8	7.9	7.8	7.9	8.0	8.0	8.1	8.1	7.9	7.8
Male	13.2	11.1	10.4	10.4	10.4	10.5	10.6	10.6	10.8	10.8	10.8	1.0
Female	8.1	6.3	5.9	6.0	5.9	5.9	5.9	5.9	6.0	5.9	5.8	5.8

Source: "Deaths and Death Rates, by Sex and Race: 1970 to 1991," U.S. Bureau of the Census, *Statistical Abstract of the United States, 1994,* table 117, p. 89. Primary source: U.S. National Center for Health Statistics, *Vital Statistics of the United States,* annual; and *Monthly Vital Statistics Report.* Excludes deaths of nonresidents of the United States and fetal deaths. Age-adjusted death rates are prepared using the direct method, in which age-specific death rates for a population of interest are applied to a standard population distributed by age. Age adjustment eliminates the differences in observed rates between points in time or among compared population groups that result from age differences in population composition. *Note:* 1. Includes other races, not shown separately.

★ 725 ★

Deaths

European Deaths by Age-I

This table shows the total number of deaths of men and women in Europe and deaths by age, ages under 1 year to ages 40-44, latest available year.

Country/Year	All ages	-1	1-4	5-9	10-14	15-19	20-24	25-29	30-34	35-39	40-44
Europe											
Albania											
1989											
Men	10,239	1,355	601	164	94	141	179	170	147	139	146
Women	7,929	1,077	553	116	61	56	88	105	95	90	98
Austria											
1990											
Men	38,386	395	86	48	44	265	435	389	451	465	793
Women	44,566	314	69	31	26	79	114	137	162	225	397
Belgium											
1984[2]											
Men	57,307	689	156	92	97	319	559	505	598	700	784
Women	53,766	450	149	66	74	146	168	207	262	355	492
Bulgaria											
1990											
Men	59,780	909	240	134	168	337	428	461	623	925	1,584
Women	48,828	645	173	105	87	155	154	173	282	398	616
Channel Islands											
Guernsey											
1991											
Men	318	6	1	--	--	3	1	4	2	2	4
Women	296	1	--	--	--	1	--	--	--	1	4
Jersey											
1988											
Men	415	7	--	1	1	1	4	1	2	2	3
Women	395	4	--	--	1	--	1	1	1	2	1
Czechoslovakia											
1990											
Men	96,731	1,401	204	181	179	501	692	735	1,064	1,889	2,917
Women	87,054	968	176	109	121	243	203	228	391	692	1,082
Denmark											
1989[3]											
Men	30,499	288	60	26	34	116	197	222	303	409	655
Women	28,948	204	41	25	22	51	78	82	125	222	410

[Continued]

★ 725 ★

European Deaths by Age-I
[Continued]

Country/Year	All ages	-1	1-4	5-9	10-14	15-19	20-24	25-29	30-34	35-39	40-44
Estonia 1990[4]											
Men	9,424	166	59	42	38	99	142	171	213	269	360
Women	10,106	110	49	22	15	33	36	38	51	91	111
Faroe Islands 1989											
Men	226	8	2	--	3	2	2	3	--	1	4
Women	145	7	1	--	--	--	1	--	1	1	2
Finland 1989[5]											
Men	24,513	217	35	38	47	175	252	293	417	554	862
Women	24,597	169	43	17	16	50	62	81	122	202	305
France 1989[6,7]											
Men	272,664	3,284	696	363	426	1,700	3,264	3,504	3,947	5,114	7,225
Women	253,537	2,315	463	276	292	678	903	1,168	1,421	2,092	2,986
Germany Fed. Rep. of 1990											
Men	330,439	2,954	589	340	281	1,307	2,736	3,027	3,297	3,917	5,287
Women	382,896	2,122	462	258	189	496	1,001	1,090	1,382	2,133	2,875
(Former) German Dem. Rep. 1989											
Men	91,090	911	193	183	128	469	729	868	1,106	1,549	1,466
Women	114,621	597	166	98	60	209	266	318	507	636	675
Gibraltar 1984[8]											
Men	126	2	--	--	--	--	--	--	--	1	--
Women	126	1	--	--	--	1	2	--	1	2	1
Greece 1985											
Men	48,452	960	140	98	101	344	453	424	379	470	562
Women	44,434	687	86	64	64	123	143	129	171	242	305
Hungary 1990											
Men	76,936	1,055	141	103	141	410	546	632	1,215	2,092	2,581
Women	68,724	808	105	87	84	170	191	199	471	832	1,119

[Continued]

★ 725 ★

European Deaths by Age-I
[Continued]

Country/Year	All ages	-1	1-4	5-9	10-14	15-19	20-24	25-29	30-34	35-39	40-44
Iceland											
1990											
Men	910	17	4	2	3	12	16	17	11	12	15
Women	794	11	--	1	1	4	1	6	3	7	9
Ireland											
1990[9]											
Men	17,052	253	54	38	31	101	153	108	121	142	259
Women	14,851	181	33	25	26	54	44	60	57	94	131
Isle of Man											
1989											
Men	507	5	--	--	1	4	7	1[1]	7	1[1]	11[12]
Women	481	--	2	1	--	--	1	1[1]	2	1[1]	11[12]
Italy											
1988											
Men	281,149	3,020	420	332	489	1,713	2,557	2,420	2,244	2,618	3,935
Women	258,277	2,282	329	229	302	576	781	843	927	1,439	2,234
Liechtenstein											
1987											
Men	98	1	--	1	--	--	1	1	1[1]	3	1[12]
Women	82	--	1	--	--	--	--	--	--	3	2[12]
Lithuania											
1990[4]											
Men	20,605	313	120	79	62	180	293	415	496	625	788
Women	19,155	268	64	47	35	74	57	85	143	202	297
Luxembourg											
1989											
Men	1,998	25	4	5	2	10	21	29	27	26	35
Women	1,986	21	1	--	5	4	7	9	7	13	22
Malta											
1989											
Men	1,313	34	1	2	1	12	9	7	15	11	28
Women	1,297	24	2	1	--	2	3	3	5	13	20
Monaco											
1983											
Men	245	2	--	--	1	2	--	1	--	1	1
Women	203	--	--	--	--	1	--	1	--	--	--

[Continued]

★ 725 ★

European Deaths by Age-I
[Continued]

Country/Year	All ages	-1	1-4	5-9	10-14	15-19	20-24	25-29	30-34	35-39	40-44
Netherlands 1990[10]											
Men	66,628	810	165	104	103	299	433	516	574	718	1,170
Women	62,196	587	144	61	93	131	189	242	313	446	744
Norway 1990[11]											
Men	23,866	252	57	31	39	139	153	175	207	261	378
Women	22,155	167	35	22	24	49	41	77	76	128	195
Poland 1990											
Men	209,333	5,014	836	565	577	1,489	2,125	2,544	4,451	6,317	7,734
Women	179,107	3,723	589	362	346	483	454	640	1,249	2,089	2,889
Portugal 1990											
Men	53,439	739	204	147	200	647	767	728	753	858	1,059
Women	49,676	540	134	108	121	176	219	238	285	383	513
Romania 1990											
Men	131,824	4,794	1,518	617	584	977	1,404	1,290	2,235	3,214	3,809
Women	115,262	3,677	1,238	394	325	427	561	537	919	1,358	1,696
San Marino 1989											
Men	105	2	--	--	--	1	--	1	2	1	--
Women	68	3	--	--	--	--	1	--	--	--	1
Spain 1986											
Men	162,961	3,801	1	1	1	1,382	2,014	1,846	1,663	2,200	2,848
Women	147,452	2,729	1	1	1	538	631	650	700	990	1,333
Sweden 1990											
Men	49,054	421	74	46	42	181	267	297	320	412	707
Women	46,107	318	46	31	40	74	96	127	151	223	405
Switzerland 1990											
Men	32,492	316	77	38	39	222	398	462	435	421	574
Women	31,247	258	46	30	29	72	110	146	159	200	299

[Continued]

European Deaths by Age-I
[Continued]

Country/Year	All ages	-1	1-4	5-9	10-14	15-19	20-24	25-29	30-34	35-39	40-44
Ukraine											
1988[4]											
Men	274,232	6,203	2,021	1,110	918	1,960	3,334	4,476	5,477	7,014	6,751
Women	326,493	4,436	1,561	701	541	942	1,010	1,333	1,740	2,646	2,722
United Kingdom											
1990											
Men	314,601	3,614	674	376	406	1,487	2,197	2,262	2,092	2,692	4,299
Women	327,198	2,658	489	249	273	534	700	901	1,066	1,663	2,800
(Former) USSR											
1989[4]											
Men	1,400,409	90,459	[1]	8,695	6,772	14,369	23,063	34,666	42,289	49,506	47,618
Women	1,474,126	68,012	[1]	5,122	3,670	6,375	7,307	9,836	12,442	16,161	17,190
Yugoslavia											
1989											
Men	113,819	4,272	623	349	314	616	1,014	1,187	1,525	2,288	2,683
Women	101,664	3,639	544	250	196	312	401	496	682	973	1,267

Source: Selected from "Deaths by age, sex and urban/rural residence: latest available year," United Nations, *Demographic Yearbook*, 1991, Table 19, pp. 368+. *Notes:* 1. The number in the preceding column includes this age group(s). 2. Including armed forces stationed outside the country, but excluding alien armed forces stationed in the area. 3. Excluding Faeroe Island and Greenland. 4. Excluding infants born alive after less than 28 weeks' gestation, of less than 1,000 grams in weight and 35 centimeters in length, who die within seven days of birth. 5. Including nationals temporarily outside the country. 6. Including armed forces stationed outside the country. 7. For ages five years and over, age classification based on year of birth rather than exact date of birth. 8. For medically certified. Excluding armed forces. 9. Deaths registered within one year of occurrence. 10. Including residents outside the country if listed in a Netherlands population register. 11. Including residents temporarily outside the country. 12. Includes ages 45-49.

Deaths

European Deaths by Age-II

This table shows the total number of deaths of men and women in Europe and deaths by age, ages 45+, latest available year.

Country/Year	All ages	45-49	50-54	55-59	60-64	65-69	70-74	75-79	80-84	85+	Unknown
Europe											
Albania											
1989											
Men	10,239	231	418	577	757	977	1,106	1,227	882	922	6
Women	7,929	119	171	219	356	557	670	1,209	968	1,318	3
Austria											
1990											
Men	38,386	1,262	1,505	2,235	3,501	4,436	3,603	6,530	6,431	5,512	--
Women	44,566	599	779	1,098	1,755	3,410	3,257	7,647	10,435	14,032	--

[Continued]

★ 726 ★

European Deaths by Age-II
[Continued]

Country/Year	All ages	45-49	50-54	55-59	60-64	65-69	70-74	75-79	80-84	85 +	Unknown
Belgium											
1984[2]											
Men	57,307	1,375	2,300	3,741	5,656	5,284	9,296	10,018	8,373	6,758	7
Women	53,766	787	1,184	1,928	2,876	2,914	6,336	9,593	11,717	14,058	4
Bulgaria											
1990											
Men	59,780	1,992	2,952	4,583	6,509	8,421	6,389	9,529	7,950	5,646	--
Women	48,828	809	1,207	2,174	3,463	5,567	5,059	9,357	9,760	8,644	--
Channel Islands											
Guernsey											
1991											
Men	318	7	7	11	29	36	48	49	48	60	--
Women	296	2	2	4	17	24	20	55	57	108	--
Jersey											
1988											
Men	415	11	14	16	45	49	58	200	1	1	--
Women	395	3	10	13	18	28	37	275	1	1	--
Czechoslovakia											
1990											
Men	96,731	3,936	4,990	7,452	11,056	14,434	9,462	15,515	12,353	7,770	--
Women	87,054	1,439	1,862	3,305	5,459	9,341	7,933	16,881	18,389	18,232	--
Denmark											
1989[3]											
Men	30,499	780	1,077	1,603	2,446	3,617	4,251	5,322	4,409	4,634	--
Women	28,948	509	723	1,061	1,515	2,374	3,015	4,383	5,241	8,867	--
Estonia											
1990[4]											
Men	9,424	462	705	898	1,182	1,012	878	1,066	922	728	12
Women	10,106	166	274	375	685	960	975	1,723	2,036	2,342	14
Faroe Islands											
1989											
Men	226	6	5	11	18	22	37	39	27	36	--
Women	145	2	--	4	6	9	13	23	32	43	--
Finland											
1989[5]											
Men	24,513	832	1,152	1,741	2,591	2,853	3,159	3,755	3,087	2,473	--
Women	24,597	334	454	641	1,111	1,814	2,732	4,488	5,414	6,542	--
France											
1989[6,7]											
Men	272,664	7,299	10,677	16,863	23,842	29,513	24,049	38,393	43,216	49,289	--
Women	253,537	3,019	4,354	6,783	9,843	14,179	14,385	31,554	50,378	106,538	--

[Continued]

★ 726 ★

European Deaths by Age-II
[Continued]

Country/Year	All ages	45-49	50-54	55-59	60-64	65-69	70-74	75-79	80-84	85+	Unknown
Germany											
Fed. Rep. of											
1990											
Men	330,439	9,516	16,828	21,243	30,389	35,698	31,239	55,766	55,851	50,172	2
Women	382,896	4,841	7,698	9,670	15,753	27,534	28,956	66,144	88,088	122,201	3
(Former) German											
Dem. Rep.											
1989											
Men	91,090	3,370	5,473	6,904	7,653	9,176	7,504	15,612	15,580	12,216	--
Women	114,621	1,662	2,592	3,358	5,370	9,338	9,503	23,245	27,238	28,783	--
Gibraltar											
1984[8]											
Men	126	1	3	6	11	9	16	27	11	39	--
Women	126	2	13	14	25	18	17	15	6	8	--
Greece											
1985											
Men	48,452	1,141	1,818	2,971	3,580	4,392	7,146	8,440	7,592	7,440	1
Women	44,434	630	1,001	1,556	1,905	3,145	5,695	7,978	8,877	11,633	--
Hungary											
1990											
Men	76,936	3,757	4,673	6,777	8,839	10,262	7,112	11,311	3,937	6,352	--
Women	68,724	1,534	2,093	3,112	4,745	7,172	6,403	12,837	13,326	13,436	--
Iceland											
1990											
Men	910	19	22	49	60	102	116	133	128	172	--
Women	794	15	23	33	47	51	83	125	100	274	--
Ireland											
1990[9]											
Men	17,052	335	459	840	1,398	2,111	2,681	3,186	2,585	2,197	--
Women	14,851	216	296	468	807	1,294	1,790	2,604	2,830	3,841	--
Isle of Man											
1989											
Men	507	17	[1]	40	[1]	128	[1]	197	[1]	90	--
Women	481	10	[1]	26	[1]	88	[1]	158	[1]	182	--
Italy											
1988											
Men	281,149	6,713	10,604	18,410	27,909	32,083	36,215	50,874	42,026	36,567	--
Women	258,277	3,524	5,502	8,516	13,591	18,663	25,475	45,594	52,601	74,869	--
Liechtenstein											
1987											
Men	98	1[12]	14	[1]	26	[1]	32	[1]	18	[1]	--
Women	82	2[12]	2	[1]	5	[1]	25	[1]	44	[1]	--

[Continued]

★ 726 ★

European Deaths by Age-II
[Continued]

Country/Year	All ages	45-49	50-54	55-59	60-64	65-69	70-74	75-79	80-84	85+	Unknown
Lithuania											
1990[4]											
Men	20,605	1,093	1,445	1,910	2,203	2,120	1,612	2,005	2,561	2,254	31
Women	19,155	427	550	888	1,341	1,686	1,627	2,942	3,415	4,991	16
Luxembourg											
1989											
Men	1,998	57	91	147	195	225	226	339	299	235	--
Women	1,986	29	39	66	106	157	182	339	430	549	--
Malta											
1989											
Men	1,313	33	42	78	129	168	180	214	207	142	--
Women	1,297	12	24	56	96	111	169	206	248	302	--
Monaco											
1983											
Men	245	6	5	19	10	12	31	45	59	50	--
Women	203	1	5	6	7	7	18	37	45	75	--
Netherlands											
1990[10]											
Men	66,628	1,515	2,147	3,612	5,216	8,116	9,639	10,993	9,872	10,626	--
Women	62,196	916	1,219	1,883	2,834	4,352	5,835	9,084	12,034	21,089	--
Norway											
1990[11]											
Men	23,866	457	536	945	1,597	2,702	3,671	4,177	3,832	4,257	--
Women	22,155	249	281	460	850	1,445	2,367	3,495	4,477	7,717	--
Poland											
1990											
Men	209,333	7,992	13,218	19,339	24,659	25,879	19,500	27,217	23,579	16,298	--
Women	179,107	2,963	4,970	8,174	12,767	17,693	16,775	30,565	34,635	37,741	--
Portugal											
1990											
Men	53,439	1,321	2,124	3,250	4,569	6,170	6,915	8,751	7,793	6,444	--
Women	49,676	739	1,088	1,623	2,360	3,738	5,181	8,448	10,321	13,461	--
Romania											
1990											
Men	131,824	5,018	8,758	11,546	14,379	15,530	10,725	18,484	15,666	11,276	--
Women	115,262	2,213	3,952	5,769	8,437	12,247	10,941	21,667	20,723	18,181	--
San Marino											
1989											
Men	105	--	1	5	12	11	15	17	13	24	--
Women	68	--	--	3	3	1	7	18	11	20	--
Spain											
1986											
Men	162,961	4,104	7,513	11,043	15,421	17,011	92,115	1	1	1	--

[Continued]

★ 726 ★

European Deaths by Age-II
[Continued]

Country/Year	All ages	45-49	50-54	55-59	60-64	65-69	70-74	75-79	80-84	85+	Unknown
Women	147,452	1,924	3,263	4,959	7,125	10,008	112,602	[1]	[1]	[1]	--
Sweden											
1990											
Men	49,054	976	1,166	1,859	2,960	4,926	6,986	9,178	9,030	9,206	--
Women	46,107	590	658	1,076	1,621	2,887	4,403	7,104	9,695	16,562	--
Switzerland											
1990											
Men	32,492	758	1,029	1,579	2,323	3,325	3,848	5,282	5,407	5,959	--
Women	31,247	466	567	755	1,192	1,753	2,493	4,426	6,435	11,811	--
Ukraine											
1988[4]											
Men	274,232	14,496	20,539	27,196	34,958	25,907	26,904	36,833	27,795	20,700	--
Women	326,493	6,119	9,203	13,983	24,836	28,315	38,513	64,610	61,203	62,079	--
United Kingdom											
1990											
Men	314,601	6,034	9,473	15,575	26,408	42,157	46,301	57,541	49,910	41,103	--
Women	327,198	3,866	5,852	9,598	16,752	27,439	34,580	52,577	63,780	101,421	--
(Former) USSR											
1989[4]											
Men	1,400,409	67,580	120,467	137,850	184,862	121,766	114,166	148,844	106,840	78,451	2,146
Women	1,474,126	26,462	51,225	67,607	117,585	128,347	156,664	266,491	249,401	263,339	890
Yugoslavia											
1989											
Men	113,819	4,053	7,265	11,333	13,058	13,182	8,857	16,790	14,300	10,031	79
Women	101,664	1,954	3,371	5,443	7,963	10,916	8,933	19,029	18,075	17,161	59

Source: Selected from "Deaths by age, sex and urban/rural residence: latest available year," United Nations, *Demographic Yearbook*, 1991, Table 19, pp. 368+. *Notes:* 1. The number in the preceding column includes this age group(s). 2. Including armed forces stationed outside the country, but excluding alien armed forces stationed in the area. 3. Excluding Faeroe Island and Greenland. 4. Excluding infants born alive after less than 28 weeks' gestation, of less than 1,000 grams in weight and 35 centimeters in length, who die within seven days of birth. 5. Including nationals temporarily outside the country. 6. Including armed forces stationed outside the country. 7. For ages five years and over, age classification based on year of birth rather than exact date of birth. 8. For medically certified. Excluding armed forces. 9. Deaths registered within one year of occurrence. 10. Including residents outside the country if listed in a Netherlands population register. 11. Including residents temporarily outside the country. 12. Includes ages 40-44.

★ 727 ★

Deaths

European Maternal Mortality Rates: 1980-1990

This table shows maternal deaths per 100,000 live births in Europe during the period 1980-1990.

[Maternal deaths per 100,000 live births.]

Country	Maternal deaths per 100,000
Europe	
Austria	7
Belgium	9
Bulgaria	25
Czech Republic	
Czechoslovakia	8
Denmark	4
Finland	7
France	12
Germany[1]	
Federal Rep. of Germany	8
former German Dem. Rep.	17
Greece	7
Hungary	15
Ireland[2]	6
Italy	9
Malta	36
Netherlands	8
Norway	4
Poland	13
Portugal	9
Romania	149
Spain	11
Sweden	3
Switzerland	4
United Kingdom[3]	7
USSR	48
Yugoslavia	16

Source: Selected from "Indicators on health and child-bearing," *The World's Women: Trends and Statistics 1970-1990*, United Nations, 1991, Table 5, p. 67. Primary source: World Health Organization, "Maternal mortality rates: a tabulation of available information (second edition)," (Geneva, FHE/86.3). *Notes:* 1. Pre-unification. 2. Deaths registered within one year of occurrence. 3. England and Wales only.

★ 728 ★
Deaths

Firearm Deaths to Age 34: 1991

This table shows the death rate per 100,000 population by firearms for children, youth, and young adults in 1991.

[Death rate per 100,000 population. X Not applicable.]

Item	Under 5 years old	5 to 9 years old	10 to 14 years old	15 to 19 years old	20 to 24 years old	25 to 29 years old	30 to 34 years old
Female							
White	0.4	0.3	1.0	4.6	5.1	4.9	5.5
Black	1.5	0.5	3.0	12.7	17.7	16.5	13.9
Accidents							
White	0.1	0.1	0.1	0.2	0.2	0.1	0.1
Black	0.4	0.1	0.2	0.2	X	0.1	0.1
Suicide							
White	X	X	0.4	2.1	2.0	2.4	2.8
Black	X	X	0.1	0.8	0.7	1.9	0.7
Homicide							
White	0.3	0.2	0.5	2.2	2.7	2.3	2.4
Black	1.1	0.4	2.7	11.2	16.8	14.4	13.1
Male							
White	0.5	0.5	4.6	29.1	34.6	29.0	26.0
Black	1.4	1.5	11.5	140.5	184.3	129.4	94.8
Accidents							
White	0.1	0.3	1.6	2.9	1.6	1.0	0.8
Black	0.2	0.6	2.0	6.3	4.7	2.2	1.2
Suicide							
White	X	X	1.5	13.6	17.7	15.3	14.9
Black	X	X	1.1	9.0	14.4	13.4	10.5
Homicide							
White	0.3	0.3	1.4	11.8	14.9	12.3	10.1
Black	1.1	0.9	8.2	123.6	164.4	113.4	82.9

Source: "Firearm Mortality Among Children, Youth, and Young Adults, 1 to 34 Years Old: 1991," U.S. Bureau of the Census, *Statistical Abstract of the United States, 1994*, table 137, p. 101. Primary source: U.S. National Center for Health Statistics, *Advance Data from Vital and Health Statistics*, No. 231. Deaths classified according to the ninth revision of the *International Classification of Diseases.*

★ 729 ★

Deaths

Heart Disease Deaths: 1970-1991

This table shows death rates from heart disease by sex and age for the years 1970 to 1991.

[Deaths per 100,000 population in specified age group.]

Age at death and selected type of heart disease	Male					Female				
	1970	1980	1985	1990	1991	1970	1980	1985	1990	1991
Total U.S. rate[1]	422.5	368.6	342.8	297.6	292.6	304.5	305.1	304.3	281.8	279.5
25 to 34 years old	15.2	11.4	11.5	10.3	10.7	7.7	5.3	5.0	5.0	5.3
35 to 44 years old	103.2	68.7	58.4	48.1	47.4	32.2	21.4	18.3	15.1	16.0
45 to 54 years old	376.4	282.6	236.9	183.0	179.3	109.9	84.5	73.8	61.0	59.5
55 to 64 years old	987.2	746.8	651.9	537.3	520.8	351.6	272.1	250.3	215.7	210.0
65 to 74 years old	2,170.3	1,728.0	1,508.4	1,250.0	1,219.1	1,082.7	828.6	745.3	616.8	600.6
75 to 84 years old	4,534.8	3,834.3	3,498.0	2,968.2	2,850.9	3,120.8	2,497.0	2,245.2	1,893.8	1,836.9
85 years and over	8,426.2	8,752.7	8,123.7	7,418.4	7,262.4	7,591.8	7,350.5	6,935.7	6,478.1	6,362.5
Persons 45 to 54 years										
Ischemic heart	338.0	217.3	170.6	123.8	119.6	84.0	52.2	43.6	33.6	33.4
Rheumatic heart	11.4	3.1	1.9	1.1	1.0	10.6	4.3	2.8	1.9	1.8
Hypertensive heart[2]	4.6	8.3	8.5	7.6	8.0	4.0	5.5	4.7	4.3	4.0
Persons 55 to 64 years										
Ischemic heart	904.6	581.1	479.9	375.4	360.3	299.1	189.0	164.5	135.4	133.1
Rheumatic heart	21.5	6.2	4.3	3.4	3.0	20.8	9.2	6.3	4.7	4.6
Hypertensive heart[2]	11.7	21.8	19.8	18.1	18.4	9.1	13.3	12.3	10.9	10.4
Persons 65 to 74 years										
Ischemic heart	2,010.0	1,355.5	1,130.9	898.5	870.2	978.0	605.3	514.7	415.2	398.9
Rheumatic heart	31.9	11.8	8.7	7.1	6.3	30.2	18.6	13.3	10.5	10.4
Hypertensive heart[2]	30.6	44.3	38.9	33.2	31.5	24.8	36.2	29.1	25.9	24.6
Persons 75 to 84 years										
Ischemic heart	4,222.7	2,953.7	2,544.2	2,129.6	2,032.3	2,866.3	1,842.7	1,530.3	1,287.6	1,236.9
Rheumatic heart	34.8	16.7	14.7	12.3	12.8	34.3	25.4	23.8	22.5	22.2
Hypertensive heart[2]	80.8	90.7	79.4	67.9	68.4	83.9	101.1	79.5	69.7	68.7
Persons 85 years and over										
Ischemic heart	7,781.5	6,501.6	5,748.1	5,120.7	4,964.5	6,951.5	5,280.6	4,711.0	4,257.8	4,145.9
Rheumatic heart	34.7	19.5	18.0	18.7	22.7	39.2	25.8	27.6	33.3	31.8
Hypertensive heart[2]	182.0	180.3	153.1	154.3	155.2	223.5	250.8	217.0	212.1	214.7

Source: "Death Rates From Heart Disease, by Sex and Age: 1970 to 1991," U.S. Bureau of the Census, *Statistical Abstract of the United States, 1994,* table 131, p. 98. Primary source: U.S. National Center for Health Statistics, *Vital Statistics of the United States,* annual; and unpublished data. Excludes deaths of nonresidents of the United States. Beginning 1980, deaths classified according to the ninth revision of the *International Classification of Diseases.* For earlier years, classified according to the revision in use at the time. *Notes:* 1. Includes persons under 25 years old not shown separately. 2. With or without renal disease.

★ 730 ★
Deaths

High Maternal Mortality Rates Worldwide

This table shows maternal deaths per 100,000 live births in the countries where maternal mortality rates are over 200. Maternal mortality rates show a greater disparity between developed and developing countries than any other health indicator. Abortion is a major cause of maternal mortality in developing countries. Of the one-half million women around the world who die each year from pregnancy-related causes, about 200,000 die from illegal abortions.

Country	Maternal deaths per 100,000
Africa	
Northern Africa:	
Egypt	318
Morocco	300
Sudan	660
Tunisia	310
Sub-Saharan Africa	
Botswana	200-300
Burkina Faso	810
Cameroon	300
Central African Republic	600
Chad	860
Congo	1,000
Ghana	1,000
Madagascar	240
Niger	420
Nigeria	800
Rwanda	210
Senegal	600
Sierra Leone	450
Somalia	1,100
Uganda	300
Tanzania	340
Zimbabwe	480
Latin America/Caribbean	
Bolivia	480
Haiti	230
Paraguay	365
Asia and Pacific	
Afghanistan	690
Bangladesh	600
Bhutan	1,710
India	340
Indonesia	450

[Continued]

★ 730 ★

High Maternal Mortality Rates Worldwide
[Continued]

Country	Maternal deaths per 100,000
Nepal	830
Pakistan	400-600
Papua New Guinea	900
Syria	
Syrian Arab Republic	280
Turkey	210

Source: "Maternal mortality rates over 200 per 100,000 live births are still found in many countries or areas," *The World's Women: Trends and Statistics 1970-1990*, United Nations, 1991, Table 4.5, p. 58. Primary source: World Health Organization estimates.

★ 731 ★

Deaths

High Mortality Rates Among Young Girls Worldwide

This table shows mortality rates among boys and girls aged 2 to 5 years in the countries of the world where exceptionally high mortality rates have been found in this age group. In many developing countries, girls face nutritional discrimination in addition to other types of discrimination.

Country	Deaths per year per 1,000 population aged 2-5 years	
	Girls	Boys
Pakistan	54.4	36.9
Haiti	61.2	47.8
Bangladesh	68.6	57.7
Thailand	26.8	17.3
Syria	14.6	9.3
Colombia	24.8	20.5
Costa Rica	8.1	4.8
Nepal	60.7	57.7
Dominican Republic	20.2	17.2
Philippines	21.9	19.1
Sri Lanka	18.7	16.3
Peru	30.8	28.8
Mexico	16.7	14.7
Panama	8.7	7.6
Turkey	19.5	18.4

[Continued]

★ 731 ★

High Mortality Rates Among Young Girls Worldwide
[Continued]

Country	Deaths per year per 1,000 population aged 2-5 years	
	Girls	Boys
Korea		
Republic of	12.7	11.8
Venezuela	8.4	7.6

Source: "Higher mortality rates among girls have been found in demographic and health surveys in a significant number of countries," *The World's Women: Trends and Statistics 1970-1990,* United Nations, 1991, Table 4.7, p. 60. Primary source: Compiled by UNICEF from national survey reports of the World Fertility Survey programme.

★ 732 ★

Deaths

Infant Deaths: 1970-1993

This table shows the total number of deaths and the total number of infant deaths under one year of age in thousands, and the rates per 1,000 registered live births, for the years 1970-1993. Infant mortality rates have been generally decreasing since the early 1960's.

[Numbers in thousands. Rate per 1,000 registered live births.]

Year	Number		Rate	
	Total	Infant	Total	Infant
1970	1,921	75	9.5	20.0
1971	1,928	68	9.3	19.1
1972	1,964	60	9.4	18.5
1973	1,973	56	9.3	17.7
1974	1,934	53	9.1	16.7
1975	1,893	51	8.8	16.1
1976	1,909	48	8.8	15.2
1977	1,900	47	8.6	14.1
1978	1,928	46	8.7	13.8
1979	1,914	46	8.5	13.1
1980	1,990	46	8.8	12.6
1981	1,978	43	8.6	11.9
1982	1,975	42	8.5	11.5
1983	2,019	41	8.6	11.2
1984	2,039	40	8.6	10.8
1985	2,086	40	8.8	10.6
1986	2,105	39	8.8	10.4
1987	2,123	38	8.8	10.1
1988	2,168	39	8.9	10.0
1989	2,150	40	8.7	9.8
1990	2,148	38	8.6	9.2

[Continued]

★ 732 ★

Infant Deaths: 1970-1993
[Continued]

Year	Number		Rate	
	Total	Infant	Total	Infant
1991	2,170	37	8.6	8.9
1992	2,177	34	8.5	8.5
1993	2,268	33	8.8	8.3

Source: Selected from "Live Births, Deaths, Marriages, and Divorces: 1950 to 1992," U.S. Bureau of the Census, *Statistical Abstract of the United States, 1994*, table 90, p. 75. 1993 data are provisional statistics from *Monthly Vital Statistics Report*, 42(12), May 13, 1994, p. 1. Primary source: U.S. National Center for Health Statistics, *Vital Statistics of the United States*, annual, *Monthly Vital Statistics Report*, and unpublished data.

★ 733 ★

Deaths

Latin America/Caribbean Deaths by Age-I

This table shows the total number of deaths of men and women in Latin America and the Caribbean and deaths by age, ages under 1 year to ages 40-44, latest available year.

Country/Year	All ages	-1	1-4	5-9	10-14	15-19	20-24	25-29	30-34	35-39	40-44
Latin America/Caribbean											
Argentina											
1988											
Men	140,666	9,998	1,354	656	667	1,293	1,558	1,593	1,913	2,604	3,756
Women	112,283	7,463	1,144	440	412	689	752	890	1,213	1,728	2,063
Bahamas											
1989											
Men	824	67	10	5	9	14	35	50	42	37	47
Women	635	44	11	5	2	8	7	19	26	16	22
Barbados											
1989											
Men	1,090	22	4	4	9	16	23	24	12	23	22
Women	1,187	14	4	--	--	10	9	10	15	15	22
Belize											
1989											
Men	414	69	17	6	4	8	16	17	10	6	7
Women	348	63	20	8	8	4	11	10	4	5	10
Brazil											
1989											
Men	499,660	59,011	10,658	4,962	4,984	12,866	19,149	19,593	20,491	21,002	21,972
Women	335,479	44,080	8,681	3,170	2,908	4,339	5,576	6,200	7,481	8,914	10,436

[Continued]

★ 733 ★

Latin America/Caribbean Deaths by Age-I
[Continued]

Country/Year	All ages	-1	1-4	5-9	10-14	15-19	20-24	25-29	30-34	35-39	40-44
British Virgin Islands											
1988											
Men	37	5	1	1	1	--	1	1	2	--	--
Women	22	2	1	1	1	--	--	--	--	--	3
Cayman Islands											
1988											
Men	55	2	1	--	--	--	2	--	3	--	3
Women	55	--	1	--	--	--	--	1	1	2	--
Chile											
1990											
Men	43,626	2,767	502	256	249	584	968	1,147	1,151	1,214	1,554
Women	34,808	2,148	396	143	138	251	277	357	439	502	730
Colombia[6]											
1989											
Men	92,393	7,849	2,329	1,091	1,064	3,617	6,511	6,436	5,211	4,283	3,372
Women	62,301	5,967	2,046	735	624	1,166	1,335	1,451	1,394	1,646	1,702
Costa Rica											
1990											
Men	6,530	704	117	54	63	119	178	190	187	200	177
Women	4,836	546	85	45	46	49	50	64	93	117	108
Cuba											
1989											
Men	38,060	1,223	260	179	217	653	873	859	709	844	1,019
Women	29,296	826	202	106	140	428	467	452	380	523	767
Dominica											
1989											
Men	251	17	2	2	3	2	1	9	7	2	7
Women	246	11	3	1	--	--	2	4	5	5	4
Dominican Republic											
1985											
Men	15,248	3,443	1,011	253	166	282	456	414	369	368	381
Women	12,596	2,968	950	217	145	232	263	245	264	273	291
Ecuador[7]											
1989											
Men	28,840	4,908	1,894	597	526	711	996	1,017	939	962	939
Women	22,896	3,943	1,801	450	335	488	535	488	516	554	600

[Continued]

★ 733 ★

Latin America/Caribbean Deaths by Age-I
[Continued]

Country/Year	All ages	-1	1-4	5-9	10-14	15-19	20-24	25-29	30-34	35-39	40-44
El Salvador											
1989											
Men	16,574	2,134	857	299	266	834	1,308	942	762	668	637
Women	11,192	1,663	819	278	187	308	282	219	229	221	305
Falkland Islands											
1983											
Men	13	--	--	--	--	2	--	1	1	--	--
Women	5	--	--	--	--	--	--	--	--	--	--
French Guinea											
1985 [2]											
Men	280	--	31	5	3	5	12	10	14	12	14
Women	204	--	35	--	--	3	5	7	5	2	6
Guadeloupe											
1986 [2]											
Men	1,218	56	13	7	10	22	27	20	29	35	36
Women	1,020	42	8	4	8	6	7	17	12	33	20
Guatemala											
1988											
Men	36,104	9,676	5,799	1,205	643	763	1,098	1,082	1,086	1,124	940
Women	28,733	7,402	5,465	1,086	491	542	702	654	657	759	643
Honduras											
1983											
Men	10,877	1,477	847	294	153	223	397	393	326	261	287
Women	8,427	1,280	853	222	118	134	217	209	206	189	201
Jamaica											
1982											
Men	5,417	320	156	52	42	126	[1]	125	[1]	183	[1]
Women	5,444	270	165	44	41	119	[1]	118	[1]	173	[1]
Martinique[2]											
1990											
Men	1,184	21	6	--	2	14	18	35	25	21	40
Women	1,036	25	7	3	3	1	11	8	20	9	14
Mexico[4]											
1987											
Men	224,878	34,021	10,100	3,512	3,361	6,586	9,126	9,223	8,438	8,625	8,472
Women	173,194	26,665	9,122	2,526	1,971	2,591	3,098	3,202	3,318	4,023	4,325

[Continued]

★ 733 ★

Latin America/Caribbean Deaths by Age-I
[Continued]

Country/Year	All ages	-1	1-4	5-9	10-14	15-19	20-24	25-29	30-34	35-39	40-44
Montserrat											
1986											
Men	65	--	--	1	1	1	1	1	1	--	1
Women	58	1	--	2	--	1	--	1	--	--	--
Netherlands Antilles											
1981											
Men	444	51	1	5	4	8	8	11	5	9	13
Women	449	44	1	2	2	4	5	1	2	5	6
Nicaragua											
1987											
Men	6,885	676	245	111	96	671	759	476	321	278	246
Women	4,171	541	192	63	52	122	132	118	108	131	117
Panama											
1989											
Men	5,719	606	169	79	64	127	207	218	201	165	180
Women	3,838	441	148	52	35	72	64	75	81	82	102
Paraguay											
1987											
Men	6,977	1,109	371	122	90	157	207	145	163	159	204
Women	6,220	956	341	99	77	98	92	109	136	171	176
Peru											
1985[3]											
Men	48,639	11,134	5,304	1,099	790	1,042	1,332	1,172	1,037	1,153	1,164
Women	44,344	9,326	5,326	1,031	676	860	1,006	928	949	1,107	974
Puerto Rico											
1989											
Men	15,243	545	56	35	56	166	291	454	546	592	613
Women	10,744	407	56	26	42	72	87	122	156	156	201
Saint Kitts and Nevis											
1989											
Men	244	15	4	5	--	2	1	7	4	8	3
Women	240	7	3	1	1	1	1	2	6	3	3
Saint Lucia											
1989											
Men	416	35	9	3	4	8	10	10	13	9	17
Women	415	21	10	1	8	9	7	5	13	5	9

[Continued]

★ 733 ★

Latin America/Caribbean Deaths by Age-I
[Continued]

Country/Year	All ages	-1	1-4	5-9	10-14	15-19	20-24	25-29	30-34	35-39	40-44
St. Vincent and the Grenadines 1989											
Men	386	35	6	5	3	9	5	13	11	4	9
Women	326	20	9	2	--	5	2	2	4	7	3
Suriname 1981											
Men	1,171	157	42	15	19	31	26	24	19	24	50
Women	1,174	112	39	14	11	15	13	8	12	25	26
Trinidad and Tobago 1989											
Men	4,500	154	59	29	25	67	108	143	128	117	141
Women	3,713	101	39	23	22	29	56	59	55	57	83
Uruguay 1988 [4]											
Men	16,871	677	101	[1]	104	[1]	261	[1]	306	[1]	504[5]
Women	14,029	488	83	[1]	77	[1]	107	[1]	163	[1]	335[5]
Venezuela 1989[3]											
Men	48,912	7,137	1,293	647	614	1,514	1,968	1,883	1,687	1,593	1,642
Women	35,849	5,185	1,123	440	389	541	602	670	809	884	1,022
Virgin Islands 1987											
Men	299	28	2	--	1	6	14	12	10	15	15
Women	259	18	4	1	--	1	2	5	4	8	18

Source: Selected from "Deaths by age, sex and urban/rural residence: latest available year," United Nations, *Demographic Yearbook*, 1991, Table 19, pp. 368+. *Notes:* 1. The number in the preceding column includes this age group(s). 2. Excluding deaths of infants dying before registration of birth. 3. Excluding Indian jungle population. 4. Excluding deaths of unknown sex. 5. Includes ages 45-49. 6. Based on burial permits. 7. Excluding nomadic Indian tribes.

★ 734 ★

Deaths

Latin America/Caribbean Deaths by Age-II

This table shows the total number of deaths of men and women in Latin America and the Caribbean and deaths by age, ages 45+, latest available year.

Country/Year	All ages	45-49	50-54	55-59	60-64	65-69	70-74	75-79	80-84	85+	Unknown
Latin America/Caribbean											
Argentina											
1988											
Men	140,666	5,155	7,530	10,951	13,872	15,694	16,982	17,551	14,240	12,228	1,071
Women	112,283	2,724	3,698	5,299	7,246	9,138	12,429	16,357	16,833	21,178	587
Bahamas											
1989											
Men	824	50	60	51	56	64	68	60	51	45	3
Women	635	22	36	34	38	50	63	80	61	90	1
Barbados											
1989											
Men	1,090	37	28	46	61	102	149	189	171	148	--
Women	1,187	19	30	33	57	83	142	183	207	333	1
Belize											
1989											
Men	414	12	14	20	29	26	33	35	79	1	6
Women	348	6	7	13	16	16	25	35	79	1	8
Brazil											
1989											
Men	499,660	24,407	28,959	32,348	37,792	39,515	41,233	40,148	31,976	27,374	1,220
Women	335,479	12,578	15,495	18,678	23,213	26,416	32,172	34,919	33,197	36,736	290
British Virgin Islands											
1988											
Men	37	--	--	3	3	3	2	4	6	5	2
Women	22	1	1	1	--	--	3	2	4	5	--
Cayman Islands											
1988											
Men	55	1	1	6	3	6	7	6	7	7	--
Women	55	2	2	--	4	5	4	9	8	16	--
Chile											
1990											
Men	43,626	1,981	2,351	2,948	3,985	4,308	4,777	5,141	4,158	3,585	--
Women	34,808	990	1,281	1,777	2,511	2,889	3,778	4,858	4,941	6,402	--
Colombia[6]											
1989											
Men	92,393	3,467	3,830	4,696	5,722	6,285	6,878	7,060	5,455	5,574	1,663
Women	62,301	2,156	2,749	3,496	4,475	5,122	6,019	6,499	5,613	7,407	699
Costa Rica											
1990											
Men	6,530	214	258	331	418	537	578	685	652	800	68
Women	4,836	129	183	219	307	336	426	601	575	824	33

[Continued]

★ 734 ★

Latin America/Caribbean Deaths by Age-II
[Continued]

Country/Year	All ages	45-49	50-54	55-59	60-64	65-69	70-74	75-79	80-84	85+	Unknown
Cuba											
1989											
Men	38,060	1,309	1,624	1,981	2,634	3,490	4,302	5,354	5,015	5,489	26
Women	29,296	892	1,147	1,405	2,019	2,435	3,255	4,325	4,261	5,259	7
Dominica											
1989											
Men	251	2	6	17	14	18	43	34	27	25	13
Women	246	4	8	12	11	21	36	29	34	52	4
Dominican Republic											
1985											
Men	15,248	432	610	648	872	819	1,130	875	945	1,774	--
Women	12,596	377	514	456	575	593	767	661	825	1,980	--
Ecuador[7]											
1989											
Men	28,840	979	1,130	1,351	1,518	1,653	1,880	2,120	1,970	2,630	120
Women	22,896	642	732	809	1,083	1,182	1,420	1,740	1,921	3,561	96
El Salvador											
1989											
Men	16,574	653	678	759	805	879	934	990	880	1,098	191
Women	11,192	353	375	448	619	791	775	920	842	1,450	108
Falkland Islands											
1983											
Men	13	2	1	1	2	2	--	--	1	--	--
Women	5	--	--	--	1	1	--	1	--	2	--
French Guinea											
1985 [2]											
Men	280	19	19	10	19	30	32	20	24	1	--
Women	204	9	8	10	8	12	25	23	46	--	--
Guadeloupe											
1986 [2]											
Men	1,218	49	57	101	112	118	159	131	107	128	1
Women	1,020	28	35	48	53	82	105	133	131	247	1
Guatemala											
1988											
Men	36,104	1,025	1,271	1,349	1,551	1,629	1,791	1,531	1,166	1,375	--
Women	28,733	678	808	971	1,168	1,113	1,494	1,330	1,265	1,505	--
Honduras											
1983											
Men	10,877	247	273	303	360	342	423	392	340	3,539	--
Women	8,427	170	208	227	293	304	355	348	334	2,559	--
Jamaica											
1982											
Men	5,417	329	[1]	755	[1]	1,415	[1]	1,876	[1]	[1]	38

[Continued]

★ 734 ★

Latin America/Caribbean Deaths by Age-II
[Continued]

Country/Year	All ages	45-49	50-54	55-59	60-64	65-69	70-74	75-79	80-84	85+	Unknown
Women	5,444	334	[1]	690	[1]	1,055	[1]	2,413	[1]	[1]	22
Martinique[2]											
1990											
Men	1,184	39	50	74	120	130	137	174	138	138	2
Women	1,036	13	24	44	62	87	97	133	176	297	2
Mexico[4]											
1987											
Men	224,878	9,418	10,182	11,605	12,868	13,430	13,770	16,005	13,732	19,464	2,940
Women	173,194	5,388	6,616	8,268	9,994	11,345	12,002	14,757	14,837	27,123	2,026
Montserrat											
1986											
Men	65	2	4	1	5	7	7	8	12	11	1
Women	58	2	--	1	3	4	8	5	10	19	1
Netherlands Antilles											
1981											
Men	444	11	21	24	35	37	73	63	35	30	--
Women	449	8	23	20	21	36	54	61	68	86	--
Nicaragua											
1987											
Men	6,885	234	241	273	2,150	[1]	[1]	[1]	[1]	[1]	108
Women	4,171	141	177	193	2,007	[1]	[1]	[1]	[1]	[1]	77
Panama											
1989											
Men	5,719	182	228	290	369	453	571	615	441	505	49
Women	3,838	120	132	182	200	279	380	399	323	647	24
Paraguay											
1987											
Men	6,977	239	303	407	440	555	583	1,677	[1]	[1]	46
Women	6,220	173	186	268	335	411	472	2,077	[1]	[1]	43
Peru											
1985[3]											
Men	48,639	1,487	1,695	1,994	2,332	2,438	2,592	2,934	2,646	3,548	1,746
Women	44,344	1,203	1,300	1,497	1,768	1,950	2,209	2,471	2,842	5,275	1,646
Puerto Rico											
1989											
Men	15,243	597	655	801	1,114	1,460	1,642	1,865	1,496	2,196	63
Women	10,744	263	307	463	682	937	1,166	1,507	1,462	2,621	11
Saint Kitts and Nevis											
1989											
Men	244	4	6	15	22	25	42	32	22	24	3
Women	240	9	7	8	14	17	32	34	36	54	1

[Continued]

★ 734 ★

Latin America/Caribbean Deaths by Age-II

[Continued]

Country/Year	All ages	45-49	50-54	55-59	60-64	65-69	70-74	75-79	80-84	85+	Unknown
Saint Lucia											
1989											
Men	416	15	15	26	40	29	45	47	45	36	--
Women	415	13	14	13	34	37	43	47	51	75	--
St. Vincent and											
the Grenadines											
1989											
Men	386	9	8	27	31	27	46	54	40	41	3
Women	326	7	7	18	11	29	38	31	45	82	4
Suriname											
1981											
Men	1,171	43	51	80	64	75	116	97	72	89	77
Women	1,174	36	38	48	72	65	82	88	84	131	255
Trinidad and Tobago											
1989											
Men	4,500	172	247	323	415	505	572	551	393	344	7
Women	3,713	152	191	248	292	396	413	491	419	587	--
Uruguay											
1988 [4]											
Men	16,871	504[5]	1,386	[1]	2,976	[1]	4,245	[1]	6,193	[1]	118
Women	14,029	335[5]	706	[1]	1,385	[1]	2,707	[1]	7,922	[1]	56
Venezuela											
1989 [3]											
Men	48,912	1,878	2,403	3,073	3,672	3,840	4,012	3,982	2,751	3,153	170
Women	35,849	1,119	1,465	1,878	2,470	2,715	3,090	3,613	3,175	4,620	39
Virgin Islands											
1987											
Men	299	19	13	15	24	30	33	20	29	13	--
Women	259	10	14	10	19	17	26	34	23	45	--

Source: Selected from "Deaths by age, sex and urban/rural residence: latest available year," United Nations, *Demographic Yearbook*, 1991, Table 19, pp. 368+. *Notes:* 1. The number in the preceding column includes this age group(s). 2. Excluding deaths of infants dying before registration of birth. 3. Excluding Indian jungle population. 4. Excluding deaths of unknown sex. 5. Includes ages 40-44. 6. Based on burial permits. 7. Excluding nomadic Indian tribes.

★ 735 ★

Deaths

Latin America/Caribbean Maternal Mortality Rates: 1980-1990

This table shows maternal deaths per 100,000 live births in Latin America and the Caribbean for the period 1980-1990.

[Maternal deaths per 100,000 live births.]

Country	Maternal deaths per 100,000
Latin America and the Caribbean	
Argentina	60
Bahamas, The	18
Barbados	71
Bolivia	480
Brazil	120
Chile	50
Colombia	110
Costa Rica	24
Cuba	47
Dominican Republic	74
Ecuador	160[1]
El Salvador	70
Guatemala	76
Haiti	230
Honduras	50
Jamaica	110
Mexico	91
Nicaragua	47
Panama	57
Paraguay	365
Peru	89[2]
Puerto Rico	13
Suriname	82
Trinidad and Tobago	54
Uruguay	43
Venezuela	59[2]

Source: Selected from "Indicators on health and child-bearing," *The World's Women: Trends and Statistics 1970-1990*, United Nations, 1991, Table 5, p. 68. Primary source: World Health Organization, "Maternal mortality rates: a tabulation of available information (second edition)," (Geneva, FHE/86.3). *Notes:* 1. Excluding nomadic Indian tribes. 2. Excluding Indian jungle population.

★ 736 ★
Deaths

Leading Causes of Death by Age: 1991

This table shows the total number of deaths and the death rate per 100,000 population for the leading causes of death at specific ages.

[NA Not available.]

Age and Leading Cause of Death	Number of Deaths			Rate per 100,000 Population		
	Total	Male	Female	Total	Male	Female
All Ages						
All races[2]	2,169,518	1,121,665	1,047,853	860.3	912.1	811.0
White	1,868,904	956,497	912,407	886.2	926.2	847.7
Black	269,525	147,331	122,194	864.9	998.7	744.5
Leading causes of death						
Heart disease	720,862	359,814	361,048	285.9	292.6	279.5
Malignant neoplasms (cancer)	514,657	272,380	242,277	204.1	221.5	187.5
Cerebrovascular disease (stroke)	143,481	56,714	86,767	56.9	46.1	67.2
Chronic obstructive pulmonary disease	90,650	50,485	40,165	35.9	41.1	31.2
Accidents	89,347	59,730	29,617	35.4	48.6	22.9
Motor vehicle	43,536	29,947	13,589	17.3	24.4	10.5
Pneumonia	77,860	36,214	41,646	30.9	29.4	32.2
Diabetes	48,951	21,096	27,855	19.4	17.2	21.6
Suicide	30,810	24,769	NA	12.2	20.1	NA
HIV infection[3]	29,555	26,046	NA	11.7	21.2	NA
Homicide and legal intervention	26,513	20,768	NA	10.5	16.9	NA
1 to 4 Years Old						
All causes	7,214	4,045	3,169	47.4	52.0	42.7
Leading causes of death						
Accidents	2,665	1,566	1,099	17.5	20.1	14.8
Motor vehicle	902	491	411	5.9	6.3	5.5
Congenital anomalies	871	469	402	5.7	6.0	5.4
Malignant neoplasms (cancer)	526	288	238	3.5	3.7	3.2
Homicide and legal intervention	428	235	193	2.8	3.0	2.6
Heart disease	332	178	154	2.2	2.3	2.1
Pneumonia and influenza	207	125	82	1.4	1.6	1.1
5 to 14 Years Old						
All causes	8,479	5,272	3,207	23.6	28.7	18.3

[Continued]

★ 736 ★

Leading Causes of Death by Age: 1991
[Continued]

Age and Leading Cause of Death	Number of Deaths			Rate per 100,000 Population		
	Total	Male	Female	Total	Male	Female
Leading causes of death						
Accidents	3,660	2,493	1,167	10.2	13.6	6.7
Malignant neoplasms (cancer)	1,106	650	456	3.1	3.5	2.6
Congenital anomalies	487	263	224	1.4	1.4	1.3
Homicide and legal intervention	519	337	182	1.4	1.8	1.0
Heart disease	281	151	130	0.8	0.8	0.7
Pneumonia and influenza	135	69	66	0.4	0.4	0.4
15 to 24 Years Old						
All causes	36,452	27,549	8,903	100.1	148.0	50.0
Leading causes of death						
Accidents	15,278	11,534	3,744	42.0	62.0	21.0
Motor vehicle	11,664	8,468	3,196	32.0	45.5	18.0
Homicide and legal intervention	8,159	6,923	1,236	22.4	37.2	6.9
Suicide	4,751	4,073	678	13.1	21.9	3.8
Malignant neoplasms (cancer)	1,814	1,083	731	5.0	5.8	4.1
Heart disease	990	641	349	2.7	3.4	2.0
HIV infection[3]	613	452	161	1.7	2.4	0.9
25 to 44 Years Old						
All causes	147,750	104,261	43,489	179.9	255.2	105.3
Leading causes of death						
Accidents	26,526	20,561	5,965	32.3	50.3	14.4
Motor vehicle	15,082	11,142	3,940	18.4	27.3	9.5
Malignant neoplasms (cancer)	22,228	10,164	12,064	27.1	24.9	29.2
HIV infection[3]	21,747	19,263	2,484	26.5	47.1	6.0
Heart disease	15,822	11,497	4,325	19.3	28.1	10.5
Homicide and legal intervention	12,372	9,770	2,602	15.1	23.9	6.3
Suicide	12,281	9,836	2,445	14.9	24.1	5.9
45 to 64 Years Old						
All causes	368,754	227,464	141,290	788.9	1,011.2	582.6

[Continued]

★ 736 ★

Leading Causes of Death by Age: 1991
[Continued]

Age and Leading Cause of Death	Number of Deaths			Rate per 100,000 Population		
	Total	Male	Female	Total	Male	Female
Leading causes of death						
Malignant neoplasms (cancer)	134,117	72,193	61,924	286.9	320.9	255.4
Heart disease	105,359	74,258	31,101	225.4	330.1	128.3
Cerebrovascular (stroke)	14,464	7,791	6,673	30.9	34.6	27.5
Accidents	13,693	9,750	3,943	29.3	43.3	16.3
Motor vehicle	6,616	4,458	2,158	14.2	19.8	8.9
Chronic obstructive pulmonary disease	12,769	6,874	5,895	27.3	30.6	24.3
Chronic liver disease and cirrhosis	10,497	7,301	3,196	22.5	32.5	13.2
Diabetes	10,045	5,129	4,916	21.5	22.8	20.3
65 Years Old and Over						
All causes	1,563,527	731,629	831,898	4,924.0	5,719.9	4,387.0
Leading causes of death						
Heart disease	597,267	272,619	324,648	1,881.0	2,131.3	1,712.0
Malignant neoplasms (cancer)	354,768	187,944	166,824	1,117.3	1,469.3	879.7
Cerebrovascular (stroke)	125,139	46,887	78,252	394.1	366.6	412.7
Chronic obstructive pulmonary disease	76,412	42,814	33,598	240.6	334.7	177.2
Pneumonia and influenza	68,962	30,710	38,252	217.2	240.1	201.7
Diabetes	36,528	14,593	21,935	115.0	114.1	115.7
Accidents	26,444	13,163	13,281	83.3	102.9	70.0
Motor vehicle	7,044	3,956	3,088	22.2	30.9	16.3

Source: "Deaths, by Age and Leading Cause: 1991," U.S. Bureau of the Census, *Statistical Abstract of the United States, 1994,* table 127, p. 95. Primary source: U.S. National Center for Health Statistics, *Vital Statistics of the United States,* annual; and unpublished data. Excludes deaths of nonresidents of the United States. Deaths classified according to ninth revision of *International Classification of Diseases. Notes:* 1. Includes those deaths with age not stated. 2. Includes other races not shown separately. 3. Human immunodeficiency virus.

★ 737 ★

Deaths

Lung Cancer Deaths: 1973-1990

This table shows age-adjusted death rates per 100,000 population from lung cancer by race and sex for the years 1973-1990. Lung cancer mortality rates among women continue to rise, and in 1986 lung cancer became the leading cause of cancer deaths among women. In 1994 cancer of the lung, prostate, breast, and colon/rectum were expected to account for 55% of all cancer deaths.

[Incidence rate per 100,000 population, age adjusted.]

Year	All Races			White			Black		
	Total	Men	Women	Total	Men	Women	Total	Men	Women
1973	34.8	62.4	13.3	34.3	61.6	13.3	40.8	75.1	13.0
1974	36.0	64.1	14.3	35.5	63.2	14.3	42.5	78.5	14.2
1975	36.8	65.1	15.2	36.3	64.2	15.3	43.3	79.7	14.9
1976	38.1	66.7	16.4	37.7	65.7	16.5	44.7	82.0	15.9
1977	39.2	68.2	17.3	38.6	66.8	17.4	47.8	87.8	17.3
1978	40.4	69.5	18.6	39.9	68.2	18.7	48.5	88.8	17.9
1979	41.1	70.1	19.4	40.5	68.8	19.5	49.4	89.7	19.2
1980	42.5	71.5	20.9	41.9	70.0	21.0	51.8	92.7	21.4
1981	43.0	71.7	21.7	42.3	70.0	21.8	53.1	95.5	21.9
1982	44.2	72.9	23.0	43.6	71.2	23.2	54.6	97.9	23.0
1983	44.9	72.9	24.4	44.3	71.2	24.6	55.7	98.0	25.0
1984	45.8	73.9	25.1	45.1	72.0	25.4	56.9	102.1	24.5
1985	46.6	74.1	26.4	46.0	72.3	26.8	57.5	101.6	26.0
1986	47.1	74.3	27.2	46.4	72.4	27.5	58.3	102.6	27.0
1987	48.1	75.1	28.3	47.4	73.2	28.5	59.8	104.6	28.4
1988	48.6	74.8	29.4	48.0	73.0	29.8	59.9	104.1	29.3
1989	49.3	74.7	30.8	48.7	72.6	31.2	61.6	106.7	30.3
1990	50.2	75.6	31.7	49.6	73.5	32.1	62.8	107.6	31.9

Source: Selected from "Age-Adjusted Lung Cancer Incidence and Mortality Rates, by Race and Sex, United States, 1973-1990," *Statistical Bulletin* 75(3), Jul-Sep 1994, Table 1, p. 20. Primary source: National Cancer Institute, *Cancer Statistics Review, 1973-1990,* 1993. Adjusted on basis of age distribution of the U.S. total population, 1970.

★ 738 ★
Deaths

Maternal and Infant Deaths: 1970-1991

This table shows infant mortality rates (deaths per 1,000 live births) and maternal mortality rates (deaths per 100,000 live births from deliveries and complications of pregnancy, childbirth, and puerperium) by race for the years 1970 to 1991.

Item and year	Infant deaths[1]				Maternal deaths[2]			
	Total	White	Black/other	Black	Total	White	Black/other	Black
1970	20.0	17.8	30.9	32.6	21.5	14.4	55.9	59.8
1980	12.6	11.0	19.1	21.4	9.2	6.7	19.8	21.5
1981	11.9	10.5	17.8	20.0	8.5	6.3	17.3	20.4
1982	11.5	10.1	17.3	19.6	7.9	5.8	16.4	18.2
1983	11.2	9.7	16.8	19.2	8.0	5.9	16.3	18.3
1984	10.8	9.4	16.1	18.4	7.8	5.4	16.9	19.7
1985	10.3	9.3	15.8	18.2	7.8	5.2	18.1	20.4
1986	10.4	8.9	15.7	18.0	7.2	4.9	16.0	18.8
1987	10.1	8.6	15.4	17.9	6.6	5.1	12.0	14.2
1988	10.0	8.5	15.0	17.6	8.4	5.9	17.4	19.5
1989	9.8	8.2	15.2	17.7	7.9	5.6	16.5	18.4
1990	9.2	7.6	15.5	18.0	8.2	5.4	19.1	22.4
1991	8.9	7.3	15.1	17.6	7.9	5.8	15.6	18.3

Source: Selected from "Infant, Maternal, and Neonatal Mortality Rates and Fetal Mortality Ratios, by Race: 1970 to 1991," U.S. Bureau of the Census, *Statistical Abstract of the United States, 1994,* table 120, p. 91. *Notes:* 1. Represents deaths of infants under 1 year old, exclusive of fetal deaths. 2. Per 100,000 live births from deliveries and complications of pregnancy, childbirth, and the puerperium. Beginning 1979, deaths are classified according to the ninth revision of the *International Classification of Diseases*; earlier years classified according to the revision in use at the time.

★ 739 ★
Deaths

Middle Eastern Deaths by Age-I

This table shows the total number of deaths of men and women in the Middle East and deaths by age, ages under 1 year to ages 40-44, latest available year.

Country/Year	All ages	-1	1-4	5-9	10-14	15-19	20-24	25-29	30-34	35-39	40-44
Middle East											
Iran Islamic Rep. of 1986											
Men	132,019	9,714	14,319	6,353	4,171	9,574	10,216	5,114	3,862	2,861	3,148
Women	58,042	6,338	4,875	2,022	1,430	2,329	2,547	2,226	2,053	1,611	1,727

[Continued]

★ 739 ★

Middle Eastern Deaths by Age-I
[Continued]

Country/Year	All ages	-1	1-4	5-9	10-14	15-19	20-24	25-29	30-34	35-39	40-44
Jordan											
1980[2]											
Men	3,941	545	315	131	106	106	108	91	88	100	133
Women	2,377	507	302	89	39	48	58	49	57	66	82
Kuwait											
1986											
Men	2,731	453	105	65	30	62	76	91	101	86	124
Women	1,659	388	68	43	26	22	23	44	27	46	53
Syria											
Syrian Arab Rep.											
1984[3]											
Men	17,224	1,653	2,163	976	605	577	244	290	272	266	396
Women	14,855	1,468	2,141	1,744	795	467	333	285	252	221	305

Source: Selected from "Deaths by age, sex and urban/rural residence: latest available year," United Nations, *Demographic Yearbook*, 1991, Table 19, pp. 368+. *Notes:* 1. The number in the preceding column includes this age group(s). 2. Excluding data for Jordanian territory under occupation since June 1967 by Israeli military forces. Excluding foreigners but including registered Palestinian refugees. 3. Excluding deaths for which cause is unknown.

★ 740 ★

Deaths

Middle Eastern Deaths by Age-II

This table shows the total number of deaths of men and women in the Middle East and deaths by age, ages 45+, latest available year.

Country/Year	All ages	45-49	50-54	55-59	60-64	65-69	70-74	75-79	80-84	85+	Unknown
Middle East											
Iran											
Islamic Rep. of											
1986											
Men	132,019	3,948	5,792	7,266	10,676	35,045	1	1	1	1	--
Women	58,042	1,912	2,548	3,027	4,643	18,754	1	1	1	1	--
Jordan											
1980[2]											
Men	3,941	172	252	222	248	1,315	1	1	1	1	9
Women	2,377	56	91	100	127	703	1	1	1	1	3
Kuwait											
1986											
Men	2,731	162	215	202	201	155	161	111	107	180	44
Women	1,659	55	82	65	106	104	112	104	105	180	6

[Continued]

★ 740 ★

Middle Eastern Deaths by Age-II
[Continued]

Country/Year	All ages	45-49	50-54	55-59	60-64	65-69	70-74	75-79	80-84	85+	Unknown
Syria Syrian Arab Rep. 1984[3]											
Men	17,224	512	1,097	678	1,211	1,164	1,500	1,001	1,106	1,513	--
Women	14,855	313	629	369	679	638	1,060	890	1,050	1,216	--

Source: Selected from "Deaths by age, sex and urban/rural residence: latest available year," United Nations, *Demographic Yearbook,* 1991, Table 19, pp. 368+. *Notes:* 1. The number in the preceding column includes this age group(s). 2. Excluding data for Jordanian territory under occupation since June 1967 by Israeli military forces. Excluding foreigners but including registered Palestinian refugees. 3. Excluding deaths for which cause is unknown.

★ 741 ★
Deaths

Middle East/North African Maternal Mortality Rates: 1980-1990

This table shows maternal deaths per 100,000 live births in the Middle East and North Africa for the period 1980-1990.

[Maternal deaths per 100,000 live births.]

Country	Maternal deaths per 100,000
Middle East/North Africa	
Algeria[1]	140
Egypt	318
Kuwait	4
Libya	
Libyan Arab Jamahiriya	80[1]
Morocco	300[2]
Syria	
Syrian Arab Republic	280
Tunisia	310[3]
Turkey	210

Source: Selected from "Indicators on health and child-bearing," *The World's Women: Trends and Statistics 1970-1990,* United Nations, 1991, Table 5, p. 69. Primary source: World Health Organization, "Maternal mortality rates: a tabulation of available information (second edition)," (Geneva, FHE/86.3). *Notes:* 1. 1977/78. 2. 1974/75. 3. 1970/72.

★ 742 ★

Deaths

North American Deaths by Age-I

This table shows the total number of deaths of men and women in North America and deaths by age, ages under 1 year to ages 40-44, latest available year.

Country/Year	All ages	-1	1-4	5-9	10-14	15-19	20-24	25-29	30-34	35-39	40-44
North America											
Bermuda											
1990											
Men	249	4	2	3	--	5	6	4	3	9	11
Women	196	3	--	1	1	--	--	3	6	4	3
Canada											
1989[1]											
Men	104,108	1,606	330	210	245	1,033	1,315	1,527	1,620	1,788	2,105
Women	86,857	1,189	265	162	157	331	460	555	705	904	1,247
Greenland											
1987											
Men	281	13	9	3	7	19	25	12	8	10	12
Women	164	16	3	--	--	3	8	7	5	4	7
United States											
1989											
Men	1,114,190	22,361	4,110	2,510	2,914	11,263	15,902	19,932	24,222	26,742	28,586
Women	1,036,276	17,294	3,182	1,803	1,687	4,307	5,016	6,998	9,372	11,120	14,471

Source: Selected from "Deaths by age, sex and urban/rural residence: latest available year," United Nations, *Demographic Yearbook*, 1991, Table 19, pp. 368+. *Notes:* 1. Including Canadian residents temporarily in the United States, but excluding Canadian residents temporarily in Canada.

★ 743 ★

Deaths

North American Deaths by Age-II

This table shows the total number of deaths of men and women in North America and deaths by age, ages 45+, latest available year.

Country/Year	All ages	45-49	50-54	55-59	60-64	65-69	70-74	75-79	80-84	85+	Unknown
North America											
Bermuda											
1990											
Men	249	13	14	14	21	26	31	35	20	28	--
Women	196	2	6	5	11	20	21	37	23	50	--

[Continued]

★ 743 ★

North American Deaths by Age-II
[Continued]

Country/Year	All ages	45-49	50-54	55-59	60-64	65-69	70-74	75-79	80-84	85+	Unknown
Canada											
1989[2]											
Men	104,108	2,646	3,736	6,240	9,442	12,596	14,130	15,508	13,473	14,554	4
Women	86,857	1,665	2,143	3,350	5,174	7,579	9,462	12,476	13,803	25,225	5
Greenland											
1987											
Men	281	10	23	25	26	20	20	17	16	6	--
Women	164	4	7	14	15	13	13	15	16	14	--
United States											
1989											
Men	1,114,190	32,718	42,105	62,981	96,628	129,847	148,559	157,090	135,580	149,735	405
Women	1,036,276	18,139	25,304	38,493	61,956	89,250	113,568	144,135	162,401	307,623	157

Source: Selected from "Deaths by age, sex and urban/rural residence: latest available year," United Nations, *Demographic Yearbook*, 1991, Table 19, pp. 368+. *Notes:* 1. Including Canadian residents temporarily in the United States, but excluding Canadian residents temporarily in Canada.

★ 744 ★
Deaths

North American Maternal Mortality Rates: 1980-1990

This table shows maternal deaths per 100,000 live births in North America during the period 1980-1990.

[Maternal deaths per 100,000 live births.]

Country	Maternal deaths per 100,000
North America	
Canada	4
United States	8

Source: Selected from "Indicators on health and child-bearing," *The World's Women: Trends and Statistics 1970-1990*, United Nations, 1991, Table 5, p. 67. Primary source: World Health Organization, "Maternal mortality rates: a tabulation of available information (second edition)," (Geneva, FHE/86.3).

★ 745 ★

Deaths

Oceanian Deaths by Age-I

This table shows the total number of deaths of men and women in Oceania and deaths by age, ages under 1 year to ages 40-44, latest available year.

Country/Year	All ages	-1	1-4	5-9	10-14	15-19	20-24	25-29	30-34	35-39	40-44
Oceania											
American Samoa 1988											
Men	130	10	5	1	1	4	8	3	4	5	7
Women	67	7	2	2	1	4	3	1	1	1	2
Australia 1990											
Men	64,660	1,224	256	150	135	676	950	998	976	966	1,357
Women	55,402	921	168	88	94	265	298	325	375	499	705
Cook Islands 1988											
Men	57	2	--	1	--	4	1	3	--	--	4
Women	37	2	--	--	--	1	1	--	--	1	--
Fiji 1987											
Men	1,890	106	47	23	19	29	62	64	55	74	96
Women	1,288	83	32	23	16	25	35	49	28	35	39
Guam 1986[2]											
Men	286	18	2	5	3	14	12	8	6	10	9
Women	165	13	3	--	4	4	1	2	--	4	3
Marshall Islands 1989											
Men	102	16	6	2	1	1	4	5	2	4	4
Women	49	13	4	1	1	1	2	--	6	--	1
New Caledonia 1982											
Men	538	49	27	8	7	13	18	18	12	18	23
Women	376	35	15	12	2	2	2	8	10	5	8
New Zealand 1990											
Men	13,971	296	81	36	39	214	296	216	189	195	261
Women	12,560	204	39	20	23	85	79	88	95	112	185
Norfolk Island 1988											
Men	6	--	--	--	--	--	--	--	1	--	--

[Continued]

★ 745 ★

Oceanian Deaths by Age-I
[Continued]

Country/Year	All ages	-1	1-4	5-9	10-14	15-19	20-24	25-29	30-34	35-39	40-44
Women	3	--	--	--	--	--	--	--	--	--	--
Northern Mariana Islands 1989											
Men	83	2	1	1	1	6	5	6	4	4	2
Women	39	--	--	1	--	1	1	--	2	1	1
Pacific Islands Palau 1985											
Men	56	10	--	1	--	2	--	2	1	2	2
Women	39	4	--	1	--	--	1	2	1	1	
Samoa 1980											
Men	286	22	12	2	9	10	9	8	6	10	9
Women	189	13	11	6	7	6	5	5	2	8	7
Tokelau 1982											
Men	5	--	--	--	--	--	--	--	--	--	--
Women	11	--	2	--	--	--	--	--	--	--	--

Source: Selected from "Deaths by age, sex and urban/rural residence: latest available year," United Nations, *Demographic Yearbook*, 1991, Table 19, pp. 368+. *Notes:* 1. The number in the preceding column includes this age group(s). 2. Including U.S. military personnel, their dependents and contract employees.

★ 746 ★
Deaths

Oceanian Deaths by Age-II

This table shows the total number of deaths of men and women in Oceania and deaths by age, ages 45+, latest available year.

Country/Year	All ages	45-49	50-54	55-59	60-64	65-69	70-74	75-79	80-84	85+	Unknown
Oceania											
American Samoa 1988											
Men	130	8	6	14	14	12	9	11	5	3	--
Women	67	2	4	6	9	8	8	3	1	2	--
Australia 1990											
Men	64,660	1,575	2,253	3,503	5,899	8,217	8,976	10,429	8,468	7,642	10
Women	55,402	892	1,310	1,791	3,018	4,671	6,173	8,650	9,361	15,797	1

[Continued]

★ 746 ★

Oceanian Deaths by Age-II
[Continued]

Country/Year	All ages	45-49	50-54	55-59	60-64	65-69	70-74	75-79	80-84	85+	Unknown
Cook Islands											
1988											
Men	57	1	3	7	2	1	8	9	11	1	--
Women	37	--	5	1	4	4	6	2	10	1	--
Fiji											
1987											
Men	1,890	149	172	187	160	175	180	107	75	78	32
Women	1,288	103	105	105	115	115	114	80	86	76	24
Guam											
1986[2]											
Men	286	13	20	30	32	35	21	24	16	8	--
Women	165	2	9	19	22	17	20	14	13	15	--
Marshall Islands											
1989											
Men	102	6	9	5	8	8	10	11	1	1	--
Women	49	2	1	7	2	3	1	14	1	1	--
New Caledonia											
1982											
Men	538	21	37	50	50	60	54	33	26	14	--
Women	376	12	16	24	35	35	42	43	34	36	--
New Zealand											
1990											
Men	13,971	334	469	763	1,223	1,696	1,965	2,252	1,891	1,555	--
Women	12,560	260	362	505	739	1,082	1,460	1,834	2,151	3,237	--
Norfolk Island											
1988											
Men	6	--	--	1	--	1	1	--	2	--	--
Women	3	--	--	--	--	--	2	--	1	--	--
Northern Mariana Islands											
1989											
Men	83	5	5	7	6	7	6	6	5	4	--
Women	39	--	1	8	4	3	4	5	1	6	--
Pacific Islands											
Palau											
1985											
Men	56	1	3	9	4	4	5	5	4	1	--
Women	39	1	--	1	3	7	5	6	3	3	--

[Continued]

★ 746 ★

Oceanian Deaths by Age-II
[Continued]

Country/Year	All ages	45-49	50-54	55-59	60-64	65-69	70-74	75-79	80-84	85+	Unknown
Samoa											
1980											
Men	286	16	19	18	35	27	18	17	9	20	10
Women	189	6	10	13	11	13	18	12	12	20	6
Tokelau											
1982											
Men	5	1	--	--	1	--	--	--	1	2	--
Women	11	--	--	--	--	2	2	2	--	3	--

Source: Selected from "Deaths by age, sex and urban/rural residence: latest available year," United Nations, *Demographic Yearbook*, 1991, Table 19, pp. 368+.
Notes: 1. The number in the preceding column includes this age group(s). 2. Including U.S. military personnel, their dependents and contract employees.

★ 747 ★

Deaths

Oceanian Maternal Mortality Rates: 1980-1990

This table shows maternal deaths per 100,000 live births in Oceania for the period 1980-1990.

[Maternal deaths per 100,000 live births.]

Country	Maternal deaths per 100,000
Oceania	
Australia	5
Fiji	41
New Caledonia	160
New Zealand	14
Papua New Guinea	900
Solomon Islands	10
Vanuatu	107

Source: Selected from "Indicators on health and child-bearing," *The World's Women: Trends and Statistics 1970-1990*, United Nations, 1991, Table 5, p. 69. Primary source: World Health Organization, "Maternal mortality rates: a tabulation of available information (second edition)," (Geneva, FHE/86.3).

★ 748 ★

Deaths

Sub-Saharan Africa Maternal Mortality Rates: 1980-1990

This table shows maternal deaths per 100,000 live births in Sub-Saharan Africa for the period 1980-1990.

[Maternal deaths per 100,000 live births.]

Country	Maternal deaths per 100,000
Sub-Saharan Africa	
Botswana	200-300
Burkina Faso	810
Cameroon[1]	300
Cape Verde	107
Central African Republic	600
Chad	860[2]
Congo	1,000[2]
Ghana	1,000
Kenya	170[1]
Madagascar	240
Malawi	100[3]
Mauritius	126
Niger	420
Nigeria	800
Rwanda	210[4]
Senegal	600
Sierra Leone	450
Somalia	1,100
South Africa	83[5]
Sudan	660
Tanzania	340[6]
Uganda	300
Zambia	151
Zimbabwe	480[7]

Source: Selected from "Indicators on health and child-bearing," *The World's Women: Trends and Statistics 1970-1990*, United Nations, 1991, Table 5, p. 67. Primary source: World Health Organization, "Maternal mortality rates: a tabulation of available information (second edition)," (Geneva, FHE/86.3). *Notes:* 1. 1977/78. 2. 1970/72. 3. All health institutions. 4. All hospitals. 5. From 267 hospitals. 6. From 48 hospitals. 7. 1974/75.

★ 749 ★

Deaths

Suicide Rates: 1980-1991

This table shows suicide rates per 100,000 population, by sex, race, and age group, for the years 1980 to 1991.

[Rates per 100,000 population.]

Age	Male						Female					
	White			Black			White			Black		
	1980	1990	1991	1980	1990	1991	1980	1990	1991	1980	1990	1991
All ages[2]	19.9	22.0	21.7	10.3	12.0	12.1	5.9	5.3	5.2	2.2	2.3	1.9
10 to 14 years	1.4	2.3	2.4	0.5	1.6	2.0	0.3	0.9	0.8	0.1	[1]	[1]
15 to 19 years	15.0	19.3	19.1	5.6	11.5	12.2	3.3	4.0	4.2	1.6	1.9	[1]
20 to 24 years	27.8	26.8	26.5	20.0	19.0	20.7	5.9	4.4	4.3	3.1	2.6	1.8
25 to 34 years	25.6	25.6	26.1	21.8	21.9	21.1	7.5	6.0	5.8	4.1	3.7	3.3
35 to 44 years	23.5	25.3	24.7	15.6	16.9	15.2	9.1	7.4	7.2	4.6	4.0	2.9
45 to 54 years	24.2	24.8	25.3	12.0	14.8	14.3	10.2	7.5	8.3	2.8	3.2	3.0
55 to 64 years	25.8	27.5	26.8	11.7	10.8	13.0	9.1	8.0	7.1	2.3	2.6	2.1
65 to 74 years	32.5	34.2	32.6	11.1	14.7	13.8	7.0	7.2	6.4	1.7	2.6	2.4
75 to 84 years	45.5	60.2	56.1	10.5	14.4	21.6	5.7	6.7	6.0	1.4	[1]	[1]
85 years and over	52.8	70.3	75.1	18.9	[1]	[1]	5.8	5.4	6.6	0.1	[1]	[1]

Source: "Suicides Rates, by Sex, Race, and Age Group,: 1980 to 1991," U.S. Bureau of the Census, *Statistical Abstract of the United States, 1994,* table 136, p. 101. Primary source: U.S. National Center for Health Statistics, *Monthly Vital Statistics Report;* and unpublished data. Excludes deaths of nonresidents of the United States. Beginning 1980, deaths classified according to the ninth revision of the *International Classification of Diseases.* For earlier years, classified according to the revision in use at the time. *Notes:* 1. Base figure to small to meet statistical standards for reliability of a derived figure. 2. Includes other age groups not shown separately.

★ 750 ★

Deaths

Suicides: 1970-1991

This table shows total number of suicides and method used by sex for the years 1970 to 1991.

Method	Male						Female					
	1970	1980	1985	1989	1990	1991	1970	1980	1985	1989	1990	1991
Total	16,629	20,505	23,145	24,102	24,724	24,769	6,851	6,364	6,308	6,130	6,182	6,041
Firearms[1]	9,704	12,937	14,809	15,680	16,285	16,120	2,068	2,459	2,554	2,498	2,600	2,406
Percent of total	58%	63%	64%	65%	66%	65%	30%	39%	41%	41%	42%	40%
Poisoning[2]	3,299	2,997	3,319	3,211	3,221	3,316	3,285	2,456	2,385	2,232	2,203	2,228

[Continued]

★ 750 ★

Suicides: 1970-1991
[Continued]

Method	Male						Female					
	1970	1980	1985	1989	1990	1991	1970	1980	1985	1989	1990	1991
Hanging and strangulation[3]	2,422	2,997	3,532	3,708	3,688	3,751	831	694	732	776	756	810
Other[4]	1,204	1,574	1,485	1,503	1,530	1,582	667	755	637	624	623	597

Source: "Suicides, by Sex and Method Used: 1970 to 1991," U.S. Bureau of the Census, *Statistical Abstract of the United States, 1994,* table 135, p. 100. Primary source: U.S. National Center for Health Statistics, *Vital Statistics of the United States,* annual; and unpublished data. Excludes deaths of nonresidents of the United States. Beginning 1979, deaths classified according to the ninth revision of the *International Classification of Diseases.* For earlier years, classified according to the revision in use at the time. *Notes:* 1. Includes explosives in 1970. 2. Includes solids, liquids, and gases. 3. Includes suffocation. 4. Beginning 1980, includes explosives.

★ 751 ★

Deaths

Traffic Accident Deaths: 1975-1990

This table presents data on driver fatalities in 1975 and 1990 and shows the changes that took place during that period. The number of female driver fatalities annually jumped 65% during this period, while the number of men being killed each year went down about 1%. The increase in female driver fatalities is attributed to increases in the number of licensed drivers and in the number of miles driven. In 1975 female drivers drove an average of 5,877 miles annually, compared to 9,438 in 1990.

Driver Age Group	Driver Fatalities by Age and Sex (Actual Counts)						
	1975			1990			1975-1990
	Female drivers	Male drivers	Fem.-Male ratio	Female drivers	Male drivers	Fem.-Male ratio	Ratio change
16-19 years	556	3,483	0.160	775	2,434	0.318	99.5%
20-24 years	634	4,256	0.149	809	3,397	0.238	59.9%
25-29 years	456	2,780	0.164	756	2,925	0.258	57.6%
30-34 years	307	1,688	0.182	618	2,349	0.263	44.7%
35-39 years	267	1,263	0.211	515	1,791	0.288	36.0%
40-44 years	240	1,025	0.234	451	1,296	0.348	48.6%
45-49 years	239	986	0.242	350	970	0.361	48.9%
50-54 years	220	979	0.225	282	789	0.357	59.0%
55-59 years	208	827	0.252	261	679	0.384	52.8%
60-64 years	201	730	0.275	275	689	0.399	45.0%
65-69 years	167	621	0.269	277	623	0.445	65.3%
70 years +	281	1,202	0.234	762	1,631	0.467	99.8%
Total	3,776	19,840	0.190	6,131	19,573	0.313	64.6%

Source: Ezio C. Cerrelli, "Female Drivers in Fatal Crashes, Recent Trends," U.S. Department of Transportation, National Highway Traffic Safety Administration, NHTSA Technical Report, DOT HS 808 106, January 1994, Table D, p. 27, "Driver Fatalities by Age and Sex (Actual Counts)."

★ 752 ★

Deaths

Traffic Accident Deaths: 1990

This table presents data on automobile crashes and driver fatalities by various characteristics of drivers in 1990. Female drivers accounted for 48.6% of all licensed drivers. Females drove an estimated 9,450 miles annually, compared to 16,500 miles for males. Male drivers made up 62.1% of all drivers involved in crashes in 1990 (females 37.9%). Of the 57,675 drivers involved in fatal crashes, male drivers accounted for 44,000 (76.3%) and female drivers for 13,675 (23.7%).

[VMT = Vehicle Miles of Travel.]

Driver Age Group	Licensed drivers (1,000)	Average annual travel	Total miles of travel (millions)	Drivers in all crashes (1,000)	Drivers in fatal crashes	Driver fatal-ities	Crash Inv. rate[1] (per VMT)	Fat. Inv. rate[1] (per VMT)	Fatality rate[1] (per VMT)	Crash Inv. rate[1] per (LIC.)	Fat.Inv. rate[1] (per LIC.)	Fatality rate[1] (per LIC.)
15-19 years	4,336	7,387	32,030	618	1,850	775	1,920	5.78	2.4	143	0.43	1.18
20-24 years	8,093	11,807	95,554	660	1,950	809	691	2.04	0.8	82	0.24	0.10
25-29 years	9,656	11,191	108,060	603	1,858	756	558	1.72	0.7	62	0.19	0.08
30-34 years	10,071	10,785	108,616	538	1,595	618	495	1.47	0.6	53	0.16	0.06
35-39 years	9,371	11,437	107,176	456	1,301	515	425	1.21	0.5	49	0.14	0.05
40-44 years	8,295	11,021	91,419	372	1,111	451	407	1.22	0.5	45	0.13	0.05
45-49 years	6,378	9,956	63,499	267	745	350	420	1.17	0.6	42	0.12	0.05
50-54 years	5,108	8,693	44,404	173	622	282	390	1.40	0.6	34	0.12	0.06
55-59 years	4,582	7,681	35,194	149	488	261	423	1.39	0.7	33	0.11	0.06
60-64 years	4,497	6,706	30,157	126	491	275	418	1.63	0.9	28	0.11	0.06
65-69 years	4,109	5,885	24,181	110	488	277	455	2.02	1.1	27	0.12	0.07
70-74 years	3,107	4,673	14,519	89	475	276	613	3.27	1.9	29	0.15	0.09
75-79 years	2,084	3,570	7,440	56	383	246	753	5.15	3.3	27	0.18	0.12
80-84 years	1,078	3,300	3,557	29	226	170	815	6.35	4.8	27	0.21	0.16
85 years +	456	1,615	736	14	92	70	1,901	12.49	9.5	31	0.20	0.15
Total	81,221	9,438	766,544	4,260	13,675	6,131	556	1.78	0.8	52	0.17	0.08

Source: Ezio C. Cerrelli, "Crash Data and Rates for Age-Sex Groups of Drivers, 1990," U.S. Department of Transportation, National Highway Traffic Safety Administration, Research Note, May 1992, Table B, "1990 Female Driver Crash and Fatality Data." *Note:* 1. Rates per 100,000,000 VMT and per 1,000 licensed drivers.

Fertility

★ 753 ★

Asian and Near Eastern Fertility Rates: 1995-2020

This table shows projections of the total fertility rates in Asia and the Near East in 1995, 2000, 2005, 2010, 2015, and 2020. Total fertility rate is the average number of children that would be born per woman if all women lived to the end of their childbearing years and bore children according to a given set of age-specific fertility rates. Of the world's 20 poorest nations, only Bangladesh has been registering a fertility decline. From 1975 to 1990, fertility declined from 7 to 4.5 there.*

[NA Not available.]

Country	1995	2000	2005	2010	2015	2020
Asia	3.0	2.8	2.7	2.5	2.5	2.4
Asia, excluding Near East	2.9	2.7	2.6	2.5	2.4	2.3
Afghanistan	6.2	5.9	5.5	5.1	4.7	4.3
Bangladesh	4.4	4.0	3.6	3.3	3.1	2.8
Bhutan	5.4	5.1	4.8	4.5	4.1	3.8
Brunei	3.4	3.3	3.2	3.1	3.0	3.0
Burma	3.6	3.3	3.0	2.8	2.6	2.4
Cambodia	5.8	5.8	5.5	5.2	4.9	4.6
China						
Mainland	1.8	1.8	1.8	1.8	1.8	1.8
Taiwan	1.8	1.8	1.8	1.8	1.8	1.8
Hong Kong	1.4	1.5	1.5	1.5	1.6	1.6
India	3.4	3.0	2.8	2.6	2.4	2.3
Indonesia	2.7	2.5	2.4	2.3	2.2	2.1
Iran	6.3	5.9	5.4	4.9	4.5	4.0
Japan	1.6	1.6	1.6	1.6	1.6	1.6
Laos	6.0	5.4	4.8	4.2	3.7	3.2
Macau	1.5	1.6	1.6	1.6	1.6	1.6
Malaysia	3.5	3.3	3.2	3.0	2.9	2.8
Maldives	6.2	5.6	5.0	4.4	3.9	3.4
Mongolia	4.3	3.9	3.6	3.3	3.0	2.8
Nepal	5.2	4.7	4.2	3.8	3.4	3.1
North Korea	2.3	2.2	2.1	2.0	2.0	1.9
Pakistan	6.4	5.9	5.5	5.0	4.5	4.1
Philippines	3.3	2.9	2.6	2.4	2.3	2.2
Singapore	1.9	1.8	1.8	1.8	1.8	1.8
South Korea	1.7	1.7	1.7	1.7	1.7	1.7
Sri Lanka	2.0	1.9	1.8	1.8	1.8	1.8
Thailand	2.0	1.9	1.9	1.8	1.8	1.8

[Continued]

★ 753 ★

Asian and Near Eastern Fertility Rates: 1995-2020
[Continued]

Country	1995	2000	2005	2010	2015	2020
Vietnam	3.2	2.8	2.5	2.3	2.2	2.1
Near East	4.8	4.5	4.2	3.9	3.7	3.4
Bahrain	3.9	3.7	3.5	3.3	3.1	3.0
Cyprus	2.3	2.2	2.1	2.1	2.0	2.0
Gaza Strip	7.3	6.6	5.9	5.2	4.6	4.0
Iraq	6.6	5.8	5.3	4.8	4.3	3.9
Israel	2.8	2.7	2.5	2.4	2.3	2.2
Jordan	5.5	4.6	3.9	3.3	2.9	2.6
Kuwait	3.9	3.7	3.8	3.8	3.9	3.8
Lebanon	3.3	3.0	2.7	2.5	2.4	2.3
Oman	6.5	6.2	5.9	5.6	5.2	4.9
Qatar	3.6	2.9	2.6	2.4	2.2	2.1
Saudi Arabia	6.6	6.4	6.2	5.9	5.5	5.2
Syria	6.6	6.0	5.4	4.9	4.3	3.8
Turkey	3.1	2.8	2.5	2.4	2.2	2.2
United Arab Emirates	4.5	4.2	3.9	3.5	3.3	3.0
West Bank	4.0	3.3	2.8	2.5	2.3	2.2
Yemen	7.1	6.7	6.3	5.8	5.3	4.8

Source: Selected from "Total Fertility Rates by Country or Area: 1985 to 2020," U.S. Bureau of the Census, *World Population Profile: 1994*, 1994, Table 7, p. A-23. Primary source: U.S. Bureau of the Census, International Data Base.

★ 754 ★

Fertility

European Fertility Rates: 1995-2020

This table shows projections of the total fertility rates in Europe in 1995, 2000, 2005, 2010, 2015, and 2020. Total fertility rate is the average number of children that would be born per woman if all women lived to the end of their childbearing years and bore children according to a given set of age-specific fertility rates.

[NA Not available.]

Country	1995	2000	2005	2010	2015	2020
Europe	1.7	1.7	1.7	1.7	1.7	1.7
Albania	2.7	2.4	2.2	2.1	1.9	1.9
Andorra	1.7	1.7	1.7	1.7	1.7	1.7
Austria	1.5	1.5	1.5	1.5	1.6	1.6
Belgium	1.6	1.6	1.6	1.6	1.6	1.6
Bulgaria	1.7	1.7	1.7	1.7	1.7	1.7

[Continued]

★ 754 ★

European Fertility Rates: 1995-2020
[Continued]

Country	1995	2000	2005	2010	2015	2020
Czech Republic	1.8	1.8	1.8	1.8	1.8	1.8
Denmark	1.7	1.7	1.7	1.7	1.7	1.7
Faroe Islands	2.4	2.2	2.1	2.0	1.9	1.8
Finland	1.8	1.8	1.8	1.8	1.8	1.8
France	1.8	1.8	1.8	1.8	1.8	1.8
Germany	1.5	1.5	1.5	1.5	1.5	1.6
Gibraltar	2.3	2.1	2.0	1.9	1.9	1.8
Greece	1.5	1.5	1.5	1.5	1.6	1.6
Guernsey	1.7	1.8	1.8	1.8	1.8	1.8
Hungary	1.8	1.8	1.8	1.8	1.8	1.8
Iceland	2.1	1.8	1.8	1.8	1.8	1.8
Ireland	2.0	1.8	1.8	1.8	1.8	1.8
Isle of Man	1.8	1.8	1.8	1.8	1.8	1.8
Italy	1.4	1.5	1.5	1.5	1.6	1.6
Jersey	1.4	1.5	1.5	1.5	1.6	1.6
Liechtenstein	1.5	1.5	1.5	1.5	1.6	1.6
Luxembourg	1.7	1.7	1.7	1.7	1.7	1.7
Malta	1.9	1.8	1.8	1.8	1.8	1.8
Monaco	1.7	1.7	1.7	1.7	1.7	1.7
Netherlands	1.6	1.5	1.5	1.5	1.6	1.6
Norway	1.8	1.5	1.5	1.5	1.6	1.6
Poland	1.9	1.8	1.8	1.8	1.8	1.8
Portugal	1.5	1.5	1.5	1.5	1.6	1.6
Romania	1.8	1.8	1.8	1.8	1.8	1.8
San Marino	1.5	1.5	1.5	1.5	1.6	1.6
Slovakia	1.9	1.8	1.8	1.8	1.8	1.8
Spain	1.4	1.5	1.5	1.5	1.6	1.6
Sweden	2.0	1.8	1.8	1.8	1.8	1.8
Switzerland	1.6	1.6	1.6	1.6	1.6	1.6
United Kingdom	1.8	1.8	1.8	1.8	1.8	1.8

Source: Selected from "Total Fertility Rates by Country or Area: 1985 to 2020," U.S. Bureau of the Census, *World Population Profile: 1994*, 1994, Table 7, p. A-25. Primary source: U.S. Bureau of the Census, International Data Base.

★ 755 ★

Fertility

Fertility Rates and Race of Child: 1970-1991

This table shows the total fertility rate and the fertility rate for whites and blacks based on race of child and registered births. The total fertility rate is the number of births that 1,000 women would have in their lifetime if, at each year of age, they experienced the birth rates occurring in the specified year. A total fertility rate of 2,110 represents "replacement level" fertility for the total population under current mortality conditions (assuming no net immigration). The 1990-91 total fertility rates were higher than any seen in the United States since the early 1970s.

[X is not available.]

Annual average and year	Total	White	Black and other
1970-1974	2,094	1,997	2,680
1975-79	1,774	1,685	2,270
1980-84	1,819	1,731	2,262
1985-88	1,870	1,769	2,339
1970	2,480	2,385	3,067
1971	2,267	2,161	2,920
1972	2,010	1,907	2,628
1973	1,879	1,783	2,443
1974	1,835	1,749	2,339
1975	1,774	1,686	2,276
1976	1,738	1,652	2,223
1977	1,790	1,703	2,279
1978	1,760	1,668	2,265
1979	1,808	1,716	2,310
1980	1,840	1,749	2,323
1981	1,815	1,726	2,275
1982	1,829	1,742	2,265
1983	1,803	1,718	2,225
1984	1,806	1,719	2,224
1985	1,843	1,754	2,263
1986	1,836	1,742	2,282
1987	1,871	1,767	2,349
1988	1,932	1,814	2,463
1989	2,014	1,895	2,526
1990	2,081	1,963	2,578
1991	2,071	X	X

Source: Selected from "Total Fertility Rate and Intrinsic Rate of Natural Increase: 1960 to 1990," U.S. Bureau of the Census, *Statistical Abstract of the United States, 1994*, table 94, p. 78; "Summary of Annual Data on demographic, Social, and Economic Characteristics: 1985-1992, 1980, and 1970," and U.S. Bureau of the Census, *Current Population Reports*, "Population Profile of the United States 1993," Table A-1, p. 48. Primary source: U.S. National Center for Health Statistics, *Vital Statistics of the United States*, annual, and unpublished data.

★ 756 ★

Fertility

Latin American/Caribbean Fertility Rates: 1995-2020

This table shows projections of the total fertility rates in Latin America and the Caribbean in 1995, 2000, 2005, 2010, 2015, and 2020. Total fertility rate is the average number of children that would be born per woman if all women lived to the end of their childbearing years and bore children according to a given set of age-specific fertility rates. Brazil, one of the six most populous countries in the world in 1994, has the world's largest Roman Catholic population. In a survey conducted there in June 1994, 88% of respondents said they don't follow church teachings on birth control. Among women aged 25 to 44, the "don't follow" group was 90%.

[NA Not available.]

Country	1995	2000	2005	2010	2015	2020
Latin America/Caribbean	2.8	2.6	2.4	2.2	2.1	2.1
Anguilla	3.1	3.0	2.9	2.8	2.7	2.6
Antigua and Barbuda	1.7	1.7	1.7	1.7	1.7	1.7
Argentina	2.7	2.5	2.4	2.3	2.2	2.1
Aruba	1.8	1.8	1.8	1.8	1.8	1.8
Bahamas, The	1.9	1.8	1.8	1.8	1.8	1.8
Barbados	1.8	1.8	1.8	1.8	1.8	1.8
Belize	4.3	3.6	3.1	2.7	2.5	2.3
Bolivia	4.1	3.6	3.2	2.9	2.7	2.5
Brazil	2.4	2.1	2.0	1.9	1.9	1.8
British Virgin Islands	2.3	2.2	NA	NA	NA	NA
Cayman Islands	1.4	1.3	NA	NA	NA	NA
Chile	2.5	2.4	2.4	2.3	2.3	2.2
Colombia	2.4	2.2	2.0	1.9	1.9	1.9
Costa Rica	3.0	2.8	2.6	2.5	2.4	2.3
Cuba	1.8	1.8	1.8	1.8	1.8	1.8
Dominica	2.0	1.9	1.8	1.8	1.8	1.8
Dominican Republic	2.7	2.4	2.2	2.1	2.1	2.0
Ecuador	3.0	2.6	2.4	2.2	2.1	2.1
El Salvador	3.7	3.3	3.0	2.7	2.5	2.4
French Guiana	3.5	3.3	3.1	2.9	2.8	2.7
Grenada	3.9	3.5	3.2	2.9	2.7	2.5
Guadeloupe	2.0	1.8	1.8	1.7	1.7	1.7
Guatemala	4.6	4.0	3.5	3.0	2.7	2.5
Guyana	2.2	2.1	1.9	1.9	1.8	1.8
Haiti	5.8	5.2	4.5	3.9	3.3	2.9
Honduras	4.6	3.8	3.2	2.8	2.5	2.3
Jamaica	2.4	2.1	2.0	1.9	1.9	1.9
Martinique	1.9	1.8	1.8	1.8	1.8	1.8
Mexico	3.1	2.8	2.6	2.4	2.3	2.2
Montserrat	2.0	1.7	NA	NA	NA	NA

[Continued]

★ 756 ★

Latin American/Caribbean Fertility Rates: 1995-2020
[Continued]

Country	1995	2000	2005	2010	2015	2020
Netherlands Antilles	1.9	1.8	1.8	1.8	1.8	1.8
Nicaragua	4.2	3.5	3.0	2.6	2.4	2.2
Panama	2.8	2.6	2.4	2.3	2.2	2.2
Paraguay	4.2	3.9	3.5	3.2	3.0	2.8
Peru	3.0	2.6	2.4	2.2	2.1	2.1
Puerto Rico	2.0	1.8	1.8	1.8	1.8	1.8
Saint Kitts and Nevis	2.6	2.4	2.2	2.1	2.1	2.0
Saint Lucia	2.4	2.2	2.1	2.0	2.0	2.0
Saint Vincent and the Grenadines	2.0	1.9	1.8	1.8	1.8	1.8
Suriname	2.7	2.5	2.3	2.2	2.1	2.0
Trinidad and Tobago	2.3	2.1	2.0	1.9	1.9	1.8
Turks and Caicos Islands	2.3	1.6	NA	NA	NA	NA
Uruguay	2.4	2.3	2.2	2.1	2.1	2.0
Venezuela	3.0	2.7	2.5	2.3	2.2	2.2
Virgin Islands	2.4	2.0	NA	NA	NA	NA

Source: Selected from "Total Fertility Rates by Country or Area: 1985 to 2020," U.S. Bureau of the Census, *World Population Profile: 1994*, 1994, Table 7, p. A-24. Primary source: U.S. Bureau of the Census, International Data Base. Introductory remarks about the Catholic population in Brazil are from James Brooke, "With Church Preaching in Vain, Brazilians Embrace Birth Control," *The New York Times*, September 2, 1994, p. A1+.

★ 757 ★
Fertility

North African Fertility Rates: 1995-2020

This table shows projections of the total fertility rates in North Africa in 1995, 2000, 2005, 2010, 2015, and 2020. Total fertility rate is the average number of children that would be born per woman if all women lived to the end of their childbearing years and bore children according to a given set of age-specific fertility rates. The future trend in world fertility is expected to continue downward, with women bearing an average of 2.5 children each by the year 2020.

[NA Not available.]

Country	1995	2000	2005	2010	2015	2020
North Africa	4.0	3.5	3.2	2.9	2.7	2.5
Algeria	3.7	3.2	2.8	2.5	2.3	2.2
Egypt	4.2	3.8	3.4	3.1	2.9	2.7
Libya	6.3	6.0	5.7	5.3	5.0	4.6
Morocco	3.7	3.1	2.7	2.5	2.3	2.2

[Continued]

★ 757 ★

North African Fertility Rates: 1995-2020
[Continued]

Country	1995	2000	2005	2010	2015	2020
Tunisia	2.7	2.3	2.1	2.1	2.0	2.0
Western Sahara	6.9	6.6	NA	NA	NA	NA

Source: Selected from "Total Fertility Rates by Country or Area: 1985 to 2020," U.S. Bureau of the Census, *World Population Profile: 1994*, 1994, Table 7, p. A-23. Primary source: U.S. Bureau of the Census, International Data Base.

★ 758 ★

Fertility

North American Fertility Rates: 1995-2020

This table shows projections of the total fertility rates in North America in 1995, 2000, 2005, 2010, 2015, and 2020. Total fertility rate is the average number of children that would be born per woman if all women lived to the end of their childbearing years and bore children according to a given set of age-specific fertility rates.

[NA Not available.]

Country	1995	2000	2005	2010	2015	2020
North America						
Bermuda	1.8	1.8	NA	NA	NA	NA
Canada	1.8	1.8	1.8	1.8	1.8	1.8
Greenland	2.3	2.1	2.0	1.9	1.9	1.8
Saint Pierre and Miquelon	1.7	1.6	NA	NA	NA	NA
United States	2.1	2.1	2.1	2.1	2.1	2.1

Source: Selected from "Total Fertility Rates by Country or Area: 1985 to 2020," U.S. Bureau of the Census, *World Population Profile: 1994*, 1994, Table 7, p. A-24. Primary source: U.S. Bureau of the Census, International Data Base.

★ 759 ★

Fertility

Oceanian Fertility Rates: 1995-2020

This table shows projections of the total fertility rates in Oceania in 1995, 2000, 2005, 2010, 2015, and 2020. Total fertility rate is the average number of children that would be born per woman if all women lived to the end of their childbearing years and bore children according to a given set of age-specific fertility rates.

[NA Not available.]

Country	1995	2000	2005	2010	2015	2020
Oceania	2.4	2.3	2.2	2.1	2.1	2.0
American Samoa	4.3	3.9	NA	NA	NA	NA
Australia	1.8	1.8	1.8	1.8	1.8	1.8
Cook Islands	3.3	3.1	NA	NA	NA	NA
Federated States of Micronesia	4.0	3.8	NA	NA	NA	NA
Fiji	2.9	2.7	2.5	2.4	2.3	2.2
French Polynesia	3.3	3.1	3.0	2.8	2.7	2.6
Guam	2.3	1.8	NA	NA	NA	NA
Kiribati	3.7	NA	NA	NA	NA	NA
Marshall Islands	6.9	6.6	6.3	6.0	5.6	5.3
New Caldeonia	2.6	2.4	2.3	2.2	2.1	2.1
New Zealand	2.0	1.8	1.8	1.8	1.8	1.8
Papua New Guinea	4.6	4.1	3.6	3.3	3.0	2.7
Solomon Islands	5.6	4.8	4.0	3.4	2.9	2.6
Tonga	3.6	3.3	NA	NA	NA	NA
Trust Territory of the Pacific Islands (Palau)	2.9	2.4	NA	NA	NA	NA
Tuvalu	3.1	3.1	3.0	2.9	2.8	2.7
Vanuatu	4.1	3.5	3.0	2.6	2.4	2.2
Wallis and Futuna	3.1	NA	NA	NA	NA	NA
Western Samoa	4.0	3.5	3.1	2.7	2.5	2.3

Source: Selected from "Total Fertility Rates by Country or Area: 1985 to 2020," U.S. Bureau of the Census, *World Population Profile: 1994*, 1994, Table 7, p. A-26. Primary source: U.S. Bureau of the Census, International Data Base.

★ 760 ★

Fertility

Sub-Saharan African Fertility Rates: 1995-2020

This table shows projections of the total fertility rates in Sub-Saharan Africa in 1995, 2000, 2005, 2010, 2015, and 2020. Total fertility rate is the average number of children that would be born per woman if all women lived to the end of their childbearing years and bore children according to a given set of age-specific fertility rates. Nine of the 10 highest fertility countries in the world are in Sub-Saharan Africa. More than 40 Sub-Saharan African countries are in the high fertility category, but their combined populations represent less than 10% of the world's total population. The influence of high fertility rates will continue to be reflected in the age composition of the population. Children ages 0 to 4 years will greatly outnumber the elderly in 2020.

[NA Not available.]

Country	1995	2000	2005	2010	2015	2020
Sub-Saharan Africa						
Angola	6.4	6.1	5.6	5.2	4.7	4.2
Benin	6.7	6.3	5.9	5.4	4.8	4.3
Botswana	3.9	3.1	2.6	2.3	2.2	2.1
Burkina	6.9	6.5	6.0	5.4	4.9	4.3
Burundi	6.6	6.3	5.8	5.3	4.8	4.4
Cameroon	5.8	5.6	5.4	5.2	5.0	4.7
Cape Verde	6.2	5.7	5.1	4.5	3.9	3.5
Central African Republic	5.4	5.1	4.7	4.4	4.0	3.7
Chad	5.3	5.1	4.8	4.5	4.1	3.8
Comoros	6.7	6.3	5.9	5.4	4.9	4.3
Congo	5.2	4.8	4.4	4.0	3.6	3.2
Cote d'Ivoire	6.6	6.2	5.7	5.1	4.5	3.9
Djibouti	6.2	5.8	5.4	5.0	4.5	4.1
Equatorial Guinea	5.2	4.9	4.7	4.4	4.1	3.8
Ethiopia	6.8	6.4	5.9	5.4	4.9	4.4
Gabon	3.9	3.7	3.5	3.4	3.2	3.0
Gambia, The	6.2	5.9	5.5	5.1	4.7	4.4
Ghana	6.1	5.8	5.4	5.0	4.7	4.3
Guinea	5.8	5.5	5.1	4.7	4.3	3.9
Guinea-Bissau	5.4	5.0	4.6	4.2	3.8	3.4
Kenya	5.8	5.0	4.2	3.6	3.1	2.8
Lesotho	4.4	3.9	3.5	3.1	2.8	2.6
Liberia	6.3	6.0	5.6	5.2	4.8	4.4
Madagascar	6.6	6.3	5.8	5.3	4.9	4.4
Malawi	7.4	6.9	6.5	6.0	5.4	4.9
Mali	7.3	6.9	6.5	6.1	5.6	5.2
Mauritania	6.9	6.5	6.1	5.6	5.0	4.5
Mauritius	2.2	2.1	2.1	2.0	2.0	1.9
Mayotte	6.7	6.3	5.9	5.4	4.9	4.4
Mozambique	6.2	5.8	5.4	5.0	4.6	4.1

[Continued]

★ 760 ★

Sub-Saharan African Fertility Rates: 1995-2020

[Continued]

Country	1995	2000	2005	2010	2015	2020
Namibia	6.3	6.0	5.6	5.1	4.6	4.1
Niger	7.4	7.0	6.6	6.2	5.8	5.3
Nigeria	6.3	6.0	5.5	5.1	4.6	4.2
Reunion	2.8	2.6	2.5	2.4	2.3	2.2
Rwanda	8.1	7.6	7.1	6.4	5.7	5.0
Saint Helena	1.1	1.1	NA	NA	NA	NA
Sao Tome and Principe	4.4	3.9	3.4	3.0	2.7	2.5
Senegal	6.0	5.7	5.4	5.0	4.7	4.4
Seychelles	2.2	2.0	1.9	1.9	1.9	1.9
Sierra Leone	5.9	5.6	5.2	4.8	4.4	4.0
Somalia	7.1	6.5	6.0	5.4	4.8	4.2
South Africa	4.4	4.2	4.1	3.9	3.6	3.4
Sudan	6.0	5.5	4.9	4.4	3.8	3.4
Swaziland	6.1	5.9	5.6	5.4	5.1	4.9
Tanzania	6.2	5.9	5.5	5.2	4.8	4.4
Togo	6.8	6.5	6.0	5.6	5.1	4.6
Uganda	7.0	6.7	6.3	5.8	5.4	4.9
Zaire	6.7	6.4	6.0	5.6	5.2	4.7
Zambia	6.6	6.3	5.9	5.4	5.0	4.5
Zimbabwe	4.9	4.1	3.4	2.9	2.5	2.3

Source: Selected from "Total Fertility Rates by Country or Area: 1985 to 2020," U.S. Bureau of the Census, *World Population Profile: 1994,* 1994, Table 7, p. A-22. Primary source: U.S. Bureau of the Census, International Data Base.

★ 761 ★

Fertility

World's Largest Fertility Decline: 1985 to 1994

This table shows births per woman in 1985 and 1994 and the decline during that period for the ten countries with the largest fertility decline. These countries have been very successful at lowering high fertility rates, reducing average fertility levels by at least 1 child per woman.

[Population and events in thousands.]

Country	Births per woman		
	1985	1994	Decline '85-'94
Botswana	5.9	4.1	1.8
Tunisia	4.5	2.9	1.6
Jordan	7.1	5.6	1.5
Nicaragua	5.7	4.3	1.4
Zimbabwe	6.4	5.1	1.3

[Continued]

★ 761 ★

World's Largest Fertility Decline: 1985 to 1994
[Continued]

Country	Births per woman		
	1985	1994	Decline '85-'94
Morocco	5.1	3.8	1.3
Kenya	7.1	5.9	1.2
Peru	4.3	3.1	1.2
Ecuador	4.2	3.1	1.1
Bangladesh	5.5	4.5	1.0

Source: "Ten Countries with Largest Fertility Decline: 1985 to 1994," U.S. Bureau of the Census, *World Population Profile: 1994*, 1994, Figure 27, p. 30. Primary source: U.S. Bureau of the Census, International Data Base.

★ 762 ★

Fertility

Yugoslavian and Soviet Union Fertility Rates: 1995-2020

This table shows projections of the total fertility rates in the former Yugoslavia and the former Soviet Union in 1995, 2000, 2005, 2010, 2015, and 2020. Total fertility rate is the average number of children that would be born per woman if all women lived to the end of their childbearing years and bore children according to a given set of age-specific fertility rates. The U.S. view is that the Socialist Federal Republic of Yugoslavia has dissolved and no successor state represents its continuation. Macedonia has proclaimed independent statehood, but has not been recognized as a state by the U.S. Serbia and Montenegro have asserted the formation of a joint independent state, but this entity has not been recognized as a state by the U.S.

[NA Not available.]

Country	1995	2000	2005	2010	2015	2020
(Former) Yugoslovakia	1.8	1.8	1.8	1.8	1.8	1.7
Bosnia and Herzegovina	1.6	1.6	1.6	1.6	1.6	1.6
Croatia	1.6	1.6	1.6	1.6	1.6	1.6
Macedonia	2.0	2.0	2.0	1.9	1.9	1.8
Slovenia	1.7	1.6	1.6	1.6	1.6	1.6
(Former) Soviet Union	2.2	2.1	2.0	2.0	1.9	1.9
BALTICS	2.0	1.9	1.9	1.8	1.8	1.8
Estonia	2.0	1.9	1.9	1.8	1.8	1.8
Latvia	2.0	1.9	1.9	1.8	1.8	1.8
Lithuania	2.0	1.9	1.9	1.8	1.8	1.8
COMMONWEALTH OF INDEPENDENT STATES	2.2	2.1	2.0	2.0	1.9	1.9
Armenia	3.1	2.6	2.4	2.2	2.1	2.0
Azerbaijan	2.6	2.4	2.2	2.1	2.0	2.0
Belarus	1.9	1.8	1.8	1.8	1.8	1.7
Kazakhstan	2.4	2.3	2.2	2.1	2.0	2.0
Kyrgystan	3.3	3.1	2.9	2.7	2.5	2.4

[Continued]

★ 762 ★

Yugoslavian and Soviet Union Fertility Rates: 1995-2020
[Continued]

Country	1995	2000	2005	2010	2015	2020
Moldova	2.2	2.1	2.0	1.9	1.9	1.8
Russia	1.8	1.8	1.8	1.8	1.7	1.7
Tajikistan	4.6	4.1	3.7	3.4	3.1	2.8
Turkmenistan	3.7	3.4	3.1	2.9	2.7	2.5
Ukraine	1.8	1.8	1.8	1.8	1.7	1.7
Uzbekistan	3.7	3.4	3.1	2.9	2.7	2.5
GEORGIA	2.2	2.1	2.0	1.9	1.9	1.9

Source: Selected from "Total Fertility Rates by Country or Area: 1985 to 2020," U.S. Bureau of the Census, *World Population Profile: 1994*, 1994, Table 7, p. A-25. Primary source: U.S. Bureau of the Census, International Data Base.

Fetal and Infant Deaths

★ 763 ★

Female Infant Mortality in Asia

This table shows the number of female infant deaths per 1,000 female births in selected developing Asian countries or areas in 1992.

[Female infant deaths per 1,000 female births.]

Country	Female infant deaths per 1,000
Singapore	5
Hong Kong	6
China (Taiwan)	6
South Korea	20
Sri Lanka	21
Malaysia	22
China (Mainland)	31
Philippines	45
Vietnam	46
Indonesia	66
India	81
Nepal	89
Bangladesh	103

[Continued]

★ 763 ★

Female Infant Mortality in Asia
[Continued]

Country	Female infant deaths per 1,000
Pakistan	104
Afghanistan	156

Source: "Infant Mortality Rates Reflect the Wide Variety of Conditions," U.S. Bureau of the Census, *Statistical Brief: Statistical Indicators on Women: An Asian Perspective,* November 1993, p. 2.

★ 764 ★

Fetal and Infant Deaths

Infant Mortality in Asia and the Near East: 1994

This table shows infant deaths per 1,000 live births for both sexes and for males and females in Asia and the Near East in 1994.

[Infant deaths per 1,000 live births.]

Country	Infant deaths per 1,000 live births		
	Both sexes	Male	Female
World	65	65	64
Developing countries	72	72	71
Developed countries	15	17	13
Asia	68	66	70
Asia, excluding Near East	69	66	71
Afghanistan	156	161	151
Bangladesh	107	115	99
Bhutan	121	119	123
Brunei	25	27	23
Burma	64	70	57
Cambodia	111	119	102
China			
Mainland	52	40	66
Taiwan	6	6	6
Hong Kong	6	6	6
India	78	78	79
Indonesia	67	73	61
Iran	60	61	60
Japan	4	5	4
Laos	102	112	91
Macau	6	6	5

[Continued]

★ 764 ★

Infant Mortality in Asia and the Near East: 1994
[Continued]

Country	Infant deaths per 1,000 live births		
	Both sexes	Male	Female
Malaysia	26	30	21
Maldives	54	53	55
Mongolia	43	49	38
Nepal	84	85	82
North Korea	28	31	24
Pakistan	102	103	100
Philippines	51	58	43
Singapore	6	6	5
South Korea	22	20	24
Sri Lanka	22	24	20
Thailand	37	40	34
Vietnam	46	47	45
Near East	56	59	52
Bahrain	19	22	16
Cyprus	9	10	8
Gaza Strip	37	38	36
Iraq	67	73	61
Israel	9	10	8
Jordan	32	35	30
Kuwait	13	14	11
Lebanon	40	44	35
Oman	37	39	34
Qatar	22	26	18
Saudi Arabia	52	54	50
Syria	43	43	42
Turkey	49	53	45
United Arab Emirates	22	25	18
West Bank	34	36	32
Yemen	113	118	108

Source: Selected from "Infant Mortality Rates and Life Expectancy at Birth, by Country or Area and Sex: 1994," U.S. Bureau of the Census, *World Population Profile: 1994*, 1994, Table 8, p. A-28. Primary source: U.S. Bureau of the Census, International Data Base.

★ 765 ★

Fetal and Infant Deaths

Infant Mortality in Developed Countries: 1993

This table shows infant mortality (death rate per 1,000 live births) in selected developed countries in 1993. Although the U.S. infant mortality rate has been declining since the early part of this century, the United States was still in 18th place among developed nations.

[Infant mortality rate per 1,000 live births.]

Country	Rate
Finland	4.4
Japan (1992)	4.5
Sweden	4.8
Denmark	5.7
Ireland	6.0
Germany (1992)	6.2
Norway (1991)	6.2
Switzerland	6.2
Netherlands	6.3
Austria	6.5
United Kingdom (1992)	6.6
Canada (1990)	6.8
Australia (1992)	7.0
France (1991)	7.3
Italy	7.4
Spain	7.6
Belgium	8.0
United States	8.3

Source: Judith Yavarkovsky, "Statistical Information, Please," *Statistical Bulletin*, Vol. 76(1), January-March 1995, p. 36, "Infant Mortality in Selected Developed Countries 1993." Primary source: *Population and Vital Statistics Report*, Series A, Vol. XLVI, No. 3, United Nations, July 1, 1994 (provisional data.).

★ 766 ★
Fetal and Infant Deaths

Infant Mortality in Europe: 1994

This table shows infant deaths per 1,000 live births for both sexes and for males and females in Europe in 1994.

[Infant deaths per 1,000 live births.]

Country	Infant deaths per 1,000 live births		
	Both sexes	Male	Female
World	65	65	64
Developing countries	72	72	71
Developed countries	15	17	13
Europe	9	10	8
Albania	30	31	28
Andorra	8	9	7
Austria	7	8	6
Belgium	7	8	6
Bulgaria	12	14	10
Czech Republic	9	11	8
Denmark	7	8	6
Faroe islands	8	9	7
Finland	5	5	5
France	7	8	6
Germany	7	7	6
Gibraltar	8	9	7
Greece	9	9	8
Guernsey	7	8	5
Hungary	13	14	11
Iceland	4	4	4
Ireland	7	8	7
Isle of Man	8	9	7
Italy	8	8	7
Jersey	5	6	4
Liechtenstein	5	5	5
Luxembourg	7	8	6
Malta	8	9	7
Monaco	7	8	6
Netherlands	6	7	5
Norway	6	7	6
Poland	13	15	11
Portugal	10	11	8
Romania	20	22	18
San Marino	6	7	5
Slovakia	10	12	9

[Continued]

★ 766 ★

Infant Mortality in Europe: 1994
[Continued]

Country	Infant deaths per 1,000 live births		
	Both sexes	Male	Female
Spain	7	8	6
Sweden	6	6	5
Switzerland	7	7	6
United Kingdom	7	8	6

Source: Selected from "Infant Mortality Rates and Life Expectancy at Birth, by Country or Area and Sex: 1994," U.S. Bureau of the Census, *World Population Profile: 1994*, 1994, Table 8, p. A-30. Primary source: U.S. Bureau of the Census, International Data Base.

★ 767 ★

Fetal and Infant Deaths

Infant Mortality in Latin America/Caribbean: 1994

This table shows infant deaths per 1,000 live births for both sexes and for males and females in Latin America and the Caribbean in 1994.

[Infant deaths per 1,000 live births.]

Country	Infant deaths per 1,000 live births		
	Both sexes	Male	Female
World	65	65	64
Developing countries	72	72	71
Developed countries	15	17	13
Latin America and the Caribbean	43	47	38
Anguilla	18	23	12
Antigua and Barbuda	19	21	15
Argentina	29	33	26
Aruba	8	10	7
Bahamas, The	34	35	32
Barbados	20	23	18
Belize	36	40	31
Bolivia	74	82	65
Brazil	60	64	55
British Virgin Islands	20	23	16
Cayman Islands	8	10	7
Chile	15	17	14
Colombia	28	32	25
Costa Rica	11	11	11
Cuba	10	11	9
Dominica	10	13	7
Dominican Republic	52	56	47

[Continued]

★ 767 ★

Infant Mortality in Latin America/Caribbean: 1994
[Continued]

Country	Infant deaths per 1,000 live births		
	Both sexes	Male	Female
Ecuador	39	44	34
El Salvador	41	47	34
French Guiana	16	17	15
Grenada	12	14	11
Guadeloupe	9	10	8
Guatemala	54	58	50
Guyana	49	53	44
Haiti	109	116	101
Honduras	45	49	41
Jamaica	17	19	15
Martinique	10	11	9
Mexico	27	33	22
Montserrat	12	14	9
Netherlands Antilles	10	10	9
Nicaragua	53	62	43
Panama	17	18	15
Paraguay	25	27	23
Peru	54	59	49
Puerto Rico	14	15	13
Saint Kitts and Nevis	20	22	18
Saint Lucia	19	20	17
Saint Vincent and the Grenadines	17	18	16
Suriname	31	37	26
Trinidad and Tobago	17	19	14
Turks and Caicos Islands	13	15	11
Uruguay	17	19	15
Venezuela	28	31	25
Virgin Islands	13	15	10

Source: Selected from "Infant Mortality Rates and Life Expectancy at Birth, by Country or Area and Sex: 1994," U.S. Bureau of the Census, *World Population Profile: 1994*, 1994, Table 8, p. A-29. Primary source: U.S. Bureau of the Census, International Data Base.

★ 768 ★

Fetal and Infant Deaths

Infant Mortality in North Africa: 1994

This table shows infant deaths per 1,000 live births for both sexes and for males and females in North Africa.

[Infant deaths per 1,000 live births.]

Country	Infant deaths per 1,000 live births		
	Both sexes	Male	Female
World	65	65	64
Developing countries	72	72	71
Developed countries	15	17	13
North Africa	63	66	60
Algeria	52	55	49
Egypt	76	78	75
Libya	63	68	59
Morocco	50	55	44
Tunisia	34	40	29
Western Sahara	152	157	145

Source: Selected from "Infant Mortality Rates and Life Expectancy at Birth, by Country or Area and Sex: 1994," U.S. Bureau of the Census, *World Population Profile: 1994*, 1994, Table 8, p. A-28. Primary source: U.S. Bureau of the Census, International Data Base.

★ 769 ★

Fetal and Infant Deaths

Infant Mortality in North America: 1994

This table shows infant deaths per 1,000 live births for both sexes and for males and females in North America in 1994.

[Infant deaths per 1,000 live births.]

Country	Infant deaths per 1,000 live births		
	Both sexes	Male	Female
World	65	65	64
Developing countries	72	72	71
Developed countries	15	17	13
North America	8	9	7
Bermuda	13	15	11
Canada	7	8	6
Greenland	27	33	21

[Continued]

★ 769 ★

Infant Mortality in North America: 1994

[Continued]

Country	Infant deaths per 1,000 live births		
	Both sexes	Male	Female
Saint Pierre and Miquelon	12	14	9
United States	8	9	7

Source: Selected from "Infant Mortality Rates and Life Expectancy at Birth, by Country or Area and Sex: 1994," U.S. Bureau of the Census, *World Population Profile: 1994*, 1994, Table 8, p. A-30. Primary source: U.S. Bureau of the Census, International Data Base.

★ 770 ★

Fetal and Infant Deaths

Infant Mortality in Oceania: 1994

This table shows infant deaths per 1,000 live births for both sexes and for males and females in Oceania in 1994.

[Infant deaths per 1,000 live births. NA Not available.]

Country	Infant deaths per 1,000 live births		
	Both sexes	Male	Female
World	65	65	64
Developing countries	72	72	71
Developed countries	15	17	13
Oceania	26	26	25
American Samoa	19	22	16
Australia	7	8	6
Cook Islands	25	28	21
Federated States of Micronesia	37	42	32
Fiji	18	20	16
French Polynesia	15	17	12
Guam	15	18	13
Kiribati	98	107	90
Marshall Islands	49	51	48
Nauru	41	NA	NA
New Caledonia	15	18	12
New Zealand	9	9	8
Northern Mariana Islands	38	43	33
Papua New Guinea	63	63	64
Solomon Islands	28	32	24
Tonga	21	NA	NA
Trust Territory of the Pacific Islands (Palau)	25	29	21
Tuvalu	27	32	26

[Continued]

★ 770 ★

Infant Mortality in Oceania: 1994
[Continued]

Country	Infant deaths per 1,000 live births		
	Both sexes	Male	Female
Vanuatu	68	73	63
Wallis and Futuna	26	27	26
Western Samoa	37	42	32

Source: Selected from "Infant Mortality Rates and Life Expectancy at Birth, by Country or Area and Sex: 1994," U.S. Bureau of the Census, *World Population Profile: 1994*, 1994, Table 8, p. A-30. Primary source: U.S. Bureau of the Census, International Data Base.

★ 771 ★

Fetal and Infant Deaths

Infant Mortality in Sub-Saharan Africa: 1994

This table shows infant deaths per 1,000 live births for both sexes and for males and females in Sub-Saharan Africa.

[Infant deaths per 1,000 live births.]

Country	Infant deaths per 1,000 live births		
	Both sexes	Male	Female
World	65	65	64
Developing countries	72	72	71
Developed countries	15	17	13
Africa	91	97	85
Sub-Saharan Africa	95	102	89
Angola	145	157	133
Benin	110	119	101
Botswana	39	42	37
Burkina	118	125	112
Burundi	114	124	103
Cameroon	77	84	70
Cape Verde	58	63	52
Central African Republic	137	146	128
Chad	132	129	135
Comoros	80	88	71
Congo	111	118	104
Cote d'Ivoire	95	103	86
Djibouti	111	120	102
Equatorial Guinea	103	110	95
Ethiopia	106	115	98

[Continued]

★ 771 ★

Infant Mortality in Sub-Saharan Africa: 1994
[Continued]

Country	Infant deaths per 1,000 live births		
	Both sexes	Male	Female
Gabon	95	107	83
Gambia, The	124	136	111
Ghana	83	90	76
Guinea	139	151	127
Guinea-Bissau	120	129	111
Kenya	74	78	71
Lesotho	70	72	67
Liberia	113	122	105
Madagascar	89	96	82
Malawi	141	149	133
Mali	106	113	100
Mauritania	85	88	82
Mauritius	18	22	15
Mayotte	80	88	71
Mozambique	129	140	117
Namibia	62	70	54
Niger	111	118	104
Nigeria	75	78	72
Reunion	8	9	7
Rwanda	119	126	111
Saint Helena	37	40	35
Sao Tome and Principe	64	68	59
Senegal	76	79	72
Seychelles	12	15	9
Sierra Leone	142	158	126
Somalia	126	136	116
South Africa	47	45	49
Sudan	80	80	79
Swaziland	93	103	84
Tanzania	110	121	98
Togo	89	96	82
Uganda	112	120	105
Zaire	111	121	100
Zambia	85	89	81
Zimbabwe	74	80	68

Source: Selected from "Infant Mortality Rates and Life Expectancy at Birth, by Country or Area and Sex: 1994," U.S. Bureau of the Census, *World Population Profile: 1994*, 1994, Table 8, p. A-27. Primary source: U.S. Bureau of the Census, International Data Base.

★ 772 ★

Fetal and Infant Deaths

Infant Mortality in Yugoslavia and the Soviet Union: 1994

This table shows infant deaths per 1,000 live births for both sexes and for males and females in the former Yugoslavia and the former Soviet Union in 1994. The U.S. view is that the Socialist Federal Republic of Yugoslavia has dissolved and no successor state represents its continuation. Macedonia has proclaimed independent statehood, but has not been recognized as a state by the U.S. Serbia and Montenegro have asserted the formation of a joint independent state, but this entity has not been recognized as a state by the U.S.

[Infant deaths per 1,000 live births.]

Country	Infant deaths per 1,000 live births		
	Both sexes	Male	Female
World	65	65	64
Developing countries	72	72	71
Developed countries	15	17	13
(Former) Yugoslavia	17	18	16
Bosnia and Herzegovina	13	14	11
Croatia	9	10	8
Macedonia	28	29	27
Serbia and Montenegro	21	22	20
Slovenia	8	9	7
(Former) Soviet Union	34	38	29
BALTICS	19	21	16
Estonia	19	23	16
Latvia	22	25	18
Lithuania	17	18	16
COMMONWEALTH OF INDEPENDENT STATES	35	39	30
Armenia	27	30	24
Azerbaijan	35	38	32
Belarus	19	22	15
Kazakhstan	41	46	36
Kyrgystan	47	53	41
Moldova	30	34	26
Russia	27	31	23
Tajikistan	62	69	55
Turkmenistan	70	78	62
Ukraine	21	24	18
Uzbekistan	53	60	46
GEORGIA	23	26	20

Source: Selected from "Infant Mortality Rates and Life Expectancy at Birth, by Country or Area and Sex: 1994," U.S. Bureau of the Census, *World Population Profile: 1994*, 1994, Table 8, p. A-30. Primary source: U.S. Bureau of the Census, International Data Base.

Life Expectancy

★ 773 ★

Expectation of Life at Birth and Other Ages: 1979-1991

This table gives average life expectancy at birth and at various ages, in years, for the years 1979 through 1991, totals and by race.

[In years.]

Age and Sex	Total[1]			White			Black		
	1979-1981	1990	1991	1979-1981	1990	1991	1979-1981	1990	1991
At birth									
Male	70.1	71.8	72.0	70.8	72.7	72.9	64.1	64.5	64.6
Female	77.6	78.8	78.9	78.2	79.4	79.6	72.9	73.6	73.8
Age 20									
Male	51.9	53.3	53.4	52.5	54.0	54.1	46.4	46.7	46.9
Female	59.0	59.8	59.9	59.4	60.3	60.4	54.9	55.3	55.4
Age 40									
Male	33.6	35.1	35.3	34.0	35.6	35.8	29.5	30.1	30.3
Female	39.8	40.6	40.7	40.2	41.0	41.1	36.3	36.8	36.9
Age 50									
Male	25.0	26.4	26.6	25.3	26.7	26.9	22.0	22.5	22.7
Female	30.7	31.3	31.5	31.0	31.6	31.8	27.8	28.2	28.3
Age 65									
Male	14.2	15.1	15.3	14.3	15.2	15.4	13.3	13.2	13.4
Female	18.4	18.9	19.1	18.6	19.1	19.2	17.1	17.2	17.2

Source: Selected from "Selected Life Table Values: 1979 to 1991," U.S. Bureau of the Census, *Statistical Abstract of the United States, 1994*, table 115, p. 87. Primary source: U.S. National Center for Health Statistics, *U.S. Life Tables and Actuarial Tables, 1959-61, 1969-71, and 1979-81; Vital Statistics of the United States*, annual, and unpublished data. *Note:* 1. Inclues other races not shown separately.

★ 774 ★

Life Expectancy

Expectation of Life at Birth: 1970-1992

This table shows life expectancy at birth in years for those born from 1970 to 1992, totals and by race.

[In years.]

Year	Total			White			Black and Other			Black		
	Total	Male	Female	Total	Male	Female	Total	Male	Female	Total	Male	Female
1970	70.8	67.1	74.7	71.7	68.0	75.6	65.3	61.3	69.4	64.1	60.0	68.3
1975	72.6	68.8	76.6	73.4	69.5	77.3	68.0	63.7	72.4	66.8	62.4	71.3
1980	73.7	70.0	77.4	74.4	70.7	78.1	69.5	65.3	73.6	68.1	63.8	72.5
1981	74.1	70.4	77.8	74.8	71.1	78.4	70.3	66.2	74.4	68.9	64.5	73.2
1982	74.5	70.8	78.1	75.1	71.5	78.7	70.9	66.8	74.9	69.4	65.1	73.6
1983	74.6	71.0	78.1	75.2	71.6	78.7	70.9	67.0	74.7	69.4	65.2	73.5
1984	74.7	71.1	78.2	75.3	71.8	78.7	71.1	67.2	74.9	69.5	65.3	73.6
1985	74.7	71.1	78.2	75.3	71.8	78.7	71.0	67.0	74.8	69.3	65.0	73.4
1986	74.7	71.2	78.2	75.4	71.9	78.8	70.9	66.8	74.9	69.1	64.8	73.4
1987	74.9	71.4	78.3	75.6	72.1	78.9	71.0	66.9	75.0	69.1	64.7	73.4
1988	74.9	71.4	78.3	75.6	72.2	78.9	70.8	66.7	74.8	68.9	64.4	73.2
1989	75.1	71.7	78.5	75.9	72.5	79.2	70.9	66.7	74.9	68.8	64.3	73.3
1990	75.4	71.8	78.8	76.1	72.7	79.4	71.2	67.0	75.2	69.1	64.5	73.6
1991	75.5	72.0	78.9	76.3	72.9	79.6	71.5	67.3	75.5	69.3	64.6	73.8
1992 (prelim.)	75.7	72.3	79.0	76.5	73.2	79.7	71.8	67.8	75.6	69.8	65.5	73.9

Source: Selected from "Expectation of Life at Birth, 1970 to 1992, and Projections, 1995 to 2010," U.S. Bureau of the Census, *Statistical Abstract of the United States, 1994,* table 114, p. 87. Primary source: U.S. National Center for Health Statistics, *Vital Statistics of the United States,* annual, and *Monthly Vital Statistics Reports.*

★ 775 ★

Life Expectancy

Expectation of Life at Birth: 1995-2010

This table gives projections of life expectancy at birth in years for those born from 1995 to 2010, totals and by race.

[In years.]

Year	Total			White			Black and Other			Black		
	Total	Male	Female	Total	Male	Female	Total	Male	Female	Total	Male	Female
1995	76.3	72.8	79.7	77.0	73.7	80.3	72.5	68.2	76.8	70.3	65.8	74.8
2000	76.7	73.2	80.2	77.6	74.3	80.9	72.9	68.3	77.5	70.2	65.3	75.1
2005	77.3	73.8	80.7	78.2	74.9	81.4	73.6	69.1	78.1	70.7	65.9	75.5
2010	77.9	74.5	81.3	78.8	75.6	82.0	74.3	69.9	78.7	71.3	66.5	76.0

Source: Selected from "Expectation of Life at Birth, 1970 to 1992, and Projections, 1995 to 2010," U.S. Bureau of the Census, *Statistical Abstract of the United States, 1994,* table 114, p. 87. Primary source: U.S. Bureau of the Census, *Current Population Reports,* P25-1104.

★ 776 ★

Life Expectancy

Expectation of Life by Age in 1990

This table gives expectation of life in years in 1991, by age in 1990 by race.

[In years.]

Age in 1990 (years)	Total	White		Black	
		Male	Female	Male	Female
At birth	75.4	72.7	79.4	64.5	73.6
1	75.1	72.3	78.9	64.8	73.8
2	74.1	71.4	78.0	63.9	72.9
3	73.1	70.4	77.0	62.9	71.9
4	72.2	69.4	76.0	62.0	71.0
5	71.2	68.5	75.0	61.0	70.0
6	70.2	67.5	74.1	60.1	69.0
7	69.2	66.5	73.1	59.1	68.1
8	68.2	65.5	72.1	58.1	67.1
9	67.3	64.5	71.1	57.1	66.1
10	66.3	63.5	70.1	56.1	65.1
11	65.3	62.6	69.1	55.1	64.1
12	64.3	61.6	68.1	54.2	63.1
13	63.3	60.6	67.1	53.2	62.1
14	62.3	59.6	66.2	52.2	61.2
15	61.3	58.6	65.2	51.3	60.2
16	60.4	57.7	64.2	50.3	59.2
17	59.4	56.7	63.2	49.4	58.2
18	58.5	55.8	62.3	48.5	57.3
19	57.5	54.9	61.3	47.6	56.3
20	56.6	54.0	60.3	46.7	55.3
21	55.7	53.0	59.3	45.9	54.4
22	54.7	52.1	58.4	45.0	53.4
23	53.8	51.2	57.4	44.1	52.5
24	52.8	50.3	56.4	43.3	51.5
25	51.9	49.3	55.4	42.4	50.6
26	51.0	48.4	54.5	41.6	49.6
27	50.0	47.5	53.5	40.7	48.7
28	49.1	46.6	52.5	39.9	47.7
29	48.1	45.6	51.6	39.0	46.8
30	47.2	44.7	50.6	38.2	45.9
31	46.3	43.8	49.6	37.4	45.0
32	45.3	42.9	48.7	36.5	44.0
33	44.4	41.9	47.7	35.7	43.1
34	43.5	41.0	46.7	34.9	42.2
35	42.6	40.1	45.8	34.1	41.3
36	41.6	39.2	44.8	33.3	40.4
37	40.7	38.3	43.8	32.5	39.5
38	39.8	37.4	42.9	31.7	38.6
39	38.9	36.5	41.9	30.9	37.7

[Continued]

★ 776 ★

Expectation of Life by Age in 1990

[Continued]

Age in 1990 (years)	Total	White		Black	
		Male	Female	Male	Female
40	38.0	35.6	41.0	30.1	36.8
41	37.0	34.7	40.0	29.3	35.9
42	36.1	33.8	39.1	28.5	35.0
43	35.2	32.9	38.1	27.7	34.1
44	34.3	32.0	37.2	27.0	33.3
45	33.4	31.1	36.2	26.2	32.4
46	32.5	30.2	35.3	25.4	31.5
47	31.6	29.3	34.4	24.7	30.7
48	30.7	28.4	33.5	24.0	29.8
49	29.9	27.6	32.5	23.2	29.0
50	29.0	26.7	31.6	22.5	28.2
51	28.1	25.8	30.7	21.8	27.4
52	27.3	25.0	29.9	21.1	26.6
53	26.4	24.2	29.0	20.4	25.8
54	25.6	23.3	28.1	19.7	25.0
55	24.8	22.5	27.2	19.0	24.2
56	24.0	21.7	26.4	18.4	23.4
57	23.2	21.0	25.5	17.8	22.7
58	22.4	20.2	24.7	17.1	22.0
59	21.6	19.4	23.8	16.5	21.2
60	20.8	18.7	23.0	15.9	20.5
61	20.1	18.0	22.2	15.4	19.8
62	19.4	17.3	21.4	14.8	19.1
63	18.6	16.6	20.6	14.3	18.5
64	17.9	15.9	19.8	13.7	17.8
65	17.2	15.2	19.1	13.2	17.2
70	13.9	12.1	15.4	10.7	14.1
75	10.9	9.4	12.0	8.6	11.2
80	8.3	7.1	9.0	6.7	8.6
85 +	6.1	5.2	6.4	5.0	6.3

Source: Selected from "Expectation of Life and Expected Deaths, by Race, Sex, and Age: 1991," U.S. Bureau of the Census, *Statistical Abstract of the United States, 1994,* table 116, p. 88. Primary source: U.S. National Center for Health Statistics, *Vital Statistics of the United States,* annual, and unpublished data.

★ 777 ★

Life Expectancy

Expectation of Life in 1993

This table recaps life expectancy for the total population and for females in 1979-1981, 1990, 1991, and 1992 (provisional), as calculated by the National Center for Health Statistics. It also shows 1993 figures as estimated by the Metropolitan Life Insurance Company. According to MetLife, 1993 showed a slight decline in expectation of life. Newborns could expect to live 75.4 years on average; for baby girls the figure was 78.7 years, and for baby boys, 72.0 years. Each of these values represented a decline of 0.3 years from the 1992 provisional figures. This decrease is attributed to a rise in the absolute number of deaths and a corresponding increase in mortality rates. That increase came from all major forms of death as well as from AIDS. AIDS deaths most frequently occur between ages 20 and 44. Still, in 1993 "women continue to have a significant longevity advantage over men."

[In years.]

Age	1979-81	1990	1991	1992	1993
Total Population					
0	73.9	75.4	75.5	75.7	75.4
15	60.2	61.3	61.5	61.6	61.3
25	50.8	51.9	52.1	52.2	51.9
35	41.4	42.6	42.7	42.8	42.5
45	32.3	33.4	33.6	33.7	33.5
55	23.9	24.8	24.9	25.1	24.8
65	16.5	17.2	17.4	17.5	17.2
75	10.5	10.9	11.1	11.1	10.9
85	6.0	6.1	6.2	6.3	6.0
Female					
0	77.6	78.8	78.9	79.0	78.7
15	63.8	64.7	64.8	64.9	64.6
25	54.2	55.0	55.1	55.2	54.9
35	44.5	45.3	45.5	45.5	45.3
45	35.2	35.9	36.0	36.1	35.9
55	26.4	27.0	27.1	27.2	26.9
65	18.4	18.9	19.1	19.1	18.9
75	11.6	12.0	12.1	12.1	11.9
85	6.4	6.4	6.5	6.7	6.4

Source: "Expectation of Life (in Years) United States, 1979-81 to 1993," *Statistical Bulletin,* 75(3), July-Sept 1994, p. 13. Primary source: U.S. National Center for Health Statistics and calculations by Metropolitan Life Insurance Company.

★ 778 ★

Life Expectancy

Expectation of Life in Asia and the Near East: 1994

This table shows life expectancy at birth in years for those born in 1994 in Asia and the Near East.

[Life expectancy at birth in years.]

Country	Life expectancy at birth (years)		
	Both sexes	Male	Female
World	62	61	64
Developing countries	61	59	62
Developed countries	74	71	78
Asia	63	62	64
Asia, excluding Near East	62	61	63
Afghanistan	45	46	44
Bangladesh	55	55	55
Bhutan	51	51	50
Brunei	71	69	73
Burma	60	58	62
Cambodia	49	48	51
China			
Mainland	68	67	69
Taiwan	75	72	79
Hong Kong	80	77	84
India	59	58	59
Indonesia	61	59	63
Iran	66	65	67
Japan	79	76	82
Laos	52	50	53
Macau	80	77	82
Malaysia	69	66	72
Maldives	65	63	66
Mongolia	66	64	69
Nepal	53	52	53
North Korea	70	67	73
Pakistan	57	57	58
Philippines	65	63	68
Singapore	76	73	79
South Korea	71	67	74
Sri Lanka	72	69	74
Thailand	68	65	72
Vietnam	65	63	68

[Continued]

★ 778 ★

Expectation of Life in Asia and the Near East: 1994

[Continued]

Country	Life expectancy at birth (years)		
	Both sexes	Male	Female
Near East	67	65	69
Bahrain	74	71	76
Cyprus	76	74	79
Gaza Strip	68	66	69
Iraq	66	65	67
Israel	78	76	80
Jordan	72	70	74
Kuwait	75	73	77
Lebanon	69	67	72
Oman	68	66	70
Qatar	73	70	75
Saudi Arabia	68	66	70
Syria	66	65	68
Turkey	71	69	73
United Arab Emirates	72	70	74
West Bank	70	69	72
Yemen	51	50	53

Source: Selected from "Infant Mortality Rates and Life Expectancy at Birth, by Country or Area and Sex: 1994," U.S. Bureau of the Census, *World Population Profile: 1994,* 1994, Table 8, p. A-28. Primary source: U.S. Bureau of the Census, International Data Base.

★ 779 ★

Life Expectancy

Expectation of Life in Europe: 1994

This table shows life expectancy at birth in years for those born in 1994 in Europe.

[Life expectancy at birth in years.]

Country	Life expectancy at birth (years)		
	Both sexes	Male	Female
World	62	61	64
Developing countries	61	59	62
Developed countries	74	71	78
Europe	76	73	79
Albania	73	70	77
Andorra	78	76	82
Austria	77	73	80

[Continued]

★ 779 ★

Expectation of Life in Europe: 1994
[Continued]

Country	Life expectancy at birth (years)		
	Both sexes	Male	Female
Belgium	77	74	80
Bulgaria	73	70	77
Czech Republic	73	69	77
Denmark	76	73	79
Faroe islands	78	75	82
Finland	76	72	80
France	78	74	82
Germany	76	73	80
Gibraltar	76	73	79
Greece	78	75	80
Guernsey	78	75	81
Hungary	71	67	76
Iceland	79	77	81
Ireland	76	73	79
Isle of Man	76	74	79
Italy	78	74	81
Jersey	77	74	80
Liechtenstein	77	74	81
Luxembourg	77	73	81
Malta	77	75	79
Monaco	78	74	82
Netherlands	78	75	81
Norway	77	74	81
Poland	73	69	77
Portugal	75	72	79
Romania	72	69	75
San Marino	81	77	85
Slovakia	73	69	77
Spain	78	74	81
Sweden	78	75	81
Switzerland	78	75	82
United Kingdom	77	74	80

Source: Selected from "Infant Mortality Rates and Life Expectancy at Birth, by Country or Area and Sex: 1994," U.S. Bureau of the Census, *World Population Profile: 1994*, 1994, Table 8, p. A-29. Primary source: U.S. Bureau of the Census, International Data Base.

★ 780 ★

Life Expectancy

Expectation of Life in Latin America/Caribbean: 1994

This table shows life expectancy at birth in years for those born in 1994 in Latin America and the Caribbean.

[Life expectancy at birth in years.]

Country	Life expectancy at birth (years)		
	Both sexes	Male	Female
World	62	61	64
Developing countries	61	59	62
Developed countries	74	71	78
Latin America and the Caribbean	68	64	71
Anguilla	74	71	77
Antigua and Barbuda	73	71	75
Argentina	71	68	75
Aruba	76	73	80
Bahamas, The	72	68	75
Barbados	74	71	77
Belize	68	66	70
Bolivia	63	61	66
Brazil	62	57	67
British Virgin Islands	73	71	75
Cayman Islands	77	75	79
Chile	75	72	78
Colombia	72	69	75
Costa Rica	78	76	80
Cuba	77	75	79
Dominica	77	74	80
Dominican Republic	68	66	71
Ecuador	70	67	73
El Salvador	67	64	70
French Guiana	75	72	79
Grenada	70	68	73
Guadeloupe	77	74	80
Guatemala	64	62	67
Guyana	65	62	68
Haiti	45	43	47
Honduras	68	65	70
Jamaica	74	72	77
Martinique	78	75	81
Mexico	73	69	77
Montserrat	76	74	78
Netherlands Antilles	76	74	79

[Continued]

★ 780 ★

Expectation of Life in Latin America/Caribbean: 1994
[Continued]

Country	Life expectancy at birth (years)		
	Both sexes	Male	Female
Nicaragua	64	61	67
Panama	75	72	78
Paraguay	73	72	75
Peru	66	63	68
Puerto Rico	74	70	78
Saint Kitts and Nevis	66	63	69
Saint Lucia	69	67	72
Saint Vincent and the Grenadines	72	71	74
Suriname	69	67	72
Trinidad and Tobago	71	68	73
Turks and Caicos Islands	75	73	77
Uruguay	74	71	77
Venezuela	73	70	76
Virgin Islands	75	74	77

Source: Selected from "Infant Mortality Rates and Life Expectancy at Birth, by Country or Area and Sex: 1994," U.S. Bureau of the Census, *World Population Profile: 1994*, 1994, Table 8, p. A-29. Primary source: U.S. Bureau of the Census, International Data Base.

★ 781 ★

Life Expectancy

Expectation of Life in North Africa: 1994

This table shows life expectancy at birth in years for those born in 1994 for both sexes and males and females in North Africa.

[Life expectancy at birth in years.]

Country	Infant deaths per 1,000 live births		
	Both sexes	Male	Female
World	62	61	64
Developing countries	61	59	62
Developed countries	74	71	78
North Africa	65	63	66
Algeria	68	67	69
Egypt	61	59	63
Libya	64	62	66
Morocco	68	66	70

[Continued]

★ 781 ★

Expectation of Life in North Africa: 1994

[Continued]

Country	Infant deaths per 1,000 live births		
	Both sexes	Male	Female
Tunisia	73	71	75
Western Sahara	46	45	47

Source: Selected from "Infant Mortality Rates and Life Expectancy at Birth, by Country or Area and Sex: 1994," U.S. Bureau of the Census, *World Population Profile: 1994,* 1994, Table 8, p. A-28. Primary source: U.S. Bureau of the Census, International Data Base.

★ 782 ★

Life Expectancy

Expectation of Life in North America: 1994

This table shows life expectancy at birth in years for those born in 1994 in North America.

[Life expectancy at birth in years.]

Country	Life expectancy at birth (years)		
	Both sexes	Male	Female
World	62	61	64
Developing countries	61	59	62
Developed countries	74	71	78
North America	76	73	80
Bermuda	75	73	77
Canada	78	75	82
Greenland	67	63	71
Saint Pierre and Miquelon	76	74	78
United States	76	73	79

Source: Selected from "Infant Mortality Rates and Life Expectancy at Birth, by Country or Area and Sex: 1994," U.S. Bureau of the Census, *World Population Profile: 1994,* 1994, Table 8, p. A-29. Primary source: U.S. Bureau of the Census, International Data Base.

★ 783 ★

Life Expectancy

Expectation of Life in Oceania: 1994

This table shows life expectancy at birth in years for those born in 1994 in Oceania.

[Life expectancy at birth in years. NA Not available.]

Country	Life expectancy at birth (years)		
	Both sexes	Male	Female
World	62	61	64
Developing countries	61	59	62
Developed countries	74	71	78
Oceania	70	68	73
American Samoa	73	71	75
Australia	78	74	81
Cook Islands	71	69	73
Federated States of Micronesia	68	66	70
Fiji	65	63	68
French Polynesia	71	68	73
Guam	74	72	76
Kiribati	54	53	56
Marshall Islands	63	62	65
Nauru	67	NA	NA
New Caledonia	74	70	77
New Zealand	76	73	80
Northern Mariana Islands	67	66	69
Papua New Guinea	56	56	57
Solomon Islands	70	68	73
Tonga	68	NA	NA
Trust Territory of the Pacific Islands (Palau)	71	69	73
Tuvalu	63	62	64
Vanuatu	59	58	61
Wallis and Futuna	72	71	72
Western Samoa	68	66	70

Source: Selected from "Infant Mortality Rates and Life Expectancy at Birth, by Country or Area and Sex: 1994," U.S. Bureau of the Census, *World Population Profile: 1994*, 1994, Table 8, p. A-29. Primary source: U.S. Bureau of the Census, International Data Base.

★ 784 ★

Life Expectancy

Expectation of Life in Sub-Saharan Africa: 1994

This table shows life expectancy at birth in years for those born in 1994 for both sexes and for males and females in Sub-Saharan Africa.

[Life expectancy at birth in years.]

Country	Life expectancy at birth (years)		
	Both sexes	Male	Female
World	62	61	64
Developing countries	61	59	62
Developed countries	74	71	78
Africa	53	51	54
Sub-Saharan Africa	51	49	53
Angola	46	44	48
Benin	52	50	54
Botswana	63	60	66
Burkina	47	46	48
Burundi	40	38	42
Cameroon	57	55	59
Cape Verde	63	61	65
Central African Republic	43	41	44
Chad	41	40	42
Comoros	58	56	60
Congo	48	46	49
Cote d'Ivoire	49	47	51
Djibouti	49	47	51
Equatorial Guinea	52	50	54
Ethiopia	53	51	54
Gabon	55	52	58
Gambia, The	50	48	52
Ghana	56	54	58
Guinea	44	42	46
Guinea-Bissau	47	46	49
Kenya	53	51	55
Lesotho	62	60	64
Liberia	58	55	60
Madagascar	54	52	56
Malawi	40	39	41
Mali	46	44	48
Mauritania	48	45	51
Mauritius	71	67	75
Mayotte	58	56	60
Mozambique	48	47	50

[Continued]

★ 784 ★

Expectation of Life in Sub-Saharan Africa: 1994
[Continued]

Country	Life expectancy at birth (years)		
	Both sexes	Male	Female
Namibia	62	59	64
Niger	45	43	46
Nigeria	55	54	57
Reunion	74	71	77
Rwanda	40	39	41
Saint Helena	75	73	77
Sao Tome and Principe	63	61	65
Senegal	57	55	58
Seychelles	70	66	73
Sierra Leone	46	44	49
Somalia	55	54	55
South Africa	65	62	68
Sudan	54	53	55
Swaziland	56	52	61
Tanzania	43	42	45
Togo	57	55	59
Uganda	37	37	38
Zaire	47	46	49
Zambia	44	44	45
Zimbabwe	42	40	44

Source: Selected from "Infant Mortality Rates and Life Expectancy at Birth, by Country or Area and Sex: 1994," U.S. Bureau of the Census, *World Population Profile: 1994*, 1994, Table 8, p. A-27. Primary source: U.S. Bureau of the Census, International Data Base.

★ 785 ★

Life Expectancy

Expectation of Life in Yugoslavia and the Soviet Union: 1994

This table shows life expectancy at birth in years for those born in 1994 in the former Yugoslavia and the former Soviet Union. The U.S. view is that the Socialist Federal Republic of Yugoslavia has dissolved and no successor state represents its continuation. Macedonia has proclaimed independent statehood, but has not been recognized as a state by the U.S. Serbia and Montenegro have asserted the formation of a joint independent state, but this entity has not been recognized as a state by the U.S.

[Life expectancy at birth in years.]

Country	Life expectancy at birth (years)		
	Both sexes	Male	Female
World	62	61	64
Developing countries	61	59	62
Developed countries	74	71	78
(Former) Yugoslavia	74	71	77
Bosnia and Herzegovina	75	72	78
Croatia	74	70	77
Macedonia	74	72	76
Serbia and Montenegro	74	71	76
Slovenia	74	70	78
(Former) Soviet Union	69	65	74
BALTICS	70	66	76
Estonia	70	65	75
Latvia	69	64	75
Lithuania	71	67	76
COMMONWEALTH OF INDEPENDENT STATES	69	65	74
Armenia	72	69	76
Azerbaijan	71	67	75
Belarus	71	66	76
Kazakhstan	68	63	73
Kyrgystan	68	64	72
Moldova	68	65	72
Russia	69	64	74
Tajikistan	69	66	72
Turkmenistan	65	62	69
Ukraine	70	65	75
Uzbekistan	69	65	72
GEORGIA	73	69	77

Source: Selected from "Infant Mortality Rates and Life Expectancy at Birth, by Country or Area and Sex: 1994," U.S. Bureau of the Census, *World Population Profile: 1994*, 1994, Table 8, p. A-29. Primary source: U.S. Bureau of the Census, International Data Base.

Marital Status

★ 786 ★

Asian and Near Eastern Married Women: 1990-2000

This table shows the total population of women and the number of currently married women of reproductive age (15 to 49 years) in Asia and the Near East in midyear 1990 and 1994 and projected for 1995 and 2000.

[Midyear population in thousands.]

Country	Women				Currently married women			
	1990	1994	1995	2000	1990	1994	1995	2000
Asia, excluding Near East								
Afghanistan	3,452	3,821	4,275	5,878	2,778	3,079	3,448	4,747
Bangladesh	25,926	29,574	30,565	35,675	21,658	24,734	25,573	29,938
Brunei	63	72	74	84	40	46	47	54
Burma	10,244	11,200	11,463	12,875	6,337	7,011	7,184	8,103
China								
Mainland	308,049	325,810	329,694	345,163	191,654	219,057	225,952	250,908
Taiwan	5,536	5,952	6,038	6,379	3,764	4,107	4,183	4,484
Hong Kong	1,505	1,539	1,544	1,530	987	1,060	1,073	1,085
India	208,699	227,136	231,901	257,723	167,910	184,190	188,332	209,310
Indonesia	48,926	54,037	55,364	61,535	34,741	38,437	39,428	44,478
Iran	12,011	13,955	14,381	17,033	9,098	10,571	10,888	12,858
Japan	31,462	31,054	30,999	29,368	18,670	18,306	18,364	17,758
Macau	129	140	142	151	75	89	92	101
Malaysia	4,518	4,943	5,039	5,640	2,845	3,189	3,270	3,638
Maldives	47	53	55	67	35	40	42	50
Nepal	4,293	4,817	4,962	5,750	3,518	3,925	4,041	4,693
Pakistan	24,861	27,995	28,614	32,797	18,414	20,723	21,177	24,270
Philippines	16,269	18,163	18,653	21,039	10,182	11,466	11,800	13,488
Singapore	794	816	818	814	457	493	499	501
South Korea	12,167	12,872	13,032	13,816	7,293	8,075	8,265	9,098
Sri Lanka	4,660	4,991	5,073	5,466	2,833	3,089	3,149	3,426
Thailand	15,169	16,474	16,806	18,086	9,438	10,570	10,843	11,915
Vietnam	16,987	18,789	19,275	21,746	10,299	11,707	12,070	13,754
Near East								
Bahrain	111	126	130	149	72	83	86	99
Cyprus	177	181	182	188	122	126	126	128
Gaza Strip	130	151	157	191	84	97	100	122
Iraq	3,915	4,302	4,492	5,496	2,665	2,930	3,064	3,786
Israel	1,039	1,257	1,284	1,366	667	816	834	895
Jordan	723	876	907	1,091	480	596	621	754

[Continued]

★ 786 ★

Asian and Near Eastern Married Women: 1990-2000

[Continued]

Country	Women				Currently married women			
	1990	1994	1995	2000	1990	1994	1995	2000
Kuwait	504	422	447	590	338	280	297	392
Lebanon	817	940	971	1,112	466	538	560	676
Qatar	78	90	93	108	56	64	65	73
Syria	2,660	3,138	3,269	4,026	1,762	2,101	2,193	2,712
Turkey	13,795	15,381	15,783	17,892	10,140	11,403	11,731	13,425
United Arab Emirates	433	560	593	760	336	422	443	549
West Bank	297	345	357	416	195	228	236	277

Source: Selected from "All Women and Currently Married Women of Reproductive Age (15 to 49 Years), by Country or Area: 1990 to 2000," U.S. Bureau of the Census, *World Population Profile: 1994*, 1994, Table 5, p. A-15. Primary source: U.S. Bureau of the Census, International Data Base. The category "currently married women" includes women in consensual unions. Estimates are based on component projections of the female population and the percent of women who are married or in consensual unions in each 5-year age group from the most recent source in the International Data Base. Countries with no data available on marital status or no component projections are omitted from the table.

★ 787 ★

Marital Status

European Married Women: 1990-2000

This table shows the total population of women and the number of currently married women of reproductive age (15 to 49 years) in Europe in midyear 1990 and 1994 and projected for 1995 and 2000.

[Midyear population in thousands.]

Country	Women				Currently married women			
	1990	1994	1995	2000	1990	1994	1995	2000
Europe								
Albania	814	844	857	926	599	627	637	690
Austria	1,966	1,981	1,986	1,992	1,220	1,267	1,278	1,292
Belgium	2,438	2,467	2,467	2,418	1,712	1,767	1,771	1,742
Bulgaria	2,144	2,130	2,123	2,059	1,644	1,624	1,623	1,588
Czech Republic	2,594	2,669	2,673	2,591	1,740	1,765	1,774	1,771
Denmark	1,310	1,303	1,293	1,232	671	683	680	669
Faroe Islands	11	11	11	12	7	7	7	8
Finland	1,258	1,271	1,267	1,216	675	689	688	649
France	14,155	14,458	14,484	14,124	8,750	9,194	9,261	9,124
Germany	19,399	19,255	19,278	19,288	12,390	12,743	12,834	12,982
Gibraltar	7	8	8	8	5	5	5	5
Greece	2,397	2,583	2,613	2,660	1,677	1,822	1,845	1,901
Guernsey	16	16	16	16	10	11	11	12
Hungary	2,542	2,583	2,584	2,520	1,733	1,731	1,739	1,743
Iceland	65	67	68	70	35	37	38	39

[Continued]

★ 787 ★

European Married Women: 1990-2000
[Continued]

Country	Women				Currently married women			
	1990	1994	1995	2000	1990	1994	1995	2000
Ireland	851	889	901	940	471	494	500	523
Isle of Man	16	18	18	18	10	11	11	12
Italy	14,553	14,640	14,638	14,190	9,284	9,615	9,701	9,712
Liechtenstein	8	9	9	9	5	5	5	5
Luxembourg	97	103	103	102	65	70	70	70
Netherlands	3,967	4,005	4,004	3,882	2,215	2,338	2,360	2,335
Norway	1,056	1,068	1,065	1,044	586	613	616	617
Poland	9,389	9,861	9,989	10,247	6,485	6,715	6,786	6,875
Portugal	2,617	2,729	2,745	2,785	1,773	1,879	1,900	1,982
Romania	5,586	5,736	5,777	5,773	3,976	4,090	4,130	4,222
Slovakia	1,328	1,396	1,412	1,453	889	923	934	973
Spain	9,757	10,108	10,154	10,137	5,521	5,865	5,938	6,244
Sweden	2,048	2,052	2,041	1,985	911	929	926	910
Switzerland	1,734	1,776	1,774	1,754	1,052	1,105	1,109	1,105
United Kingdom	14,138	14,107	14,096	13,814	9,351	9,607	9,621	9,411

Source: Selected from "All Women and Currently Married Women of Reproductive Age (15 to 49 Years), by Country or Area: 1990 to 2000," U.S. Bureau of the Census, *World Population Profile: 1994*, 1994, Table 5, p. A-17. Primary source: U.S. Bureau of the Census, International Data Base. The category "currently married women" includes women in consensual unions. Estimates are based on component projections of the female population and the percent of women who are married or in consensual unions in each 5-year age group from the most recent source in the International Data Base. Countries with no data available on marital status or no component projections are omitted from the table.

★ 788 ★
Marital Status

Latin American/Caribbean Married Women: 1990-2000

This table shows the total population of women and the number of currently married women of reproductive age (15 to 49 years) in Latin America and the Caribbean in midyear 1990 and 1994 and projected for 1995 and 2000.

[Midyear population in thousands.]

Country	Women				Currently married women			
	1990	1994	1995	2000	1990	1994	1995	2000
Latin America/Caribbean								
Anguilla	2	2	2	2	1	1	1	1
Argentina	7,705	8,256	8,410	9,001	4,793	5,079	5,156	5,552
Aruba	19	19	19	19	9	10	10	10
Bahamas, The	74	82	84	91	40	46	47	52
Barbados	70	72	72	74	33	35	36	37
Belize	42	48	49	59	18	21	22	26

[Continued]

★ 788 ★

Latin American/Caribbean Married Women: 1990-2000
[Continued]

Country	Women				Currently married women			
	1990	1994	1995	2000	1990	1994	1995	2000
Bolivia	1,695	1,896	1,948	2,219	993	1,118	1,151	1,322
Brazil	39,466	43,219	44,132	47,806	23,660	26,252	26,867	29,531
Chile	3,486	3,685	3,735	3,978	2,027	2,166	2,198	2,345
Colombia	9,022	9,830	10,019	10,991	4,937	5,530	5,672	6,310
Costa Rica	773	855	875	984	466	524	537	603
Cuba	3,003	3,065	3,058	3,075	1,958	2,076	2,094	2,142
Dominica	23	25	26	28	11	13	13	16
Dominican Republic	1,841	2,037	2,084	2,331	1,186	1,342	1,380	1,570
Ecuador	2,462	2,769	2,846	3,238	1,510	1,718	1,771	2,044
El Salvador	1,236	1,415	1,458	1,625	735	841	870	1,015
French Guiana	29	34	36	42	9	11	12	14
Grenada	21	21	21	22	9	9	9	10
Guadeloupe	109	117	119	124	35	40	41	45
Guatemala	2,176	2,480	2,561	2,986	1,428	1,625	1,679	1,971
Guyana	195	196	196	199	99	101	101	105
Haiti	1,363	1,426	1,450	1,626	705	729	737	787
Honduras	1,077	1,245	1,290	1,526	650	753	781	931
Jamaica	631	671	682	756	140	159	164	194
Martinique	104	109	110	114	32	36	37	42
Mexico	21,559	23,980	24,569	27,450	12,857	14,553	14,988	17,141
Netherlands Antilles	53	52	51	52	23	24	24	24
Nicaragua	833	980	1,017	1,218	496	586	609	733
Panama	617	680	695	768	350	391	401	451
Paraguay	1,095	1,237	1,277	1,498	641	729	752	874
Peru	5,419	6,068	6,234	7,063	3,187	3,605	3,715	4,276
Puerto Rico	954	1,007	1,007	1,003	551	588	587	586
Saint Kitts and Nevis	9	10	11	12	2	2	2	3
Saint Lucia	35	38	38	42	18	20	20	23
Saint Vincent and the Grenadines	29	31	32	36	14	15	16	19
Trinidad and Tobago	330	352	359	397	169	183	186	204
Uruguay	740	774	782	811	454	473	479	504
Venezuela	4,770	5,360	5,505	6,219	2,669	3,022	3,112	3,561

Source: Selected from "All Women and Currently Married Women of Reproductive Age (15 to 49 Years), by Country or Area: 1990 to 2000," U.S. Bureau of the Census, *World Population Profile: 1994*, 1994, Table 5, p. A-16. Primary source: U.S. Bureau of the Census, International Data Base. The category "currently married women" includes women in consensual unions. Estimates are based on component projections of the female population and the percent of women who are married or in consensual unions in each 5-year age group from the most recent source in the International Data Base. Countries with no data available on marital status or no component projections are omitted from the table.

★ 789 ★

Marital Status

Marital Status by Age: 1990 Census-I

This table shows total population aged 15 years and over, total female population aged 15 years and over, and marital status in five categories of the female population aged 15 years and over as reported in the 1990 census. Now married, except separated, includes persons whose current marriage has not ended through widowhood, divorce, or separation (regardless of previous marital history). The category may also include couples who live together or persons in common-law marriages if they consider this category most appropriate. Widowed includes widows and widowers who have not remarried. Divorced includes persons who are legally divorced and who have not remarried. Separated includes persons legally separated or otherwise absent from their spouse because of marital discord. Included are persons who have been deserted or who have parted because they no longer want to live together but who have not obtained a divorce. Never married includes all persons who have never been married, including persons whose only marriage(s) was annulled.

Age	Total pop.	Marital status				
		Now married, exc. separated	Widowed	Divorced	Separated	Never married
Total, both sexes	195,142,002	106,925,341	14,499,528	16,584,043	4,573,237	52,559,853
15 to 64 years	163,900,171	90,308,651	3,492,036	14,951,810	4,232,658	50,915,016
65 to 69 years	10,111,735	6,780,252	1,976,604	713,083	151,340	490,456
70 to 74 years	7,994,823	4,761,154	2,312,855	436,525	92,465	391,824
75 to 79 years	6,121,369	3,002,340	2,466,831	267,853	55,805	328,540
80 to 84 years	3,933,739	1,440,810	2,097,975	135,945	26,329	232,680
85 to 89 years	2,060,247	502,679	1,358,824	57,152	10,493	131,099
90 to 99 years	982,612	126,401	764,941	20,790	3,839	66,641
100 years and over	37,306	3,054	29,462	885	308	3,597
65 years and over	31,241,831	16,616,690	11,007,492	1,632,233	340,579	1,644,837
85 years and over	3,080,165	632,134	2,153,227	78,827	14,640	201,337
Female						
Total	101,324,687	53,144,096	12,121,939	9,626,577	2,676,840	23,755,235
15 to 64 years	82,648,029	45,926,078	2,895,949	8,599,714	2,496,997	22,729,291
65 to 69 years	5,579,428	3,156,720	1,650,331	432,079	81,343	258,955
70 to 74 years	4,585,517	2,097,168	1,937,477	271,218	48,643	231,011
75 to 79 years	3,721,601	1,234,518	2,071,316	173,630	28,951	213,186
80 to 84 years	2,567,645	534,247	1,761,052	92,840	13,358	166,148
85 to 89 years	1,446,211	160,368	1,139,765	40,953	5,368	99,757
90 to 99 years	746,851	33,856	641,207	15,549	1,993	54,246
100 years and over	29,405	1,141	24,842	594	187	2,641
65 years and over	18,676,658	7,218,018	9,225,990	1,026,863	179,843	1,025,944
85 years and over	2,222,467	195,365	1,805,814	57,096	7,548	156,644

Source: U.S. Bureau of the Census. 1990 Census of Population, prepared from the Census Analysis System.

★ 790 ★

Marital Status

Marital Status by Age: 1990 Census-II

This table shows total population aged 15 years and over, total female population aged 15 years and over, and marital status in five categories of the female population aged 15 years and over as reported in the 1990 census, in percent.

Age	Total pop.	Marital status				
		Now married, exc. separated	Widowed	Divorced	Separated	Never married
Total, both sexes	100.0%	100.0%	100.0%	100.0%	100.0%	100.0%
15 to 64 years	84.0%	84.5%	24.1%	90.2%	92.6%	96.9%
65 to 69 years	5.2%	6.3%	13.6%	4.3%	3.3%	0.9%
70 to 74 years	4.1%	4.5%	16.0%	2.6%	2.0%	0.7%
75 to 79 years	3.1%	2.8%	17.0%	1.6%	1.2%	0.6%
80 to 84 years	2.0%	1.3%	14.5%	0.8%	0.6%	0.4%
85 to 89 years	1.1%	0.5%	9.4%	0.3%	0.2%	0.2%
90 to 99 years	0.5%	0.1%	5.3%	0.1%	0.1%	0.1%
100 years and over	0.0%	0.0%	0.2%	0.0%	0.0%	0.0%
65 years and over	16.0%	15.5%	75.9%	9.8%	7.4%	3.1%
85 years and over	1.6%	0.6%	14.9%	0.5%	0.3%	0.4%
Female						
Total	100.0%	100.0%	100.0%	100.0%	100.0%	100.0%
15 to 64 years	81.6%	86.4%	23.9%	89.3%	93.3%	95.7%
65 to 69 years	5.5%	5.9%	13.6%	4.5%	3.0%	1.1%
70 to 74 years	4.5%	3.9%	16.0%	2.8%	1.8%	1.0%
75 to 79 years	3.7%	2.3%	17.1%	1.8%	1.1%	0.9%
80 to 84 years	2.5%	1.0%	14.5%	1.0%	0.5%	0.7%
85 to 89 years	1.4%	0.3%	9.4%	0.4%	0.2%	0.4%
90 to 99 years	0.7%	0.1%	5.3%	0.2%	0.1%	0.2%
100 years and over	0.0%	0.0%	0.2%	0.0%	0.0%	0.0%
65 years and over	18.4%	13.6%	76.1%	10.7%	6.7%	4.3%
85 years and over	2.2%	0.4%	14.9%	0.6%	0.3%	0.7%

Source: U.S. Bureau of the Census. 1990 Census of Population, prepared from the Census Analysis System.

★791★

Marital Status

Marital Status by Race and Hispanic Origin: 1970-1993

This table shows the total population in millions, the marital status of the total population in millions, and figures in millions for males and females by race and Hispanic origin from 1970 to 1993.

[As of March, except as noted. Persons 18 years old and over.]

Marital status, race, and Hispanic origin	Total (millions)				Male				Female			
	1970	1980	1990	1993	1970	1980	1990	1993	1970	1980	1990	1993
Total[1]	132.5	159.5	181.8	187.1	62.5	75.7	86.9	89.7	70.0	83.85	95.0	97.4
Never married	21.4	32.3	40.4	42.3	11.8	18.0	22.4	23.6	9.6	14.3	17.9	18.6
Married	95.0	104.6	112.6	114.5	47.1	51.8	55.8	56.8	47.9	52.8	56.7	57.7
Widowed	11.8	12.7	13.8	13.7	2.1	2.0	2.3	2.5	9.7	10.8	11.5	11.2
Divorced	4.3	9.9	15.1	16.7	1.6	3.9	6.3	6.8	2.7	6.0	8.8	9.9
Percent of total	100.0%	100.0%	100.0%	100.0%	100.0%	100.0%	100.0%	100.0%	100.0%	100.0%	100.0%	100.0%
Never married	16.2%	20.3%	22.2%	22.6%	18.9%	23.8%	25.8%	26.3%	13.7%	17.1%	18.9%	19.1%
Married	71.7%	65.5%	61.9%	61.2%	75.3%	68.4%	64.3%	63.4%	68.5%	63.0%	59.7%	59.2%
Widowed	8.9%	8.0%	7.6%	7.3%	3.3%	2.6%	2.7%	2.8%	13.9%	12.8%	12.1%	11.5%
Divorced	3.2%	6.2%	8.3%	8.9%	2.5%	5.2%	7.2%	7.6%	3.9%	7.1%	9.3%	10.1%
Percent standardized for age[2]												
Never married	14.1%	16.5%	20.6%	22.0%	16.5%	18.7%	23.3%	24.9%	12.1%	14.5%	18.2%	19.4%
Married	74.2%	69.3%	63.7%	62.2%	77.6%	72.9%	66.5%	64.3%	70.8%	65.9%	61.2%	60.1%
Widowed	8.3%	7.6%	6.9%	6.7%	3.3%	2.7%	2.7%	3.1%	13.0%	12.1%	10.8%	10.0%
Divorced	3.4%	6.6%	8.7%	9.1%	2.6%	5.6%	7.6%	7.7%	4.1%	7.6%	9.8%	10.4%
White, total	118.2	139.5	155.5	158.7	55.9	66.7	74.8	76.6	62.2	72.8	80.6	82.1
Never married	18.4	26.4	31.6	32.4	10.2	15.0	18.0	18.6	8.2	11.4	13.6	13.8
Married	85.8	93.8	99.5	100.9	42.7	46.7	49.5	50.3	43.1	47.1	49.9	50.6
Widowed	10.3	10.9	11.7	11.5	1.7	1.6	1.9	2.0	8.6	9.3	9.8	9.5
Divorced	3.7	8.3	12.6	14.0	1.3	3.4	5.4	5.8	2.3	5.0	7.3	8.2
Percent of total	100.0%	100.0%	100.0%	100.0%	100.0%	100.0%	100.0%	100.0%	100.0%	100.0%	100.0%	100.0%
Never married	15.6%	18.9%	20.3%	20.4%	18.2%	22.5%	24.1%	24.3%	13.2%	15.7%	16.9%	16.8%
Married	72.6%	67.2%	64.0%	63.6%	76.3%	70.0%	66.2%	65.7%	69.3%	64.7%	61.9%	61.6%
Widowed	8.7%	7.8%	7.5%	7.2%	3.1%	2.5%	2.6%	2.6%	13.8%	12.8%	12.2%	11.6%
Divorced	3.1%	6.0%	8.1%	8.8%	2.4%	5.0%	7.2%	7.5%	3.8%	6.8%	9.0%	10.0%
Black, total	13.0	16.6	20.3	21.3	5.9	7.4	9.1	9.6	7.1	9.2	11.2	11.7
Never married	2.7	5.1	7.1	8.0	1.4	2.5	3.5	3.9	1.2	2.5	3.6	4.1
Married	8.3	8.5	9.3	9.2	3.9	4.1	4.5	4.4	4.4	4.5	4.8	4.8
Widowed	1.4	1.6	1.7	1.8	0.3	0.3	0.3	0.4	1.1	1.3	1.4	1.4
Divorced	0.6	1.4	2.1	2.2	0.2	0.5	0.8	0.8	0.4	0.9	1.3	1.4
Percent of total	100.0%	100.0%	100.0%	100.0%	100.0%	100.0%	100.0%	100.0%	100.0%	100.0%	100.0%	100.0%
Never married	20.6%	30.5%	35.1%	37.6%	24.3%	34.3%	38.4%	40.8%	17.4%	27.4%	32.5%	34.9%
Married	64.1%	51.4%	45.8%	43.4%	66.9%	54.6%	49.2%	46.1%	61.7%	48.7%	43.0%	41.1%
Widowed	11.0%	9.8%	8.5%	8.6%	5.2%	4.2%	3.7%	4.4%	15.8%	14.3%	12.4%	12.0%
Divorced	4.4%	8.4%	10.6%	10.5%	3.6%	7.0%	8.8%	8.6%	5.0%	9.5%	12.0%	12.0%
Hispanic, total[3]	5.1	7.9	13.6	14.9	2.4	3.8	6.7	7.4	2.6	4.1	6.8	7.5
Never married	0.9	1.9	3.7	4.2	0.5	1.0	2.2	2.4	0.4	0.9	1.5	1.7
Married	3.6	5.2	8.4	9.0	1.8	2.5	4.1	4.4	1.8	2.6	4.3	4.6

[Continued]

★ 791 ★

Marital Status by Race and Hispanic Origin: 1970-1993
[Continued]

Marital status, race, and His- panic origin	Total (millions)				Male				Female			
	1970	1980	1990	1993	1970	1980	1990	1993	1970	1980	1990	1993
Widowed	0.3	0.4	0.5	0.7	0.1	0.1	0.1	0.1	0.2	0.3	0.4	0.5
Divorced	0.2	0.5	1.0	1.1	0.1	0.2	0.4	0.5	0.1	0.3	0.6	0.6
Percent of total	100.0%	100.0%	100.0%	100.0%	100.0%	100.0%	100.0%	100.0%	100.0%	100.0%	100.0%	100.0%
Never married	18.6%	24.1%	27.2%	27.9%	21.2%	27.3%	32.1%	32.5%	16.2%	21.1%	22.5%	23.3%
Married	71.8%	65.6%	61.7%	60.4%	73.8%	67.1%	60.9%	59.7%	70.0%	64.3%	62.4%	61.1%
Widowed	5.6%	4.4%	4.0%	4.4%	2.3%	1.6%	1.5%	1.7%	8.7%	7.1%	6.5%	7.0%
Divorced	3.9%	5.8%	7.0%	7.3%	2.7%	4.0%	5.5%	6.1%	5.1%	7.6%	8.5%	8.6%

Source: Selected from "Marital Status of the Population, by Sex, Race, and Hispanic Origin: 1970 to 1993," U.S. Bureau of the Census, *Statistical Abstract of the United States 1994*, Table 59, p. 55. Primary source: U.S. Bureau of the Census, *1970 Census of Population*, vol. I, part 1, and *Current Population Reports*, P20-450, and earlier reports; and unpublished data. Excludes members of Armed Forces except those living off post or with their families on post. Except as noted, based on Current Population Survey. *Notes:* 1. Includes persons of other races, not shown separately. 2. 1960 age distribution used as standard; standardization improves comparability over time by removing effects of changes in age distribution of population. 3. Hispanic persons may be of any race. 1970 data as of April and based on census.

★ 792 ★
Marital Status

Marital Status of the African Population

This table presents statistics on the female population of Africa by marital status, latest available year. Marital status is the personal status of each individual in relation to the marriage laws or customs of the country. Single means never married. Widowed and divorced persons are not remarried.

[Figures for "All ages" unless otherwise noted. NA Not available.]

Country	Year	Total female population	Single	Married	Widowed	Divorced	Unknown
Africa							
Burkina Faso[1]	1985	2,226,332	266,826	1,656,560	265,779	25,655	11,512
Burundi	1988	2,600,515	1,486,641	931,502	128,095	54,277	NA
Egypt[1,2,3]	1986	13,552,381	2,776,728	8,871,002	1,723,873	180,776	NA
Equatorial Guinea	1983	92,091	29,564	47,327	12,028	1,491	335
Mali[1]	1987	2,189,770	296,037	1,635,443	201,780	30,860	25,650
Sudan[1]	1983	4,977,746	953,086	3,243,159	511,621	158,775	111,105
Swaziland	1986	359,480	269,208	79,884	8,782	496	6
Zaire[4]	1984	14,808,908	9,156,204	4,357,293	647,706	382,735	29,441

Source: Selected from "Population by marital status, age and sex: 1980-1989," *Demographic Yearbook, 1990*, United Nations, 1992, Table 41, pp. 894+. Also in source: figures by age group. *Notes:* 1. Ages 15+. Persons of unknown age are excluded. 2. For Egyptian nationals only. 3. For 16 years and over. 4. Consensually married = 235,529.

★ 793 ★

Marital Status

Marital Status of the Asian and Near Eastern Population

This table presents statistics on the female population of Asia and the Near East by marital status, latest available year. Marital status is the personal status of each individual in relation to the marriage laws or customs of the country. Single means never married. Widowed and divorced persons are not remarried. Figures are given for those countries for which information was available.

[Figures for "All ages" unless otherwise noted. NA Not available.]

Country	Year	Total female population	Single	Married	Widowed	Divorced	Unknown
Asia, excluding Near East							
China[1]	1987	375,898,100	86,622,800	254,466,700	33,871,000	937,600	NA
Iran							
Islam, Rep. of	1986	13,151,808	2,492,937	9,294,453	1,119,816	101,898	142,704
Maldives	1985	46,873	6,049	32,558	2,554	5,646	66
Vietnam[1,3]	1989	20,879,424	5,566,131	12,487,489	2,417,185	178,437	29,523
Near East							
Iraq[1]	1987	4,232,272	1,149,681	2,449,674	403,693	44,462	184,762
Israel	1987	1,506,000	355,300	1,150,700[2]	NA	NA	NA
Kuwait	1988	494,376	139,844	318,556	28,083	7,893	NA
Qatar	1986	121,227	67,930	47,863	3,795	1,269	370
Turkey	1985	15,721,775	3,420,643	10,827,214	1,346,078	126,683	1,157

Source: Selected from "Population by marital status, age and sex: 1980-1989," *Demographic Yearbook, 1990*, United Nations, 1992, Table 41, pp. 894+. Also in source: figures by age group. *Notes:* 1. Ages 15+. Persons of unknown age are excluded. 2. Ever married. 3. Separated = 200,659.

★ 794 ★

Marital Status

Marital Status of the European Population

This table presents statistics on the female population of Europe by marital status, latest available year. Marital status is the personal status of each individual in relation to the marriage laws or customs of the country. Single means never married. Widowed and divorced persons are not remarried. Figures are given for those countries for which information was available.

[Figures for "All ages" unless otherwise noted. NA Not available.]

Country	Year	Total female population	Single	Married	Widowed	Divorced	Separated
Europe							
Bulgaria[1]	1985	4,515,347	1,359,759	2,494,175	476,987	132,870	15,367
Channel Islands[2]							
Jersey	1989	42,723	17,100	18,260	4,479	2,008	876
Czechoslovakia	1989	8,027,612	2,806,748	3,836,666	973,719	410,479	NA

[Continued]

★ 794 ★

Marital Status of the European Population
[Continued]

Country	Year	Total female population	Single	Married	Widowed	Divorced	Separated
Denmark	1988	2,601,258	1,054,232	1,084,167[3]	284,755	178,104	[3]
Finland	1987	2,545,734	1,054,302	1,057,730	283,992	149,710	NA
France	1989	28,727,412	11,664,101	12,549,630	3,253,729	1,259,952	NA
Germany							
Fed. Rep. of	1988	32,021,988	10,999,609	14,963,946	4,607,074	1,451,359	NA
(Former) G. Dem. Rep.	1988	8,701,830	2,909,527	4,076,662	1,129,872	585,769	NA
Hungary	1989	5,477,816	1,747,593	2,600,458	785,458	344,307	NA
Iceland	1989	125,800	64,854	45,486	8,183	5,539	1,738
Ireland	1988	1,770,700	923,000	673,700	149,300	24,700[4]	[4]
Liechtenstein	1987	14,187	6,512	6,115	1,091	469	NA
Luxembourg	1990	193,840	70,074	92,044[5]	13,861	17,481[5]	[5]
Malta	1985	175,586	82,779	78,249	12,893	1,665[6]	[6]
Netherlands	1989	7,511,363	3,013,989	3,459,695	697,548	340,131	NA
Norway	1990	2,139,836	882,449	898,785	228,412	100,499	29,691
San Marino	1989	11,698	4,058	6,401	1,186	53	NA
Spain	1986	19,595,252	8,520,232	9,010,292	1,856,308	50,560	157,860
Sweden	1988	4,283,008	1,841,678	1,656,166	456,323	328,841	NA
Switzerland	1988	3,391,052	1,344,331	1,552,736	330,157	163,828	NA
United Kingdom	1989	29,329,699	11,073,913	13,434,775	3,316,785	1,504,226	NA
USSR	1989	112,663,560	15,715,127	68,316,222[7]	19,560,726	8,478,461[7]	[7]

Source: Selected from "Population by marital status, age and sex: 1980-1989," *Demographic Yearbook, 1990*, United Nations, 1992, Table 41, pp. 894+. Also in source: figures by age group. *Notes:* 1. Consensually married = 36,189. 2. Married and separated. 3. 1,084,167 = Married and separated. 4. 24,700 = divorced and separated. 5. 92,044 = Married and consensually married; 17,481 = Divorced and separated; 380 = unknown. 6. 1,665 = Divorced and separated. 7. Ages 16+. Persons of unknown age are excluded. 68,316,222 = Married and consensually married. 8,478,461 = Divorced and separated. Unknown = 593,024.

791

★ 795 ★

Marital Status

Marital Status of the Latin American/Caribbean Population

This table presents statistics on the female population of Latin America and the Caribbean by marital status, latest available year. Marital status is the personal status of each individual in relation to the marriage laws or customs of the country. Single means never married. Widowed and divorced persons are not remarried. Figures are given for those countries for which information was available.

[Figures for "All ages" unless otherwise noted. NA Not available.]

Country	Year	Total female population	Single	Married	Widowed	Divorced	Unknown
Latin America and the Caribbean							
Bolivia[1,5]	1988	1,803,800	513,500	952,600	151,000	66,500	3,600
Cayman Islands[2]	1989	12,983	6,475	5,100	607	498	NA
Falkland Islands	1986	884	352	409	123[7]	7	7
Guatemala[1,3]	1990	2,444,937	576,166	964,607	220,531	139,607	NA
Haiti[4]	1988	2,847,270	1,682,332	312,395	109,453	3,477	NA
Uruguay[6]	1987	1,516,220	661,554	571,869	146,611	40,392	NA

Source: Selected from "Population by marital status, age and sex: 1980-1989," *Demographic Yearbook, 1990,* United Nations, 1992, Table 41, pp. 894+. Also in source: figures by age group. *Notes:* 1. Ages 15+. Persons of unknown age are excluded. 2. Separated = 303. 3. Consensually married = 544,026. 4. Consensually married = 580,109; Separated = 159,504. 5. Consensually married = 116,700. Divorced includes separated. 6. Consensually married = 68,742. Separated = 27,052. 7. 123 = widowed, divorced, and separated.

★ 796 ★

Marital Status

Marital Status of the North American Population

This table presents statistics on the female population of North America by marital status, latest available year. Marital status is the personal status of each individual in relation to the marriage laws or customs of the country. Single means never married. Widowed and divorced persons are not remarried.

[Figures for "All ages" unless otherwise noted. NA Not available.]

Country	Year	Total female population	Single	Married	Widowed	Divorced	Unknown
North America							
Canada	1989	13,293,900	5,244,100	6,397,700[1]	1,093,100	559,000	NA
Greenland	1988	24,849	15,855	6,932	1,317	745	NA
United States[2]	1990	126,379,000	49,260,000	53,256,000	11,477,000	8,845,000	693,000

Source: Selected from "Population by marital status, age and sex: 1980-1989," *Demographic Yearbook, 1990,* United Nations, 1992, Table 41, pp. 894+. Also in source: figures by age group. *Notes:* 1. Married and separated. 2. Separated = 2,848,000.

★ 797 ★

Marital Status

Marital Status of the Oceanian Population

This table presents statistics on the female population of Oceania by marital status, latest available year. Marital status is the personal status of each individual in relation to the marriage laws or customs of the country. Single means never married. Widowed and divorced persons are not remarried. Figures are given for those countries for which information was available.

[Figures for "All ages" unless otherwise noted. NA Not available.]

Country	Year	Total female population	Single	Married	Widowed	Divorced	Separated
Oceania							
Australia	1990	8,554,994	3,573,609	3,905,700	685,010	390,675	NA
New Caledonia	1989	80,311	50,711	23,514[1]	4,344	1,742[1]	[1]
Niue	1986	1,260	744[2]	443	67	6	--
Norfolk Island[3]	1986	542	78	358	54	33	17
Northern Mariana Islands[4]	1980	4,591	1,574	2,572	299	146	--
Pitcairn[5]	1988	32	11	15	4	NA	NA
Tonga	1986	46,312	28,873	15,129	1,785	479[6]	[6]
Vanuatu	1989	69,035	40,366	25,138[6]	2,363	485	NA

Source: Selected from "Population by marital status, age and sex: 1980-1989," *Demographic Yearbook, 1990,* United Nations, 1992, Table 41, pp. 894+. Also in source: figures by age group. *Notes:* 1. 23,514 = married and consensually married; 1,742 = divorced and separated. 2. 744 = Single and consensually married. 3. Ages 15+. Persons of unknown age are excluded. Unknown = 2. 4. Ages 15+. Persons of unknown age are excluded. 5. Consensually married = 2. 6. 25,138 = married and consensually married. Unknown = 683.

★ 798 ★

Marital Status

Never Married: 1970 and 1992

This table shows the percentage of women in their age group who had never been married in 1970 and 1992. Among women in their late twenties and early thirties, the proportions never married tripled between 1970 and 1992.

Year and Age	Women	Men
1970		
30 to 34 years	6.2%	9.4%
25 to 29 years	10.5%	19.1%
20 to 24 years	35.8%	54.7%
1992		
30 to 34 years	18.8%	29.4%

[Continued]

★ 798 ★

Never Married: 1970 and 1992
[Continued]

Year and Age	Women	Men
25 to 29 years	33.2%	48.7%
20 to 24 years	65.7%	80.3%

Source: "Percent Never Married, by Sex and Age: 1970 and 1992," U.S. Bureau of the Census, *Current Population Reports*, "Population Profile of the United States 1993," Figure 19, p. 20.

★ 799 ★

Marital Status

North African Married Women: 1990-2000

This table shows the total population of women and the number of currently married women of reproductive age (15 to 49 years) in North Africa in midyear 1990 and 1994 and projected for 1995 and 2000.

[Midyear population in thousands.]

Country	Women				Currently married women			
	1990	1994	1995	2000	1990	1994	1995	2000
North Africa								
Algeria	5,740	6,651	6,899	8,255	3,310	3,873	4,023	4,829
Egypt	12,467	14,184	14,651	16,742	8,507	9,544	9,821	11,309
Morocco	6,270	7,056	7,272	8,431	3,934	4,475	4,623	5,411
Tunisia	1,964	2,199	2,260	2,578	1,155	1,317	1,360	1,587

Source: Selected from "All Women and Currently Married Women of Reproductive Age (15 to 49 Years), by Country or Area: 1990 to 2000," U.S. Bureau of the Census, *World Population Profile: 1994*, 1994, Table 5, p. A-14. Primary source: U.S. Bureau of the Census, International Data Base. The category "currently married women" includes women in consensual unions. Estimates are based on component projections of the female population and the percent of women who are married or in consensual unions in each 5-year age group from the most recent source in the International Data Base. Countries with no data available on marital status or no component projections are omitted from the table.

★ 800 ★

Marital Status

North American Married Women: 1990-2000

This table shows the total population of women and the number of currently married women of reproductive age (15 to 49 years) in North America in midyear 1990 and 1994 and projected for 1995 and 2000.

[Midyear population in thousands.]

Country	Women				Currently married women			
	1990	1994	1995	2000	1990	1994	1995	2000
North America								
Canada	7,154	7,453	7,511	7,630	4,389	4,654	4,704	4,779
Greenland	15	15	15	16	6	6	6	7
United States	65,802	67,787	68,376	69,970	41,700	43,597	44,005	44,717

Source: Selected from "All Women and Currently Married Women of Reproductive Age (15 to 49 Years), by Country or Area: 1990 to 2000," U.S. Bureau of the Census, *World Population Profile: 1994*, 1994, Table 5, p. A-16. Primary source: U.S. Bureau of the Census, International Data Base. The category "currently married women" includes women in consensual unions. Estimates are based on component projections of the female population and the percent of women who are married or in consensual unions in each 5-year age group from the most recent source in the International Data Base. Countries with no data available on marital status or no component projections are omitted from the table.

★ 801 ★

Marital Status

Oceanian Married Women: 1990-2000

This table shows the total population of women and the number of currently married women of reproductive age (15 to 49 years) in Oceania in midyear 1990 and 1994 and projected for 1995 and 2000.

[Midyear population in thousands.]

Country	Women				Currently married women			
	1990	1994	1995	2000	1990	1994	1995	2000
Oceania								
Australia	4,489	4,742	4,789	4,928	2,568	2,785	2,830	2,951
Fiji	188	198	201	221	124	130	132	144
French Polynesia	49	53	55	61	21	24	25	28
New Caledonia	44	48	49	53	23	26	26	29
New Zealand	861	876	878	864	497	519	523	525
Solomon Islands	71	84	88	107	46	54	57	70
Tuvalu	2	3	3	3	1	1	1	1

[Continued]

★ 801 ★

Oceanian Married Women: 1990-2000
[Continued]

Country	Women				Currently married women			
	1990	1994	1995	2000	1990	1994	1995	2000
Vanuatu	35	40	42	48	22	26	26	31
Western Samoa	43	47	48	57	23	27	28	34

Source: Selected from "All Women and Currently Married Women of Reproductive Age (15 to 49 Years), by Country or Area: 1990 to 2000," U.S. Bureau of the Census, *World Population Profile: 1994*, 1994, Table 5, p. A-18. Primary source: U.S. Bureau of the Census, International Data Base. The category "currently married women" includes women in consensual unions. Estimates are based on component projections of the female population and the percent of women who are married or in consensual unions in each 5-year age group from the most recent source in the International Data Base. Countries with no data available on marital status or no component projections are omitted from the table.

★ 802 ★

Marital Status

Sub-Saharan African Married Women: 1990-2000

This table shows the total population of women and the number of currently married women of reproductive age (15 to 49 years) in Sub-Saharan Africa in midyear 1990 and 1994 and projected for 1995 and 2000.

[Midyear population in thousands.]

Country	Women				Currently married women			
	1990	1994	1995	2000	1990	1994	1995	2000
Sub-Saharan Africa								
Angola	1,895	2,186	2,242	2,578	1,396	1,614	1,657	1,903
Benin	1,064	1,209	1,249	1,475	857	975	1,007	1,191
Botswana	294	339	351	418	122	142	147	177
Burkina	2,035	2,272	2,334	2,647	1,692	1,888	1,939	2,192
Burundi	1,268	1,372	1,404	1,582	818	881	895	972
Cameroon	2,590	2,952	3,053	3,590	1,772	1,999	2,063	2,428
Cape Verde	86	97	100	118	23	26	27	32
Chad	1,232	1,326	1,353	1,498	1,012	1,089	1,111	1,230
Comoros	101	116	120	144	67	77	80	96
Cote d'Ivoire	2,691	3,076	3,175	3,710	2,053	2,348	2,424	2,831
Ethiopia	11,478	13,092	13,542	15,754	9,130	10,412	10,768	12,504
Gabon	259	268	271	288	214	221	223	238
Guinea	1,386	1,493	1,530	1,743	1,284	1,383	1,418	1,615
Kenya	5,264	6,299	6,453	7,477	3,691	4,422	4,531	5,263
Lesotho	411	466	481	559	279	315	325	377
Liberia	507	648	670	793	350	448	463	547
Madagascar	2,605	2,967	3,066	3,628	1,726	1,963	2,029	2,391
Malawi	2,086	2,142	2,148	2,393	1,602	1,643	1,646	1,821
Mali	1,826	2,022	2,081	2,420	1,433	1,575	1,619	1,880
Mauritania	427	485	501	594	268	304	314	372

[Continued]

★ 802 ★

Sub-Saharan African Married Women: 1990-2000

[Continued]

Country	Women				Currently married women			
	1990	1994	1995	2000	1990	1994	1995	2000
Mauritius	296	314	319	337	179	192	195	208
Mayotte	17	20	20	25	13	15	16	19
Mozambique	3,390	4,056	4,236	4,877	2,544	3,052	3,189	3,673
Nigeria	18,957	21,539	22,264	26,276	14,871	16,838	17,388	20,505
Reunion	163	175	178	192	75	86	89	100
Rwanda	1,540	1,745	1,799	2,070	1,029	1,131	1,157	1,288
Senegal	1,754	2,007	2,072	2,420	1,345	1,538	1,590	1,867
Seychelles	18	20	20	22	7	8	8	10
South Africa	9,648	10,707	10,988	12,536	4,641	5,214	5,363	6,140
Sudan	6,038	6,633	6,783	8,097	4,431	4,860	4,964	5,915
Swaziland	204	223	231	272	74	80	83	99
Tanzania	5,659	6,354	6,524	7,304	4,097	4,579	4,698	5,250
Togo	832	951	984	1,177	653	744	769	916
Uganda	3,859	4,264	4,363	4,839	2,805	3,087	3,154	3,476
Zaire	8,465	9,488	9,774	11,332	6,466	7,224	7,441	8,631
Zambia	1,799	1,999	2,059	2,298	1,241	1,353	1,384	1,517
Zimbabwe	2,308	2,540	2,597	2,929	1,530	1,667	1,701	1,905

Source: Selected from "All Women and Currently Married Women of Reproductive Age (15 to 49 Years), by Country or Area: 1990 to 2000," U.S. Bureau of the Census, *World Population Profile: 1994*, 1994, Table 5, p. A-14. Primary source: U.S. Bureau of the Census, International Data Base. The category "currently married women" includes women in consensual unions. Estimates are based on component projections of the female population and the percent of women who are married or in consensual unions in each 5-year age group from the most recent source in the International Data Base. Countries with no data available on marital status or no component projections are omitted from the table.

★ 803 ★

Marital Status

Yugoslavian and Soviet Union Married Women: 1990-2000

This table shows the total population of women and the number of currently married women of reproductive age (15 to 49 years) in the former Yugoslavia and the former Soviet Union in midyear 1990 and 1994 and projected for 1995 and 2000. The U.S. view is that the Socialist Federal Republic of Yugoslavia has dissolved and no successor state represents its continuation. Macedonia has proclaimed independent statehood, but has not been recognized as a state by the U.S. Serbia and Montenegro have asserted the formation of a joint independent state, but this entity has not been recognized as a state by the U.S.

[Midyear population in thousands.]

Country	Women				Currently married women			
	1990	1994	1995	2000	1990	1994	1995	2000
(Former) Yugoslavia								
Bosnia and Herzegovina	1,195	1,241	1,256	1,296	818	865	879	918
Croatia	1,136	1,145	1,153	1,153	802	810	815	815
Macedonia	548	575	582	606	374	394	400	419

[Continued]

★ 803 ★

Yugoslavian and Soviet Union Married Women: 1990-2000
[Continued]

Country	Women				Currently married women			
	1990	1994	1995	2000	1990	1994	1995	2000
Serbia and Montenegro	2,538	2,619	2,643	2,695	1,759	1,812	1,831	1,874
Slovenia	489	496	500	501	344	348	351	354
(Former) Soviet Union								
BALTICS								
Estonia	384	397	402	417	242	249	252	260
Latvia	654	663	669	696	413	419	423	434
Lithuania	928	946	954	990	603	620	626	647
COMMONWEALTH OF INDEPENDENT STATES								
Armenia	844	876	888	926	574	600	608	626
Azerbaijan	1,828	1,967	2,012	2,199	1,126	1,250	1,284	1,403
Belarus	2,466	2,550	2,583	2,667	1,692	1,757	1,780	1,815
Kazakhstan	4,183	4,430	4,513	4,755	2,733	2,907	2,968	3,118
Kyrgystan	1,026	1,133	1,164	1,302	675	753	777	864
Moldova	1,105	1,142	1,159	1,208	774	796	807	831
Russia	36,026	37,553	38,157	39,182	24,360	25,229	25,601	25,887
Tajikistan	1,193	1,357	1,406	1,654	810	936	972	1,136
Turkmenistan	872	981	1,012	1,156	547	625	674	741
Ukraine	12,307	12,497	12,627	12,808	8,510	8,647	8,740	8,807
Uzbekistan	4,787	5,382	5,559	6,413	3,226	3,670	3,799	4,363
GEORGIA	1,353	1,404	1,423	1,480	882	924	939	975

Source: Selected from "All Women and Currently Married Women of Reproductive Age (15 to 49 Years), by Country or Area: 1990 to 2000," U.S. Bureau of the Census, *World Population Profile: 1994*, 1994, Table 5, p. A-17. Primary source: U.S. Bureau of the Census, International Data Base. The category "currently married women" includes women in consensual unions. Estimates are based on component projections of the female population and the percent of women who are married or in consensual unions in each 5-year age group from the most recent source in the International Data Base.

Marriages and Divorces

★ 804 ★

African Divorces

This table shows the total number of divorces in selected African countries for the years 1987 through 1991 (as available). Divorce rates, the number of final divorce decrees granted under civil law per 1,000 mid-year population, are also shown.

Country	Number					Rate				
	1987	1988	1989	1990	1991	1987	1988	1989	1990	1991
Africa										
Libya										
Libyan Arab Jamahiriya[1]	2,889	2,264	--	--	--	0.79	0.60	--	--	--
Mauritius										
Island of	842	740	711	692	--	0.84	0.73	0.69	0.67	--
Reunion	694	629	780	753	--	1.23	1.10	1.35	1.27	--
St. Helena										
excl. dependents	7	13	17	5	--	--	--	--	--	--
Seychelles	--	--	45	47	86	--	--	--	--	--
Tunisia	8,381	10,395	12,695	--	--	1.10	1.34	1.60	--	--

Source: Selected from "Divorces and crude divorce rates: 1987-1991," United Nations, *Demographic Yearbook*, 1991, Table 25, pp. 508-511. Data exclude annulments and legal separations unless otherwise specified. Rates are shown only for countries or areas having at least a total 100 divorces in a given year. 1991 data are provisional. *Note:* 1. Data are estimated to be incomplete (less than 90%).

★ 805 ★

Marriages and Divorces

African Marriages by Age-I

This table shows the total number of marriages in selected African countries for the latest available year and the number of marriages by age of the bride and groom, for brides and grooms aged under 15 through age 34. The legal age of marriage is also shown.

Country	Age[1]	All ages	Under 15	15-19	20-24	25-29	30-34
Algeria							
1980[2]							
Groom	--	128,424	5,966	[4]	40,731	47,811	15,035
Bride	--	128,424	283	54,867	45,276	16,722	4,631

[Continued]

★ 805 ★

African Marriages by Age-I
[Continued]

Country	Age[1]	All ages	Under 15	15-19	20-24	25-29	30-34
Botswana							
1986							
Groom	--	1,638	--	--	35	502	519
Bride	--	1,638	--	82	597	536	223
Egypt							
1986[3]							
Groom	18	405,830	24,000	[4]	108,803	142,004	70,770
Bride	16	405,830	163,980	[4]	141,440	58,064	19,204
Mauritius							
Island of Mauritius							
1990							
Groom	16	11,252	--	172	2,449	4,325	2,238
Bride	16	11,252	2	2,439	4,302	2,482	1,078
Reunion							
1990							
Groom	--	3,716	--	44	1,034	1,390	560
Bride	--	3,716	--	464	1,503	978	385
Tunisia							
1989							
Groom	20	55,163	--	239	11,246	23,864	12,603
Bride	17	55,163	--	11,845	24,756	12,080	3,906

Source: Selected from "Marriages by age of bridegroom and by age of bride: latest available year," United Nations, *Demographic Yearbook*, 1991, Table 24, pp. 497+. Data are legal (recognized) marriages performed and registered. *Notes:* 1. Age below which marriage is unlawful or invalid without dispensation by competent authority. 2. For Algerian population only. 3. Including marriages resumed after "revocable divorce" (among Moslem population), which approximates legal separation. 4. Includes ages under 15 through 19.

★ 806 ★

Marriages and Divorces

African Marriages by Age-II

This table shows the total number of marriages in selected African countries for the latest available year and the number of marriages by age of the bride and groom, for brides and grooms aged 35-60+. The legal age of marriage is also shown.

Country	Age[1]	All ages	35-39	40-44	45-49	50-54	55-59	60+	Unknown
Algeria									
1980[2]									
Groom	--	128,424	5,955	3,657	2,735	5,284	[4]	[4]	1,250
Bride	--	128,424	1,934	1,403	869	513	[4]	[4]	1,926

[Continued]

★ 806 ★

African Marriages by Age-II
[Continued]

Country	Age[1]	All ages	35-39	40-44	45-49	50-54	55-59	60+	Unknown
Botswana									
1986									
Groom	--	1,638	251	137	4	4	194	4	--
Bride	--	1,638	89	111	4	4	4	4	--
Egypt									
1986[3]									
Groom	18	405,830	24,494	10,120	7,680	5,376	4,862	7,577	144
Bride	16	405,830	9,373	4,123	2,850	1,637	1,165	3,961	33
Mauritius									
Island of Mauritius									
1990									
Groom	16	11,252	1,020	466	225	148	93	116	--
Bride	16	11,252	500	221	100	60	33	35	--
Reunion									
1990									
Groom	--	3,716	293	130	78	57	43	87	--
Bride	--	3,716	157	82	52	35	17	43	--
Tunisia									
1989									
Groom	20	55,163	3,376	1,040	671	614	478	1,032	--
Bride	17	55,163	1,381	485	224	162	152	169	--

Source: Selected from "Marriages by age of bridegroom and by age of bride: latest available year," United Nations, *Demographic Yearbook*, 1991, Table 24, pp. 497+. Data are legal (recognized) marriages performed and registered. *Notes:* 1. Age below which marriage is unlawful or invalid without dispensation by competent authority. 2. For Algerian population only. 3. Including marriages resumed after "revocable divorce" (among Moslem population), which approximates legal separation. 4. Figure in preceding column includes this age group.

★ 807 ★

Marriages and Divorces

African Marriages: 1987-1991

This table shows the total number of marriages in Africa and the marriage rate, for available years between 1987 and 1991. Rates are the number of legal (recognized) marriages performed and registered per 1,000 mid-year population. Rates are shown only for countries or areas having at least a total of 100 marriages in a given year.

Country	Number					Rate				
	1987	1988	1989	1990	1991	1987	1988	1989	1990	1991
Africa										
Botswana	1,862	--	--	--	--	1.6	--	--	--	--
Libya										
Libyan Arab										
Jamahiriya[1]	17,862	16,989	--	--	--	4.9	4.5	--	--	--
Mauritius[2]	11,201	11,283	11,040	11,252	11,295	11.2	11.1	10.8	10.9	10.6
Rodrigues[2]	191	170	157	173	--	5.2	4.7	4.2	4.6	--
Reunion	3,001	3,354	3,553	3,831	--	5.3	5.8	6.0	6.4	--
St. Helena										
excl. dependents	28	32	23	--	--	--	--	--	--	--
Sao Tome and Principe[1]	56	49	--	--	--	--	--	--	--	--
Seychelles[2]	622	--	777	1,037	931	9.4	--	11.6	15.4	13.5
Swaziland[3]	2,270	2,556	3,115	--	--	3.2	3.5	4.1	--	--
Tunisia	49,452	50,026	55,163	55,612	--	6.5	6.4	7.0	6.9	--

Source: Selected from "Marriages and crude marriage rates, by urban/rural residence: 1987-1991," United Nations, *Demographic Yearbook*, 1991, Table 23, pp. 490+. 1991 figures are provisional. *Notes:* 1. Data are estimated to be incomplete (less than 90%). 2. Data are estimated to be virtually complete (at least 90%). 3. Marriages solemnized by Christian rite only.

★ 808 ★

Marriages and Divorces

Age at Marriage and Previous Marital Status: 1980-1988

This table shows the percent distribution of marriages by age of the woman and previous marital status, in 1980 and 1988.

Previous marital status	Total	Under 20 years old	20-24 years old	25-29 years old	30-34 years old	35-44 years old	45-64 years old	65 years old and over
Women								
All marriages[1]								
1980	100.0%	21.1%	37.1%	18.7%	9.3%	7.8%	5.0%	1.0%
1988	100.0%	11.8%	31.5%	24.1%	13.2%	12.6%	5.8%	1.0%
First marriages[2]								
1980	100.0%	30.4%	47.3%	16.0%	4.0%	1.6%	0.6%	0.1%
1988	100.0%	17.7%	43.3%	26.1%	8.5%	3.7%	0.7%	0.1%

[Continued]

★ 808 ★
Age at Marriage and Previous Marital Status: 1980-1988
[Continued]

Previous marital status	Total	Under 20 years old	20-24 years old	25-29 years old	30-34 years old	35-44 years old	45-64 years old	65 years old and over
Remarriages[2,3]								
1980	100.0%	1.7%	15.3%	24.4%	20.6%	20.8%	14.3%	2.9%
1988	100.0%	0.7%	9.1%	20.5%	21.9%	29.5%	15.4%	2.8%
Previously divorced[4]								
1980	100.0%	1.7%	16.7%	26.7%	22.5%	21.6%	10.0%	0.6%
1988	100.0%	0.8%	9.8%	22.2%	23.3%	30.7%	12.5%	0.6%

Source: Selected from "Percent Distribution of Marriages, by Age, Sex, and Previous Marital Status: 1980 to 1988," U.S. Bureau of the Census, *Statistical Abstract of the United States, 1994,* table 141, p. 103. Data cover marriage registration area. Based on a sample and subject to sampling variability. *Notes:* 1. Includes marriage order not stated. 2. Excludes data for Iowa. 3. Includes remarriages of previously widowed. 4. Excludes remarriages in Michigan, Ohio, and South Carolina.

★ 809 ★
Marriages and Divorces
Asian Divorces

This table shows the total number of divorces in selected Asian countries for the years 1987 through 1991. Divorce rates, the number of final divorce decrees granted under civil law per 1,000 mid-year population, are also shown.

Country	Number					Rate				
	1987	1988	1989	1990	1991	1987	1988	1989	1990	1991
Asia										
Armenia	4,240	3,997	4,134	--	--	1.23	1.18	1.26	--	--
Azerbaijan	8,511	9,226	11,436	--	--	1.24	1.32	1.61	--	--
Bahrain	626	615	726	590	--	1.37	1.30	1.49	1.17	--
Brunei Darussalam	198	190	190	--	--	0.85	0.79	0.76	--	--
Cyprus	326	312	335	350	300	0.48	0.45	0.48	0.50	0.42
Georgia	6,766	7,082	7,358	--	--	1.28	1.32	1.35	--	--
Hong Kong	5,055	--	--	5,551	--	0.90	--	--	0.96	--
Iran Islamic Rep. of	33,433	33,114	33,943	37,827	--	0.65	0.63	0.63	0.69	--
Israel[2]	5,218	5,592	5,829	6,000	--	1.19	1.26	1.29	1.29	--
Japan[3]	158,227	153,600	157,811	157,608	--	1.29	1.25	1.28	1.27	--
Jordan[4]	3,709	4,646	4,694	--	--	1.02	1.24	1.21	--	--
Kazakhstan	46,466	45,942	45,772	--	--	2.84	2.78	2.75	--	--
Korea Rep. of[1,5]	38,283	36,479	32,474	--	--	0.92	0.87	0.77	--	--
Kuwait	2,697	2,834	2,987	--	--	1.44	1.45	1.46	--	--
Kyrgyzstan	7,810	8,207	8,231	--	--	1.86	1.92	1.90	--	--

[Continued]

★ 809 ★

Asian Divorces
[Continued]

Country	Number					Rate				
	1987	1988	1989	1990	1991	1987	1988	1989	1990	1991
Macau	37	33	70	95	--	--	--	--	--	--
Maldives	--	--	--	1,706	--	--	--	--	7.93	--
Mongolia	1,000	1,700	1,000	--	--	0.51	0.84	0.48	--	--
Qatar	337	385	406	359	1.03	0.90	0.89	0.74	--	
Singapore	2,339	2,536	--	--	4,419	0.89	0.96	--	--	1.60
Sri Lanka[1]	3,194	2,732	--	--	--	0.19	0.16	--	--	--
Syria										
Syrian Arab Rep.[6]	7,249	8,486	8,568	8,335	--	0.66	0.75	0.73	0.69	--
Tajikistan	7,344	7,509	7,576	--	--	1.50	1.49	1.46	--	--
Turkey	18,305	22,513	25,376	--	--	0.34	0.41	0.45	--	--
Turkmenistan	4,909	4,956	4,940	--	--	1.44	1.42	1.38	--	--
Uzbekistan	29,169	30,965	29,953	--	--	1.51	1.57	1.49	--	--

Source: Selected from "Divorces and crude divorce rates: 1987-1991," United Nations, *Demographic Yearbook*, 1991, Table 25, pp. 508-511. Data exclude annulments and legal separations unless otherwise specified. Rates are shown only for countries or areas having at least a total 100 divorces in a given year. 1991 data are provisional. *Notes:* 1. Data are estimated to be incomplete (less than 90%). 2. Including data for East Jerusalem and Israeli residents in certain other territories under occupation by Israeli military forces since June 1967. 3. For Japanese nationals in Japan only; however, rates computed on total population. 4. Excluding data for Jordanian territory under occupation since June 1967 by Israeli military forces. Excluding foreigner but including registered Palestinian refugess. 5. Excluding alien armed forces, civilian aliens employed by armed forces, and foreign diplomatic personnel and their dependents. 6. Excluding nomads; however, rates computed on total population.

★ 810 ★
Marriages and Divorces

Asian Marriages by Age-I

This table shows the total number of marriages in selected Asian countries for the latest available year and the number of marriages by age of the bride and groom, for brides and grooms aged under 15 through age 34. The legal age of marriage is also shown (when provided by source).

Country	Age[1]	All ages	Under 15	15-19	20-24	25-29	30-34
Asia							
Armenia							
1989							
Groom	--	27,257	6	731	11,313	9,682	2,795
Bride	--	27,257	393	8,883	11,185	3,578	1,415
Azerbaijan							
1989							
Groom	--	71,874	18	829	29,164	28,656	7,170
Bride	--	71,874	422	17,418	33,012	12,923	4,022

[Continued]

★ 810 ★

Asian Marriages by Age-I
[Continued]

Country	Age[1]	All ages	Under 15	15-19	20-24	25-29	30-34
Bahrain							
1990							
Groom	--	2,942	--	52	966	1,087	388
Bride	--	2,942	40	732	1,255	507	238
Brunei Darussalam							
1986							
Groom	[9]	1,673	--	73	628	552	252
Bride	[9]	1,673	12	181	523	534	312
Cyprus							
1989[3]							
Groom	17	5,597	--	47	1,752	2,195	910
Bride	15	5,597	996	[2]	2,428	1,264	441
Georgia							
1989							
Groom	--	38,288	131	2,068	13,431	11,929	5,068
Bride	--	38,288	1,015	9,615	14,609	6,721	2,849
Hong Kong							
1989							
Groom	16	43,947	--	259	5,373	16,868	10,207
Bride	16	43,947	--	1,447	12,452	16,648	5,249
Israel							
1989[4]							
Groom	[10]	32,303	1,090	[2]	11,640	12,232	4,143
Bride	[10]	32,303	7,432	[2]	15,135	6,162	1,886
Japan							
1990[5]							
Groom	18	653,415	7,704	[2]	120,572	282,951	143,637
Bride	16	653,415	22,457	[2]	236,677	283,370	62,761
Jordan							
1989[6]							
Groom	18	31,508	--	1,566	12,038	11,512	3,249
Bride	16	31,508	--	12,655	12,690	4,427	1,005
Kazakhstan							
1989							
Groom	--	165,380	20	6,242	83,301	42,420	14,104
Bride	--	165,380	2,989	40,015	72,013	24,288	10,565

[Continued]

★ 810 ★

Asian Marriages by Age-I
[Continued]

Country	Age[1]	All ages	Under 15	15-19	20-24	25-29	30-34
Korea							
Rep. of							
1989							
Groom	18	309,872	--	865	40,247	198,541	53,245
Bride	16	309,872	--	8,328	156,497	120,911	15,109
Kuwait							
1989							
Groom	18	11,051	356	[2]	4,113	3,562	1,446
Bride	15	11,051	71	3,377	4,705	1,624	616
Kyrgyzstan							
1989							
Groom	--	41,790	--	918	23,127	11,294	2,753
Bride	--	41,790	416	12,034	19,887	4,996	1,862
Macau							
1990							
Groom	--	1,794	--	1	193	760	536
Bride	--	1,794	--	25	496	796	353
Philippines							
1989							
Groom	16	393,514	--	32,708	149,876	124,482	46,855
Bride	14	393,514	1,108	101,178	155,057	85,048	28,793
Qatar							
1990							
Groom	--	1,370	66	[2]	502	479	186
Bride	--	1,370	451	[2]	569	234	71
Singapore							
1988							
Groom	[9]	24,853	--	97	4,908	11,607	5,500
Bride	[9]	24,853	--	1,266	10,773	8,895	2,633
Sri Lanka							
1985[7]							
Groom	--	128,858	1	669	41,434	46,880	25,141
Bride	--	128,858	408	20,494	65,680	26,658	10,061
Tajikistan							
1989							
Groom	--	47,616	31	963	30,954	10,390	2,190
Bride	--	47,616	225	18,362	21,675	4,201	1,430

[Continued]

★ 810 ★

Asian Marriages by Age-I
[Continued]

Country	Age[1]	All ages	Under 15	15-19	20-24	25-29	30-34
Turkey							
1988[8]							
Groom	17	448,144	--	38,062	190,855	149,091	38,892
Bride	15	448,144	1,553	160,437	188,270	65,041	17,440
Turkmenistan							
1989							
Groom	--	34,890	50	1,006	22,170	8,317	1,665
Bride	--	34,890	271	5,336	20,713	6,171	1,221
Uzbekistan							
1989							
Groom	--	200,681	295	4,266	135,880	39,552	8,628
Bride	--	200,681	13,982	62,079	93,126	17,697	6,420

Source: Selected from "Marriages by age of bridegroom and by age of bride: latest available year," United Nations, *Demographic Yearbook*, 1991, Table 24, pp. 497+. Data are legal (recognized) marriages performed and registered. *Notes:* 1. Age below which marriage is unlawful or invalid without dispensation by competent authority. 2. Figure in preceding column includes this age group. 3. For government controlled areas. 4. Including data for East Jerusalem and Israeli residents in certain other territories under occupation by Israeli military forces since June 1967. 5. For Japanese nationals in Japan only. For grooms and brides married for the first time whose marriages occurred and were registered in the same year. 6. Excluding data for Jordanian territory under occupation since June 1967 by Israeli military forces. Excluding foreigners but including registered Palestinian refugees. 7. For under 16 and 16-19 years, as appropriate. 8. For provincial capitals and district centers only. 9. Varies among major civil divisions, or ethnic or religious groups. 10. No minimum age has been fixed for males.

★ 811 ★

Marriages and Divorces

Asian Marriages by Age-II

This table shows the total number of marriages in selected Asian countries for the latest available year and the number of marriages by age of the bride and groom, for brides and grooms aged under 35-60+. The legal age of marriage is also shown (when provided by source).

Country	Age[1]	All ages	35-39	40-44	45-49	50-54	55-59	60+	Unknown
Asia									
Armenia									
1989									
Groom	--	27,257	909	432	328	395	257	407	2
Bride	--	27,257	676	305	231	233	157	201	--
Azerbaijan									
1989									
Groom	--	71,874	2,151	939	634	805	598	909	1
Bride	--	71,874	1,572	677	403	534	346	541	4

[Continued]

★ 811 ★

Asian Marriages by Age-II
[Continued]

Country	Age[1]	All ages	35-39	40-44	45-49	50-54	55-59	60+	Unknown
Bahrain 1990									
Groom	--	2,942	187	80	40	111	2	2	31
Bride	--	2,942	68	27	15	18	2	2	42
Brunei Darussalam 1986									
Groom	9	1,673	80	40	19	9	5	15	--
Bride	9	1,673	82	9	13	2	2	3	--
Cyprus 1989[3]									
Groom	17	5,597	283	149	80	66	45	70	--
Bride	15	5,597	211	116	74	23	15	29	--
Georgia 1989									
Groom	--	38,288	2,358	952	578	581	453	739	--
Bride	--	38,288	1,272	587	359	451	368	442	--
Hong Kong 1989									
Groom	16	43,947	3,143	1,269	729	900	1,429	3,770	--
Bride	16	43,947	1,580	821	689	1,119	1,628	2,314	--
Israel 1989[4]									
Groom	10	32,303	1,540	656	302	208	157	306	29
Bride	10	32,303	851	335	149	104	79	126	44
Japan 1990[5]									
Groom	18	653,415	51,997	24,058	10,229	5,569	3,463	3,228	7
Bride	16	653,415	22,340	12,411	6,930	3,532	1,760	1,175	2
Jordan 1989[6]									
Groom	18	31,508	1,125	614	496	359	228	317	4
Bride	16	31,508	356	184	84	43	30	18	16
Kazakhstan 1989									
Groom	--	165,380	6,605	3,379	2,218	2,603	1,449	3,004	35
Bride	--	165,380	5,418	2,616	1,810	2,204	1,193	2,213	56

[Continued]

★ 811 ★

Asian Marriages by Age-II
[Continued]

Country	Age[1]	All ages	35-39	40-44	45-49	50-54	55-59	60+	Unknown
Korea									
Rep. of									
1989									
Groom	18	309,872	7,871	3,597	2,166	1,411	1,929	[2]	--
Bride	16	309,872	4,192	2,062	1,349	743	681	[2]	--
Kuwait									
1989									
Groom	18	11,051	567	295	239	148	138	177	10
Bride	15	11,051	305	143	52	72	41	37	8
Kyrgyzstan									
1989									
Groom	--	41,790	1,247	569	448	481	330	611	12
Bride	--	41,790	878	408	294	363	243	400	9
Macau									
1990									
Groom	--	1,794	178	70	17	13	13	13	--
Bride	--	1,794	79	17	12	7	5	4	--
Philippines									
1989									
Groom	16	393,514	17,994	7,809	4,790	9,000	[2]	[2]	--
Bride	14	393,514	11,087	4,663	2,617	3,947	[2]	[2]	16
Qatar									
1990									
Groom	--	1,370	64	31	10	11	7	12	--
Bride	--	1,370	29	8	3	2	--	--	--
Singapore									
1988									
Groom	[9]	24,853	1,640	558	233	136	73	101	--
Bride	[9]	24,853	816	272	105	49	20	24	--
Sri Lánka									
1985[7]									
Groom	--	128,858	9,250	2,635	1,157	652	463	576	--
Bride	--	128,858	3,380	967	560	295	202	153	--
Tajikistan									
1989									
Groom	--	47,616	1,058	483	398	415	294	423	--
Bride	--	47,616	630	282	194	234	126	242	--

[Continued]

★ 811 ★

Asian Marriages by Age-II

[Continued]

Country	Age[1]	All ages	35-39	40-44	45-49	50-54	55-59	60+	Unknown
Turkey 1988[8]									
Groom	17	448,144	12,372	5,428	3,626	2,661	2,947	4,159	--
Bride	15	448,144	6,575	3,137	1,811	1,312	1,165	1,355	--
Turkmenistan 1989									
Groom	--	34,890	682	289	219	182	113	191	--
Bride	--	34,890	470	193	153	142	78	138	--
Uzbekistan 1989									
Groom	--	200,681	4,213	2,035	1,551	1,575	1,011	1,621	--
Bride	--	200,681	2,785	1,191	845	989	569	922	--

Source: Selected from "Marriages by age of bridegroom and by age of bride: latest available year," United Nations, *Demographic Yearbook*, 1991, Table 24, pp. 497+. Data are legal (recognized) marriages performed and registered. *Notes:* 1. Age below which marriage is unlawful or invalid without dispensation by competent authority. 2. Figure in preceding column includes this age group. 3. For government controlled areas. 4. Including data for East Jerusalem and Israeli residents in certain other territories under occupation by Israeli military forces since June 1967. 5. For Japanese nationals in Japan only. For grooms and brides married for the first time whose marriages occurred and were registered in the same year. 6. Excluding data for Jordanian territory under occupation since June 1967 by Israeli military forces. Excluding foreigners but including registered Palestinian refugees. 7. For under 16 and 16-19 years, as appropriate. 8. For provincial capitals and district centers only. 9. Varies among major civil divisions, or ethnic or religious groups. 10. No minimum age has been fixed for males.

★ 812 ★

Marriages and Divorces

Asian Marriages: 1987-1991

This table shows the total number of marriages in Asia and the marriage rate, for available years between 1987 and 1991. Rates are the number of legal (recognized) marriages performed and registered per 1,000 mid-year population. Rates are shown only for countries or areas having at least a total of 100 marriages in a given year.

Country	Number					Rate				
	1987	1988	1989	1990	1991	1987	1988	1989	1990	1991
Asia										
Armenia	30,259	26,581	27,257	--	--	8.8	7.9	8.3	--	--
Azerbaijan	68,031	68,887	71,874	--	--	9.9	9.9	10.1	--	--
Bahrain	2,919	3,110	3,033	2,942	--	6.4	6.6	6.2	5.8	--
Bangladesh	1,177,019	1,183,710	--	--	--	11.5	11.3	--	--	--
Brunei Darussalam	1,845	1,794	1,783	--	--	7.9	7.4	7.2	--	--
Cyprus[2]	5,954	3,304	5,597	6,500	7,000	8.7	4.8	8.1	9.3	9.9
Hong Kong	48,561	45,238	43,947	47,168	--	8.6	8.0	7.6	8.1	--
Israel[3]	30,116	31,218	32,303	32,500	--	6.9	7.0	7.1	7.0	--
Japan[4]	696,173	707,716	708,316	722,138	742,281	5.7	5.8	5.8	5.8	6.0
Kazakhstan	160,909	162,962	165,380	--	--	9.8	9.9	10.0	--	--

[Continued]

★ 812 ★

Asian Marriages: 1987-1991
[Continued]

Country	Number					Rate				
	1987	1988	1989	1990	1991	1987	1988	1989	1990	1991
Korea										
Rep. of[1]	366,937	368,119	309,872	--	--	8.8	8.8	7.3	--	--
Kyrgyzstan	40,161	40,490	41,790	--	--	9.6	9.5	9.7	--	--
Macau	2,472	2,282	1,728	1,794	--	5.8	5.2	3.9	3.7	--
Malaysia[1,5]										
Peninsular Malaysia	42,456	44,904	--	--	--	3.1	3.2	--	--	--
Maldives	--	--	--	2,280	--	--	--	--	10.6	--
Mongolia	19,100	21,800	15,600	--	--	9.7	10.8	7.5	--	--
Philippines[1]	400,760	393,514	302,109	--	--	7.0	6.7	5.0	--	--
Qatar	1,349	1,333	1,330	1,370	--	4.1	3.1	2.9	2.8	--
Singapore[6,7]	23,404	24,853	--	--	24,791	9.0	9.4	--	--	9.0
Sri Lanka[1]	129,571	130,889	141,533	--	--	7.9	7.9	8.4	--	--
Syria										
Syrian Arab Rep.[8]	102,626	99,323	102,557	91,346	--	9.4	8.8	8.8	7.5	--
Tajikistan	46,233	46,933	47,616	--	--	9.5	9.3	9.2	--	--
Thailand	--	391,124	406,134	461,280	--	--	7.2	7.4	8.2	--
Turkmenistan	31,484	33,008	34,890	--	--	9.2	9.4	9.8	--	--
Uzbekistan	189,557	193,856	200,681	--	--	9.8	9.8	10.0	--	--

Source: Selected from "Marriages and crude marriage rates, by urban/rural residence: 1987-1991," United Nations, *Demographic Yearbook*, 1991, Table 23, pp. 490+. 1991 figures are provisional. *Notes:* 1. Data are estimated to be incomplete (less than 90%). 2. For government controlled areas. 1990 data are provisional. 3. Including data for East Jerusalem and Israeli residents in certain other territories under occupation by Israeli military forces since June 1967. 4. For Japanese nationals in Japan only, but rates computed on total population. 5. Non-Moslem civil marriages and Christian ritual marriages only. 6. Rates computed on population excluding transients afloat and non-locally domiciled military and civilian services personnel and their dependents. 7. Registration of Kandyan marriages is complete; registration of Moslem and general marriages is incomplete. 8. Excluding nomads; however, rates computed on total population.

★ 813 ★
Marriages and Divorces

Average Age at Marriage Worldwide

This table shows the average age of women at first marriage in countries where the average age at first marriage for women is still below 20 years. Data refer mainly to the early 1980s. When women begin working as homemakers at a very young age, they tend not to finish secondary school or work outside the home.

Country	Avg. age at 1st marriage
Africa	
Benin	18.2
Burkina Faso	17.4
Cameroon	17.5
Comoros	19.5

[Continued]

★ 813 ★

Average Age at Marriage Worldwide
[Continued]

Country	Avg. age at 1st marriage
Cote d'Ivoire	17.8
Ethiopia	17.7
Ghana	19.3
Lesotho	19.6
Malawi	17.8
Mali	18.1
Mauritania	19.2
Mozambique	17.6
Nigeria	18.7
Senegal	17.7
Zambia	19.4
Latin America/Caribbean	
Cuba	19.9
Asia	
Afghanistan	17.8
Bangladesh	16.7
India	18.7
Iran (Islamic Rep. of)	19.7
Nepal	17.9
Pakistan	19.8
United Arab Emirates	18.0
Yemen	17.8

Source: "Where average age at first marriage for women is still below 20 years," *The World's Women: Trends and Statistics 1970-1990*, United Nations, 1991, Table 1.7, p. 14. Primary source: Population Division of the United Nations Secretariat and World Fertility Survey.

★ 814 ★

Marriages and Divorces

Breakups of Two-Parent Families

This table shows the percentage of poor and not-poor two-parent families that discontinued within two years of forming during the mid-1980s. Economic stress can cause families to break up. When two-parent families do break up, low income and unemployment often result. About 1 in every 12 two-parent families that existed at the beginning of a typical two-year period no longer existed two years later. The family joined a different household that already existed, or the spouses separated, or one died. The usual result was that a new single-parent family came into being. Of every four mother-child families, one did not exist two years later. This type of family usually discontinued as a result of marriage (a new two-parent family formed) or when the mother and her children joined a household that already existed, such as a household maintained by the mother's parents.

Family type	Poor	Not poor
Total	13%	7%
White	12%	7%
Black	21%	11%
Hispanic origin (of any race)	11%	9%

Source: Selected from U.S. Bureau of the Census, *Population Profile of the United States: 1993,* Special Studies Series P23-185, Figure 17, p. 18, "Percent of Poor Two-Parent Families that Discontinued Within 2 Years: Mid-1980's." Two-year family changes are estimated by combining results from the 1984 and 1985 SIPP panels, which cover two different biennial periods between December 1983 and April 1987. Poverty status refers to the beginning of 2-year periods.

★ 815 ★

Marriages and Divorces

Divorce Rates in 5 Countries: 1920-1985

This table shows rates of final civil divorce decrees granted in five countries from 1920 to 1985. Divorce rates had begun rising even before liberalized laws went into effect in the 1970s. Rates climbed until the 1980s, then stabilized at fairly high levels. Rates in the United States have been consistently higher than in the other four countries. The low Swedish rate should be understood in a context in which marriage and divorce behavior is "informal."

[Rates per 1,000 mid-year population. NA Not available.]

Country	1920-1924	1930-1934	1940	1950	1960	1970	1975	1980	1985
England and Wales	0.07	0.1	0.18	0.7	0.51	1.17	2.43	3.01	3.20
France	0.67	0.51	0.28	0.84	0.61	0.79	1.27	1.59	1.95
Germany	0.59	0.67	0.75	NA	NA	NA	NA	NA	NA
West Germany	NA	NA	NA	1.57	0.83	1.24	1.73	1.56	2.10

[Continued]

★ 815 ★

Divorce Rates in 5 Countries: 1920-1985
[Continued]

Country	1920-1924	1930-1934	1940	1950	1960	1970	1975	1980	1985
Sweden	0.25	0.40	0.55	1.14	1.20	1.61	3.14	2.41	2.37
United States	1.48	1.47	2.00	2.55	2.18	3.51	4.82	5.19	4.96

Source: "Divorce Rates, 1920-1985," Mary Ann Glendon, *The Transformation of Family Law: State, Law and Family in the United States and Western Europe,* (Chicago and London: U. of Chicago Press). Primary source: United Nations Demographic Yearbooks, 1953, 1962, 1968, 1972, 1980, 1986 (New York: United Nations).

★ 816 ★

Marriages and Divorces

European Divorces

This table shows the total number of divorces in selected European countries for the years 1987 through 1991. Divorce rates, the number of final divorce decrees granted under civil law per 1,000 mid-year population, are also shown.

Country	Number					Rate				
	1987	1988	1989	1990	1991	1987	1988	1989	1990	1991
Europe										
Albania	2,537	2,597	2,628	--	--	0.82	0.83	0.82	--	--
Austria[1]	14,639	14,924	15,489	16,282	--	1.93	1.96	2.03	2.11	--
Belarus	30,507	32,111	34,573	--	--	3.02	2.98	3.38	--	--
Bulgaria[2]	11,687	12,359	12,611	11,341	--	1.30	1.38	1.40	1.26	--
Channel Islands	358	403	358	--	382	2.63	2.88	2.60	--	2.67
Guernsey	153	165	172	196	173	2.76	2.77	2.89	3.29	2.94
Jersey	205	238	186	--	209	2.55	2.97	2.25	--	2.48
Czechoslovakia	39,522	38,922	39,680	40,922	37,259	2.54	2.49	2.54	2.61	2.39
Denmark[3]	14,381	14,717	15,152	--	--	2.80	2.87	2.95	--	--
Estonia	6,128	5,924	5,916	5,785	--	3.96	3.80	3.77	3.68	--
Faeroe Islands	45	43	52	--	--	--	--	--	--	--
Finland[4]	10,110	12,146	14,365	--	--	2.05	2.45	2.89	--	--
France[5]	106,527	106,096	105,295	105,813	--	1.91	1.90	1.87	1.87	--
Germany[6]										
Fed. Rep. of	129,850	128,729	126,628	122,869	--	2.12	2.09	2.04	1.94	--
Former G. Dem. Rep.	50,640	49,380	50,063	--	--	3.04	2.96	3.01	--	--
Hungary	29,846	23,853	24,935	24,863	--	2.85	2.28	2.40	2.40	--
Iceland[7]	477	459	520	479	580	1.94	1.84	2.06	1.88	2.25
Isle of Man	305	183	190	--	--	4.75	2.74	2.80	--	--
Italy[8]	27,072	25,092	30,314	27,836	--	0.47	0.44	0.53	0.48	--
Latvia	10,709	10,890	11,249	--	--	4.05	4.08	4.19	--	--
Liechtenstein	--	--	29	--	--	--	--	--	--	--
Lithuania	11,726	11,682	12,295	--	--	3.24	3.20	3.33	--	--
Luxembourg	739	779	855	--	--	1.99	2.09	2.27	--	--

[Continued]

★ 816 ★

European Divorces
[Continued]

Country	Number					Rate				
	1987	1988	1989	1990	1991	1987	1988	1989	1990	1991
Netherlands	27,788	27,870	28,250	28,419	28,300	1.89	1.89	1.90	1.90	1.88
Moldova										
Rep. of	11,598	12,085	12,401	--	--	2.70	2.80	2.85	--	--Norway
Poland	49,707	48,211	47,189	42,436	35,000	1.32	1.27	1.24	1.11	0.91
Portugal	8,948	9,022	9,657	9,216	10,649	0.90	0.91	0.98	0.93	1.01
Romania	34,110	36,775	36,008	32,966	--	1.49	1.59	1.55	1.42	--
Russia										
Russian Federation	580,106	573,863	582,500	--	--	3.98	3.90	3.94	--	--
San Marino	22	23	22	--	--	--	--	--	--	--
Spain	--	--	--	--	23,063	--	--	--	--	0.59
Sweden	18,426	17,746	18,862	19,357	19,000	2.19	2.10	2.22	2.26	2.20
Switzerland	11,552	12,731	12,720	13,183	--	1.76	1.93	1.91	1.96	--
Ukraine	184,720	185,357	193,676	192,800	--	3.60	3.59	3.74	3.71	--
United Kingdom	164,208	165,043	163,942	165,658	--	2.88	2.89	2.86	2.88	--
Yugoslavia	22,907	23,127	22,761	19,418	--	0.98	0.98	0.96	0.81	--

Source: Selected from "Divorces and crude divorce rates: 1987-1991," United Nations, *Demographic Yearbook*, 1991, Table 25, pp. 508-511. Data exclude annulments and legal separations unless otherwise specified. Rates are shown only for countries or areas having at least a total 100 divorces in a given year. 1991 data are provisional. *Notes:* 1. Excluding aliens temporarily in the area. 2. Including Bulgarian nationals outside the country, but excluding aliens in the area. 3. Excluding Faeroe Islands and Greenland. 4. Including nationals temporarily outside the country. 5. Rates computed on population including armed forces stationed outside the country, but excluding alien armed forces living in military camps within the country. 6. All data shown pertaining to Germany prior to October 3, 1990 are indicated separately for the Federal Republic of Germany and the former German Democratic Republic based on their respective territories at the time indicated. 7. For the de jure population. 8. Data from civil registers which are incomplete or of unknown completeness.

★ 817 ★

Marriages and Divorces

European Marriages by Age-I

This table shows the total number of marriages in selected European countries for the latest available year and the number of marriages by age of the bride and groom, for brides and grooms aged under 15 through age 34. The legal age of marriage is also shown (when provided in source document).

Country	Age[1]	All ages	Under 15	15-19	20-24	25-29	30-34
Europe							
Albania							
1989							
Groom	18	27,655	331	[2]	7,670	13,951	4,261
Bride	16	27,655	5,521	[2]	15,644	5,078	1,017
Austria							
1990[3]							
Groom	18	45,212	--	877	11,784	16,656	7,268
Bride	16	45,212	--	3,385	18,178	13,082	4,882

[Continued]

★ 817 ★

European Marriages by Age-I
[Continued]

Country	Age[1]	All ages	Under 15	15-19	20-24	25-29	30-34
Belarus							
1989							
Groom	18	97,929	435	3,594	51,555	21,597	8,327
Bride	18	97,929	2,986	22,687	40,465	14,000	3,915
Belgium							
1985[4]							
Groom	18	57,551	1,258	[2]	28,389	16,479	4,815
Bride	15	57,551	7,826	[2]	31,873	10,039	3,393
Bulgaria							
1990[5,6]							
Groom	18	59,874	401	3,115	31,723	14,136	5,005
Bride	18	59,874	--	22,765	24,627	6,379	2,636
Czechoslovakia							
1990							
Groom	16	131,388	--	9,934	65,514	30,235	9,767
Bride	16	131,388	--	42,479	56,441	15,002	6,207
Denmark							
1989[7]							
Groom	18	30,894	--	131	3,925	9,969	6,413
Bride	15	30,894	--	666	7,498	10,334	5,089
Estonia							
1990							
Groom	--	11,774	--	836	4,782	2,409	1,238
Bride	--	11,774	--	2,731	4,222	1,682	1,027
Finland							
1989[8]							
Groom	18	24,569	--	316	5,609	9,399	4,402
Bride	17	24,569	--	1,237	8,515	8,200	3,115
France							
1990[9,10]							
Groom	18	287,099	--	1,200	63,643	113,564	49,494
Bride	15	287,099	1	9,552	108,065	91,533	35,728
Germany							
Fed. Rep. of[11]							
1990							
Groom	18	414,475	3,018	[2]	81,586	158,052	79,666
Bride	18	414,475	18,247	[2]	143,111	140,537	52,460

[Continued]

★817★

European Marriages by Age-I
[Continued]

Country	Age[1]	All ages	Under 15	15-19	20-24	25-29	30-34
Former G. Dem. Rep.[11]							
1989							
Groom	18	130,989	--	2,484	45,799	42,252	14,525
Bride	18	130,989	--	12,765	60,469	28,177	11,216
Greece							
1985							
Groom	18	63,709	7	1,065	16,537	24,529	11,312
Bride	14	63,709	342	16,089	24,476	12,870	4,645
Hungary							
1990							
Groom	16	66,405	--	3,751	31,920	14,569	6,097
Bride	16	66,405	2	18,257	29,261	7,513	3,891
Iceland							
1990[12]							
Groom	18	1,154	--	5	219	459	239
Bride	18	1,154	--	20	383	418	161
Ireland							
1989							
Groom	14	18,174	--	207	4,689	8,432	3,090
Bride	12	18,174	--	680	7,326	7,326	1,866
Italy							
1988							
Groom	16	318,296	--	3,195	77,923	144,471	56,022
Bride	16	318,296	--	31,961	145,618	95,358	25,711
Latvia							
1989							
Groom	--	24,496	166	1,438	10,762	4,784	2,324
Bride	--	24,496	631	4,920	9,044	3,652	2,015
Lithuania							
1990							
Groom	--	36,310	2,672	[2]	17,913	7,512	2,972
Bride	--	36,310	8,791	[2]	15,688	4,824	2,463
Luxembourg							
1989[12]							
Groom	18	2,184	--	32	489	830	397
Bride	15	2,184	--	153	771	719	287

[Continued]

★817★

European Marriages by Age-I
[Continued]

Country	Age[1]	All ages	Under 15	15-19	20-24	25-29	30-34
Malta							
1989[10]							
Groom	16	2,485	--	52	748	1,164	347
Bride	14	2,485	--	243	1,229	715	176
Moldova							
Rep. of							
1989							
Groom	--	39,928	110	1,435	21,653	8,793	2,956
Bride	--	39,928	1,269	11,331	16,354	4,594	2,334
Netherlands							
1990							
Groom	18	95,649	459	[2]	19,349	38,357	18,404
Bride	18	95,649	2,926	[2]	35,936	31,216	12,722
Norway							
1990[9,13]							
Groom	16	21,926	--	149	4,140	8,191	4,639
Bride	16	21,926	--	806	7,779	7,318	3,082
Poland							
1990							
Groom	21	255,369	--	12,400	124,619	69,619	22,541
Bride	16	255,369	--	56,195	130,718	34,148	13,792
Portugal							
1990[14]							
Groom	16	71,654	74	2,927	29,142	24,706	7,079
Bride	16	71,654	1,339	12,310	32,607	15,651	4,239
Romania							
1990							
Groom	18	192,652	7,769	[2]	106,039	40,250	17,028
Bride	16	192,652	57,323	[2]	94,857	16,698	8,759
Russia							
Russian Federation							
1989							
Groom	18	1,384,307	12,168	68,288	628,115	297,586	136,124
Bride	18	1,384,307	61,891	317,626	477,429	200,405	115,820
Spain							
1983[15]							
Groom	14	196,155	80	8,611	80,387	73,606	17,686
Bride	12	196,155	320	33,245	102,816	40,287	8,797

[Continued]

★ 817 ★

European Marriages by Age-I
[Continued]

Country	Age[1]	All ages	Under 15	15-19	20-24	25-29	30-34
Sweden 1900[16]							
Groom	18	43,442	--	201	5,399	13,291	9,319
Bride	18	43,442	--	1,120	10,349	13,906	6,511
Switzerland 1900							
Groom	18	46,603	--	107	7,002	17,837	10,371
Bride	17	46,603	1	1,111	14,266	17,373	6,904
Ukraine 1989							
Groom	18	489,330	3,633	23,073	247,585	96,156	40,149
Bride	17	489,330	43,007	117,985	168,661	59,754	32,855
United Kingdom 1989[17]							
Groom	16	392,042	--	8,234	113,813	123,491	56,442
Bride	16	392,042	--	29,863	152,804	100,531	41,989
Yugoslavia 1989							
Groom	18	158,544	1	3,528	59,386	55,493	20,709
Bride	18	158,544	9	37,499	68,857	29,892	9,714

Source: Selected from "Marriages by age of bridegroom and by age of bride: latest available year," United Nations, *Demographic Yearbook*, 1991, Table 24, pp. 497+. Data are legal (recognized) marriages performed and registered. *Notes:* 1. Age below which marriage is unlawful or invalid without dispensation by competent authority. 2. Figure in preceding column includes this age group. 3. Excluding aliens temporarily in the area. 4. Including armed forces stationed outside the country and alien armed forces in the area unless marriage performed by local foreign authority. 5. For under 18 and 18-19 years, as appropriate. 6. Including Bulgarian nationals outside the country, but excluding aliens in the area. 7. Excluding Faeroe Islands and Greenland. 8. Marriages in which the bride was domiciled in Finland only. 9. Age classification based on year of birth rather than exact date of birth. 10. Including armed forces stationed outside the country. 11. All data shown pertaining to Germany prior to October 3, 1990 are indicated separately for the Federal Republic of Germany and the former German Democratic Republic based on their respective territories at the time indicated. 12. For the de jure population. 13. Marriages in which the groom was domiciled in Norway only. 14. For under 17 and 17-19 years, as appropriate. 15. Civil marriages only. Canonical marriages are void for males under 16 years of age and for females under 14 years of age. 16. Including residents outside the country. 17. For under 16 and 16-19 years, as appropriate.

★ 818 ★

Marriages and Divorces

European Marriages by Age-II

This table shows the total number of marriages in selected European countries for the latest available year and the number of marriages by age of the bride and groom, for brides and grooms aged 35-60+. The legal age of marriage is also shown (when provided).

Country	Age[1]	All ages	35-39	40-44	45-49	50-54	55-59	60+	Unknown
Europe									
Albania									
1989									
Groom	18	27,655	859	287	141	154	2	2	--
Bride	16	27,655	246	69	33	43	2	2	--
Austria									
1990[3]									
Groom	18	45,212	3,053	2,001	1,601	895	457	620	--
Bride	16	45,212	2,146	1,525	1,054	536	200	224	--
Belarus									
1989									
Groom	18	97,929	3,982	2,295	1,454	1,492	981	2,212	5
Bride	18	97,929	3,607	2,004	1,306	1,425	867	1,664	3
Belgium									
1985[4]									
Groom	18	57,551	2,514	1,260	953	1,212	2	671	--
Bride	15	57,551	1,771	946	670	760	2	273	--
Bulgaria									
1990[5]									
Groom	18	59,874	2,365	1,352	649	397	278	453	--
Bride	18	59,874	1,437	842	492	236	203	257	--
Czechoslovakia									
1990									
Groom	16	131,388	5,880	3,990	2,469	1,313	972	1,314	--
Bride	16	131,388	4,149	3,135	2,011	975	472	517	--
Denmark									
1989[6]									
Groom	18	30,894	3,673	2,495	1,464	891	517	472	944
Bride	15	30,894	2,603	1,829	1,149	541	246	238	701
Estonia									
1990									
Groom	--	11,774	809	578	311	295	213	302	1
Bride	--	11,774	676	509	303	270	169	185	--
Finland									
1989[7]									
Groom	18	24,569	2,105	1,198	671	354	240	275	--

[Continued]

★ 818 ★

European Marriages by Age-II
[Continued]

Country	Age[1]	All ages	35-39	40-44	45-49	50-54	55-59	60+	Unknown
Bride	17	24,569	1,558	924	473	265	128	154	--
France 1990[8,9]									
Groom	18	287,099	23,393	15,007	7,650	4,959	3,374	4,815	--
Bride	15	287,099	18,018	11,327	5,406	3,405	1,865	2,199	--
Germany Fed. Rep. of[10] 1990									
Groom	18	414,475	34,901	19,624	14,701	10,809	5,008	7,110	--
Bride	18	414,475	22,904	13,741	10,575	7,089	2,815	2,996	--
Former G. Dem. Rep.[10] 1989									
Groom	18	130,989	9,289	4,764	5,045	3,363	1,703	1,765	--
Bride	18	130,989	6,990	3,671	3,817	2,330	871	683	--
Greece 1985									
Groom	18	63,709	4,584	1,843	1,282	889	641	1,017	3
Bride	14	63,709	2,209	1,005	808	515	373	374	3
Hungary 1990									
Groom	16	66,405	3,679	2,067	1,459	921	693	1,249	--
Bride	16	66,405	2,823	1,647	1,205	711	448	647	--
Iceland 1990[11]									
Groom	18	1,154	82	50	36	25	25	14	--
Bride	18	1,154	65	46	30	18	7	6	--
Ireland 1989									
Groom	14	18,174	978	356	144	67	48	126	37
Bride	12	18,174	559	168	67	46	35	62	39
Italy 1988									
Groom	16	318,296	17,559	7,463	4,026	2,506	1,832	3,299	--
Bride	16	318,296	8,971	4,070	2,437	1,612	1,146	1,412	--
Latvia 1989									
Groom	--	24,496	1,456	1,014	798	611	438	705	--
Bride	--	24,496	1,255	852	744	521	357	504	1

[Continued]

★ 818 ★

European Marriages by Age-II
[Continued]

Country	Age[1]	All ages	35-39	40-44	45-49	50-54	55-59	60+	Unknown
Lithuania									
1990									
Groom	--	36,310	1,469	1,035	766	643	444	883	1
Bride	--	36,310	1,353	939	685	592	399	573	3
Luxembourg									
1989[11]									
Groom	18	2,184	198	102	56	35	23	22	--
Bride	15	2,184	108	66	42	28	8	2	--
Malta									
1989[9]									
Groom	16	2,485	91	43	22	8	6	4	--
Bride	14	2,485	58	36	15	6	4	3	--
Moldova									
1989									
Groom	--	39,928	1,589	761	603	582	411	1,029	6
Bride	--	39,928	1,319	656	558	530	349	623	11
Netherlands									
1990									
Groom	18	95,649	7,858	4,561	2,586	1,647	1,020	1,408	--
Bride	18	95,649	5,369	3,227	1,984	1,105	493	671	--
Norway									
1990[9,12]									
Groom	16	21,926	2,110	1,268	665	330	209	225	--
Bride	16	21,926	1,387	750	440	184	80	100	--
Poland									
1990									
Groom	21	255,369	9,552	5,091	2,553	2,423	2,244	4,327	--
Bride	16	255,369	7,530	4,475	2,396	2,140	1,682	2,293	--
Portugal									
1990									
Groom	16	71,654	2,500	1,327	865	771	646	1,617	--
Bride	16	71,654	1,802	1,028	746	610	483	839	--
Romania									
1990									
Groom	18	192,652	8,395	4,185	2,459	2,241	1,574	2,712	--
Bride	16	192,652	5,466	3,104	2,086	1,711	1,152	1,496	--

[Continued]

★ 818 ★

European Marriages by Age-II
[Continued]

Country	Age[1]	All ages	35-39	40-44	45-49	50-54	55-59	60+	Unknown
Russia									
Russian Federation									
1989									
Groom	18	1,384,307	76,740	43,879	28,576	32,736	20,022	39,974	99
Bride	18	1,384,307	67,813	38,251	26,855	30,246	17,792	30,075	104
Spain									
1983[13]									
Groom	14	196,155	5,732	2,500	1,754	1,417	1,234	3,148	--
Bride	12	196,155	3,465	1,639	1,384	1,244	1,047	1,911	--
Sweden									
1900[14]									
Groom	18	43,442	4,796	3,211	2,208	1,113	590	686	2,628
Bride	18	43,442	3,382	2,473	1,482	644	279	331	2,965
Switzerland									
1900									
Groom	18	46,603	4,459	2,673	1,791	1,015	676	672	--
Bride	17	46,603	3,021	1,744	1,108	563	285	227	--
Ukraine									
1989									
Groom	18	489,330	22,545	13,062	9,919	11,245	6,297	15,648	18
Bride	17	489,330	19,364	11,469	9,447	10,121	5,424	11,229	14
United Kingdom									
1989									
Groom	16	392,042	29,582	21,829	13,348	8,981	6,015	10,307	--
Bride	16	392,042	22,914	17,376	10,785	6,387	3,198	6,195	--
Yugoslavia									
1989									
Groom	18	158,544	7,836	3,320	1,955	1,624	1,358	3,163	171
Bride	18	158,544	4,631	2,231	1,486	1,301	970	1,767	187

Source: Selected from "Marriages by age of bridegroom and by age of bride: latest available year," United Nations, *Demographic Yearbook,* 1991, Table 24, pp. 497+. Data are legal (recognized) marriages performed and registered. *Notes:* 1. Age below which marriage is unlawful or invalid without dispensation by competent authority. 2. Figure in preceding column includes this age group. 3. Excluding aliens temporarily in the area. 4. Including armed forces stationed outside the country and alien armed forces in the area unless marriage performed by local foreign authority. 5. Including Bulgarian nationals outside the country, but excluding aliens in the area. 6. Excluding Faeroe Islands and Greenland. 7. Marriages in which the bride was domiciled in Finland only. 8. Age classification based on year of birth rather than exact date of birth. 9. Including armed forces stationed outside the country. 10. All data shown pertaining to Germany prior to October 3, 1990 are indicated separately for the Federal Republic of Germany and the former German Democratic Republic based on their respective territories at the time indicated. 11. For the de jure population. 12. Marriages in which the groom was domiciled in Norway only. 13. Civil marriages only. Canonical marriages are void for males under 16 years of age and for females under 14 years of age. 14. Including residents outside the country. 17. For under 16 and 16-19 years, as appropriate.

★ 819 ★

Marriages and Divorces

European Marriages: 1987-1991

This table shows the total number of marriages in Europe and the marriage rate, for available years between 1987 and 1991. Rates are the number of legal (recognized) marriages performed and registered per 1,000 mid-year population. Rates are shown only for countries or areas having at least a total of 100 marriages in a given year.

Country	Number					Rate				
	1987	1988	1989	1990	1991	1987	1988	1989	1990	1991
Europe										
Albania	27,370	28,174	27,655	--	--	8.9	9.0	8.6	--	--
Andorra	125	125	66	153	--	2.6	2.5	--	3.0	--
Austria[1]	76,205	35,361	42,523	45,212	43,960	10.1	4.7	5.6	5.9	5.6
Belarus	102,053	96,064	97,929	--	--	10.1	8.9	9.6	--	--
Belgium[2]	56,770	59,093	63,528	64,658	60,832	5.8	6.0	6.5	6.6	6.2
Bulgaria[3]	64,429	62,617	63,263	59,874	48,820	7.2	7.0	7.0	6.7	5.4
Channel Islands	1,099	1,140	1,103	--	1,050	8.1	8.2	7.7	--	7.4
Guernsey	447	445	452	403	403	8.1	7.5	7.6	6.8	6.8
Jersey	652	695	651	--	647	8.1	8.7	7.9	--	7.7
Czechoslovakia	122,168	118,951	117,787	131,388	104,692	7.8	7.6	7.5	8.4	6.7
Denmark[4]	31,132	32,088	30,780	31,293	30,747	6.1	6.3	6.0	6.1	6.0
Estonia	13,434	12,973	12,644	11,774	--	8.7	8.3	8.1	7.5	--
Faeroe Islands	205	260	230	--	--	4.4	5.5	4.9	--	--
Finland[5]	26,259	25,933	24,569	24,150	23,573	5.3	5.2	4.9	4.8	4.7
France[6]	265,177	271,124	279,900	287,099	281,000	4.8	4.9	5.0	5.1	5.0
Germany[7]										
Fed. Rep. of	382,564	397,738	398,608	414,475	400,794	6.3	6.5	6.4	6.6	6.5
Former German Dem. Rep.	141,283	137,165	130,989	--	--	8.5	8.2	7.9	--	--
Gibraltar[8]	724	739	754	781	--	24.6	24.6	24.6	25.3	--
Greece	62,899	52,414	59,955	59,125	--	6.3	5.2	6.0	5.9	--
Hungary	66,082	65,907	66,949	66,405	60,348	6.3	6.3	6.4	6.4	5.7
Iceland[9]	1,160	1,294	1,176	1,154	1,280	4.7	5.2	4.7	4.5	5.0
Ireland	18,309	18,382	18,174	--	--	5.2	5.2	5.2	--	--
Isle of Man	430	446	483	--	--	6.7	6.7	7.1	--	--
Italy	305,328	318,296	311,613	311,739	--	5.3	5.5	5.4	5.4	--
Latvia	25,477	25,296	24,496	--	--	9.6	9.5	9.1	--	--
Liechtenstein	338	--	315	--	--	12.3	--	11.3	--	--
Lithuania	35,122	34,906	34,630	36,310	34,241	9.7	9.6	9.4	9.8	9.2
Luxembourg[9]	1,958	2,079	2,184	2,312	--	5.3	5.6	5.8	6.2	--
Malta[10]	2,437	2,531	2,485	2,609	--	7.1	7.3	7.1	7.4	--
Moldova										
Rep. of	39,084	39,745	39,928	--	--	9.1	9.2	9.2	--	--
Netherlands	87,400	87,843	90,248	95,649	95,500	6.0	6.0	6.1	6.4	6.3
Norway[11]	21,081	21,744	20,755	21,926	--	5.0	5.2	4.9	5.2	--
Poland	252,819	246,791	255,643	255,369	237,000	6.7	6.5	6.7	6.7	6.1
Portugal	67,948	71,098	73,195	71,654	71,808	6.9	7.2	7.4	7.3	6.8

[Continued]

★ 819 ★

European Marriages: 1987-1991

[Continued]

Country	Number					Rate				
	1987	1988	1989	1990	1991	1987	1988	1989	1990	1991
Romania	168,079	172,527	177,943	192,652	--	7.3	7.5	7.7	8.3	--
Russian Federation	1,442,622	1,397,445	1,384,307	--	--	9.9	9.5	9.4	--	--
San Marino	198	181	169	--	--	8.7	8.0	7.4	--	--
Spain	210,098	214,898	--	214,805	--	5.4	5.5	--	5.5	--
Sweden	41,223	44,229	108,919	40,477	40,000	4.9	5.2	12.8	4.7	4.7
Switzerland	43,063	45,716	45,066	46,603	46,000	6.6	6.9	6.8	6.9	6.9
Ukraine	512,985	455,770	489,330	482,800	--	10.0	8.8	9.5	9.3	--
United Kingdom	397,937	394,049	392,042	--	--	7.0	6.9	6.8	--	--
Yugoslavia	163,469	160,419	158,544	149,498	--	7.0	6.8	6.7	6.3	--

Source: Selected from "Marriages and crude marriage rates, by urban/rural residence: 1987-1991," United Nations, *Demographic Yearbook*, 1991, Table 23, pp. 490+. 1991 data are provisional. *Notes:* 1. Excluding aliens temporarily in the area. 2. Including armed forces stationed outside the country and alien armed forces in the area unless marriage performed by local foreign authority. 3. Including Bulgarian nationals outside the country, but excluding aliens in the area. 4. Excluding Faeroe Islands and Greenland. 5. Marriages in which the bride was domiciled in Finland only. 6. Including armed forces stationed outside the country. Rates computed on population including armed forces stationed outside the country, but excluding alien armed forces living in military camps within the country. 7. All data shown pertaining to Germany prior to October 3, 1990 are indicated separately for the Federal Republic of Germany and the former German Democratic Republic based on their respective territories at the time indicated. 8. Rates computed on population excluding armed forces. 9. For the de jure population. 10. Computed on population including civilian nationals temporarily outside the country. 11. Marriages in which the groom was domiciled in Norway only.

★ 820 ★

Marriages and Divorces

Ever Divorced: 1975 and 1990

This table shows the percentage of ever-married women who were divorced after their first marriage, by age, in June 1975 and June 1990. Assuming a continuation of recent divorce trends, the 1990 data suggest that about 4 out of 10 first marriages may end in divorce. This is somewhat less than the 5 out of 10 that was suggested by earlier surveys. Even with this anticipated decline in divorce, the percentage of marriages in the United States that end in divorce is expected to continue to be among the highest in the world.[1].

Age	Women divorced	
	1975	1990
20 to 24 years old	11.2%	12.5%
25 to 29 years old	17.1%	19.2%
30 to 34 years old	19.8%	28.1%
35 to 39 years old	21.5%	34.1%
40 to 44 years old	20.5%	35.8%
45 to 49 years old	21.0%	35.2%
50 to 54 years old	18.0%	29.5%

Source: Selected from U.S. Bureau of the Census, *Population Profile of the United States: 1993*, Special Studies Series P23-185, Figure 22, p. 23, "Percent of Ever-Married Women Divorced After First Marriage, by Age: June 1975 and June 1990." *Note:* 1. United Nations (1988). *1985/86 Statistical Yearbook*, New York NY.

★ 821 ★

Marriages and Divorces

Ever Married: 1975 and 1990

This table shows the percentage of women who had ever been married, by age, in June 1975 and June 1990. The most notable declines in the percent of women ever married were for those in their twenties and early thirties. Projections based on 1990 data suggest that 90% of women will marry at some time in their lives, down from 95%, which has historically been the percentage reached by most age groups of women. Only about 3 out of 4 black women will ever marry, compared to 9 out of 10 of white women. Four out of 10 first marriages will end in divorce.

Age	Women Ever Married	
	1975	1990
20 to 24 years old	62.5%	38.5%
25 to 29 years old	87.2%	69.0%
30 to 34 years old	93.1%	82.2%
35 to 39 years old	95.5%	89.4%
40 to 44 years old	95.8%	92.0%
45 to 49 years old	95.9%	94.4%
50 to 54 years old	95.8%	95.5%

Source: Selected from U.S. Bureau of the Census, *Population Profile of the United States: 1993*, Special Studies Series P23-185, Figure 21, p. 22, "Percent of Women Ever Married, by Age: June 1975 and June 1990."

★ 822 ★

Marriages and Divorces

Lowest Divorce Rates Worldwide

This table shows the divorce rate per 1,000 population for the 13 countries with the lowest divorce rate in 1988.

[Divorce rate per 1,000 population.]

Country	Rate
Brazil	0.2
Grenada	0.2
Guatemala	0.2
Saint Kitts and Nevis and Anguilla	0.2
Saint Vincent	0.2
Haiti	0.1
Iraq	0.1
Mauritania	0.1
Sri Lanka	0.1
Western Samoa	0.1
Malaysia	0.02

[Continued]

826

★ 822 ★

Lowest Divorce Rates Worldwide
[Continued]

Country	Rate
Zaire	0.02
Mozambique	0.01

Source: Selected from George Kurian, *The New Book of World Rankings*, Facts on File, Inc., New York, 1991, pp. 30-31, table entitled "Divorce Rate." Primary source: *U.N. Demographic Yearbook.*

★ 823 ★

Marriages and Divorces

Highest Divorce Rates Worldwide

This table shows the divorce rate per 1,000 population for the 11 countries with the highest divorce rate in 1988.

[Divorce rate per 1,000 population.]

Country	Rate
Maldives	25.5
Liechtenstein	7.3
Peru	6.0
United States	4.8
Puerto Rico	4.0
Bermuda	3.8
Cuba	3.1
East Germany	2.9
Canada	2.8
Denmark	2.8
United Kingdom	2.8

Source: Selected from George Kurian, *The New Book of World Rankings*, Facts on File, Inc., New York, 1991, pp. 30-31, table entitled "Divorce Rate." Primary source: *U.N. Demographic Yearbook.*

★ 824 ★

Marriages and Divorces

Latin American/Caribbean Divorces

This table shows the total number of divorces in selected Latin American and Caribbean countries for the years 1987 through 1991. Divorce rates, the number of final divorce decrees granted under civil law per 1,000 mid-year population, are also shown.

Country	Number					Rate				
	1987	1988	1989	1990	1991	1987	1988	1989	1990	1991
Latin America and the Caribbean										
Antigua and Barbuda	43	--	--	--	--	--	--	--	--	--
Aruba	214	196	--	--	--	3.57	3.22	--	--	--
Bahamas[1]	425	364	275	--	--	1.77	1.49	1.10	--	--
Barbados	363	385	416	--	--	1.43	1.51	1.63	--	--
Belize	82	91	114	--	95	--	--	0.62	--	--
Brazil	30,772	33,437	66,070	--	--	0.22	0.23	0.45	--	--
British Virgin Islands	15	0	--	--	--	--	--	--	--	--
Cayman Islands	--	--	76	91	--	--	--	--	--	--
Chile	5,152	5,413	5,337	6,048	--	0.41	0.42	0.41	0.46	--
Costa Rica	2,899	2,482	2,916	3,282	--	1.04	0.87	1.00	1.10	--
Cuba	32,600	35,668	37,647	37,284	43,485	3.16	3.42	3.58	3.51	4.05
Dominica	--	--	--	29	--	--	--	--	--	--
Ecuador[2]	4,075	4,424	5,663	--	--	0.41	0.43	0.54	--	--
El Salvador	2,519	2,316	2,239	--	--	0.50	0.45	0.43	--	--
Falkland Islands	--	4	--	--	--	--	--	--	--	--
Guatemala	1,502	1,614	--	--	--	0.18	0.18	--	--	--
Jamaica	920	863	672	--	--	0.39	0.36	0.28	--	--
Martinique	357	374	297	264	--	1.03	1.07	0.83	0.73	--
Mexico	45,323	47,671	47,963	54,012	--	0.56	0.57	0.57	0.63	--
Netherlands Antilles	471	438	416	409	--	2.47	2.30	2.19	2.15	
Nicaragua	842	1,547	1,891	866	--	0.24	0.43	0.50	0.22	--
Panama[3]	1,505	1,731	1,872	--	--	0.66	0.74	0.79	--	--
Puerto Rico	14,611	13,930	13,838	13,695	--	4.26	4.02	3.96	3.80	--
Saint Lucia	35	44	44	--	--	--	--	--	--	--
Trinidad and Tobago	1,163	1,074	1,075	--	--	0.96	0.89	0.89	--	--
Uruguay[4]	4,611	6,376	--	--	--	1.51	2.08	--	--	--
Venezuela[5]	22,665	24,774	21,876	--	--	1.26	1.34	1.16	--	--
Virgin Islands	263	--	--	--	332	2.48	--	--	--	2.81

Source: Selected from "Divorces and crude divorce rates: 1987-1991," United Nations, *Demographic Yearbook*, 1991, Table 25, pp. 508-511. Data exclude annulments and legal separations unless otherwise specified. Rates are shown only for countries or areas having at least a total 100 divorces in a given year. 1991 data are provisional. *Notes:* 1. Petitions for divorce entered in courts. 2. Excluding nomadic Indian tribes. 3. Excluding tribal Indian population, numbering 62,187 in 1960. 4. Excluding annulments. 5. Excluding Indian jungle population.

★ 825 ★

Marriages and Divorces

Latin American/Caribbean Marriages by Age-I

This table shows the total number of marriages in selected Latin American and Caribbean countries for the latest available year and the number of marriages by age of the bride and groom, for brides and grooms aged under 15 through age 34. The legal age of marriage is also shown.

Country	Age[1]	All ages	Under 15	15-19	20-24	25-29	30-34
Latin America/Caribbean							
Argentina							
1989							
Groom	16	161,422	34	9,141	63,783	51,188	16,794
Bride	14	161,422	1,128	39,937	65,075	30,103	10,024
Bahamas							
1989							
Groom	15	2,131	--	18	471	715	378
Bride	15	2,131	3	152	672	621	339
Barbados							
1989							
Groom	18	2,047	--	5	260	625	447
Bride	16	2,047	--	34	490	711	386
Brazil							
1989							
Groom	--	827,928	40	65,897	360,160	244,924	83,102
Bride	--	827,928	6,212	281,152	309,425	140,513	45,717
Chile							
1990							
Groom	14	98,702	1	4,826	38,728	33,271	11,852
Bride	12	98,702	416	19,632	40,619	23,188	8,024
Colombia							
1986[2]							
Groom	14	70,350	142	2,689	22,912	22,207	9,444
Bride	12	70,350	497	15,180	27,089	14,071	5,126
Costa Rica							
1990							
Groom	15	22,703	3	1,689	8,428	6,472	2,765
Bride	15	22,703	152	6,156	8,132	4,261	1,796
Cuba							
1989							
Groom	16	85,535	--	7,079	28,296	20,424	8,146
Bride	14	85,535	809	20,016	27,866	14,832	5,767
Dominican Republic							
1984							
Groom	16	30,985	9	831	6,336	8,273	5,414

[Continued]

★ 825 ★

Latin American/Caribbean Marriages by Age-I
[Continued]

Country	Age[1]	All ages	Under 15	15-19	20-24	25-29	30-34
Bride	15	30,985	4,400	9	8,955	6,825	4,121
Ecuador							
1989[3]							
Groom	14	62,996	22	7,673	24,019	16,586	7,022
Bride	12	62,996	1,116	20,136	22,327	10,585	4,212
El Salvador							
1989[4]							
Groom	16	20,816	--	1,292	6,757	5,116	2,799
Bride	14	20,816	200	4,394	6,988	4,030	1,989
Guadeloupe							
1986[5]							
Groom	20	1,692	--	5	295	652	331
Bride	19	1,692	142	9	653	443	187
Guatemala							
1988							
Groom	16	46,155	32	7,288	17,262	8,469	4,228
Bride	14	46,155	1,394	17,751	12,310	5,243	3,115
Honduras							
1983							
Groom	14	19,875	15	1,518	9,034	3,901	2,340
Bride	12	19,875	760	4,798	9,229	2,407	1,244
Martinique							
1988[5]							
Groom	--	1,558	--	2	173	556	352
Bride	--	1,558	--	52	466	492	231
Mexico							
1986							
Groom	18	578,895	208	96,078	244,172	135,654	47,301
Bride	18	578,895	9,843	213,125	210,399	82,201	28,635
Panama							
1989[6]							
Groom	14	11,173	--	401	2,999	3,150	1,675
Bride	12	11,173	113	1,628	3,693	2,542	1,180
Paraguay							
1987							
Groom	14	17,741	--	672	6,117	5,313	2,452
Bride	12	17,741	359	5,674	5,399	2,858	1,399

[Continued]

★ 825 ★

Latin American/Caribbean Marriages by Age-I

[Continued]

Country	Age[1]	All ages	Under 15	15-19	20-24	25-29	30-34
Puerto Rico 1989							
Groom	18	31,642	--	3,604	10,832	7,312	3,464
Bride	12	31,642	394	7,105	10,521	6,023	2,833
Trinidad and Tobago 1989							
Groom	7	6,794	--	191	1,826	2,223	1,072
Bride	7	6,794	36	1,195	2,337	1,611	666
Uruguay 1987							
Groom	14	22,728	1,552	9	7,936	6,128	2,776
Bride	12	22,728	5,472	9	7,908	4,296	1,940
Venezuela 1989[8]							
Groom	21	111,970	18	12,991	41,088	29,356	13,188
Bride	18	111,970	2,571	32,713	37,505	21,059	9,137
Virgin Islands 1987							
Groom	--	1,906	1	18	245	486	424
Bride	--	1,906	2	83	435	535	375

Source: Selected from "Marriages by age of bridegroom and by age of bride: latest available year," United Nations, *Demographic Yearbook*, 1991, Table 24, pp. 497+. Data are legal (recognized) marriages performed and registered. *Notes:* 1. Age below which marriage is unlawful or invalid without dispensation by competent authority. 2. Except for Bogota, data are not to be considered as necessarily representative of the country. 3. Excluding nomadic Indian tribes. 4. Including residents outside the country. 5. Age classification based on year of birth rather than exact date of birth. 6. Excluding tribal population. 7. Varies among major civil divisions, or ethnic or religious groups. 8. Excluding Indian jungle population. 9. Figure in preceding column includes this age group.

★ 826 ★

Marriages and Divorces

Latin American/Caribbean Marriages by Age-II

This table shows the total number of marriages in selected Latin American and Caribbean countries for the latest available year and the number of marriages by age of the bride and groom, for brides and grooms aged 35-60+. The legal age of marriage is also shown.

Country	Age[1]	All ages	35-39	40-44	45-49	50-54	55-59	60+	Unknown
Latin America/Caribbean									
Argentina 1989									
Groom	16	161,422	6,143	3,134	1,965	1,752	1,527	4,199	1,762
Bride	14	161,422	4,128	2,323	1,667	1,589	1,348	2,163	1,937

[Continued]

★ 826 ★

Latin American/Caribbean Marriages by Age-II
[Continued]

Country	Age[1]	All ages	35-39	40-44	45-49	50-54	55-59	60+	Unknown
Bahamas 1989									
Groom	15	2,131	223	136	82	40	32	30	6
Bride	15	2,131	154	94	51	21	11	7	6
Barbados 1989									
Groom	18	2,047	291	170	82	44	47	76	--
Bride	16	2,047	167	108	73	30	17	31	--
Brazil 1989									
Groom	--	827,928	29,403	13,985	8,608	6,488	5,035	10,268	--
Bride	--	827,928	19,614	9,999	6,054	3,855	2,345	3,042	--
Chile 1990									
Groom	14	98,702	4,138	1,862	1,160	754	566	1,544	--
Bride	12	98,702	2,998	1,400	849	564	372	640	--
Colombia 1986[2]									
Groom	14	70,350	3,800	1,807	1,151	960	781	4,214	243
Bride	12	70,350	2,020	1,070	737	603	533	3,289	135
Costa Rica 1990									
Groom	15	22,703	1,316	639	404	269	177	386	155
Bride	15	22,703	880	473	258	134	80	159	222
Cuba 1989									
Groom	16	85,535	5,300	3,616	2,899	2,264	1,875	5,305	331
Bride	14	85,535	3,865	3,085	2,520	1,973	1,522	2,972	308
Dominican Republic 1984									
Groom	16	30,985	3,226	2,120	1,454	898	598	755	1,071
Bride	15	30,985	2,315	1,307	827	441	212	207	1,375
Ecuador 1989[3]									
Groom	14	62,996	3,087	1,608	919	713	475	872	--
Bride	12	62,996	1,908	1,085	644	390	268	325	88

[Continued]

★ 826 ★

Latin American/Caribbean Marriages by Age-II
[Continued]

Country	Age[1]	All ages	35-39	40-44	45-49	50-54	55-59	60+	Unknown
El Salvador									
1989[4]									
Groom	16	20,816	1,653	1,048	686	482	336	517	130
Bride	14	20,816	1,143	708	429	280	164	198	293
Guadeloupe									
1986[5]									
Groom	20	1,692	158	57	46	148	[9]	[9]	--
Bride	19	1,692	93	48	36	90	[9]	[9]	--
Guatemala									
1988									
Groom	16	46,155	2,557	1,717	1,302	1,015	789	1,496	--
Bride	14	46,155	1,975	1,394	1,052	743	498	680	--
Honduras									
1983									
Groom	14	19,875	1,192	754	419	309	177	216	--
Bride	12	19,875	627	350	199	129	63	69	--
Martinique									
1988[5]									
Groom	--	1,558	173	88	56	158	[9]	[9]	--
Bride	--	1,558	130	59	38	90	[9]	[9]	--
Mexico									
1986									
Groom	18	578,895	20,654	11,041	6,986	15,959	[9]	[9]	842
Bride	18	578,895	13,192	7,140	4,644	8,140	[9]	[9]	1,576
Panama									
1989[6]									
Groom	14	11,173	898	577	416	289	230	453	85
Bride	12	11,173	631	443	289	221	163	168	102
Paraguay									
1987									
Groom	14	17,741	1,159	703	453	264	200	397	11
Bride	12	17,741	801	483	281	176	124	172	15
Puerto Rico									
1989									
Groom	18	31,642	1,968	1,333	963	628	1,538	[9]	--
Bride	12	31,642	1,679	1,125	715	475	772	[9]	--

[Continued]

★ 826 ★

Latin American/Caribbean Marriages by Age-II
[Continued]

Country	Age[1]	All ages	35-39	40-44	45-49	50-54	55-59	60+	Unknown
Trinidad and Tobago									
1989									
Groom	7	6,794	498	332	182	140	116	213	1
Bride	7	6,794	377	197	143	97	44	89	2
Uruguay									
1987									
Groom	14	22,728	1,316	1,304	9	1,708	9	9	8
Bride	12	22,728	1,028	1,024	9	1,036	9	9	24
Venezuela									
1989[8]									
Groom	21	111,970	6,826	3,436	1,930	1,202	825	1,110	--
Bride	18	111,970	4,459	2,122	1,083	586	353	382	--
Virgin Islands									
1989									
Groom	--	1,906	285	197	248	2	9	9	--
Bride	--	1,906	226	134	115	9	9	9	--

Source: Selected from "Marriages by age of bridegroom and by age of bride: latest available year," United Nations, *Demographic Yearbook*, 1991, Table 24, pp. 497+. Data are legal (recognized) marriages performed and registered. *Notes:* 1. Age below which marriage is unlawful or invalid without dispensation by competent authority. 2. Except for Bogota, data are not to be considered as necessarily representative of the country. 3. Excluding nomadic Indian tribes. 4. Including residents outside the country. 5. Age classification based on year of birth rather than exact date of birth. 6. Excluding tribal population. 7. Varies among major civil divisions, or ethnic or religious groups. 8. Excluding Indian jungle population. 9. Figure in preceding column includes this age group.

★ 827 ★

Marriages and Divorces

Latin American/Caribbean Marriages: 1987-1991

This table shows the total number of marriages in Latin American and the Caribbean, and the marriage rate, for available years between 1987 and 1991. Rates are the number of legal (recognized) marriages performed and registered per 1,000 mid-year population. Rates are shown only for countries or areas having at least a total of 100 marriages in a given year.

Country	Number					Rate				
	1987	1988	1989	1990	1991	1987	1988	1989	1990	1991
Latin America and the Caribbean										
Antigua and Barbuda	343	--	--	--	--	4.5	--	--	--	--
Argentina	--	--	--	186,337	--	--	--	--	5.8	--
Aruba	380	390	--	--	--	6.3	6.4	--	--	--
Bahamas	1,888	2,167	2,131	2,182	--	7.9	8.9	8.6	8.6	--
Barbados	1,523	1,856	2,047	--	--	6.0	7.3	8.0	--	--
Belize	1,074	1,089	1,138	--	1,202	6.1	6.1	6.2	--	6.3
Brazil	930,893	951,236	827,928	--	--	6.6	6.6	5.6	--	--
British Virgin Islands	189	176	--	--	--	15.5	14.2	--	--	--

[Continued]

★ 827 ★

Latin American/Caribbean Marriages: 1987-1991

[Continued]

Country	Number					Rate				
	1987	1988	1989	1990	1991	1987	1988	1989	1990	1991
Cayman Islands	279	254	267	274	--	12.2	10.5	10.3	10.0	--
Chile	95,531	103,484	103,710	98,702	--	7.6	8.1	8.0	7.5	--
Costa Rica	21,743	22,918	22,984	22,703	--	7.8	8.0	7.9	7.6	--
Cuba	78,146	82,431	85,535	101,572	161,160	7.6	7.9	8.1	9.6	15.0
Dominica	--	--	--	225	--	--	--	--	2.7	--
Ecuador	61,301	66,468	62,996	64,532	--	6.2	6.5	6.0	6.7	--
El Salvador	22,327	21,314	20,787	23,167	--	4.4	4.2	4.0	4.4	--
Guatemala	44,669	46,155	--	--	--	5.3	5.3	--	--	--
Jamaica	--	10,429	11,145	13,037	--	--	4.4	4.7	5.4	--
Martinique	1,527	1,558	1,571	1,572	--	4.4	4.4	4.4	4.3	--
Mexico	604,425	625,919	628,162	633,424	--	7.4	7.6	7.4	7.4	--
Netherlands Antilles	1,283	1,275	1,226	1,267	--	6.7	6.7	6.5	6.7	--
Nicaragua	11,703	--	--	--	--	3.3	--	--	--	--
Panama[1]	11,188	11,060	11,173	12,467	--	4.9	4.8	4.7	5.2	--
Paraguay[2]	17,741	--	--	--	--	4.5	--	--	--	--
Puerto Rico	33,285	32,214	31,642	33,080	--	9.7	9.3	9.1	9.2	--
Saint Lucia	414	402	396	--	--	2.9	2.8	2.7	--	--
Saint Vincent and the Grenadines	--	462	--	--	--	--	4.1	--	--	--
Trinidad and Tobago	7,602	7,327	6,794	--	--	6.3	6.0	5.6	--	--
Uruguay	22,728	21,528	--	--	--	7.5	7.0	--	--	--
Venezuela[3]	105,058	113,125	111,970	--	--	5.8	6.1	5.9	--	--
Virgin Islands	1,906	--	--	--	2,855	18.0	--	--	--	24.2

Source: Selected from "Marriages and crude marriage rates, by urban/rural residence: 1987-1991," United Nations, *Demographic Yearbook*, 1991, Table 23, pp. 490+. 1991 figures are provisional. *Notes:* 1. Excluding tribal Indian population. 2. Data are estimated to be incomplete (less than 90%). 3. Excluding Indian jungle population, estimated at 100,830 in 1961.

★ 828 ★

Marriages and Divorces

Least Marrying Countries

This table shows the marriage rate per 1,000 population for the 10 countries with the lowest marriage rate in 1988.

[Marriage rate per 1,000 population.]

Country	Rate
Mali	2.8
Rwanda	2.7
Antigua	2.6
Madagascar	2.6

[Continued]

★ 828 ★

Least Marrying Countries
[Continued]

Country	Rate
Togo	2.3
Malaysia	1.7
Equatorial Guinea	0.8
Haiti	0.7
Mozambique	0.7
Afghanistan	0.4

Source: Selected from George Kurian, *The New Book of World Rankings*, Facts on File, Inc., New York, 1991, pp. 30-31, table entitled "Marriage Rates." Primary source: *U.N. Demographic Yearbook.*

★ 829 ★

Marriages and Divorces

Most Marrying Countries

This table shows the marriage rate per 1,000 population for the 10 countries with the highest marriage rate in 1988.

[Marriage rate per 1,000 population.]

Country	Rate
Anguilla	22.2
Virgin Islands	12.9
Benin	12.8
British Virgin Islands	12.7
Bermuda	12.2
Guam	11.3
Mauritius	11.0
Liechtenstein	10.8
American Samoa	10.7
Pakistan	10.7

Source: Selected from George Kurian, *The New Book of World Rankings*, Facts on File, Inc., New York, 1991, pp. 30-31, table entitled "Marriage Rates." Primary source: *U.N. Demographic Yearbook.*

Marriages and Divorces

Marriage Experience: 1975-1990-I

This table shows the distributions of women by age and for the white population, according to whether they had ever been married, divorced after first marriage, or remarried after divorce. The data are from the four most recent marriage history surveys (1975, 1980, 1985, and 1990). Women 25 to 54 years old are included because these age groups include women whose marriage experiences to date reflect the range of change in trends during the 25-year period. It was considered unlikely that a major influence on divorce trends would be exerted by women over age 54.

[NA Not available.]

Category	All races				White			
	1975	1980	1985	1990	1975	1980	1985	1990
Percent ever married								
20 to 24	62.5%	49.5%	43.3%	38.5%	64.9%	52.2%	46.6%	41.3%
25 to 29	87.2%	78.6%	74.0%	69.0%	88.8%	81.0%	77.4%	73.2%
30 to 34	93.1%	89.9%	85.8%	82.2%	93.9%	91.6%	88.1%	85.6%
35 to 39	95.5%	94.3%	91.6%	89.4%	96.2%	95.3%	93.1%	91.4%
40 to 44	95.8%	95.1%	94.6%	92.0%	95.9%	95.8%	95.6%	93.4%
45 to 49	95.9%	95.9%	94.4%	94.4%	95.9%	96.4%	95.1%	95.1%
50 to 54	95.8%	95.3%	95.2%	95.5%	96.0%	95.8%	95.4%	96.1%
Percent divorced after first marriage								
20 to 24	11.2%	14.2%	13.9%	12.5%	11.3%	14.7%	14.4%	12.8%
25 to 29	17.1%	20.7%	21.0%	19.2%	17.7%	21.0%	21.5%	19.8%
30 to 34	19.8%	26.2%	29.3%	28.1%	20.0%	25.8%	29.0%	28.6%
35 to 39	21.5%	27.2%	32.0%	34.1%	21.2%	26.7%	32.0%	34.6%
40 to 44	20.5%	26.1%	32.1%	35.8%	19.7%	25.5%	32.0%	35.2%
45 to 49	21.0%	23.1%	29.0%	35.2%	20.3%	22.7%	28.4%	35.5%
50 to 54	18.0%	21.8%	25.7%	29.5%	16.8%	21.0%	24.6%	28.5%
Percent remarried after divorce								
20 to 24	47.9%	45.5%	44.3%	38.1%	50.1%	47.0%	46.0%	39.3%
25 to 29	60.2%	53.4%	55.3%	51.8%	62.0%	56.4%	58.3%	52.8%
30 to 34	64.4%	60.9%	61.4%	59.6%	67.5%	63.3%	64.3%	61.4%
35 to 39	69.5%	64.9%	63.0%	65.0%	70.9%	66.9%	64.9%	66.5%
40 to 44	69.7%	67.4%	64.7%	67.1%	71.9%	68.6%	67.5%	69.5%
45 to 49	69.6%	69.2%	67.9%	65.9%	70.7%	70.4%	69.6%	67.2%
50 to 54	73.5%	72.0%	68.2%	63.0%	73.4%	72.6%	68.4%	65.4%

Source: "Marriage Experience for Women, by Age, Race, and Hispanic Origin: 1975, 1980, 1985, and 1990," U.S. Bureau of the Census, Current Population Reports, P23-180, *Marriage, Divorce, and Remarriage in the 1990's*, table B, p. 3.

★ 831 ★

Marriages and Divorces

Marriage Experience: 1975-1990-II

This table shows the distributions of women by age for the black and Hispanic origin populations, according to whether they had ever been married, divorced after first marriage, or remarried after divorce. The data are from the four most recent marriage history surveys (1975, 1980, 1985, and 1990).

[NA Not available. B base less than 0.]

Category	Black				Hispanic origin[1]		
	1975	1980	1985	1990	1980	1985	1990
Percent ever married							
20 to 24	47.5%	33.3%	23.9%	23.5%	55.4%	56.7%	45.8%
25 to 29	76.5%	62.3%	53.4%	45.0%	80.2%	78.4%	69.6%
30 to 34	87.1%	77.9%	70.9%	61.1%	88.3%	88.0%	83.0%
35 to 39	90.1%	87.4%	80.7%	74.9%	91.2%	91.6%	88.9%
40 to 44	95.1%	89.7%	86.1%	82.1%	94.2%	90.3%	92.8%
45 to 49	95.4%	92.5%	88.4%	89.7%	94.4%	91.1%	91.7%
50 to 54	94.6%	92.1%	93.4%	91.9%	95.0%	92.5%	91.8%
Percent divorced after first marriage							
20 to 24	10.6%	10.5%	11.0%	9.6%	9.4%	11.0%	6.8%
25 to 29	15.3%	20.25	18.2%	17.8%	13.9%	14.8%	13.5%
30 to 34	20.5%	31.4%	34.4%	26.6%	21.1%	19.2%	19.9%
35 to 39	22.7%	32.9%	34.6%	35.8%	21.9%	26.3%	29.7%
40 to 44	27.4%	33.7%	36.9%	45.1%	19.7%	22.8%	26.6%
45 to 49	26.9%	29.0%	36.0%	39.8%	23.9%	24.3%	24.6%
50 to 54	29.7%	29.0%	33.7%	39.2%	22.5%	21.8%	22.9%
Percent remarried after divorce							
20 to 24	B	B	B	B	B	B	B
25 to 29	43.1%	27.9%	25.4%	44.4%	B	50.5%	49.5%
30 to 34	41.8%	42.0%	41.1%	42.0%	58.3%	44.9%	45.9%
35 to 39	62.6%	50.6%	44.8%	54.0%	45.2%	57.1%	51.2%
40 to 44	57.1%	58.4%	45.4%	50.3%	B	50.6%	53.9%
45 to 49	61.7%	62.7%	54.6%	55.0%	B	78.9%	51.0%
50 to 54	73.7%	72.7%	64.3%	50.2%	B	B	62.2%

Source: "Marriage Experience for Women, by Age, Race, and Hispanic Origin: 1975, 1980, 1985, and 1990," U.S. Bureau of the Census, Current Population Reports, P23-180, *Marriage, Divorce, and Remarriage in the 1990's,* table B, p. 3. *Note:* 1. May be of any race. No data available for 1975.

★ 832 ★

Marriages and Divorces

Marriage Rates and Age of Bride and Groom: 1970-1988

This table shows marriage rates per 1,000 population 15 years old and over in specified group by previous marital status. It also shows the median age in years at marriage for bride and groom by their previous marital status.

[Rate per 1,000 population 15 years old and over in specified group.]

Year	Marriage Rates						Median Age at Marriage (years)					
	Women			Men			Women			Men		
							First marriage	Remarriage		First marriage	Divorced	Widowed
	Single	Divorced	Widowed	Single	Divorced	Widowed		Divorced	Widowed			
1970	93.4	123.3	10.2	80.4	204.5	40.6	20.6	30.1	51.2	22.5	34.5	58.7
1975	75.9	117.2	8.3	61.5	189.8	40.4	20.8	30.2	52.4	22.7	33.6	59.4
1980	66.0	91.3	6.7	54.7	142.1	32.2	21.8	31.0	53.6	23.6	34.0	61.2
1985	61.5	81.8	5.7	50.1	121.6	27.7	23.0	32.8	54.6	24.8	36.1	62.7
1986	59.7	79.5	5.5	49.1	117.8	26.8	23.3	33.1	54.3	25.1	36.6	62.9
1987	58.9	80.7	5.4	48.8	115.7	26.1	23.6	33.3	53.9	25.3	36.7	62.8
1988	58.4	78.6	5.3	48.3	109.7	25.1	23.7	33.6	53.9	25.5	37.0	63.0

Source: "Marriage Rates and Median Age of Bride and Groom, by Previous Marital Status: 1970 to 1988," U.S. Bureau of the Census, *Statistical Abstract of the United States, 1994*, table 142, p. 103. Data cover marriage registration area. Figures for previously divorced and previously widowed exclude data for Michigan and Ohio for all years, for South Carolina beginning 1975, and for the District of Columbia for 1970. Based on a sample and subject to sampling variability.

★ 833 ★

Marriages and Divorces

Marriages and Divorces: 1970-1993

This table shows the total number of marriages and divorces in thousands, and the rates per 1,000 population, for the years 1970 through 1993.

[Numbers in thousands. Rate per 1,000 population.]

Year	Number		Rate	
	Marriages[1]	Divorces[2]	Marriages[1]	Divorces[2]
1970	2,159	708	10.6	3.5
1971	2,190	773	10.6	3.7
1972	2,282	845	10.9	4.0
1973	2,284	915	10.8	4.3
1974	2,230	977	10.5	4.6
1975	2,153	1,036	10.0	4.8
1976	2,155	1,083	9.9	5.0
1977	2,178	1,091	9.9	5.0
1978	2,282	1,130	10.3	5.1
1979	2,331	1,181	10.4	5.3
1980	2,390	1,189	10.6	5.2
1981	2,422	1,213	10.6	5.3
1982	2,456	1,170	10.6	5.1
1983	2,446	1,158	10.5	5.0

[Continued]

★ 833 ★

Marriages and Divorces: 1970-1993
[Continued]

Year	Number		Rate	
	Marriages[1]	Divorces[2]	Marriages[1]	Divorces[2]
1984	2,477	1,169	10.5	5.0
1985	2,413	1,190	10.1	5.0
1986	2,407	1,178	10.0	4.9
1987	2,403	1,166	9.9	4.8
1988	2,396	1,167	9.8	4.8
1989[3]	2,404	1,163	9.7	4.7
1990[3]	2,448	1,175	9.8	4.7
1991[3]	2,371	1,187	9.4	4.7
1992[3]	2,362	1,215	9.3	4.8
1993[3]	2,334	1,187	9.0	4.6

Source: Selected from "Live Births, Deaths, Marriages, and Divorces: 1950 to 1992," U.S. Bureau of the Census, *Statistical Abstract of the United States, 1994,* table 90, p. 75. 1993 figures are provisional statistics from *Monthly Vital Statistics Report,* 42(12), May 13, 1994, p. 1. Primary source: U.S. National Center for Health Statistics, *Vital Statistics of the United States,* annual, *Monthly Vital Statistics Report,* and unpublished data. *Notes:* 1. Includes estimates for some States for 1976 and 1977 and marriage licenses for some States for all years except 1973 and 1975. Beginning 1978, includes nonlicensed marriages in California. 2. Includes reported annulments and some estimated State figures for all years. 3. Preliminary.

★ 834 ★

Marriages and Divorces

Middle Eastern Marriages: 1987-1990

This table shows the total number of marriages in the Middle East and the marriage rate, for available years between 1987 and 1991. Rates are the number of legal (recognized) marriages performed and registered per 1,000 mid-year population. Rates are shown only for countries or areas having at least a total of 100 marriages in a given year. No 1991 data were available.

Country	Number				Rate				
	1987	1988	1989	1990	1987	1988	1989	1990	
Middle East									
Iran[1]									
Islamic Rep. of	346,652	361,945	458,708	454,963	--	6.8	6.9	8.5	8.3	--
Iraq	95,534	145,885	--	--	--	5.8	8.5	--	--	--
Jordan[2]	23,208	28,247	31,508	--	--	6.4	7.5	8.1	--	--
Kuwait	9,842	10,283	11,051	--	--	5.3	5.2	5.4	--	--
Turkey[1,3]	436,065	448,144	450,763	--	--	8.2	8.2	7.9	--	--

Source: Selected from "Marriages and crude marriage rates, by urban/rural residence: 1987-1991," United Nations, *Demographic Yearbook,* 1991, Table 23, pp. 490+. *Notes:* 1. Data are estimated to be incomplete (less than 90%). 2. Excluding data for Jordanian territory under occupation since 1967 by Israeli military forces. Excluding foreigners, but including registered Palestinian refugees. 3. For provincial capitals and district centers only; however, rates computed on total population.

★ 835 ★

Marriages and Divorces

North American Divorces

This table shows the total number of divorces in selected North American countries for the years 1987 through 1991 (as available). Divorce rates, the number of final divorce decrees granted under civil law per 1,000 mid-year population, are also shown.

Country	Number					Rate				
	1987	1988	1989	1990	1991	1987	1988	1989	1990	1991
North America										
Bermuda	186	183	172	--	--	3.24	3.08	2.86	--	--
Canada	78,160	--	80,716	--	--	3.05	--	3.08	--	--
Greenland	151	95	132	--	--	2.79	--	2.38	--	--
United States	1,166,000	1,154,764	1,163,000	1,175,000	1,187,000	4.80	4.71	4.70	4.70	4.73

Source: Selected from "Divorces and crude divorce rates: 1987-1991," United Nations, *Demographic Yearbook*, 1991, Table 25, pp. 508-511. Data exclude annulments and legal separations unless otherwise specified. Rates are shown only for countries or areas having at least a total 100 divorces in a given year. 1991 data are provisional.

★ 836 ★

Marriages and Divorces

North American Marriages by Age-I

This table shows the total number of marriages in selected North American countries for the latest available year and the number of marriages by age of the bride and groom, for brides and grooms aged under 15 through age 34. The legal age of marriage is also shown.

Country	Age[1]	All ages	Under 15	15-19	20-24	25-29	30-34
North America							
Canada							
1989							
Groom	2	190,640	2	2,203	44,839	67,302	32,113
Bride	2	190,640	7	10,335	66,788	56,854	24,766
United States							
1989[3,4,5]							
Groom	2	1,852,275	7,765	75,961	497,398	503,901	292,072
Bride	2	1,852,275	50,893	167,465	583,641	447,175	243,678

Source: Selected from "Marriages by age of bridegroom and by age of bride: latest available year," United Nations, *Demographic Yearbook*, 1991, Table 24, pp. 497+. Data are legal (recognized) marriages performed and registered. *Notes:* 1. Age below which marriage is unlawful or invalid without dispensation by competent authority. 2. Varies among major civil divisions, or ethnic or religious groups. 3. Marriages performed in varying number of states. These data are not to be considered as necessarily representative of the country. 4. Based on returns of sample marriage records. 5. For under 18 and 18-19 years, as appropriate.

★ 837 ★

Marriages and Divorces

North American Marriages by Age-II

This table shows the total number of marriages in selected North American countries for the latest available year and the number of marriages by age of the bride and groom, for brides and grooms aged 35-60+. The legal age of marriage is also shown.

Country	Age[1]	All ages	35-39	40-44	45-49	50-54	55-59	60+	Unknown
North America									
Canada									
1989									
Groom	2	190,640	16,138	9,824	5,997	3,793	2,804	5,243	382
Bride	2	190,640	12,497	7,541	4,470	2,513	1,695	3,012	162
United States									
1989[3,4,5]									
Groom	2	852,275	280,301	[6]	110,117	[6]	50,087	34,673	--
Bride	2	1,852,275	233,438	[6]	77,767	[6]	29,189	19,029	--

Source: Selected from "Marriages by age of bridegroom and by age of bride: latest available year," United Nations, *Demographic Yearbook*, 1991, Table 24, pp. 497+. Data are legal (recognized) marriages performed and registered. *Notes:* 1. Age below which marriage is unlawful or invalid without dispensation by competent authority. 2. Varies among major civil divisions, or ethnic or religious groups. 3. Marriages performed in varying number of states. These data are not to be considered as necessarily representative of the country. 4. Based on returns of sample marriage records. 5. For under 18 and 18-19 years, as appropriate. 6. Figure in preceding column includes this age group.

★ 838 ★

Marriages and Divorces

North American Marriages: 1987-1991

This table shows the total number of marriages in North America and the marriage rate, for available years between 1987 and 1991. Rates are the number of legal (recognized) marriages performed and registered per 1,000 mid-year population. Rates are shown only for countries or areas having at least a total of 100 marriages in a given year.

Country	Number					Rate				
	1987	1988	1989	1990	1991	1987	1988	1989	1990	1991
North America										
Bermuda	786	868	877	907	--	13.7	14.6	14.6	15.0	--
Canada	182,151	187,860	190,640	--	--	7.1	7.2	7.3	--	--
Greenland	385	376	396	--	--	7.1	6.9	7.1	--	--
United States	2,403,378	2,395,926	2,404,000	2,448,000	2,371,000	9.9	9.8	9.7	9.8	9.4

Source: Selected from "Marriages and crude marriage rates, by urban/rural residence: 1987-1991," United Nations, *Demographic Yearbook*, 1991, Table 23, pp. 490+. 1991 figures are provisional.

★ 839 ★

Marriages and Divorces

Oceanian Divorces

This table shows the total number of divorces in selected Oceanian countries for the years 1987 through 1991 (as available). Divorce rates, the number of final divorce decrees granted under civil law per 1,000 mid-year population, are also shown.

Country	Number					Rate				
	1987	1988	1989	1990	1991	1987	1988	1989	1990	1991
Oceania										
American Samoa	--	42	--	--	--	--	--	--	--	--
Australia[1]	39,725	41,007	41,383	42,635	--	2.44	2.48	2.46	2.49	--
Guam[2]	1,279	--	--	--	--	10.12	--	--	--	--
New Caledonia	166	--	--	--	--	1.05	--	--	--	--
New Zealand	8,709	8,674	8,555	9,036	9,133	2.65	2.63	2.58	2.70	2.70

Source: Selected from "Divorces and crude divorce rates: 1987-1991," United Nations, *Demographic Yearbook*, 1991, Table 25, pp. 508-511. Data exclude annulments and legal separations unless otherwise specified. Rates are shown only for countries or areas having at least a total 100 divorces in a given year. 1991 data are provisional. *Notes:* 1. Excluding full-blooded aborigines estimated at 49,036 in June 1966. 2. Including U.S. military personnel, their dependents and contract employees.

★ 840 ★

Marriages and Divorces

Oceanian Marriages by Age-I

This table shows the total number of marriages in selected Oceanian countries for the latest available year and the number of marriages by age of the bride and groom, for brides and grooms aged under 35-60+. The legal age of marriage is also shown (when provided).

Country	Age[1]	All ages	35-39	40-44	45-49	50-54	55-59	60+	Unknown
Oceania									
Australia									
1990									
Groom	18	116,959	9,850	6,320	3,913	2,458	1,640	2,956	--
Bride	15	116,959	7,365	4,718	3,032	1,717	861	1,612	4
Fiji									
1987									
Groom	18	6,039	319	186	110	63	44	68	1
Bride	16	6,039	187	85	57	40	19	9	1
Guam									
1987[2]									
Groom	17	1,512	158	100	43	30	24	19	1
Bride	17	1,512	135	49	19	19	5	4	--

[Continued]

★ 840 ★

Oceanian Marriages by Age-I
[Continued]

Country	Age[1]	All ages	35-39	40-44	45-49	50-54	55-59	60+	Unknown
New Zealand 1989									
Groom	16	22,733	1,821	1,228	732	511	390	671	--
Bride	16	22,733	1,365	956	574	328	198	388	--

Source: Selected from "Marriages by age of bridegroom and by age of bride: latest available year," United Nations, *Demographic Yearbook*, 1991, Table 24, pp. 497+. Data are legal (recognized) marriages performed and registered. *Notes:* 1. Age below which marriage is unlawful or invalid without dispensation by competent authority. 2. Including U.S. military personnel, their dependents and contract employees.

★ 841 ★

Marriages and Divorces

Oceanian Marriages by Age-I

This table shows the total number of marriages in selected Oceanian countries for the latest available year and the number of marriages by age of the bride and groom, for brides and grooms aged under 16 through age 34. The legal age of marriage is also shown (when provided).

Country	Age[1]	All ages	Under 16	16-19	20-24	25-29	30-34
Oceania							
Australia 1990							
Groom	18	116,959	24	1,460	30,278	38,702	19,358
Bride	15	116,959	10	7,288	44,201	31,678	14,473
Fiji 1987							
Groom	18	6,039	--	397	2,421	1,726	704
Bride	16	6,039	--	1,870	2,456	915	400
Guam 1987[2]							
Groom	17	1,512	--	9	415	454	259
Bride	17	1,512	1	43	538	447	252
New Zealand 1989							
Groom	16	22,733	--	280	5,882	7,458	3,760
Bride	16	22,733	--	1,261	8,890	6,124	2,649

Source: Selected from "Marriages by age of bridegroom and by age of bride: latest available year," United Nations, *Demographic Yearbook*, 1991, Table 24, pp. 497+. Data are legal (recognized) marriages performed and registered. *Notes:* 1. Age below which marriage is unlawful or invalid without dispensation by competent authority. 2. Including U.S. military personnel, their dependents and contract employees.

★ 842 ★

Marriages and Divorces

Oceanian Marriages: 1987-1991

This table shows the total number of marriages in Oceania and the marriage rate, for available years between 1987 and 1991. Rates are the number of legal (recognized) marriages performed and registered per 1,000 mid-year population. Rates are shown only for countries or areas having at least a total of 100 marriages in a given year.

Country	Number					Rate				
	1987	1988	1989	1990	1991	1987	1988	1989	1990	1991
Oceania										
American Samoa	319	342	--	--	--	8.6	9.1	--	--	--
Australia	114,113	116,816	117,176	116,959	--	7.0	7.1	7.0	6.8	--
Cook Islands	91	122	--	--	--	--	6.9	--	--	--
Fiji	6,039	6,892	--	--	--	8.4	9.3	--	--	--
French Polynesia	1,246	1,264	1,093	--	--	6.8	6.7	5.7	--	--
Guam[1]	1,512	--	--	--	--	12.0	--	--	--	--
New Caledonia	729	--	--	--	--	4.6	--	--	--	--
New Zealand	24,443	23,485	22,733	23,341	23,065	7.5	7.1	6.9	7.0	6.8
Norfolk Island	--	25	--	--	--	--	--	--	--	--
Northern Mariana Islands	--	--	713	--	--	--	--	28.5	--	--
Tongo	573	347	592	696	--	6.0	3.6	6.2	7.3	--

Source: Selected from "Marriages and crude marriage rates, by urban/rural residence: 1987-1991," United Nations, *Demographic Yearbook*, 1991, Table 23, pp. 490+. 1991 data are provisional. *Note:* 1. Incl. U.S. military personnel, their dependents & contract employees.

★ 843 ★

Marriages and Divorces

Will Divorce: 1990

This table shows the percentage of ever-married women between the ages of 20 and 54 whose first marriage had ended in divorce by June 1990. The table also shows the percentage of these marriages that was predicted to end in divorce if the parties' future experience were similar to that of older cohorts during 1975 to 1980 and 1985 to 1990. The data seem to indicate that women born during the early and middle baby-boom years are likely to have higher eventual percents divorced than their predecessors or successors. The low divorce prospects for the younger women may be due to the fact that these women are more likely to marry later than the older women.

[Universe is ever-married women 20 to 54.]

Age	Ended in divorce by June 1990	May end in divorce if their future experience is similar to older cohorts during[1]	
		1975-1980	1985-1990
20 to 24	12.5%	49.2%	37.6%
25 to 29	19.2%	46.4%	39.0%
30 to 34	28.1%	46.25	40.8%
35 to 39	34.1%	44.8%	42.0%
40 to 44	35.8%	41.9%	39.9%
45 to 49	35.2%	38.7%	36.2%
50 to 54	29.5%	32.0%	30.2%

Source: "Percent of Women Whose First Marriage Ended in Divorce and May Eventually End in Divorce: June 1990," U.S. Bureau of the Census, Current Population Reports, P23-180, *Marriage, Divorce, and Remarriage in the 1990's,*" Table C, p. 5. *Note:* 1. Increments through age 65.

★ 844 ★

Marriages and Divorces

Will Divorce Again: 1990

This table shows the percentage of women whose second marriage ended in redivorce and may eventually end in redivorce if their future experience is similar to older cohorts during the periods 1980 to 1985 and 1985 to 1990. In 1990, about 3.1 million women aged 15 to 65 had ended their first two marriages in divorce. These women represented 5% of all ever-married women and 29% of all women who remarried after their first divorce. By contrast, in 1990, 17.2 million women 15 to 65 years old had ended a first marriage by divorce, representing about 28% of all ever-married women. According to the source, previous studies indicate that redivorce is somewhat more likely than first divorce, and redivorce occurs sooner after remarriage than first divorce occurs after first marriage[1].

[X Not applicable.]

Age	Ended in redivorce by June 1990	May end in redivorce if their future experience is similar to older cohorts during:	
		1975-1980	1985-1990
20 to 24	13.1%	62.1%	46.8%
25 to 29	17.8%	57.1%	42.4%
30 to 34	22.7%	57.6%	42.8%
35 to 39	28.5%	55.6%	40.1%
40 to 44	30.6%	49.4%	38.5%
45 to 49	36.4%	49.8%	40.9%
50 to 54	34.5%	45.7%	38.3%
55 to 59	31.1%	38.3%	31.1%
60 to 65	27.0%	X	X

Source: "Percent of Women Whose Second Marriage Ended in Redivorce and May Eventually End in Redivorce: June 1990," U.S. Bureau of the Census, Current Population Reports, P23-180, *Marriage, Divorce, and Remarriage in the 1990's*," Table D, p. 7. Universe is women 20 to 65 married two or more times whose first marriage ended in divorce. *Notes:* 1. Castro Martin, Teresa, and Larry L. Bumpass (1989). "Recent Trends and Differentials in Marital Disruption." *Demography*, Vol. 26, No. 1, pp. 37-51.

Population

★ 845 ★

Asian and Near Eastern Young and Elderly Population: 1990

This table gives the total female population in thousands, in Asia and the Near East in 1990. It shows the percentage who were under age 15 and the percentage who were 60 years old and over in 1990.

[Numbers in thousands, except percent.]

Country	Female population	Under age 15	60 years and over
Asia, excluding Near East			
Afghanistan	8,042	42%	5%
Bahrain	210	39%	4%
Bangladesh	56,033	44%	4%
Bhutan	732	40%	6%
Cambodia	732	40%	6%
China	551,124	26%	10%
Hong Kong	2,828	22%	14%
India	412,328	37%	7%
Indonesia	90,517	34%	7%
Korea			
Dem. People's Rep.	11,539	36%	7%
Republic of	21,742	26%	9%
Malaysia	8,602	35%	6%
Mongolia	1,110	41%	6%
Myanmar	20,942	36%	7%
Nepal	9,318	42%	5%
Pakistan	58,798	46%	4%
Papua New Guinea	1,930	42%	5%
Philippines	31,046	39%	6%
Singapore	1,328	22%	9%
Sri Lanka	8,575	32%	8%
Thailand	27,751	32%	7%
Vietnam	34,265	38%	7%
Near East			
Bahrain	210	39%	4%
Cyprus	352	25%	15%
Iraq	9,278	46%	5%
Israel	2,292	30%	13%
Jordan	2,078	48%	4%

[Continued]

848

★ 845 ★

Asian and Near Eastern Young and Elderly Population:
1990
[Continued]

Country	Female population	Under age 15	60 years and over
Kuwait	897	45%	3%
Lebanon	1,525	34%	8%
Oman	698	47%	5%
Qatar	138	46%	3%
Saudi Arabia	6,450	49%	5%
Syrian Arab Republic	6,176	48%	4%
Turkey	27,072	35%	7%
United Arab Emirates	518	46%	3%
Yemen	5,447	45%	5%

Source: Selected from *The World's Women: Trends and Statistics 1970-1990*, United Nations, 1991, Table 1, p. 22.

★ 846 ★

Population

Childless Women: 1992

This table shows total number of women in thousands by marital status and gives the percentage of those who were childless in 1992 by race and age.

[As of June. Numbers in thousands.]

Characteristic	Total no. of women (1,000)	Women by no. of children ever born	
		Total	None
All Races[1]			
Women ever married	37,260	100%	18%
15 to 19 years old	339	100%	44%
20 to 24 years old	3,064	100%	38%
25 to 29 years old	6,780	100%	28%
30 to 34 years old	9,050	100%	17%
35 to 39 years old	9,337	100%	12%
40 to 44 years old	8,690	100%	11%
Women never married	21,354	100%	81%
15 to 19 years old	7,847	100%	95%
20 to 24 years old	6,023	100%	80%
25 to 29 years old	3,259	100%	70%
30 to 34 years old	2,199	100%	64%
35 to 39 years old	1,300	100%	65%
40 to 44 years old	726	100%	75%

[Continued]

★ 846 ★

Childless Women: 1992
[Continued]

Characteristic	Total no. of women (1,000)	Women by no. of children ever born	
		Total	None
White			
Women ever married	32,165	100%	19%
15 to 19 years old	313	100%	45%
20 to 24 years old	2,708	100%	40%
25 to 29 years old	5,929	100%	28%
30 to 34 years old	7,799	100%	17%
35 to 39 years old	7,993	100%	13%
40 to 44 years old	7,422	100%	12%
Women never married	15,993	100%	88%
15 to 19 years old	6,191	100%	96%
20 to 24 years old	4,674	100%	87%
25 to 29 years old	2,287	100%	80%
30 to 34 years old	1,476	100%	77%
35 to 39 years old	837	100%	82%
40 to 44 years old	529	100%	88%
Black			
Women ever married	3,585	100%	11%
15 to 19 years old	16	100%	[2]
20 to 24 years old	238	100%	22%
25 to 29 years old	608	100%	19%
30 to 34 years old	858	100%	12%
35 to 39 years old	934	100%	7%
40 to 44 years old	930	100%	7%
Women never married	4,432	100%	53%
15 to 19 years old	1,297	100%	88%
20 to 24 years old	1,097	100%	47%
25 to 29 years old	813	100%	41%
30 to 34 years old	634	100%	31%
35 to 39 years old	412	100%	30%
40 to 44 years old	179	100%	34%

Source: Selected from "Childless Women and Children Ever Born, by Race, Age, and Marital Status: 1992," U.S. Bureau of the Census, *Statistical Abstract of the United States, 1994*, table 105, p. 82. Also in source, number of children ever born (one and two or more). Primary sources: U.S. Bureau of the Census, *Current Population Reports*, series P20; and unpublished data. Covers civilian noninstitutional population. *Notes:* 1. Includes other races, not shown separately. 2. Base figure too small to meet statistical standards for reliability.

★ 847 ★
Population

Children Ever Born: 1992

This table shows total number of women in thousands, and gives the percentage of those who ever had one child or two or more children, by marital status and race, in 1992.

[As of June. Numbers in thousands.]

Characteristic	Total no. of women (1,000)	Women by number of children ever born		
		Total	One	Two or more
All Races[1]				
Women ever married	37,260	100%	23%	59%
15 to 19 years old	339	100%	46%	10%
20 to 24 years old	3,064	100%	34%	28%
25 to 29 years old	6,780	100%	30%	43%
30 to 34 years old	9,050	100%	23%	60%
35 to 39 years old	9,337	100%	19%	69%
40 to 44 years old	8,690	100%	18%	71%
Women never married	21,354	100%	10%	9%
15 to 19 years old	7,847	100%	4%	1%
20 to 24 years old	6,023	100%	13%	7%
25 to 29 years old	3,259	100%	13%	17%
30 to 34 years old	2,199	100%	15%	22%
35 to 39 years old	1,300	100%	13%	22%
40 to 44 years old	726	100%	11%	15%
White				
Women ever married	32,165	100%	23%	58%
15 to 19 years old	313	100%	47%	8%
20 to 24 years old	2,708	100%	35%	26%
25 to 29 years old	5,929	100%	30%	41%
30 to 34 years old	7,799	100%	23%	60%
35 to 39 years old	7,993	100%	19%	68%
40 to 44 years old	7,422	100%	17%	72%
Women never married	15,993	100%	7%	5%
15 to 19 years old	6,191	100%	3%	1%
20 to 24 years old	4,674	100%	9%	4%
25 to 29 years old	2,287	100%	10%	10%
30 to 34 years old	1,476	100%	13%	10%
35 to 39 years old	837	100%	8%	10%
40 to 44 years old	529	100%	6%	6%
Black				
Women ever married	3,585	100%	23%	66%
15 to 19 years old	16	100%	[2]	[2]
20 to 24 years old	238	100%	28%	50%

[Continued]

★ 847 ★

Children Ever Born: 1992
[Continued]

Characteristic	Total no. of women (1,000)	Women by number of children ever born		
		Total	One	Two or more
25 to 29 years old	608	100%	27%	54%
30 to 34 years old	858	100%	22%	66%
35 to 39 years old	934	100%	22%	71%
40 to 44 years old	930	100%	22%	72%
Women never married	4,432	100%	20%	27%
15 to 19 years old	1,297	100%	9%	4%
20 to 24 years old	1,097	100%	29%	23%
25 to 29 years old	813	100%	23%	37%
30 to 34 years old	634	100%	21%	49%
35 to 39 years old	412	100%	24%	47%
40 to 44 years old	179	100%	26%	41%

Source: Selected from "Childless Women and Children Ever Born, by Race, Age, and Marital Status: 1992," U.S. Bureau of the Census, *Statistical Abstract of the United States, 1994*, table 105, p. 82. Primary sources: U.S. Bureau of the Census, *Current Population Reports*, series P20; and unpublished data. Covers civilian noninstitutional population. *Notes:* 1. Includes other races, not shown separately. 2. Base figure too small to meet statistical standards for reliability.

★ 848 ★

Population

Developed Countries' Young and Elderly Population: 1990

This table gives the total female population in thousands, in developed countries 1990. It shows the percentage who were under age 15 and the percentage who were 60 years old and over in 1990.

[Numbers in thousands, except percent.]

Country	Female population	Under age 15	60 years and over
Developed Countries			
Albania	1,575	32%	9%
Australia	8,391	22%	17%
Austria	3,908	16%	24%
Belgium	5,080	17%	23%
Bulgaria	4,546	19%	21%
Canada	13,393	20%	18%
Czechoslovakia	8,032	22%	19%
Denmark	2,600	16%	23%
Finland	2,561	18%	22%
France	28,748	19%	22%

[Continued]

★ 848 ★

Developed Countries' Young and Elderly Population:
1990
[Continued]

Country	Female population	Under age 15	60 years and over
Germany[1]			
Fed. Rep. of Germany	31,436	14%	25%
former German Dem. Rep.	8,689	18%	23%
Greece	5,098	19%	21%
Hungary	5,463	19%	22%
Iceland	126	25%	16%
Ireland	1,853	27%	16%
Israel	2,292	30%	13%
Italy	29,453	16%	22%
Japan	62,758	18%	19%
Luxembourg	188	16%	22%
Malta	179	22%	16%
Netherlands	7,455	17%	20%
New Zealand	1,705	22%	17%
Norway	2,131	18%	24%
Poland	19,661	24%	17%
Portugal	5,320	20%	20%
Romania	11,781	23%	17%
Spain	19,964	20%	21%
Sweden	4,226	16%	26%
Switzerland	3,338	16%	23%
United Kingdom	29,148	18%	23%
United States	127,668	20%	19%
U.S.S.R.	151,660	24%	19%
Yugoslavia	12,051	22%	16%

Source: Selected from *The World's Women: Trends and Statistics 1970-1990,* United Nations, 1991, Table 1, p. 22. *Note:* 1. Data as of the end of June 1990, before unification.

★ 849 ★

Population

Elderly Population Worldwide

This table shows the countries of the world where women aged 60 and over make up 19% or more of the population. In every place in the world except Africa, the proportion of women aged 60 and over is rising because of longer life expectancy and the bearing of fewer children.

Country or Area	Female pop. aged 60+
Austria	24%
Belgium	23%
Bulgaria	21%
Czechoslovakia	19%
Denmark	23%
Finland	22%
France	22%
Germany	
Fed. Rep. of Germany	25%
former German Dem. Rep.	23%
Greece	21%
Hungary	22%
Italy	22%
Japan	19%
Luxembourg	22%
Netherlands	20%
Norway	24%
Portugal	20%
Spain	21%
Sweden	26%
Switzerland	23%
United Kingdom	23%
United States	19%
U.S.S.R.	19%

Source: "Where women aged 60 and over make up 19% or more of the female population," *The World's Women: Trends and Statistics 1970-1990*, United Nations, 1991, Table 1.5, p. 13. Primary source: Statistical Office and Population Division of the United Nations Secretariat.

★ 850 ★

Population

Elderly Population, Characteristics: 1980-1993

This table shows the total population age 65 years old and over, male, female, and black populations age 65 years old (in millions), and characteristics of these groups.

[As of March, except as noted.]

Characteristic	Total				Male				Female			
	1980	1985	1990	1993	1980	1985	1990	1993	1980	1985	1990	1993
Total[1]	24.2	26.8	29.6	30.9	9.9	11.0	12.3	12.8	14.2	15.8	17.2	18.0
White	21.9	24.2	26.5	27.5	9.0	9.9	11.0	11.4	12.9	14.3	15.4	16.1
Black	2.0	2.2	2.5	2.7	0.8	0.9	1.0	1.1	1.2	1.3	1.5	1.6
Percent below poverty level[2]	15.2%	12.4%	11.4%	12.9%	11.1%	8.7%	7.8%	8.9%	17.9%	15.0%	13.9%	15.7%
Marital status												
Single	5.5%	5.2%	4.6%	4.4%	4.9%	5.3%	4.2%	4.4%	5.9%	5.1%	4.9%	4.4%
Married	55.4%	55.2%	56.1%	56.6%	78.0%	77.2%	76.5%	76.8%	39.5%	39.9%	41.4%	42.2%
Spouse present	53.6%	53.4%	54.1%	54.7%	76.1%	75.0%	74.2%	74.6%	37.9%	38.3%	39.7%	40.6%
Spouse absent	1.8%	1.8%	2.0%	1.9%	1.9%	2.2%	2.3%	2.2%	1.7%	1.6%	1.7%	1.6%
Widowed	35.7%	35.6%	34.2%	33.7%	13.5%	13.8%	14.2%	14.3%	51.2%	50.7%	48.6%	47.6%
Divorced	3.5%	4.0%	5.0%	5.3%	3.6%	3.7%	5.0%	4.5%	3.4%	4.3%	5.1%	5.8%
Family status												
In families[3]	67.6%	67.3%	66.7%	67.5%	83.0%	82.4%	81.9%	81.6%	56.8%	56.7%	55.8%	57.4%
Nonfamily house-holders	31.2%	31.1%	31.9%	31.2%	15.7%	15.4%	16.6%	16.4%	42.0%	42.1%	42.8%	41.7%
Secondary individuals	1.2%	1.6%	1.4%	1.3%	1.3%	2.2%	1.5%	1.9%	1.1%	1.1%	1.4%	0.9%
Living arrangements												
Living in household	99.8%	99.6%	99.7%	99.9%	99.9%	99.5%	99.9%	99.9%	99.7%	99.6%	99.5%	99.9%
Living alone	30.3%	30.2%	31.0%	30.3%	14.9%	14.7%	15.7%	15.5%	41.0%	41.1%	42.0%	40.8%
Spouse present	53.6%	53.4%	54.1%	54.0%	76.1%	75.0%	74.3%	73.7%	37.9%	38.3%	39.7%	40.1%
Live with some-one else	15.9%	15.9%	14.6%	15.5%	8.9%	9.8%	9.9%	10.7%	20.8%	20.2%	17.8%	19.0%
Not in household[4]	0.2%	0.4%	0.3%	0.1%	0.1%	0.5%	0.1%	0.1%	0.3%	0.4%	0.5%	0.1%
Years of school completed												
8 years or less	43.1%	35.4%	28.5%	24.1%	45.3%	37.2%	30.0%	25.0%	41.6%	34.1%	27.5%	23.5%
1-3 yrs high school	16.2%	16.5%	16.1%	15.6%[5]	15.5%	15.7%	15.7%	14.9%[5]	16.7%	17.0%	16.4%	16.1%[5]
4 yrs high school	24.0%	29.0%	32.9%	34.2%[6]	21.4%	26.4%	29.0%	29.7%[6]	25.8%	30.7%	35.6%	37.4%[6]
1-3 yrs college	8.2%	9.8%	10.9%	14.1%[7]	7.5%	9.1%	10.8%	14.3%[7]	8.6%	10.3%	11.0%	13.9%[7]
4 yrs+ college	8.6%	9.4%	11.6%	12.0%[8]	10.3%	11.5%	14.5%	16.1%[8]	7.4%	8.0%	9.5%	9.0%[8]
Labor force participation[9]												
Employed	12.2%	10.4%	11.5%	10.9%	18.4%	15.3%	15.9%	15.1%	7.8%	7.0%	8.4%	7.9%

[Continued]

★ 850 ★

Elderly Population, Characteristics: 1980-1993
[Continued]

Characteristic	Total				Male				Female			
	1980	1985	1990	1993	1980	1985	1990	1993	1980	1985	1990	1993
Unemployed	0.4%	0.3%	0.4%	0.4%	0.6%	0.5%	0.5%	0.5%	0.3%	0.2%	0.3%	0.3%
Not in labor force	87.5%	89.2%	88.1%	88.7%	81.0%	84.2%	83.6%	84.4%	91.9%	92.7%	91.3%	91.8%

Source: "Persons 65 years Old and Over—Characteristics, by Sex: 1980 to 1993," U.S. Bureau of the Census, *Statistical Abstract of the United States 1994*, Table 48, p. 47. Primary source: Except as noted, U.S. Bureau of the Census, *Current Population Reports*, P20-450, and earlier reports; P60-185 and earlier reports; and unpublished data. *Notes:* 1. Includes other races, not shown separately. 2. Poverty status based on income in preceding year. 3. Excludes those living in unrelated subfamilies. 4. In group quarters other than institutions. 5. Represents those who completed ninth to twelfth grade, but have no high school diploma. 6. High school graduate. 7. Some college or associate degree. 8. Bachelor's or advanced degree. 9. Annual averages of monthly figures. Source: U.S. Bureau of Labor Statistics, *Employment and Earnings*, January issues.

★ 851 ★

Population

Elderly Population: 1980-1992

This table shows the total population age 65 years old and over and the female population age 65 years and over, by age group.

[In thousands. As of April, except 1992, as of July.]

Age group and Sex	Number (1,000)			Percent distribution		
	1980	1990	1992	1980	1990	1992
Persons 65 and over	25,549	31,079	32,285	100.0%	100.0%	100.0%
65 to 69 years	8,782	10,066	9,977	34.3%	32.4%	30.9%
70 to 74 years	6,798	7,980	8,483	26.6%	25.7%	26.3%
75 to 79 years	4,794	6,103	6,415	18.8%	19.6%	19.9%
80 to 84 years	2,935	3,909	4,150	11.5%	12.6%	12.9%
85 years old and over	2,240	3,021	3,259	8.8%	9.7%	10.1%
Females, 65 and over	15,245	18,586	19,240	100.0%	100.0%	100.0%
65 to 69 years	4,880	5,558	5,503	31.9%	29.9%	28.6%
70 to 74 years	3,945	4,580	4,833	25.9%	24.6%	25.1%
75 to 79 years	2,946	3,714	3,862	19.3%	20.0%	20.1%
80 to 84 years	1,916	2,553	2,693	12.6%	13.7%	14.0%
85 years old and over	1,559	2,180	2,349	10.3%	11.7%	12.2%

Source: Selected from "Population 65 Years Old and Over, by Age Group and Sex, 1980 to 1992, and Projections, 2000," U.S. Bureau of the Census, *Statistical Abstract of the United States 1994*, Table 47, p. 47. Primary source: U.S. Bureau of the Census, *Current Population Reports*, P25-1095 and P25-1104.

★ 852 ★

Population

Latin American/Caribbean Young and Elderly Population: 1990

This table gives the total female population in thousands, in Latin America and the Caribbean in 1990. It shows the percentage who were under age 15 and the percentage who were 60 years old and over in 1990.

[Numbers in thousands, except percent.]

Country	Female population	Under age 15	60 years and over
Latin America and the Caribbean			
Argentina	16,320	29%	15%
Bahamas, The (1985)	119	33%	7%
Barbados	136	24%	16%
Bolivia	3,709	43%	5%
Brazil	75,376	35%	7%
Chile	6,668	30%	10%
Colombia	15,840	36%	7%
Costa Rica	1,491	36%	7%
Cuba	5,076	22%	12%
Dominican Republic	3,526	38%	6%
Ecuador	5,358	40%	6%
El Salvador	2,677	43%	6%
Guadeloupe	174	25%	14%
Guatemala	4,550	45%	5%
Guyana	518	34%	7%
Haiti	3,312	38%	6%
Honduras	2,546	44%	5%
Jamaica	1,268	34%	9%
Martinique	170	23%	15%
Mexico	44,393	36%	6%
Nicaragua	1,931	45%	5%
Panama	1,188	35%	7%
Paraguay	2,111	40%	6%
Peru	11,083	39%	6%
Puerto Rico	1,903	27%	13%
Saint Lucia	72	43%	9%
Suriname	204	34%	7%
Trinidad and Tobago	643	31%	9%
Uruguay	1,590	25%	18%
Venezuela	9,781	38%	6%

Source: Selected from *The World's Women: Trends and Statistics 1970-1990*, United Nations, 1991, Table 1, p. 22.

★ 853 ★

Population

Middle East/North African Young and Elderly Population: 1990

This table gives the total female population in thousands, in the Middle East and North Africa in 1990. It shows the percentage who were under age 15 and the percentage who were 60 years old and over in 1990.

[Numbers in thousands, except percent.]

Country	Female population	Under age 15	60 years and over
Middle East/North Africa			
Algeria	12,678	44%	6%
Egypt	26,617	40%	7%
Iran	27,801	43%	5%
Iraq	9,278	46%	5%
Jordan	2,078	48%	4%
Kuwait	897	45%	3%
Lebanon	1,525	34%	8%
Libya			
Libyan Arab Jamahiriya	2,163	47%	4%
Morocco	12,556	40%	6%
Oman	698	47%	5%
Saudi Arabia	6,450	49%	5%
Syria			
Syrian Arab Republic	6,176	48%	4%
Tunisia	4,036	37%	6%
Turkey	27,072	35%	7%
United Arab Emirates	518	46%	3%
Yemen	5,447	45%	5%

Source: Selected from *The World's Women: Trends and Statistics 1970-1990*, United Nations, 1991, Table 1, p. 22.

★ 854 ★

Population

Most Females in Population Worldwide

This table shows the female percentage of the population in the 10 countries with the highest percentage of females.

Country	Female percentage of pop.
Cape Verde	53.7%
Monaco	53.4%
Soviet Union	53.4%
Swaziland	53.3%
East Germany	53.0%
Botswana	52.9%
Grenada	52.9%
Antigua	52.8%
Saint Lucia	52.8%
South Yemen	52.7%

Source: Selected from George Kurian, *The New Book of World Rankings*, Facts on File, Inc., New York, 1991, pp. 30-31, table entitled "Females in Population." Primary source: *U.N. Demographic Yearbook.*

★ 855 ★

Population

Ratio of Elderly Males to Females: 1990

This table shows the number of men per 100 women aged 65 and over in 1990.

Age	Men per 100 women
65-69	81
70-74	74
75-79	64
80-84	53
85-89	42
90-94	33
95-99	27
100+	27

Source: Selected from "Our Nation's Elderly—A Portrait," *Census and You*, December 1992, p. 6, table entitled "Many More Women Than Men Live to Very Old Ages." Primary source: *Sixty-Five Plus in America*, P-23, No. 178.

★ 856 ★

Population

Ratio of Females to Males Worldwide

This table shows the countries of the world where there are fewer than 95 women per 100 men. While women outnumber men in most regions of the world, fewer than half of the world's people were women in 1990. In some areas, this is because social and cultural factors deny girls and women the same advantages of nutrition and health care that men receive. In some countries, female infanticide, widow burning, and dowry deaths still exist. Abortion on the basis of preference for males is also occurring. India passed a law in 1994 providing for a fine of about $320 and penalties of up to three years in prison for those found guilty of administering or submitting to pre-natal tests only to determine the sex of a fetus[1].

Country or Area	Women per 100 men
Developed regions	
Albania	94.3
Africa	
Libyan Arab Jamahiriya	90.8
Asia and Pacific	
Eastern Asia	
China	94.3
Hong Kong	93.9
South-eastern Asia	
Brunei Darussalam	93.8
Southern Asia	
Afghanistan	94.5
Bangladesh	94.1
Bhutan	93.3
India	93.5
Nepal	94.8
Pakistan	92.1
Western Asia	
Bahrain	68.8[2]
Jordan	94.8
Kuwait	75.2[2]
Oman	90.6[2]
Qatar	59.8[2]
Saudi Arabia	84.0[1]
Turkey	94.8
United Arab Emirates	48.3[1]

[Continued]

★ 856 ★

Ratio of Females to Males Worldwide
[Continued]

Country or Area	Women per 100 men
Oceania	
Papua New Guinea	92.8
Vanuatu	91.7

Source: "Where there are fewer than 95 women per 100 men," *The World's Women: Trends and Statistics 1970-1990*, United Nations, 1991, Table 1.1, p. 11. Primary source: Statistical Office and Population Division of the United Nations Secretariat. Related reading: Irene Sege, "The Grim Mystery of World's Missing Women," *Boston Globe*, February 3, 1992, pp. 23+. *Notes:* 1. John F. Burns, "India Fights Abortion of Female Fetuses," *The New York Times*, August 27, 1994, p. 5 Y. 2. Oil-producing countries which also have large male immigrant populations.

★ 857 ★

Population

Ratio of Females to Males Worldwide: Fewest Men

This table shows the 20 countries of the world with the fewest men per 100 women in 1988.

Country	M per 100 F
USSR	89.9
Somalia	91.2
Barbados	91.4
North Yemen	91.4
East Germany	91.6
Botswana	91.7
Austria	91.7
Lesotho	92.6
West Germany	92.6
Hungary	93.2
Portugal	93.3
Finland	94.2
Lebanon	94.4
Italy	94.6
Mali	94.7
Central Arab Republic	94.8
Puerto Rico	94.9
Luxembourg	95.1
Czechoslovakia	95.1
United States	95.2

Source: "Fewest men per 100 women, 1988," *The Economist book of vital world statistics: a complete guide to the world in figures*, The Economist Books Ltd., London, 1990, p. 25.

★ 858 ★

Population

Ratio of Females to Males Worldwide: Most Men

This table shows the 20 countries of the world with the most men per 100 women in 1988.

Country	M per 100 F
United Arab Emirates	206.8
Qatar	167.3
Bahrain	145.3
Kuwait	132.9
Saudi Arabia	119.1
Oman	110.4
Libya	110.1
Pakistan	108.6
Papua New Guinea	107.8
Bhutan	107.2
India	107.0
Hong Kong	106.5
Bangladesh	106.3
Albania	106.0
China	106.0
Afghanistan	105.9
Turkey	105.4
Nepal	105.4
Jordan	105.4
Iraq	103.9

Source: "Most men per 100 women, 1988," *The Economist book of vital world statistics: a complete guide to the world in figures,* The Economist Books Ltd., London, 1990, p. 25.

★ 859 ★

Population

Ratio of Males to Females in Asia

This table shows the number of men per 100 women in 32 Asian countries or areas in 1992. It also shows the median age of the women in those countries. The developing nations of Asia (east of Iran) and the Pacific are home to the majority of the world's women. Women are outnumbered by men in most Asian countries.

Country or area	Sex ratio (men per 100 women)	Median age of women
China		
Mainland	106	26
Taiwan	106	28
India	107	22
Indonesia	100	23
Pakistan	106	18
Bangladesh	108	18
Vietnam	96	22
Philippines	99	21
Thailand	102	24
South Korea	101	28
Burma	100	22
Nepal	105	18
Malaysia	100	22
Sri Lanka	100	26
Afghanistan	108	18
Cambodia	91	20
Hong Kong	106	33
Laos	97	18
Papua New Guinea	107	18
Singapore	103	31
Mongolia	100	19
Bhutan	106	20
Fiji	102	22
Solomon Islands	104	16
Maldives	106	17
Western Samoa	107	19
Vanuatu	108	18
Micronesia	105	20
Tonga	102	18
Kiribati	105	20
Marshall Islands	105	15
Cook Islands	102	18

Source: Selected from "An Overview of the 32 Countries or Areas: 1992," U.S. Bureau of the Census, *Statistical Brief: Statistical Indicators on Women: An Asian Perspective*, November 1993, p. 2.

★ 860 ★

Population

Ratio of Males to Females: 1970-1990

This table shows the ratio of females to males by age group as of April 1, 1970, 1980, and 1990.

[Number of males per 100 females. Total resident population.]

Age	1970	1980	1990
All ages	94.5	95.1	95.3
Under 14 years	103.9	104.6	104.9
14 to 24 years	98.7	101.9	104.6
25 to 44 years	95.5	97.4	98.9
45 to 64 years	91.6	90.7	92.5
65 years and over	72.1	67.6	67.2

Source: Selected from "Ratio of Males to Females, by Age Group, 1950 to 1992, and Projections, 2000 and 2025, U.S. Bureau of the Census, *Statistical Abstract of the United States 1994*, Table 14, p. 15. Primary source: U.S. Bureau of the Census, *U.S. Census of Population: 1970*, vol I, part B; *Current Population Reports*, P25-1095 and P25-1104; and unpublished data.

★ 861 ★

Population

Resident Population by Age: 1970-1990-I

This table shows the total population of the United States, total population by age, and the female and male populations by age, ages under 5 years through 44 years, from the 1970 through the 1990 censuses.

[In thousands. As of April 1.]

Year	Total, all all years	Under 5 years	5-9 years	10-14 years	15-19 years	20-24 years	25-29 years	30-34 years	35-39 years	40-44 years
1970, total[1]	203,235	17,163	19,969	20,804	19,084	16,383	13,486	11,437	11,113	11,988
Female	104,309	8,413	9,794	10,206	9,443	8,458	6,859	5,838	5,697	6,166
Male	98,926	8,750	10,175	10,598	9,641	7,925	6,626	5,599	5,416	5,823
1980, total	226,546	16,348	16,700	18,242	21,168	21,319	19,521	17,561	13,965	11,669
Female	116,493	7,986	8,161	8,926	10,413	10,655	9,816	8,884	7,104	5,961
Male	110,053	8,362	8,539	9,316	10,755	10,663	9,705	8,677	6,862	5,708
1990, total[2]	248,710	18,758	18,035	17,060	17,882	19,132	21,328	21,833	19,846	17,589
Female	127,471	9,159	8,803	8,322	8,709	9,389	10,625	10,971	10,013	8,913
Male	121,239	9,599	9,232	8,739	9,173	9,743	10,702	10,862	9,833	8,676

Source: Selected from "Resident Population, by Age and Sex: 1970 to 1992," U.S. Bureau of the Census, *Statistical Abstract of the United States 1994*, Table 13, p. 14. Primary source: U.S. Bureau of the Census, *Current Population Reports*, P25-917 and P25-1095; and unpublished data. Data excludes Armed Forces overseas. *Notes:* 1. Official count. The revised 1970 resident population count is 203,302,031; the difference of 66,733 is due to errors found after release of the official series. 2. Data for the population by age for April 1, 1990 are modified counts. The review of detailed 1990 information indicated that respondents tended to provide their age as of the date of completion of the questionnaire, not their age as of April 1, 1990. In addition, there may have been a tendency for respondents to round up their age if they were close to having a birthday.

★ 862 ★

Population

Resident Population by Age: 1970-1990-II

This table shows the female and male populations of the United States by age, ages 45-85 and over, ages 5-13, 14-17, 18-24, and median ages, from the 1970 through the 1990 censuses.

[In thousands. As of April 1.]

Year	45-49 years	50-54 years	55-59 years	60-64 years	65-74 years	75-84 years	85 years and over	5-13 years	14-17 years	18-24 years	Median age (year)
1970, total[1]	12,124	11,111	9,979	8,623	12,443	6,122	1,408	36,675	15,851	23,714	28.0
Female	6,269	5,759	5,210	4,593	7,002	3,684	919	17,987	7,782	12,131	29.3
Male	5,855	5,351	4,769	4,030	5,440	2,437	489	18,687	8,069	11,583	26.8
1980, total	11,090	11,710	11,615	10,088	15,581	7,729	2,240	31,159	16,247	30,022	30.0
Female	5,702	6,089	6,133	5,418	8,824	4,862	1,559	15,237	7,950	14,969	31.3
Male	5,388	5,621	5,482	4,670	6,757	2,867	682	15,923	8,298	15,054	28.8
1990, total[2]	13,744	11,313	10,487	10,625	18,045	10,012	3,021	31,826	13,340	26,942	32.8
Female	7,004	5,820	5,479	5,679	10,139	6,267	2,180	15,532	6,483	13,208	34.0
Male	6,739	5,493	5,008	4,947	7,907	3,745	841	16,295	6,857	13,734	31.6

Source: Selected from "Resident Population, by Age and Sex: 1970 to 1992," U.S. Bureau of the Census, *Statistical Abstract of the United States 1994,* Table 13, p. 14. Primary source: U.S. Bureau of the Census, *Current Population Reports,* P25-917 and P25-1095; and unpublished data. Data excludes Armed Forces overseas. *Notes:* 1. Official count. The revised 1970 resident population count is 203,302,031; the difference of 66,733 is due to errors found after release of the official series. 2. Data for the population by age for April 1, 1990 are modified counts. The review of detailed 1990 information indicated that respondents tended to provide their age as of the date of completion of the questionnaire, not their age as of April 1, 1990. In addition, there may have been a tendency for respondents to round up their age if they were close to having a birthday.

★ 863 ★

Population

Sub-Saharan African Young and Elderly Population: 1990

This table gives the total female population in thousands, in Sub-Saharan Africa in 1990. It shows the percentage who were under age 15 and the percentage who were 60 years old and over in 1990.

[Numbers in thousands, except percent.]

Country	Female population	Under age 15	60 years and over
Sub-Saharan Africa			
Angola	5,084	44%	5%
Benin	2,407	47%	5%
Botswana	671	47%	5%
Burkina	4,546	43%	5%
Burundi	2,780	45%	6%
Cameroon	5,701	43%	7%

[Continued]

★ 863 ★

Sub-Saharan African Young and Elderly Population:
1990
[Continued]

Country	Female population	Under age 15	60 years and over
Cape Verde	201	39%	7%
Central African Republic	1,495	42%	7%
Chad	2,878	42%	6%
Comoros	262	46%	5%
Congo	1,010	43%	6%
Cote d'Ivoire	6,211	50%	4%
Dijibouti	202	46%	4%
Equatorial Guinea	224	41%	7%
Ethiopia	23,550	45%	5%
Gabon	594	32%	10%
Gambia	435	43%	5%
Ghana	7,564	45%	5%
Guinea	3,479	43%	5%
Guinea-Bissau	507	40%	7%
Kenya	12,555	52%	5%
Lesotho	921	42%	6%
Liberia	1,263	46%	5%
Madagascar	6,049	45%	5%
Malawi	4,279	45%	5%
Mali	4,809	45%	5%
Mauritania	1,024	44%	5%
Mauritius	558	28%	8%
Mozambique	7,937	43%	6%
Namibia	942	45%	6%
Niger	3,585	47%	5%
Nigeria	57,009	48%	4%
Reunion	307	30%	9%
Rwanda	3,657	49%	4%
Senegal	3,722	44%	5%
Seychelles (1986)	33	35%	11%
Sierra Leone	2,112	44%	6%
Somalia	3,952	46%	4%
South Africa	17,731	36%	7%
Sudan	12,540	45%	5%
Swaziland	400	47%	5%
Tanzania	13,816	48%	4%
Togo	1,747	45%	5%

[Continued]

★ 863 ★

Sub-Saharan African Young and Elderly Population: 1990
[Continued]

Country	Female population	Under age 15	60 years and over
Uganda	9,295	48%	4%
Zaire	18,188	45%	5%
Zambia	4,285	48%	4%
Zimbabwe	4,903	44%	5%

Source: Selected from *The World's Women: Trends and Statistics 1970-1990*, United Nations, 1991, Table 1, p. 22.

★ 864 ★

Population

Urban and Rural Populations by Age: 1990

This table shows the female population by age according to the 1990 census and shows how many women lived in urban and rural areas and on farms.

Age	U.S.	Urban	Rural	Rural farm
Female	127,537,494	96,728,990	30,808,504	1,869,217
Under 3 years	5,328,627	4,088,192	1,240,435	59,718
3 and 4 years	3,585,008	2,705,456	879,552	44,298
5 to 9 years	8,836,345	6,500,511	2,335,834	129,853
10 to 14 years	8,363,399	6,018,548	2,344,851	145,437
15 to 17 years	4,874,273	3,515,024	1,359,249	87,376
18 and 19 years	3,719,669	2,920,398	799,271	43,634
20 to 24 years	9,176,002	7,462,924	1,713,078	74,466
25 to 29 years	10,614,778	8,422,946	2,191,832	89,898
30 to 34 years	11,142,783	8,570,346	2,572,437	119,055
35 to 39 years	10,061,512	7,576,140	2,485,372	126,642
40 to 44 years	8,950,913	6,678,890	2,272,023	131,538
45 to 49 years	7,118,795	5,238,422	1,880,373	132,676
50 to 54 years	5,920,436	4,353,040	1,567,396	128,400
55 to 59 years	5,481,587	4,036,069	1,445,518	131,611
60 to 64 years	5,682,160	4,250,202	1,431,958	123,675
65 to 74 years	10,225,733	7,767,760	2,457,973	189,660
75 years and over	8,455,474	6,624,122	1,831,352	111,280
Median age				
All persons	33.0	32.6	34.1	39.8

[Continued]

★ 864 ★

Urban and Rural Populations by Age: 1990

[Continued]

Age	U.S.	Urban	Rural	Rural farm
Male	31.8	31.3	33.4	39.2
Female	34.2	33.9	34.9	40.5

Source: Selected from "Age, Sex, Ability to Speak English, and Disability: 1990," U.S. Bureau of the Census, 1990 Census of Population, *Social and Economic Characteristics, United States*, 1990 CP-2-1, Table 15, p. 15.

Population Estimates and Projections

★ 865 ★

Asian Population: 2000

This table shows estimates of the total population of Asian countries in the year 2000 and estimates the number of women aged 15-49 (childbearing age) in 2000.

[Population in thousands.]

Country	Total	Women 15-49
Afghanistan	26,511	6,046
Bangladesh	150,589	36,389
Bhutan	1,906	436
Cambodia	10,046	2,460
China	1,299,180	345,578
Hong Kong	6,336	1,718
India	1,041,540	253,492
Indonesia	218,661	59,102
Korea, Dem. People's Rep.	26,117	7,242
Korea, Republic of	46,403	13,202
Laos	5,463	1,241
Malaysia	21,983	5,709
Mongolia	2,847	692
Myanmar	51,129	13,326
Nepal	24,084	5,654
Pakistan	162,409	36,722
Papua New Guinea	4,845	1,170
Philippines	77,473	20,064
Singapore	2,997	814
Sri Lanka	19,416	5,366

[Continued]

★ 865 ★

Asian Population: 2000
[Continued]

Country	Total	Women 15-49
Thailand	63,670	18,398
Vietnam	82,427	22,101

Source: Selected from John A. Ross, W. Parker Mauldin, Steven R. Green, et al., *Family Planning and Child Survival Programs as Assessed in 1991*, The Population Council, 1992, Table 1, p. 30, "Selected Demographic Characteristics, Developing and Developed Countries."

★ 866 ★

Population Estimates and Projections

Developed Countries' Population: 2000

This table shows estimates of the total population of developed countries in the year 2000 and estimates the number of women aged 15-49 (childbearing age) in 2000.

[Population in thousands.]

Country	Total	Women 15-49
Albania	3,795	993
Australia	18,855	4,829
Austria	7,613	1,868
Belgium	9,832	2,350
Bulgaria	9,071	2,131
Canada	28,488	7,297
Czechoslovakia	16,179	4,079
Denmark	5,153	1,222
Finland	5,077	1,222
France	58,145	14,041
Germany	76,962	18,006
Greece	10,193	2,402
Hungary	10,531	2,566
Ireland	4,086	1,061
Israel	5,321	1,352
Italy	57,195	13,894
Japan	128,470	29,276
Netherlands	15,829	3,901
New Zealand	3,662	933
Norway	4,331	1,042
Poland	40,366	10,364
Portugal	10,587	2,684
Romania	24,346	6,057
Spain	40,667	10,154
Sweden	8,560	1,875
Switzerland	6,762	1,592
United Kingdom	58,393	13,792

[Continued]

★ 866 ★

Developed Countries' Population: 2000
[Continued]

Country	Total	Women 15-49
United States	266,096	67,979
U.S.S.R.[1]	308,363	77,534
Yugoslavia[2]	24,900	6,237

Source: Selected from John A. Ross, W. Parker Mauldin, Steven R. Green, et al., *Family Planning and Child Survival Programs as Assessed in 1991*, The Population Council, 1992, Table 1, p. 30, "Selected Demographic Characteristics, Developing and Developed Countries." *Notes:* 1. According to the U.S. Bureau of the Census, International Data Base, the population of the former Soviet Union was 296,000,000 in 1994. Source: "Population, Vital Events, and Rates, by Country or Area: 1994," U.S. Bureau of the Census, *World Population Profile: 1994*, 1994, Table 4, p. A-12. 2. According to the U.S. Bureau of the Census, International Data Base, the population of the Former Yugoslavia was 24,295,000 in 1994. Source: "Population, Vital Events, and Rates, by Country or Area: 1994," U.S. Bureau of the Census, *World Population Profile: 1994*, 1994, Table 4, p. A-12. The U.S. view is that the Socialist Federal Republic of Yugoslavia has dissolved and no successor state represents its continuation. Macedonia has proclaimed independent statehood, but has not been recognized as a state by the U.S. Serbia and Montenegro have asserted the formation of a joint independent state, but this entity has not been recognized as a state by the U.S.

★ 867 ★

Population Estimates and Projections

Elderly Population: 2000

This table shows a projection of the population age 65 years old and over and a projection of the female population, by age group.

[In thousands. As of July.]

Age group and Sex	Number 2000	% distrib. 2000
Persons 65 years and over	35,322	100.0%
65 to 69 years	9,594	27.2%
70 to 74 years	8,957	25.4%
75 to 79 years	7,507	21.3%
80 to 84 years	4,931	14.0%
85 years old and over	4,333	12.3%
Females 65 years and over	20,719	100.0%
65 to 69 years	5,173	25.0%
70 to 74 years	4,993	24.1%
75 to 79 years	4,369	21.1%
80 to 84 years	3,089	14.9%
85 years old and over	3,095	14.9%

Source: Selected from "Population 65 Years Old and Over, by Age Group and Sex, 1980 to 1992, and Projections, 2000," U.S. Bureau of the Census, *Statistical Abstract of the United States 1994*, Table 47, p. 47. Primary source: U.S. Bureau of the Census, *Current Population Reports*, P25-1095 and P25-1104. Data are for middle series, assuming an ultimate total fertility rate = 2,150; life expectancy in 2050 = 82.6 years; and annual net immigration = 880,000.

★ 868 ★

Population Estimates and Projections

Estimates of the World's Population: 1990

This table shows total population of both sexes by age for world regions, as estimated for 1990. Female population is also shown.

[Population in millions.]

World Region	Both Sexes				Female			
	All ages	-15	15-64	65+	All ages	-15	15-64	65+
World total	5,292	1,710	3,254	328	2,628	835	1,605	188
Africa	642	289	334	19	323	144	169	11
Eastern Africa	197	93	99	5	99	46	50	3
Middle Africa	70	32	36	2	35	16	18	1
Northern Africa	141	58	77	5	70	28	38	3
Southern Africa	41	16	24	2	21	8	12	1
Western Africa	194	91	98	5	98	45	50	3
Latin America	448	161	266	21	225	79	134	12
Caribbean	34	11	21	2	17	5	11	1
Central America	118	46	68	4	59	22	34	2
South America	297	105	177	15	149	52	89	8
Northern America	276	59	182	34	141	29	92	20
Asia[1,2]	3,113	1,023	1,934	156	1,520	497	939	83
Eastern Asia[1]	1,336	344	908	84	652	166	439	47
Southern Asia	1,201	463	688	49	580	224	332	24
South Eastern Asia	445	162	264	17	223	80	133	10
Western Asia[2]	132	53	74	5	64	26	35	3
Europe[1,2]	498	98	334	67	255	48	167	41
Oceania	26.5	7.0	17.1	2.4	13.2	3.4	8.4	1.4
Australia and New Zealand	20.3	4.5	13.6	2.2	10.2	2.2	6.7	1.3
Melanesia	5.3	2.1	3.0	0.1	2.6	1.0	1.4	0.1
Micronesia	0.4	0.1	0.2	0.0	0.2	0.1	0.1	0.0
Polynesia	0.6	0.2	0.3	0.0	0.3	0.1	0.1	0.0
(Former) Soviet Union	289	73	187	28	152	36	96	20

Source: Selected from "Estimates of population and its percentage distribuion, by age and sex and sex ratio for all ages for the world, macro regions and regions: 1990," United Nations, *Demographic Yearbook*, 1991, Table 2. All figures are estimates of the order of magnitude and are subject to a substantial margin of error. *Notes:* 1. Excluding the former USSR, shown separately. 2. The European portion of Turkey is included with Western Asia rather than Europe.

★ 869 ★

Population Estimates and Projections

Hispanic and Non-Hispanic Populations: 1995-2050

This table shows estimates of the resident population and percent distribution, by Hispanic origin and non-Hispanic origin, projected for 1995 to 2050. National population estimates are derived by using decennial census data as benchmarks and data available from various agencies such as the National Center for Health Statistics (births and deaths) and the Immigration and Naturalization Service.

[In thousands. As of July.]

Origin and Sex	Population					Percent distribution		
	1995	2000	2005	2010	2025	2000	2010	2025
Hispanic Origin	26,798	31,166	35,702	40,525	56,927	100.0%	100.0%	100.0%
Female	13,188	15,388	17,679	20,115	28,396	49.4%	49.6%	49.9%
Male	13,610	15,777	18,022	20,410	28,531	50.6%	50.4%	50.1%
Non-Hispanic White	193,900	197,872	200,842	203,441	209,863	100.0%	100.0%	100.0%
Female	99,184	101,025	102,370	103,538	106,501	51.1%	50.9%	50.7%
Male	94,716	96,846	98,472	99,903	103,362	48.9%	49.1%	49.3%
Non-Hispanic Black	31,648	33,741	35,793	37,930	44,705	100.0%	100.0%	100.0%
Female	16,689	17,802	18,901	20,040	23,616	52.8%	52.8%	52.8%
Male	14,958	15,939	16,891	17,890	21,089	47.2%	47.2%	47.2%
Non-Hispanic American Indian, Eskimo, Aleut	1,927	2,055	2,190	2,336	2,796	100.0%	100.0%	100.0%
Female	979	1,045	1,115	1,190	1,426	50.9%	50.9%	51.0%
Male	948	1,010	1,075	1,146	1,370	49.1%	49.1%	49.0%
Non-Hispanic Asian, Pacific Islander	9,161	11,407	13,759	16,199	24,046	100.0%	100.0%	100.0%
Female	4,708	5,879	7,099	8,361	12,386	51.5%	51.6%	51.5%
Male	4,453	5,529	6,660	7,838	11,660	48.5%	48.4%	48.5%

Source: Selected from "Projections of Hispanic and Non-Hispanic Populations, by Age and Sex: 1995 to 2025," U.S. Bureau of the Census, *Statistical Abstract of the United States 1994*, Table 24, p. 25. Primary source: U.S. Bureau of the Census, *Current Population Reports*, P25-1104. Data are for middle series, assuming an ultimate total fertility rate = 2,150; life expectancy in 2050 = 82.6 years; and annual net immigration = 880,000.

★ 870 ★

Population Estimates and Projections

Latin America/Caribbean Population: 2000

This table shows estimates of the total population of Latin America/ Caribbean countries in the year 2000 and estimates the number of women aged 15-49 (childbearing age) in 2000.

[Population in thousands.]

Country	Total	Women 15-49
Argentina	36,238	8,962
Bolivia	9,724	2,283
Brazil	179,487	47,771
Chile	15,272	4,008
Colombia	39,397	10,860
Costa Rica	3,711	976
Cuba	11,504	3,012
Dominican Republic	8,621	2,251
Ecuador	13,319	3,427
El Salvador	6,739	1,657
Guatemala	12,222	2,836
Guyana	891	260
Haiti	8,003	1,984
Honduras	6,846	1,660
Jamaica	2,735	769
Mexico	107,233	29,171
Nicaragua	5,261	1,257
Panama	2,893	764
Paraguay	5,538	1,382
Peru	26,276	6,865
Puerto Rico	3,836	973
Trinidad and Tobago	1,484	400
Uruguay	3,274	808
Venezuela	24,715	6,408

Source: Selected from John A. Ross, W. Parker Mauldin, Steven R. Green, et al., *Family Planning and Child Survival Programs as Assessed in 1991*, The Population Council, 1992, Table 1, p. 28, "Selected Demographic Characteristics, Developing and Developed Countries."

★ 871 ★

Population Estimates and Projections

Middle East/North African Population: 2000

This table shows estimates of the total population of Middle East and North African countries in the year 2000 and estimates the number of women aged 15-49 (childbearing age) in 2000.

[Population in thousands.]

Country	Total	Women 15-49
Algeria	32,904	8,237
Egypt	64,210	16,374
Iran	68,759	16,982
Iraq	26,339	5,965
Jordan	5,558	1,283
Kuwait	2,639	652
Lebanon	3,327	876
Libya	6,500	1,399
Morocco	31,559	8,095
Oman	2,176	444
Saudi Arabia	20,697	4,127
Syria	17,826	4,014
Tunisia	9,924	2,651
Turkey	66,789	17,170
United Arab Emirates	1,951	360
Yemen	16,648	3,668

Source: Selected from John A. Ross, W. Parker Mauldin, Steven R. Green, et al., *Family Planning and Child Survival Programs as Assessed in 1991*, The Population Council, 1992, Table 1, p. 30, "Selected Demographic Characteristics, Developing and Developed Countries."

★ 872 ★

Population Estimates and Projections

Resident Population by Age and Race: 1992-I

This table shows the total population of the United States, total population by age, and the female and male populations by age, ages under 5 years through 44 years, by race, as estimated for 1992.

[In thousands. As of July.]

1992, sex, and race	Total, all years	Under 5 years	5-9 years	10-14 years	15-19 years	20-24 years	25-29 years	30-34 years	35-39 years	40-44 years
All Races	255,082	19,512	18,349	18,100	17,074	19,050	20,189	22,273	21,099	18,805
Female	130,589	9,526	8,954	8,829	8,312	9,345	10,049	11,166	10,618	9,518
Male	124,493	9,986	9,396	9,271	8,762	9,706	10,140	11,107	10,481	9,287
White	212,912	15,454	14,688	14,436	13,622	15,430	16,520	18,471	17,601	15,857
Female	108,567	7,526	7,150	7,022	6,612	7,525	8,150	9,163	8,764	7,938
Male	104,344	7,928	7,538	7,416	7,010	7,905	8,370	9,308	8,837	7,919

[Continued]

★ 872 ★

Resident Population by Age and Race: 1992-I
[Continued]

1992, sex, and race	Total, all years	Under 5 years	5-9 years	10-14 years	15-19 years	20-24 years	25-29 years	30-34 years	35-39 years	40-44 years
Black	31,635	3,099	2,782	2,782	2,638	2,686	2,714	2,794	2,565	2,139
Female	16,645	1,531	1,372	1,374	1,303	1,365	1,418	1,485	1,368	1,150
Male	14,990	1,568	1,410	1,408	1,335	1,321	1,296	1,308	1,197	989
American Indian, Eskimo, Aleut	2,134	219	215	214	185	185	181	185	166	142
Female	1,076	107	106	106	91	88	89	94	85	73
Male	1,059	111	109	108	94	97	92	91	81	69
Asian, Pacific Islander	8,401	740	665	666	629	749	774	824	767	667
Female	4,301	361	326	328	306	366	392	424	401	357
Male	4,100	379	338	338	323	383	382	400	366	311

Source: Selected from "Resident Population, by Age and Race: 1980 to 1992," U.S. Bureau of the Census, *Statistical Abstract of the United States 1994*, Tables 20, pp. 20. Primary source: U.S. Bureau of the Census, *Current Population Reports*, P25-1095; and unpublished data.

★ 873 ★

Population Estimates and Projections

Resident Population by Age and Race: 1992-II

This table shows the total population of the United States, total population by age, and the female and male populations by age and race, ages 45-85 and over, 5-13 years, 14-17 years, and 18-24 years, as estimated for 1992.

[In thousands. As of July.]

1992, sex, and race	Total, all years	45-49 years	50-54 years	55-59 years	60-64 years	65-74 years	75-84 years	85 yrs. and over	5-13 years	14-17 years	18-24 years
All Races	255,082	15,361	12,056	10,487	10,441	18,460	10,565	3,259	33,005	13,648	25,919
Female	130,589	7,820	6,198	5,464	5,550	10,336	6,555	2,349	16,105	6,632	12,703
Male	124,493	7,541	5,858	5,022	4,891	8,126	4,010	909	16,901	7,016	13,217
White	212,912	13,225	10,354	9,073	9,155	16,468	9,581	2,975	26,381	10,887	20,910
Female	108,567	6,670	5,276	4,682	4,820	9,176	5,939	2,154	12,838	5,278	10,194
Male	104,344	6,555	5,078	4,391	4,335	7,292	3,642	821	13,543	5,610	10,716
Black	31,635	1,541	1,256	1,059	982	1,559	801	238	5,032	2,109	3,747
Female	16,645	838	691	592	560	916	514	168	2,483	1,038	1,894
Male	14,990	703	565	467	423	644	287	70	2,549	1,072	1,853
American Indian, Eskimo, Aleut	2,134	110	84	67	55	78	37	12	389	153	256
Female	1,076	56	44	35	29	43	23	8	192	75	123
Male	1,059	53	40	32	26	34	15	4	196	78	133

[Continued]

★ 873 ★

Resident Population by Age and Race: 1992-II
[Continued]

1992, sex, and race	Total, all years	45-49 years	50-54 years	55-59 years	60-64 years	65-74 years	75-84 years	85 yrs. and over	5-13 years	14-17 years	18-24 years
Asian, Pacific Islander	8,401	485	362	288	249	356	146	34	1,206	498	1,005
Female	4,301	255	188	155	141	200	80	20	592	242	491
Male	4,100	230	174	133	107	155	66	14	613	257	513

Source: Selected from "Resident Population, by Age and Race: 1980 to 1992," U.S. Bureau of the Census, *Statistical Abstract of the United States 1994*, Table 20, p. 20. Primary source: U.S. Bureau of the Census, *Current Population Reports*, P25-1095; and unpublished data.

★ 874 ★

Population Estimates and Projections

Resident Population by Age: 1993-2050

This table shows middle series resident population projections by age and sex, 1993 to 2050. National population estimates are derived by using decennial census data as benchmarks and data available from various agencies such as the National Center for Health Statistics (births and deaths) and the Immigration and Naturalization Service.

[In thousands. As of July.]

Year	Total	Under 5 years	5 to 13 years	14 to 17 years	18 to 24 years	25 to 34 years	35 to 44 years	45 to 54 years	55 to 64 years	65 to 74 years	75 to 84 years	85 years and over
Female												
Middle series												
1993	132,006	9,712	16,298	6,703	12,820	21,402	20,369	14,177	11,110	10,433	6,590	2,391
1994	133,393	9,813	16,514	6,843	12,687	21,107	20,806	14,816	11,097	10,517	6,698	2,494
1995	134,749	9,837	16,707	7,087	12,507	20,835	21,238	15,447	11,140	10,544	6,814	2,593
2000	141,140	9,473	17,811	7,681	12,734	19,178	22,697	18,477	12,369	10,166	7,458	3,095
2005	147,165	9,425	17,948	8,230	13,878	18,491	21,702	21,028	15,027	10,065	7,802	3,570
2010	153,245	9,756	17,637	8,438	14,839	19,188	20,038	22,468	17,949	11,235	7,583	4,114
2020	166,045	10,693	18,835	8,303	14,943	21,849	20,060	19,896	21,848	16,348	8,605	4,662
2030	178,303	11,054	20,216	9,131	15,606	21,851	22,746	19,947	19,421	19,903	12,705	5,721
2040	189,456	11,689	20,978	9,585	16,939	23,129	22,773	22,627	19,576	17,794	15,640	8,724
2050	199,933	12,374	22,282	10,016	17,530	24,787	24,057	22,647	22,224	18,076	14,141	11,799
Male												
Middle series												
1993	125,921	10,204	17,126	7,099	13,311	21,420	20,003	13,560	10,017	8,217	4,038	924
1994	127,318	10,316	17,353	7,244	13,159	21,118	20,458	14,174	10,035	8,344	4,150	965
1995	128,685	10,344	17,556	7,503	12,958	20,835	20,911	14,777	10,101	8,420	4,274	1,005
2000	135,101	9,958	18,738	8,129	13,177	19,059	22,425	17,692	11,321	8,385	4,980	1,238
2005	141,121	9,908	18,895	8,716	14,360	18,301	21,372	20,193	13,842	8,559	5,463	1,512
2010	147,187	10,262	18,575	8,949	15,382	18,991	19,620	21,631	16,603	9,744	5,574	1,855
2020	159,897	11,263	19,866	8,816	15,513	21,703	19,601	18,989	20,414	14,561	6,874	2,297
2030	171,690	11,635	21,312	9,691	16,197	21,721	22,294	18,988	18,008	18,081	10,643	3,122
2040	182,049	12,289	22,091	10,161	17,571	22,998	22,361	21,597	18,125	16,174	13,566	5,116
2050	192,098	13,008	23,460	10,614	18,181	24,675	23,681	21,690	20,696	16,552	12,446	7,094

Source: Selected from "Resident Population Projections, by Age and Sex: 1993 to 2050," U.S. Bureau of the Census, *Statistical Abstract of the United States 1994*, Table 16, p. 16. Primary source: U.S. Bureau of the Census, *Current Population Reports*, P25-1104.

★ 875 ★

Population Estimates and Projections

Resident Population by Hispanic Origin: 1992-I

This table shows the total population of the United States, total population by age, and the female and male populations by age, ages under 5 years through 44 years, by Hispanic origin, as estimated for 1992.

[In thousands. As of July.]

Hispanic origin	Total, all years	Under 5 years	5-9 years	10-14 years	15-19 years	20-24 years	25-29 years	30-34 years	35-39 years	40-44 years
HISPANIC ORIGIN	24,238	2,809	2,325	2,169	2,068	2,344	2,447	2,268	1,867	1,460
Female	11,904	1,372	1,138	1,060	997	1,069	1,133	1,080	910	728
Male	12,334	1,437	1,187	1,109	1,071	1,275	1,314	1,188	957	731
NON-HISPANIC										
White	190,802	12,904	12,574	12,464	11,730	13,294	14,291	16,406	15,906	14,530
Female	97,718	6,280	6,115	6,057	5,701	6,553	7,120	8,182	7,939	7,277
Male	93,084	6,624	6,459	6,406	6,029	6,741	7,172	8,224	7,967	7,253
Black	30,316	2,942	2,653	2,666	2,530	2,559	2,577	2,666	2,456	2,056
Female	15,992	1,455	1,309	1,318	1,251	1,306	1,354	1,424	1,315	1,109
Male	14,324	1,487	1,344	1,349	1,279	1,253	1,224	1,242	1,141	948
American Indian, Eskimo, Aleut	1,850	181	183	184	160	157	154	159	145	125
Female	939	89	90	91	79	76	77	81	75	65
Male	911	92	93	93	81	81	77	77	70	60
Asian, Pacific Islander	7,876	676	614	618	586	695	720	774	725	634
Female	4,036	330	302	304	285	341	366	399	379	339
Male	3,839	346	313	314	301	355	354	375	346	295

Source: Selected from "Resident Population, by Age and Hispanic Origin: 1980 to 1992," U.S. Bureau of the Census, *Statistical Abstract of the United States 1994*, Tables 21, p. 21. Primary source: U.S. Bureau of the Census, *Current Population Reports*, P25-1095; and unpublished data. In the 1990 census, the Bureau of the Census collected data on the Hispanic origin population in the United States by using a self-identification question. Persons of Spanish/Hispanic origin are those who classified themselves in one of the specific Hispanic origin categories listed on the questionnaire—Mexican, Puerto Rican, Cuban, or Other Spanish/Hispanic origin. A space was added for the respondent to write in the entry for the Other Spanish/Hispanic category. It should be noted that Hispanic persons may be of any race. National population estimates are derived by using decennial census data as benchmarks and data available from various agencies such as the National Center for Health Statistics (births and deaths) and the Immigration and Naturalization Service.

★ 876 ★

Population Estimates and Projections

Resident Population by Hispanic Origin: 1992-II

This table shows the total population of the United States, total population by age, and the female and male populations by Hispanic origin, ages 45-85 and over, 5-13 years, 14-17 years, years, as estimated for 1992.

[In thousands. As of July.]

Hispanic origin	Total, all years	45-49 years	50-54 years	55-59 years	60-64 years	65-74 years	75-84 years	85 yrs. and over	5-13 years	14-17 years	18-24 years
HISPANIC ORIGIN	24,238	1,084	824	681	595	812	376	110	4,083	1,633	3,189
Female	11,904	552	427	359	320	457	231	71	1,998	795	1,471
Male	12,334	532	397	322	275	356	145	38	2,086	838	1,718
NON-HISPANIC											
White	190,802	12,235	9,601	8,446	8,605	15,715	9,229	2,871	22,665	9,397	17,999
Female	97,718	6,167	4,886	4,352	4,525	8,755	5,724	2,086	11,019	4,552	8,854
Male	93,084	6,069	4,715	4,094	4,080	6,961	3,507	785	11,645	4,845	9,146
Black	30,316	1,482	1,211	1,024	952	1,521	785	234	4,809	2,023	3,577
Female	15,992	808	667	573	543	892	503	165	2,374	994	1,814
Male	14,324	674	544	451	409	628	282	69	2,435	1,028	1,763
American Indian, Eskimo, Aleut	1,850	98	76	61	50	72	35	11	332	133	219
Female	939	51	40	32	27	39	21	7	164	66	107
Male	911	48	36	29	23	32	14	4	168	68	112
Asian, Pacific Islander	7,876	461	345	274	238	342	140	33	1,116	463	934
Female	4,036	243	179	147	135	192	76	19	549	225	458
Male	3,839	219	166	127	102	150	64	13	567	238	477

Source: Selected from "Resident Population, by Age and Hispanic Origin: 1980 to 1992," U.S. Bureau of the Census, *Statistical Abstract of the United States 1994*, Tables 21, p. 21. In the 1990 census, the Bureau of the Census collected data on the Hispanic origin population in the United States by using a self-identification question. Persons of Spanish/Hispanic origin are those who classified themselves in one of the specific Hispanic origin categories listed on the questionnaire—Mexican, Puerto Rican, Cuban, or Other Spanish/Hispanic origin. A space was added for the respondent to write in the entry for the Other Spanish/Hispanic category. It should be noted that Hispanic persons may be of any race. National population estimates are derived by using decennial census data as benchmarks and data available from various agencies such as the National Center for Health Statistics (births and deaths) and the Immigration and Naturalization Service. Primary source: U.S. Bureau of the Census, *Current Population Reports*, P25-1095; and unpublished data.

★ 877 ★

Population Estimates and Projections

Resident Population by Race: 1995-2050

This table shows estimates of the population and percent distribution, by sex and race, projected for 1995 to 2050. National population estimates are derived by using decennial census data as benchmarks and data available from various agencies such as the National Center for Health Statistics (births and deaths) and the Immigration and Naturalization Service.

[In thousands. As of July.]

Sex and Race	Population					Percent distribution		
	1995	2000	2005	2010	2025	2000	2010	2025
Total	263,434	276,241	288,286	300,431	338,338	100.0%	100.0%	100.0%
Female	134,749	141,140	147,165	153,245	172,326	51.1%	51.0%	50.9%
Male	128,685	135,101	141,121	147,187	166,012	48.9%	49.0%	49.1%
White	218,334	226,267	233,343	240,297	261,531	100.0%	100.0%	100.0%
Female	111,195	115,022	118,433	121,792	132,209	50.8%	50.7%	50.6%
Male	107,140	111,245	114,911	118,505	129,322	49.2%	49.3%	49.4%
Black	33,117	35,469	37,793	40,224	48,005	100.0%	100.0%	100.0%
Female	17,420	18,667	19,906	21,197	25,291	52.6%	52.7%	52.7%
Male	15,697	16,802	17,886	19,027	22,713	47.4%	47.3%	47.3%
American Indian, Eskimo, Aleut	2,226	2,380	2,543	2,719	3,278	100.0%	100.0%	100.0%
Female	1,123	1,203	1,287	1,377	1,664	50.5%	50.6%	50.8%
Male	1,103	1,177	1,256	1,342	1,614	49.5%	49.4%	49.2%
Asian, Pacific Islander	9,756	12,125	14,608	17,191	25,524	100.0%	100.0%	100.0%
Female	5,011	6,248	7,540	8,878	13,161	51.5%	51.6%	51.6%
Male	4,745	5,877	7,068	8,312	12,363	48.5%	48.4%	48.4%

Source: Selected from "Projections of Resident Population, by Age, Sex, and Race: 1995 to 2025," U.S. Bureau of the Census, *Statistical Abstract of the United States 1994*, Table 23, p. 24. Primary source: U.S. Bureau of the Census, *Current Population Reports*, P25-1104. Data are for middle series, assuming an ultimate total fertility rate = 2,150; life expectancy in 2050 = 82.6 years; and annual net immigration = 880,000.

★ 878 ★

Population Estimates and Projections

Sub-Saharan African Population: 2000

This table shows estimates of the total population of Sub-Saharan African countries in the year 2000 and estimates the number of women aged 15-49 (childbearing age) in 2000.

[Population in thousands.]

Country	Total	Women 15-49
Angola	13,295	3,015
Benin	6,369	1,403
Botswana	1,822	424
Burkina Faso	12,092	2,706
Burundi	7,358	1,710
Cameroon	16,701	3,563
Central African Republic	4,074	922
Chad	7,337	1,693
Congo	3,167	706
Cote D'Ivoire	17,600	3,643
Ethiopia	66,364	14,582
Gabon	1,612	352
Ghana	20,564	4,687
Guinea	7,830	1,706
Guinea-Bissau	1,197	277
Kenya	35,060	7,709
Lesotho	2,370	555
Liberia	3,575	771
Madagascar	16,627	3,754
Malawi	12,458	2,731
Mali	12,685	2,825
Mauritania	2,702	610
Mauritius	1,201	351
Mozambique	20,493	4,724
Namibia	2,437	546
Niger	10,752	2,359
Nigeria	149,621	33,521
Rwanda	10,200	2,240
Senegal	9,716	2,235
Sierra Leone	5,437	1,232
Somalia	9,736	2,202
South Africa	43,666	11,034
Sudan	33,625	7,644
Tanzania	39,639	8,491
Togo	4,861	1,086
Uganda	26,958	5,801
Zaire	49,190	11,072

[Continued]

★ 878 ★

Sub-Saharan African Population: 2000
[Continued]

Country	Total	Women 15-49
Zambia	12,267	2,675
Zimbabwe	13,123	3,193

Source: Selected from John A. Ross, W. Parker Mauldin, Steven R. Green, et al., *Family Planning and Child Survival Programs as Assessed in 1991*, The Population Council, 1992, Table 1, p. 28, "Selected Demographic Characteristics, Developing and Developed Countries."

Chapter 11
PUBLIC LIFE

★ 879 ★

Appointments to Civilian Positions by President Bush

This table shows numbers and percents of President George Bush's appointments of women to full-time civilian positions requiring Senate confirmation for the years 1989-1992. Excluded are positions in the Foreign Service (non-career ambassador positions to overseas posts are covered), the National Oceanic and Atmospheric Administration Corps, and the Public Health Service Corps. Included are one recess appointee and three incumbents from the Reagan Administration whom President Bush announced he was retaining in office.

Appointees	1989	1990	1991	1992	1989-92
Women	84	49	49	33	215
Percent of all appointees	21.2%	17.6%	21.3%	18.9%	19.9%

Source: Selected from Rogelio Garcia, "Women Nominated and Appointed to Full-Time Civilian Positions by President George Bush, 1989-92," CRS Report to Congress, 93-542 GOV, May 26, 1993, Table 1, p. CRS-1.

★ 880 ★

Politics and Government

Appointments to Civilian Positions by President Reagan

This table shows numbers and percents of President Ronald Reagan's appointments of women to full-time civilian positions requiring Senate confirmation for the years 1989-1992. Excluded are positions in the Foreign Service (non-career ambassador positions to overseas posts are covered), the National Oceanic and Atmospheric Administration Corps, and the Public Health Service Corps. Included are one recess appointee and three incumbents from the Reagan Administration whom President Bush announced he was retaining in office.

Appointees	1981	1982	1983	1984	1981-84
Women	47	28	37	38	150
Percent of all appointees	8.9%	10.9%	17.8%	19.7%	12.6%

Source: Selected from Rogelio Garcia, "Women Nominated and Appointed to Full-Time Civilian Positions by President George Bush, 1989-92," CRS Report to Congress, 93-542 GOV, May 26, 1993, Table 2, p. CRS-1.

★ 881 ★

Politics and Government

Gender Gap in 1990 and 1992 Elections

Throughout the 1980s, fewer women than men voted for the victorious Republican presidential candidates. In 1992 women showed a stronger preference than men did for Bill Clinton, but the gender gap was smaller (4 percentage points compared to 6-9 percentage points) than in the victorious Republican elections. Women in 1992 were less likely than men to vote for Ross Perot. The gender gap was also evident in elections to State offices. This table shows voting choices of women and men in the 1992 presidential election and in hotly contested 1992 and 1990 elections for selected state offices with the largest gender gaps (14 to 16 percentage points), according to voter research and surveys. The races with the largest gender gaps tended to be those with a Democratic woman candidate.

Office, Year, and Candidate	Women	Men	Results
President, 1992			
Bill Clinton	45%	41%	Won
George Bush	37%	38%	Lost
Ross Perot	17%	21%	Lost

[Continued]

★ 881 ★

Gender Gap in 1990 and 1992 Elections
[Continued]

Office, Year, and Candidate	Women	Men	Results
Senate, 1992			
California			
Barbara Boxer (D)	57%	43%	Won
Bruce Herschensohn (R)	37%	51%	Lost
Dianne Feinstein (D)	64%	50%	Won
John Seymour (R)	33%	46%	Lost
Oregon			
Les AuCoin (D)	56%	40%	Lost
Bob Packwood (R)	44%	60%	Won
Governor, 1990			
California			
Dianne Feinstein (D)	58%	42%	Lost
Pete Wilson (R)	42%	58%	Won
Oregon			
Barbara Roberts (D)	56%	40%	Won
Dave Frohnmayer (R)	29%	45%	Lost
Texas			
Ann Richards (D)	59%	44%	Won
Clayton Williams (R)	41%	56%	Lost

Source: Center for the American Woman and Politics (CAWP), National Information Bank on Women in Public Office, Eagleton Institute of Politics, Rutgers University, *Fact Sheet*.

★ 882 ★

Politics and Government

Heads of Government Worldwide

This table presents statistics about women heads of government around the world.

Item	Number/Percent
Number of the 159 United Nations member States that were headed by women at the end of 1990:[1]	6
Percentage of the world's cabinet ministers who were women at the end of 1990:	3.5%
Number of countries in the world where women held no ministerial positions at the end of 1990:	93
Number of countries where women held more than 20% of ministerial-level government positions at the end of 1990:[2]	3
Percentage of Sweden's parliament seats held by women in 1995:[3]	41%
Percentage of legislative seats held by women in the Seychelles in 1993:[4]	46%
Percentage of legislative seats held by women in 54 European and North American countries:	
1985	16%
1994	11%

Source: Selected from *The World's Women: Trends and Statistics 1970-1990*, United Nations, 1991, p. 31. *Notes:* 1. Iceland, Ireland, Nicaragua, Norway, Dominica, and the Philippines. 2. Bhutan, Dominica, and Norway. 3. Making it the western legislature with the highest proportion of elected women. 4. The Seychelles are in the Indian Ocean off Africa's eastern coast. The Seychelles has the world's highest percentage of women in its legislature.

★ 883 ★

Politics and Government

Ministerial Positions Worldwide

This table shows the percentage of ministerial-level positions held by women around the world in 1987-1988. Figures are shown only for those countries where women have achieved at least 10% of ministerial-level positions.

Country	Minister positions
Developed regions	
Austria	11%
Canada	13%
Denmark	14%
Finland	12%
Germany	
Fed. Rep. of Germany	10%
former German Dem. Rep.	10%
Norway	37%
Romania	12%
Sweden	17%
Switzerland	11%
Africa	
Burkina Faso	12%
Burundi	10%
Senegal	13%
Tanzania	16%
Latin America/Caribbean	
Dominica	22%
Guatemala	12%
Uruguay	13%
Asia and Pacific	
Bhutan	25%
Philippines	11%

Source: "Where women have achieved at least 10 percent of ministerial-level positions," *The World's Women: Trends and Statistics 1970-1990*, United Nations, 1991, table 2.1, p. 32. Primary source: Division for the Advancement of Women, Centre for Social Development and Humanitarian Affairs of the United Nations Secretariat and United States National Standards Association.

★ 884 ★

Politics and Government

Parliamentary Representation Worldwide

This table shows the percentage of parliamentary positions held by women around the world in 1987 in countries where women made up less than 4% of parliamentary representation.

Country	Parliamentary representation
Developed regions	
Japan	1.4%
Malta	2.9%
Africa	
Algeria	2.4%
Comoros	0.0%
Djibouti	0.0%
Egypt	3.9%
Equatorial Guinea	3.3%
Kenya	1.7%
Madagascar	1.5%
Mali	3.7%
Morocco	0.0%
South Africa	3.5%
Sudan	0.7%
Swaziland	2.0%
Zaire	3.5%
Zambia	2.9%
Latin America/Caribbean	
Antigua and Barbuda	0.0%
Barbados	3.7%
Belize	3.6%
Bolivia	3.8%
Ecuador	1.4%
El Salvador	3.3%
Paraguay	1.7%
Uruguay	0.0%
Venezuela	3.9%
Asia and Pacific	
Bhutan	1.3%
Cyprus	1.8%
Iran Islamic Rep. of	1.5%

[Continued]

★ 884 ★

Parliamentary Representation Worldwide
[Continued]

Country	Parliamentary representation
Korea	
Republic of	2.5%
Lebanon	0.0%
Papua New Guinea	0.0%
Singapore	3.8%
Solomon Islands	0.0%
Thailand	3.5%
Tonga	0.0%
Turkey	3.0%
United Arab Emirates	0.0%
Vanuatu	0.0%
Yemen	0.0%

Source: "Where women make up less than 4 per cent of parliamentary representation," *The World's Women: Trends and Statistics 1970-1990,* United Nations, 1991, table 2.4, p. 33. Primary source: Inter-Parliamentary Union (Geneva).

★ 885 ★

Politics and Government

Political Party Identification: 1952-1986

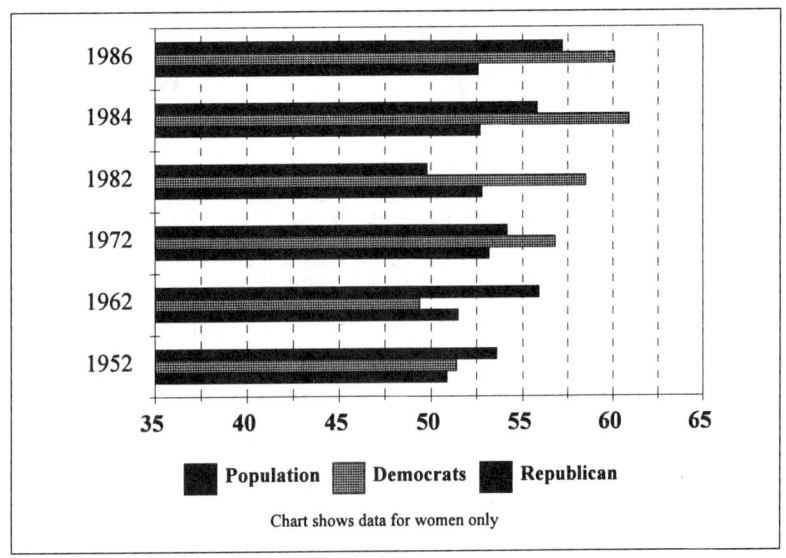

This table shows the composition of the voting age population and of persons identifying themselves as Republicans and Democrats by sex, 1952-1986.

Year	Voting age population		Democrats		Republicans	
	Male	Female	Male	Female	Male	Female
1952	49.1%	50.9%	48.6%	51.4%	46.4%	53.6%
1962	48.5%	51.5%	50.6%	49.4%	44.1%	55.9%
1972	46.8%	53.2%	43.2%	56.8%	45.8%	54.2%
1982	47.2%	52.8%	41.5%	58.5%	50.2%	49.8%
1984	47.3%	52.7%	39.1%	60.9%	44.2%	55.8%
1986	47.4%	52.6%	39.9%	60.1%	42.8%	57.2%

Source: "Composition of the Voting Age Population and of Persons Identifying Themselves as Republicans and Democrats by Sex, 1952-1986," Jennifer D. Williams, *CRS Report for Congress: The "Gender Gap": Differences Between Men and Women in Political Attitudes and Voting Behavior in the 1980s,* September 28, 1989, Table 10, p. CRS-46. Primary sources: Voting age population statistics are from U.S. Bureau of the Census, *Current Population Reports,* Series P-20. Party identification data are from the American National Election Study, Center for Political Studies, University of Michigan.

★ 886 ★

Politics and Government

Political Party Identification: 1970-1988

This table shows the political parties that men and women identified themselves with between 1970 and 1988. Women are more likely than men to identify with the two major parties, while larger percentages of men consider themselves to be independents.

Category	1970	1972	1974	1976	1978	1980	1982	1984	1986	1988
Male										
Democratic	43%	37%	35%	37%	38%	37%	39%	33%	37%	29%
Independent	34%	40%	42%	41%	43%	39%	34%	38%	37%	41%
Republican	23%	23%	22%	22%	18%	22%	26%	27%	25%	28%
Apolitical	1%	1%	1%	1%	2%	2%	2%	1%	2%	2%
Female										
Democratic	45%	43%	41%	43%	41%	44%	49%	40%	43%	39%
Independent	29%	32%	31%	31%	34%	31%	27%	31%	30%	32%
Republican	25%	24%	24%	26%	22%	23%	23%	27%	26%	27%
Apolitical	1%	2%	3%	1%	3%	2%	2%	2%	2%	2%
Difference	0	2.5	2.0	1.0	-.5	3.0	6.5	3.5	2.5	5.5

Source: Selected from "Party Identification by Sex, 1952-1988," Jennifer D. Williams, *CRS Report for Congress: The "Gender Gap": Differences Between Men and Women in Political Attitudes and Voting Behavior in the 1980s,* September 28, 1989, Table 9, p. CRS-44. Primary sources: Data are from the American National Election Study, Center for Political Studies, University of Michigan. These surveys designate eight categories of party identification, which are collapsed into four categories in this table. Democrats comprise the survey categories of weak Democrats and strong Democrats; independents comprise the independent-Democrat, independent-independent, and independent-Republication categories; Republicans include the weak Republican and strong Republican categories; and the apolitical category is the same as in the surveys. The "other" category used in the surveys is not included here. Preliminary data for 1988 were provided by Santa Traugott, Project Manager, American National Election Study. A positive number indicates that more women than men identified themselves as Democratic. A negative number means that more women than men identified themselves as Republican. Difference = [(% women Democratic minus % men Democratic) minus (% women Republican minus % men Republican)] / 2.

★ 887 ★

Politics and Government

Voter Turnout by Race and Origin: 1984-1992

This table shows the percent and number of the voting-age population who reported voting in recent presidential elections, by race and Hispanic origin. The number of female voters exceeded the number of male voters.

[Number who reported voting in millions.]

Race or Origin	% of voting-age pop. who reported voting		No. who reported voting (millions)	
	women	Men	Women	Men
1992				
Black	56.7%	50.8%	6.6	4.8
Hispanic	30.9%	26.8%	2.3	1.9
White	64.5%	62.6%	52.9	47.6
1988				
Black	54.2%	48.2%	5.9	4.2
Hispanic	30.1%	27.4%	2.0	1.8
White	59.8%	58.3%	47.7	42.7
1984				
Black	59.2%	51.7%	6.1	4.2
Hispanic	33.1%	32.1%	1.7	1.4
White	62.0%	60.8%	47.7	42.4

Source: Center for the American Woman and Politics (CAWP), Eagleton Institute of Politics, Rutgers University. Primary source: U.S. Bureau of the Census, *Current Population Reports*, Series P20.

★ 888 ★

Politics and Government

Voter Turnout: 1964-1984

This table shows voter turnout by sex for presidential election years 1964 through 1984. Women have long constituted a majority of the electorate because they have been a majority of the voting age population.

Year	Percent reported voting		Composition of the electorate[1]	
	Men	Women	Men	Women
1964	71.9%	67.0%	48.9%	51.1%
1968	69.8%	66.0%	48.1%	51.9%
1972	64.1%	62.0%	47.7%	52.3%
1976	59.6%	58.8%	47.4%	52.6%

[Continued]

★ 888 ★

Voter Turnout: 1964-1984
[Continued]

Year	Percent reported voting		Composition of the electorate[1]	
	Men	Women	Men	Women
1980	59.1%	59.4%	47.0%	53.0%
1984	59.0%	60.8%	46.5%	53.5%

Source: "Voter Turnout by Sex, Presidential Election Years," Jennifer D. Williams, *CRS Report for Congress: The "Gender Gap": Differences Between Men and Women in Political Attitudes and Voting Behavior in the 1980s,* September 28, 1989, Table 11, p. CRS-50. Primary source: U.S. Bureau of the Census, *Current Population Reports,* Series P-20. *Note:* 1. Men's votes and women's votes as percentages of total votes cast.

★ 889 ★

Politics and Government

Voter Turnout: 1980-1992

This table shows voting-age population and the percent reporting they voted during presidential election years, 1980-1992.

[Voting-age population in millions.]

Characteristic	Voting-age population (millions)							Percent reporting they voted			
	1980	1982	1984	1986	1988	1990	1992	1980	1984	1988	1992
Total	157.1	165.5	170.0	173.9	178.1	182.1	185.7	59.2%	59.9%	57.4%	61.3%
Male	74.1	78.0	80.3	82.4	84.5	86.6	88.6	59.1%	59.0%	56.4%	60.2%
Female	83.0	87.4	89.6	91.5	93.6	95.5	97.1	59.4%	60.8%	58.3%	62.3%

Source: Selected from "Voting-Age Population, Percent Reporting Registered, and Voted: 1978 to 1992, U.S. Department of Commerce, *Statistical Abstract of the United States 1994,* Table 448, p. 287. Primary source: U.S. Bureau of the Census, *Current Population Reports,* Series P20-466, and earlier reports.

★ 890 ★

Politics and Government

Votes for Representatives: 1984-1994

This table shows percentages of men and women who voted for Democratic and Republican members of the House of Representatives in election years 1984 through 1994. Men are more likely to vote Republican than are women. The eight-point gap between men and women voters in the 1994 election was the largest measured in the Congressional elections included here. In 1994, for the first time in 40 years, Republicans won control of both House and Senate.

Voter description	1984		1986		1988		1990		1992		1994	
	Dem.	Rep.	Dem.	Rep.	Dem.	Rep.	Dem.	Rep.	Dem.	Rep.	Dem.	Rep.
Total vote for House	51%	49%	52%	48%	54%	46%	52%	48%	54%	46%	50%	50%
Men	48%	52%	51%	49%	52%	48%	51%	49%	52%	48%	46%	54%
Women	54%	46%	54%	46%	57%	43%	54%	46%	55%	45%	54%	46%
White men	43%	57%	47%	53%	47%	53%	48%	52%	49%	51%	38%	62%
White women	49%	51%	50%	50%	52%	48%	52%	48%	51%	49%	45%	55%
Black men	90%	10%	84%	16%	82%	18%	79%	21%	84%	16%	85%	15%
Black women	94%	6%	88%	12%	88%	12%	80%	20%	92%	8%	90%	10%
Men 18-29 yrs.	47%	53%	48%	52%	52%	48%	48%	51%	52%	48%	52%	48%
Women 18-29 yrs.	56%	44%	54%	46%	55%	45%	55%	45%	58%	42%	56%	44%
Men 30-44 yrs.	52%	48%	52%	48%	51%	49%	52%	48%	51%	49%	43%	57%
Women 30-44 yrs.	56%	44%	52%	48%	57%	43%	54%	46%	54%	46%	51%	49%
Men 45-59 yrs.	47%	53%	50%	50%	49%	51%	48%	52%	50%	50%	46%	54%
Women 45-59 yrs.	52%	48%	58%	42%	57%	43%	53%	47%	54%	46%	56%	44%
Men 60 and older	46%	54%	51%	49%	54%	46%	52%	48%	56%	44%	49%	51%
Women 60 and older	51%	49%	53%	47%	56%	44%	54%	46%	57%	43%	53%	47%
Married men	46%	54%	50%	50%	50%	50%	49%	51%	48%	52%	44%	56%
Married women	52%	48%	53%	47%	53%	47%	51%	49%	51%	49%	48%	52%
Unmarried men	53%	47%	54%	46%	54%	46%	56%	44%	58%	42%	52%	48%
Unmarried women	59%	41%	58%	42%	63%	37%	61%	39%	63%	37%	66%	34%
Men without a high school diploma	59%	41%	56%	44%	60%	40%	59%	41%	67%	33%	60%	40%
Women without a high school diploma	61%	39%	57%	43%	66%	34%	60%	40%	65%	35%	70%	30%
Male high school graduate	49%	51%	57%	43%	56%	44%	56%	44%	59%	41%	48%	52%
Female high school graduate	52%	48%	53%	47%	57%	43%	56%	44%	57%	43%	55%	45%
Men with some college	45%	55%	50%	50%	50%	50%	50%	50%	51%	49%	44%	56%
Women with some college	53%	47%	51%	49%	55%	45%	53%	47%	55%	45%	50%	50%
Male college grads.	47%	53%	46%	54%	46%	54%	48%	52%	47%	53%	45%	55%

[Continued]

★ 890 ★

Votes for Representatives: 1984-1994

[Continued]

Voter description	1984		1986		1988		1990		1992		1994	
	Dem.	Rep.	Dem.	Rep.	Dem.	Rep.	Dem.	Rep.	Dem.	Rep.	Dem.	Rep.
Female college grads.	55%	45%	57%	43%	55%	45%	55%	45%	54%	48%	53%	47%

Source: Selected from "Portrait of the Electorate: Who Voted for Whom in the House," *The New York Times National*, November 13, 1994, p. 15 Y. Primary sources: 1994 data were collected by Mitofsky International based on questionnaires completed by 5,260 voters leaving polling places around the country on election day. 1990 and 1992 data were collected by Voter Research and Surveys based on questionnaires completed by 15,490 voters in 1992 and 19,888 voters in 1990. Data for other years were based on surveys of voters conducted by The New York Times and CBS News: 11,645 in 1988, 8,994 in 1986, 9,174 in 1984, and 7,855 in 1982.

★ 891 ★

Politics and Government

Women in Elective Offices: 1975-1995

This table shows the percentages of people in elective offices who were women, by level of office, 1975-1995.

Level of Office	1975	1977	1979	1981	1983	1985	1987	1989	1991	1993	1994	1995
U.S. Congress	4%	4%	3%	4%	4%	5%	5%	5%	6%	10%	10%	10%
Statewide Elective	10%	10%	11%	11%	11%	14%	14%	14%	18%	22%	23%	26%
State Legislatures	8%	9%	10%	12%	13%	15%	16%	17%	18%	21%	21%	21%
County Governing Boards[1]	3%	4%	5%	6%	8%	8% (1984)	9%	9% (1988)	NA	NA	NA	NA
Mayors and Municipal Councils	4%	8%	10%	10%	NA	14%[2]	NA	NA	NA	NA[3]	NA	NA

Source: Center for the American Woman and Politics (CAWP), National Information Bank on Women in Public Office, Eagleton Institute of Politics, Rutgers University, *Fact Sheet*. Primary source: U.S. Bureau of the Census, *Current Population Reports*, Series P20-466, and earlier reports. *Notes:* 1. The three states without county governing boards are CT, RI, and VT. 2. Includes data from Washington DC. States for which data were incomplete and therefore not included are: IL, IN, KY, MO, PA, WI. 3. While data for the more than 100,000 officials serving in towns and cities of all sizes have not been collected since 1985, figures are available for cities with populations over 10,000. According to the National League of Cities, of the 23,729 mayors and municipal council members (and their equivalents) serving in cities with populations over 10,000 in April 1993, 4,657 or 19.6% were women.

★ 892 ★

Politics and Government

Women in State Legislatures, Best and Worst States: 1995

This table shows the ten states with the highest percentages and the ten states with the lowest percentages of women state legislators.

State	% Women
Highest	
Washington	39.5%
Nevada	34.9%
Colorado	31.0%
New Hampshire	30.2%
Arizona	30.0%
Vermont	29.4%
Maryland	28.7%
Idaho	28.6%
Kansas	27.9%
Maine	26.9%
Lowest	
Alabama	3.6%
Kentucky	8.0%
Louisiana	9.7%
Oklahoma	10.7%
Virginia	11.4%
Mississippi	11.5%
Pennsylvania	11.9%
South Carolina	12.4%
New Jersey	12.5%
Arkansas	12.6%

Source: Center for the American Woman and Politics (CAWP), National Information Bank on Women in Public Office, Eagleton Institute of Politics, Rutgers University, *Fact Sheet.*

★ 893 ★

Politics and Government

Women in State Legislatures: 1969-1995

This table shows the number of women legislators and their percentage of total legislators for the years 1969-1995. Of the total 1,535 women in state legislatures in 1995, 846 were Democrats, 673 were Republicans, 12 were Nonpartisans, and 4 were Independents. Since 1969, the number of women serving in state legislatures has increased five-fold.

Year	Women Legislators	% of Total Legislators
1969	301	4.0%
1971	344	4.5%
1973	424	5.6%
1975	604	8.0%
1977	688	9.1%
1979	770	10.3%
1981	908	12.1%
1983	991	13.3%
1985	1,103	14.8%
1987	1,170	15.7%
1989	1,270	17.0%
1991	1,368	18.3%
1992	1,375	18.4%
1993	1,524	20.5%
1994	1,547	20.8%
1995	1,535	20.7%

Source: Center for the American Woman and Politics (CAWP), National Information Bank on Women in Public Office, Eagleton Institute of Politics, Rutgers University, *Fact Sheet*.

★ 894 ★

Politics and Government

Women in Statewide Elective Offices: 1995

This table shows the number of women holding statewide elective executive offices, by office, in 1995. A record 84 women held these offices, 25.9% of the 324 available positions.[1,2] Thirty-six were Democrats, forty-five were Republicans, and 3 were elected in nonpartisan races. As of 1995 women had been elected to these offices in 46 of the nation's 50 states (the exceptions are Maine, New Hampshire, North Carolina, and West Virginia).

Office	No. of women
Governor	1
Lieutenant governor	19
Comptrollers/controllers	3
Chief state education officials	11
Public service commissioners	3

Source: Center for the American Woman and Politics (CAWP), National Information Bank on Women in Public Office, Eagleton Institute of Politics, Rutgers University, *Fact Sheet. Notes:* 1. Women appointed in 1993 and then elected statewide in November 1994 to executive posts, are included in these numbers. In addition, these figures included Rebecca M. Cook (D-MO), who was appointed as secretary of state on December 16, 1994, to fill a vacancy. Cook replaced Judith Morarty (D), who was impeached. 2. These figures do not include: officials in appointive state cabinet-level positions; officials elected to executive posts by the legislature; members of the judicial branch; or elected members of university Boards of Trustees or Boards of Education.

★ 895 ★

Politics and Government

Women in the U.S. Congress: 1979-1995

This table shows the total number of women in the U.S. Congress and the number who were senators and representatives, by their party affiliation, for the 96th through the 104th congresses.

Congress and Dates	Women in Senate			Women in House			Total Women		
	Total	Democrats	Republicans	Total	Democrats	Republicans	Total	Democrats	Republicans
96th, 1979-1981	1	0	1	16	11	5	17	11	6
97th, 1981-1983	2	0	2	21	11	1	23	11	12
98th, 1983-1985	2	0	2	22	13	9	24	13	11
99th, 1985-1987	2	0	2	23	12	11	25	12	13
100th, 1987-1989	2	1	1	23	12	11	25	13	12

[Continued]

★ 895 ★

Women in the U.S. Congress: 1979-1995
[Continued]

Congress and Dates	Women in Senate			Women in House			Total Women		
	Total	Democrats	Republicans	Total	Democrats	Republicans	Total	Democrats	Republicans
101st, 1989-1991	2	1	1	29	16	13	31	17	14
102nd, 1991-1993	4[1]	3	1	29[2]	20	9	33[2]	23	10
103rd, 1993-1995	7[3]	5	2	47[2]	35	12	54[2]	40	14
104th, 1995-1997	8	5	3	47[2]	30	17	55[2]	35	2

Source: Center for the American Woman and Politics (CAWP), National Information Bank on Women in Public Office, Eagleton Institute of Politics, Rutgers University, *Fact Sheet. Notes:* 1. On election day in 1992, three women served in the Senate; two were elected and one was appointed. On November 3, Dianne Feinstein won a special election to complete two years of a term; she was sworn in on November 10, 1992. 2. Does not include a Republican Delegate to the House from Washington, DC. 3. Includes Kay Bailey Hutchison (R-TX), who won a special election on June 5, 1993, to serve out the remaining year and one half of a term.

★ 896 ★

Politics and Government

Women of Color in Elective Office: 1995

This table shows characteristics of women in the U.S. Congress, statewide elective offices, and in state legislatures in 1995. "Women of color" is used to refer to African American, Asian American/Pacific Islander, Latina, and Native American women as a group. Of the 55 women serving in the 104th U.S. Congress, 14, or 25.5% were women of color, and an African American woman served as Delegate to the House from Washington, DC. Of the 84 women serving in statewide elective offices, 5, or 6.0% were women of color. Of the 1,535 women state legislators serving nationwide, 219, or 14.3% were women of color—54 senators and 165 representatives.

Office	Total	Democrats	Republicans	African-American	Asian Amer./ Pac. Isl.	Latina	Native Americans
U.S. Congresswomen	15[1]	14	1	11[1]	1	3	0
Statewide elective executives	5	4	1	2	1	2	0
State legislators	219[2]	210	7	167	11	34	7

Source: Center for the American Woman and Politics (CAWP), National Information Bank on Women in Public Office, Eagleton Institute of Politics, Rutgers University, *Fact Sheet. Notes:* 1. Includes 1 African American Delegate to the House from Washington, DC. 2. Includes 2 independents.

Volunteers

★ 897 ★

Asked to Volunteer and Did So

This table shows the percentage of respondents to a survey who reported that they were asked to volunteer in the past year and the percentage who actually volunteered. Respondents were four times as likely to volunteer if they were asked than if they were not asked to do so. Information was obtained from in-home personal interviews conducted by The Gallup Organization from April 22 to May 15, 1994, with a representative national sample of 1,509 adult Americans aged 18 or older. The very wealthy (those with incomes above $200,000) were not targeted.

Characteristic	Asked to volunteer	Did volunteer	Not asked to volunteer	Did volunteer
Total	44.5%	81.8%	54.4%	20.5%
Male	40.2%	83.2%	59.0%	17.8%
Female	48.4%	80.8%	50.2%	23.5%

Source: Selected from "Respondents who were asked to volunteer in the past year and actual volunteer behavior: 1993," *Giving and Volunteering in the United States*, Independent Sector, 1994, Table 4.10, p. 80. Respondents who did not answer or did not know were not considered in this table.

★ 898 ★
Volunteers

Involvement in Church, School, Community

The Ms. Foundation for Women and the Center for Policy Alternatives collaborated on a project involving six focus groups and a nationwide poll to find out what were the concerns of all women and to identify those that were specific to certain groups of women. This table shows the responses of women to questions about their involvement in activities outside of family and work. Retired women and African American women who volunteer are most likely to be involved in religious activities. Hispanic women are more likely than women from other ethnic groups to be involved in community activities—84% of those surveyed belong to a voluntary organization. Asian American women are least involved—55% list no voluntary activities.

Characteristic	Yes
Involved in at least one activity outside of family and work.	64%
Full-time working women	65%
Homemakers	65%
Retired women	59%

[Continued]

★ 898 ★

Involvement in Church, School, Community
[Continued]

Characteristic	Yes
Part-time working women	72%
Spend more than 20 hours per week volunteering.	29%
Spend between 11 and 20 hours per week volunteering.	33%
Spend 10 hours or less each week volunteering.	38%

Source: Womens Voices: A Polling Report, A Joint Project of the Ms. Foundation for Women and Center for Policy Alternatives, p. 29.

★ 899 ★
Volunteers

Mother Volunteered

This table shows the percentage of respondents to a survey who reported that their parents volunteered when the respondent was young, 1992 and 1994. The table also shows whether the respondent is a volunteer. Information was obtained from in-home personal interviews conducted by The Gallup Organization from April 22 to May 15, 1994, with a representative national sample of 1,509 adult Americans aged 18 or older. The very wealthy (those with incomes above $200,000) were not targeted.

Parent's volunteer status	1994		1992	
	All respondents	Respondents who volunteered	All respondents	Respondents volunteered
Parents volunteered	43.8%	61.8%	44.6%	68.5%
Both mother and father	22.9%	68.8%	25.2%	74.9%
Mother only	17.0%	52.8%	16.2%	59.9%
Father only	3.9%	60.0%	3.2%	61.5%
Neither parent volunteered	47.0%	36.7%	45.6%	38.6%
Don't know/no answer	9.2%	36.7%	9.8%	30.4%

Source: Selected from "Parents Volunteering When Respondent Was Young Compared with Current Volunteering: 1992 and 1994," *Giving and Volunteering in the United States,* Independent Sector, 1994, Table 4.2, p. 65.

★ 900 ★

Volunteers

Volunteers: 1988-1994

This table shows the percentage of men and women who reported volunteering in the last month and in the previous 12 months, 1988, 1990, 1992, and 1994. Information was obtained from in-home personal interviews conducted by The Gallup Organization from April 22 to May 15, 1994, with a representative national sample of 1,509 adult Americans aged 18 or older. The very wealthy (those with incomes above $200,000) were not targeted.

Gender	March 1994		March 1992		March 1990		March 1988	
	Prev. 12 mos.	Prev. month	Prev. 12 mo.	Prev. month	Prev. 12 mo.	Prev. mo.	Prev. 12 mo.	Prev. mo.
All	48%	39%	51%	39%	54%	43%	45%	39%
Male	44%	36%	49%	35%	52%	41%	44%	37%
Female	51%	42%	53%	42%	56%	45%	47%	41%

Source: Selected from "Demographic characteristics of population 18 years and older volunteering in previous month and 12 months: 1992 and 1994," *Giving and Volunteering in the United States*, Independent Sector, 1994, Table 1.10, p. 41.

Chapter 12
RELIGION

Catholic Sisters/Missionaries

★ 901 ★

Catholic Missionaries Overseas: 1992

This table shows the total number of U.S. Catholic missionaries overseas by world region, and the number who were women, 1992.

Region	Missionaries	
	Total	Women
Africa	949	466
Near East	59	16
Far East	1,163	396
Oceania	512	257
North America	257	152
Caribbean Islands	431	193
Central America	810	371
South America	1,286	631
Total	5,467	2,482

Source: Selected from "Missionary Activity of the Church: United States Overseas Missionaries," *The Catholic Almanac,* Our Sunday Visitor Publishing, 1994, p. 524. Primary source: *1992-1993 Report on U.S. Catholic Overseas Mission.*

★ 902 ★

Catholic Sisters/Missionaries

Catholic Missionary Sisters: 1980-1992

Total number of Catholic missionary sisters overseas, 1980-1992.

Year	Sisters
1980	2,592
1981	2,574
1982	2,560
1983	2,540
1984	2,492
1985	2,505
1986	2,481
1987	2,505
1988	2,495
1989	2,473
1990	2,347
1991	2,264
1992	2,222

Source: Selected from "U.S. Overseas Missionaries, 1960-1992," *1993 Catholic Almanac,* p. 526. Also in source: Number of priests, deacons, brothers, and parishes by major city/diocese in each state.

★ 903 ★

Catholic Sisters/Missionaries

Number of Canadian Catholic Sisters: 1991

This table shows the total number of Catholic sisters in Canada by civil province.

Civil Province	Sisters
Newfoundland	421
Prince Edward Island	197
Nova Scotia	877
New Brunswick	979
Quebec	20,258
Ontario	4,242
Manitoba	836
Saskatchewan	682
Alberta	825
British Columbia	468
Yukon Territory	
Whitehorse	6

[Continued]

★ 903 ★

Number of Canadian Catholic Sisters: 1991
[Continued]

Civil Province	Sisters
Northwest Territories MacKenzie-Ft. Smith	30
Total	29,821

Source: Selected from "Statistics of the Catholic Church in Canada," *1994 Catholic Almanac*, Our Sunday Visitor Publishing, 1994, p. 381. Primary source: *Canadian Conference of Catholic Bishops, Statistics of the Catholic Church in Canada, 1991-1992 Report*, published January, 1993.

★ 904 ★
Catholic Sisters/Missionaries

Number of Catholic Sisters by State: 1992

Total number of Catholic sisters by state and outlying U.S. areas as of January 1, 1993.

State/Diocese	Sisters
Alabama	386
Alaska	86
Arizona	562
Arkansas	364
California	5,768
Colorado	867
Connecticut	1,987
Delaware	348
District of Columbia	1,010
Florida	1,408
Georgia	317
Hawaii	277
Idaho	116
Illinois	6,776
Indiana	2,257
Iowa	1,745
Kansas	1,725
Kentucky	2,151
Louisiana	1,367
Maine	595
Maryland	1,388
Massachusetts	5,213
Michigan	3,454
Minnesota	3,007

[Continued]

★ 904 ★

Number of Catholic Sisters by State: 1992
[Continued]

State/Diocese	Sisters
Mississippi	356
Missouri	3,313
Montana	177
Nebraska	725
Nevada	102
New Hampshire	927
New Jersey	4,189
New Mexico	625
New York	9,332
North Carolina	249
North Dakota	450
Ohio	5,241
Oklahoma	324
Oregon	692
Pennsylvania	10,201
Rhode Island	922
South Carolina	167
South Dakota	579
Tennessee	318
Texas	3,310
Utah	99
Vermont	292
Virginia	566
Washington	1,102
West Virginia	326
Wisconsin	4,479
Wyoming	47
Puerto Rico	1,202
American Samoa,	
Samoa-Pago Pago	14
Carolines-Marshalls	39
Guam	104
No. Mariana Islands	22
U.S. Virgin Islands	20
Total	94,022

Source: Selected from "Catholic Population of the United States," *1994 Catholic Almanac*, p. 428. Also in source: Number of priests, deacons, brothers, and parishes by major city/diocese in each state.

★ 905 ★

Catholic Sisters/Missionaries

Number of Catholic Sisters: 1992 and 1993

Total number of Catholic sisters in 1992 and 1993.

Year	Total
1992	97,751
1993	92,621
Decrease, 1992-1993	5,130

Source: Selected from "Statistical Summary of the Church in the U.S.," *1994 Catholic Almanac*, p. 436.

Religious Practices, Preferences, and Attitudes

★ 906 ★

African Denominations and Membership

This table shows the total population of selected African countries, the female population, the total membership of the largest religious denominations, and the number of members who were female, latest available year.

Country/ denomination	Census date	Total population	Females
Africa			
Egypt	1986	48,205,049	23,549,752
Moslem		45,368,453	22,169,912
Christian		2,829,349	1,377,959
Mauritius	1983	964,762	484,614
Hindu		297,555	149,818
Islam		123,999	61,758
Sanatanist		99,535	49,901
Rodrigues	1983	33,082	16,530
Catholic		31,518	15,847
Saint Helena	1987	5,500	2,831
Church of England		4,756	2,423
Jehovah Witness		268	155
South Africa	1980	25,016,525	12,296,077
Nederduitsc		3,782,510	1,862,250

[Continued]

★ 906 ★

African Denominations and Membership
[Continued]

Country/ denomination	Census date	Total population	Females
Catholic		2,406,699	1,170,545
Other religions		4,674,704	2,383,002
Unknown		4,405,311	2,089,306

Source: Selected from "Population by Religion and Sex: Each Census, 1979-1988," *1988 Demographic Yearbook,* pp. 671-81 (New York: United Nations, 1990).

★ 907 ★

Religious Practices, Preferences, and Attitudes

Asian Denominations and Membership

This table shows the total population of selected Asian countries, the female population, the total membership of the largest religious denominations, and the number of members who were female, latest available year.

[NA Not available.]

Country/ denomination	Census date	Total population	Females
Asia			
Bangladesh	1981	87,119,965	42,200,774
Moslem		75,486,980	36,557,601
Hindu		10,570,245	5,125,589
India	1981	665,287,849	321,357,426
Hindu		549,724,717	265,359,428
Moslem		75,571,514	36,551,871
Israel	1983	4,037,620	2,026,030
Jews		3,349,997	1,687,272
Moslem		526,639	257,995
Jordan	1979	2,132,997	1,017,156
Moslem		2,036,407	971,945
Korea			
Republic of	1985	40,419,652	20,192,088
Buddhist		8,059,624	4,318,727
No religion		23,216,356	10,944,809
Macau	1981	222,525	NA
Buddhist		100,350	NA
No religion		102,209	NA

[Continued]

★ 907 ★

Asian Denominations and Membership
[Continued]

Country/ denomination	Census date	Total population	Females
Malaysia	1980	10,886,713	5,463,099
Moslem		6,106,105	3,107,834
Buddhist		2,064,949	1,036,915
Sabah	1980	950,556	455,061
Islam		487,627	231,957
Sarawak	1980	1,233,103	615,103
Christian		351,361	176,968
Moslem		324,575	161,901
Pakistan	1981	84,253,644	40,020,967
Moslem		81,450,057	NA
Sri Lanka	1981	14,846,750	7,278,496
Buddhist		10,288,325	5,040,259
Hindu		2,297,806	1,118,928

Source: Selected from "Population by Religion and Sex: Each Census, 1979-1988," *1988 Demographic Yearbook*, pp. 671-81 (New York: United Nations, 1990).

★ 908 ★

Religious Practices, Preferences, and Attitudes

Catholic Marriages Performed: 1992

This table shows the total number of Catholic marriages performed by state in 1992.

State	Marriages
Alabama	861
Alaska	273
Arizona	2,954
Arkansas	
Little Rock	649
California	33,121
Colorado	2,913
Connecticut	7,488
Delaware	
Wilmington	1,203
District of Colombia	2,666
Florida	10,153
Georgia	1,334

[Continued]

★ 908 ★

Catholic Marriages Performed: 1992
[Continued]

State	Marriages
Hawaii	
Honolulu	1,124
Idaho	
Boise	580
Illinois	20,995
Indiana	5,283
Iowa	4,401
Kansas	2,737
Kentucky	2,707
Louisiana	7,614
Maine	
Portland	1,857
Maryland	
Baltimore	5,186
Massachusetts	16,957
Michigan	13,470
Minnesota	8,027
Mississippi	797
Missouri	5,841
Montana	844
Nebraska	2,434
Nevada	
Reno-Las Vegas	814
New Hampshire	
Manchester	1,743
New Jersey	17,868
New Mexico	2,225
New York	38,555
North Carolina	1,499
North Dakota	1,246
Ohio	14,735
Oklahoma	1,110
Oregon	1,565
Pennsylvania	22,269
Rhode Island	
Providence	2,741
South Carolina	
Charleston	719
South Dakota	1,034
Tennessee	1,192

[Continued]

★ 908 ★

Catholic Marriages Performed: 1992
[Continued]

State	Marriages
Texas	16,564
Utah	
Salt Lake City	419
Vermont	
Burlington	903
Virginia	2,881
Washington	3,150
West Virginia	
Wheeling-Charleston	753
Wisconsin	13,215
Wyoming	
Cheyenne	372
Military Archdiocese	2,240
U.S. Total 1993	316,675
U.S. Total 1992	322,550
U.S. Total 1983	347,445

Source: Selected from "Receptions into the Church and Marriages in the United States, *The Catholic Almanac*, Our Sunday Visitor Publishing, 1994, p. 434-35. Primary source: *The Official Catholic Director, 1993*. Figures as of January 1, 1993.

★ 909 ★

Religious Practices, Preferences, and Attitudes

European Denominations and Membership

This table shows the total population of selected European countries, the female population, the total membership of the largest religious denominations, and the number of members who were female, latest available year.

[NA Not available.]

Country/ denomination	Census date	Total population	Females
Europe			
Austria	1981	7,555,338	3,982,912
Catholic		6,398,192	3,417,261
Finland	1985	4,910,664	2,532,884
Lutheran		4,381,534	2,311,562
Ireland	1981	3,443,405	1,714,051
Catholic		3,203,574	1,599,550

[Continued]

★ 909 ★

European Denominations and Membership
[Continued]

Country/ denomination	Census date	Total population	Females
Liechtenstein	1982	26,380	13,376
Catholic		22,467	NA
Portugal	1981	7,836,504	NA
Catholic		6,352,705	NA
United Kingdom			
Northern Ireland	1981	1,481,959	756,742
Catholic		414,532	211,315
Other Christians		281,472	143,915

Source: Selected from "Population by Religion and Sex: Each Census, 1979-1988," *1988 Demographic Yearbook*, pp. 671-81 (New York: United Nations, 1990).

★ 910 ★

Religious Practices, Preferences, and Attitudes

Latin America/Caribbean Denominations and Membership

This table shows the total population of selected Latin American and Caribbean countries, the female population, the total membership of the largest religious denominations, and the number of members who were female, latest available year.

[NA Not available.]

Country/ denomination	Census date	Total population	Females
Latin America/Caribbean			
Bahamas	1980	209,505	107,731
Baptist		67,193	35,431
Catholic		39,397	19,539
Barbados	1980	244,228	128,457
Anglican		96,894	52,653
No religion		42,721	15,354
Belize	1980	142,847	70,948
Catholic		88,587	43,945
Methodist		8,632	4,340
Brazil	1980	119,011,052	59,868,219
Catholic		114,606,475	57,821,375
No religion		1,953,096	749,277

[Continued]

★ 910 ★

Latin America/Caribbean Denominations and Membership
[Continued]

Country/ denomination	Census date	Total population	Females
British Virgin Islands	1980	10,985	5,368
Methodist		4,997	2,426
Anglican		2,302	1,106
Dominica	1981	73,795	37,041
Catholic		56,770	28,789
Methodist		3,663	1,796
Grenada	1981	89,088	46,145
Catholic		52,820	27,340
Anglican		15,226	7,724
Guyana	1980	758,619	382,778
Hindu		281,119	140,118
Agnostic		108,787	55,320
Haiti	1982	5,053,792	2,605,422
Catholic		4,057,496	2,076,958
Baptist		491,329	257,744
Jamaica	1982	2,172,879	1,109,417
Church of God		400,379	225,239
No religion		385,517	141,326
Mexico	1980	66,846,833	33,807,526
Catholic		61,916,757	31,443,532
Protestant		2,201,609	1,140,245
Montserrat	1980	11,519	5,983
Anglican		3,676	1,873
Methodist		2,742	1,440
Netherlands Antilles	1981	231,932	119,784
Catholic		197,115	NA
Protestant		7,369	NA
Peru	1981	17,005,210	8,515,343
Catholic		15,150,572	7,574,319
Saint Kitts and Nevis	1980	43,309	22,469
Anglican		14,111	7,135
Methodist		12,473	6,495
Saint Lucia	1980	113,409	58,900
Catholic		97,075	50,616
Seventh Day Adventist		4,909	2,645

[Continued]

★ 910 ★

Latin America/Caribbean Denominations and Membership
[Continued]

Country/ denomination	Census date	Total population	Females
Saint Vincent and the Grenadines	1980	97,845	50,436
Agnostic		40,682	20,617
Methodist		20,454	10,370
Trinidad and Tobago	1980	1,055,763	529,529
Catholic		347,740	175,003
Hindu		262,917	129,447
Turks and Caicos Islands	1980	4,510	2,375
Baptist		1,807	967
Methodist		864	432

Source: Selected from "Population by Religion and Sex: Each Census, 1979-1988," *1988 Demographic Yearbook*, pp. 671-81 (New York: United Nations, 1990).

★ 911 ★

Religious Practices, Preferences, and Attitudes

Oceanian Denominations and Membership

This table shows the total population of selected Oceanian countries, the female population, the total membership of the largest religious denominations, and the number of members who were female, latest available year.

[NA Not available.]

Country/ denomination	Census date	Total population	Females
Oceania			
Australia	1981	14,576,330	7,309,254
Church of England		3,810,469	1,965,652
Catholic		3,786,505	1,924,361
Fiji	1986	715,375	352,807
Christian		378,452	186,021
Hindu		273,088	135,275
New Zealand	1986	3,263,283	1,646,616
Anglican		791,850	423,384
Presbyterian		587,517	307,407
Papua New Guinea	1980	2,079,128	989,933
Catholic		718,352	339,832
Lutheran		548,973	262,586
United Church		272,469	129,775

[Continued]

★ 911 ★

Oceanian Denominations and Membership
[Continued]

Country/denomination	Census date	Total population	Females
Samoa	1981	156,349	75,322
Other Christians		74,031	35,728
Catholic		33,997	16,523
Vanuatu	1979	111,251	52,177
Presbyterians		40,843	19,169
Anglican		16,778	7,872

Source: Selected from "Population by Religion and Sex: Each Census, 1979-1988," *1988 Demographic Yearbook*, pp. 671-81 (New York: United Nations, 1990).

★ 912 ★

Religious Practices, Preferences, and Attitudes

Religious Preferences of Women Entering College: 1994

This table shows the percentages of entering college freshmen women who reported a preference for various religious denominations. For this survey, the national population included 2,700 institutions. The data are based on responses from 237,777 freshmen entering 461 two- and four-year institutions in 1994.

Denomination	Type of Institution				
	All institutions	All 2-year colleges	All 4-year colleges	All universities	All black colleges
Student's Religious Preference					
Baptist	18.0%	21.9%	19.3%	10.3%	60.2%
Buddhist	0.4%	0.2%	0.4%	0.6%	0.1%
Eastern Orthodox	0.4%	0.0%	0.4%	0.8%	0.0%
Episcopal	2.0%	1.6%	2.1%	2.6%	1.2%
Islamic	0.3%	0.1%	0.4%	0.5%	0.1%
Jewish	1.7%	0.7%	1.3%	4.0%	0.0%
LDS (Mormon)	0.5%	0.7%	0.4%	0.5%	0.1%
Lutheran	6.2%	4.7%	6.8%	7.0%	0.4%
Methodist	9.1%	10.2%	8.4%	8.7%	7.3%
Presbyterian	4.1%	3.3%	3.9%	5.2%	1.0%
Quaker	0.2%	0.3%	0.2%	0.2%	0.0%
Roman Catholic	29.9%	28.5%	29.6%	32.5%	10.1%
Seventh Day Adventist	0.3%	0.2%	0.4%	0.2%	0.7%
United Church of Christ	1.6%	1.3%	1.9%	1.6%	1.3%
Other Christian	9.5%	9.6%	10.2%	8.1%	6.6%
Other religion	4.4%	5.8%	3.8%	3.3%	4.5%
None	11.4%	10.8%	10.5%	13.9%	5.4%

[Continued]

★ 912 ★

Religious Preferences of Women Entering College: 1994
[Continued]

Denomination	Type of Institution				
	All institutions	All 2-year colleges	All 4-year colleges	All universities	All black colleges
Student Born-Again Christian?					
No	68.7%	65.0%	66.7%	77.7%	43.8%
Yes	31.3%	35.0%	33.3%	22.3%	56.2%

Source: Selected from "Weighted National Norms for Freshman Women, Fall 1994: Student's Religious Preference" Astin, A.W. et al., *The American Freshman: National Norms for Fall 1994,* 1994, p. 50.

★ 913 ★

Religious Practices, Preferences, and Attitudes

The Churches' Stands on Abortion

This table presents statistics on the views of major religious groups on abortion.

Item	Membership
Presbyterian Church	
One of the most strongly pro-abortion rights Protestant denominations, membership:	> 3 million
Southern Baptist Convention	
Working toward legislation and/or a constitutional amendment to prohibit abortions except to save the life of the mother.	14.5 million
American Baptist Churches	
Membership divided on abortion question. Left up to individual.	1.5 million
United Methodist	
Reluctant to approve abortion but respect the well-being of the mother.	9.1 million

[Continued]

★ 913 ★

The Churches' Stands on Abortion
[Continued]

Item	Membership
Evangelical Lutheran Church	
Adopted resolution calling on church leaders to help "couples and individuals explore all issues."	5.2 million
Lutheran Church, Missouri Synod	
Holds that the unborn "are persons in the sight of God from the time of conception."	2.6 million
Episcopal Church	
Respects individual conscience.	2.5 million
African Methodist Episcopal Church	
No official position, but most members said to believe "abortion is usually wrong except where a greater wrong would be involved," such as ... rape... incest ...mother's life in jeopardy.	2.2 million
Assemblies of God	
Affirmed in 1985 that life begins at conception.	2.1 million
United Church of Christ	
Upholds the "right of women to have ... safe, legal abortions as one option among others."	1.6 million
Jehovah's Witnesses	
Abortion is murder except when necessary to save the life of the mother.	750,000
Unitarian Universalist Association	
Supports "the right to choose contraception and abortion as legitimate aspects of the right to privacy."	170,000

[Continued]

★ 913 ★

The Churches' Stands on Abortion
[Continued]

Item	Membership
Friends	
In 1970 urged "the repeal of all laws limiting the circumstances under which a woman may have an abortion."	> 110,000
Latter-Day Saints (Mormons)	
Opposes abortion.	3.8 million
Roman Catholic Church	
Life begins at the moment of conception and abortion is murder.	
United States	52 million
Worldwide	900 million
Greek Orthodox Church	
Life begins at the moment of conception.	1.9 million
Russian Orthodox Church	
Same as Greek Orthodox.	1 million
Reform Judaism	
Abortion is permitted when the life or health of the mother is threatened. This can mean the "spiritual or psychological" life of the mother.	1.3 million
Conservative Judaism	
Views close to Reform Judaism.	1.2 million
Orthodox Judaism	
Against abortion except when life or health of mother is in jeopardy.	1 million

[Continued]

★ 913 ★

The Churches' Stands on Abortion
[Continued]

Item	Membership
Islam	
Abortion allowed for any reason in the first 40 days of pregnancy; for no reason thereafter, except to safe the life of the mother.	
North American	2.6 million
Worldwide	860 million
Hinduism	
Abortion allowed only in cases of rape, incest, or to save mother's life. However, abortion in India is legal and widely accepted. Membership (worldwide)	735 million
Sikhism	
Opinions divided, but because Sikhs believe in rebirth, is not a burning controversy. Membership (worldwide):	16.6 million
Buddhism	
Opinions divided, but Buddhists belive in rebirth.	
United States	100,000
Worldwide	300 million
Shintoism	
No position on abortion. Most Japanese believe the decision is a personal matter.	100 million

Source: Selected from Mark Weston, "Faith and Abortion: Where the World's Major Religions Disagree," *Washington Post*, January 23, 1990, pp. 12-15. Membership figures are for the United States and were taken from the 1989 World Almanac.

Women Clergy

★914★

African-American Pastors

This table presents numbers of female and male pastors and associate pastors in metroplitan Detroit churches belonging to seven historically African-American denominations. Only one, the Church of God in Christ, officially bars woman pastors. The other six, which attract 46% of all black worshipers, have no restrictive policies on woman pastors. African-American women now account for four out of every 10 black seminarians, compared to one out of 10 in 1985. Women account for fewer than 4% of black clergy in 2,150 churches of the historically black faiths.[1].

Church	Male pastors	Female pastors	Male assoc. pastors	Female assoc. pastors
National Baptist Convention USA (221 churches)	211	0	97	3
Progressive Baptist Convention USA (35 churches)	32	0	32	2
National Baptist Convention of American (18 churches)	12	0	3	2
African Methodist Episcopal Church (41 churches)	31	8	15	30
Christian Methodist Episcopal Church (19 churches)	15	3	4	5
African Methodist Episcopal Zion Church (12 churches	11	1	2	0
Church of God in Christ (122 churches)	117	0	15	0

Source: Kate DeSmet, "The Pain of the Woman Pastor," *The Detroit News and Free Press*, February 5, 1995, p. A1, A10. Primary source: *1995 Church Directory*, compiled by the Christian Communication Council. *Notes:* 1. C. Eric Lincoln and Lawrence H. Mamiya, *The Black Church in the African American Experience* (Duke University Press, 1990).

Chapter 13
SEXUALITY

Sexual Practices, Preferences, and Attitudes

★ 915 ★

Achieving Orgasm

The table below shows the responses of women and men to a survey question about whether they achieve orgasm during lovemaking.

Frequency	Women total	Career women	Home-makers	Men
N =	1,398	631	273	1,341
Always	15%	18%	13%	65%
Often	46%	49%	38%	28%
Sometimes	23%	23%	27%	3%
Rarely	8%	4%	10%	2%
Never	8%	6%	12%	2%
Always + Often	61%	67%	51%	93%
Rarely + Never	16%	10%	22%	4%

Source: "I Have Orgasm During Lovemaking," Samuel S. Janus, PhD, and Cynthia L. Janus, MD, *The Janus Report on Sexual Behavior*, (New York: John Wiley & Sons, Inc., 1993), Table 3.28, p. 86. Between 1988 and 1992, the authors distributed 4,550 questionnaires to subjects at a variety of sites. The sample design was planned to conform to the population distribution of the United States in the areas of sex, age, region, income, education, and marital status. Returned questionnaires totaled 3,260. Of these, 495 were discarded. Satisfactorily completed questionnaires totaled 2,765: 1,418 women and 1,347 men. This table further designates women as career women or homemakers.

★ 916 ★
Sexual Practices, Preferences, and Attitudes

Are One-Night Stands Degrading?

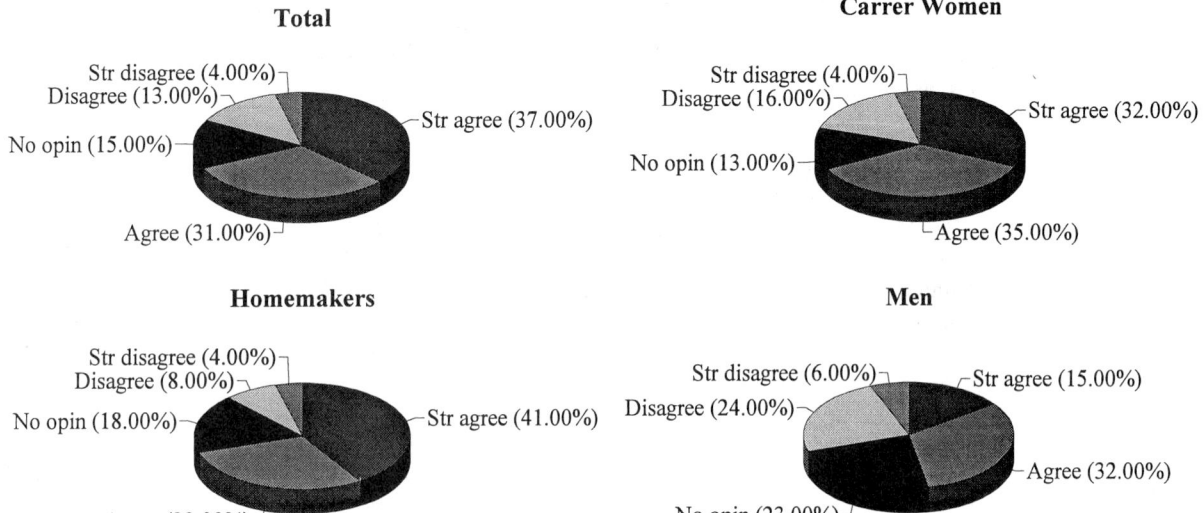

The table below shows the responses of women and men to a survey question about whether they consider one-night stands to be degrading. According to the authors, "anonymous sex has apparently achieved considerable acceptance into the psyche of American women."

Responses	Women total	Career women	Home-makers	Men
N =	1,411	634	273	1,341
One-night stands are degrading.				
Strongly agree	37%	32%	41%	15%
Agree	31%	35%	29%	32%
No opinion	15%	13%	18%	23%
Disagree	13%	16%	8%	24%
Strongly disagree	4%	4%	4%	6%
Strongly agree + Agree	68%	67%	70%	47%
Disagree + Strongly disagree	17%	20%	12%	30%

Source: "I Find One-Night Stands To Be Degrading", Samuel S. Janus, PhD, and Cynthia L. Janus, MD, *The Janus Report on Sexual Behavior*, (New York: John Wiley & Sons, Inc., 1993), Table 3.19, p. 75. Between 1988 and 1992, the authors distributed 4,550 questionnaires to subjects at a variety of sites. The sample design was planned to conform to the population distribution of the United States in the areas of sex, age, region, income, education, and marital status. Returned questionnaires totaled 3,260. Of these, 495 were discarded. Satisfactorily completed questionnaires totaled 2,765: 1,418 women and 1,347 men. This table further designates women as career women or homemakers.

★ 917 ★

Sexual Practices, Preferences, and Attitudes

Attraction

The table below shows the responses of married and divorced women and men to a survey question about what originally attracted them about their mates.

Responses	Married		Divorced	
	Women	Men	Women	Men
N =	803	770	125	120
Attracted by...				
Looks	17%	26%	15%	33%
Personality	44%	49%	39%	42%
Sexiness	5%	9%	21%	4%
Wealth	1%	2%	1%	0%
Warmth	26%	12%	20%	16%
Power	3%	1%	3%	1%
Humor	4%	1%	1%	4%

Source: "I Was Initially Attracted to my Spouse/Partner by His/Her:," Samuel S. Janus, PhD, and Cynthia L. Janus, MD, *The Janus Report on Sexual Behavior,* (New York: John Wiley & Sons, Inc., 1993), Table 6.2, p. 175. Between 1988 and 1992, the authors distributed 4,550 questionnaires to subjects at a variety of sites. The sample design was planned to conform to the population distribution of the United States in the areas of sex, age, region, income, education, and marital status. Returned questionnaires totaled 3,260. Of these, 495 were discarded. Satisfactorily completed questionnaires totaled 2,765: 1,418 women and 1,347 men.

★ 918 ★

Sexual Practices, Preferences, and Attitudes

Caution in Sex

The table below shows the responses of women and men, by age, to a survey question about whether they have become more cautious about sex in the last few years. The authors attribute this caution to fear of sexually transmitted diseases and AIDS.

Response	Ages (Years)									
	18 to 26		27 to 38		39 to 50		51 to 64		65+	
	F	M	F	M	F	M	F	M	F	M
N =	274	256	380	357	302	284	234	229	224	217
I have become more cautious.										
a. Strongly agree	31%	29%	29%	24%	20%	19%	14%	22%	31%	19%
b. Agree	48%	54%	43%	52%	44%	50%	42%	52%	25%	55%
c. No opinion	14%	10%	13%	7%	16%	11%	18%	8%	21%	5%
d. Disagree	6%	5%	13%	15%	17%	17%	21%	14%	22%	14%
e. Strongly disagree	1%	2%	2%	2%	3%	3%	5%	4%	1%	7%

[Continued]

★ 918 ★

Caution in Sex
[Continued]

Response	18 to 26 F	18 to 26 M	27 to 38 F	27 to 38 M	39 to 50 F	39 to 50 M	51 to 64 F	51 to 64 M	65+ F	65+ M
Affirmative (lines a + b)	79%	83%	72%	76%	64%	69%	56%	74%	56%	74%
Negative (lines d + e)	7%	7%	15%	17%	20%	20%	26%	18%	23%	21%

Source: "In the Past Few Years I Have Become More Cautious About Sex", Samuel S. Janus, PhD, and Cynthia L. Janus, MD, *The Janus Report on Sexual Behavior*, (New York: John Wiley & Sons, Inc., 1993), Table 2.4, p. 33. Between 1988 and 1992, the authors distributed 4,550 questionnaires to subjects at a variety of sites. The sample design was planned to conform to the population distribution of the United States in the areas of sex, age, region, income, education, and marital status. Returned questionnaires totaled 3,260. Of these, 495 were discarded. Satisfactorily completed questionnaires totaled 2,765: 1,418 women and 1,347 men.

★ 919 ★

Sexual Practices, Preferences, and Attitudes

Cohabitation

The table below shows the responses of married and divorced women and men to a survey question about whether they lived with their spouse before marriage and for how many years. The authors concluded that the failure of marriages following cohabitation indicates that extended periods of cohabitation could be detrimental to a resulting marriage.

Responses	Married	Divorced	Women Married	Women Divorced	Men Married	Men Divorced
N =	1,571	245	801	125	770	120
Yes	43%	56%	39%	67%	47%	44%
No	57%	44%	61%	33%	53%	56%
How long?						
N =	676	139				
One year or less	49%	22%				
2-5 years	44%	72%				
6-10 years	6%	5%				
More than 10 years	1%	1%				

Source: "Did You Live with Your Spouse Before Marrying" and "How Many Years Did You Live Together (Before Marrying)?," Samuel S. Janus, PhD, and Cynthia L. Janus, MD, *The Janus Report on Sexual Behavior*, (New York: John Wiley & Sons, Inc., 1993), Tables 6.4 and 6.5, p. 177. Between 1988 and 1992, the authors distributed 4,550 questionnaires to subjects at a variety of sites. The sample design was planned to conform to the population distribution of the United States in the areas of sex, age, region, income, education, and marital status. Returned questionnaires totaled 3,260. Of these, 495 were discarded. Satisfactorily completed questionnaires totaled 2,765: 1,418 women and 1,347 men.

★ 920 ★

Sexual Practices, Preferences, and Attitudes

Frequency of Achieving Orgasm

The table below shows the responses of women and men, by age, to a survey question about how often they achieve orgasm during lovemaking. According to the authors of the study, "women view orgasm as important; men regard it as crucial."

Frequency	Ages (Years)									
	18 to 26		27 to 38		39 to 50		51 to 64		65+	
	F	M	F	M	F	M	F	M	F	M
N =	265	254	373	352	293	283	231	226	221	213
a. Always	18%	68%	16%	68%	14%	60%	21%	77%	8%	55%
b. Often	39%	25%	51%	26%	52%	34%	44%	18%	42%	38%
c. Sometimes	22%	3%	18%	3%	22%	4%	22%	1%	37%	4%
d. Rarely	8%	1%	9%	1%	7%	1%	10%	2%	4%	1%
e. Never	13%	3%	6%	2%	5%	1%	3%	2%	9%	2%
Frequently (lines a + b)	57%	93%	67%	94%	66%	94%	65%	95%	50%	93%
At least sometimes (lines a through c)	79%	96%	85%	97%	88%	98%	87%	96%	87%	97%

Source: "I Have Orgasm During Lovemaking", Samuel S. Janus, PhD, and Cynthia L. Janus, MD, *The Janus Report on Sexual Behavior,* (New York: John Wiley & Sons, Inc., 1993), Table 2.2, p. 27. Between 1988 and 1992, the authors distributed 4,550 questionnaires to subjects at a variety of sites. The sample design was planned to conform to the population distribution of the United States in the areas of sex, age, region, income, education, and marital status. Returned questionnaires totaled 3,260. Of these, 495 were discarded. Satisfactorily completed questionnaires totaled 2,765: 1,418 women and 1,347 men.

★ 921 ★

Sexual Practices, Preferences, and Attitudes

Frequency of Homosexual Activity

The table below shows the frequency of occasions of homosexual activity on the part of women and men who responded YES to a survey question about whether they have had homosexual experiences.

Frequency	Women, total	Career women	Home-makers	Men
N =	235	146	26	294
a. Once	6%	7%	4%	5%
b. Occasionally	67%	63%	84%	56%
c. Frequently	6%	4%	7%	13%

[Continued]

★ 921 ★

Frequency of Homosexual Activity
[Continued]

Frequency	Women, total	Career women	Home-makers	Men
d. Ongoing	21%	26%	5%	26%
Active (lines c + d)	27%	30%	12%	39%

Source: "Have You Had Homosexual Experiences? Yes Responses", Samuel S. Janus, PhD, and Cynthia L. Janus, MD, *The Janus Report on Sexual Behavior*, (New York: John Wiley & Sons, Inc., 1993), Table 3.15, p. 70. Between 1988 and 1992, the authors distributed 4,550 questionnaires to subjects at a variety of sites. The sample design was planned to conform to the population distribution of the United States in the areas of sex, age, region, income, education, and marital status. Returned questionnaires totaled 3,260. Of these, 495 were discarded. Satisfactorily completed questionnaires totaled 2,765: 1,418 women and 1,347 men. This table further designates women as career women or homemarkers.

★ 922 ★

Sexual Practices, Preferences, and Attitudes

Frequency of Masturbation

The table below shows the responses of women and men, by age, to a survey question about how often they indulge in masturbation.

Frequency	Ages (Years)									
	18 to 26		27 to 38		39 to 50		51 to 64		65+	
	F	M	F	M	F	M	F	M	F	M
N =	266	253	378	353	294	281	233	226	213	214
a. Daily	2%	6%	3%	9%	2%	7%	1%	9%	0%	1%
b. Several times weekly	6%	18%	11%	19%	12%	16%	7%	23%	2%	16%
c. Weekly	10%	19%	16%	25%	16%	19%	12%	22%	2%	27%
d. Monthly	9%	8%	17%	9%	17%	12%	16%	4%	23%	6%
e. Rarely	29%	23%	33%	26%	37%	30%	34%	18%	38%	27%
f. Never	44%	26%	20%	12%	16%	16%	30%	24%	35%	23%
Active (lines a + b)	8%	24%	14%	28%	14%	23%	8%	32%	2%	17%
At least monthly (lines a through d)	27%	51%	47%	62%	47%	54%	36%	58%	27%	50%

Source: "I Masturbate on Average", Samuel S. Janus, PhD, and Cynthia L. Janus, MD, *The Janus Report on Sexual Behavior*, (New York: John Wiley & Sons, Inc., 1993), Table 2.3, p. 31. Between 1988 and 1992, the authors distributed 4,550 questionnaires to subjects at a variety of sites. The sample design was planned to conform to the population distribution of the United States in the areas of sex, age, region, income, education, and marital status. Returned questionnaires totaled 3,260. Of these, 495 were discarded. Satisfactorily completed questionnaires totaled 2,765: 1,418 women and 1,347 men.

★ 923 ★

Sexual Practices, Preferences, and Attitudes

Frequency of Sexual Activity

The table below shows the responses of women and men, by age, to a survey question about the frequency of all their sexual activity.

Frequency	Ages (Years)									
	18 to 26		27 to 38		39 to 50		51 to 64		65+	
	F	M	F	M	F	M	F	M	F	M
N =	268	254	380	353	295	282	230	227	221	212
a. Daily	13%	15%	8%	16%	10%	15%	4%	12%	1%	14%
b. A few times weekly	33%	38%	41%	44%	29%	39%	28%	51%	40%	39%
c. Weekly	22%	19%	27%	23%	29%	29%	33%	18%	33%	16%
d. Monthly	15%	15%	12%	8%	11%	9%	8%	11%	4%	20%
e. Rarely	17%	13%	12%	9%	21%	8%	27%	8%	22%	11%
Active (lines a + b)	46%	53%	49%	60%	39%	54%	32%	63%	41%	53%
At least weekly (lines a through c)	68%	72%	76%	83%	68%	83%	65%	81%	74%	69%

Source: "Frequency of all Sexual Activity Is", Samuel S. Janus, PhD, and Cynthia L. Janus, MD, *The Janus Report on Sexual Behavior*, (New York: John Wiley & Sons, Inc., 1993), Table 2.1, p. 25. Between 1988 and 1992, the authors distributed 4,550 questionnaires to subjects at a variety of sites. The sample design was planned to conform to the population distribution of the United States in the areas of sex, age, region, income, education, and marital status. Returned questionnaires totaled 3,260. Of these, 495 were discarded. Satisfactorily completed questionnaires totaled 2,765: 1,418 women and 1,347 men.

★ 924 ★

Sexual Practices, Preferences, and Attitudes

Group Sex

The table below shows the responses of women and men to a survey question about how they viewed group sex. According to the authors, when respondents were interviewed, it was learned that group sex starts because it appeals to men. Most women at first have to be urged to try the activity. Later, when women find they enjoy group sex, their mates begin to lose interest in it.

Responses	Women	Men
N =	1,412	1,342
Group sex is...		
Very normal	1%	3%
All right	7%	14%
Unusual	22%	38%
Kinky	68%	43%
Never heard of it	2%	2%

[Continued]

★ 924 ★

Group Sex
[Continued]

Responses	Women	Men
Have had personal experience with it.	8%	14%

Source: "Rating Scale: Group Sex," Samuel S. Janus, PhD, and Cynthia L. Janus, MD, *The Janus Report on Sexual Behavior*, (New York: John Wiley & Sons, Inc., 1993), Table 4.11, p. 127. Between 1988 and 1992, the authors distributed 4,550 questionnaires to subjects at a variety of sites. The sample design was planned to conform to the population distribution of the United States in the areas of sex, age, region, income, education, and marital status. Returned questionnaires totaled 3,260. Of these, 495 were discarded. Satisfactorily completed questionnaires totaled 2,765: 1,418 women and 1,347 men.

★ 925 ★

Sexual Practices, Preferences, and Attitudes

Number of Sex Partners

The table below shows the responses of women and men to a survey question about how many different people they have had sexual relations with.

Response	Women total	Career women	Home-makers	Men
N =	1,391	628	262	1,332
Number of partners.				
None	3%	1%	4%	1%
1 to 10	42%	33%	48%	28%
11 to 30	39%	46%	32%	32%
31 to 60	9%	10%	11%	21%
61 to 100	3%	3%	3%	8%
101 +	4%	7%	2%	10%
1 to 30	81%	79%	80%	60%
61 and over	7%	10%	5%	18%

Source: "How Many Different Individuals (Including Spouses) Have You Had Sexual Relations With?," Samuel S. Janus, PhD, and Cynthia L. Janus, MD, *The Janus Report on Sexual Behavior*, (New York: John Wiley & Sons, Inc., 1993), Table 3.39, p. 95. Between 1988 and 1992, the authors distributed 4,550 questionnaires to subjects at a variety of sites. The sample design was planned to conform to the population distribution of the United States in the areas of sex, age, region, income, education, and marital status. Returned questionnaires totaled 3,260. Of these, 495 were discarded. Satisfactorily completed questionnaires totaled 2,765: 1,418 women and 1,347 men. This table further designates women as career women or homemakers.

★ 926 ★

Sexual Practices, Preferences, and Attitudes

Number of Sex Partners by Age and Race

This table shows the number of women aged 15-44 who had ever had intercourse and the percentage with various lifetime numbers of sexual partners, according to the 1988 National Survey of Family Growth.

[Numbers in thousands, except percent.]

Characteristic	Ever had intercourse	Number of partners				
		1	2 or more	4 or more	6 or more	more than 10
Total	51,146	33.2%	66.8%	40.8%	23.1%	8.3%
Marital status						
Currently married[1]	32,127	39.5%	60.5%	34.3%	18.3%	6.3%
Formerly married	6,498	14.2%	85.8%	62.7%	39.1%	15.8%
Never married	12,521	26.5%	73.5%	46.3%	27.2%	9.6%
Age						
15-17	2,067	45.1%	54.9%	27.0%	12.9%	4.4%
18-19	2,789	39.5%	60.5%	32.2%	14.1%	4.7%
20-24	8,103	29.4%	70.6%	38.0%	21.1%	6.0%
25-29	10,237	28.3%	71.8%	45.5%	24.8%	9.2%
30-34	10,703	29.1%	70.8%	46.3%	26.3%	10.5%
35-39	9,372	33.8%	66.2%	43.7%	26.8%	10.1%
40-44	7,875	43.4%	56.7%	32.9%	19.8%	6.6%
Poverty status[2]						
0-99%	7,076	27.2%	72.7%	45.5%	25.6%	8.8%
100-199%	9,488	33.4%	66.6%	40.4%	20.8%	7.6%
200% or more	34,582	34.4%	65.6%	39.8%	23.1%	8.3%
Race/ethnicity						
Non-Hispanic white	37,970	33.1%	66.9%	41.2%	23.9%	9.0%
Non-Hispanic black	6,673	18.5%	81.5%	51.5%	24.5%	6.8%
Hispanic	4,703	47.6%	52.4%	29.3%	17.5%	5.8%
Other	1,800	50.5%	49.5%	22.9%	15.1%	6.0%

Source: Kathryn Kost and Jacqueline Darroch Forrest,"American Women's Sexual Behavior and Exposure to Risk of Sexually Transmitted Diseases," *Family Planning Perspectives,* Vol. 24(6), November/December 1992, pp. 244-254, Table 1, p. 246, "Among U.S. women aged 15-44 who have ever had intercourse, percentage of women with various lifetime numbers of sexual partners, by selected characteristics, 1988 National Survey of Family Growth (NSFG)." *Notes:* 1. Includes both those who are formally married and those in a consensual union. 2. Expressed as the percentage above or below the federally designated poverty level.

★ 927 ★

Sexual Practices, Preferences, and Attitudes

Partners of the Same Sex

This table presents statistics about men and women who reported having sexual partners of the same sex in the last year. Data is from a study of 3,432 Americans from 18 to 59 years of age conducted by a team of researchers based at the University of Chicago. The team reported that 2.8% of the men and 1.4% of the women had identified themselves as homosexual or bisexual, having had a partner of the same sex in the last year. When questioned about their entire adulthood, 16.4% of the men and 6.2% of the women said they had had at least one partner of the same sex.

Characteristic	Men	Women
Persons who reported having sexual partners of the same sex in the last year:		
Location		
Top 12 largest cities	10.2%	2.1%
Suburbs of top 12 cities	2.7%	1.2%
Rural	1.0%	0.6%
Total	2.6%[1]	1.1%
Education		
College graduate	3.5%	2.5%
Some college	3.0%	1.1%
High school graduate	1.4%	0.8%
Less than high school	3.1%	0.9%

Source: David W. Dunlap, "Gay Survey Raises a New Question," *The New York Times,* October 18, 1994, p. A10. Primary source: *The Social Organization of Sexuality,* University of Chicago Press, 1994. *Note:* 1. 2.6% shown in newspaper article's table; 2.8% discussed in article.

★ 928 ★

Sexual Practices, Preferences, and Attitudes

Premarital Sex

The table below shows the responses of married and divorced women and men to a survey question about whether they had sexual experience before marriage.

Amount	Married		Divorced	
	Women	Men	Women	Men
N =	802	772	127	122
Sexual experience...				
Very much	16%	31%	20%	37%
Much	21%	34%	21%	39%

[Continued]

★ 928 ★

Premarital Sex
[Continued]

Amount	Married		Divorced	
	Women	Men	Women	Men
Little	29%	18%	26%	13%
Very little	18%	9%	17%	1%
None	16%	8%	16%	10%
Very much + Much	37%	65%	41%	76%
Little + Very little	47%	27%	43%	14%

Source: "I Had Sexual Experience Before Marriage," Samuel S. Janus, PhD, and Cynthia L. Janus, MD, *The Janus Report on Sexual Behavior*, (New York: John Wiley & Sons, Inc., 1993), Table 6.3, p. 176. Between 1988 and 1992, the authors distributed 4,550 questionnaires to subjects at a variety of sites. The sample design was planned to conform to the population distribution of the United States in the areas of sex, age, region, income, education, and marital status. Returned questionnaires totaled 3,260. Of these, 495 were discarded. Satisfactorily completed questionnaires totaled 2,765: 1,418 women and 1,347 men.

★ 929 ★

Sexual Practices, Preferences, and Attitudes

Sex Ever or in the Last Three Months: 1982-1988

This table shows the percentage of women who had ever had intercourse and who had had intercourse in the previous three months, by marital status and age group, according to the 1982 and 1988 National Survey of Family Growth.

Age group	All women				Never married[1]				Formerly married[1]	
	Ever had intercourse		Last 3 months		Ever had intercourse		Last three months		Last 3 months	
	1982	1988	1982	1988	1982	1988	1982	1988	1982	1988
15-44	86.4%	88.5%	77.4%	77.6%	59.3%	65.5%	44.9%	49.0%	67.8%	60.8%
15-19	47.1%	53.2%	40.0%	42.5%	42.1%	49.5%	34.3%	38.5%	[2]	[2]
20-24	85.7%	86.4%	75.5%	75.8%	72.3%	74.8%	54.4%	59.9%	85.9%	63.2%
25-29	96.7%	94.8%	89.3%	85.4%	83.8%	79.9%	60.3%	61.1%	78.9%	63.8%
30-34	98.0%	98.0%	89.7%	88.2%	81.3%	84.8%	52.5%	53.6%	70.3%	67.5%
35-39	97.9%	97.9%	88.8%	86.5%	67.5%	78.1%	42.4%	50.8%	60.7%	62.6%
40-44	98.2%	98.9%	85.5%	84.3%	63.0%	84.5%	22.9%[3]	33.6%	52.4%	48.9%

Source: Jacqueline Darroch Forrest and Susheela Singh, "The Sexual and Reproductive Behavior of American Women, 1982-1988," *Family Planning Perspectives*, Vol. 22(5), September/October 1990, pp. 206-214, Table 3, p. 208, "Percentage of women who had ever had intercourse and who had had intercourse in the previous three months, by marital status and age-group, 1982 and 1988 NSFG." *Notes:* 1. Not cohabiting. 2. Fewer than 20 respondents. 3. Denotes proportion with relative standard error of 30% or more.

★ 930 ★

Sexual Practices, Preferences, and Attitudes

Sexual Self-Assessment

The table below shows the responses of women and men to a survey question
about how they see themselves in terms of their sexuality. The authors believe
that the difference between women's and men's perceptions of their places on
the sexual spectrum corresponded with the stereotype of men being more
sexually adventurous and open than women.

Responses	Women	Men
N = Total married and divorced groups of respondents	927	892
Sexually, I consider myself to be...		
Very proper	4%	3%
Proper	19%	14%
Moderate	42%	31%
Liberal	27%	44%
Very liberal	8%	8%
Very proper + Proper	23%	17%
Liberal + Very liberal	35%	52%

Source: "Sexually, I Consider Myself to Be:," Samuel S. Janus, PhD, and Cynthia L. Janus, MD, *The
Janus Report on Sexual Behavior*, (New York: John Wiley & Sons, Inc., 1993), Table 6.15, p. 187.
Between 1988 and 1992, the authors distributed 4,550 questionnaires to subjects at a variety of sites.
The sample design was planned to conform to the population distribution of the United States in the
areas of sex, age, region, income, education, and marital status. Returned questionnaires totaled
3,260. Of these, 495 were discarded. Satisfactorily completed questionnaires totaled 2,765: 1,418
women and 1,347 men.

★ 931 ★

Sexual Practices, Preferences, and Attitudes

Simultaneous Orgasm

The table below shows the responses of women and men to a survey
question about whether they believe that simultaneous orgasm is necessary
for gratifying sex.

Response	Women total	Career women	Home-makers	Men
N =	1,398	635	270	1,338
Simultaneous orgasm a must.				
Strongly agree	3%	3%	4%	7%
Agree	11%	9%	18%	17%
No opinion	10%	7%	14%	12%
Disagree	52%	51%	47%	52%
Strongly disagree	24%	30%	17%	12%
Strongly agree + Agree	14%	12%	22%	24%
Disagree + Strongly disagree	76%	81%	64%	64%

Source: "Simultaneous Orgasm Is a Must for Gratifying Sex," Samuel S. Janus, PhD, and
Cynthia L. Janus, MD, *The Janus Report on Sexual Behavior*, (New York: John Wiley & Sons,
Inc., 1993), Table 3.24, p. 80. Between 1988 and 1992, the authors distributed 4,550
questionnaires to subjects at a variety of sites. The sample design was planned to conform to the
population distribution of the United States in the areas of sex, age, region, income, education,
and marital status. Returned questionnaires totaled 3,260. Of these, 495 were discarded.
Satisfactorily completed questionnaires totaled 2,765: 1,418 women and 1,347 men. This table
further designates women as career women or homemakers.

★932★

Sexual Practices, Preferences, and Attitudes

Variety of Sex Techniques

The table below shows the responses of women and men to a survey question about whether they believe that a large variety of sex techniques is necessary for maximum sexual pleasure.

Responses	Women total	Career women	Home-makers	Men
N =	1,395	638	277	1,336
A large variety of sex techniques a must for maximum pleasure.				
Strongly agree	7%	7%	8%	13%
Agree	29%	28%	34%	36%
No opinion	16%	15%	15%	17%
Disagree	39%	42%	36%	30%
Strongly disagree	9%	8%	7%	4%
Strongly agree + Agree	36%	35%	42%	49%
Disagree + Strongly disagree	48%	50%	43%	34%

Source: "A Large Variety of Sex Techniques Is a Must for Maximum Pleasure", Samuel S. Janus, PhD, and Cynthia L. Janus, MD, *The Janus Report on Sexual Behavior*, (New York: John Wiley & Sons, Inc., 1993), Table 3.23, p. 79. Between 1988 and 1992, the authors distributed 4,550 questionnaires to subjects at a variety of sites. The sample design was planned to conform to the population distribution of the United States in the areas of sex, age, region, income, education, and marital status. Returned questionnaires totaled 3,260. Of these, 495 were discarded. Satisfactorily completed questionnaires totaled 2,765: 1,418 women and 1,347 men. This table further designates women as career women or homemakers.

Teenagers

★ 933 ★

Sex Ever, Teenagers by Race/Ethnicity and Poverty Level: 1982-1988

This table shows the percentage of women aged 15-19 who had ever had sexual intercourse, by race/ethnicity and poverty level, according to age-group and according to the 1982 and 1988 National Survey of Family Growth.

Race/ethnicity and poverty level	Age 15-19		Age 15-17		Age 18-19	
	1982	1988	1982	1988	1982	1988
Total	47.1%	53.2%	32.6%	38.4%	64.1%	74.4%
Race/ethnicity						
Non-Hispanic white	44.5%	52.4%	29.8%	36.2%	60.8%	74.3%
Non-Hispanic black	59.0%	60.8%	44.4%	50.5%	79.1%	78.0%
Hispanic	50.6%	48.5%	35.6%	36.1%	70.1%	70.0%
Poverty level						
Less than 200%	55.6%	56.5%	45.7%	41.6%	65.0%	80.9%
Greater than or equal to 200%	39.7%	50.1%	23.0%	35.0%	63.0%	69.0%

Source: Jacqueline Darroch Forrest and Susheela Singh, "The Sexual and Reproductive Behavior of American Women, 1982-1988," *Family Planning Perspectives*, Vol. 22(5), September/October 1990, pp. 206-214, Table 4, p. 208, "Percentage of women aged 15-19 who had ever had intercourse, by race/ethnicity and poverty level, according to age-group, 1982 and 1988."

★ 934 ★

Teenagers

Teenage Sexual Activity

Some statistics about teenage sexual activity, gathered by The Alan Guttmacher Institute.

Item	Number/Percent
Percent of women who have had intercourse before age 18	56%
Percent of women in early 1970s	35%
Number of black women who report having had intercourse by age 16.5	50%

[Continued]

★ 934 ★

Teenage Sexual Activity
[Continued]

Item	Number/Percent
Number of women who had sex before age 14 who report that sex was experienced involuntarily	7 in 10
Number of women who had sex before age 15 who report that sex was experienced involuntarily	6 in 10
Number of sexually experienced teenage women who wait almost 18 months before first intercourse and having sex with a second sexual partner	50%
Number of sexually active 15-17-year-old women who have had 2 or more partners	55%
Number of sexually active 15-17-year-old women who have had at least 6 sex partners	13%

Source: Selected from "Teenage Reproductive Health in the United States," The Alan Guttmacher Institute, *Facts In Brief.*

Chapter 14
SPORTS AND RECREATION

Exercise

★ 935 ★

Exercise Activities

This table shows the percent of women and men who have participated in selected forms of exercise during the past two weeks. Activities are ranked by the percent of men participating in 1990. Men reported participating in more exercises.

Activity	Percent participating	
	Men	Women
1. Walking for exercise	40%	48%
2. Gardening or yard work	31%	22%
3. Calisthenics or general exercise	20%	17%
4. Weight lifting or training	14%	4%
5. Biking	12%	10%
6. Jogging or running	12%	5%
7. Swimming or water exercise	9%	8%
8. Basketball	9%	1%
9. Dancing other than aerobics	7%	9%
10. Aerobics or aerobic dancing	3%	10%

Source: Selected from John P. Robinson and Geoffrey Godbey, "Has Fitness Peaked?," *American Demographics*, September 1993, pp. 36+, p. 42, table entitled "Dancing Girls." Primary source: Authors' calculations from the National Health Interview Surveys.

General Participation

★ 936 ★

Sports Participation: 1992

This table lists twenty-six sports activities. For each activity, the table shows the total number of participants in thousands, how many are male and how many are female, what percentage of participants in the particular sport are male and female, and what percentage of the total number of sports participants are involved in the particular sport. These figures were prepared for the National Sporting Goods Association based on a sample of 10,000 households.

[Numbers in thousands, except percent.]

Sport	Total	Male	Female
Total	229,906	111,522	118,385
	100.0%	48.5%	51.5%
	100.0%	100.0%	100.0%
Aerobic exercising	27,834	5,076	22,758
	100.0%	18.2%	81.8%
	12.1%	4.6%	19.2%
Backpacking/	9,698	6,021	3,676
wilderness camping	100.0%	62.1%	37.9%
	4.2%	5.4%	3.1%
Baseball	15,140	12,476	2,664
	100.0%	82.4%	17.6%
	6.6%	11.2%	2.3%
Basketball	28,181	20,566	7,615
	100.0%	73.0%	27.0%
	12.3%	18.4%	6.4%
Bicycle riding	54,632	28,000	26,632
	100.0%	51.3%	48.7%
	23.8%	25.1%	22.5%
Bowling	42,494	21,768	20,726
	100.0%	51.2%	48.8%
	18.5%	19.5%	17.5%
Calisthenics	11,475	5,046	6,428
	100.0%	44.0%	56.0%
	5.0%	4.5%	5.4%
Camping	47,328	25,671	21,657
(vacation/overnight)	100.0%	54.2%	45.8%
	20.6%	23.0%	18.3%

[Continued]

★ 936 ★

Sports Participation: 1992
[Continued]

Sport	Total	Male	Female
Exercise walking	67,822	23,204	44,619
	100.0%	34.2%	65.8%
	29.5%	20.8%	37.7%
Exercise with equipment	39,360	19,068	20,292
	100.0%	48.4%	51.6%
	17.1%	17.1%	17.1%
Fishing fresh water	41,656	28,190	13,467
	100.0%	67.7%	32.3%
	18.1%	25.3%	11.4%
Fishing salt water	12,607	8,757	3,851
	100.0%	69.5%	30.5%
	5.5%	7.9%	3.3%
Football	13,494	11,707	1,787
	100.0%	86.8%	13.2%
	5.9%	10.5%	1.5%
Golf	24,021	18,459	5,562
	100.0%	76.8%	23.2%
	10.4%	16.6%	4.7%
Hiking	21,619	11,588	10,031
	100.0%	53.6%	46.4%
	9.4%	10.4%	8.5%
Hunting with firearms	17,819	15,960	1,859
	100.0%	89.6%	10.4%
	7.8%	14.3%	1.6%
Racquetball	6,560	4,840	1,720
	100.0%	73.8%	26.2%
	2.9%	4.3%	1.5%
Running/jogging	21,932	12,711	9,222
	100.0%	58.0%	42.0%
	9.5%	11.4%	7.8%
Skiing alpine/downhill	10,782	6,484	4,298
	100.0%	60.1%	39.9%
	4.7%	5.8%	3.6%
Skiing cross country	3,470	1,752	1,718
	100.0%	50.5%	49.5%
	1.5%	1.6%	1.5%

[Continued]

★ 936 ★

Sports Participation: 1992
[Continued]

Sport	Total	Male	Female
Soccer	10,619	7,179	3,439
	100.0%	67.6%	32.4%
	4.6%	6.4%	2.9%
Softball	19,187	11,837	7,350
	100.0%	61.7%	38.3%
	8.3%	10.6%	6.2%
Swimming	63,146	29,837	33,309
	100.0%	47.3%	52.7%
	27.5%	26.8%	28.1%
Target shooting	12,309	9,812	2,496
	100.0%	79.7%	20.3%
	5.4%	8.8%	2.1%
Tennis	17,323	9,965	7,358
	100.0%	57.5%	42.5%
	7.5%	8.9%	6.2%
Volleyball	22,130	11,414	10,716
	100.0%	51.6%	48.4%
	9.6%	10.2%	9.1%

Source: *Sports Participation in 1992: Series I*, The NPD Group, Inc., New York, 1993.

★ 937 ★

General Participation

Tennis

This table shows the number of men and women aged 12 and over who reported playing tennis in surveys conducted in 1988, 1989, and 1982.

[In millions.]

Year	Played at least once			Played 4 or more times			Played 21 or more times		
	Total	Male	Female	Total	Male	Female	Total	Male	Female
1992	22.6	12.5	10.1	13.7	8.1	5.6	5.9	3.7	2.2
1989	21.2	12.0	9.3	14.2	8.4	5.8	6.1	3.9	2.2
1988	20.4	11.3	9.1	12.8	7.3	5.5	5.8	3.5	2.3

Source: *"How Many Americans Play Tennis?" Tennis Participation Today: Highlights from a New National Study of American Tennis Players, 1992*, Tennis Industry Association.

★ 938 ★

General Participation

Tennis Players' Other Activities

This table shows the sports and fitness activities participated in four or more times during 1992 by people who reported also playing tennis.

[In millions.]

Activity/Gender	Percent
Female	
Walking	61%
Bicycling	58%
Aerobics	48%
Exercise machines	45%
Running	44%
Male	
Basketball	52%
Exercise machines	50%
Bicycling	48%
Running	48%
Volleyball	39%

Source: "What Tennis Competes With." *Tennis Participation Today: Highlights from a New National Study of American Tennis Players, 1992*, Tennis Industry Association.

Girl Scouts

★ 939 ★

Profiles of Girl Scouts

This table presents statistics gleaned from a survey of of 1,300 Girl Scouts. There are approximately 3.4 million Girl Scouts in 210,607 troops, including USA Girl Scouts Overseas in 73 countries, whose members come from U.S. military and civilian families living abroad.

Description	Number/percent
Race/Ethnicity of Sample	
White	84%
Black	9%
American Indian or	
Alaskan Native	2%
Asian	1%
Other	3%
Not sure	2%

[Continued]

★ 939 ★

Profiles of Girl Scouts
[Continued]

Description	Number/percent
Household Income	
Percent who live in neighborhoods where median household income is less than $35,000	50%
American Indian/Alaskan Native	85%
Household uses food stamps	9%
American Indian/Alaskan Native	16%
Unemployed adult in family	12%
American Indian/Alaskan Native	16%
Religious Background	
Protestant	45%
Catholic	31%
Jewish	3%
No religion	5%
Other	1%
Not sure	14%
Latchkey Homes	
No adult home at least a few times a week	43%
Black	56%
Hispanic	53%
White	41%
Urban	49%
Suburban	39%
Rural	42%
Academic Achievement	
Mostly A's	27%
Mostly A's or B's	44%
Other Non-Classroom Activities	
Arts	77%
Sports	74%
Clubs/organizations	46%
3 or more activities other than Scouting	66%
Family Tradition	
Scouts whose mothers were Girl Scouts:	
White	47%
Black	23%
Hispanic	37%

[Continued]

★ 939 ★

Profiles of Girl Scouts
[Continued]

Description	Number/percent
Benefits of Scouting	
A lot of fun	65%
Black girls	85%
Urban girls	73%
Somewhat fun	21%
Helped make new friends	
A lot	52%
Somewhat	25%
Provided you with an all-girl group to spend time with	
A lot	51%
Somewhat	29%
Taught you about things like good health, safety etc.	
A lot	51%
Somewhat	28%
Helped you gain new skills	
A lot	46%
Somewhat	33%
Helped you do something good for your community	
A lot	46%
Somewhat	32%
Taught you how to cooperate with other people	
A lot	46%
Somewhat	31%
Leadership	
(Senior Girl Scouts)	
Lead troop in activity:	
Sometimes	72%
Very often	34%
Lead school class in activity:	
Sometimes	45%
Very often	15%
Make decisions about what goes on in troop:	
Very often	66%

[Continued]

★ 939 ★

Profiles of Girl Scouts
[Continued]

Description	Number/percent
Make decisions about what goes on in school classroom:	
Very often	25%
Feel troop leader very often listens to what they have to say:	74%
Feel classroom teacher very often listens to what they have to say:	42%
Moral Values	
Girls Scouts vs national cross-section of girls	
Would not cheat on an important test:	
Girl Scouts	70%
National sample	50%
Tell principal your best friend destroyed school property if principal asks:	
Girl Scouts	43%
Black Girl Scouts	62%
National sample	25%
Long-term boyfriend wants to have sex. You would say yes in this situation.	
Girl Scouts	9%
National sample	22%
Someone hands you a drink at a party. You refuse to drink.	
Girl Scouts	66%
National sample	50%

Source: Sylvia J. Brown, Ph.D., and Michael Conn, *Girl Scouts: Who We Are, What We Think: Executive Summary*, Fall 1990.

High School

★ 940 ★

Favorite Sports

This table lists the ten most played sports among high school girls in 1993-1994 by the number of participants in the sport, according to the National Federation of State High School Associations.

Sport	Participants
01. Basketball	412,576
02. Track & field (outdoor)	345,700
03. Volleyball	327,616
04. Softball (fast pitch)	257,118
05. Soccer	166,173
06. Tennis	136,239
07. Cross country	124,700
08. Swimming & diving	102,652
09. Field hockey	53,747
10. Softball (slow pitch)	41,118

Source: "Ten Most Popular Girls Sports," National Federation of State High School Associations, fact sheet. *Note:* 1. Shown in table entitled "High School Athletics Participation.

★ 941 ★

High School

High School Athletics Participation: 1993-1994

This table lists types of sports and shows the number of schools offering the sport and the number of boys and girls participating in the sport, as reported to the National Federation of State High School Assocations (NFSHSA). Shown in parentheses after the name of the sport are the number of states reporting for boys and the number of states reporting for girls. According to the NFSHSA, 3,748,530 boys and 2,124,755 girls competed for 17,250 high schools in the 1993-1994 school year, with a boy or girl who played multiple sports being counted for as many sports as he or she played[5].

[X Not available.]

Sport	Boys		Girls		Total No. of participants
	Schools	Participants	Schools	Participants	
Adapted sports[1]					
Floor hockey (1/1)	33	X	33	X	187
Soccer (1/1)	30	X	30	X	204
Softball (1/1)	28	X	28	X	188
Archery (2/3)	7	49	11	70	119
Badminton (5/7)	183[3]	3,053	347[3]	7,310	10,363
Baseball (48/12)	13,962	438,846	80	353[4]	439,199

[Continued]

★ 941 ★

High School Athletics Participation: 1993-1994
[Continued]

Sport	Boys		Girls		Total No. of
	Schools	Participants	Schools	Participants	participants
Basketball (51/51)	16,451	530,068	16,016	412,576	942,644
Bowling (12/14)	657	7,480	630	6,860	14,340
Canoeing (1/1)	6	161	6	148	309
Competitive Spirit					
Squads (12/17)	85[3]	213[4]	1,422	27,555	27,768
Crew (8/8)	38	1,116	36	1,121	2,237
Cross Country (51/51)	10,693	162,188	10,142	124,700	286,888
Decathlon (7/4)	130	417	7	21	438
Equestrian (2/4)	19	105	28	214	319
Fencing (6/6)	58	1,121	43	613	1,734
Field Hockey (1/19)	1	1[4]	1,452	53,747	53,748
Football					
11-man (51/19)	13,029	903,971	70	334[4]	904,305
9-man (5/0)	264	6,715	X	X	6,715
8-man (14/1)	590	12,761	1	1[4]	12,762
6-man (6/1)	155	4,687	1	16[4]	4,703
Golf (50/47)	10,605[3]	131,207	4,957[3]	36,601[4]	167,808
Gymnastics (18/35)	202	2,409	1,582	20,029	22,438
Heptathlon (1/4)	1	1	43	157	158
Ice Hockey (15/10)	935	22,032	39	194[4]	22,226
Judo (1/0)	21	184	X	X	184
Lacrosse (13/14)	474	22,003	334	12,342[4]	34,345
Pentathlon (0/1)	X	X	62	104	104
Riflery (12/10)	161	1,706	96	590	2,296
Skiing					
Cross Country (11/11)	340	3,796	321	3,260	7,056
Alpine (14/14)	377	5,521	359	3,641	9,162
Soccer (48/48)	7,445	255,538	5,463	166,173[4]	421,711
Softball					
Fast pitch (4/44)	62	1,228	10,243	257,118	258,346
Slow pitch (2/13)	16	198	1,925	41,118	41,316
Swimming & diving (47/47)	4,595	81,328[4]	4,643[3]	102,652[4]	183,980
Team tennis[2] (1/1)	313	X	313	X	11,119
Tennis (51/51)	9,069[3]	135,702	8,780[3]	136,239[4]	271,941
Track & Field					
Indoor (21/21)	1,746	40,866	1,608	34,533	75,399
Outdoor (51/51)	14,192	419,758	14,027	345,700	765,458
Volleyball (22/50)	1,207[3]	26,208[4]	12,403	327,616	353,824

[Continued]

★ 941 ★

High School Athletics Participation: 1993-1994
[Continued]

Sport	Boys		Girls		Total No. of participants
	Schools	Participants	Schools	Participants	
Water Polo (5/6)	412	10,562	259	2,225[4]	12,787
Weight Lifting (12/10)	469	15,780	129	2,486[4]	18,266
Wrestling (47/27)	8,538	223,433	220	783[4]	224,216
Other	43	555	67	1,115	1,670

Source: "1994 High School Athletics Participation Survey Conducted by The National Federation of State High School Associations Based on Competition at the High School Level in the 1993-1994 School Year," National Federation of State High School Associations, fact sheet. *Notes:* 1. Number of schools offering coeducational programs adapted for participants with disabilities. 2. Number of schools offering coeducational team tennis. 3. Includes some co-educational teams. 4. Includes girls playing on boys' teams and boys playing on girls' teams. 5. Jane Gottesman, "Is Cheerleading a Sneaky Way Around Title IX?," *The New York Times,* October 23, 1994, p. 28 Y.

★ 942 ★

High School

Sports Participation: 1971-1994

This table shows the number of female participants in high school sports from 1971 through 1994, according to the National Federation of State High School Associations.

Year	Participants
1971	294,015
1972-73	817,073
1973-74	1,300,169
1975-76	1,645,039
1977-78	2,083,040
1978-79	1,854,400
1979-80	1,750,264
1980-81	1,853,789
1981-82	1,810,671
1982-83	1,779,972
1983-84	1,747,346
1984-85	1,757,884
1985-86	1,807,121
1986-87	1,836,356
1987-88	1,849,684
1988-89	1,839,352
1989-90	1,858,659
1990-91	1,892,316
1991-92	1,940,801
1992-93	1,997,489
1993-94	2,124,755[1]

Source: "Athletics Participation Survey Totals," National Federation of State High School Associations, fact sheet. *Note:* 1. Does not include 11,695 participants in coeducational sports.

Leisure

★ 943 ★

Activities of College-Age Women-I

This table shows the percentages of entering college freshmen women who reported that they engaged in various activities during the past year. Data is shown by type of institution entered. The percentage of freshmen who frequently smoke cigarettes rose for the sixth time in seven years. The percent who reported drinking beer reached an all-time low, as did the percent who said they drank wine or hard liquor. The percent who reported performing volunteer work rose for the fifth straight year, while the percentage who expected to do volunteer work in college declined. For this survey, the national population included 2,700 institutions. The data are based on responses from 237,777 freshmen entering 461 two- and four-year institutions in 1994.

Activity	Type of Institution				
	All institutions	All 2-year colleges	All 4-year colleges	All universities	All black colleges
Attended a religious service	85.5%	80.8%	88.6%	86.3%	93.9%
Participated in demonstration	41.6%	40.2%	44.4%	38.3%	55.1%
Didn't complete homework on time	62.3%	59.5%	64.1%	62.9%	62.0%
Tutored another student	51.5%	37.3%	56.0%	63.0%	54.6%
Studied with other students	87.7%	81.9%	89.6%	92.1%	85.4%
Smoked cigarettes	12.6%	17.9%	9.9%	10.1%	1.3%
Drank beer	48.1%	49.6%	44.6%	52.5%	20.1%
Drank wine or liquor	53.5%	52.8%	51.9%	57.4%	37.3%
Stayed up all night	80.8%	77.4%	82.3%	82.8%	84.9%
Spoke another language at home	6.9%	5.6%	6.8%	9.1%	3.5%
Felt overwhelmed	30.9%	25.0%	33.5%	34.5%	27.2%
Felt depressed	11.5%	12.2%	11.6%	10.3%	15.5%
Performed volunteer work	72.7%	62.5%	76.5%	80.1%	69.9%
Played a musical instrument	39.6%	33.2%	42.1%	43.8%	38.0%
Discussed politics	13.6%	7.7%	15.3%	18.8%	13.2%
Visited art gallery or museum	59.4%	47.8%	63.1%	68.8%	55.2%
Discussed religion	22.9%	16.6%	26.5%	25.0%	31.3%

Source: Selected from "Weighted National Norms for Freshman Women, Fall 1994: Activities Engaged in During the Past Year," Astin, A.W. et al., *The American Freshman: National Norms for Fall 1994*, 1994, p. 47.

★ 944 ★
Leisure

Activities of College-Age Women-II

This table shows the percentages of entering college freshmen women who reported spending six or more hours per week in the last year on various activities. For this survey, the national population included 2,700 institutions. The data are based on responses from 237,777 freshmen entering 461 two- and four-year institutions in 1994.

Activity	Type of Institution				
	All institutions	All 2-year colleges	All 4-year colleges	All universities	All black colleges
Six or more hours per week in the last year spent on:					
socializing with friends	75.1%	70.4%	76.2%	79.6%	65.7%
talking with teacher outside class	5.1%	4.9%	5.4%	4.8%	8.2%
exercising or sports	38.9%	32.6%	40.5%	44.8%	27.2%
partying	27.0%	27.9%	25.5%	28.4%	23.3%
volunteer work	8.0%	7.0%	8.4%	8.6%	11.1%
student clubs and groups	17.0%	12.4%	18.7%	20.3%	18.9%
watching TV	26.3%	29.5%	25.6%	22.9%	46.7%
reading for pleasure	13.8%	14.2%	14.1%	12.8%	15.3%

Source: Selected from "Weighted National Norms for Freshman Women, Fall 1994: Hours Per Week in the Last Year Spent On" Astin, A.W. et al., *The American Freshman: National Norms for Fall 1994*, 1994, p. 49.

★ 945 ★
Leisure

Attendance at Arts Activities: 1982-1992

This table shows the difference in arts attendance rates between 1982 and 1992. An attendance rate is the percentage of the adult population that indicated attending an arts event (or visiting an art museum, etc.) at least once in the last 12 months divided by the adult population,.

Gender	Jazz	Classical music	Opera	Musicals	Plays	Ballet	Art museums	Reading literature
Male	+1.6%	+0.2%	+0.6%	-1.5%	+1.6%	+0.9%	+5.5%	-1.7%
Female	+0.4%	-1.1%	+0.2%	-0.9%	+1.7%	+0.1%	+3.8%	-2.8%

Source: Selected from "1982-1992 Differences in Arts Attendance Rates by Demographic Factors," National Endowment for the Arts, Research Division Note #51, February 16, 1994, Table 3. Primary source: U.S. Bureau of the Census 1992 Survey on Public Participation in the Arts.

★ 946 ★
Leisure

Attendance at Arts Activities: 1992-I

This table shows the percentage of the adult population that indicated attending an arts event (or visiting an art museum, etc.) at least once in the last 12 months divided by the adult population. Jazz was the only arts activity in which men were slightly more likely than women to attend live performances.

[Adult population in millions.]

Item	Adult pop.	Jazz	Classical music	Opera	Musicals	Plays	Ballet	Art museums	Reading literature	Sample size
Grand mean:	185.8	10.6%	12.5%	3.3%	17.4%	13.5%	4.7%	26.7%	54.0%	12,736
Male	89.0	11.9%	11.5%	3.3%	15.1%	12.3%	3.6%	26.5%	47.2%	5,598
Female	96.8	9.4%	13.4%	3.5%	19.6%	14.6%	5.6%	26.9%	60.2%	7,129

Source: Selected from "1992 Attendance Rates for Arts Activities by Demographic Factors," National Endowment for the Arts, Research Division Note #51, February 16, 1994, Table 1. Primary source: U.S. Bureau of the Census 1992 Survey on Public Participation in the Arts.

★ 947 ★
Leisure

Attendance at Arts Activities: 1992-II

This table shows the percentage of the adult population that indicated attending an arts activity at least once in the last 12 months divided by the adult population.

[Adult population in millions.]

Item	Adult pop.	Dance	Art fair	Historic park	Books	Read plays	Read poetry	Read novels	Listen poet. reading	Listen novel reading	Sample size
Grand mean:	185.8	7.1%	40.7%	34.5%	60.9%	5.3%	17.1%	48.5%	8.3%	7.4%	12,736
Male	89.0	6.7%	35.4%	34.9%	55.5%	4.8%	12.3%	45.5%	7.7%	6.9%	5,598
Female	96.8	7.5%	45.6%	34.1%	65.9%	5.9%	20.9%	58.1%	9.0%	7.9%	7,129

Source: Selected from "Attendance Rates for Various Arts Activities by Demographic Factors: 1992," National Endowment for the Arts, Research Division Note #27, October 1993, Appendix A.2.

★ 948 ★

Leisure

Cable Network Preferences

This table shows characteristics of the U.S. adult population and gives numbers concerning preferences in cable networks in 1993.

[Numbers in thousands.]

Item	Total U.S. pop	Men Total	Women		
			Total	% of all women	% of total item
All adults	186,039	88,760	97,279	100.0%	52.3%
Cable Networks					
A&E (Arts & Entertainment)	29,877	16,257	13,619	14.0%	45.6%
American Movie Classics	18,479	8,555	9,924	10.2%	53.7%
BET (Black Entertainment TV)	6,545	3,327	3,218	3.3%	49.2%
CMT (Country Music TV)	10,496	5,182	5,314	5.5%	50.6%
CNBC	8,965	5,094	3,871	4.0%	43.2%
CNN	68,569	36,593	31,976	32.9%	46.6%
Comedy Central	9,621	5,780	3,841	3.9%	39.6%
Court TV	2,908	1,431	1,477	1.5%	50.8%
C-SPAN	15,084	8,932	6,152	6.3%	40.8%
The Discovery Channel	45,488	24,299	21,189	21.8%	46.6%
E! Entertainment TV	5,368	2,448	2,920	3.0%	54.4%
ESPN	47,131	32,205	14,926	15.3%	31.7%
The Family Channel	28,818	11,985	16,833	17.3%	58.4%
Headline News	28,312	16,244	12,069	12.4%	42.6%
Lifetime	22,639	9,151	13,488	13.9%	59.6%
MTV	24,779	13,740	11,038	11.3%	44.5%
Nick at Nite	16,164	7,432	8,732	9.0%	54.0%
Nickelodeon	18,217	7,817	10,399	10.7%	57.1%
Nostalgia Channel	2,351	1,126	1,225	1.3%	52.1%
Prevue Guide Channel	10,079	5,090	4,989	5.1%	49.5%
TBS	42,942	23,248	19,694	20.2%	45.9%
The Travel Channel	3,835	2,007	1,828	1.9%	47.7%
TLC: The Learning Channel	5,636	3,000	2,636	2.7%	46.8%
TNN: The Nashville Network	26,145	13,591	12,554	12.9%	48.0%
TNT (Turner Network TV)	43,471	22,794	20,677	21.3%	47.6%
USA Network	41,336	21,360	19,976	20.5%	48.3%

[Continued]

★ 948 ★

Cable Network Preferences
[Continued]

Item	Total U.S. pop	Men Total	Women Total	Women % of all women	Women % of total item
VH-1	14,921	7,950	6,971	7.2%	46.7%
The Weather Channel	40,629	20,265	20,364	20.9%	50.1%

Source: Selected from *Mediamark Research Multimedia Audiences Report*, Spring 1993, M-3, p. 3. Data based on 20,124 interviews conducted between March 1992 and January 1993.

★ 949 ★

Leisure

Desire to Attend More Arts Performances: 1992

This table shows the responses of adults to the question: "If you could go to any of these events as often as you wanted, which ones would you go to more often than you do now?"

[Adult population in millions.]

Item	Adult pop.	Jazz	Classical music	Opera	Musicals	Plays	Ballet	Dance	Art museum/ galleries
Grand mean:	185.8	25.2%	25.4%	11.0%	36.2%	33.4%	18.3%	23.8%	41.5%
Male	89.0	29%	24%	9%	30%	30%	10%	17%	40%
Female	96.8	22%	27%	13%	42%	37%	26%	30%	42%

Source: Selected from "Desire to Attend More Arts Performances by Demographic Factors," National Endowment for the Arts, Research Division Note #27, October 1993, Appendix E.2.

★ 950 ★

Leisure

Lessons in Arts Activities: 1992

This table shows the percentage of the adult population that indicated having ever taken lessons in an arts activity.

[Adult population in millions.]

Item	Adult pop.	Music lesson	Visual arts	Ballet	Dance	Creative writing	Art appreciate	Music appreciate
Grand mean:	185.8	39.6%	17.7%	7.0%	15.8%	15.6%	22.9%	18.1%
Male	89.0	36%	17%	1%	10%	15%	23%	17%
Female	96.8	43%	18%	12%	22%	16%	22%	19%

Source: Selected from "Lessons/Classes for Various Arts Activities by Demographic Factors," National Endowment for the Arts, Research Division Note #27, October 1993, Appendix C.4.

★ 951 ★

Leisure

Listening to Broadcast and Recorded Media: 1982-1992-I

This table shows the differences in the percentage of the adult population that indicated viewing or listening to an arts broadcast or recording at least once in the last 12 months divided by the adult population, between 1982 and 1992. According to *The New York Times*, "Among those who call themselves lovers of classical music, women are more likely to attend live performances, while men outnumber women when it comes to buying music."

Gender	Jazz			Classical music		
	TV	Radio	Record	TV	Radio	Record
Grand mean:	+8%	+10%	0%	0%	+11%	+1%
Male	+3%	+10%	+2%	-1%	+11%	+2%
Female	+2%	+10%	0%	+1%	+10%	+1%

Source: Selected from "1982-1992 Differences in Broadcast and recorded Media Rates by Demographic Variables," National Endowment for the Arts, Research Division Note #52, February 16, 1994, Table 3. Primary source: U.S. Bureau of the Census 1992 Survey on Public Participation in the Arts. Related reading: Diana Jean Schemo, "For Musical Appreciation, Sexes Go Their Own Ways, *The New York Times*, November 15, 1994, p. B1 Y.

★ 952 ★

Leisure

Listening to Broadcast and Recorded Media: 1982-1992-II

This table shows the differences in the percentage of the adult population that indicated viewing or listening to an arts broadcast or recording at least once in the last 12 months divided by the adult population, between 1982 and 1992.

Gender	Opera			Musicals			Plays		Dance	Visual
	TV	Radio	Record	TV	Radio	Record	TV	Radio	TV	Art-TV
Grand mean:	-1%	+2%	-1%	-5%	-1%	-3%	-10%	-1%	+2%	+9%
Male	0%	+1%	0%	-7%	-2%	-2%	-10%	-1%	+4%	+9%
Female	-5%	+2%	-1%	-5%	0%	-4%	-9%	-1%	0%	+8%

Source: Selected from "1982-1992 Differences in Broadcast and recorded Media Rates by Demographic Variables," National Endowment for the Arts, Research Division Note #52, February 16, 1994, Table 3. Primary source: U.S. Bureau of the Census 1992 Survey on Public Participation in the Arts.

★ 953 ★

Leisure

Listening to Broadcast and Recorded Media: 1992-I

This table shows the percentage of the adult population that indicated viewing or listening to an arts broadcast or recording at least once in the last 12 months divided by the adult population.

[Adult population in millions.]

Gender	Adult pop.	Jazz			Classical Music			Opera		
		TV	Radio	Record	TV	Radio	Record	TV	Radio	Record
Grand mean:	185.8	20.9%	28.2%	20.6%	25.1%	30.8%	23.8%	11.6%	8.7%	6.9%
Male	89.0	23%	31%	23%	23%	31%	23%	11%	8%	7%
Female	96.8	19%	26%	19%	27%	31%	24%	12%	9%	7%

Source: Selected from "1992 Broadcast and Recorded Media Rates by Demographic Variables," National Endowment for the Arts, Research Division Note #52, February 16, 1994, Table 1. Primary source: U.S. Bureau of the Census 1992 Survey on Public Participation in the Arts.

★ 954 ★

Leisure

Listening to Broadcast and Recorded Media: 1992-II

This table shows the percentage of the adult population that indicated viewing or listening to an arts broadcast or recording at least once in the last 12 months divided by the adult population.

[Adult population in millions.]

Gender	Adult pop.	Musicals			Plays		Dance TV	Visual art-TV
		TV	Radio	Record	TV	Radio		
Grand mean:	185.8	15.1%	3.5%	5.7%	16.8%	2.8%	18.8%	31.6%
Male	89.0	14%	3%	5%	16%	3%	16%	32%
Female	96.8	17%	4%	6%	18%	3%	21%	31%

Source: Selected from "1992 Broadcast and Recorded Media Rates by Demographic Variables," National Endowment for the Arts, Research Division Note #52, February 16, 1994, Table 1. Primary source: U.S. Bureau of the Census 1992 Survey on Public Participation in the Arts.

★ 955 ★

Leisure

Magazines, Newspapers, Television, and Online Data Services: 1993

This table shows characteristics of the U.S. adult population and gives numbers concerning readership of newspapers, readership of magazines and television viewing, and use of online data services (Compuserve and Prodigy).

[Numbers in thousands.]

Item	Total U.S. pop	Men Total	Women		
			Total	% of total women	% of total item
All adults	186,039	88,760	97,279	100.0%	52.3%
Household heads	108,049	73,691	34,358	35.3%	31.8%
Homemakers	110,079	24,742	85,337	87.7%	77.5%
Compuserve	1,020	753	267	0.3%	26.2%
Prodigy	2,465	1,572	893	0.9%	36.2%
Daily Newspapers					
Read any	109,176	53,979	55,197	56.7%	50.6%
Read one daily	86,971	41,208	45,763	47.0%	52.6%
Read two or more dailies	22,205	12,771	9,434	9.7%	42.5%
Sunday Newspapers					
Read any	122,028	58,565	63,464	65.2%	52.0%
Read one Sunday	108,206	51,621	56,586	58.2%	52.3%

[Continued]

★ 955 ★

Magazines, Newspapers, Television, and Online Data Services:
1993
[Continued]

Item	Total U.S. pop	Men Total	Women		
			Total	% of total women	% of total item
Read two or more Sundays	13,822	6,944	6,878	7.1%	49.8%
Heavy magazines-Heavy TV	49,313	23,448	25,866	26.6%	52.5%
Heavy magazines-Light TV	43,704	20,931	22,773	23.4%	52.1%
Light magazines-Heavy TV	43,705	20,931	22,773	23.4%	52.1%
Light magazines-Light TV	49,317	23,450	25,867	26.6%	52.5%

Source: Selected from *Mediamark Research Multimedia Audiences Report*, Spring 1993, M-3, p. 2. Data based on 20,124 interviews conducted between March 1992 and January 1993.

★ 956 ★
Leisure

Media Exposure: 1993

This table shows mean levels of media exposures of females by various demographic characteristics. A total of 22,468 adults were included in the survey and the data is projectable to the population aged 18 and over. The data describe the following: Magazines: Average number of magazines read, as reported in two separate personal interviews. Newspapers: Average number of weekday newspaper issues read in two weekdays and weekend/Sunday newspapers read in two weeks. Radio: Average number of quarter hours listened to in two weekdays, all day radio, drive time radio, and mid-day radio. Television: Average number of half hours viewed in two weeks, all day TV, prime time TV, fringe (early and late) TV, and daytime TV. Cable television: Average number of half hours viewed in last seven days among those who can receive cable TV.

Characteristic	Magazines read	Newspapers read	Radio quarter hours			Television half hours				Cable half hours
			All day	Drive time	Mid-day	All day	Prime time	Fringe	Daytime	hours
Total females	6.0	2.9	23.3	11.7	8.1	99.2	32.9	22.1	22.7	20.5
Mothers	6.7	2.8	25.3	12.9	8.6	87.8	30.1	18.0	20.8	22.4
Employed mothers	6.7	2.8	23.7	12.1	8.6	87.0	28.9	18.1	21.0	18.8
Age										
18-24	7.1	2.3	31.9	14.7	10.5	80.5	24.9	18.7	22.7	21.5
25-34	6.5	2.7	25.3	12.8	8.8	90.6	30.1	17.9	21.4	22.0
35-44	6.8	3.0	24.2	12.4	8.7	79.5	29.7	16.3	16.8	21.1
45-54	6.3	3.3	23.9	12.6	8.6	99.6	36.9	22.3	19.1	20.0
55-64	5.3	3.3	17.8	9.3	6.0	119.8	37.9	28.4	27.1	20.0
65+	3.9	3.0	16.8	8.5	5.6	132.0	39.5	32.0	30.9	18.0
Education										
Graduated college	7.1	3.6	21.1	11.2	7.0	72.7	28.7	16.1	12.0	18.6
Attended college	7.0	3.2	26.3	13.1	9.4	92.3	32.9	19.3	20.2	22.9
Graduated high school	6.1	2.9	23.5	11.8	8.2	106.0	34.6	23.9	24.4	21.3
Did not grad. hs	3.7	2.0	21.2	10.5	7.2	116.9	33.6	26.8	31.3	17.8
Employment										
Employed	6.7	3.0	25.6	13.1	8.9	86.1	31.2	18.6	17.3	21.4
Full time	6.7	3.0	26.0	13.4	9.0	84.6	30.8	18.2	16.7	21.0

[Continued]

★ 956 ★

Media Exposure: 1993
[Continued]

Characteristic	Magazines read	Newspapers read	Radio quarter hours			Television half hours				Cable half hours
			All day	Drive time	Mid-day	All day	Prime time	Fringe	Daytime	
Part time	6.9	3.1	23.1	11.8	8.0	94.5	33.2	20.8	20.6	23.3
Not employed	5.0	2.7	20.1	9.8	6.9	117.1	35.3	26.8	29.9	19.3
Occupation										
Professional/manager	7.2	3.5	24.5	13.0	8.4	74.6	29.3	15.8	12.8	18.9
Technical/clerical/sales	6.7	3.1	26.2	13.4	9.2	87.5	32.4	18.5	17.5	23.2
Precision/craft	7.6	3.0	28.0	14.4	10.6	81.2	29.6	17.5	14.9	23.5
Other employed	6.2	2.5	25.6	12.7	8.8	95.6	31.2	21.7	21.6	20.6
Marital status										
Single	7.0	2.6	29.0	13.7	9.7	91.3	28.4	20.4	22.9	21.4
Married	6.1	3.1	22.1	11.5	7.9	96.2	33.5	21.0	20.8	21.3
Divorced/separated/ widowed	5.1	2.7	21.5	10.8	7.1	111.9	35.0	25.6	26.6	17.9
Parents	6.7	2.8	25.3	12.9	8.6	87.8	30.1	18.0	20.8	22.4
Race										
White	5.9	3.0	22.9	11.7	8.1	96.9	33.8	21.5	20.9	20.9
Black	6.9	2.8	26.9	12.5	8.0	120.3	30.0	26.7	35.8	18.9
Other	4.5	2.0	21.2	10.4	7.5	80.5	21.2	19.9	19.7	16.5

Source: Selected from "Mean Levels of Media Exposures, Females," *The 1993 Study of Media and Markets*, Simmons Market Research Bureau, 1994, Table 1.

★ 957 ★
Leisure

Musical Preferences: 1992

This table shows the responses of adults to the question: "Tell me which of these types of music you like to listen to?"

[Adult population in millions.]

Item	Adult pop.	Jazz	Classical music	Opera	Musicals	Blues	Big band	Folk	Country/ Western	Rock	Mood/ easy
Grand mean:	185.8	33.9%	33.3%	12.1%	27.5%	40.3%	34.8%	22.7%	51.8%	43.5%	48.9%
Male	89.0	38%	32%	10%	24%	44%	34%	23%	52%	48%	44%
Female	96.8	30%	35%	14%	31%	37%	36%	23%	52%	39%	53%

Source: Selected from "Preference Rates for Selected Types of Music by Demographic Factors," National Endowment for the Arts, Research Division Note #27, October 1993, Appendix E.4.

★ 958 ★

Leisure

Not Enough Leisure Time

This table shows the responses of 1,000 Michigan residents to a survey question about the activities they would like to participate in but do not have enough time for.

Activity	Women	Men
I need more time for...		
Work	13%	12%
Sleep	45%	40%
Family	52%	47%
Keeping fit	65%	50%
Just me	72%	60%

Source: Vickie Elmer and Michael Betzold, "Men and Women Both Say They Want More," *Detroit Free Press*, February 27, 1995, p. 1+. Primary source: February surveys of 1,000 Michigan residents for Free Press/WXYZ-TV by EPIC-MRA, Lansing.

★ 959 ★

Leisure

Participation in Arts Activities: 1992-I

This table shows the percentage of the adult population that indicated participating in an arts activity at least once in the last 12 months divided by the adult population.

[Adult population in millions.]

Item	Adult pop.	Play jazz	Play classical music	Sing opera	Sing musicals	Sing choir	Act in plays	Ballet	Dance
Grand mean:	185.8	1.7%	4.2%	1.1%	3.8%	6.4%	1.6%	0.2%	8.1%
Male	89.0	2%	3%	1%	3%	5%	2%	0%	8%
Female	96.8	1%	5%	1%	5%	7%	2%	0.4%	8%

Source: Selected from "Personal Participation Rates for Various Arts Activities by Demographic Factors," National Endowment for the Arts, Research Division Note #27, October 1993, Appendix C.2.

★ 960 ★
Leisure

Participation in Arts Activities: 1992-II

This table shows the percentage of the adult population that indicated having ever taken lessons in various arts activities.

[Adult population in millions.]

Item	Adult pop.	Pottery	Needle-work	Photo-graphy	Painting	Creative writing	Compose	Buy art work	Own art work
Grand mean:	185.8	8.4%	24.8%	11.6%	9.6%	7.4%	2.1%	22.1%	7.2%
Male	89.0	8%	5%	13%	9%	7%	3%	22%	7%
Female	96.8	9%	43%	10%	10%	8%	1%	22%	7%

Source: Selected from "Personal Participation Rates for Various Arts Activities by Demographic Factors," National Endowment for the Arts, Research Division Note #27, October 1993, Appendix C.2.

★ 961 ★
Leisure

Participation in Leisure Activities: 1992

This table shows the number of hours spent watching television on an average day by adults and the percentage of the adult population that indicated participating in various leisure activities during the last 12 months.

[Adult population in millions.]

Item	Adult pop.	TV hours	Movies	Sports events	Amuse-ment park	Exercise	Play sports	Outdoor	Charity	Home improvement	Gardening
Grand mean:	185.8	3.0	59.0%	36.8%	50.2%	59.7%	38.8%	34.1%	32.6%	47.6%	54.7%
Male	89.0	2.8	60%	44%	51%	61%	50%	39%	30%	53%	46%
Female	96.8	3.1	59%	30%	50%	59%	29%	29%	34%	42%	62%

Source: Selected from "Participation Rates in Other Leisure Activities by Demographic Factors," National Endowment for the Arts, Research Division Note #27, October 1993, Appendix D.2.

★ 962 ★

Leisure

Radio Format Preferences

This table shows characteristics of the U.S. adult population and gives numbers concerning preferences in radio formats in 1993.

[Numbers in thousands.]

Item	Total U.S. pop	Men Total	Women		
			Total	% of all women	% of total item
All adults	186,039	88,760	97,279	100.0%	52.3%
Radio formats					
Adult contemporary	36,620	16,212	20,408	21.0%	55.7%
All news	9,291	5,319	3,973	4.1%	42.8%
AOR/Progressive rock	29,197	17,253	11,944	12.3%	40.9%
Black	4,695	2,116	2,579	2.7%	54.9%
CHR/rock	31,374	14,542	16,832	17.3%	53.6%
Classic rock	13,009	7,839	5,170	5.3%	39.7%
Classical	4,170	2,073	2,097	2.2%	50.3%
Country	41,796	21,006	20,790	21.4%	49.7%
Easy listening	3,096	1,379	1,718	1.8%	55.5%
Full service	4,154	2,346	1,809	1.9%	43.5%
Golden oldies	19,465	9,663	9,801	10.1%	50.4%
Jazz	4,475	2,601	1,874	1.9%	41.9%
MOR/Nostalgia	6,484	2,988	3,496	3.6%	53.9%
News/Talk	28,404	15,855	12,550	12.9%	44.2%
Religious	7,351	2,948	4,403	4.5%	59.9%
Soft contemporary	8,284	3,391	4,894	5.0%	59.1%
Urban contemporary	12,117	5,938	6,239	6.4%	51.2%

Source: Selected from *Mediamark Research Multimedia Audiences Report*, Spring 1993, M-3, p. 3. Data based on 20,124 interviews conducted between March 1992 and January 1993.

★ 963 ★

Leisure

Radio Network Preferences

This table shows characteristics of the U.S. adult population and gives numbers concerning preferences in radio networks in 1993.

[Numbers in thousands.]

Item	Total U.S. pop	Men Total	Women Total	Women % of all women	Women % of total item
All adults	186,039	88,760	97,279	100.0%	52.3%
Radio Networks					
ABC Excel	11,896	6,834	5,062	5.2%	42.6%
ABC Galaxy	7,831	3,740	4,091	4.2%	52.2%
ABC Genesis	17,046	8,440	8,607	8.8%	50.5%
ABC Platinum	24,782	13,243	11,539	11.9%	46.6%
ABC Prime	36,293	19,255	17,038	17.5%	46.9%
AURN	3,946	1,596	2,350	2.4%	59.6%
CBS	16,677	9,065	7,612	7.8%	45.6%
CBS Spectrum	24,592	13,056	11,536	11.9%	46.9%
Concert Music Network	2,197	1,231	966	1.0%	44.0%
Internet	86,808	43,576	43,232	44.4%	49.8%
Katz Radio Group	77,799	39,801	37,998	39.1%	48.8%
Mutual	20,322	10,731	9,591	9.9%	47.2%
NBC	11,294	5,672	5,622	5.8%	49.8%
Power	13,480	7,568	5,912	6.1%	43.9%
The Source	14,160	8,161	6,000	6.2%	42.4%
STRZ Entertainment	2,937	1,264	1,672	1.7%	56.9%
Super	16,323	8,457	7,867	8.1%	48.2%
Ultimate	16,636	8,346	8,290	8.5%	49.8%
Wall Street Journal Network	8,555	5,084	3,471	3.6%	40.6%

Source: Selected from *Mediamark Research Multimedia Audiences Report*, Spring 1993, M-3, p. 3. Data based on 20,124 interviews conducted between March 1992 and January 1993.

★ 964 ★

Leisure

Subscribers to Online Services

This table shows the breakdown of subscribers to various online services by gender. While women make up more than half the U.S. population, they comprise only 26% of consumer online services subscriptions. CompuServe has the fewest women subscribers. Eighty-eight percent of its 2.7 million subscribers are male. Seventy-seven percent of GEnie's 120,000 users are male. Prodigy has made the biggest effort marketing to families; 40% of its 2.1 million members are women.

Online Service	Men	Women
CompuServe	88%	12%
GEnie	77%	23%
America Online	70%	30%
Prodigy	60%	40%
Average	74%	26%

Source: "The Gender Gap: Use of Online Services by Men & Women," *Electronic Information Report*, March 17, 1995, p. 3. Primary source: *Economics of Online Publishing*, SIMBA Information Inc., Wilton, CT.

★ 965 ★

Leisure

Television and Teenagers

Advocates for Youth reports on "Media Effects on Adolescent Sexuality." They report that by the time American teenagers graduate from high school, they will have spent 15,000 hours watching television, compared to 12,000 hours spent in the classroom.[1] This table shows some of their findings as they relate primarily to female teens.

Item	Number/percent
Number of sexual acts per hour shown on prime-time television, including deep kissing and petting[2]	3
Number of acts of intercourse shown on prime-time television that are between married couples	1 in 6
Number of sexual acts per hour shown on daytime serials, the programs favored by junior and high school students	3.5

[Continued]

★ 965 ★

Television and Teenagers
[Continued]

Item	Number/percent
Number of sexual acts or references including intercourse, prostitution, and rape that could be viewed annually by an adolescent female[3]	1,500
Number of acts of sexual intercourse that were counted in a study of 50 hours of daytime serials[4]	156
Number of references to contraception or safer sex included in the 50 hours	5
Number of references to HIV/AIDS	1

Source: Selected from Media Effects on Adolescent Sexuality," Advocates for Youth, fact sheet compiled by Chelsey Goddard, January 1995. *Notes:* 1. Strasburger VC, "Children, adolescents, and the media: five crucial issues," *Adolescent Medicine: Adolescents and the Media*, Philadelphia, PA: vol. 4(3), Hanley & Belfus, 1993: 479-494. 2. Greenberg BS, Stanley C, Siemicki M, et al., "Sex content on soaps and prime-television series most viewed by adolescents," *Media, Sex and the Adolescent*, Creskill, NJ: Hampton, 1993:" 29-44. 3. Greenberg BS, Linsangan R, "Gender differences in adolescents' media use, exposure to sexual content and parental mediation," *Media, Sex and the Adolescent*, Creskill, NJ: Hampton, 1993: 134-144. 4. Greenberg BS, Busselle RW, "Soap operas and sexual activity," Prepared for the Kaiser Family Foundation for presentation at the SOAP SUMMIT, 10/21/94.

The Economics of Sports

★ 966 ★

Sports Business

Financial World (FW) magazine's first annual report on the economics of sports was issued on February 14, 1995. This table shows figures from that issue that relate to women's sports.

Item	Number/Percent
Tennis[1]	
Growth of prize money since 1990	
Men	59%
Total	$60 million
Women	52%
Total	$35 million
Increase in attendance at Women's Tennis Association tours, 1986-1993	30%
Total, 1993	3.2 million

[Continued]

★ 966 ★

Sports Business
[Continued]

Item	Number/Percent
Martina Navratilova's winnings in a 19-year career	$20 million
Sailing[2]	
Cost to participate in the America's Cup, minimum: 1995 Women's Challenge budget	$13 million $20 million
Figure Skating[3]	
Figure skating's rank as a sport among American women and their teenage daughters	No. 1
TV Coverage, 1994 Winter Olympics: Ladies' technical program audience Share	127 million 48.5
Basketball[3]	
Number of girls between the ages of 7 and 11 who played some kind of organized basketball: 1985 1993	700,000 1.9 million

Source: FW, February 14, 1995, various articles detailed in footnotes below. *Notes:* 1. "It's thirty-all," *FW*, February 14, 1995, pp. 62+. 2. "The cup runneth over," *FW*, February 14, 1995, pp. 72+. 3. "Ladies, don't touch that dial: Television has discovered an amazing fact: Where women go, men will follow," *FW*, February 14, 1995, pp. 99+.

LIST OF SOURCES CONSULTED

Advocates for Youth (formerly the Center for Population Options). Provides information, education, and advocacy to youth-serving agencies and professionals, policy makers, and the media. 1025 Vermont Avenue, NW, Suite 200, Washington, DC 20005. Telephone (202)347-5700.

—*Teenage Pregnancy and Too-Early Childbearing: Public Costs, Personal Consequences.* 6th Edition, 1992.

AIDS & Public Policy Journal. 4X/Yr. ISSN 0887-3852. Academic/scholarly publication addressing the social, political, ethical, and legal issues in public health and health policy, especially as they relate to AIDS. University Publishing Group, Inc., 107 E. Church St., Frederick, MD 21701. Telephone (800)654-8188.

America. Weekly. ISSN 0002-7049. Published by the Jesuits of the United States and Canada. America Press, Inc., 106 West 56th Street, New York, NY 10019.

American Association of Retired Persons. Fact Sheets. 601 E Street, NW, Washington, DC 20049. Telephone (800)222-8185.

American College Testing Program. *Reference Norms for Spring 1994 ACT Tested H.S. Graduates. ACT High School Profile Report HS Graduating Class 1994: National Report for Females.* Code 990-002. *ACT High School Profile Report HS Graduating Class 1994: National Report for Males.* Code 990-001. 2201 North Dodge Street, P.O. Box 168, Iowa City, IA 52243. Telephone (319)337-1000.

American Demographics. Monthly. ISSN 0163-4089. American Demographics, Inc., 127 W. State Street, Ithaca, NY 14850. Telephone (607)273-6343.

American Institute of Chemical Engineers. *AIChE 1994 Salary Survey Report.* 1994. 345 East 47th Street, New York, NY 10017. Telephone (212)705-7338.

American Institute of Physics. *AIP Report*. American Institute of Physics, Education and Employment Statistics Division, One Physics Ellipse, College Park, MD 20740-3843. Telephone (301)209-3070.

—*Physics in the High Schools II: Findings from the 1989-90 Nationwide Survey of Secondary School Teachers of Physics*, by Michael Neuschatz and Lori Alpert. AIP Report, Pub. No. R-390, April 1994. ISBN 1-56396-350-7. Single copies free.

—*1992 Salaries: Society Membership Survey*, by Jean M. Curtin and Raymond Y. Chu. 1993. ISBN 1-56396-289-6. Single copies free.

American Jewish Year Book 1991. David Singer, ed. Volume 91. ISBN 0-8276-0402-5. (New York: The American Jewish Committee, 1991).

The American Journal of Drug and Alcohol Abuse. Quarterly. Medical journal. ISSN 0095-2990. Marcel Dekker, Inc., 270 Madison Ave., New York, NY 10016. Telephone (212)696-9000.

American Journal of Orthopsychiatry. Quarterly. ISSN 0002-9432. Journal on an interdisciplinary and interprofessional approach to mental health treatment. American Orthopsychiatric Assn., 330 Seventh Ave., 18th Floor, New York, NY 10001. Telephone (212)564-5930.

American Journal of Public Health. Monthly. ISSN 0090-0036. Public health journal. American Public Health Assn., 1015 15th St. NW, Ste. 300, Washington, DC 20005. Telephone (202)789-5600.

Anderson, Ronald E. (ed.). *Computers in American Schools 1992: An Overview*. A National Report from the International IEA Computers in Education Study. Based on work supported by the National Science Foundation. Order from IEA Computers in Education Study, 909 Social Sciences Bldg., University of Minnesota, 267 19th Ave. S., Minneapolis, MN 55455. Telephone (612)624-3824.

Architectural Record. 14X/Yr. Magazine focusing on architecture. McGraw-Hill, Inc., 1221 Avenue of the Americas, New York, NY 10020. Telephone (212)512-4686.

Archives of Internal Medicine. Semimonthly. Educational/clinical journal for internists, cardiologists, gastroenterologists, and other internal medicine subspecialists. American Medical Assn., 515 N. State St., Chicago, IL 60610. Telephone (312)464-5000.

Astin, Alexander W., William S. Korn, Linda J. Sax, and Kathryn M. Machoney. (1994). *The American Freshman: National Norms for Fall 1994*. ISBN 1-878477-15-3.Los Angeles: Higher Education Research Institution, UCLA. Copies may be purchased from the Higher Education Research Institute, Graduate School of Education & Information Studies, 3005 Moore Hall, University of California, Los Angeles, CA 90024-1521. Telephone (310)825-1925; Fax 206-2228.

The Atlantic Monthly. Monthly. ISSN 0276-9077. General interest magazine. The Atlantic Monthly Co., 745 Boylston St., Boston, MA 02116. Telephone (617)536-9500.

Better Homes and Gardens. Monthly. ISSN 0006-0151. Meredith Corporation, 1716 Locust Street, Des Moines, IA 50309-3023.

British Journal of Addiction. ISSN 0952-0481. After 1993: *Addiction.* 12X/Yr. ISSN 0965-2140. Academic/scholarly publication. Carfax Publishing Co., P.O. Box 25, Abingdon, Oxon. OX14 EUE, England. Telephone 44-235-555335. FAX 44-235-553559.

Cancer. Semimonthly. ISSN 0008-543X. Oncology journal publishing original articles on clinical aspects of cancer, surgical and medical therapy, and interdisciplinary research. J.B. Lippincott Co., 227 E. Washington Sq., Philadelphia, PA 19106. Telephone (215)238-4492.

Catholic Almanac. 1993 and 1994 editions. ISBN 0-87973-269-5 (1993). ISBN 0-87973-271-7 (1994). Felician A. Foy, ed. (Huntington, IN: Our Sunday Visitor Publishing Division, 1993).

Center for the American Women and Politics (CAWP), Eagleton Institute of Politics, Rutgers University, New Brunswick, NJ 08901. Telephone (908)828-2210. Fax (908)932-6778.

The Chronicle of Higher Education. Weekly. ISSN 0009-5982. 1255 23rd St., N.W., Washington, D.C. 20037.

Congressional Research Service. Washington, DC. Conducts research, analyzes legislation, and provides information at the request of U.S. Congress committees, members, and staffs. To obtain copies of CRS Reports, contact your Member of Congress. Telephone (202)224-3121.

—Cooper, Edith Fairman, "Alcohol Use and Abuse by Women." September 13, 1991. CRS Report for Congress 91-680 SPR.

—Eddy, Mark, "Minority and Women-Owned Business Programs of the Federal Government." March 18, 1993. CRS Report for Congress, 93-331 GOV.

—Garcia, Rogelio, "Women Nominated and Appointed to Full-Time Civilian Positions by President George Bush, 1989-92." May 26, 1993. CRS Report for Congress, 93-542 GOV.

—Levine, Linda, "The 'Glass Ceiling:' Access of Women and Minorities to Management Positions." August 19, 1991. CRS Report for Congress, 91-623 E.

—Levine, Linda, "Pay Equity Legislation in the 102d Congress." Updated January 6, 1993 (Archived). CRS Issue Brief. Order Code IB91080.

—McCallion, Gail, "A Demographic Portrait of Older Workers." September 27, 1988. CRS Report for Congress 88-636 E.

—Thomas, Rosita M., "Abortion: National and State Public Opinion Polls." October 24, 1989. CRS Report for Congress, 89-591 GOV.

—Whittier, Charles H., "Abortion in World Religions." May 1988. CRS Report for Congress, 88-357 GOV.

—Williams, Jennifer D., "The 'Gender Gap': Differences Between Men and Women in Political Attitudes and Voting Behavior in the 1980s." September 28, 1989. CRS Report for Congress, 89-547 GOV.

Consumer Reports. Monthly. ISSN 0010-7174. Provides consumers with information on goods, services, health, and personal finance. Consumers Union of U.S., Inc., 101 Truman Ave., Yonkers, NY 10703-1057.

Detroit Free Press. Daily. General newspaper. Knight-Ridder, Inc., 321 W. Lafayette Blvd., Detroit, MI 48231. Telephone (313)222-6400.

Ebony. Monthly. General editorial magazine geared toward African Americans. Johnson Publishing Co., Inc., 820 S. Michigan Ave., Chicago, IL 60605. Telephone (312)322-9200.

The Economist Book of Vital World Statistics: A Complete Guide to the World in Figures. ISBN 0-09-174652-3. (London: Hutchinson Business Books Limited, 1990).

Electronic Information Report. 46X/Yr. Newsletter. Formerly (until February 1994): *Information and Database Publishing*. ISSN 0197-0178. SIMBA-Communications Trends, 213 Danbury Rd., Box 7430, Wilton, CT 06897-7430. Telephone (203)834-0033.

FW. Financial World. Biweekly (25X/yr.). ISSN 0015-2064. Financial World Partners, 1328 Broadway, New York, NY 10001-2116. Telephone (212)594-5030.

FairTest National Center for Fair & Open Testing. An advocacy organization "working to end the abuses, misuses and flaws of standardized testing." "Special emphasis is placed on eliminating the racial, class, gender, and cultural barriers to equal opportunity posed by standardized tests." Publishes the *Examiner*. 342 Broadway, Cambridge, MA 02139. Telephone (617)864-4810.

Family Planning Perspectives. Bimonthly. ISSN 0014-7354. The Alan Guttmacher Institute, an independent, nonprofit corporation for research, policy analysis, and public education. 111 Fifth Avenue, New York, NY 10003. Telephone (212)254-5656. Fax (212)254-9891.

Girl Scouts of the United States of America. *Girl Scouts: Who We Are, What We Think*. Executive Summary. Fall 1990. A research study conducted for Girl Scouts of the United States of America by Louis Harris and Associates, Inc. Girl Scouts of the USA, 830 Third Avenue, New York, NY 10022.

Glendon, Mary Ann. *The Transformation of Family Law: State, Law, and Family in the United States and Western Europe*. (Chicago: University of Chicago Press, 1977).

Gomby, Deanna S., and Patricia H. Shiono, "Estimating the Number of Substance-Exposed Infants," *The Future of Children*, a publication of the Center for the Future of Children, The David and Lucille Packard Foundation, Spring, 1991. Available from CSAP National Resource Center for the Prevention of Perinatal Abuse of Alcohol and Other Drugs, 9302 Lee Highway, Fairfax, VA 22031. Telephone (703)218-5600. Fax (703)218-5701. CSAP National Resource Center's information base is available on-line through the Perinatal Research and Education Management Information System (PREMIS).

Hastings, Elizabeth Hann, and Philip K. Hastings, eds., *Index to International Public Opinion, 1992-1993*. ISBN 0-313-29057-1. (Westport, CT: Greenwood Press, 1994).

Haugaard, Jeffrey J., "Sexual Abuse in Families." LCI Working Paper #93-03. January 1993. Chapter to appear in *Handbook of Developmental Family Psychology and Psychopathology*, L. L'Abate, ed. Bronfenbrenner Life Course Institute, Cornell University, College of Human Ecology, Martha Van Rensselaer Hall, Ithaca, NY 14853.

Impact. A Newsletter of Chemical Health in Minnesota. Quarterly. Minnesota Prevention Resource Center, 2829 Verndale Avenue, Anoka, MN 55303. Telephone (612)427-5310.

Independent Sector. *Giving and Volunteering in the United States*. Findings from a National Survey. 1994 Edition. ISSN 1040-4082. Independent Sector, 1828 L Street, N.W., Suite 1200, Washington, DC 20036.

The International Journal of Addictions. 14X/Yr. ISSN 0020-773X. Medical journal reporting individual and community problems brought on by drug, alcohol, and tobacco use, abuse, and dependency. Also considers legal and social aspects of addiction. Marcel Dekker, Inc., 270 Madison Ave., New York, NY 10016. Telephone (212)696-9000.

International Labour Office. *Year Book of Labour Statistics*. ISBN 92-2-007347-1. 1994. Statistical data from more than 180 countries and territories are provided on such subjects as population, employment, hours of work, wages, consumer prices, household budgets, etc. Information is given in English and French. The *Year Book* is supplemented by the *Bulletin of Labour Statistics*, published quarterly with eight supplements. International Labour Office, Geneva, Switzerland. 2 volumes.

Janus, Samuel S., PhD, and Cynthia L. Janus, MD, *The Janus Report on Sexual Behavior: The First Broad-Scale Scientific National Survey Since Kinsey*. ISBN 0-471-52540-5. (New York: John Wiley & Sons, Inc., 1993).

Journal of Alcohol and Drug Education. ISSN 0090-1482. Academic/scholarly publication. American Alcohol and Drug Information Foundation, C/o MICAP, Box 10212, Lansing, MI 48901. Telephone (517)484-2636.

Journal of Consulting and Clinical Psychology. Bimonthly. ISSN 0022-006X. Journal presenting research on techniques of diagnosis and treatment in disordered behavior and studies of populations of clinical interest. American Psychological Assn., 750 First St., NE, Washington, DC 20002-4242. Telephone (202)336-5500.

Journal of Drug Education. Quarterly. Journal on the behavioral consequences of drug use and abuse for education and health professionals, social service and Armed Forces personnel. Baywood Publishing Co., Inc., 26 Austin Ave., PO Box 337, Amityville, NY 11701. Telephone (516)691-1270.

Journal of Family Issues. 4X/yr. ISSN 0192-513X. Focuses on family studies. Sage Publications, Inc., 211 W. Hillcrest Dr., Newbury Park, CA 91320. Telephone (805)499-0721.

Journal of Personality and Social Psychology. Monthly. ISSN 0022-3514. Journal presenting research in three major areas: attitudes and social cognition; interpersonal relations and group processes; and personality processes and individual differences. American Psychological Assn., 750 First St. NE, Washington, DC 20002-4242. Telephone (202)336-5500.

Journal of Primary Prevention. ISSN 0278-095X. Academic/scholarly journal presenting theoretical, empirical, and methodological research on preventative intervention in human services. Discusses innovative programs and concepts. Human Sciences Press, Inc., 233 Spring St., New York, NY 10013-1578. Telephone (212)620-8000.

Journal of Studies on Alcohol. Bimonthly. ISSN 0096-882X. Journal containing original research reports about alcohol, its use and misuse, and its biomedical, behavioral, and sociocultural effects. Rutgers Center of Alcohol Studies, P.O. Box 969, Piscataway, NJ 08855. Telephone (908)932-2190.

Journal of the National Cancer Institute. Semimonthly. ISSN 0027-8874. Health service journal on cancer. U.S. Government Printing Office, Superintendent of Documents, Washington, DC 20402-9322. Telephone (202)783-3238.

Kilgore, Nancy. *Every Eighteen Seconds: A Journey Through Domestic Violence.* (Volcano, CA: Volcano Press, 1992).

Kurian, George Thomas. *The New Book of World Rankings.* ISBN 0-8160-1931-2. (New York: Facts on File, 1991). ISBN 0-8160-1931-2.

The Lancet (North American Edition). Weekly. Medical journal. Contents identical to British edition. Williams & Wilkins, 428 E. Preston St., Baltimore, MD 21202. Telephone (410)528-8553.

Market: Europe. 16X yr. ISSN 1050-9410. W-Two Publications, Ltd., 202 The Commons, Suite 401, Ithaca, NY 14850-9942. Telephone (607)277-0934.

Marshall, Ray. *The State of Families, 3: Losing Direction.* Families, Human Resource Development, and Economic Performance. Third in a series commissioned by Family Service America to illustrate the conditions facing American families. (Milwaukee: Family Service America, 1991.)

Martin, Laura C. *A Life Without Fear.* A Guide to Preventing Sexual Assault. (Nashville: Rutledge Hill Press, 1992).

Mayer, Adele. *Women Sex Offenders: Treatment and Dynamics.* ISBN 1-55691-063-0.(Holmes Beach, FL: Learning Publications, Inc., 1992).

Mediamark Research Inc. *Mediamark Research Multimedia Audiences Report: Spring 1993.* 444 N. Michigan Avenue, Suite 3530, Chicago, IL 60611. Telephone (312)329-0901. Fax (312)329-0443.

Ms. Bimonthly. ISSN 0047-8318. Lang Communications, 230 Park Avenue, New York, NY 10169.

Ms. Foundation for Women. *Women's Voices: A Joint Project, A Polling Report* and *A Policy Guide:* , Ms. Foundation for Women and Center for Policy Alternatives. Information packet and sheets. September 1992. Available from Ms. Foundation for Women, 141 Fifth Avenue 6-S, New York, NY 10010. Telephone (212)353-8580.

National Commission on AIDS. *AIDS: An Expanding Tragedy.* The Final Report of the National Commission on AIDS. Copies of reports may be ordered through the CDC National AIDS Clearinghouse, P.O. Box 6003, Rockville, MD 20849-6003. Telephone (800)458-5231 (voice) or (800)243-7012 (TDD).

National Education Association. Research Division. NEA, 1201 16th Street, N.W., Washington, DC 20036-3290. Telephone (202)822-7442; Fax (202)822-7697. Copies are available from NEA Professional Library, P.O. Box 509, West Haven, CT 06516. Telephone 1-800-229-4200.

—*Status of the American Public School Teacher 1990-1991.*

—*Rankings of the States 1994.*

National Education Goals Panel. 1993. *The National Education Goals Report: Volume One: The National Report: Building a Nation of Learners.* For sale by the U.S. Government Printing Office, Superintendent of Documents, Washington, DC 20402-9328.

National Endowment for the Arts. The Nancy Hanks Center, 1100 Pennsylvania Ave. NW, Washington, DC 20506. Telephone (202)682-5400.

—*Arts Participation in America: 1982-1992.* Research Division Report #27. Prepared by Jack Faucett Associates. October 1993.

—*Dancemakers: A Study Report on Choreographers in Four American Cities.* Research Division Report #28. ISBN 0-16-042946-3. Prepared by Dick Netzer and Ellen Parker based on a survey conducted by Alyce Dissette and Richard J. Orend. October 1993.

—"Demographic Differences in Arts Attendance: 1982-1992." Research Division Note #51. February 16, 1994.

—"Demographic Differences in Arts Participation via Broadcast and Recorded Media: 1982-1992." Research Division Note #52. February 16, 1994.

—*Trends in Artist Occupations: 1970-1990.* Research Division Report #29. ISBN 0-16-045347-X. Prepared by Diane C. Ellis and John C. Beresford. August 1994.

National Federation of State High School Associations, 11724 NW Plaza Circle, P.O. Box 20626, Kansas City, MO 64195-0626.

National Live Stock and Meat Board. *Eating in America Today II (EAT).* Research conducted by the Nutritional Marketing Division of MRCA Information Services through their ongoing survey, purchased by the National Live Stock and Meat Board to evaluate consumers actual food intake (eating habits) compared to their attitudes. National Live Stock and Meat Board, 444 North Michigan Avenue, Chicago, IL 60611. Telephone (312)670-9200. Fax (312)467-9729.

National Restaurant Association. Washington, DC.

—News Release, April 7, 1994. "Nine Out of Ten Colleges Offer Meatless Alternatives at Every Meal as Interest in Vegetarianism Grows Among Students." Contact Wendy Webster, Manager, Media Relations, National Restaurant Association, 1200 Seventeenth Street, N.W., Washington, DC 20036-3097. Telephone (202)331-5938.

—*Foodservice Employee Profile: 1993*. (CS467). For a copy, telephone (800)424-5156, ext. 5375, or (202)973-5375.

National Victim Center. Conducts research and maintains a resource library. Sponsors INFO-LINK, a toll-free source of information and referral for victims of crime, concerned citizens, public policymakers, and allied professionals dedicated to improving victims' rights and services. Telephone 1-800-FYI-CALL.

National Sporting Goods Association. International Headquarters, 1699 Wall St., Mt. Prospect, IL 60056-5780. Telephone (708)439-4000. Fax (708)439-0111.

—*The Sporting Goods Market in 1993: With Demographics for 1992 Based on Interviews with 80,000 American Households*. ISSN 0193-8401. A statistical study of retail sales for representative categories of sporting goods and recreational equipment. 1993.

—*Sports Participation in 1992*. Series I: A statistical study of sports participation for twenty-five sports activities. ISSN 0882-8210.

The New England Journal of Medicine. Weekly. ISSN 0028-4795. Journal for the medical profession. Massachusetts Medical Society, 10 Shattuck St., Boston, MA 02115-6094. Telephone (617)734-9800.

The New York Times. Daily. 229 W. 43rd St., New York, NY 10036. (212)556-1234.

Newsweek. Weekly. ISSN 0028-9604. 251 West 57th Street, New York, NY 10019-1894.

NOW Legal Defense and Education Fund. *Secrets in Public: Sexual Harassment in Our Schools*. A Report on the Results of a Seventeen Magazine Survey. A Joint Project of NOW Legal Defense and Education Fund and Wellesley College Center for Research on Women. March 1993. Available from the Wellesley College Center for Research on Women, telephone (607)283-2507.

The Numbers News. Monthly. ISSN 0732-1597. Timely news on market trends. A Publication of American Demographics, Inc. P.O. Box 68, Ithaca, NY 14851. Telephone (800)828-1133. Fax (607)273-3196.

Obstetrics and Gynecology. Monthly. Professional journal focusing on medical and surgical treatment of female conditions, obstetrics management, and clinical evaluation of drugs and instruments. Elsevier Science Publishing Co., Inc., 655 Avenue of the Americas, New York, NY 10010. Telephone (212)633-3977.

Older Women's League (OWL). 666 Eleventh Street, NW, Suite 700, Washington, DC 20001. Telephone (202)783-6686.

Pediatrics. Monthly. Medical journal reporting on pediatrics. American Academy of Pediatrics, Inc., 141 NW Point Blvd., PO Box 927, Elk Grove Village, IL 60007-0927. Telephone (708)228-5005.

Pillemer, Karl, and J. Jill Suitor, "Violence and Violent Feelings: What Causes Them Among Family Caregivers?" LCI Working Paper #92-03. Accepted for publication in *Journal of Gerontology*. Bronfenbrenner Life Course Institute, Cornell University, College of Human Ecology, Martha Van Rensselaer Hall, Ithaca, NY 14853.

Lawrence A. Pfaff and Associates. *Study Reveals Gender Differences in Management and Leadership Skills*. Study Summary. 1995. Lawrence A. Pfaff and Associates, 3506 Lovers Lane, Suite 3, Kalamazoo, MI 49001. Telephone (616)344-2242. Fax (616)344-2054.

Polakow, Valerie, *Lives on the Edge: Single Mothers and Their Children in the Other America*. (Chicago: The University of Chicago Press, 1993).

Population Bulletin. Published 4X yr. and distributed to members of the Population Reference Bureau. ISSN 0032-468X. 1875 Connecticut Ave. NW, Suite 520, Washington, DC 20009. Telephone (202)483-1100.

—Dennis A. Ahlburg and Carol J. Devita, "New Realities of the American Family," *Population Bulletin*, Vol 47, No. 2, August 1992.

—Frances Goldscheider and Calvin Goldscheider, "Leaving and Returning Home in 20th Century America," *Population Bulletin*, Vol. 48, No. 4, March 1994.

—William P. O'Hare, Kelvin M. Pollard, Taynia L. Mann, and Mary M. Kent, "African Americans in the 1990s," *Population Bulletin*, July 1991.

—Abdel R. Oman and Farzaneh Roudi, "The Middle East Population Puzzle," *Population Bulletin*, Vol. 48, No. 1, July 1993.

Post-Dispatch. Daily. Pulitzer Publishing Co., 900 N. Tucker Blvd., Saint Louis, MO 63101. (314)340-8000.

Ryka ROSE (Regaining One's Self-Esteem) Foundation. A non-profit organization created in 1992 to help end violence against women. P.O. Box 157, Islington, MA 02090. Telephone (617)762-9900.

Shroff, Kersi B., "Divorce, Maintenance and Child Support Laws in Australia, Canada, England and New Zealand." Law Library of Congress, American-British Law Division LL90-65. To obtain a copy of this report, contact your Member of Congress. Telephone (202)224-3121.

Simmons Market Research Bureau, Inc. *The 1993 Study of Media and Markets*. Based on a total of 22,468 adults and projectable to the population 18 years and over living in the coterminous 48 states of the United States. 420 Lexington, Avenue, New York, NY 10170; Telephone (212)916-8900.

Sisters in Crime. Formed in 1986 "to combat discrimination against women in the mystery field, educate publishers and the general public as to inequalities in the treatment of female authors, and to raise the level of awareness of their contribution to the field. P.O. Box 442124, Lawrence, KS 66044-8933. Telephone (913)842-1325.

Special Libraries Association. *SLA Biennial Salary Survey 1995*. 1994. ISBN 0-87111-423-2. 1700 18th Street, N.W., Washington, D.C. 20009.

Sporting Goods Manufacturing Association. *The U.S. Athletic Footwear Market Today*. 1993 Edition. Athletic Footwear Association, 200 Castlewood Drive, North Palm Beach, FL 33408. Telephone (407)840-1161.

State Rankings. ISBN 0-9625531-2-3. 1992. (Lawrence, KS: Morgan Quitno Corporation, 1992).

Statistical Bulletin. Quarterly. ISSN 0741-9767. Journal featuring health statistics, demography, and health care costs. Metropolitan Life Insurance Co., PO Box 64187, Baltimore, MD 21264-0025. Telephone (410)528-4227.

Tennis Industry Association. *Tennis Participation Today: Highlights from a New National Study of American Tennis Players, 1992*. Three national studies of tennis participation (1988, 1989, and 1992) have been conducted for the Tennis Industry Association by Audits & Surveys, New York. 200 Castlewood Drive, North Palm Beach, FL 33408. Telephone (407)840-1127.

Thurgood, D.H., and J.E. Clarke. 1995. *Summary Report 1993: Doctorate Recipients from United States Universities*. Washington, D.C. National Academy Press. The report gives the results of data collected in the *Survey of Earned Doctorates*, sponsored by five federal agencies: NSF, NIH, US. Dept. of Ed., and USDA and conducted by the NRC.

Toubia, Nahid, *Female Genital Mutilation: A Call for Global Action.* 1993. Available from Women, Ink., 777 United Nations Plaza, NY, NY 10017. Telephone (212)687-8633.

United Nations. *1988 Demographic Yearbook.* Annual. 1990. A central source for demographic data from approximately 220 countries. Special section on population by religion and sex. United Nations Publishing Division, United Nations, New York, NY 10017. (800)253-9646. *1990 Demographic Yearbook.* 1992. *1991 Demographic Yearbook.* 1992.

United Nations. *Statistical Yearbook.* Annual. 39th issue. ISBN 92-1-061159-4. A comprehensive compendium of vital internationally comparable data for the analysis of socio-economic development at the world, regional, and national levels. Data available as of December 31, 1993.

—*The World's Women 1970-1990: Trends and Statistics.* 1991.

U.S. Advisory Commission on Intergovernmental Relations. *Changing Public Attitudes on Government and Taxes.* A Commission Survey. 1994. The ACIR was created by Congress in 1959 to monitor the operation of the American federal system and to recommend improvements. 800 K Street, NW, Suite 450, South Building, Washington, DC 20575. Telephone (202)653-5540. Fax (202)653-5429.

U.S. Bureau of the Census. Economics and Statistics Administration, Washington DC. For sale by the U.S. Government Printing Office, Superintendent of Documents, Washington, DC 20402-9328 (unless otherwise noted).

—Bennefield, Robert L., *Dynamics of Economic Well-Being: Health Insurance, 1990 to 1992.* Current Population Reports, P70-37.

—Bruno, Rosalind R., and Andrea Adams., *School Enrollment-Social and Economic Characteristics of Students: October 1993.* Current Population Reports, P20-479.

—Campbell, Paul R., *Population Projections for States, by Age, Race, and Sex: 1993 to 2020.* Current Population Reports, P25-1111. 1994.

—*Census and You.* Monthly news from the U.S. Bureau of the Census.

—Current Population Reports, P23-180. *Marriage, Divorce, and Remarriage in the 1990's.*

—Current Population Reports, P23-185. *Population Profile of the United States: 1993.*

—Garcia, Jesus M., *The Hispanic Population in the United States: March 1992*, Current Population Reports, P20-465RV.

—*Social and Economic Characteristics: United States.* 1990 Census of Population, CP-2-1. Issued November 1993.

—Sutterlin, Rebecca and Robert A. Kominski, *Dollars for Scholars: Postsecondary Costs and Financing, 1990-1991.* Current Population Reports, P70-39.

—Statistical Brief 93-18. Issued November 1993. Free.

—*Statistical Abstract of the United States: 1994.* (114th edition.) Presents the most important statistical information gathered by all branches of the federal government.

U.S. Congress. House. Committee on Ways and Means. *1991 Green Book: Background Material and Data on Programs Within the Jurisdiction of the Committee on Ways and Means.* May 7, 1991. For sale by the U.S. Government Printing Office, Superintendent of Documents, Washington, DC 20402-9328.

U.S. Congress. Senate. Committee on the Judiciary.

—*Fighting Crime in America: An Agenda for the 1990's.* A Majority Staff Report Prepared for the Use of the Committee on the Judiciary. March 12, 1991.

—*Legislation to Reduce the Growing Problem of Violent Crime Against Women.* Hearing before the Committee on the Judiciary, United States Senate, One Hundred First Congress, Second Session. June 20, 1990, Part I, Serial No. J-101-80.

—*Turning the Act Into Action: The Violence Against Women Law.* Senator Joseph R. Biden Jr., United States Senate, October 1994.

U.S. Department of Education. National Center for Education Statistics. For sale by the U.S. Government Printing Office, Superintendent of Documents, Washington, DC 20402-9328. Some publications are available free from the Office of Educational Research and Improvement, Washington, D.C. 20208-5721.

—*Degrees and Other Awards Conferred by Institutions of Higher Education: 1991-92.* July 1994. NCES 94-053.

—*Dropout Rates in the United States: 1993.* NCES 94-669. September 1994.

—NAEP 1992 Reading Report Card for the Nation and the States. Data from the National and Trial State Assessments. For ordering information write: Education Information Branch, Office of Educational Research and Improvement, U.S. Dept. of Education, 555 New Jersey Avenue, NW, Washington, DC 20208-5641. Telephone 1-800-424-1616. ISBN 0-88685-147-5.

—Persistence and Attainment in Postsecondary Education for Beginning AY 1989-90 Students as of Spring 1992. November 1993. NCES 94-477.

—Salaries of Full-Time Instructional Faculty on 9- and 10-Month Contracts in Institutions of Higher Education, 1982-83 Through 1992-93. December 1993. NCES 93-475.

—Trends in Enrollment in Higher Education, by Racial/Ethnic Category: Fall 1982 Through Fall 1992. March 1994. NCES-94-104.

—Undergraduates Who Work While Enrolled in Postsecondary Education: 1989-90. September 1994. NCES 94-311.

—Vocational Education in G-7 Countries: Profiles and Data. Research and Development Report. September 1994. U.S. Department of Education, Office of Educational Research and Improvement. NCES 94-005.

U.S. Department of Education. Office of Educational Research and Improvement. National Center for Education Statistics. *Projections of Education Statistics to 2003*. December 1992. NCES 92-218. ISSN 0-16-038250-5. For sale by the U.S. Government Printing Office, Superintendent of Documents, Washington, DC 20402-9328.

U.S. Department of Health & Human Services. Centers for Disease Control and Prevention, National Center for Health Statistics, 6525 Belcrest Road, Hyattsville, MD 20782.

—Alcohol, Drug Abuse, and Mental Health Administration. *Alcohol Alert*. No. 10, PH 290, October 1990, "Alcohol and Women." *Alcohol, Tobacco, and Other Drugs May Harm the Unborn*. DHHS Publication No. (ADM)90-1711. Printed 1990, Reprinted 1994. Distributed by the Office for Substance Abuse Prevention's National Clearinghouse for Alcohol and Drug Information, P.O. Box 2345, Rockville, MD 20847-2345. Telephone 1-800-729-6686.

—Administration for Children and Families. Children's Bureau. *Analysis of 1989 Child Welfare Data*. Prepared by the staff of Caliber Associates in conjunction with staff at MAXIMUS, Inc. April 1993.

—CDC National Aids Clearinghouse. A reference, referral, and distribution service for HIV/AIDS-related information. P.O. Box 6003, Rockville, MD 20849-6003. Telephone (800)458-5231.

—*Health United States 1992.* 1993.

—*Monthly Vital Statistics Report.*

—National Institute on Drug Abuse. *National Survey Results on Drug Use from the Monitoring the Future Study, 1975-1992.* Volume I: Secondary School Students. 1993. *Women & Drug Abuse: You and Your Community Can Help.*

U.S. Department of Justice.

—Bureau of Justice Assistance. "Family Violence: Interventions for the Justice System." Program Brief. October 1993, NCJ-144532.

—Bureau of Justice Statistics. *Bulletin.* "Prisoners in 1993," "Felony Sentences in State Courts, 1992," and "Capital Punishment 1993." BJS Publications and some others are available from BJS Clearinghouse, P.O. Box 179, BJS-236, Annapolis Junction, MD 20701-0179.

—Bureau of Justice Statistics. *Correctional Populations in the United States, 1992.* January 1995. NCJ-146413.

—Bureau of Justice Statistics. *Criminal Victimization in the United States, 1991.* December 1992, NCJ-139563.

—Bureau of Justice Statistics. Selected Findings. "Violence Between Intimates." November 1994. NCJ-149259.

—Bureau of Justice Statistics. Special Report. "Women in Jail 1989." March 1992.

—Bureau of Justice Statistics. Special Report. "Murder in Families." July 1994.

—Bureau of Justice Statistics. *Survey of State Prison Inmates, 1991.* Available from the National Institute of Justice, P.O. Box 6000, Rockville, MD 20850. Telephone 800-851-3420.

—1992. *Child Rape Victims, 1992.* Patrick A. Langan, Ph.D., and Caroline Wolf Harlow, Ph.D. Richard Florence of the Justice Research and Statistics Association collected State rape data through a telephone survey of State Statistical Analysis Centers and police officials of the District of Columbia, Nevada, and Wyoming. Office of Justice Programs, Bureau of Justice Statistics, June 1994, NCJ-147001.

—National Institute of Justice. Research in Brief. "The Cycle of Violence." October 1992.

—National Victims Resource Center. Conducts personalized searches of the National Institute of Justice/NCJRS data base. Provides and information packet entitled "Criminal Justice Information Package-Domestic Violence Statistics." Write or phone at the Office for Victims of Crime, Office of Justice Programs, Box 6000, Rockville, MD 20850. Telephone 1-800-627-NVRC (6872).

—Office of Justice Programs. *Comprehensive Strategy for Serious, Violent, and Chronic Juvenile Offenders.* Program Summary. Second printing, June 1994. and *School Crime: A National Crime Victimization Survey Report.* September 1991, NCJ-131645. Copies available from Juvenile Justice Clearinghouse, P.O. Box 6000, Rockville, MD 20850. Telephone 800-638-8736.

—Office of Justice Programs. *Violence Against Women: A National Crime Victimization Survey Report.* January 1994. NCJ-145325.

—1992. *Crime in the United States.* Uniform Crime Reports. Annual. Federal Bureau of Investigation, Washington,. D.C. 20535. For sale by the U.S. Government Printing Office, Superintendent of Documents, Washington, DC 20402-9328.

—National Institute of Justice. Research in Brief. *Drug Use Forecasting: 1991 Annual Report.* December 1992. NCJ 137776.

U.S. Department of Labor. Glass Ceiling Commission. March 1995. *Good for Business: Making Full Use of the Nation's Human Capital: The Environmental Scan.* ISBN 0-16-045547-2. Copies of the report are available from the following sources:

—Printed copies from the U.S. Government Printing Office and its regional bookstores. Telephone (202)783-3238.

—Microfiche copies are available from the National Technical Information Service, 5285 Port Royal Road, Springfield, VA 22161. Telephone (703)487-4690.

—Electronic copies are available from the Internet via the World Wide Web server and GOPHER, thanks to a partnership with Cornell University. Access code for WWW is http://www.ilr.cornell.edu. Access code for GOPHER is 128:253.61.155.

—To request research papers from the Glass Ceiling Commission, send to: Glass Ceiling Commission, U.S. Department of Labor, 200 Constitution Ave., NW-Room C-2313. Fax (202)219-7368.

U.S. Department of Labor. Bureau of Labor Statistics. Washington, D.C. 20212. *Monthly Labor Review*. Monthly. ISSN 0098-1818. Washington, D.C. 20212. Telephone (202)606-5900.

—Robert Cage, "How does rental assistance influence spending behavior?" May 1994 (reprint).

—"Consumer Expenditures in 1993." Report 885, December 1994.

—Howard V. Hayghe and Suzanne M. Bianchi, "Married mothers' work patterns: the job-family compromise." June 1994.

—*Labor Composition and U.S. Productivity Growth, 1948-90*. Bulletin 2426, December 1993.

—"Usual Weekly Earnings of Wage and Salary Workers: Fourth Quarter 1994." News. USDL 95-43.

—"Work and Family: Promotions Among Women." Data from the National Longitudinal Surveys. Report 868, March 1994.

U.S. Department of Labor. Women's Bureau. Washington, D.C. 20212.

—*1993 Handbook on Women Workers: Trends & Issues*. 1994.

—*Facts on Working Women: Women Workers: Outlook to 2005*. No. 92-1, January 1992.

—*Working Women Count! A Report to the Nation*. 1994. ISBN 0-16-045393-3. For sale by the U.S. Government Printing Office, Superintendent of Documents, Washington, DC 20402-9328.

U.S. Department of Transportation. National Highway Traffic Safety Administration. National Center for Statistics & Analysis (NRD-31), 400 7th Street, S.W., Washington, DC 20590. Telephone (202)366-4198.

——Cerrelli, Ezio C. "Crash Data and Rates for Age-Sex Groups of Drivers, 1990. Research Note. May 1992.

——*Female Drivers in Fatal Crashes: Recent Trends.* January 1994. DOT HS 808 106. Available from the National Technical Information Service, Springfield, VA 22161.

U.S. Equal Employment Opportunity Commission. 1801 L Street, N.W., Washington, D.C. 20507. Telephone (202)663-4949.

——Indicators of Equal Employment Opportunity-Status and Trends. September 1993.

——*Job Patterns for Minorities & Women in Private Industry 1993.* 1994.

——*Job Patterns for Minorities and Women in State and Local Government 1993.* 1994.

United States General Accounting Office. First copies of reports are available free. Write US-GAO, Box 6015, Gaithersburg, MD 20884-6015.

——*DOD Service Academies: More Actions Needed to Eliminate Sexual Harassment.* January 1994. GAO/NSIAD-94-6.

——*Operation Desert Storm: Race and Gender Comparison of Deployed Forces with All Active Duty Forces.* June 1992. GAO/NSIAD-92-111FS.

——*Women in the Military: Deployment in the Persian Gulf War.* Report to the Secretary of Defense. July 1993. GAO/NSIAD-93-93.

U.S. Merit Systems Protection Board. *A Question of Equity: Women and the Glass Ceiling.* A Report to the President and the Congress of the United States. 1992. Available free from U.S. Merit Systems Protection Board, 1120 Vermont Avenue, NW, Washington, D.C. 20419.

USA Today. Daily. General newspaper with national perspective. ISSN 0734-7456. Gannett Co., Inc., 1 Gannett Dr., White Plains, NY 10604-3498. Telephone (914)694-9300.

USA Weekend. Weekly. Editorial offices: 1000 Wilson Blvd., Arlington, VA 22229-0012. Telephone (703)276-6445.

Utne Reader. Bimonthly. Reading digest covering politics, international issues, the arts, science, and social issues. Lens Publishing Co., Inc., The Fawkes Bldg., 1624 Harmon Pl., Ste. 330, Minneapolis, MN 55403. Telephone (612)338-5040.

The Washington Post. Daily. 1150 15th St., NW, Washington, DC 20071. Telephone (202)334-6000.

Watson, R.R., ed., *Drug and Alcohol Abuse Reviews, Vol. 7: Alcohol, Cocaine, and Accidents*. (Totowa, NJ: Humana Press Inc., 1995)

Williams, Linda Meyer, and David Finkelhor, "Paternal Caregiving and Incest: A Test of a Biosocial Model." Unpublished manuscript. 1993. Distributed by Family Research Laboratory, University of New Hampshire, Durham, NH 03824.

Wilson Library Bulletin. Monthly. ISSN 0043-5651. Magazine for library professionals. The H.W. Wilson Co., 950 University Ave., Bronx, NY 10452. Telephone (718)588-8400.

Women's Sports & Fitness. 8X/yr. ISSN 8750-653X. The official magazine of the Women's Sports Foundation. Women's Sports & Fitness, Inc., 2025 Pearl St., Boulder, CO 80302.

Women Work! The National Network for Women's Employment. *Women Work, Poverty Persists: A Status Report on Displaced Homemakers & Single Mothers in the United States*. Women Work! 1625 K Street, NW, Suite 300, Washington, DC 20006. Telephone (202)467-6346.

Working Woman. Monthly. January issue includes an annual salary survey. Lang Communications, Inc., 230 Park Ave., 7th Fl., New York, NY 10169. Telephone (800)234-9675.

World Bank. *Social Indicators of Development 1994*. ISBN 0-8018-4788-5. Published annually on diskette and in book form. For information, contact The World Bank, 1818 H Street N.W., Washington, D.C. 20433. Telephone (202)473-1155. (Baltimore: Johns Hopkins University Press: 1994).

World Health Organization. *Maternal and Perinatal Infections: Report of a WHO Consultation*. Records the results of a WHO consultation to evaluate the public health significance of maternal and perinatal infections in developing countries. 1991. WHO/MCH/91.10. Order no. 1930033. World Health Organization, Publications Center USA, 49 Sheridan Avenue, Albany, NY 12219.

World Press Review. Monthly. ISSN 0195-8895. Foreign press digest, subtitle: News and Views from Around the World. World Press Review, 200 Madison Ave., New York, NY 10016. Telephone (212)889-5155.

World Watch. Bimonthly. Magazine reporting on ecological protection and economic development worldwide. Worldwatch Institute, 1776 Massachusetts Ave., NW, Washington, DC 20036. Telephone (202)452-1999.

Yearbook of American & Canadian Churches 1993. Kenneth Bedell, ed. Annual. ISBN 0687-46648-2. (Nashville: Abingdon Press, 1993).

Subject and Geographic Index

The *Subject and Geographic Index* indexes general table topics as well as "line items" within tables. The primary reference number appearing after subject index terms are page numbers. Reference numbers in brackets are entry numbers. All subject terms in this index apply to the United States unless modified by *worldwide* or by a country name. Tables listed under the heading *United States* present international comparisons that include the United States. Tables appearing under the heading *North America* present international comparisons that may include the United States.

The *Library of Congress Subject Headings* and *Women: An Alphabetical Microthesaurus of Terms Selected from the Legislative Indexing of Vocabulary* (Congressional Research Service: CRS Report for Congress 88-710 L; November 21, 1988 revision) were used as a general guide for the selection of headings in this index but were not followed in all cases.

Abortion, pp. 191, 610-611, 613, 616 [197, 638-639, 641, 643]
— Africa, pp. 620-621 [648-649]
— and adoption, p. 3 [4]
— Asia, pp. 621-622 [650-651]
— attitudes, pp. 2-3, 5-9, 31, 43, 45-46, 71 [2-10, 35, 43, 46, 75]
— Brazil, p. 614 [642]
— China, p. 614 [642]
— churches' positions, p. 915 [913]
— deaths, p. 618 [645]
— England, p. 614 [642]
— Europe, pp. 623-624 [652-653]
— locations, p. 617 [644]
— North America, p. 627 [654-655]
— Oceania, pp. 628-629 [656-657]
— opinions about, pp. 1, 34, 36 [1, 39-40]
— postabortion reaction, p. 630 [660]
— risks, p. 618 [645]
— Romania, pp. 345, 614 [357, 642]
— Russia, p. 614 [642]
— South Africa, p. 614 [642]
— South America, pp. 629-630 [658-659]
— teenagers, p. 612 [640]
— Turkey, p. 614 [642]
— Wales, p. 614 [642]
— worldwide, pp. 619-620 [646-647]
Abuse, pp. 143, 150, 171, 178 [148, 157, 180, 185]
— prison inmates, pp. 108, 118-120, 123-124, 126 [113, 124-126, 129-130, 132]
— sexual, pp. 148, 348, 407 [155, 359, 425]
— spouse, p. 180 [187]
Accidents
See also: Automobiles; Motor vehicle accidents
— deaths, pp. 700, 712, 727 [723, 728, 736]
ACT scores, pp. 337-338 [347-348]
Acting and actors, pp. 555, 957 [582, 959]
— income, p. 453 [470]

Acute conditions, p. 376 [388]
Administrative occupations, pp. 570-571 [600-601]
Adoption, pp. 189-192 [194-198]
— and abortion, p. 3 [4]
Advertising
— and smoking, p. 98 [102]
Aerobics, pp. 936-937 [935-936]
Affirmative action
— opinions on, p. 39 [41]
Afghanistan
— age at first marriage, p. 812 [813]
— births, p. 631 [661]
— contraception, p. 659 [686]
— deaths, pp. 689, 714, 756 [716, 730, 763-764]
— employment, p. 519 [542]
— enrollment in school, pp. 271-272, 274-275 [285-288]
— enrollment in vocational school, p. 277 [289]
— fertility rates, p. 744 [753]
— illiteracy, p. 252 [269]
— infant deaths, p. 756 [763-764]
— life expectancy, p. 772 [778]
— literacy, p. 251 [268]
— marital status, p. 782 [786]
— marriages, pp. 812, 836 [813, 828]
— maternal deaths, pp. 689, 714 [716, 730]
— median age, p. 863 [859]
— occupations, p. 519 [542]
— population projections, p. 868 [865]
— population, pp. 782, 848 [786, 845]
— ratio of females to males, p. 860 [856]
— ratio of males to females, pp. 862-863 [858-859]
— teachers, p. 558 [584]
Africa
See also: Central African Republic; Middle East/North Africa; North Africa; South Africa; Sub-Saharan Africa
— abortions, pp. 620-621 [648-649]

Africa continued:
— age at first marriage, p. 811 [813]
— births to unmarried mothers, p. 637 [666]
— births, p. 658 [685]
— Catholic missionaries, p. 902 [901]
— clitoridectomy, pp. 171, 375 [180, 387]
— deaths, pp. 684, 686, 714, 764 [712-713, 730, 771]
— divorce, pp. 714, 799 [730, 804]
— educational attainment, p. 249 [267]
— employment and occupations, p. 518 [541]
— enrollment in school, pp. 262-263, 265, 267 [280-283]
— enrollment in vocational school, p. 269 [284]
— female-headed households, p. 207 [215]
— government, pp. 886-887 [883-884]
— HIV/AIDS, p. 404 [422]
— infant deaths, p. 764 [771]
— labor force, p. 534 [559]
— life expectancy, p. 779 [784]
— literacy, p. 249 [267]
— marital status, p. 789 [792]
— marriages, pp. 799-800, 802 [805-807]
— maternal deaths, p. 714 [730]
— population, p. 871 [868]
— religious denominations, p. 906 [906]
— teachers, p. 553 [580]
— time spent getting water, p. 183 [190]
— wages in agriculture, p. 450 [465]
— wages in construction, p. 450 [466]
— wages in manufacturing, p. 451 [467]
— wages in mining, p. 452 [468]
— wages in transport, p. 452 [469]
African American population *See:* Black population
Age of population
— 1970-1990 censuses, pp. 864-865 [860-862]
— 1992 estimates, pp. 874-875, 878 [872-873, 876]
— 35 and over in college, p. 281 [292]
— accident deaths, p. 683 [711]
— age of cocaine users, p. 130 [136]
— and sexual intercourse, pp. 930, 934 [929, 933]
— arrestees, p. 101 [105]
— births by obstetric procedure, p. 647 [674]
— births to teenage mothers, pp. 633-635 [663-665]
— births to unmarried mothers, p. 639 [668]
— brides and grooms, p. 839 [832]
— by Hispanic origin in 1992, pp. 877-878 [875-876]
— cancer deaths, p. 696 [720]
— childless women, p. 849 [846]
— contraceptive use, p. 675 [701]
— criminals, p. 113 [118]
— deaths, pp. 698-699 [721-722]
— earnings of full-time workers, p. 460 [478]
— elderly in poverty, p. 508 [529]
— elderly population worldwide, p. 854 [849]
— elderly, pp. 855-856, 859, 870 [850-851, 855, 867]
— enrolled in school, p. 283 [294]
— ever divorced, pp. 837-838 [830-831]
— ever married, pp. 837-838 [830-831]
— ever remarried, pp. 837-838 [830-831]

Age of population continued:
— firearm deaths, p. 712 [728]
— heart disease deaths, p. 713 [729]
— hospital utilization, p. 397 [413]
— householders, p. 211 [219]
— in labor force, pp. 542, 546 [566, 571]
— in prison, p. 127 [133]
— income of older women, p. 508 [530]
— jail inmates, p. 111 [116]
— labor force, pp. 541, 543 [565, 567]
— living arrangements, pp. 209, 212, 215 [217, 220, 223]
— marital status, pp. 786-787 [789-790]
— marriage ending in divorce, p. 846 [843]
— marriage ending in redivorce, p. 847 [844]
— married before age 20 (worldwide), p. 811 [813]
— married women, p. 802 [808]
— media exposure, p. 955 [956]
— median age of first alcohol and marijuana use, p. 129 [134]
— median age of first use of cocaine, p. 130 [135]
— median age, p. 865 [862]
— mothers delivering by cesarean section, p. 640 [669]
— mothers who smoke, p. 646 [673]
— mothers with medical risk factors, p. 644 [672]
— mothers, pp. 632, 650 [662, 676]
— motor vehicle accident victims, pp. 742-743 [751-752]
— murder defendants and victims, p. 152 [159]
— not enrolled in school, p. 286 [295]
— number of sex partners, p. 928 [926]
— projections, p. 876 [874]
— sexual harassment, p. 330 [340]
— single mothers, p. 224 [234]
— single women, p. 220 [229]
— suicide victims, p. 741 [749]
— urban and rural, p. 867 [864]
— victims of crime, pp. 146, 160, 163, 173-174 [153, 169, 173, 181-182]
— victims of violence, pp. 155, 683 [163, 711]
— voters for U.S. representatives, p. 893 [890]
— with chronic conditions, p. 378 [391]
— with injuries, p. 382 [395]
— women divorced after first marriage, pp. 825, 837-838 [820, 830-831]
— women ever married, p. 826 [821]
— women having abortions, pp. 610, 613, 616 [638, 641, 643]
— women suffering fetal losses, p. 610 [638]
— women with children, p. 851 [847]
Agnostic religon, pp. 912-913 [910]
Agriculture
— wages (Africa), p. 450 [465]
— wages (Asia), p. 454 [471]
— wages (Europe), p. 469 [489]
— wages (Latin America/Caribbean), p. 480 [498]
Agriculture and mining employment, p. 561 [588]
Aid to Families with Dependent Children *See:* Government assistance programs
AIDS, pp. 353, 403 [362, 421]
See: See also HIV/AIDS
— effect on sexual behavior, p. 922 [918]

Numbers following p. or pp. are page references. Numbers in [ ] are table references.

AIDS continued:
— in metropolitan areas, p. 346 [358]
— testing (opinions about), p. 71 [75]
Air Force Academy
— sexual harassment, pp. 605-609 [633-637]
Alabama
   See also: Birmingham, Alabama
— Catholic marriages, p. 908 [908]
— Catholic sisters, p. 904 [904]
— child rape victims, pp. 138-139 [142-143]
— college enrollment, p. 280 [291]
— elective offices, p. 895 [892]
— imprisonment, p. 114 [119]
— prisoners under sentence of death, p. 115 [120]
— teacher salaries, p. 496 [518]
— WIC Program grants, p. 445 [458]
Alaska
— Catholic marriages, p. 908 [908]
— Catholic sisters, p. 904 [904]
— college enrollment, p. 280 [291]
— teacher salaries, p. 495 [518]
— WIC Program grants, p. 446 [458]
Albania
— births, p. 641 [670]
— deaths, pp. 702, 706, 759 [725-726, 766]
— divorce, p. 814 [816]
— employment, pp. 520, 538 [543, 563]
— enrollment in school, pp. 289-291, 293 [296-299]
— enrollment in vocational school, p. 294 [300]
— fertility rates, p. 745 [754]
— infant deaths, p. 759 [766]
— life expectancy, p. 773 [779]
— marital status, p. 783 [787]
— marriages, pp. 815, 820, 824 [817-819]
— occupations, p. 520 [543]
— population projections, p. 869 [866]
— population, pp. 783, 852 [787, 848]
— ratio of females to males, p. 860 [856]
— ratio of males to females, p. 862 [858]
— teachers, p. 564 [592]
Alcohol, pp. 178, 348-349, 353, 390 [185, 359-360, 362, 404]
— and eating disorders, p. 357 [367]
— and injuries, p. 351 [361]
— and violence, pp. 165-166 [174-175]
— assistance funds for victims, p. 159 [168]
— jail inmates, p. 108 [113]
— use by arrestees, p. 129 [134]
— use by college students, pp. 354-355, 947 [364-365, 943]
— use by criminals, p. 113 [118]
— use by high school seniors, p. 314 [320]
— use by juveniles, pp. 143, 145 [148, 151-152]
— use during pregnancy, pp. 354, 414 [363, 432]
— Victims of Crimes Act funding, p. 159 [167]
Algeria
— births, p. 654 [681]
— contraception, p. 667 [692]
— deaths, pp. 684, 686, 733, 762 [712-713, 741, 768]
— employment, p. 518 [541]

Algeria continued:
— enrollment in school, pp. 263, 265, 267 [281-283]
— enrollment in vocational school, p. 269 [284]
— fertility rates, p. 749 [757]
— government, p. 887 [884]
— illiteracy, p. 249 [267]
— infant deaths, p. 762 [768]
— labor force, p. 534 [559]
— life expectancy, p. 776 [781]
— literacy, p. 257 [274]
— marital status, p. 794 [799]
— marriages, pp. 799-800 [805-806]
— maternal deaths, p. 733 [741]
— occupations, p. 518 [541]
— population projections, p. 874 [871]
— population, pp. 220, 794, 858 [228, 799, 853]
Allowances, p. 423 [442]
Alzheimer's disease, pp. 377-378 [389-390]
American Indian/Eskimo/Aleut population
— 1992 estimates, pp. 874-875, 877-878 [872-873, 875-876]
— ACT scores, p. 337 [347]
— alcohol abuse, p. 349 [360]
— and alcohol, p. 353 [362]
— birth rates, p. 632 [662]
— births to teenage mothers, p. 649 [675]
— births to unmarried mothers, p. 649 [675]
— births, p. 649 [675]
— college enrollment, p. 279 [290]
— degrees conferred, pp. 235, 237, 239 [249, 252, 255]
— displaced homemakers, pp. 196, 504-506 [203, 524-527]
— earnings, pp. 491, 494 [514, 517]
— educational attainment, pp. 248, 512 [265, 533]
— employment, p. 529 [554]
— Federal government, p. 566 [594-595]
— in elective offices, p. 898 [896]
— in poverty, p. 512 [533]
— income, p. 420 [438]
— low birth weight, p. 649 [675]
— occupations, pp. 570-571 [600-601]
— physics students, p. 296 [301]
— prenatal care, p. 649 [675]
— SAT scores, p. 342 [354]
— single mothers' poverty status, pp. 514-515 [536-537]
— single mothers, p. 513 [534-535]
— spouse murders, p. 152 [159]
— veterans, p. 604 [632]
American Samoa
— births, p. 655 [683]
— contraception, p. 669 [696]
— deaths, pp. 736-737, 763 [745-746, 770]
— divorce, p. 843 [839]
— enrollment in school, pp. 307-310 [312-315]
— enrollment in vocational school, p. 311 [316]
— fertility rates, p. 751 [759]
— households, p. 216 [224]
— infant deaths, p. 763 [770]
— life expectancy, p. 778 [783]
— marriages, pp. 836, 845 [829, 842]

Numbers following p. or pp. are page references. Numbers in [ ] are table references.

Amniocentesis, p. 647 [674]
Amphetamines
— use by juveniles, p. 145 [151]
— use by prison inmates, p. 137 [141]
Amusement parks
— visits, p. 958 [961]
Andorra
— births, p. 641 [670]
— fertility rates, p. 745 [754]
— infant deaths, p. 759 [766]
— life expectancy, p. 773 [779]
— marriages, p. 824 [819]
Anemia
— mothers, p. 644 [672]
Anglican religion, pp. 911-914 [910-911]
Angola
— births, p. 656 [684]
— deaths, p. 764 [771]
— employment, p. 518 [541]
— enrollment in school, pp. 262-263, 265, 267 [280-283]
— enrollment in vocational school, p. 269 [284]
— fertility rates, p. 752 [760]
— illiteracy, p. 249 [267]
— infant deaths, p. 764 [771]
— life expectancy, p. 779 [784]
— literacy, p. 258 [276]
— marital status, p. 796 [802]
— occupations, p. 518 [541]
— population projections, p. 880 [878]
— population, pp. 796, 865 [802, 863]
Anguilla
— births, p. 643 [671]
— fertility rates, p. 748 [756]
— infant deaths, p. 760 [767]
— life expectancy, p. 775 [780]
— marital status, p. 784 [788]
— marriages, p. 836 [829]
— population, p. 784 [788]
Announcers, p. 555 [582]
— income, p. 453 [470]
Anorexia nervosa, p. 357 [367]
Antigua and Barbuda
— births, p. 643 [671]
— contraception, pp. 664-665 [690-691]
— deaths, p. 760 [767]
— divorce, p. 828 [824]
— enrollment in school, pp. 298-299 [303-304]
— fertility rates, p. 748 [756]
— government, p. 887 [884]
— infant deaths, p. 760 [767]
— life expectancy, p. 775 [780]
— marriages, pp. 834-835 [827-828]
— population, p. 859 [854]
Architects and architecture, p. 555 [581-582]
— degrees, pp. 231, 233, 236, 244 [245, 247, 251, 259]
— income, p. 453 [470]
Argentina
— births to unmarried mothers, p. 637 [666]

Argentina continued:
— births, p. 643 [671]
— cigarette smoking, p. 372 [382]
— deaths, pp. 717, 722, 726, 760 [733-735, 767]
— employment, p. 521 [544]
— enrollment in school, pp. 296, 298-299, 301 [302-305]
— enrollment in vocational school, p. 302 [306]
— fertility rates, p. 748 [756]
— illiteracy, p. 256 [273]
— infant deaths, p. 760 [767]
— labor force, p. 539 [564]
— life expectancy, p. 775 [780]
— literacy, p. 255 [272]
— marital status, p. 784 [788]
— marriages, pp. 829, 831, 834 [825-827]
— maternal deaths, p. 726 [735]
— occupations, p. 521 [544]
— population projections, p. 873 [870]
— population, pp. 218, 784, 857 [226, 788, 852]
— teachers, p. 568 [598]
Arizona
See also: Phoenix, Arizona
— Catholic marriages, p. 908 [908]
— Catholic sisters, p. 904 [904]
— college enrollment, p. 280 [291]
— elective offices, p. 895 [892]
— imprisonment, p. 114 [119]
— prisoners under sentence of death, p. 115 [120]
— teacher salaries, p. 495 [518]
— WIC Program grants, p. 445 [458]
Arkansas
— Catholic marriages, p. 908 [908]
— Catholic sisters, p. 904 [904]
— child rape victims, p. 139 [143]
— college enrollment, p. 280 [291]
— elective offices, p. 895 [892]
— teacher salaries, p. 496 [518]
— WIC Program grants, p. 445 [458]
Armenia
— births, p. 642 [670]
— contraception, p. 674 [700]
— divorce, p. 803 [809]
— enrollment in school, p. 275 [288]
— fertility rates, p. 754 [762]
— infant deaths, p. 766 [772]
— life expectancy, p. 781 [785]
— marital status, p. 798 [803]
— marriages, pp. 804, 807, 810 [810-812]
— population, p. 798 [803]
Arrestees
— charges, p. 102 [106-107]
Arson
— imprisonment, pp. 108, 124 [113, 130]
— juvenile offenses, p. 143 [148]
Art and arts
— art fairs, p. 949 [947]
— art museums, pp. 948-949, 951 [945-946, 949]
— artists' income, pp. 453, 459 [470, 476]

Numbers following p. or pp. are page references. Numbers in [ ] are table references.

Art and arts continued:
— artists, pp. 555, 557 [582-583]
— attendance at events, pp. 948-949, 951 [945-947, 949]
— broadcast, pp. 952-954 [951-954]
— lessons, p. 952 [950]
— ownership, p. 958 [960]
— participation, pp. 957-958 [959-960]
Arthritis, p. 378 [391]
Artificial insemination
— attitudes of nuns, p. 45 [46]
Artificial joints, p. 409 [427]
Aruba
— births, p. 643 [671]
— divorce, p. 828 [824]
— fertility rates, p. 748 [756]
— infant deaths, p. 760 [767]
— life expectancy, p. 775 [780]
— marital status, p. 784 [788]
— marriages, p. 834 [827]
— population, p. 784 [788]
Asia/Near East
   See also: Near East
— abortions, pp. 621-622 [650-651]
— age at first marriage, p. 812 [813]
— allocation of time, pp. 186, 188 [191-192]
— births to unmarried mothers, p. 636 [666]
— births, pp. 631, 658 [661, 685]
— cigarette smoking, p. 370 [380]
— contraception, pp. 659-660 [686-687]
— deaths, pp. 689-690, 692, 755-756 [716-718]
— divorce, p. 803 [809]
— educational attainment, p. 252 [269]
— employment, pp. 519, 535 [542, 560]
— enrollment in school, pp. 271-272, 274-275 [285-288]
— enrollment in vocational school, p. 277 [289]
— female-headed households, p. 207 [215]
— fertility rates, p. 744 [753]
— HIV/AIDS, p. 401 [419]
— housework, pp. 186, 188 [191-192]
— illiteracy, p. 252 [269]
— infant deaths, pp. 755-756 [763-764]
— labor force, pp. 522, 524, 536 [545, 547, 561]
— life expectancy, p. 772 [778]
— literacy, p. 252 [269]
— marital status, p. 790 [793]
— marriages, pp. 804, 807, 810 [810-812]
— maternal deaths, p. 689 [716]
— population projections, p. 868 [865]
— population, pp. 848, 871 [845, 868]
— ratio of females to males, p. 860 [856]
— ratio of males to females, p. 863 [859]
— religious denominations, p. 907 [907]
— teachers, p. 558 [584]
— time spent getting water, p. 184 [190]
— wages in agriculture, p. 454 [471]
— wages in construction, p. 454 [472]
— wages in manufacturing, p. 455 [473]
— wages in mining, p. 457 [474]

Asia/Near East continued:
— wages in transport, p. 457 [475]
Asian and Pacific Islander population
— 1992 estimates, pp. 874-875, 877-878 [872-873, 875-876]
— ACT scores, p. 337 [347]
— birth rates, p. 632 [662]
— births to teenage mothers, p. 649 [675]
— births to unmarried mothers, p. 649 [675]
— births, p. 649 [675]
— college enrollment, p. 279 [290]
— degrees conferred, pp. 235, 237, 239 [249, 252, 255]
— displaced homemakers, pp. 196, 504-506 [203, 524-527]
— earnings, pp. 491, 494 [514, 517]
— educational attainment, pp. 248, 512 [265, 533]
— employment, p. 529 [554]
— executives' income, pp. 79-80, 92 [83-84, 96]
— executives, pp. 77-78, 87-88 [80-82, 91-92]
— families, p. 200 [207]
— Federal Government employment, p. 566 [594-595]
— in elective offices, p. 898 [896]
— in poverty, p. 512 [533]
— income, p. 420 [438]
— labor force, pp. 533, 543 [558, 567]
— low birth weight, p. 649 [675]
— occupations, pp. 570-571 [600-601]
— prenatal care, p. 649 [675]
— SAT scores, p. 342 [354]
— sexual harassment, p. 331 [341]
— single mothers' poverty status, pp. 514-515 [536-537]
— single mothers, p. 513 [534-535]
— spouse murders, p. 152 [159]
— veterans, p. 604 [632]
— volunteerism, p. 899 [898]
Assault
   See also: Abuse; Sexual assault
— arrests, p. 102 [106]
— assistance funds for victims, pp. 158-159 [166-168]
— imprisonment, pp. 108, 123-124, 126 [113, 129-130, 132]
— juvenile offenses, p. 143 [148]
— perpetrators, pp. 104, 113 [109, 118]
— prison inmates, p. 118 [124]
— victims, pp. 153, 155, 157, 173, 176 [160-161, 163-165, 181, 183]
Asthma, p. 378 [391]
Astronomy *See:* Physics/Astronomy
Atherosclerosis
— deaths, p. 700 [723]
Athletes, p. 432 [451]
Athletic footwear sales, p. 447 [461]
Audio/video equipment
— gift preference, p. 12 [13]
Australia
— allocation of time, pp. 184, 186 [191-192]
— births to unmarried mothers, p. 636 [666]
— births, p. 655 [683]
— cigarette smoking, p. 373 [384]
— college professors, p. 559 [585]
— contraception, p. 669 [696]
— deaths, pp. 736-737, 739, 758, 763 [745-747, 765, 770]

Subject and Geographic Index

Australia continued:
— divorce, p. 843 [839]
— employment, p. 520 [543]
— enrollment in school, pp. 307-310 [312-315]
— female-headed households, p. 207 [215]
— fertility rates, p. 751 [759]
— housework, pp. 184, 186, 188 [191-193]
— infant deaths, pp. 758, 763 [765, 770]
— labor force, p. 537 [562]
— life expectancy, p. 778 [783]
— marital status, pp. 793, 795 [797, 801]
— marriages, pp. 843-845 [840-842]
— maternal deaths, p. 739 [747]
— occupations, p. 520 [543]
— population projections, p. 869 [866]
— population, pp. 795, 852 [801, 848]
— religion, p. 913 [911]
— teachers, p. 575 [604]
— wages in construction, p. 486 [508]
— wages in manufacturing, p. 486 [509]
— wages in mining, p. 487 [510]
— wages in transport, p. 487 [511]
Austria
— births to unmarried mothers, p. 636 [666]
— births, p. 641 [670]
— cigarette smoking, p. 371 [381]
— computers in school, p. 228 [239]
— contraception, p. 662 [688]
— deaths, pp. 702, 706, 711, 758-759 [725-727, 765-766]
— divorce, p. 814 [816]
— education, p. 335 [345]
— elderly population, p. 854 [849]
— employment, pp. 520, 538 [543, 563]
— enrollment in school, pp. 289-291, 293 [296-299]
— enrollment in vocational school, p. 294 [300]
— female-headed households, p. 207 [215]
— fertility rates, p. 745 [754]
— government, p. 886 [883]
— infant deaths, pp. 758-759 [765-766]
— labor force, p. 537 [562]
— life expectancy, p. 773 [779]
— marital status, p. 783 [787]
— marriages, pp. 815, 820, 824 [817-819]
— maternal deaths, p. 711 [727]
— occupations, p. 520 [543]
— population projections, p. 869 [866]
— population, pp. 783, 852 [787, 848]
— ratio of males to females, p. 861 [857]
— religion, p. 910 [909]
— teachers, p. 564 [592]
— violence against women, p. 179 [186]
Authors, p. 555 [582]
— income, p. 453 [470]
Automobiles
— accidents, pp. 123, 180 [129, 187]
— theft, pp. 102, 108, 124 [107, 113, 130]
Azerbaijan
— births, p. 642 [670]

Azerbaijan continued:
— contraception, p. 674 [700]
— divorce, p. 803 [809]
— enrollment in school, p. 275 [288]
— fertility rates, p. 754 [762]
— infant deaths, p. 766 [772]
— life expectancy, p. 781 [785]
— marital status, p. 798 [803]
— marriages, pp. 804, 807, 810 [810-812]
— population, p. 798 [803]
Backpacking, p. 937 [936]
Bahamas, The
— births to unmarried mothers, p. 637 [666]
— births, p. 643 [671]
— contraception, pp. 664, 666 [690-691]
— deaths, pp. 717, 722, 726, 760 [733-735, 767]
— divorce, p. 828 [824]
— enrollment in school, pp. 298-299, 301 [303-305]
— fertility rates, p. 748 [756]
— infant deaths, p. 760 [767]
— labor force, p. 539 [564]
— life expectancy, p. 775 [780]
— marital status, p. 784 [788]
— marriages, pp. 829, 832, 834 [825-827]
— maternal deaths, p. 726 [735]
— population, pp. 218, 784, 857 [226, 788, 852]
— religion, p. 911 [910]
— teachers, p. 568 [598]
Bahrain
— births, p. 632 [661]
— contraception, p. 660 [686]
— deaths, pp. 689-690, 757 [716-718, 764]
— divorce, p. 803 [809]
— employment, p. 519 [542]
— enrollment in school, pp. 271-272, 274-275 [285-288]
— enrollment in vocational school, p. 277 [289]
— fertility rates, p. 745 [753]
— households, p. 216 [224]
— illiteracy, p. 260 [277]
— infant deaths, p. 757 [764]
— labor force, p. 536 [561]
— life expectancy, p. 773 [778]
— literacy, p. 257 [274]
— marital status, p. 782 [786]
— marriages, pp. 805, 808, 810 [810-812]
— maternal deaths, p. 689 [716]
— occupations, p. 519 [542]
— population, pp. 782, 848 [786, 845]
— ratio of females to males, p. 860 [856]
— ratio of males to females, p. 862 [858]
— teachers, p. 558 [584]
Ballet
— attendance, pp. 948-949, 951 [945-946, 949]
— lessons, p. 952 [950]
— participation, p. 957 [959]
Baltics
— births, p. 658 [685]
Bangladesh
— age at first marriage, p. 812 [813]

Numbers following p. or pp. are page references. Numbers in [ ] are table references.

Bangladesh continued:
— births, p. 631 [661]
— cigarette smoking, p. 370 [380]
— contraception, pp. 659-660 [686-687]
— deaths, pp. 689-690, 692, 714, 755-756 [716-718, 730, 763-764]
— deaths of children, p. 715 [731]
— employment, pp. 519, 535 [542, 560]
— enrollment in school, pp. 271-272, 274-275 [285-288]
— enrollment in vocational school, p. 277 [289]
— fertility rates, p. 744 [753]
— fertility, p. 754 [761]
— illiteracy, p. 252 [269]
— infant deaths, pp. 755-756 [763-764]
— labor force, p. 536 [561]
— life expectancy, p. 772 [778]
— literacy, p. 251 [268]
— marital status, p. 782 [786]
— marriages, p. 810 [812]
— maternal deaths, pp. 689, 714 [716, 730]
— median age, p. 863 [859]
— occupations, p. 519 [542]
— population projections, p. 868 [865]
— population, pp. 782, 848 [786, 845]
— ratio of females to males, p. 860 [856]
— ratio of males to females, pp. 862-863 [858-859]
— religion, p. 907 [907]
— teachers, p. 558 [584]
Baptist religion, pp. 911-913 [910]
Barbados
— births, p. 643 [671]
— contraception, pp. 664, 666 [690-691]
— deaths, pp. 717, 722, 726, 760 [733-735, 767]
— divorce, p. 828 [824]
— employment, p. 521 [544]
— enrollment in school, pp. 296, 298-299, 301 [302-305]
— female-headed households, p. 207 [215]
— fertility rates, p. 748 [756]
— government, p. 887 [884]
— illiteracy, p. 256 [273]
— infant deaths, p. 760 [767]
— labor force, p. 539 [564]
— life expectancy, p. 775 [780]
— marital status, p. 784 [788]
— marriages, pp. 829, 832, 834 [825-827]
— maternal deaths, p. 726 [735]
— occupations, p. 521 [544]
— population, pp. 784, 857 [788, 852]
— ratio of males to females, p. 861 [857]
— religion, p. 911 [910]
— teachers, p. 568 [598]
"Barbie" doll, p. 426 [444]
Barbiturates
— use by juveniles, p. 145 [151]
— Use by prison inmates, p. 137 [141]
Baseball, p. 937 [936]
Basketball, pp. 936-937, 962 [935-936, 966]
Belarus
— abortions, p. 623 [652]

Belarus continued:
— births, p. 642 [670]
— contraception, p. 675 [700]
— deaths, p. 766 [772]
— divorce, p. 814 [816]
— enrollment in school, pp. 289-291, 293 [296-299]
— enrollment in vocational school, p. 294 [300]
— fertility rates, p. 754 [762]
— infant deaths, p. 766 [772]
— life expectancy, p. 781 [785]
— marital status, p. 798 [803]
— marriages, pp. 816, 820, 824 [817-819]
— population, p. 798 [803]
Belgium
— allocation of time, pp. 185-186 [191-192]
— births, p. 641 [670]
— cigarette smoking, p. 371 [381]
— contraception, pp. 662, 678 [688, 704]
— deaths, pp. 702, 707, 711, 758-759 [725-727, 765-766]
— education, p. 335 [345]
— elderly population, p. 854 [849]
— employment, pp. 520, 538 [543, 563]
— enrollment in school, pp. 289-291, 293 [296-299]
— enrollment in vocational school, p. 294 [300]
— female-headed households, p. 207 [215]
— fertility rates, p. 745 [754]
— households, p. 205 [213]
— housework, pp. 185-186 [191-192]
— infant deaths, pp. 758-759 [765-766]
— labor force, p. 537 [562]
— life expectancy, p. 774 [779]
— marital status, p. 783 [787]
— marriages, pp. 816, 820, 824 [817-819]
— maternal deaths, p. 711 [727]
— occupations, p. 520 [543]
— population projections, p. 869 [866]
— population, pp. 783, 852 [787, 848]
— wages in agriculture, p. 469 [489]
— wages in construction, p. 470 [490]
— wages in manufacturing, p. 472 [491]
— wages in mining, p. 474 [492]
Belize
— abortions, p. 627 [654]
— births to unmarried mothers, p. 637 [666]
— births, p. 643 [671]
— contraception, pp. 664, 666 [690-691]
— deaths, pp. 717, 722, 760 [733-734, 767]
— divorce, p. 828 [824]
— employment, p. 521 [544]
— enrollment in school, pp. 296, 298-299 [302-304]
— enrollment in vocational school, p. 302 [306]
— fertility rates, p. 748 [756]
— government, p. 887 [884]
— illiteracy, p. 256 [273]
— infant deaths, p. 760 [767]
— life expectancy, p. 775 [780]
— marital status, p. 784 [788]
— marriages, p. 834 [827]

Numbers following p. or pp. are page references. Numbers in [ ] are table references.

Belize continued:
— occupations, p. 521 [544]
— population, p. 784 [788]
— religion, p. 911 [910]
Benin
— age at first marriage, p. 811 [813]
— births, p. 656 [684]
— clitoridectomy, p. 375 [387]
— contraception, pp. 671, 673 [698-699]
— deaths, p. 764 [771]
— employment, p. 518 [541]
— enrollment in school, pp. 262-263, 265, 267 [280-283]
— enrollment in vocational school, p. 269 [284]
— fertility rates, p. 752 [760]
— illiteracy, p. 249 [267]
— infant deaths, p. 764 [771]
— life expectancy, p. 779 [784]
— literacy, p. 258 [276]
— marital status, p. 796 [802]
— marriages, p. 836 [829]
— occupations, p. 518 [541]
— population projections, p. 880 [878]
— population, pp. 219, 796, 865 [227, 802, 863]
Bermuda
— abortions, pp. 619, 627 [646, 654-655]
— births, p. 655 [682]
— deaths, pp. 734, 762 [742-743, 769]
— divorce, pp. 827, 841 [823, 835]
— enrollment in school, pp. 304-305 [307-308, 310]
— fertility rates, p. 750 [758]
— households, p. 205 [213]
— infant deaths, p. 762 [769]
— life expectancy, p. 777 [782]
— marriages, pp. 836, 842 [829, 838]
— teachers, p. 569 [599]
Bhutan
— births, p. 631 [661]
— deaths, pp. 689, 714, 756 [716, 730, 764]
— employment, p. 519 [542]
— enrollment in school, pp. 272, 275 [286, 288]
— fertility rates, p. 744 [753]
— government, pp. 886-887 [883-884]
— illiteracy, p. 252 [269]
— infant deaths, p. 756 [764]
— life expectancy, p. 772 [778]
— maternal deaths, pp. 689, 714 [716, 730]
— median age, p. 863 [859]
— occupations, p. 519 [542]
— population projections, p. 868 [865]
— population, p. 848 [845]
— ratio of females to males, p. 860 [856]
— ratio of males to females, pp. 862-863 [858-859]
— teachers, p. 558 [584]
Bicycling, pp. 936-937 [935-936]
Big band music, p. 956 [957]
Biological/life sciences
— degrees, pp. 231, 233, 236, 244 [245, 247, 251, 259]
— faculty, p. 582 [611]

Birmingham, Alabama
See also: Alabama
— AIDS, p. 346 [358]
— alcohol, p. 129 [134]
— arrestees, pp. 101-102 [105-107]
— drugs, pp. 129-132, 134 [134-139]
— school dropouts, p. 103 [108]
Birth control pill, pp. 675, 677, 681-683 [701-702, 708-710]
Births and birth rates, pp. 610-611, 632, 650-651 [638-639, 662, 676-677]
— Asia, p. 631 [661]
— attended, p. 652 [678]
— cesarean section, p. 640 [669]
— cost of cesarean delivery, p. 428 [446]
— cost of vaginal delivery, p. 429 [447]
— Europe, p. 641 [670]
— Latin America/Caribbean, p. 643 [671]
— median birth weight, p. 652 [678]
— mothers who smoke, p. 646 [673]
— mothers with medical risk factors, p. 644 [672]
— multiple, p. 653 [679-680]
— Near East, p. 631 [661]
— North Africa, p. 654 [681]
— North America, p. 655 [682]
— obstetric procedures, p. 647 [674]
— Oceania, p. 655 [683]
— out of wedlock, p. 195 [200]
— Sub-Saharan Africa, p. 656 [684]
— teenage mothers, pp. 440, 633-635, 649 [454, 663-665, 675]
— unmarried mothers (worldwide), p. 636 [666]
— unmarried mothers, pp. 638-639, 649 [667-668, 675]
Bisexual women
— HIV/AIDS, p. 405 [423]
Black population
— 1992 estimates, pp. 874-875, 877-878 [872-873, 875-876]
— abortions, p. 616 [643]
— ACT scores, p. 337 [347]
— adoption, pp. 189-190, 192 [194, 196, 198]
— and alcohol, p. 353 [362]
— approval ratings of President Reagan, p. 32 [36]
— arrestees, p. 101 [105]
— attitudes of clergy, p. 48 [47]
— birth rates, p. 632 [662]
— births by medical risk factors, p. 644 [672]
— births by mother's smoking status, p. 646 [673]
— births by obstetric procedure, p. 647 [674]
— births to teenage mothers, pp. 633-635, 649 [663-665, 675]
— births to unmarried mothers, pp. 195, 638-639, 649 [200, 667-668, 675]
— births, pp. 649-650, 652 [675-676, 678]
— cancer deaths, p. 730 [737]
— cancer, pp. 358, 361-362, 367, 695 [368-370, 376, 719]
— cholesterol levels, p. 380 [393]
— cigarette smoking, p. 368 [378]
— clergy, p. 919 [914]
— college enrollment, p. 279 [290]
— college freshmen, p. 947 [943]
— contraception, p. 682 [709]

Numbers following p. or pp. are page references. Numbers in [ ] are table references.

Black population continued:
— contraceptive use, p. 675 [701]
— criminals, p. 176 [183]
— death rates, p. 698 [721]
— deaths, pp. 699-701, 731 [722-724, 738]
— degrees conferred, pp. 235, 237, 239 [249, 252, 255]
— displaced homemakers, pp. 196, 504-506 [203, 524-527]
— divorce, p. 838 [831]
— drug use by arrestees, p. 130 [136]
— drug use, p. 132 [138]
— earnings, pp. 460, 467, 491, 494 [478, 485, 514, 517]
— educational attainment, pp. 248, 512 [265, 533]
— elderly in poverty, p. 508 [529]
— elderly, pp. 214, 855 [222, 850]
— employment, p. 529 [554]
— executives' income, pp. 86, 91-92 [89, 94-96]
— executives, pp. 87-88, 90, 93 [90-93, 97]
— families, pp. 199, 201-202 [206, 208-209]
— family breakups, p. 813 [814]
— Federal Government employment, p. 566 [594-595]
— fertility rates, p. 747 [755]
— firearm deaths, p. 712 [728]
— government assistance, pp. 424, 510 [443, 531]
— health care coverage, pp. 393-394 [408-410]
— high school dropouts, p. 316 [322-323]
— HIV positive prison inmates, p. 403 [421]
— homicide, p. 712 [728]
— imprisonment, pp. 111, 116, 122, 127 [116, 122, 128, 133]
— in elective offices, p. 898 [896]
— in poverty, p. 512 [533]
— income of married-couple families, p. 421 [439]
— income of older women, p. 508 [530]
— income, pp. 417, 420 [435, 438]
— infant deaths, p. 731 [738]
— job promotions, pp. 530-531 [556-557]
— labor force, pp. 526, 533, 543 [551, 558, 567]
— leisure, p. 948 [944]
— life expectancy, pp. 767-769 [773-776]
— living arrangements, p. 212 [220]
— low birth weight, p. 649 [675]
— marital status, pp. 212, 788 [220, 791]
— marriages, p. 838 [831]
— maternal deaths, p. 731 [738]
— media exposure, p. 955 [956]
— median earnings, pp. 484, 496 [506, 519]
— military personnel, pp. 588-593, 599-600, 602 [618-623, 627-628, 630]
— mothers in prison, p. 112 [117]
— mothers working, pp. 546, 549 [572, 575]
— multiple births, p. 653 [680]
— murder defendants and victims, p. 152 [159]
— number of sex partners, p. 928 [926]
— occupations, pp. 570-571 [600-601]
— parents working, p. 548 [574]
— physics students, pp. 246, 296 [262, 301]
— political views, p. 71 [74-75]
— prenatal care, p. 649 [675]
— prisoners under sentence of death, p. 115 [120]

Black population continued:
— religious preferences, p. 914 [912]
— SAT scores, p. 342 [354]
— school enrollment, pp. 283, 286 [294-295]
— self assessments, p. 73 [77]
— self esteem, p. 72 [76]
— sex discrimination in employment, p. 523 [546]
— sexual harassment, p. 331 [341]
— single mothers, pp. 513-515 [534-537]
— suicide, pp. 712, 741 [728, 749]
— teenage contraceptive use, p. 680 [707]
— teenage sexual activity, p. 934 [933-934]
— veterans, p. 604 [632]
— victims of crime, pp. 146, 160, 163, 173-174, 176 [153, 169, 173, 181-183]
— victims of violence, p. 151 [158]
— volunteerism, p. 899 [898]
— voter turnout, pp. 891, 893 [887, 890]
— wages, pp. 461, 479, 497-498, 500, 502 [479, 496, 520-523]
— wealth, p. 507 [528]
— work disabilities, p. 562 [589]
Blues (music), p. 956 [957]
Bolivia
— births, p. 643 [671]
— cigarette smoking, p. 372 [382]
— contraception, pp. 664, 666 [690-691]
— deaths, pp. 714, 726, 760 [730, 735, 767]
— employment, p. 521 [544]
— enrollment in school, pp. 296, 298, 300-301 [302-305]
— fertility rates, p. 748 [756]
— government, p. 887 [884]
— illiteracy, p. 256 [273]
— infant deaths, p. 760 [767]
— labor force, p. 539 [564]
— life expectancy, p. 775 [780]
— literacy, p. 255 [272]
— marital status, pp. 785, 792 [788, 795]
— maternal deaths, pp. 714, 726 [730, 735]
— occupations, p. 521 [544]
— population projections, p. 873 [870]
— population, pp. 218, 785, 857 [226, 788, 852]
Books
— gift preference, p. 12 [13]
Bosnia and Herzegovina
— births, p. 642 [670]
— fertility rates, p. 754 [762]
— infant deaths, p. 766 [772]
— life expectancy, p. 781 [785]
— marital status, p. 797 [803]
— population, p. 797 [803]
Botswana
— abortions, p. 620 [648]
— births, p. 656 [684]
— contraception, pp. 671, 673 [698-699]
— deaths, pp. 714, 740, 764 [730, 748, 771]
— employment, p. 518 [541]
— enrollment in school, pp. 263, 265, 267 [281-283]
— enrollment in vocational school, p. 269 [284]

Numbers following p. or pp. are page references. Numbers in [ ] are table references.

Botswana continued:
— female-headed households, p. 207 [215]
— fertility rates, p. 752 [760]
— fertility, p. 753 [761]
— illiteracy, p. 249 [267]
— infant deaths, p. 764 [771]
— labor force, p. 534 [559]
— life expectancy, p. 779 [784]
— literacy, p. 258 [276]
— marital status, p. 796 [802]
— marriages, pp. 800-802 [805-807]
— maternal deaths, pp. 714, 740 [730, 748]
— occupations, p. 518 [541]
— population projections, p. 880 [878]
— population, pp. 219, 796, 859, 865 [227, 802, 854, 863]
— ratio of males to females, p. 861 [857]
— time spent getting water, p. 183 [190]
— wages in agriculture, p. 450 [465]
Bowling, p. 937 [936]
Brain cancer, p. 365 [373]
Brazil
— abortion, p. 614 [642]
— births, p. 643 [671]
— cigarette smoking, p. 372 [382]
— college professors, p. 559 [585]
— contraception, pp. 664, 666 [690-691]
— deaths, pp. 717, 722, 726, 760 [733-735, 767]
— divorce, pp. 826, 828 [822, 824]
— employment, p. 521 [544]
— enrollment in school, pp. 296, 298, 300-301 [302-305]
— fertility rates, p. 748 [756]
— illiteracy, p. 256 [273]
— infant deaths, p. 760 [767]
— labor force, p. 539 [564]
— life expectancy, p. 775 [780]
— literacy, p. 255 [272]
— marital status, p. 785 [788]
— marriages, pp. 829, 832, 834 [825-827]
— maternal deaths, p. 726 [735]
— occupations, p. 521 [544]
— population projections, p. 873 [870]
— population, pp. 218, 785, 857 [226, 788, 852]
— religion, p. 911 [910]
— teachers, p. 568 [598]
Breast cancer, pp. 358, 361-366, 695 [368-375, 719]
— and diet, p. 386 [400]
Breast implants, p. 409 [427]
— lawsuit, p. 94 [98]
British Virgin Islands
— births, p. 643 [671]
— deaths, pp. 718, 722, 760 [733-734, 767]
— divorce, p. 828 [824]
— enrollment in school, pp. 296, 298, 300 [302-304]
— enrollment in vocational school, p. 303 [306]
— fertility rates, p. 748 [756]
— infant deaths, p. 760 [767]
— life expectancy, p. 775 [780]
— marriages, pp. 834, 836 [827, 829]

British Virgin Islands continued:
— religion, p. 912 [910]
Bronchitis, p. 378 [391]
Brunei Darussalam
— births, p. 631 [661]
— deaths, p. 756 [764]
— divorce, p. 803 [809]
— employment, p. 519 [542]
— enrollment in school, pp. 271-272, 274-275 [285-288]
— enrollment in vocational school, p. 277 [289]
— fertility rates, p. 744 [753]
— illiteracy, p. 252 [269]
— infant deaths, p. 756 [764]
— labor force, p. 536 [561]
— life expectancy, p. 772 [778]
— marital status, p. 782 [786]
— marriages, pp. 805, 808, 810 [810-812]
— occupations, p. 519 [542]
— population, p. 782 [786]
— ratio of females to males, p. 860 [856]
— teachers, p. 558 [584]
Buddhist religion, pp. 907-908 [907]
Bulgaria
— abortions, pp. 620, 623-624 [647, 652-653]
— allocation of time, pp. 185, 187 [191-192]
— births to unmarried mothers, p. 636 [666]
— births, p. 641 [670]
— contraception, p. 662 [688]
— deaths, pp. 702, 707, 711, 759 [725-727, 766]
— divorce, p. 814 [816]
— elderly population, p. 854 [849]
— employment, p. 520 [543]
— enrollment in school, pp. 289-290, 292-293 [296-299]
— enrollment in vocational school, p. 294 [300]
— fertility rates, p. 745 [754]
— housework, pp. 185, 187 [191-192]
— infant deaths, p. 759 [766]
— labor force, p. 537 [562]
— life expectancy, p. 774 [779]
— marital status, pp. 783, 790 [787, 794]
— marriages, pp. 816, 820, 824 [817-819]
— maternal deaths, p. 711 [727]
— occupations, p. 520 [543]
— population projections, p. 869 [866]
— population, pp. 783, 852 [787, 848]
— teachers, p. 564 [592]
Bulimia nervosa, pp. 357, 390 [367, 404]
Burglary
— arrests, p. 102 [106]
— imprisonment, pp. 108, 123-124, 126 [113, 129-130, 132]
— juvenile offenses, p. 143 [148]
— perpetrators, p. 104 [109]
Burkina
— age at first marriage, p. 811 [813]
— births, p. 656 [684]
— clitoridectomy, p. 375 [387]
— contraception, pp. 671, 673 [698-699]
— deaths, pp. 714, 740, 764 [730, 748, 771]

Numbers following p. or pp. are page references. Numbers in [ ] are table references.

Burkina continued:
— employment, p. 518 [541]
— enrollment in school, pp. 262-263, 265, 267 [280-283]
— enrollment in vocational school, p. 269 [284]
— fertility rates, p. 752 [760]
— government, p. 886 [883]
— HIV/AIDS, p. 404 [422]
— illiteracy, p. 249 [267]
— infant deaths, p. 764 [771]
— life expectancy, p. 779 [784]
— literacy, p. 258 [276]
— marital status, pp. 789, 796 [792, 802]
— maternal deaths, pp. 714, 740 [730, 748]
— occupations, p. 518 [541]
— population projections, p. 880 [878]
— population, pp. 796, 865 [802, 863]
— teachers, p. 553 [580]
— time spent getting water, p. 183 [190]

Burma
  See also: Myanmar
— births, p. 631 [661]
— deaths, p. 756 [764]
— fertility rates, p. 744 [753]
— infant deaths, p. 756 [764]
— life expectancy, p. 772 [778]
— marital status, p. 782 [786]
— median age, p. 863 [859]
— population, p. 782 [786]
— ratio of males to females, p. 863 [859]

Burundi
— births, p. 656 [684]
— contraception, pp. 671, 673 [698-699]
— deaths, p. 764 [771]
— employment, p. 518 [541]
— enrollment in school, pp. 262-263, 265, 267 [280-283]
— enrollment in vocational school, p. 269 [284]
— fertility rates, p. 752 [760]
— government, p. 886 [883]
— HIV/AIDS, p. 404 [422]
— illiteracy, p. 249 [267]
— infant deaths, p. 764 [771]
— labor force, p. 534 [559]
— life expectancy, p. 779 [784]
— literacy, p. 258 [276]
— marital status, pp. 789, 796 [792, 802]
— occupations, p. 518 [541]
— population projections, p. 880 [878]
— population, pp. 219, 796, 865 [227, 802, 863]
— teachers, p. 553 [580]

Bush, George (President)
— appointed offices, p. 882 [879]

Business management degrees, pp. 231, 233, 236, 244 [245, 247, 251, 259]

Business owners, p. 100 [104]

Cable network preferences, p. 950 [948]

Calcium
— recommended consumption, p. 388 [401]

California
  See also: Los Angeles, California; San Diego, California
— abortions, p. 617 [644]

California continued:
— Catholic marriages, p. 908 [908]
— Catholic sisters, p. 904 [904]
— college enrollment, p. 280 [291]
— executives' income, p. 85 [88]
— imprisonment, p. 114 [119]
— politics, p. 883 [881]
— prisoners under sentence of death, p. 115 [120]
— teacher salaries, p. 495 [518]
— WIC Program grants, p. 444 [458]

Calisthenics, pp. 936-937 [935-936]

Cambodia
— births, p. 631 [661]
— deaths, p. 756 [764]
— employment, p. 519 [542]
— fertility rates, p. 744 [753]
— illiteracy, p. 252 [269]
— infant deaths, p. 756 [764]
— life expectancy, p. 772 [778]
— literacy, p. 251 [268]
— median age, p. 863 [859]
— occupations, p. 519 [542]
— population projections, p. 868 [865]
— population, p. 848 [845]
— ratio of males to females, p. 863 [859]

Cameroon
— age at first marriage, p. 811 [813]
— births, p. 656 [684]
— contraception, pp. 671, 673 [698-699]
— deaths, pp. 714, 740, 764 [730, 748, 771]
— employment, p. 518 [541]
— enrollment in school, pp. 262-263, 265, 267 [280-283]
— enrollment in vocational school, p. 269 [284]
— fertility rates, p. 752 [760]
— illiteracy, p. 249 [267]
— infant deaths, p. 764 [771]
— labor force, p. 534 [559]
— life expectancy, p. 779 [784]
— marital status, p. 796 [802]
— maternal deaths, pp. 714, 740 [730, 748]
— occupations, p. 518 [541]
— population projections, p. 880 [878]
— population, pp. 219, 796, 865 [227, 802, 863]

Camping, p. 937 [936]

Canada
— abortions, p. 627 [654-655]
— allocation of time, pp. 184, 186 [191-192]
— attitudes toward working mothers, p. 21 [24]
— births, p. 655 [682]
— Catholic sisters, p. 903 [903]
— cigarette smoking, p. 373 [383]
— contraception, pp. 668-669, 678 [694-695, 704]
— deaths, pp. 734-735, 758, 762 [742-744, 765, 769]
— divorce, pp. 827, 841 [823, 835]
— educational attainment, p. 261 [278]
— employment, p. 520 [543]
— enrollment in school, pp. 304-305, 312 [307-310, 317]
— female-headed households, p. 207 [215]

Numbers following p. or pp. are page references. Numbers in [ ] are table references.

Canada continued:
— fertility rates, p. 750 [758]
— government, p. 886 [883]
— housework, pp. 184, 186 [191-192]
— infant deaths, pp. 758, 762 [765, 769]
— labor force, p. 537 [562]
— life expectancy, p. 777 [782]
— marital status, pp. 792, 795 [796, 800]
— marriages, pp. 841-842 [836-838]
— maternal deaths, p. 735 [744]
— occupations, p. 520 [543]
— population projections, p. 869 [866]
— population, pp. 795, 852 [800, 848]
— rape, p. 171 [180]
— teachers, p. 569 [599]
Cancer, p. 363 [371]
— and diet, p. 386 [400]
— breast, pp. 358, 361-362, 366, 695 [368-370, 374, 719]
— colorectal, p. 366 [374]
— deaths, pp. 365, 683, 696, 700, 727 [373, 711, 720, 723, 736]
— incidence, p. 364 [372]
— lung, pp. 366-367, 730 [374, 376, 737]
— risks, p. 365 [373]
— sites, pp. 364, 366 [372, 375]
Cape Verde
— births, p. 656 [684]
— deaths, pp. 684, 686, 740, 764 [712-713, 748, 771]
— employment, p. 518 [541]
— enrollment in school, pp. 262-263, 265 [280-282]
— enrollment in vocational school, p. 269 [284]
— fertility rates, p. 752 [760]
— illiteracy, p. 249 [267]
— infant deaths, p. 764 [771]
— life expectancy, p. 779 [784]
— marital status, p. 796 [802]
— maternal deaths, p. 740 [748]
— occupations, p. 518 [541]
— population, pp. 796, 859, 866 [802, 854, 863]
Cardiac disease, p. 644 [672]
Career advancement, pp. 55, 64 [53, 66]
CAT scans, p. 411 [429]
Cataracts, p. 378 [391]
Catholics, pp. 906-907, 910-914 [906, 909-911]
— contraceptive use, p. 680 [706]
— marriages, p. 908 [908]
— missionaries (worldwide), p. 902 [901]
— sisters (Canada), p. 903 [903]
— sisters, pp. 903-904, 906 [902, 904-905]
Cayman Islands
— births, p. 643 [671]
— deaths, pp. 718, 722, 760 [733-734, 767]
— divorce, p. 828 [824]
— fertility rates, p. 748 [756]
— infant deaths, p. 760 [767]
— life expectancy, p. 775 [780]
— marital status, p. 792 [795]
— marriages, p. 835 [827]
Central African Republic
   See also: Africa; Middle East/North Africa; North Africa;
   South Africa; Sub-Saharan Africa

Central African Republic continued:
— births, p. 656 [684]
— clitoridectomy, p. 375 [387]
— deaths, pp. 714, 740, 764 [730, 748, 771]
— employment, p. 518 [541]
— enrollment in school, pp. 262-263, 265, 267 [280-283]
— enrollment in vocational school, p. 269 [284]
— fertility rates, p. 752 [760]
— HIV/AIDS, p. 404 [422]
— illiteracy, p. 249 [267]
— infant deaths, p. 764 [771]
— life expectancy, p. 779 [784]
— literacy, p. 258 [276]
— maternal deaths, pp. 714, 740 [730, 748]
— occupations, p. 518 [541]
— population projections, p. 880 [878]
— population, pp. 219, 866 [227, 863]
— ratio of males to females, p. 861 [857]
— teachers, p. 553 [580]
Cerebrovascular disease
— deaths, p. 727 [736]
Cervix
— cancer, pp. 364, 366 [372, 375]
— incompetent, p. 644 [672]
Cesarean delivery, pp. 411-412, 640 [431, 669]
— cost, p. 428 [446]
Chad
— births, p. 656 [684]
— clitoridectomy, p. 375 [387]
— deaths, pp. 714, 740, 764 [730, 748, 771]
— employment, p. 518 [541]
— enrollment in school, pp. 263, 265, 267 [281-283]
— enrollment in vocational school, p. 269 [284]
— fertility rates, p. 752 [760]
— illiteracy, p. 249 [267]
— infant deaths, p. 764 [771]
— life expectancy, p. 779 [784]
— literacy, p. 258 [276]
— marital status, p. 796 [802]
— maternal deaths, pp. 714, 740 [730, 748]
— occupations, p. 518 [541]
— population projections, p. 880 [878]
— population, pp. 796, 866 [802, 863]
— teachers, p. 553 [580]
Channel Islands
   See also: Guernsey; Jersey
— abortions, p. 623 [652]
— deaths, pp. 702, 707 [725-726]
— divorce, p. 814 [816]
— marital status, p. 790 [794]
— marriages, p. 824 [819]
Charitable contributions, pp. 430, 443 [448-449, 457]
Chemical engineers
— salary, p. 492 [515]
Chemistry faculty, p. 582 [611]
Chicago, Illinois
   See also: Illinois
— AIDS, p. 346 [358]

Numbers following p. or pp. are page references. Numbers in [ ] are table references.

Chicago, Illinois continued:
— alcohol, p. 129 [134]
— arrestees, pp. 101-102 [105-107]
— drugs, pp. 129-132, 134 [134-135, 137-139]
— school dropouts, p. 103 [108]
Child abuse, p. 147 [154]
— assistance funds for victims, pp. 158-159 [166-168]
— imprisonment, pp. 108, 124 [113, 130]
Child care
— expenditures, p. 431 [450]
— opinions about, p. 43 [43]
— problems, p. 527 [552]
— time spent, pp. 223, 225-226 [233, 236-237]
Child support, p. 424 [443]
Children
— adoptive, p. 198 [205]
— attitudes toward (Japan), p. 25 [30]
— discipline, p. 224 [235]
— firearm deaths, p. 712 [728]
— in female-headed households, p. 197 [204]
— in married-couple households, p. 198 [205]
— in substitute care, p. 194 [199]
— living arrangements, p. 196 [202]
— number, p. 851 [847]
— of displaced homemakers, p. 196 [203]
— presence in households, p. 210 [218]
— sexual abuse, pp. 148, 407 [155, 425]
Chile
— abortions, pp. 619, 629-630 [646, 658-659]
— births to unmarried mothers, p. 637 [666]
— births, p. 643 [671]
— cigarette smoking, p. 372 [382]
— college professors, p. 559 [585]
— contraception, p. 664 [690]
— deaths, pp. 718, 722, 726, 760 [733-735, 767]
— divorce, p. 828 [824]
— employment, p. 521 [544]
— enrollment in school, pp. 296, 298, 300-301 [302-305]
— enrollment in vocational school, p. 303 [306]
— female-headed households, p. 207 [215]
— fertility rates, p. 748 [756]
— illiteracy, p. 256 [273]
— infant deaths, p. 760 [767]
— labor force, p. 540 [564]
— life expectancy, p. 775 [780]
— literacy, p. 255 [272]
— marital status, p. 785 [788]
— marriages, pp. 829, 832, 835 [825-827]
— maternal deaths, p. 726 [735]
— occupations, p. 521 [544]
— population projections, p. 873 [870]
— population, pp. 218, 785, 857 [226, 788, 852]
China
— abortion, p. 614 [642]
— births, p. 631 [661]
— cigarette smoking, p. 370 [380]
— contraception, pp. 659, 661, 678 [686-687, 704]
— deaths, pp. 689, 755-756 [716, 763-764]

China continued:
— employment, pp. 519, 535 [542, 560]
— enrollment in school, pp. 271-272, 274-275 [285-288]
— enrollment in vocational school, p. 277 [289]
— fertility rates, p. 744 [753]
— illiteracy, p. 252 [269]
— infant deaths, pp. 755-756 [763-764]
— life expectancy, p. 772 [778]
— literacy, p. 251 [268]
— marital status, pp. 782, 790 [786, 793]
— maternal deaths, p. 689 [716]
— median age, p. 863 [859]
— occupations, p. 519 [542]
— population projections, p. 868 [865]
— population, pp. 782, 848 [786, 845]
— ratio of females to males, p. 860 [856]
— ratio of males to females, pp. 862-863 [858-859]
— teachers, p. 558 [584]
Chiropractic degrees, pp. 239, 241 [255-256]
Chlamydia
  See also: Sexually transmitted diseases
— teenagers, p. 382 [396]
Cholesterol levels, p. 380 [393]
Choreographers
— income, p. 459 [476]
Christian religion, pp. 906, 908, 913 [906-907, 911]
Chronic conditions, p. 378 [391]
— deaths, pp. 700, 727 [723, 736]
Church of England, pp. 906, 913 [906, 911]
Church of God, p. 912 [910]
Cigarette smoking, pp. 368-369, 390 [377-379, 404]
— advertising, p. 98 [102]
— Asia, p. 370 [380]
— college freshmen, p. 947 [943]
— during pregnancy, pp. 414, 633 [432, 663]
— Europe, p. 371 [381]
— expenditures, p. 443 [457]
— Latin America/Caribbean, p. 372 [382]
— Middle East, p. 374 [386]
— Near East, p. 370 [380]
— North Africa, p. 374 [386]
— North America, p. 373 [383]
— Oceania, p. 373 [384]
— Sub-Saharan Africa, p. 374 [385]
— use by juveniles, p. 145 [152]
Circumcision *See:* Clitoridectomy
Cirrhosis deaths, pp. 700, 727 [723, 736]
Civil Rights
— opinions on, p. 39 [41]
Classical music, pp. 948-949, 951 [945-946, 949]
— listening or viewing, pp. 952-953, 956 [951, 953, 957]
— participation, p. 957 [959]
— radio format preferences, p. 959 [962]
Clerical occupations, pp. 570-571 [600-601]
Clitoridectomy
— Africa, pp. 171, 375 [180, 387]
— Kenya, p. 171 [180]
Clothing
— cost, p. 449 [464]

Subject and Geographic Index

Clothing continued:
— expenditures, pp. 441, 443, 449 [456-457, 463]
— gift preference, p. 12 [13]
— pantyhose, p. 448 [462]
Cocaine, pp. 353, 356 [362, 366]
— use by arrestees, pp. 130-131 [135-137]
— use by juveniles, p. 144 [150]
— use by prison inmates, p. 137 [141]
— use during pregnancy, p. 414 [432]
Cohabitation, p. 923 [919]
Colds, p. 376 [388]
College enrollment *See:* Education
College professors
See also: Teachers
— salaries, p. 476 [494]
— trends in employment, p. 560 [586]
— worldwide, p. 559 [585]
Colombia
— births, p. 643 [671]
— cigarette smoking, p. 372 [382]
— contraception, pp. 664, 666 [690-691]
— deaths, pp. 718, 722, 726, 760 [733-735, 767]
— deaths of children, p. 715 [731]
— employment, p. 521 [544]
— enrollment in school, pp. 296, 298, 300-301 [302-305]
— enrollment in vocational school, p. 303 [306]
— fertility rates, p. 748 [756]
— illiteracy, p. 256 [273]
— infant deaths, p. 760 [767]
— labor force, p. 540 [564]
— life expectancy, p. 775 [780]
— literacy, p. 255 [272]
— marital status, p. 785 [788]
— marriages, pp. 829, 832 [825-826]
— maternal deaths, p. 726 [735]
— occupations, p. 521 [544]
— population projections, p. 873 [870]
— population, pp. 218, 785, 857 [226, 788, 852]
— teachers, p. 568 [598]
— violence against women, p. 179 [186]
Colon cancer, pp. 364, 366 [372, 375]
Colorado
— Catholic marriages, p. 908 [908]
— Catholic sisters, p. 904 [904]
— college enrollment, p. 280 [291]
— drugs, p. 130 [136]
— elective offices, p. 895 [892]
— imprisonment, p. 115 [119]
— teacher salaries, p. 495 [518]
— WIC Program grants, p. 445 [458]
Colorectal cancer, p. 366 [374]
Communications degrees, pp. 231, 233, 236, 244 [245, 247, 251, 259]
Comoros
— age at first marriage, p. 811 [813]
— births, p. 656 [684]
— deaths, p. 764 [771]
— employment, p. 518 [541]

Comoros continued:
— enrollment in school, pp. 262-263, 265, 267 [280-283]
— enrollment in vocational school, p. 269 [284]
— fertility rates, p. 752 [760]
— government, p. 887 [884]
— illiteracy, p. 249 [267]
— infant deaths, p. 764 [771]
— labor force, p. 534 [559]
— life expectancy, p. 779 [784]
— marital status, p. 796 [802]
— occupations, p. 518 [541]
— population, pp. 219, 796, 866 [227, 802, 863]
— teachers, p. 553 [580]
Composers, p. 555 [582]
— income, p. 453 [470]
Compuserve users, p. 954 [955]
Computer science
— degrees, pp. 231, 233, 236, 244 [245, 247, 251, 259]
— faculty, p. 582 [611]
Computers
— in school, pp. 227-231 [238-240, 243-244]
— Internet, p. 960 [963]
— occupations, pp. 570-571 [600-601]
— use by secretaries, p. 583 [612]
— use of online data services, pp. 99, 954, 961 [103, 955, 964]
— use out of school, pp. 229-230 [241-242]
Condom, pp. 675, 677, 682 [701-702, 709]
— female, p. 385 [399]
Congenital anomalies
— deaths, p. 727 [736]
Congo
— births, p. 656 [684]
— deaths, pp. 714, 740, 764 [730, 748, 771]
— employment, p. 518 [541]
— enrollment in school, pp. 262-263, 265, 267 [280-283]
— enrollment in vocational school, p. 269 [284]
— female-headed households, p. 207 [215]
— fertility rates, p. 752 [760]
— HIV/AIDS, p. 404 [422]
— illiteracy, p. 250 [267]
— infant deaths, p. 764 [771]
— life expectancy, p. 779 [784]
— literacy, p. 258 [276]
— maternal deaths, pp. 714, 740 [730, 748]
— occupations, p. 518 [541]
— population projections, p. 880 [878]
— population, pp. 219, 866 [227, 863]
— teachers, p. 553 [580]
Connecticut
— Catholic marriages, p. 908 [908]
— Catholic sisters, p. 904 [904]
— college enrollment, p. 280 [291]
— imprisonment, p. 114 [119]
— teacher salaries, p. 495 [518]
— WIC Program grants, p. 445 [458]
Constipation, p. 378 [391]
Construction
— employment, p. 561 [588]

Numbers following p. or pp. are page references. Numbers in [ ] are table references.

Construction continued:
— occupations, pp. 570-571 [600-601]
— wages (Africa), p. 450 [466]
— wages (Asia), p. 454 [472]
— wages (Europe), p. 470 [490]
— wages (Latin America/Caribbean), p. 481 [499]
— wages (Oceania), p. 486 [508]
Contraception, pp. 95, 385 [99, 399]
— Africa, pp. 667-668, 671, 673 [692-693, 698-699]
— and religious affiliation, p. 680 [706]
— Asia/Near East, pp. 659-660 [686-687]
— Europe, pp. 662-663 [688-689]
— Latin America/Caribbean, pp. 664-665 [690-691]
— methods, pp. 675, 677, 681-683 [701-702, 708-710]
— Norplant, p. 679 [705]
— North America, pp. 668-669 [694-695]
— Oceania, pp. 669-670 [696-697]
— Soviet Union, p. 674 [700]
— teenagers, p. 680 [707]
— worldwide, pp. 677-678 [703-704]
Cook Islands
— births, p. 655 [683]
— contraception, p. 669 [696]
— deaths, pp. 736, 738, 763 [745-746, 770]
— enrollment in school, pp. 307-308, 310 [312-313, 315]
— fertility rates, p. 751 [759]
— infant deaths, p. 763 [770]
— life expectancy, p. 778 [783]
— marriages, p. 845 [842]
— median age, p. 863 [859]
— ratio of males to females, p. 863 [859]
— teachers, p. 575 [604]
Core curriculum, p. 315 [321]
Corporations
— executives' income, pp. 79-80, 85, 91-92 [83-84, 88, 94-96]
— executives, pp. 77-78, 82, 84, 87-88, 90, 93 [80-82, 85-87, 90-93, 97]
Costa Rica
— births to unmarried mothers, p. 637 [666]
— births, p. 643 [671]
— contraception, pp. 664, 666 [690-691]
— deaths, pp. 718, 722, 726, 760 [733-735, 767]
— deaths of children, p. 715 [731]
— divorce, p. 828 [824]
— employment, p. 521 [544]
— enrollment in school, pp. 296, 298, 300-301 [302-305]
— enrollment in vocational school, p. 303 [306]
— fertility rates, p. 748 [756]
— illiteracy, p. 256 [273]
— infant deaths, p. 760 [767]
— labor force, p. 540 [564]
— life expectancy, p. 775 [780]
— literacy, p. 255 [272]
— marital status, p. 785 [788]
— marriages, pp. 829, 832, 835 [825-827]
— maternal deaths, p. 726 [735]
— occupations, p. 521 [544]
— population projections, p. 873 [870]

Costa Rica continued:
— population, pp. 218, 785, 857 [226, 788, 852]
— wages in agriculture, p. 480 [498]
— wages in construction, p. 481 [499]
— wages in manufacturing, p. 481 [500]
— wages in mining, p. 482 [501]
— wages in transport, p. 482 [502]
Cote d'Ivoire
— age at first marriage, p. 812 [813]
— births, p. 656 [684]
— cigarette smoking, p. 374 [385]
— clitoridectomy, p. 375 [387]
— contraception, pp. 671, 673, 677 [698-699, 703]
— deaths, p. 764 [771]
— employment, p. 518 [541]
— enrollment in school, pp. 262-263, 265, 267 [280-283]
— enrollment in vocational school, p. 269 [284]
— fertility rates, p. 752 [760]
— HIV/AIDS, p. 404 [422]
— illiteracy, p. 250 [267]
— infant deaths, p. 764 [771]
— life expectancy, p. 779 [784]
— literacy, p. 258 [276]
— marital status, p. 796 [802]
— occupations, p. 518 [541]
— population projections, p. 880 [878]
— population, pp. 796, 866 [802, 863]
— time spent getting water, p. 183 [190]
Counselors, pp. 570-571 [600-601]
Counterfeiting, p. 143 [148]
Country/western music, p. 956 [957]
Crafts
— occupations, pp. 570-571 [600-601]
— persons, p. 555 [582]
Croatia
— births, p. 642 [670]
— fertility rates, p. 754 [762]
— infant deaths, p. 766 [772]
— life expectancy, p. 781 [785]
— marital status, p. 797 [803]
— population, p. 797 [803]
Cuba
— abortions, pp. 620, 627 [647, 654]
— age at first marriage, p. 812 [813]
— births, p. 643 [671]
— contraception, p. 664 [690]
— deaths, pp. 718, 723, 726, 760 [733-735, 767]
— divorce, pp. 827-828 [823-824]
— employment, p. 521 [544]
— enrollment in school, pp. 296, 298, 300-301 [302-305]
— enrollment in vocational school, p. 303 [306]
— female-headed households, p. 207 [215]
— fertility rates, p. 748 [756]
— illiteracy, p. 256 [273]
— infant deaths, p. 760 [767]
— labor force, p. 540 [564]
— life expectancy, p. 775 [780]
— literacy, p. 255 [272]

Numbers following p. or pp. are page references. Numbers in [ ] are table references.

Cuba continued:
— marital status, p. 785 [788]
— marriages, pp. 829, 832, 835 [825-827]
— maternal deaths, p. 726 [735]
— occupations, p. 521 [544]
— population projections, p. 873 [870]
— population, pp. 218, 785, 857 [226, 788, 852]
— teachers, p. 568 [598]
Cyprus
— births, p. 632 [661]
— deaths, pp. 690, 693, 757 [717-718, 764]
— divorce, p. 803 [809]
— employment, p. 519 [542]
— enrollment in school, pp. 271-272, 274-275 [285-288]
— enrollment in vocational school, p. 277 [289]
— fertility rates, p. 745 [753]
— government, p. 887 [884]
— infant deaths, p. 757 [764]
— labor force, p. 536 [561]
— life expectancy, p. 773 [778]
— marital status, p. 782 [786]
— marriages, pp. 805, 808, 810 [810-812]
— occupations, p. 519 [542]
— population, pp. 782, 848 [786, 845]
— teachers, p. 558 [584]
— wages in agriculture, p. 454 [471]
— wages in construction, p. 454 [472]
— wages in manufacturing, p. 455 [473]
— wages in mining, p. 457 [474]
— wages in transport, p. 457 [475]
Czech Republic *See:* Czechoslovakia
Czechoslovakia
— abortions, pp. 620, 623-624 [647, 652-653]
— allocation of time, pp. 185, 187 [191-192]
— births, p. 641 [670]
— cigarette smoking, p. 371 [381]
— contraception, p. 662 [688]
— deaths, pp. 702, 707, 711, 759 [725-727, 766]
— divorce, p. 814 [816]
— elderly population, p. 854 [849]
— employment, pp. 520, 538 [543, 563]
— enrollment in school, pp. 289-290, 292-293 [296-299]
— enrollment in vocational school, p. 294 [300]
— female-headed households, p. 207 [215]
— fertility rates, p. 746 [754]
— housework, pp. 185, 187 [191-192]
— infant deaths, p. 759 [766]
— labor force, p. 537 [562]
— life expectancy, p. 774 [779]
— marital status, pp. 783, 790 [787, 794]
— marriages, pp. 816, 820, 824 [817-819]
— maternal deaths, p. 711 [727]
— occupations, p. 520 [543]
— population projections, p. 869 [866]
— population, pp. 783, 852 [787, 848]
— ratio of males to females, p. 861 [857]
— teachers, p. 564 [592]
— wages in manufacturing, p. 472 [491]

Czechoslovakia continued:
— wages in mining, p. 474 [492]
Dallas, Texas
— AIDS, p. 346 [358]
— alcohol, p. 129 [134]
— arrestees, pp. 101-102 [105-107]
— drugs, pp. 129-132, 134 [134-139]
— school dropouts, p. 103 [108]
Dance and dancers, p. 555 [582]
— attendance, pp. 949, 951 [947, 949]
— income, p. 453 [470]
— lessons, p. 952 [950]
— listening or viewing, pp. 953-954 [952, 954]
— participation, pp. 936, 957 [935, 959]
Dating violence, p. 140 [144]
Death, pp. 698-699, 701 [721-722, 724]
— accidents, p. 683 [711]
— Africa, pp. 684, 686 [712-713]
— and health care coverage, pp. 393-394 [408-409]
— Asia, pp. 690, 692 [717-718]
— by age, p. 727 [736]
— cancer, pp. 365, 696 [373, 720]
— causes, pp. 700, 727 [723, 736]
— Europe, pp. 702, 706 [725-726]
— fetal, pp. 610-611 [638-639]
— firearms, p. 712 [728]
— girls (worldwide), p. 715 [731]
— heart disease, p. 713 [729]
— HIV/AIDS, pp. 687-688 [714-715]
— infant (Africa), p. 764 [771]
— infant (Asia), p. 755 [763]
— infant (Asia/Near East), p. 756 [764]
— infant (developed countries), p. 758 [765]
— infant (Europe), p. 759 [766]
— infant (Latin America/Caribbean), p. 760 [767]
— infant (North Africa), p. 762 [768]
— infant (North America), p. 762 [769]
— infant (Oceania), p. 763 [770]
— infant (Soviet Union), p. 766 [772]
— infant (Yugoslavia), p. 766 [772]
— infant, pp. 700, 716, 731 [723, 732, 738]
— Latin America/Caribbean, pp. 717, 722 [733-734]
— lung cancer, p. 730 [737]
— maternal (Africa), p. 733 [741]
— maternal (Asia), p. 689 [716]
— maternal (Europe), p. 711 [727]
— maternal (Latin America/Caribbean), p. 726 [735]
— maternal (Middle East), p. 733 [741]
— maternal (North America), p. 735 [744]
— maternal (Oceania), p. 739 [747]
— maternal (worldwide), pp. 714, 740 [730, 748]
— maternal, p. 731 [738]
— Middle East, pp. 731-732 [739-740]
— motor vehicle accidents, pp. 742-743 [751-752]
— Near East, pp. 690, 692 [717-718]
— North America, p. 734 [742-743]
— Oceania, pp. 736-737 [745-746]
— risk by income, p. 420 [437]

Numbers following p. or pp. are page references. Numbers in [ ] are table references.

1000

Death continued:
— suicide, p. 741 [749-750]
Death penalty
— opinions on, p. 39 [41]
Deformities, p. 378 [391]
Degrees, p. 235 [250]
— associates', pp. 231-233, 236, 244 [245-247, 251, 259]
— bachelors', pp. 234, 247 [248, 264]
— by race/ethnicity, pp. 235, 237 [249, 252]
— doctors', pp. 238-239, 323 [253-254, 332]
— first-professional, pp. 239, 241-243 [255-258]
— masters', p. 245 [260]
— mathematics, p. 246 [261]
— science, p. 247 [263]
Delaware
— abortions, p. 617 [644]
— Catholic marriages, p. 908 [908]
— Catholic sisters, p. 904 [904]
— child rape victims, p. 139 [143]
— college enrollment, p. 280 [291]
— teacher salaries, p. 495 [518]
— WIC Program grants, p. 446 [458]
Denmark
— abortions, p. 623 [652]
— births to unmarried mothers, p. 636 [666]
— births, p. 641 [670]
— cigarette smoking, p. 371 [381]
— contraception, p. 662 [688]
— deaths, pp. 702, 707, 711, 758-759 [725-727, 765-766]
— divorce, pp. 814, 827 [816, 823]
— elderly population, p. 854 [849]
— employment, pp. 520, 538 [543, 563]
— enrollment in school, pp. 289-290, 292-293 [296-299]
— enrollment in vocational school, p. 294 [300]
— fertility rates, p. 746 [754]
— government, p. 886 [883]
— households, p. 205 [213]
— infant deaths, pp. 758-759 [765-766]
— labor force, p. 537 [562]
— life expectancy, p. 774 [779]
— marital status, pp. 783, 791 [787, 794]
— marriages, pp. 816, 820, 824 [817-819]
— maternal deaths, p. 711 [727]
— occupations, p. 520 [543]
— population projections, p. 869 [866]
— population, pp. 783, 852 [787, 848]
— wages in manufacturing, p. 472 [491]
Dental implants, p. 409 [427]
Dentist contacts, p. 398 [414]
Dentistry degrees, pp. 239, 241 [255-256]
Depressants
— use by juveniles, p. 145 [151]
— use by prison inmates, p. 137 [141]
Dermatitis, p. 378 [391]
Designers, p. 555 [582]
— income, p. 453 [470]
Destruction of property
— arrests, p. 102 [106]

Detroit, Michigan
— AIDS, p. 346 [358]
— alcohol, p. 129 [134]
— arrestees, pp. 101-102 [105-107]
— drugs, pp. 129-132, 134 [134-139]
— school dropouts, p. 103 [108]
Diabetes, p. 378 [391]
— deaths, pp. 700, 727 [723, 736]
— mothers, p. 644 [672]
Diaphragm, pp. 675, 677 [701-702]
Diet and dieting, pp. 388-390, 392 [401-405, 407]
— protection against cancer, p. 386 [400]
Digestive system problems, p. 376 [388]
Disabilities, p. 379 [392]
— work, p. 562 [589]
Discipline of children, p. 224 [235]
Discrimination in employment, pp. 56-57, 64 [55-56, 66]
Displaced homemakers, p. 196 [203]
— median income, p. 504 [524-525]
— poverty status, pp. 505-506 [526-527]
District of Columbia
— Catholic marriages, p. 908 [908]
— Catholic Sisters, p. 904 [904]
— child rape victims, p. 139 [143]
— college enrollment, p. 280 [291]
— drugs, p. 131 [136]
— imprisonment, p. 114 [119]
— teacher salaries, p. 495 [518]
— WIC Program grants, p. 446 [458]
Divinity degrees, pp. 239, 241 [255-256]
Divorce and divorced people, pp. 788, 813, 825, 839, 846-847, 922-923, 929 [791, 814, 820, 833, 843-844, 917, 919, 928]
— Africa, p. 799 [804]
— and smoking, p. 368 [377]
— Asia, p. 803 [809]
— contraception, p. 681 [708]
— elderly, p. 855 [850]
— Europe, p. 814 [816]
— householders, p. 211 [219]
— in eleven countries, p. 827 [823]
— in thirteen countries, p. 826 [822]
— Latin America/Caribbean, p. 828 [824]
— North America, p. 841 [835]
— Oceania, p. 843 [839]
— reasons, p. 221 [230]
— women divorced after first marriage, pp. 837-838 [830-831]
Djibouti
— births, p. 656 [684]
— clitoridectomy, p. 375 [387]
— deaths, p. 764 [771]
— enrollment in school, pp. 262, 264-265 [280-282]
— enrollment in vocational school, p. 269 [284]
— fertility rates, p. 752 [760]
— government, p. 887 [884]
— infant deaths, p. 764 [771]
— life expectancy, p. 779 [784]
— population, p. 866 [863]
Doctors of medicine, p. 575 [605]
Doctors' degrees, p. 237 [252]
— indebtedness for, p. 438 [452]

Numbers following p. or pp. are page references. Numbers in [ ] are table references.

Doctors' degrees continued:
— sources of financial support, p. 440 [455]
Dominica
— births, p. 643 [671]
— contraception, pp. 664, 666 [690-691]
— deaths, pp. 718, 723, 760 [733-734, 767]
— divorce, p. 828 [824]
— employment, p. 521 [544]
— enrollment in school, pp. 296, 298, 300-301 [302-305]
— enrollment in vocational school, p. 303 [306]
— female-headed households, p. 207 [215]
— fertility rates, p. 748 [756]
— government, pp. 885-886 [882-883]
— illiteracy, p. 256 [273]
— infant deaths, p. 760 [767]
— labor force, p. 540 [564]
— life expectancy, p. 775 [780]
— marital status, p. 785 [788]
— marriages, p. 835 [827]
— occupations, p. 521 [544]
— population, p. 785 [788]
— religion, p. 912 [910]
— teachers, p. 568 [598]
Dominican Republic
— births, p. 643 [671]
— contraception, pp. 664, 666 [690-691]
— deaths, pp. 718, 723, 726, 760 [733-735, 767]
— deaths of children, p. 715 [731]
— employment, p. 521 [544]
— enrollment in school, pp. 296, 298, 300-301 [302-305]
— enrollment in vocational school, p. 303 [306]
— fertility rates, p. 748 [756]
— illiteracy, p. 256 [273]
— infant deaths, p. 760 [767]
— labor force, p. 540 [564]
— life expectancy, p. 775 [780]
— literacy, p. 255 [272]
— marital status, p. 785 [788]
— marriages, pp. 829, 832 [825-826]
— maternal deaths, p. 726 [735]
— occupations, p. 521 [544]
— population projections, p. 873 [870]
— population, pp. 785, 857 [788, 852]
Down's syndrome, p. 378 [390]
Dropouts, p. 103 [108]
— arrestees, p. 103 [108]
— high school, pp. 316, 318 [322-325]
Drugs, pp. 178, 353 [185, 362]
— and HIV/AIDS, pp. 399-400, 402, 407 [415-416, 420, 425]
— arrests, p. 102 [106]
— criminals, pp. 104, 113 [109, 118]
— families of prison inmates, p. 122 [128]
— imprisonment, pp. 108, 123-124, 126 [113, 129-130, 132]
— opinions about drug testing, p. 71 [75]
— prison inmates, p. 118 [124]
— use by arrestees, pp. 129-132, 134 [134-139]
— use by jail inmates, p. 135 [140]
— use by juveniles, pp. 143-145 [148-151]

Drugs continued:
— use by prison inmates, p. 137 [141]
— use by women 15-44, p. 356 [366]
— use during pregnancy, p. 414 [432]
Earnings
See also: Income; Salaries
— black population, p. 467 [485]
— displaced workers, p. 480 [497]
— Federal Government employees, p. 494 [517]
— government employees, p. 491 [514]
— labor force, pp. 468-469 [487-488]
— waitresses, p. 586 [617]
— women with work disabilities, p. 562 [589]
East Germany
See also: Germany; West Germany
— divorce, p. 827 [823]
— population, p. 859 [854]
— ratio of males to females, p. 861 [857]
East Timor
— employment, p. 519 [542]
— occupations, p. 519 [542]
Easy listening music, pp. 956, 959 [957, 962]
Eating disorders
See also: Anorexia; Bulimia
— and alcoholism, p. 357 [367]
Eclampsia, p. 644 [672]
Economy
— attitudes and opinions, pp. 11, 30-31, 36, 39, 42-43, 59 [11, 34-35, 40-43, 58]
Ecuador
— births, p. 643 [671]
— contraception, pp. 664, 666 [690-691]
— deaths, pp. 718, 723, 726, 761 [733-735, 767]
— divorce, p. 828 [824]
— employment, p. 521 [544]
— enrollment in school, pp. 296, 298, 300-301 [302-305]
— enrollment in vocational school, p. 303 [306]
— fertility rates, p. 748 [756]
— fertility, p. 754 [761]
— government, p. 887 [884]
— illiteracy, p. 256 [273]
— infant deaths, p. 761 [767]
— labor force, p. 540 [564]
— life expectancy, p. 775 [780]
— literacy, p. 255 [272]
— marital status, p. 785 [788]
— marriages, pp. 830, 832, 835 [825-827]
— maternal deaths, p. 726 [735]
— occupations, p. 521 [544]
— population projections, p. 873 [870]
— population, pp. 218, 785, 857 [226, 788, 852]
Education
See also: Educational attainment
— ACT scores, pp. 337-338 [347-348]
— advanced placement mathematics examinations, p. 319 [327]
— advanced placement science examinations, p. 320 [328]
— aid, p. 418 [436]
— aspirations of students, pp. 313, 321 [319, 329]

Numbers following p. or pp. are page references. Numbers in [ ] are table references.

Education continued:
— college enrollment, pp. 279, 281 [290, 292]
— computers in school, pp. 227-231 [238-240, 243-244]
— core curriculum, p. 315 [321]
— cost, p. 439 [453]
— degree attainment, p. 261 [279]
— degrees conferred (projections), pp. 239, 243 [254, 258]
— degrees conferred, pp. 231-239, 241-242, 244-245 [245-253, 255-257, 259-260]
— doctors' degrees, p. 323 [332]
— elderly, p. 855 [850]
— enrollment (Africa), pp. 262-263, 265, 267, 269 [280-284]
— enrollment (Asia), pp. 271-272, 274-275, 277 [285-289]
— enrollment (Europe), pp. 289-291, 293-294 [296-300]
— enrollment (Latin America/Caribbean), pp. 296, 298-299, 301-302 [302-306]
— enrollment (North America), pp. 304-305 [307-310]
— enrollment (Oceania), pp. 307-311 [312-316]
— enrollment in seminaries, p. 312 [318]
— enrollment, p. 312 [317]
— expenditures, p. 443 [457]
— faculty salaries, p. 478 [495]
— fellowships, p. 418 [436]
— high school dropouts, p. 318 [324]
— high school programs, p. 319 [326]
— jail inmates, pp. 106, 111 [112, 116]
— LSAT scores, p. 338 [349]
— mathematics degrees, p. 246 [261]
— medical school, p. 322 [331]
— mothers of children enrolled in nursery school, p. 306 [311]
— National Assessment of Educational Progress scores, pp. 339-340, 344 [350, 352, 356]
— National Merit Semifinalists, p. 339 [351]
— opinions about, pp. 31, 43, 59 [35, 43, 58]
— physics faculty, p. 576 [607]
— physics, pp. 246, 296 [262, 301]
— prison inmates, p. 127 [133]
— SAT scores, pp. 341-343 [353-355]
— science and engineering faculty, p. 582 [611]
— science degrees, p. 247 [263]
— student opinions, p. 74 [78]
— teaching sisters, p. 584 [613]
— time to complete baccalaureate degree, p. 247 [264]
— victims of crime, pp. 160, 163, 173-174 [169, 173, 181-182]
— vocational, p. 323 [333]
— working while enrolled in college, p. 553 [579]
Educational attainment, pp. 248-249, 286 [265-266, 295]
— Africa, p. 249 [267]
— and earnings, pp. 461-462, 468, 497-498 [479-480, 487, 520-521]
— and income (displaced homemakers), p. 504 [525]
— and income (single mothers), p. 513 [535]
— and job promotions, pp. 530-531 [556-557]
— Asia, p. 252 [269]
— black population in the labor force, p. 526 [551]
— displaced homemakers, p. 196 [203]
— Europe, p. 254 [271]
— executives, pp. 87, 90, 93 [90, 93, 97]

Educational attainment continued:
— householders, p. 512 [533]
— labor force, p. 528 [553]
— Latin America/Caribbean, p. 256 [273]
— Near East, p. 260 [277]
— Oceania, p. 258 [275]
— worldwide, p. 261 [278]
Egypt
— births, p. 654 [681]
— cigarette smoking, p. 374 [385-386]
— clitoridectomy, p. 375 [387]
— contraception, pp. 667-668 [692-693]
— deaths, pp. 684, 686, 714, 733, 762 [712-713, 730, 741, 768]
— employment, p. 518 [541]
— enrollment in school, pp. 262, 264-265, 267 [280-283]
— enrollment in vocational school, p. 269 [284]
— fertility rates, p. 749 [757]
— government, p. 887 [884]
— illiteracy, p. 250 [267]
— infant deaths, p. 762 [768]
— labor force, p. 534 [559]
— life expectancy, p. 776 [781]
— literacy, p. 257 [274]
— marital status, pp. 789, 794 [792, 799]
— marriages, pp. 800-801 [805-806]
— maternal deaths, pp. 714, 733 [730, 741]
— occupations, p. 518 [541]
— population projections, p. 874 [871]
— population, pp. 220, 794, 858 [228, 799, 853]
— religion, p. 906 [906]
— teachers, p. 553 [580]
— wages in agriculture, p. 450 [465]
— wages in construction, p. 450 [466]
— wages in manufacturing, p. 451 [467]
— wages in mining, p. 452 [468]
— wages in transport, p. 452 [469]
El Salvador
— births, p. 643 [671]
— contraception, pp. 664, 666 [690-691]
— deaths, pp. 719, 723, 726, 761 [733-735, 767]
— divorce, p. 828 [824]
— employment, p. 521 [544]
— enrollment in school, pp. 296, 298, 300-301 [302-305]
— enrollment in vocational school, p. 303 [306]
— female-headed households, p. 207 [215]
— fertility rates, p. 748 [756]
— government, p. 887 [884]
— illiteracy, p. 256 [273]
— infant deaths, p. 761 [767]
— labor force, p. 540 [564]
— life expectancy, p. 775 [780]
— literacy, p. 255 [272]
— marital status, p. 785 [788]
— marriages, pp. 830, 833, 835 [825-827]
— maternal deaths, p. 726 [735]
— occupations, p. 521 [544]
— population projections, p. 873 [870]
— population, pp. 218, 785, 857 [226, 788, 852]

Numbers following p. or pp. are page references. Numbers in [ ] are table references.

El Salvador continued:
— teachers, p. 568 [598]
— wages in manufacturing, p. 481 [500]
Elderly people
— abuse
— Asia, p. 848 [845]
— assistance funds for victims, p. 159 [167]
— income, p. 417 [435]
— Latin America/Caribbean, p. 857 [852]
— living arrangements, pp. 213-214 [221-222]
— marital status, pp. 786-787 [789-790]
— Middle East, p. 858 [853]
— Near East, p. 848 [845]
— North Africa, p. 858 [853]
— Sub-Saharan Africa, p. 865 [863]
Electronic fetal monitoring, p. 647 [674]
Employment, p. 566 [594-595]
— Africa, p. 518 [541]
— after recession, p. 516 [538]
— and child care problems, p. 527 [552]
— Asia and the Pacific, p. 519 [542]
— changing jobs, p. 517 [540]
— college professors, p. 560 [586]
— college students, p. 282 [293]
— developed countries, p. 520 [543]
— jail inmates, pp. 106, 110 [112, 115]
— Latin America/Caribbean, p. 521 [544]
— private sector, p. 529 [554]
— since 1969, p. 517 [539]
— welfare mothers, p. 544 [569]
— while enrolled in college, p. 553 [579]
Engineers and engineering, pp. 570-571 [600-601]
— degrees conferred, pp. 231, 233, 236, 244 [245, 247, 251, 259]
— faculty, p. 582 [611]
England
See also: Great Britain
— abortion, p. 614 [642]
— college professors, p. 559 [585]
— divorce, p. 813 [815]
— rape, p. 162 [171]
— salaries of chemical engineers, p. 492 [515]
English language and literature
— degrees, pp. 231, 233, 236, 244 [245, 247, 251, 259]
Enrollment *See:* Education
Entertainment expenditures, p. 443 [457]
Environmental science faculty, p. 582 [611]
Equal Employment Opportunity Commission, p. 149 [156]
Equal Rights Amendment
— opinions about, p. 34 [39]
Equatorial Guinea
— births, p. 656 [684]
— deaths, p. 764 [771]
— employment, p. 518 [541]
— enrollment in school, pp. 264-265 [281-282]
— enrollment in vocational school, p. 269 [284]
— fertility rates, p. 752 [760]
— government, p. 887 [884]
— illiteracy, p. 250 [267]

Equatorial Guinea continued:
— infant deaths, p. 764 [771]
— life expectancy, p. 779 [784]
— marital status, p. 789 [792]
— marriages, p. 836 [828]
— occupations, p. 518 [541]
— population, p. 866 [863]
Eritrea
— clitoridectomy, p. 375 [387]
Estonia
— abortions, p. 623 [652]
— births, p. 642 [670]
— contraception, p. 674 [700]
— deaths, p. 766 [772]
— divorce, p. 814 [816]
— enrollment in school, p. 293 [299]
— fertility rates, p. 754 [762]
— infant deaths, p. 766 [772]
— life expectancy, p. 781 [785]
— marital status, p. 798 [803]
— marriages, pp. 816, 820, 824 [817-819]
— population, p. 798 [803]
Ethiopia
— age at first marriage, p. 812 [813]
— births, p. 657 [684]
— clitoridectomy, p. 375 [387]
— contraception, pp. 671, 677 [698, 703]
— deaths, p. 764 [771]
— employment, p. 518 [541]
— enrollment in school, pp. 262, 264, 266-267 [280-283]
— enrollment in vocational school, p. 269 [284]
— fertility rates, p. 752 [760]
— illiteracy, p. 250 [267]
— infant deaths, p. 764 [771]
— life expectancy, p. 779 [784]
— literacy, p. 258 [276]
— marital status, p. 796 [802]
— occupations, p. 518 [541]
— population projections, p. 880 [878]
— population, pp. 219, 796, 866 [227, 802, 863]
— teachers, p. 553 [580]
Europe
— abortions, pp. 623-624 [652-653]
— births, pp. 641, 658 [670, 685]
— cigarette smoking, p. 371 [381]
— contraception, pp. 662-663 [688-689]
— deaths, pp. 702, 706, 711, 759 [725-727, 766]
— divorce, p. 814 [816]
— educational attainment, p. 254 [271]
— employment, p. 538 [563]
— enrollment in school, pp. 289-291, 293 [296-299]
— enrollment in vocational school, p. 294 [300]
— fertility rates, p. 745 [754]
— HIV/AIDS, p. 401 [419]
— housework, p. 188 [193]
— infant deaths, p. 759 [766]
— life expectancy, p. 773 [779]
— literacy, p. 254 [271]

Numbers following p. or pp. are page references. Numbers in [ ] are table references.

Europe continued:
— marital status, pp. 783, 790 [787, 794]
— marriages, pp. 815, 820, 824 [817-819]
— maternal deaths, p. 711 [727]
— population, pp. 783, 871 [787, 868]
— rape, p. 162 [171]
— religious denominations, p. 910 [909]
— teachers, p. 564 [592]
— wages in agriculture, p. 469 [489]
— wages in construction, p. 470 [490]
— wages in manufacturing, p. 472 [491]
— wages in mining, p. 474 [492]
— wages in transport, p. 475 [493]
Euthanasia
— attitudes of nuns, p. 45 [46]
Executives
— earnings, p. 86 [89]
— major corporations, p. 82 [85-86]
— private industry, pp. 77-80, 84-85, 87-88, 90-93 [80-84, 87-88, 90-97]
Exercise, p. 936 [935]
— participation, p. 958 [961]
— teenage girls, p. 391 [406]
— walking, p. 938 [936]
Expectation of life *See:* Life expectancy
Expenditures
— child care, p. 431 [450]
— health care, p. 447 [460]
— husband and wife, p. 443 [457]
— renters, p. 441 [456]
— single parents, p. 443 [457]
Faeroe Islands
— abortions, p. 619 [646]
— births, p. 641 [670]
— deaths, pp. 703, 707, 759 [725-726, 766]
— divorce, p. 814 [816]
— fertility rates, p. 746 [754]
— infant deaths, p. 759 [766]
— life expectancy, p. 774 [779]
— marital status, p. 783 [787]
— marriages, p. 824 [819]
— population, p. 783 [787]
Falkland Islands
— deaths, pp. 719, 723 [733-734]
— divorce, p. 828 [824]
— enrollment in school, pp. 298, 300 [303-304]
— marital status, p. 792 [795]
Families, p. 199 [206]
— attitudes towards, p. 14 [15]
— discontinuation of, p. 813 [814]
— female-headed, p. 197 [204]
— government assistance programs, p. 510 [531]
— income, p. 417 [435]
— married-couple, p. 198 [205]
— poverty status, p. 511 [532]
— two-parent, p. 195 [201]
— types, pp. 200-204, 208 [207-212, 216]
Farms, pp. 570-571, 867 [600-601, 864]
Fathers, p. 196 [202]
— single, p. 208 [216]

Fathers continued:
— work, pp. 195, 548 [201, 574]
Federal Government
— employment, pp. 565-566 [593-595]
— salaries, p. 494 [517]
Feminist movement
— opinions of Canadians, p. 20 [23]
Fertility, p. 747 [755]
— Asia/Near East, p. 744 [753]
— Europe, p. 745 [754]
— Latin America/Caribbean, p. 748 [756]
— North Africa, p. 749 [757]
— North America, p. 750 [758]
— Oceania, p. 751 [759]
— Soviet Union, p. 754 [762]
— Sub-Saharan Africa, p. 752 [760]
— world, p. 753 [761]
— Yugoslavia, p. 754 [762]
Fetal Alcohol Syndrome, p. 349 [360]
Figure skating, p. 962 [966]
Fiji
— births, p. 655 [683]
— cigarette smoking, p. 373 [384]
— contraception, pp. 669-670 [696-697]
— deaths, pp. 736, 738-739, 763 [745-747, 770]
— employment, pp. 519, 535 [542, 560]
— enrollment in school, pp. 307-310 [312-315]
— enrollment in vocational school, p. 311 [316]
— fertility rates, p. 751 [759]
— illiteracy, p. 258 [275]
— infant deaths, p. 763 [770]
— labor force, p. 536 [561]
— life expectancy, p. 778 [783]
— marital status, p. 795 [801]
— marriages, pp. 843-845 [840-842]
— maternal deaths, p. 739 [747]
— median age, p. 863 [859]
— occupations, p. 519 [542]
— population, p. 795 [801]
— ratio of males to females, p. 863 [859]
— religion, p. 913 [911]
— teachers, p. 575 [604]
Finance, insurance, real estate
— employment, p. 561 [588]
Finland
— abortions, pp. 623-624 [652-653]
— allocation of time, pp. 185-186 [191-192]
— births to unmarried mothers, p. 636 [666]
— births, p. 641 [670]
— cigarette smoking, p. 371 [381]
— contraception, p. 662 [688]
— deaths, pp. 703, 707, 711, 758-759 [725-727, 756-767]
— divorce, p. 814 [816]
— education, p. 335 [345]
— elderly population, p. 854 [849]
— employment, pp. 520, 538 [543, 563]
— enrollment in school, pp. 289-290, 292-293 [296-299]
— enrollment in vocational school, p. 294 [300]

Numbers following p. or pp. are page references. Numbers in [ ] are table references.

Finland continued:
— fertility rates, p. 746 [754]
— government, p. 886 [883]
— housework, pp. 185-186 [191-192]
— infant deaths, pp. 758-759 [765-766]
— labor force, p. 537 [562]
— life expectancy, p. 774 [779]
— marital status, pp. 783, 791 [787, 794]
— marriages, pp. 816, 820, 824 [817-819]
— maternal deaths, p. 711 [727]
— occupations, p. 520 [543]
— population projections, p. 869 [866]
— population, pp. 783, 852 [787, 848]
— ratio of males to females, p. 861 [857]
— religion, p. 910 [909]
— wages in agriculture, p. 470 [489]
— wages in construction, p. 471 [490]
— wages in manufacturing, p. 472 [491]
— wages in mining, p. 474 [492]
Fishing, pp. 570-571, 938 [600-601, 936]
Florida
— Catholic marriages, p. 908 [908]
— Catholic sisters, p. 904 [904]
— child rape victims, p. 139 [143]
— college enrollment, p. 280 [291]
— imprisonment, p. 114 [119]
— prisoners under sentence of death, p. 115 [120]
— teacher salaries, p. 495 [518]
— WIC Program grants, p. 444 [458]
Flowers
— gift preference, p. 12 [13]
Flu, pp. 376, 727 [388, 736]
Foam (contraceptive), p. 675 [701]
Folk music, p. 956 [957]
Food
— consumption, pp. 388-389 [402-403]
— expenditures, p. 443 [457]
— gift preference, p. 12 [13]
Food service employees, p. 567 [596-597]
Food Stamps *See:* Government assistance programs
Football, p. 938 [936]
Foreign languages and literature
— degrees, pp. 231, 233, 236, 244 [245, 247, 251, 259]
Foreign students
— physics, pp. 246, 296 [262, 301]
Forestry, pp. 570-571 [600-601]
Forgery arrests, p. 102 [106]
France
— abortions, pp. 623-624 [652-653]
— allocation of time, pp. 185, 187 [191-192]
— births to unmarried mothers, p. 637 [666]
— births, p. 641 [670]
— cigarette smoking, p. 371 [381]
— contraception, pp. 662-663 [688-689]
— deaths, pp. 703, 707, 711, 758-759 [725-727, 765-766]
— divorce, pp. 813-814 [815-816]
— educational attainment, p. 261 [278]
— education, p. 335 [345]

France continued:
— elderly population, p. 854 [849]
— employment, pp. 520, 538 [543, 563]
— enrollment in school, pp. 289-290, 292-293, 312 [296-299, 317]
— enrollment in vocational school, p. 294 [300]
— female-headed households, p. 207 [215]
— fertility rates, p. 746 [754]
— households, p. 205 [213]
— housework, pp. 185, 187 [191-192]
— infant deaths, pp. 758-759 [765-766]
— labor force, p. 537 [562]
— life expectancy, p. 774 [779]
— marital status, pp. 783, 791 [787, 794]
— marriages, pp. 816, 821, 824 [817-819]
— maternal deaths, p. 711 [727]
— occupations, p. 520 [543]
— population projections, p. 869 [866]
— population, pp. 783, 852 [787, 848]
— rape, p. 162 [171]
— teachers, p. 564 [592]
— wages in construction, p. 471 [490]
— wages in manufacturing, p. 472 [491]
— wages in mining, p. 474 [492]
Fraud
— arrests, p. 102 [106]
— imprisonment, pp. 108, 123-124, 126 [113, 129-130, 132]
— perpetrators, p. 104 [109]
French Guiana
— abortions, p. 629 [658]
— births to unmarried mothers, p. 637 [666]
— births, p. 643 [671]
— deaths, pp. 719, 723, 761 [733-734, 767]
— employment, p. 521 [544]
— enrollment in school, pp. 297-298, 300 [302-304]
— enrollment in vocational school, p. 303 [306]
— female-headed households, p. 208 [215]
— fertility rates, p. 748 [756]
— illiteracy, p. 256 [273]
— infant deaths, p. 761 [767]
— labor force, p. 540 [564]
— life expectancy, p. 775 [780]
— marital status, p. 785 [788]
— occupations, p. 521 [544]
— population, p. 785 [788]
French Polynesia
— births, p. 655 [683]
— cigarette smoking, p. 373 [384]
— deaths, p. 763 [770]
— employment, p. 519 [542]
— enrollment in school, pp. 307-310 [312-315]
— enrollment in vocational school, p. 311 [316]
— fertility rates, p. 751 [759]
— infant deaths, p. 763 [770]
— labor force, p. 536 [561]
— life expectancy, p. 778 [783]
— marital status, p. 795 [801]
— marriages, p. 845 [842]
— occupations, p. 519 [542]

Numbers following p. or pp. are page references. Numbers in [ ] are table references.

French Polynesia continued:
— population, p. 795 [801]
— teachers, p. 575 [604]
Functional Information Technology Test (FITT), pp. 227-228 [238-239]
Gabon
— births, p. 657 [684]
— deaths, p. 765 [771]
— employment, p. 518 [541]
— enrollment in school, pp. 262, 264, 266-267 [280-283]
— enrollment in vocational school, p. 269 [284]
— fertility rates, p. 752 [760]
— illiteracy, p. 250 [267]
— infant deaths, p. 765 [771]
— life expectancy, p. 779 [784]
— literacy, p. 259 [276]
— marital status, p. 796 [802]
— occupations, p. 518 [541]
— population projections, p. 880 [878]
— population, pp. 219, 796, 866 [227, 802, 863]
Gambia, The
— births, p. 657 [684]
— clitoridectomy, p. 375 [387]
— deaths, p. 765 [771]
— employment, p. 518 [541]
— enrollment in school, pp. 262, 264, 266 [280-282]
— enrollment in vocational school, p. 269 [284]
— fertility rates, p. 752 [760]
— illiteracy, p. 250 [267]
— infant deaths, p. 765 [771]
— life expectancy, p. 779 [784]
— occupations, p. 518 [541]
— population, p. 866 [863]
Games
— gift preference, p. 12 [13]
Gardening, pp. 936, 958 [935, 961]
Gaza Strip
See also: Palestine
— births, p. 632 [661]
— fertility rates, p. 745 [753]
— infant deaths, p. 757 [764]
— life expectancy, p. 773 [778]
— marital status, p. 782 [786]
— population, p. 782 [786]
Genital herpes
See also: Sexually transmitted diseases
— mothers, p. 644 [672]
— teenagers, p. 382 [396]
Genital mutilation *See:* Clitoridectomy
Georgia (country of)
— births, p. 658 [685]
— divorce, p. 803 [809]
— enrollment in school, p. 276 [288]
— marriages, pp. 805, 808 [810-811]
Georgia (State of)
— Catholic marriages, p. 908 [908]
— Catholic sisters, p. 904 [904]
— college enrollment, p. 280 [291]

Georgia (State of) continued:
— imprisonment, p. 114 [119]
— teacher salaries, p. 495 [518]
— WIC Program grants, p. 445 [458]
Germany
See also: East Germany; West Germany
— allocation of time, pp. 185, 187 [191-192]
— attitudes toward working women, p. 24 [28-29]
— births to unmarried mothers, p. 637 [666]
— births, p. 641 [670]
— cigarette smoking, p. 371 [381]
— college professors, p. 559 [585]
— computers in school, p. 228 [239]   ·
— contraception, p. 662 [688]
— deaths, pp. 703, 708, 711, 758-759 [725-727, 765-766]
— divorce, pp. 813-814 [815-816]
— educational attainment, p. 261 [278]
— education, p. 335 [345]
— elderly population, p. 854 [849]
— employment, pp. 520, 538 [543, 563]
— enrollment in school, pp. 289-290, 292-293, 312 [296-299, 317]
— enrollment in vocational school, p. 294 [300]
— fertility rates, p. 746 [754]
— government, p. 886 [883]
— housework, pp. 185, 187 [191-192]
— infant deaths, pp. 758-759 [765-766]
— labor force, p. 537 [562]
— life expectancy, p. 774 [779]
— marital status, pp. 783, 791 [787, 794]
— marriages, pp. 816, 821, 824 [817-819]
— maternal deaths, p. 711 [727]
— occupations, p. 520 [543]
— opinions on equal rights, p. 22 [25]
— opinions on politics, p. 22 [26]
— population projections, p. 869 [866]
— population, pp. 783, 853 [787, 848]
— reasons for working, p. 23 [27]
— teachers, p. 564 [592]
— wages in manufacturing, p. 472 [491]
Ghana
— age at first marriage, p. 812 [813]
— births, p. 657 [684]
— cigarette smoking, p. 374 [385]
— clitoridectomy, p. 375 [387]
— contraception, pp. 671, 673 [698-699]
— deaths, pp. 714, 740, 756 [730, 748, 771]
— employment, p. 518 [541]
— enrollment in school, pp. 262, 264, 266-267 [280-283]
— enrollment in vocational school, p. 269 [284]
— female-headed households, p. 207 [215]
— fertility rates, p. 752 [760]
— illiteracy, p. 250 [267]
— infant deaths, p. 765 [771]
— labor force, p. 534 [559]
— life expectancy, p. 779 [784]
— literacy, p. 259 [276]
— maternal deaths, pp. 714, 740 [730, 748]
— occupations, p. 518 [541]

Numbers following p. or pp. are page references. Numbers in [ ] are table references.

Ghana continued:
— population projections, p. 880 [878]
— population, p. 866 [863]
— time spent getting water, p. 183 [190]
GI Bill, p. 418 [436]
Gibraltar
— births, p. 641 [670]
— deaths, pp. 703, 708, 759 [725-726, 766]
— enrollment in school, pp. 289-290, 292 [296-298]
— enrollment in vocational school, p. 295 [300]
— fertility rates, p. 746 [754]
— infant deaths, p. 759 [766]
— life expectancy, p. 774 [779]
— marital status, p. 783 [787]
— marriages, p. 824 [819]
— population, p. 783 [787]
— wages in construction, p. 471 [490]
— wages in manufacturing, p. 472 [491]
— wages in transport, p. 475 [493]
Gift preferences, p. 12 [13]
Girl Scouts, p. 940 [939]
Golf, p. 938 [936]
Gonorrhea
  See also: Sexually transmitted diseases
— teenagers, p. 382 [396]
Government
— appointed offices, pp. 882-883 [879-880]
— attitudes toward, p. 44 [44]
— elective offices, pp. 883, 894-898 [881, 891-896]
— employment, pp. 566, 585 [595, 614]
— heads of state worldwide, p. 885 [882]
— ministerial-level positions worldwide, p. 886 [883]
— parliamentary positions worldwide, p. 887 [884]
— salaries of employees, pp. 491, 494 [514, 517]
Government assistance programs
Government assistance programs, pp. 395, 424, 441, 510, 512, 544 [411, 443, 456, 531, 533, 569]
— Food stamps, p. 510 [531]
— homeless people, p. 206 [214]
— Medicare and Medicaid, pp. 393-394 [408-410]
— public housing, p. 510 [531]
— Supplemental Security Income, pp. 422, 510 [441, 531]
— teenage mothers, pp. 440, 446 [454, 459]
— WIC, p. 444 [458]
Great Britain
  See also: England; Ireland; Wales
— salaries of chemical engineers, p. 492 [515]
Greece
— abortions, pp. 619, 623-624 [646, 652-653]
— births, p. 641 [670]
— cigarette smoking, p. 371 [381]
— deaths, pp. 703, 708, 711, 759 [725-727, 766]
— elderly population, p. 854 [849]
— employment, pp. 520, 538 [543, 563]
— enrollment in school, pp. 289-290, 292-293 [296-299]
— enrollment in vocational school, p. 295 [300]
— fertility rates, p. 746 [754]
— illiteracy, p. 254 [271]

Greece continued:
— infant deaths, p. 759 [766]
— labor force, p. 537 [562]
— life expectancy, p. 774 [779]
— literacy, p. 253 [270]
— marital status, p. 783 [787]
— marriages, pp. 817, 821, 824 [817-819]
— maternal deaths, p. 711 [727]
— occupations, p. 520 [543]
— population projections, p. 869 [866]
— population, pp. 783, 853 [787, 848]
— rape, p. 162 [171]
— teachers, p. 564 [592]
— wages in manufacturing, p. 472 [491]
Greenland
— abortions, pp. 620, 627 [647, 654]
— births, p. 655 [682]
— deaths, pp. 734-735, 762 [742-743, 769]
— divorce, p. 841 [835]
— fertility rates, p. 750 [758]
— households, p. 205 [213]
— infant deaths, p. 762 [769]
— life expectancy, p. 777 [782]
— marital status, pp. 792, 795 [796, 800]
— marriages, p. 842 [838]
— population, p. 795 [800]
Grenada
— births, p. 643 [671]
— contraception, pp. 664, 666 [690-691]
— deaths, p. 761 [767]
— divorce, p. 826 [822]
— enrollment in school, pp. 297-298, 300 [302-304]
— female-headed households, p. 208 [215]
— fertility rates, p. 748 [756]
— illiteracy, p. 256 [273]
— infant deaths, p. 761 [767]
— life expectancy, p. 775 [780]
— marital status, p. 785 [788]
— population, pp. 785, 859 [788, 854]
— religion, p. 912 [910]
Groceries
— method of payment, p. 427 [445]
Guadeloupe
— abortions, p. 619 [646]
— births to unmarried mothers, p. 637 [666]
— births, p. 643 [671]
— contraception, p. 664 [690]
— deaths, pp. 719, 723, 761 [733-734, 767]
— employment, p. 521 [544]
— enrollment in school, pp. 297-298, 300 [302-304]
— enrollment in vocational school, p. 303 [306]
— female-headed households, p. 208 [215]
— fertility rates, p. 748 [756]
— illiteracy, p. 256 [273]
— infant deaths, p. 761 [767]
— labor force, p. 540 [564]
— life expectancy, p. 775 [780]
— marital status, p. 785 [788]

Numbers following p. or pp. are page references. Numbers in [ ] are table references.

Guadeloupe continued:
— marriages, pp. 830, 833 [825-826]
— occupations, p. 521 [544]
— population, pp. 785, 857 [788, 852]

Guam
— births to unmarried mothers, p. 637 [666]
— births, p. 655 [683]
— Catholic sisters, p. 905 [904]
— contraception, p. 669 [696]
— deaths, pp. 736, 738, 763 [745-746, 770]
— divorce, p. 843 [839]
— employment, p. 519 [542]
— enrollment in school, pp. 307-310 [312-315]
— fertility rates, p. 751 [759]
— infant deaths, p. 763 [770]
— life expectancy, p. 778 [783]
— marriages, pp. 836, 843-845 [829, 840-842]
— occupations, p. 519 [542]
— teachers, p. 575 [604]

Guatemala
— allocation of time, pp. 185, 187 [191-192]
— births, p. 643 [671]
— cigarette smoking, p. 372 [382]
— contraception, pp. 664, 666 [690-691]
— deaths, pp. 719, 723, 726, 761 [733-735, 767]
— divorce, pp. 826, 828 [822, 824]
— employment, p. 521 [544]
— enrollment in school, pp. 297-298, 300-301 [302-305]
— enrollment in vocational school, p. 303 [306]
— fertility rates, p. 748 [756]
— government, p. 886 [883]
— housework, pp. 185, 187 [191-192]
— illiteracy, p. 256 [273]
— infant deaths, p. 761 [767]
— labor force, p. 540 [564]
— life expectancy, p. 775 [780]
— literacy, p. 255 [272]
— marital status, pp. 785, 792 [788, 795]
— marriages, pp. 830, 833, 835 [825-827]
— maternal deaths, p. 726 [735]
— occupations, p. 521 [544]
— population projections, p. 873 [870]
— population, pp. 218, 785, 857 [226, 788, 852]
— teachers, p. 568 [598]

Guernsey
See also: Channel Islands; Jersey
— births, p. 641 [670]
— deaths, pp. 702, 707, 759 [725-726, 766]
— divorce, p. 814 [816]
— fertility rates, p. 746 [754]
— infant deaths, p. 759 [766]
— life expectancy, p. 774 [779]
— marital status, p. 783 [787]
— marriages, p. 824 [819]
— population, p. 783 [787]

Guinea
— births, p. 657 [684]
— clitoridectomy, p. 375 [387]

Guinea continued:
— deaths, p. 765 [771]
— employment, p. 518 [541]
— enrollment in school, pp. 264, 266-267 [281-283]
— enrollment in vocational school, p. 269 [284]
— fertility rates, p. 752 [760]
— illiteracy, p. 250 [267]
— infant deaths, p. 765 [771]
— life expectancy, p. 779 [784]
— literacy, p. 259 [276]
— marital status, p. 796 [802]
— occupations, p. 518 [541]
— population projections, p. 880 [878]
— population, pp. 219, 796, 866 [227, 802, 863]
— teachers, p. 554 [580]

Guinea-Bissau
— births, p. 657 [684]
— clitoridectomy, p. 375 [387]
— deaths, p. 765 [771]
— employment, p. 518 [541]
— enrollment in school, pp. 262, 264, 266-267 [280-283]
— enrollment in vocational school, p. 269 [284]
— fertility rates, p. 752 [760]
— illiteracy, p. 250 [267]
— infant deaths, p. 765 [771]
— life expectancy, p. 779 [784]
— occupations, p. 518 [541]
— population projections, p. 880 [878]
— population, p. 866 [863]

Guyana
— births, p. 643 [671]
— cigarette smoking, p. 372 [382]
— contraception, pp. 664, 666 [690-691]
— deaths, p. 761 [767]
— employment, p. 521 [544]
— enrollment in school, pp. 297-298, 300-301 [302-305]
— enrollment in vocational school, p. 303 [306]
— female-headed households, p. 208 [215]
— fertility rates, p. 748 [756]
— illiteracy, p. 256 [273]
— infant deaths, p. 761 [767]
— life expectancy, p. 775 [780]
— marital status, p. 785 [788]
— occupations, p. 521 [544]
— population projections, p. 873 [870]
— population, pp. 218, 785, 857 [226, 788, 852]
— religion, p. 912 [910]
— teachers, p. 568 [598]

Haiti
— births, p. 643 [671]
— contraception, pp. 664, 666 [690-691]
— deaths, pp. 714, 726, 761 [730, 735, 767]
— deaths of children, p. 715 [731]
— divorce, p. 826 [822]
— employment, p. 521 [544]
— enrollment in school, pp. 297-298, 300-301 [302-305]
— enrollment in vocational school, p. 303 [306]
— fertility rates, p. 748 [756]

Numbers following p. or pp. are page references. Numbers in [ ] are table references.

1009

Haiti continued:
— HIV/AIDS, p. 404 [422]
— illiteracy, p. 256 [273]
— infant deaths, p. 761 [767]
— labor force, p. 540 [564]
— life expectancy, p. 775 [780]
— literacy, p. 255 [272]
— marital status, pp. 785, 792 [788, 795]
— marriages, p. 836 [828]
— maternal deaths, pp. 714, 726 [730, 735]
— occupations, p. 521 [544]
— population projections, p. 873 [870]
— population, pp. 218, 785, 857 [226, 788, 852]
— religion, p. 912 [910]
— teachers, p. 568 [598]
Hallucinogens, p. 137 [141]
— use by juveniles, p. 144 [149]
— use by prison inmates, p. 137 [141]
Hanging deaths, p. 741 [750]
Hawaii
— abortions, p. 617 [644]
— Catholic marriages, p. 909 [908]
— Catholic sisters, p. 904 [904]
— college enrollment, p. 280 [291]
— teacher salaries, p. 495 [518]
— WIC Program grants, p. 445 [458]
Hay fever, p. 378 [391]
Health and health care
— attitudes about, pp. 31, 43, 59 [35, 43, 58]
— costs, p. 447 [460]
— coverage, pp. 393-396 [408-412]
— expenditures, pp. 441, 443 [456-457]
— occupations, pp. 570-571 [600-601]
— opinions of British, p. 17 [19]
Health professions degrees, pp. 231, 233, 236, 244 [245, 247, 251, 259]
Hearing impairments, p. 378 [391]
Heart conditions, p. 378 [391]
— deaths, pp. 700, 713, 727 [723, 729, 736]
— heart attack risk, p. 416 [434]
Heart valves, p. 409 [427]
Hemoglobinopathy, p. 644 [672]
Hemorrhoids, p. 378 [391]
Hernia, p. 378 [391]
Heroin
— use by arrestees, p. 131 [137]
— use by juveniles, p. 144 [150]
— use by prison inmates, p. 137 [141]
High blood pressure, p. 378 [391]
High school
  See also: Education
— core curriculum, p. 315 [321]
— dropouts, pp. 316, 318 [322-323, 325]
— student aspirations, pp. 313, 321 [319, 329]
— student opinions, p. 74 [78]
— students' occupational expectations, p. 321 [330]
— students' values, p. 75 [79]
Higher education
  See also: Education
— students' alcohol use, p. 354 [364]

Higher education continued:
— tenure status of faculty, p. 586 [616]
Hiking, p. 938 [936]
Hindu religion, pp. 906-908, 912-913 [906-907, 910-911]
Hip joints, p. 409 [427]
Hispanic origin population
— 1992 estimates, pp. 877-878 [875-876]
— abortions, p. 616 [643]
— ACT scores, p. 337 [347]
— adoption, pp. 190, 192 [196, 198]
— arrestees, p. 101 [105]
— attitudes, p. 44 [45]
— birth rates, p. 632 [662]
— births to teenage mothers, pp. 633, 649 [663, 675]
— births to unmarried mothers, pp. 639, 649 [668, 675]
— births, p. 649 [675]
— cholesterol levels, p. 380 [393]
— college enrollment, p. 279 [290]
— contraception, p. 682 [709]
— degrees conferred, pp. 235, 237, 239 [249, 252, 255]
— displaced homemakers, pp. 196, 504-506 [203, 524-527]
— divorce, p. 838 [831]
— drug use by arrestees, p. 130 [136]
— drugs, p. 132 [138]
— earnings, pp. 460, 491, 494 [478, 514, 517]
— educational attainment, pp. 248, 512 [265, 533]
— elderly in poverty, p. 508 [529]
— elderly, p. 214 [222]
— employment, p. 529 [554]
— executives' income, pp. 85, 92 [88, 96]
— executives, pp. 84, 87-88 [87, 91-92]
— families, pp. 199, 204 [206, 212]
— family breakups, p. 813 [814]
— Federal Government employment, p. 566 [594-595]
— government assistance, p. 424 [443]
— high school dropouts, p. 316 [322-323]
— HIV positive prison inmates, p. 403 [421]
— imprisonment, pp. 111, 122, 127 [116, 128, 133]
— in elective offices, p. 898 [896]
— in poverty, p. 512 [533]
— income of older women, p. 508 [530]
— income, pp. 417, 420 [435, 438]
— labor force, pp. 530, 533, 543, 574 [555, 558, 567, 603]
— low birth weight, p. 649 [675]
— marital status, p. 788 [791]
— marriages, p. 838 [831]
— median earnings, pp. 484, 496 [506, 519]
— military personnel, pp. 588-593, 599-600, 602 [618-623, 627-628, 630]
— mothers in prison, p. 112 [117]
— mothers working, p. 546 [572]
— number of sex partners, p. 928 [926]
— occupations, pp. 570-571 [600-601]
— parents working, p. 548 [574]
— physics students, pp. 246, 296 [262, 301]
— population projections, p. 872 [869]
— prenatal care, p. 649 [675]
— SAT scores, p. 342 [354]

Numbers following p. or pp. are page references. Numbers in [ ] are table references.

Hispanic origin population continued:
— school enrollment, pp. 283, 286 [294-295]
— sex discrimination in employment, p. 523 [546]
— sexual harassment, p. 331 [341]
— single mothers' poverty status, pp. 514-515 [536-537]
— single mothers, p. 513 [534-535]
— teenage contraceptive use, p. 680 [707]
— teenage sexual activity, p. 934 [933]
— veterans, p. 604 [632]
— victims of crime, pp. 146, 160, 163, 173-174 [153, 169, 173, 181-182]
— volunteerism, p. 899 [898]
— voter turnout, p. 891 [887]
— wages, pp. 461, 498, 500, 502 [479, 521-523]
— work disabilities, p. 562 [589]
Historic parks
— attendance, p. 949 [947]
History degrees, pp. 231, 233, 236, 244 [245, 247, 251, 259]
HIV/AIDS, pp. 400, 402, 407 [417, 420, 425]
— Africa, p. 404 [422]
— and drugs, pp. 356, 399, 405 [366, 415, 423]
— and pregnancy, p. 401 [418]
— attitudes of nuns on use of condoms, p. 45 [46]
— deaths, pp. 687-688, 700, 727 [714-715, 723, 736]
— Haiti, p. 404 [422]
— prison inmates, p. 403 [421]
— teenagers, p. 382 [396]
— Thailand, p. 171 [180]
— transmission, pp. 400, 406 [416, 424]
— worldwide, p. 401 [419]
Holy See
— teachers, p. 564 [592]
Home economics degrees, pp. 231, 233, 236, 244 [245, 247, 251, 259]
Home improvement, p. 958 [961]
Homeless people, pp. 178, 206 [185, 214]
Homicide, pp. 154, 178, 180, 683, 700, 712, 727 [162, 185, 187, 711, 723, 728, 736]
— arrests, p. 102 [106]
— assistance funds for survivors, p. 159 [168]
— prison inmates, p. 118 [124]
— Victims of Crimes Act funding, p. 159 [167]
Homosexuality, pp. 924, 929 [921, 927]
See also: Lesbians
Honduras
— births, p. 643 [671]
— contraception, pp. 664, 666 [690-691]
— deaths, pp. 719, 723, 726, 761 [733-735, 767]
— employment, p. 521 [544]
— enrollment in school, pp. 297-298, 300-301 [302-305]
— enrollment in vocational school, p. 303 [306]
— female-headed households, p. 208 [215]
— fertility rates, p. 748 [756]
— illiteracy, p. 256 [273]
— infant deaths, p. 761 [767]
— life expectancy, p. 775 [780]
— literacy, p. 255 [272]
— marital status, p. 785 [788]

Honduras continued:
— marriages, pp. 830, 833 [825-826]
— maternal deaths, p. 726 [735]
— occupations, p. 521 [544]
— population projections, p. 873 [870]
— population, pp. 218, 785, 857 [226, 788, 852]
Hong Kong
— abortions, pp. 619, 621 [646, 650]
— births to unmarried mothers, p. 637 [666]
— births, p. 631 [661]
— cigarette smoking, p. 370 [380]
— college professors, p. 559 [585]
— contraception, pp. 659, 661 [686-687]
— deaths, pp. 689-690, 693, 755-756 [716-718, 763-764]
— divorce, p. 803 [809]
— employment, pp. 519, 535 [542, 560]
— enrollment in school, pp. 271-272, 274, 276 [285-288]
— enrollment in vocational school, p. 277 [289]
— female-headed households, p. 208 [215]
— fertility rates, p. 744 [753]
— illiteracy, p. 252 [269]
— infant deaths, pp. 755-756 [763-764]
— labor force, p. 536 [561]
— life expectancy, p. 772 [778]
— literacy, p. 251 [268]
— marital status, p. 782 [786]
— marriages, pp. 805, 808, 810 [810-812]
— maternal deaths, p. 689 [716]
— median age, p. 863 [859]
— occupations, p. 519 [542]
— population projections, p. 868 [865]
— population, pp. 782, 848 [786, 845]
— ratio of females to males, p. 860 [856]
— ratio of males to females, pp. 862-863 [858-859]
— teachers, p. 558 [584]
— wages in manufacturing, p. 455 [473]
Hospital utilization, pp. 171, 396-397 [180, 412-413]
— and Valium, p. 353 [362]
— procedures performed, p. 411 [429]
— victims of crime, p. 177 [184]
— victims, p. 180 [187]
Households
— black families, p. 202 [209]
— government assistance programs, p. 510 [531]
— income, p. 417 [435]
— poverty status, p. 511 [532]
— wealth, p. 507 [528]
— worldwide, pp. 205, 216 [213, 224]
Housework, pp. 183, 223, 225-226 [189, 233, 236-237]
— worldwide, pp. 184, 186 [191-192]
Housing expenditures, p. 443 [457]
Hungary
— abortions, pp. 620, 623-624 [647, 652-653]
— allocation of time, pp. 185, 187 [191-192]
— births, p. 641 [670]
— cigarette smoking, p. 371 [381]
— contraception, pp. 662-663, 678 [688-689, 704]
— deaths, pp. 703, 708, 711, 759 [725-727, 766]

Numbers following p. or pp. are page references. Numbers in [ ] are table references.

Subject and Geographic Index

1011

Hungary continued:
— divorce, p. 814 [816]
— elderly population, p. 854 [849]
— employment, pp. 520, 538 [543, 563]
— enrollment in school, pp. 289-290, 292-293 [296-299]
— enrollment in vocational school, p. 295 [300]
— fertility rates, p. 746 [754]
— housework, pp. 185, 187 [191-192]
— illiteracy, p. 254 [271]
— infant deaths, p. 759 [766]
— labor force, p. 537 [562]
— life expectancy, p. 774 [779]
— literacy, p. 253 [270]
— marital status, pp. 783, 791 [787, 794]
— marriages, pp. 817, 821, 824 [817-819]
— maternal deaths, p. 711 [727]
— occupations, p. 520 [543]
— population projections, p. 869 [866]
— population, pp. 783, 853 [787, 848]
— ratio of males to females, p. 861 [857]
— teachers, p. 564 [592]
Hunting, p. 938 [936]
Hydramnios, p. 644 [672]
Hypertension, pp. 378, 644 [391, 672]
Hysterectomy, p. 411 [429]
Iceland
— abortions, pp. 623-624 [652-653]
— births, p. 641 [670]
— deaths, pp. 704, 708, 759 [725-726, 766]
— divorce, p. 814 [816]
— employment, pp. 520, 538 [543, 563]
— enrollment in school, pp. 289-290, 292-293 [296-299]
— enrollment in vocational school, p. 295 [300]
— fertility rates, p. 746 [754]
— government, p. 885 [882]
— infant deaths, p. 759 [766]
— labor force, p. 537 [562]
— life expectancy, p. 774 [779]
— marital status, pp. 783, 791 [787, 794]
— marriages, pp. 817, 821, 824 [817-819]
— occupations, p. 520 [543]
— population, pp. 783, 853 [787, 848]
Idaho
— abortions, p. 617 [644]
— Catholic marriages, p. 909 [908]
— Catholic sisters, p. 904 [904]
— child rape victims, p. 139 [143]
— college enrollment, p. 280 [291]
— elective offices, p. 895 [892]
— prisoners under sentence of death, p. 115 [120]
— teacher salaries, p. 496 [518]
— WIC Program grants, p. 445 [458]
Illinois
See also: Chicago, Illinois
— Catholic marriages, p. 909 [908]
— Catholic sisters, p. 904 [904]
— college enrollment, p. 280 [291]
— executives' income, p. 85 [88]

Illinois continued:
— imprisonment, p. 114 [119]
— prisoners under sentence of death, p. 115 [120]
— teacher salaries, p. 495 [518]
— WIC Program grants, p. 444 [458]
Illiteracy See: Literacy
Imprisonment, pp. 105-106, 108, 110-111, 114, 116, 123-124, 127, 154 [110, 112-113, 115-116, 119, 122, 129-130, 133, 162]
— abuse history of inmates, pp. 118-120 [124-126]
— criminal history of inmates, pp. 106, 121 [111, 127]
— drugs, p. 137 [141]
— family history of inmates, p. 122 [128]
— HIV positive inmates, p. 403 [421]
— juveniles, p. 143 [148]
— mothers, p. 112 [117]
— offenses and sentences of inmates, p. 126 [132]
— prior sentences of inmates, pp. 109, 126 [114, 131]
— sentences of inmates, p. 117 [123]
— under sentence of death, pp. 115-116 [120-121]
Incest, pp. 140-141, 147-148, 408 [145, 154-155, 426]
— and abortion, pp. 5, 616 [5, 643]
— assistance funds for victims, p. 159 [168]
Income, p. 420 [438]
See also: Earnings; Salaries
— and risk of dying, p. 420 [437]
— Asian/Pacific Islander families, p. 200 [207]
— black families, p. 201 [208]
— by occupation, p. 463 [481]
— corporate executives, pp. 79-80, 85, 91-92 [83-84, 88, 94-96]
— death rates by, p. 698 [721]
— executives, p. 86 [89]
— families and households, p. 417 [435]
— families, pp. 201, 204 [208, 212]
— full-time workers, p. 422 [440]
— Hispanic origin families, p. 204 [212]
— household, p. 459 [477]
— jail inmates, p. 106 [112]
— married-couple families, p. 421 [439]
— median earnings, pp. 484, 496 [506, 519]
— nurses, p. 485 [507]
— older women, p. 508 [530]
— physical therapists, p. 485 [507]
— physician assistants, p. 485 [507]
— physics teachers, p. 579 [609]
— ratio of male-female earnings, p. 484 [505]
— registered nurses, pp. 485, 580 [507, 610]
— victims of crime, pp. 160, 163, 173-174 [169, 173, 181-182]
Incompetent cervix, p. 644 [672]
India
— abortions, pp. 619, 621-622 [646, 650-651]
— age at first marriage, p. 812 [813]
— births, pp. 631, 658 [661, 685]
— cigarette smoking, p. 370 [380]
— contraception, pp. 659, 661 [686-687]
— deaths, pp. 689, 714, 755-756 [716, 730, 763-764]
— dowry deaths, p. 179 [186]
— employment, p. 519 [542]
— enrollment in school, pp. 271-272, 274, 276 [285-288]

Numbers following p. or pp. are page references. Numbers in [ ] are table references.

1012

India continued:
— enrollment in vocational school, p. 277 [289]
— fertility rates, p. 744 [753]
— illiteracy, p. 252 [269]
— infant deaths, pp. 755-756 [763-764]
— labor force, p. 536 [561]
— life expectancy, p. 772 [778]
— literacy, p. 251 [268]
— marital status, p. 782 [786]
— maternal deaths, pp. 689, 714 [716, 730]
— median age, p. 863 [859]
— occupations, p. 519 [542]
— population projections, p. 868 [865]
— population, pp. 782, 848 [786, 845]
— ratio of females to males, p. 860 [856]
— ratio of males to females, pp. 862-863 [858-859]
— religion, p. 907 [907]
— teachers, p. 558 [584]
— time spent getting water, p. 184 [190]
— violence, p. 171 [180]
Indiana
   See also: Indianapolis, Indiana
— Catholic marriages, p. 909 [908]
— Catholic sisters, p. 904 [904]
— college enrollment, p. 280 [291]
— imprisonment, p. 114 [119]
— teacher salaries, p. 495 [518]
— WIC Program grants, p. 445 [458]
Indianapolis, Indiana
— arrestees, p. 102 [106-107]
— drugs, p. 131 [136]
— school dropouts, p. 103 [108]
Indigestion, p. 378 [391]
Indonesia
— allocation of time, pp. 186, 188 [191-192]
— births, p. 631 [661]
— cigarette smoking, p. 370 [380]
— contraception, pp. 659, 661 [686-687]
— deaths, pp. 689, 714, 755-756 [716, 730, 763-764]
— employment, pp. 519, 535 [542, 560]
— enrollment in school, pp. 271-272, 274, 276 [285-288]
— enrollment in vocational school, p. 277 [289]
— fertility rates, p. 744 [753]
— housework, pp. 186, 188 [191-192]
— illiteracy, p. 252 [269]
— infant deaths, pp. 755-756 [763-764]
— labor force, p. 536 [561]
— life expectancy, p. 772 [778]
— literacy, p. 251 [268]
— marital status, p. 782 [786]
— maternal deaths, pp. 689, 714 [716, 730]
— median age, p. 863 [859]
— occupations, p. 519 [542]
— population projections, p. 868 [865]
— population, pp. 782, 848 [786, 845]
— ratio of males to females, p. 863 [859]
— teachers, p. 558 [584]
Induced labor, p. 647 [674]
Infections, p. 376 [388]
Influenza, p. 376 [388]

Influenza deaths, p. 727 [736]
Inhalants
— use by juveniles, p. 144 [149]
Injuries, pp. 376, 381-382 [388, 394-395]
— involvement of alcohol, p. 351 [361]
Insurance
   See also: Health care
— expenditures, p. 443 [457]
Intrauterine device, p. 675 [701]
Iowa
— Catholic marriages, p. 909 [908]
— Catholic sisters, p. 904 [904]
— college enrollment, p. 280 [291]
— teacher salaries, p. 495 [518]
— WIC Program grants, p. 445 [458]
Iran
— age at first marriage, p. 812 [813]
— births, p. 631 [661]
— contraception, p. 659 [686]
— deaths, pp. 731-732, 756 [739-740, 764]
— divorce, p. 803 [809]
— employment, p. 519 [542]
— enrollment in school, pp. 271-272, 274, 276 [285-288]
— enrollment in vocational school, p. 277 [289]
— fertility rates, p. 744 [753]
— government, p. 887 [884]
— illiteracy, p. 252 [269]
— infant deaths, p. 756 [764]
— labor force, p. 536 [561]
— life expectancy, p. 772 [778]
— literacy, pp. 251, 257 [268, 274]
— marital status, pp. 782, 790 [786, 793]
— marriages, p. 840 [834]
— occupations, p. 519 [542]
— population projections, p. 874 [871]
— population, pp. 220, 782, 858 [228, 786, 853]
— teachers, p. 558 [584]
Iran-Contra Affair
— opinions about, p. 36 [40]
Iraq
— births, p. 632 [661]
— cigarette smoking, pp. 371, 374 [380, 386]
— contraception, p. 660 [686]
— deaths, p. 757 [764]
— divorce, p. 826 [822]
— employment, p. 519 [542]
— enrollment in school, pp. 271, 273-274, 276 [285-288]
— enrollment in vocational school, p. 277 [289]
— fertility rates, p. 745 [753]
— households, p. 216 [224]
— illiteracy, p. 260 [277]
— infant deaths, p. 757 [764]
— labor force, p. 536 [561]
— life expectancy, p. 773 [778]
— literacy, pp. 252, 257 [268, 274]
— marital status, pp. 782, 790 [786, 793]
— marriages, p. 840 [834]
— occupations, p. 519 [542]

Numbers following p. or pp. are page references. Numbers in [ ] are table references.

Iraq continued:
— population projections, p. 874 [871]
— population, pp. 220, 782, 848, 858 [228, 786, 845, 853]
— ratio of males to females, p. 862 [858]
— teachers, p. 558 [584]
— violence against women, p. 179 [186]
Ireland
— births, p. 641 [670]
— cigarette smoking, p. 371 [381]
— contraception, p. 662 [688]
— deaths, pp. 704, 708, 711, 758-759 [725-727, 765-766]
— education, p. 335 [345]
— employment, pp. 520, 538 [543, 563]
— enrollment in school, pp. 289-290, 292-293 [296-299]
— enrollment in vocational school, p. 295 [300]
— fertility rates, p. 746 [754]
— government, p. 885 [882]
— infant deaths, pp. 758-759 [765-766]
— labor force, p. 537 [562]
— life expectancy, p. 774 [779]
— marital status, pp. 784, 791 [787, 794]
— marriages, pp. 817, 821, 824 [817-819]
— maternal deaths, p. 711 [727]
— occupations, p. 520 [543]
— population projections, p. 869 [866]
— population, pp. 784, 853 [787, 848]
— religion, pp. 910-911 [909]
— wages in manufacturing, p. 473 [491]
— wages in mining, p. 474 [492]
Islam religion, pp. 906, 908 [906-907]
Isle of Man
— births, p. 641 [670]
— deaths, pp. 704, 708, 759 [725-726, 766]
— divorce, p. 814 [816]
— fertility rates, p. 746 [754]
— infant deaths, p. 759 [766]
— life expectancy, p. 774 [779]
— marital status, p. 784 [787]
— marriages, p. 824 [819]
— population, p. 784 [787]
Israel
— abortions, pp. 621-622 [650-651]
— births, p. 632 [661]
— cigarette smoking, p. 371 [380]
— college professors, p. 559 [585]
— deaths, pp. 690, 693, 757 [717-718, 764]
— divorce, p. 803 [809]
— employment, p. 519 [542]
— enrollment in school, pp. 271, 273-274, 276 [285-288]
— enrollment in vocational school, p. 277 [289]
— fertility rates, p. 745 [753]
— illiteracy, p. 260 [277]
— infant deaths, p. 757 [764]
— labor force, p. 536 [561]
— life expectancy, p. 773 [778]
— literacy, pp. 252-253 [268, 270]
— marital status, pp. 782, 790 [786, 793]
— marriages, pp. 805, 808, 810 [810-812]

Israel continued:
— maternal deaths, p. 689 [716]
— occupations, p. 519 [542]
— population projections, p. 869 [866]
— population, pp. 782, 848, 853 [786, 845, 848]
— religion, p. 907 [907]
— teachers, p. 558 [584]
Italy
— abortions, pp. 623-624 [652-653]
— births, p. 641 [670]
— cigarette smoking, p. 371 [381]
— contraception, pp. 662-663 [688-689]
— deaths, pp. 704, 708, 711, 758-759 [725-727, 765-766]
— divorce, p. 814 [816]
— educational attainment, p. 261 [278]
— education, p. 335 [345]
— elderly population, p. 854 [849]
— employment, pp. 520, 539 [543, 563]
— enrollment in school, pp. 289-290, 292-293, 312 [296-299, 317]
— enrollment in vocational school, p. 295 [300]
— fertility rates, p. 746 [754]
— illiteracy, p. 254 [271]
— infant deaths, pp. 758-759 [765-766]
— labor force, p. 537 [562]
— life expectancy, p. 774 [779]
— literacy, p. 253 [270]
— marital status, p. 784 [787]
— marriages, pp. 817, 821, 824 [817-819]
— maternal deaths, p. 711 [727]
— occupations, p. 520 [543]
— population projections, p. 869 [866]
— population, pp. 784, 853 [787, 848]
— rape, p. 162 [171]
— ratio of males to females, p. 861 [857]
IUD, p. 675 [701]
Ivory Coast *See:* Cote d'Ivoire
Jamaica
— births, p. 643 [671]
— contraception, pp. 664, 666 [690-691]
— deaths, pp. 719, 723, 726, 761 [733-735, 767]
— divorce, p. 828 [824]
— employment, p. 521 [544]
— enrollment in school, pp. 297-298, 300, 302 [302-305]
— enrollment in vocational school, p. 303 [306]
— female-headed households, p. 208 [215]
— fertility rates, p. 748 [756]
— illiteracy, p. 256 [273]
— infant deaths, p. 761 [767]
— life expectancy, p. 775 [780]
— marital status, p. 785 [788]
— marriages, p. 835 [827]
— maternal deaths, p. 726 [735]
— occupations, p. 521 [544]
— population projections, p. 873 [870]
— population, pp. 218, 785, 857 [226, 788, 852]
— religion, p. 912 [910]
— teachers, p. 568 [598]
Japan
— abortions, p. 622 [650-651]

Numbers following p. or pp. are page references. Numbers in [ ] are table references.

Japan continued:
— attitudes toward children, p. 25 [30]
— attitudes toward working women, p. 27 [31]
— births, p. 631 [661]
— cigarette smoking, p. 370 [380]
— college professors, p. 559 [585]
— computers in school, p. 228 [239]
— contraception, pp. 659, 661 [686-687]
— deaths, pp. 690, 693, 756, 758 [717-718, 764-765]
— divorce, p. 803 [809]
— educational attainment, p. 261 [278]
— elderly population, p. 854 [849]
— employment, p. 520 [543]
— enrollment in school, pp. 271, 273-274, 276, 312 [285-288, 317]
— enrollment in vocational school, p. 277 [289]
— fertility rates, p. 744 [753]
— government, p. 887 [884]
— housework, p. 188 [193]
— illiteracy, p. 253 [269]
— infant deaths, pp. 756, 758 [764-765]
— labor force, p. 537 [562]
— life expectancy, p. 772 [778]
— marital status, p. 782 [786]
— marriages, pp. 805, 808, 810 [810-812]
— occupations, p. 520 [543]
— population projections, p. 869 [866]
— population, pp. 782, 853 [786, 848]
— rape, p. 162 [171]
— reasons for working, p. 28 [32]
— teachers, p. 558 [584]
— wages in agriculture, p. 454 [471]
— wages in construction, p. 455 [472]
— wages in manufacturing, p. 456 [473]
— wages in mining, p. 457 [474]
— wages in transport, p. 458 [475]

Jazz
— attendance, pp. 948-949, 951 [945-946, 949]
— listening or viewing, pp. 952-953, 956 [951, 953, 957]
— participation, p. 957 [959]
— radio format preferences, p. 959 [962]

Jehovah Witness religion, p. 906 [906]

Jersey
See also: Channel Islands; Guernsey
— abortions, p. 623 [652]
— births, p. 641 [670]
— deaths, pp. 702, 707, 759 [725-726, 766]
— divorce, p. 814 [816]
— fertility rates, p. 746 [754]
— infant deaths, p. 759 [766]
— life expectancy, p. 774 [779]
— marital status, p. 790 [794]
— marriages, p. 824 [819]

Jewelry
— gift preference, p. 12 [13]

Jews
— contraceptive use, p. 680 [706]
— religion, p. 907 [907]

Job commitment, p. 53 [51]

Job promotions, pp. 530-531 [556-557]

Job Training Partnership Act, p. 418 [436]

Jogging, p. 936 [935]

Jordan
— births, p. 632 [661]
— contraception, pp. 660-661 [686-687]
— deaths, pp. 732, 757 [739-740, 764]
— divorce, p. 803 [809]
— employment, p. 519 [542]
— enrollment in school, pp. 271, 273-274, 276 [285-288]
— enrollment in vocational school, p. 277 [289]
— fertility rates, p. 745 [753]
— fertility, p. 753 [761]
— households, p. 216 [224]
— illiteracy, p. 260 [277]
— infant deaths, p. 757 [764]
— labor force, p. 536 [561]
— life expectancy, p. 773 [778]
— literacy, pp. 252, 257 [268, 274]
— marital status, p. 782 [786]
— marriages, pp. 805, 808, 840 [810-811, 834]
— occupations, p. 519 [542]
— population projections, p. 874 [871]
— population, pp. 220, 782, 848, 858 [228, 786, 845, 853]
— ratio of females to males, p. 860 [856]
— ratio of males to females, p. 862 [858]
— religion, p. 907 [907]
— teachers, p. 558 [584]

Juveniles
— alcohol use, p. 145 [151-152]
— delinquency trends, p. 141 [146]
— drug use, pp. 144-145 [149-151]
— in custody, p. 143 [148]
— prostitution, p. 142 [147]
— steroid use, p. 145 [152]
— tobacco use, p. 145 [152]
— victims of crimes, p. 146 [153]

Kansas
— Catholic marriages, p. 909 [908]
— Catholic sisters, p. 904 [904]
— child rape victims, p. 139 [143]
— college enrollment, p. 280 [291]
— elective offices, p. 895 [892]
— teacher salaries, p. 495 [518]
— WIC Program grants, p. 445 [458]

Kansas City, Missouri
— AIDS, p. 346 [358]
— alcohol, p. 129 [134]
— arrestees, pp. 101-102 [105-107]
— drugs, pp. 129-132, 134 [134-139]
— school dropouts, p. 103 [108]

Kazakhstan
— births, p. 642 [670]
— contraception, p. 675 [700]
— deaths, p. 766 [772]
— divorce, p. 803 [809]
— enrollment in school, p. 276 [288]
— fertility rates, p. 754 [762]
— infant deaths, p. 766 [772]
— life expectancy, p. 781 [785]

Numbers following p. or pp. are page references. Numbers in [ ] are table references.

Kazakhstan continued:
— marital status, p. 798 [803]
— marriages, pp. 805, 808, 810 [810-812]
— population, p. 798 [803]
Kentucky
— Catholic marriages, p. 909 [908]
— Catholic sisters, p. 904 [904]
— college enrollment, p. 280 [291]
— elective offices, p. 895 [892]
— imprisonment, p. 115 [119]
— teacher salaries, p. 495 [518]
— WIC Program grants, p. 445 [458]
Kenya
— births, p. 657 [684]
— clitoridectomy, pp. 171, 375 [180, 387]
— contraception, pp. 671, 673 [698-699]
— deaths, pp. 740, 765 [748, 771]
— employment, p. 518 [541]
— enrollment in school, pp. 262, 264, 266-267 [280-283]
— enrollment in vocational school, p. 269 [284]
— fertility rates, p. 752 [760]
— fertility, p. 754 [761]
— government, p. 887 [884]
— HIV/AIDS, p. 404 [422]
— illiteracy, p. 250 [267]
— infant deaths, p. 765 [771]
— life expectancy, p. 779 [784]
— literacy, p. 259 [276]
— marital status, p. 796 [802]
— maternal deaths, p. 740 [748]
— occupations, p. 518 [541]
— population projections, p. 880 [878]
— population, pp. 219, 796, 866 [227, 802, 863]
— time spent getting water, p. 184 [190]
— wages in agriculture, p. 450 [465]
— wages in construction, p. 451 [466]
— wages in manufacturing, p. 451 [467]
— wages in mining, p. 452 [468]
— wages in transport, p. 452 [469]
Kidnaping
— imprisonment for, pp. 108, 124 [113, 130]
Kidney disease, p. 365 [373]
— deaths, p. 700 [723]
Kiribati
— births, p. 655 [683]
— cigarette smoking, p. 373 [384]
— contraception, p. 669 [696]
— deaths, p. 763 [770]
— enrollment in school, pp. 308-309 [313-314]
— enrollment in vocational school, p. 311 [316]
— fertility rates, p. 751 [759]
— infant deaths, p. 763 [770]
— life expectancy, p. 778 [783]
— median age, p. 863 [859]
— ratio of males to females, p. 863 [859]
Knee joints, p. 409 [427]
Korea
See also: North Korea; South Korea
— cigarette smoking, p. 370 [380]

Korea continued:
— deaths, pp. 689-690, 693 [716-718]
— deaths of children, p. 716 [731]
— divorce, p. 803 [809]
— employment, p. 519 [542]
— enrollment in school, pp. 271, 273-274, 276 [285-288]
— enrollment in vocational school, p. 277 [289]
— government, p. 888 [884]
— illiteracy, p. 253 [269]
— labor force, p. 536 [561]
— marriages, pp. 806, 809, 811 [810-812]
— maternal deaths, p. 689 [716]
— occupations, p. 519 [542]
— population projections, p. 868 [865]
— population, p. 848 [845]
— religion, p. 907 [907]
— teachers, p. 558 [584]
— wages in agriculture, p. 454 [471]
— wages in construction, p. 455 [472]
— wages in manufacturing, p. 456 [473]
— wages in mining, p. 457 [474]
— wages in transport, p. 458 [475]
Kuwait
— births, p. 632 [661]
— cigarette smoking, pp. 371, 374 [380, 386]
— contraception, p. 660 [686]
— deaths, pp. 689, 732-733, 757 [716, 739-741, 764]
— divorce, p. 803 [809]
— employment, p. 519 [542]
— enrollment in school, pp. 271, 273-274, 276 [285-288]
— enrollment in vocational school, p. 278 [289]
— fertility rates, p. 745 [753]
— households, p. 216 [224]
— illiteracy, p. 260 [277]
— infant deaths, p. 757 [764]
— life expectancy, p. 773 [778]
— literacy, pp. 252, 257 [268, 274]
— marital status, pp. 783, 790 [786, 793]
— marriages, pp. 806, 809, 840 [810-811, 834]
— maternal deaths, pp. 689, 733 [716, 741]
— occupations, p. 519 [542]
— population projections, p. 874 [871]
— population, pp. 783, 849, 858 [786, 845, 853]
— ratio of females to males, p. 860 [856]
— ratio of males to females, p. 862 [858]
— teachers, p. 558 [584]
— violence against women, p. 179 [186]
Kyrgyzstan
— births, p. 642 [670]
— contraception, p. 675 [700]
— divorce, p. 803 [809]
— enrollment in school, p. 276 [288]
— fertility rates, p. 754 [762]
— infant deaths, p. 766 [772]
— life expectancy, p. 781 [785]
— marital status, p. 798 [803]
— marriages, pp. 806, 809, 811 [810-812]
— population, p. 798 [803]

Numbers following p. or pp. are page references. Numbers in [ ] are table references.

Labor force
— 1950-2000, p. 546 [571]
— Africa, p. 534 [559]
— Asia and the Pacific, p. 536 [561]
— developed countries, p. 537 [562]
— educational attainment and earnings, p. 468 [487]
— educational attainment, p. 528 [553]
— elderly, p. 855 [850]
— job promotions, pp. 530-531 [556-557]
— Latin America/Caribbean, p. 539 [564]
— multiple jobholders, p. 524 [548]
— nontraditional work, p. 323 [333]
— part-time, p. 525 [549]
— perceived responsibility for improving job performance,
   p. 58 [57]
— perceived usefulness of job skills, p. 64 [67]
— projections, pp. 533, 542-543 [558, 566-567]
— skilled trades, p. 526 [550]
— union membership, p. 544 [568]
— with disabilities, p. 379 [392]
— work experience and earnings, p. 469 [488]
— worker training, p. 551 [577]
— years of experience, p. 528 [553]
Laos
— births, p. 631 [661]
— deaths, pp. 689, 756 [716, 764]
— employment, p. 519 [542]
— enrollment in school, pp. 271, 273-274, 276 [285-288]
— enrollment in vocational school, p. 278 [289]
— fertility rates, p. 744 [753]
— illiteracy, p. 253 [269]
— infant deaths, p. 756 [764]
— life expectancy, p. 772 [778]
— literacy, p. 251 [268]
— maternal deaths, p. 689 [716]
— median age, p. 863 [859]
— occupations, p. 519 [542]
— population projections, p. 868 [865]
— ratio of males to females, p. 863 [859]
— teachers, p. 558 [584]
Larceny
— arrests, p. 102 [106]
— imprisonment, pp. 108, 123-124, 126 [113, 129-130, 132]
— juvenile offenses, p. 143 [148]
— perpetrators, p. 104 [109]
— victims, p. 160 [169]
Larynx cancer, p. 365 [373]
Latin America/Caribbean
   See also: South America
— age at first marriage, p. 812 [813]
— allocation of time, pp. 185, 187 [191-192]
— births to unmarried mothers, p. 637 [666]
— births, pp. 643, 658 [671, 685]
— cigarette smoking, p. 372 [382]
— contraception, pp. 664-665 [690-691]
— deaths, pp. 714, 717, 722, 726, 760 [730, 733-735, 767]
— divorce, p. 828 [824]
— educational attainment, p. 256 [273]

Latin America/Caribbean continued:
— employment and occupations, p. 521 [544]
— employment, p. 521 [544]
— enrollment in school, pp. 296, 298-299, 301 [302-305]
— enrollment in vocational school, p. 302 [306]
— female-headed households, p. 207 [215]
— fertility rates, p. 748 [756]
— government, pp. 886-887 [883-884]
— HIV/AIDS, p. 401 [419]
— housework, pp. 185, 187 [191-192]
— infant deaths, p. 760 [767]
— labor force, pp. 522, 524, 539 [545, 547, 564]
— life expectancy, p. 775 [780]
— literacy, p. 256 [273]
— marital status, pp. 784, 792 [788, 795]
— marriages, pp. 829, 831, 834 [825-827]
— maternal deaths, pp. 714, 726 [730, 735]
— occupations, p. 521 [544]
— population projections, p. 873 [870]
— population, pp. 218, 784, 857, 871 [226, 788, 852, 868]
— religious denominations, p. 911 [910]
— teachers, p. 568 [598]
— wages in agriculture, p. 480 [498]
— wages in construction, p. 481 [499]
— wages in manufacturing, p. 481 [500]
— wages in mining, p. 482 [501]
— wages in transport, p. 482 [502]
Latvia
— births, p. 642 [670]
— contraception, p. 674 [700]
— deaths, p. 766 [772]
— divorce, p. 814 [816]
— enrollment in school, p. 293 [299]
— fertility rates, p. 754 [762]
— infant deaths, p. 766 [772]
— life expectancy, p. 781 [785]
— marital status, p. 798 [803]
— marriages, pp. 817, 821, 824 [817-819]
— population, p. 798 [803]
— wages in agriculture, p. 470 [489]
— wages in manufacturing, p. 473 [491]
Law
— breast implant case settlement, p. 94 [98]
— degrees, pp. 231, 233, 236, 239, 241, 244 [245, 247, 251, 255-256,
   259]
Law School Admission Test scores, p. 338 [349]
Lebanon
— births, p. 632 [661]
— contraception, p. 660 [686]
— deaths, p. 757 [764]
— employment, p. 519 [542]
— enrollment in school, pp. 271, 273-274, 276 [285-288]
— enrollment in vocational school, p. 278 [289]
— fertility rates, p. 745 [753]
— government, p. 888 [884]
— illiteracy, p. 260 [277]
— infant deaths, p. 757 [764]
— life expectancy, p. 773 [778]

Numbers following p. or pp. are page references. Numbers in [ ] are table references.

Lebanon continued:
— literacy, pp. 252, 257 [268, 274]
— marital status, p. 783 [786]
— occupations, p. 519 [542]
— population projections, p. 874 [871]
— population, pp. 220, 783, 849, 858 [228, 786, 845, 853]
— ratio of males to females, p. 861 [857]
— teachers, p. 558 [584]
Lesbians, pp. 924, 929 [921, 927]
   See also: Homosexuality
— attitudes toward, p. 71 [75]
— HIV/AIDS, p. 405 [423]
Lesotho
— age at first marriage, p. 812 [813]
— births, p. 657 [684]
— contraception, pp. 671, 673 [698-699]
— deaths, p. 765 [771]
— employment, p. 518 [541]
— enrollment in school, pp. 264, 266, 268 [281-283]
— enrollment in vocational school, p. 269 [284]
— fertility rates, p. 752 [760]
— illiteracy, p. 250 [267]
— infant deaths, p. 765 [771]
— labor force, p. 534 [559]
— life expectancy, p. 779 [784]
— literacy, p. 259 [276]
— marital status, p. 796 [802]
— occupations, p. 518 [541]
— population projections, p. 880 [878]
— population, pp. 219, 796, 866 [227, 802, 863]
— ratio of males to females, p. 861 [857]
— teachers, p. 554 [580]
Liberia
— births, p. 657 [684]
— clitoridectomy, p. 375 [387]
— contraception, pp. 671, 673 [698-699]
— deaths, p. 765 [771]
— employment, p. 518 [541]
— enrollment in school, pp. 262, 264, 266, 268 [280-283]
— enrollment in vocational school, p. 269 [284]
— fertility rates, p. 752 [760]
— illiteracy, p. 250 [267]
— infant deaths, p. 765 [771]
— life expectancy, p. 779 [784]
— literacy, p. 259 [276]
— marital status, p. 796 [802]
— occupations, p. 518 [541]
— population projections, p. 880 [878]
— population, pp. 219, 796, 866 [227, 802, 863]
— teachers, p. 554 [580]
Librarians, pp. 570-571 [600-601]
— salaries, pp. 467, 483 [486, 503-504]
Library science degrees, pp. 231, 233, 236, 244 [245, 247, 251, 259]
Libya
— births, p. 654 [681]
— deaths, pp. 684, 686, 733, 762 [712-713, 741, 768]
— divorce, p. 799 [804]

Libya continued:
— employment, p. 518 [541]
— enrollment in school, pp. 262, 264, 266, 268 [280-283]
— enrollment in vocational school, p. 269 [284]
— fertility rates, p. 749 [757]
— illiteracy, p. 250 [267]
— infant deaths, p. 762 [768]
— life expectancy, p. 776 [781]
— literacy, p. 257 [274]
— marriages, p. 802 [807]
— maternal deaths, p. 733 [741]
— occupations, p. 518 [541]
— population projections, p. 874 [871]
— population, p. 858 [853]
— ratio of females to males, p. 860 [856]
— ratio of males to females, p. 862 [858]
Liechtenstein
— births, p. 641 [670]
— deaths, pp. 704, 708, 759 [725-726, 766]
— divorce, pp. 814, 827 [816, 823]
— fertility rates, p. 746 [754]
— infant deaths, p. 759 [766]
— life expectancy, p. 774 [779]
— marital status, pp. 784, 791 [787, 794]
— marriages, pp. 824, 836 [819, 829]
— population, p. 784 [787]
— religion, p. 911 [909]
Life expectancy, pp. 767-769, 771 [773-774, 776-777]
— Africa, pp. 776, 779 [781, 784]
— and Alzheimer's disease risk, p. 377 [389]
— Asia/Near East, p. 772 [778]
— Europe, p. 773 [779]
— Latin America/Caribbean, p. 775 [780]
— North America, p. 777 [782]
— Oceania, p. 778 [783]
— projections, p. 768 [775]
— Soviet Union, p. 781 [785]
— Yugoslavia, p. 781 [785]
Literacy
— Africa, pp. 249, 257-258 [267, 274, 276]
— Asia, pp. 251-252 [268-269]
— developed countries, p. 253 [270]
— Europe, p. 254 [271]
— Latin America/Caribbean, pp. 255-256 [272-273]
— Middle East, p. 257 [274]
— Near East, p. 260 [277]
— Oceania, p. 258 [275]
Lithuania
— abortions, pp. 623-624 [652-653]
— births, p. 642 [670]
— contraception, p. 674 [700]
— deaths, pp. 704, 709, 766 [725-726, 772]
— divorce, p. 814 [816]
— enrollment in school, p. 293 [299]
— fertility rates, p. 754 [762]
— infant deaths, p. 766 [772]
— life expectancy, p. 781 [785]
— marital status, p. 798 [803]

Numbers following p. or pp. are page references. Numbers in [ ] are table references.

Lithuania continued:
— marriages, pp. 817, 822, 824 [817-819]
— population, p. 798 [803]
Liver disease, p. 365 [373]
— deaths, p. 727 [736]
Living arrangements, pp. 208, 211 [216, 219]
— Asian/Pacific Islander population, p. 200 [207]
— black families, p. 201 [208]
— children of incarcerated mothers, p. 112 [117]
— elderly, pp. 213-214, 855 [221-222, 850]
— families and nonfamilies, p. 203 [211]
— families, pp. 201-202, 204 [208, 210, 212]
— Hispanic origin families, p. 204 [212]
— persons 15 years and over, pp. 209, 212 [217, 220]
— presence of children, p. 210 [218]
— prison inmates, p. 122 [128]
— reasons for leaving home, p. 217 [225]
— single women, p. 220 [229]
— worldwide, p. 207 [215]
— young adults, p. 215 [223]
Los Angeles, California
— AIDS, p. 346 [358]
— alcohol, p. 129 [134]
— arrestees, pp. 101-102 [105-107]
— drugs, pp. 129-131, 133-134 [134-139]
— school dropouts, p. 103 [108]
Louisiana
   See also: New Orleans, Louisiana
— Catholic marriages, p. 909 [908]
— Catholic sisters, p. 904 [904]
— college enrollment, p. 280 [291]
— elective offices, p. 895 [892]
— imprisonment, p. 114 [119]
— teacher salaries, p. 496 [518]
— WIC Program grants, p. 445 [458]
Low birth weight, pp. 649, 652 [675, 678]
LSAT scores, p. 338 [349]
LSD *See:* Hallucinogens
Lung disease, pp. 364-367, 644, 730 [372-376, 672, 737]
Lutheran religion, pp. 910, 913 [909, 911]
Luxembourg
— births, p. 641 [670]
— deaths, pp. 704, 709, 759 [725-726, 766]
— divorce, p. 814 [816]
— elderly population, p. 854 [849]
— employment, pp. 520, 539 [543, 563]
— enrollment in school, pp. 289, 291-293 [296-299]
— enrollment in vocational school, p. 295 [300]
— female-headed households, p. 207 [215]
— fertility rates, p. 746 [754]
— infant deaths, p. 759 [766]
— labor force, p. 538 [562]
— life expectancy, p. 774 [779]
— marital status, pp. 784, 791 [787, 794]
— marriages, pp. 817, 822, 824 [817-819]
— occupations, p. 520 [543]
— population, pp. 784, 853 [787, 848]
— ratio of males to females, p. 861 [857]

Luxembourg continued:
— teachers, p. 564 [592]
— wages in construction, p. 471 [490]
— wages in manufacturing, p. 473 [491]
Lymphoma, pp. 364-366 [372-373, 375]
Macau
— births, p. 631 [661]
— deaths, pp. 691, 693, 756 [717-718, 764]
— divorce, p. 804 [809]
— fertility rates, p. 744 [753]
— illiteracy, p. 253 [269]
— infant deaths, p. 756 [764]
— life expectancy, p. 772 [778]
— marital status, p. 782 [786]
— marriages, pp. 806, 809, 811 [810-812]
— population, p. 782 [786]
— religion, p. 907 [907]
— wages in manufacturing, p. 456 [473]
Macedonia
— births, p. 642 [670]
— fertility rates, p. 754 [762]
— infant deaths, p. 766 [772]
— life expectancy, p. 781 [785]
— marital status, p. 797 [803]
— population, p. 797 [803]
Machine operators, pp. 570-571 [600-601]
Madagascar
— births, p. 657 [684]
— contraception, pp. 671, 673 [698-699]
— deaths, pp. 714, 740, 765 [730, 748, 771]
— employment, p. 518 [541]
— enrollment in school, pp. 264, 266, 268 [281-283]
— enrollment in vocational school, p. 269 [284]
— fertility rates, p. 752 [760]
— government, p. 887 [884]
— illiteracy, p. 250 [267]
— infant deaths, p. 765 [771]
— life expectancy, p. 779 [784]
— literacy, p. 259 [276]
— marital status, p. 796 [802]
— marriages, p. 835 [828]
— maternal deaths, pp. 714, 740 [730, 748]
— occupations, p. 518 [541]
— population projections, p. 880 [878]
— population, pp. 219, 796, 866 [227, 802, 863]
— teachers, p. 554 [580]
Magazines, p. 954 [955]
Maine
— Catholic marriages, p. 909 [908]
— Catholic sisters, p. 904 [904]
— college enrollment, p. 280 [291]
— elective offices, p. 895 [892]
— teacher salaries, p. 495 [518]
— WIC Program grants, p. 445 [458]
Malawi
— age at first marriage, p. 812 [813]
— births, p. 657 [684]
— contraception, pp. 671, 673 [698-699]

Numbers following p. or pp. are page references. Numbers in [ ] are table references.

1019

Subject and Geographic Index

Malawi continued:
— deaths, pp. 740, 765 [748, 771]
— employment, p. 518 [541]
— enrollment in school, pp. 264, 266, 268 [281-283]
— enrollment in vocational school, p. 269 [284]
— female-headed households, p. 207 [215]
— fertility rates, p. 752 [760]
— HIV/AIDS, p. 404 [422]
— illiteracy, p. 250 [267]
— infant deaths, p. 765 [771]
— labor force, p. 534 [559]
— life expectancy, p. 779 [784]
— literacy, p. 259 [276]
— marital status, p. 796 [802]
— maternal deaths, p. 740 [748]
— occupations, p. 518 [541]
— population projections, p. 880 [878]
— population, pp. 219, 796, 866 [227, 802, 863]
Malaysia
— births, p. 631 [661]
— cigarette smoking, p. 370 [380]
— contraception, pp. 659, 661 [686-687]
— deaths, pp. 689, 691, 693, 755, 757 [716-718, 763-764]
— divorce, p. 826 [822]
— employment, p. 519 [542]
— enrollment in school, pp. 271, 273-274, 276 [285-288]
— enrollment in vocational school, p. 278 [289]
— fertility rates, p. 744 [753]
— illiteracy, p. 253 [269]
— infant deaths, pp. 755, 757 [763-764]
— labor force, p. 536 [561]
— life expectancy, p. 772 [778]
— literacy, p. 251 [268]
— marital status, p. 782 [786]
— marriages, pp. 811, 836 [812, 828]
— maternal deaths, p. 689 [716]
— median age, p. 863 [859]
— occupations, p. 519 [542]
— population projections, p. 868 [865]
— population, pp. 782, 848 [786, 845]
— ratio of males to females, p. 863 [859]
— religion, p. 908 [907]
— teachers, p. 558 [584]
Maldives
— births, p. 631 [661]
— deaths, pp. 691, 694, 757 [717-718, 764]
— divorce, pp. 804, 827 [809, 823]
— employment, pp. 519, 535 [542, 560]
— enrollment in school, pp. 271, 273-274 [285-287]
— enrollment in vocational school, p. 278 [289]
— fertility rates, p. 744 [753]
— infant deaths, p. 757 [764]
— labor force, p. 536 [561]
— life expectancy, p. 772 [778]
— marital status, pp. 782, 790 [786, 793]
— marriages, p. 811 [812]
— median age, p. 863 [859]
— occupations, p. 519 [542]

Maldives continued:
— population, p. 782 [786]
— ratio of males to females, p. 863 [859]
Males
— ratio of males to females, pp. 859, 864 [855, 860]
— sterilization, p. 683 [710]
Mali
— age at first marriage, p. 812 [813]
— births, p. 657 [684]
— clitoridectomy, p. 375 [387]
— contraception, pp. 671, 673, 677 [698-699, 703]
— deaths, p. 765 [771]
— employment, p. 518 [541]
— enrollment in school, pp. 264, 266, 268 [281-283]
— enrollment in vocational school, p. 269 [284]
— fertility rates, p. 752 [760]
— government, p. 887 [884]
— illiteracy, p. 250 [267]
— infant deaths, p. 765 [771]
— labor force, p. 534 [559]
— life expectancy, p. 779 [784]
— literacy, p. 259 [276]
— marital status, pp. 789, 796 [792, 802]
— marriages, p. 835 [828]
— occupations, p. 518 [541]
— population projections, p. 880 [878]
— population, pp. 219, 796, 866 [227, 802, 863]
— ratio of males to females, p. 861 [857]
Malta
— births, p. 641 [670]
— deaths, pp. 704, 709, 711, 759 [725-727, 766]
— employment, pp. 520, 539 [543, 563]
— enrollment in school, pp. 289, 291-293 [296-299]
— enrollment in vocational school, p. 295 [300]
— fertility rates, p. 746 [754]
— government, p. 887 [884]
— illiteracy, p. 254 [271]
— infant deaths, p. 759 [766]
— labor force, p. 538 [562]
— life expectancy, p. 774 [779]
— literacy, p. 257 [274]
— marital status, p. 791 [794]
— marriages, pp. 818, 822, 824 [817-819]
— maternal deaths, p. 711 [727]
— occupations, p. 520 [543]
— population, p. 853 [848]
— teachers, p. 564 [592]
Malvinas *See:* Falkland Islands
Managers, pp. 570-571 [600-601]
— employment, p. 578 [608]
— skills, p. 54 [52]
Manslaughter
— imprisonment, pp. 108, 123-124, 126, 154 [113, 129-130, 132, 162]
Manufacturing
— employment, p. 561 [588]
— wages (Africa), p. 451 [467]
— wages (Asia), p. 455 [473]
— wages (Europe), p. 472 [491]

Numbers following p. or pp. are page references. Numbers in [ ] are table references.

Subject and Geographic Index

Manufacturing continued:
— wages (Latin America/Caribbean), p. 481 [500]
— wages (Oceania), p. 486 [509]
Marijuana, pp. 353, 356, 390 [362, 366, 404]
— use by arrestees, pp. 129, 131 [134, 137]
— use by juveniles, p. 144 [149]
— use by prison inmates, p. 137 [141]
— use during pregnancy, p. 414 [432]
Marital status
— 1990 census, pp. 786-787 [789-790]
— abortions, p. 616 [643]
— Africa, pp. 789, 794, 796 [792, 799, 802]
— and childlessness, p. 849 [846]
— and children, p. 851 [847]
— and contraceptive use, p. 675 [701]
— and job promotions, pp. 530-531 [556-557]
— Asia/Near East, pp. 782, 790 [786, 793]
— black population, p. 788 [791]
— by race and Hispanic origin, p. 788 [791]
— crime victims, p. 153 [160]
— elderly, p. 855 [850]
— Europe, pp. 783, 790 [787, 794]
— family householders, p. 197 [204]
— Hispanic origin population, p. 788 [791]
— homeless people, p. 206 [214]
— householders, p. 211 [219]
— jail inmates, p. 111 [116]
— Latin America/Caribbean, pp. 784, 792 [788, 795]
— never married, p. 793 [798]
— North America, pp. 792, 795 [796, 800]
— Oceania, pp. 793, 795 [797, 801]
— prison inmates, p. 127 [133]
— Soviet Union, p. 797 [803]
— victims of crime, pp. 160, 163, 173-174 [169, 173, 181-182]
— voters for U.S. representatives, p. 893 [890]
— Yugoslavia, p. 797 [803]
Marriage, pp. 802, 839, 846 [808, 832-833, 843]
— Africa, pp. 799-800, 802 [805-807]
— Asia, pp. 804, 807, 810 [810-812]
— attitudes, p. 13 [14]
— before age 20 (worldwide), p. 811 [813]
— Catholic, p. 908 [908]
— Europe, pp. 815, 820, 824 [817-819]
— in ten countries, pp. 835-836 [828-829]
— Latin America/Caribbean, pp. 829, 831, 834 [825-827]
— marital satisfaction, p. 222 [231]
— Middle East, p. 840 [834]
— North America, pp. 841-842 [836-838]
— Oceania, pp. 843-845 [840-842]
— women divorced after first marriage, pp. 825, 837-838 [820, 830-831]
— women ever married, pp. 826, 837-838 [821, 830-831]
Married men
— contraception, p. 681 [708]
Married people, pp. 212, 788, 922-923, 929 [220, 791, 917, 919, 928]
— age and previous marital status, pp. 802, 839 [808, 832]
— childless, p. 849 [846]

Married people continued:
— contraception, p. 681 [708]
— elderly, p. 855 [850]
— families, pp. 202-203, 208 [209-211, 216]
— government assistance programs, p. 510 [531]
— in households, pp. 210-211 [218-219]
— income, pp. 417, 421 [435, 439]
— number of sex partners, p. 928 [926]
— poverty status, p. 511 [532]
— use of husband's surname, p. 15 [17]
— with children, p. 851 [847]
Marshall Islands
— births, p. 655 [683]
— deaths, pp. 736, 738, 763 [745-746, 770]
— fertility rates, p. 751 [759]
— infant deaths, p. 763 [770]
— life expectancy, p. 778 [783]
— median age, p. 863 [859]
— ratio of males to females, p. 863 [859]
Martinique
— abortions, p. 627 [654]
— births to unmarried mothers, p. 637 [666]
— births, p. 643 [671]
— contraception, p. 664 [690]
— deaths, pp. 719, 724, 761 [733-734, 767]
— divorce, p. 828 [824]
— employment, p. 521 [544]
— enrollment in school, pp. 297-298, 300 [302-304]
— enrollment in vocational school, p. 303 [306]
— female-headed households, p. 208 [215]
— fertility rates, p. 748 [756]
— illiteracy, p. 256 [273]
— infant deaths, p. 761 [767]
— labor force, p. 540 [564]
— life expectancy, p. 775 [780]
— marital status, p. 785 [788]
— marriages, pp. 830, 833, 835 [825-827]
— occupations, p. 521 [544]
— population, pp. 785, 857 [788, 852]
Maryland
— Catholic marriages, p. 909 [908]
— Catholic sisters, p. 904 [904]
— college enrollment, p. 280 [291]
— elective offices, p. 895 [892]
— imprisonment, p. 114 [119]
— teacher salaries, p. 495 [518]
— WIC Program grants, p. 445 [458]
Massachusetts
— Catholic marriages, p. 909 [908]
— Catholic sisters, p. 904 [904]
— college enrollment, p. 280 [291]
— imprisonment, p. 114 [119]
— teacher salaries, p. 495 [518]
— WIC Program grants, p. 445 [458]
Masturbation, p. 925 [922]
— attitudes of nuns, p. 45 [46]
Mathematics
— advanced placement examinations, p. 319 [327]

Numbers following p. or pp. are page references. Numbers in [ ] are table references.

Mathematics continued:
— degrees conferred, pp. 231, 233, 236, 244 [245, 247, 251, 259]
— faculty, p. 582 [611]
— proficiency, p. 339 [350]
Mauritania
— age at first marriage, p. 812 [813]
— births, p. 657 [684]
— clitoridectomy, p. 375 [387]
— contraception, pp. 671, 678 [698, 703]
— deaths, p. 765 [771]
— divorce, p. 826 [822]
— employment, p. 518 [541]
— enrollment in school, pp. 264, 266, 268 [281-283]
— enrollment in vocational school, p. 269 [284]
— fertility rates, p. 752 [760]
— illiteracy, p. 250 [267]
— infant deaths, p. 765 [771]
— life expectancy, p. 779 [784]
— literacy, p. 259 [276]
— marital status, p. 796 [802]
— occupations, p. 518 [541]
— population projections, p. 880 [878]
— population, pp. 219, 796, 866 [227, 802, 863]
Mauritius
— births to unmarried mothers, p. 637 [666]
— births, p. 657 [684]
— cigarette smoking, p. 374 [385]
— contraception, pp. 671, 673, 678 [698-699, 704]
— deaths, pp. 685-686, 740, 765 [712-713, 748, 771]
— divorce, p. 799 [804]
— employment, p. 518 [541]
— enrollment in school, pp. 262, 264, 266, 268 [280-283]
— enrollment in vocational school, p. 269 [284]
— fertility rates, p. 752 [760]
— illiteracy, p. 250 [267]
— infant deaths, p. 765 [771]
— life expectancy, p. 779 [784]
— marital status, p. 797 [802]
— marriages, pp. 800-802, 836 [805-807, 829]
— maternal deaths, p. 740 [748]
— occupations, p. 518 [541]
— population projections, p. 880 [878]
— population, pp. 219, 797, 866 [227, 802, 863]
— religion, p. 906 [906]
— teachers, p. 554 [580]
Mayotte
— births, p. 657 [684]
— fertility rates, p. 752 [760]
— infant deaths, p. 765 [771]
— life expectancy, p. 779 [784]
— marital status, p. 797 [802]
— population, p. 797 [802]
Medicaid See: Government assistance programs
Medical care
— victims of crime, p. 177 [184]
Medical device implants, p. 409 [427]
Medicare See: Government assistance programs
Medicine degrees, pp. 239, 241 [255-256]
Melanoma, pp. 364-365 [372-373]

Menstruation
— attitudes toward, p. 17 [19]
Methodist religion, pp. 911-913 [910]
Mexico
— births, p. 643 [671]
— cigarette smoking, p. 372 [382]
— college professors, p. 559 [585]
— contraception, pp. 665-666 [690-691]
— deaths, pp. 719, 724, 726, 761 [733-735, 767]
— deaths of children, p. 715 [731]
— divorce, p. 828 [824]
— employment, p. 521 [544]
— enrollment in school, pp. 297-298, 300, 302 [302-305]
— enrollment in vocational school, p. 303 [306]
— fertility rates, p. 748 [756]
— illiteracy, p. 256 [273]
— infant deaths, p. 761 [767]
— labor force, p. 540 [564]
— life expectancy, p. 775 [780]
— literacy, p. 255 [272]
— marital status, p. 785 [788]
— marriages, pp. 830, 833, 835 [825-827]
— maternal deaths, p. 726 [735]
— occupations, p. 521 [544]
— population projections, p. 873 [870]
— population, pp. 218, 785, 857 [226, 788, 852]
— religion, p. 912 [910]
— teachers, p. 568 [598]
Michigan
See also: Detroit, Michigan
— Catholic marriages, p. 909 [908]
— Catholic sisters, p. 904 [904]
— child rape victims, p. 139 [143]
— college enrollment, p. 280 [291]
— imprisonment, p. 114 [119]
— teacher salaries, p. 495 [518]
— WIC Program grants, p. 445 [458]
Micronesia (Federated States of)
— births, p. 655 [683]
— deaths, p. 763 [770]
— fertility rates, p. 751 [759]
— households, p. 216 [224]
— infant deaths, p. 763 [770]
— life expectancy, p. 778 [783]
— median age, p. 863 [859]
— ratio of males to females, p. 863 [859]
Middle East/North Africa
— cigarette smoking, p. 374 [386]
— deaths, pp. 731-733 [739-741]
— literacy, p. 257 [274]
— marriages, p. 840 [834]
— maternal deaths, p. 733 [741]
— population projections, p. 874 [871]
— population, pp. 220, 858 [228, 853]
Migraine, p. 378 [391]
Military academies
— sexual harassment, pp. 605-609 [633-637]
Military Archdiocese
— Catholic marriages, p. 908 [908]

Numbers following p. or pp. are page references. Numbers in [ ] are table references.

1022

Military personnel, pp. 588-593, 602-604 [618-623, 630-632]
— by branch, p. 601 [629]
— by rank, pp. 599-600 [627-628]
— degrees, pp. 231, 233, 236, 244 [245, 247, 251, 259]
— performance, p. 596 [625]
— pilot training, p. 598 [626]
— wartime conditions, p. 595 [624]
Mining
— wages (Africa), p. 452 [468]
— wages (Asia), p. 457 [474]
— wages (Europe), p. 474 [492]
— wages (Latin America/Caribbean), p. 482 [501]
— wages (Oceania), p. 487 [510]
Minnesota
— Catholic marriages, p. 909 [908]
— Catholic sisters, p. 904 [904]
— college enrollment, p. 280 [291]
— teacher salaries, p. 495 [518]
— WIC Program grants, p. 445 [458]
Mississippi
— Catholic marriages, p. 909 [908]
— Catholic sisters, p. 905 [904]
— college enrollment, p. 280 [291]
— elective offices, p. 895 [892]
— imprisonment, p. 114 [119]
— prisoners under sentence of death, p. 115 [120]
— teacher salaries, p. 496 [518]
— WIC Program grants, p. 445 [458]
Missouri
See also: Kansas City, Missouri; St. Louis, Missouri
— Catholic marriages, p. 909 [908]
— Catholic sisters, p. 905 [904]
— college enrollment, p. 280 [291]
— imprisonment, p. 114 [119]
— prisoners under sentence of death, p. 115 [120]
— teacher salaries, p. 496 [518]
— WIC Program grants, p. 445 [458]
Moldova
— births, p. 642 [670]
— contraception, p. 675 [700]
— divorce, p. 815 [816]
— enrollment in school, p. 293 [299]
— fertility rates, p. 755 [762]
— infant deaths, p. 766 [772]
— life expectancy, p. 781 [785]
— marital status, p. 798 [803]
— marriages, pp. 818, 822, 824 [817-819]
— population, p. 798 [803]
Monaco
— births, p. 641 [670]
— deaths, pp. 704, 709, 759 [725-726, 766]
— enrollment in school, pp. 289, 291-292 [296-298]
— enrollment in vocational school, p. 295 [300]
— fertility rates, p. 746 [754]
— households, p. 205 [213]
— infant deaths, p. 759 [766]
— life expectancy, p. 774 [779]
— population, p. 859 [854]

Money
— gift preference, p. 12 [13]
Mongolia
— births, p. 631 [661]
— deaths, pp. 689, 691, 694, 757 [716-718, 764]
— divorce, p. 804 [809]
— employment, pp. 519, 535 [542, 560]
— enrollment in school, pp. 271, 273-274, 276 [285-288]
— enrollment in vocational school, p. 278 [289]
— fertility rates, p. 744 [753]
— infant deaths, p. 757 [764]
— life expectancy, p. 772 [778]
— marriages, p. 811 [812]
— maternal deaths, p. 689 [716]
— median age, p. 863 [859]
— occupations, p. 519 [542]
— population projections, p. 868 [865]
— population, p. 848 [845]
— ratio of males to females, p. 863 [859]
— teachers, p. 558 [584]
Montana
— Catholic marriages, p. 909 [908]
— Catholic sisters, p. 905 [904]
— college enrollment, p. 280 [291]
— teacher salaries, p. 496 [518]
— WIC Program grants, p. 445 [458]
Montserrat
— births, p. 643 [671]
— contraception, pp. 665-666 [690-691]
— deaths, pp. 720, 724, 761 [733-734, 767]
— enrollment in school, pp. 297-298, 300 [302-304]
— enrollment in vocational school, p. 303 [306]
— fertility rates, p. 748 [756]
— infant deaths, p. 761 [767]
— life expectancy, p. 775 [780]
— religion, p. 912 [910]
Morality
— attitudes, p. 9 [10]
Morocco
— births, p. 654 [681]
— contraception, pp. 667-668 [692-693]
— deaths, pp. 714, 733, 762 [730, 741, 768]
— employment, p. 518 [541]
— enrollment in school, pp. 262, 264, 266, 268 [280-283]
— enrollment in vocational school, p. 269 [284]
— fertility rates, p. 749 [757]
— fertility, p. 754 [761]
— government, p. 887 [884]
— illiteracy, p. 250 [267]
— infant deaths, p. 762 [768]
— labor force, p. 534 [559]
— life expectancy, p. 776 [781]
— literacy, p. 257 [274]
— marital status, p. 794 [799]
— maternal deaths, pp. 714, 733 [730, 741]
— occupations, p. 518 [541]
— population projections, p. 874 [871]
— population, pp. 220, 794, 858 [228, 799, 853]

Numbers following p. or pp. are page references. Numbers in [ ] are table references.

Morocco continued:
—teachers, p. 554 [580]
Moslem religion, pp. 906-908 [906-907]
Mothers, p. 196 [202]
—births by age and medical risk factors, p. 644 [672]
—births by age and obstetric procedure, p. 647 [674]
—births by age and smoking status, p. 646 [673]
—births by age of, pp. 632, 650 [662, 676]
—births to teenagers, p. 649 [675]
—births to unmarried mothers (worldwide), p. 636 [666]
—births to unmarried mothers, pp. 638-639, 649 [667-668, 675]
—cesarean delivery, p. 640 [669]
—children enrolled in nursery school, p. 306 [311]
—in prison, p. 112 [117]
—low birth weight babies, p. 649 [675]
—on welfare, p. 544 [569]
—receiving prenatal care, p. 649 [675]
—single, pp. 208, 224 [216, 234]
—teenage, pp. 633-635 [663-665]
—triplets, p. 653 [679]
—twins, p. 653 [679-680]
—unmarried, p. 223 [232]
—work, pp. 195, 546-550 [201, 572-576]
Motor vehicle accidents
—deaths, pp. 727, 742-743 [736, 751-752]
Movies, p. 958 [961]
Mozambique
—age at first marriage, p. 812 [813]
—births, p. 657 [684]
—deaths, p. 765 [771]
—divorce, p. 827 [822]
—employment, p. 518 [541]
—enrollment in school, pp. 262, 264, 266, 268 [280-283]
—enrollment in vocational school, p. 269 [284]
—fertility rates, p. 752 [760]
—illiteracy, p. 250 [267]
—infant deaths, p. 765 [771]
—life expectancy, p. 779 [784]
—literacy, p. 259 [276]
—marital status, p. 797 [802]
—marriages, p. 836 [828]
—occupations, p. 518 [541]
—population projections, p. 880 [878]
—population, pp. 219, 797, 866 [227, 802, 863]
—teachers, p. 554 [580]
—time spent getting water, p. 184 [190]
Multiple births, p. 653 [679-680]
Murder
—defendants, p. 152 [159]
—imprisonment, pp. 108, 123-124, 126, 154 [113, 129-130, 132, 162]
—perpetrators, p. 104 [109]
—victims, p. 152 [159]
Music and musicals
—attendance at events, pp. 948-949 [945-946]
—attendance, pp. 948-949, 951 [945-946, 949]
—lessons, p. 952 [950]
—listening or viewing, pp. 953-954, 956 [952-954, 957]

Music and musicals continued:
—musicians' income, p. 453 [470]
—musicians, p. 555 [582]
—participation, p. 957 [959]
—radio format preferences, p. 959 [962]
Myanmar
See also: Burma
—deaths, p. 689 [716]
—employment, p. 519 [542]
—enrollment in school, pp. 273-274, 276 [286-288]
—enrollment in vocational school, p. 278 [289]
—illiteracy, p. 253 [269]
—maternal deaths, p. 689 [716]
—occupations, p. 519 [542]
—population projections, p. 868 [865]
—population, p. 848 [845]
—wages in construction, p. 455 [472]
—wages in manufacturing, p. 456 [473]
—wages in mining, p. 457 [474]
—wages in transport, p. 458 [475]
Namibia
—births, p. 657 [684]
—contraception, pp. 671, 673 [698-699]
—deaths, p. 765 [771]
—employment, p. 518 [541]
—enrollment in school, pp. 262, 264, 266, 268 [280-283]
—enrollment in vocational school, p. 270 [284]
—fertility rates, p. 753 [760]
—infant deaths, p. 765 [771]
—life expectancy, p. 780 [784]
—occupations, p. 518 [541]
—population projections, p. 880 [878]
—population, pp. 219, 866 [227, 863]
—teachers, p. 554 [580]
National Assessment of Educational Progress
—mathematics scores, p. 339 [350]
—reading scores, p. 340 [352]
—science scores, p. 344 [356]
National Merit Semifinalists, p. 339 [351]
Native American population *See:* American Indian/Eskimo/ Aleut population
Natural scientists, pp. 570-571 [600-601]
Nauru
—births, p. 655 [683]
—enrollment in school, pp. 307-309 [312-314]
—enrollment in vocational school, p. 311 [316]
—households, p. 216 [224]
—infant deaths, p. 763 [770]
—life expectancy, p. 778 [783]
Naval Academy
—sexual harassment, pp. 605-609 [633-637]
Near East
See also: Asia/Near East; Middle East; Middle East/North Africa
—births, p. 658 [685]
—Catholic missionaries, p. 902 [901]
—cigarette smoking, p. 370 [380]
—contraception, pp. 659-660 [686-687]

Numbers following p. or pp. are page references. Numbers in [ ] are table references.

Near East continued:
— deaths, pp. 690, 692 [717-718]
— educational attainment, p. 260 [277]
— fertility rates, p. 744 [753]
— infant deaths, p. 756 [764]
— life expectancy, p. 772 [778]
— literacy, p. 260 [277]
— marital status, pp. 782, 790 [786, 793]
— population, pp. 782, 848 [786, 845]

Nebraska
— Catholic marriages, p. 909 [908]
— Catholic sisters, p. 905 [904]
— child rape victims, p. 139 [143]
— college enrollment, p. 280 [291]
— teacher salaries, p. 496 [518]
— WIC Program grants, p. 445 [458]

Nederduitsc religion, p. 906 [906]

Needlework, p. 958 [960]

Nepal
— age at first marriage, p. 812 [813]
— allocation of time, pp. 186, 188 [191-192]
— births, p. 631 [661]
— cigarette smoking, p. 370 [380]
— contraception, pp. 659, 661 [686-687]
— deaths, pp. 689, 715, 755, 757 [716, 730, 763-764]
— deaths of children, p. 715 [731]
— employment, p. 519 [542]
— enrollment in school, pp. 271, 273-274, 276 [285-288]
— enrollment in vocational school, p. 278 [289]
— fertility rates, p. 744 [753]
— housework, pp. 186, 188 [191-192]
— illiteracy, p. 253 [269]
— infant deaths, pp. 755, 757 [763-764]
— labor force, p. 536 [561]
— life expectancy, p. 772 [778]
— literacy, p. 251 [268]
— marital status, p. 782 [786]
— maternal deaths, pp. 689, 715 [716, 730]
— median age, p. 863 [859]
— occupations, p. 519 [542]
— population projections, p. 868 [865]
— population, pp. 782, 848 [786, 845]
— ratio of females to males, p. 860 [856]
— ratio of males to females, pp. 862-863 [858-859]
— teachers, p. 558 [584]
— time spent getting water, p. 184 [190]

Netherlands
— abortions, pp. 619, 623-624 [646, 652-653]
— allocation of time, pp. 185, 187 [191-192]
— births, p. 641 [670]
— cigarette smoking, p. 371 [381]
— college professors, p. 559 [585]
— computers in school, p. 228 [239]
— contraception, pp. 662, 678 [688, 704]
— deaths, pp. 705, 709, 711, 758-759 [725-727, 765-766]
— divorce, p. 815 [816]
— education, p. 335 [345]
— elderly population, p. 854 [849]

Netherlands continued:
— employment, pp. 520, 539 [543, 563]
— enrollment in school, pp. 289, 291-293 [296-299]
— enrollment in vocational school, p. 295 [300]
— fertility rates, p. 746 [754]
— households, p. 205 [213]
— housework, pp. 185, 187 [191-192]
— infant deaths, pp. 758-759 [765-766]
— labor force, p. 538 [562]
— life expectancy, p. 774 [779]
— marital status, pp. 784, 791 [787, 794]
— marriages, pp. 818, 822, 824 [817-819]
— maternal deaths, p. 711 [727]
— occupations, p. 520 [543]
— population projections, p. 869 [866]
— population, pp. 784, 853 [787, 848]
— wages in manufacturing, p. 473 [491]
— wages in transport, p. 475 [493]

Netherlands Antilles
— births, p. 643 [671]
— deaths, pp. 720, 724, 761 [733-734, 767]
— divorce, p. 828 [824]
— employment, p. 521 [544]
— enrollment in school, pp. 297-298 [302-303]
— enrollment in vocational school, p. 303 [306]
— female-headed households, p. 208 [215]
— fertility rates, p. 749 [756]
— infant deaths, p. 761 [767]
— life expectancy, p. 775 [780]
— literacy, p. 255 [272]
— marital status, p. 785 [788]
— marriages, p. 835 [827]
— occupations, p. 521 [544]
— population, p. 785 [788]
— religion, p. 912 [910]

Nevada
— abortions, p. 617 [644]
— Catholic marriages, p. 909 [908]
— Catholic sisters, p. 905 [904]
— college enrollment, p. 280 [291]
— elective offices, p. 895 [892]
— prisoners under sentence of death, p. 115 [120]
— teacher salaries, p. 495 [518]
— WIC Program grants, p. 445 [458]

New Caledonia
— births, p. 655 [683]
— cigarette smoking, p. 373 [384]
— deaths, pp. 736, 738-739, 763 [745-747, 770]
— divorce, p. 843 [839]
— enrollment in school, pp. 308-310 [313-315]
— enrollment in vocational school, p. 311 [316]
— fertility rates, p. 751 [759]
— infant deaths, p. 763 [770]
— labor force, p. 536 [561]
— life expectancy, p. 778 [783]
— marital status, pp. 793, 795 [797, 801]
— marriages, p. 845 [842]
— maternal deaths, p. 739 [747]

Numbers following p. or pp. are page references. Numbers in [ ] are table references.

Subject and Geographic Index

New Caledonia continued:
— population, p. 795 [801]
— teachers, p. 575 [604]
New Hampshire
— Catholic marriages, p. 909 [908]
— Catholic sisters, p. 905 [904]
— college enrollment, p. 280 [291]
— elective offices, p. 895 [892]
— teacher salaries, p. 495 [518]
— WIC Program grants, p. 445 [458]
New Jersey
— Catholic marriages, p. 909 [908]
— Catholic sisters, p. 905 [904]
— college enrollment, p. 280 [291]
— elective offices, p. 895 [892]
— imprisonment, p. 114 [119]
— teacher salaries, p. 495 [518]
— WIC Program grants, p. 445 [458]
New Mexico
— Catholic marriages, p. 909 [908]
— Catholic sisters, p. 905 [904]
— college enrollment, p. 280 [291]
— teacher salaries, p. 496 [518]
— WIC Program grants, p. 445 [458]
New Orleans, Louisiana
— AIDS, p. 346 [358]
— alcohol, p. 129 [134]
— arrestees, pp. 101-102 [105-107]
— drugs, pp. 129-131, 133-134 [134-139]
— school dropouts, p. 103 [108]
New York
— abortions, p. 617 [644]
— Catholic marriages, p. 909 [908]
— Catholic sisters, p. 905 [904]
— college enrollment, p. 280 [291]
— executives' income, p. 85 [88]
— imprisonment, p. 114 [119]
— teacher salaries, p. 495 [518]
— WIC Program grants, p. 444 [458]
New York, New York
— AIDS, p. 346 [358]
— alcohol, p. 129 [134]
— arrestees, pp. 101-103 [105-107]
— drugs, pp. 129-134 [134-139]
— school dropouts, p. 103 [108]
New Zealand
See also: Oceania
— abortions, pp. 628-629 [656-657]
— births to unmarried mothers, p. 637 [666]
— births, p. 655 [683]
— cigarette smoking, p. 373 [384]
— contraception, p. 669 [696]
— deaths, pp. 736, 738-739, 763 [745-747, 770]
— divorce, p. 843 [839]
— education, p. 335 [345]
— employment, p. 520 [543]
— enrollment in school, pp. 308-310 [313-315]
— enrollment in vocational school, p. 311 [316]

New Zealand continued:
— female-headed households, p. 207 [215]
— fertility rates, p. 751 [759]
— infant deaths, p. 763 [770]
— labor force, p. 538 [562]
— life expectancy, p. 778 [783]
— marital status, p. 795 [801]
— marriages, pp. 844-845 [840-842]
— maternal deaths, p. 739 [747]
— occupations, p. 520 [543]
— population projections, p. 869 [866]
— population, pp. 795, 853 [801, 848]
— religion, p. 913 [911]
— teachers, p. 575 [604]
— wages in construction, p. 486 [508]
— wages in manufacturing, p. 486 [509]
— wages in mining, p. 487 [510]
— wages in transport, p. 487 [511]
Newspapers
— book reviews, p. 97 [101]
— reading, p. 954 [955]
Nicaragua
— births, p. 643 [671]
— contraception, p. 665 [690]
— deaths, pp. 720, 724, 726, 761 [733-735, 767]
— divorce, p. 828 [824]
— employment, p. 521 [544]
— enrollment in school, pp. 297-298, 300, 302 [302-305]
— enrollment in vocational school, p. 303 [306]
— fertility rates, p. 749 [756]
— fertility, p. 753 [761]
— government, p. 885 [882]
— households, p. 216 [224]
— illiteracy, p. 256 [273]
— infant deaths, p. 761 [767]
— life expectancy, p. 776 [780]
— literacy, p. 255 [272]
— marital status, p. 785 [788]
— marriages, p. 835 [827]
— maternal deaths, p. 726 [735]
— occupations, p. 521 [544]
— population projections, p. 873 [870]
— population, pp. 218, 785, 857 [226, 788, 852]
— teachers, p. 568 [598]
Niger
— births, p. 657 [684]
— clitoridectomy, p. 375 [387]
— contraception, pp. 671, 673 [698-699]
— deaths, pp. 714, 740, 765 [730, 748, 771]
— employment, p. 518 [541]
— enrollment in school, pp. 262, 264, 266, 268 [280-283]
— enrollment in vocational school, p. 270 [284]
— fertility rates, p. 753 [760]
— illiteracy, p. 250 [267]
— infant deaths, p. 765 [771]
— life expectancy, p. 780 [784]
— literacy, p. 259 [276]
— maternal deaths, pp. 714, 740 [730, 748]

Numbers following p. or pp. are page references. Numbers in [ ] are table references.

Niger continued:
— occupations, p. 518 [541]
— population projections, p. 880 [878]
— population, p. 866 [863]
— teachers, p. 554 [580]
Nigeria
— age at first marriage, p. 812 [813]
— births, p. 657 [684]
— cigarette smoking, p. 374 [385]
— clitoridectomy, p. 375 [387]
— contraception, pp. 672-673 [698-699]
— deaths, pp. 714, 740, 765 [730, 748, 771]
— employment, p. 518 [541]
— enrollment in school, pp. 264, 266, 268 [281-283]
— enrollment in vocational school, p. 270 [284]
— fertility rates, p. 753 [760]
— illiteracy, p. 250 [267]
— infant deaths, p. 765 [771]
— labor force, p. 534 [559]
— life expectancy, p. 780 [784]
— literacy, p. 259 [276]
— marital status, p. 797 [802]
— maternal deaths, pp. 714, 740 [730, 748]
— occupations, p. 518 [541]
— population projections, p. 880 [878]
— population, pp. 219, 797, 866 [227, 802, 863]
— teachers, p. 554 [580]
Niue
— enrollment in school, pp. 308-309 [313-314]
— marital status, p. 793 [797]
Norfolk Island
— deaths, pp. 736, 738 [745-746]
— marital status, p. 793 [797]
— marriages, p. 845 [842]
Norplant, pp. 95, 679 [99, 705]
North Africa
See also: Africa; Central African Republic; Middle East/
North Africa; South Africa; Sub-Saharan Africa
— births, pp. 654, 658 [681, 685]
— cigarette smoking, p. 374 [386]
— contraception, pp. 667-668 [692-693]
— fertility rates, p. 749 [757]
— infant deaths, p. 762 [768]
— life expectancy, p. 776 [781]
— marital status, p. 794 [799]
— maternal deaths, p. 733 [741]
— population projections, p. 874 [871]
— population, pp. 220, 794, 858 [228, 799, 853]
North America
— abortions, p. 627 [654-655]
— allocation of time, pp. 184, 186 [191-192]
— births, pp. 655, 658 [682, 685]
— Catholic missionaries, p. 902 [901]
— cigarette smoking, p. 373 [383]
— contraception, pp. 668-669 [694-695]
— deaths, pp. 734-735, 762 [742-744, 769]
— divorce, p. 841 [835]
— enrollment in school, pp. 304-305 [307-310]

North America continued:
— fertility rates, p. 750 [758]
— HIV/AIDS, p. 401 [419]
— housework, pp. 184, 186, 188 [191-193]
— infant deaths, p. 762 [769]
— life expectancy, p. 777 [782]
— marital status, pp. 792, 795 [796, 800]
— marriages, pp. 841-842 [836-838]
— maternal deaths, p. 735 [744]
— population, pp. 795, 871 [800, 868]
— teachers, p. 569 [599]
North Carolina
— Catholic marriages, p. 909 [908]
— Catholic sisters, p. 905 [904]
— child rape victims, p. 139 [143]
— college enrollment, p. 280 [291]
— imprisonment, p. 114 [119]
— prisoners under sentence of death, p. 115 [120]
— teacher salaries, p. 496 [518]
— WIC Program grants, p. 445 [458]
North Dakota
— Catholic marriages, p. 909 [908]
— Catholic sisters, p. 905 [904]
— child rape victims, pp. 138-139 [142-143]
— college enrollment, p. 280 [291]
— teacher salaries, p. 496 [518]
— WIC Program grants, p. 446 [458]
North Korea
See also: Korea
— births, p. 631 [661]
— fertility rates, p. 744 [753]
— infant deaths, p. 757 [764]
— life expectancy, p. 772 [778]
North Yemen
See also: South Yemen; Yemen
— contraception, p. 678 [703]
— ratio of males to females, p. 861 [857]
Northern Mariana Islands
— births, p. 655 [683]
— infant deaths, p. 763 [770]
— life expectancy, p. 778 [783]
— marital status, p. 793 [797]
— marriages, p. 845 [842]
Norway
— abortions, p. 623 [652]
— allocation of time, pp. 185, 187 [191-192]
— births to unmarried mothers, p. 637 [666]
— births, p. 641 [670]
— cigarette smoking, p. 371 [381]
— contraception, pp. 662-663 [688-689]
— deaths, pp. 705, 709, 711, 758-759 [725-727, 765-766]
— education, p. 335 [345]
— elderly population, p. 854 [849]
— employment, pp. 520, 539 [543, 563]
— enrollment in school, pp. 289, 291-293 [296-299]
— enrollment in vocational school, p. 295 [300]
— female-headed households, p. 207 [215]
— fertility rates, p. 746 [754]

Subject and Geographic Index

Numbers following p. or pp. are page references. Numbers in [ ] are table references.

1027

Norway continued:
— government, pp. 885-886 [882-883]
— households, p. 205 [213]
— housework, pp. 185, 187 [191-192]
— infant deaths, pp. 758-759 [765-766]
— labor force, p. 538 [562]
— life expectancy, p. 774 [779]
— marital status, pp. 784, 791 [787, 794]
— marriages, pp. 818, 822, 824 [817-819]
— maternal deaths, p. 711 [727]
— occupations, p. 520 [543]
— population projections, p. 869 [866]
— population, pp. 784, 853 [787, 848]
— teachers, p. 564 [592]
— wages in manufacturing, p. 473 [491]
— wages in transport, p. 475 [493]
Nuclear power
— opinions on, p. 39 [41]
Nuns
— opinions of, p. 45 [46]
Nursery school enrollment, p. 306 [311]
    See also: Education
Nurses, p. 580 [610]
— income, p. 485 [507]
Occupations, pp. 570-571 [600-601]
— 20 leading occupations, p. 465 [483]
— Africa, p. 518 [541]
— architecture, p. 555 [581]
— artists, pp. 453, 555, 557 [470, 582-583]
— Asia and the Pacific, p. 519 [542]
— by disability status, p. 562 [589]
— college professors, pp. 559, 561 [585, 587]
— developed countries, p. 520 [543]
— distribution, p. 563 [590]
— elementary and secondary schools, p. 563 [591]
— fastest growing, p. 573 [602]
— Federal Government, pp. 565-566 [593-595]
— food service, p. 567 [596-597]
— government, p. 585 [614]
— high school students' expectations, p. 321 [330]
— Hispanic females, p. 574 [603]
— income, p. 463 [481]
— Latin America/Caribbean, p. 521 [544]
— military personnel, p. 603 [631]
— physicians, p. 575 [605]
— private sector managerial and professional, p. 578 [608]
— ratio of median weekly earnings, p. 466 [484]
— registered nurses, p. 580 [610]
— secretaries, p. 583 [612]
— teachers (Africa), p. 553 [580]
— teachers (Asia), p. 558 [584]
— teachers (Europe), p. 564 [592]
— teachers (Latin America/Caribbean), p. 568 [598]
— teachers (North America), p. 569 [599]
— teachers (Oceania), p. 575 [604]
— teachers, pp. 563, 576, 579, 585-586 [591, 606, 609, 615-616]
— wages, p. 500 [522]
— waitresses, p. 586 [617]

Oceania
— abortions, pp. 628-629 [656-657]
— births, pp. 655, 658 [683, 685]
— Catholic missionaries, p. 902 [901]
— cigarette smoking, p. 373 [384]
— contraception, pp. 669-670 [696-697]
— deaths, pp. 736-737, 739, 763 [745-747, 770]
— divorce, p. 843 [839]
— educational attainment, p. 258 [275]
— enrollment in school, pp. 307-310 [312-315]
— enrollment in vocational school, p. 311 [316]
— fertility rates, p. 751 [759]
— HIV/AIDS, p. 401 [419]
— infant deaths, p. 763 [770]
— life expectancy, p. 778 [783]
— literacy, p. 258 [275]
— marital status, pp. 793, 795 [797, 801]
— marriages, pp. 843-845 [840-842]
— maternal deaths, p. 739 [747]
— population, pp. 795, 871 [801, 868]
— ratio of females to males, p. 861 [856]
— religious denominations, p. 913 [911]
— teachers, p. 575 [604]
— wages in construction, p. 486 [508]
— wages in manufacturing, p. 486 [509]
— wages in mining, p. 487 [510]
— wages in transport, p. 487 [511]
Ohio
— Catholic marriages, p. 909 [908]
— Catholic sisters, p. 905 [904]
— college enrollment, p. 280 [291]
— drugs, p. 130 [136]
— imprisonment, p. 114 [119]
— teacher salaries, p. 495 [518]
— WIC Program grants, p. 444 [458]
Oklahoma
— Catholic marriages, p. 909 [908]
— Catholic sisters, p. 905 [904]
— college enrollment, p. 280 [291]
— elective offices, p. 895 [892]
— imprisonment, p. 114 [119]
— prisoners under sentence of death, p. 115 [120]
— teacher salaries, p. 496 [518]
— WIC Program grants, p. 445 [458]
Oligohydramnios, p. 644 [672]
Olive oil
— benefits, p. 386 [400]
Oman
— births, p. 632 [661]
— contraception, p. 660 [686]
— deaths, p. 757 [764]
— employment, p. 519 [542]
— enrollment in school, pp. 271, 273-274, 276 [285-288]
— enrollment in vocational school, p. 278 [289]
— fertility rates, p. 745 [753]
— infant deaths, p. 757 [764]
— life expectancy, p. 773 [778]
— literacy, pp. 252, 257 [268, 274]

Numbers following p. or pp. are page references. Numbers in [ ] are table references.

1028

Oman continued:
— occupations, p. 519 [542]
— population projections, p. 874 [871]
— population, pp. 849, 858 [845, 853]
— ratio of females to males, p. 860 [856]
— ratio of males to females, p. 862 [858]
Online services, pp. 99, 961 [103, 964]
Opera
— attendance, pp. 948-949, 951 [945-946, 949]
— listening or viewing, pp. 953, 956 [952-953, 957]
— participation, p. 957 [959]
Operation Desert Shield/Desert Storm
— military personnel, pp. 588-593 [618-623]
Operations, p. 411 [429]
Optometry degrees, pp. 239, 241 [255-256]
Oregon
   See also: Portland, Oregon
— Catholic marriages, p. 909 [908]
— Catholic sisters, p. 905 [904]
— college enrollment, p. 281 [291]
— politics, p. 883 [881]
— teacher salaries, p. 495 [518]
— WIC Program grants, p. 445 [458]
Orgasm, pp. 920, 924, 932 [915, 920, 931]
Orthopedic impairments, p. 378 [391]
Osteopathic Medicine degrees, pp. 239, 241 [255-256]
Ovarian cancer, pp. 364, 366 [372, 375]
— and diet, p. 386 [400]
Pacemakers, p. 409 [427]
Pacific Islands
— enrollment in school, p. 310 [315]
Painters and painting, p. 555 [582]
— income, p. 453 [470]
— participation, p. 958 [960]
Pakistan
— age at first marriage, p. 812 [813]
— births, p. 631 [661]
— cigarette smoking, p. 370 [380]
— contraception, pp. 659, 661 [686-687]
— deaths, pp. 689, 691, 694, 715, 756-757 [716-718, 730, 763-764]
— deaths of children, p. 715 [731]
— employment, pp. 519, 535 [542, 560]
— enrollment in school, pp. 273-274, 276 [286-288]
— enrollment in vocational school, p. 278 [289]
— fertility rates, p. 744 [753]
— households, p. 216 [224]
— illiteracy, p. 253 [269]
— infant deaths, pp. 756-757 [763-764]
— labor force, p. 536 [561]
— life expectancy, p. 772 [778]
— literacy, p. 251 [268]
— marital status, p. 782 [786]
— marriages, p. 836 [829]
— maternal deaths, pp. 689, 715 [716, 730]
— median age, p. 863 [859]
— occupations, p. 519 [542]
— population projections, p. 868 [865]
— population, pp. 782, 848 [786, 845]

Pakistan continued:
— ratio of females to males, p. 860 [856]
— ratio of males to females, pp. 862-863 [858-859]
— religion, p. 908 [907]
— teachers, p. 558 [584]
— time spent getting water, p. 184 [190]
Palau
— births, p. 655 [683]
— deaths, pp. 737-738 [745-746]
Palestine
   See also: Gaza Strip
— enrollment in school, pp. 271, 273-274, 276 [285-288]
— enrollment in vocational school, p. 278 [289]
— teachers, p. 558 [584]
Panama
— abortions, p. 627 [654]
— births, p. 643 [671]
— contraception, pp. 665-666 [690-691]
— deaths, pp. 720, 724, 726, 761 [733-735, 767]
— deaths of children, p. 715 [731]
— divorce, p. 828 [824]
— employment, p. 521 [544]
— enrollment in school, pp. 297, 299-300, 302 [302-305]
— enrollment in vocational school, p. 303 [306]
— female-headed households, p. 208 [215]
— fertility rates, p. 749 [756]
— illiteracy, p. 256 [273]
— infant deaths, p. 761 [767]
— labor force, p. 540 [564]
— life expectancy, p. 776 [780]
— literacy, p. 255 [272]
— marital status, p. 785 [788]
— marriages, pp. 830, 833, 835 [825-827]
— maternal deaths, p. 726 [735]
— occupations, p. 521 [544]
— population projections, p. 873 [870]
— population, pp. 218, 785, 857 [226, 788, 852]
— teachers, p. 568 [598]
Pancreatic cancer, p. 364 [372]
Pantyhose sales, p. 448 [462]
Papua New Guinea
— births, p. 656 [683]
— cigarette smoking, pp. 370, 373 [380, 384]
— contraception, pp. 670, 677 [696, 703]
— deaths, pp. 689, 715, 739, 763 [716, 730, 747, 770]
— employment, p. 519 [542]
— enrollment in school, pp. 308-310 [313-315]
— enrollment in vocational school, p. 311 [316]
— fertility rates, p. 751 [759]
— government, p. 888 [884]
— illiteracy, p. 258 [275]
— infant deaths, p. 763 [770]
— life expectancy, p. 778 [783]
— maternal deaths, pp. 689, 715, 739 [716, 730, 747]
— median age, p. 863 [859]
— occupations, p. 519 [542]
— population projections, p. 868 [865]
— population, p. 848 [845]

Numbers following p. or pp. are page references. Numbers in [ ] are table references.

Subject and Geographic Index

Papua New Guinea continued:
— ratio of females to males, p. 861 [856]
— ratio of males to females, pp. 862-863 [858-859]
— religion, p. 913 [911]
— teachers, p. 575 [604]
Paraguay
— births, p. 643 [671]
— contraception, pp. 665-666 [690-691]
— deaths, pp. 714, 720, 724, 726, 761 [730, 733-735, 767]
— employment, p. 521 [544]
— enrollment in school, pp. 297, 299-300, 302 [302-305]
— enrollment in vocational school, p. 303 [306]
— fertility rates, p. 749 [756]
— government, p. 887 [884]
— illiteracy, p. 256 [273]
— infant deaths, p. 761 [767]
— labor force, p. 540 [564]
— life expectancy, p. 776 [780]
— literacy, p. 255 [272]
— marital status, p. 785 [788]
— marriages, pp. 830, 833, 835 [825-827]
— maternal deaths, pp. 714, 726 [730, 735]
— occupations, p. 521 [544]
— population projections, p. 873 [870]
— population, pp. 218, 785, 857 [226, 788, 852]
— wages in agriculture, p. 480 [498]
— wages in construction, p. 481 [499]
— wages in manufacturing, p. 481 [500]
— wages in mining, p. 482 [501]
— wages in transport, p. 482 [502]
Parole violation arrests, p. 102 [106]
Part-time work, p. 525 [549]
— multiple jobholders, p. 524 [548]
Pay equity
— opinions about, pp. 31, 43, 59 [35, 43, 58]
PCP *See:* Hallucinogens
Pell Grants, p. 418 [436]
Pennsylvania
  See also: Philadelphia, Pennsylvania
— Catholic marriages, p. 909 [908]
— Catholic sisters, p. 905 [904]
— child rape victims, p. 139 [143]
— college enrollment, p. 281 [291]
— elective offices, p. 895 [892]
— imprisonment, p. 114 [119]
— prisoners under sentence of death, p. 115 [120]
— teacher salaries, p. 495 [518]
— WIC Program grants, p. 445 [458]
Penumonia deaths, p. 727 [736]
Performing arts degrees, pp. 231, 233, 236, 244 [245, 247, 251, 259]
Perfume
— gift preference, p. 12 [13]
Periodic abstinence, p. 677 [702]
Persian Gulf War, pp. 595-596 [624-625]
— opinions on, pp. 36, 39 [40-41]
Peru
— allocation of time, pp. 185, 187 [191-192]

Peru continued:
— births, p. 643 [671]
— cigarette smoking, p. 372 [382]
— contraception, pp. 665, 667 [690-691]
— deaths, pp. 720, 724, 726, 761 [733-735, 767]
— deaths of children, p. 715 [731]
— divorce, p. 827 [823]
— employment, p. 521 [544]
— enrollment in school, pp. 297, 299-300, 302 [302-305]
— enrollment in vocational school, p. 303 [306]
— female-headed households, p. 208 [215]
— fertility rates, p. 749 [756]
— fertility, p. 754 [761]
— housework, pp. 185, 187 [191-192]
— illiteracy, p. 256 [273]
— infant deaths, p. 761 [767]
— labor force, p. 540 [564]
— life expectancy, p. 776 [780]
— literacy, p. 255 [272]
— marital status, p. 785 [788]
— maternal deaths, p. 726 [735]
— occupations, p. 521 [544]
— population projections, p. 873 [870]
— population, pp. 218, 785, 857 [226, 788, 852]
— religion, p. 912 [910]
— teachers, p. 568 [598]
Pharmacy degrees, pp. 239, 241 [255-256]
Philadelphia, Pennsylvania
  See also: Pennsylvania
— AIDS, p. 346 [358]
— alcohol, p. 129 [134]
— arrestees, pp. 101-103 [105-107]
— drugs, pp. 129-134 [134-139]
— school dropouts, p. 103 [108]
Philippines
— births to unmarried mothers, p. 637 [666]
— births, p. 631 [661]
— contraception, pp. 659, 661 [686-687]
— deaths, pp. 689, 691, 694, 755, 757 [716-718, 763-764]
— deaths of children, p. 715 [731]
— employment, pp. 519, 535 [542, 560]
— enrollment in school, pp. 271, 273-274, 276 [285-288]
— fertility rates, p. 744 [753]
— government, pp. 885-886 [882-883]
— illiteracy, p. 253 [269]
— infant deaths, pp. 755, 757 [763-764]
— labor force, p. 536 [561]
— life expectancy, p. 772 [778]
— literacy, p. 251 [268]
— marital status, p. 782 [786]
— marriages, pp. 806, 809, 811 [810-812]
— maternal deaths, p. 689 [716]
— median age, p. 863 [859]
— occupations, p. 519 [542]
— population projections, p. 868 [865]
— population, pp. 782, 848 [786, 845]
— ratio of males to females, p. 863 [859]
— teachers, p. 558 [584]

Numbers following p. or pp. are page references. Numbers in [ ] are table references.

Philosophy degrees, pp. 231, 233, 236, 244 [245, 247, 251, 259]
Phoenix, Arizona
   See also: Arizona
—AIDS, p. 346 [358]
—alcohol, p. 129 [134]
—arrestees, pp. 101-103 [105-107]
—drugs, pp. 129-134 [134-139]
—school dropouts, p. 103 [108]
Photography, pp. 453, 555 [470, 582]
—gift preference, p. 12 [13]
—participation, p. 958 [960]
Physical sciences degrees, pp. 231, 233, 236, 244 [245, 247, 251, 259]
Physical therapists
—income, p. 485 [507]
Physician contacts, pp. 396, 398 [412, 414]
Physicians, p. 575 [605]
Physics/Astronomy
—faculty, pp. 576, 582 [607, 611]
—minorities in, pp. 246, 296 [262, 301]
—salaries, pp. 488, 493 [512, 516]
Pill *See:* Birth control pill
Pitcairn
—marital status, p. 793 [797]
Plays
—attendance, pp. 948-949, 951 [945-946, 949]
—listening or viewing, pp. 953-954 [952, 954]
Pneumonia deaths, p. 700 [723]
Podiatry degrees, pp. 239, 241 [255-256]
Poisoning deaths, p. 741 [750]
Poland
—abortions, p. 623 [652]
—allocation of time, pp. 185, 187 [191-192]
—births, p. 641 [670]
—cigarette smoking, p. 371 [381]
—contraception, p. 662 [688]
—deaths, pp. 705, 709, 711, 759 [725-727, 766]
—divorce, p. 815 [816]
—employment, pp. 520, 539 [543, 563]
—enrollment in school, pp. 289, 291-293 [296-299]
—enrollment in vocational school, p. 295 [300]
—female-headed households, p. 207 [215]
—fertility rates, p. 746 [754]
—housework, pp. 185, 187 [191-192]
—illiteracy, p. 254 [271]
—infant deaths, p. 759 [766]
—labor force, p. 538 [562]
—life expectancy, p. 774 [779]
—marital status, p. 784 [787]
—marriages, pp. 818, 822, 824 [817-819]
—maternal deaths, p. 711 [727]
—occupations, p. 520 [543]
—population projections, p. 869 [866]
—population, pp. 784, 853 [787, 848]
—teachers, p. 564 [592]
Police
—crime reports, p. 169 [177]
—response to crime, p. 168 [176]

Politics
—abortion, pp. 2-3 [3-4]
—appointed offices, pp. 882-883 [879-880]
—approval ratings of presidents, pp. 32-33 [36-37]
—attitudes, pp. 34, 44 [38, 45]
—elective offices, pp. 883, 894-898 [881, 891-896]
—opinions on issues, pp. 34, 36, 39 [39-41]
—opinions on parties, p. 42 [42]
—party identification, pp. 889-890 [885-886]
—views of college freshmen, p. 71 [74-75]
—voter turnout, pp. 891-893 [887-890]
Population
—1970-1990 censuses, pp. 864-865 [860-862]
—1992 estimates, pp. 874-875, 877-878 [872-873, 875-876]
—Africa, pp. 794, 796, 858, 865 [799, 802, 853, 863]
—Asia/Near East, p. 782 [786]
—Asia, p. 848 [845]
—developed countries, p. 852 [848]
—elderly, pp. 855-856 [850-851]
—Europe, p. 783 [787]
—Latin America/Caribbean, pp. 784, 857 [788, 852]
—Middle East, p. 858 [853]
—most females worldwide, p. 859 [854]
—North America, p. 795 [800]
—Oceania, p. 795 [801]
—projections, p. 542 [566]
—Soviet Union, p. 797 [803]
—urban (Latin America/Caribbean), p. 218 [226]
—urban (Middle East/North Africa), p. 220 [228]
—urban (Sub-Saharan Africa), p. 219 [227]
—urban and rural, p. 867 [864]
—world, pp. 658, 871 [685, 868]
—Yugoslavia, p. 797 [803]
Population projections
—1993-2050, p. 876 [874]
—1995-2050, pp. 872, 879 [869, 877]
—Africa, p. 874 [871]
—Asia, p. 868 [865]
—developed countries, p. 869 [866]
—elderly, p. 870 [867]
—Latin America/Caribbean, p. 873 [870]
—Middle East, p. 874 [871]
—Sub-Saharan Africa, p. 880 [878]
Portland, Oregon
   See also: Oregon
—AIDS, p. 347 [358]
—alcohol, p. 129 [134]
—arrestees, pp. 101-103 [105-107]
—Catholic marriages, p. 909 [908]
—drugs, pp. 129-133, 135 [134-139]
—school dropouts, p. 103 [108]
Portugal
—births to unmarried mothers, p. 637 [666]
—births, p. 641 [670]
—cigarette smoking, p. 371 [381]
—contraception, pp. 662-663 [688-689]
—deaths, pp. 705, 709, 711, 759 [725-727, 766]
—divorce, p. 815 [816]

Numbers following p. or pp. are page references. Numbers in [ ] are table references.

Portugal continued:
— education, p. 335 [345]
— elderly population, p. 854 [849]
— employment, pp. 520, 539 [543, 563]
— enrollment in school, pp. 289, 291-293 [296-299]
— enrollment in vocational school, p. 295 [300]
— fertility rates, p. 746 [754]
— illiteracy, p. 254 [271]
— infant deaths, p. 759 [766]
— labor force, p. 538 [562]
— life expectancy, p. 774 [779]
— literacy, p. 253 [270]
— marital status, p. 784 [787]
— marriages, pp. 818, 822, 824 [817-819]
— maternal deaths, p. 711 [727]
— occupations, p. 520 [543]
— population projections, p. 869 [866]
— population, pp. 784, 853 [787, 848]
— rape, p. 162 [171]
— ratio of males to females, p. 861 [857]
— religion, p. 911 [909]
— teachers, p. 564 [592]
— wages in construction, p. 471 [490]
— wages in manufacturing, p. 473 [491]
— wages in transport, p. 475 [493]
Pottery making, p. 958 [960]
Poverty, pp. 511-512 [532-533]
— Asian and Pacific Islander families, p. 200 [207]
— black families, p. 201 [208]
— elderly, pp. 508, 855 [529, 850]
— families, pp. 201, 204 [208, 212]
— Hispanic origin families, p. 204 [212]
— older women, p. 508 [530]
Precision production occupations, pp. 570-571 [600-601]
Precision production trades
— degrees conferred, pp. 231, 233, 236, 244 [245, 247, 251, 259]
Pregnancy
— abuse, pp. 178, 180 [185, 187]
— and alcohol, p. 354 [363]
— and drugs, p. 414 [432]
— ectopic, p. 412 [430]
— HIV/AIDS, p. 401 [418]
— older women, p. 412 [431]
— prenatal care, p. 649 [675]
— risk by contraceptive method, p. 677 [702]
— ultrasound, p. 410 [428]
Presbyterian religion, pp. 913-914 [911]
Principals
— elementary and secondary schools, p. 563 [591]
Printmakers, p. 555 [582]
Prison *See:* Imprisonment
Prisoners *See:* Imprisonment
Probation, pp. 102, 126 [106, 131]
Prodigy users, p. 954 [955]
Prostitution, p. 407 [425]
— arrests, p. 102 [107]
— in Thailand, p. 171 [180]
— juvenile, p. 142 [147]

Protective services degrees, pp. 231, 233, 236, 244 [245, 247, 251, 259]
Protein consumption, p. 390 [405]
Protestant religion, p. 912 [910]
— contraceptive use, p. 680 [706]
Psychology degrees, pp. 231, 233, 236, 244 [245, 247, 251, 259]
Public administration
— degrees, pp. 231, 233, 236, 244 [245, 247, 251, 259]
— employment, p. 561 [588]
Public housing *See:* Government assistance programs
Public peace disturbance arrests, p. 102 [107]
Puerto Rico
— births to unmarried mothers, p. 637 [666]
— births, p. 644 [671]
— Catholic sisters, p. 905 [904]
— contraception, p. 665 [690]
— deaths, pp. 720, 724, 726, 761 [733-735, 767]
— divorce, pp. 827-828 [823-824]
— employment, p. 521 [544]
— enrollment in school, p. 302 [305]
— female-headed households, p. 208 [215]
— fertility rates, p. 749 [756]
— illiteracy, p. 256 [273]
— infant deaths, p. 761 [767]
— labor force, p. 540 [564]
— life expectancy, p. 776 [780]
— literacy, p. 255 [272]
— marital status, p. 785 [788]
— marriages, pp. 831, 833, 835 [825-827]
— maternal deaths, p. 726 [735]
— occupations, p. 521 [544]
— population projections, p. 873 [870]
— population, pp. 218, 785, 857 [226, 788, 852]
— ratio of males to females, p. 861 [857]
— WIC Program grants, p. 446 [458]
Punishment
— discipline of children, p. 224 [235]
— opinions about, p. 6 [6]
Qatar
— births, p. 632 [661]
— contraception, p. 660 [686]
— deaths, pp. 692, 694, 757 [717-718, 764]
— divorce, p. 804 [809]
— employment, p. 519 [542]
— enrollment in school, pp. 271, 273, 275-276 [285-288]
— enrollment in vocational school, p. 278 [289]
— fertility rates, p. 745 [753]
— illiteracy, p. 260 [277]
— infant deaths, p. 757 [764]
— life expectancy, p. 773 [778]
— literacy, p. 252 [268]
— marital status, pp. 783, 790 [786, 793]
— marriages, pp. 806, 809, 811 [810-812]
— occupations, p. 519 [542]
— population, pp. 783, 849 [786, 845]
— ratio of females to males, p. 860 [856]
— ratio of males to females, p. 862 [858]
— teachers, p. 558 [584]

Numbers following p. or pp. are page references. Numbers in [ ] are table references.

Rabbinical and Talmudic Studies degrees, pp. 239, 241 [255-256]

Racial discrimination
— opinions about, p. 71 [75]

Racquetball, p. 938 [936]

Radio, pp. 952-955 [951-954, 956]
— format preferences, p. 959 [962]
— network preferences, p. 960 [963]

Rape, pp. 150, 161-162, 178 [157, 170-171, 185]
— and abortion, pp. 5, 616 [5, 643]
— college women, p. 355 [365]
— imprisonment, pp. 108, 123-124, 126 [113, 129-130, 132]
— in Canada, p. 171 [180]
— perpetrators, pp. 104, 113 [109, 118]
— prison inmates, pp. 118, 120 [124, 126]
— victims, pp. 138-139, 153, 155, 157, 173, 176 [142-143, 160-161, 164-165, 181, 183]

Reading, p. 955 [956]
— expenditures, p. 443 [457]
— participation, pp. 948-949, 954 [945-947, 955]

Reagan, Ronald (President)
— appointed offices, p. 883 [880]

Rectal cancer, pp. 364, 366 [372, 375]

Registered nurses, p. 580 [610]
— income, p. 485 [507]

Religion
— abortion, p. 915 [913]
— and abortion, p. 616 [643]
— attendance at services, p. 947 [943]
— attitudes of clergy, p. 48 [47]
— attitudes of nuns, p. 45 [46]
— black clergy, p. 919 [914]
— Catholic missionaries (worldwide), p. 902 [901]
— degrees conferred, pp. 231, 233, 236, 244 [245, 247, 251, 259]
— divinity degrees conferred, pp. 239, 241 [255-256]
— enrollment in seminaries, p. 312 [318]
— membership (Africa), p. 906 [906]
— membership (Asia), p. 907 [907]
— membership (Europe), p. 910 [909]
— membership (Latin America/Caribbean), p. 911 [910]
— membership (Oceania), p. 913 [911]
— preferences of college freshmen, p. 914 [912]
— Rabbinical and Talmudic Studies degrees, pp. 239, 241 [255-256]
— sisters (Canada), p. 903 [903]
— sisters, pp. 903-904, 906 [902, 904-905]
— teaching sisters, p. 584 [613]
— volunteerism, p. 899 [898]

Religious music, p. 959 [962]

Renal disease, p. 644 [672]

Renters, p. 211 [219]
— expenditures, p. 441 [456]

Respiratory problems, p. 376 [388]

Retail trade employment, p. 561 [588]

Reunion
— abortions, pp. 620-621 [648-649]
— births to unmarried mothers, p. 637 [666]
— births, p. 657 [684]

Reunion continued:
— contraception, p. 672 [698]
— deaths, pp. 685-686, 765 [712-713, 771]
— divorce, p. 799 [804]
— employment, p. 518 [541]
— enrollment in school, pp. 262, 264, 266 [280-282]
— enrollment in vocational school, p. 270 [284]
— female-headed households, p. 207 [215]
— fertility rates, p. 753 [760]
— illiteracy, p. 250 [267]
— infant deaths, p. 765 [771]
— labor force, p. 534 [559]
— life expectancy, p. 780 [784]
— marital status, p. 797 [802]
— marriages, pp. 800-802 [805-807]
— occupations, p. 518 [541]
— population, pp. 797, 866 [802, 863]

Rh factor, p. 644 [672]

Rhinitis, p. 378 [391]

Rhode Island
— Catholic marriages, p. 909 [908]
— Catholic sisters, p. 905 [904]
— child rape victims, p. 139 [143]
— college enrollment, p. 281 [291]
— teacher salaries, p. 495 [518]
— WIC Program grants, p. 445 [458]

Rhythm method of contraception, p. 675 [701]

Robbery
— arrests, p. 102 [107]
— imprisonment, pp. 108, 123-124, 126 [113, 129-130, 132]
— perpetrators, pp. 104, 113 [109, 118]
— prison inmates, p. 118 [124]
— victims, pp. 153, 155, 157, 173, 176 [160-161, 164-165, 181, 183]

Rock music, pp. 956, 959 [957, 962]

Rodrigues
— deaths, pp. 685-686 [712-713]
— marriages, p. 802 [807]
— religion, p. 906 [906]

Roe versus Wade
— opinions about, pp. 3, 9 [4, 10]

Romania
— abortion, pp. 345, 614, 620 [357, 642, 647]
— births, p. 641 [670]
— cigarette smoking, p. 371 [381]
— contraception, p. 662 [688]
— deaths, pp. 705, 709, 711, 759 [725-727, 766]
— divorce, p. 815 [816]
— employment, pp. 520, 539 [543, 563]
— enrollment in school, pp. 289, 291-293 [296-299]
— enrollment in vocational school, p. 295 [300]
— fertility rates, p. 746 [754]
— government, p. 886 [883]
— infant deaths, p. 759 [766]
— life expectancy, p. 774 [779]
— marital status, p. 784 [787]
— marriages, pp. 818, 822, 825 [817-819]
— maternal deaths, p. 711 [727]
— occupations, p. 520 [543]

Subject and Geographic Index

Romania continued:
— population projections, p. 869 [866]
— population, pp. 784, 853 [787, 848]
— teachers, p. 564 [592]
RU-486
— opinions about, p. 3 [4]
Running/jogging, p. 938 [936]
Russia
   See also: Soviet Union
— abortion, p. 614 [642]
— births, p. 642 [670]
— college professors, p. 559 [585]
— contraception, p. 675 [700]
— deaths, p. 766 [772]
— divorce, p. 815 [816]
— enrollment in school, p. 293 [299]
— fertility rates, p. 755 [762]
— infant deaths, p. 766 [772]
— life expectancy, p. 781 [785]
— marital status, p. 798 [803]
— marriages, pp. 818, 823, 825 [817-819]
— population, p. 798 [803]
Rwanda
— births, p. 657 [684]
— contraception, pp. 672-673, 678 [698-699, 703]
— deaths, pp. 714, 740, 765 [730, 748, 771]
— employment, p. 518 [541]
— enrollment in school, pp. 262, 264, 266, 268 [280-283]
— enrollment in vocational school, p. 270 [284]
— female-headed households, p. 207 [215]
— fertility rates, p. 753 [760]
— HIV/AIDS, p. 404 [422]
— illiteracy, p. 250 [267]
— infant deaths, p. 765 [771]
— labor force, p. 534 [559]
— life expectancy, p. 780 [784]
— literacy, p. 259 [276]
— marital status, p. 797 [802]
— marriages, p. 835 [828]
— maternal deaths, pp. 714, 740 [730, 748]
— occupations, p. 518 [541]
— population projections, p. 880 [878]
— population, pp. 219, 797, 866 [227, 802, 863]
— teachers, p. 554 [580]
Sailing, p. 962 [966]
Saint Helena
— abortions, p. 620 [648]
— births, p. 657 [684]
— deaths, pp. 685-686, 765 [712-713, 771]
— divorce, p. 799 [804]
— enrollment in school, pp. 262, 264, 266, 268 [280-283]
— enrollment in vocational school, p. 270 [284]
— fertility rates, p. 753 [760]
— infant deaths, p. 765 [771]
— life expectancy, p. 780 [784]
— marriages, p. 802 [807]
— religion, p. 906 [906]
— teachers, p. 554 [580]

Saint Kitts and Nevis
— births, p. 644 [671]
— contraception, pp. 665, 667 [690-691]
— deaths, pp. 720, 724, 761 [733-734, 767]
— divorce, p. 826 [822]
— employment, p. 521 [544]
— enrollment in school, pp. 297, 299-300, 302 [302-305]
— female-headed households, p. 208 [215]
— fertility rates, p. 749 [756]
— illiteracy, p. 256 [273]
— infant deaths, p. 761 [767]
— life expectancy, p. 776 [780]
— marital status, p. 785 [788]
— occupations, p. 521 [544]
— population, pp. 218, 785 [226, 788]
— religion, p. 912 [910]
— teachers, p. 568 [598]
Saint Lucia
— births, p. 644 [671]
— contraception, pp. 665, 667 [690-691]
— deaths, pp. 720, 725, 761 [733-734, 767]
— divorce, p. 828 [824]
— employment, p. 521 [544]
— enrollment in school, pp. 297, 299-300, 302 [302-305]
— enrollment in vocational school, p. 303 [306]
— female-headed households, p. 208 [215]
— fertility rates, p. 749 [756]
— illiteracy, p. 256 [273]
— infant deaths, p. 761 [767]
— life expectancy, p. 776 [780]
— marital status, p. 785 [788]
— marriages, p. 835 [827]
— occupations, p. 521 [544]
— population, pp. 785, 857, 859 [788, 852, 854]
— religion, p. 912 [910]
— teachers, p. 568 [598]
Saint Pierre and Miquelon
— births, p. 655 [682]
— enrollment in school, pp. 304-305 [307-309]
— fertility rates, p. 750 [758]
— infant deaths, p. 763 [769]
— life expectancy, p. 777 [782]
Saint Vincent and the Grenadines
— births, p. 644 [671]
— contraception, pp. 665, 667 [690-691]
— deaths, p. 761 [767]
— divorce, p. 826 [822]
— employment and occupations, p. 521 [544]
— enrollment in school, pp. 297, 299-301 [302-305]
— enrollment in vocational school, p. 303 [306]
— female-headed households, p. 208 [215]
— fertility rates, p. 749 [756]
— illiteracy, p. 256 [273]
— infant deaths, p. 761 [767]
— life expectancy, p. 776 [780]
— marital status, p. 785 [788]
— marriages, p. 834 [827]
— population, p. 785 [788]

Numbers following p. or pp. are page references. Numbers in [ ] are table references.

Saint Vincent and the Grenadines continued:
— religion, p. 911 [910]
— teachers, p. 569 [598]
Salaries
See also: Earnings; Income
— by occupation, p. 488 [513]
— chemical engineers, p. 492 [515]
— college professors, p. 476 [494]
— faculty, p. 478 [495]
— full-time workers, pp. 460, 462 [478, 480]
— in 20 leading occupations, p. 465 [483]
— librarians, p. 483 [503]
— library directors, p. 483 [504]
— physics doctorates, p. 493 [516]
— physics, p. 488 [512]
— ratio of median weekly earnings, p. 466 [484]
— Special Libraries Association members, p. 467 [486]
— union members, p. 464 [482]
Sales occupations, pp. 570-571 [600-601]
Samoa
— Catholic sisters, p. 905 [904]
— deaths, pp. 737, 739 [745-746]
— employment, p. 519 [542]
— enrollment in school, pp. 308-310 [313-315]
— enrollment in vocational school, p. 311 [316]
— labor force, p. 536 [561]
— occupations, p. 519 [542]
— religion, p. 914 [911]
— teachers, p. 575 [604]
San Antonio, Texas
See also: Texas
— AIDS, p. 347 [358]
— alcohol, p. 129 [134]
— arrestees, pp. 101-103 [105-107]
— drugs, pp. 129-133, 135 [134-139]
— school dropouts, p. 103 [108]
San Diego, California
See also: California
— AIDS, p. 347 [358]
— alcohol, p. 129 [134]
— arrestees, pp. 101-103 [105-107]
— drugs, pp. 129-133, 135 [134-139]
— school dropouts, p. 103 [108]
San Marino
— births, p. 641 [670]
— deaths, pp. 705, 709, 759 [725-726, 766]
— divorce, p. 815 [816]
— enrollment in school, pp. 289, 291-292 [296-298]
— enrollment in vocational school, p. 295 [300]
— fertility rates, p. 746 [754]
— infant deaths, p. 759 [766]
— life expectancy, p. 774 [779]
— marital status, p. 791 [794]
— marriages, p. 825 [819]
Sanatanist religion, p. 906 [906]
Sao Tome and Principe
— births, p. 657 [684]
— employment, p. 518 [541]

Sao Tome and Principe continued:
— enrollment in school, pp. 263-264, 266 [280-282]
— enrollment in vocational school, p. 270 [284]
— fertility rates, p. 753 [760]
— illiteracy, p. 250 [267]
— infant deaths, p. 765 [771]
— labor force, p. 534 [559]
— life expectancy, p. 780 [784]
— marriages, p. 802 [807]
— occupations, p. 518 [541]
Saudi Arabia
— births, p. 632 [661]
— deaths, p. 757 [764]
— employment, p. 519 [542]
— enrollment in school, pp. 271, 273, 275-276 [285-288]
— enrollment in vocational school, p. 278 [289]
— fertility rates, p. 745 [753]
— illiteracy, p. 260 [277]
— infant deaths, p. 757 [764]
— life expectancy, p. 773 [778]
— literacy, pp. 252, 257 [268, 274]
— occupations, p. 519 [542]
— population projections, p. 874 [871]
— population, pp. 849, 858 [845, 853]
— ratio of females to males, p. 860 [856]
— ratio of males to females, p. 862 [858]
— teachers, p. 559 [584]
Scholarships, p. 418 [436]
— athletic, p. 432 [451]
— receipt by jail inmates, p. 106 [112]
School dropouts *See:* Dropouts
Science
— advanced placement examinations, p. 320 [328]
— faculty, p. 582 [611]
— teachers, pp. 576, 579 [606, 609]
Sculptors, p. 555 [582]
Secretaries, p. 583 [612]
Self esteem
— college freshmen, p. 73 [77]
— teenagers, p. 72 [76]
Seminary enrollment, p. 312 [318]
Senegal
— age at first marriage, p. 812 [813]
— births, p. 657 [684]
— cigarette smoking, p. 374 [385]
— clitoridectomy, p. 375 [387]
— contraception, pp. 672-673 [698-699]
— deaths, pp. 714, 740, 765 [730, 748, 771]
— employment, p. 518 [541]
— enrollment in school, pp. 263-264, 266, 268 [280-283]
— enrollment in vocational school, p. 270 [284]
— fertility rates, p. 753 [760]
— government, p. 886 [883]
— illiteracy, p. 250 [267]
— infant deaths, p. 765 [771]
— life expectancy, p. 780 [784]
— literacy, p. 259 [276]
— marital status, p. 797 [802]

Subject and Geographic Index

Senegal continued:
— maternal deaths, pp. 714, 740 [730, 748]
— occupations, p. 518 [541]
— population projections, p. 880 [878]
— population, pp. 219, 797, 866 [227, 802, 863]
— teachers, p. 554 [580]
— time spent getting water, p. 184 [190]
Septicemia deaths, p. 700 [723]
Serbia and Montenegro
— births, p. 642 [670]
— infant deaths, p. 766 [772]
— life expectancy, p. 781 [785]
— marital status, p. 798 [803]
— population, p. 798 [803]
Service industry, p. 567 [596-597]
— employment, p. 561 [588]
— occupations, pp. 570-571 [600-601]
Seventh Day Adventist religion, p. 912 [910]
Sex, pp. 920-922, 924-928, 930-934 [915-918, 920, 922-926, 929-933]
— abuse of prison inmates, pp. 118-120 [124-126]
— abuse, pp. 148, 348, 407 [155, 359, 425]
— activity of teenagers, pp. 928, 930, 934 [926, 929, 933-934]
— crimes, pp. 102, 140-141 [107, 145]
— homosexuality, pp. 924, 929 [921, 927]
— premarital, p. 929 [928]
Sex discrimination, p. 68 [72]
— in employment, pp. 149, 523 [156, 546]
— opinions about, p. 36 [40]
— opinions of British, pp. 18-20 [20-22]
Sex roles, p. 50 [49]
— attitudes of teenagers, p. 48 [48]
Sexual assault
See also: Sex
— imprisonment, pp. 108, 123-124, 126 [113, 129-130, 132]
Sexual behavior surveys, pp. 221, 681, 920-934 [230, 708, 915-933]
Sexual harassment, pp. 59, 150 [58, 157]
— at school, pp. 51, 325-334 [50, 334-344]
— in the military, pp. 605-609 [633-637]
Sexually transmitted diseases
See also: Genital herpes
— and ectopic pregnancy, p. 412 [430]
— fear of, p. 922 [918]
— teenagers, p. 382 [396]
— worldwide, pp. 383, 385 [397-398]
Seychelles
— abortions, pp. 619-621 [646, 648-649]
— births to unmarried mothers, p. 637 [666]
— births, p. 657 [684]
— deaths, pp. 685, 687, 765 [712-713, 771]
— divorce, p. 799 [804]
— employment, p. 518 [541]
— enrollment in school, pp. 263-264, 266, 268 [280-283]
— enrollment in vocational school, p. 270 [284]
— fertility rates, p. 753 [760]
— government, p. 885 [882]
— illiteracy, p. 250 [267]

Seychelles continued:
— infant deaths, p. 765 [771]
— labor force, p. 534 [559]
— life expectancy, p. 780 [784]
— marital status, p. 797 [802]
— marriages, p. 802 [807]
— occupations, p. 518 [541]
— population, pp. 219, 797, 866 [227, 802, 863]
— teachers, p. 554 [580]
Shoes, p. 448 [462]
Shopping, p. 96 [100]
Sierra Leone
— births, p. 657 [684]
— clitoridectomy, p. 375 [387]
— contraception, p. 677 [703]
— deaths, pp. 714, 740, 765 [730, 748, 771]
— employment, p. 518 [541]
— enrollment in school, pp. 264, 266, 268 [281-283]
— enrollment in vocational school, p. 270 [284]
— fertility rates, p. 753 [760]
— illiteracy, p. 250 [267]
— infant deaths, p. 765 [771]
— life expectancy, p. 780 [784]
— literacy, p. 259 [276]
— maternal deaths, pp. 714, 740 [730, 748]
— occupations, p. 518 [541]
— population projections, p. 880 [878]
— population, p. 866 [863]
— teachers, p. 554 [580]
Silicone implants, p. 409 [427]
— lawsuit, p. 94 [98]
Singapore
— abortions, pp. 620, 622 [647, 650-651]
— births, p. 631 [661]
— cigarette smoking, p. 370 [380]
— contraception, pp. 659, 661, 678 [686-687, 704]
— deaths, pp. 689, 692, 694, 755, 757 [716-718, 763-764]
— divorce, p. 804 [809]
— employment, pp. 520, 535 [542, 560]
— enrollment in school, pp. 271, 273, 275-276 [285-288]
— enrollment in vocational school, p. 278 [289]
— fertility rates, p. 744 [753]
— government, p. 888 [884]
— illiteracy, p. 253 [269]
— infant deaths, pp. 755, 757 [763-764]
— labor force, p. 536 [561]
— life expectancy, p. 772 [778]
— literacy, p. 251 [268]
— marital status, p. 782 [786]
— marriages, pp. 806, 809, 811 [810-812]
— maternal deaths, p. 689 [716]
— median age, p. 863 [859]
— occupations, p. 520 [542]
— population projections, p. 868 [865]
— population, pp. 782, 848 [786, 845]
— ratio of males to females, p. 863 [859]
— teachers, p. 559 [584]
— wages in agriculture, p. 454 [471]

Numbers following p. or pp. are page references. Numbers in [ ] are table references.

1036

Singapore continued:
— wages in construction, p. 455 [472]
— wages in manufacturing, p. 456 [473]
— wages in transport, p. 458 [475]
Singing, p. 957 [959]
Single men
— contraception, p. 681 [708]
Single people, pp. 14, 220, 224, 788, 793 [16, 229, 234, 791, 798]
— childless, p. 849 [846]
— contraception, p. 681 [708]
— elderly, p. 855 [850]
— families, p. 208 [216]
— in households, p. 211 [219]
— income, p. 417 [435]
— living arrangements, p. 203 [211]
— median income, p. 513 [534-535]
— number of sex partners, p. 928 [926]
— poverty status, pp. 514-515 [536-537]
— sexual activity, p. 930 [929]
— teenage mothers, pp. 633, 635 [663, 665]
— with children, pp. 210, 851 [218, 847]
Sinusitis, p. 378 [391]
Skiing, p. 938 [936]
Skin cancer, p. 365 [373]
Slovakia
— births, p. 641 [670]
— enrollment in school, p. 293 [299]
— fertility rates, p. 746 [754]
— infant deaths, p. 759 [766]
— life expectancy, p. 774 [779]
— marital status, p. 784 [787]
— population, p. 784 [787]
Slovenia
— births, p. 642 [670]
— enrollment in school, p. 289 [296]
— fertility rates, p. 754 [762]
— infant deaths, p. 766 [772]
— life expectancy, p. 781 [785]
— marital status, p. 798 [803]
— population, p. 798 [803]
Smoking *See:* Cigarette smoking
Soccer, p. 939 [936]
Social sciences degrees, pp. 231, 233, 236, 244 [245, 247, 251, 259]
Social Security, pp. 441, 508 [456, 530]
— receipt by jail inmates, p. 106 [112]
Softball, p. 939 [936]
Solomon Islands
— births, p. 656 [683]
— contraception, p. 670 [696]
— deaths, pp. 739, 763 [747, 770]
— enrollment in school, pp. 308-309 [313-314]
— enrollment in vocational school, p. 311 [316]
— fertility rates, p. 751 [759]
— government, p. 888 [884]
— infant deaths, p. 763 [770]
— life expectancy, p. 778 [783]
— marital status, p. 795 [801]

Solomon Islands continued:
— maternal deaths, p. 739 [747]
— median age, p. 863 [859]
— population, p. 795 [801]
— ratio of males to females, p. 863 [859]
Somalia
— births, p. 657 [684]
— clitoridectomy, p. 375 [387]
— deaths, pp. 714, 740, 765 [730, 748, 771]
— employment, p. 518 [541]
— enrollment in school, pp. 263-264, 266, 268 [280-283]
— enrollment in vocational school, p. 270 [284]
— fertility rates, p. 753 [760]
— illiteracy, p. 250 [267]
— infant deaths, p. 765 [771]
— life expectancy, p. 780 [784]
— literacy, p. 259 [276]
— maternal deaths, pp. 714, 740 [730, 748]
— occupations, p. 518 [541]
— population projections, p. 880 [878]
— population, p. 866 [863]
— ratio of males to females, p. 861 [857]
South Africa
See also: Africa; Central African Republic; Middle East/North Africa; North Africa; Sub-Saharan Africa
— abortion, p. 614 [642]
— births, p. 657 [684]
— contraception, p. 672 [698]
— deaths, pp. 740, 765 [748, 771]
— employment, p. 518 [541]
— fertility rates, p. 753 [760]
— government, p. 887 [884]
— infant deaths, p. 765 [771]
— labor force, p. 534 [559]
— life expectancy, p. 780 [784]
— marital status, p. 797 [802]
— maternal deaths, p. 740 [748]
— occupations, p. 518 [541]
— population projections, p. 880 [878]
— population, pp. 219, 797, 866 [227, 802, 863]
— religion, p. 906 [906]
South America
See also: Latin America/Caribbean
— abortions, pp. 629-630 [658-659]
— Catholic missionaries, p. 902 [901]
South Carolina
— Catholic marriages, p. 909 [908]
— Catholic sisters, p. 905 [904]
— child rape victims, pp. 138-139 [142-143]
— college enrollment, p. 281 [291]
— elective offices, p. 895 [892]
— imprisonment, p. 114 [119]
— teacher salaries, p. 496 [518]
— WIC Program grants, p. 445 [458]
South Dakota
— abortions, p. 617 [644]
— Catholic marriages, p. 909 [908]
— Catholic sisters, p. 905 [904]

Numbers following p. or pp. are page references. Numbers in [ ] are table references.

Subject and Geographic Index

South Dakota continued:
— college enrollment, p. 281 [291]
— teacher salaries, p. 496 [518]
— WIC Program grants, p. 445 [458]
South Korea
  See also: Korea; North Korea
— births, p. 631 [661]
— college professors, p. 559 [585]
— contraception, pp. 659, 661 [686-687]
— employment, p. 535 [560]
— fertility rates, p. 744 [753]
— infant deaths, pp. 755, 757 [763-764]
— life expectancy, p. 772 [778]
— marital status, p. 782 [786]
— median age, p. 863 [859]
— population, p. 782 [786]
— ratio of males to females, p. 863 [859]
South Yemen
  See also: North Yemen; Yemen
— literacy, pp. 252, 257 [268, 274]
— population, p. 859 [854]
Soviet Union, p. 754 [762]
  See also: Russia
— abortions, p. 620 [647]
— allocation of time, pp. 185, 187 [191-192]
— births, pp. 642, 658 [670, 685]
— cigarette smoking, p. 372 [381]
— contraception, p. 674 [700]
— deaths, pp. 702, 706, 711, 766 [725-727, 772]
— elderly population, p. 854 [849]
— employment, pp. 521, 539 [543, 563]
— enrollment in school, pp. 290-292, 294 [296-299]
— enrollment in vocational school, p. 295 [300]
— housework, pp. 185, 187-188 [191-193]
— infant deaths, p. 766 [772]
— life expectancy, p. 781 [785]
— marital status, p. 791 [794]
— maternal deaths, p. 711 [727]
— occupations, p. 521 [543]
— population projections, p. 869 [866]
— population, pp. 853, 859, 871 [848, 854, 868]
— ratio of males to females, p. 861 [857]
— teachers, p. 565 [592]
Spain
— births, p. 641 [670]
— cigarette smoking, p. 371 [381]
— contraception, pp. 662-663 [688-689]
— deaths, pp. 705, 709, 711, 758, 760 [725-727, 765-766]
— divorce, p. 815 [816]
— education, p. 335 [345]
— elderly population, p. 854 [849]
— employment, pp. 520, 539 [543, 563]
— enrollment in school, pp. 289, 291-292, 294 [296-299]
— enrollment in vocational school, p. 295 [300]
— fertility rates, p. 746 [754]
— illiteracy, p. 254 [271]
— infant deaths, pp. 758, 760 [765-766]
— labor force, p. 538 [562]

Spain continued:
— life expectancy, p. 774 [779]
— literacy, p. 253 [270]
— marital status, pp. 784, 791 [787, 794]
— marriages, pp. 818, 823, 825 [817-819]
— maternal deaths, p. 711 [727]
— occupations, p. 520 [543]
— population projections, p. 869 [866]
— population, pp. 784, 853 [787, 848]
— teachers, p. 564 [592]
Spending
— athletic scholarships, p. 432 [451]
— sporting goods, p. 449 [463]
Spermicides, p. 677 [702]
Sports and sports equipment
— athletic footwear sales, p. 447 [461]
— athletic scholarships, p. 432 [451]
— economics of, p. 962 [966]
— equipment, pp. 12, 449 [13, 463]
— high school participation, pp. 944, 946 [940-942]
— participation, pp. 937, 958 [936, 961]
Sri Lanka
— births, p. 631 [661]
— cigarette smoking, p. 370 [380]
— contraception, pp. 659, 661 [686-687]
— deaths, pp. 689, 692, 694, 755, 757 [716-718, 763-764]
— deaths of children, p. 715 [731]
— divorce, pp. 804, 826 [809, 822]
— employment, pp. 520, 535 [542, 560]
— enrollment in school, pp. 273, 275-276 [286-288]
— enrollment in vocational school, p. 278 [289]
— fertility rates, p. 744 [753]
— illiteracy, p. 253 [269]
— infant deaths, pp. 755, 757 [763-764]
— labor force, p. 536 [561]
— life expectancy, p. 772 [778]
— literacy, p. 251 [268]
— marital status, p. 782 [786]
— marriages, pp. 806, 809, 811 [810-812]
— maternal deaths, p. 689 [716]
— median age, p. 863 [859]
— occupations, p. 520 [542]
— population projections, p. 868 [865]
— population, pp. 782, 848 [786, 845]
— ratio of males to females, p. 863 [859]
— religion, p. 908 [907]
— teachers, p. 559 [584]
— wages in agriculture, p. 454 [471]
— wages in manufacturing, p. 456 [473]
St. Louis, Missouri
  See also: Missouri
— AIDS, p. 347 [358]
— alcohol, p. 129 [134]
— arrestees, pp. 101-103 [105-107]
— drugs, pp. 129-133, 135 [134-139]
— school dropouts, p. 103 [108]
State government
— employment, p. 585 [614]

Numbers following p. or pp. are page references. Numbers in [ ] are table references.

State government continued:
— salaries of employees, p. 491 [514]
Stepfathers, p. 196 [202]
Stepmothers, p. 196 [202]
Sterilization, pp. 675, 682-683 [701, 709-710]
Steroids
— use by juveniles, p. 145 [152]
Stimulants
— use by juveniles, p. 145 [151]
— use by prison inmates, p. 137 [141]
Strangulation, p. 741 [750]
Stress
— and sexual harassment, p. 609 [637]
Stroke deaths, pp. 700, 727 [723, 736]
Sub-Saharan Africa
  See also: Africa; Central African Republic; Middle East/
  North Africa; North Africa; South Africa
— births, p. 658 [685]
— cigarette smoking, p. 374 [385]
— contraception, pp. 671, 673 [698-699]
— deaths, pp. 714, 740, 764 [730, 748, 771]
— fertility rates, p. 752 [760]
— HIV/AIDS, p. 401 [419]
— infant deaths, p. 764 [771]
— labor force, pp. 522, 524 [545, 547]
— life expectancy, p. 779 [784]
— marital status, p. 796 [802]
— maternal deaths, pp. 714, 740 [730, 748]
— population projections, p. 880 [878]
— population, pp. 219, 796, 865 [227, 802, 863]
Substitute care, pp. 122, 194 [128, 199]
Sudan
— births, p. 657 [684]
— clitoridectomy, p. 375 [387]
— contraception, pp. 672, 674 [698-699]
— deaths, pp. 714, 740, 765 [730, 748, 771]
— employment, p. 518 [541]
— enrollment in school, pp. 263-264, 266, 268 [280-283]
— enrollment in vocational school, p. 270 [284]
— female-headed households, p. 207 [215]
— fertility rates, p. 753 [760]
— government, p. 887 [884]
— illiteracy, p. 250 [267]
— infant deaths, p. 765 [771]
— life expectancy, p. 780 [784]
— literacy, p. 259 [276]
— marital status, pp. 789, 797 [792, 802]
— maternal deaths, pp. 714, 740 [730, 748]
— occupations, p. 518 [541]
— population projections, p. 880 [878]
— population, pp. 219, 797, 866 [227, 802, 863]
— teachers, p. 554 [580]
Suicide, pp. 683, 712, 727, 741 [711, 728, 736, 749-750]
— attitudes of nuns, p. 45 [46]
Supplemental Security Income *See:* Government assistance
  programs
Suriname
— births, p. 644 [671]

Suriname continued:
— deaths, pp. 721, 725-726, 761 [733-735, 767]
— employment, p. 522 [544]
— enrollment in school, pp. 297, 299-300, 302 [302-305]
— enrollment in vocational school, p. 303 [306]
— fertility rates, p. 749 [756]
— illiteracy, p. 256 [273]
— infant deaths, p. 761 [767]
— labor force, p. 540 [564]
— life expectancy, p. 776 [780]
— maternal deaths, p. 726 [735]
— occupations, p. 522 [544]
— population, p. 857 [852]
Swaziland
— births, p. 657 [684]
— cigarette smoking, p. 374 [385]
— contraception, pp. 672, 674 [698-699]
— deaths, p. 765 [771]
— employment, p. 518 [541]
— enrollment in school, pp. 263-264, 266, 268 [280-283]
— enrollment in vocational school, p. 270 [284]
— fertility rates, p. 753 [760]
— government, p. 887 [884]
— illiteracy, p. 250 [267]
— infant deaths, p. 765 [771]
— life expectancy, p. 780 [784]
— marital status, pp. 789, 797 [792, 802]
— marriages, p. 802 [807]
— occupations, p. 518 [541]
— population, pp. 797, 859, 866 [802, 854, 863]
— teachers, p. 554 [580]
— wages in agriculture, p. 450 [465]
— wages in construction, p. 451 [466]
— wages in manufacturing, p. 451 [467]
— wages in mining, p. 452 [468]
— wages in transport, p. 453 [469]
Sweden
— abortions, pp. 623-624 [652-653]
— births to unmarried mothers, p. 637 [666]
— births, p. 641 [670]
— cigarette smoking, p. 371 [381]
— college professors, p. 560 [585]
— contraception, pp. 662-663, 678 [688-689, 704]
— deaths, pp. 705, 710-711, 758, 760 [725-727, 765-766]
— divorce, pp. 814-815 [815-816]
— education, p. 335 [345]
— elderly population, p. 854 [849]
— employment, pp. 521, 539 [543, 563]
— enrollment in school, pp. 289, 291-292, 294 [296-299]
— enrollment in vocational school, p. 295 [300]
— female-headed households, p. 207 [215]
— fertility rates, p. 746 [754]
— government, pp. 885-886 [882-883]
— households, p. 205 [213]
— infant deaths, pp. 758, 760 [765-766]
— labor force, p. 538 [562]
— life expectancy, p. 774 [779]
— marital status, pp. 784, 791 [787, 794]

Sweden continued:
— marriages, pp. 819, 823, 825 [817-819]
— maternal deaths, p. 711 [727]
— occupations, p. 521 [543]
— population projections, p. 869 [866]
— population, pp. 784, 853 [787, 848]
— wages in agriculture, p. 470 [489]
— wages in construction, p. 471 [490]
— wages in manufacturing, p. 473 [491]
— wages in mining, p. 475 [492]
— wages in transport, p. 476 [493]
Swimming, pp. 936, 939 [935-936]
Switzerland
— births, p. 641 [670]
— cigarette smoking, p. 371 [381]
— contraception, p. 662 [688]
— deaths, pp. 705, 710-711, 758, 760 [725-727, 765-766]
— divorce, p. 815 [816]
— elderly population, p. 854 [849]
— employment, pp. 521, 539 [543, 563]
— enrollment in school, pp. 289, 291-292, 294 [296-299]
— enrollment in vocational school, p. 295 [300]
— female-headed households, p. 207 [215]
— fertility rates, p. 746 [754]
— government, p. 886 [883]
— households, p. 205 [213]
— infant deaths, pp. 758, 760 [765-766]
— labor force, p. 538 [562]
— life expectancy, p. 774 [779]
— marital status, pp. 784, 791 [787, 794]
— marriages, pp. 819, 823, 825 [817-819]
— maternal deaths, p. 711 [727]
— occupations, p. 521 [543]
— population projections, p. 869 [866]
— population, pp. 784, 853 [787, 848]
— teachers, p. 565 [592]
— wages in agriculture, p. 470 [489]
— wages in manufacturing, p. 473 [491]
— wages in transport, p. 476 [493]
Syphilis
See also: Sexually transmitted diseases
— teenagers, p. 382 [396]
Syria
— births, p. 632 [661]
— contraception, pp. 660-661 [686-687]
— deaths, pp. 689, 715, 732-733, 757 [716, 730, 739-741, 764]
— deaths of children, p. 715 [731]
— divorce, p. 804 [809]
— employment, p. 520 [542]
— enrollment in school, pp. 272-273, 275-276 [285-288]
— enrollment in vocational school, p. 278 [289]
— fertility rates, p. 745 [753]
— illiteracy, p. 260 [277]
— infant deaths, p. 757 [764]
— labor force, p. 536 [561]
— life expectancy, p. 773 [778]
— literacy, pp. 252, 257 [268, 274]
— marital status, p. 783 [786]

Syria continued:
— marriages, p. 811 [812]
— maternal deaths, pp. 689, 715, 733 [716, 730, 741]
— occupations, p. 520 [542]
— population projections, p. 874 [871]
— population, pp. 220, 783, 858 [228, 786, 853]
— teachers, p. 559 [584]
Syrian Arab Republic *See:* Syria
Taiwan
— births, p. 631 [661]
Tajikistan
— births, p. 642 [670]
— contraception, p. 675 [700]
— divorce, p. 804 [809]
— enrollment in school, p. 276 [288]
— fertility rates, p. 755 [762]
— infant deaths, p. 766 [772]
— life expectancy, p. 781 [785]
— marital status, p. 798 [803]
— marriages, pp. 806, 809, 811 [810-812]
— population, p. 798 [803]
Tanzania
— births, p. 657 [684]
— clitoridectomy, p. 375 [387]
— contraception, pp. 672, 674 [698-699]
— deaths, pp. 714, 740, 765 [730, 748, 771]
— employment, p. 518 [541]
— enrollment in school, pp. 264, 266, 268 [281-283]
— fertility rates, p. 753 [760]
— government, p. 886 [883]
— HIV/AIDS, p. 404 [422]
— infant deaths, p. 765 [771]
— life expectancy, p. 780 [784]
— marital status, p. 797 [802]
— maternal deaths, pp. 714, 740 [730, 748]
— occupations, p. 518 [541]
— population projections, p. 880 [878]
— population, pp. 219, 797, 866 [227, 802, 863]
— teachers, p. 554 [580]
Target shooting, p. 939 [936]
Taxes
— opinions about, p. 11 [11]
Teachers, pp. 561, 570-571, 585 [587, 600-601, 615]
— art, pp. 453, 555 [470, 582]
— at third level (Africa), p. 553 [580]
— at third level (Asia), p. 558 [584]
— at third level (Europe), p. 564 [592]
— at third level (Latin America/Caribbean), p. 568 [598]
— at third level (North America), p. 569 [599]
— at third level (Oceania), p. 575 [604]
— elementary and secondary schools, p. 563 [591]
— reasons for leaving teaching, p. 336 [346]
— religious, p. 584 [613]
— salaries, pp. 453, 478, 495 [470, 495, 518]
— sexual harassment, p. 327 [336]
— tenure status, p. 586 [616]
Technical occupations, pp. 570-571 [600-601]
Teenagers
— abortions, p. 612 [640]

Numbers following p. or pp. are page references. Numbers in [ ] are table references.

Teenagers continued:
— activities of college freshmen, pp. 947-948 [943-944]
— alcohol use, p. 314 [320]
— and exercise, p. 391 [406]
— Asia, p. 848 [845]
— attitudes, p. 48 [48]
— births to unmarried mothers, p. 639 [668]
— cigarette smoking, p. 98 [102]
— contraception, pp. 679-680 [705, 707]
— firearm deaths, p. 712 [728]
— income, p. 423 [442]
— Latin America/Caribbean, p. 857 [852]
— Middle East, p. 858 [853]
— mothers, pp. 440, 446 [454, 459]
— Near East, p. 848 [845]
— North Africa, p. 858 [853]
— self esteem, p. 72 [76]
— sexual activity, pp. 930, 934 [929, 933-934]
— sexual partners, p. 928 [926]
— sexually transmitted diseases, p. 382 [396]
— single mothers' poverty status, p. 514 [536]
— Sub-Saharan Africa, p. 865 [863]
Television, p. 955 [956]
— cable network preferences, p. 950 [948]
— teenagers, pp. 948, 961 [944, 965]
— viewing, pp. 952-954, 958 [951, 953-954, 961]
Tennessee
— Catholic marriages, p. 909 [908]
— Catholic sisters, p. 905 [904]
— college enrollment, p. 281 [291]
— imprisonment, p. 115 [119]
— prisoners under sentence of death, p. 115 [120]
— teacher salaries, p. 496 [518]
— WIC Program grants, p. 445 [458]
Tennis, pp. 939-940, 962 [936-938, 966]
Test scores
— ACT, pp. 337-338 [347-348]
— Functional Information Technology Test (FITT), pp. 227-228 [238-239]
— NAEP (Reading), p. 340 [352]
— NAEP, pp. 339, 344 [350, 356]
— SAT, pp. 342-343 [354-355]
Texas
   See also: Dallas, Texas; San Antonio, Texas
— Catholic marriages, p. 910 [908]
— Catholic sisters, p. 905 [904]
— college enrollment, p. 281 [291]
— drugs, p. 131 [136]
— executives' income, p. 85 [88]
— imprisonment, p. 114 [119]
— politics, p. 883 [881]
— prisoners under sentence of death, p. 115 [120]
— teacher salaries, p. 495 [518]
— WIC Program grants, p. 444 [458]
Thailand
— births, p. 631 [661]
— cigarette smoking, p. 370 [380]
— contraception, pp. 659, 661 [686-687]

Thailand continued:
— deaths, pp. 689, 692, 695, 757 [716-718, 764]
— deaths of children, p. 715 [731]
— employment, pp. 520, 535 [542, 560]
— enrollment in school, pp. 272-273, 275-276 [285-288]
— enrollment in vocational school, p. 278 [289]
— fertility rates, p. 744 [753]
— government, p. 888 [884]
— HIV/AIDS, p. 171 [180]
— illiteracy, p. 253 [269]
— infant deaths, p. 757 [764]
— labor force, p. 536 [561]
— life expectancy, p. 772 [778]
— literacy, p. 251 [268]
— marital status, p. 782 [786]
— marriages, p. 811 [812]
— maternal deaths, p. 689 [716]
— median age, p. 863 [859]
— occupations, p. 520 [542]
— population projections, p. 869 [865]
— population, pp. 782, 848 [786, 845]
— prostitution, p. 171 [180]
— ratio of males to females, p. 863 [859]
— teachers, p. 559 [584]
— violence against women, p. 179 [186]
— wages in construction, p. 455 [472]
— wages in manufacturing, p. 456 [473]
— wages in mining, p. 457 [474]
— wages in transport, p. 458 [475]
Theater attendance, pp. 948-949, 951 [945-946, 949]
Theft
— arrests, p. 102 [106]
— imprisonment, pp. 108, 123-124, 126 [113, 129-130, 132]
— juvenile offenses, p. 143 [148]
— perpetrators, p. 104 [109]
— victims, pp. 153, 155, 157, 160, 174 [160-161, 164-165, 169, 182]
Thryoid cancer, p. 365 [373]
Tinnitus, p. 378 [391]
Tocolysis, p. 647 [674]
Togo
— births, p. 657 [684]
— clitoridectomy, p. 375 [387]
— contraception, pp. 672, 674 [698-699]
— deaths, p. 765 [771]
— employment, p. 518 [541]
— enrollment in school, pp. 263-264, 266, 268 [280-283]
— enrollment in vocational school, p. 270 [284]
— fertility rates, p. 753 [760]
— illiteracy, p. 250 [267]
— infant deaths, p. 765 [771]
— labor force, p. 534 [559]
— life expectancy, p. 780 [784]
— literacy, p. 259 [276]
— marital status, p. 797 [802]
— marriages, p. 836 [828]
— occupations, p. 518 [541]
— population projections, p. 880 [878]
— population, pp. 797, 866 [802, 863]

Togo continued:
— teachers, p. 554 [580]
Tokelau
— deaths, pp. 737, 739 [745-746]
— enrollment in school, pp. 308-309 [313-314]
— enrollment in vocational school, p. 311 [316]
Tonga
— births, p. 656 [683]
— cigarette smoking, p. 373 [384]
— contraception, p. 670 [696]
— deaths, p. 763 [770]
— employment, p. 520 [542]
— enrollment in school, pp. 308-310 [313-315]
— enrollment in vocational school, p. 311 [316]
— fertility rates, p. 751 [759]
— government, p. 888 [884]
— infant deaths, p. 763 [770]
— labor force, p. 536 [561]
— life expectancy, p. 778 [783]
— marital status, p. 793 [797]
— median age, p. 863 [859]
— occupations, p. 520 [542]
— ratio of males to females, p. 863 [859]
— teachers, p. 575 [604]
Tongo
— marriages, p. 845 [842]
Toys, p. 426 [444]
Traffic offense arrests, p. 102 [107]
Tranquilizers, p. 353 [362]
— use by juveniles, p. 145 [151]
Transport
— wages (Africa), p. 452 [469]
— wages (Asia), p. 457 [475]
— wages (Europe), p. 475 [493]
— wages (Latin America/Caribbean), p. 482 [502]
— wages (Oceania), p. 487 [511]
Transportation
— degrees, pp. 231, 233, 236, 244 [245, 247, 251, 259]
— expenditures, p. 443 [457]
Transportation and utilities employment, p. 561 [588]
Travel
— average annual miles, pp. 742-743 [751-752]
— gift preference, p. 12 [13]
Trinidad and Tobago
— births, p. 644 [671]
— cigarette smoking, p. 372 [382]
— contraception, pp. 665, 667 [690-691]
— deaths, pp. 721, 725-726, 761 [733-735, 767]
— divorce, p. 828 [824]
— employment, p. 522 [544]
— enrollment in school, pp. 297, 299-300, 302 [302-305]
— enrollment in vocational school, p. 303 [306]
— female-headed households, p. 208 [215]
— fertility rates, p. 749 [756]
— illiteracy, p. 256 [273]
— infant deaths, p. 761 [767]
— labor force, p. 540 [564]
— life expectancy, p. 776 [780]

Trinidad and Tobago continued:
— literacy, p. 255 [272]
— marital status, p. 785 [788]
— marriages, pp. 831, 834-835 [825-827]
— maternal deaths, p. 726 [735]
— occupations, p. 522 [544]
— population projections, p. 873 [870]
— population, pp. 218, 785, 857 [226, 788, 852]
— religion, p. 913 [910]
Triplets, p. 653 [679]
Tunisia
— abortions, pp. 619-620 [646, 648]
— births, p. 654 [681]
— cigarette smoking, p. 374 [386]
— contraception, pp. 667-668 [692-693]
— deaths, pp. 685, 687, 714, 733, 762 [712-713, 730, 741, 768]
— divorce, p. 799 [804]
— employment, p. 518 [541]
— enrollment in school, pp. 263-264, 266, 268 [280-283]
— enrollment in vocational school, p. 270 [284]
— fertility rates, p. 750 [757]
— fertility, p. 753 [761]
— illiteracy, p. 250 [267]
— infant deaths, p. 762 [768]
— labor force, p. 534 [559]
— life expectancy, p. 777 [781]
— literacy, p. 257 [274]
— marital status, p. 794 [799]
— marriages, pp. 800-802 [805-807]
— maternal deaths, pp. 714, 733 [730, 741]
— occupations, p. 518 [541]
— population projections, p. 874 [871]
— population, pp. 220, 794, 858 [228, 799, 853]
— teachers, p. 554 [580]
Turkey
— abortion, p. 614 [642]
— births, p. 632 [661]
— cigarette smoking, pp. 371, 374 [380, 386]
— contraception, pp. 660-661 [686-687]
— deaths, pp. 689, 715, 733, 757 [716, 730, 741, 764]
— deaths of children, p. 715 [731]
— divorce, p. 804 [809]
— education, p. 335 [345]
— employment, p. 520 [542]
— enrollment in school, pp. 272-273, 275-276 [285-288]
— enrollment in vocational school, p. 278 [289]
— fertility rates, p. 745 [753]
— government, p. 888 [884]
— illiteracy, p. 260 [277]
— infant deaths, p. 757 [764]
— labor force, p. 536 [561]
— life expectancy, p. 773 [778]
— literacy, pp. 252, 257 [268, 274]
— marital status, pp. 783, 790 [786, 793]
— marriages, pp. 807, 810, 840 [810-811, 834]
— maternal deaths, pp. 689, 715, 733 [716, 730, 741]
— occupations, p. 520 [542]
— population projections, p. 874 [871]

Numbers following p. or pp. are page references. Numbers in [ ] are table references.

Turkey continued:
— population, pp. 220, 783, 849, 858 [228, 786, 845, 853]
— ratio of females to males, p. 860 [856]
— ratio of males to females, p. 862 [858]
— teachers, p. 559 [584]
— wages in agriculture, p. 470 [489]
— wages in construction, p. 471 [490]
— wages in manufacturing, p. 473 [491]
— wages in mining, p. 475 [492]
— wages in transport, p. 476 [493]
Turkmenistan
— births, p. 642 [670]
— contraception, p. 675 [700]
— divorce, p. 804 [809]
— enrollment in school, p. 276 [288]
— fertility rates, p. 755 [762]
— infant deaths, p. 766 [772]
— life expectancy, p. 781 [785]
— marital status, p. 798 [803]
— marriages, pp. 807, 810-811 [810-812]
— population, p. 798 [803]
Turks and Caicos Islands
— births, p. 644 [671]
— enrollment in school, pp. 299-300 [303-304]
— fertility rates, p. 749 [756]
— infant deaths, p. 761 [767]
— life expectancy, p. 776 [780]
— religion, p. 913 [910]
Tuvalu
— births, p. 656 [683]
— contraception, p. 670 [696]
— enrollment in school, pp. 308-309 [313-314]
— enrollment in vocational school, p. 311 [316]
— fertility rates, p. 751 [759]
— infant deaths, p. 763 [770]
— life expectancy, p. 778 [783]
— marital status, p. 795 [801]
— population, p. 795 [801]
Twins, p. 653 [679-680]
Uganda
— births, p. 657 [684]
— clitoridectomy, p. 375 [387]
— contraception, pp. 672, 674, 678 [698-699, 703]
— deaths, pp. 714, 740, 765 [730, 748, 771]
— employment, p. 518 [541]
— enrollment in school, pp. 264, 266, 268 [281-283]
— enrollment in vocational school, p. 270 [284]
— fertility rates, p. 753 [760]
— HIV/AIDS, p. 404 [422]
— illiteracy, p. 250 [267]
— infant deaths, p. 765 [771]
— life expectancy, p. 780 [784]
— literacy, p. 259 [276]
— marital status, p. 797 [802]
— maternal deaths, pp. 714, 740 [730, 748]
— occupations, p. 518 [541]
— population projections, p. 880 [878]
— population, pp. 219, 797, 867 [227, 802, 863]

Uganda continued:
— teachers, p. 554 [580]
Ukraine
— abortions, p. 624 [652]
— births, p. 642 [670]
— contraception, p. 675 [700]
— deaths, pp. 706, 710, 766 [725-726, 772]
— divorce, p. 815 [816]
— enrollment in school, pp. 289, 291-292, 294 [296-299]
— enrollment in vocational school, p. 295 [300]
— fertility rates, p. 755 [762]
— infant deaths, p. 766 [772]
— life expectancy, p. 781 [785]
— marital status, p. 798 [803]
— marriages, pp. 819, 823, 825 [817-819]
— population, p. 798 [803]
Ulcers, p. 378 [391]
Ultrasound, pp. 410-411, 647 [428-429, 674]
Union membership, p. 544 [568]
— median earnings, p. 464 [482]
United Arab Emirates
— age at first marriage, p. 812 [813]
— births, p. 632 [661]
— deaths, p. 757 [764]
— employment, p. 520 [542]
— enrollment in school, pp. 272-273, 275-276 [285-288]
— enrollment in vocational school, p. 278 [289]
— fertility rates, p. 745 [753]
— government, p. 888 [884]
— illiteracy, p. 260 [277]
— infant deaths, p. 757 [764]
— labor force, p. 537 [561]
— life expectancy, p. 773 [778]
— marital status, p. 783 [786]
— occupations, p. 520 [542]
— population projections, p. 874 [871]
— population, pp. 220, 783, 849, 858 [228, 786, 845, 853]
— ratio of females to males, p. 860 [856]
— ratio of males to females, p. 862 [858]
— teachers, p. 559 [584]
United Church, p. 913 [911]
United Kingdom
   See also: England; Ireland; Wales
— abortions, p. 624 [652-653]
— allocation of time, pp. 185, 187 [191-192]
— births to unmarried mothers, p. 637 [666]
— births, p. 641 [670]
— cigarette smoking, p. 372 [381]
— contraception, pp. 663, 678 [688-689, 704]
— deaths, pp. 706, 710-711, 760 [725-727, 766]
— divorce, pp. 815, 827 [816, 823]
— educational attainment, p. 261 [278]
— education, p. 335 [345]
— elderly population, p. 854 [849]
— employment, pp. 521, 539 [543, 563]
— enrollment in school, pp. 290-292, 294, 312 [296-299, 317]
— enrollment in vocational school, p. 295 [300]
— female-headed households, p. 207 [215]

United Kingdom continued:
— fertility rates, p. 746 [754]
— households, p. 205 [213]
— housework, pp. 185, 187 [191-192]
— infant deaths, pp. 758, 760 [765-766]
— labor force, p. 538 [562]
— life expectancy, p. 774 [779]
— marital status, pp. 784, 791 [787, 794]
— marriages, pp. 819, 823, 825 [817-819]
— maternal deaths, p. 711 [727]
— occupations, p. 521 [543]
— opinions about sex discrimination, p. 20 [22]
— opinions on sexual harassment, pp. 18-19 [20-21]
— population projections, p. 869 [866]
— population, pp. 784, 853 [787, 848]
— religion, p. 911 [909]
— teachers, p. 565 [592]
— wages in agriculture, p. 470 [489]
— wages in manufacturing, p. 473 [491]
— wages in transport, p. 476 [493]
United States
— abortion, pp. 345, 620, 627 [357, 647, 654]
— allocation of time, pp. 185-186 [191-192]
— births to unmarried mothers, p. 637 [666]
— births, p. 655 [682]
— cigarette smoking, p. 373 [383]
— contraception, pp. 668-669 [694-695]
— deaths, pp. 734-735, 758, 763 [742-744, 765, 769]
— divorce, pp. 814, 827, 841 [815, 823, 835]
— education, p. 335 [345]
— elderly population, p. 854 [849]
— employment, p. 521 [543]
— enrollment in school, pp. 304-305, 312 [307-310, 317]
— female-headed households, p. 207 [215]
— fertility rates, p. 750 [758]
— households, p. 205 [213]
— housework, pp. 185-186 [191-192]
— infant deaths, pp. 758, 763 [765, 769]
— labor force, p. 538 [562]
— life expectancy, p. 777 [782]
— literacy, p. 254 [270]
— marital status, pp. 792, 795 [796, 800]
— marriages, pp. 841-842 [836-838]
— maternal deaths, p. 735 [744]
— occupations, p. 521 [543]
— population projections, p. 870 [866]
— population, pp. 795, 853 [800, 848]
— ratio of males to females, p. 861 [857]
— teacher salaries, p. 495 [518]
— teachers, p. 569 [599]
U.S. Air Force
— pilot training, p. 598 [626]
Uruguay
— births, p. 644 [671]
— cigarette smoking, p. 372 [382]
— deaths, pp. 721, 725-726, 761 [733-735, 767]
— divorce, p. 828 [824]
— employment, p. 522 [544]

Uruguay continued:
— enrollment in school, pp. 297, 299-300, 302 [302-305]
— enrollment in vocational school, p. 303 [306]
— female-headed households, p. 208 [215]
— fertility rates, p. 749 [756]
— government, pp. 886-887 [883-884]
— illiteracy, p. 257 [273]
— infant deaths, p. 761 [767]
— labor force, p. 540 [564]
— life expectancy, p. 776 [780]
— literacy, p. 255 [272]
— marital status, pp. 785, 792 [788, 795]
— marriages, pp. 831, 834-835 [825-827]
— maternal deaths, p. 726 [735]
— occupations, p. 522 [544]
— population projections, p. 873 [870]
— population, pp. 218, 785, 857 [226, 788, 852]
USSR *See:* Russia; Soviet Union
Utah
— abortions, p. 617 [644]
— Catholic marriages, p. 910 [908]
— Catholic sisters, p. 905 [904]
— college enrollment, p. 281 [291]
— teacher salaries, p. 496 [518]
— WIC Program grants, p. 445 [458]
Uzbekistan
— births, p. 642 [670]
— contraception, p. 675 [700]
— deaths, p. 766 [772]
— divorce, p. 804 [809]
— enrollment in school, p. 277 [288]
— fertility rates, p. 755 [762]
— infant deaths, p. 766 [772]
— life expectancy, p. 781 [785]
— marital status, p. 798 [803]
— marriages, pp. 807, 810-811 [810-812]
— population, p. 798 [803]
Vaginal birth, p. 412 [431]
— cost, p. 429 [447]
Valium, p. 353 [362]
Values
— high school students, p. 75 [79]
Vanuatu
— births, p. 656 [683]
— contraception, p. 670 [696]
— deaths, pp. 739, 764 [747, 770]
— enrollment in school, pp. 308-309 [313-314]
— enrollment in vocational school, p. 311 [316]
— fertility rates, p. 751 [759]
— government, p. 888 [884]
— infant deaths, p. 764 [770]
— life expectancy, p. 778 [783]
— marital status, pp. 793, 796 [797, 801]
— maternal deaths, p. 739 [747]
— median age, p. 863 [859]
— population, p. 796 [801]
— ratio of females to males, p. 861 [856]
— ratio of males to females, p. 863 [859]

Vanuatu continued:
— religion, p. 914 [911]
Varicose veins, p. 378 [391]
Vasectomy, pp. 682-683 [709-710]
Venezuela
— allocation of time, pp. 185, 187 [191-192]
— births, p. 644 [671]
— cigarette smoking, p. 372 [382]
— contraception, pp. 665, 667 [690-691]
— deaths, pp. 721, 725-726, 761 [733-735, 767]
— deaths of children, p. 716 [731]
— divorce, p. 828 [824]
— employment, p. 522 [544]
— enrollment in school, pp. 297, 299, 301-302 [302-305]
— enrollment in vocational school, p. 303 [306]
— female-headed households, p. 208 [215]
— fertility rates, p. 749 [756]
— government, p. 887 [884]
— housework, pp. 185, 187 [191-192]
— illiteracy, p. 257 [273]
— infant deaths, p. 761 [767]
— labor force, p. 540 [564]
— life expectancy, p. 776 [780]
— literacy, p. 255 [272]
— marital status, p. 785 [788]
— marriages, pp. 831, 834-835 [825-827]
— maternal deaths, p. 726 [735]
— occupations, p. 522 [544]
— population projections, p. 873 [870]
— population, pp. 218, 785, 857 [226, 788, 852]
Vermont
— Catholic marriages, p. 910 [908]
— Catholic sisters, p. 905 [904]
— college enrollment, p. 281 [291]
— elective offices, p. 895 [892]
— teacher salaries, p. 495 [518]
— WIC Program grants, p. 446 [458]
Veterans, p. 604 [632]
Veterinary Medicine degrees, pp. 239, 241 [255-256]
Victims
See also: Victims of crimes
— crime at school, p. 146 [153]
— dating violence, p. 140 [144]
— violence (worldwide), p. 179 [186]
— violence, pp. 165-166 [174-175]
Victims of crimes, pp. 113, 153, 155, 157, 160, 162-163, 170, 173-174, 176-177 [118, 160-161, 163-165, 169, 172-173, 178-179, 181-184]
— assistance funds, pp. 158-159 [166-168]
— at school, p. 146 [153]
— child rape, pp. 138-139 [142-143]
— police reports, p. 169 [177]
— police response, p. 168 [176]
Victims of Crimes Act, pp. 158-159 [166-168]
Vietnam
— births, p. 631 [661]
— cigarette smoking, p. 370 [380]
— contraception, pp. 659, 661 [686-687]

Vietnam continued:
— deaths, pp. 689, 755, 757 [716, 763-764]
— employment, pp. 520, 535 [542, 560]
— enrollment in school, pp. 272-273, 275, 277 [285-288]
— enrollment in vocational school, p. 278 [289]
— fertility rates, p. 745 [753]
— illiteracy, p. 253 [269]
— infant deaths, pp. 755, 757 [763-764]
— life expectancy, p. 772 [778]
— marital status, pp. 782, 790 [786, 793]
— maternal deaths, p. 689 [716]
— median age, p. 863 [859]
— occupations, p. 520 [542]
— population projections, p. 869 [865]
— population, pp. 782, 848 [786, 845]
— ratio of males to females, p. 863 [859]
— teachers, p. 559 [584]
Violence, p. 180 [187]
— at school, p. 146 [153]
— costs, p. 178 [185]
— imprisonment, pp. 106, 108, 118, 121, 123-124, 126, 154 [111, 113, 124, 127, 129-130, 132, 162]
— juvenile perpetrators, p. 143 [148]
— murder, p. 152 [159]
— opinions about, pp. 31, 43 [35, 43]
— perpetrators, pp. 104, 113 [109, 118]
— police reports, p. 169 [177]
— police response, p. 168 [176]
— prison inmates, p. 118 [124]
— victims (worldwide), p. 179 [186]
— victims, pp. 138-140, 150-151, 153, 155, 157-159, 162-163, 165-166, 170, 173-174, 176-177 [142-144, 157-158, 160-161, 163-168, 172-175, 178-179, 181-184]
Virgin Islands (U.S.)
— births, p. 644 [671]
— Catholic sisters, p. 905 [904]
— deaths, pp. 721, 725, 761 [733-734, 767]
— divorce, p. 828 [824]
— employment, p. 522 [544]
— enrollment in school, pp. 297, 299, 301-302 [302-305]
— fertility rates, p. 749 [756]
— infant deaths, p. 761 [767]
— labor force, p. 540 [564]
— life expectancy, p. 776 [780]
— marriages, pp. 831, 834-836 [825-827, 829]
— occupations, p. 522 [544]
— population, p. 218 [226]
— teachers, p. 569 [598]
Virginia
— Catholic marriages, p. 910 [908]
— Catholic sisters, p. 905 [904]
— college enrollment, p. 281 [291]
— elective offices, p. 895 [892]
— imprisonment, p. 114 [119]
— teacher salaries, p. 495 [518]
— WIC Program grants, p. 445 [458]
Visual arts
— degrees conferred, pp. 231, 233, 236, 244 [245, 247, 251, 259]

Subject and Geographic Index

Numbers following p. or pp. are page references. Numbers in [ ] are table references.

Visual arts continued:
— lessons, p. 952 [950]
Visual impairments, p. 378 [391]
Volleyball, p. 939 [936]
Volunteer workers, pp. 899-901, 958 [897-900, 961]
Voting age population, pp. 889, 891-892 [885, 887-889]
Waitresses, p. 586 [617]
Wales
— abortion, p. 614 [642]
— divorce, p. 813 [815]
Walking, p. 936 [935]
Wallis and Futuna
— births, p. 656 [683]
— fertility rates, p. 751 [759]
— infant deaths, p. 764 [770]
— life expectancy, p. 778 [783]
War
— opinions on, pp. 34, 36, 39 [39-41]
Washington
— Catholic marriages, p. 910 [908]
— Catholic sisters, p. 905 [904]
— college enrollment, p. 281 [291]
— elective offices, p. 895 [892]
— imprisonment, p. 114 [119]
— teacher salaries, p. 495 [518]
— WIC Program grants, p. 445 [458]
Washington, DC
— Catholic marriages, p. 908 [908]
— drugs, p. 131 [136]
Wealth
— households, p. 507 [528]
Weapons
— and spouse abuse, p. 180 [187]
— arrests, p. 102 [107]
— deaths, p. 712 [728]
— handgun control, p. 71 [75]
— imprisonment, pp. 108, 123-124 [113, 129-130]
— opinions on, p. 39 [41]
— suicide, p. 741 [750]
— use by criminals, p. 104 [109]
— use by spouses, p. 166 [175]
— used in crimes, pp. 157, 177 [165, 184]
Weight, pp. 415-416 [433-434]
Weight lifting, p. 936 [935]
Welfare
  See also: Government assistance programs
— receipt by jail inmates, p. 106 [112]
West Bank
— births, p. 632 [661]
— fertility rates, p. 745 [753]
— infant deaths, p. 757 [764]
— life expectancy, p. 773 [778]
— marital status, p. 783 [786]
— population, p. 783 [786]
West Germany
  See also: East Germany; Germany
— contraception, p. 678 [704]
— households, p. 205 [213]

West Germany continued:
— ratio of males to females, p. 861 [857]
West Virginia
— abortions, p. 617 [644]
— Catholic marriages, p. 910 [908]
— Catholic sisters, p. 905 [904]
— college enrollment, p. 281 [291]
— teacher salaries, p. 495 [518]
— WIC Program grants, p. 445 [458]
Western Sahara
— births, p. 654 [681]
— fertility rates, p. 750 [757]
— infant deaths, p. 762 [768]
— life expectancy, p. 777 [781]
Western Samoa
— births, p. 656 [683]
— contraception, p. 670 [696]
— divorce, p. 826 [822]
— fertility rates, p. 751 [759]
— households, p. 216 [224]
— illiteracy, p. 258 [275]
— infant deaths, p. 764 [770]
— life expectancy, p. 778 [783]
— marital status, p. 796 [801]
— median age, p. 863 [859]
— population, p. 796 [801]
— ratio of males to females, p. 863 [859]
Wholesale trade employment, p. 561 [588]
WIC Program *See:* Government assistance programs
Widowed people, p. 788 [791]
— and smoking, p. 368 [377]
— elderly, p. 855 [850]
— householders, p. 211 [219]
Wisconsin
— Catholic marriages, p. 910 [908]
— Catholic sisters, p. 905 [904]
— child rape victims, p. 139 [143]
— college enrollment, p. 281 [291]
— teacher salaries, p. 495 [518]
— WIC Program grants, p. 445 [458]
Work, p. 545 [570]
— attitudes toward (Canada), p. 21 [24]
— attitudes toward (Germany), pp. 23-24 [27-29]
— attitudes toward (Japan), pp. 27-28 [31-32]
— attitudes toward, pp. 56, 59-63, 65-68, 70 [54, 59, 61-65, 68-73]
— experience and earnings, p. 469 [488]
— married mothers, pp. 546-547, 550 [572-573, 576]
— mothers, p. 549 [575]
— parents, p. 548 [574]
Work disabilities, p. 562 [589]
Writers and writing
— lessons, p. 952 [950]
— mysteries, p. 97 [101]
— participation, p. 958 [960]
Wyoming
— abortions, p. 617 [644]
— Catholic marriages, p. 910 [908]
— Catholic sisters, p. 905 [904]

Numbers following p. or pp. are page references. Numbers in [ ] are table references.

Wyoming continued:
— college enrollment, p. 281 [291]
— teacher salaries, p. 495 [518]
— WIC Program grants, p. 446 [458]
Yemen
  See also: North Yemen; South Yemen
— age at first marriage, p. 812 [813]
— births, p. 632 [661]
— contraception, pp. 660-661 [686-687]
— deaths, p. 757 [764]
— employment, p. 520 [542]
— enrollment in school, pp. 272-273, 275, 277 [285-288]
— enrollment in vocational school, p. 278 [289]
— fertility rates, p. 745 [753]
— government, p. 888 [884]
— illiteracy, p. 260 [277]
— infant deaths, p. 757 [764]
— labor force, p. 537 [561]
— life expectancy, p. 773 [778]
— occupations, p. 520 [542]
— population projections, p. 874 [871]
— population, pp. 220, 849, 858 [228, 845, 853]
— teachers, p. 559 [584]
Yugoslavia
— abortions, p. 620 [647]
— allocation of time, pp. 185, 187 [191-192]
— births, p. 642 [670]
— cigarette smoking, p. 372 [381]
— deaths, pp. 706, 710-711, 766 [725-727, 772]
— divorce, p. 815 [816]
— employment, pp. 521, 539 [543, 563]
— enrollment in school, pp. 290-292, 294 [296-299]
— enrollment in vocational school, p. 295 [300]
— fertility rates, p. 754 [762]
— housework, pp. 185, 187 [191-192]
— infant deaths, p. 766 [772]
— labor force, p. 538 [562]
— life expectancy, p. 781 [785]
— literacy, p. 254 [270]
— marriages, pp. 819, 823, 825 [817-819]
— maternal deaths, p. 711 [727]
— occupations, p. 521 [543]
— population projections, p. 870 [866]
— population, p. 853 [848]
— teachers, p. 565 [592]
Zaire
— births, p. 657 [684]
— clitoridectomy, p. 376 [387]
— contraception, p. 678 [703]
— deaths, p. 765 [771]
— divorce, p. 827 [822]
— employment, p. 518 [541]
— enrollment in school, pp. 265-266, 268 [281-283]
— enrollment in vocational school, p. 270 [284]
— fertility rates, p. 753 [760]
— government, p. 887 [884]
— HIV/AIDS, p. 404 [422]
— illiteracy, p. 250 [267]

Zaire continued:
— infant deaths, p. 765 [771]
— life expectancy, p. 780 [784]
— literacy, p. 259 [276]
— marital status, pp. 789, 797 [792, 802]
— occupations, p. 518 [541]
— population projections, p. 880 [878]
— population, pp. 219, 797, 867 [227, 802, 863]
Zambia
— age at first marriage, p. 812 [813]
— births, p. 657 [684]
— cigarette smoking, p. 374 [385]
— contraception, pp. 672, 674 [698-699]
— deaths, p. 765 [771]
— employment, p. 519 [541]
— enrollment in school, pp. 265, 267-268 [281-283]
— enrollment in vocational school, p. 270 [284]
— female-headed households, p. 207 [215]
— fertility rates, p. 753 [760]
— government, p. 887 [884]
— HIV/AIDS, p. 404 [422]
— illiteracy, p. 251 [267]
— infant deaths, p. 765 [771]
— labor force, p. 534 [559]
— life expectancy, p. 780 [784]
— literacy, p. 259 [276]
— marital status, p. 797 [802]
— maternal deaths, p. 740 [748]
— occupations, p. 519 [541]
— population projections, p. 881 [878]
— population, pp. 219, 797, 867 [227, 802, 863]
Zimbabwe
— births, p. 657 [684]
— contraception, pp. 672, 674 [698-699]
— deaths, pp. 685, 687, 714, 740, 765 [712-713, 730, 748, 771]
— employment, p. 519 [541]
— enrollment in school, pp. 265, 267-268 [281-283]
— enrollment in vocational school, p. 270 [284]
— fertility rates, p. 753 [760]
— fertility, p. 753 [761]
— HIV/AIDS, p. 404 [422]
— illiteracy, p. 251 [267]
— infant deaths, p. 765 [771]
— life expectancy, p. 780 [784]
— literacy, p. 259 [276]
— marital status, p. 797 [802]
— maternal deaths, pp. 714, 740 [730, 748]
— occupations, p. 519 [541]
— population projections, p. 881 [878]
— population, pp. 797, 867 [802, 863]
— teachers, p. 554 [580]

Numbers following p. or pp. are page references. Numbers in [ ] are table references.